KT-578-865

The Oxford Italian Minidictionary

Second Edition
with new phrasefinder

ITALIAN–ENGLISH
ENGLISH–ITALIAN

ITALIANO–INGLESE
INGLESE–ITALIANO

OXFORD
UNIVERSITY PRESS

OXFORD
UNIVERSITY PRESS

Great Clarendon Street, Oxford OX2 6DP

Oxford University Press is a department of the University of Oxford.
It furthers the University's objective of excellence in research, scholarship,
and education by publishing worldwide in

Oxford New York

Athens Auckland Bangkok Bogotá Buenos Aires Calcutta
Cape Town Chennai Dar es Salaam Delhi Florence Hong Kong Istanbul
Karachi Kuala Lumpur Madrid Melbourne Mexico City Mumbai
Nairobi Paris São Paulo Singapore Taipei Tokyo Toronto Warsaw

with associated companies in Berlin Ibadan

Oxford is a registered trade mark of Oxford University Press
in the UK and in certain other countries

Published in the United States
by Oxford University Press Inc., New York

British Library Cataloguing in Publication Data

Data available

Library of Congress Cataloging in Publication Data

Data available

ISBN 0–19–860253–7

ISBN 0–19–860291–X (Italian cover edition only)

10 9 8 7 6 5

Printed in Great Britain by
Charles Letts (Scotland) Ltd
Dalkeith, Scotland

Contents / Indice

First Edition/Prima edizione
Editor/Redazione
Joyce Andrews

Second Edition/Seconda edizione
Editors/Redazione
Debora Mazza, Donatella Boi, Sonia Tinagli-Baxter
Peter Terrell, Jane Goldie, Francesca Logi, Carla Zipoli

Copy Editors/Segreteria di redazione
Jacqueline Gregan, Daphne Trotter

Project management by/A cura di
LEXUS

Phrasefinder/Trovafrasi
Loredana Riu, Neil and Roswitha Morris

Preface/Prefazione

This new edition of the *Oxford Italian-English Minidictionary* is an updated and expanded version of the dictionary edited by Joyce Andrews. Colloquial words and phrases figure largely, as do neologisms. Noteworthy additions include terms from special areas such as computing and business that have become a familiar feature of current language. The dictionary also includes a unique **Phrasefinder**, which groups together all the essential phrases you will need for everyday conversation. The section is thematically arranged and covers 8 key topics: *going places, keeping in touch, food and drink, places to stay, shopping and money, sports and leisure, good timing* and *conversion charts*.

Questa nuova edizione del *mini dizionario Oxford Italiano-Inglese* è il risultato di un lavoro di ampliamento e aggiornamento della precedente edizione curata da Joyce Andrews. Un'attenzione particolare è stata rivolta a vocaboli ed espressioni colloquiali di coniazione recente e a termini relativi a settori specifici, quali l'informatica e il commercio, divenuti ricorrenti nella lingua di tutti i giorni. Il dizionario comprende anche un prezioso **"Trovafrasi"** che contiene tutte le espressioni essenziali per l'uso quotidiano della lingua. La sezione è ordinata per temi e copre 8 argomenti fondamentali: *in viaggio, comunicazioni, mangiare e bere, dove alloggiare, spese e soldi, sport e tempo libero, l'ora giusta e tabelle di conversione.*

Proprietary terms/Marchi registrati

This dictionary includes some words which are, or are asserted to be, proprietary names or trade marks. Their inclusion does not imply that they have acquired for legal purposes a non-proprietary or general significance, nor is any other judgement implied concerning their legal status. In cases where the editor has some evidence that a word is used as proprietary name or trade mark this is indicated by the symbol ®, but no judgement concerning the legal status of such words is made or implied thereby.

Questo dizionario include alcune parole che sono o vengono considerate marchi registrati. La loro presenza non implica che abbiano acquisito legalmente un significato generale, né si suggerisce alcun altro giudizio riguardo il loro stato giuridico. Qualora il redattore abbia trovato testimonianza dell'uso di una parola come marchio registrato, quest'ultima è stata contrassegnata dal simbolo ®, ma nessun giudizio riguardo lo stato giuridico di tale parola viene espresso o suggerito in tal modo.

Introduction

In order to give the maximum information about English and Italian in the space available, this new dictionary uses certain space-saving conventions.

A swung dash ~ is used to replace the headword within the entry.

Where the headword contains a vertical bar | the swung dash replaces only the part of the headword that comes in front of the |. For example: **efficien|te** *a* efficient. **~za** *nf* efficiency (the second bold word reads **efficienza**).

Indicators are provided to guide the user to the best translation for a specific sense of a word. Types of indicator are:

field labels (see the list on pp ix-x), which indicate a general area of usage (commercial, computing, photography etc);

sense indicators, eg: **bore** *n* (*of gun*) calibro *m*; (*person*) seccatore, -trice *mf*;

typical subjects of verbs, eg: **bond** *vt* (*glue:*) attaccare;

typical objects of verbs, placed after the translation of the verb, eg; **boost** *vt* stimolare (*sales*); sollevare (*morale*);

nouns that typically go together with certain adjectives, eg: **rich** *a* ricco; (*food*) pesante.

A solid black circle means that the same word is being translated as a different part of speech, eg. **partition** *n* ... ● *vt* ...

English pronunciation is given for the Italian user in the International Phonetic Alphabet (see p viii)

Italian stress is shown by a ' placed in front of the stressed syllable in a word.

Square brackets are used around parts of an expression which can be omitted without altering the sense.

Introduzione

Allo scopo di fornire il maggior numero possibile di informazioni in inglese e in italiano, questo nuovo dizionario ricorre ad alcune convenzioni per sfruttare al massimo lo spazio disponibile.

Un trattino ondulato ~ è utilizzato al posto del lemma all'interno della voce.

Qualora il lemma contenga una barra verticale |, il trattino ondulato sostituisce solo la parte del lemma che precede |. Ad esempio: **dark|en** *vt* oscurare. **~ness** *n* buio *m* (la seconda parola in neretto va letta **darkness**).

Degli indicatori vengono forniti per indirizzare l'utente verso la traduzione corrispondente al senso voluto di una parola. I tipi di indicatori sono:

etichette semantiche (vedi la lista a pp ix-x), indicanti l'ambito specifico in cui la parola viene generalmente usata in quel senso (commercio, informatica, fotografia ecc);

indicatori di significato, es.: **redazione** *nf* ⟨*ufficio*⟩ editorial office; ⟨*di testi*⟩ editing;

soggetti tipici di verbi, es.: **trovarsi** *vr* ⟨*luogo:*⟩ be;

complementi oggetti tipici di verbi, collocati dopo la traduzione dello stesso verbo, es: **superare** *vt* overtake ⟨*veicolo*⟩; pass ⟨*esame*⟩;

sostantivi che ricorrono tipicamente con certi aggettivi, es.: **solare** *a* ⟨*energia, raggi*⟩ solar; ⟨*crema*⟩ sun.

Un pallino nero indica che la stessa parola viene tradotta come una diversa parte del discorso, es. **calcolatore** *a* ... ● *nm* ...

La pronuncia inglese è data usando l'Alfabetico Fonetico Internazionale (vedi p viii).

L'accento tonico nelle parole italiane è indicato dal segno ' collocato davanti alla sillaba accentata.

Delle parentesi quadre racchiudono parti di espressioni che possono essere omesse senza alterazioni di senso.

Pronunciation of Italian

Vowels:

a   is broad like *a* in *father*: **casa**.

e   has two sounds: closed like *ey* in *they*: **sera**; open like *e* in *egg*: **sette**.

i   is like *ee* in *feet*: **venire**.

o   has two sounds: closed like *o* in *show*: **bocca**; open like *o* in *dog*: **croma**.

u   is like *oo* in *moon*: **luna**.

When two or more vowels come together each vowel is pronounced separately: **buono**; **baia**.

Consonants:

b, d, f, l, m, n, p, t, v are pronounced as in English. When these are double they are sounded distinctly: **bello**.

c   before **a, o** or **u** and before consonants is like *k* in *king*: **cane**.
    before **e** or **i** is like *ch* in *church*: **cena**.

ch   is also like *k* in *king*: **chiesa**.

g   before **a, o,** or **u** is hard like *g* in *got*: **gufo**.
    before **e** or **i** is like *j* in *jelly*: **gentile**.

gh   is like *g* in *gun*: **ghiaccio**.

gl   when followed by **a, e, o, u** is like *gl* in *glass*: **gloria**.

gli   is like *lli* in *million*: **figlio**.

gn   is like *ni* in *onion*: **bagno**.

h   is silent.

ng   is like *ng* in *finger* (not *singer*): **ringraziare**.

r   is pronounced distinctly.

s   between two vowels is like *s* in *rose*: **riso**.
    at the beginning of a word it is like *s* in *soap*: **sapone**.

sc   before **e** or **i** is like *sh* in *shell*: **scienza**.

z   sounds like *ts* within a word: **fazione**; like *dz* at the beginning: **zoo**.

The stress is shown by the sign ' printed before the stressed syllable.

Pronuncia inglese

SIMBOLI FONETICI

Vocali e dittonghi

æ bad	ʊ put	aʊ now
ɑː ah	uː too	aʊə flour
e wet	ə ago	ɔɪ coin
ɪ sit	ɜː work	ɪə here
iː see	eɪ made	eə hair
ɒ got	əʊ home	ʊə poor
ɔː door	aɪ five	
ʌ cup	aɪə fire	

Consonanti

b boy	l leg	t ten
d day	m man	tʃ chip
dʒ page	n new	θ three
f foot	ŋ sing	ð this
g go	p pen	v verb
h he	r run	w wet
j yes	s speak	z his
k coat	ʃ ship	ʒ pleasure

Note: ' precede la sillaba accentata.
La vocale nasale in parole quali *nuance* è indicata nella trascrizione fonetica come ɒ̃: njuːɒ̃s.

Abbreviations/Abbreviazioni

adjective	*a*	aggettivo
abbreviation	*abbr*	abbreviazione
administration	*Admin*	amministrazione
adverb	*adv*	avverbio
aeronautics	*Aeron*	aeronautica
American	*Am*	americano
anatomy	*Anat*	anatomia
archaeology	*Archaeol*	archeologia
architecture	*Archit*	architettura
astrology	*Astr*	astrologia
attributive	*attrib*	attributo
automobiles	*Auto*	automobile
auxiliary	*aux*	ausiliario
biology	*Biol*	biologia
botany	*Bot*	botanica
British English	*Br*	inglese britannico
Chemistry	*Chem*	chimica
commerce	*Comm*	commercio
computers	*Comput*	informatica
conjunction	*conj*	congiunzione
cooking	*Culin*	cucina
definite article	*def art*	articolo determinativo
	ecc	eccetera
electricity	*Electr*	elettricità
et cetera	*etc*	
feminine	*f*	femminile
familiar	*fam*	familiare
figurative	*fig*	figurato
formal	*fml*	formale
geography	*Geog*	geografia
geology	*Geol*	geologia
grammar	*Gram*	grammatica
humorous	*hum*	umoristico
indefinite article	*indef art*	articolo indeterminativo
interjection	*int*	interiezione
interrogative	*inter*	interrogativo
invariable	*Inv*	invariabile
(no plural form)		
law	*Jur*	legge/giuridico
literary	*liter*	letterario
masculine	*m*	maschile
mathematics	*Math*	matematica
mechanics	*Mech*	meccanica
medicine	*Med*	medicina

masculine or feminine	*mf*	maschile o femminile
military	*Mil*	militare
music	*Mus*	musica
noun	*n*	sostantivo
nautical	*Naut*	nautica
pejorative	*pej*	peggiorativo
personal	*pers*	personale
photography	*Phot*	fotografia
physics	*Phys*	fisica
plural	*pl*	plurale
politics	*Pol*	politica
possessive	*poss*	possessivo
past participle	*pp*	participio passato
prefix	*pref*	prefisso
preposition	*prep*	preposizione
present tense	*pres*	presente
pronoun	*pron*	pronome
psychology	*Psych*	psicologia
past tense	*pt*	tempo passato
	qcno	qualcuno
	qcsa	qualcosa
proprietary term	®	marchio registrato
rail	*Rail*	ferrovia
reflexive	*refl*	riflessivo
religion	*Relig*	religione
relative pronoun	*rel pron*	pronome relativo
somebody	*sb*	
school	*Sch*	scuola
singular	*sg*	singolare
slang	*sl*	gergo
something	*sth*	
technical	*Techn*	tecnico
telephone	*Teleph*	telefono
theatrical	*Theat*	teatrale
television	*TV*	televisione
typography	*Typ*	tipografia
university	*Univ*	università
auxiliary verb	*v aux*	verbo ausiliare
intransitive verb	*vi*	verbo intransitivo
reflexive verb	*vr*	verbo riflessivo
transitive verb	*vt*	verbo transitivo
transitive and intransitive	*vt/i*	verbo transitivo e intransitivo
vulgar	*vulg*	volgare
cultural equivalent	≈	equivalenza culturale

Aa

a (**ad** before vowel prep to; (stato in luogo, tempo, età) at; (con mese, città) in; (mezzo, modo) by; **dire qcsa a qcno** tell sb sth; **alle tre** at three o'clock; **a vent'anni** at the age of twenty; **a Natale** at Christmas; **a dicembre** in December; **ero al cinema** I was at the cinema; **vivo a Londra** I live in London; **a due a due** two by two; **a piedi** on o by foot; **maglia a maniche lunghe** long-sleeved sweater; **casa a tre piani** house with three floors; **giocare a tennis** play tennis; **50 km all'ora** 50 km an hour; **2 000 lire al chilo** 2,000 lire a kilo; **al mattino/alla sera** in the morning/evening; **a venti chilometri/due ore da qui** twenty kilometres/two hours away

a'bate nm abbot

abbacchi'ato a downhearted

ab'bacchio nm [young] lamb

abbagli'ante a dazzling ●nm headlight, high beam

abbagli'are vt dazzle. **ab'baglio** nm blunder; **prendere un ~** make a blunder

abbai'are vi bark

abba'ino nm dormer window

abbando'na|re vt abandon; leave (luogo); give up (piani ecc). **~rsi** vr let oneself go; **~rsi a** give oneself up to (ricordi ecc). **~to** a abandoned. **abban'dono** nm abandoning; fig abandon; (stato) neglect

abbassa'mento nm (di temperatura, acqua, prezzi) drop

abbas'sar|e vt lower; turn down (radio, TV); **~e i fari** dip the headlights. **~si** vr stoop; (sole ecc) sink; fig demean oneself

ab'basso adv below ●int down with

abba'stanza adv enough; (alquanto) quite

ab'batter|e vt demolish; shoot down (aereo); put down (animale); topple (regime); (fig: demoralizzare) dishearten. **~si** vr (cadere) fall; fig be discouraged

abbatti'mento nm (morale) despondency

abbat'tuto a despondent, down-in-the-mouth

abbel'lir|e vt embellish. **~si** vr adorn oneself

abbeve'ra|re vt water. **~'toio** nm drinking trough

abbi'ente a well-to-do

abbiglia'mento nm clothes pl; (industria) clothing industry, rag trade

abbigli'ar|e vt dress. **~si** vr dress up

abbina'mento nm combining

abbi'nare vt combine; match (colori)

abbindo'lare vt cheat

abbocca'mento nm interview; (conversazione) talk

abboc'care vi bite; (tubi) join; fig swallow the bait

abboc'cato a (vino) fairly sweet

abbof'farsi vr stuff oneself

abbona'mento nm subscription; (ferroviario ecc) season-ticket; **fare l'~** take out a subscription

abbo'na|re vt make a subscriber. **~rsi** vr subscribe (a to); take out a season-ticket (a for) (teatro, stadio). **~to, -a** nmf subscriber

abbon'dan|te a abundant; (quantità) copious; (nevicata) heavy; (vestiario) roomy. **~te di** abounding in. **~'te'mente** adv ⟨mangiare⟩ copiously. **~za** nf abundance

abbon'dare vi abound

abbor'da|bile a ⟨persona⟩ approachable; ⟨prezzo⟩ reasonable. **~ggio** nm Mil boarding. **~re** vt board ⟨nave⟩; approach ⟨persona⟩; ⟨fam: attaccar bottone a⟩ chat up; tackle ⟨compito ecc⟩

abbotto'na|re vt button up. **~'tura** nf [row of] buttons. **~to** a fig tight-lipped

abboz'zare vt sketch [out]; **~ un sorriso** give a hint of a smile. **ab'bozzo** nm sketch

abbracci'are vt embrace; hug, embrace ⟨persona⟩; take up ⟨professione⟩; fig include. **ab'braccio** nm hug

abbrevi'a|re vt shorten; ⟨ridurre⟩ curtail; abbreviate ⟨parola⟩. **~zi'one** nf abbreviation

abbron'zante nm sun-tan lotion

abbron'za|re vt bronze; tan ⟨pelle⟩. **~rsi** vr get a tan. **~to** a tanned. **~'tura** nf [sun-]tan

abbrusto'lire vt toast; roast ⟨caffè ecc⟩

abbruti'mento nm brutalization. **abbru'tire** vt brutalize. **abbru'tirsi** vr become brutalized

abbuf'fa|rsi vr fam stuff oneself. **~ta** nf blowout

abbuo'nare vt reduce

abbu'ono nm allowance; Sport handicap

abdi'ca|re vi abdicate. **~zi'one** nf abdication

aber'rante a aberrant

aberrazi'one nf aberration

a'bete nm fir

abi'etto a despicable

'abi|le a able; ⟨idoneo⟩ fit; ⟨astuto⟩ clever. **~ità** nf inv ability; ⟨idoneità⟩ fitness; ⟨astuzia⟩ cleverness. **~'mente** adv ably; ⟨con astuzia⟩ cleverly

abili'ta|re vt qualify. **~to** a qualified. **~zi'one** nf qualification; ⟨titolo⟩ diploma

abis'sale a abysmal. **a'bisso** nm abyss

abi'tabile a inhabitable

abi'tacolo nm Auto passenger compartment

abi'tante nmf inhabitant

abi'ta|re vi live. **~to** a inhabited ●nm built-up area. **~zi'one** nf house

'abito nm ⟨da donna⟩ dress; ⟨da uomo⟩ suit. **~ da cerimonia/da sera** formal/evening dress

abitu'a|le a usual, habitual. **~'mente** adv usually

abitu'a|re vt accustom. **~si a** vr get used to

abitu'dinario, -a a of fixed habits ●nmf person of fixed habits

abi'tudine nf habit; **d'~** usually; **per ~** out of habit; **avere l'~ di fare qcsa** be in the habit of doing sth

abnegazi'one nf self-sacrifice

ab'norme a abnormal

abo'li|re vt abolish; repeal ⟨legge⟩. **~zi'one** nf abolition; repeal

abomi'nevole a abominable

abo'rigeno, -a a & nmf aboriginal

abor'rire vt abhor

abor'ti|re vi miscarry; ⟨volontariamente⟩ have an abortion; fig fail. **~vo** a abortive. **a'borto** nm miscarriage; ⟨volontario⟩ abortion. **~sta** a pro-choice

abrasi'one nf abrasion. **abra'sivo** a & nm abrasive

abro'ga|re vt repeal. **~zi'one** nf repeal

'abside nf apse

abu'lia nf apathy. **a'bulico** a apathetic

abu'sa|re vi **~ di** abuse; over-indulge in ⟨alcol⟩; ⟨approfittare di⟩ take advantage of; ⟨violentare⟩ rape. **~ivo** a illegal

a'buso nm abuse. **~ di confidenza** breach of confidence

a.C. abbr ⟨avanti Cristo⟩ BC

'acca nf fam **non ho capito un'~** I understood damn all

acca'demi|a nf academy. **A~a di**

Belle Arti Academy of Fine Arts. **~co, -a** *a* academic ● *nmf* academician

acca'd|ere *vi* happen; **accada quel che accada** come what may. **~uto** *nm* event

accalappi'are *vt* catch; *fig* allure

accal'carsi *vr* crowd

accal'dairsi *vr* get overheated; *fig* get excited. **~to a** overheated

accalo'rarsi *vr* get excited

accampa'mento *nm* camp. **accam'pare** *vt* *fig* put forth. **accoam'parsi** *vr* camp

accani'mento *nm* tenacity; *(odio)* rage

acca'ni|rsi *vr* persist; *(infierire)* rage. **~to** *a* persistent; *(odio)* fierce; *fig* inveterate

ac'canto *adv* near; **~** *a prep* next to

accanto'nare *vt* set aside; *Mil* billet

accaparra'mento *nm* hoarding; *Comm* cornering

accapar'ra|re *vt* hoard. **~rsi** *vr* grab; *corner* (mercato). **~'tore, ~'trice** *nmf* hoarder

accapigli'arsi *vr* scuffle; *(litigare)* squabble

accappa'toio *nm* bathrobe; *(per spiaggia)* beachrobe

accappo'nare *vt* **fare ~ la pelle a** qcno make sb's flesh creep

accarez'zare *vt* caress, stroke; *fig* cherish

accartocci'ar|e *vt* scrunch up. **~si** *vr* curl up

acca'sarsi *vr* get married

accasci'arsi *vr* flop down; *fig* lose heart

accata'stare *vt* pile up

accatti'vante *a* beguiling

accatti'varsi *vr* **~ le simpatie/la stima/l'affetto di** qcno gain sb's sympathy/respect/affection

accatto'naggio *nm* begging. **accat'tone, -a** *nmf* beggar

accaval'lar|e *vt* cross (gambe). **~si** *vr* pile up; *fig* overlap

acce'cante *a* (luce) blinding

acce'care *vt* blind ● *vi* go blind

ac'cedere *vi* **~ a** enter; *(acconsentire)* comply with

accele'ra|re *vi* accelerate ● *vt* speed up, accelerate; **~re il passo** quicken one's pace. **~to** *a* rapid. **~'tore** *nm* accelerator. **~zi'one** *nf* acceleration

ac'cender|e *vt* light; turn on (luce, TV ecc); *fig* inflame; **ha da ~?** have you got a light?. **~si** *vr* catch fire; *(illuminarsi)* light up; (TV ecc) turn on; *fig* become inflamed

accendi'gas *nm inv* gas lighter; *(su cucina)* automatic ignition

accen'dino *nm* lighter

accendi'sigari *nm* cigar-lighter

accen'nare *vt* indicate; hum (melodia) ● *vi* **~ a** beckon to; *fig* hint at; *(far l'atto di)* make as if to; **accenna a piovere** it looks like rain. **ac'cenno** *nm* gesture; *(con il capo)* nod; *fig* hint

accensi'one *nf* lighting; *(di motore)* ignition

accen'ta|re *vt* accent; *(con accento tonico)* stress. **~zi'one** *nf* accentuation. **ac'cento** *nm* accent; *(tonico)* stress

accentra'mento *nm* centralizing

accen'trare *vt* centralize

accentu'a|re *vt* accentuate. **~rsi** *vr* become more noticeable. **~to** *a* marked

accerchia'mento *nm* surrounding

accerchi'are *vt* surround

accerta'mento *nm* check

accer'tare *vt* ascertain; *(controllare)* check; assess (reddito)

ac'ceso *a* lighted; (radio, TV ecc) on; (colore) bright

acces'sibile *a* accessible; (persona) approachable; (spesa) reasonable

ac'cesso *nm* access; (Med: di rabbia) fit; **vietato l'~** no entry

acces'sorio *a* accessory; (secondario) of secondary importance ● *nm* accessory; **accessori** *pl* (rifiniture) fittings

ac'cetta *nf* hatchet

accet'tabile *a* acceptable

accet'tare *vt* accept; (*aderire a*) agree to

accettazi'one *nf* acceptance; (*luogo*) reception. ~ [bagagli] check-in. [banco] ~ check-in [desk]

ac'cetto *a* agreeable; essere bene ~ be very welcome

accezi'one *nf* meaning

acchiap'pare *vt* catch

acchito *nm* di primo ~ at first

acciac'care *vt* crush; *fig* prostrate. ~to, -a *a* essere ~to ache all over. acci'acco *nm* infirmity; acciacchi *pl* aches and pains

acciai'eria *nf* steelworks

acci'aio *nm* steel; ~ inossidabile stainless steel

acciden'tale *a* accidental. ~l'mente *adv* accidentally. ~to *a* (*terreno*) uneven

acci'dente *nm* accident; *Med* stroke; non capisce/non vede un ~ *fam* he doesn't understand/can't see a damn thing. acci'denti! *int* damn!

accigli'arsi *vr* frown. ~to *a* frowning

ac'cingersi *vr* ~ a be about to

acci'picchia *int* good Lord!

acciuf'fare *vt* catch

acci'uga *nf* anchovy

accla'mare *vt* applaud; (*eleggere*) acclaim. ~zi'one *nf* applause

acclima'tare *vt* acclimatize. ~si *vr* get acclimatized

ac'cludere *vt* enclose. ~so *a* enclosed

accocco'larsi *vr* squat

accogli'ente *a* welcoming; (*confortevole*) cosy. ~za *nf* welcome

ac'cogliere *vt* receive; (*conpiacere*) welcome; (*contenere*) hold

accol'larsi *vr* take on (*responsabilità, debiti, doveri*). accol'lato *a* high-necked

accoltel'lare *vt* knife

accomia'tare *vt* dismiss. ~si *vr* take one's leave (da of)

accomo'dante *a* accommodating

accomo'dare *vt* (*riparare*) mend; (*disporre*) arrange. ~si *vr* make oneself at home; si accomodi! come in!; (*si sieda*) take a seat!

accompagna'mento *nm* accompaniment; (*seguito*) retinue

accompa'gnare *vt* accompany; ~re qcno a casa see sb home; ~re qcno alla porta show sb out. ~'tore, ~'trice *nmf* companion; (*di comitiva*) escort; *Mus* accompanist

accomu'nare *vt* pool

acconci'are *vt* arrange. ~'tura *nf* hair-style; (*ornamento*) headdress

accondiscen'dente *a* too obliging. ~za *nf* excessive desire to please

accondi'scendere *vi* ~ a condescend; comply with (*desiderio*); (*acconsentire*) consent to

acconsen'tire *vi* consent

acconten'tare *vt* satisfy. ~si *vr* be content (di with)

ac'conto *nm* deposit; in ~ on account; lasciare un ~ leave a deposit

accop'pare *vt fam* bump off

accoppia'mento *nm* coupling; (*di animali*) mating

accoppi'are *vt* couple; mate (*animali*). ~rsi *vr* pair off; mate. ~ta *nf* (*scommessa*) bet placed on two horses for first and second place

acco'rato *a* sorrowful

accorci'are *vt* shorten. ~si *vr* get shorter

accor'dare *vt* concede; match (*colori ecc*); *Mus* tune. ~si *vr* agree

ac'cordo *nm* agreement; *Mus* chord; (*armonia*) harmony; andare d'~ get on well; d'~! agreed!; essere d'~ agree; prendere accordi con qcno make arrangements with sb

ac'corgersi *vr* ~ di notice; (*capire*) realize

accorgi'mento *nm* shrewdness; (*espediente*) device

ac'correre *vi* hasten

accor'tezza *nf* (*previdenza*) forethought

ac'corto *a* shrewd; **mai ~** incautious

accosta'mento *nm* (*di colori*) combination

acco'sta|re *vt* draw close to; approach (*persona*); set ajar (*porta ecc*). **~si** *vr* **~si a** come near to

accovacci'ar|si *vr* crouch, squat down. **~to a** squatting

accoz'zaglia *nf* jumble; (*di persone*) mob

accoz'zare *vt* **~ colori** mix colours that clash

accredita'mento *nm* credit; **~ tramite bancogiro** Bank Giro Credit

accredi'tare *vt* confirm (*notizia*); *Comm* credit

ac'cresc|ere *vt* increase. **~ersi** *vr* grow larger. **~i'tivo** *a* augmentative

accucci'ar|si *vr* (*cane:*) lie down; (*persona:*) crouch

accu'dire *vi* **~ a** attend to

accumu'la|re *vt* accumulate. **~rsi** *vr* pile up, accumulate. **~tore** *nm* accumulator; *Auto* battery. **~zi'one** *nf* accumulation. **ac'cumulo** *nm* (*di merce*) build-up

accura'tezza *nf* care

accu'rato *a* careful

ac'cusa *nf* accusation; *Jur* charge; **essere in stato di ~** *Jur* have been charged; **la Pubblica A~** *Jur* the public prosecutor

accu'sa|re *vt* accuse; *Jur* charge; complain of (*dolore*); **~re ricevuta di** *Comm* acknowledge receipt of. **~to, -a** *nmf* accused. **~tore** *nm* *Jur* prosecutor

a'cerbo *a* sharp; (*immaturo*) unripe

'acero *nm* maple

a'cerrimo *a* implacable

ace'tone *nm* nail polish remover

a'ceto *nm* vinegar

A.C.I. *abbr* (**Automobile Club d'Italia**) Italian Automobile Association

acidità *nf* acidity. **~ di stomaco** acid stomach

'acido *a* acid; (*persona*) sour ● *nm* acid

a'cidulo *a* slightly sour

'acino *nm* berry; (*chicco*) grape

'acne *nf* acne

'acqua *nf* water; **fare ~** *Naut* leak; **~ in bocca!** *fig* mum's the word!. **~ di Colonia** eau de Cologne. **~ corrente** running water. **~ dolce** fresh water. **~ minerale** mineral water. **~ minerale gassata** fizzy mineral water. **~ naturale** still mineral water. **~ potabile** drinking water. **~ salata** salt water. **~ tonica** tonic water

acqua'forte *nf* etching

ac'quaio *nm* sink

acquama'rina *a* aquamarine

acqua'rello *nm* = **acquerello**

ac'quario *nm* aquarium; *Astr* Aquarius

acqua'santa *nf* holy water

acqua'scooter *nm inv* water-scooter

ac'quatico *a* aquatic

acquat'tarsi *vr* crouch

acqua'vite *nf* brandy

acquaz'zone *nm* downpour

acque'dotto *nm* aqueduct

'acqueo a vapore ~ water vapour

acque'rello *nm* water-colour

acqui'rente *nmf* purchaser

acqui'si|re *vt* acquire. **~to a** acquired. **~zi'one** *nf* attainment

acqui'st|are *vt* purchase; (*ottenere*) acquire. **ac'quisto** *nm* purchase, **uscire per gli acquisti** go shopping; **fare ~i** shop

acqui'trino *nm* marsh

acquo'lina *nf* **far venire l'~ in bocca a qcno** make sb's mouth water

ac'quoso *a* watery

'acre *a* acrid; (*al gusto*) sour; *fig* harsh

a'crilico *nm* acrylic

a'croba|ta *nmf* acrobat. **~'zia** *nf* acrobatics *pl*

a'cronimo *nm* acronym

acu'ir|e vt sharpen. **~si** vr become more intense

a'culeo nm sting; Bot prickle

a'cume nm acumen

acumi'nato a pointed

a'custic|a nf acoustics pl. **~o a** acoustic

acu'tezza nf acuteness

acutiz'zarsi vr become worse

a'cuto a sharp; (suono) shrill; (freddo, odore) intense; Gram, Math, Med acute ● nm Mus high note

adagi'ar|e vt lay down. **~si** vr lie down

a'dagio adv slowly ● nm Mus adagio; (proverbio) adage

adattabilità nf adaptability

adatta'mento nm adaptation; **avere spirito di ~** be adaptable

adatta'r|e vt adapt; (aggiustare) fit. **~rsi** vr adapt. **~'tore** nm adaptor. **a'datto a** suitable (a for); (giusto) right

addebita'mento nm debit. **~ diretto** direct debit

addebi'tare vt debit; ascribe (colpa)

ad'debito nm charge

addensa'mento nm thickening; (di persone) gathering

adden'sar|e vt thicken. **~si** vr thicken; (affollarsi) gather

adden'tare vt bite

adden'trarsi vr penetrate

ad'dentro adv deeply; **essere ~ in** be in on

addestra'mento nm training

adde'strar|e vt train. **~si** vr train

ad'detto, -a a assigned ● nm employee; (diplomatico) attaché; **addetti** pl ai lavori persons involved in the work. **~ stampa** information officer, press officer

addiaccio nm **dormire all'~** sleep in the open

addi'etro adv (indietro) back; (nel passato) before

ad'dio nm & int goodbye. **~ al celibato** stag night, stag party

addirit'tura adv (perfino) even;

(assolutamente) absolutely; **~!** really!

ad'dirsi vr **~ a** suit

addi'tare vt point at; (in mezzo a un gruppo) point out; fig point to

addi'tivo a & nm additive

addizio'nale a additional. **~'mente** adv additionally

addizio'nare vt add [up]. **addizi'one** nf addition

addob'bare vt decorate. **ad'dobbo** nm decoration

addol'cir|e vt sweeten; tone down (colore); fig soften. **~si** vr fig mellow

addolo'ra|re vt grieve. **~rsi** vr be upset (per by). **~to a** pained, distressed

ad'dom|e nm abdomen. **~i'nale** a abdominal; [muscoli] **addominali** pl abdominals

addomesti'ca|re vt tame. **~'tore** nm tamer

addormen'ta|re vt put to sleep. **~rsi** vr go to sleep. **~to a** asleep; fig slow

addos'sar|e vt **~e a** (appoggiare) lean against; (attribuire) lay on. **~si** vr (ammassarsi) crowd; shoulder (responsabilità ecc)

ad'dosso adv on; **~ a** prep on; (molto vicino) right next to; **mettere gli occhi ~ a** qcno/qcsa hanker after sb/sth; **non mettermi le mani ~!** keep your hands off me!; **stare ~ a** qcno fig be on sb's back

ad'durre vt produce (prova, documento); give (pretesto, esempio)

adegua'mento nm adjustment

adegua'r|e vt adjust. **~rsi** vr conform. **~to a** adequate; (conforme) consistent

a'dempi|ere vt fulfil. **~'mento** nm fulfilment

ade'noidi nfpl adenoids

ade'ren|te a adhesive; (vestito) tight ● nmf follower. **~za** nf adhesion. **~ze** npl connections

ade'rire vi **~ a** stick to, adhere

to; support ‹sciopero, petizione›; agree to ‹richiesta›

adesca'mento nm Jur soliciting

ade'scare vt bait; fig entice

adesi'one nf adhesion; fig agreement

ade'sivo a adhesive ● nm sticker; Auto bumper sticker

a'desso adv now; ‹poco fa› just now; ‹tra poco› any moment now; **da ~ in poi** from now on; **per ~** for the moment

adia'cente a adjacent; **~ a** next to

adi'bire vt **~ a** put to use as

'adipe nm adipose tissue

adi'ra|rsi vr get irate. **~to** a irate

a'dire vt resort to; **~ le vie legali** take legal proceedings

'adito nm **dare ~ a** give rise to

adocchi'are vt eye; ‹con desiderio› covet

adole'scen|te a & nmf adolescent. **~za** nf adolescence. **~zi'ale** a adolescent

adom'brar|e vt darken; fig veil. **~si** vr ‹offendersi› take offence

adope'rar|e vt use. **~si** vr take trouble

ado'rabile a adorable

ado'ra|re vt adore. **~zi'one** nf adoration

ador'nare vt adorn

adot't|are vt adopt. **~ivo** a adoptive. **adozi'one** nf adoption

ad prep = **a** ‹davanti a vocale›

adrena'lina nf adrenalin

adri'atico a Adriatic ● nm **l'A~** the Adriatic

adu'la|re vt flatter. **~tore**, **~trice** nmf flatterer. **~zi'one** nf flattery

adulte'ra|re vt adulterate. **~to** a adulterated

adul'terio nm adultery. **a'dultero**, **-a** a adulterous ● nm adulterer ● nf adulteress

a'dulto, **-a** a & nmf adult; ‹maturo› mature

adu'nanza nf assembly

adu'na|ro vt gather. **~ta** nf Mil parade

a'dunco a hooked

ae'rare vt air ‹stanza›

a'ereo a aerial; ‹dell'aviazione› air attrib ● nm aeroplane, plane

ae'robic|a nf aerobics. **~o** a aerobic

aerodi'namic|a nf aerodynamics sg. **~o** a aerodynamic

aero'nautic|a nf aeronautics sg; Mil Air Force. **~o** a aeronautical

aero'plano nm aeroplane

aero'porto nm airport

aero'scalo nm cargo and servicing area

aero'sol nm inv aerosol

'afa nf sultriness

af'fabil|e a affable. **~ità** nf affability

affaccen'da|rsi vr busy oneself ‹a with›. **~to** a busy

affacci'arsi vr show oneself; **~ alla finestra** appear at the window

affa'ma|re vt starve [out]. **~to** a starving

affan'na|re vt leave breathless. **~rsi** vr busy oneself ‹agitarsi› get worked up. **~to** a breathless; dal respiro **~to** wheezy. **affanno** nm breathlessness; fig worry

af'fare nm matter; Comm transaction, deal; ‹occasione› bargain; **affari** pl business; **non sono affari tuoi** fam it's none of your business. **affa'rista** nmf wheeler-dealer

affasci'nante a fascinating; ‹persona, sorriso› bewitching

affasci'nare vt bewitch; fig charm

affatica'mento nm fatigue

affati'car|e vt tire; ‹sfinire› exhaust. **~si** vr tire oneself out; ‹affannarsi› strive

af'fatto adv completely; **non...** not... at all; **niente ~!** not at all!

affer'ma|re vt affirm; ‹sostenere› assert. **~rsi** vr establish oneself

affermativa'mente adv in the affirmative

afferma'tivo a affirmative

affermazi'one nf assertion; ‹successo› achievement

affer'rar|e vt seize; catch ⟨oggetto⟩; (capire) grasp; **~e al volo** fig be quick on the uptake. **~si** vr **~si a** grasp at

affet'ta|re vt slice; (ostentare) affect. **~to** a sliced; ⟨sorriso, maniere⟩ affected ● nm cold meat, sliced meat. **~zi'one** nf affectation

affet'tivo a affective; **rapporto ~** emotional tie

af'fetto[1] nm affection; **con ~** affectionately

af'fetto[2] a **~ da** suffering from

affettuosità nf inv ⟨gesto⟩ affectionate gesture

affettu'oso a affectionate

affezio'na|rsi vr **~rsi a** grow fond of. **~to** a devoted (a to)

affian'car|e vt put side by side; Mil flank; fig support. **~si** vr come side by side; fig stand together; **~si a qcno** fig help sb out

affiata'mento nm harmony

affia'ta|rsi vr get on well together. **~to** a close-knit; **una coppia ~ta** a very close couple

affibbi'are vt **~ qcsa a qcno** saddle sb with sth; **~ un pugno a qcno** let fly at sb

affi'dabil|e a dependable. **~ità** nf dependability

affida'mento nm (Jur: dei minori) custody; **fare ~ su qcno** rely on sb; **non dare ~** not inspire confidence

affi'dar|e vt entrust. **~si** vr **~si a** rely on

affievo'lirsi vr grow weak

af'figgere vt affix

affi'lare vt sharpen

affili'ar|e vt affiliate. **~si** vr become affiliated

affi'nare vt sharpen; (perfezionare) refine

affinché conj so that, in order that

af'fin|e a similar. **~ità** nf affinity

affiora'mento nm emergence; Naut surfacing

affio'rare vi emerge; fig come to light

af'fisso nm bill; Gram affix

affitta'camere nm inv landlord ● nf inv landlady

affit'tare vt (dare in affitto) let; (prendere in affitto) rent; **'affittasi'** 'to let', 'for rent'

af'fitt|o nm rent; **contratto d'~o** lease; **dare in ~o** let; **prendere in ~o** rent. **~u'ario, -a** nmf Jur lessee

af'fligger|e vt torment. **~si** vr distress oneself

af'fli|tto a distressed. **~zi'one** nf distress; fig affliction

afflosci'arsi vr become floppy; (accasciarsi) flop down; ⟨morale:⟩ decline

afflu'en|te a & nm tributary. **~za** nf flow; (di gente) crowd

afflu'ire vi flow; fig pour in

af'flusso nm influx

affo'ga|re vt/i drown; Culin poach; **~re in** fig be swamped with. **~to** a ⟨persona⟩ drowned; ⟨uova⟩ poached. **~to al caffè** nm ice cream with hot espresso poured over it

affol'la|re vt, **~rsi** vr crowd. **~to** a crowded

affonda'mento nm sinking

affon'dare vt/i sink

affossa'mento nm pothole

affran'ca|re vt redeem ⟨bene⟩; stamp ⟨lettera⟩; free ⟨schiavo⟩. **~rsi** vr free oneself. **~'trice** nf franking machine. **~'tura** nf stamping; (di spedizione) postage

af'franto a prostrated; (esausto) worn out

af'fresco nm fresco

affret'ta|re vt speed up. **~rsi** vr hurry. **~ta'mente** adv hastily. **~to** a hasty

affron'tar|e vt face; confront ⟨il nemico⟩; meet ⟨le spese⟩. **~si** vr clash

af'fronto nm affront, insult; **fare un ~ a qcno** insult sb

affumi'ca|re vt fill with smoke; Culin smoke. **~to** a ⟨prosciutto, formaggio⟩ smoked

affuso'la|re vt taper [off]. **~to** a tapering

afo'risma *nm* aphorism

a'foso *a* sultry

'Africa *nf* Africa. **afri'cano, -a** *a* & *nmf* African

afrodi'siaco *a* & *nm* aphrodisiac

a'genda *nf* diary

agen'dina *nf* pocket-diary

a'gente *nm* agent; **agenti** *pl* atmosferici atmospheric agents. **~ di cambio** stockbroker. **~ di polizia** policeman

agen'zia *nf* agency; *(filiale)* branch office; *(banca)* branch. **~ di viaggi** travel agency. **~ immobiliare** estate agency

agevo'lare *vt* facilitate. **~zi'one** *nf* facilitation

a'gevole *a* easy; *(strada)* smooth. **~'mente** *adv* easily

agganci'are *vt* hook up; *Rail* couple. **~si** *vr* *(vestito:)* hook up

ag'geggio *nm* gadget

agget'tivo *nm* adjective

agghiacci'ante *a* terrifying

agghiacci'are *vt* *fig* ~ qcno make sb's blood run cold. **~si** *vr* freeze

agghin'darle *vt* *fam* dress up. **~si** *vr* *fam* doll oneself up. **~to** *a* dressed up

aggiorna'mento *nm* up-date

aggior'narle *vt* *(rinviare)* postpone; *(mettere a giorno)* bring up to date. **~si** *vr* get up to date. **~to** *a* up-to-date; *(versione)* updated

aggi'rarle *vt* surround; *(fig:ingannare)* trick. **~si** *vr* hang about; **~si su** *(discorso ecc:)* be about; *(somma:)* be around

aggiudi'carle *vt* award; *(all'asta)* knock down. **~si** *vr* win

aggi'un|gere *vt* add. **~ta** *nf* addition. **~tivo** *a* supplementary. **~to** *a* added ● *a* & *nm* *(assistente)* assistant

aggiu'starle *vt* mend; *(sistemare)* settle; *(fam: mettere a posto)* fix. **~si** *vr* adapt; *(mettersi in ordine)* tidy oneself up; *(decidere)* sort things out; *(tempo:)* clear up

agglomera'mento *nm* conglomeration

agglome'rato *nm* built-up area

aggrap'parle *vt* grasp. **~si** *vr* **~si a** cling to

aggra'vante *Jur* *nf* aggravation ● *a* aggravating

aggra'var|e *vt* *(peggiorare)* make worse; increase *(pena)*; *(appesantire)* weigh down. **~si** *vr* worsen

aggrazi'ato *a* graceful

aggre'dire *vt* attack

aggre'ga|re *vt* add; *(associare a un gruppo ecc)* admit. **~rsi** *vr* **~rsi a** join. **~to** *a* associated ● *nm* aggregate; *(di case)* block

aggressi'one *nf* aggression; *(atto)* attack

aggres'sivo *a* aggressive. **~ività** *nf* aggressiveness. **~ore** *nm* aggressor

aggrin'zare, aggrin'zire *vt* wrinkle

aggrot'tare *vt* **~ le ciglia/la fronte** frown

aggrovigli'a|re *vt* tangle. **~rsi** *vr* get entangled; *fig* get complicated. **~to** *a* entangled; *fig* confused

agguan'tare *vt* catch

aggu'ato *nm* ambush; *(tranello)* trap; **stare in ~** lie in wait

agguer'rito *a* fierce

agia'tezza *nf* comfort

agi'ato *a* *(persona)* well off; *(vita)* comfortable

a'gibile *a* *(palazzo)* fit for human habitation. **~ità** *nf* fitness for human habitation

a'gille *a* agile. **~ità** *nf* agility

'agio *nm* ease; **mettersi a proprio ~** make oneself at home

a'gire *vi* act; *(comportarsi)* behave; *(funzionare)* work; **~ su** affect

agi'tarle *vt* shake; wave *(mano)*; *(fig: turbare)* trouble. **~rsi** *vr* toss about; *(essere inquieto)* be restless; *(mare:)* get rough. **~to** *a* restless; *(mare)* rough. **~tore, ~'trice** *nmf* *(persona)* agitator. **~zi'one** *nf* agitation; **mettere in ~zione** qcno make sb worried

'agli = a + gli

'aglio nm garlic

a'gnello nm lamb

agno'lotti nmpl ravioli sg

a'gnostico, -a a & nmf agnostic

'ago nm needle

ago'ni|a nf agony. **~z'zare** vi be on one's deathbed

ago'nistic|a nf competition. **~o** a competitive

agopun'tura nf acupuncture

a'gosto nm August

a'grari|a nf agriculture. **~o** a agricultural ● nm landowner

a'gricolo a agricultural. **~'tore** nm farmer. **~'tura** nf agriculture

agri'foglio nm holly

agritu'rismo nm farm holidays, agro-tourism

'agro a sour

agroalimen'tare a food attrib

agro'dolce a bitter-sweet; Culin sweet-and-sour; **in** ~ sweet and sour

agrono'mia nf agronomy

a'grume nm citrus fruit; (pianta) citrus tree

aguz'zare vt sharpen; ~ **le orecchie** prick up one's ears; ~ **la vista** look hard

aguz'zino nm slave-driver; (carceriere) jailer

ahimè int alas

'ai = a + i

'Aia nf L'~ The Hague

'aia nf threshing-floor

Aids nmf Aids

ai'rone nm heron

ai'tante a sturdy

aiu'ola nf flower-bed

aiu'tante nmf assistant ● nm Mil adjutant. ~ **di campo** aide-de-camp

aiu'tare vt help

ai'uto nm help, aid; (assistente) assistant

aiz'zare vt incite; ~ **contro** set on

al = a + il

'ala nf wing; **fare** ~ make way

ala'bastro nm alabaster

'alacre a brisk

a'lano nm Great Dane

'alba nf dawn

Alba'n|ia nf Albania. **a~ese** a & nmf Albanian

albeggi'are vi dawn

albe'ra|to a wooded; (viale) tree-lined. **~'tura** nf Naut masts pl.

albe'rello nm sapling

al'berg|o nm hotel. **~o diurno** hotel where rooms are rented during the daytime. **~a'tore, ~a'trice** nmf hotel-keeper. **~hi'ero** a hotel attrib

'albero nm tree; Naut mast; Mech shaft. **~ genealogico** family tree. ~ **maestro** Naut mainmast. ~ **di Natale** Christmas tree

albi'cocc|a nf apricot. **~o** nm apricot-tree

al'bino nm albino

'albo nm register; (libro ecc) album; (per avvisi) notice board

'album nm album. ~ **da disegno** sketch-book

al'bume nm albumen

'alce nm elk

'alcol nm alcohol; Med spirit; (liquori forti) spirits pl; **darsi all'**~ take to drink. **al'colici** nmpl alcoholic drinks. **al'colico** a alcoholic. **alco'lismo** nm alcoholism. **~iz'zato, -a** a & nmf alcoholic

alco'test® nm inv Breathalyser®

al'cova nf alcove

al'cun, al'cuno a & pron any; **non ha** ~ **amico** he hasn't any friends, he has no friends. **alcuni** pl some, a few; **~i suoi amici** some of his friends

alea'torio a unpredictable

a'letta nf Mech fin

alfa'betico a alphabetical

alfabetizzazi'one nf ~ **della popolazione** teaching people to read and write

alfa'beto nm alphabet

alfi'ere nm (negli scacchi) bishop

al'fine adv eventually, in the end

'alga nf seaweed

'algebra nf algebra

Alge'ri|a *nf* Algeria. **a~no, -a** *a & nmf* Algerian

all'ante *nm* glider

'alibi *nm inv* alibi

alie'na|re *vt* alienate. **~rsi** *vr* become estranged; **~rsi le simpatie di** qcno lose sb's good will. **~to, -a** *a* alienated ● *nmf* lunatic

a'lieno, -a *nmf* alien ● *a* è **~ da invidia** envy is foreign to him

alimen'ta|re *vt* feed; *fig* foment ● *a* food *attrib*; *(abitudine)* dietary ● *nm* **~ri** *pl* food-stuffs. **~'tore** *nm* power unit. **~zi'one** *nf* feeding

ali'mento *nm* food; **alimenti** *pl* food; *Jur* alimony

a'liquota *nf* share; *(di imposta)* rate

ali'scafo *nm* hydrofoil

'alito *nm* breath

'alla = **a + la**

allaccia'mento *nm* connection

allacci'ar|e *vt* fasten *(cintura)*; lace up *(scarpe)*; do up *(vestito)*; *(collegare)* connect; form *(amicizia)*. **~si** *vr* do up, fasten *(vestito, cintura)*

allaga'mento *nm* flooding

alla'gar|e *vt* flood. **~si** *vr* become flooded

allampa'nato *a* lanky

allarga'mento *nm (di strada, ricerche)* widening

allar'gar|e *vt* widen; open *(braccia, gambe)*; let out *(vestito ecc)*; *fig* extend. **~si** *vr* widen

allar'mante *a* alarming

allar'ma|re *vt* alarm. **~to** *a* panicky

al'larme *nm* alarm; **dare l'~** raise the alarm; **falso ~** *fig* false alarm. **~ aereo** air raid warning

allar'mis|mo *nm* alarmism. **~ta** *nmf* alarmist

allatta'mento *nm (di animale)* suckling; *(di neonato)* feeding

allat'tare *vt* suckle *(animale)*; feed *(neonato)*

'alle = **a + le**

alle'a|nza *nf* alliance. **~to, -a** *a* allied ● *nmf* ally

alle'ar|e *vt* unite. **~si** *vr* form an alliance

alle'gare[1] *vt* *Jur* allege

alle'gare[2] *vt (acchiudere)* enclose; set on edge *(denti)*. **~to** *a* enclosed ● *nm* enclosure; in **~to** attached, appended. **~zi'one** *nf* *Jur* allegation

allegge'rir|e *vt* lighten; *fig* alleviate. **~si** *vr* become lighter; *(vestirsi leggero)* put on lighter clothes

allego'ria *nf* allegory. **alle'gorico** *a* allegorical

allegra'mente *adv* breezily

alle'gria *nf* gaiety

al'legro *a* cheerful; *(colore)* bright; *(brillo)* tipsy ● *nm Mus* allegro

alle'luia *int* hallelujah!

allena'mento *nm* training

alle'na|re *vt*, **~rsi** *vr* train. **~'tore, ~'trice** *nmf* trainer, coach

allen'tar|e *vt* loosen; *fig* relax. **~si** *vr* become loose; *Mech* work loose

aller'gia *nf* allergy. **al'lergico** *a* allergic

al'lerta *nf* **stare ~** be alert, be on the alert

allesti'mento *nm* preparation. **~ scenico** *Theat* set

alle'stire *vt* prepare; stage *(spettacolo)*; *Naut* fit out

allet'tante *a* alluring

allet'tare *vt* entice

alleva'mento *nm* breeding; *(progresso)* bringing up; *(luogo)* farm; *(per piante)* nursery; **pollo di ~** battery chicken

alle'vare *vt* bring up *(bambini)*; breed *(animali)*; grow *(piante)*

allevi'are *vt* alleviate; *fig* lighten

alli'bito *a* astounded

allibra'tore *nm* bookmaker

allie'tar|e *vt* gladden. **~si** *vr* rejoice

alli'evo, -a *nmf* pupil ● *nm Mil* cadet

alliga'tore *nm* alligator

allinea'mento *nm* alignment

alline'ar|e *vt* line up; *Typ* align; *Fin* adjust. **~si** *vr* fall into line

'**allo** = a + lo

al'**locco** nm Zool tawny owl

al'**lodola** nf [sky]lark

alloggi'**are** vt 〈persona:〉 put up; 〈casa:〉 provide accommodation for; Mil billet ● vi put up, stay; Mil be billeted. al'**loggio** nm 〈appartamento〉 flat; Mil billet

allontana'**mento** nm removal

allonta'**nar|e** vt move away; 〈licenziare〉 dismiss; avert 〈pericolo〉. **~si** vr go away

al'**lora** adv then; 〈in quel tempo〉 at that time; 〈in tal caso〉 in that case; **d'~ in poi** from then on; **e ~?** what now?; 〈e con ciò?〉 so what?; **fino ~** until then

al'**loro** nm laurel; Culin bay

'**alluce** nm big toe

alluci'**na|nte** a fam incredible; sostanza **~nte** hallucinogen. **~to, -a** nmf fam space cadet. **~zi'one** nf hallucination

allucino'**geno** a 〈sostanza〉 hallucinatory

al'**ludere** vi **~ a** allude to

allu'**minio** nm aluminium

allun'**gar|e** vt lengthen; stretch [out] 〈gamba〉; extend 〈tavolo〉; 〈diluire〉 dilute; **~e il collo** crane one's neck. **~e le mani su** qcno touch sb up. **~e il passo** quicken one's step. **~si** vr grow longer; 〈crescere〉 grow taller; 〈sdraiarsi〉 lie down

allusi'**one** nf allusion

allu'**sivo** a allusive

alluvio'**nale** a alluvial

alluvi'**one** nf flood

al'**meno** adv at least; **[se] ~ venisse il sole!** if only the sun would come out!

a'**logeno** nm halogen ● a **lampada alogena** halogen lamp

a'**lone** nm halo

'**Alpi** nfpl **le ~** the Alps

alpi'**nis|mo** nm mountaineering. **~ta** nmf mountaineer

al'**pino** a Alpine ● nm Mil **gli alpini** the Alpine troops

al'**quanto** a a certain amount of ● adv rather of

alt int stop

alta'**lena** nf swing; 〈tavola in bilico〉 see-saw

alta'**lenare** vi fig vacillate

al'**tale** nm altar

alta'**mente** adv highly

al'**tare** nm altar

alta'**rino** nm **scoprire gli altarini di** qcno reveal sb's guilty secrets

alte'**rar|e** vt alter; adulterate 〈vino〉; 〈falsificare〉 falsify. **~rsi** vr be altered; 〈cibo:〉 go bad; 〈merci:〉 deteriorate; 〈arrabbiarsi〉 get angry. **~to** a 〈vino〉 adulterated. **~zi'one** nf alteration; 〈di vino〉 adulteration

al'**terco** nm altercation

alter'**nanza** nf alternation

alter'**na|re** vt, **~rsi** vr alternate. **~'tiva** a alternative. **~'tivo** a alternate. **~to** a alternating. **~'tore** nm Electr alternator

al'**tern|o** a alternate; **a giorni ~i** every other day

al'**tero** a haughty

al'**tezza** nf height; 〈profondità〉 depth; 〈suono〉 pitch; 〈di tessuto〉 width; 〈titolo〉 Highness; **essere all'~ di** be on a level with; fig be up to

altezzos|a'**mente** adv haughtily. **~ità** nf haughtiness

altez'**zoso** a haughty

al'**ticcio** a tipsy, merry

al'**tipiano** nm plateau

alti'**tudine** nf altitude

'**alto** a high; 〈di statura〉 tall; 〈profondo〉 deep; 〈suono〉 high-pitched; 〈tessuto〉 wide; Geog northern; **a notte alta** in the middle of the night; **avere degli alti e bassi** have some ups and downs; **ad alta fedeltà** high-fidelity; **a voce alta, ad alta voce** in a loud voice; 〈leggere〉 aloud; **essere in ~ mare** be on the high seas. **alta finanza** nf high finance. **alta moda** nf high fashion. **alta tensione** nf high voltage ● adv high; **in ~** at the top; 〈guardare:〉 up; **mani in ~!** hands up!

alto'forno nm blast-furnace

altolà int halt there!

altolo'cato a highly placed

altopar'lante nm loudspeaker

altopi'ano nm plateau

altret'tanto a & pron as much; (pl) as many ● adv likewise; **buona fortuna! – grazie, ~** good luck! – thank you, the same to you

altri'menti adv otherwise

'altro a other; **un ~, un'altra** another; **l'altr'anno** last year; **domani l'~** the day after tomorrow; **l'ho visto l'~ giorno** I saw him the other day ● pron other [one]; **un ~, un'altra** another [one]; **ne vuoi dell'~?** would you like some more?; **l'un l'~** one another; **nessun ~** nobody else; **gli altri** (la gente) other people ● nm something else; **non fa ~ che lavorare** he does nothing but work; **deside-ra ~?** (in negozio) anything else?; **più che ~, sono stanco** I'm tired more than anything; **se non ~** at least; **senz'~** certainly; **tra l'~** what's more; **~ che!** and how!

altro'ieri nm **l'~** the day before yesterday

al'tronde adv **d'~** on the other hand

al'trove adv elsewhere

al'trui a other people's ● nm other people's belongings pl

altru'ismo nm altruism. **~ta** nmf altruist

al'tura nf high ground; Naut deep sea

a'lunno, -a nmf pupil

alve'are nm hive

al'za|re vt lift, raise; (costruire) build; Naut hoist; **~re le spalle** shrug one's shoulders; **~re i tac-chi** fig take to one's heels. **~rsi** vr rise; (in piedi) stand up; (da letto) get up; **~rsi in piedi** get to one's feet. **~ta** nf lifting; (aumento) rise; (da letto) getting up; Archit elevation. **~to** a up

a'mabile a lovable; (vino) sweet

a'maca nf hammock

amalga'mar|e vt, **~si** vr amalga-mate

a'mante a **~ di** fond of ● nm lover ● nf mistress, lover

ama'rena nf sour black cherry

ama'retto nm macaroon

a'ma|re vt love; be fond of, like (musica, sport ecc). **~to, -a** a loved ● nmf beloved

ama'rezza nf bitterness; (dolore) sorrow

a'maro a bitter ● nm bitterness; (liquore) bitters pl

ama'rognolo a rather bitter

ama'tore, -'trice nmf lover

ambasci'a|ta nf embassy; (mes-saggio) message. **~tore, -'trice** nm ambassador ● nf ambassa-dress

ambe'due a & pron both

ambien'ta|le a environmental. **~lista** a & nmf environmentalist

ambien'tar|e vt acclimatize; set (personaggio, film ecc). **~si** vr get acclimatized

ambi'ente nm environment; (stan-za) room; fig milieu

ambigu'ità nf inv ambiguity; (di persona) shadiness

am'biguo a ambiguous; (persona) shady

am'bire vi **~ a** aspire to

'ambito nm sphere

ambiva'len|te a ambivalent. **~za** nf ambivalence

ambizi'o|ne nf ambition. **~so** a ambitious

'ambra nf amber. **am'brato** a am-ber

ambu'lante a wandering; **vendi-tore ~** hawker

ambu'lanza nf ambulance

ambula'torio nm (di medico) sur-gery; (di ospedale) out-patients' [department]

a'meba nf amoeba

'amen int amen

a'meno a pleasant

A'merica nf America. **~ del Sud** South America. **ameri'cano, -a** a & nmf American

ame'tista *nf* amethyst

ami'anto *nm* asbestos

ami'chevole *a* friendly

ami'cizia *nf* friendship; fare ~ con qcno make friends with sb; amicizie *pl* (amici) friends

a'mico, -a *nmf* friend; ~ del cuore bosom friend

'amido *nm* starch

ammac'ca|re *vt* dent; bruise ⟨frutto⟩. ~rsi *vr* ⟨metallo:⟩ get dented; ⟨frutto:⟩ bruise. ~to *a* dented; ⟨frutto⟩ bruised. ~tura *nf* dent; (livido) bruise

ammae'stra|re *vt* (istruire) teach; train ⟨animale⟩. ~to *a* trained

ammai'nare *vt* lower ⟨bandiera⟩; furl ⟨vele⟩

amma'la|rsi *vr* fall ill. ~to, -a *a* ill ● *nmf* sick person; (paziente) patient

ammali'are *vt* bewitch

am'manco *nm* deficit

ammanet'tare *vt* handcuff

ammani'cato *a* essere ~ have connections

amma'raggio *nm* splashdown

amma'rare *vi* put down on the sea; ⟨nave spaziale:⟩ splash down

ammas'sar|e *vt* amass. ~si *vr* crowd together. am'masso *nm* mass; (mucchio) pile

ammat'tire *vi* go mad

ammaz'zar|e *vt* kill. ~si *vr* (suicidarsi) kill oneself; (rimanere ucciso) be killed

am'menda *nf* amends *pl*; (multa) fine; fare ~ di qcsa make amends for sth

am'messo *pp di* am'mettere ● *conj* ~ che supposing that

am'mettere *vt* admit; (riconoscere) acknowledge; (supporre) suppose

ammic'care *vi* wink

ammini'stra|re *vt* administer; (gestire) run. ~tivo *a* administrative. ~tore, ~trice *nmf* administrator; (di azienda) manager; (di società) director. ~tore delegato managing director. ~zi'one *nf* ad-

ministration; fatti di ordinaria ~zione *fig* routine matters

ammi'ragli|o *nm* admiral. ~'ato *nm* admiralty

ammi'ra|re *vt* admire. ~to a re-stare/essere ~to be full of admiration. ~'tore, ~'trice *nmf* admirer. ~zi'one *nf* admiration.

ammi'revole *a* admirable

ammis'sibile *a* admissible

ammissi'one *nf* admission; (approvazione) acknowledgement

ammobili'a|re *vt* furnish. ~to *a* furnished

am'modo *a* proper ● *adv* properly

am'mollo *nm* in ~ soaking

ammo'niaca *nf* ammonia

ammoni'mento *nm* warning; (di rimprovero) admonishment

ammo'ni|re *vt* warn; (rimproverare) admonish. ~'tore *a* admonishing. ~zi'one *nf Sport* warning

ammon'tare *vi* ~ a amount to ● *nm* amount

ammonticchi'are *vt* heap up

ammorbi'dente *nm* (per panni) softener

ammorbi'dir|e *vt*, ~si *vr* soften

ammorta'mento *nm Comm* amortization

ammor'tare *vt* pay off (spesa); *Comm* amortize (debito)

ammortiz'za|re *vt Comm* = ammortare; *Mech* damp. ~'tore *nm* shock-absorber

ammosci'ar|e *vt* make flabby. ~si *vi* get flabby

ammucchi'a|re *vt*, ~rsi *vr* pile up. ~ta *nf* (sl: orgia) orgy

ammuf'fi|re *vi* go mouldy. ~to *a* mouldy

ammuti'na|mento *nm* mutiny

ammuti'narsi *vr* mutiny

ammuto'lire *vi* be struck dumb

amne'sia *nf* amnesia

amni'stia *nf* amnesty

'amo *nm* hook; *fig* bait

amo'rale *a* amoral

a'more *nm* love; fare l'~ make love; per l'amor di Dio/del cielo! for heaven's sake!; andare d'~ e

d'accordo get on like a house on fire; **~ proprio** self-respect; **è un ~** *(persona)* he/she is a darling; **per ~ di** for the sake of; **amori** *pl* love affairs. **~ggi'are** *vi* flirt.

amo'revole *a* loving

a'morfo *a* shapeless; *(persona)* colourless, grey

amo'roso *a* a loving; *(sguardo ecc)* amorous; *(lettera, relazione)* love

ampi'ezza *nf* *(di esperienza)* breadth; *(di stanza)* spaciousness; *(di gonna)* fullness; *(importanza)* scale

'ampio *a* ample; *(esperienza)* wide; *(stanza)* spacious; *(vestito)* loose; *(gonna)* full; *(pantaloni)* baggy

am'plesso *nm* embrace

amplia'mento *nm* *(di casa, porto)* enlargement; *(di strada)* widening

ampli'are *vt* broaden *(conoscenze)*

amplifi'ca|re *vt* amplify; *fig* magnify. **~'tore** *nm* amplifier. **~zi'one** *nf* amplification

am'polla *nf* cruet

ampol'loso *a* pompous

ampu'ta|re *vt* amputate. **~zi'one** *nf* amputation

amu'leto *nm* amulet

anabbagli'ante *a* *Auto* dipped ● *nmpl* **anabbaglianti** dipped headlights

anacro'nis|mo *nm* anachronism. **~tico** *a* **essere ~** be an anachronism

a'nagrafe *nf* *(ufficio)* registry office; *(registro)* register of births, marriages and deaths

ana'grafico *a* **dati** *nmpl* **anagrafici** personal data

ana'gramma *nm* anagram

anal'colico *a* non-alcoholic ● *nm* soft drink, non-alcoholic drink

a'nale *a* anal

analfa'be|ta *a & nmf* illiterate. **~tismo** *nm* illiteracy

anal'gesico *nm* painkiller

a'nalisi *nf inv* analysis; *Med* test. **~ grammaticale/del periodo/logica** parsing. **~ del sangue** blood test

ana'li|sta *nmf* analyst. **~tico** *a* analytical. **~z'zare** *vt* analyse; *Med* test

anal'lergico *a* hypoallergenic

analo'gia *nf* analogy. **a'nalogo** *a* analogous

'ananas *nm inv* pineapple

anar'chi|a *nf* anarchy. **a'narchico, -a** *a* anarchic ● *nmf* anarchist. **~smo** *nm* anarchism

A.N.A.S. *nf abbr* **(Azienda Nazionale Autonoma delle Strade)** *national road maintenance authority*

anato'mia *nf* anatomy. **ana'tomico** *a* anatomical; *(sedia)* contoured, ergonomic

'anatra *nf* duck

ana'troccolo *nm* duckling

'anca *nf* hip; *(di animale)* flank

ance'strale *a* ancestral

'anche *conj* also, too; *(persino)* even; **~ se** even if; **~ domani** tomorrow also o too, also tomorrow

anchilo'sato *a fig* stiff

an'cora *adv* still, yet; *(di nuovo)* again; *(di più)* some more; **~ una volta** once more

'anco|ra *nf* anchor; **gettare l'~ra** drop anchor. **~'raggio** *nm* anchorage. **~'rare** *vt* anchor

anda'mento *nm* *(del mercato, degli affari)* trend

an'dante *a* *(corrente)* current; *(di poco valore)* cheap ● *nm* *Mus* andante

an'da|re *vi* go; *(funzionare)* work; **~ via** *(partire)* leave; *(macchia:)* come out; **~ [bene]** *(confarsi)* suit; *(taglia:)* fit; **ti va bene alle tre?** does three o'clock suit you?; **non mi va di mangiare** I don't feel like eating; **~ di fretta** be in a hurry; **~ fiero di** be proud of; **~ di moda** be in fashion; **va' in** **[là]!** come on!; **come va?** how are things?; **~** a male go off; **~ a fuoco** go up in flames; **va spedito** **[entro]** stamattina it must be sent this morning; **ne va del mio lavoro** my job is at stake; **come è andata**

a finire? how did it turn out?;
cosa vai dicendo? what are you
talking about? ~rsene go away;
(morire) pass away ● nm going; a
lungo ~re eventually
'andito nm passage
an'drone nm entrance
a'neddoto nm anecdote
ane'lare vt ~ a long for. a'nelito
nm longing
a'nello nm ring; (di catena) link
ane'mia nf anaemia. a'nemico a
anaemic
a'nemone nm anemone
aneste'sia nf anaesthesia; (sostanza) anaesthetic. ~'sta nmf
anaesthetist. ane'stetico a & nm
anaesthetic
an'fibi nmpl (stivali) army boots
an'fibio nm (animale) amphibian
● a amphibious
anfite'atro nm amphitheatre
'anfora nf amphora
an'fratto nm ravine
an'gelico a angelic
'angelo nm angel. ~ custode
guardian angel
angli'c|ano a Anglican. ~ismo
nm Anglicism
an'glofilo, -a a a & nmf Anglophile
an'glofono, -a nmf English-
speaker
anglo'sassone a & nmf Anglo-
Saxon
ango'la|re a angular. ~zi'one nf
angle shot
'angolo nm corner; Math angle. ~
[di] cottura kitchenette
ango'loso a angular
an'gosci|a nf anguish. ~'are vt
torment. ~'ato a agonized. ~'oso
a (disperato) anguished; (che dà
angoscia) distressing
angu'illa nf eel
an'guria nf water-melon
an'gusti|a nf (ansia) anxiety; (pe-
nuria) poverty. ~'are vt distress.
~'arsi vr be very worried (per
about)
an'gusto a narrow

'anice nm anise; Culin aniseed;
(liquore) anisette
ani'dride nf ~ carbonica carbon
dioxide
'anima nf soul; non c'era ~ viva
there was not a soul about; all'~!
good grief!; un'~ in pena a soul in
torment. ~ gemella soul mate
ani'ma|le a nm animal; ~li
domestici pl pets. ~'lesco a animal
ani'ma|re vt give life to; (ravviva-
re) enliven; (incoraggiare) encourage. ~rsi vr come to life; (acca-
lorarsi) become animated. ~to
a animate; (discussione) animated;
(paese) lively. ~'tore, ~'trice nmf
leading spirit; Cinema animator.
~zi'one nf animation
'animo nm (mente) mind; (indole)
disposition; (cuore) heart; perdersi d'~ lose heart; farsi ~ take
heart. ~sità nf animosity
ani'moso a brave; (ostile) hostile
'anitra nf = anatra
annac'qua|re vt anche fig water
down. ~to a watered down
annaffi'a|re vt water. ~'toio nm
watering-can
an'nali nmpl annals
anna'spare vi flounder
an'nata nf year; (importo annuale)
annual amount; (di vino) vintage
annebbia'mento nm fog build-up;
fig clouding
annebbi'ar|e vt cloud (vista, men-
te). ~si vr become foggy; (vista,
mente:) grow dim
annega'mento nm drowning
anne'ga|re vt/i drown
anne'ri|re vt/i blacken. ~si vr be-
come black
annessi'one nf (di nazione) an-
nexation
an'nesso pp di annettere ● a attached; (stato) annexed
an'nettere vt add; (accludere) enclose; annex (stato)
annichi'lire vt annihilate
anni'darsi vr nest
annienta'mento nm annihilation

annien'tar|e vt annihilate. ~si vr abase oneself

anniver'sario a & nm anniversary. ~ di matrimonio wedding anniversary

'anno nm year; Buon A~! Happy New Year!; quanti anni ha? how old are you?; Tommaso ha dieci anni Thomas is ten [years old]. ~ bisestile leap year

anno'dar|e vt knot; do up (cintura); fig form. ~si vr become knotted

annoi'a|re vt bore; (recare fastidio) annoy. ~rsi vr get bored; (condizione) be bored. ~to a bored

anno'ta|re vt note down; annotate (testo). ~zi'one nf note

annove'rare vt number

annu'a|le a annual, yearly. ~rio nm year-book

annu'ire vi nod; (acconsentire) agree

annulla'mento nm annulment; (di appuntamento) cancellation

annul'lar|e vt annul; cancel (appuntamento); (togliere efficacia a) undo; disallow (gol); (distruggere) destroy. ~si vr cancel each other out

annunci'a|re vt announce; (preannunciare) foretell. ~tore, ~trice nmf announcer. ~zi'one nf Annunciation

an'nuncio nm announcement; (pubblicitario) advertisement; (notizia) news. annunci pl economici classified advertisements

'annuo a annual, yearly

annu'sare vt sniff

annuvo'lar|e vt cloud. ~si vr cloud over

'ano nm anus

anoma'lia nf anomaly

a'nomalo a anomalous

anoni'mato nm mantenere l'~ remain anonymous

a'nonimo, -a a anonymous ● nmf (pittore, scrittore) anonymous painter/writer

anores'sia nf Med anorexia

ano'ressico, -a nmf anorexic

anor'mal|e a abnormal ● nmf deviant, abnormal person. ~ità nf inv abnormality

'ansa nf handle; (di fiume) bend

an'sare vi pant

'ansia, ansietà nf anxiety; stare/ essere in ~ per be anxious about

ansi'oso a anxious

antago'nis|mo nm antagonism. ~ta nmf antagonist

an'tartico a & nm Antarctic

ante'cedente a preceding ● nm precedent

ante'fatto nm prior event

ante'guerra a pre-war ● nm pre-war period

ante'nato, -a nmf ancestor

an'tenna nf Radio, TV aerial; (di animale) antenna; Naut yard. ~ parabolica satellite dish

ante'porre vt put before

ante'prima nf preview; vedere qcsa in ~ have a sneak preview of sth

anteri'ore a front attrib; (nel tempo) previous

antiade'rente ⟨padella⟩ nonstick

anti'aereo a anti-aircraft attrib

antial'lergico a hypoallergenic

antia'tomico a rifugio ~ fallout shelter

antibi'otico a & nm antibiotic

anti'caglia nf ⟨oggetto⟩ piece of old junk

antica'mente adv in ancient times, long ago

anti'camera nf ante-room; far ~ be kept waiting

antichità nf inv antiquity; (oggetto) antique

antici'clone nm anticyclone

antici'pa|re vt advance; Comm pay in advance; (prevedere) anticipate; (prevenire) forestall ● vi be early. ~ta'mente adv in advance. ~zi'one nf anticipation; (notizia) advance news

an'ticipo nm advance; (caparra)

deposit; **in ~** early; *(nel lavoro)* ahead of schedule

an'tico *a* ancient; *(mobile ecc)* antique; *(vecchio)* old; **all'antica** old-fashioned ●*nmpl* **gli antichi** the ancients

anticoncezio'nale *a* & *nm* contraceptive

anticonfor'mis|mo *nm* unconventionality. **~ta** *nmf* nonconformist. **~tico** *a* unconventional, nonconformist

anticonge'lante *a* & *nm* antifreeze

anti'corpo *nm* antibody

anticostituzio'nale *a* unconstitutional

anti'crimine *a* *inv* *(squadra)* crime *attrib*

antidemo'cratico *a* undemocratic

antidolo'rifico *nm* painkiller

an'tidoto *nm* antidote

anti'droga *a* *inv* *(campagna)* anti-drugs; *(squadra)* drug *attrib*

antie'stetico *a* ugly

antifa'scismo *nm* anti-fascism

antifa'scista *a* & *nmf* anti-fascist

anti'forfora *a* *inv* dandruff *attrib*

anti'furto *nm* anti-theft device; *(allarme)* alarm ●*a* *inv* *(sistema)* anti-theft

anti'gelo *nm* antifreeze; *(para-brezza)* defroster

antigi'enico *a* unhygienic

An'tille *nfpl* **le ~** the West Indies

an'tilope *nf* antelope

antin'cendio *a* *inv* **allarme ~** fire alarm; **porta ~** fire door

anti'nebbia *nm* *inv* *Auto (faro)* ~ foglamp, foglight

antinfiamma'torio *a* & *nm* anti-inflammatory

antinucle'are *a* anti-nuclear

antio'rario *a* anti-clockwise

anti'pasto *nm* hors d'oeuvre, starter

antipa'tia *nf* antipathy. **anti'patico** *a* unpleasant

an'tipodi *nmpl* antipodes; **essere agli ~** *fig* be poles apart

antiquari'ato *nm* antique trade

anti'quario, -a *nmf* antique dealer

anti'quato *a* antiquated

anti'ruggine *nm* *inv* rust-inhibitor

anti'rughe *a* *inv* anti-wrinkle *attrib*

anti'scippo *a* *inv* theft-proof

anti'semita *a* anti-Semitic

anti'settico *a* & *nm* antiseptic

antisoci'ale *a* anti-social

antista'minico *nm* antihistamine

anti'stante *a* *prep* in front of

anti'tarlo *nm* *inv* woodworm treatment

antiterro'ristico *a* antiterrorist *attrib*

an'titesi *nf* *inv* antithesis

antolo'gia *nf* anthology

'antro *nm* cavern

antropolo'gia *nf* anthropology. **antro'pologo, -a** *nmf* anthropologist

anu'lare *nm* ring-finger

'anzi *conj* in fact; *(o meglio)* or better still; *(al contrario)* on the contrary

anziani'tà *nf* old age; *(di servizio)* seniority

anzi'ano, -a *a* old, elderly; *(di grado ecc)* senior ●*nmf* elderly person

anzi'ché *conj* rather than

anzi'tempo *adv* prematurely

anzi'tutto *adv* first of all

a'orta *nf* aorta

apar'titico *a* unaligned

apa'tia *nf* apathy. **a'patico** *a* apathetic

'ape *nf* bee; **nido** *nm* **di api** honeycomb

aperi'tivo *nm* aperitif

aperta'mente *adv* openly

a'perto *a* open; **all'aria aperta** in the open air; **all'~** open-air

aper'tura *nf* opening; *(inizio)* beginning; *(ampiezza)* spread; *(di arco)* span; *Pol* overtures *pl*; *Phot* aperture; **~ mentale** openness

'apice *nm* apex

apicol'tura *nf* beekeeping

ap'nea *nf* immersione in ~ free diving

a'polide *a* stateless ● *nmf* stateless person

a'postolo *nm* apostle

apostro'fare *vt* (*mettere un apostrofo a*) write with an apostrophe; reprimand (*persona*)

a'postrofo *nm* apostrophe

appaga'mento *nm* fulfilment

appa'ga|re *vt* satisfy. **~rsi** *vr* **~rsi di** be satisfied with

appai'are *vt* pair; mate (*animali*)

appallotto'lare *vt* roll into a ball

appalta'tore *nm* contractor

ap'palto *nm* contract; **dare in ~** contract out

appan'naggio *nm* (*in denaro*) annuity; *fig* prerogative

appan'nar|e *vt* mist (*vetro*); dim (*vista*). **~si** *vr* mist over; (*vista*) grow dim

appa'rato *nm* apparatus; (*pompa*) display

apparecchi'a|re *vt* prepare ● *vi* lay the table. **~'tura** *nf* (*impianti*) equipment

appa'recchio *nm* apparatus; (*congegno*) device; (*radio, tv ecc*) set; (*aeroplano*) aircraft. **~ acustico** hearing aid

appa'ren|te *a* apparent. **~te-'mente** *adv* apparently. **~za** *nf* appearance; **in ~za** apparently

appa'ri|re *vi* appear; (*sembrare*) look. **~'scente** *a* striking; *pej* gaudy **~zi'one** *nf* apparition

apparta'mento *nm* flat, apartment *Am*

appar'ta|rsi *vr* withdraw. **~to** *a* secluded

apparte'nenza *nf* membership

apparte'nere *vi* belong

appassio'nante *a* (*storia, argomento*) exciting

appassio'na|re *vt* excite; (*commuovere*) move. **~rsi** *vr* **~rsi a** become excited by. **~to** *a* passionate; **~to di** (*entusiastico*) fond of

appas'sir|e *vi* wither. **~si** *vr* fade

appel'larsi *vr* ~ **a** appeal to

ap'pello *nm* appeal; (*chiamata per nome*) rollcall; (*esami* exam session); **fare l'~** call the roll

ap'pena *adv* just; (*a fatica*) hardly ● *conj* [**non**] ~ as soon as, no sooner... than

ap'pendere *vt* hang [up]

appendi'abiti *nm inv* hat-stand, hallstand

appen'dice *nf* appendix. **appendi-'cite** *nf* appendicitis

Appen'nini *nmpl* **gli** ~ the Apennines

appesan'tir|e *vt* weigh down. **~si** *vr* become heavy

ap'peso *pp di* **appendere** ● *a* hanging; (*impiccato*) hanged

appe'ti|to *nm* appetite; **aver ~to** be hungry; **buon ~to!** enjoy your meal!. **~'toso** *a* appetizing; *fig* tempting

appezza'mento *nm* plot of land

appia'nar|e *vt* level; *fig* smooth over. **~si** *vr* improve

appiat'tir|e *vt* flatten. **~si** *vr* flatten oneself

appic'care *vt* ~ **il fuoco** a set fire to

appicci'car|e *vt* stick; **~e a** (*fig: appioppare*) palm off on ● *vi* be sticky. **~si** *vr* stick; (*cose:*) stick together; **~si a qcno** *fig* stick to sb like glue

appiccica'ticcio *a* sticky; *fig* clingy

appicci'coso *a* sticky; *fig* clingy

appie'dato *a* **sono rimasto** ~ I don't have the car; **sono rimasto** ~ I was stranded

appi'eno *adv* fully

appigli'arsi *vr* ~ **a** get hold of; (*fig* stick to. **ap'piglio** *nm* finger-hold; (*per piedi*) foothold; *fig* pretext

appiop'pare *vt* ~ **a** palm off on; (*fam: dare*) give

appiso'larsi *vr* doze off

applau'dire *vt/i* applaud. **ap'plau-so** *nm* applause

appli'cabile *a* applicable

appli'ca|re *vt* apply; enforce (*legge ecc*). **~rsi** *vr* apply oneself. **~'tore**

nm applicator. **~zi'one** *nf* application; *(di legge)* enforcement

appoggi'ar|e *vt* lean (a against); *(mettere)* put; *(sostenere)* back. **~si** *vr* **~si a** lean against; *fig* rely on. **ap'poggio** *nm* support

appol'lai'arsi *vr fig* perch

ap'porre *vt* affix

appor'tare *vt* bring; *(causare)* cause. **ap'porto** *nm* contribution

apposita'mente *adv* especially

ap'posito *a* proper

ap'posta *adv* on purpose; *(espressamente)* specially

apposta'mento *nm* ambush; *(caccia)* lying in wait

appo'star|e *vt* post *(soldati)*. **~si** *vr* lie in wait

ap'prend|ere *vt* understand; *(imparare)* learn. **~i'mento** *nm* learning

appren'di|sta *nmf* apprentice. **~'stato** *nm* apprenticeship

apprensi'one *nf* apprehension; **essere in ~** be anxious about. **appren'sivo** *a* apprehensive

ap'presso *adv & prep (vicino)* near; *(dietro)* behind; **come ~** as follows

appre'star|e *vt* prepare. **~si** *vr* get ready

apprez'za|bile *a* appreciable. **~'mento** *nm* appreciation; *(giudizio)* opinion

apprez'za|re *vt* appreciate. **~to a** *(apprezzato)* appreciated

ap'proccio *nm* approach

appro'dare *vi* land; **~ a** *fig* come to; **non ~ a nulla** come to nothing. **ap'prodo** *nm* landing; *(luogo)* landing-stage

approfit'tar|e *vi* take advantage *(di* of*)*, profit *(di* by*)*. **~'tore**, **~'trice** *nmf* chancer

approfondi'mento *nm* deepening; **di ~** *(fig: esame)* further

approfon'dir|e *vt* deepen. **~rsi** *vr (divario:)* widen. **~to a** *(studio, ricerca)* in-depth

appropri'a|rsi *vr (essere adatto a)* suit; **~rsi di** take possession of.

~to *a* appropriate. **~zi'one** *nf Jur* appropriation. **~zione indebita** *Jur* embezzlement

approssi'ma|re *vt* **~re per eccesso/difetto** round up/down. **~rsi** *vr* draw near. **~tiva'mente** *adv* approximately. **~'tivo** *a* approximate. **~zi'one** *nf* approximation

appro'va|re *vt* approve of; approve *(legge)*. **~zi'one** *nf* approval

approvvigiona'mento *nm* supplying; **approvvigionamenti** *pl* provisions

approvvigio'nar|e *vt* supply. **~si** *vr* stock up

appunta'mento *nm* appointment, date *fam*; **fissare un ~** make an appointment; **darsi ~** decide to meet

appun'tar|e *vt (annotare)* take notes; *(fissare)* fix; *(con spillo)* pin; *(appuntire)* sharpen. **~si** *vr* **su** *(teoria:)* be based on

appun'ti|re *vt* sharpen. **~to a** *(mento)* pointed

ap'punto¹ *nm* note; *(piccola critica)* niggle

ap'punto² *adv* exactly; **per l'~!** exactly!; **stavo ~ dicendo...** I was just saying...

appu'rare *vt* verify

a'pribile *a* that can be opened

apribot'tiglie *nm inv* bottle-opener

a'prile *nm* April; **il primo d'~** April Fools' Day

a'prir|e *vt* open; turn on *(luce, acqua ecc)*; *(con chiave)* unlock; open up *(ferita ecc)*. **~si** *vr* open; *(spaccarsi)* split; *(confidarsi)* confide **(con** in*)*

apri'scatole *nm inv* tin-opener

aqua'planing *nm* **andare in ~** aquaplane

'aquila *nf* eagle; **non è un'~al** he is no genius!. **~'lino** *a* aquiline

aqui'lone *nm (giocattolo)* kite

ara'besco *nm* arabesque; *hum* scribble

A'rabia Sau'dita *nf* l'**~** Saudi Arabia

'arabo, -a a Arab; ⟨lingua⟩ Arabic ● *nmf* Arab ● *nm* ⟨lingua⟩ Arabic

a'rachide *nf* peanut

ara'gosta *nf* lobster

a'rancia *nf* orange. **~'ata** *nf* orangeade. **~o** *nm* orange-tree; ⟨colore⟩ orange. **~'one** a & *nm* orange

a'rare *vt* plough. **~tro** *nm* plough

ara'tura *nf* ploughing

a'razzo *nm* tapestry

arbi'trar|e *vt* arbitrate in; Sport referee. **~ietà** *nf* arbitrariness. **~io** a arbitrary

ar'bitrio *nm* will; **è un ~** it's very high-handed

'arbitro *nm* arbiter; Sport referee; ⟨nel baseball⟩ umpire

ar'busto *nm* shrub

'arca *nf* ark; ⟨cassa⟩ chest

ar'ca|ico a archaic. **~'ismo** *nm* archaism

ar'cangelo *nm* archangel

ar'cata *nf* arch; ⟨serie di archi⟩ arcade

archeolo'gia *nf* archaeology. **~o'logico** a archaeological. **~'ologo, -a** *nmf* archaeologist

ar'chetto *nm* Mus bow

archit'ettare *vt* fig devise; **cosa state architettando?** *fig* what are you plotting?

archi'tet|to *nm* architect. **~'tonico** a architectural. **~'tura** *nf* architecture

archivi'are *vt* file; Jur close

ar'chivio *nm* archives *pl*; Comput file

archi'vista *nmf* filing clerk

ar'cigno a grim

arci'pelago *nm* archipelago

arci'vescovo *nm* archbishop

'arco *nm* arch; Math arc; ⟨arma, Mus⟩ bow; **nell'~ di una giornata/due mesi** in the space of a day/two months

arcoba'leno *nm* rainbow

arcu'ar|e *vt* bend. **~rsi** *vr* bend. **~to** a bent, curved; ⟨schiena di gatto⟩ arched

ar'dente a burning; *fig* ardent. **~'mente** *adv* ardently

'ardere *vt/i* burn

ar'desia *nf* slate

ar'di|re *vi* dare. **~to** a dar. ⟨coraggioso⟩ bold; ⟨sfacciato⟩ impudent

ar'dore *nm* ⟨calore⟩ heat; *fig* ardour

'arduo a arduous; ⟨ripido⟩ steep

'area *nf* area. **~ di rigore** ⟨in calcio⟩ penalty area. **~ di servizio** service area

a'rena *nf* arena

are'narsi *vr* run aground; ⟨fig: trattative⟩ reach deadlock; **mi sono arenato** I'm stuck

'argano *nm* winch

argen'tato a silver-plated

argente'ria *nf* silver[ware]

ar'gento *nm* silver

ar'gilla *nf* clay. **~'loso** a ⟨terreno⟩ clayey

argi'nare *vt* embank; *fig* hold in check, contain

'argine *nm* embankment; ⟨diga⟩ dike

argomen'tare *vi* argue

argo'mento *nm* argument; ⟨motivo⟩ reason; ⟨soggetto⟩ subject

argu'ire *vt* deduce

ar'gu|to a witty. **~zia** *nf* wit; ⟨battuta⟩ witticism

'aria *nf* air; ⟨aspetto⟩ appearance; Mus tune; **andare all'~** *fig* come to nothing; **avere l'~...** look...; **corrente d'~** draught; **mandare all'~ qcsa** *fig* ruin sth

aridità *nf* aridity, dryness

'arido a arid

arieggi'ar|e *vt* air. **~to** a airy

ari'ete *nm* ram. **A~** Astr Aries

ari'etta *nf* ⟨brezza⟩ breeze

a'ringa *nf* herring

ari'oso a ⟨locale⟩ light and airy

aristo'cra|tico, -a a aristocratic ● *nmf* aristocrat. **~zia** *nf* aristocracy

arit'metica *nf* arithmetic

arlec'chino *nm* Harlequin; *fig* buffoon

'arma *nf* weapon; **armi** *pl* arms; ⟨forze armate⟩ [armed] forces;

chiamare alle armi call up; **sotto le armi** in the army; **alle prime armi** *fig* inexperienced, fledg[e]-ling. **~ da fuoco** firearm. **~ impropria** makeshift weapon. **~ a doppio taglio** *fig* double-edged sword

armadi'etto *nm* locker, cupboard

ar'madio *nm* cupboard; (*guarda-roba*) wardrobe

armamen'tario *nm* tools *pl*; *fig* paraphernalia

arma'mento *nm* armament; *Naut* fitting out

ar'ma|re *vt* arm; (*equipaggiare*) fit out; *Archit* reinforce. **~rsi** *vr* arm oneself (**di** with). **~ta** *nf* army; (*flotta*) fleet. **~'tore** *nm* shipowner. **~'tura** *nf* framework; (*impalcatura*) scaffolding; (*di guerriero*) armour

armeggi'are *vi fig* manoeuvre

armi'stizio *nm* armistice

armo'ni|a *nf* harmony. **ar'monica** *nf* **~ [a bocca]** mouth organ. **ar'monico** *a* harmonic. **~'oso** *a* harmonious

armoniz'zar|e *vt* harmonize ● *vi* match. **~si** *vr* (*colori:*) go together, match

ar'nese *nm* tool; (*oggetto*) thing; (*congegno*) gadget; **male in ~** in bad condition

'arnia *nf* beehive

a'roma *nf* aroma; **aromi** *pl* herbs. **~tera'pia** *nf* aromatherapy

aro'matico *a* aromatic

aromatiz'zare *vt* flavour

'arpa *nf* harp

ar'peggio *nm* arpeggio

ar'pia *nf* harpy

arpi'one *nm* hook; (*pesca*) harpoon

arrabat'tarsi *vr* do all one can

arrabbi'a|rsi *vr* get angry. **~to** *a* angry. **~'tura** *nf* rage; **prendersi un'~tura** fly into a rage

arraf'fare *vt* grab

arrampi'ca|rsi *vr* climb [up]. **~ta** *nf* climb. **~'trice** *nmf*

climber. **~'tore sociale** social climber

arran'care *vi* limp, hobble; *fig* struggle, limp along

arrangia'mento *nm* arrangement

arrangi'ar|e *vt* arrange. **~si** *vr* manage; **~si alla meglio** get by; **ar'rangiati** get on with it!

arra'parsi *vr fam* get randy

arre'care *vt* bring; (*causare*) cause

arreda'mento *nm* interior decoration; (*l'arredare*) furnishing; (*mobili ecc*) furnishings *pl*

arre'da|re *vt* furnish. **~'tore, ~'trice** *nmf* interior designer. **ar'redo** *nm* furnishings *pl*

ar'rendersi *vr* surrender

arren'devo|le *a* (*persona*) yielding. **~'lezza** *nf* softness

arre'star|e *vt* arrest; (*fermare*) stop. **~si** *vr* halt. **ar'resto** *nm* stop; *Med, Jur* arrest; **la dichiaro in [stato d']arresto** you are under arrest; **mandato di arresto** warrant. **arresti** *pl* **domiciliari** *Jur* house arrest

arre'tra|re *vt/i* withdraw; pull back (*giocatore*). **~to** *a* (*paese ecc*) backward; (*Mil: posizione*) rear; **numero ~to** (*di rivista*) back number; **del lavoro ~to** a backlog of work ● *nm* (*di stipendio*) back pay

arre'trati *nmpl* arrears

arricchi'mento *nm* enrichment

arric'chi|re *vt* enrich. **~rsi** *vr* get rich. **~to, -a** *nmf* nouveau riche

arricci'are *vt* curl; **~ il naso** turn up one's nose

ar'ringa *nf* harangue; *Jur* closing address

arrischi'a|rsi *vr* dare. **~to** *a* risky; (*imprudente*) rash

arri'va|re *vi* arrive; **~re a** (*raggiungere*) reach; (*ridursi*) be reduced to. **~to, -a** *a* successful; **ben ~to!** welcome! ● *nmf* successful person

arrive'derci *int* goodbye; **~ a domani** see you tomorrow

arri'vis|mo *nm* social climbing;

(nel lavoro) careerism. **~ta** *nmf* social climber; *(nel lavoro)* careerist

ar'rivo *nm* arrival; *Sport* finish

arro'gan|te *a* arrogant. **~za** *nf* arrogance

arro'garsi *vr* **~ il diritto di fare qcsa** take it upon oneself to do sth

arrossa'mento *nm* reddening

arros'sa|re *vt* make red, redden *(occhi).* **~si** *vr* go red

arros'sire *vi* blush, go red

arro'stire *vt* roast; toast *(pane);* *(ai ferri)* grill. **ar'rosto** *a & nm* roast

arroto'lare *vt* roll up

arroton'dar|e *vt* round; *Math ecc* round off. **~si** *vr* become round; *(persona:)* get plump

arrovel'larsi *vr* **~ il cervello** rack one's brains

arroven'ta|re *vt* make red-hot. **~rsi** *vr* become red-hot. **~to** *a* red-hot

arruf'fa|re *vt* ruffle; *fig* confuse. **~to** *a (capelli)* ruffled

arruffianarsi *vr* **~ qcno** *fig* butter sb up

arruggi'ni|re *vt* rust. **~rsi** *vr* go rusty; *fig (fisicamente)* stiffen up; *(conoscenze:)* go rusty. **~to** *a* rusty

arruola'mento *nm* enlistment

arruo'lar|e *vt/i,* **~si** *vr* enlist

arse'nale *nm* arsenal; *(cantiere)* [naval] dockyard

ar'senico *nm* arsenic

'arso *pp di* ardere ● *a* burnt; *(arido)* dry. **ar'sura** *nf* burning heat; *(sete)* parching thirst

'arte *nf* art; *(abilità)* craftsmanship; **le belle arti** the fine arts. **arti figurative** figurative arts

arte'fa|re *vt* adulterate *(vino);* disguise *(voce).* **~tto** *a* fake; *(vino)* adulterated

ar'tefice *nmf* craftsman; craftswoman; *fig* author

ar'teria *nf* artery. **~ [stradale]** arterial road

arteriosclo'rosi *nf* arteriosclerosis, hardening of the arteries

'artico *a & nm* Arctic

artico'la|re *a* articular ● *vt* articulate; *(suddividere)* divide. **~rsi** *vr fig* **~rsi in** consist of. **~to** *a Auto* articulated; *fig* well-constructed. **~zi'one** *nf Anat* articulation

ar'ticolo *nm* article. **~ di fondo** leader

artifici'ale *a* artificial

arti'fici|o *nm* artifice; *(affettazione)* affectation; **~'oso** *a* artful; *(affettato)* affected

artigia'na|le *a* made by hand; *hum* amateurish. **~'mente** *adv* with craftsmanship; *hum* amateurishly

artigia|'nato *nm* craftsmanship; *(ceto)* craftsmen *pl.* **~'ano, -a** *nm* craftsman ● *nf* craftswoman

artigli'ere *nm* artilleryman. **~e'ria** *nf* artillery

ar'tiglio *nm* claw; *fig* clutch

ar'tist|a *nmf* artist. **~ica'mente** *adv* artistically. **~ico** *a* artistic

'arto *nm* limb

ar'trite *nf* arthritis

ar'trosi *nf* rheumatism

arzigogo'lato *a* fantastic, bizarre

ar'zillo *a* sprightly

a'scella *nf* armpit

ascen'den|te *a* ascending ● *nm (antenato)* ancestor; *(influenza)* ascendancy; *Astr* ascendant

ascensi'one *nf* ascent; **l'A~** the Ascension

ascen'sore *nm* lift, elevator *Am*

a'scesa *nf* ascent; *(al trono)* accession; *(al potere)* rise

a'scesso *nm* abscess

a'sceta *nmf* ascetic

'ascia *nf* axe

asciugabianche'ria *nm inv (stenditoio)* clothes horse

asciugaca'pelli *nm inv* hair dryer, hairdrier

asciuga'mano *nm* towel

asciu'gar|e *vt* dry. **~si** *vr* dry oneself; *(diventare asciutto)* dry up

asci'utto *a* dry; *(magro)* wiry; *(risposta)* curt; **essere all'~** *fig* be hard up

ascol'ta|re vt listen to ● vi listen.
~ **'tore**, ~ **'trice** nmf listener

a'scolto nm listening; **dare ~ a**
listen to; **mettersi in ~** Radio
tune in

asfal'tare vt asphalt

a'sfalto nm asphalt

asfis'si|a nf asphyxia. ~ **'ante** a
⟨caldo⟩ oppressive; ⟨fig: persona⟩
annoying. ~ **'are** vt asphyxiate; fig
annoy

'Asia nf Asia. **asi'atico, -a** a & nmf
Asian

a'silo nm shelter; ⟨d'infanzia⟩
nursery school. ~ **nido** day
nursery. ~ **politico** political asylum

asim'metrico a asymmetrical

'asino nm donkey; ⟨fig: persona
stupida⟩ ass

'asma nf asthma. **a'smatico** a
asthmatic

asoci'ale a asocial

'asola nf buttonhole

a'sparagi nmpl asparagus sg

a'sparago nm asparagus spear

asperità nf inv harshness; ⟨di
terreno⟩ roughness

aspet'ta|re vt wait for; ⟨prevedere⟩
expect; ~ **re un bambino** be ex-
pecting [a baby]; **fare ~ qcno**
keep sb waiting ● vi wait. ~ **rsi** vr
expect. ~ **'tiva** nf expectation

a'spetto[1] nm appearance; ⟨di
problema⟩ aspect; **di bell'~** good-
looking

a'spetto[2] nm **sala ~ d'~** waiting
room

aspi'rante a aspiring; ⟨pompa⟩
suction attrib ● nmf ⟨a un posto⟩
applicant; ⟨al trono⟩ aspirant; **gli
aspiranti al titolo** the contenders
for the title

aspira'polvere nm inv vacuum
cleaner

aspi'ra|re vt inhale; Mech suck in
● vi ~ **re a** aspire to. ~ **'tore** nm ex-
tractor fan. ~ **zi'one** nf inhalation;
Mech suction; ⟨ambizione⟩ ambition

aspi'rina nf aspirin

aspor'tare vt take away

aspra'mente adv ⟨duramente⟩ se-
verely

a'sprezza nf ⟨al gusto⟩ sourness;
⟨di clima⟩ severity; ⟨di suono⟩
harshness; ⟨di odore⟩ pungency

'aspro a ⟨al gusto⟩ sour; ⟨clima⟩ severe; ⟨suono, parole⟩ harsh;
⟨odore⟩ pungent; ⟨litigio⟩ bitter

assag'gi'are vt taste. ~ **'gini** nmpl
Culin samples. **as'saggio** nm tast-
ing; ⟨piccola quantità⟩ taste

as'sai adv very; ⟨moltissimo⟩ very
much; ⟨abbastanza⟩ enough

assa'li|re vt attack. ~ **'tore**, ~ **'trice**
nmf assailant

as'salto nm attack; **prendere d'~**
storm ⟨città⟩; fig mob ⟨persona⟩;
hold up ⟨banca⟩

assapo'rare vt savour

assassi'nare vt murder, assassi-
nate; fig murder

assas'sin|io nm murder, assassi-
nation. ~ **o, -a** a murderous ● nm
murderer ● nf murderess

'asse nf board ● nm Techn axle;
Math axis. ~ **da stiro** ironing
board

asselcon'dare vt satisfy; ⟨favori-
re⟩ support

assedi'are vt besiege. **as'sedio**
nm siege

asse'gna|mento nm allotment;
fare ~ su rely on

asse'gna|re vt allot; award ⟨pre-
mio⟩. ~ **'tario** nmf recipient.
~ **zi'one** nf ⟨di alloggio, borsa di stu-
dio⟩ allocation; ⟨di premio⟩ award

as'segno nm allowance; ⟨banca-
rio⟩ cheque; **contro ~** cash on delivery. ~ **circolare** bank draft.
assegni pl familiari family allowance. ~ **non trasferibile** cheque
made out to 'account payee

assem'blea nf assembly; ⟨adu-
nanza⟩ gathering

assembra'mento nm gathering

assen'nato a sensible

as'senso nm assent

assen'tarsi *vr* go away; (*da stanza*) leave the room

as'sen|te *a* absent; (*distratto*) absent-minded ● *nmf* absentee.
~te'ismo *nm* absenteeism.
~te'ista *nmf* frequent absentee.
~za *nf* absence; (*mancanza*) lack

asse'rire *vt* assert. **~tivo** *a* assertive. **~zi'one** *nf* assertion

assesso'rato *nm* department

asses'sore *nm* councillor

assesta'mento *nm* settlement

asse'star|e *vt* arrange; **~e un colpo** deal a blow. **~si** *vr* settle oneself

asse'tato *a* parched

as'setto *a* order; *Naut, Aeron* trim

assicu'ra|re *vt* assure; *Comm* insure; register (*posta*); (*fissare*) secure; (*accertare*) ensure. **~rsi** *vr* (*con contratto*) insure oneself; (*legarsi*) fasten oneself; **~rsi che** make sure that. **~tivo** *a* insurance *attrib*. **~tore, ~trice** *nmf* insurance agent ● *a* insurance *attrib*. **~zi'one** *nf* (*contratto*) insurance

assidera'mento *nm* exposure. **asside'rato** *a Med* suffering from exposure; (*fam*) frozen

assidu|a'mente *adv* assiduously. **~ità** *nf* assiduity

as'siduo *a* assiduous; (*cliente*) regular

assil'lante *a* (*persona, pensiero*) nagging

assil'lare *vt* pester

as'sillo *nm* worry

assimi'la|re *vt* assimilate. **~zi'one** *nf* assimilation

as'sise *nfpl* assizes; **Corte d'A~** Court of Assize[s]

assi'sten|te *nmf* assistant. **~te sociale** social worker. **~te di volo** flight attendant. **~za** *nf* assistance; (*presenza*) presence. **~za sociale** social work

assistenzi'a|le *a* welfare *attrib*. **~'lismo** *nm* welfare

as'sistere *vt* assist; (*curare*) nurse

● *vi* **~ a** (*essere presente*) be present at; watch (*spettacolo ecc*)

'asso *nm* ace; **piantare in ~** leave in the lurch

associ'a|re *vt* join; (*collegare*) associate. **~rsi** *vr* join forces; *Comm* enter into partnership. **~rsi** *a* join; subscribe to (*giornale ecc*). **~zi'one** *nf* association

assoget'tar|e *vt* subject. **~si** *vr* submit

asso'lato *a* sunny

assol'dare *vt* recruit

as'solo *nm Mus* solo

as'solto *pp di* **assolvere**

assoluta'mente *adv* absolutely

assolu'tismo *nm* absolutism

asso'lu|to *a* absolute. **~zi'one** *nf* acquittal; *Relig* absolution

as'solvere *vt* perform (*compito*); *Jur* acquit; *Relig* absolve

assomigli'ar|e *vi* **~e a** be like, resemble. **~si** *vr* resemble each other

assom'marsi *vr* combine; **~ a** qcsa add to sth

asso'nanza *nf* assonance

asson'nato *a* drowsy

asso'pirsi *vr* doze off

assor'bente *a & nm* absorbent. **~ igienico** sanitary towel

assor'bire *vt* absorb

assor'da|re *vt* deafen. **~nte** *a* deafening

assorti'mento *nm* assortment

assor'ti|re *vt* match (*colori*). **~to** *a* assorted; (*colori, persone*) matched

as'sorto *a* engrossed

assottigli'ar|e *vt* make thin; (*aguzzare*) sharpen; (*ridurre*) reduce. **~si** *vr* grow thin; (*finanze:*) be whittled away

assue'fa|re *vt* accustom. **~rsi** *vr* **~rsi a** get used to. **~tto** *a* (*a caffè, aspirina*) immune to the effects; (*a droga*) addicted. **~zi'one** *nf* (*a caffè, aspirina*) immunity to the effects; (*a droga*) addiction

as'sumere *vt* assume; take on (*im-*

piegato); ~ **informazioni** make inquiries

as'sunto *pp di* **assumere** ● *nm* task. **assunzi'one** *nf (di impiegato)* employment

assurdità *nf inv* absurdity; ~ *pl* nonsense

as'surdo *a* absurd

'asta *nf* pole; *Mech* bar; *Comm* auction; **a mezz'~** at half-mast

a'stemio *a* abstemious

aste'nersi *vr* abstain (**da** from). **~si'one** *nf* abstention

aste'nuto, -a *nmf* abstainer

aste'risco *nm* asterisk

astig'ma|tico *a* astigmatic. **~'tismo** *nm* astigmatism

asti'nenza *nf* abstinence; **crisi di** ~ cold turkey

'asti|o *nm* rancour; **avere ~o contro** qcno bear sb a grudge. **~'oso** *a* resentful

a'stratto *a* abstract

astrin'gente *a & nm* astringent

'astro *nm* star

astrolo'gia *nf* astrology. **a'strologo, -a** *nmf* astrologer

astro'nauta *nmf* astronaut

astro'nave *nf* spaceship

astrono'mia *nf* astronomy. **~o'nomico** *a* astronomical. **a'stronomo** *nm* astronomer

astrusità *nf* abstruseness

a'stuccio *nm* case

a'stu|to *a* shrewd; *(furbo)* cunning. **~zia** *nf* shrewdness; *(azione)* trick

ate'ismo *nm* atheism

A'tene *nf* Athens

'ateo, -a *a & nmf* atheist

a'tipico *a* atypical

at'lant|e *nm* atlas. **~ico** *a* Atlantic; **l'[Oceano] A~ico** the Atlantic [Ocean]

at'let|a *nmf* athlete. **~ica** *nf* athletics *sg*. **~ica leggera** track and field events. **~ica pesante** weight-lifting, boxing, wrestling, *etc.* **~ico** *a* athletic

atmo'sfer|a *nf* atmosphere. **~ico** *a* atmospheric

a'tomic|a *nf* atom bomb. **~o** *a* atomic

'atomo *nm* atom

'atrio *nm* entrance hall

a'troc|e *a* atrocious; *(terrible)* dreadful. **~ità** *nf inv* atrocity

atrofiz'zarsi *vr Med, fig* atrophy

attaccabot'toni *nmf inv* [crashing] bore

attacca'brighe *nmf inv* troublemaker

attacca'mento *nm* attachment

attacca'panni *nm inv* [coat-] hanger; *(a muro)* clothes hook

attac'car|e *vt* attach; *(legare)* tie; *(appendere)* hang; *(cucire)* sew on; *(contagiare)* pass on; *(assalire)* attack; *(iniziare)* start ● *vi* stick; *(diffondersi)* catch on. **~si** *vr* cling; *(affezionarsi)* become attached; *(litigare)* quarrel

attacca'ticcio *a* sticky

at'tacco *nm* attack; *(punto d'unione)* junction

attar'darsi *vr* stay late; *(indugiare)* linger

attec'chire *vi* take; *(moda ecc.)* catch on

atteggia'mento *nm* attitude

atteggi'ar|e *vt* assume. **~si** *vr* ~**si a** pose as

attem'pato *a* elderly

at'tender|e *vt* wait for ● *vi* ~ **a** attend to. **~si** *vr* expect

atten'dibil|e *a* reliable. **~ità** *nf* reliability

atte'nersi *vr* ~ **a** stick to

attenta'mente *adv* attentively

atten'ta|re *vi* ~ **re a** make an attempt on. **~to** *nm* act of violence; *(contro politico ecc)* assassination attempt. **~'tore, ~'trice** *nmf (a scopo politico)* terrorist

at'tento *a* attentive; *(accurato)* careful; ~! look out!; **stare** ~ pay attention

attenu'ante *nf* extenuating circumstance

attenu'a|re *vt* attenuate; *(minimizzare)* minimize; subdue *(colori,*

ecc⟩; calm ⟨*dolore*⟩; soften ⟨*colpo*⟩.
~rsi *vr* diminish. **~zi'one** *nf*
lessening

attenzi'one *nf* attention; **~!** watch
out!

atter'ra|ggio *nm* landing. **~re** *vt*
knock down ● *vi* land

atter'rir|e *vt* terrorize. **~si** *vr* be
terrified

at'tes|a *nf* waiting; (*aspettativa*)
expectation; **in ~a di** waiting for.
~o *pp di* **attendere**

atte'sta|re *vt* state; (*certificare*)
certify. **~to** *nm* certificate. **~zi-
'one** *nf* certificate; (*dichiarazione*)
declaration

'**attico** *nm* attic

at'tiguo *a* adjacent

attil'lato *a* ⟨*vestito*⟩ close-fitting

'**attimo** *nm* moment

atti'nente *a* ~ **a** pertaining to

at'tingere *vt* draw; *fig* obtain

atti'rare *vt* attract

atti'tudine *nf* (*disposizione*) aptitude; (*atteggiamento*) attitude

atti'v|are *vt* activate. **~ismo** *nm*
activism. **~ista** *nmf* activist.
attività *nf inv* activity; *Comm* assets *pl*. **~o** *a* active; *Comm* produc-
tive ● *nm* assets *pl*

attiz'za|re *vt* poke; *fig* stir up.
~'toio *nm* poker

'**atto** *nm* act; (*azione*) action;
Comm, *Jur* deed; (*certificato*) certificate; **atti** *pl* (*di società ecc*) proceedings; **mettere in ~** put into
effect

at'tonito *a* astonished

attorcigli'ar|e *vt* twist. **~si** *vr* get
twisted

at'tore *nm* actor

attorni'ar|e *vt* surround. **~si** *vr*
~si di surround oneself with

at'torno *adv* around, about ● *prep*
~ a around, about

attrac'care *vt/i* dock

attra'ente *a* attractive

at'tra|rre *vt* attract. **~rsi** *vr* be at-
tracted to each other. **~t'tiva** *nf*
charm. **~zi'one** *nf* attraction.

~zioni *pl* **turistiche** tourist at-
tractions

attraversa'mento *nm* (*di strada*)
crossing. **~ pedonale** pedestrian
crossing, crosswalk *Am*

attraver'sare *vt* cross; (*passare*)
go through

attra'verso *prep* through; (*obliquamente*) across

attrez'za|re *vt* equip; *Naut* rig.
~rsi *vr* kit oneself out; **~'tura** *nf*
equipment; *Naut* rigging

at'trezzo *nm* tool; **attrezzi** *pl*
equipment; *Sport* appliances *pl*;
Theat props *pl*

attribu'ir|e *vt* attribute. **~si** *vr* as-
cribe to oneself; **~si il merito di**
claim credit for

attri'bu|to *nm* attribute. **~zi'one**
nf attribution

at'trice *nf* actress

at'trito *nm* friction

attu'abile *a* feasible

attu'al|e *a* present; (*di attualità*)
topical; (*effettivo*) actual. **~ità** *nf*
topicality; (*avvenimento*) news;
programma di ~ità current affairs programme. **~iz'zare** *vt* up-
date. **~'mente** *adv* at present

attu'ar|e *vt* carry out. **~rsi** *vr* be
realized. **~zi'one** *nf* carrying out

attu'tire *vt* deaden; **~ il colpo** soften the blow

au'dac|e *a* daring, bold; (*insolente*)
audacious. **~ia** *nf* daring, boldness; (*insolenza*) audacity

'**audience** *nf inv* (*telespettatori*)
audience

'**audio** *nm* audio

audiovi'sivo *a* audiovisual

audi'torio *nm* auditorium

audizi'one *nf* audition; *Jur* hearing

'**auge** *nm* height; **essere in ~** be
popular

augu'rar|e *vt* wish. **~si** *vr* hope.
au'gurio *nm* wish; (*presagio*)
omen; **auguri!** all the best!; (*a
Natale*) Happy Christmas!; **tanti
auguri** best wishes

'**aula** *nf* classroom; (*università*)

lecture-hall; (*sala*) hall. **~ magna** (*in università*) great hall. **~ del tribunale** courtroom

aumen'tare *vt/i* increase. **au'mento** *nm* increase; (*di stipendio*) [pay] rise

au'reola *nf* halo

au'rora *nf* dawn

auscul'tare *vt Med* auscultate

ausili'are *a & nmf* auxiliary

auspicabile *a* **è ~ che...** it is to be hoped that...

auspi'care *vt* hope for

au'spicio *nm* omen; **auspici** (*pl: protezione*) auspices

austerità *nf* austerity

au'stero *a* austere

Au'strali|a *nf* Australia. **a~'ano, -a** *a & nmf* Australian

'Austria *nf* Austria. **au'striaco, -a** *a & nmf* Austrian

autar'chia *nf* autarchy. **au'tarchico** *a* autarchic

autenti'c|are *vt* authenticate. **~ità** *nf* authenticity

au'tentico *a* authentic; (*vero*) true

au'tista *nm* driver

'auto *nf inv* car

'auto+ *pref* self+

autoabbron'zante *nm* self-tan ● *a* self-tanning

autoambu'lanza *nf* ambulance

autoartico'lato *nm* articulated lorry

autobio|gra'fia *nf* autobiography. **~'grafico** *a* autobiographical

auto'botte *nf* tanker

'autobus *nm inv* bus

auto'carro *nm* lorry

autocommiserazi'one *nf* self-pity

autoconcessio'nario *nm* car dealer

auto'critica *nf* self-criticism

autodi'datta *nmf* self-educated person, autodidact

autodi'fesa *nf* self-defence

auto'gol *nm inv* own goal

au'tografo *a & nm* autograph

autolesio'nis|mo *nm fig* self-destruction. **~tico** *a* self-destructive

auto'linea *nf* bus line

au'toma *nm* robot

automatica'mente *adv* automatically

auto'matico *a* automatic ● *nm* (*bottone*) press-stud; (*fucile*) automatic

automatiz'za|re *vt* automate. **~zi'one** *nf* automation

auto'mezzo *nm* motor vehicle

auto'mobi|le *nf* [motor] car. **~'lismo** *nm* motoring. **~'lista** *nmf* motorist. **~'listico** *a* ⟨*industria*⟩ automobile *attrib*

autonoma'mente *adv* autonomously

autono'mia *nf* autonomy; *Auto* range; (*di laptop, cellulare*) battery life. **au'tonomo** *a* autonomous

auto'psia *nf* autopsy

auto'radio *nf inv* car radio; (*veicolo*) radio car

au'tore, -'trice *nmf* author; (*di pitture*) painter; (*di furto ecc*) perpetrator; **quadro d'~** genuine master

auto'revo|le *a* authoritative; (*che ha influenza*) influential. **~'lezza** *nf* authority

autori'messa *nf* garage

autori|tà *nf inv* authority. **~'tario** *a* autocratic. **~'tarismo** *nm* authoritarianism

autori'tratto *nm* self-portrait

autoriz'za|re *vt* authorize. **~zi'one** *nf* authorization

auto'scontro *nm inv* bumper car, dodgem

autoscu'ola *nf* driving school

auto'stop *nm* hitch-hiking; **fare l'~** hitch-hike. **~'pista** *nmf* hitch-hiker

auto'strada *nf* motorway

autostra'dale *a* motorway *attrib*

autosuffici'en|te *a* self-sufficient. **~za** *nf* self-sufficiency

autotrasporta'|tore, ~'trice *nm*, haulier, carrier

auto'treno *nm* articulated lorry, roadtrain

autove'icolo *nm* motor vehicle

auto'velox *nm inv* speed camera

autovet'tura *nf* motor vehicle

autun'nale *a* autumn[al]

au'tunno *nm* autumn

aval'lare *vt* endorse, back *(cambiale)*; *fig* endorse

a'vallo *nm* endorsement

avam'braccio *nm* forearm

avangu'ardia *nf* vanguard; *fig* avant-garde; **essere all'~** be in the forefront; *Techn* be at the leading edge

a'vanti *adv (in avanti)* forward; *(davanti)* in front; *(prima)* before; **~!** *(entrate)* come in!; *(suvvia)* come on!; *(su semaforo)* come on!, walk *Am*; **va' ~!** go ahead!; **andare ~** *(precedere)* go ahead; *(orologio:)* be fast; **● e indietro** backwards and forwards **● a** *(precedente)* before **● prep ~ a** before; *(in presenza di)* in the presence of

avanti'eri *adv* the day before yesterday

avanza'mento *nm* progress; *(promozione)* promotion

avan'zare *vi* advance; *(progredire)* progress; *(essere d'avanzo)* be left [over] **● vt** advance; *(superare)* surpass; *(promuovere)* promote. **~rsi** *vr* advance; *(avvicinarsi)* approach. **~ta** *nf* advance. **~to** *a* advanced; *(nella notte)* late; **in età ~ta** elderly. **a'vanzo** *nm* remainder; *Comm* surplus; **avanzi** *pl* *(rovine)* remains; *(di cibo)* left-overs

ava'ri|a *nf (di motore)* engine failure. **~'ato** *a (frutta, verdura)* rotten; *(carne)* tainted

ava'rizia *nf* avarice. **a'varo, -a** *a* stingy **● nmf** miser

a'vena *nf* oats *pl*

a'vere *vt* have; *(ottenere)* get; *(indossare)* wear; *(provare)* feel; **ho trent'anni** I'm thirty; **ha avuto il posto** he got the job; **~ fame/freddo** be hungry/cold; **ho mal di denti** I've got toothache; **cos'ha a che fare con lui?** what has it got to do

with him?; **~ da fare** be busy; **che hai?** what's the matter with you?; **nei hai per molto?** will you be long?; **quanti ne abbiamo oggi?** what date is it today?; **avercela con qcno** have it in for sb **● v aux** have; **non l'ho visto** I haven't seen him; **lo hai visto?** have you seen him?; **l'ho visto ieri** I saw him yesterday **● nm** *averi pl* wealth *sg*

avia'tore *nm* flyer, aviator. **~zi'one** *nf* aviation; *Mil* Air Force

avidità *nf* avidness. **'avido** *a* avid

'avo, -a *nmf* ancestor

avo'cado *nm inv* avocado

a'vorio *nm* ivory

Avv. *abbr* avvocato

avva'lersi *vr* avail oneself **(of** di)

avvalla'mento *nm* depression

avvalo'rare *vt* bear out *(tesi)*; endorse *(documento)*; *(accrescere)* enhance

avvam'pare *vi* flare up; *(arrossire)* blush

avvantaggi'ar|e *vt* favour. **~si** *vr* **~si di** benefit from; *(approfittare)* take advantage of

avve'd|ersi *vr (accorgersi)* notice; *(capire)* realize. **~uto** *a* shrewd

avvelena'mento *nm* poisoning

avvele'na|re *vt* poison. **~rsi** *vr* poison oneself. **~to** *a* poisoned

avve'nente *a* attractive

avveni'mento *nm* event

avve'nire *vi* happen; *(aver luogo)* take place

avve'ni|re *nm* future. **~'ristico** *a* futuristic

avven'ta|rsi *vr* fling oneself. **~to** *a (decisione)* rash

av'vento *nm* advent; *Relig* Advent

avven'tore *nm* regular customer

avven'tu|ra *nf* adventure; *(amorosa)* affair; **d'~** *(film)* adventure *attrib.* **~'rarsi** *vr* venture. **~ri'ero, -a** *nm* adventurer **●** *nf* adventuress. **~'roso** *a* adventurous

avve'rabile *a (previsione)* that may come true. **~rsi** *vr* come true

av'verbio nm adverb

avver'sar|e vt oppose. **~io, -a** opposing ● nmf opponent

avversi|'one nf aversion. **~tà** nf inv adversity

av'verso a (sfavorevole) adverse; (contrario) averse

avver'tenza nf (cura) care; (avvertimento) warning; (avviso) notice; (premessa) foreword; **avvertenze** pl (istruzioni) instructions

avverti'mento nm warning

avver'tire vt warn; (informare) inform; (sentire) feel

avvez'zar|e vt accustom. **~si** vr accustom oneself. **av'vezzo** a **av'vezzo** a used to

avvia'mento nm starting; Comm goodwill

avvi'a|re vt start. **~rsi** vr set out. **~to** a under way; **bene ~to** thriving

avvicenda'mento nm (in agricoltura) rotation; (nel lavoro) replacement

avvicen'darsi vr take turns, alternate

avvicina'mento nm approach

avvici'nar|e vt bring near; approach (persona). **~si** vr come nearer, approach; **~si a** come nearer to, approach

avvi'lente a demoralizing; (umiliante) humiliating

avvili'mento nm despondency; (degradazione) degradation

avvi'li|re vt dishearten; (degradare) degrade. **~rsi** vr lose heart; (degradarsi) degrade oneself. **~to** a disheartened; (degradato) degraded

avvilup'par|e vt envelop. **~si** vr wrap oneself up; (aggrovigliarsi) get entangled

avvi'nazzato a drunk

avvin'cente a (libro ecc) enthralling. **av'vincere** vt enthral

avvinghi'ar|e vt clutch. **~si** vr cling

av'vio nm start-up; **dare l'~** a qcsa get sth under way; **prendere l'~** get under way

avvi'sare vt inform; (mettere in guardia) warn

av'viso nm notice; (annuncio) announcement; (avvertimento) warning; (pubblicitario) advertisement; **a mio ~** in my opinion. **~ di garanzia** Jur notification that one is to be the subject of a legal inquiry

avvi'stare vt catch sight of

avvi'tare vt screw in; screw down (coperchio)

avviz'zire vi wither

avvo'cato nm lawyer; fig advocate. **~tura** nf legal profession

av'volger|e vt wrap [up]. **~si** vr wrap oneself up

avvol'gibile nm roller blind

avvol'toio nm vulture

aza'lea nf azalea

azi'en|da nf business, firm. **~ agricola** farm. **~ di soggiorno** tourist bureau. **~dale** a (politica, dirigente) company attrib; (giornale) in-house

azio'na'mento nm operation

azio'nare vt operate

azio'nario a share attrib

azi'one nf action; Fin share; **d'~** (romanzo, film) action[-packed].

azio'nista nmf shareholder

a'zoto nm nitrogen

azzan'nare vt seize with its teeth; sink its teeth into (gamba)

azzar'd|are vt risk. **~arsi** vr dare. **~ato** a risky; (precipitoso) rash.

az'zardo nm hazard; **gioco d'azzardo** game of chance

azzec'care vt hit; (fig: indovinare) guess

azzuf'farsi vr come to blows

az'zur|ro a & nm blue; **il principe ~** Prince Charming. **~rognolo** a bluish

Bb

bab'beo *a* foolish ● *nm* idiot
'babbo *nm fam* dad, daddy. **B~ Natale** Father Christmas
bab'buccia *nf* slipper
babbu'ino *nm* baboon
ba'bordo *nm Naut* port side
baby'sitter *nmf inv* baby-sitter; **fare la ~** babysit
ba'cato *a* wormeaten
'bacca *nf* berry
baccalà *nm inv* dried salted cod
bac'cano *nm* din
bac'cello *nm* pod
bac'chetta *nf* rod; *(magica)* wand; *(di direttore d'orchestra)* baton; *(di tamburo)* drumstick
ba'checa *nf* showcase; *(in ufficio)* notice board. **~ elettronica** *Comput* bulletin board
bacia'mano *nm* kiss on the hand; **fare il ~ a qcno** kiss sb's hand
baci'arle *vt* kiss. **~si** *vr* kiss [each other]
ba'cillo *nm* bacillus
baci'nella *nf* basin
ba'cino *nm* basin; *Anat* pelvis; *(di porto)* dock; *(di minerali)* field
'bacio *nm* kiss
'baco *nm* worm. **~ da seta** silkworm
ba'cucco *a* **un vecchio ~** a senile old man
'bada *nf* **tenere qcno a ~** keep sb at bay
ba'dare *vi* take care (**a** of); *(fare attenzione)* look out; **bada ai fatti tuoi!** mind your own business!
ba'dia *nf* abbey
ba'dile *nm* shovel
'badminton *nm* badminton
'baffi *nmpl* moustache *sg*; *(di animale)* whiskers; **mi fa un baffo** I don't give a damn; **ridere sotto i ~** laugh up one's sleeve
baf'futo *a* moustached

ba'gagli *nmpl* luggage, baggage. **~'aio** *nm Rail* luggage van; *Auto* boot
ba'gaglio *nm* luggage; **un ~** a piece of luggage. **~ a mano** hand luggage, hand baggage
baggia'nata *nf* **non dire baggianate** don't talk nonsense
bagli'ore *nm* glare; *(improvviso)* flash; *(fig: di speranza)* glimmer
ba'gnante *nmf* bather
ba'gna|re *vt* wet; *(inzuppare)* soak; *(immergere)* dip; *(innaffiare)* water; *(mare, lago:)* wash; *(fiume:)* flow through. **~rsi** *vr* get wet; *(al mare ecc)* swim, bathe.
bagnasci'uga *nm inv* edge of the water, waterline
ba'gnato *a* wet
ba'gnino, -a *nmf* life guard
'bagno *nm* bath; *(stanza)* bathroom; *(gabinetto)* toilet; *(in casa)* toilet, bathroom; *(al mare)* swim, bathe; **bagni** *pl* *(stabilimento)* lido; **fare il ~** have a bath; *(nel mare ecc)* [have a] swim or bathe; **andare in ~** go to the bathroom or toilet; **mettere a ~** soak. **~ turco** Turkish bath
bagnoma'ria *nm* **cuocere a ~** cook in a double saucepan
bagnoschi'uma *nm inv* bubble bath
'baia *nf* bay
baio'netta *nf* bayonet
'baita *nf* mountain chalet
bala'ustra, balaus'trata *nf* balustrade
balbet'ta|re *vt/i* stammer; *(bambino:)* babble. **~io** *nm* stammering; babble
bal'buzie *nf* stutter. **~'onte** *a* stuttering ● *nmf* stutterer
Bal'can|i *nmpl* Balkans. **b~ico** *a* Balkan
balco'nata *nf Theat* balcony, dress circle
balcon'cino *nm* **reggiseno a ~** underwired bra
bal'cone *nm* balcony
baldac'chino *nm* canopy; **letto a ~** four-poster bed

bal'dan|za *nf* boldness. **~'zoso** *a* bold

bal'doria *nf* revelry; **far ~** have a riotous time

Bale'ari *nfpl* **le [isole] ~** the Balearics, the Balearic Islands

ba'lena *nf* whale

bale'nare *vi* lighten; *fig* flash; **mi è balenata un'idea** I've just had an idea

bale'niera *nf* whaler

ba'leno *nm* **in un ~** in a flash

ba'lera *nf* dance hall

'balia *nf* wetnurse

ba'lia *nf* **in ~ di** at the mercy of

ba'listico *a* ballistic; **perito ~** ballistics expert

'balla *nf* bale; (*fam: frottola*) tall story

bal'labile *a* good for dancing to

bal'la|re *vi* dance. **~ta** *nf* ballad

balla'toio *nm* (*nelle scale*) landing

balle'rino, -a *nmf* dancer; (*classico*) ballet dancer; **ballerina** (*classica*) ballet dancer, ballerina

bal'letto *nm* ballet

bal'lista *nmf fam* ball-shitter

'ballo *nm* dance; (*il ballare*) dancing; **sala da ~** ballroom; **essere in ~** (*lavoro, vita:*) be at stake; (*persona:*) be committed; **tirare qcno in ~** involve sb

ballonzo'lare *vi* skip about

ballot'taggio *nm* second count (*of votes*)

balne|a|re *a* bathing *attrib*. **stagione ~** swimming season. **stazione ~** seaside resort. **~zi'one** *nf* **è vietata la ~zione** no swimming

ba'lordo *a* foolish; (*stordito*) stunned; **tempo ~** nasty weather

'balsamo *nm* balsam; (*per capelli*) conditioner; (*lenimento*) remedy

'baltico *a* Baltic. **il [mar] B~** the Baltic [Sea]

balu'ardo *nm* bulwark

'balza *nf* crag; (*di abito*) flounce

bal'zano *a* (*idea*) weird

bal'zare *vi* bounce; (*saltare*) jump; **~ in piedi** leap to one's feet.

'balzo *nm* bounce; (*salto*) jump;

prendere la palla al balzo seize an opportunity

bam'bagia *nf* cotton wool; **vivere nella ~** *fig* be in clover

bambi'nata *nf* childish thing to do/say

bam'bi|no, -a *nmf* child; (*appena nato*) baby; **avere un ~no** have a baby. **~'none, -a** *nmf pej* big or overgrown child

bam'boccio *nm* chubby child; (*sciocco*) simpleton; (*fantoccio*) rag doll

'bambo|la *nf* doll. **~'lotto** *nm* male doll

bambù *nm* bamboo

ba'nal|e *a* banal; **~ità** *nf inv* banality; **~iz'zare** *vt* trivialize

ba'nan|a *nf* banana. **~o** *nm* banana-tree

'banca *nf* bank. **~ [di] dati** data-bank

banca'rella *nf* stall

ban'cario, -a *a* banking *attrib*; **trasferimento ~** bank transfer ● *nmf* bank employee

banca'rotta *nf* bankruptcy; **fare ~** go bankrupt

banchet'tare *vi* banquet. **ban-'chetto** *nm* banquet

banchi'ere *nm* banker

ban'china *nf Naut* quay; (*in stazione*) platform; (*di strada*) path; **~ non transitabile** soft verge

ban'chisa *nf* floe

'banco *nm* (*di scuola*) desk; (*di negozio*) counter; (*di officina*) bench; (*di gioco, banca*) bank; (*di mercato*) stall; (*degli imputati*) dock; **sotto ~** under the counter; **medicinale da ~** over the counter medicines. **~ informazioni** information desk. **~ di nebbia** fog bank

'bancomat® *nm inv* autobank, cashpoint; (*carta*) bank card, cash card

ban'cone *nm* counter; (*in bar*) bar

banco'nota *nf* banknote, bill *Am*; **banco'note** *pl* paper currency '**banda** *nf* band; *(di delinquenti)* gang. ~ **d'atterraggio** landing strip. ~ **rumorosa** rumble strip

bande'ruola *nf* weathercock; *Naut* pennant

bandie|ra *nf* flag; **cambiare ~ra** change sides, switch allegiances. **~rina** *nf (nel calcio)* corner flag. **~rine** *pl* hunting *sg*

ban'di|re *vt* banish; *(pubblicare)* publish; *fig* dispense with *(formalità, complimenti)*. **~to** *nm* bandit. **~'tore** *nm (di aste)* auctioneer

'**bando** *nm* proclamation; **~ di concorso** job advertisement *(published in an official gazette for a job for which a competitive examination has to be taken)*

bar *nm inv* bar

'**bara** *nf* coffin

ba'rac|ca *nf* hut; *(catapecchia)* hovel; **mandare avanti la ~ca** keep the ship afloat. **~'cato** *nm* person living in a makeshift shelter. **~'chino** *nm (di gelati, giornali)* kiosk; *Radio* CB radio. **~'cone** *nm (roulotte)* circus caravan; *(in luna park)* booth. **~'copoli** *nf inv* shanty town

bara'onda *nf* chaos; **non fare ~** don't make a mess

ba'rare *vi* cheat

'**baratro** *nm* chasm

barat'tare *vt* barter. **ba'ratto** *nm* barter

ba'rattolo *nm* jar; *(di latta)* tin

'**barba** *nf* beard; *(fam: noia)* bore; **farsi la ~** shave; **è una ~** *(noia)* it's boring

barbabi'etola *nf* beetroot. **~ da zucchero** sugar-beet

bar'barico *a* barbaric. **bar'barie** *nf* barbarity. '**barbaro** *a* barbarous ● *nm* barbarian

'**barbecue** *nm inv* barbecue

barbi'ere *nm* barber; *(negozio)* barber's

barbi'turico *nm* barbiturate

bar'bone *nm (vagabondo)* vagrant; *(cane)* poodle

bar'boso *a fam* boring

barbu'gliare *vi* mumble

bar'buto *a* bearded

'**barca** *nf* boat; **una ~ di** *fig* a lot of. **~ a motore** motorboat. **~ da pesca** fishing boat. **~ a remi** rowing boat, rowboat *Am*. **~ di salvataggio** lifeboat. **~ a vela** sailing boat, sailboat *Am*. **~i'olo** *nm* boatman

barcame'narsi *vr* manage

barcol'lare *vi* stagger

bar'cone *nm* barge; *(di ponte)* pontoon

bar'dare *vt* harness. **~si** *vr hum* dress up

ba'rel|la *nf* stretcher. **~li'ere** *nm* stretcher-bearer

'**Barents: il mare di ~** the Barents Sea

bari'centro *nm* centre of gravity

ba'ri|le *nm* barrel. **~'lotto** *nm fig* tub of lard

ba'rista *nm* barman ● *nf* barmaid

ba'ritono *nm* baritone

bar'lume *nm* glimmer; **un ~ di speranza** a glimmer of hope

'**barman** *nm inv* barman

'**baro** *nm* cardsharper

ba'rocco *a & nm* baroque

ba'rometro *nm* barometer

ba'rone *nm* baron; **i baroni** *fig* the top brass. **baro'nessa** *nf* baroness

'**barra** *nf* bar; *(lineetta)* stroke; *Naut* tiller. **~ spazio** *Comput* space bar. **~ strumenti** *Comput* tool bar

bar'rare *vt* block off *(strada)*

barri'care *vt* barricade. **~ta** *nf* barricade

barri'era *nf* barrier; *(stradale)* road-block; *Geol* reef. **~ razziale** colour bar

bar'ri|re *vi* trumpet. **~to** *nm* trumpeting

barzel'letta *nf* joke; **~ sporca** *o* **spinta** dirty joke

basa'mento *nm* base

ba'sare *vt* base. **~si** *vr* **~si su** be based on; **mi baso su ciò che ho visto** I'm going on [the basis of] what I saw

'basco, -a nmf & a Basque ● nm (copricapo) beret

'base nf basis; (fondamento) foundation; Mil base; Pol rank and file; **a ~ di** containing; **in ~ a** on the basis of. **~ dati** database

'baseball nm baseball

ba'setta nf sideburn

basi'lare a basic

ba'silica nf basilica

ba'silico nm basil

ba'sista nm grass roots politician; (di un crimine) mastermind

'basket nm basketball

bas'sezza nf lowness; (di statura) shortness; (viltà) vileness

bas'sista nmf bassist

'basso a low; (di statura) short; (acqua) shallow; (televisione) quiet; (vile) despicable; **parlare a bassa voce** speak quietly, speak in a low voice; **la bassa Italia** southern Italy ● nm lower part; Mus bass. **guardare in ~** look down

basso'fondo nm (pl **bassifondi**) shallows pl; **bassifondi** pl (quartieri poveri) slums

bassori'lievo nm bas-relief

bas'sotto nm dachshund

ba'stardo, -a a bastard; (di animale) mongrel ● nmf bastard; (animale) mongrel

ba'stare vi be enough; (durare) last; **basta!** that's enough!, that'll do!; **basta che** (purché) provided that; **basta così** that's enough; **basta così?** is that enough?, will that do?; (in negozio) will there be anything else?; **basta andare alla posta** you only have to go to the post office

Basti'an con'trario nm contrary old so-and-so

basti'one nm bastion

basto'nare vt beat

baston'cino nm (da sci) ski pole. **~ di pesce** fish finger, fish stick Am

ba'stone nm stick; (da golf) club; (da passeggio) walking stick

ba'tosta nf blow

bat'taglia nf battle; (lotta) fight. **~'are** vi battle; fig fight

bat'taglio nm (di campana) clapper; (di porta) knocker

battagli'one nm battalion

bat'tello nm boat; (motonave) steamer

bat'tente nm (di porta) wing; (di finestra) shutter; (battaglio) knocker

'batter|e vt beat; (percorrere) scour; thresh (grano); break (record) ● vi (bussare, urtare) knock; (cuore) beat; (ali ecc) flap; Tennis serve; **~e a macchina** type; **~e gli occhi** blink; **~e le mani** clap [one's hands]; **~e le ore** strike the hours. **~si** vr fight

bat'teri nmpl bacteria

batte'ria nf battery; Mus drums pl

bat'terio nm bacterium. **~'logico** a bacteriological

batte'rista nmf drummer

bat'tesimo nm baptism, christening

battez'zare vt baptize, christen

battiba'leno nm **in un ~** in a flash

batti'becco nm squabble

batticu'ore nm palpitation; **mi venne il ~** I was scared

bat'tigia nf water's edge

batti'mano nm applause

batti'panni nm inv carpetbeater

batti'stero nm baptistery

batti'strada nm inv outrider; (di pneumatico) tread; Sport pacesetter

battitap'peto nm inv carpet sweeper

'battito nm (del cuore) [heart]beat; (alle tempie) throbbing; (di orologio) ticking; (della pioggia) beating

bat'tuta nf beat; (colpo) knock; (spiritosaggine) wisecrack; (osservazione) remark; Mus bar; Tennis service; Theat cue; (dattilografia) stroke

ba'tuffolo nm flock

ba'ule nm trunk

'bava *nf* dribble; (*di cane ecc*) slobber; **aver la ~ alla bocca** foam at the mouth

bava'glino *nm* bib

ba'vaglio *nm* gag

'bavero *nm* collar

ba'zar *nm inv* bazaar

baz'zecola *nf* trifle

bazzi'care *vt/i* haunt

be'arsi *vr* delight (**di** in)

beati'tudine *nf* bliss. **be'ato** *a* blissful; *Relig* blessed; **beato te!** lucky you!

beauty-'case *nm inv* toilet bag

bebè *nm inv* baby

bec'caccia *nf* woodcock

bec'ca|re *vt* peck; *fig* catch. **~rsi** *vr* (*litigare*) quarrel. **~ta** *nf* peck

beccheggi'are *vi* pitch

bec'chino *nm* grave-digger

'bec|co *nm* beak; (*di caffettiera ecc*) spout. **~'cuccio** *nm* spout

be'fana *nf* Epiphany; (*donna brutta*) old witch

'beffa *nf* hoax; **farsi beffe di qcno** mock sb. **bef'fardo** *a* derisory; (*persona*) mocking

beffar|e *vt* mock. **~si** *vr* **~si di** make fun of

'bega *nf* quarrel; **è una bella ~** it's really annoying

be'gonia *nf* begonia

beige *a & nm* beige

be'la|re *vi* bleat. **~to** *nm* bleating

'belga *a & nmf* Belgian

'Belgio *nm* Belgium

'bella *nf* (*in carte, Sport*) decider

bel'lezza *nf* beauty; **che ~!** how lovely!; **chiudere/finire in ~** end on a high note

'belli|co *a* war *attrib*. **~'coso** *a* warlike. **~ge'rante** *a & nmf* belligerent

'bello *a* nice; (*di aspetto*) beautiful; (*uomo*) handsome; (*moralmente*) good; **cosa fai di ~ stasera?** what are you up to tonight?; **oggi fa ~** it's a nice day; **una bella cifra** a lot; **un bel piatto di pasta** a big plate of pasta; **nel bel mezzo** right in the middle; **un bel niente**

absolutely nothing; **bell'e fatto** over and done with; **bell'amico!** [a] fine friend he is/you are!; **questa è bella!** that's a good one!; **scamparla bella** have a narrow escape ● *nm* (*bellezza*) beauty; (*innamorato*) sweetheart; **sul più ~** at the crucial moment; **il ~ è che...** the funny thing is that...

'belva *nf* wild beast

be'molle *nm Mus* flat

ben *vedi* **bene**

benché *conj* though, although

'benda *nf* bandage; (*per occhi*) blindfold. **ben'dare** *vt* bandage; blindfold (*occhi*)

'bene *adv* well; **ben ~** thoroughly; **~!** good!; **star ~** (*di salute*) be well; (*vestito, stile:*) suit; (*finanziariamente*) be well off; **non sta ~** (*non è educato*) it's not nice; **sta/va ~!** all right!; **ti sta ~!** [it] serves you well!; **ti auguro ~** I wish you well; **di ~ in meglio** better and better; **fare ~** (*aver ragione*) do the right thing; **fare ~ a** (*cibo:*) be good for; **una persona per ~** a good person; **per ~** (*fare*) properly; **è ben difficile** it's very difficult; **come tu ben sai** as you well know; **lo credo ~** I can well believe it! ● *nm* good; **per il tuo ~** for your own good. **beni** *nmpl* (*averi*) property *sg*; **un ~ di famiglia** a family heirloom

bene'detto *a* blessed

bene'di|re *vt* bless. **~zi'one** *nf* blessing

benedu'cato *a* well-mannered

benefat'to|re, -'trice *nm* benefactor ● *nf* benefactress

benefi'care *vt* help

benefi'cenza *nf* charity

benefici'ar|e *vi* **~e di** profit by. **~io, -a** *a & nmf* beneficiary. **bene'ficio** *nm* benefit. **be'nefico** *a* beneficial; (*di beneficenza*) charitable

bene'placito *nm* consent, approval

be'nessere *nm* well-being

bene'stante *a* well-off ● *nmf* well-off person

bene'stare *nm* consent

benevo'lenza *nf* benevolence. be'nevolo *a* benevolent

ben'fatto *a* well-made

'beni *nmpl* property *sg*; *Fin* assets; ~ di consumo consumer goods

benia'mino *nm* favourite

be'nigno *a* kindly; *Med* benign

beninfor'mato *a* well-informed

benintenzio'nato, -a *a* well-meaning ● *nmf* well-meaning person

benin'teso *adv* needless to say, of course

benpen'sante *a & nmf* self-righteous

benser'vito *nm* dare il ~ a qcno give sb the sack

bensì *conj* but rather

benve'nuto *a & nm* welcome

ben'visto *a* essere ~ go down well (da with)

benvo'lere *vt* farsi ~ da qcno win sb's affection; prendere qcno in ~ take a liking to sb; essere benvoluto da tutti to be well-liked by everyone

ben'zina *nf* petrol, gas *Am*; far ~ get petrol. ~ verde unleaded petrol. benzi'naio, -a *nmf* petrol station attendant

'bere *vt* drink; (*assorbire*) absorb; *fig* swallow ● *nm* drinking; (*bevande*) drinks *pl*

berga'motto *nm* bergamot

ber'lina *nf Auto* saloon

Ber'lino *nm* Berlin

ber'muda *nfpl* (*pantaloni*) Bermuda shorts

ber'noccolo *nm* bump; (*disposizione*) flair

ber'retto *nm* beret, cap

bersagli'are *vt fig* bombard. ber'saglio *nm* target

be'stemmi|a *nf* swear-word; (*maledizione*) oath; (*sproposito*) blasphemy. ~'are *vi* swear

'besti|a *nf* animal; (*persona brutale*) beast; (*persona sciocca*) fool;

andare in ~a *fam* blow one's top. ~'ale *a* bestial; (*espressione, violenza*) brutal; (*fam: freddo, fame*) terrible. ~alità *nf inv* bestiality; *fig* nonsense. ~'ame *nm* livestock

'bettola *nf fig* dive

be'tulla *nf* birch

be'vanda *nf* drink

bevi'|tore, -'trice *nmf* drinker

be'vut|a *nf* drink. ~o *pp di* bere

bi'ada *nf* fodder

bianche'ria *nf* linen. ~ intima underwear

bi'anco *a* white; (*foglio, pagina ecc*) blank ● *nm* white; mangiare in ~ not eat any fried or heavy foods; andare in ~ *fam* not score; in ~ e nero (*film, fotografia*) black and white, monochrome; passare una notte in ~ have a sleepless night

bian'core *nm* (*bianchezza*) whiteness

bianco'spino *nm* hawthorn

biasci'care *vt* (*mangiare*) eat noisily; (*parlare*) mumble

biasi'mare *vt* blame. bi'asimo *nm* blame

'Bibbia *nf* Bible

bibe'ron *nm inv* [baby's] bottle

'bibita *nf* [soft] drink

'biblico *a* biblical

bibliogra'fia *nf* bibliography

biblio'te|ca *nf* library; (*mobile*) bookcase. ~'cario, -a *nmf* librarian

bicarbo'nato *nm* bicarbonate. ~ di sodio bicarbonate of soda

bicchi'ere *nm* glass

bicchie'rino *nm fam* tipple

bici'cletta *nf* bicycle; andare in ~ ride a bicycle

bico'lore *a* two-coloured

bidè *nm inv* bidet

bi'dello, -a *nmf* janitor, [school] caretaker

bido'nata *nf fam* swindle

bi'done *nm* bin; (*fam: truffa*) swindle; fare un ~ a qcno *fam* stand sb up

bien'nale *a* biennial

bi'ennio *nm* two-year period

bi'etola *nf* beet

bifo'cale *a* bifocal

bi'folco, -a *nmf fig* boor

bifor'c|arsi *vr* fork. **~azi'one** *nf* fork. **~uto** *a* forked

biga'mia *nf* bigamy. **'bigamo, -a** *a* bigamous ● *nmf* bigamist

bighello'nare *vi* loaf around. **bighel'lone** *nm* loafer

bigiotte'ria *nf* costume jewellery; *(negozio)* jeweller's

bigliet't|aio *nm* booking clerk; *(sui treni)* ticket-collector. **~e'ria** *nf* ticket-office; *Theat* box-office

bigli'et|to *nm* ticket; *(lettera breve)* note; *(cartoncino)* card; *(di banca)* banknote. **~to da visita** business card. **~'tone** *nm* *(fam: soldi)* big one

bignè *nm inv* cream puff

bigo'dino *nm* roller

bi'gotto *nm* bigot

bi'kini *nm inv* bikini

bi'lanci|a *nf* scales *pl*; *(di orologio, Comm)* balance; **B~a** *Astr* Libra. **~'are** *vt* balance; *fig* weigh. **~o** *nm* budget; *Comm* balance sheet; **fare il ~o** balance the books; *fig* take stock

'bile *nf* bile; *fig* rage

bili'ardo *nm* billiards *sg*

bi'lico *nm* equilibrium; **in ~** in the balance

bi'lingue *a* bilingual

bili'one *nm* billion

bilo'cale *a* two-room

'bimbo, -a *nmf* child

bimen'sile *a* fortnightly

bime'strale *a* bimonthly

bi'nario *nm* track; *(piattaforma)* platform

bi'nocolo *nm* binoculars *pl*

bio'chimica *nf* biochemistry

biodegra'dabile *a* biodegradable

bio'etica *nf* bioethics

bio'fisica *nf* biophysics

biogra'fia *nf* biography. **bio'grafico** *a* biographical. **bi'ografo, -a** *nmf* biographer

biolo'gia *nf* biology. **bio'logico** *a* biological. **bi'ologo, -a** *nmf* biologist

bi'ond|a *nf* blonde. **~o** *a* blond ● *nm* fair colour; *(uomo)* fair-haired man

bio'sfera *nf* biosphere

bi'ossido *nm* **~ di carbonio** carbon dioxide

biparti'tismo *nm* two-party system

'birba *nf*, **bir'bante** *nm* rascal, rogue. **bir'bone** *a* wicked

biri'chino, -a *a* naughty ● *nmf* little devil

bi'rillo *nm* skittle

'birr|a *nf* beer; **a tutta ~a** *fig* flat out. **~a chiara** lager. **~a scura** brown ale. **~e'ria** *nf* beer-house; *(fabbrica)* brewery

bis *nm inv* encore

bi'saccia *nf* haversack

bi'sbetic|a *nf* shrew. **~o** *a* bad-tempered

bisbigli'are *vt/i* whisper. **bi'sbiglio** *nm* whisper

'bisca *nf* gambling-house

'biscia *nf* snake

bi'scotto *nm* biscuit

bisessu'ale *a* & *nmf* bisexual

bise'stile *a* **anno ~** leap year

bisetti'mana'nale *a* fortnightly

bi'slacco *a* peculiar

bis'nonno, -a *nmf* great-grand-father; great-grandmother

biso'gn|are *vi* **~a agire subito** we must act at once; **~a farlo** it is necessary to do it; **non ~a venire** you don't have to come. **~o** *nm* need; *(povertà)* poverty; **aver ~o di** need. **~oso** *a* needy; *(povero)* poor; **~oso di** in need of

bi'sonte *nm* bison

bi'stecca *nf* steak

bisticci'are *vi* quarrel. **bi'sticcio** *nm* quarrel; *(gioco di parole)* pun

bistrat'tare *vt* mistreat

'bisturi *nm inv* scalpel

bi'torzolo *nm* lump

'bitter *nm inv* (bitter) aperitif

bi'vacco *nm* bivouac

'bivio *nm* crossroads; *(di strada)* fork

bizan'tino *a* Byzantine

'bizza *nf* tantrum; **fare le bizze** ⟨*bambini:*⟩ play up

biz'zarro *a* bizarre

biz'zeffe *adv* **a ~** galore

blan'dire *vt* soothe; *(allettare)* flatter. 'blando *a* mild

bla'sone *nm* coat of arms

blate'rare *vi* blether, blather

'blatta *nf* cockroach

blin'da|re *vt* armour-plate. **~to** *a* armoured

blitz *nm inv* blitz

bloc'car|e *vt* block; *(isolare)* cut off; *Mil* blockade; *Comm* freeze. **~si** *vr Mech* jam

blocca'sterzo *nm* steering lock

'blocco *nm* block; *Mil* blockade; *(dei fitti)* restriction; *(di carta)* pad; *(unione)* coalition; **in ~** *Comm* in bulk. **~ stradale** road-block

bloc-'notes *nm inv* writing pad

blu *a & nm* blue

blue-'jeans *nmpl* jeans

bluff *nm inv* *(carte, fig)* bluff. bluf'fare *vi* *(carte, fig)* bluff

'blusa *nf* blouse

'boa *nm* boa [constrictor]; *(sciarpa)* [feather] boa ● *nf Naut* buoy

bo'ato *nm* rumbling

bo'bina *nf* spool; *(di film)* reel; *Electr* coil

'bocca *nf* mouth; **a ~ aperta** *fig* dumbfounded; **in ~ al lupo!** *fam* break a leg!; **fare la respirazione ~ a ~ a qcno** give sb mouth to mouth resuscitation *or* the kiss of life

boc'caccia *nf* grimace; **far boccacce** make faces

boc'caglio *nm* nozzle

boc'cale *nm* jug; *(da birra)* tankard

bocca'porto *nm Naut* hatch

boc'cata *nf (di fumo)* puff; **prendere una ~ d'aria** get a breath of fresh air

boc'cetta *nf* small bottle

boccheggi'are *vi* gasp

boc'chino *nm* cigarette holder; *(di pipa, Mus)* mouthpiece

'bocc|ia *nf (palla)* bowl; **~e** *pl (gioco)* bowls *sg*

bocci'a|re *vt (agli esami)* fail; *(respingere)* reject; *(alle bocce)* hit; **essere ~to** fail; *(ripetere)* repeat a year. **~'tura** *nf* failure

bocci'olo *nm* bud

boc'cone *nm* morsel

boc'cone *nm* mouthful; *(piccolo pasto)* snack

boc'coni *adv* face downwards

'boia *nm* executioner

boi'ata *nf fam* rubbish

boicot'tare *vt* boycott

bo'lero *nm* bolero

'bolgia *nf (caos)* bedlam

'bolide *nm* meteor; **passare come un ~** shoot past [like a rocket]

Bo'livi|a *nf* Bolivia. **b~'ano,** *a a* & *nmf* Bolivian

'bolla *nf* bubble; *(pustola)* blister

bol'la|re *vt* stamp; *fig* brand. **~to** *a fig* branded; **carta ~ta** *paper with stamp showing payment of duty*

bol'iente *a* boiling [hot]

bol'let|ta *nf* bill; **essere in ~ta** be hard up. **~'tino** *nm* bulletin; *Comm* list

bol'lino *nm* coupon

bol'li|re *vt/i* boil. **~to** *nm* boiled meat. **~'tore** *nm* boiler; *(per l'acqua)* kettle. **~'tura** *nf* boiling

'bollo *nm* stamp

bol'lore *nm* boil; *(caldo)* intense heat; *fig* ardour

'bomba *nf* bomb; **a prova di ~** bomb-proof

bombarda'mento *nm* shelling; *(con aerei)* bombing; *fig* bombardment. **~ aereo** air raid

bombar'd|are *vt* shell; *(con aerei)* bomb; *fig* bombard. **~i'ere** *nm* bomber

bom'betta *nf* bowler [hat]

'bombola *nf* cylinder. **~ di gas** gas bottle, gas cylinder

bombo'lone *nm* doughnut

bomboni'era *nf* wedding keepsake

bo'naccia *nf Naut* calm

bonacci'one, -a *nmf* goodnatured person ● *a* good-natured

bo'nario *a* kindly

bo'nifica *nf* land reclamation. **bonifi'care** *vt* reclaim

bo'nifico *nm Comm* discount; *(bancario)* [credit] transfer

bontà *nf* goodness; *(gentilezza)* kindness

'bora *nf* bora *(cold north-east wind in the upper Adriatic)*

borbot'tare *vi* mumble; *(stomaco:)* rumble. **~io** *nm* mumbling; *(di stomaco)* rumbling

borchia *nf* stud. **~ato** *a* studded

bor'dare *vt* border. **~tura** *nf* border

bor'deaux *a inv (colore)* claret

bor'dello *nm* brothel; *fig* bedlam; *(disordine)* mess

'bordo *nm* border; *(estremità)* edge; **a** **~** *Naut, Aeron* on board

bor'gata *nf* hamlet

bor'ghese *a* bourgeois; *(abito* civilian; **in ~** in civilian dress; *(poliziotto)* in plain clothes

borghe'sia *nf* middle classes *pl*

'borgo *nm* village; *(quartiere)* district

'boria *nf* conceit. **~'oso** *a* conceited

bor'lotto *nm* [**fagiolo**] **~** borlotto bean

boro'talco *nm* talcum powder

bor'raccia *nf* flask

'borsa *nf* bag; *(borsetta)* handbag; *(valori)* Stock Exchange. **~ dell'acqua calda** hot-water bottle. **~ a frigo** cool-box. **~a della spesa** shopping bag. **~ di studio** scholarship. **~ai'olo** *nm* pickpocket. **~el'lino** *nm* purse. **bor'sista** *nmf Fin* speculator; *Sch* scholarship holder

bor'sello *nm* *(portamonete)* purse; *(borsetto)* man's handbag

~tta *nf* handbag. **~tto** *nm* man's handbag

bo'scaglia *nf* woodlands *pl*

boscai'olo *nm* woodman; *(guardaboschi)* forester

'bosco *nm* wood. **bo'scoso** *a* wooded

'bossolo *nm* cartridge case

bo'tanica *nf* botany. **~o** *a* botanical ● *nm* botanist

'botola *nf* trapdoor

'botta *nf* blow; *(rumore)* bang; **fare a botte** come to blows. **~ e risposta** *fig* thrust and counterthrust

'botte *nf* barrel

bot'te|ga *nf* shop; *(di artigiano)* workshop. **~'gaio, -a** *nmf* shopkeeper. **~'ghino** *nm Theatr* boxoffice; *(del lotto)* lottery-shop **~e'ria** *nf* wine shop

bot'tino *nm* loot; *Mil* booty

'botto *nm* bang; **di ~** all of a sudden

bot'tone *nm* button; *Bot* bud

bo'vino *a* bovine; **bovini** *pl* cattle

box *nm inv (per cavalli)* loosebox; *(recinto per bambini)* play-pen

'boxe *nf* boxing

'bozza *nf* draft; *Typ* proof; *(bernoccolo)* bump. **boz'zetto** *nm* sketch

'bozzolo *nm* cocoon

brac'care *vt* hunt

brac'cetto *nm* **a ~** arm in arm

braccia'le *nm* bracelet; *(fascia)* armband. **~'letto** *nm* bracelet; *(di orologio)* watch-strap

bracci'ante *nm* day labourer

bracci'ata *nf (nel nuoto)* stroke

'braccio *nm (pl nf* **braccia**) arm; *(di fiume, pl* **bracci**) arm. **~'olo** *nm (di sedia)* arm[rest]; *(da nuoto)* armband

'bracco *nm* hound

bracconi'ere *nm* poacher

bracie *nf* embers *pl;* **alla ~e** chargrilled. **~i'ere** *nm* brazier. **~'ola** *nf* chop

'brado *a* **allo stato ~** in the wild

'**brama** *nf* longing. **bra'mare** *vt* long for. **bramo'sia** *nf* yearning

'**branca** *nf* branch

'**branchia** *nf* gill

'**branco** *nm* (*di cani*) pack; (*pej: di persone*) gang

branco'iare *vi* grope

'**branda** *nf* camp-bed

bran'dello *nm* scrap; **a brandelli** in tatters

bran'dire *vt* brandish

'**brano** *nm* piece; (*di libro*) passage

Bra'sil|e *nm* Brazil. **b~i'ano, -a** *a* & *nmf* Brazilian

bra'vata *nf* bragging

'**bravo** *a* good; (*abile*) clever; (*coraggioso*) brave; **~!** well done!. **bra'vura** *nf* skill

'**breccia** *nf* breach; **sulla ~** very successful, at the top

bre'saola *nf* dried, salted beef sliced thinly and eaten cold

bre'tella *nf* shoulder-strap; **bretelle** *pl* (*di calzoni*) braces

'**breve** *a* brief, short; **in ~** briefly; **tra ~** shortly

brevet'tare *vt* patent. **bre'vetto** *nm* patent; (*attestato*) licence

brevità *nf* shortness

'**brezza** *nf* breeze

'**bricco** *nm* jug

bric'cone *nm* blackguard; *hum* rascal

bricio|la *nf* crumb; *fig* grain. **~o** *nm* fragment

'**briga** *nf* (*fastidio*) trouble; (*lite*) quarrel; **attaccar ~** pick a quarrel; **prendersi la ~ di fare qcsa** go to the trouble of doing sth

brigadi'ere *nm* (*dei carabinieri*) sergeant

bri'gante *nm* bandit; *hum* rogue

bri'gare *vi* intrigue

bri'gata *nf* brigade; (*gruppo*) group

briga'tista *nmf* *Pol* member of the Red Brigades

'**briglia** *nf* rein; **a ~ sciolta** at breakneck speed

bril'lante *a* brilliant; (*scintillante*) sparkling ● *nm* diamond

bril'lare *vi* shine; (*metallo:*) glitter; (*scintillare*) sparkle

'**brillo** *a* tipsy

'**brina** *nf* hoar-frost

brin'dare *vi* toast; **~ a qcno** drink a toast to sb

'**brindisi** *nm inv* toast

bri'tannico *a* British

'**brivido** *nm* shiver; (*di paura ecc*) shudder; (*di emozione*) thrill

brizzo'lato *a* greying

'**brocca** *nf* jug

broc'cato *nm* brocade

'**broccoli** *nmpl* broccoli *sg*

'**broda** *nf* *pej* dishwater

'**brodo** *nm* broth; (*per cucinare*) stock. **~ ristretto** consommé

'**broglio** *nm* **~ elettorale** gerrymandering

bron'chite *nf* bronchitis

'**broncio** *nm* sulk; **fare il ~** sulk

bronto'l|are *vi* grumble; (*tuono ecc:*) rumble. **~io** *nm* grumbling; (*di tuono*) rumbling. **~one, -a** *nmf* grumbler

'**bronzo** *nm* bronze

bros'sura *nf* **edizione in ~** paperback

bru'care *vt* (*pecora:*) graze

bruciacchi'are *vt* scorch

brucia'pelo *adv* **a ~** point-blank

bruci'a|re *vt* burn; (*scottare*) scald; (*incendiare*) set fire to ● *vi* burn; (*scottare*) scald. **~rsi** *vr* burn oneself. **~to** *a* burnt; *fig* burnt-out. **~tore** *nm* burner. **~'tura** *nf* burn.

bruci'ore *nm* burning sensation

'**bruco** *nm* grub

bru'folo *nm* spot

brughi'era *nf* heath

bru'li|care *vi* swarm; **~hio** *nm* swarming

'**brullo** *a* bare

'**bruma** *nf* mist

'**bruno** *a* brown; (*occhi, capelli*) dark

brusca'mente *adv* (*di colpo*) suddenly

bru'schetta *nf* toasted bread rubbed with garlic and sprinkled with olive oil '**brusco** *a* sharp; *(persona)* brusque, abrupt; *(improvviso)* sudden

bru'sio *nm* buzzing

bru'tal|e *a* brutal. **~ità** *nf inv* brutality. **~iz'zare** *vt* brutalize. '**bruto** *a & nm* brute

brut'tezza *nf* ugliness

'**brut**|to *a* ugly; *(tempo, tipo, situazione, affare)* nasty; *(cattivo)* bad; **~ta copia** rough copy; **~to tiro** dirty trick. **~tura** *nf* ugly thing

'**buca** *nf* hole; *(avvallamento)* hollow. **~ delle lettere** *(a casa)* letter box

buca'neve *nm inv* snowdrop

bu'car|e *vt* make a hole in; *(pungere)* prick; punch *(biglietti)* ● *vi* have a puncture. **~si** *vr* prick oneself; *(con droga)* shoot up

bu'cato *nm* washing

'**buccia** *nf* peel, skin

bucherel'lare *vt* riddle

'**buco** *nm* hole

bu'dello *nm (pl f* **budella**) bowel

bu'dino *nm* pudding

'**bue** *nm (pl* **buoi**) ox; **carne di ~** beef

bu'falo *nm* buffalo

bu'fera *nf* storm; *(di neve)* blizzard

buf'fetto *nm* cuff

'**buffo** *a* funny; *Theat* comic ● *nm* funny thing. **~'nata** *nf (scherzo)* joke. **buf'fone** *nm* buffoon; **fare il buffone** play the fool

bu'gi|a [[¹]] *nf* lie; *(a pietosa* white lie. **~'ardo, -a** *a & nmf* liar

bugi'gattolo *nm* cubby-hole

'**buio** *a* dark ● *nm* darkness, **al ~** in the dark; **~ pesto** pitch dark

'**bulbo** *nm* bulb; *(dell'occhio)* eyeball

Bulga'ria *nf* Bulgaria. '**bulgaro, -a** *a & nmf* Bulgarian

buli'mia *nf* bulimia. **bu'limico** *a* bulimic

'**bullo** *nm* bully

bul'lone *nm* bolt

'**bunker** *nm inv* bunker

buona'fede *nf* good faith

buona'notte *int* good night

buona'sera *int* good evening

buon'giorno *int* good morning; *(di pomeriggio)* good afternoon

buon'grado: di ~ *adv* willingly

buon'gusto *nm* good taste

buon'gu|staio, -a *nmf* gourmet. **buon'gusto** *nm* good taste

bu'ono *a* good; *(momento)* right; **dar ~** *(convalidare)* accept; **alla buona** easy-going; *(cena)* informal; **buona notte/sera** good night/evening; **buon compleanno/Natale!** happy birthday/merry Christmas!; **~ senso** common sense; **di buon'ora** early; **una buona volta** once and for all; **buona parte di** the best part of; **tre ore buone** three good hours ● *nm* good; *(in film)* goody; *(tagliando)* voucher; *(titolo)* bond; **con le buone** gently; **~ sconto** money-off coupon ● *nmf* **buono, - a a nulla** dead loss

buontem'pone, -a *nmf* happy-go-lucky person

buonu'more *nm* good temper

buonu'scita *nf* retirement bonus; *(di dirigente)* golden handshake

burat'tino *nm* puppet

'**burbero** *a* surly; *(nei modi)* rough

bu'rocra|te *nm* bureaucrat. **buro'cratico** *a* bureaucratic. **~'zia** *nf* bureaucracy

bur'ra|sca *nf* storm. **~'scoso** *a* stormy

'**burro** *nm* butter

bur'rone *nm* ravine

bu'scar|e *vt*, **~si** *vr* catch; **~le** *fam* get a hiding

bus'sare *vt* knock

'**bussola** *nf* compass; **perdere la ~** lose one's bearings

'**busta** *nf* envelope; *(astuccio)* case. **~ paga** pay packet. **~'rella** *nf* bribe. **bu'stina** *nf (di tè)* tea bag; *(per medicine)* sachet

'**busto** *nm* bust; *(indumento)* corset

but'tar|e *vt* throw; **~e giù** *(demolire)* knock down; *(inghiottire)* gulp down; scribble down *(scritto)*; *fam* put on *(pasta)*; *(scoraggiare)* dishearten; **~e via** throw away.

~**si** *vr* throw oneself; (*saltare*) jump

butte'rato *a* pock-marked

buz'zurro *nm fam* yokel

Cc

caba'ret *nm inv* cabaret

ca'bina *nf Naut, Aeron* cabin; (*balneare*) beach hut. ~ **elettorale** polling booth. ~ **di pilotaggio** cockpit. ~ **telefonica** telephone box. **cabi'nato** *nm* cabin cruiser

ca'cao *nm* cocoa

'cacca *nf fam* pooh

'caccia *nf* hunt; (*con fucile*) shooting; (*inseguimento*) chase; (*selvaggina*) game ● *nm inv Aeron* fighter; *Naut* destroyer

cacciabombardi'ere *nm* fighter-bomber

cacciagi'one *nf* game

cacci'a|re *vt* hunt; (*mandar via*) chase away; (*scacciare*) drive out; (*ficcare*) shove ● *vi* go hunting. ~**rsi** *vr* (*nascondersi*) hide; (*andare a finire*) get to; ~**rsi nei guai** get into trouble; **alla** ~**'tora** *a* Culin chasseur. ~**'tore, ~'trice** *nmf* hunter. ~**tore di frodo** poacher

caccia'vite *nm inv* screwdriver

ca'chet *nm inv Med* capsule; (*colorante*) colour rinse; (*stile*) cachet

'cachi *nm inv* (*albero, frutta*) persimmon

'cacio *nm* (*formaggio*) cheese

'caco *nm fam* (*frutto*) persimmon

'cactus *nm inv* cactus

ca'da|vere *nm* corpse. ~**'verico** *a fig* deathly pale

ca'dente *a* falling; (*casa*) crumbling

ca'denza *nf* cadence; (*ritmo*) rhythm; *Mus* cadenza

ca'dere *vi* fall; (*capelli ecc:*) fall out; (*capitombolare*) tumble; (*vestito ecc:*) hang; **far** ~ (*di mano*)

drop; ~ **dal sonno** feel very sleepy; **lasciar** ~ drop; **dalle nuvole** *fig* be taken aback

ca'detto *nm* cadet

ca'duta *nf* fall; (*di capelli*) loss; *fig* downfall

caffè *nm inv* coffee; (*locale*) café. ~ **corretto** espresso coffee with a dash of liqueur. ~ **lungo** weak black coffee. ~ **macchiato** coffee with a dash of milk. ~ **ristretto** extra-strong espresso coffee. ~ **solubile** instant coffee. ~**'ina** *nf* caffeine. ~**'latte** *nm inv* white coffee.

caffetti'era *nf* coffee-pot

cafo'naggine *nf* boorishness

cafo'nata *nf* boorishness

ca'fone, -a *nmf* boor

ca'gare *vi fam* crap

cagio'nare *vt* cause

cagio'nevole *a* delicate

cagli'ar|e *vi*, ~**si** *vr* curdle

'cagna *nf* bitch

ca'gnara *nf fam* din

ca'gnesco *a* **guardare qcno in** ~ scowl at sb

'cala *nf* creek

cala'brone *nm* hornet

cala'maio *nm* inkpot

cala'mari *nmpl* squid *sg*

cala'mita *nf* magnet

calamità *nf inv* calamity

ca'lar|e *vi* come down; (*vento:*) drop; (*diminuire*) fall; (*tramontare*) set ● *vt* (*abbassare*) lower; (*nei lavori a maglia*) decrease ● *nm* (*di luna*) waning. ~**si** *vr* lower oneself

'calca *nf* throng

cal'cagno *nm* heel

cal'care[1] *nm* limestone

cal'care[2] *vt* tread; (*premere*) press [down]; ~ **la mano** *fig* exaggerate; ~ **le orme di qcno** *fig* follow in sb's footsteps

'calce[1] *nf* lime

'calce[2] *nm* **in** ~ at the foot of the page

calce'struzzo *nm* concrete

cal'cetto *nm Sport* five-a-side [football]

calci'a|re *vt* kick. ~'tore *nm* footballer

cal'cina *nf* mortar

calci'naccio *nm* (*pezzo di intonaco*) flake of plaster

'calcio¹ *nm* kick; *Sport* football; (*di arma da fuoco*) butt; **dare un ~ a** kick. ~ **d'angolo** corner [kick]

'calcio² *nm* (*chimica*) calcium

'calco *nm* (*con carta*) tracing; (*arte*) cast

calco'la|re *vt* calculate, (*considerare*) consider. ~'tore *nm* calculating ●*nm* calculator; (*macchina elettronica*) computer

'calcolo *nm* calculation; *Med* stone

cal'daia *nf* boiler

caldar'rosta *nf* roast chestnut

caldeggi'are *vt* support

'caldo *a* warm; (*molto caldo*) hot ●*nm* heat; **avere ~** be warm/hot; **fa ~** it is warm/hot

calen'dario *nm* calendar

ca'libro *nm* calibre; (*strumento*) callipers *pl*; **di grosso ~** (*persona*) top *attrib*

'calice *nm* goblet; *Relig* chalice

ca'ligine *nm* fog; (*industriale*) smog

calligra'fia *nf* handwriting; (*cinese*) calligraphy

cal'lista *nmf* chiropodist. 'callo *nm* corn, have il callo a become hardened to. cal'loso *a* callous

'calma *nf* calm. cal'mante *a* calming ●*nm* sedative. cal'mare *vt* calm [down] (*lenire*) soothe cal'marsi *vr* calm down; (*vento*) drop; (*dolore*) die down. calmo *a* calm

'calo *nm Comm* fall; (*di volume*) shrinkage; (*di peso*) loss

calorosa'mente *adv* (*cordialmente*) warmly

ca'lore *nm* heat; (*moderato*) warmth; **in ~** (*animale*) on heat. calo'roso *a* warm

calo'ria *nf* calorie

ca'lorico *a* calorific

calo'rifero *nm* radiator

calpe'stare *vt* trample [down]; *fig* trample on (*diritti, sentimenti*); **vietato ~ l'erba** keep off the grass

calpe'stio *nm* (*passi*) footsteps

ca'lunni|a *nf* slander. ~'are *vt* slander. ~'oso *a* slanderous

ca'lura *nf* heat

cal'vario *nm* Calvary; *fig* trial

cal'vizie *nf* baldness. 'calvo *a* bald

calz|a *nf* (*da donna*) stocking; (*da uomo*) sock. ~a'maglia *nf* tights *pl*; (*per danza*) leotard

cal'zante *a fig* fitting

cal'za|re *vt* (*indossare*) wear; (*mettersi*) put on ●*vi* fit

calza'scarpe *nm inv* shoehorn

calza'tura *nf* footwear

calzatu'rificio *nm* shoe factory

cal'zetta *nf* **è una mezza ~** *fig* he's no use

calzet'tone *nm* knee-length woollen sock. cal'zino *nm* sock

calzo'l|aio *nm* shoemaker. ~e'ria *nf* (*negozio*) shoe shop

calzon'cini *nmpl* shorts. ~ **da bagno** swimming trunks

cal'zone *nm Culin* folded pizza with tomato and mozzarella or ricotta inside

cal'zoni *nmpl* trousers, pants *Am*

camale'onte *nm* chameleon

cambi'ale *nf* bill of exchange

cambia'mento *nm* change

cambi'ar|e *vt/i* change; move (*casa*); (*fare cambio di*) exchange; **~e rotta** *Naut* alter course. ~**si** *vr* change. **'cambio** *nm* change; (*Comm, scambio*) exchange; *Mech* gear; **dare il cambio a** relieve sb; **in cambio di** in exchange for

'camera *nf* room; (*mobili*) [bedroom] suite; *Phot* camera; *Pol, Comm* Chamber. **~ ardente** funeral parlour. **~ d'aria** inner tube. **C~ di Commercio** Chamber of Commerce. **C~ dei Deputati** *Pol* ≈ House of Commons. **~ doppia** double room. ~ **da letto** bedroom. ~ **matrimoniale** double room. ~ **oscura** darkroom. ~ **singola** single room

came'rata¹ nf (dormitorio) dormitory; Mil barrack room

came'ra|ta² nmf (amico) mate; Pol comrade. **~'tismo** nm comradeship

cameri'era nf maid; (di ristorante) waitress; (in albergo) chambermaid; (di bordo) stewardess

cameri'ere nm manservant; (di ristorante) waiter; (di bordo) steward

came'rino nm dressing-room

'camice nm overall. **cami'cetta** nf blouse. **ca'micia** nf shirt; **uovo in camicia** poached egg. **camicia di notte** nightdress

cami'netto nm fireplace

ca'mino nm chimney; (focolare) fireplace

'camion nm inv lorry Br, truck

camion'cino nm van

camio'netta nf jeep

camio'nista nmf lorry driver Br, truck driver

cam'mello nm camel; (tessuto) camel-hair ● a inv (colore) camel

cam'meo nm cameo

cammi'na|re vi walk; (auto, orologio:) go. **~ta** nf walk; **fare una ~ta** go for a walk. **cam'mino** nm way; **essere in cammino** be on the way; **mettersi in cammino** set out

camo'milla nf camomile; (bevanda) camomile tea

ca'morra nf local mafia

ca'moscio nm chamois; (pelle) suede

cam'pagna nf country; (paesaggio) countryside; Comm, Mil campaign; **in ~** in the country. **~ elettorale** election campaign. **~ pubblicitaria** marketing campaign. **campa'gnolo, -a** a rustic ● nm countryman ● nf countrywoman

cam'pale a field attrib; **giornata ~** fig strenuous day

cam'pa|na nf bell; (di vetro) belljar. **~'nella** nf (di tenda) curtain ring. **~'nello** nm door-bell; (cicalino) buzzer

campa'nile nm belfry

campani'lismo nm parochialism

campani'lista nmf person with a parochial outlook

cam'panula nf Bot campanula

cam'pare vi live; (a stento) get by

cam'pato a **~ in aria** unfounded

campeggi'a|re vi camp; (spiccare) stand out. **~'tore, ~'trice** nmf camper. **cam'peggio** nm camping; (terreno) campsite

cam'pestre a rural

'camping nm inv campsite

campio'nari|o nm [set of] samples ● a samples; **fiera ~a** trade fair

campio'nato nm championship

campiona'tura nf (di merce) range of samples

campi'on|e nm champion; Comm sample; (esemplare) specimen. **~'essa** nf ladies' champion

'campo nm field; (accampamento) camp. **~ da calcio** football pitch. **~ di concentramento** concentration camp. **~ da golf** golf course. **~ da tennis** tennis court

camuf'far|e vt disguise. **~si** vr disguise oneself

'Cana|da nm Canada. **~'dese** a & nmf Canadian

ca'naglia nf scoundrel; (plebaglia) rabble

ca'nal|e nm channel; (artificiale) canal. **~iz'zare** vt channel (acque). **~izzazi'one** nf channelling; (rete) pipes pl

'canapa nf hemp

cana'rino nm canary

cancel'la|re vt cross out; (con la gomma) rub out; fig wipe out; (annullare) cancel; Comput delete, erase. **~'tura** nf erasure. **~zi'one** nf cancellation; Comput deletion

cancelle'ria nf chancellery; (articoli per scrivere) stationery

cancelli'ere nm chancellor; (di tribunale) clerk

can'cello nm gate

cance'ro|geno nm carcinogen ●a carcinogenic. **~'roso** a cancerous

can'crena nf gangrene

'cancro nm cancer. **C~** Astr Cancer

candeg'gi|na nf bleach. **~'are** vt bleach. **oan'doggio** nm bleaching

can'de|la nf candle; Auto spark plug; **~'labro** nm candelabra. **~li'ere** nm candlestick

cande'lotto nm (di dinamite) stick

candida'mente adv candidly

candi'da|rsi vr stand as a candidate. **~to, -a** nmf candidate. **~'tura** nf Pol candidacy; (per lavoro) application

'candido a snow-white; (sincero) candid; (puro) pure

can'dito a candied

can'dore nm whiteness; fig innocence

'cane nm dog; (di arma da fuoco) cock; **un tempo da cani** foul weather. **~ da caccia** hunting dog

ca'nestro nm basket

cangi'ante a iridescent; **seta ~** shot silk

can'guro nm kangaroo

ca'nile nm kennel; (di allevamento) kennels pl. **~ municipale** dog pound

ca'nino a & nm canine

canna nf reed; (da zucchero) cane; (di fucile) barrel; (bastone) stick; (di bicicletta) crossbar; (asta) rod; (fam: hascish) joint; **povero in ~** destitute. **~ da pesca** fishing-rod

can'nella nf cinnamon

can'neto nm bed of reeds

canni'ba|le nm cannibal. **~'lismo** nm cannibalism

cannocchi'ale nm telescope

canno'nata nf cannon shot; **è una ~** fig it's brilliant

cannon'cino nm (dolce) cream horn

can'none nm cannon; fig ace

can'nuccia nf [drinking] straw; (di pipa) stem

ca'noa nf canoe

'canone nm canon; (affitto) rent; **equo ~** fair rents act

ca'noni|co nm canon. **~z'zare** vt canonize. **~zzazi'one** nf canonization

ca'noro a melodious

ca'notta nf (estiva) vest top

canot'taggio nm canoeing; (voga) rowing

canotti'era nf singlet

canotti'ere nm oarsman

ca'notto nm [rubber] dinghy

cano'vaccio nm (trama) plot; (straccio) duster

can'tante nmf singer

can't|are vt/i sing. **~au'tore, ~a'trice** nmf singer-songwriter. **~icchi'are** vt sing softly; (a bocca chiusa) hum

canti'ere nm yard; Naut shipyard; (di edificio) construction site. **~ navale** naval dockyard

canti'lena nf singsong; (ninnananna) lullaby

can'tina nf cellar; (osteria) wine shop

'canto¹ nm singing; (canzone) song; Relig chant; (poesia) poem

'canto² nm (angolo) corner; (lato) side; **dal ~ mio** for my part; **d'altro ~** on the other hand

canto'nata nf prendere una ~ fig be sadly mistaken

can'tone nm canton; (angolo) corner

can'tuccio nm nook

canzo'na|re vt tease. **~'torio** a teasing. **~'tura** nf teasing

can'zo|ne nf song. **~'netta** nf fam pop song. **~ni'ere** nm songbook

'caos nm chaos. **ca'otico** a chaotic

C.A.P. nm abbr (Codice di Avviamento Postale) post code, zip code Am

ca'pac|e a able; (esperto) skilled;

(*stadio, contenitore*) big; **~e di** (*disposto a*) capable of; **~ità** *nf inv* ability; (*attitudine*) skill; (*capienza*) capacity

capaci'tarsi *vr* **~ di** (*rendersi conto*) understand; (*accorgersi*) realize

ca'panna *nf* hut

capan'nello *nm* **fare ~ intorno a** qcno/qcsa gather round sb/sth

capan'none *nm* shed; *Aeron* hangar

ca'parbio *a* obstinate

ca'parra *nf* deposit

capa'tina *nf* short visit; **fare una ~ in città/da** qcno pop into town/ in on sb

ca'pello *nm* hair; **~li** *pl* (*capigliatura*) hair *sg*. **~'lone** *nm* hippie. **~'luto** *a* hairy

capez'zale *nm* bolster; *fig* bedside

ca'pezzolo *nm* nipple

capi'en|te *a* capacious. **~za** *nf* capacity

capiglia'tura *nf* hair

ca'pire *vt* understand; **~ male** misunderstand; **si capisce!** naturally!; **sì, ho capito** yes, I see

capi'ta|le *a* *Jur* capital; (*principale*) main ● *nf* (*città*) capital ● *nm Comm* capital. **~'lismo** *nm* capitalism. **~'lista** *nmf* capitalist. **~'listico** *a* capitalist

capitane'ria *nf* **~ di porto** port authorities *pl*

capi'tano *nm* captain

capi'tare *vi* (*giungere per caso*) come; (*accadere*) happen

capi'tello *nm Archit* capital

capito'la|re *vi* capitulate. **~zi'one** *nf* capitulation

ca'pitolo *nm* chapter

capi'tombolo *nm* headlong fall; **fare un ~** tumble down

'capo *nm* head; (*chi comanda*) boss *fam*; (*di vestiario*) item; *Geog* cape; (*in tribù*) chief; (*parte estrema*) top; **a ~** (*in dettato*) new paragraph; **da ~** over again; **in ~ a un mese** within the month; **giramento di ~** dizziness; **mal di ~** head-

ache; **~ d'abbigliamento** item of clothing. **~ d'accusa** *Jur* charge, count. **~ di bestiame** head of cattle

capo'banda *nm Mus* bandmaster; (*di delinquenti*) ringleader

ca'poccia *nm* (*fam: testa*) nut

capocci'one, -a *nmf fam* brainbox

capo'danno *nm* New Year's Day

capofa'miglia *nmf* head of the family

capo'fitto *nm* **a ~** headlong

capo'giro *nm* giddiness

capola'voro *nm* masterpiece

capo'linea *nm* terminus

capo'lino *nm* **fare ~** peep in

capolu'ogo *nm* main town

capo'rale *nm* lance-corporal

capo'squadra *nmf Sport* team captain

capo'stipite *nmf* (*di famiglia*) progenitor

capo'tavola *nmf* head of the table

capo'treno *nm* guard

capouf'ficio *nmf* head clerk

capo'verso *nm* first line

capo'vol|gere *vt* overturn; *fig* reverse. **~gersi** *vr* overturn; (*barca:*) capsize; *fig* be reversed. **~to** *pp* *di* **capovolgere** ● *a* upside-down

'cappa *nf* cloak; (*di camino*) cowl; (*di cucina*) hood

cap'pel|la *nf* chapel. **~'lano** *nm* chaplain

cap'pello *nm* hat. **~ a cilindro** top hat

'cappero *nm* caper

'cappio *nm* noose

cap'pone *nm* capon

cap'potto *nm* [over]coat

cappuc'cino *nm* (*frate*) Capuchin; (*bevanda*) white coffee

cap'puccio *nm* hood; (*di penna stilografica*) cap

'capra *nf* goat. **ca'pretto** *nm* kid

ca'priccio *nm* whim; (*bizzarria*) freak; **fare i capricci** have tantrums. **~'oso** *a* capricious; (*bambino*) naughty

Capri'corno nm Astr Capricorn
capri'ola nf somersault
capri'olo nm roe-deer
'capro nm [billy-]goat. **~ espiatorio** scapegoat. **ca'prone** nm [billy] goat
'capsula nf capsule; (di proiettile) cap; (di dente) crown
cap'tare vt Radio, TV pick up; catch (attenzione)
cara'bina nf carbine
carabini'ere nm carabiniere; **carabini'eri** pl Italian police force (which is a branch of the army)
ca'raffa nf carafe
Ca'raibi nmpl (zona) Caribbean sg; (isole) Caribbean Islands; **il mar dei ~** the Caribbean [Sea]
cara'mella nf sweet
cara'mello nm caramel
ca'rato nm carat
ca'ratte|re nm character, (caratteristica) characteristic; Typ letter; **di buon ~re** good-natured. **~'ristico, -a** a characteristic; (pittoresco) quaint ● nf characteristic. **~riz'zare** vt characterize
carbon'cino nm (per disegno) charcoal
car'bone nm coal
carboniz'zare vt burn to a cinder
carbu'rante nm fuel
carbura'tore nm carburettor
car'cassa nf carcass; fig old wreck
carce'ra|rio a prison attrib. **~to, -a** nmf prisoner. **~zi'one** nf imprisonment. **~zione preventiva** preventive detention
'carcer|e nm prison, (punizione) imprisonment. **~i'ere, -a** nmf gaoler
carci'ofo nm artichoke
car'diaco a cardiac
cardi'nale a & nm cardinal
'cardine nm hinge
cardio|chi'rurgo nm heart surgeon **~lo'gia** nf cardiology. **cardi'ologo** nm heart specialist. **~'tonico** nm heart stimulant
'cardo nm thistle
ca'rena nf Naut bottom

ca'ren|te a **~te di** lacking in. **~za** nf lack; (scarsità) scarcity
care'stia nf famine; (mancanza) dearth
ca'rezza nf caress; **fare una ~ a** caress
cari'arsi vi decay. **~to** a decayed
'carica nf office; Mil, Electr charge; fig drive. **cari'care** vt load; Mil, Electr charge; wind up (orologio). **~'tore** nm (per proiettile) magazine
carica'tu|ra nf caricature. **~'rale** a grotesque. **~'rista** nmf caricaturist
'carico a loaded (**di** with); (colore) strong; (orologio) wound [up]; (batteria) charged ● nm load; (di nave) cargo; (il caricare) loading; **a ~ di** Comm to be charged to; (persona) dependent on
'carie nf [tooth] decay
ca'rino a pretty; (piacevole) agreeable
ca'risma nf charisma. **caris'matico** a charismatic
carità nf charity; **per ~à!** (come rifiuto) God forbid!. **~a'tevole** a charitable
carnagi'one nf complexion
car'naio nm fig shambles
car'nale a carnal; **cugino ~** first cousin
'carne nf flesh; (alimento) meat; **~ di manzo/maiale/vitello** beef/pork/veal
car'nefi|ce nm executioner. **~'cina** nf slaughter
carne'vale nm carnival. **~'lesco** a carnival
car'nivoro nm carnivore ● a carnivorous
car'noso a fleshy
'caro, -a a dear; **cari saluti** kind regards ● nmf fam darling, dear; **i miei cari** my nearest and dearest
ca'rogna nf carcass; fig bastard
caro'sello nm merry-go-round
ca'rota nf carrot
caro'vana nf caravan; (di veicoli) convoy

caro'vita nm high cost of living

'carpa nf carp

carpenti'ere nm carpenter

car'pire vt seize; (con difficoltà) extort

car'pone, car'poni adv on all fours

car'rabile a suitable for vehicles; **passo ~** vedi **carraio**

car'raio a **passo ~** entrance to driveway, garage etc where parking is forbidden

carreggi'ata nf roadway; **doppia ~** dual carriageway, divided highway Am

carrel'lata nf TV pan

car'rello nm trolley; (di macchina da scrivere) carriage; Aeron undercarriage; Cinema, TV dolly. **~ d'atterraggio** Aeron landing gear

car'retto nm cart

carri'era nf career; **di gran ~ra** at full speed; **fare ~ra** get on. **~'rismo** nm careerism

carri'ola nf wheelbarrow

'carro nm cart. **~ armato** tank. **~ attrezzi** breakdown vehicle, wrecker Am. **~ funebre** hearse. **~ merci** truck

car'rozza nf carriage; Rail car, coach. **~ cuccette** sleeping car. **~ ristorante** restaurant car

carroz'zella nf (per bambini) pram; (per invalidi) wheelchair

carrozze'ria nf bodywork; (officina) bodyshop

carroz'zina nf pram; (pieghevole) push-chair, stroller Am

carroz'zone nm (di circo) caravan

'carta nf paper; (da gioco) card; (statuto) charter; Geog map. **~ d'argento** ≈ senior citizens' railcard. **~ assorbente** blotting-paper. **~ di credito** credit card. **~ geografica** map. **~ d'identità** identity card. **~ igienica** toilet-paper. **~ di imbarco** boarding card or pass. **~ da lettere** writing-paper. **~ da parati** wallpaper. **~ stagnola** silver paper; Culin aluminium foil. **~ straccia** waste

paper. **~ stradale** road map. **~ velina** tissue-paper. **~ verde** Auto green card. **~ vetrata** sandpaper

cartacar'bone nf carbon paper

carta'ccia nf waste paper

carta'modello nm paper pattern

cartamo'neta nf paper money

carta'pesta nf papier mâché

carta'straccia nf waste paper

cartave'trare vt sand [down]

car'tella nf (per documenti ecc) briefcase; (di cartone) folder; (di scolaro) satchel. **~la clinica** medical record. **~'lina** nf document wallet, folder

cartel'lino nm (etichetta) label; (dei prezzi) price-tag; (di presenza) time-card; **timbrare il ~** clock in; (all'uscita) clock out

cartel'lo nm sign; (pubblicitario) poster; (stradale) road sign; (di protesta) placard; Comm cartel. **~'lone** nm poster; Theat bill

carti'era nf paper-mill

carti'lagine nf cartilage

car'tina nf map

car'toccio nm paper bag; **al ~** Culin baked in foil

carto'|laio, -a nmf stationer. **~le'ria** nf stationer's. **~libre'ria** nf stationer's and book shop

carto'lina nf postcard; **~ postale** postcard

carto'mante nmf fortune-teller

carton'cino nm (materiale) card

car'tone nm cardboard; (arte) cartoon. **~ animato** [animated] cartoon

car'tuccia nf cartridge

'casa nf house; (abitazione propria) home; (ditta) firm; **amico di ~** family friend; **andare a ~** go home; **essere di ~** be like one of the family; **fatto in ~** home-made; **padrone di ~** (di pensione ecc) landlord; (proprietario) house owner. **~ di cura** nursing home. **~ popolare** council house. **~ dello studente** hall of residence

ca'sacca nf military coat; (giacca) jacket

ca'saccio *adv* a ~ at random

casa'ling|a *nf* housewife. ~o *a* domestic; (*fatto in casa*) home-made; (*amante della casa*) home-loving; (*semplice*) homely

ca'scante *a* falling; (*floscio*) flabby

ca'sca|re *vi* fall [down]. ~ta *nf* (*di acqua*) waterfall

ca'schetto *nm* [capelli a] ~ bob

ca'scina *nf* farm building

'casco *nm* crash-helmet; (*asciuga-capelli*) [hair-]drier; ~ di banane bunch of bananas

caseggi'ato *nm* block of flats *Br*, apartment block

casei'ficio *nm* dairy

ca'sella *nf* pigeon-hole. ~ postale post office box; *Comput* mailbox

casel'lante *nmf* (*per treni*) signal-man

casel'lario *nm* ~ giudiziario record of convictions; avere il ~ giudiziario vergine have no criminal record

ca'sello [autostra'dale] *nm* [motorway] toll booth

case'reccio *a* home-made

ca'serma *nf* barracks *pl*; (*dei carabinieri*) [police] station

casi'nista *nmf* *fam* muddler. ca'sino *nm* *fam* (*bordello*) brothel; (*fig: confusione*) racket; (*disordine*) mess; un casino di loads of

casinò *nm inv* casino

ca'sistica *nf* (*classificazione*) case records *pl*

'caso *nm* chance; (*fatto, circostanza, Med, Gram*) case; a ~ at random; ~ mai if need be; far ~ a pay attention to; non far ~ a take no account of; per ~ by chance. ~ [giudiziario] [legal] case

caso'lare *nm* farmhouse

'caspita *int* good gracious!

'cassa *nf* till; *Comm* cash; (*luogo di pagamento*) cash desk; (*mobile*) chest; (*istituto bancario*) bank. ~ automatica prelievi cash dispenser, automatic teller. ~ da

morto coffin. ~ toracica *Anat* ribcage

cassa'forte *nf* safe

cassa'panca *nf* linen chest

casseru'ola *nf* saucepan

cas'setta *nf* case; (*per registratore*) cassette. ~ delle lettere postbox, letterbox. ~ di sicurezza strong-box

cas'set|to *nm* drawer. ~'tone *nm* chest of drawers

cassi'ere, -a *nmf* cashier; (*di supermercato*) checkout assistant, checkout operator; (*di banca*) teller

'casta *nf* caste

ca'stagn|a *nf* chestnut. casta-'gneto *nm* chestnut grove. ~o *nm* chestnut[-tree]

ca'stano *a* chestnut

ca'stello *nm* castle; (*impalcatura*) scaffold

casti'gare *vt* punish

casti'gato *a* (*casto*) chaste

ca'stigo *nm* punishment

casti'tà *nf* chastity. 'casto *a* chaste

ca'storo *nm* beaver

ca'strare *vt* castrate

casu'al|e *a* chance *attrib*. ~'mente *adv* by chance

ca'supola *nf* little house

cata'clisma *nm* *fig* upheaval

cata'comba *nf* catacomb

cata'fascio *nm* andare a ~ go to rack and ruin

cata'litico *a* marmitta catalitica *Auto* catalytic converter

cataliz'za|re *vt* *fig* heighten. ~'tore *nm* *Auto* catalytic converter

catalo'gare *vt* catalogue. ca'talo-go *nm* catalogue

catama'rano *nm* (*da diporto*) catamaran

cata'pecchia *nf* hovel; *fam* dump

catapul'tar|e *vt* (*scaraventare fuori*) eject. ~si *vr* (*precipitarsi*) dive

catarifran'gente *nm* reflector

ca'tarro *nm* catarrh

ca'tasta *nf* pile

ca'tasto *nm* land register

ca'tastrofe *nf* catastrophe. **cata-'strofico** *a* catastrophic

cate'chismo *nm* catechism

cate|go'ria *nf* category. ~'gorico *a* categorical

ca'tena *nf* chain. ~ montuosa mountain range. **catene** *pl* da neve tyre-chains. **cate'naccio** *nm* bolt

cate|'nella *nf* (collana) chain. ~'nina *nf* chain

cate'ratta *nf* cataract

ca'terva *nf* una ~ di heaps of

cati'nell|a *nf* basin; **piovere a ~e** bucket down

ca'tino *nm* basin

ca'torcio *nm fam* old wreck

ca'trame *nm* tar

'cattedra *nf* (tavolo di insegnante) desk; (di università) chair

catte'drale *nf* cathedral

catti'veria *nf* wickedness; (azione) wicked action

cattività *nf* captivity

cat'tivo *a* bad; (bambino) naughty

catto|'cesimo *nm* Catholicism

cat'tolico, -a *a & nmf* [Roman] Catholic

cat'tu|ra *nf* capture. ~'rare *vt* capture

caucciù *nm* rubber

'causa *nf* cause; *Jur* lawsuit; **far ~ a** qcno sue sb. **cau'sare** *vt* cause

'caustico *a* caustic

cauta'mente *adv* cautiously

cau'tela *nf* caution

caute'lar|e *vt* protect. ~si *vr* take precautions

cauteriz'z|are *vt* cauterize. ~i'o-ne *nf* cauterization

'cauto *a* cautious

cauzi'one *nf* security; (per libertà provvisoria) bail

'cava *nf* quarry; *fig* mine

caval'ca|re *vt* ride; (stare a caval-cioni) sit astride. ~ta *nf* ride; (cor-teo) cavalcade. ~'via *nm* flyover

cavalci'oni: a ~ *adv* astride

cavali'ere *nm* rider; (titolo) knight; (accompagnatore) escort; (al ballo) partner

cavalle'resco *a* chivalrous. ~'ria

nf chivalry; *Mil* cavalry. ~'rizzo, -a *nm* horseman ●*nf* horsewoman

caval'letta *nf* grasshopper

caval'letto *nm* trestle; (di macchi-na fotografica) tripod; (di pittore) easel

caval'lina *nf* (ginnastica) horse

ca'vallo *nm* horse; (misura di po-tenza) horsepower; (scacchi) knight; (dei pantaloni) crotch; **a ~** on horseback; **andare a ~** go horse-riding. **~ a dondolo** rocking-horse

caval'lone *nm* (ondata) roller

caval'luccio ma'rino *nm* sea horse

ca'var|e *vt* take out; (di dosso) take off; ~**sela** get away with it; **se la cava** bene he's doing all right

cava'tappi *nm inv* corkscrew

ca'ver|na *nf* cave. ~'noso *a* (voce) deep

'cavia *nf* guinea-pig

cavi'ale *nm* caviar

ca'viglia *nf* ankle

cavil'lare *vi* quibble. ca'villo *nm* quibble

cavità *nf inv* cavity

'cavo *a* hollow ●*nm* cavity; (di metallo) cable; *Naut* rope

cavo'lata *nf fam* rubbish

cavo'letto *nm* ~ **di Bruxelles** Brussels sprout

cavolfi'ore *nm* cauliflower

'cavolo *nm* cabbage; ~! *fam* sugar!

caz'zo *int vulg* fuck!

caz'zott|o *nm* punch; **prendere a** qcno a ~i beat sb up

cazzu'ola *nf* trowel

c/c *abbr* (conto corrente) c/a

CD-Rom *nm inv* CD-Rom

ce *pers pron* (a noi) (to) us ●*adv* there; ~ **ne sono molti** there are many

'cece *nm* chick-pea

cecità *nf* blindness

ceco, -a *a & nmf* Czech; **la Repub-blica Ceca** the Czech Republic

Cecoslo'vacc|hia *nf* Czechoslo-vakia. c~o, -a *a & nmf* Czechoslo-vak '**cedere** *vi* (*arrendersi*) surrender; (*concedere*) yield; (*sprofondare*) subside ● *vt* give up; make over (*proprietà ecc*). **ce'devole** *a* (*terreno ecc*) soft; *fig* yielding. **cedi'mento** nm (*di terreno*) subsidence

'**cedola** nf coupon

'**cedro** nm (*albero*) cedar; (*frutto*) citron

C.E.E. nf abbr (**Comunità Economica Europea**) E[E]C

'**ceffo** nm (*muso*) snout; (*pej: persona*) mug

cef'fone nm slap

ce'lar|e vt conceal. **~si** vr hide

cele'bra|re vt celebrate. **~zi'one** nf celebration

ce'lebr|e a famous. **~ità** nf inv celebrity

celere a swift

ce'leste a (*divino*) heavenly ● a & nm (*colore*) sky-blue

celi'bato nm celibacy

'**celibe** a single ● nm bachelor

'**cella** nf cell

'**cellofan** nm inv cellophane: *Culin* cling film

'**cellula** nf cell. **~ fotoelettrica** electronic eye

cellu'lare nm (*telefono*) cellular phone ● a (*furgone*) **~** nm police van. [*telefono*] **~** nm cellular phone

cellu'lite nf cellulite

cellu'loide a celluloid

cellu'losa nf cellulose

'**celt|a** nm Celt. **~ico** a Celtic

cemen'tare vt cement. **ce'mento** nm cement. **cemento armato** reinforced concrete

'**cena** nf dinner; (*leggera*) supper

ce'nacolo nm circle

ce'nare vi have dinner

cencio nm rag; (*per spolverare*) duster. **~oso** a in rags

'**cenere** nf ash; (*di carbone ecc*) cinders

ce'netta nf (*cena semplice*) informal dinner

'**cenno** nm sign; (*col capo*) nod; (*con la mano*) wave; (*allusione*) hint; (*breve resoconto*) mention

ce'none nm il **~ di Capodanno/ Natale** special New Year's Eve/ Christmas Eve dinner

censi'mento nm census

cen's|ore nm censor. **~ura** nf censorship. **~u'rare** vt censor

centelli'nare vt sip

cente'n|ario, -a a & nmf centenarian ● nm (*commemorazione*) centenary. **~'nale** a centennial

cen'tesimo a hundredth ● nm (*di dollaro*) cent; **non avere un ~** be penniless

cen'ti|grado a centigrade. **~metro** nm centimetre

centi'naio nm hundred

'**cento** a & nm a or one hundred; **per ~** per cent

cento'metrista nmf *Sport* one hundred metres runner

cento'mila a or one hundred thousand

cen'trale a central ● nf (*di società ecc*) head office. **~ atomica** atomic power station. **~ elettrica** power station. **~ nucleare** nuclear power station. **~ telefonica** [telephone] exchange

centra'li|na nf *Teleph* switchboard. **~nista** nmf operator

centra'lino nm *Teleph* exchange; (*di albergo ecc*) switchboard

centra'li|smo nm centralism. **~z'zare** vt centralize

cen'trare vt **~ qcsa** hit sth in the centre; (*fissare nel centro*) centre; *fig* hit on the head (*idea*)

cen'trifu|ga nf spin-drier. **~ [asciugaverdure]** shaker. **~'gare** vt *Techn* centrifuge; (*lavatrice:*) spin

cen'trino nm doily

'**centro** nm centre. **~ [città]** city centre. **~ commerciale** shopping centre, mall. **~ sociale** community centre

'**ceppo** nm (*di albero*) stump; (*da ardere*) log; (*fig: gruppo*) stock

'cera nf wax; (aspetto) look. **~ per il pavimento** floor-polish

ce'ramica nf (arte) ceramics; (materia) pottery; (oggetto) piece of pottery

ce'rato a (tela) waxed

cerbi'atto nm fawn

'cerca nf **andare in ~ di** look for

cercaper'sone nm inv beeper

cer'care vt look for ● vi ~ **di** try to

'cerchi|**a** nf circle. **~'are** vt circle (parola). **~'ato** a (occhi) black-ringed. **~'etto** nm (per capelli) hairband

'cerchi|**o** nm circle; (giocattolo) hoop. **~'one** nm alloy wheel

cere'ale nm cereal

cere'brale a cerebral

'cereo a waxen

ce'retta nf depilatory wax

ceri'moni|**a** nf ceremony. **~'ale** nm ceremonial. **~'oso** a ceremonious

ce'rino nm [wax] match

cerni'era nf hinge; (di borsa) clasp. **~ lampo** zip[-fastener], zipper Am

'cernita nf selection

'cero nm candle

ce'rone nm grease-paint

ce'rotto nm [sticking] plaster

'certa'mente adv certainly

cer'tezza nf certainty

certifi'ca|**re** vt certify. **~to** nm certificate

'certo a certain; (notizia) definite; (indeterminativo) some; **sono ~ di riuscire** I am certain to succeed; **a una certa età** at a certain age; **certi giorni** some days; **un ~ signor Giardini** a Mr Giardini; **una certa Anna** somebody called Anna; **certa gente** pej some people; **ho certi dolori** I'm in such pain!. **certi** pron pl some; (alcune persone) some people ● adv of course; **sapere per ~** know for certain, know for sure; **di ~** surely; **~ che si!** of course!

cer'vel|**lo** nm brain. **~'lone, -a** nmf hum genius. **~'lotico** a (macchinoso) over-elaborate

'cervo nm deer

ce'sareo a Med Caesarean

cesel'la|**re** vt chisel. **~to** a chiselled. **ce'sello** nm chisel

ce'soie nfpl shears

ce'spuglio nm bush. **~'oso** a (terreno) bushy

ces'sa|**re** vi stop, cease ● vt stop. **~re** nm **il fuoco** ceasefire. **~zi'one** nf cessation

cessi'one nf handover

'cesso sl (gabinetto) bog, john Am; (fig: locale, luogo) dump

'cesta nf [large] basket. **ce'stello** nm (per lavatrice) drum

cesti'nare vt throw away. **ce'stino** nm [small] basket; (per la carta straccia) waste-paper basket. **'cesto** nm basket

'ceto nm [social] class

'cetra nf lyre

cetrio'lino nm gherkin. **cetri'olo** nm cucumber

cfr abbr (**confronta**) cf.

che pron rel (persona: soggetto) who; (persona: oggetto) that, who, whom fml; (cosa, animale) that, which; **questa è la casa ~ ho comprato** this is the house [that] I've bought; **il ~ mi sorprende** which surprises me; **dal ~ deduco che...** from which I gather that...; **avere di ~ vivere** have enough to live on; **grazie! – non c'è di!** thank you! – don't mention it!; **il giorno ~ ti ho visto** fam the day I saw you ● a inter what; (esclamativo: con aggettivo) how; (con nome) what a; **~ macchina prendiamo, la tua o la mia?** which car are we taking, yours or mine?; **~ bello!** how nice!; **~ idea!** what an idea!; **~ bella giornata!** what a lovely day! ● pron inter what; **a ~ pensi?** what are you thinking about? ● conj that; (con comparazioni) than; **credo ~ abbia ragione** I think [that] he is right; **era così commosso ~ non riusciva a parlare** he was so moved [that] he couldn't speak; **aspetto ~ telefoni** I'm waiting for him to phone; **è da**

un po' ~ **non lo vedo** it's been a while since I saw him; **mi piace più Roma** ~ **Milano** I like Rome better than Milan; ~ **ti piaccia o no** whether you like it or not; ~ **io sappia** as far as I know

checché *indef pron* whatever

chemiotera'pia *nf* chemotherapy

chero'sene *nm* paraffin

cheru'bino *nm* cherub

cheti'chella: alla ~ *adv* silently

'cheto *a* quiet

chi *rel pron* whoever; *(coloro che)* people who; **ho trovato** ~ **ti può aiutare** I found somebody who can help you; **c'è** ~ **dice che...** some people say that...; **senti** ~ **parla!** listen to who's talking! ● *pron inter (soggetto)* who; *(oggetto, con preposizione)* who, whom *fml*; *(possessivo)* ~ **whose;** ~ **sei?** who are you?; ~ **hai incontrato?** who did you meet?; **di** ~ **sono questi libri?** whose books are these?; **con** ~ **parli?** who are you talking to?; **a** ~ **lo dici!** tell me about it!

chi'acchie|ra *nf* chat; *(pettegolezzo)* gossip. ~'**rare** *vi* chat; *(far pettegolezzi)* gossip. ~'**rato** *a* **essere** ~**rato** *(persona:)* be the subject of gossip; ~**re** *pl* chitchat; **far** quattro ~**re** have a chat; ~'**rone, -a** *a* talkative ● *nmf* chatterer

chia'ma|re *vt* call; *(far venire)* send for; **come ti chiami?** what's your name?; **mi chiamo Roberto** my name is Robert; ~**re alle armi** call up. ~**rsi** *vr* be called. ~**ta** *nf* call; *Mil* call-up

chi'appa *nf fam* cheek

chiara'mente *adv* clearly

chia'rezza *nf* clarity; *(limpidezza)* clearness

chiarifi'ca|re *vt* clarify. ~'**tore** *a* clarificatory. ~**zi'one** *nf* clarification

chiari'mento *nm* clarification

chia'rir|e *vt* make clear; *(spiegare)* clear up. ~**si** *vr* become clear

chi'aro *a* clear; *(luminoso)* bright;

(colore) light. **chia'rore** *nm* glimmer

chiaroveg'gente *a* clear-sighted ● *nmf* clairvoyant

chi'as|so *nm* din. ~'**soso** *a* rowdy

chi'av|e *nf* key; **chiudere a** ~**e** lock. ~**e inglese** monkey-wrench. ~**i'stello** *nm* latch

chiaz|za *nf* stain. ~'**zare** *vt* stain

chic *a inv* chic

chicches'sia *pron* anybody

'chicco *nm* grain; *(di caffè)* bean; *(d'uva)* grape

chi'eder|e *vt* ask; *(per avere)* ask for; *(esigere)* demand. ~**si** *vr* wonder

chi'esa *nf* church

chi'esto *pp* di **chiedere**

'chiglia *nf* keel

'chilo *nm* kilo

chilo'grammo *nm* kilogram[me]

chilome'traggio *nm* Auto mileage

chilo'metrico *a* in kilometres

chi'lometro *nm* kilometre

chi'mera *nf fig* illusion

'chimic|a *nf* chemistry. ~**o, -a** *a* chemical ● *nmf* chemist

'china *nf (declivio)* slope; **inchiostro di** ~ Indian ink

chi'nar|e *vt* lower. ~**si** *vr* stoop

chincaglie'rie *nfpl* knick-knacks

chinesitera'pia *nf* physiotherapy

chi'nino *nm* quinine

'chino *a* bent

chi'notto *nm* sparkling soft drink

chi'occia *nf* sitting hen

chi'occiola *nf* snail; **scala a** ~ spiral staircase

chi'odo *nm* nail; *(idea fissa)* obsession. ~ **di garofano** clove

chi'oma *nf* head of hair; *(fogliame)* foliage

chi'osco *nm* kiosk; *(per giornali)* news-stand

chi'ostro *nm* cloister

chiro'man|te *nmf* palmist. ~'**zia** *nf* palmistry

chirur'gia *nf* surgery. **chi'rurgico** *a* surgical. **chi'rurgo** *nm* surgeon

chissà *adv* who knows; ~ **quando**

arriverà I wonder when he will arrive

chi'tar|ra *nf* guitar. **~'rista** *nmf* guitarist

chi'uder|e *vt* shut, close; (*con la chiave*) lock; turn off (*luce, acqua ecc*); (*per sempre*) close down (*negozio, fabbrica ecc*); (*recingere*) enclose ● *vi* shut, close. **~si** *vr* shut; (*tempo:*) cloud over; (*ferita:*) heal over; *fig* withdraw into oneself

chi'unque *pron* anyone, anybody ● *rel pron* whoever

chi'usa *nf* enclosure; (*di canale*) lock; (*conclusione*) close

chi'u|so *pp di* **chiudere** ● *a* shut; (*tempo*) overcast; (*persona*) reserved. **~'sura** *nf* closing; (*sistema*) lock; (*allacciatura*) fastener. **~sura lampo** zip, zipper *Am*

ci *pron* (*personale*) us; (*riflessivo*) ourselves; (*reciproco*) each other; (*a ciò, di ciò ecc*) about it; **non ci disturbare** don't disturb us; **aspettateci** wait for us; **ci ha detto tutto** he told us everything; **ce lo manderanno** they'll send it to us; **ci considereremo...** we consider ourselves...; **ci laviamo le mani** we wash our hands; **ci odiamo** we hate each other; **non ci penso** I never think about it; **pensaci!** think about it! ● *adv* (*qui*) here; (*lì*) there; (*moto per luogo*) through it; **ci siamo** we are here; **ci siete?** are you there?; **ci siamo passati tutti** we all went through it; **c'è** there is; **ce ne sono molti** there are many; **ci vuole pazienza** it takes patience; **non ci vedo/sento** I can't see/hear

cia'bat|ta *nf* slipper. **~'tare** *vi* shuffle

ciabat'tino *nm* cobbler

ci'alda *nf* wafer

cial'trone *nm* (*mascalzone*) scoundrel

ciam'bella *nf* *Culin* ring-shaped cake; (*salvagente*) lifebelt; (*gonfiabile*) rubber ring

cianci'are *vi* gossip

cianfru'saglie *nfpl* knick-knacks

ci'ao *int fam* (*all' arrivo*) hello!, hi!; (*alla partenza*) bye-bye!, cheerio!

ciar'la|re *vi* chat. **~'tano** *nm* charlatan

cias'cuno *a* each ● *pron* everyone, everybody; (*distributivo*) each [one]; **per ~** each

ci'bar|e *vt* feed. **~ie** *nfpl* provisions. **~ si** *vr* eat; **~si di** live on

ciber'netico *a* cybernetic

'cibo *nm* food

ci'cala *nf* cicada

cica'lino *nm* buzzer

cica'tri|ce *nf* scar. **~z'zante** *nm* ointment

cicatriz'zarsi *vr* heal [up]. **cicatrizzazi'one** *nf* healing

'cicca *nf* cigarette end; (*fam: sigaretta*) fag; (*fam: gomma*) [chewing] gum

cic'chetto *nm fam* (*bicchierino*) nip; (*rimprovero*) telling-off

cic'cia *nf fam* fat, flab. **~'one, -a** *nmf fam* fatty, fatso

cice'rone *nm* guide

cicla'mino *nm* cyclamen

ci'clis|mo *nm* cycling. **~ta** *nmf* cyclist

'ciclo *nm* cycle; (*di malattia*) course

ciclomo'tore *nm* moped

ci'clone *nm* cyclone

ci'cogna *nf* stork

ci'coria *nf* chicory

ci'eco, -a *a* blind ● *nm* blind man ● *nf* blind woman

ci'elo *nm* sky; *Relig* heaven; **santo ~**! good heavens!

'cifra *nf* figure; (*somma*) sum; (*monogramma*) monogram; (*codice*) code

ci'fra|re *vt* embroider with a monogram; (*codificare*) code. **~to** *a* monogrammed; coded

'ciglio *nm* (*bordo*) edge; (*pl nf* **ciglia**: *delle palpebre*) eyelash

'cigno *nm* swan

cigo'l|are vt squeak. **~io** nm squeak.

'**Cile** nm Chile

ci'lecca nf far **~** miss

ci'leno, -a a & nmf Chilean

cili'egi|a nf cherry. **~o** nm cherry [tree]

cilin'drata nf cubic capacity, c.c.; **macchina di alta ~** highpowered car

ci'lindro nm cylinder; (cappello) top hat

'**cima** nf top; (fig: persona) genius; **da ~ a fondo** from top to bottom

ci'melio nm relic

cimen'tar|e vt put to the test. **~si** vr (provare) try one's hand

'**cimice** nf bug; (puntina) drawing pin, thumbtack Am

cimini'era nf chimney; Naut funnel

cimi'tero nm cemetery

ci'murro nm distemper

'**Cina** nf China

cin cin! int cheers!

cincischi'are vi fiddle

'**cine** nm fam cinema

cine'asta nmf film maker

'**cinema** nm inv cinema. **cine'presa** nf cine-camera

ci'nese a & nmf Chinese

cine'teca nf (raccolta) film collection

ci'netico a kinetic

'**cingere** vt (circondare) surround

cinghia nf strap; (cintura) belt

singhi'ale nm wild boar; **pelle di ~** pigskin

cinguett'|are vi twitter. **~io** nm twittering

'**cinico** a cynical

ci'niglia nf (tessuto) chenille

ci'nismo nm cynicism

ci'nofilo a (unità) dog-loving

cin'quanta a & nm fifty. **cinquan'tenne** a & nmf fifty-year-old. **cinquan'tesimo** a fiftieth. **cinquan'tina** nf una cinquantina di about fifty

'**cinque** a & nm five

cinquecen'tesco a sixteenth-century

cinque'cento a five hundred **●nm il C~** the sixteenth century

cinque'mila a & nm five thousand

'**cinta** nf (di pantaloni) belt; **muro di ~** [boundary] wall. **cin'tare** vt enclose

'**cintola** nf (di pantaloni) belt

cin'tura nf belt. **~ di salvataggio** lifebelt. **~ di sicurezza** Aeron, Auto seat-belt

cintu'rino nm **~ dell'orologio** watch-strap

ciò pron this; that; **~ che** what; **~ nondimeno** nevertheless

ci'occa nf lock

ciocco'la|ta nf chocolate; (bevanda) [hot] chocolate. **~tino** nm chocolate. **~to** nm chocolate. **~to al latte/fondente** milk/plain chocolate

cioè adv that is

ciond'ol|are vi dangle. **ci'ondolo** nm pendant. **~oni** adv fig hanging about

ciono'stante adv nonetheless

ci'otola nf bowl

ci'ottolo nm pebble

ci'polla nf onion; (bulbo) bulb

ci'presso nm cypress

'**cipria** nf [face] powder

'**Cipro** nf Cyprus. **cipri'ota** a & nmf Cypriot

'**circa** adv & prep about

'**circo** nm circus

circo'la|re a circular **●nf** circular; (di metropolitana) circle line **●vi** circulate. **~'torio** a Med circulatory. **~zi'one** nf circulation; (traffico) traffic

'**circolo** nm circle; (società) club

circon'ci|dere vt circumcise. **~si'one** nf circumcision

circon'dar|e vt surround. **~io** nm (amministrativo) administrative district. **~si di** vr surround oneself with

circonfe'renza nf circumference. **~ dei fianchi** hip measurement

circonvallazi'one nf ring road

circo'scritto a limited

circoscrizi'one nf area. ~ **eletto-rale** constituency

circo'spetto a wary

circospezi'one nf con ~ warily

circo'stante a surrounding

circo'stanza nf circumstance; (occasione) occasion

circu'ire vt (ingannare) trick

cir'cuito nm circuit

circumnavi'ga|re vt circumnavigate. **~zi'one** nf circumnavigation

'ciste nf inv cyst

ci'sterna nf cistern; (serbatoio) tank

'cisti nf inv cyst

ci'ta|re vt (riportare brani ecc) quote; (come esempio) cite; Jur summons. **~zi'one** nf quotation; Jur summons sg

citofo'nare vi buzz. **ci'tofono** nm entry phone; (in ufficio, su aereo ecc) intercom

ci'trullo nmf fam dimwit

città nf inv town; (grande) city

citta'della nf citadel

citta|di'nanza nf citizenship; (popolazione) citizens pl. **~'dino, -a** nmf citizen; (abitante di città) city dweller

ciucci'are vt fam suck. **ci'uccio** nm fam dummy

ci'uco nm ass

ci'uffo nm tuft

ci'urma nf Naut crew

ci'vet|ta nf owl; (fig: donna) flirt; [auto] ~ta unmarked police car. **~'tare** vi flirt. **~te'ria** nf coquettishness

'civico a civic

ci'vil|e a civil. **~iz'zare** vt civilize. **~iz'zato** a (paese) civilized. **~izzazi'one** nf civilization. **~'mente** adv civilly

civiltà nf inv civilization; (cortesia) civility

'clacson nm inv horn. **clacso-'nare** vi beep the horn, hoot

cla'mo|re nm clamour; **fare** ~**re** cause a sensation. **~rosa'mente** adv (sbagliare) sensationally.

~'roso a noisy; (sbaglio) sensational

clan nm inv clan; fig clique

clandestina'mente adv secretly. **~ità** nf secrecy

clande'stino a clandestine; **movimento** ~ underground movement; **passeggero** ~ stowaway

clari'netto nm clarinet

'classe nf class. ~ **turistica** tourist class

classi'cis|mo nm classicism. **~ta** nmf classicist

'classico a classical; (tipico) classic ● nm classic

clas'sifi|ca nf classification; Sport results pl. **~'care** vt classify. **~'carsi** vr be placed. **~ca'tore** nm (cartella) folder. **~cazi'one** nf classification

clas'sista nmf class-conscious person

'clausola nf clause

claustro|fo'bia nf claustrophobia. **~'fobico** a claustrophobic

clau'sura nf Relig enclosed order

clavi'cembalo nm harpsichord

cla'vicola nf collar-bone

cle'men|te a merciful; (tempo) mild. **~za** nf mercy

cleri'cale a clerical. **'clero** nm clergy

clic nm Comput click; **fare** ~ **su** click on

cli'en|te nmf client; (di negozio) customer. **~'tela** nf customers pl

'clima nm climate. **cli'matico** a climatic; **stazione climatica** health resort

'clinica nf clinic. **clinico** a clinical ● nm clinician

clo'aca nf sewer

'cloro nm chlorine. **~'formio** nm chloroform

clou a inv i **momenti** ~ the highlights

coabi'ta|re vi live together. **~zi'one** nf cohabitation

coagu'la|re vt, **~rsi** vr coagulate. **~zi'one** nf coagulation

coaliz|i'one *nf* coalition. **~'zarsi** *vr* unite

co'atto *a Jur* compulsory

'cobra *nm inv* cobra

coca'ina *nf* cocaine. **cocai'nomane** *nmf* cocaine addict

cocci'nella *nf* ladybird

'coccio *nm* earthenware; (*frammento*) fragment

cocci|u'taggine *nf* stubbornness. **~'uto** *a* stubborn

'cocco *nm* coconut palm; *fam* love; **noce di ~** *nf* coconut

cocco'drillo *nm* crocodile

cocco'lare *vt* cuddle

co'cente *a* (*sole*) burning

'cocktail *nm inv* (*ricevimento*) cocktail party

co'comero *nm* watermelon

co'cuzzolo *nm* top; (*di testa, cappello*) crown

'coda *nf* tail; (*di abito*) train; (*fila*) queue; **fare la ~** queue [up], stand in line *Am*. **~ di cavallo** (*acconciatura*) ponytail. **~ dell'occhio** corner of one's eye **~ di paglia** guilty conscience

co'dardo, -a *a* cowardly ● *nmf* coward

'codice *nm* code. **~ di avviamento postale** postal code, zip code *Am*. **~ a barre** bar-code. **~ fiscale** tax code. **~ della strada** highway code.

codifi'care *vt* codify

coe'rente *a* consistent. **coe'renza** *nf* consistency

coesi'one *nf* cohesion

coe'sistere *vi* coexist

coe'taneo, -a *a & nmf* contemporary

cofa'netto *nm* casket. **'cofano** *nm* (*forziere*) chest; *Auto* bonnet, hood *Am*

'cogliere *vt* pick; (*sorprendere*) catch; (*afferrare*) seize; (*colpire*) hit

co'gnato, -a *nmf* brother-in-law; sister-in-law

cognizi'one *nf* knowledge

co'gnome *nm* surname

'coi = **con** + **i**

coinci'denza *nf* coincidence; (*di treno ecc*) connection

coin'cidere *vi* coincide

coinqui'lino *nm* flatmate

coin'vol|gere *vt* involve. **~gi'mento** *nm* involvement. **~to** *a* involved

'coito *nm* coitus

col = **con** + **il**

colà *adv* there

cola|'brodo *nm inv* strainer; **ridotto a un ~brodo** *fam* full of holes. **~'pasta** *nm inv* colander

co'la|re *vt* strain; (*versare lentamente*) drip ● *vi* (*gocciolare*) drip; (*perdere*) leak; **~re a picco** *Naut* sink. **~ta** *nf* (*di metallo*) casting; (*di lava*) flow

colazi'one *nf* (*del mattino*) breakfast; (*di mezzogiorno*) lunch; **prima ~** breakfast; **far ~** have breakfast/lunch. **~ al sacco** packed lunch

co'lei *pron f* the one

co'lera *nm* cholera

coleste'rolo *nm* cholesterol

colf *nf abbr* (**collaboratrice familiare**) home help

'colica *nf* colic

co'lino *nm* [tea] strainer

'colla *nf* glue; (*di farina*) paste. **~ di pesce** gelatine

collabo'ra|re *vi* collaborate. **~'tore, ~'trice** *nmf* collaborator. **~zi'one** *nf* collaboration

col'lana *nf* necklace; (*serie*) series

col'lant *nm* tights *pl*

col'lare *nm* collar

col'lasso *nm* collapse

collau'dare *vt* test. **col'laudo** *nm* test

'colle *nm* hill

col'lega *nmf* colleague

collega'mento *nm* connection; *Mil* liaison; *Radio ecc* link. **colle'gare** *vt* connect. **~si** *vr* *TV, Radio* link up

collegi'ale *nmf* boarder ● *a* (*responsabilità, decisione*) collective

col'legio nm (convitto) boarding-school. ~ **elettorale** constituency

'**collera** nf anger; **andare in** ~ get angry. **col'lerico** a irascible

col'letta nf collection

collet|tività nf inv community. ~'**tivo** a collective; (interesse) general; **biglietto** ~'**tivo** group ticket

col'letto nm collar

collezi|o'nare vt collect. ~'**one** nf collection. ~**o'nista** nmf collector

colli'mare vi coincide

col'li|na nf hill. ~'**noso** a (terreno) hilly

col'lirio nm eyewash

collisi'one nf collision

'**collo** nm neck; (pacco) package; **a** ~ **alto** high-necked. ~ **del piede** instep

colloca'mento nm placing; (impiego) employment

collo'ca|re vt place. ~**rsi** vr take one's place. ~**zi'one** nf placing

colloqui'ale a (termine) colloquial. **col'loquio** nm conversation; (udienza ecc) interview; (esame) oral [exam]

collusi'one nf collusion

colluttazi'one nf scuffle

col'mare vt fill [to the brim]; bridge (divario) ~ **qcno di gentilezze** overwhelm sb with kindness. '**colmo** a full ● nm top; fig height; **al colmo della disperazione** in the depths of despair; **questo è il colmo!** (con indignazione) this is the last straw!; (con stupore) I don't believe it!

co'lomb|a nf dove. ~**o** nm pigeon

co'loni|a[1] nf colony; ~**a [estiva]** (per bambini) holiday camp. ~**'ale** a colonial

co'lonia[2] nf **[acqua di]** ~ [eau de] Cologne

co'lonico a (terreno, casa) farm

coloniz'za|re vt colonize. ~'**tore**, ~'**trice** nmf colonizer

co'lon|na nf column. ~ **sonora** sound-track. ~ **vertebrale** spine. ~'**nato** nm colonnade

colon'nello nm colonel

co'lono nm tenant farmer

colo'rante nm colouring

colo'rare vt colour; colour in (disegno)

co'lore nm colour; **a colori** in colour; **di** ~ coloured. **colo'rito** a coloured; (viso) rosy; (racconto) colourful ● nm complexion

co'loro pron pl the ones

colos'sale a colossal. **co'losso** nm colossus

'**colpa** nf fault; (biasimo) blame; (colpevolezza) guilt; (peccato) sin; **dare la** ~ **a** blame; **essere in** ~ be at fault; **per** ~ **di** because of. **col'pevole** a guilty ● nmf culprit

col'pire vt hit, strike; ~ **nel segno** hit the nail on the head

'**colpo** nm blow; (di arma da fuoco) shot; (urto) knock; (emozione) shock; Med, Sport stroke; (furto) raid; **di** ~ suddenly; **far** ~ make a strong impression; **far venire un** ~ **a qcno** fig give sb a fright; **perdere colpi** (motore:) keep missing; **a** ~ **d'occhio** at a glance; **a** ~ **sicuro** for certain. ~ **d'aria** chill. ~ **basso** blow below the belt. ~ **di scena** coup de théâtre. ~ **di sole** sunstroke; **colpi pl di sole** (su capelli) highlights. ~ **di stato** coup [d'état]. ~ **di telefono** ring; **dare un** ~ **di telefono a qn** give sb a ring. ~ **di testa** [sudden] impulse. ~ **di vento** gust of wind

col'poso a **omicidio** ~ manslaughter

col'tella|ta nf stab. **col'tello** nm knife

colti'va|re vt cultivate. ~'**tore**, ~'**trice** nmf farmer. ~**zi'one** nf farming; (di piante) growing

'**colto** pp di **cogliere** ● a cultured

'**coltre** nf blanket

col'tura nf cultivation

co'lui pron inv m the one

'**coma** nm inv coma; **in** ~ in a coma

comanda'mento nm commandment

coman'dante nm commander; Naut, Aeron captain

coman'dare vt command; Mech control ●vi be in charge. **co'mando** nm command; (di macchina) control

co'mare nf (madrina) godmother

combaci'are vi fit together; (testimonianze:) concur

combat'tente a fighting ●nm combatant. **ex ~** ex-serviceman

com'bat|tere vt/i fight. **~ti'mento** nm fight; Mil battle; **fuori ~timento** (pugilato) knocked out. **~'tuto** a (gara) hard fought

combi'na|re vt/i arrange; (mettere insieme) combine, (fam. fare) do, **cosa stai ~ndo?** what are you doing?. **~rsi** vr combine; (mettersi d'accordo) come to an agreement. **~zi'one** nf combination; (caso) coincidence; **per ~zione** by chance

com'briccola nf gang

combu'sti|bile a combustible ●nm fuel. **~'one** nf combustion

com'butta nf gang; **in ~** in league

'come adv like; (in qualità di) as; (interrogativo, esclamativo) how; **questo vestito è ~ il tuo** this dress is like yours; **~ stai?** how are you?; **~ va?** how are things?; **~ mai?** how come?; **~?** what?; **non sa ~ fare** he doesn't know what to do; **~ sta bene!** how well he looks!; **~ no!** that will be right!; **~ tu sai** as you know; **fa ~ vuoi** do as you like; **~ se** as if ●conj (non appena) as soon as

co'meta nf comet

'comico, -a a comic[al]; (teatro) comic ●nm funny side ●nmf (attore) comedian, comic actor ●nf (a torte in faccia) slapstick sketch

co'mignolo nm chimney-pot

cominci'are vt/i begin, start; **a ~ da oggi** from today; **per ~** to begin with

comi'tato nm committee

comi'tiva nf party, group

co'mizio nm meeting

com'mando nm inv commando

com'med|ia nf comedy; (opera teatrale) play; fig sham. **~a musicale** musical. **~'ante** nmf comedian; fig pej phoney. **~'ografo, -a** nmf playwright

commemo'ra|re vt commemorate. **~zi'one** nf commemoration

commen'sale nmf fellow diner

commen'ta|re vt comment on; (annotare) annotate. **~ario** nm commentary. **~a'tore, ~a'trice** nmf commentator. **com'mento** nm comment

commerci'a|le a commercial; (relazioni, trattative) trade; (attività) business. **centro ~le** shopping centre. **~'lista** nmf business consultant; (contabile) accountant. **~liz'zare** vt market. **~lizzazi'one** nf marketing

commerci'ante nmf trader, merchant; (negoziante) shopkeeper. **~ all'ingrosso** wholesaler

commerci'are vi **~ in** deal in

com'mercio nm commerce; (internazionale) trade; (affari) business; **in ~** (prodotto) on sale. **~ all'ingrosso** wholesale trade. **~ al minuto** retail trade

com'messo, -a pp di **commettere** ●nmf shop assistant. **~ viaggiatore** commercial traveller ●nf (ordine) order

comme'stibile a edible. **commestibili** nmpl groceries

com'mettere vt commit; make (sbaglio)

commi'ato nm leave; **prendere ~ da** take leave of

commise'rar|e vt commiserate. **~si** vr feel sorry for oneself

commissari'ato nm (di polizia) police station

commis's|ario nm [police] superintendent; (membro di commissione) commissioner; Sport steward; Comm commission agent. **~ario d'esame** examiner. **~i'one** nf (incarico) errand; (comitato ecc) commission; (Comm: di merce) order; **~i'oni** pl (acquisti) **fare ~i'oni** go shopping. **~i'one d'esa-**

me board of examiners. **C~ione Europea** European Commission
commit'tente *nmf* purchaser
com'mo|sso *pp di* **commuovere** ● *a* moved. **~'vente** *a* moving
commozi'one *nf* emotion. ~ **cerebrale** concussion
commu'over|e *vt* touch, move. **~si** *vr* be touched
commu'tare *vt* change; *Jur* commute
comò *nm inv* chest of drawers
comoda'mente *adv* comfortably
como'dino *nm* bedside table
comodità *nf inv* comfort; *(convenienza)* convenience
'comodo *a* comfortable; *(conveniente)* convenient; *(spazioso)* roomy; *(facile)* easy; **stia** ~**!** I don't get up!; **far** ~ be useful ● *nm* comfort; **fare il proprio** ~ do as one pleases
compae'sano, -a *nmf* fellow countryman
com'pagine *nf (squadra)* team
compa'gnia *nf* company; *(gruppo)* party; **fare** ~ **a qcno** keep sb company; **essere di** ~ be sociable. ~ **aerea** airline
com'pagno, -a *nmf* companion; *(Comm, Sport, in coppia)* partner; *Pol* comrade. ~ **di scuola** schoolmate
compa'rabile *a* comparable
compa'ra|re *vt* compare. **~'tivo** *a* & *nm* comparative. **~zi'one** *nf* comparison
com'pare *nm (padrino)* godfather; *(testimone di matrimonio)* witness
compa'rire *vi* appear; *(spiccare)* stand out; ~ **in giudizio** appear in court
com'parso, -a *pp di* **comparire** ● *nf* appearance; *Cinema* extra; *Theat* walk-on
compartecipazi'one *nf* sharing; *(quota)* share
comparti'mento *nm* compartment; *(amministrativo)* department
compas'sato *a* calm and collected
compassi'one *nf* compassion;

aver ~ **per** feel pity for; **far** ~ arouse pity. **~'nevole** *a* compassionate
com'passo *nm* [pair of] compasses *pl*
compa'tibil|e *a (conciliabile)* compatible; *(scusabile)* excusable. **~ità** *nf* compatibility. **~'mente** *adv* **~mente con i miei impegni** if my commitments allow
compa'tire *vt* pity; *(scusare)* make allowances for
compatri'ota *nmf* compatriot
compat'tezza *nf (di materia)* compactness. **com'patto** *a* compact; *(denso)* dense; *(solido)* solid; *fig* united
compene'trare *vt* pervade
compen'sar|e *vt* compensate; *(supplire)* make up for. **~si** *vr* balance each other out
compen'sato *nm (legno)* plywood
compensazi'one *nf* compensation
com'penso *nm* compensation; *(retribuzione)* remuneration; **in** ~ *(in cambio)* in return; *(d'altra parte)* on the other hand; *(invece)* instead
'comper|a *nf* purchase; **far** ~**e** do some shopping
compe'rare *vt* buy
compe'ten|te *a* competent. **~za** *nf* competence; *(responsabilità)* responsibility
com'petere *vi* compete; ~ **a** *(compito:)* be the responsibility of
competi|tività *nf* competitiveness. **~'tivo** *a (prezzo, carattere)* competitive. **~'tore, ~'trice** *nmf* competitor. **~zi'one** *nf* competition
compia'cen|te *a* obliging. **~za** *nf* obligingness
compia'c|ere *vt/i* please. **~ersi** *vr (congratularsi)* congratulate. **~ersi di** *(degnarsi)* condescend. **~i'mento** *nm* satisfaction; *pej* smugness. **~i'uto** *a* satisfied; *(aria, sorriso)* smug
compi'an|gere *vt* pity; *(per lutto)*

ecc) sympathize with. **~to** *a* lamented ● *nm* grief

'compier|e *vt* (*concludere*) complete; commit (*delitto*); **~e gli anni** have one's birthday. **~si** *vr* end; (*avverarsi*) come true

compi'la|re *vt* compile; fill in (*modulo*). **~zi'one** *nf* compilation

compi'mento *nm* **portare a ~ qcsa** conclude sth

com'pire *vt* = **compiere**

compi'tare *vt* spell

com'pito[1] *a* polite

'compito[2] *nm* task; *Sch* homework

compi'ut|o *a* **avere 30 anni ~i** be over 30

comple'anno *nm* birthday

complemen'tare *a* complementary; (*secondario*) subsidiary

comple'mento *nm* complement; *Mil* draft. **~ oggetto** direct object

comples|si'tà *nf* complexity. **~siva'mente** *adv* on the whole. **~'sivo** *a* comprehensive; (*totale*) total. **com'plesso** *a* complex; (*difficile*) complicated ● *nm* complex; (*di cantanti ecc*) group; (*di circostanze, fattori*) combination; **in ~so** on the whole

completa'mente *adv* completely

comple'tare *vt* complete

com'pleto *a* complete; (*pieno*) full [up]; **essere al ~** (*teatro:*) be sold out; **la famiglia al ~** the whole family ● *nm* (*vestito*) suit; (*insieme di cose*) set

compli'ca|re *vt* complicate. **~rsi** *vr* become complicated. **~to** complicated. **~zi'one** *nf* complication; **salvo complicazioni** all being well

'complic|e *nmf* accomplice ● *a* (*sguardo*) knowing. **~ità** *nf* complicity

complimen'tar|e *vt* compliment. **~si** *vr* **~si con** congratulate

compli'menti *nmpl* (*ossequi*) regards, (*congratulazioni*) congratulations; **far ~** stand on ceremony

compli'mento *nm* compliment

complot'tare *vi* plot. **com'plotto** *nm* plot

compo'nente *a* & *nm* component ● *nmf* member

compo'nibile *a* (*cucina*) fitted; (*mobili*) modular

componi'mento *nm* composition; (*letterario*) work

com'por|re *vt* compose; (*ordinare*) put in order; *Typ* set. **~si** *vr* **~si di** be made up of

comporta'mento *nm* behaviour

compor'tar|e *vt* involve; (*consentire*) allow. **~si** *vr* behave

composi'tore, -'trice *nmf* composer; *Typ* compositor. **~zi'one** *nf* composition

com'posta *nf* stewed fruit; (*concime*) compost

compo'stezza *nf* composure

com'posto *pp di* **comporre** ● *a* composed; (*costituito*) comprising; **stai ~!** sit properly! ● *nm* *Chem* compound

compra|re *vt* buy. **~'tore, -'trice** *nmf* buyer

compra'vendita *nf* buying and selling

compren|dere *vt* understand; (*includere*) comprise. **~'sibile** *a* understandable. **~sibil'mente** *adv* understandably. **~si'one** *nf* understanding. **~'sivo** *a* understanding; (*che include*) inclusive.

com'preso *pp di* **comprendere** ● *a* included; **tutto compreso** (*prezzo*) all-in

com'pressa *nf* compress; (*pastiglia*) tablet

compressi'one *nf* compression

com'presso *pp di* **comprimere** ● *a* compressed

com'primere *vt* press; (*reprimere*) repress

compro'me|sso *pp di* **compromettere** ● *nm* compromise. **~t'tente** *a* compromising. **~ttere** *vt* compromise

comproprietà *nf* multiple ownership

compro'vare *vt* prove

com'punto a contrite

compu'tare vt calculate

com'puter nm computer. **~iz'zare** vt computerize. **~iz'zato** a computerized

computiste'ria nf book-keeping. **'computo** nm calculation

comu'nale a municipal

co'mune a common; (condiviso) mutual; (ordinario) ordinary ● nm borough, council; (amministrativo) commune; **fuori del ~** out of the ordinary. **~'mente** adv commonly

comuni'ca|re vt communicate; pass on (malattia); Relig administer Communion to. **~rsi** vr receive Communion. **~'tiva** nf communicativeness. **~'tivo** a communicative. **~to** nm communiqué. **~to stampa** press release. **~zi'one** nf communication; Teleph [phone] call; **avere la ~zione** get through; **dare la ~zione** a qcno put sb through

comuni'one nf communion; Relig [Holy] Communion

comu'nis|mo nm communism. **~ta** a & nmf communist

comunità nf inv community. **C~ [Economica] Europea** European [Economic] Community

co'munque conj however ● adv anyhow

con prep with; (mezzo) by; **~ facilità** easily; **~ mia grande gioia** to my great delight; **è gentile ~ tutti** he is kind to everyone; **col treno** by train; **~ questo tempo** in this weather

co'nato nm **~ di vomito** retching

'conca nf basin; (valle) dell

concate'na|re vt link together. **~zi'one** nf connection

'concavo a concave

con'ce|dere vt grant; award (premio); (ammettere) admit. **~si** vr allow oneself (pausa)

concentra'mento nm concentration

concen'tra|re vt, **~rsi** vr concen-

trate. **~to** a concentrated ● nm **~to di pomodoro** tomato purée. **~zi'one** nf concentration

concepi'mento nm conception

conce'pire vt conceive (bambino); (capire) understand; (figurarsi) conceive of; devise (piano ecc)

con'cernere vt concern

concer'tar|e vt Mus harmonize; (organizzare) arrange. **~si** vr agree

concer'tista nmf concert performer. **con'certo** nm concert; (composizione) concerto

concessio'nario nm agent

concessi'one nf concession

con'cesso pp di concedere

con'cetto nm concept; (opinione) opinion

concezi'one nf conception; (idea) concept

con'chiglia nf [sea] shell

'concia nf tanning; (di tabacco) curing

conci'a|re vt cure (tabacco); **~re qcno per le feste** give sb a good hiding. **~rsi** vr (sporcarsi) get dirty; (vestirsi male) dress badly. **~to** a (pelle, cuoio) tanned

concili'abile a compatible

concili'ante a conciliatory

concili'a|re vt reconcile; settle (contravvenzione); (favorire) induce. **~rsi** vr go together; (mettersi d'accordo) become reconciled. **~zi'one** nf reconciliation; Jur settlement

con'cilio nm Relig council; (riunione) assembly

conci'mare vt feed (pianta). **con'cime** nm manure; (chimico) fertilizer

concisi'one nf conciseness. **con'ciso** a concise

conci'tato a excited

concitta'dino, -a nmf fellow citizen

con'clu|dere vt conclude; (finire con successo) achieve. **~dersi** vr come to an end. **~si'one** nf conclusion; **in ~sione** (insomma) in short. **~'sivo** *a* conclusive. **~so** *pp di* **concludere**

concomi'tanza *nf* (*di circostanze, fatti*) combination

concor'da|nza *nf* agreement. **~re** *vt* agree; *Gram* make agree. **~to** *nm* agreement; *Jur, Comm* arrangement

con'cord|e *a* in agreement; (*unanime*) unanimous

concor'ren|te *a* a concurrent; (*rivale*) competing ● *nmf Comm, Sport* competitor; (*candidato*) candidate. **~za** *nf* competition. **~zi'ale** *a* competitive

con'cor|rere *vi* (*contribuire*) concur; (*andare insieme*) go together; (*competere*) compete. **~so** *pp di* **concorrere** ● *nm* competition; **fuori ~so** not in the official competition. **~so di bellezza** beauty contest

concreta'mente *adv* concretely

concre'tare *vt* (*concludere*) achieve. **~tiz'zare** *vt* put into concrete form (*idea, progetto*)

con'creto *a* concrete; **in ~** in concrete terms

concussi'one *nf* extortion

con'danna *nf* sentence; **pronunziare una ~** pass a sentence. **condan'nare** *vt* condemn; *Jur* sentence. **condan'nato, -a** *nmf* convict

conden'sa|re *vt*, **~rsi** *vr* condense. **~zi'one** *nf* condensation

condi'mento *nm* seasoning; (*salsa*) dressing. **con'dire** *vt* flavour; dress (*insalata*)

condiscen'den|te *a* indulgent; *pej* condescending. **~za** *nf* indulgence; *pej* condescension

condi'videre *vt* share

condizio'na|le *a & nm* conditional ● *nf Jur* suspended sentence. **~'mento** *nm Psych* conditioning

condizio'na|re *vt* condition. **~to a** *a* conditional. **~'tore** *nm* air conditioner

condizi'one *nf* condition; **a ~ che** on condition that

condogli'anze *nfpl* condolences; **fare le ~** a offer condolences to

condomini'ale *a* (*spese*) common. **condo'minio** *nm* joint ownership; (*edificio*) condominium

condo'nare *vt* remit. **con'dono** *nm* remission

con'dotta *nf* conduct; (*circoscrizione di medico*) district; (*di gara ecc*) management; (*tubazione*) piping

con'dotto *pp di* **condurre** ● *a* **medico ~** district doctor ● *nm* pipe; *Anat* duct

condu'cente *nm* driver

con'du|rre *vt* lead; drive (*veicoli*); (*accompagnare*) take; conduct (*gas, elettricità ecc*); (*gestire*) run. **~rsi** *vr* behave. **~'tore, -'trice** *nmf TV* presenter; (*di veicolo*) driver ● *nm Electr* conductor. **~t'tura** *nf* duct

confabu'lare *vi* have a confab

confa'cente *a* suitable. **con'farsi** *vr* confarsi a suit

confederazi'one *nf* confederation

confe'renz|a *nf* (*discorso*) lecture; (*congresso*) conference. **~a stampa** news conference. **~i'ere, -a** *nmf* lecturer

confe'rire *vt* (*donare*) give ● *vi* confer

con'ferma *nf* confirmation. **confer'mare** *vt* confirm

confes'sa|re *vt*, **~rsi** *vr* confess. **~io'nale** *a & nm* confessional. **~i'one** *nf* confession. **~ore** *nm* confessor

con'fetto *nm* sugared almond

confet'tura *nf* jam

confezio'na|re *vt* manufacture; make (*abiti*); package (*merci*). **~to a** (*vestiti*) off-the-peg; (*gelato*) wrapped

confezi'one *nf* manufacture; (*di abiti*) tailoring; (*di pacchi*) packaging; **confezioni** *pl* clothes. **~ regalo** gift pack

confic'car|e *vt* thrust. **~si** *vr* run into

confi'd|are *vi* **~are in** trust ● *vt*

confide. **~arsi** *vr* **~arsi con** confide in. **~ente ●** confident **● nmf** confidant

confi'denz|a *nf* confidence; *(familiarità)* familiarity; **prendersi delle ~** take liberties. **~'iale** *a* confidential; *(rapporto, tono)* familiar

configu'ra|re *vt* Comput configure. **~zi'one** *nf* configuration

confi'nante *a* neighbouring

confi'na|re *vi (relegare)* confine **● vi ~re con** border on. **~rsi** *vr* withdraw. **~to** *a* confined

con'fin|e *nm* border; *(tra terreni)* boundary. **~o** *nm* political exile

con'fis|ca *nf (di proprietà)* forfeiture. **~'scare** *vt* confiscate

con'flitt|o *nm* conflict. **~u'ale** *a* adversarial

conflu'enza *nf* confluence; *(di strade)* junction

conflu'ire *vi (fiumi:)* flow together; *(strade:)* meet

con'fonder|e *vt* confuse; *(turbare)* confound; *(imbarazzare)* embarrass. **~si** *vr (mescolarsi)* mingle; *(turbarsi)* become confused; *(sbagliarsi)* be mistaken

confor'ma|re *vt*, **~rsi** *vr* conform. **~zi'one** *nf* conformity **(a** with); *(del terreno)* composition

con'forme *a* according. **~'mente** *adv* accordingly

confor'mi|smo *nm* conformity. **~sta** *nmf* conformist. **~tà** *nf (a norma)* conformity

confor'tante *a* comforting

confor't|are *vt* comfort. **~evole** *a (comodo)* comfortable. **con'forto** *nm* comfort

confron'tare *vt* compare

con'fronto *nm* comparison; **in ~ a** by comparison with; **nei tuoi confronti** towards you; **senza ~** far and away

confusio'nario *a (persona)* muddle-headed. **~'one** *nf* confusion; *(baccano)* racket; *(disordine)* mess; *(imbarazzo)* embarrassment. **con'fuso** *pp di* confondere

● a confused; *(indistinto)* indistinct; *(imbarazzato)* embarrassed

confu'tare *vt* confute

conge'dar|e *vt* dismiss; Mil discharge. **~si** *vr* take one's leave

con'gedo *nm* leave; **essere in ~** be on leave. **~ malattia** sick leave. **~ maternità** maternity leave

conge'gnare *vt* devise; *(mettere insieme)* assemble. **con'gegno** *nm* device

congela'mento *nm* freezing; Med frost-bite

conge'la|re *vt* freeze. **~to** *a (cibo)* deep-frozen. **~'tore** *nm* freezer

congeni'ale *a* congenial

con'genito *a* congenital

congestio'na|re *vt* congest. **~to** *a (traffico)* congested; *(viso)* flushed. **congesti'one** *nf* congestion

conget'tura *nf* conjecture

congi'unger|e *vt* join; combine *(sforzi)*. **~si** *vr* join

congiunti'vite *nf* conjunctivitis

congi'untivo *nm* subjunctive

congi'unto *pp di* congiungere **● a** joined **● nm** relative

congiun'tu|ra *nf* joint; *(circostanza)* juncture; *(situazione)* situation. **~'rale** *a* economic

congiunzi'one *nf* Gram conjunction

congi'u|ra *nf* conspiracy. **~'rare** *vi* conspire

conglome'rato *nm* conglomerate; *fig* conglomeration; *(da costruzione)* concrete

congratu'la|rsi *vr* **~rsi con** qcno **per** congratulate sb on. **~zi'oni** *nfpl* congratulations

con'grega *nf* band

congre'ga|re *vt*, **~rsi** *vr* congregate. **~zi'one** *nf* congregation

con'gresso *nm* congress

'congruo *a* proper; *(giusto)* fair

conguagli'are *vt* balance. **congu'aglio** *nm* balance

coni'are *vt* coin

'conico *a* conical

co'nifera *nf* conifer

co'niglio *nm* rabbit

coniu'gale *a* marital; (*vita*) married

coniu'ga|re *vt* conjugate. **~rsi** *vr* get married. **~zi'one** *nf* conjugation

'coniuge *nmf* spouse

connazio'nale *nmf* compatriot

connessi'one *nf* connection. **con'nesso** *pp di* **connettere**

con'nettere *vt* connect ● *vi* think rationally

conni'vente *a* conniving

conno'ta|re *vt* connote. **~to** *nm* distinguishing feature; **~ti** *pl* description

con'nubio *nm fig* union

'cono *nm* cone

cono'scen|te *nmf* acquaintance. **~za** *nf* knowledge; (*persona*) acquaintance; (*sensi*) consciousness; **perdere ~za** lose consciousness; **riprendere ~za** regain consciousness, come to

co'nosc|ere *vt* know; (*essere a conoscenza di*) be acquainted with; (*fare la conoscenza di*) meet. **~i'tore, ~i'trice** *nmf* connoisseur. **~i'uto** *pp di* **conoscere** ● *a* well-known

con'quist|a *nf* conquest. **conqui'stare** *vt* conquer; *fig* win

consa'cra|re *vt* consecrate; ordain (*sacerdote*); (*dedicare*) dedicate. **~rsi** *vr* devote oneself. **~zi'one** *nf* consecration

consangu'ineo, ~a *nmf* blood-relation

consa'pevol|e *a* conscious. **~'lez-za** *nf* consciousness. **~l'mente** *adv* consciously

'con°cio *a* conscious

consecu'tivo *a* consecutive; (*seguente*) next

con'segna *nf* delivery; (*merce*) consignment; (*custodia*) care; (*di prigioniero*) handover; (*Mil: ordine*) orders *pl*; (*Mil: punizione*) confinement; **pagamento alla ~** cash on delivery

conse'gnare *vt* deliver; (*affidare*)

give in charge; *Mil* confine to barracks

consegu'en|te *a* consequent. **~za** *nf* consequence; **di ~za** (*perciò*) consequently

consegui'mento *nm* achievement

consegu'ire *vt* achieve ● *vi* follow

con'senso *nm* consent

consensu'ale *a* consensus-based

con'sen|tire *vi* consent ● *vt* allow

con'serto *a* **a braccia conserte** with one's arms folded

con'serva *nf* preserve; (*di frutta*) jam; (*di agrumi*) marmalade. **~ di pomodoro** tomato sauce

conser'var|e *vt* preserve; (*mantenere*) keep. **~rsi** *vr* keep; **~si in salute** keep well

conserva'tore, -'trice *nmf Pol* conservative

conserva'torio *nm* conservatory

conservazi'one *nf* preservation; **a lunga ~** long-life

conside'ra|re *vt* consider; (*stimare*) regard. **~to a** (*stimato*) esteemed. **~zi'one** *nf* consideration; (*osservazione, riflessione*) remark

conside'revole *a* considerable

consigli'abile *a* advisable

consigli'ar|e *vt* advise; (*raccomandare*) recommend. **~'arsi** *vr* **~arsi con qcno** ask sb's advice. **~'ere, -a** *nmf* adviser; (*membro di consiglio*) councillor

con'siglio *nm* advice; (*ente*) council. **~ d'amministrazione** board of directors. **C~ dei Ministri** Cabinet

consi'sten|te *a* substantial; (*spesso*) thick; (*fig: argomento*) valid. **~za** *nf* consistency; (*spessore*) thickness

con'sistere *vi* **~ in** consist of

consoci'ata *nf* (*azienda*) associate company

conso'lar|e[1] *vt* console; (*rallegrare*) cheer. **~si** *vr* console oneself

conso'lare[2] *a* consular. **~to** *nm* consulate

consolazi'one *nf* consolation; (*gioia*) joy

con'sole *nf inv* *(tastiera)* console
'console *nm* consul
consoli'dar|e *vt,* **~si** *vr* consolidate
conso'nante *nf* consonant
'consono *a* consonant
con'sorte *nmf* consort
con'sorzio *nm* consortium
con'stare *vi* ~ **di** consist of; *(risultare)* appear; **a quanto mi consta** as far as I know; **mi consta che** it appears that
consta'ta|re *vt* ascertain. **~zi'one** *nf* observation
consu'e|to *a & nm* usual. **~tudi'nario** *a* *(diritto)* common; *(persona)* set in one's ways. **~'tudine** *nf* habit; *(usanza)* custom
consu'len|te *nmf* consultant. **~za** *nf* consultancy
consul'ta|re *vt* consult. **~rsi con** consult with. **~zi'one** *nf* consultation
consul't|ivo *a* consultative. **~orio** *nm* clinic
consu'ma|re *vt* *(usare)* consume; wear out *(abito, scarpe)*; consummate *(matrimonio)*; commit *(delitto)*. **~rsi** *vr* consume; *(abito, scarpe)* wear out; *(struggersi)* pine
consu'mato *a* *(politico)* seasoned; *(scarpe, tappeto)* worn
consuma'tore, -'trice *nmf* consumer. **~zi'one** *nf* *(bibita)* drink; *(spuntino)* snack
consu'mis|mo *nm* consumerism. **~ta** *nmf* consumerist
con'sumo *nm* consumption; *(di abito, scarpe)* wear; *(uso)* use; **generi di ~** consumer goods *or* items. **~ [di carburante]** [fuel] consumption
consun'tivo *a* *(bilancio)* final statement
conta'balle *nmf fam* storyteller
con'tabil|e *a* book-keeping ● *nmf* accountant. **~ità** *nf* accounting; **tenere la ~ità** keep the accounts
contachi'lometri *nm inv* mileometer, odometer *Am*

conta'dino, -a *nmf* farm-worker; *(medievale)* peasant
contagi'|are *vt* infect. **con'tagio** *nm* infection. **~'oso** *a* infectious
conta'gocce *nm inv* dropper
contami'na|re *vt* contaminate. **~zi'one** *nf* contamination
con'tante *nm* cash; **pagare in contanti** pay cash
con'tare *vt/i* count; *(tenere conto di)* take into account; *(proporsi)* intend
conta'scatti *nm inv* *Teleph* time-unit counter
conta'tore *nm* meter
contat'tare *vt* contact. **con'tatto** *nm* contact
'conte *nm* count
conteggi'are *vt* put on the bill ● *vi* calculate. **con'teggio** *nm* calculation. **conteggio alla rovescia** countdown
con'te|gno *nm* behaviour; *(atteggiamento)* attitude. **~'gnoso** *a* dignified
contem'pla|re *vt* contemplate; *(fissare)* gaze at. **~zi'one** *nf* contemplation
con'tempo *nm* **nel ~** in the meantime
contempo|ranea'mente *adv* at once. **~'raneo, -a** *a & nmf* contemporary
conten'dente *nmf* competitor. **con'tendere** *vi* compete; *(litigare)* quarrel ● *vt* contend
conte'n|ere *vt* contain; *(reprimere)* repress. **~ersi** *vr* contain oneself. **~l'tore** *nm* container
conten'tarsi *vr* ~ **di** be content with
conten'tezza *nf* joy
conten'tino *nm* placebo
con'tento *a* glad; *(soddisfatto)* contented
conte'nuto *nm* contents *pl*; *(soggetto)* content
contenzi'oso *nm* legal department
con'tes|a *nf* disagreement; *Sport*

contest. **~o** pp di **contendere** ● a contested

con'tessa nf countess

conte'sta|re vt contest; Jur notify. **~'tario** a anti-establishment. **~'tore**, **~'trice** nmf protester. **~zi'one** nf (disputa) dispute

con'testo nm context

con'tiguo a adjacent

continen'tale a continental. **conti'nente** nm continent

conti'nenza nf continence

contin'gen|te nm contingent; (quota) quota. **~za** nf contingency

continua'mente adv (senza interruzione) continuously; (frequentemente) continually

continu'are vt/i continue; (riprendere) resume. **~a'tivo** a permanent. **~azi'one** nf continuation. **~ità** nf continuity

con'tinu|o a continuous; (molto frequente) continual. **corrente ~a** direct current; **di ~o** continually

'**conto** nm calculation; (in banca, negozio) account; (di ristorante ecc) bill; (stima) consideration; **a conti fatti** all things considered; **far ~ di** (supporre) suppose; (proporsi) intend; **far ~ su** rely on; **in fin dei conti** when all is said and done; **per ~ di** on behalf of; **per ~ mio** (a mio parere) in my opinion; (da solo) on my own; **starsene per ~ proprio** be on one's own; **rendersi ~ di qcsa** realize sth; **sul ~ di qcno** (voci, informazioni) about sb; **tener ~ di qcsa** take sth into account; **tenere da ~ qcsa** look after sth; **fare i conti con qcno** fig sort sb out. **~ corrente** current account, checking account Am. **~ alla rovescia** countdown

con'torcer|e vt twist. **~si** vr twist about

contor'nare vt surround

con'torno nm contour; Culin vegetables pl

contorsi'one nf contortion. **con'torto** pp di **contorcere** ● a twisted

contrabban'|dare vt smuggle. **~di'ere**, **-a** nmf smuggler. **contrab'bando** nm contraband

contrab'basso nm double bass

contraccambi'are vt return. **contrac'cambio** nm return

contracce|t'tivo nm contraceptive. **~zi'one** nf contraception

contrac'col|po nm rebound; (di arma da fuoco) recoil; fig repercussion

con'trada nf (rione) district

contrad'detto pp di **contraddire**

contrad'di|re vt contradict. **~t'torio** a contradictory. **~zi'one** nf contradiction

contraddi'stin|guere vt differentiate. **~to** a distinct

contra'ente nmf contracting party

contra'ereo a anti-aircraft

contraf'fa|re vt disguise; (imitare) imitate; (falsificare) forge. **~tto** a forged. **~zi'one** nf disguising; (imitazione) imitation; (falsificazione) forgery

con'tralto nm countertenor ● nf contralto

contrap'peso nm counterbalance

contrap'por|re vt counter; (confrontare) compare. **~si** vr contrast; **~si a** be opposed to

contraria'mente adv contrary (a to)

contrari'are vt oppose; (infastidire) annoy. **~rsi** vr get annoyed. **~età** nf inv adversity; (ostacolo) set-back

con'trario a contrary, opposite; (direzione) opposite; (sfavorevole) unfavourable ● nm contrary, opposite; **al ~** on the contrary

con'trarre vt contract

contras'se'gnare vt mark. **~'segno** nm mark; **[in] ~segno** (spedizione) cash on delivery, COD

contra'stante a contrasting

contra'stare vt oppose; (contestare) contest ● vi clash. **con'trasto** nm contrast; (litigio) dispute

contrattac'care vt counter

attack. **contrat'tacco** nm counter-attack

contrat'ta|re vt/i negotiate; (mercanteggiare) bargain. **~zi'one** nf (salariale) bargaining

contrat'tempo nm hitch

con'tratt|o pp di contrarre ● nm contract. **~o a termine** fixed-term contract. **~u'ale** a contractual

contravve'n|ire vi contravene. **~zi'one** nf contravention; (multa) fine

contrazi'one nf contraction; (di prezzi) reduction

contribu'ente nmf contributor; (del fisco) taxpayer

contribu'ire vi contribute. **contri'buto** nm contribution

'contro prep against; **~ di me** against me ● nm **il pro e il ~** the pros and cons pl

contro'battere vt counter

controbilanci'are vt counterbalance

controcor'rente a (idee, persona) non-conformist ● adv upriver; fig upstream

controffen'siva nf counter-offensive

controfi'gura nf stand-in

controfir'mare vt countersign

controindicazi'one nf Med contraindication

control'la|re vt control; (verificare) check; (collaudare) test. **~rsi** vr have self-control. **~to** a controlled

con'trol|lo nm control; (verifica) check; Med check-up. **~lo delle nascite** birth control. **~lore** nm controller; (sui treni ecc) [ticket] inspector. **~lore di volo** air-traffic controller

contro'luce nf **in ~** against the light

contro'mano adv in the wrong direction

contromi'sura nf countermeasure

contropi'ede nm **prendere in ~** catch off guard

controprodu'cente a self-defeating

con'trordin|e nm counter order; **salvo ~i** unless I/you hear to the contrary

contro'senso nm contradiction in terms

controspio'naggio nm counter-espionage

contro'vento adv against the wind

contro'vers|ia nf controversy; Jur dispute. **~o** a controversial

contro'voglia adv unwillingly

contu'macia nf default; **in ~** in one's absence

contun'dente a (corpo, arma) blunt

contur'ba|nte a perturbing

contusi'one nf bruise

convale'scen|te a convalescent. **~za** nf convalescence; **essere in ~za** be convalescing

con'vali|da nf validation. **~'dare** vt confirm; validate (atto, biglietto)

con'vegno nm meeting; (congresso) congress

conve'nevol|e a suitable; **~i** pl pleasantries

conveni'en|te a convenient; (prezzo) attractive (vantaggioso) advantageous. **~za** nf convenience; (interesse) advantage; (di prezzo) attractiveness

conve'nire vi (riunirsi) gather; (concordare) agree; (ammettere) admit; (essere opportuno) be convenient ● vt agree on; **ci conviene andare** it is better to go; **non mi conviene stancarmi** I'd better not tire myself out

con'vento nm (di suore) convent; (di frati) monastery

conve'nuto a fixed

convenzi|o'nale a conventional. **~'one** nf convention

conver'gen|te a converging. **~za** nf fig confluence

con'vergere *vi* converge

conver'sa|re *vi* converse. **~zi'one** *nf* conversation

conversi'one *nf* conversion

con'verso *pp di* **convergere**

conver'tibile *nf Auto* convertible

conver'ti|re *vt* convert. **~rsi** *vr* be converted. **~to, -a** *nmf* convert

con'vesso *a* convex

convin'cente *a* convincing

convin|cere *vt* convince. **~to a** convinced. **~zi'one** *nf* conviction

con'vitto *nm* boarding school

convi'ven|te *nm* common-law husband ● *nf* common-law wife. **~za** *nf* cohabitation. **con'vivere** *vi* live together

convivi'ale *a* convivial

convo'ca|re *vt* convene. **~zi'one** *nf* convening

convogli'are *vt* convey; (*navi*) convoy. **con'voglio** *nm* convoy; (*ferroviario*) train

convulsi'one *nf* convulsion. **con'vulso** *a* convulsive; (*febbrile*) feverish

coope'ra|re *vi* co-operate. **~'tiva** *nf* co-operative. **~zi'one** *nf* co-operation

coordina'mento *nm* co-ordination

coordi'na|re *vt* co-ordinate. **~ta** *nf Math* coordinate. **~zi'one** *nf* co-ordination

co'perchio *nm* lid; (*copertura*) cover

co'perta *nf* blanket; (*copertura*) cover, *Naut* deck

co•per'tina *nf* cover; (*di libro*) dustjacket

co'perto *pp di* **coprire** ● *a* covered; (*cielo*) overcast ● *nm* (*a tavola*) place; (*prezzo del coperto*) cover charge; **al ~** under cover

coper'tone *nm* tarpaulin; (*gomma*) tyre

coper'tura *nf* covering; *Comm*, *Fin* cover

'copia *nf* copy; **bella/brutta ~** fair/rough copy. **~ su carta** hardcopy. **copi'are** *vt* copy

copi'one *nm* script

copi'oso *a* plentiful

'coppa *nf* (*calice*) goblet; (*per gelato ecc*) dish; *Sport* cup. **~ [di] gelato** ice-cream (*served in a dish*)

cop'petta *nf* (*di ceramica*, *vetro*) bowl; (*di gelato*) small tub

'coppia *nf* couple; (*in carte*) pair

co'prente *a* (*cipria*, *vernice*) covering

copri'capo *nm* headgear

coprifu'oco *nm* curfew

copri'letto *nm* bedspread

copripiu'mino *nm* duvet cover

co'pri|re *vt* cover; drown (*suono*); hold (*carica*). **~si** *vr* (*vestirsi*) cover up; *fig* cover oneself; (*cielo*) become overcast

coque *sf* **alla ~** (*uovo*) soft-boiled

co'raggio *nm* courage; (*sfacciataggine*) nerve; **~o!** come on. **~'oso** *a* courageous

co'rale *a* choral

co'rallo *nm* coral

co'rano *nm* Koran

co'raz|za *nf* armour; (*di animali*) shell. **~'zata** *nf* battleship. **~'zato** *a* (*nave*) armour-clad

corbelle'ria *nf* nonsense; (*sproposito*) blunder

'corda *nf* cord; (*spago*, *Mus*) string; (*fune*) rope; (*cavo*) cable; **essere giù di ~** be depressed; **dare ~ a** qcno encourage sb. **corde** *pl* **vocali** vocal cords

cor'data *nf* roped party

cordi'al|e *a* cordial ● *nm* (*bevanda*) cordial; **saluti ~i** best wishes. **~ità** *nf* cordiality

cor'doglio *nm* grief; (*lutto*) mourning

cor'done *nm* cord; (*schieramento*) cordon. **~ ombelicale** umbilical cord

core|ogra'fia *nf* choreography. **~'ografo, -a** *nmf* choreographer

cori'andoli *nmpl* confetti *sg*

cori'andolo *nm* (*spezia*) coriander

cori'car|e *vt* put to bed. **~si** *vr* go to bed

co'rista *nmf* choir member

cor'nacchia *nf* crow

corna *vedi* **corno**

corna'musa *nf* bagpipes *pl*

'cornea *nf* cornea

cor'nett|a *nf Mus* cornet; (*del telefono*) receiver. **~o** *nm* (*brioche*) croissant

cor'ni|ce *nf* frame. **~ci'one** *nm* cornice

'corno *nm* (*pl nf* **corna**) horn; **fare le corna a qcno** be unfaithful to sb; **fare le corna** (*per scongiuro*) touch wood. **cor'nuto** *a* horned ●*nm* (*fam: marito tradito*) cuckold; (*insulto*) bastard

'coro *nm* chorus; *Relig* choir

co'rolla *nf* corolla

co'rona *nf* crown; (*di fiori*) wreath; (*rosario*) rosary. **~'mento** *nm* (*di impresa*) crowning. **coro'nare** *vt* crown; (*sogno*) fulfil

cor'petto *nm* bodice

'corpo *nm* body; (*Mil, diplomatico*) corps *inv*; **a ~ a ~** man to man; **andare di ~** move one's bowels. **~ di ballo** corps de ballet. **~ insegnante** teaching staff. **~ del reato** incriminating item

corpo'rale *a* corporal

corporati'vismo *nm* corporatism

corpora'tura *nf* build

corporazi'one *nf* corporation

cor'poreo *a* bodily

cor'poso *a* full-bodied

corpu'lento *a* stout

cor'puscolo *nm* corpuscle

corre'dare *vt* equip

corre'dino *nm* (*per neonato*) layette

cor'redo *nm* (*nuziale*) trousseau

cor'reggere *vt* correct; lace (*bevanda*)

corre'lare *vt* correlate

cor'rente *a* running; (*in vigore*) current; (*frequente*) everyday; (*inglese ecc*) fluent ●*nf* current; (*d'aria*) draught; **essere al ~** be up to date. **~'mente** *adv* (*parlare*) fluently

'correre *vi* run; (*affrettarsi*) hurry; *Sport* race; (*notizie:*) circulate; **~**

dietro a run after ●*vt* run; **~ un pericolo** run a risk; **lascia ~!** don't bother!

corre|tta'mente *adv* correctly.

cor'retto *pp di* **correggere** ●*a* correct; (*caffè*) with a drop of alcohol. **~zi'one** *nf* correction. **~zione di bozze** proof-reading

cor'rida *nf* bullfight

corri'doio *nm* corridor; *Aeron* aisle

corri|'dore, -'trice *nmf* racer; (*a piedi*) runner

corri'era *nf* coach, bus

corri'ere *nm* courier; (*posta*) mail; (*spedizioniere*) carrier

corri'mano *nm* bannister

corrispet'tivo *nm* amount due

corrispon|'den|te *a* corresponding ●*nmf* correspondent. **~za** *nf* correspondence; **scuola/corsi per ~za** correspondence course; **vendite per ~za** mail-order [shopping]. **corri'spondere** *vi* correspond; (*stanza:*) communicate; **corrispondere a** (*contraccambiare*) return

corri'sposto *a* (*amore*) reciprocated

corrobo'rare *vt* strengthen; *fig* corroborate

cor'roder|e *vt*, **~si** *vr* corrode

cor'rompere *vt* corrupt; (*con denaro*) bribe

corrosi'one *nf* corrosion. **corro'sivo** *a* corrosive

cor'roso *pp di* **corrodere**

cor'rotto *pp di* **corrompere** ●*a* corrupt

corrucci'a|rsi *vr* be vexed. **~to** *a* upset

corru'gare *vt* wrinkle; **~ la fronte** knit one's brows

corruzi'one *nf* corruption; (*con denaro*) bribery

'corsa *nf* running; (*rapida*) dash; *Sport* race; (*di treno ecc*) journey; **di ~** at a run; **fare una ~** run

cor'sia *nf* gangway; (*di ospedale*) ward; *Auto* lane; (*di supermercato*) aisle

cor'sivo nm italics pl
'corso pp di **correre** ● nm course; (strada) main street; Comm circulation; **lavori in ~** work in progress; **nel ~ di** during. **~ d'acqua** watercourse
'corte nf [courtyard]; (Jur, regale) court; **fare la ~ a qcno** court sb. **~ d'appello** court of appeal
cor'teccia nf bark
corteggia'mento nm courtship
coreteggia're vt court. **~'tore** nm admirer
cor'teo nm procession
cor'te|se a courteous. **~'sia** nf courtesy; **per ~sia** please
cortigi'ano, -a nmf courtier ● nf courtesan
cor'tile nm courtyard
cor'tina nf curtain; (schermo) screen
'corto a short; **per farla corta** in short; **essere a ~ di** be short of. **~ circuito** nm short [circuit]
cortome'traggio nm Cinema short
cor'vino a jet-black
'corvo nm raven
'cosa nf thing; (faccenda) matter; inter, rel what; [**che**] **~** what; **nessuna ~** nothing; **ogni ~** everything; **per prima ~** first of all; **tante cose** so many things; (augurio) all the best
'cosca nf clan
'coscia nf thigh; Culin leg
cosci'en|te a conscious. **~za** nf conscience; (consapevolezza) consciousness
co'scrit'to nm conscript. **~zi'one** nf conscription
così adv so; (in questo modo) like this, like that; (perciò) therefore; **le cose stanno ~** that's how things stand; **fermo ~!** hold it; **proprio ~!** exactly!; **basta ~!** that will do!; **ah, è ~?** it's like that, is it?; **~ so-so;** **e ~ via** and so on; **per ~ dire** so to speak; **più di ~** any more, **una ~ cara ragazza!** such a nice girl!; **è stato ~**

generoso da aiutarti he was kind enough to help you ● conj (allora) so ● a inv (tale) like that, such; **una ragazza ~** a girl like that, such a girl
cosicché conj and so
cosid'detto a so-called
co'smesi nf cosmetics
co'smetico a & nm cosmetic
'cosmico a cosmic
'cosmo nm cosmos
cosmopo'lita a cosmopolitan
co'spargere vt sprinkle; (disseminare) scatter
co'spetto nm **al ~ di** in the presence of
co'spicuo a conspicuous; (somma ecc) considerable
cospi'ra|re vi conspire. **~'tore,** **~'trice** nmf conspirator. **~zi'one** nf conspiracy
'costa nf coast, coastline; Anat rib
costà adv there
co'stan|te a & nf constant. **~za** nf constancy
co'stare vi cost; **quanto costa?** how much is it?
co'stata nf chop
costeggi'are vt (per mare) coast; (per terra) skirt
co'stei pers pron vedi **costui**
costellazi'one nf constellation
coster'na|to a dismayed. **~zi'one** nf consternation
costi'er|a nf stretch of coast. **~o** a coastal
costi'pa|to a constipated. **~zi'one** nf constipation; (raffreddore) bad cold
costitu'ir|e vt constitute; (formare) form; (nominare) appoint. **~si** vr Jur give oneself up
costituzio'nale a constitutional.
costituzi'one nf constitution; (fondazione) setting up
'costo nm cost; **ad ogni ~** at all costs; **a nessun ~** on no account
'costola nf rib; (di libro) spine
costo'letta nf cutlet
co'storo pron vedi **costui**
co'stoso a costly

co'stretto *pp di* **costringere**

co'stri|ngere *vt* compel; (*stringere*) constrict. **~'tivo** *a* coercive. **~zi'one** *nf* constraint

costru'ire *vt* build, construct. **~'tivo** *a* constructive. **~zi'one** *nf* building, construction

co'stui, co'stei, *pl* **co'storo** *prons* (*soggetto*) he, she, *pl* they; (*complemento*) him, her, *pl* them

co'stume *nm* (*usanza*) custom; (*condotta*) morals *pl*; (*indumento*) costume. **~ da bagno** swim-suit; (*da uomo*) swimming trunks

co'tenna *nf* pigskin; (*della pancetta*) rind

coto'letta *nf* cutlet

co'tone *nm* cotton. **~ idrofilo** cotton wool, absorbent cotton *Am*

'cotta *nf* (*fam: innamoramento*) crush

'cottimo *nm* **lavorare a ~** *do* piece-work

'cotto *pp di* **cuocere** ● *a* done; (*fam: infatuato*) in love; (*fam: sbronzo*) drunk; **ben ~** (*carne*) well done

'cotton fi'oc® *nm inv* cotton bud

cot'tura *nf* cooking

co'vare *vt* hatch; sicken for (*malattia*); harbour (*odio*) ● *vi* smoulder

'covo *nm* den

co'vone *nm* sheaf

'cozza *nf* mussel

coz'zare *vi* **~ contro** bump into.

'cozzo *nm* *fig* clash

C.P. *abbr* (**Casella Postale**) PO Box

'crampo *nm* cramp

'cranio *nm* skull

cra'tere *nm* crater

cra'vatta *nf* tie; (*a farfalla*) bow-tie

cre'anza *nf* politeness; **mala ~** bad manners

cre'a|re *vt* create; (*causare*) cause. **~tività** *nf* creativity. **~'tivo** *a* creative. **~to** *nm* creation. **~'tore,** **~'trice** *nmf* creator. **~zi'one** *nf* creation

crea'tura *nf* creature; (*bambino*) baby; **povera ~!** poor thing!

cre'den|te *nmf* believer. **~za** *nf* belief; *Comm* credit; (*mobile*) sideboard. **~zi'ali** *nfpl* credentials

'creder|e *vt* believe; (*pensare*) think ● *vi* **~e in** believe in; **credo di sì** I think so; **non ti credo** I don't believe you. **~si** *vr* think oneself to be; **si crede uno scrittore** he flatters himself he is a writer. **cre'dibile** *a* credible.

credibilità *nf* credibility

'credi|to *nm* credit; (*stima*) esteem; **comprare a ~to** buy on credit. **~tore,** **~'trice** *nmf* creditor

'credo *nm inv* credo

credulità *nf* credulity

'credu|lo *a* credulous. **~'lone, -a** *nmf* simpleton

'crema *nf* cream; (*di uova e latte*) custard. **~ idratante** moisturizer. **~ pasticciera** egg custard. **~ solare** suntan lotion

cre'ma|re *vt* cremate. **~'torio** *nm* crematorium. **~zi'one** *nf* cremation

crème cara'mel *nf* crème caramel

creme'ria *nf* dairy (*also selling ice cream and cakes*)

Crem'lino *nm* Kremlin

'crepa *nf* crack

cre'paccio *nm* cleft; (*di ghiacciaio*) crevasse

crepacu'ore *nm* heart-break

crepa'pelle: a ~ *adv* fit to burst; **ridere a ~** split one's sides with laughter

cre'pare *vi* crack; (*fam: morire*) kick the bucket; **~ dal ridere** laugh fit to burst

crepa'tura *nf* crevice

crêpe *nf inv* pancake

crepi'tare *vi* crackle

cre'puscolo *nm* twilight

cre'scendo *nm* crescendo

'cresc|ere *vi* grow; (*aumentare*) increase ● *vt* (*allevare*) bring up; (*aumentare*) increase. **~ita** *nf* growth; (*aumento*) increase. **~i'uto** *pp di* **crescere**

'cresi|ma *nf* confirmation. **~'mare** *vt* confirm

'crespo *a* ‹capelli› frizzy ● *nm* crêpe

'cresta *nf* crest; ‹cima› peak

'creta *nf* clay

'Creta *nf* Crete

cre'tino, -a *a* stupid ● *nmf* idiot

cric *nm* jack

'cricca *nf* gang

cri'ceto *nm* hamster

crimi'nal|e *a & nmf* criminal. **~ità** *nf* crime. **'crimine** *nm* crime

orimi'noso *a* criminal

'crin|e *nm* horsehair. **~i'era** *nf* mane

'cripta *nf* crypt

crisan'temo *nm* chrysanthemum

'crisi *nf inv* crisis; *Med* fit

cristal'lino *nm* crystalline

cristalliz'zar|e *vt, ~si* *vr* crystallize; ‹fig: parola, espressione:› become part of the language

cri'stallo *nm* crystal

Cristia'nesimo *nm* Christianity

cristi'ano, -a *a & nmf* Christian

'Cristo *nm* Christ; **un povero c~** *a* poor beggar

cri'terio *nm* criterion; ‹buon senso› [common] sense

'criti|ca *nf* criticism; ‹recensione› review. **criti'care** *vt* criticize. **~co** *a* critical ● *nm* critic. **~cone, -a** *nmf* faultfinder

crivel'lare *vt* riddle (**di** with)

ori'vello *nm* sieve

croc'cante *a* crisp ● *nm* type of crunchy nut biscuit

oroc'chetta *nf* croquette

'croce *nf* cross; **a occhio e ~** roughly; **fare testa e ~** spin a coin. **C~ Rossa** Red Cross

croce'via *nm inv* crossroads *sg*

croci'ata *nf* crusade

cro'cicchio *nm* crossroads *sg*

croci'era *nf* cruise; *Archit* crossing

croci'fi|ggere *vt* crucify. **~ssi'one** *nf* crucifixion. **~sso** *pp* of **crocifiggere** ● *a* crucified ● *nm* crucifix

crogio'larsi *vr* bask

crogi[u]'olo *nm* crucible; *fig* melting pot

crol'lare *vi* collapse; ‹prezzi:› slump. **'crollo** *nm* collapse; ‹dei prezzi› slump

cro'mato *a* chromium-plated. **'cromo** *nm* chrome. **cromo'soma** *nm* chromosome

'oronaca *nf* chronicle; ‹di giornale› news; *TV, Radio* commentary; **fatto di ~** news item. **~ nera** crime news

'cronico *a* chronic

cro'nista *nmf* reporter

crono'logico *a* chronological

crono'traggio *nm* timing

cronome'trare *vt* time

cro'nometro *nm* chronometer

'crosta *nf* crust; ‹di formaggio› rind; ‹di ferita› scab; ‹quadro› daub

cro'staceo *nm* shellfish

cro'stata *nf* tart

cro'stino *nm* crouton

crucci'arsi *vr* worry. **'cruccio** *nm* worry

cruci'ale *a* crucial

cruci'verba *nm inv* crossword [puzzle]

cru'del|e *a* cruel. **~tà** *nf inv* cruelty

'crudo *a* raw; ‹rigido› harsh

cru'ento *a* bloody

cru'miro *nm* blackleg, scab

'orusoa *nf* bran

cru'scotto *nm* dashboard

'Cuba *nf* Cuba

cu'betto *nm* **~ di ghiaccio** ice cube

'cubico *a* cubic

cubi'tal|e *a* **a caratteri ~i** in enormous letters

'cubo *nm* cube

cuc'cagna *nf* abundance; ‹baldoria› merry-making; **paese della ~** land of plenty

cuc'cetta *nf* ‹su un treno› couchette; *Naut* berth

cucchia'ino *nm* teaspoon

cucchi'a|io *nm* spoon; **al ~io** *(dolce)* creamy. **~l'ata** *nf* spoonful

'**cuccia** *nf* dog's bed; **fa la ~!** lie down!

cuccio'lata *nf* litter

'**cucciolo** *nm* puppy

cu'cina *nf* kitchen; *(il cucinare)* cooking; *(cibo)* food; *(apparecchio)* cooker; **far da ~** cook; **libro di ~** cook[ery] book. **~ a gas** gas cooker

cuci'n|are *vt* cook. **~ino** *nm* kitchenette

cu'ci|re *vt* sew; **macchina per ~re** sewing-machine. **~to** *nm* sewing. **~'tura** *nf* seam

cucù *nm inv* cuckoo

'**cuculo** *nm* cuckoo

'**cuffia** *nf* bonnet; *(da bagno)* bathing-cap; *(ricevitore)* headphones *pl*

cu'gino, -a *nmf* cousin

'**cui** *pron rel (persona: con prep)* who, whom *fml*; *(cose, animali: con prep)* which; *(tra articolo e nome)* whose; **la persona con ~ ho parlato** the person [who] I spoke to; **la ditta per ~ lavoro** the company I work for, the company for which I work; **l'amico il ~ libro è stato pubblicato** the friend whose book was published; **in ~** *(dove)* where; *(quando)* that; **per ~** *(perciò)* so; **la città in ~ vivo** the city I live in, the city where I live; **il giorno in ~ l'ho visto** the day [that] I saw him

culi'nari|a *nf* cookery. **~o** *a* culinary

'**culla** *nf* cradle. **cul'lare** *vt* rock

culmi'na|nte *a* culminating. **~re** *vi* culminate. '**culmine** *nm* peak

'**culo** *nm vulg* arse; *(fortuna)* luck

'**culto** *nm* cult; *Relig* religion; *(adorazione)* worship

cul'tu|ra *nf* culture. **~ra generale** general knowledge. **~'rale** *a* cultural

cultu'ris|mo *nm* body-building. **~ta** *nmf* body-builder

cumula'tivo *a* cumulative; **biglietto ~** group ticket

'**cumulo** *nm* pile; *(mucchio)* heap; *(nuvola)* cumulus

'**cuneo** *nm* wedge

cu'netta *nf* gutter

cu'ocere *vt/i* cook; fire *(ceramica)*

cu'oco, -a *nmf* cook

cu'oio *nm* leather. **~ capelluto** scalp

cu'ore *nm* heart; **cuori** *pl (carte)* hearts; **nel profondo del ~** in one's heart of hearts; **di [buon] ~** *(persona)* kind-hearted; **nel ~ della notte** in the middle of the night; **stare a ~ a qcno** be very important to sb

cupi'digia *nf* greed

'**cupo** *a* gloomy; *(suono)* deep

'**cupola** *nf* dome

'**cura** *nf* care; *(amministrazione)* management; *Med* treatment; **a ~ di** edited by; **in ~** under treatment. **~ dimagrante** *[slimming]* diet. **cu'rante** *a* **medico curante** GP, doctor

cu'rar|e *vt* take care of; *Med* treat; *(guarire)* cure; edit *(testo)*. **~si** *vr* take care of oneself; *Med* follow a treatment; **~si di** *(badare a)* mind

cu'rato *nm* parish priest

cura'tore, -'trice *nmf* trustee; *(di testo)* editor

'**curia** *nf* curia

curio's|are *vi* be curious; *(mettere il naso)* pry *(in into); (nei negozi)* look around. **~ità** *nf inv* curiosity. **curi'oso** *a* curious; *(strano)* odd

cur'sore *nm Comput* cursor

'**curva** *nf* curve; *(stradale)* bend. **~ a gomito** U-bend. **cur'vare** *vt* curve; *(strada:)* bend. **cur'varsi** *vr* bend. '**curvo** *a* curved; *(piegato)* bent

cusci'netto *nm* pad; *Mech* bearing

cu'scino *nm* cushion; *(guanciale)* pillow. **~ d'aria** air cushion

'**cuspide** *nf* spire

cu'stod|e *nm* caretaker. **~e giudiziario** official receiver. **~ia**

nf care; *Jur* custody; (*astuccio*) case. **~ia cautelare** remand.
custo'dire *vt* keep; (*badare*) look after

cu'taneo *a* skin *attrib*

'cute *nf* skin

cu'ticola *nf* cuticle

Dd

da *prep* from; (*con verbo passivo*) by; (*moto a luogo*) to; (*moto per luogo*) through; (*stato in luogo*) at; (*temporale*) since; (*continuativo*) for; (*causale*) with; (*in qualità di*) as; (*come*) like; (*con caratteristica*) with; **da Roma a Milano** from Rome to Milan; **staccare un quadro dalla parete** take a picture off the wall; **i bambini dai 5 ai 10 anni** children between 5 and 10; **vedere qcsa da vicino/lontano** see sth from up close/from a distance; **scritto a** written by; **andare dal panettiere** go to the baker's; **passo da te più tardi** I'll come over to your place later; **passiamo da qui** let's go this way; **un appuntamento dal dentista** an appointment at the dentist's; **il treno passa da Venezia** the train goes through Venice; **dall'anno scorso** since last year; **vivo qui in da due anni** I've been living here for two years; **da domani** from tomorrow; **piangere dal dolore** cry with pain; **ho molto da fare** I have a lot to do; **occhiali da sole** sunglasses; **qualcosa da mangiare** something to eat; **un uomo dai capelli scuri** a man with dark hair; **è un oggetto da poco** it's not worth much; **l'ho fatto da solo** I did it by myself; **si è fatto da sé** he is a self-made man; **non è da lui** it's not like him

dac'capo *adv* again; (*dall'inizio*) from the beginning

dacché *conj* since

'dado *nm* dice; *Culin* stock cube; *Techn* nut

daf'fare *nm* work

'dagli = da + gli. **'dai** = da + i

'dai *int* come on!

'daino *nm* deer; (*pelle*) buckskin

dal = da + il. **'dalla** = da + la. **'dalle** = da + le. **'dallo** = da + lo

'dalia *nf* dahlia

dal'tonico *a* colour-blind

'dama *nf* lady; (*nei balli*) partner; (*gioco*) draughts *sg*

dami'gella *nf* (*di sposa*) bridesmaid

damigi'ana *nf* demijohn

dam'meno *adv* **non essere ~** (*di qcno*) be no less good (than sb)

da'naro *nm* = **denaro**

dana'roso *a* (*fam: ricco*) loaded

da'nese *a* Danish ● *nmf* Dane ● *nm* (*lingua*) Danish

Dani'marca *nf* Denmark

dan'na|re *vt* damn; **far ~re qcno** drive sb mad. **~to** *a* damned. **~zi'one** *f* damnation

danneggia'mento *nm* damage. **~'are** *vt* damage; (*nuocere*) harm

'danno *nm* damage; (*a persona*) harm. **dan'noso** *a* harmful

Da'nubio *nm* Danube

'danza *nf* dance; (*il danzare*) dancing. **dan'zare** *vi* dance

dapper'tutto *adv* everywhere

dap'poco *a* worthless

dap'prima *adv* at first

'dardo *nm* dart

'dar|e *vt* give; sit (*esame*); have (*festa*); **~ qcsa a qcno** give sb sth; **~ da mangiare a qcno** give sb something to eat; **~ il benvenuto a qcno** welcome sb; **~ la buonanotte a qcno** say good night to sb; **~ del tu/del lei a qcno** address sb as "tu"/"lei"; **~ del cretino a qcno** call sb an idiot; **~ qcsa per scontato** take sth for granted; **cosa danno alla TV stasera?** what's on TV tonight? ● *vi* **nel-**

l'occhio be conspicuous; ~ alla **testa** go to one's head; ~ **su** (finestra, casa) look on to; ~ **sui** o **ai nervi a qcno** get on sb's nerves ● nm Comm debit. ~**si** vr (scambiarsi) give each other; (mettersi) **si da fare** get down to it; **si è dato tanto da fare!** he went to so much trouble!; ~**si a** (cominciare) take up; ~**si al bere** take to drink; ~**si per** (malato, assente) pretend to be; ~**si per vinto** give up; **può ~si** maybe

'**darsena** nf dock

'**data** nf date. ~ **di emissione** date of issue. ~ **di nascita** date of birth. ~ **di scadenza** cut-off date

da'ta|re vt date; **a ~re da** as from. ~**to a** dated

dato a given; (dedito) addicted; ~ **che** seeing that, given that ● nm datum. ~ **di fatto** well-established fact; **dati** pl data. **da'tore** nm giver. **datore, datrice** nmf di lavoro employer

'**dattero** nm date

dattilogra'f|are vt type. ~**ia** nf typing. **datti'lografo, -a** nmf typist

dattilo'scritto a (copia) typewritten

dat'torno adv **togliersi ~** clear off

da'vanti adv before; (dirimpetto) opposite; (di fronte) in front ● a inv front ● nm front; ~ **a** prep before, in front of

davan'zale nm window sill

da'vanzo adv more than enough

dav'vero adv really; **per ~** in earnest; **dici ~?** honestly?

'**dazio** nm duty; (ufficio) customs pl

d.C. abbr (dopo Cristo) AD

'**dea** nf goddess

debel'lare vt defeat

debili'ta|nte a weakening. ~**re** vt weaken. ~**rsi** vr become debilitated. ~**zi'one** nf debilitation

debita'mente adv duly

'**debi|to** a due; **a tempo ~** in due course ● nm debt. ~'**tore**, ~'**trice** nmf debtor

'**debo|le** a weak; (luce) dim; (suono) faint ● nm weak point; (preferenza) weakness. ~'**lezza** nf weakness

debor'dare vi overflow

debosci'ato a debauched

debut'ta|nte nm (attore) actor making his début ● nf actress making her début. ~**re** vi make one's début. **de'butto** nm début

deca'den|te a decadent. ~'**tismo** nm decadence. ~**za** nf decline; Jur loss. **deca'dere** vi lapse. **decadi'mento** nm (delle arti) decline

decaffei'nato a decaffeinated ● nm decaffeinated coffee, decaf fam

decan'tare vt (lodare) praise

decapi'ta|re vt decapitate; behead (condannato). ~**zi'one** nf decapitation; beheading

decappot'tabile a convertible

de'ce|dere vi (morire) die. ~'**duto** a deceased

decele'rare vt decelerate, slow down

decen'nale a ten-yearly. **de'cennio** nm decade

de'cen|te a decent. ~'**temente** adv decently. ~**za** nf decency

decentra'mento nm decentralization

de'cesso nm death; **atto di ~** death certificate

de'ci|dere vt decide; settle (questione). ~**si** vr make up one's mind

deci'frare vt decipher; (documenti cifrati) decode

deci'male a decimal

deci'mare vt decimate

'**decimo** a tenth

de'cina nf Math ten; **una ~ di** (circa dieci) about ten

deci'sa'mente adv definitely, decidedly

decisio'nale a decision-making

deci'si|one nf decision. ~'**sivo** a decisive. **de'ciso** pp di **decidere** ● a decided

decla'ma|re vt/i declaim. **~'torio** a (stile) declamatory

declas'sare vt downgrade

decli'na|re vt decline; **~re ogni responsabilità** disclaim all responsibility ●vi go down; (tramontare) set. **~zi'one** nf Gram declension. **de'clino** nm decline; **in declino** (popolarità:) on the decline

decodificazi'one nf decoding

decol'lare vi take off

décolle'té nm inv décolleté, low neckline

de'collo nm take-off

decolo'ra|nte nm bleach. **~re** vt bleach

decolorazi'one nf bleaching

decom'po|rre vt, **~rsi** vr decompose. **~sizi'one** nf decomposition

deconcen'trarsi vr become distracted

deconge'lare vt defrost

decongestio'nare vt Med, fig relieve congestion in

deco'ra|re vt decorate. **~'tivo** a decorative. **~to** a (ornato) decorated. **~'tore**, **~'trice** nmf decorator. **~zi'one** nf decoration

de'coro nm decorum

decorosa'mente adv decorously. **decoroso** a dignified

decor'renza nf **~ dal...** starting from...

de'correre vi pass; **a ~ da** with effect from. **de'corso** pp di decorrere ●nm passing; Med course

de'crepito a decrepit

decre'scente a decreasing. **de'crescere** vi decrease; (prezzi:) go down; (acque:) subside

decre'tare vt decree. **de'creto** nm decree. **decreto legge** decree which has the force of law

'dedalo nm maze

'dedica nf dedication

dedi'car|e vt dedicate. **~si** vr dedicate oneself

'dedi|to a **~ a** given to; (assorto) engrossed in, addicted to (vizi). **~zi'one** nf dedication

de'dotto pp di **dedurre**

dedu'cibile a (tassa) allowable

de'du|rre vt deduce; (sottrarre) deduct. **~'tivo** a deductive. **~zi'one** nf deduction

defal'care vt remit

defe'rire vt Jur remit

defezi|o'nare vi (abbandonare) defect. **~'one** nf defection

defici'en|te a (mancante) deficient; Med mentally deficient ●nmf mental defective; pej halfwit. **~za** nf deficiency; (lacuna) gap; Med mental deficiency

'deficit nm inv deficit. **~'tario** a (bilancio) deficit attrib

defi'larsi vr (scomparire) slip away

défilé nm inv fashion show

defi'ni|re vt (risolvere) settle. **~tiva'mente** adv for good. **~'tivo** a definitive. **~to** a definite. **~zi'one** nf definition; (soluzione) settlement

deflazi'one nf deflation

deflet'tore nm Auto quarterlight

deflu'ire vi (liquidi:) flow away; (persone:) stream out

de'flusso nm (di marea) ebb

defor'mar|e vt deform (arto); fig distort. **~si** vr lose its shape. **de'forme** a deformed. **~ità** nf deformity

defor'ma|to a warped. **~zi'one** nf (di fatti) distortion; **è una ~zione professionale** put it down to the job

defrau'dare vt defraud

de'funto, **-a** a & nmf deceased

degene'ra|re vi degenerate. **~to** a degenerate. **~zi'one** nf degeneration. **de'genere** a degenerate

de'gen|te a bedridden ●nmf patient. **~za** nf confinement

'degli = **di + gli**

deglu'tire vt swallow

de'gna|re vt **~e qcno di uno sguardo** deign to look at sb. **~si** vr deign, condescend

'degno a worthy; (meritevole) deserving

degrada'mento nm degradation

degra'dante *a* demeaning

degra'da|re *vt* degrade. **~rsi** *vr* lower oneself; ⟨*città*⟩ fall into a state of disrepair. **~zi'one** *nf* degradation

de'grado *nm* damage; **~ ambientale** *nm* environmental damage

degu'sta|re *vt* taste. **~zi'one** *nf* tasting

'dei = di + i. **'del** = di + il

dela'tore, -'trice *nmf* [police] informer. **~zi'one** *nf* informing

'delega *nf* proxy

dele'ga|re *vt* delegate. **~to** *nm* delegate. **~zi'one** *nf* delegation

dele'terio *a* harmful

del'fino *nm* dolphin; ⟨*stile di nuoto*⟩ butterfly [stroke]

de'libera *nf* bylaw

delibe'ra|re *vt/i* deliberate; **~ su** in rule on/in. **~to** *a* deliberate

delicata'mente *adv* delicately

delica'tezza *nf* delicacy; ⟨*fragilità*⟩ frailty; ⟨*tatto*⟩ tact

deli'cato *a* delicate; ⟨*salute*⟩ frail; ⟨*suono, colore*⟩ soft

delimi'tare *vt* delimit

deline'a|re *vt* outline. **~rsi** *vr* be outlined; *fig* take shape. **~to** *a* defined

delin'quen|te *nmf* delinquent. **~za** *nf* delinquency

deli'rante *a Med* delirious; ⟨*assurdo*⟩ insane

deli'rare *vi* be delirious. **de'lirio** *nm* delirium; *fig* frenzy

de'litt|o *nm* crime. **~u'oso** *a* criminal

de'lizi|a *nf* delight. **~'are** *vt* delight. **~'oso** *a* delightful; ⟨*cibo*⟩ delicious

'della = di + la. **'delle** = di + le. **'dello** = di + lo

'delta *nm inv* delta

delta'piano *nm* hang-glider; **fare ~** go hang-gliding

delucidazi'one *nf* clarification

delu'dente *a* disappointing

de'lu|dere *vt* disappoint. **~si'one** *nf* disappointment. **de'luso** *a* disappointed

dema'gogico *a* popularity-seeking, demagogic

demar'ca|re *vt* demarcate. **~zi'one** *nf* demarcation

de'men|te *a* demented. **~za** *nf* dementia. **~zi'ale** *a* ⟨*assurdo*⟩ zany

demilitariz'za|re *vt* demilitarize. **~zi'one** *nf* demilitarization

demistificazi'one *nf* debunking

demo'cra|tico *a* democratic. **~'zia** *nf* democracy

democristi'ano, -a *a & nmf* Christian Democrat

demogra'fia *nf* demography. **demo'grafico** *a* demographic

demo'li|re *vt* demolish. **~zi'one** *nf* demolition

'demone *nm* demon. **de'monio** *nm* demon

demoraliz'zar|e *vt* demoralize. **~si** *vr* become demoralized

de'mordere *vi* give up

demoti'vato *a* demotivated

de'nari *nmpl* ⟨*nelle carte*⟩ diamonds

de'naro *nm* money

deni'gra|re *vt* denigrate. **~'torio** *a* denigratory

denomi'na|re *vt* name. **~'tore** *nm* denominator. **~zi'one** *nf* denomination; **~zione di origine controllata** mark *guaranteeing the quality of a wine*

deno'tare *vt* denote

densità *nf inv* density. **'denso** *a* thick, dense

den'ta|le *a* dental. **~rio** *a* dental. **~ta** *nf* bite. **~'tura** *nf* teeth *pl*

'dente *nm* tooth; ⟨*di forchetta*⟩ prong; **al ~** *Culin* just slightly firm. **~ del giudizio** wisdom tooth. **~ di latte** milk tooth. **denti'era** *nf* dentures *pl*, false teeth *pl*

denti'fricio *nm* toothpaste

den'tista *nmf* dentist

'dentro *adv* in, inside; ⟨*in casa*⟩ indoors; **da ~** from within; **qui ~** in here ● *prep* in, inside; ⟨*di tempo*⟩ within, by ● *nm* inside

denuclearizzazi'one *nf* denuclearization

denu'dar|e *vt* bare. **~si** *vr* strip

de'nunci|a, de'nunzia *nf* denunciation; *(alla polizia)* reporting; *(dei redditi)* [income] tax return. **~'are** *vt* denounce; *(accusare)* report

denu'tri|to *a* underfed. **~zi'one** *nf* malnutrition

deodo'rante *a* & *nm* deodorant

dépendance *nf inv* outbuilding

depe'ri|bile *a* perishable. **~'mento** *nm* wasting away; *(di merci)* deterioration. **~re** *vi* waste away

depi'la|re *vt* depilate. **~rsi** *vr* shave *(gambe)*; pluck *(sopracciglia)*. **~'torio** *nm* depilatory

deplo'rabile *a* deplorable

deplo'r|are *vt* deplore; *(dolersi di)* grieve over. **~evole** *a* deplorable

de'porre *vt* put down; lay down *(armi)*; lay *(uova)*; *(da una carica)* depose; *(testimoniare)* testify

depor'ta|re *vt* deport. **~to, -a** *nmf* deportee. **~zi'one** *nf* deportation

deposi'tar|e *vt* deposit; *(lasciare in custodia)* leave; *(in magazzino)* store. **~io, -a** *nmf (di segreto)* repository. **~si** *vr* settle

de'posito *nm* deposit; *(luogo)* warehouse; *Mil* depot. **~ ba-gagli** left-luggage office. **~zi'one** *nf* deposition; *(da una carica)* removal

depra'va|re *vt* deprave. **~to** *a* depraved. **~zi'one** *nf* depravity

depre'ca|bile *a* appalling. **~re** *vt* deprecate

depre'dare *vt* plunder

depressi'one *nf* depression. **de'presso** *pp di* **deprimere** ● *a* depressed

deprez'zar|e *vt* depreciate. **~si** *vr* depreciate

depri'mente *a* depressing

de'prim|ere *vt* depress. **~si** *vr* become depressed

depu'ra|re *vt* purify. **~'tore** *nm* purifier

depu'ta|re *vt* delegate. **~to, -a** *nmf* Member of Parliament, MP

deraglia'mento *nm* derailment

deragli'are *vi* go off the lines; **far ~** derail

'derby *nm inv Sport* local Derby

deregolamentazi'one *nf* deregulation

dere'litto *a* derelict

dere'tano *nm* backside, bottom

de'ri|dere *vt* deride. **~si'one** *nf* derision. **~'sorio** *a* derisory

de'riva *nf* drift; andare alla **~** drift

deri'va|re *vi* **~ re da** *(provenire)* derive from ● *vt* derive; *(sviare)* divert. **~zi'one** *nf* derivation; *(di fiume)* diversion

dermato|lo'gia *nf* dermatology. **~'logico** *a* dermatological. **der-ma'tologo, -a** *nmf* dermatologist

'deroga *nf* dispensation. **dero'ga-re** *vi* derogare a depart from

der'rat|a *nf* merchandise. **~e ali-mentari** foodstuffs

deru'bare *vt* rob

descrit'tivo *a* descriptive. **des-'critto** *pp di* **descrivere**

des'cri|vere *vt* describe. **~'vibile** *a* describable. **~zi'one** *nf* description

de'serto *a* uninhabited ● *nm* desert

deside'rabile *a* desirable

deside'rare *vt* wish; *(volere)* want; *(intensamente)* long for; *(bramare)* desire; **desidera?** what would you like?, can I help you?; **lasciare a ~** leave a lot to be desired

desi'de|rio *nm* wish; *(brama)* desire; *(intenso)* longing. **~'roso** *a* desirous; *(bramoso)* longing

desi'gnare *vt* designate; *(fissare)* fix

desi'nenza *nf* ending

de'sistere *vi* **~ da** desist from

'desktop 'publishing *nm inv* desktop publishing

deso'lante *a* distressing

deso'la|re *vt* distress. **~to** *a* desolate; *(spiacente)* sorry. **~zi'one** *nf* desolation

'despota *nm* despot

de'star|e *vt* waken; *fig* awaken. **~si** *vr* waken; *fig* awaken

desti'na|re *vt* destine; (*nominare*) appoint; (*assegnare*) assign; (*indirizzare*) address. **~'tario** *nm* (*di lettera, pacco*) addressee. **~zi'one** *nf* destination; *fig* purpose

de'stino *nm* destiny; (*fato*) fate

destitu'ire *vt* dismiss. **~zi'one** *nf* dismissal

'desto *a* liter awake

'destra *nf* (*parte*) right; (*mano*) right hand; **prendere a ~** turn right

destreggi'ar|e *vi*, **~si** *vr* manoeuvre

de'strezza *nf* dexterity; (*abilità*) skill

'destro *a* right; (*abile*) skilful

detei'nato *a* tannin-free

dete'n|ere *vt* hold; (*polizia:*) detain. **~uto, -a** *nmf* prisoner. **~zi'one** *nf* detention

deter'gente *a* cleaning; (*latte, crema*) cleansing ● *nm* detergent; (*per la pelle*) cleanser

deteriora'mento *nm* deterioration

deterio'rar|e *vt* cause to deteriorate. **~si** *vr* deteriorate

determi'nante *a* decisive

determi'nar|e *vt* determine. **~rsi** *vr* **~rsi a** resolve to. **~'tezza** *nf* determination. **~to** *a* (*risoluto*) determined; (*particolare*) specific. **~zi'one** *nf* determination; (*decisione*) decision

deter'rente *a & nm* deterrent

deter'sivo *nm* detergent. **~ per i piatti** washing-up liquid

dete'stare *vt* detest, hate

deto'nare *vi* detonate

de'tra|rre *vt* deduct (**da** from). **~zi'one** *nf* deduction

detri'mento *nm* detriment; **a ~ di** to the detriment of

de'trito *nm* debris

'detta *nf* **a ~ di** according to

dettagli'ante *nmf* Comm retailer

dettagli'a|re *vt* detail. **~ta'mente** *adv* in detail

det'taglio *nm* detail; **al ~** Comm retail

det'ta|re *vt* dictate; **~re legge** *fig* lay down the law. **~ to** *nm*, **~'tura** *nf* dictation

'detto *a* said; (*chiamato*) called; (*soprannominato*) nicknamed; **~ fatto** no sooner said than done ● *nm* saying

detur'pare *vt* disfigure

deva'sta|re *vt* devastate. **~to** *a* devastated. **~zi'one** *nf* devastation; *fig* ravages *pl*

devi'a|re *vi* deviate ● *vt* divert. **~zi'one** *nf* deviation; (*stradale*) diversion

devitaliz'zare *vt* deaden (*dente*)

devo'lu|to *pp di* devolvere ● *a* devolved. **~zi'one** *nf* devolution

de'volvere *vt* devolve

de'vo|to *a* devout; (*affezionato*) devoted. **~zi'one** *nf* devotion

di *prep* of; (*partitivo*) some; (*scritto da*) by; (*parlare, pensare ecc*) about; (*con causa, mezzo*) with; (*con provenienza*) from; (*in comparazioni*) than; (*con infinito*) to; **la casa di mio padre/dei miei genitori** my father's house/my parents' house; **compra del pane** buy some bread; **hai del pane?** do you have any bread?; **un film di guerra** a war film; **piangere di dolore** cry with pain; **coperto di neve** covered with snow; **sono di Genova** I'm from Genoa; **uscire di casa** leave one's house; **più alto di te** taller than you; **è ora di partire** it's time to go; **crede di aver ragione** he thinks he's right; **dire di sì** say yes; **di domenica** on Sundays; **di sera** in the evening; **una pausa di un'ora** an hour's break; **un corso di due mesi** a two-month course

dia'bet|e *nm* diabetes. **~ico, -a** *a & nmf* diabetic

dia'bolico *a* diabolical

dia'dema *nm* diadem; (*di donna*) tiara

di'afano *a* diaphanous

dia'framma *nm* diaphragm; (*divisione*) screen

di'agnos|i *nf inv* diagnosis. **~ti'care** *vt* diagnose

diago'nale *a & nf* diagonal

dia'gramma *nm* diagram

dia'lett|o *a* dialect. **dia'letto** *nm* dialect

dialo'gante a unità ~ *Comput* interactive terminal

di'alogo *nm* dialogue

dia'mante *nm* diamond

di'ametro *nm* diameter

di'amine *int* **che** ~... what on earth...

diaposi'tiva *nf* slide

di'ario *nm* diary

diar'rea *nf* diarrhoea

di'avolo *nm* devil; **va al** ~ go to hell!; **che** ~ **fai?** what the hell are you doing?

di'batt|ere *vt* debate. **~ersi** *vr* struggle. **~ito** *nm* debate; (*meno formale*) discussion

dica'stero *nm* office

di'cembre *nm* December

dice'ria *nf* rumour

dichia'ra|re *vt* state; (*ufficialmente*) declare. **~rsi** *vr* **si dichiara innocente** he says he's innocent. **~zi'one** *nf* statement; (*documento, di guerra*) declaration

dician'nove *a & nm* nineteen

dicias'sette *a & nm* seventeen

dici'otto *a & nm* eighteen

dici'tura *nf* wording

didasca'lia *nf* (*di film*) subtitle; (*di illustrazione*) caption

di'datti|ca *nf* didactics. **~o** *a* didactic; (*televisione*) educational

di'dentro *adv* inside

didi'etro *adv* behind ● *nm hum* hindquarters *pl*

di'eci *a & nm* ten

die'cina *nf* = **decina**

'diesel *a & nf inv* diesel

di'esis *nm inv* sharp

di'eta *nf* diet; **essere a** ~ be on

a diet. **die'tetico** *a* diet. **die'tista** *nmf* dietician. **die'tologo** *nmf* dietician

di'etro *adv* behind ● *prep* behind; (*dopo*) after ● *a* back; (*di zampe*) hind ● *nm* back; **le stanze di** ~ the back rooms; **le zampe di** ~ the hind legs

dietro'front *nm inv* about-turn; *fig* U-turn

di'fatti *adv* in fact

di'fen|dere *vt* defend. **~dersi** *vr* defend oneself. **~'siva** *nf* **stare sulla ~'siva** be on the defensive. **~'sivo** *a* defensive. **~'sore** *nm* defender; **avvocato ~'sore** defence counsel

di'fes|a *nf* defence; **prendere le ~e di qcno** come to sb's defence. **~o** *pp di* **difendere**

difet't|are *vi* be defective; **~are di** lack. **~ivo** *a* defective

di'fet|to *nm* defect; (*morale*) fault, flaw; (*mancanza*) lack; (*in tessuto, abito*) flaw; **essere in ~to** be at fault; **far ~to** be lacking. **~'toso** *a* defective; (*abito*) flawed

diffa'ma|re *vt* (*con parole*) slander; (*per iscritto*) libel. **~'torio** *a* slanderous; (*per iscritto*) libellous. **~zi'one** *nf* slander; (*scritta*) libel

diffe'ren|te *a* different. **~za** *nf* difference; **a ~za di** unlike; **non fare ~za** make no distinction (*fra* between). **~zi'ale** *a & nm* differential

differenzi'ar|e *vt* differentiate. **~si** *vr* **~si da** differ from

diffe'ri|re *vt* postpone ● *vi* be different. **~ta** *nf* **in ~ta** *TV* prerecorded

diffi'cile *a* difficult; (*duro*) hard; (*improbabile*) unlikely ● *nm* difficulty. **~'mente** *adv* with difficulty

diffi'coltà *nf inv* difficulty

dif'fida *nf* warning

diffi'd|are *vi* **~are di** distrust ● *vt* warn. **~ente** *a* mistrustful. **~enza** *nf* mistrust

dif'fond|ere *vt* spread; diffuse (*calore, luce ecc*). **~si** *vr* spread.

diffusi'one *nf* diffusion; *(di giornale)* circulation

dif'fu|so *pp di* **diffondere** ●*a* common; *(malattia)* widespread; *(luce)* diffuse. **~'sore** *nm (per asciugacapelli)* diffuser

difi'lato *adv* straight; *(subito)* straightaway

'diga *nf* dam; *(argine)* dike

dige'ribile *a* digestible

dige'rire *vt* digest; *fam* stomach. **~sti'one** *nf* digestion. **~'stivo** *a* digestive ●*nm* digestive; *(dopo cena)* liqueur

digi'tale *a* digital; *(delle dita)* finger *attrib* ●*nf (flore)* foxglove

digi'tare *vt* key in

digiu'nare *vi* fast

digi'uno *a* **essere ~** have an empty stomach ●*nm* fast; **a ~** *(bere ecc)* on an empty stomach

digni|tà *nf* dignity. **~'tario** *nm* dignitary. **~'toso** *a* dignified

digressi'one *nf* digression

digri'gnare *vi* **~ i denti** grind one's teeth

dila'gare *vi* flood; *fig* spread

dilani'are *vt* tear to pieces

dilapi'dare *vt* squander

dila'ta|re *vt*, **~rsi** *vr* dilate; *(metallo, gas:)* expand. **~zi'one** *nf* dilation

dilazio'nabile *a* postponable

dilazi|o'nare *vt* delay. **~'one** *nf* delay

dilegu'ar|e *vt* disperse. **~si** *vr* disappear

di'lemma *nm* dilemma

dilet'tan|te *nmf* amateur. **~'tistico** *a* amateurish

dilet'tare *vt* delight

di'letto, -a *a* beloved ●*nm (piacere)* delight ●*nmf (persona)* beloved

dili'gen|te *a* diligent; *(lavoro)* accurate. **~za** *nf* diligence

dilu'ire *vt* dilute

dilun'gar|e *vt* prolong. **~si** *vr* **~si su** dwell on *(argomento)*

diluvi'are *vi* pour [down]. **di'luvio** *nm* downpour; *fig* flood

dima'gr|ante *a* slimming, diet. **~i'mento** *nm* loss of weight. **~ire** *vi* slim

dime'nar|e *vt* wave; wag *(coda)*. **~si** *vr* be agitated

dimensi'one *nf* dimension; *(misura)* size

dimenti'canza *nf* forgetfulness; *(svista)* oversight

dimenti'car|e *vt*, **~si** *vr* **[di]** forget. **dimentico** *a* **dimentico di** *(che non ricorda)* forgetful of

di'messo *pp di* **dimettere** ●*a* humble; *(trasandato)* shabby; *(voce)* low

dimesti'chezza *nf* familiarity

di'metter|e *vt* dismiss; *(da ospedale ecc)* discharge. **~si** *vr* resign

dimez'zare *vt* halve

diminu'ire *vt/i* diminish; *(in maglia)* decrease. **~'tivo** *a* & *nm* diminutive. **~zi'one** *nf* decrease; *(riduzione)* reduction

dimissi'oni *nfpl* resignation *sg*; **dare le ~** resign

di'mo|ra *nf* residence. **~'rare** *vi* reside

dimo'strante *nmf* demonstrator

dimo'stra|re *vt* demonstrate; *(provare)* prove; *(mostrare)* show. **~rsi** *vr* prove [to be]. **~'tivo** *a* demonstrative. **~zi'one** *nf* demonstration; *Math* proof

di'nam|ica, -a *a* dynamic ●*nf* dynamics. *sg*. **dina'mismo** *nm* dynamism

dinami'tardo *a* **attentato ~** bomb attack

dina'mite *nf* dynamite

'dinamo *nf inv* dynamo

di'nanzi *adv* in front ●*prep* **~ a** in front of

di'nastia *nf* dynasty

di'niego *nm* denial

dinocco'lato *a* lanky

dino'sauro *nm* dinosaur

din'torn|i *nmpl* outskirts; **nei ~i di** in the vicinity of. **~o** *adv* around

'dio *nm (pl* **'dei)** god; **D~** God

di'ocesi *nf inv* diocese

dipa'nare *vt* wind into a ball; *fig* unravel

diparti'mento *nm* department

dipen'den|te *a* depending ● *nmf* employee. **~za** *nf* dependence; (*edificio*) annexe

di'pendere *vi* **~ da** depend on; (*provenire*) derive from; **dipende** it depends

di'pinger|e *vt* paint; (*descrivere*) describe. **~si** *vr* (*truccarsi*) make up. **di'pinto** *pp di* **dispingere** ● *a* painted ● *nm* painting

di'plo|ma *nm* diploma. **~'marsi** *vr* graduate

diplo'matico *a* diplomatic ● *nm* diplomat; (*pasticcino*) millefeuille (*with alcohol*)

diplo'mato *nmf/a* person with school qualification ● *a* qualified

diploma'zia *nf* diplomacy

di'porto *nm* **Imbarcazione da ~** pleasure craft

dira'dar|e *vt* thin out; make less frequent (*visite*). **~si** *vr* thin out; (*nebbia*) clear

dira'ma|re *vt* issue ● *vi*. **~rsi** *vr* branch out; (*diffondersi*) spread. **~zi'one** *nf* (*di strada*) fork

'dire *vt* say; (*raccontare, riferire*) tell; **~ quello che si pensa** speak one's mind; **voler ~** mean; **volevo ben ~!** I wondered!; **~ di sì/no** say yes/no; **si dice che...** rumour has it that...; **come si dice "casa" in Inglese?** what's the English for "casa"?; **questo nome mi dice qualcosa** the name rings a bell; **che ne dici di...?** how about...?; **non c'è che ~** there's no disputing that; **o ~ che...** to think that...; **a dir poco/tanto** at least/most ● *vi* **~ bene/male di** speak highly/ill of sb; **dica pure** (*in negozio*) how can I help you?; **dici sul serio?** are you serious?; **per modo di ~** in a manner of speaking

diretta'mente *adv* directly

diret'tissima *nf* **per ~** *Jur* without

going through the normal procedures

diret'tissimo *nm* fast train

diret'tiva *nf* directive

di'retto *pp di* **dirigere** ● *a* direct. **~ a** (*inteso*) meant for. **essere ~ a** be heading for. **in diretta** (*trasmissione*) live ● *nm* (*treno*) through train

diret'|tore, -'trice *nm* manager; manageress; (*di scuola*) headmaster; headmistress. **~tore d'orchestra** conductor

direzi'one *nf* direction; (*di società*) management; *Sch* headmaster's/ headmistress's office (*primary school*)

diri'gen|te *a* ruling ● *nmf* executive; *Pol* leader. **~za** *nf* management. **~zi'ale** *a* management *attrib*, managerial

di'riger|e *vt* direct; conduct (*orchestra*); run (*impresa*). **~si ~ verso** head for

dirim'petto *adv* opposite ● *prep* **~ a** facing

di'ritt|o¹, dritto *a* straight; (*destro*) right ● *adv* straight; **andare ~** go straight on ● *nm* right side; *Tennis* forehand; **fare un ~** (*a maglia*) knit one

di'ritt|o² *nm* right; *Jur* law. **~i** *pl d'autore** royalties

dirit'tura *nf* straight line; *fig* honesty. **~ d'arrivo** *Sport* home straight

diroc'cato *a* tumbledown

dirom'pente *a fig* explosive

dirot'ta|re *vt* reroute (*treno, aereo*), (*illegalmente*) hijack; **di'vert** (*traffico*) ● *vi* alter course. **~'tore, ~'trice** *nmf* hijacker

di'rotto *a* (*pioggia*) pouring; (*pianto*) uncontrollable; **piovere a ~** rain heavily

di'rupo *nm* precipice

dis'abile *nmf* disabled person

disabi'tato *a* uninhabited

disabitu'arsi *vr* **~ a** get out of the habit of

disac'cordo *nm* disagreement

disadat'tato, -a *a* maladjusted ● *nmf* misfit

disa'dorno *a* unadorned

disa'gevole *a* (*scomodo*) uncomfortable

disagi'ato *a* poor; (*vita*) hard

di'sagio *nm* discomfort; (*difficoltà*) inconvenience; (*imbarazzo*) embarrassment; **sentirsi a ~** feel uncomfortable; **disagi** *pl* (*privazioni*) hardships

disappro'va|re *vt* disapprove of. **~zi'one** *nf* disapproval

disap'punto *nm* disappointment

disar'mante *a fig* disarming

disar'mare *vt/i* disarm. **di'sarmo** *nm* disarmament

disa'strato, -a *a* devastated ● *nmf* disaster victim

di'sastro *nm* disaster; (*fam: grande confusione*) mess; (*fam: persona*) disaster area. **disa'stroso** *a* disastrous

disat'ten|to *a* inattentive. **~zi'one** *nf* inattention; (*svista*) oversight

disatti'vare *vt* de-activate

disa'vanzo *nm* deficit

disavven'tura *nf* misadventure

dis'brigo *nm* dispatch

dis'capito *nm* **a ~ di** to the detriment of

dis'carica *nf* scrap-yard

discen'den|te *a* descending ● *nmf* descendant. **~za** *nf* descent; (*discendenti*) descendants *pl*

di'scendere *vt/i* descend; (*dal treno*) get off; (*da cavallo*) dismount; (*sbarcare*) land. **~ da** (*trarre origine da*) be a descendant of

di'scepolo, -a *nmf* disciple

di'scernere *vt* discern

di'sces|a *nf* descent; (*pendio*) slope; **~a in picchiata** (*di aereo*) nosedive; **essere in ~a** (*strada:*) go downhill. **~a libera** (*in sci*) downhill race. **disce'sista** *nmf* (*sciatore*) downhill skier. **~so** *pp di* **discendere**

dis'chetto *nm* Comput diskette

dischi'uder|e *vt* open; (*svelare*) disclose. **~si** *vr* open up

disci'oglier|e *vt*. **~si** *vr* dissolve; (*neve:*) thaw; (*fondersi*) melt. **disci'olto** *pp di* **disciogliere**

disci'pli|na *nf* discipline. **~'nare** *a* discipline. ● *vt* discipline. **~'nato** *a* disciplined

'disco *nm* disc; Comput disk; Sport discus; Mus record; **ernia del ~** slipped disc. **~ fisso** Comput hard disk. **~ volante** flying saucer

discogra'fia *nf* (*insieme di incisioni*) discography. **disco'grafico** *a* (*industria*) record attrib, recording; **casa discografica** record company, recording company

'discolo *nmf* rascal ● *a* unruly

disco'lpar|e *vt* clear. **~si** *vr* clear oneself

disco'noscere *vt* disown (*figlio*)

discontinuità *nf* (*nel lavoro*) irregularity. **discon'tinuo** *a* intermittent; (*fig:* impegno, rendimento) uneven

discor'dan|te *a* discordant. **~za** *nf* mismatch

discor'dare *vi* (*opinioni:*) conflict. **dis'corde** *a* clashing. **dis'cordia** *nf* discord; (*dissenso*) dissension

discor'rere *vi* talk (**di** about). **~'sivo** *a* colloquial. **dis'corso** *pp di* **discorrere** ● *nm* speech; (*conversazione*) talk

dis'costo *a* distant ● *adv* far away; **stare ~** stand apart

disco'te|ca *nf* disco; (*raccolta*) record library. **~'caro** *nmf pej* disco freak

discre'pan|te *a* contradictory. **~za** *nf* discrepancy

dis'cre|to *a* discreet; (*moderato*) moderate; (*abbastanza buono*) fairly good. **~zi'one** *nf* discretion; (*giudizio*) judgement; **a ~zione di** at the discretion of

discrimi'nante *a* extenuating

discrimi'na|re *vt* discriminate. **~'torio** *a* (*atteggiamento*) discriminatory. **~zi'one** *nf* discrimination

discussi'one *nf* discussion; (*alter-*

co) argument. **dis'cusso** *pp di*
discutere ● *a* controversial
dis'cutere *vt* discuss; *(formale)*
debate; *(litigare)* argue; **~ sul**
prezzo bargain. **discu'tibile** *a* debatable; *(gusto)* questionable
disde'gnare *vt* disdain. **dis'degno**
nm disdain
dis'dett|a *nf* retraction; *(sfortuna)*
bad luck; *Comm* cancellation. **~o**
pp di **disdire**
disdi'cevole *a* unbecoming
dis'dire *vt* retract; *(annullare)* cancel
diseduca'tivo *a* boorish, uncouth
dise'gna|re *vt* draw; *(progettare)*
design. **~'tore, ~'trice** *nmf* designer. **di'segno** *nm* drawing;
(progetto, linea) design
diser'bante *nm* herbicide, weed-
killer **●** *a* herbicidal, weed-killing
disere'da|re *vt* disinherit. **~to** *a*
dispossessed **●** *nmf* **i ~ti** the dispossessed
diser|'tare *vt/i* desert; **~tare la**
scuola stay away from school.
~'tore *nm* deserter. **~zi'one** *nf* de-
sertion
disfaci'mento *nm* decay
dis'fa|re *vt* undo; strip *(letto)*;
(smantellare) take down; *(annientare)* defeat; **~re le valigie** unpack
[one's bags]. **~rsi** *vr* fall to pieces;
(sciogliersi) melt; **~rsi di** *(liberarsi di)* get rid of; **~rsi in lacrime**
dissolve into tears. **~tta** *a* defeat.
• **tto** *a/fig* worn out
disfat'tismo *nm* defeatism. **~ta** *a*
& *nmf* defeatist
disfunzi'one *nf* disorder
dis'gelo *nm* thaw
dis'grazi|a *nf* misfortune; *(inci-
dente)* accident; *(sfavore)* disgrace.
~ata'mente *adv* unfortunately.
~'ato, -a *a* unfortunate **●** *nmf*
wretch
disgre'gar|e *vt* break up. **~si** *vr*
disintegrate
disgu'ido *nm* **~ postale** mistake
in delivery
disgu'st|are *vt* disgust. **~arsi** *nf*

~arsi di be disgusted by.
dis'gusto *nm* disgust. **~oso** *a* disgusting
disidra'ta|re *vt* dehydrate. **~to** *a*
dehydrated
disil'lu|dere *vt* disenchant. **~si'o-**
ne *nf* disenchantment. **~so** *a* dis-
illusioned
disimbal'lare *vt* unpack
disimpa'rare *vt* forget
disimpe'gnar|e *vt* release; *(com-
piere)* fulfil; redeem *(oggetto dato
in pegno)*. **~si** *vr* disengage
oneself; *(cavarsela)* manage.
disim'pegno *nm (locale)* vestibule
disincan'tato *a (disilluso)* disillu-
sioned
disinfe'sta|re *vt* disinfest.
~zi'one *nf* disinfestation
disinfet'tante *a* & *nm* disinfectant
disinfe|t'tare *vt* disinfect. **~zi'one**
nf disinfection
disinfor'mato *a* uninformed
disini'bito *a* uninhibited
disinne'scare *vt* defuse *(mina)*.
disin'nesco *nm (di bomba)* bomb
disposal
disinse'rire *vt* disconnect
disinte'gra|re *vt, ~rsi* *vr* disinte-
grate. **~zi'one** *nf* disintegration
disinteres'sarsi *vr* **~ di** take no
interest in. **disinte'resse** *nm* in-
difference; *(oggettività)* disinter-
estedness
disintossi'ca|re *vt* detoxify. **~rsi**
vr come off drugs **~zi'one** *nf* giving up alcohol/drugs
disin'volto *a* natural. **disinvol-**
'tura *nf* confidence
disles'sia *nf* dyslexia. **dis'lessico**
a dyslexic
disli'vello *nm* difference in height;
fig inequality
dislo'care *vt* *Mil* post
dismenor'rea *nf* dysmenorrhoea
dismi'sura *nf* excess; **a ~** excessively
disobbedi'ente *a* disobedient
disobbe'dire *vt* disobey
disoccu'pa|to, -a *a* unemployed

● *nm* unemployed person. **~zi'o-ne** *nf* unemployment

disonestà *nf* dishonesty. **diso'nesto** *a* dishonest

disono'rare *vt* dishonour. **diso'nore** *nm* dishonour

di'sopra *adv* above ● *a* upper ● *nm* top

disordi'na|re *vt* disarrange. **~ta'mente** *adv* untidily. **~to** *a* untidy; (*sregolato*) immoderate. **di'sordine** *nm* disorder, untidiness; (*sregolatezza*) debauchery

disorganiz'zare *vt* disorganize. **~to** *a* disorganized. **~zi'one** *nf* disorganization

disorienta'mento *nm* disorientation

disorien'ta|re *vt* disorientate. **~rsi** *vr* lose one's bearings. **~to** *a* *fig* bewildered

di'sotto *adv* below ● *a* lower ● *nm* bottom

dis'paccio *nm* dispatch

dispa'rato *a* disparate

'dispari *a* odd, uneven. **~tà** *nf inv* disparity

dis'parte *adv* in **~** apart; **stare in ~** stand aside

dis'pendi|o *nm* (*spreco*) waste. **~'oso** *a* expensive

dis'pen|sa *nf* pantry; (*distribuzione*) distribution; (*mobile*) cupboard; *Jur* exemption; *Relig* dispensation; (*pubblicazione periodica*) number. **~'sare** *vt* distribute; (*esentare*) exonerate

dispe'ra|re *vi* despair (**di** of). **~rsi** *vr* despair. **~ta'mente** (*piangere*) desperately. **~to** *a* desperate. **~zi'one** *nf* despair

dis'per|dere *vt*, **~dersi** *vr* scatter, disperse. **~si'one** *nf* dispersion; (*di truppe*) dispersal. **~'sivo** *a* disorganized. **~so** *pp di* **disperdere** ● *a* scattered; (*smarrito*) lost ● *nm* missing soldier

dis'pet|to *nm* spite; **a ~ di** in spite of; **fare un ~ a qcno** spite sb. **~'toso** *a* spiteful

dispia'ce|re *nm* upset; (*rammari-*

co) regret; (*dolore*) sorrow; (*preoccupazione*) worry ● *vi* **mi dispiace** I'm sorry; **non mi dispiace** I don't dislike it; **se non ti dispiace** if you don't mind. **~'uto** *a* upset; (*dolente*) sorry

dispo'nibil|e *a* available; (*gentile*) helpful. **~ità** *nf* availability; (*gentilezza*) helpfulness

dis'por|re *vt* arrange ● *vi* dispose; (*stabilire*) order; **~re di** have at one's disposal. **~si** *vr* (*in fila*) line up

disposi'tivo *nm* device

disposizi'one *nf* disposition; (*ordine*) order; (*libera disponibilità*) disposal. **dis'posto** *pp di* **disporre** ● *a* ready; (*incline*) disposed; **essere ben disposto verso** be favourably disposed towards

di'spotico *a* despotic. **dispo'tismo** *nm* despotism

dispregia'tivo *a* disparaging

disprez'zare *vt* despise. **dis'prezzo** *nm* contempt

'disputa *nf* dispute

dispu'ta|re *vi* dispute; (*gareggiare*) compete. **~si** *vr* **~si qcsa** contend for sth

dissacra'torio *a* debunking

dissangua'mento *nm* loss of blood

dissangu'a|re *vt*, **~rsi** *vr* bleed. **~rsi** *vr fig* become impoverished. **~to** *a* bloodless; *fig* impoverished

dissa'pore *nm* disagreement

dissec'car|e *vt*, **~rsi** *vr* dry up

dissemi'nare *vt* disseminate; (*notizie*) spread

dis'senso *nm* dissent; (*disaccordo*) disagreement

dissente'ria *nf* dysentery

dissen'tire *vi* disagree (**da** with)

dissertazi'one *nf* dissertation

disser'vizio *nm* poor service

disse'sta|re *vt* upset; *Comm* damage. **~to** *a* (*strada*) uneven. **dis'sesto** *nm* ruin

disse'tante *a* a thirst-quenching

disse'ta|re *vt* **~re qcno** quench sb's thirst

dissi'dente *a & nmf* dissident

dis'sidio *nm* disagreement

dis'simile *a* unlike, dissimilar

dissimu'lare *vt* conceal; (*fingere*) dissimulate

dissi'pa|re *vt* dissipate; (*sperperare*) squander. **~rsi** *vr* ⟨*nebbia:*⟩ clear; ⟨*dubbio:*⟩ disappear. **~to** *a* dissipated. **~zi'one** *nf* squandering

dissoci'ar|e *vt*, **~si** *vr* dissociate

disso'dare *vt* till

dis'solto *pp di* **dissolvere**

disso'luto *a* dissolute

dis'solver|e *vt*, **~si** *vr* dissolve; (*disperdere*) dispel

disso'nanza *nf* dissonance

dissua'dere *vt* dissuade. **~si'one** *nf* dissuasion. **~'sivo** *a* dissuasive

distac'car|e *vt* detach; *Sport* leave behind. **~si** *vr* be detached.

di'stacco *nm* detachment; (*separazione*) separation; *Sport* lead

di'stan|te *a* far away; (*fig: person*) detached ● *adv* far away. **~za** *nf* distance. **~zi'are** *vt* space out; *Sport* outdistance

di'stare *vi* be distant; **quanto dista?** how far is it?

di'sten|dere *vt* stretch out (*p rte del corpo*); (*spiegare*) spread; (*deporre*) lay. **~dersi** *vr* stretch; (*sdraiarsi*) lie down; (*rilassarsi*) relax. **~si'one** *nf* stretching; (*rilassamento*) relaxation; *Pol* détente. **~'sivo** *a* relaxing

di'steso, -a *pp di* **distendere** ● *nf* expanse

distil'la|re *vt/i* distil. **~zi'one** *nf* distillation. **~e'ria** *nf* distillery

di'stingue|re *vt* distinguish. **~si** *vr* distinguish oneself. **distin'guibile** *a* distinguishable

di'stinta *nf Comm* list. **~ di pagamento** receipt. **~ di versamento** paying-in slip

distinta'mente *adv* (*separatamente*) individually, separately; (*chiaramente*) clearly

distin'tivo *a* distinctive ● *nm* badge

di'stin|to, -a *pp di* **distinguere** ● *a* distinct; (*signorile*) distinguished; **~ti saluti** Yours faithfully. **~zi'one** *nf* distinction

di'stogliere *vt* **~ da** (*allontanare*) remove from; (*dissuadere*) dissuade from. **di'stolto** *pp di* **distogliere**

di'storcere *vt* twist

distorsi'one *nf Med* sprain; (*alterazione*) distortion

di'stra|rre *vt* distract; (*divertire*) amuse. **~rsi** *vr* get distracted; (*svagarsi*) amuse oneself; **non ti distrarre!** pay attention!. **~rsi** *vr* (*deconcentrarsi*) be distracted. **~tta'mente** *adv* absently. **~tto** *pp di* **distrarre** ● *a* absent-minded; (*disattento*) inattentive. **~zi'one** *nf* absent-mindedness; (*errore*) inattention; (*svago*) amusement

di'stretto *nm* district

distribu'|ire *vt* distribute; (*disporre*) arrange; deal ⟨*carte*⟩. **~'tore** *nm* distributor; (*di benzina*) petrol pump; (*automatico*) slot-machine. **~zi'one** *nf* distribution

distri'car|e *vt* disentangle; **~si** *vr* *fig* get out of it

di'strugge|re *vt* destroy. **~t'tivo** *a* destructive; (*critica*) negative. **~tto** *pp di* **distruggere** ● *a* destroyed; **un uomo ~tto** a broken man. **~zi'one** *nf* destruction

distur'bar|e *vt* disturb; (*sconvolgere*) upset. **~si** *vr* trouble oneself.

di'sturbo *nm* bother; (*indisposizione*) trouble; *Med* problem; *Radio, TV* interference; **disturbi** *pl Radio, TV* static. **disturbi di stomaco** stomach trouble

disubbidi'en|te *a* disobedient. **~za** *nf* disobedience

disubbi'dire *vi* **~ a** disobey

disugu'agli'anza *nf* disparity. **~'ale** *a* unequal; (*irregolare*) irregular

disu'mano *a* inhuman

di'suso nm cadere in ~ fall into disuse

di'tale nm thimble

di'tata nf poke; (impronta) fingermark

'dito nm (pl nf dita) finger; (di vino, acqua) finger. ~ del piede toe

'ditta nf firm

dit'tafono nm dictaphone

ditta'tor|e nm dictator. ~i'ale a dictatorial. **ditta'tura** nf dictatorship

dit'tongo nm diphthong

di'urno a daytime; spettacolo ~ matinée

'diva nf diva

diva'ga|re vi digress. ~zi'one nf digression

divam'pare vi burst into flames; fig spread like wildfire

di'vano nm settee, sofa. ~ letto sofa bed

divari'care vt open

di'vario nm discrepancy; un ~ di opinioni a difference of opinion

dive'n|ire vi = diventare. ~uto pp di divenire

diven'tare vi become; (lentamente) grow; (rapidamente) turn

di'verbio nm squabble

diver'gen|te a divergent. ~za nf divergence; ~za di opinioni difference of opinion. **di'vergere** vi diverge

diversa'mente adv (altrimenti) otherwise; (in modo diverso) differently

diversifi'ca|re vt diversify. ~rsi vr differ, be different. ~zi'one nf diversification

diver|si'one nf diversion. ~sità nf inv difference. ~sivo nm diversion. **di'verso** a different; diversi pl (parecchi) several ●pron several [people]

diver'tente a amusing. **diverti'mento** nm amusement

diver'tir|e vt amuse. ~si vr enjoy oneself

divi'dendo nm dividend

di'vider|e vt divide; (condividere) share. ~si vr (separarsi) separate

divi'eto nm prohibition; ~ di sosta no parking

divinco'larsi vr wriggle

divinità nf inv divinity. **di'vino** a divine

di'visa nf uniform; Comm currency

divisi'one nf division

di'vismo nm worship; (atteggiamento) superstar mentality

di'vi|so pp di dividere. ~'sore nm divisor. ~'sorio a dividing; muro ~sorio partition wall

'divo, -a nmf star

divo'rar|e vt devour. ~si vr ~si da be consumed with

divorzi'a|re vi divorce. ~to, -a nmf divorcee. **di'vorzio** nm divorce

divul'ga|re vt divulge; (rendere popolare) popularize. ~rsi vr spread. ~'tivo a popular. ~zi'one nf popularization

dizio'nario nm dictionary

dizi'one nf diction

do nm Mus (chiave, nota) C

'doccia nf shower; (grondaia) gutter; fare la ~ have a shower

do'cen|te a teaching ●nmf teacher; (di università) lecturer. ~za nf university teacher's qualification

docile a docile

documen'tar|e vt document. ~si vr gather information (su about)

documen'tario a & nm documentary

documen'ta|to a (persona) well-informed, (persona) well-informed. ~zi'one nf documentation

docu'mento nm document

dodi'cesimo a & nm twelfth. **'dodici** a & nm twelve

do'gan|a nf customs pl; (dazio) duty. **doga'nale** a customs. ~i'ere nm customs officer

'doglie nfpl labour pains

'dogma nm dogma. **dog'matico** a dogmatic. ~'tismo nm dogmatism 'dolce *a* sweet; ⟨clima⟩ mild; ⟨voce, consonante⟩ soft; ⟨acqua⟩ fresh ● *nm* ⟨portata⟩ dessert; ⟨torta⟩ cake; **non mangio dolci** I don't eat sweet things. ~'mente *adv* sweetly. dol'cezza *nf* sweetness; ⟨di clima⟩ mildness

dolce'vita *a inv* ⟨maglione⟩ roll-neck

dolci'ario *a* confectionery

dolci'astro *a* sweetish

dolcifi'cante *nm* sweetener ● *a* sweetening

dolci'umi *nmpl* sweets

do'lente *a* painful; ⟨spiacente⟩ sorry

do'le|re *vi* ache, hurt; ⟨dispiacere⟩ regret. ~rsi *vr* regret; ⟨protestare⟩ complain; ~rsi di be sorry for

'dollaro *nm* dollar

'dolo *nm* Jur malice; ⟨truffa⟩ fraud

Dolo'miti *nfpl* le ~ the Dolomites

do'lore *nm* pain; ⟨morale⟩ sorrow. dolo'roso *a* painful

do'loso *a* malicious

do'manda *nf* question; ⟨richiesta⟩ request; ⟨scritta⟩ application; *Comm* demand; **fare una ~ a qcno** ask (sb) a question. ~ di impiego job application

doman'dar|e *vt* ask; ⟨esigere⟩ demand; ~e qcsa a qcno ask sb for sth. ~si *vr* wonder

do'mani *adv* tomorrow; ~ sera tomorrow evening ● *nm* il ~ the future; a ~ see you tomorrow

do'ma|re *vt* tame; *fig* control ⟨emozioni⟩. ~tore *nm* tamer

domat'tina *adv* tomorrow morning

do'meni|ca *nf* Sunday. ~'cale *a* Sunday *attrib*

do'mestico, -a *a* domestic ● *nm* servant ● *nf* maid

domicili'are *a* **arresti domiciliari** *Jur* house arrest

domicili'arsi *vr* settle

domi'cilio *nm* domicile; ⟨abitazione⟩ home; **recapitiamo a ~** we do home deliveries

domi'na|re *vt* dominate; ⟨controllare⟩ control ● *vi* rule over; ⟨prevalere⟩ be dominant. ~rsi *vr* control oneself. ~'tore, ~'trice *nmf* ruler ~zi'one *nf* domination

do'minio *nm* control; *Pol* dominion; ⟨ambito⟩ field; di ~ pubblico common knowledge

don *nm inv* ⟨ecclesiastico⟩ Father

do'na|re *vt* give; donate ⟨sangue, organo⟩ ● *vi* ~re a ⟨giovare esteticamente⟩ suit. ~'tore, ~'trice *nmf* donor. ~zi'one *nf* donation

dondo'l|are *vt* swing; ⟨cullare⟩ rock ● *vi* sway. ~arsi *vr* swing. ~io *nm* rocking. 'dondolo *nm* swing; cavallo/sedia a dondolo rocking-horse/chair

dongio'vanni *nm inv* Romeo

'donna *nf* woman. ~ di servizio domestic help

don'naccia *nf pej* whore

donnai'olo *nm* philanderer.

'donnola *nf* weasel

'dono *nm* gift

'dopo *prep* after; ⟨a partire da⟩ since ● *adv* after, afterwards; ⟨più tardi⟩ later; ⟨in seguito⟩ later on; ~ di me after me

dopo'barba *nm inv* aftershave

dopo'cena *nm inv* evening

dopodiché *adv* after which

dopodo'mani *adv* the day after tomorrow

dopogu'erra *nm inv* post-war period

dopo'pranzo *nm inv* afternoon

dopo'sci *a & nm inv* après-ski

doposcu'ola *nm inv* after-school activities *pl*

dopo 'shampoo *nm inv* conditioner ● *a inv* conditioning

dopo'sole *nm inv* aftersun cream ● *a inv* aftersun

dopo'tutto *adv* after all

doppi'aggio *nm* dubbing

doppia'mente *adv* ⟨in misura doppia⟩ doubly

doppi'a|re *vt* *Naut* double; *Sport* lap; *Cinema* dub. ~'tore, ~'trice *nmf* dubber '**doppio** *a & adv* double. **~ clic** *nm Comput* double click. **~ fallo** *nm Tennis* double fault. **~ gioco** *nm* double-dealing. **~ mento** *nm* double chin. **~ senso** *nm* double entendre. **doppi vetri** *nmpl* double glazing ●*nm* double, twice the quantity; *Tennis* **Doubles** *pl.* **~ misto** *Tennis* mixed doubles ●*adv* double

doppi'one *nm* duplicate

doppio'petto *a* double-breasted

dop'pista *nmf Tennis* doubles player

do'ra|re *vt* gild; *Culin* brown. **~to** *a* gilt; *(color oro)* golden. **~'tura** *nf* gilding

dormicchi'are *vi* doze

dormigli'one, -a *nmf* sleepyhead; *fig* lazy-bones

dor'mi|re *vi* sleep; *(essere addormentato)* be asleep; *fig* be asleep. **~ta** *nf* good sleep. **~'tina** *nf* nap. **~'torio** *nm* dormitory

dormi'veglia *nm* **essere in ~** be half asleep

●**dor'sale** *a* dorsal ●*nf (di monte)* ridge

'**dorso** *nm* back; *(di libro)* spine; *(di monte)* crest; *(nel nuoto)* backstroke

do'saggio *nm* dosage

do'sare *vt* dose; *fig* measure; **~ le parole** weigh one's words

dosa'tore *nm* measuring jug

'**dose** *nf* dose; **in buona ~** *fig* in good measure. **~ eccessiva** overdose

dossi'er *nm inv (raccolta di dati, fascicolo)* file

'**dosso** *nm (dorso)* back; **levarsi di ~ gli abiti** take off one's clothes

do'ta|re *vt* endow; *(di accessori)* equip. **~to** *a (persona)* gifted; *(fornito)* equipped. **~zi'one** *nf (attrezzatura)* equipment; **in ~zione** at one's disposal

'**dote** *nf* dowry; *(qualità)* gift

'**dotto** *a* learned ●*nm* scholar; *Anat* duct

dotto'rato *nm* doctorate. **dot'tore, ~'ressa** *nmf* doctor

dot'trina *nf* doctrine

'**dove** *adv* where; **di ~ sei?** where do you come from; **fin ~?** how far?; **per ~?** which way?

do'vere *vi (obbligo)* have to, must; **devo andare** I have to go, I must go; **devo venire anch'io?** do I have to come too?; **avresti dovuto dirmelo** you should have told me, you ought to have told me; **devo sedermi un attimo** I must sit down for a minute, I need to sit down for a minute; **dev'essere successo qualcosa** something must have happened; **come si deve** properly ●*vt (essere debitore di, derivare)* owe; **essere dovuto a** be due to ●*nm* duty; **per ~** out of duty.

dove'roso *a* only right and proper

do'vunque *adv (dappertutto)* everywhere; *(in qualsiasi luogo)* anywhere ●*conj* wherever

do'vuto *a* due; *(debito)* proper

doz'zi|na *f* dozen. **~'nale** *a* cheap

dra'gare *vt* dredge

'**drago** *nm* dragon

dramm|a *nm* drama. **dram'matico** *a* dramatic. **~atiz'zare** *vt* dramatize. **~a'turgo** *nm* playwright. **dram'mone** *nm (film)* tear-jerker

drappeggi'are *vt* drape. **drap'peggio** *nm* drapery

drap'pello *nm Mil* squad; *(gruppo)* band

'**drastico** *a* drastic

dre'na|ggio *nm* drainage. **~re** *vt* drain

drib'blare *vt (in calcio)* dribble. '**dribbling** *nm inv (in calcio)* dribble

dritta *nf (mano destra)* right hand; *Naut* starboard; *(informazione)* pointer, tip; **a ~ e a manca** *(dappertutto)* left, right and centre

'**dritto** *a* = **diritto** ●*nmf fam* crafty so-and-so

driz'zar|e *vt* straighten; (*rizzare*) prick up. **~si** *vr* straighten [up]; (*alzarsi*) raise

'dro|ga *nf* drug. **~'gare** *vt* drug. **~'garsi** *vr* take drugs. **~'gato, -a** *nmf* drug addict

droghe'ria *nf* grocery. **~'iere, -a** *nmf* grocer

drome'dario *nm* dromedary

'dubbi|o *a* (*ambiguo*) dubious ● *nm* doubt; (*sospetto*) suspicion; **mettere in ~o** doubt; **essere fuori ~o** be beyond doubt; **essere in ~o** be doubtful. **~'oso** *a* doubtful

dubita|re *vt* doubt; **~re** *di* doubt; (*diffidare*) mistrust; **dubito che venga** I doubt whether he'll come. **~'tivo** *a* (*ambiguo*) ambiguous

duca, du'chessa *nmf* duke; duchess

'due *a & nm* two

due'cento *a & nm* two hundred

du'ello *nm* duel

due'mila *a & nm* two thousand

due'pezzi *nm inv* (*bikini*) bikini

du'etto *nm* duo; *Mus* duet

'duna *nf* dune

'dunque *conj* therefore; (*allora*) well [then]

'duo *nm inv* duo; *Mus* duet

'duomo *nm* cathedral

'duplex *nm Teleph* party line

dupli'ca|re *vt* duplicate. **~to** *nm* duplicate. **'duplice** *a* double; **in duplice** in duplicate

dura'mente *adv* (*lavorare*) hard; (*rimproverare*) harshly

du'rante *prep* during

du'ra|re *vi* last; (*cibo:*) keep; (*resistere*) hold out. **~ata** *nf* duration. **~a'turo, ~evole** *a* lasting, enduring

du'rezza *nf* hardness; (*di carne*) toughness; (*di voce, padre*) harshness

'duro, -a *a* hard; (*persona, carne*) tough; (*voce*) harsh; (*pane*) stale; **tieni ~!** (*resistere*) hang in there!

● *nmf* (*persona*) tough person, toughie *fam*

du'rone *nm* hardened skin

'duttile *a* (*materiale*) ductile; (*carattere*) malleable

Ee

e, ed *conj* and

'ebano *nm* ebony

eb'bene *conj* well [then]

eb'brezza *nf* inebriation; (*euforia*) elation; **guida in stato di ~** drink-driving, drunken driving. **'ebbro** *a* inebriated; **ebbro di gioia** delirious with joy

'ebete *a* stupid

ebollizi'one *nf* boiling

e'braico *a* Hebrew ● *nm* (*lingua*) Hebrew. **e'br|eo, -a** *a* Jewish ● *nmf* Jew; Jewess

'Ebridi *nfpl* **le ~** the Hebrides

eca'tombe *nf* **fare un'~** wreak havoc

ecc *abbr* (*eccetera*) etc

ecce'den|te *a* (*peso, bagaglio*) excess. **~za** *nf* excess; (*d'avanzo*) surplus; **avere qcsa in ~za** have an excess of sth; **bagagli in ~za** excess baggage. **~za di cassa** surplus. **ec'cedere** *vt* exceed ● *vi* go too far; **eccedere nel mangiare** overeat; **essedere nel bere** drink to excess

eccel'len|te *a* excellent. **~za** *nf* excellence; (*titolo*) Excellency; **per ~za** par excellence. **ec'cellere** *vi* excel (**in** at)

eccentricità *nf* eccentricity. **ec'centrico, -a** *a & nmf* eccentric

eccessiva'mente *adv* excessively. **ec'cesso** *nm* excess; **andare agli eccessi** go to extremes; **all'~** to excess. **~ di velocità** speeding

ec'cetera *adv* et cetera

ec'cetto *prep* except; **~ che** (*a*

meno che⟩ unless. **eccettu'are** *vt* except

eccezio'nal|e *a* exceptional. **~'mente** *adv* exceptionally; ⟨*contrariamente alla regola*⟩ as an exception

eccezi'one *nf* exception; *Jur* objection; **a ~ di** with the exception of

eccita'mento *nm* excitement

ecci'tante *a* exciting; ⟨*sostanza*⟩ stimulant ● *nm* stimulant

ecci'ta|re *vt* excite. **~rsi** *vr* get excited. **~to** *a* excited

eccitazi'one *nf* excitement

ecclesi'astico *a* ecclesiastical ● *nm* priest

'ecco *adv* ⟨*qui*⟩ here; ⟨*là*⟩ there; **~!** exactly!; **~ fatto** there we are; **~ la tua borsa** here is your bag; **~ [li] mio figlio** there is my son; **~mi** here I am; **~ tutto** that is all

ec'come *adv & int* and how!

echeggi'are *vi* echo

e'clissi *nf inv* eclipse

'eco *nmf* (*pl m* **echi**) echo

ecogra'fia *nf* scan

ecolo'gia *nf* ecology. **eco'logico** *a* ecological; ⟨*prodotto*⟩ environmentally friendly

e commerci'ale *nf* ampersand

econo'm|ia *nf* economy; ⟨*scienza*⟩ economics; **fare ~ia** economize ⟨*di* on⟩. **eco'nomico** *a* economic; ⟨*a buon prezzo*⟩ cheap. **~ista** *nmf* economist; **save** ⟨*tempo, denaro*⟩ economize; save ⟨*tempo, denaro*⟩

e'conomo, -a *a* thrifty ● *nmf* ⟨*di collegio*⟩ bursar

é'cru *a inv* raw

'Ecu *nm inv* ECU, ecu

ec'zema *nm* eczema

ed *conj vedi* **e**

'edera *nf* ivy

e'dicola *nf* [newspaper] kiosk

edifi'cabile *a* ⟨*area, terreno*⟩ classified as suitable for development

edifi'cante *a* edifying

edifi'care *vt* build; ⟨*indurre al bene*⟩ edify

edi'ficio *nm* building; *fig* structure

e'dile *a* building *attrib*

edi'lizi|a *nf* building trade. **~o** *a* building *attrib*

edi|'tore, -'trice *a* publishing ● *nmf* publisher; ⟨*curatore*⟩ editor. **~to'ria** *nf* publishing. **~tori'ale** *a* publishing ● *nm* ⟨*articolo*⟩ editorial, leader

edizi'one *nf* edition; ⟨*di manifestazione*⟩ performance. **~ ridotta** abridg[e]ment. **~ della sera** ⟨*di telegiornale*⟩ evening news

edu'ca|re *vt* educate; ⟨*allevare*⟩ bring up. **~'tivo** *a* educational. **~to** *a* polite. **~tore, ~trice** *nmf* educator. **~zi'one** *nf* education; ⟨*di bambini*⟩ upbringing; ⟨*buone maniere*⟩ [good] manners *pl.* **~zione fisica** physical education

e'felide *nf* freckle

effemi'nato *a* effeminate

efferve'scente *a* effervescent; ⟨*frizzante*⟩ fizzy; ⟨*aspirina*⟩ soluble

effettiva'mente *adv* **è troppo tardi – ~** it's too late – so it is

effet'tivo *a* actual; ⟨*efficace*⟩ effective; ⟨*personale*⟩ permanent; *Mil* regular ● *nm* ⟨*somma totale*⟩ sum total

ef'fetto *nm* effect; ⟨*impressione*⟩ impression; **in ~i** in fact; **a tutti gli ~i** to all intents and purposes; **~i personali** personal belongings. **~u'are** *vt* effect; carry out ⟨*controllo, sondaggio*⟩. **~u'arsi** *vr* take place

effi'cac|e *a* effective. **~ia** *nf* effectiveness

effici'en|te *a* efficient. **~za** *nf* efficiency

ef'fimero *a* ephemeral

effusi'one *nf* effusion

E'geo *nm* **l'~** the Aegean [Sea]

E'gitto *nm* Egypt. **egizi'ano, -a a &** *nmf* Egyptian. **egizi'ano, -a &**

'egli *pers pron* he; **~ stesso** he himself

ego'centrico, -a *a* egocentric ● *nmf* egocentric person

ego'is|mo *nm* selfishness. **~ta** *a* selfish ●*nmf* selfish person. **~tico** *a* selfish

e'gregio *a* distinguished; **E~ Signore** Dear Sir

eguali'tario *a* & *nm* egalitarian

eiaculazi'one *nf* ejaculation

elabo'ra|re *vt* elaborate; process ⟨*dati*⟩. **~to a** elaborate. **~zi'one** *nf* elaboration; ⟨*di dati*⟩ processing. **~zione [di] testi** word processing

elar'gire *vt* lavish

elastici'tà *nf* elasticity. **~z'zato** *a* ⟨*stoffa*⟩ elasticated. **e'lastico** *a* elastic; ⟨*tessuto*⟩ stretch; ⟨*orario, mente*⟩ flexible; ⟨*persona*⟩ easygoing ●*nm* elastic; ⟨*fascia*⟩ rubber band

ele'fante *nm* elephant

ele'gan|te *a* elegant. **~za** *nf* elegance

e'leggere *vt* elect. **eleg'gibile** *a* eligible

elemen'tare *a* elementary; **scuola ~** primary school

ele'mento *nm* element; **elementi** *pl* ⟨*fatti*⟩ data; ⟨*rudimenti*⟩ elements

ele'mosina *nf* charity; **chiedere l'~** beg. **elemosi'nare** *vt/i* beg

elen'care *vt* list

e'lenco *nm* list. **~ abbonati** telephone directory. **~ telefonico** telephone directory

elet'tivo *a* ⟨*carica*⟩ elective. **e'letto, -a** *pp di* **eleggere** ●*a* chosen ●*nmf* ⟨*nominato*⟩ elected member, **per pochi eletti** for the chosen few

eletto'ra|le *a* electoral. **~to** *nm* electorate

elet'tore, -'trice *nmf* voter

elet'trauto *nm* garage for electrical repairs

elettri'cista *nm* electrician

elettri|cità *nf* electricity. **e'lettrico** *a* electric. **~z'zante** *a* ⟨*notizia, gara*⟩ electrifying. **~z'zare** *vt* fig electrify. **~z'zato** *a* fig electrified

elettrocardio'gramma *nm* electrocardiogram

e'lettrodo *nm* electrode

elettrodo'mestico *nm* [electrical] household appliance

elet'trone *nm* electron

elet'tronico, -a *a* electronic ●*nf* electronics

ele'va|re *vt* raise; ⟨*promuovere*⟩ promote; ⟨*erigere*⟩ erect; ⟨*fig: migliorare*⟩ better; **~ al quadrato/cubo** square/cube. **~rsi** *vr* rise; ⟨*edificio*⟩ stand. **~to a** high. **~zi'one** *nf* elevation

elezi'one *nf* election

'elica *nf* Naut screw, propeller; Aeron propeller; ⟨*del ventilatore*⟩ blade

ell'cottero *nm* helicopter

elimi'na|re *vt* eliminate. **~'toria** *nf* Sport preliminary heat. **~zi'one** *nf* elimination

é'li|te *nf* inv élite. **~'tista** *a* élitist

'ella *pers pron* she

ellepi *nm* inv LP

el'metto *nm* helmet

elogi'are *vt* praise. **e'logio** *nm* praise; ⟨*discorso, scritto*⟩ eulogy

elo'quen|te *a* eloquent; *fig* telltale. **~za** *nf* eloquence

e'lu|dere *vt* evade; evade ⟨*sorveglianza, controllo*⟩. **~'sivo** *a* elusive

el'vetico *a* Swiss

emaci'ato *a* emaciated

'E-mail *nf* e-mail

ema'na|re *vt* give off; pass ⟨*legge*⟩ ●*vi* emanate. **~zi'one** *nf* giving off, ⟨*di legge*⟩ enactment

emanci'pa|re *vt* emancipate. **~rsi** *vr* become emancipated. **~to a** emancipated. **~zi'one** *nf* emancipation

emargi'na|to *nm* marginalized person. **~zi'one** *nf* marginalization

ema'toma *nm* haematoma

em'bargo *nm* embargo

em'ble|ma *nm* emblem. **~'matico** *a* emblematic

embo'lia *nf* embolism

embrio'nale *a* Biol, fig embryonic. **embri'one** *nm* embryo

emen|da'mento *nm* amendment. **~'dare** *vt* amend

emer'gen|te *a* emergent. **~za** *nf* emergency; **in caso di ~za** in an emergency

e'mergere *vi* emerge; ⟨*sottomarino:*⟩ surface; (*distinguersi*) stand out

e'merito *a* ⟨*professore*⟩ emeritus; **un ~ imbecille** a prize idiot

e'merso *pp di* **emergere**

e'messo *pp di* **emettere**

e'mettere *vt* emit; give out ⟨*luce, suono*⟩; let out ⟨*grido*⟩; (*mettere in circolazione*) issue

emi'crania *nf* migraine

emi'gra|re *vi* emigrate. **~to, -a** *nmf* immigrant. **~zi'one** *nf* emigration

emi'nen|te *a* eminent. **~za** *nf* eminence

e'miro *nm* emir

emis'fero *nm* hemisphere

emis'sario *nm* emissary

emissi'one *nf* emission; (*di denaro*) issue; (*trasmissione*) broadcast

emit'tente *a* issuing; (*trasmittente*) broadcasting ● *nf* **Radio** transmitter

emor'ragia *nf* haemorrhage

emor'roidi *nfpl* piles

emotività *nf* emotional make-up.

emo'tivo *a* emotional

emozio'na|nte *a* exciting; (*commovente*) moving. **~re** *vt* excite; (*commuovere*) move. **~rsi** *vr* become excited; (*commuoversi*) be moved. **~to** *a* excited; (*commosso*) moved. **emozi'one** *nf* emotion; (*agitazione*) excitement

'empio *a* impious; (*spietato*) pitiless; (*malvagio*) wicked

em'pirico *a* empirical

em'porio *nm* emporium; (*negozio*) general store

emu'la|re *vt* emulate. **~zi'one** *nf* emulation

emulsi'one *nf* emulsion

en'ciclica *nf* encyclical

enciclope'dia *nf* encyclopaedia

encomi'are *vt* commend. **en'comio** *nm* commendation

en'demico *a* endemic

endo've|na *nf* intravenous injection. **~'noso** *a* intravenous; **per via ~nosa** intravenously

E.N.I.T. *nm abbr* (**Ente Nazionale Italiano per il Turismo**) Italian State Tourist Office

ener'getico *a* ⟨*risorse, crisi*⟩ energy attrib; ⟨*alimento*⟩ energy-giving **ener'gia** *nf* energy. **e'nergico** *a* energetic; (*efficace*) strong

ener'gumeno *nm* Neanderthal

'enfasi *nf* emphasis

en'fati|co *a* emphatic. **~z'zare** *vt* emphasize

e'nigma *nm* enigma. **enig'matico** *a* enigmatic. **enig'mistica** *nf* puzzles *pl*

en'nesimo *a* **Math** nth; *fam* umpteenth

e'norm|e *a* enormous. **~e'mente** *adv* massively. **~ità** *nf inv* enormity; (*assurdità*) absurdity

eno'teca *nf* wine-tasting shop

'ente *nm* board; (*società*) company; (*filosofia*) being

entità *nf inv* (*filosofia*) entity; (*gravità*) seriousness; (*dimensione*) extent

entou'rage *nm inv* entourage

en'trambi *a & pron* both

en'tra|re *vi* go in, enter; **~re in** go into; (*stare in, trovar posto in*) fit into; (*arruolarsi*) join; **~rci** (*avere a che fare*) have to do with; **tu che c'entri?** what has it got to do with you? **~ta** *nf* entry, entrance; **~te** *pl* **Comm** takings; (*reddito*) income *sg*

'entro *prep* (*tempo*) within

entro'terra *nm inv* hinterland

entusias'mante *a* fascinating, exciting

entusias'mar|e *vt* arouse enthusiasm in. **~si** *vr* be enthusiastic (**per** about)

entusi'as|mo *nm* enthusiasm. **~ta** *a* enthusiastic ● *nmf* enthusiast. **~tico** *a* enthusiastic

enume'ra|re *vt* enumerate. **~zi-'one** *nf* enumeration
enunci'a|re *vt* enunciate. **~zi'one** *nf* enunciation
epa'tite *nf* hepatitis
'epico *a* epic
epide'mia *nf* epidemic
epi'dermide *nf* epidermis
Epifa'nia *nf* Epiphany
epi'gramma *nm* epigram
epil|es'sia *nf* epilepsy. **epi'lettico, -a** *a & nmf* epileptic
e'pilogo *nm* epilogue
epi'sodi|co *a* episodic; **caso ~co** one-off case. **~o** *nm* episode
e'piteto *nm* epithet
'epoca *nf age; (periodo)* period; **a quell'~** in those days; **auto d'~** vintage car
ep'pure *conj* [and] yet
epu'rare *vt* purge
equa'tore *nm* equator. **equatori-'ale** *a* equatorial
equazi'one *nf* equation
e'questre *a* equestrian; **circo ~** circus
equi'latero *a* equilateral
equili'bra|re *vt* balance. **~to** *a (persona)* well-balanced. **equi-'librio** *nm* balance; *(buon senso)* common sense; *(di bilancia)* equilibrium
equili'brismo *nm* **fare ~** do a balancing act
e'quino *a* horse *attrib*
equi'nozio *nm* equinox
equipaggia'mento *nm* equipment
equipaggi'are *vt* equip; *(di persone)* man
equi'paggio *nm* crew; *Aeron* cabin crew
equipa'rare *vt* make equal
é'quipe *nf inv* team
equità *nf* equity
equitazi'one *nf* riding
equiva'len|te *a & nm* equivalent. **~za** *nf* equivalence
equiva'lere *vi* **~ a** be equivalent to
equivo'care *vi* misunderstand

e'quivoco *a* equivocal; *(sospetto)* suspicious; **un tipo ~** a shady character ● *nm* misunderstanding
'equo *a* fair, just
'era *nf* era
'erba *nf* grass; *(aromatica, medicinale)* herb. **~ cipollina** chives *pl*.
er'baccia *nf* weed. **er'baceo** *a* herbaceous
erbi'cida *nm* weed-killer
erbo'rist|a *nmf* herbalist. **~e'ria** *nf* herbalist's shop
er'boso *a* grassy
er'culeo *a (forza)* herculean
e'red|e *nmf* heir; heiress. **~ità** *nf inv* inheritance; *Biol* heredity. **~i'tare** *vt* inherit. **~itarietà** *nf* heredity. **~i'tario** *a* hereditary
ere'mita *nm* hermit
ere'sia *nf* heresy. **e'retico, -a** *a* heretical ● *nmf* heretic
e're|tto *pp di* **erigere** ● *a* erect. **~zi'one** *nf* erection; *(costruzione)* building
er'gastolo *nm* life sentence; *(luogo)* prison
'erica *nf* heather
e'rigere *vt* erect; *(fig: fondare)* found
eri'tema *nm (cutaneo)* inflammation; *(solare)* sunburn
ermel'lino *nm* ermine
ermetica'mente *adv* hermetically. **er'metico** *a* hermetic; *(a tenuta d'aria)* airtight
'ernia *nf* hernia
e'rodere *vt* erode
e'ro|e *nm* hero. **~ico** *a* heroic. **~ismo** *nm* heroism
ero'ga|re *vt* distribute; *(fornire)* supply. **~zi'one** *nf* supply
ero'ina *nf* heroine; *(droga)* heroin
erosi'one *nf* erosion
e'rotico *a* erotic. **ero'tismo** *nm* eroticism
er'rante *a* wandering. **er'rare** *vi* wander; *(sbagliare)* be mistaken
er'rato *a (sbagliato)* mistaken
'erre *nf* **~ moscia** burr
erronea'mente *adv* mistakenly

er'rore nm error, mistake; (di stampa) misprint; **essere in ~** be wrong

'erta nf **stare all'~** be on the alert

eru'di|rsi vr get educated. **~to** a learned

erut'tare vt (vulcano:) erupt ● vi (ruttare) belch. **eruzi'one** nf eruption; Med rash

esacer'bare vt exacerbate

esage'ra|re vt exaggerate ● vi exaggerate; (nel comportamento) go over the top; **~re nel mangiare** eat too much. **~ta'mente** adv excessively. **~to** a exaggerated; (prezzo) exorbitant ● nm **è un ~to** he exaggerates. **~zi'one** nf exaggeration; **è costato un'~zio-ne** it cost the earth

esa'lare vt/i exhale

esal'ta|re vt exalt; (entusiasmare) elate. **~to** a (fanatico) fanatical ● nm fanatic. **~zi'one** nf exaltation; (in discorso) fervour

e'same nm examination; **dare un ~** take an exam; **prendere in ~** examine. **~ del sangue** blood test. **esami pl di maturità** ≈ A-levels

esami'na|re vt examine. **~tore**, **~trice** nmf examiner

e'sangue a bloodless

e'sanime a lifeless

esaspe'rante a exasperating

esaspe'ra|re vt exasperate. **~rsi** vr get exasperated. **~zi'one** nf exasperation

esat|ta'mente adv exactly. **~tez-za** nf exactness; (precisione) precision; (di risposta, risultato) accuracy

e'satto pp di **esigere** ● a exact; (risposta, risultato) correct; (orologio) right; **hai l'ora esatta?** do you have the right time?; **sono le due esatte** it's two o'clock exactly

esat'tore nm collector

esau'dire vt grant; fulfil (speranze)

esau'riente a exhaustive

esau'ri|re vt exhaust. **~rsi** vr ex-

haust oneself; (merci ecc:) run out. **~to** a exhausted; (merci) sold out; (libro) out of print; **fare il tutto ~to** (spettacolo:) play to a full house

'esca nf bait

escande'scenz|a nf outburst; **dare in ~e** lose one's temper

escla'ma|re vi exclaim. **~tivo** a exclamatory. **~zi'one** nf exclamation

es'clu|dere vt exclude; rule out (possibilità, ipotesi). **~si'one** nf exclusion. **~'siva** nf exclusive right, sole right; **in ~siva** exclusive. **~siva'mente** adv exclusively. **~'sivo** a exclusive. **~so** pp di **escludere** ● **a non è ~so che ci sia** it's not out of the question that he'll be there

escogi'tare vt contrive

escre'mento nm excrement

escursi'one nf excursion; (scorreria) raid; (di temperatura) range

ese'cra|bile a abominable. **~re** vt abhor

esecu|'tivo a & nm executive. **~tore**, **~trice** nmf executor; Mus performer. **~zi'one** nf execution; Mus performance

esegu'ire vt carry out; Jur execute; Mus perform

e'sempio nm example; **ad o per ~** for example; **dare l'~** a qcno set sb an example; **fare un ~** give an example. **esem'plare** a examplary ● nm specimen; (di libro) copy. **esemplifi'care** vt exemplify

esen'ta|re vt exempt. **~si** vr free oneself. **e'sente** a exempt. **esente da imposta** duty-free. **esente da IVA** VAT-exempt

esen'tasse a duty-free

e'sequie nfpl funeral rites

eser'cente nmf shopkeeper

eserci'ta|re vt exercise; (addestra-re) train; (fare uso di) exert; (professione) practise. **~rsi** vr practise. **~zi'one** nf exercise; Mil drill

e'sercito nm army

eser'cizio *nm* exercise; (*pratica*) practice; *Comm* financial year; (*azienda*) business; **essere fuori ~** be out of practice

esi'bi|re *vt* show off; produce ⟨*documenti*⟩. **~rsi** *vr Theat* perform; *fig* show off. **~zi'one** *nf Theat* performance; (*di documenti*) production

esibizio'nis|mo *nm* showing off. **~ta** *nmf* exhibitionist

esi'gen|te *a* exacting; (*pignolo*) fastidious. **~za** *nf* demand; (*bisogno*) need. **e'sigere** *vt* demand; (*riscuotere*) collect

e'siguo *a* meagre

esila'ra|nte *a* exhilarating

'esile *a* slender; ⟨*voce*⟩ thin

esili'a|re *vt* exile. **~rsi** *vr* go into exile. **~to, -a** *a* exiled ● *nmf* exile.
e'silio *nm* exile

e'simere *vt* release. **~si** *vr* **~si da** get out of

esi'sten|te *a* existing. **~za** *nf* existence. **~zi'ale** *a* existential.
~zia'lismo *nm* existentialism

e'sistere *vi* exist

esi'tante *a* hesitating; ⟨*voce*⟩ faltering

esi'ta|re *vi* hesitate. **~zi'one** *nf* hesitation

'esito *nm* result; **avere buon ~** be a success

'esodo *nm* exodus

e'sofago *nm* oesophagus

esone'rare *vt* exempt. **e'sonero** *nm* exemption

esor'bi|tante *a* exorbitant

esorciz'zare *vt* exorcize

esordi'ente *nmf* person making his/her *début*. **e'sordio** *nm* opening; (*di attore*) *début*. **esor'dire** *vi début*

esor'tare *vt* (*pregare*) beg; (*incitare*) urge

eso'terico *a* esoteric

e'sotico *a* exotic

aspa'drillas *nfpl* espadrilles

es'pan|dere *vt* expand. **~dersi** *vr* expand; (*diffondersi*) extend
~si'one *nf* expansion. **~sivo** *a* expansive; ⟨*persona*⟩ friendly

espatri'are *vi* leave one's country.
es'patrio *nm* expatriation

espedi'ent|e *nm* expedient; **vivere di ~i** live by one's wits

es'pellere *vt* expel

esperi'enza *nf* experience; **parlare per ~enza** speak from experience. **~'mento** *nm* experiment

es'perto, -a *a* & *nmf* expert

espi'a|re *vt* atone for. **~'torio** *a* expiatory

espi'rare *vt/i* breathe out

espli'care *vt* carry on

esplicita'mente *adv* explicitly.
es'plicito *a* explicit

es'plodere *vi* explode ● *vt* fire

esplo'ra|re *vt* explore. **~'tore, ~'trice** *nmf* explorer; **giovane ~tore** boy scout. **~zi'one** *nf* exploration

esplo'si|one *nf* explosion. **~'vivo** *a* & *nm* explosive

espo'nente *nm* exponent

es'por|re *vt* expose; display ⟨*merci*⟩; (*spiegare*) expound; exhibit ⟨*quadri ecc*⟩. **~si** *vr* (*compromettersi*) compromise oneself; (*al sole*) expose oneself; (*alle critiche*) lay oneself open

espor'ta|re *vt* export. **~'tore, ~'trice** *nmf* exporter. **~zi'one** *nf* export

esposizi'one *nf* (*mostra*) exhibition; (*in vetrina*) display; (*spiegazione ecc*) exposition; (*posizione, fotografia*) exposure. **es'posto** *pp di* **esporre** ● *a* exposed; **esposto a** (*rivolto*) facing ● *nm* statement

espressa'mente *adv* expressly; **non l'ha detto ~** he didn't put it in so many words

espressi'one *nf* expression.
~'sivo *a* expressive

es'presso *pp di* **esprimere** ● *a* express ● *nm* (*lettera*) express letter; (*treno*) express train; (*caffè*) espresso; **per ~** (*spedire*) [by] express [post]

es'primer|e *vt* express. **~si** *vr* express oneself

espropri'a|re vt dispossess. **~zi'one** nf Jur expropriation. **es'proprio** nm expropriation

espulsi'one nf expulsion. **es'pulso** pp di **espellere**

es'senza nf essence. **~i'ale** a essential ●nm important thing. **~ial'mente** a essentially

'essere vi be; **c'è** there is; **ci sono** there are; **che ora è?** what time is it? – it's ten o'clock; **chi è?** – **sono io** who is it? – it's me; **ci sono!** (ho capito) I've got it!; **ci siamo!** (siamo arrivati) here we are at last!; **è stato detto che** it has been said that; **siamo in due** there are two of us; **questa camicia è da lavare** this shirt is to be washed; **non è da te** it's not like you; **~ di** (provenire da) be from; **~ per** (favorevole) be in favour of; **se fossi in te,...** if I were you,...; **sarà!** if you say so!; **come sarebbe a dire?** what are you getting at? ●v aux have; (in passivi) be; **siamo arrivati** we have arrived; **ci sono stato ieri** I was there yesterday; **sono nato a Torino** I was born in Turin; **è riconosciuto come...** he is recognized as... ●nm being. **~ umano** human being. **~ vivente** living creature

essic'cato a dried

'esso, -a pers pron he, she; (cosa, animale) it

est nm east

'estasi nf ecstasy; **andare in ~ per** go into raptures over. **~'are** vt enrapture

e'state nf summer

esten'dere vt extend. **~dersi** vr spread; (allungarsi) stretch. **~si'one** nf extension; (ampiezza) expanse; Mus range. **~'sivo** a extensive

estenu'ante a exhausting

estenu'a|re vt wear out; deplete (risorse, casse). **~rsi** vr wear oneself out

esteri'or|e a & nm exterior.

~'mente adv externally; (di persone) outwardly

esterna'mente adv on the outside

ester'nare vt express, show

e'sterno a external; **per uso ~** for external use only ●nm (allievo) day-boy; Archit exterior; (scala) outside; (in film) location shot

'estero a foreign ●nm foreign countries pl; **all'~** abroad

esterre'fatto a horrified

e'steso pp di **estendere** ●a extensive; (diffuso) widespread; **per ~** (scrivere) in full

e'stetic|a nf aesthetics sg. **~a'mente** adv aesthetically. **~o, -a** a aesthetic; (chirurgia, chirurgo) plastic. **este'tista** nf beautician

'estimo nm estimate

e'stin|guere vt extinguish. **~guersi** vr die out. **~to, -a** pp di **estinguere** ●nmf deceased. **~'tore** nm [fire] extinguisher. **~zi'one** nf extinction; (di incendio) putting out

estir'pa|re vt uproot; extract (dente); fig eradicate (crimine, malattia). **~zi'one** nf eradication; (di dente) extraction

e'stivo a summer

e'stor|cere vt extort. **~si'one** nf extortion. **~to** pp di **estorcere**

estradizi'one nf extradition

e'straneo, -a a extraneous; (straniero) foreign ●nmf stranger

estrani'ar|e vt estrange. **~si** vr become estranged

e'stra|rre vt extract; (sorteggiare) draw. **~tto** pp di **estrarre** ●nm extract; (brano) excerpt; (documento) abstract. **~tto conto** statement [of account], bank statement. **~zi'one** nf extraction; (a sorte) draw

estrema'mente adv extremely

estre'mis|mo nm extremism. **~ta** nmf extremist

estremità nf inv extremity; (di una corda) end ●nfpl Anat extremities

e'stremo a extreme; (ultimo) last;
misure estreme drastic measures; l'E~ Oriente the Far East
● nm (limite) extreme. estremi pl
(di documento) main points; (di
reato) essential elements; essere
agli estremi be at the end of one's
tether
'estro nm (disposizione artistica)
talent; (ispirazione) inspiration;
(capriccio) whim. e'stroso a tal-
ented; (capriccioso) unpredictable
estro'mettere vt expel
estro'verso a extroverted ● nm
extrovert
estu'ario nm estuary
esube'ran|te a exuberant. ~za nf
exuberance
'esule nmf exile
esul'tante a exultant
esul'tare vi rejoice
esu'mare vt exhume
età nf inv age; raggiungere la
maggiore ~ come of age; un
uomo di mezz'~ a middle-aged
man
'etere nm ether. e'tereo a ethereal
eterna'mente adv eternally
eternità nf eternity; è un'~ che
non la vedo I haven't seen her for
ages
e'terno a eternal; (questione, problema) age-old; in ~ fam for ever
etero'geneo a diverse, heteroge-
neous
eterosessu'ale nmf heterosexual
'etic|a nf ethics. ~o a ethical
eti'chetta¹ nf label; (con il prezzo)
price-tag
eti'chetta² nf (cerimoniale) etiquette
etichet'tare vt label
eti'lometro nm Breathalyzer®
etimolo'gia nf etymology
Eti'opia nf Ethiopia
'etnico a ethnic. etnolo'gia nf eth-
nology
'etrusco a ● nmf Etruscan
'ettaro nm hectare
'etto, etto'grammo nm hundred
grams, ≈ quarter pound

euca'lipto nm eucalyptus
eucari'stia nf Eucharist
eufe'mismo nm euphemism
eufo'ria nf elation; Med euphoria.
eu'forico a elated; Med euphoric
Euro'city nm international Inter-
city
eurodepu'tato nm Euro MP, MEP
Eu'ropa nf Europe. euro'peo, -a a
& nmf European
eutana'sia nf euthanasia
evacu'a|re vt evacuate. ~zi'one nf
evacuation
e'vadere vt evade; (sbrigare) deal
with ● vi ~ da escape from
evane'scente a vanishing
evan'gel|ico a evangelical. evan-
ge'lista nm evangelist. ~o nm =
vangelo
evapo'ra|re vi evaporate. ~zi'one
nf evaporation
evasi'one nf escape; (fiscale) evasion; fig escapism. eva'sivo a evasive
e'vaso pp di evadere ● nm fugitive
eva'sore nm ~ fiscale tax evader
eveni'enza nf eventuality
e'vento nm event
eventu'al|e a possible. ~ità nf inv
eventuality
evi'den|te a evident; è ~ che it
is obvious that. ~te'mente adv
evidently. ~za nf evidence; mettere in ~za emphasize; mettersi in
~za make oneself conspicuous
evidenzi'a|re vt highlight. ~'tore
nm (penna) highlighter
evi'tare vt avoid; (risparmiare)
spare
evo'care vt evoke
evo'lu|to pp di evolvere ● a
evolved; (progredito) progressive;
(civiltà, nazione) advanced; una
donna evoluta a modern woman.
~zi'one nf evolution; (di ginnasta,
aereo) circle
e'volvere vt develop; ~si vi
evolve
ev'viva int hurray; ~ il Papa! long
live the Pope!; gridare ~ cheer
ex+ pref ex+, former

'extra *a inv* extra; *(qualità)* first-class ● *nm inv* extra

extracomuni'tario *a* non-EC

extraconiu'gale *a* extramarital

extrater'restre *nmf* extra-terrestrial

Ff

fa¹ *nm inv Mus (chiave, nota)* F

fa² *adv* ago; **due mesi ~** two months ago

fabbi'sogno *nm* requirements *pl*, needs *pl*

'fabbri|ca *nf* factory

fabbri'cabile *a (area, terreno)* that can be built on

fabbri'cante *nm* manufacturer

fabbri'ca|re *vt* build; *(produrre)* manufacture; *(fig: inventare)* fabricate. **~to** *nm* building. **~zi'one** *nf* manufacturing; *(costruzione)* building

'fabbro *nm* blacksmith

fac'cend|a *nf* matter; **~e** *pl (lavori domestici)* housework *sg*. **~i'ere** *nm* wheeler-dealer

fac'chino *nm* porter

'facci|a *nf* face; *(di foglio)* side; **~a a ~a** face to face; **~a tosta** cheek; **voltar ~a** change sides; **di ~a** *(palazzo)* opposite; **alla ~a di** *(fam: a dispetto di)* in spite of. **~'ata** *nf* façade; *(di foglio)* side; *(fig: esteriorità)* outward appearance

fa'ceto *a* facetious; **tra il serio e il ~** half joking

fa'chiro *nm* fakir

'facil|e *a* easy; *(affabile)* easy-going; **essere ~e alle critiche** be quick to criticize; **essere ~e al riso** laugh a lot; **~e a farsi** easy to do; **è ~e che piova** it's likely to rain. **~ità** *nf inv* ease; *(disposizione)* aptitude; **avere ~ità di parola** express oneself well

facili'ta|re *vt* facilitate. **~zi'one** *nf* facility; **~zioni** *pl* special terms

facil'mente *adv (con facilità)* easily; *(probabilmente)* probably

faci'lone *a* slapdash. **~'ria** *nf* slapdash attitude

facino'roso *a* violent

facol'tà *nf inv* faculty; *(potere)* power. **~'tivo** *a* optional; **fermata ~tiva** request stop

facol'toso *a* wealthy

fac'simile *nm* facsimile

fac'totum *nmf* man/girl Friday, factotum

'faggio *nm* beech

fagi'ano *nm* pheasant

fagio'lino *nm* French bean

fagi'olo *nm* bean; **a ~** *(arrivare, capitare)* at the right time

fagoci'tare *vt* gobble up *(società)*

fa'gotto *nm* bundle; *Mus* bassoon

'faida *nf* feud

fai da te *nm* do-it-yourself, DIY

fal'cata *nf* stride

'falc|e *nf* scythe. **fal'cetto** *nm* sickle. **~i'are** *vt* cut; *fig* mow down. **~ia'trice** *nf* [lawn-]mower

'falco *nm* hawk

fal'cone *nm* falcon

'falda *nf* stratum; *(di neve)* flake; *(di cappello)* brim; *(pendio)* slope

fale'gname *nm* carpenter. **~'ria** *nf* carpentry

'falla *nf* leak

fal'lace *a* deceptive

'fallico *a* phallic

falli'men|tare *a* disastrous; *Jur* bankruptcy. **falli'mento** *nm Fin* bankruptcy; *fig* failure

fal'li|re *vi Fin* go bankrupt; *fig* fail ● *vt* miss *(colpo)*. **~to, -a** *a* unsuccessful; *Fin* bankrupt ● *nmf* failure; *Fin* bankrupt

'fallo *nm* fault; *(errore)* mistake; *Sport* foul; *(imperfezione)* flaw; **senza ~** without fail

falò *nm inv* bonfire

fal'sar|e *vt* alter; *(falsificare)* falsify. **~io, -io** *nmf* forger; *(di documenti)* counterfeiter

falsifi'ca|re *vt* fake; *(contraffare)*

forge. **~zi'one** *nf* (*di documento*) falsification

falsità *nf* falseness

'falso *a* false; (*sbagliato*) wrong; ⟨*opera d'arte ecc*⟩ fake; ⟨*gioielli, oro*⟩ imitation ● *nm* forgery; **giurare il ~** commit perjury

'fama *nf* fame; (*reputazione*) reputation

'fame *nf* hunger; **aver ~** be hungry; **tare la ~** barely scrape a living. **fa'melico** *a* ravenous

famige'rato *a* infamous

fa'miglia *nf* family

famili'ar|e *a* family *attrib*; (*ben noto*) familiar; (*senza cerimonie*) informal ● *nmf* relative, relation ~**ità** *nf* familiarity; (*informalità*) informality. **~iz'zarsi** *vr* familiarize oneself

fa'moso *a* famous

fa'nale *nm* lamp; *Auto ecc* light. **fanali** *pl* **posteriori** *Auto* rear lights

fa'natico, -a *a* fanatical; **essere ~ di calcio/cinema** be a football/cinema fanatic ● *nmf* fanatic. **fana'tismo** *nm* fanaticism

fanci'ulla *nf* young girl. **~'lezza** *nf* childhood. **~lo** *nm* young boy

fan'donia *nf* lie; **fandonie!** nonsense!

fan'fara *nf* fanfare; (*complesso*) brass band

fanfaro'nata *nf* brag. **fanfa'rone, -a** *nmf* braggart

fan'ghiglia *nf* mud. **'fango** *nm* mud. **fan'goso** *a* muddy

fannul'lone, -a *nmf* idler

fantasci'enza *nf* science fiction

fanta'sia *nf* fantasy; (*immaginazione*) imagination; (*capriccio*) fancy; (*di tessuto*) pattern. **~'oso** *a* ⟨*stilista, ragazzo*⟩ imaginative; (*resoconto*) improbable

fan'tasma *nm* ghost

fantasti'c|are *vi* day-dream. **~he'ria** *nf* day-dream. **fan'tastico** *a* fantastic; (*racconto*) fantasy

'fante *nm* infantryman; (*nelle carte*) jack. **~'ria** *nf* infantry

fan'tino *nm* jockey

fan'toccio *nm* puppet

fanto'matico *a* (*inafferrabile*) phantom *attrib*

fara'butto *nm* trickster

fara'ona *nf* (*uccello*) guinea-fowl

far'ci|re *vt* stuff; fill ⟨*torta*⟩. ~**to** *a* stuffed; (*dolce*) filled

far'dello *nm* bundle; *fig* burden

'fare *vt* do; make ⟨*dolce, letto ecc*⟩; (*recitare la parte di*) play; (*trascorrere*) spend; ~ **una pausa/un sogno** have a break/a dream; ~ **colpo su impress;** ~ **paura a** frighten; ~ **piacere a** please; **farla finita** put an end to it; ~ **l'insegnante** be a teacher; ~ **lo scemo** play the idiot; ~ **una settimana al mare** spend a week at the seaside; **3 più 3 fa 6** 3 and 3 makes 6; **quanto fa?** – how much? **10 000 lira** how much is it? – it's 10,000 lire; **far ~ qcsa a qcno** get sb to do sth; (*costringere*) make sb do sth; ~ **vedere** show; **fammi parlare** let me speak; **niente a che ~ con** nothing to do with; **non c'è niente da ~** (*per problema*) there is nothing we/you/etc. can do; **fa caldo/buio** it's warm/dark; **non fa niente** it doesn't matter; **strada facendo** on the way. **farcela** (*riuscire*) manage ● *vi* **fai in modo di venire** try and come; ~ **da act as;** ~ **per** make as if to; ~ **presto** be quick; **non fa per me** it's not for me ● *nm* way; **sul far del giorno** at daybreak. **farsi** *vr* (*diventare*) get; (*sl: drogarsi*) shoot up; **farsi avanti** come forward; **farsi i fatti propri** mind one's own business; **farsi la barba** shave; **farsi la villa** *fam* buy a villa; **farsi il ragazzo** *fam* find a boyfriend; **farsi due risate** have a laugh; **farsi male** hurt oneself; **farsi strada** (*aver successo*) make one's way in the world

fa'retto *nm* spot[light]

far'falla *nf* butterfly

farfal'lino *nm* (*cravatta*) bow tie

farfugli'are vt mutter

fa'rina nf flour. **fari'nacei** nmpl starchy food sg

fa'ringe nf pharynx

fari'noso a ⟨neve⟩ powdery; ⟨mela⟩ soft; ⟨patata⟩ floury

farma|'ceutico a pharmaceutical. **~'cia** nf pharmacy; ⟨negozio⟩ chemist's [shop]. **~cia di turno** duty chemist. **~'cista** nmf chemist. **'farmaco** nm drug

'faro nm Auto headlight; Aeron beacon; ⟨costruzione⟩ lighthouse

'farsa nf farce

'fasci|a nf band; ⟨zona⟩ area; ⟨ufficiale⟩ sash; ⟨benda⟩ bandage. **~'are** vt bandage; cling to ⟨fianchi⟩. **~a'tura** nf dressing; ⟨azione⟩ bandaging

fa'scicolo nm file; ⟨di rivista⟩ issue; ⟨libretto⟩ booklet

'fascino nm fascination

'fascio nm bundle; ⟨di fiori⟩ bunch

fa'scis|mo nm fascism. **~ta** nmf fascist

'fase nf phase

fa'stidi|o nm nuisance; ⟨scomodo⟩ inconvenience; **dar ~o** a qcno bother sb; **~i** pl ⟨preoccupazioni⟩ worries; ⟨disturbi⟩ troubles. **~'oso** a tiresome

'fasto nm pomp. **fa'stoso** a sumptuous

fa'sullo a bogus

'fata nf fairy

fa'tal|e a fatal; ⟨inevitabile⟩ fated

fata'l|ismo nm fatalism. **~ista** nmf fatalist. **~ità** nf inv fate; ⟨caso sfortunato⟩ misfortune. **~'mente** adv inevitably

fa'tica nf effort; ⟨lavoro faticoso⟩ hard work; ⟨stanchezza⟩ fatigue; **a ~** with great difficulty; **è ~ sprecata** it's a waste of time; **far ~ a fare qcsa** find it difficult to do sth; **fare ~ a finire qcsa** struggle to finish sth. **fati'caccia** nf pain

fati'ca|re vi toil; **~re a** ⟨stentare⟩ find it difficult to. **~ta** nf effort;

⟨sfacchinata⟩ grind. **fati'coso** a tiring; ⟨difficile⟩ difficult

'fato nm fate

fat'taccio nm hum foul deed

fat'tezze nfpl features

fat'tibile a feasible

'fatto pp di **fare ● a** done, made; **~ a mano/in casa** handmade/homemade **● nm** fact; ⟨azione⟩ action; ⟨avvenimento⟩ event; **bada ai fatti tuoi!** mind your own business; **sa il ~ suo** he knows his business; **di ~** in fact; **in ~ di** as regards

fat'tore nm ⟨causa, Math⟩ factor; ⟨di fattoria⟩ farm manager. **~'ria** nf farm; ⟨casa⟩ farmhouse

fatto'rino nm messenger [boy]

fattucchi'era nf witch

fat'tura nf ⟨stile⟩ cut; ⟨lavorazione⟩ workmanship; Comm invoice

fattu'ra|re vt invoice; ⟨adulterare⟩ adulterate. **~to** nm turnover, sales pl. **~zi'one** nf invoicing, billing

'fatuo a fatuous

'fauna nf fauna

fau'tore nm supporter

'fava nf broad bean

fa'vella nf speech

fa'villa nf spark

'favo|la nf fable; ⟨fiaba⟩ story; ⟨oggetto di pettegolezzi⟩ laughingstock; ⟨meraviglia⟩ dream. **~'loso** a fabulous

fa'vore nm favour; **essere a ~ di** ⟨condizioni, trattamento⟩ preferential. **~'gglia'mento** nm Jur aiding and abetting. **favo'revole** a favourable. **~vol'mente** adv favourably

favo'ri|re vt favour; ⟨promuovere⟩ promote; **vuol ~re?** ⟨a cena, pranzo⟩ will you have some?; ⟨entrare⟩ will you come in?. **~to, -a** a & nmf favourite

fax nm inv fax. **fa'xare** vt fax

fazi'one nf faction

faziosità nf bias. **fazi'oso** nm sectarian

fazzolet'tino nm ~ **[di carta]** [paper] tissue

fazzo'letto nm handkerchief; (da testa) headscarf

feb'braio nm February

febbre nf fever; **avere la ~** have o run a temperature. **~ da fieno** hay fever. **febbrici'tante** a fevered. **feb'brile** a feverish

feccia nf dregs pl

fecola nf potato flour

fecon'da|**re** vt fertilize. **~'tore** nm fertilizer. **~zi'one** nf fertilization. **~zione artificiale** artificial insemination. **fe'condo** a fertile

fede nf faith; (fiducia) trust; (anello) wedding-ring; **in buona/mala ~** in good/bad faith; **prestar ~ a** believe; **tener ~ alla parola** keep one's word. **fe'dele** a faithful ● nmf believer; (seguace) follower. **~l'mente** adv faithfully. **~ltà** nf faithfulness; **alta ~ltà** high fidelity

fodera nf pillowcase

fede'ra|**le** a federal. **~'lismo** nm federalism. **~zi'one** nf federation

fe'dina nf **avere la ~ penale sporca/pulita** have a/no criminal record

fegato nm liver; fig guts pl

felce nf fern

fe'lic|**e** a happy; (fortunato) lucky. **~ità** nf happiness

felici'ta|**rsi** vr **~rsi con** congratulate. **~zi'oni** nfpl congratulations

fe'lino a feline

felpa nf (indumento) sweatshirt

fel'pato a brushed; (passo) stealthy

feltro nm felt; (cappello) felt hat

femmin|**a** nf female. **femmi'nile** a feminine; (rivista, abbigliamento) women's; (sesso) female ● nm feminine. **~ilità** nf femininity. **femmi'nismo** nm feminism

femore nm femur

fend|**ere** vt split. **~i'tura** nf split; (in roccia) crack

feni'cottero nm flamingo

fenome'nale a phenomenal. **fe'nomeno** nm phenomenon

'feretro nm coffin

feri'ale a weekday; **giorno ~** weekday

'ferie nfpl holidays; (di università, tribunale ecc) vacation sg; **andare in ~** go on holiday

feri'mento nm wounding

fe'ri|**re** vt wound; (in incidente) injure; fig hurt. **~rsi** vr injure oneself. **~ta** nf wound. **~to** a wounded ● nm wounded person; Mil casualty

'ferma nf Mil period of service

ferma'capelli nm inv hairslide

ferma'carte nm inv paperweight

fermacra'vatta nm inv tiepin

fer'maglio nm clasp; (spilla) brooch; (per capelli) hair slide

ferma'mente adv firmly

fer'ma|**re** vt stop; (fissare) fix; Jur detain ● vi stop. **~rsi** vr stop. **~ta** nf stop. **~ta dell'autobus** bus-stop. **~ta a richiesta** request stop

fermen'ta|**re** vi ferment. **~zi'one** nf fermentation. **fer'mento** nm ferment; (lievito) yeast

fer'mezza nf firmness

'fermo a still; (veicolo) stationary; (stabile) steady; (orologio) not working ● nm Jur detention; Mech catch; **in stato di ~** in custody

fe'roc|**e** a ferocious; (bestia) wild; (freddo, dolore) unbearable. **~e'mente** adv fiercely, ferociously. **~ia** nf ferocity

fer'raglia nf scrap iron

ferra'gosto nm 15 August (bank holiday in Italy); (periodo) August holidays pl

ferra'menta nfpl ironmongery sg; **negozio di ~** ironmonger's

fer'ra|**re** vt shoe (cavallo). **~to a ~to in** (preparato in) well up in

'ferreo a iron

'ferro nm iron; (attrezzo) tool; (di chirurgo) instrument; **bistecca ai ferri** grilled steak; **di ~** (memoria) excellent; (alibi) cast-iron; **salute**

di ~ iron constitution. ~ **battuto** wrought iron. ~ **da calza** knitting needle. ~ **di cavallo** horseshoe. ~ **da stiro** iron

ferro'vecchio nm scrap merchant

ferro'vi|a nf railway. ~'**ario** a railway. ~'**ere** nm railwayman

'**fertil|e** a fertile. ~**ità** nf fertility. ~**iz'zante** nm fertilizer

fer'vente a blazing; fig fervent

'**fervere** vi ⟨preparativi:⟩ be well under way

'**fervid|o** a fervent; ~**i auguri** best wishes

fer'vore nm fervour

fesse'ria nf nonsense

'**fesso** pp di **fendere** ● a cracked; ⟨fam: sciocco⟩ foolish ● nm fam ⟨idiota⟩ fool; **far** ~ **qcno** con sb

fes'sura nf crack; ⟨per gettone ecc⟩ slot

'**festa** nf feast; ⟨giorno festivo⟩ holiday; ⟨compleanno⟩ birthday; ⟨ricevimento⟩ party; fig joy; **fare** ~ **a qcno** welcome sb; **essere in** ~ be on holiday; **far** ~ celebrate. ~**i'olo** a festive

festeggia'mento nm celebration; ⟨manifestazione⟩ festivity

festeggi'are vt celebrate; ⟨accogliere festosamente⟩ give a hearty welcome to

fe'stino nm party

festi'vità nfpl festivities. **fe'stivo** a holiday; ⟨lieto⟩ festive. **festivi** nmpl public holidays

fe'stone nm ⟨nel cucito⟩ scallop, scallop

fe'stoso a merry

fe'tente a evil smelling; fig revolting ● nmf fam bastard

fe'ticcio nm fetish

'**feto** nm foetus

fe'tore nm stench

'**fetta** nf slice; **a fette** sliced. ~ **biscottata** slices of crispy toast-like bread

fet'tuccia nf tape; ⟨con nome⟩ name tape

feu'dale a feudal. '**feudo** nm feud

FFSS abbr (**Ferrovie dello Stato**) Italian state railways

fi'aba nf fairy-tale. **fia'besco** a fairy-tale

fi'acc|a nf weariness; ⟨indolenza⟩ laziness; **battere la** ~ **a** be sluggish. **fiac'care** vt weaken. ~**o** a weak; ⟨indolente⟩ slack; ⟨stanco⟩ weary; ⟨partita⟩ dull

fi'accol|a nf torch. ~**'lata** nf torch-light procession

fi'ala nf phial

fi'amma nf flame; Naut pennant; **in fiamme** aflame. **andare in fiamme** go up in flames. ~ **ossidrica** blowtorch

fiam'mant|e a flaming; **nuovo** ~**nte** brand new. ~**ta** nf blaze

fiammeggi'are vi blaze

fiam'mifero nm match

fiam'mingo, -**a** a Flemish ● nmf Fleming ● nm ⟨lingua⟩ Flemish

fiancheggi'are vt border; fig support

fi'anco nm side; ⟨di persona⟩ hip; ⟨di animale⟩ flank; Mil wing; **al mio** ~ by my side; ~ **a** ⟨lavorare⟩ side by side

fi'asco nm flask; fig fiasco; **fare** ~ be a fiasco

fia'tare vi breathe; ⟨parlare⟩ breathe a word

fi'ato nm breath; ⟨vigore⟩ stamina; **strumenti a** ~ wind instruments; **senza** ~ breathlessly; **tutto d'un** ~ ⟨bere, leggere⟩ all in one go

'**fibbia** nf buckle

'**fibr|a** nf fibre; **fibre** pl ⟨alimentari⟩ roughage. ~ **ottica** optical fibre

ficca'naso nmf nosey parker

fic'car|e vt thrust; drive ⟨chiodo ecc⟩; ⟨fam: mettere⟩ shove. ~**si** vr thrust oneself; ⟨nascondersi⟩ hide; ~**si nei guai** get oneself into trouble

fiche nf ⟨gettone⟩ chip

'**fico** nm ⟨albero⟩ fig-tree; ⟨frutto⟩ fig. ~ **d'India** prickly pear

'**fico**, -**a** fam nmf cool sort ● a cool

fidanza'mento nm engagement

fidan'zalrsi *vr* get engaged. **~to, -a** *nmf (ufficiale)* fiancé; fiancée

fi'dalrsi *vr* **~rsi** di trust. **~to** *a* trustworthy

'fido *nm* devoted follower; *Comm* credit

fi'ducila *nf* confidence; **degno di ~a** trustworthy; **persona di ~a** reliable person; **di ~a** *(fornitore, banca)* regular, usual. **~'oso** *a* trusting

fi'ele *nm* bile; *fig* bitterness

fie'nile *nm* barn. **fi'eno** *nm* hay

fi'era *nf* fair

fie'rezza *nf (dignità)* pride. **fi'ero** *a* proud

fi'evole *a* faint; *(luce)* dim

'fifa *nf fam* jitters; **aver ~** have the jitters. **fi'fone, -a** *nmf fam* chicken

figlila *nf* daughter; **~a unica** only child. **~'astra** *nf* stepdaughter. **~'astro** *nm* stepson. **~o** *nm* son; *(generico)* child. **~o di papà** spoilt brat. **~o unico** only child

figli'occila *nf* goddaughter. **~o** *nm* godson

figli'olla *nf* girl. **~'lanza** *nf* offspring. **~lo** *nm* boy

'figo, -a *vedi* **fico, -a**

fi'gura *nf* figure; *(aspetto esteriore)* shape; *(illustrazione)* illustration; **far bella/brutta ~** make a good/ bad impression; **mi hai fatto fare una brutta ~** you made me look a fool; **che ~!** how embarrassing!. **figu'raccia** *nf* bad impression

figu'ralre *vt* represent; *(simboleggiare)* symbolize; *(immaginare)* imagine ● *vi (far figura)* cut a fine figure; *(in lista)* appear, figure. **~rsi** *vr (immaginarsi)* imagine; **~ti!** imagine that!; **posso? – [ma] ~ti!** may I? – of course!. **~'tivo** *a* figurative

figu'rina *nf (da raccolta)* ≃ cigarette card

figu,rl'nista *nmf* dress designer. **~'rino** *nm* fashion sketch. **~'rone** *nm* **fare un ~rone** make an excellent impression

'fila *nf* line; *(di soldati ecc)* file; *(di*

oggetti) row; *(coda)* queue; **di ~** in succession; **fare la ~** queue [up], stand in line *Am*; **in ~ indiana** single file

fila'mento *nm* filament

filan'tropia *nf* philanthropy

fi'lare *vt* spin; *Naut* pay out ● *vi (andarsene)* run away; *(liquido)* trickle; **fila!** *fam* scram!; **~ con** *(fam: amoreggiare)* go out with; **~ dritto** toe the line

filar'monica *nf (orchestra)* orchestra

fila'strocca *nf* rigmarole; *(per bambini)* nursery rhyme

filate'lia *nf* philately

fi'lalto *a* spun; *(ininterrotto)* running; *(continuato)* uninterrupted; **di ~to** *(subito)* immediately ● *nm* yarn. **~'tura** *nf* spinning; *(filanda)* spinning mill

fil di 'ferro *nm* wire

fi'letto *nm (bordo)* border; *(di vite)* thread; *Culin* fillet

fili'ale *a* filial ● *nf Comm* branch

fili'grana *nf* filigree; *(su carta)* watermark

film *nm inv* film. **~ giallo** thriller. **~ a lungo metraggio** feature film

fil'malre *vt* film. **~to** *nm* short film. **fil'mino** *nm* cine film

'filo *nm* thread; *(tessile)* yarn; *(metallico)* wire; *(di lama)* edge; *(venatura)* grain; *(di perle)* string; *(d'erba)* blade; *(di luce)* ray; **con un ~ di voce** in a whisper; **per e per segno** in detail, **fare il ~ a qcne** fancy sb; **perdere il ~** lose the thread. **~ spinato** barbed wire

filobus *nm inv* trolleybus

filodiffusi'one *nf* cable radio

fi'lone *nm* vein; *(di pane)* long loaf

filoso'fia *nf* philosophy. **fi'losofo, -a** *nmf* philosopher

fil'trare *vt* filter. **'filtro** *nm* filter

'filza *nf* string

fin *vedi* **fine, fino'**

fi'nalle *a* final ● *nm* end ● *nf Sport* final. **fina'lista** *nmf* finalist. **~ità** *nf inv* finality; *(scopo)* aim.

~'mente *adv* at last; (*in ultimo*) finally

fi'nanz|a *nf* finance; ~i'ario *a* financial. ~i'ere *nm* financier; (*guardia di finanza*) customs officer. ~ia'mento *nm* funding

finanzi'a|re *vt* fund, finance. ~'tore, ~'trice *nmf* backer

finché *conj* until; (*per tutto il tempo che*) as long as

'fine *a* fine; (*sottile*) thin; (*udito, vista*) keen; (*raffinato*) refined ● *nf* end; alla ~ in the end; alla fin ~ after all; in fin dei conti when all's said and done; te lo dico a fin di bene I'm telling you for your own good; senza ~ endless ● *nm* aim. ~ settimana weekend

fi'nestra *nf* window. fine'strella *nf di aiuto* Comput help window, help box. fine'strino *nm* Rail, Auto window

fi'nezza *nf* fineness; (*sottigliezza*) thinness; (*raffinatezza*) refinement

'finger|e *vt* pretend; feign (*affetto ecc*). ~si *vr* pretend to be

fini'menti *nmpl* finishing touches; (*per cavallo*) harness *sg*

fini'mondo *nm* end of the world; *fig* pandemonium

fi'ni|re *vt/i* finish, end; (*smettere*) stop; (*diventare, andare a finire*) end up; ~scila! stop it!. ~to *a* finished; (*abile*) accomplished. ~'tura *nf* finish

finlan'dese *a* Finnish ● *nmf* Finn ● *nm* (*lingua*) Finnish

Fin'landia *nf* Finland

'fino[1] *prep* ~ a till, until; (*spazio*) as far as; ~ all'ultimo to the last; fin da (*tempo*) since; (*spazio*) from; fin qui as far as here; fin troppo too much; ~ a che punto how far

'fino[2] *a* fine; (*acuto*) subtle; (*puro*) pure

fi'nocchio *nm* fennel; (*fam: omosessuale*) poof

fi'nora *adv* so far, up till now

'finta *nf* pretence, sham; Sport feint; far ~ di pretend to; far ~ di

niente act as if nothing had happened; per ~ (*per scherzo*) for a laugh

'finto, -a *pp di* fingere ● *a* false; (*artificiale*) artificial; fare il ~o tonto act dumb

finzi'one *nf* pretence

fi'occo *nm* bow; (*di neve*) flake; (*nappa*) tassel; coi fiocchi *fig* excellent. ~ di neve snowflake

fi'ocina *nf* harpoon

fi'oco *a* weak; (*luce*) dim

fi'onda *nf* catapult

fio'raio, -a *nmf* florist

fiorda'liso *nm* cornflower

fi'ordo *nm* fiord

fi'ore *nm* flower; (*parte scelta*) cream; fiori *pl* (*nelle carte*) clubs; a fior d'acqua on the surface of the water; fior di (*abbondanza*) a lot of; ha i nervi a fior di pelle his nerves are on edge; a fiori flowery

fioren'tino *a* Florentine

fio'retto *nm* (*scherma*) foil; Relig act of mortification

fio'rire *vi* flower; (*albero:*) blossom; *fig* flourish

fio'rista *nmf* florist

fiori'tura *nf* (*di albero*) blossoming

fi'otto *nm* scorrere a fiotti pour out; piove a fiotti the rain is pouring down

Fi'renze *nf* Florence

'firma *nf* signature; (*nome*) name

fir'ma|re *vt* sign. ~'tario, -a *nmf* signatory. ~to *a* (*abito, borsa*) designer *attrib*

fisar'monica *nf* accordion

fi'scale *a* fiscal

fischi'are *vi* whistle ● *vt* whistle; (*in segno di disapprovazione*) boo

fischiet't|are *vt* whistle. ~io *nm* whistling

fischi'etto *nm* whistle. 'fischio *nm* whistle

'fisco *nm* treasury; (*tasse*) taxation; il ~ the taxman

'fisica *nf* physics

fisica'mente *adv* physically

'fisico, -a *a* physical ● *nmf* physicist ● *nm* physique

'**fisima** nf whim

fisio|**lo**'**gia** nf physiology. **~**'**logico** a physiological

fisiono'**mia** nf features, face; (di paesaggio) appearance

fisiotera'**pi**|**a** nf physiotherapy. **~sta** nmf physiotherapist

fis'**sa**|**re** vt fix, fasten; (guardare fissamente) stare at; arrange (appuntamento, ora). **~rsi** vr (stabilirsi) settle; (fissare lo sguardo) stare; **~rsi su** (ostinarsi) set one's mind on; **~rsi di fare qcsa** become obsessed with doing sth. **~to** nm (persona) person with an obsession. **~zi**'**one** nf fixation; (ossessione) obsession

'**fisso** a fixed; **un lavoro ~** a regular job; **senza fissa dimora** of no fixed abode

'**fitta** nf sharp pain

fit'**tizio** a fictitious

'**fitto**[1] a thick; **~** di full of ● nm depth

'**fitto**[2] nm (affitto) rent; **dare a ~** let; **prendere a ~** rent; (noleggiare) hire

fiu'**mana** nf swollen river; fig stream

fi'**ume** nm river; fig stream

fiu'**tare** vt smell. **fi**'**uto** nm [sense of] smell; fig nose

'**flaccido** a flabby

fla'**cone** nm bottle

fla'**gello** nm scourge

fla'**grante** a flagrant; **in ~** in the act

fla'**nella** nf flannel

'**flash** nm inv Journ newsflash

'**flauto** nm flute

'**flebile** a feeble

'**flemma** nf calm; Med phlegm. **flem**'**matico** a phlegmatic

fles'**sibil**|**e** a flexible. **~ità** nf flexibility

fless|**i**'**one** nf (del busto in avanti) forward bend

'**flesso** pp di **flettere**

fless'**uoso** a supple

'**flettere** vt bend

flir'**tare** vi flirt

F.lli abbr (**fratelli**) Bros

'**floppy disk** nm inv floppy disk

'**flora** nf flora

'**florido** a flourishing

'**floscio** a limp; (flaccido) flabby

'**flotta** nf fleet. **flot**'**tiglia** nf flotilla

flu'**ente** a fluent

flu'**ido** nm fluid

flu'**ire** vi flow

fluore'**scente** a fluorescent

flu'**oro** nm fluorine

'**flusso** nm flow; Med flux; (del mare) flood[-tide]; **~ e riflusso** ebb and flow

fluttu'**ante** a fluctuating

fluttu'**a**|**re** vi (prezzi, moneta:) fluctuate. **~zi**'**one** nf fluctuation

fluvi'**ale** a river

fo'**bia** nf phobia

'**foca** nf seal

fo'**caccia** nf (pane) flat bread; (dolce) ≈ raisin bread

fo'**cale** a (distanza, punto) focal.

focaliz'**zare** vt get into focus (fotografia); focus (attenzione); define (problema)

'**foce** nf mouth

foco'**laio** nm Med focus; fig centre

foco'**lare** nm hearth; (caminetto) fireplace; Techn furnace

fo'**coso** a fiery

foder|**a** nf lining; (di libro) dustjacket; (di poltrona ecc) loose cover. **fode**'**rare** vt line; cover (libro). **~o** nm sheath

'**foga** nf impetuosity

foggi|**a** nf fashion; (maniera) manner; (forma) shape. **~**'**are** vt mould

'**fogli**|**a** nf leaf; (di metallo) foil, **~ame** nm foliage

fogli'**etto** nm (pezzetto di carta) piece of paper

'**foglio** nm sheet; (pagina) leaf. **~ elettronico** Comput spreadsheet. **~ rosa** provisional driving licence

'**fogna** nf sewer. **~**'**tura** nf sewerage

fo'**lata** nf gust

fol'clo|re nm folklore. ~'**ristico** a folk; (bizzarro) weird

folgo'ra|re vi (splendere) shine ● vt (con un fulmine) strike. ~**zi'one** nf (da fulmine, elettrica) electrocution; (idea) brainwave

'**folgore** nf thunderbolt

'**folla** nf crowd

'**folle** a mad; **in ~** Auto in neutral; **andare in ~** Auto coast

folle'mente adv madly

fol'lia nf madness; **alla ~** (amare) to distraction

'**folto** a thick

fomen'tare vt stir up

fond'ale nm Theat backdrop

fonda'men|ta nfpl foundations. ~'**tale** a fundamental. ~**to** nm (di principio, teoria) foundation

fon'da|re vt establish; base (ragionamento, accusa). ~**to** a (ragionamento) well-founded. ~**zi'one** nf establishment; ~**zioni** pl (di edificio) foundations

fon'delli nmpl **prendere qcno per i ~** fam pull sb's leg

fon'dente a (cioccolato) dark

'**fonder|e** vt/i melt; (colori:) blend. ~**si** vr melt; Comm merge. **fonde'ria** nf foundry

'**fondi** nmpl (denaro) funds; (di caffè) grounds

'**fondo** a deep; **è notte fonda** it's the middle of the night ● nm bottom; (fine) end; (sfondo) background; (indole) nature; (somma di denaro) fund; (feccia) dregs pl; **andare a ~** (nave:) sink; **da cima a ~** from beginning to end; **in ~** after all; **in ~ in ~** deep down; **fino in ~** right to the end; (capire) thoroughly. ~ **d'investimento** investment trust

fondo'tinta nm foundation cream

fon'duta nf fondue made with cheese, milk and eggs

fo'netic|a nf phonetics. ~**o** a phonetic

fon'tana nf fountain

'**fonte** nf spring; fig source ● nm font

fo'raggio nm forage

fo'ra|re vt pierce; punch (biglietto) ● vi puncture. ~**si** vr (gomma, pallone:) go soft

'**forbici** nfpl scissors

forbi'cine nfpl (per le unghie) nail scissors

for'bito a erudite

'**forca** nf fork; (patibolo) gallows pl

for'cella nf fork; (per capelli) hairpin

for'chet|ta nf fork. ~'**tata** nf (quantità) forkful

for'cina nf hairpin

'**forcipe** nm forceps pl

for'cone nm pitchfork

fo'resta nf forest. fore'stale a forest attrib

foresti'ero, -a a foreign ● nmf foreigner

for'fait nm inv fixed price; **dare ~** (abbandonare) give up

'**forfora** nf dandruff

'**forgi|a** nf forge. ~'**are** vt forge

'**forma** nf form; (sagoma) shape; Culin mould; (da calzolaio) last; **essere in ~** be in good form; **a ~ di** in the shape of; **forme** pl (del corpo) figure sg; (convenzioni) appearances

formag'gino nm processed cheese. **for'maggio** nm cheese

for'mal|e a formal. ~**ità** nf inv formality. ~**iz'zarsi** vr stand on ceremony. ~'**mente** adv formally

for'ma|re vt form; (sviluparsi) develop. ~**rsi** vr form; (di libro) format; ~**to** nm size; (di libro) format; ~**to tessera** (fotografia) passport-size

format'tare vt format

formazi'one nf formation; Sport line-up. ~ **professionale** vocational training

for'mica[1] nf ant. ~'**caio** nm anthill

For'mica[2] nf (laminato plastico) Formica®

formico'la|re vi (braccio ecc:) tingle; ~**are di** be swarming with; **mi ~a la mano** I have pins and needles in my hand. ~**io** nm swarming; (*di braccio ecc*) pins and needles *pl*

formi'dabile *a* (*tremendo*) formidable; (*eccezionale*) tremendous

for'mina *nf* mould

for'moso *a* shapely

'formula *nf* formula. **formu'lare** *vt* formulate; (*esprimere*) express

for'nace *nf* furnace; (*per laterizi*) kiln

for'naio *nm* baker; (*negozio*) bakery

for'nello *nm* stove; (*di pipa*) bowl

for'nire *vt* supply (**di** with). ~**'tore** *nm* supplier. ~**'tura** *nf* supply

'forno *nm* oven; (*panetteria*) bakery; **al** ~ roast. ~ **a microonde** microwave [oven]

'foro *nm* hole; (*romano*) forum; (*tribunale*) [law] court

'forse *adv* perhaps, maybe; **essere in** ~ be in doubt

forsen'nato, -a *a* mad ● *nmf* madman; madwoman

'forte *a* strong; (*colore*) bright; (*suono*) loud; (*resistente*) tough; (*spesa*) considerable; (*dolore*) severe; (*pioggia*) heavy; (*a tennis, calcio*) good; (*fam: simpatico*) great; (*taglia*) large ● *adv* strongly; (*parlare*) loudly; (*velocemente*) fast; (*piovere*) heavily ● *nm* (*fortezza*) fort; (*specialità*) strong point

for'tezza *nf* fortress; (*forza morale*) fortitude

fortifi'care *vt* fortify

for'tino *nm* Mil blockhouse

for'tuito *a* fortuitous; **incontro** ~ chance encounter

for'tuna *nf* fortune; (*successo*) success; (*buona sorte*) luck. **atterraggio di** ~ forced landing; **aver** ~ be lucky; **buona** ~! good luck!; **di** ~ makeshift; **per** ~ luckily.

fortu'nato *a* lucky, fortunate; (*impresa*) successful. ~**ta'mente** *adv* fortunately

fo'runcolo *nm* pimple; (*grosso*) boil

'forza *nf* strength; (*potenza*)

power; (*fisica*) force; **di** ~ by force; **a** ~ **di** by dint of; **con** ~ hard; ~**!** come on!; ~ **di volontà** will-power; ~ **maggiore** circumstances beyond one's control; **la** ~ **pubblica** the police; **per** ~ against one's will; (*naturalmente*) of course; **farsi** ~ bear up; **mare** ~ **8** force 8 gale; **bella** ~**!** *fam* big deall. **le forze armate** the armed forces. ~ **di gravità** [force of] gravity

for'zare *vt* force; (*scassare*) break open, (*sforzare*) strain; ~**to** *a* forced; (*sorriso*) strained ● *nm* convict

forzi'ere *nm* coffer

for'zuto *a* strong

fo'schia *nf* haze

'fosco *a* dark

fo'sfato *nm* phosphate

'fosforo *nm* phosphorus

'fossa *nf* pit; (*tomba*) grave. ~ **biologica** cesspool. **fos'sato** *nm* (*di fortificazione*) moat

fos'setta *nf* dimple

'fossile *nm* fossil

'fosso *nm* ditch; Mil trench

'foto *nf inv fam* photo; **fare delle** ~ take some photos

foto'cellula *nf* photocell

fotocomposizi'one *nf* filmsetting, photocomposition

foto'copia *nf* photocopy. ~**'are** *vt* photocopy. ~**a'trice** *nf* photocopier

foto finish *nm inv* photo finish

foto'genico *a* photogenic

fotogra'fare *vt* photograph. ~**'fia** *nf* (*arte*) photography; (*immagine*) photograph; **fare** ~**fie** take photographs. **foto'grafico** *a* photographic; **macchina fotografica** camera. **fo'tografo, -a** *nmf* photographer

foto'gramma *nm* frame

fotomo'dello, -a *nmf* [photographer's] model

fotomon'taggio *nm* photomontage

fotoro'manzo *nm* photo story

'fotter|e *vt* (*fam: rubare*) nick; *vulg* fuck, screw. **~sene** *vr vulg* not give a fuck

fot'tuto *a* (*fam: maledetto*) bloody

fou'lard *nm inv* scarf

fra *prep* (*in mezzo a due*) between; (*in un insieme*) among; (*tempo, distanza*) in; **detto ~ noi** between you and me; **~ sé e sé** to oneself; **~ l'altro** what's more; **~ breve** soon; **~ quindici giorni** in two weeks' time; **~ tutti, siamo in venti** there are twenty of us altogether

fracas'sar|e *vt* smash. **~si** *vr* shatter

fra'casso *nm* din; (*di cose che cadono*) crash

'fradicio *a* (*bagnato*) soaked; (*guasto*) rotten; **ubriaco ~** blind drunk

'fragil|e *a* fragile; *fig* frail. **~ità** *nf* fragility; *fig* frailty

'fragola *nf* strawberry

fra'gor|e *nm* uproar; (*di cose rotte*) clatter; (*di tuono*) rumble. **~'roso** *a* uproarious; (*tuono*) rumbling; ⟨*suono*⟩ clanging

fra'gran|te *a* fragrant. **~za** *nf* fragrance

frain'ten|dere *vt* misunderstand. **~dersi** *vr* be at cross-purposes. **~so** *pp di* **fraintendere**

frammen'tario *a* fragmentary. **fram'mento** *nm* fragment

'frana *nf* landslide; (*fam: persona*) walking disaster area. **fra'nare** *vi* slide down

franca'mente *adv* frankly

fran'cese *a* French ● *nmf* Frenchman; Frenchwoman ● *nm* (*lingua*) French

fran'chezza *nf* frankness

'Francia *nf* France

'franco' *a* frank; *Comm* free; **farla franca** get away with sth

'franco² *nm* (*moneta*) franc

franco'bollo *nm* stamp

fran'gente *nm* (*onda*) breaker; (*scoglio*) reef; (*fig: momento diffici-*

le) crisis; **in quel ~** given the situation

'frangia *nf* fringe

fra'noso *a* subject to landslides

fran'toio *nm* olive-press

frantu'mar|e, ~si *vt vr* shatter. **fran'tumi** *nmpl* splinters; **andare in frantumi** be smashed to smithereens

frappé *nm inv* milkshake

frap'por|re *vt* interpose. **~si** *vr* intervene

fra'sario *nm* vocabulary; (*libro*) phrase book

'frase *nf* sentence; (*espressione*) phrase. **~ fatta** cliché

'frassino *nm* ash[-tree]

frastagli'a|re *vt* make jagged. **~to** *a* jagged

frastor'na|re *vt* daze. **~to** *a* dazed

frastu'ono *nm* racket

'frate *nm* friar; (*monaco*) monk

fratel'lan|za *nf* brotherhood. **~stro** *nm* half-brother

fra'tel|li *nmpl* (*fratello e sorella*) brother and sister. **~o** *nm* brother

fraterniz'zare *vi* fraternize.

fra'terno *a* brotherly

frat'taglie *nfpl* (*di pollo ecc*) giblets

frat'tanto *adv* in the meantime

frat'tempo *nm* **nel ~** meanwhile, in the meantime

frat'tu|ra *nf* fracture. **~'rare** *vt*, **~'rarsi** *vr* break

fraudo'lento *a* fraudulent

frazi'one *nf* fraction; (*borgata*) hamlet

'frecci|a *nf* arrow; *Auto* indicator. **~'ata** *nf* (*osservazione pungente*) cutting remark

fredda'mente *adv* coldly

fred'dare *vt* cool; (*fig: con sguardo, battuta*) cut down; (*uccidere*) kill

fred'dezza *nf* coldness

'freddo *a & nm* cold; **aver ~** be cold; **fa ~** it's cold

freddo'loso *a* sensitive to cold, chilly

fred'dura *nf* pun

fre'ga|re *vt* rub; (*fam: truffare*)

cheat; *(fam: rubare)* swipe. **~rsene** *fam* not give a damn; **chi se ne frega!** what the heck!. **~si** *vr* rub *(occhi)*. **~ta** *nf* rub. **~'tura** *nf fam (truffa)* swindle; *(delusione)* letdown

'**fregio** *nm Archit* frieze; *(ornamento)* decoration

fre'**mente** *a* quivering

'**frem|ere** *vi* quiver. **~ito** *nm* quiver

fre'**na|re** *vt* brake; *fig* restrain; hold back *(lacrime, impazienza)* ●*vi* brake. **~rsi** *vr* check oneself. **~ta** *nf* **fare una ~ta brusca** hit the brakes

fre**ne'sia** *nf* frenzy; *(desiderio smodato)* craze. fre'**netico** *a* frenzied

'**freno** *nm* brake; *fig* check; **togliere il ~** release the brake; **usare il ~** apply the brake; **tenere a ~** restrain. **~ a mano** handbrake

frequen'**tare** *vt* frequent; attend *(scuola ecc)*; mix with *(persone)*

fre'**quen|te** *a* frequent; **di ~te** frequently. **~za** *nf* frequency; *(assiduità)* attendance

fre'**schezza** *nf* freshness; *(di temperatura)* coolness

'**fresco** *a* fresh; *(temperatura)* cool; **stai ~!** you're for it! ●*nm* coolness; *(di luogo)* cool; **mettere/tenere in ~** put/keep in a cool place

'**fretta** *nf* hurry, haste; **aver ~** be in a hurry; **far ~ a qcno** hurry sb; **in ~ e furia** in a great hurry. frettolosa'**mente** *adv* hurriedly. fretto'**loso** *a (persona)* in a hurry; *(lavoro)* rushed, hurried

fri'**abile** *a* crumbly

'**friggere** *vt* fry, **vai a farti ~!** get lost! ●*vi* sizzle

friggi'**trice** *nf* chip pan

frigi**dità** *nf* frigidity. '**frigido** *a* frigid

fri'**gnare** *vi* whine

'**frigo** *nm* fridge

frigo'**bar** *nm inv* minibar

frigo'**rifero** *a* refrigerating ●*nm* refrigerator

fringu'**ello** *nm* chaffinch

frit'**tata** *nf* omelette

frit'**tella** *nf* fritter; *(fam: macchia d'unto)* grease stain

'**fritto** *pp* di **friggere** ●*a* fried; **essere ~** be done for ●*nm* fried food. **~ misto** mixed fried fish/vegetables. frit'**tura** *nf (pietanza)* fried dish

frivo'**lezza** *nf* frivolity. '**frivolo** *a* frivolous

frizio'**nare** *vt* rub. frizi'**one** *nf* friction; *Mech* clutch; *(di pelle)* rub

friz'**zante** *a* fizzy; *(vino)* sparkling; *(aria)* bracing

'**frizzo** *nm* gibe

fro'**dare** *vt* defraud

'**frode** *nf* fraud. **~ fiscale** tax evasion

'**frollo** *a* tender; *(selvaggina)* high; *(persona)* spineless; **pasta frolla** short[crust] pastry

'**fronda** *nf* [leafy] branch; *fig* rebellion. fron'**doso** *a* leafy

fron'**tale** *a* frontal; *(scontro)* head-on

'**fronte** *nf* forehead; *(di edificio)* front; **di ~** opposite; **di ~ a** opposite, facing; *(a paragone)* compared with; **far ~ a** face ●*nm Mil, Pol* front. **~ggiare** *vt* face

fronte'**spizio** *nm* title page

fronti'**era** *nf* frontier, border

fron'**tone** *nm* pediment

'**fronzolo** *nm* frill

'**frotta** *nf (di animali)* flock

frot'**tola** *nf* fib; frot'**tole** *pl* nonsense *sg*

fru'**gale** *a* frugal

fru'**gare** *vi* rummage ●*vt* search

frul'**la|re** *vt Culin* whisk ●*vi (ali)* whirr. **~to** *nm* **~to di frutta** fruit drink with milk and crushed ice. **~'tore** *nm* [electric] mixer. frul'**lino** *nm* whisk

fru'**mento** *nm* wheat

frusci'**are** *vi* rustle

fru'scio nm rustle; (radio, giradischi) background noise; (di acque) murmur

'frusta nf whip; (frullino) whisk

fru'sta|re vt whip. ~ta nf lash. fru'stino nm riding crop

fru'stra|re vt frustrate. ~to a frustrated. ~zi'one nf frustration

'frutt|a nf fruit; (portata) dessert. frut'tare vi bear fruit ● vt yield. frut'teto nm orchard. ~i'vendolo, -a nmf greengrocer. ~o nm anche fig fruit; Fin yield; ~i di bosco fruits of the forest. ~i di mare seafood sg. ~u'oso a profitable

f.to abbr (firmato) signed

fu a (defunto) late; il ~ signor Rossi the late Mr Rossi

fuci'la|re vt shoot. ~ta nf shot

fu'cile nm rifle

fu'cina nf forge

'fucsia nf fuchsia

'fuga nf escape; (perdita) leak; Mus fugue; darsi alla ~ take to flight

fu'gace a fleeting

fug'gevole a short-lived

fuggi'asco, -a nmf fugitive

fuggi'fuggi nm stampede

fug'gi|re vi flee; (innamorati:) elope; fig fly. ~'tivo, -a nmf fugitive

'fulcro nm fulcrum

ful'gore nm splendour

fu'liggine nf soot

fulmi'nar|e vt strike by lightning; (con sguardo) look daggers at; (con scarica elettrica) electrocute. ~si vr burn out. 'fulmine nm lightning. ful'mineo a rapid

'fulvo a tawny

fumai'olo nm funnel; (di casa) chimney

fu'ma|re vt/i smoke; (in ebollizione) steam. ~'tore, ~'trice nmf smoker; non fumatori nonsmoker, non-smoking

fu'metto nm comic strip; fumetti pl comics

'fumo nm smoke; (vapore) steam;

fig hot air; andare in ~ vanish.

fu'moso a (ambiente) smoky; (discorso) vague

fu'nambolo, -a nmf tightrope walker

'fune nf rope; (cavo) cable

'funebre a funeral; (cupa) gloomy

fune'rale nm funeral

fu'nereo a (aria) funereal

fu'nesto a sad

'fungere vi ~ da act as

'fungo nm mushroom; Bot, Med fungus

funico'lare nf funicular [railway]

funi'via nf cableway

funzio'nal|e a functional. ~ità nf functionality

funziona'mento nm functioning

funzio'nare vi work, function; ~ da (fungere da) act as

funzio'nario nm official

funzi'one nf function; (carica) office; Relig service; entrare in ~ take up office

fu'oco nm fire; (fisica, fotografia) focus; far ~ fire; dar ~ a set fire to; prendere ~ catch fire. fuochi pl d'artificio fireworks. ~ di paglia nine-days' wonder

fuorché prep except

fu'ori adv out; (all'esterno) outside; (all'aperto) outdoors; andare di ~ (traboccare) spill over; essere di sé be beside oneself; essere in ~ (sporgere) stick out; far ~ fam do in; ~ luogo (inopportuno) out of place; ~ mano (out of the way); ~ moda old-fashioned; ~ pasto between meals; ~ pericolo out of danger; ~ questione out of the question; ~ uso out of use ● nm outside

fuori'bordo nm speedboat (with outboard motor)

fuori'classe nmf inv champion

fuorigi'oco nm & adv offside

fuori'legge nmf outlaw

fuori'serie a custom-made ● nf Auto custom-built model

fuori'strada nm off-road vehicle

fuorvi'are *vt* lead astray ● *vi* go astray
furbacchi'one *nm* crafty old devil
furbe'ria *nf* cunning. **fur'bizia** *nf* cunning
'**furbo** *a* cunning; (*intelligente*) clever; (*astuto*) shrewd; **bravo ~l** nice one!; **fare il ~** try to be clever
fu'rente *a* furious
fur'fante *nm* scoundrel
furgon'cino *nm* delivery van. **fur'gone** *nm* van
'**furia** *nf* fury; (*fretta*) haste; **a ~ di** by dint of. **~'bondo, ~'oso** *a* furious
fu'rore *nm* fury; (*veemenza*) frenzy; **far ~** be all the rage. **~ggi'are** *vi* be a great success
furtiva'mente *adv* covertly. **fur'tivo** *a* furtive
'**furto** *nm* theft; (*con scasso*) burglary; **commettere un ~** steal
'**fusa** *nfpl* **fare le ~** purr
fu'scello *nm* (*di legno*) twig; (*di paglia*) straw; **sei un ~** you're as light as a feather
fu'seaux *mpl* leggings
fu'sibile *nm* fuse
fusi'one *nf* fusion; **Comm** merger
'**fuso** *pp di* **fondere** ● *a* melted ● *nm* spindle; **a ~** spindle-shaped. **~ orario** time zone
fusoli'era *nf* fuselage
fu'stagno *nm* corduroy
fu'stino *nm* (*di detersivo*) box
'**fusto** *nm* (*di albero*) stem; (*tronco*) trunk; (*recipiente di metallo*) drum; (*di legno*) barrel
'**futile** *a* futile
fu'turo *a & nm* future

Gg

gab'bar|e *vt* cheat. **~si** *vr* **~si di** make fun of
'**gabbia** *nf* cage; (*da imballaggio*) crate. **~ degli imputati** dock. **~ toracica** rib cage
gabbi'ano *nm* [sea]gull
gabi'netto *nm* (*di medico*) consulting room; **Pol** cabinet; (*toletta*) lavatory; (*laboratorio*) laboratory
'**gaffe** *nf inv* blunder
gagli'ardo *a* vigorous
gai'ezza *nf* gaiety. '**gaio** *a* cheerful
'**gala** *nf* gala
ga'lante *a* gallant. **~'ria** *nf* gallantry. **galantu'omo** *nm* (*pl* **galantuomini**) gentleman
ga'lassia *nf* galaxy
gala'teo *nm* [good] manners *pl*; (*trattato*) book of etiquette
gale'otto *nm* (*rematore*) galleyslave; (*condannato*) convict
ga'lera *nf* (*nave*) galley; *fam* prison
'**galla** *nf* **Bot** gall; **a ~** *adv* afloat; **venire a ~** surface
galleggi'ante *a* floating ● *nm* craft; (*boa*) float
galleggi'are *vi* float
galle'ria *nf* (*traforo*) tunnel; (*d'arte*) gallery; **Theat** circle; (*arcata*) arcade. **~ d'arte** art gallery
'**Galles** *nm* Wales. **gal'lese** *a* welsh ● *nm* Welshman; (*lingua*) Welsh ● *nf* Welshwoman
gal'letto *nm* cockerel; **fare il ~** show off
gal'lina *nf* hen
gal'lismo *nm* machismo
'**gallo** *nm* cock
gal'lone *nm* stripe; (*misura*) gallon
galop'pare *vi* gallop. **ga'loppo** *nm* gallop, **al galoppo** at a gallop
galvaniz'zare *vt* galvanize
'**gamba** *nf* leg; (*di lettera*) stem; **a quattro gambe** on all fours;

darsela a gambe take to one's heels; **essere in** ~ (*essere forte*) be strong; (*capace*) be smart

gamba'letto *nm* pop sock

gambe'retto *nm* shrimp. **'gambero** *nm* prawn; (*di fiume*) crayfish

'gambo *nm* stem; (*di pianta*) stalk

'gamma *nf Mus* scale; *fig* range

ga'nascia *nf* jaw; **ganasce** *pl* **del freno** brake shoes

'gancio *nm* hook

'ganghero *nm* **uscire dai gangheri** *fig* get into a temper

'gara *nf* competition; (*di velocità*) race; **fare a** ~ compete. ~ **d'appalto** call for tenders

ga'rage *nm inv* garage

ga'ran|te *nmf* guarantor. ~**'tire** *vt* guarantee; (*rendersi garante*) vouch for; (*assicurare*) assure. ~**'zia** *nf* guarantee; **in** ~ under guarantee

gar'ba|re *vi* like; **non mi garba** I don't like it. ~**to** *a* courteous

'garbo *nm* courtesy; (*grazia*) grace; **con** ~ graciously

gareggi'are *vi* compete

garga'nella *nf* **a** ~ from the bottle

garga'rismo *nm* gargle; **fare i gargarismi** gargle

ga'rofano *nm* carnation

gar'rire *vi* chirp

'garza *nf* gauze

gar'zone *nm* boy. ~ **di stalla** stable-boy

gas *nm inv* gas; **dare** ~ *Auto* accelerate; **a tutto** ~ flat out. ~ **lacrimogeno** tear gas. ~ **di scarico** *pl* exhaust fumes

gas'dotto *nm* natural gas pipeline

ga'solio *nm* diesel oil

ga'sometro *nm* gasometer

gas's|are *vt* aerate; (*uccidere col gas*) gas. ~**ato** *a* gassy. ~**oso, -a** *a* gassy; (*bevanda*) fizzy ● *nf* lemonade

'gastrico *a* gastric. **ga'strite** *nf* gastritis

gastro|no'mia *nf* gastronomy. ~**'nomico** *a* gastronomic. **ga'stronomo, -a** *nmf* gourmet

'gatta *nf* **una** ~ **da pelare** a headache

gatta'buia *nf hum* clink

gat'tino, -a *nmf* kitten

'gatto, -a *nmf* cat. ~ **delle nevi** snowmobile

gat'toni *adv* on all fours

ga'vetta *nf* mess tin; **fare la** ~ rise through the ranks

gay *a inv* gay

'gazza *nf* magpie

gaz'zarra *nf* racket

gaz'zella *nf* gazelle; *Auto* police car

gaz'zetta *nf* gazette

gaz'zosa *nf* clear lemonade

'geco *nm* gecko

ge'la|re *vt/i* freeze. ~**ta** *nf* frost

gela'ta|io, -a *nmf* ice-cream seller; (*negozio*) ice-cream shop. ~**e'ria** *nf* ice-cream parlour. ~**'e'ra** *nf* ice-cream maker

gela'ti|na *nf* gelatine; (*dolce*) jelly. ~**na di frutta** fruit jelly. ~**'noso** *a* gelatinous

ge'lato *a* frozen ● *nm* ice-cream

'gelido *a* freezing

'gelo *nm* (*freddo intenso*) freezing cold; (*brina*) frost; *fig* chill

ge'lone *nm* chilblain

gelosa'mente *adv* jealously

gelo'sia *nf* jealousy. **ge'loso** *a* jealous

'gelso *nm* mulberry[-tree]

gelso'mino *nm* jasmine

gemel'laggio *nm* twinning

ge'mello, -a *a & nmf* twin; (*di polsino*) cuff-link; **Gemelli** *pl Astr* Gemini *sg*

'gem|ere *vi* groan; (*tubare*) coo. ~**ito** *nm* groan

'gemma *nf* gem; *Bot* bud

'gene *nm* gene

genea'lo'gia *nf* genealogy

gene'ra|le' *a* general; **spese** ~**i** overheads

gene'rale² *nm Mil* general

generalità *nf* (*qualità*) generality, general nature; ~ *pl* (*dati personali*) particulars

generaliz'za|re *vt* generalize.

~zi'one *nf* generalization.
general'mente *adv* generally
gene'ra|re *vt* give birth to; (*causare*) breed; *Techn* generate. ~'tore *nm Techn* generator. ~zi'one *nf* generation

'genere *nm* kind; *Biol* genus; *Gram* gender; (*letterario, artistico*) genre; (*prodotto*) product; **il ~ umano** mankind; **in ~** generally. **generi** *pl* **alimentari** provisions
generica'mente *adv* generically.
ge'nerico *a* generic; **medico generico** general practitioner
'genero *nm* son-in-law
generosità *nf* generosity. gene'roso *a* generous
'genesi *nf* genesis
ge'netico, -a *a* genetic ● *nf* genetics
gen'giva *nf* gum
geni'ale *a* ingenious; (*congeniale*) congenial
'genio *nm* genius; **andare a ~ be** to one's taste. **~ civile** civil engineering. **~ [militare]** Engineers
geni'tale *a* genital. **genitali** *nmpl* genitals
geni'tore *nm* parent
gen'naio *nm* January
'Genova *nf* Genoa
gen'taglia *nf* rabble
'gente *nf* people *pl*
gen'tile *a* kind; **G~e Signore** (*in lettere*) Dear Sir. **gen'tilezza** *nf* kindness; **per gentilezza** (*per favore*) please. **~'mente** *adv* kindly. **~'uomo** (*pl* **~'uomini**) *nm* gentleman
genu'ino *a* genuine; (*cibo, prodotto*) natural
geogra'fia *nf* geography. geo'grafico *a* geographical. ge'ografo, -a *nmf* geographer
geolo'gia *nf* geology. geo'logico *a* geological. ge'ologo, -a *nmf* geologist
ge'ometra *nmf* surveyor
geome'tria *nf* geometry. geo'metrico *a* geometric[al]
ge'ranio *nm* geranium

gerar'chia *nf* hierarchy. ge'rarchico hierarchic[al]
ge'rente *nm* manager ● *nf* manageress
'gergo *nm* slang; (*di professione ecc*) jargon
geria'tria *nf* geriatrics *sg*
Ger'mania *nf* Germany
'germe *nm* germ; (*fig: principio*) seed
germogli'are *vi* sprout. ger'moglio *nm* sprout
gero'glifico *nm* hieroglyph
'gesso *nm* chalk; (*Med, scultura*) plaster
gestazi'one *nf* gestation
gestico'lare *vi* gesticulate
gesti'one *nf* management
ge'sti|re *vi* manage. **~si** *vr* budget one's time and money
'gesto *nm* gesture; (*azione pl nf* gesta) deed
ge'store *nm* manager
Gesù *nm* Jesus. **~ bambino** baby Jesus
gesu'ita *nm* Jesuit
get'ta|re *vt* throw; (*scagliare*) fling; (*emettere*) spout; *Techn, fig* cast; **~re via** throw away. **~rsi** *vr* throw oneself; **~rsi in** (*fiume*) flow into. **~ta** *nf* throw; *Techn* casting
'getto *nm* throw; (*di liquidi, gas*) jet; **a ~ continuo** in a continuous stream; **di ~** straight off
getto'nato *a* (*canzone*) popular.
get'tone *nm* token (*per giochi*) counter
ghe'pardo *nm* cheetah
ghettiz'zare *vt* ghettoize. 'ghetto *nm* ghetto
ghiacci'aio *nm* glacier
ghiacci'a|re *vt/i* freeze. **~to** *a* frozen; (*freddissimo*) ice-cold
ghi'acc|io *nm* ice; *Auto* black ice. **~olo** *nm* icicle; (*gelato*) ice lolly
ghi'aia *nf* gravel
ghi'anda *nf* acorn
ghi'andola *nf* gland
ghigliot'tina *nf* guillotine

ghi'gnare *vi* sneer. **'ghigno** *nm* sneer

ghi'ot|to *a* greedy, gluttonous; (*appetitoso*) appetizing. **~'tone, -a** *nmf* glutton. **~tone'ria** *nf* (*qualità*) gluttony; (*cibo*) tasty morsel

ghir'landa *nf* (*corona*) wreath; (*di fiori*) garland

'ghiro *nm* dormouse; **dormire come un ~** sleep like a log

'ghisa *nf* cast iron

già *adv* already; (*un tempo*) formerly; **~!** indeed!; **~ da ieri** since yesterday

gi'acca *nf* jacket. **~ a vento** windcheater

giacché *conj* since

giac'cone *nm* jacket

gia'cere *vi* lie

giaci'mento *nm* deposit. **~ di petrolio** oil deposit

gia'cinto *nm* hyacinth

gi'ada *nf* jade

giagg'iolo *nm* iris

giagu'aro *nm* jaguar

gial'lastro *a* yellowish

gi'allo *a* & *nm* yellow; [**libro**] ~ thriller

Giap'pone *nm* Japan. **giappo'nese** *a* & *nmf* Japanese

giardi'n|aggio *nm* gardening. **~i'ere, -a** *nmf* gardener ● *nf* Auto estate car; (*sottaceti*) pickles *pl*

giar'dino *nm* garden. **~ d'infanzia** kindergarten. **~ pensile** roof-garden. **~ zoologico** zoo

giarretti'era *nf* garter

giavel'lotto *nm* javelin

gi'gan|te *a* gigantic ● *nm* giant. **~'tesco** *a* gigantic

gigantogra'fia *nf* blow-up

'giglio *nm* lily

gilè *nm inv* waistcoat

gin *nm inv* gin

gineco|lo'gia *nf* gynaecology. **~'logico** *a* gynaecological. **gine'cologo, -a** *nmf* gynaecologist

gi'nepro *nm* juniper

gi'nestra *nf* broom

gingil'larsi *vr* fiddle; (*perder tem-*

po) potter. **gin'gillo** *nm* plaything; (*ninnolo*) knick-knack

gin'nasio *nm* (*scuola*) ≈ grammar school

gin'nast|a *nmf* gymnast. **~ica** *nf* gymnastics; (*esercizi*) exercises *pl*

ginocchi'ata *nf* prendere una **~** bang one's knee

gi'nocchi|o *nm* (*pl m* **ginocchi** *o f* **ginocchia**) knee; **in ~o** on one's knees; **mettersi in ~o** kneel down; (*per supplicare*) go down on one's knees; **al ~o** (*gonna*) knee-length. **~'oni** *adv* kneeling

gio'care *vt/i* play; (*giocherellare*) toy; (*d'azzardo*) gamble; (*puntare*) stake; (*ingannare*) trick. **~rsi la carriera** throw one's career away. **~'tore, ~'trice** *nmf* player; (*d'azzardo*) gambler

gio'cattolo *nm* toy

giocherel'l|are *vi* toy; (*nervosamente*) fiddle. **~one** *a* skittish

gi'oco *nm* game; (*di bambini, Techn*) play; (*d'azzardo*) gambling; (*scherzo*) joke; (*insieme di pezzi ecc*) set; **essere in ~** be at stake; **fare il doppio ~ con** qcno double-cross sb

giocol'iere *nm* juggler

gio'coso *a* playful

gi'ogo *nm* yoke

gi'oia *nf* joy; (*gioiello*) jewel; (*appellativo*) sweetie

gioiell'i|eria *nf* jeweller's [shop]. **~i'ere, -a** *nmf* jeweller; (*negozio*) jeweller's. **gioi'ello** *nm* jewel; **gioielli** *pl* jewellery

gioi'oso *a* joyous

gio'ire *vi* **~ per** rejoice at

Gior'dania *nf* Jordan

giorna'laio, -a *nmf* newsagent, newsdealer

gior'nale *nm* [news]paper; (*diario*) journal. **~ di bordo** logbook. **~ radio** news bulletin

giornali'ero *a* daily ● *nm* (*per sciare*) day pass

giorna'lino *nm* comic

giorna'lis|mo *nm* journalism. **~ta** *nmf* journalist

giornal'mente adv daily

gior'nata nf day; (in ~ today; **vive-re alla ~** live from day to day

gi'orno nm day; **al ~** per day; **al ~ d'oggi** nowadays; **di ~** by day; **in pieno ~** in broad daylight; **un ~ sì, un ~** no every other day

gi'ostra nf merry-go-round

giova'mento nm **trarre ~ da** derive benefit from

gi'ova|ne a young; (giovanile) youthful ●nm youth, young man ●nf girl, young woman. ~**nile** a youthful. ~**notto** nm young man

giov'va|re vi ~**e** a be useful to; (far bene a) be good for. ~**si** vr ~**si di** avail oneself of

giovedì nm inv Thursday. ~ **grasso** last Thursday before Lent

gioventù nf youth; (i giovani) young people pl

giovi'ale a jovial

giovi'nezza nf youth

gira'dischi nm inv record-player

gi'raffa nf giraffe; Cinema boom

gi'randola nf (fuoco d'artificio) Catherine wheel; (giocattolo) windmill; (banderuola) weather-cock

gi'ra|re vt turn; (andare intorno, visitare) go round; Comm endorse; Cinema shoot ●vi turn; (aerei, uccelli:) circle; (andare in giro) wander; **far ~ le scatole a qcno** fam drive sb round the twist; ~**re al largo** steer clear. ~**re** vr turn [round]; **mi gira la testa** I feel dizzy. ~**ta** nf turn; Comm endorsement; (in macchina ecc) ride; **fare una ~ta** (a piedi) go for a walk; (in macchina) go for a ride

girar'rosto nm spit

gira'sole nm sunflower

gira'volta nf spin; fig U-turn

gi'rello nm (per bambini) babywalker; Culin topside

gi'revole a revolving

gi'rino nm tadpole

'giro nm turn; (circolo) circle; (percorso) round; (viaggio) tour; (passeggiata) short walk; (in macchina) drive; (in bicicletta) ride; (circolazione di denaro) circulation; **nel ~ di un mese** within a month; **prendere in ~ qcno** pull sb's leg; **senza giri di parole** without beating about the bush; **a ~ di posta** by return mail. ~ **d'affari** Comm turnover. ~ **[della] manica** armhole. **giri pl al minuto** rpm. ~ **turistico** sightseeing tour. ~ **vita** waist measurement

giro'collo nm choker; **a ~** crewneck

gi'rone nm round

gironzo'lare vi wander about

giro'tondo nm ring-a-ring-o'-roses

girova'gare vi wander about.

gi'rovago nm wanderer

'gita nf trip; **andare in ~** go on a trip. ~ **scolastica** school trip.

gi'tante nmf tripper

giù adv down; (sotto) below; (dabbasso) downstairs; **a testa in ~** a capofitto) headlong; **essere ~** be down; (di salute) be run down; ~ **di corda** down; ~ **di lì, su per ~** more or less; **non andare ~ a qcno** stick in sb's craw

gi'ub|ba nf jacket; Mil tunic. ~**botto** nm bomber jacket, jerkin

giudi'care vt judge; (ritenere) consider

gi'udice nm judge. ~ **conciliatore** justice of the peace. ~ **di gara** umpire. ~ **di linea** linesman

giu'di|zio nm judge[ment]; (opinione) opinion; (senno) wisdom; (processo) trial; (sentenza) sentence; **mettere ~** come more wise. ~**oso** a sensible

gi'ugno nm June

giu'menta nf mare

gi'unco nm reed

gi'ungere vi arrive; ~ **a** (riuscire) succeed in ●vt (unire) join

gi'ungla nf jungle

gi'unta nf addition; Mil junta; **per ~** in addition. ~ **comunale** district council

gi'unto pp di giungere ●nm Mech joint

giun'tura nf joint

giuo'care, giu'oco = **giocare, gioco**

giura'mento nm oath; **prestare ~** take the oath

giu'ra|re vt/i swear. **~to, -a** a sworn ● nmf juror

giu'ria nf jury

giu'ridico a legal

giurisdizi'one nf jurisdiction

giurispru'denza nf jurisprudence

giu'rista nmf jurist

giustifi'ca|re vt justify. **~zi'one** nf justification

giu'stizi|a nf justice. **~'are** vt execute. **~'ere** nm executioner

gi'usto a just, fair; (adatto) right; (esatto) exact ● nm (uomo retto) just man; (cosa giusta) right ● adv exactly; **~ ora** just now

glaci'ale a glacial

gla'diolo nm gladiolus

'glassa nf Culin icing

gli def art mpl (before vowel and s + consonant, gn, ps, z) the; vedi **il** ● pron (a lui) [to] him; (a esso) [to] it; (a loro) [to] them

glice'rina nf glycerine

gli'cine nm wisteria

gli'e|lo, -a pron [to] him/her/them; (forma di cortesia) [to] you; **~ chiedo** I'll ask him/her/them/ you; **glie|l'ho prestato** I've lent it to him/her/them/you. **~ne** (di ciò) [of] it; **~ne ho dato un po'** I gave him/her/them/you some

glo'ba|le a global; fig overall. **~'mente** adv globally

'globo nm globe. **~ oculare** eyeball. **~ terrestre** globe

'globulo nm globule; Med corpuscle. **~ bianco** white cell, white corpuscle. **~ rosso** red cell, red corpuscle

'glori|a nf glory. **~'arsi** vr **~arsi di** be proud of. **~'oso** a glorious

glos'sario nm glossary

glu'cosio nm glucose

'gluteo nm buttock

'gnomo nm gnome

gnorri nm **fare lo ~** play dumb

'gobb|a nf hump. **~o, -a** a hunchbacked ● nmf hunchback

'gocci|a nf drop; (di sudore) bead; **è stata l'ultima ~a** it was the last straw. **~o'lare** vi drip. **~o'lio** nm dripping

go'der|e vi (sessualmente) come; **~e di** enjoy. **~sela** have a good time. **~si** or **~si qcsa** enjoy sth

godi'mento nm enjoyment

goffa'mente adv awkwardly. **'goffo** a awkward

'gola nf throat; (ingordigia) gluttony; Geog gorge; (di camino) flue; **avere mal di ~** have a sore throat; **far ~ a qcno** tempt sb

golf nm inv jersey; Sport golf

'golfo nm gulf

golosità nf inv greediness; (cibo) tasty morsel. **go'loso** a greedy

'golpe nm inv coup

gomi'tata nf nudge

'gomito nm elbow; **alzare il ~** raise one's elbow

go'mitolo nm ball

'gomma nf rubber; (colla, da masticare) gum; (pneumatico) tyre. **~ da masticare** chewing gum

gommapi'uma nf foam rubber

gom'mista nm tyre specialist

gom'mone nm [rubber] dinghy

gom'moso a chewy

'gondol|a nf gondola. **~i'ere** nm gondolier

gonfa'lone nm banner

gonfi'abile a inflatable

gonfi'ar|e vi swell ● vt blow up; pump up (pneumatico); (esagerare) exaggerate. **~si** vr swell; (acque) rise. **'gonfio** a swollen; (pneumatico) inflated; **a gonfie vele** splendidly. **gonfi'ore** nm swelling

gongo'la|nte a overjoyed. **~re** vi be overjoyed

'gonna nf skirt. **~ pantalone** culottes pl

'gonzo nm simpleton

gorgheggi'are vi warble. **gor'gheggio** nm warble

'gorgo nm whirlpool

gorgogli'are *vi* gurgle

go'rilla *nm inv* gorilla; *(guardia del corpo)* bodyguard, minder

'gotico *a* & *nm* Gothic

gover'nante *nf* housekeeper

gover'na|re *vt* govern; *(dominare)* rule; *(dirigere)* manage; *(curare)* look after. **~'tivo** *a* government. **~'tore** *nm* governor

go'verno *nm* government; *(dominio)* rule; **al ~** in power

gracchi'are *vi* caw; *(fig: persona:)* screech

graci'dare *vi* croak

'gracile *a* delicate

gra'dasso *nm* braggart

grada'mente *adv* gradually

gradazi'one *nf* gradation. **~ alcoolica** alcohol[ic] content

gra'devol|e *a* agreeable. **~'mente** *adv* pleasantly, agreeably

gradi'mento *nm* liking; **indice di ~** *Radio, TV* popularity rating; **non è di mio ~** it's not to my liking

gradi'nata *nf* flight of steps; *(di stadio)* stand; *(di teatro)* tiers *pl*

gra'dino *nm* step

gra'di|re *vt* like; *(desiderare)* wish. **~to** *a* pleasant; *(bene accetto)* welcome

'grado *nm* degree; *(rango)* rank; **di buon ~** willingly; **essere ln ~ di fare qcsa** be in a position to do sth; *(essere capace a)* be able to do sth

gradu'ale *a* gradual

gradu'a|re *vt* graduate. **~to** *a* graded; *(provvisto di scala graduata)* graduated ● *nm* Mil noncommissioned officer. **~'toria** *nf* list. **~zi'one** *nf* graduation

'graffa *nf* clip; *(segno grafico)* brace

graf'fetta *nf* staple

graffi'a|re *vt* scratch. **~'tura** *nf* scratch

'graffio *nm* scratch

gra'fia *nf* [hand]writing; *(ortografia)* spelling

'grafic|a *nf* graphics; **~a pubblici-**

taria commercial art. **~'a'mente** *adv* in graphics, graphically. **~o** *a* graphic ● *nm* graph; *(persona)* graphic designer

gra'migna *nf* weed

gram'matic|a *nf* grammar. **~'cale** *a* grammatical

'grammo *nm* gram[me]

gran *a vedi* **grande**

'grana *nf* grain; *(formaggio)* parmesan; *(fam: seccatura)* trouble; *(fam: soldi)* readies *pl*

gra'naio *nm* barn

gra'nat|a *nf* Mil grenade; *(frutto)* pomegranate. **~l'ere** *nm* Mil grenadier

Gran Bre'tagna *nf* Great Britain

'granchio *nm* crab; *(fig: errore)* blunder; **prendere un ~** make a blunder

grandango'lare *nm* wide-angle lens

'grande *(a volte* **gran***)* *a (ampio)* large; *(grosso)* big; *(alto)* tall; *(largo)* wide; *(fig: senso morale)* great; *(grandioso)* grand; *(adulto)* grown-up; **ho una gran fame** I'm very hungry; **fa un gran caldo** it is very hot; **in ~** on a large scale; **in gran parte** to a great extent; **non è un gran che** it is nothing much; **un gran ballo** a grand ball ● *nmf (persona adulta)* grown-up; *(persona eminente)* great man/woman. **~ggi'are** *vi* **~ggiare su** tower over; *(darsi arie)* show off

gran'dezza *nf* greatness; *(ampiezza)* largeness; *(larghezza)* width, breadth; *(dimensione)* size; *(fasto)* grandeur; *(prodigalità)* lavishness; **a ~ naturale** life-size

grandi'nare *vi* hail; **grandina** it's hailing. **'grandine** *nf* hail

grandiosità *nf* grandeur. **grandi'oso** *a* grand

gran'duca *nm* grand duke

gra'nello *nm* grain; *(di frutta)* pip

gra'nita *nf* crushed ice drink

gra'nito *nm* granite

'grano *nm* grain; *(frumento)* wheat

gran'turco *nm* maize

'**granulo** nm granule

'**grappa** nf grappa; (morsa) cramp

'**grappolo** nm bunch. ~ **d'uva** bunch of grapes

gras'**setto** a bold [type]

gras'**sezza** nf fatness; (untuosità) greasiness

'**gras|so** a fat; ⟨cibo⟩ fatty; (unto) greasy; ⟨terreno⟩ rich; (grossolano) coarse ●nm fat; (sostanza) grease. ~'**soccio** a plump

'**grata** nf grating. **gra'tella**, **gra'ticola** nf Culin grill

gra'**tifica** nf bonus. ~**zi'one** nf satisfaction

grati'**na|re** vt cook au gratin. ~**to** a au gratin

'**gratis** adv free

grati'**tudine** nf gratitude. '**grato** a grateful; (gradito) pleasant

gratta'**capo** nm trouble

grattaci'**elo** nm skyscraper

grat'**tar|e** vt scratch; (raschiare) scrape; (grattugiare) grate; (fam: rubare) pinch ●vi grate. ~**si** vr scratch oneself

grat'**tugi|a** nf grater. ~'**are** vt grate

gratuita'**mente** adv free [of charge]. **gra'tuito** a free [of charge]; (ingiustificato) gratuitous

gra'**vare** vt burden ●vi ~ **su** weigh on

'**grave** a (pesante) heavy; (serio) serious; (difficile) hard; ⟨voce, suono⟩ low; (fonetica) grave; essere ~ (gravemente ammalato) be seriously ill. ~'**mente** adv seriously, gravely

gravi'**danza** nf pregnancy. '**gravido** a pregnant

gravità nf seriousness; Phys gravity

gravi'**tare** vi gravitate

gra'**voso** a onerous

'**grazi|a** nf grace; (favore) favour; Jur pardon; **entrare nelle ~e di qcno** get into sb's good books. ~'**are** vt pardon

'**grazie** int thank you!, thanks!; ~ **mille!** many thanks!, thanks a lot!

grazi'**oso** a charming; (carino) pretty

'**Grec|ia** nf Greece. **g~o**, **-a** a & nmf Greek

'**gregge** nm flock

'**greggio** a raw ●nm (petrolio) crude [oil]

grembi'**ale**, **grembi'ule** nm apron

'**grembo** nm lap; (utero) womb; fig bosom

gre'**mi|re** vt pack. ~**rsi** vr become crowded (**di** with). ~**to** a packed

'**gretto** a stingy; (di vedute ristrette) narrow-minded

'**grezzo** a = greggio

gri'**dare** vi shout; (di dolore) scream; ⟨animale:⟩ cry ●vt shout

'**grido** nm (pl m **gridi** o f **grida**) shout, cry; (di animale) cry; **l'ultimo ~** the latest fashion; **scrittore di ~** celebrated writer

'**grigio** a & nm grey

'**griglia** nf grill; **alla ~** grilled

gril'**letto** nm trigger

'**grillo** nm cricket; (fig: capriccio) whim

grimal'**dello** nm picklock

grinfia nf fig clutch

'**grin|ta** nf grit. ~'**toso** a determined

'**grinza** nf wrinkle; (di stoffa) crease

grip'**pare** vi Mech seize

gris'**sino** nm bread-stick

'**gronda** nf eaves pl

gron'**daia** nf gutter

gron'**dare** vi pour; (essere bagnato fradicio) be dripping

'**groppa** nf back

'**groppo** nm knot; **avere un ~ alla gola** have a lump in one's throat

gros'**sezza** nf size; (spessore) thickness

gros'**sista** nmf wholesaler

'**grosso** a big, large; (spesso) thick; (grossolano) coarse; (grave) serious ●nm big part; (massa) bulk; **farla grossa** do a stupid thing

grosso‖lanità *nf inv* (*qualità*) coarseness; (*di errore*) seriousness; (*azione, parola*) coarse thing. **~'lano** a coarse; (*errore*) gross

grosso'modo *adv* roughly

'grotta *nf* cave, grotto

grot'tesco a & *nm* grotesque

grovi'era *nmf* Gruyère

gro'viglio *nm* tangle; *fig* muddle

gru *nf inv* (*uccello, edilizia*) crane

'gruccia *nf* (*stampella*) crutch; (*per vestito*) hanger

gru'gni‖re *vi* grunt. **~to** *nm* grunt

'grugno *nm* snout

'grullo a silly

'grumo *nm* clot; (*di farina ecc*) lump. **gru'moso** a lumpy

'gruppo *nm* group; (*comitiva*) party. **~ sanguigno** blood group

gruvi'era *nmf* Gruyère

'gruzzolo *nm* nest-egg

guada'gnare *vt* earn; gain (*tempo, forza ecc*). **gua'dagno** *nm* gain; (*profitto*) profit; (*entrate*) earnings *pl*

gu'ado *nm* ford; **passare a ~** ford

gua'ina *nf* sheath; (*busto*) girdle

gu'aio *nm* trouble; **che ~!** that's just brilliant!; **essere nei guai** be in a fix; **guai a te se lo tocchi** don't you dare touch it!

gua'i‖re *vi* yelp. **~to** *nm* yelp

gu'ancia *nf* cheek. **~ale** *nm* pillow

gu'anto *nm* glove. **guantoni** *pl* [**da boxe**] boxing gloves

guarda'coste *nm inv* coastguard

guarda'linee *nm inv* *Sport* linesman

guar'dar‖e *vt* look at; (*osservare*) watch; (*badare a*) look after; (*dare su*) look out on ● *vi* look; (*essere orientato verso*) face. **~si** *vr* look at oneself; (*con negazione*) beware of; (*astenersi*) refrain from

guarda'rob‖a *nm inv* wardrobe; (*di locale pubblico*) cloakroom. **~'iere, -a** *nmf* cloakroom attendant

gu'ardia *nf* guard; (*poliziotto*) policeman; (*vigilanza*) watch; **es-**

sere di ~ be on guard; (*medico:*) be on duty; **fare la ~ a** keep guard over; **mettere in ~** qcno warn sb; **stare in ~** be on one's guard. **~ carceraria** prison warder. **~ del corpo** bodyguard, minder. **~ di finanza** ≈ Fraud Squad. **~ forestale** forest ranger. **~ medica** duty doctor

guardi'ano, -a *nmf* caretaker. **~ notturno** night watchman

guar'dingo a cautious

guardi'ola *nf* gatekeeper's lodge

guarigl'one *nf* recovery

gua'rire *vt* cure ● *vi* recover; (*ferita:*) heal [up]

guarnigi'one *nf* garrison

guar'ni‖re *vt* trim; *Culin* garnish. **~zi'one** *nf* trimming; *Culin* garnish; *Mech* gasket

guasta'feste *nmf inv* spoilsport

gua'star‖e *vt* spoil; (*rovinare*) ruin; break (*meccanismo*). **~si** *vr* spoil; (*andare a male*) go bad; (*tempo:*) change for the worse; (*meccanismo:*) break down. **gua'sto** a broken; (*ascensore, telefono*) out of order; (*auto*) broken down; (*cibo, dente*) bad ● *nm* breakdown; (*danno*) damage

guazza'buglio *nm* muddle

guaz'zare *vi* wallow

gu'ercio a cross-eyed

gu'erra *nf* war; (*tecnica bellica*) warfare. **~ fredda** Cold War. **~ mondiale** world war. **~afon'daio** *nm* warmonger. **~eggi'are** *vi* wage war. **guerra'resca** a (*di guerra*) war; (*bellicoso*) warlike. **~i'ero** *nm* warrior

guer'rigl‖ia *nf* guerrilla warfare. **~'ero, -a** *nmf* guerrilla

'gufo *nm* owl

'guglia *nf* spire

gu'id‖a *nf* guide; (*direzione*) guidance; (*comando*) leadership; *Auto* driving; (*tappeto*) runner; **~a a destra/sinistra** right /left hand drive. **~a telefonica** telephone directory. **~a turistica** tourist guide. **gui'dare** *vt* guide; *Auto*

drive; steer ⟨nave⟩. **~a'tore,
~a'trice** nmf driver

guin'zaglio nm leash

guiz'zare vi dart; ⟨luce:⟩ flash.
gu'izzo nm dart; ⟨di luce⟩ flash

'guscio nm shell

gu'stare vt taste ● vi like. **'gusto**
nm taste; ⟨piacere⟩ liking; **mangiare di gusto** eat heartily; **pren-
derci gusto** come to enjoy it,
develop a taste for it. **gu'stoso** a
tasty; fig delightful

guttu'rale a guttural

Hh

habitué nmf inv regular [cus-
tomer]

ham'burger nm inv hamburger

'handicap nm inv Sport handicap

handicap'pare vt handicap. **~to,
-a** nmf disabled person ● a disabled

'harem nm inv harem

'hascisc nm hashish

henné nm henna

hi-fi nm inv hi-fi

'hippy a hippy

hockey nm hockey. **~ su ghiaccio**
ice hockey. **~ su prato** hockey

hollywoodi'ano a Hollywood
attrib

ho'tel nm inv hotel

Ii

i def art mpl the; vedi **il**

i'ato nm hiatus

iber'na|re vi hibernate. **~zi'one** nf
hibernation

i'bisco nm hibiscus

'ibrido a & nm hybrid

iceberg nm inv iceberg

i'cona nf icon

Id'dio nm God

i'dea nf idea; ⟨opinione⟩ opinion;
⟨ideale⟩ ideal; ⟨indizio⟩ inkling;
⟨piccola quantità⟩ hint; ⟨intenzio-
ne⟩ intention; **cambiare ~** change
one's mind; **neanche per ~!** not
on your life!; **chiarirsi le idee** get
one's ideas straight. **~ fissa**
obsession

ide'a|le a & nm ideal. **~'lista** nmf
idealist. **~liz'zare** vt idealize

ide'a|re vt conceive. **~'tore,
~'trice** nmf originator

'idem adv the same

i'dentico a identical

identifi'cabile a identifiable

identifi'ca|re vt identify. **~zi'one**
nf identification

identi'kit nm inv identikit®

identità nf inv identity

ideolo'gia nf ideology. **ideo'logico**
a ideological

i'dilli|co a idyllic. **~o** nm idyll

idi'oma nm idiom. **idio'matico** a
idiomatic

idi'ota a idiotic ● nmf idiot.
idio'zia nf ⟨cosa stupida⟩ idiocy

idola'trare vt worship

idoleggi'are vt idolize. **'idolo** nm
idol

idoneità nf suitability; Mil fitness;
esame di ~ qualifying examination. **i'doneo** a **idoneo** a suitable
for; Mil fit for

i'drante nm hydrant

idra'ta|re vt hydrate; ⟨cosmetico:⟩
moisturize. **~nte** a ⟨crema, gel⟩
moisturizing. **~zi'one** nf moisturizing

i'draulico a hydraulic ● nm
plumber

'idrico a water attrib

idrocar'buro nm hydrocarbon

idroe'lettrico a hydroelectric

i'drofilo a vedi **cotone**

i'drogeno nm hydrogen

idromas'saggio nm ⟨sistema⟩
whirlpool bath

idrovo'lante nm seaplane

i'ella nf fam bad luck; **portare ~** be

bad luck. **iel'lato** a fam jinxed, plagued by bad luck

i'ena nf hyena

i'eri adv yesterday; ~ **l'altro, l'altro** ~ the day before yesterday; ~ **pomeriggio** yesterday afternoon; **il giornale di** ~ yesterday's paper

ietta'tore, -'trice nmf jinx. ~'**tura** nf (sfortuna) bad luck

igi'ene nf hygiene. ~**ico** a hygienic. **igie'nista** nmf hygienist

i'gnaro a unaware

i'gnobile a base; (non onorevole) dishonourable

igno'ran|te a ignorant ● nmf ignoramus. ~**za** nf ignorance

igno'rare vt (non sapere) be unaware of; (trascurare) ignore

i'gnoto a unknown

il def art m the; **il latte fa bene** milk is good for you; **il signor Magnetti** Mr Magnetti; **il dottor Piazza** Dr Piazza; **ha il naso storto** he has a bent nose; **mettiti il cappello** put your hat on; **il lunedì** on Mondays; **il 1986** 1986; **5 000 lire il chilo** 5,000 lire the o a kilo

i'lar|e a merry. ~**ità** nf hilarity

il'lazi'one nf inference

ille'cita'mente adv illicitly. **il'leci·to** a illicit

ille'gal|e a illegal. ~**ità** nf illegality. ~'**mente** adv illegally

illeg'gibile a illegible; (libro) unreadable

illegittimità nf illegitimacy. **ille'gittimo** a illegitimate

il'leso a unhurt

illette'rato, -a a a & nmf illiterate

lli'bato a chaste

illimi'tato a unlimited

illi'vidire vt bruise ● vt (per rabbia) turn livid

il'logico a illogical

il'luder|e vt deceive. ~**si** vr deceive oneself

illumi'na|re vt light [up]; fig enlighten; ~**re a giorno** floodlight. ~**rsi** vr light up. ~**zi'one** nf lighting; fig enlightenment

illumi'nismo nm Enlightenment

illusi'one nf illusion; **farsi illusioni** delude oneself

illusio'nis|mo nm conjuring. ~**ta** nmf conjurer

il'lu|so, -a pp di illudere ● a deluded ● nmf day-dreamer. ~'**sorio** a illusory

illu'stra|re vt illustrate. ~'**tivo** a illustrative. ~'**tore, ~'trice** nmf illustrator. ~**zi'one** nf illustration

il'lustre a distinguished

imbacuc'ca|re vt, ~**rsi** vr wrap up. ~**to** a wrapped up

imbal'la|ggio nm packing. ~**re** vt pack; Auto race

imbalsa'ma|re vt embalm; stuff (animale). ~**to** a embalmed; (animale) stuffed

imbam'bolato a vacant

imbaraz'zante a embarrassing

imbaraz'za|re vt embarrass; (ostacolare) encumber. ~**to** a embarrassed

imba'razzo nm embarrassment; (ostacolo) hindrance; **trarre qcno d'~** help sb out of a difficulty; **avere l'~ della scelta** be spoilt for choice. ~ **di stomaco** indigestion

imbarca'dero nm landing-stage

imbar'ca|re vt embark; (fam: rimorchiare) score. ~**rsi** vr embark, go on board. ~**zi'one** nf boat. ~**zione di salvataggio** lifeboat. **im'barco** nm embarkation, boarding; (banchina) landing stage

imba'sti|re vt tack; fig sketch. ~'**tura** nf tacking, basting

im'battersi vr ~ in run into

imbat'tibile a unbeatable. ~**uto** a unbeaten

imbavagli'are vt gag

imbec'cata nf Theat prompt

imbe'cille a stupid ● nmf Med imbecile

imbel'lire vt embellish

im'berbe a beardless; fig inexperienced

imbestia'li|re *vi*, **~rsi** *vr* fly into a rage. **~to** *a* enraged

im'bever|e *vt* imbue **(di** with). **~si** *vr* absorb

imbe'v|ibile *a* undrinkable. **~uto** *a* **~uto di** *(acqua)* soaked in; *(nozioni)* imbued with

imbian'c|are *vt* whiten ● *vi* turn white. **~hino** *nm* house painter

imbizzar'rir|e *vi*, **~si** *vr* become restless; *(arrabbiarsi)* become angry

imboc'ca|re *vt* feed; *(entrare)* enter; *fig* prompt. **~'tura** *nf* opening; *(ingresso)* entrance; *(Mus: di strumento)* mouthpiece. **im'bocco** *nm* entrance

imbo'scare *vt* hide. **~si** *vr Mil* shirk military service

imbo'scata *nf* ambush

imbottigli'are *vt* bottle. **~rsi** *vr* get snarled up in a traffic jam. **~to** *a* *(vino, acqua)* bottled

imbot'ti|re *vt* stuff; pad *(giacca)*; *Culin* fill. **~rsi** *vr* **~rsi di** *(fig: di pasticche)* stuff oneself with. **~ta** *nf* quilt. **~to** *a* *(spalle)* padded; *(cuscino)* stuffed; *(panino)* filled. **~'tura** *nf* stuffing; *(di giacca)* padding; *Culin* filling

imbracci'are *vt* shoulder *(fucile)*

imbra'nato *a* clumsy

imbrat'tar|e *vt* mark. **~si** *vr* dirty oneself

imbroc'car|e *vt* hit; **~la giusta** hit the nail on the head

imbrogli|'are *vt* muddle; *(raggirare)* cheat. **~arsi** *vr* get tangled; *(confondersi)* get confused. **im'broglio** *nm* tangle; *(pasticcio)* mess; *(inganno)* trick. **~'one, -a** *nmf* cheat

imbronci'a|re *vi*, **~rsi** *vr* sulk. **~to** *a* sulky

imbru'nire *vi* get dark; **all'~** at dusk

imbrut'tire *vt* make ugly ● *vi* become ugly

imbu'care *vt* post, mail; *(nel biliardo)* pot

imbur'rare *vt* butter

im'buto *nm* funnel

imi'ta|re *vt* imitate. **~'tore, ~'trice** *nmf* imitator, impersonator. **~zi'one** *nf* imitation

immaco'lato *a* immaculate

immagazzi'nare *vt* store

immagi'na|re *vt* imagine; *(supporre)* suppose; **s'immagini!** imagine that!. **~rio** *a* imaginary. **~zi'one** *nf* imagination. **im'magine** *nf* image; *(rappresentazione, idea)* picture

imman'cabil|e *a* unfailing. **~'mente** *adv* without fail

im'mane *a* huge; *(orribile)* terrible

imma'nente *a* immanent

immangi'abile *a* inedible

immatrico'la|re *vt* register. **~rsi** *vr* *(studente:)* matriculate. **~zi'one** *nf* registration; *(di studente)* matriculation

immaturità *nf* immaturity. **imma'turo** *a* unripe; *(persona)* immature; *(precoce)* premature

immedesi'ma|rsi *vr* **~rsi in** identify oneself with. **~zi'one** *nf* identification

immedia|ta'mente *adv* immediately. **~'tezza** *nf* immediacy. **im'medi|ato** *a* immediate

immemo'rabile *a* immemorial

immens|a'mente *adv* enormously. **~ità** *nf* immensity. **im'menso** *a* immense

immensu'rabile *a* immeasurable

im'merger|e *vt* immerse. **~si** *vr* plunge; *(sommergibile:)* dive; **~si in** immerse oneself in

immeri'tato *a* undeserved. **~evole** *a* undeserving

immersi'one *nf* immersion; *(di sommergibile)* dive. **im'merso** *pp* di *immergere*

immi'gra|nte *a & nmf* immigrant. **~re** *vi* immigrate. **~to, -a** *nmf* immigrant. **~zi'one** *nf* immigration

immi'nen|te *a* imminent. **~za** *nf* imminence

immischi'ar|e *vt* involve. **~si in** **~si** in meddle in

immis'sario *nm* tributary

immissi'one *nf* insertion

im'mobile *a* motionless

im'mobili *nmpl* real estate. **~'are** *a* **società ~are** building society, savings and loan *Am*

immobili|tà *nf* immobility. **~z'zare** *vt* immobilize; *Comm* tie up

immo'desto *a* immodest

immo'lare *vt* sacrifice

immondez'zaio *nm* rubbish tip

immon'dizia *nf* filth; *(spazzatura)* rubbish. **im'mondo** *a* filthy

immo'ral|e *a* immoral. **~ità** *nf* immorality

immorta'lare *vt* immortalize. **immor'tale** *a* immortal

immoti'vato *a (gesto)* unjustified

im'mun|e *a* exempt; *Med* immune. **~ità** *nf* immunity. **~iz'zare** *vt* immunize. **~izzazi'one** *nf* immunization

immunodefici'enza *nf* immunodeficiency

immuso'ni|rsi *vr* sulk. **~to** *a* sulky

immu'ta|bile *a* unchangeable. **~to** *a* unchanging

impacchet'tare *vt* wrap up

impacci'a|re *vt* hamper; *(disturbare)* inconvenience; *(imbarazzare)* embarrass. **~to** *a* embarrassed; *(goffo)* awkward. **im'paccio** *nm* embarrassment; *(ostacolo)* hindrance; *(situazione difficile)* awkward situation

im'pacco *nm* compress

impadro'nirsi *vr* **~ di** take possession of; *(fig: impare)* master

impa'gabile *a* priceless

impagi'nare *vt* paginate. **~zi'one** *nf* pagination

impagli'are *vt* stuff *(animale)*

impa'lato *a fig* stiff

impalca'tura *nf* scaffolding; *fig* structure

impalli'dire *vi* turn pale; *(fig: perdere d'importanza)* pale into insignificance

impa'nare *vt* *Culin* roll in breadcrumbs

impanta'narsi *vr* get bogged down

impape'rarsi *vr*, **impappi'narsi** *vr* falter, stammer

impa'rare *vt* learn

impareggi'abile *a* incomparable

imparen'ta|rsi *vr* **~ con** become related to. **~to** *a* related

'impari *a* unequal; *(dispari)* odd

impar'tire *vt* impart

imparzi'al|e *a* impartial. **~ità** *nf* impartiality

impas'sibile *a* impassive

impa'sta|re *vt* *Culin* knead; blend *(colori)*. **~'tura** *nf* kneading. **im'pasto** *nm Culin* dough; *(miscuglio)* mixture

impastic'carsi *vr* pop pills

im'patto *nm* impact

impau'rir|e *vt* frighten; **~si** *vr* become frightened

im'pavido *a* fearless

impazi'en|te *a* impatient; **~te di fare qcsa** eager to do sth. **~'tirsi** *vr* lose patience. **~za** *nf* impatience

impaz'zata *nf* **all'~** at breakneck speed

impaz'zire *vi* go mad; *(maionese:)* separate; **far ~ qcno** drive sb mad; **~ per** be crazy about; **da ~** *(mal di testa)* blinding

impec'cabile *a* impeccable

impedi'mento *nm* hindrance; *(ostacolo)* obstacle

impe'dire *vt* **~ di** prevent from; *(impacciare)* hinder; *(ostruire)* obstruct; **~ a qcno di fare qcsa** prevent sb [from] doing sth

impe'gna|re *vt* *(dare in pegno)* pawn; *(vincolare)* bind; *(prenotare)* reserve; *(assorbire)* take up ⸱ **~rsi** *vr* apply oneself; **~rsi a fare qcsa** commit oneself to doing sth. **~'tiva** *nf* referral. **~'tivo** *a* binding; *(lavoro)* demanding. **~ato** *a* engaged; *Pol* committed. **im'pegno** *nm* engagement; *Comm* commitment; *(zelo)* care

impel'lente *a* pressing

impene'trabile *a* impenetrable

impen'na|rsi *vr (cavallo:)* rear; *fig* bristle. **~ta** *nf (di prezzi)* sharp rise; (*di cavallo*) rearing; (*di moto*) wheelie

impen'sa|bile *a* unthinkable. **~to** *a* unexpected

impensie'rir|e *vt*, **~si** *vr* worry

impe'ra|nte *a* prevailing. **~re** *vi* reign; (*tendenza:*) prevail, hold sway

impera'tivo *a* & *nm* imperative

impera'tore, -'trice *nm* emperor ● *nf* empress

impercet'tibile *a* imperceptible

imperdo'nabile *a* unforgivable

imper'fe|tto *a* & *nm* imperfect. **~zi'one** *nf* imperfection

imperi'a|le *a* imperial. **~'lismo** *nm* imperialism. **~'lista** *a* imperialist. **~'listico** *a* imperialistic

imperi'oso *a* imperious; (*impellente*) urgent

impe'rizia *nf* lack of skill

imperme'abile *a* waterproof ● *nm* raincoat

imperni'ar|e *vt* pivot; (*fondare*) base. **~si** *vr* **su** be based on

im'pero *nm* empire; (*potere*) rule

imperscru'tabile *a* inscrutable

imperso'nale *a* impersonal

imperso'nare *vt* personify; (*interpretare*) act [the part of]

imper'territo *a* undaunted

imperti'nen|te *a* impertinent. **~za** *nf* impertinence

impertur'ba|bile *a* imperturbable. **~to** *a* unperturbed

imperver'sare *vt* rage

im'pervio *a* inaccessible

'impet|o *nm* impetus; (*impulso*) impulse; (*slancio*) transport. **~u'oso** *a* impetuous; (*vento*) blustering

impet'tito *a* stiff

impian'tare *vt* install; set up (*azienda*)

impi'anto *nm* plant; (*sistema*) system; (*operazione*) installation. **~ radio** *Auto* car stereo system

impia'strare *vt* plaster; (*sporcare*) dirty. **impi'astro** *nm* poultice; (*persona noiosa*) bore; (*pasticcione*) cack-handed person

impic'car|e *vt* hang. **~si** *vr* hang oneself

impicci'arsi *vr* meddle. **im'piccio** *nm* hindrance; (*seccatura*) bother. **~'one, -a** *nmf* nosey parker

impie'ga|re *vt* employ; use; spend (*tempo, denaro*); *Fin* invest. **l'autobus ha ~to un'ora** it took the bus an hour. **~rsi** *vr* get [oneself] a job

impiega'tizio *a* clerical

impie'gato, -a *nmf* employee. **~ di banca** bank clerk. **impi'ego** *nm* employment; (*posto*) job; *Fin* investment

impieto'sir|e *vt* move to pity. **~si** *vr* be moved to pity

impie'trito *a* petrified

impigli'ar|e *vt* entangle. **~si** *vr* get entangled

impigrir|e *vt* make lazy. **~si** *vr* get lazy

impla'cabile *a* implacable

impli'ca|re *vt* implicate; (*sottintendere*) imply. **~rsi** *vr* become involved. **~zi'one** *nf* implication

implicita'mente *adv* implicitly. **im'plicito** *a* implicit

implo'ra|re *vt* implore. **~zi'one** *nf* entreaty

impolve'ra|re *vt* cover with dust. **~rsi** *vr* get covered with dust. **~to** *a* dusty

impon'derabile *a* imponderable; (*causa, evento*) unpredictable

impo'nen|te *a* imposing. **~za** *nf* impressiveness

impo'nibile *a* taxable ● *nm* taxable income

impopo'lar|e *a* unpopular. **~ità** *nf* unpopularity

im'por|re *vt* impose; (*ordinare*) order. **~si** *vr* assert oneself; (*aver successo*) be successful; **~si di** (*prefiggersi di*) set oneself the task of

impor'tan|te *a* important ● *nm* important thing. **~za** *nf* importance

impor'ta|re *vt* *Comm, Comput* import; (*comportare*) cause ● *vi* matter; *(essere necessario)* be necessary. **non ~!** it doesn't matter!; **non me ne ~ niente!** I couldn't care less!. **~'tore**, **~'trice** *nmf* importer. **~zi'one** *nf* importation; *(merce importata)* import

im'porto *nm* amount

importu'nare *vt* pester. **importu'no** *a* troublesome; *(inopportuno)* untimely

imposizi'one *nf* imposition; *(imposta)* tax

imposses'sarsi *vr* ~ **di** seize

impos'sibil|e *a* impossible ● *nm* **fare l'~e** do absolutely all one can. **~ità** *nf* impossibility

im'posta[1] *nf* tax; ~ **sul reddito** income tax; ~ **sul valore aggiunto** value added tax

im'posta[2] *nf* *(di finestra)* shutter

impos'ta|re *vt (progettare)* plan; *(basare)* base; *Mus* pitch; *(imbucare)* post, mail; set out *(domanda, problema)*. **~zi'one** *nf* planning; *(di voce)* pitching

im'posto *pp di* **imporre**

impo'store, **-a** *nmf* impostor

impo'ten|te *a* powerless; *Med* impotent. **~za** *nf* powerlessness; *Med* impotence

impove'rir|e *vt* impoverish. **~si** *vr* become poor

imprati'cabile *a* impracticable; *(strada)* impassable

imprati'chir|e *vt* train. **~si** *vr* ~ **si in** *o* a get practice in

impre'ca|re *vi* curse. **~zi'one** *nf* curse

impreci's|abile *a* indeterminable. **~ato** *a* indeterminate. **~i'one** *nf* inaccuracy. **impre'ciso** *a* inaccurate

impre'gnar|e *vt* impregnate; *(imbevere)* soak; *fig* imbue. **~si** *vr* become impregnated with

imprendi'tor|e, **-'trice** *nmf* entrepreneur. **~i'ale** *a* entrepreneurial

imprepa'rato *a* unprepared

im'presa *nf* undertaking; *(gesta)* exploit; *(azienda)* firm

impre'sario *nm* impresario; *(appaltatore)* contractor

imprescin'dibile *a* inescapable

impressio'na|bile *a* impressionable. **~nte** *a* impressive; *(spaventoso)* frightening

impressio'nare *vt* impress; *(spaventare)* frighten; expose *(foto)*. **~o'narsi** *vr* be affected; *(spaventarsi)* be frightened. **~'one** *nf* impression; *(sensazione)* sensation; *(impronta)* mark; **far ~one a** qcno upset sb

impressio'nis|mo *nm* impressionism. **~ta** *nmf* impressionist

im'presso *pp di* **imprimere** ● *a* printed

impre'stare *vt* lend

impreve'dibile *a* unforeseeable; *(persona)* unpredictable

imprevi'dente *a* improvident

impre'visto *a* unforeseen ● *nm* unforeseen event; **salvo imprevisti** all being well

imprigio|na'mento *nm* imprisonment. **~'nare** *vt* imprison

im'primere *vt* impress; *(stampare)* print; *(comunicare)* impart

impro'babil|e *a* unlikely, improbable. **~ità** *nf* improbability

improdut'tivo *a* unproductive

im'pronta *nf* impression; *fig* mark. ~ **digitale** fingerprint. ~ **del piede** footprint

impro'perio *nm* insult; **improperi** *pl* abuse *sg*

im'proprio *a* improper

improvvisa'mente *adv* suddenly

improvvi'sa|re *vt/i* improvise. **~rsi** *vr* turn oneself into a. **~ta** *nf* surprise. **~to** *a (discorso)* unrehearsed. **~zi'one** *nf* improvisation

improv'viso *a* sudden; **all'~** unexpectedly

impru'dente *a* imprudent. **~za** *nf* imprudence

impu'gna|re *vt* grasp; *Jur* contest. **~tura** *nf* grip; *(manico)* handle

impulsività *nf* impulsiveness

impul'sivo *a* impulsive

im'pulso *nm* impulse; **agire d'~** act on impulse

impune'mente *adv* with impunity. **impu'nito** *a* unpunished

impun'tarsi *vr fig* dig one's heels in

impun'tura *nf* stitching

impurità *nf inv* impurity. **im'puro** *a* impure

impu'tabile *a* attributable (**a** to)

impu'ta|re *vt* attribute; (*accusare*) charge. **~to, -a** *nmf* accused. **~zi'one** *nf* charge

imputri'dire *vi* rot

in *prep* in; (*moto a luogo*) to; (*su*) on; (*entro*) within; (*mezzo*) by; (*con materiale*) made of; **essere in casa/ufficio** be at home/at the office; **in mano/tasca** in one's hand/pocket; **andare in Francia/campagna** go to France/the country; **salire in treno** get on the train; **versa la birra nel bicchiere** pour the beer into the glass; **in alto** up there; **in giornata** within the day; **nel 1997** in 1997; **una borsa in pelle** a bag made of leather, a leather bag; **in macchina** (*viaggiare, venire*) by car; **in contanti** [in] cash; **in vacanza** on holiday; **di giorno in giorno** from day to day; **se fossi in te** if I were you; **siamo in sette** there are seven of us

inabbor'dabile *a* unapproachable

i'nabil|e *a* incapable; (*fisicamente*) unfit. **~ità** *nf* incapacity

inabi'tabile *a* uninhabitable

inacces'sibile *a* inaccessible; (*persona*) unapproachable

inaccet'tabil|e *a* unacceptable. **~ità** *nf* unacceptability

inacer'bi|re *vt* embitter; exacerbate (*rapporto*). **~si** *vr* grow bitter

inaci'dir|e *vt* turn sour. **~si** *vr* go sour; (*persona*) become embittered

ina'datto *a* unsuitable

inadegu'ato *a* inadequate

inadempi'ente *nmf* defaulter. **~'mento** *nm* nonfulfilment

inaffer'rabile *a* elusive

ina'la|re *vt* inhale. **~'tore** *nm* inhaler. **~zi'one** *nf* inhalation

inalbe'rar|e *vt* hoist. **~si** (*cavallo:*) rear [up]; (*adirarsi*) lose one's temper

inalte'rabil|e *a* unchangeable; (*colore*) fast. **~to** *a* unchanged

inami'da|re *vt* starch. **~to** *a* starched

inammis'sibile *a* inadmissible

inamovi'bile *a* irremovable

inani'mato *a* inanimate; (*senza vita*) lifeless

inappa'gabile *a* unsatisfiable. **~to** *a* unfulfilled

inappel'labile *a* final

inappe'tenza *nf* lack of appetite

inappli'cabile *a* inapplicable

inappun'tabile *a* faultless

inar'car|e *vt* arch; raise (*sopracciglia*). **~si** *vr* (*legno:*) warp; (*ripiano:*) sag; (*linea:*) curve

inari'dir|e *vt* parch; empty of feelings (*persona*). **~si** *vr* dry up; (*persona:*) become empty of feelings

inartico'lato *a* inarticulate

inaspetta'mente *adv* unexpectedly. **inaspet'tato** *a* unexpected

inaspri'mento *nm* (*di carattere*) embitterment; (*di conflitto*) worsening

ina'sprir|e *vt* embitter. **~si** *vr* become embittered

inattac'cabile *a* unassailable; (*irreprensibile*) irreproachable

inatten'dibile *a* unreliable. **inat'teso** *a* unexpected

inattività *nf* inactivity. **inat'tivo** *a* inactive

inat'tuabile *a* impracticable

inau'dito *a* unheard of

inaugu'rale *a* inaugural; **viaggio ~** maiden voyage

inaugu'ra|re *vt* inaugurate; open (*mostra*); unveil (*statua*); christen (*lavastoviglie ecc*). **~zi'one** *nf* inauguration; (*di mostra*) opening; (*di statua*) unveiling

inavver'ten|za *nf* inadvertence. **~ita'mente** *adv* inadvertently

incagli'ar|e vi ground ● vt hinder. ~si vr run aground

incalco'labile a incalculable

incal'li|rsi vr grow callous; (abituarsi) become hardened. ~to a callous; (abituato) hardened

incal'za|nte a (ritmo) driving; (richiesta) urgent. ~re vt pursue; fig press

incame'rare vt appropriate

incammi'nar|e vt get going; (fig: guidare) set off. ~si vr set out

incana'lar|e vt canalize; fig channel. ~si vr converge on

incande'scen|te a incandescent; (discussione) burning. ~za nf incandescence

incan'ta|re vt enchant. ~rsi vr stand spellbound; (inceppparsi) jam. ~'tore, ~'trice nm enchanter ● nf enchantress

incan'tesimo nm spell

incan'tevole a enchanting

in'canto nm spell; fig delight; (asta) auction; **come per ~** as if by magic

incanu'ti|re vt turn white. ~to a white

inca'pac|e a incapable. ~ità nf incapability

incapo'nirsi vr be set (**a fare** on doing)

incap'pare vi ~ **in** run into

incappucci'arsi vr wrap up

incapricci'arsi vr ~ **di** take a fancy to

incapsu'lare vt seal; crown (dente)

incarce'ra|re vt imprison. ~zi'one nf imprisonment

incari'ca|re vt charge. ~rsi vr take upon oneself; **me ne incarico io** I will see to it. ~to, -a a in charge ● nmf representative. **in'carico** nm charge; **per incarico di** on behalf of

incar'na|re vt embody. ~rsi vr become incarnate. ~zi'one nf incarnation

incarta'mento nm documents pl.

incar'tare vt wrap [in paper]

incasi'nato a fam (vita) screwed up; (stanza) messed up

incas'sa|re vt pack; Mech embed; box in (mobile, frigo); (riscuotere) cash; take (colpo). ~to a set; (fiume) deeply embanked. ~**tura** nf collection; (introito) takings pl

incasto'na|re vt set. ~**tura** nf setting. ~**to** a embedded; (anello) inset (**di** with)

inca'strar|e vt fit in; (fam: in situazione) corner. ~si vr fit.

in'castro nm joint; **a incastro** (pezzi) interlocking

incate'nare vt chain

incatra'mare vt tar

incatti'vire vt turn nasty

in'cauto a imprudent

inca'va|re vt hollow out. ~to a hollow. ~**tura** nf hollow. **in'cavo** nm hollow; (scanalatura) groove

incavo'la|rsi vr fam get shirty. ~to a fam shirty

incendi'ar|e vt set fire to; fig inflame. ~si vr catch fire. ~**io, -a** a incendiary; (fig: discorso) inflammatory; (fig: bellezza) sultry ● nmf arsonist. **in'cendio** nm fire. **incendio doloso** arson

incene'ri|re vt burn to ashes; (cremare) cremate. ~**rsi** vr be burnt to ashes. ~**tore** nm incinerator

in'censo nm incense

incensu'rato a blameless; **essere ~** Jur have a clean record

incenti'vare vt motivate. **incen'tivo** nm incentive

incen'trarsi vr ~ **su** centre on

incep'par|e vt block; fig hamper. ~si vr jam

ince'rata nf oilcloth

incerot'tato a with a plaster on

incer'tezza nf uncertainty. **in'certo** a uncertain ● nm uncertainty

inces'sante a unceasing. ~**'mente** adv incessantly

in'cest|o nm incest. ~**u'oso** a incestuous

in'cetta nf buying up; **fare ~ di** stockpile

inchi'esta nf investigation
inchi'nar|e vt, **~si** vr bow. **in'chino** nm bow; (di donna) curtsy
inchio'dare vt nail; nail down ⟨coperchio⟩; **~ a letto** ⟨malattia:⟩ confine to bed
inchi'ostro nm ink
inciam'pare vi stumble; **~ in** ⟨imbattersi⟩ run into. **inci'ampo** nm hindrance
inciden'tale a incidental
inci'den|te nm ⟨episodio⟩ incident; ⟨infortunio⟩ accident. **~za** nf incidence
in'cidere vt cut; ⟨arte⟩ engrave; ⟨registrare⟩ record ● vi **~ su** ⟨gravare⟩ weigh upon
in'cinta a pregnant
incipi'ente a incipient
incipri'ar|e vt powder. **~si** vr powder one's face
in'circa adv **all'~** more or less
incisi'one nf incision; ⟨arte⟩ engraving; ⟨acquaforte⟩ etching; ⟨registrazione⟩ recording
inci'sivo a incisive ● nm ⟨dente⟩ incisor
in'ciso nm **per ~** incidentally
incita'mento nm incitement. **inci'tare** vt incite
inci'vil|e a uncivilized; ⟨maleducato⟩ impolite. **~tà** nf barbarism; ⟨maleducazione⟩ rudeness
incle'men|te a harsh. **~za** nf harshness
incli'nabile a reclining
incli'na|re vt tilt ● vi **~re** a be inclined to. **~rsi** vr list. **~to** a tilted; ⟨terreno⟩ sloping. **~zi'one** nf slope, inclination. **in'cline** a inclined
in'clu|dere vt include; ⟨allegare⟩ enclose. **~si'one** nf inclusion. **~'sivo** a inclusive. **~so** pp di **includere** ● a included; ⟨compreso⟩ inclusive; ⟨allegato⟩ enclosed
incoe'ren|te a ⟨contraddittorio⟩ inconsistent. **~za** nf inconsistency
in'cognit|a nf unknown quantity. **~o** a unknown ● nm **in ~o** incognito

incol'lar|e vt stick; ⟨con colla liquida⟩ glue. **~si** vr stick to; **~si a qcno** stick close to sb
incolle'ri|rsi vr lose one's temper. **~to** a enraged
incol'mabile a ⟨differenza⟩ unbridgeable; ⟨vuoto⟩ unfillable
incolon'nare vt line up
inco'lore a colourless
incol'pare vt blame
in'colto a uncultivated; ⟨persona⟩ uneducated
in'colume a unhurt
incom'ben|te a impending. **~za** nf task
in'combere vi **~ su** hang over; **~ a** ⟨spettare⟩ be incumbent on
incominci'are vt/i begin, start
incomo'dar|e vt inconvenience. **~si** vr trouble. **in'comodo** a uncomfortable; ⟨inopportuno⟩ inconvenient ● nm inconvenience
incompa'rabile a incomparable
incompa'tibil|e a incompatible. **~ità** nf incompatibility
incompe'ten|te a incompetent. **~za** nf incompetence
incompi'uto a unfinished
incom'pleto a incomplete
incompren'si|bile a incomprehensible. **~'one** nf lack of understanding; ⟨malinteso⟩ misunderstanding. **incom'preso** a misunderstood
inconce'pibile a inconceivable
inconcili'abile a irreconcilable
inconclu'dente a inconclusive; ⟨persona⟩ ineffectual
incondizio'nata|mente adv unconditionally. **~'nato** a unconditional
inconfes'sabile a unmentionable
inconfon'dibile a unmistakable
inconfu'tabile a irrefutable
incongru'ente a inconsistent
in'congruo a inadequate
inconsa'pevol|e a unaware; ⟨inconscio⟩ unconscious. **~'mente** adv unwittingly
in'conscio (?)
inconscia'mente adv uncon-

131   **inconsistente | indagare**

sciously. **in'conscio** *a & nm Psych* unconscious

inconsi'sten|te *a* insubstantial; *(notizia ecc)* unfounded. ~**za** *nf (di ragionamento, prove)* flimsiness

inconso'labile *a* inconsolable

inconsu'eto *a* unusual

incon'sulto *a* rash

incontami'nato *a* uncontaminated

inconte'nibile *a* irrepressible

inconten'tabile *a* insatiable; *(esigente)* hard to please

inconte'stabile *a* indisputable

inconti'nen|te *a* incontinent. ~**za** *nf* incontinence

incon'trar|e *vt* meet; encounter; meet with *(difficoltà).* ~**si** *vr* meet (con qcno sb)

incon'trario: all'~ *adv* the other way around; *(in modo sbagliato)* the wrong way around

incontra'sta|bile *a* incontrovertible. ~**to** *a* undisputed

in'contro *nm* meeting; *Sport* match. ~ **al vertice** summit meeting ● *prep* ~ **a** towards; andare **a qn** go to meet sb; *fig* meet sb half way

inconveni'ente *nm* drawback

incoraggi'a|mento *nm* encouragement. ~'**ante** *a* encouraging. ~'**are** *vt* encourage

incornici'a|re *vt* frame. ~'**tura** *nf* framing

incoro'na|re *vt* crown. ~**zi'one** *nf* coronation

incorpo'rar|e *vt* incorporate; *(mescolare)* blend. ~**si** *vr* blend; *(territori:)* merge

incorreg'gibile *a* incorrigible

in'correre *vt* ~ **in** incur; ~ **nel pericolo di...** run the risk of...

incorrut'tibile *a* incorruptible

incosci'en|te *a* unconscious; *(irresponsabile)* reckless ● *nmf* irresponsible person. ~**za** *nf* unconsciousness; recklessness

inco'stan|te *a* changeable; *(per-*

sona) fickle. ~**za** *nf* changeableness; *(di persona)* fickleness

incostituzio'nale *a* unconstitutional

incre'dibile *a* unbelievable, incredible

incredulità *nf* incredulity. **in'credulo** *a* incredulous

incremen'tare *vt* increase; *(intensificare)* step up. **incre'mento** *nm* increase. **incremento demografico** population growth

incresci'oso *a* regrettable

incre'spar|e *vt* ruffle; wrinkle *(tessuto);* make frizzy *(capelli);* ~**e la fronte** frown. ~**si** *vr (acqua:)* ripple; *(tessuto:)* wrinkle; *(capelli:)* go frizzy

incrimi'na|re *vt* indict; *fig* incriminate. ~**zi'one** *nf* indictment

incri'na|re *vt* crack; *fig* affect *(amicizia).* ~**rsi** *vr* crack; *(amicizia:)* be affected. ~'**tura** *nf* crack

incroci'a|re *vt* cross ● *vi Naut, Aeron* cruise. ~**rsi** *vr* cross. ~'**tore** *nm* cruiser

in'crocio *nm* crossing; *(di strade)* crossroads *sg*

incrol'labile *a* indestructible

incro'sta|re *vt* encrust. ~**zi'one** *nf* encrustation

incuba'|trice *nf* incubator. ~**zi'one** *nf* incubation

'incubo *nm* nightmare

in'cudine *nf* anvil

incu'rabile *a* incurable

incu'rante *a* careless

incurio'sir|e *vt* make curious. ~**si** *vr* become curious

incursi'one *nf* raid. ~ **aerea** air raid

incurva'mento *nm* bending

incur'va|re *vt,* ~**rsi** *vr* bend. ~'**tura** *nf* bending

in'cusso *pp* di **incutere**

incu'stodito *a* unguarded

in'cutere *vt* arouse; ~ **spavento a** qcno strike fear into sb

in'daco *nm* indigo

indaffa'rato *a* busy

inda'gare *vt/i* investigate

in'dagine *nf* research; (*giudizia-ria*) investigation. ~ **di mercato** market survey

indebi'tar|e *vt*, **~si** *vr* get into debt

in'debito *a* undue

indeboli'mento *nm* weakening

indebo'lir|e *vt*, **~si** *vr* weaken

inde'cen|te *a* indecent. **~za** *nf* indecency; (*vergogna*) disgrace

indeci'frabile *a* indecipherable

indecisi'one *nf* indecision. inde-'ciso *a* undecided

inde'fesso *a* tireless

indefi'ni|bile *a* indefinable. **~to** *a* indefinite

indefor'mabile *a* crushproof

in'degno *a* unworthy

inde'lebile *a* indelible

indelica'tezza *nf* indelicacy; (*azione*) tactless act. indeli'cato *a* indiscreet; (*grossolano*) indelicate

indemoni'ato *a* possessed

in'denn|e *a* uninjured; (*da malat-tia*) unaffected. **~ità** *nf inv* allow-ance; (*per danni*) compensation. **~ità di trasferta** travel allow-ance. **~iz'zare** *vt* compensate. inden'nizzo *nm* compensation

indero'gabile *a* binding

indescri'vibile *a* indescribable

inableside'ra|bile *a* undesirable. **~to** *a* (*figlio, ospite*) unwanted

indetermi'na|bile *a* indeterminable. **~'tezza** *nf* vagueness. **~to** *a* indeterminate

'Indi|a *nf* India. i~'ano, **-a** *a* & *nmf* Indian; **in fila i~'ana** in single file

indiavo'lato *a* possessed; (*vivace*) wild

indi'ca|re *vt* show, indicate; (*col dito*) point at; (*far notare*) point out; (*consigliare*) advise. **~'tivo** *a* indicative ● *nm* Gram indicative. **~'tore** *nm* indicator; Techn gauge; (*prontuario*) directory. **~zi'one** *nf* indication; (*istruzione*) direction

'indice *nm* (*dito*) forefinger; (*lan-cetta*) pointer; (*di libro, statistica*) index; (*fig: segno*) sign

indi'cibile *a* inexpressible

indietreggi'are *vi* draw back; *Mil* retreat

indi'etro *adv* back, behind; **all'~** backwards; **avanti e ~** back and forth; **essere ~** be behind; (*mentalmente*) be backward; (*con pagamenti*) be in arrears; (*di orologio*) be slow; **fare marcia ~** reverse; **rimandare ~** send back; **rimanere ~** be left behind; **torna ~!** come back!

indi'feso *a* undefended; (*inerme*) helpless

indiffe'ren|te *a* indifferent; **mi è ~te** it is all the same to me. **~za** *nf* indifference

in'digeno, **-a** *a* indigenous ● *nmf* native

indi'gen|te *a* needy. **~za** *nf* poverty

indigesti'one *nf* indigestion. indi-'gesto *a* indigestible

indi'gna|re *vt* make indignant. **~rsi** *vr* be indignant. **~to** *a* indig-nant. **~zi'one** *nf* indignation

indimenti'cabile *a* unforgettable

indipen'den|te *a* independent. **~te'mente** *adv* independently; **~temente dal tempo** regardless of the weather, whatever the weather. **~za** *nf* independence

in'dire *vt* announce

indiretta'mente *adv* indirectly. indi'retto *a* indirect

indiriz'zar|e *vt* address; (*mandare*) send; (*dirigere*) direct. **~si** *vr* di-rect one's steps. indi'rizzo *nm* ad-dress; (*direzione*) direction

indisci'pli|na *nf* lack of discipline. **~'nato** *a* undisciplined

indi'scre|to *a* indiscreet. **~zi'one** *nf* indiscretion

indiscrimi'nata'mente *adv* indis-criminately. **~'nato** *a* indiscrimi-nate

indi'scusso *a* unquestioned

indiscu'tibil|e *a* unquestionable. **~'mente** *adv* unquestionably

indispen'sabile *a* essential, indis-pensable

indispet'tir|e *vt* irritate. **~si** *vr* get irritated

indi'spo|rre *vt* antagonize. **~sto** *pp di* **indisporre ● a** indisposed. **~sizi'one** *nf* indisposition

indisso'lubile *a* indissoluble

indissolubil'mente *adv* indissolubly

indistin'guibile *a* indiscernible

indistinta'mente *adv* without exception. **indi'stinto** *a* indistinct

indistrut'tibile *a* indestructible

indistur'bato *a* undisturbed

in'divia *nf* endive

individu'a|le *a* individual. **~'lista** *nmf* individualist. **~lità** *nf* individuality. **~re** *vt* individualize; *(localizzare)* locate; *(riconoscere)* single out

indi'viduo *nm* individual

indivi'sibile *a* indivisible. **indi'viso** *a* undivided

indizi'a|re *vt* throw suspicion on. **~to, -a** *a* suspected ● *nmf* suspect. **in'dizio** *nm* sign; *Jur* circumstantial evidence

'indole *nf* nature

indo'len|te *a* indolent. **~za** *nf* indolence

indolenzi'mento *nm* stiffness

indolen'zi|rsi *vr* go stiff. **~to** *a* stiff

indo'lore *a* painless

indo'mani *nm* **l'~** the following day

Indo'nesia *nf* Indonesia

indo'rare *vt* gild

indos'sa|re *vt* wear; *(mettere addosso)* put on. **~'tore, ~'trice** *nmf* model

in'dotto *pp di* **indurre**

indottri'nare *vt* indoctrinate

indovi'n|are *vt* guess; *(predire)* foretell. **~ato** *a* successful; *(scelta)* well-chosen. **~o** *nm* riddle. **indo'vino, -a** *nmf* fortune-teller

indubbia'mente *adv* undoubtedly. **in'dubbio** *a* undoubted

indugl'ar|e *vi*, **~si** *vr* linger. **in'dugio** *nm* delay

indul'gen|te *a* indulgent. **~za** *nf* indulgence

in'dul|gere *vi* **~gere a** indulge in. **~to** *pp di* **indulgere ● nm** *Jur* pardon

indu'mento *nm* garment; **indumenti** *pl* clothes

induri'mento *nm* hardening

indu'rir|e *vt*, **~si** *vr* harden

in'durre *vt* induce

in'dustri|a *nf* industry. **~'ale** *a* industrial ● *nmf* industrialist

industrializ'za|re *vt* industrialize. **~to** *a* industrialized. **~zi'one** *nf* industrialization

industrial'mente *adv* industrially

industri'arsi *vr* try one's hardest. **~'oso** *a* industrious

induzi'one *nf* induction

inebe'tito *a* stunned

inebri'ante *a* intoxicating, exciting

inecce'pibile *a* unexceptionable

i'nedia *nf* starvation

i'nedito *a* unpublished

ineffi'cace *a* ineffective

ineffici'en|te *a* inefficient. **~za** *nf* inefficiency

ineguagli'abile *a* incomparable

inegu'ale *a* unequal; *(superficie)* uneven

inelut'tabile *a* inescapable

ine'rente *a* **~ a** concerning

i'nerme *a* unarmed; *fig* defenceless

inerpi'carsi *vr* **~ su** clamber up; *(pianta)* climb up

i'ner|te *a* inactive; *Phys* inert. **~zia** *nf* inactivity; *Phys* inertia

inesat'tezza *nf* inaccuracy. **ine'satto** *a* inaccurate; *(erroneo)* incorrect; *(non riscosso)* uncollected

inesau'ribile *a* inexhaustible

inesi'sten|te *a* non-existent. **~za** *nf* non-existence

ineso'rabile *a* inexorable

inespe'ri|enza *nf* inexperience. **ine'sperto** *a* inexperienced

inespli'cabile *a* inexplicable

ine'sploso a unexploded

inespri'mibile a inexpressible

inesti'mabile a inestimable

inetti'tudine nf ineptitude. **i'netto** a inept; **inetto a** unsuited to

ine'vaso a ⟨pratiche⟩ pending; ⟨corrispondenza⟩ unanswered

inevi'tabil|e a inevitable. **~'mente** adv inevitably

i'nezia nf trifle

infagot'tar|e vt wrap up. **~si** vr wrap [oneself] up

infal'libile a infallible

infa'ma|re vt defame. **~'torio** a defamatory

in'fam|e a infamous; ⟨fam: orrendo⟩ awful, shocking. **~ia** nf infamy

infan'garsi vr get muddy

infan'tile a ⟨letteratura, abbigliamento⟩ children's; ⟨ingenuità⟩ childlike; pej childish

in'fanzia nf childhood; ⟨bambini⟩ children pl; **prima ~** infancy

infar'cire vt pepper ⟨discorso⟩ ⟨di with⟩

infari'na|re vt flour; ⟨di⟩ sprinkle with. **~'tura** nf fig smattering

in'farto nm coronary

infasti'dir|e vt irritate. **~si** vr get irritated

infati'cabile a untiring

in'fatti conj as a matter of fact; ⟨veramente⟩ indeed

infatu'a|rsi vr become infatuated ⟨di with⟩. **~to** a infatuated. **~zi'one** nf infatuation

in'fausto a ill-omened

infe'del|e a unfaithful. **~tà** nf infaithfulness; **~** pl affairs

infe'lic|e a unhappy; ⟨inappropriato⟩ unfortunate; ⟨cattivo⟩ bad. **~ità** nf unhappiness

infel'trirsi vr get matted. **~to** a matted

inferi'or|e a ⟨più basso⟩ lower; ⟨qualità⟩ inferior ● nmf inferior. **~ità** nf inferiority

infer'meria nf infirmary; ⟨di nave⟩ sick-bay

infermi'er|a nf nurse. **~e** nm [male] nurse

infermità nf sickness. **~ mentale** mental illness. **in'fermo, -a** a sick ● nmf invalid

infer'nale a infernal; ⟨spaventoso⟩ hellish

in'ferno nm hell; **va all'~!** go to hell!

infero'cirsi vr become fierce

inferri'ata nf grating

infervo'rar|e vt arouse enthusiasm in. **~si** vr get excited

infe'stare vt infest

infet'tar|e vt infect. **~arsi** vr become infected. **~ivo** a infectious. **in'fetto** a infected. **infezi'one** nf infection

infiac'chir|e vt/i, **~si** vr weaken

infiam'mabile a [in]flammable

infiam'ma|re vt set on fire; Med, fig inflame. **~rsi** vr catch fire; Med become inflamed. **~zi'one** nf Med inflammation

in'fido a treacherous

infie'rire vi ⟨imperversare⟩ rage; **~ su** attack furiously

in'figger|e vt drive. **~si** vr **~si in** penetrate

infi'lar|e vt thread; ⟨mettere⟩ insert; ⟨indossare⟩ put on. **~si** vr slip on ⟨vestito⟩; **~si in** ⟨introdursi in⟩ slip into

infil'tra|rsi vr infiltrate. **~zi'one** nf infiltration; ⟨d'acqua⟩ seepage; ⟨Med: iniezione⟩ injection

infil'zare vt pierce; ⟨infilare⟩ string; ⟨conficcare⟩ stick

'infimo a lowest

in'fine adv finally; ⟨insomma⟩ in short

infinità nf infinity; **un'~ di** masses of. **~'mente** adv infinitely.

infi'nito a infinite; Gram infinitive ● nm infinite; Gram infinitive; Math infinity; **all'infinito** endlessly

infinocchi'are vt fam hoodwink

infischi'arsi vr **~ di** not care about; **me ne infischio** fam I couldn't care less

135 **infisso | ingerenza**

in'fisso *pp di* **infiggere** ● *nm* fixture; (*di porta, finestra*) frame
infit'tire *vt/i,* **~si** *vr* thicken
inflazi'one *nf* inflation
infles'sibile *a* inflexible. **~ità** *nf* inflexibility
inflessi'one *nf* inflexion
in'fliggere *vt* inflict. **~tto** *pp di* **infliggere**
influ'ente *a* influential. **~za** *nf* influence; *Med* influenza
influen'za|bile *a* (*mente, opinione*) impressionable. **~re** *vt* influence. **~to** *a* (*malato*) with the flu
influ'ire *vi* **~ su** influence
in'flusso *nm* influence
info'carsi *vr* catch fire; (*viso:*) go red; (*discussione:*) become heated
info'gnarsi *vr fam* get into a mess
infol'tire *vt/i* thicken
infon'dato *a* unfounded
in'fondere *vt* instil
infor'care *vt* fork up; get on (*bici*); put on (*occhiali*)
infor'male *a* informal
infor'ma|re *vt* inform. **~rsi** *vr* inquire (**di** about). **~tivo** *a* informative.
infor'matic|a *nf* computing, IT. **~o** *a* computer *attrib*
infor'mativo *a* informative. **infor'mato** *a* informed; **male informato** ill-informed. **~tore,** **~trice** *nmf* (*di polizia*) informer. **~zi'one** *nf* information (*solo sg*); **un'~zione** a piece of information
in'forme *a* shapeless
infor'nare *vt* put into the oven
infortu'narsi *vr* have an accident.
infor'tu|nio *nm* accident. **~nio sul lavoro** industrial accident. **~'nistica** *nf* study of industrial accidents
infos'sarsi *vr* sink; (*guance, occhi:*) become hollow. **~to** *a* sunken, hollow
infradici'ar|e *vt* drench. **~si** *vr* get drenched; (*diventare marcio:*) rot
infra'dito *nm inv* (*scarpe*) flip-flop
in'frang|ere *vt* break; (*in mille*

pezzi) shatter. **~ersi** *vr* break. **~'gibile** *a* unbreakable
in'franto *pp di* **infrangere** ● *a* shattered; (*fig: cuore*) broken
infra'rosso *a* infra-red
infrastrut'tura *nf* infrastructure
infrazi'one *nf* offence
infred'da|rsi *vr* catch cold.
infred'do'li|rsi *vr* feel cold. **~to** *a* cold
infrut'tuoso *a* fruitless
infuo'ca|re *vt* make red-hot. **~to** *a* burning
infu'ori *adv* **all'~** outwards; **all'~ di** except
infuri'a|re *vi* rage. **~rsi** *vr* fly into a rage. **~to** *a* blustering
infusi'one *nf* infusion. **in'fuso** *pp di* **infondere** ● *nm* infusion
Ing. *abbr* ingegnere
ingabbi'are *vt* cage; (*fig: mettere in prigione*) jail
ingaggi'are *vt* engage; sign up (*calciatori ecc*); begin (*lotta, battaglia*). **in'gaggio** *nm* engagement; (*di calciatore*) signing [up]
ingan'nar|e *vt* deceive; (*essere infedele a*) be unfaithful to. **~si** *vr* deceive oneself, **se non m'inganno** if I am not mistaken
ingan'nevole *a* deceptive. **in'gan-no** *nm* deceit; (*frode*) fraud
ingarbugli'a|re *vt* entangle; (*confondere*) confuse. **~rsi** *vr* get entangled; (*confondersi*) become confused. **~to** *a* confused
inge'gnarsi *vr* do one's best
inge'gnere *nm* engineer. **ingegne'ria** *nf* engineering
in'gegno *nm* brains *pl*; (*genio*) genius; (*abilità*) ingenuity. **~sa'mente** *adv* ingeniously
ingegnosità *nf* ingenuity. **inge'gnoso** *a* ingenious
ingelo'sir|e *vt* make jealous. **~si** *vr* become jealous
in'gente *a* huge
ingenua'mente *adv* artlessly. **~ità** *nf* ingenuousness. **in'genuo** *a* ingenuous; (*credulone*) naïve
inge'renza *nf* interference

inge'rire *vt* swallow

inges'sare *vt* put in plaster. **~'tura** *nf* plaster

Inghil'terra *nf* England

inghiot'tire *vt* swallow

in'ghippo *nm* trick

ingial'li|re *vi*, **~rsi** *vr* turn yellow. **~to** *a* yellowed

ingigan'tire *vt* magnify ● *vi*, **~si** *vr* grow to enormous proportions

inginocchi'ar|si *vr* kneel [down]. **~to** *a* kneeling. **~toio** *nm* prie-dieu

ingioiel'larsi *vr* put on one's jewels

ingiù *adv* down; **all'~** downwards; **a testa ~** head downwards

ingi'un|gere *vt* order. **~zi'one** *nf* injunction. **~zione di pagamento** final demand

ingi'uri|a *nf* insult; *(torto)* wrong; *(danno)* damage. **~'are** *vt* insult; *(fare un torto a)* wrong. **~'oso** *a* insulting

ingiusta'mente *adv* unjustly, unfairly. **ingiu'stizia** *nf* injustice. **ingi'usto** *a* unjust, unfair

in'glese *a* English ● *nm* Englishman; *(lingua)* English ● *nf* Englishwoman

ingoi'are *vt* swallow

ingol'far|e *vt* flood *(motore)*. **~si** *vr* *fig* get involved; *(motore:)* flood

ingom'bra|nte *a* cumbersome. **~re** *vt* clutter up; *fig* cram *(mente)*

in'gombro *nm* encumbrance; **essere d'~** be in the way

ingor'digia *nf* greed. **in'gordo** *a* greedy

ingor'gar|e *vt* block. **~si** *vr* be blocked [up]. **in'gorgo** *nm* blockage; *(del traffico)* jam

ingoz'zar|e *vt* gobble up; *(nutrire eccessivamente)* stuff; fatten *(animali)*. **~si** *vr* stuff oneself *(di* with)

ingra'na|ggio *nm* gear; *fig* mechanism. **~re** *vt* engage ● *vi* be in gear

ingrandi'mento *nm* enlargement

ingran'di|re *vt* enlarge; *(esagera-*

re) magnify. **~rsi** *vr* become larger; *(aumentare)* increase

ingras'sar|e *vt* fatten up; *Mech* grease ● *vi*, **~si** *vr* put on weight

ingrati'tudine *nf* ingratitude. **in'grato** *a* ungrateful; *(sgradevole)* thankless

ingrazi'arsi *vr* ingratiate oneself with

ingredi'ente *nm* ingredient

in'gresso *nm* entrance; *(accesso)* admittance; *(sala)* hall; **~ gratuito/libero** admission free; **vietato l'~** no entry; no admittance

ingros'sar|e *vt* make big; *(gonfiare)* swell ● *vi*, **~si** *vr* grow big; *(gonfiare)* swell

in'grosso **all'~** *adv* wholesale; *(pressappoco)* roughly

ingua'ribile *a* incurable

'inguine *nm* groin

ingurgi'tare *vt* gulp down

ini'bi|re *vt* inhibit; *(vietare)* forbid. **~to** *a* inhibited. **~zi'one** *nf* inhibition; *(divieto)* prohibition

iniet'tar|e *vt* inject. **~si** *vr* **~si di sangue** *(occhi:)* become bloodshot. **iniezi'one** *nf* injection

inimi'carsi *vr* make an enemy of. **inimi'cizia** *nf* enmity

inimi'tabile *a* inimitable

ininter|rotta'mente *adv* continuously. **~'rotto** *a* continuous

iniquità *nf* iniquity. **i'niquo** *a* iniquitous

inizi'al|e *a* & *nf* initial. **~'mente** *adv* initially

inizi'are *vt* begin; *(avviare)* open; **~ qcno a qcsa** initiate sb in sth ● *vi* begin

inizia'tiva *nf* initiative; **prendere l'~** take the initiative

inizi'a|to, -a *a* initiated ● *nmf* initiate; **gli ~ti** the initiated. **~'to-re, ~'trice** *nmf* initiator. **~zi'one** *nf* initiation

i'nizio *nm* beginning, start; **dare ~** a start; **avere ~** get under way

innaffi'a|re *vt* water. **~'toio** *nm* watering-can

innal'zar|e vt raise; (*erigere*) erect. **~si** vr rise

innamo'ra|rsi vr fall in love (**di** with). **~ta** nf girl-friend. **~to** a in love ● nm boy-friend

in'nanzi adv (*stato in luogo*) in front; (*di tempo*) ahead; (*avanti*) forward; (*prima*) before; **d'ora ~** from now on ● prep (*prima*) before; **~ a** in front of. **~'tutto** adv first of all; (*soprattutto*) above all

in'nato a innate

innatu'rale a unnatural

inne'gabile a undeniable

innervo'sir|e vt make nervous. **~si** vr get irritated

inne'scare vt prime. **in'nesco** nm primer

inne'stare vt graft; Mech engage; (*inserire*) insert. **in'nesto** nm graft; Mech clutch; Electr connection

inne'vato a covered in snow

'inno nm hymn. **~ nazionale** national anthem

inno'cen|te a innocent **~te'mente** adv innocently. **~za** nf innocence.

in'nocuo a innocuous

inno'va|re vt make changes in. **~'tivo** a innovative. **~'tore** a trailblazing. **~zi'one** nf innovation

innume'revole a innumerable

ino'doro a odourless

inoffen'sivo a harmless

inol'trar|e vt forward. **~si** vr advance

inol'trato a late

i'noltre adv besides

inon'da|re vt flood. **~zi'one** nf flood

inopor'tuno a idle

inoppor'tuno a untimely

inorgo'glir|e vt make proud. **~si** vr become proud

inorri'dire vt horrify ● vi be horrified

inospi'tale a inhospitable

inosser'vato a unobserved; (*non rispettato*) disregarded; **passare ~** go unnoticed

inossi'dabile a stainless

'**inox** a inv (*acciaio*) stainless

inqua'dra|re vt frame; fig put in context (*scrittore, problema*). **~rsi** vr fit into. **~'tura** nf framing

inqualifi'cabile a unspeakable

inquie'tar|e vt worry. **~si** get worried; (*impazientirsi*) get cross. **inqui'eto** a restless; (*preoccupato*) worried. **inquie'tudine** nf anxiety

inqui'lino, ~a nmf tenant

inquina'mento nm pollution

inqui'na|re vt pollute. **~to** a polluted

inqui'rente a Jur (*magistrato*) examining; **commissione ~** commission of enquiry

inqui'si|re vt/i investigate. **~to a** under investigation. **~'tore, ~'trice** a inquiring ● nmf inquisitor. **~zi'one** nf inquisition

insab'bi'are vt shelve

insa'la|ta nf salad. **~a belga** endive. **~i'era** nf salad bowl

insa'lubre a unhealthy

insa'nabile a incurable

insangui'na|re vt cover with blood. **~to** a bloody

insapo'nare vt soap

insa'po|re a tasteless. **~'rire** vt flavour

insa'puta nf **all'~ di** unknown to

insazi'abile a insatiable

insce'nare vt stage

inscin'dibile a inseparable

insedia'mento nm installation

insedi'ar|e vt install. **~si** vr install oneself

in'segna nf sign; (*bandiera*) flag; (*decorazione*) decoration; (*emblema*) insignia pl; (*stemma*) symbol. **~ luminosa** neon sign

insegna'mento nm teaching.

inse'gnante a teaching ● nmf teacher

inse'gnare vt/i teach; **~ qcsa a qcno** teach sb sth

insegui'mento nm pursuit

insegu'i|re vt pursue. **~'tore, ~'trice** nmf pursuer

inselvati'chir|e vt make wild ● vi, **~si** vr grow wild

insemi'na|re vt inseminate. **~zi'o-ne** nf insemination. **~zione artifi-ciale** artificial insemination

insena'tura nf inlet

insen'sato a senseless; (folle) crazy

insen'sibil|e a insensitive; ⟨brac-cio ecc⟩ numb. **~ità** nf insensitiv-ity

insepa'rabile a inseparable

inseri'mento nm insertion

inse'rir|e vt insert; place ⟨annun-cio⟩; Electr connect. **~si** vr **si in** get into. **in'serto** nm file; (in un film ecc) insert

inservi'ente nmf attendant

inserzi'o|ne nf insertion; (avviso) advertisement. **~'nista** nmf adver-tiser

insetti'cida nm insecticide

in'setto nm insect

insicu'rezza nf insecurity. **insi'cu-ro** a insecure

in'sidi|a nf trick; (tranello) snare. **~'are** vt/i lay a trap for. **~'oso** a insidious

insi'eme adv together; (contempo-raneamente) at the same time ● prep – **a** [together] with ● nm whole; (completo) outfit; Theat ensemble; Math set; **nell'** as a whole; **tutto ~** all together; ⟨bere⟩ at one go

in'signe a renowned

insignifi'cante a insignificant

insi'gnire vt decorate

insinda'cabile a final

insinu'ante a insinuating

insinu'a|re vt insinuate. **~rsi** vr penetrate; **~rsi in** fig creep into. **~zi'one** nf insinuation

in'sipido a insipid

insi'sten|te a insistent. **~te'men-te** adv repeatedly. **~za** nf insist-ence. **in'sistere** vi insist; (perseve-rare) persevere

insoddisfa'cente a unsatisfac-tory

insoddi'sfa|tto a unsatisfied; (scontento) dissatisfied. **~zi'one** nf dissatisfaction

insoffe'ren|te a intolerant. **~za** nf intolerance

insolazi'one nf sunstroke

inso'len|te a rude, insolent. **~za** nf rudeness, insolence; (commen-to) insolent remark

in'solito a unusual

inso'lubile a insoluble

inso'luto a unsolved; (non pagato) unpaid

insol'venza nf insolvency

in'somma adv in short; **~!** well really!; ⟨così così⟩ so so

in'sonne a sleepless. **~ia** nf in-somnia

insonno'lito a sleepy

insonoriz'zato a soundproofed

insoppor'tabile a unbearable

insor'genza nf onset

in'sorgere vi revolt, rise up; (sorgere) arise; ⟨difficoltà⟩ crop up

insormon'tabile a ⟨ostacolo, diffi-coltà⟩ insurmountable

in'sorto pp di **insorgere** ● a rebel-lious ● nm rebel

insospet'tabile a unsuspected

insospet'tir|e vt make suspicious ● vi, **~si** vr become suspicious

insoste'nibile a untenable; (in-sopportabile) unbearable

insostitu'ibile a irreplaceable

inspe'ra|bile a **una sua vittoria è ~bile** there is no hope of him win-ning. **~to** a unhoped-for

inspie'gabile a inexplicable

inspi'rare vt breathe in

in'stabil|e a unstable; ⟨tempo⟩ changeable. **~ità** nf instability; (di tempo) changeability

instal'la|re vt install. **~rsi** vr set-tle in. **~zi'one** nf installation

instan'cabile a untiring

instau'ra|re vt found. **~rsi** vr be-come established. **~zi'one** nf foundation

instra'dare vt direct

insù adv **all'~** upwards

insubordinazi'one nf insubordi-nation

insuc'cesso nm failure

insudici'ar|e vt dirty. **~si** vr get dirty

insuffici'en|te a insufficient; (inadeguato) inadequate ● nf Sch fail. **~za** nf insufficiency; (inadeguatezza) inadequacy; Sch fail. **~za cardiaca** heart failure. **~za di prove** lack of evidence

insu'lare a insular

insu'lina nf insulin

in'sulso a insipid; (sciocco) silly

insul'tare vt insult. **in'sulto** nm insult

insupe'rabile a insuperable; (eccezionale) incomparable

insurrezi'one nf insurrection

insussi'stente a groundless

intac'care vt nick; (corrodere) corrode; draw on (capitale); (danneggiare) damage

intagli'are vt carve. **in'taglio** nm carving

intan'gibile a untouchable

in'tanto adv meanwhile; (per ora) for the moment; (avversativo) but; **~ che** while

intarsi'a|re vt inlay. **~to a ~to di** inset with. **in'tarsio** nm inlay

inta'sa|re vt clog; block (traffico). **~rsi** vr get blocked. **~to** a blocked

inta'scare vt pocket

in'tatto a intact

intavo'lare vt start

inte'gra|le a whole; **edizione ~le** unabridged edition; **pane ~le** wholemeal bread. **~'mente** adv fully. **~nte** a integral. **in'tegro** a complete; (retto) upright

inte'gra|re vt integrate; (aggiungere) supplement. **~si** vr integrate. **~'tivo** a (corso) supplementary. **~zi'one** nf integration

integrità nf integrity

intelaia'tura nf framework

intel'letto nm intellect

intellettu'al|e a & nmf intellectual. **~'mente** adv intellectually

intelli'gen|te a intelligent. **~'mente** adv intelligently. **~za** nf intelligence

intelli'gibil|e a intelligible. **~'mente** adv intelligibly

intempe'ranza nf intemperance

intem'perie nfpl bad weather

inten'den|te nm superintendent. **~za nf ~za di finanza** inland revenue office

in'tender|e vt (comprendere) understand; (udire) hear; (avere intenzione) intend; (significare) mean. **~sela con** have an understanding with; **~si** vr (capirsi) understand each other; **~si di** (essere esperto) have a good knowledge of

intendi'mento nm understanding; (intenzione) intention. **~'tore, 'trice** nmf connoisseur

intene'rir|e vt soften; (commuovere) touch. **~si** vr be touched

intensa'mente adv intensely

intensifi'car|e vt, **~si** vr intensify

intensità nf inv intensity. **inten'sivo** a intensive. **in'tenso** a intense

inten'tare vt start up; **~ causa contro qcno** bring ○ institute proceedings against sb

in'tento a engrossed (a in) ● nm purpose

intenzio'nato a essere ~ a fare qcsa have the intention of doing sth

intenzio'nale a intentional. **intenzi'one** nf intention; **senza ~ne** unintentionally; **avere ~ne di fare qcsa** intend to do sth, have the intention of doing sth.

intera'gire vi interact

intera'mente adv completely, entirely

interat'tiva a interactive. **~zi'one** nf interaction

interca'lare[1] nm stock phrase

interca'lare[2] vt insert

intercambi'abile a interchangeable

interca'pedine nf cavity

inter'ce|dere vi intercede. **~ssi'one** nf intercession

intercet'ta|re vt intercept; tap (telefono). **~zi'one** nf intercep-

tion. **~zione telefonica** telephone tapping
inter'city nm inv inter-city
intercontinen'tale a intercontinental
inter'correre vi ⟨tempo:⟩ elapse; ⟨esistere⟩ exist
interco'stale a intercostal
inter'detto pp di interdire ● a astonished; ⟨proibito⟩ forbidden; **rimanere ~** be taken aback
inter'di|re vt forbid; Jur deprive of civil rights. **~zi'one** nf prohibition
interessa'mento nm interest
interes'sante a interesting; **essere in stato ~** be pregnant
interes'sa|re vt interest; ⟨riguardare⟩ concern ● vi **~re a** matter to. **~rsi** vr **~rsi a** take an interest in. **~rsi** di take care of. **~to, -a** nmf interested party ● a interested; **essere ~to** pej have an interest
inte'resse nm interest; **fare qcsa per ~** do sth out of self-interest
inter'faccia nf Comput interface
interfe'renza nf interference
interfe'r|ire vi interfere
interiezi'one nf interjection
interi'ora nfpl entrails
interi'ore a interior
inter'ludio nm interlude
intermedi'ario, -a a & nmf intermediary
inter'medio a in-between
inter'mezzo nm Theat, Mus intermezzo
intermi'nabile a interminable
intermit'ten|te a intermittent; ⟨luce⟩ flashing. **~za** nf luce a **~za** flashing light
interna'mento nm internment; ⟨in manicomio⟩ committal
inter'nare vt intern; ⟨in manicomio⟩ commit [to a mental institution]
in'terno a internal; Geog inland; ⟨interiore⟩ inner; ⟨politica⟩ national; **alunno ~** boarder ● nm interior; ⟨di condominio⟩ flat; Teleph

extension; Cinema interior shot; **all'~** inside
internazio'nale a international
in'tero a whole, entire; ⟨intatto⟩ intact; ⟨completo⟩ complete; **per ~** in full
interpel'lare vt consult
inter'por|re vt place ⟨ostacolo⟩. **~si** vr come between
interpre'ta|re vt interpret; Mus perform. **~zi'one** nf interpretation; Mus performance. **in'terprete** nmf interpreter; Mus performer
inter'ra|re vt ⟨seppellire⟩ bury; plant ⟨pianta, seme⟩. **~to** nm basement
interro'ga|re vt question; Sch test; examine ⟨studenti⟩. **~'tivo** a interrogative; ⟨sguardo⟩ questioning; **punto ~tivo** question mark ● nm question. **~'torio** a & nm questioning. **~zi'one** nf question; Sch oral [test]
inter'romper|e vt interrupt; ⟨sospendere⟩ stop; cut off ⟨collegamento⟩. **~si** vr break off
interrut'tore nm switch
interruzi'one nf interruption; **senza ~** non-stop. **~ di gravidanza** termination of pregnancy
interse'ca|re vt, **~'carsi** vr intersect. **~zi'one** nf intersection
inter'stizio nm interstice
interur'ban|a nf long-distance call. **~o** a inter-city; **telefonata ~a** long-distance call
inter'vallo nm interval; ⟨spazio⟩ space; Sch break. **intervallo pubblicitario** commercial break
interve'nire vi intervene; ⟨Med: operare⟩ operate; **~ a** take part in. **inter'vento** nm intervention; ⟨presenza⟩ presence; ⟨chirurgico⟩ operation; **pronto intervento** emergency services
inter'vista nf interview
intervi'sta|re vt interview. **~'tore, ~'trice** nmf interviewer
in'tes|a nf understanding; **cenno**

d'~a acknowledgement. ~o *pp di*
intendere ●a **resta** ~o **che...**
needless to say,...; ~**il** agreed!; ~o
a meant to; **non darsi per** ~ to
refuse to understand

inte'sta|re *vt* head; write one's
name and address at the top of
(*lettera*); *Comm* register. ~**rsi a fare qcsa** take it into one's
head to do sth. ~**'tario, -a** *nmf*
holder. ~**zi'one** *nf* heading; (*su
carta da lettere*) letterhead

intesti'nale *a* intestinal

inte'stino *a* (*lotte*) internal ●*nm*
intestine

intima'mente *adv* (*conoscere*) inti-
mately

inti'ma|re *vt* order; ~**re l'alt a
qcno** order sb to stop. ~**zi'one** *nf*
order

intimida|'torio *a* threatening.
~**zi'one** *nf* intimidation

intimi'dire *vt* intimidate

intimità *nf* cosiness. **'intimo** *a* intimate; (*interno*) innermost; (*ami-
co*) close ●*nm* (*amico*) close
friend; (*dell'animo*) heart

intimo'rire *vt* frighten. ~**rsi** *vr* get
frightened. ~**to** *a* frightened

in'tingere *vt* dip

in'tingolo *nm* sauce; (*pietanza*)
stew

intiriz'zi|re *vt* numb. ~**rsi** *vr* grow
numb. ~**to a essere** ~**to** (*dal
freddo*) be perished

intito'la|re *vt* entitle; (*dedicare*)
dedicate. ~**si** *vr* be called

intolle'rabile *a* intolerable

intona'care *vt* plaster. **in'tonaco**
nm plaster

into'na|re *vt* start to sing; tune
(*strumento*); (*accordare*) match.
~**rsi** *vr* match. ~**to a** (*persona*)
able to sing in tune; (*colore*)
matching

intonazi'one *nf* (*inflessione*) intonation; (*ironico*) tone

inton'tire *vt* daze; (*gas:*) make
dizzy ●*vi* be dazed. ~**to** *a* dazed

intop'pare *vi* ~ **in** run into

in'toppo *nm* obstacle

in'torno *adv* around ●*prep* ~ **a**
around; (*circa*) about

intorpi'di|re *vt* numb. ~**rsi** *vr* be-
come numb. ~**to** *a* torpid

intossi'ca|re *vt* poison. ~**rsi** *vr* be
poisoned. ~**zi'one** *nf* poisoning

intralci'are *vt* hamper

in'tralcio *nm* hitch; **essere d'~** be
a hindrance (a to)

intralaz'zare *vi* intrigue. **intral-
'lazzo** *nm* racket

intramon'tabile *a* timeless

intramusco'lare *a* intramuscular

intransi'gen|te *a* intransigent
uncompromising. ~**za** *nf* intran-
sigence

intransi'tivo *a* intransitive

intrappo'lato a rimanere ~ be
trapped

intrapren'den|te *a* enterprising.
~**za** *nf* initiative

intra'prendere *vt* undertake

intrat'tabile *a* very difficult

intratte'n|ere *vt* entertain. ~**ersi**
vr linger. ~**i'mento** *nm* entertainment

intrave'dere *vt* catch a glimpse of;
(*presagire*) foresee

intrecci'ar|e *vt* interweave; plait
(*capelli, corda*). ~**si** *vr* intertwine;
(*aggrovigliarsi*) become tangled;
~**e le mani** clasp one's hands

in'treccio *nm* (*trama*) plot

in'trepido *a* intrepid

intri'cato *a* tangled

intri'gante *a* scheming (*affascinante*) intriguing

intri'ga|re *vt* entangle; (*incuriosi-
re*) intrigue ●*vi* intrigue, scheme.
~**rsi** *vr* meddle. **in'trigo** *nm* plot;
intrighi *pl* intrigues

in'trinseco *a* intrinsic

in'triso a ~ di soaked in

intri'stirsi *vr* grow sad

intro'du|rre *vt* introduce; (*inseri-
re*) insert; ~**rre a** (*iniziare a*)
introduce to. ~**rsi** *vr* get in (**in**
to). ~**t'tivo** *a* (*pagine, discorso*) introductory. ~**zi'one** *nf* introduction

in'troito *nm* income, revenue; *(incasso)* takings *pl*

intro'metter|e *vt* introduce. ~si *vr* interfere; *(interporsi)* intervene. intromissi'one *nf* intervention

intro'vabile *a* that can't be found; *(prodotto)* unobtainable

intro'verso, -a *a* introverted ● *nmf* introvert

intrufo'larsi *vr* sneak in

in'truglio *nm* concoction

intrusi'one *nf* intrusion. in'truso, -a *nmf* intruder

intu'i|re *vt* perceive

intui|tiva'mente *adv* intuitively. ~'tivo *a* intuitive. in'tuito *nm* intuition. ~zi'one *nf* intuition

inuguagli'anza *nf* inequality

inu'mano *a* inhuman

inu'mare *vt* inter

inumi'dir|e *vt* dampen; moisten *(labbra)*. ~si *vr* become damp

i'nutil|e *a* useless; *(superfluo)* unnecessary. ~ità *nf* uselessness

inutiliz'za|bile *a* unusable. ~to *a* unused

inutil'mente *adv* fruitlessly

inva'dente *a* intrusive

in'vadere *vt* invade; *(affollare)* overrun

invali'd|are *vt* invalidate. ~ità *nf* disability; *Jur* invalidity. in'valido, -a *a* invalid; *(handicappato)* disabled ● *nmf* disabled person

in'vano *adv* in vain

invari'abil|e *a* invariable

invari'ato *a* unchanged

invasi'one *nf* invasion. in'vaso *pp di* invadere. inva'sore *a* invading ● *nm* invader

invecchia'mento *nm (di vino)* maturation

invecchi'are *vt/i* age

in'vece *adv* instead; *(anzi)* but; ~ di instead of

inve'ire *vi* ~ contro inveigh against

inven'd|ibile *a* unsaleable. ~uto *a* unsold

inven'tare *vt* invent

inventari'are *vt* make an inventory of. inven'tario *nm* inventory

inven|'tivo, -a *a* inventive ● *nf* inventiveness. ~'tore, ~'trice *nmf* inventor. ~zi'one *nf* invention

inver'nale *a* wintry. in'verno *nm* winter

invero'simile *a* improbable

inversa'mente *adv* inversely; ~ proporzionale in inverse proportion

inversi'one *nf* inversion; *Mech* reversal. in'verso *a* inverse; *(opposto)* opposite ● *nm* opposite

inverte'brato *a & nm* invertebrate

inver'ti|re *vt* reverse; *(capovolgere)* turn upside down. ~to, -a *nmf* homosexual

investi'ga|re *vt* investigate. ~'tore *nm* investigator. ~zi'one *nf* investigation

investi'mento *nm* investment; *(incidente)* crash

inve'sti|re *vt* invest; *(urtare)* collide with; *(travolgere)* run over; ~re qcno di invest sb with. ~'tura *nf* investiture

invet'tiva *nf* invective

invi'a|re *vt* send. ~to, -a *nmf* envoy; *(di giornale)* correspondent

invidi'a *nf* envy. ~'are *vt* envy. ~'oso *a* envious

invigo'rir|e *vt* invigorate. ~si *vr* become strong

invin'cibile *a* invincible

in'vio *nm* dispatch; *Comput* enter

invio'labile *a* inviolable

invipe'ri|rsi *vr* get nasty. ~to *a* furious

invi'sibil|e *a* invisible. ~ità *nf* invisibility

invi'tante *a (piatto, profumo)* enticing

invi'ta|re *vt* invite. ~to, -a *nmf* guest. in'vito *nm* invitation

invo'ca|re *vt* invoke; *(implorare)* beg. ~zi'one *nf* invocation

invogli'ar|e *vt* tempt; *(indurre)* induce. ~si *vr* ~si di take a fancy to

involon|taria'mente *adv* involuntarily. ~'tario *a* involuntary

invol'tino *nm Culin* beef olive

in'volto *nm* parcel; (*fagotto*) bundle

in'volucro *nm* wrapping

invulne'rabile *a* invulnerable

inzacche'rare *vt* splash with mud

inzup'par|e *vt* soak; (*intingere*) dip. **~si** *vr* get soaked

'io *pers pron* I; **chi è? – [sono] io** who is it? – [it's] me; **l'ho fatto io [stesso]** I did it myself ● *nm* l'**~** the ego

i'odio *nm* iodine

I'onio *nm* lo **~** the Ionian [Sea]

i'osa: a ~ *adv* in abundance

iperat'tivo *a* hyperactive

ipermer'cato *nm* hypermarket

iper'metrope *a* long-sighted

ipersen'sibile *a* hypersensitive

ipertensi'one *nf* high blood pressure

ip'no|si *nf* hypnosis. **~tico** *a* hypnotic. **~tismo** *nm* hypnotism. **~tiz'zare** *vt* hypnotize

ipoca'lorico *a* low-calorie

ipooon'driaco, -a *a & nmf* hypochondriac

ipocri'sia *nf* hypocrisy. **ipocrita** *a* hypocritical ● *nmf* hypocrite

ipo'te|ca *nf* mortgage. **~care** *vt* mortgage

i'potesi *nf inv* hypothesis; (*caso, eventualità*) eventuality. **ipo'tetico** *a* hypothetical. **ipotiz'zare** *vt* hypothesize

'ippico, -a *a* horse *attrib* ● *nm* riding

Ippoca'stano *nm* horse-chestnut

in'nodromo *nm* racecourse

ippo'potamo *nm* hippopotamus

'ira *nf* anger. **~'scibile** *a* irascible

i'rato *a* irate

'iride *nf Anat* iris; (*arcobaleno*) rainbow

Ir'lan|da *nf* Ireland. **~da del Nord** Northern Ireland. **i~'dese** *a* Irish ● *nm* Irishman; (*lingua*) Irish ● *nf* Irishwoman

iro'nia *nf* irony. **i'ronico** *a* ironic[al]

irradi'a|re *vt/i* radiate. **~zi'one** *nf* radiation

irraggiun'gibile *a* unattainable

irragio'nevole *a* unreasonable; (*speranza, timore*) irrational; (*assurdo*) absurd

irrazio'nal|e *a* irrational. **~ità** *a* irrationality. **~'mente** *adv* irrationally

irre'a|le *a* unreal. **~'listico** *a* unrealistic. **~'liz'zabile** *a* unattainable. **~ità** *nf* unreality

irrecupe'rabile *a* irrecoverable

irrego'lar|e *a* irregular. **~ità** *nf inv* irregularity

irremo'vibile *a fig* adamant

irrepa'rabile *a* irreparable

irrepe'ribile *a* not to be found; **sarò ~** I won't be contactable

irrepren'sibile *a* irreproachable

irrepri'mibile *a* irrepressible

irrequi'eto *a* restless

irresi'stibile *a* irresistible

irrespon'sabil|e *a* irresponsible. **~ità** *nf* irresponsibility

irrever'sibile *a* irreversible

irrevo'cabile *a* irrevocable

irricono'scibile *a* unrecognizable

irri'ga|re *vt* irrigate; (*fiume:*) flow through. **~zi'one** *nf* irrigation

irrigidi'mento *nm* stiffening

irrigi'dir|e *vt*, **~si** *vr* stiffen

irrile'vante *a* unimportant

irrimedi'abile *a* irreparable

irripe'tibile *a* unrepeatable

irri'sorio *a* derisive; (*differenza, particolare, somma*) insignificant

irri'ta|bile *a* irritable. **~nte** *a* aggravating

irri'ta|re *vt* irritate. **~rsi** *vr* get annoyed. **~to** *a* irritated; (*gola*) sore. **~zi'one** *nf* irritation

irrobu'stir|e *vt* fortify. **~si** *vr* get stronger

ir'rompere *vi* burst (**in** into)

irro'rare *vt* sprinkle

irru'ente *a* impetuous

irruzi'one *nf* fare **~** burst into

i'scritto, -a *pp di* **iscrivere** ● *a* registered ● *nmf* member; **per ~** in writing

i'scriver|e *vt* register. **~si** *vr* **~si a** register at, enrol at (*scuola*); join

⟨circolo ecc⟩. **iscrizi'one** nf registration; ⟨epigrafe⟩ inscription

i'sla|mico a Islamic. **~'mismo** nm Islam

I'slan|da nf Iceland. **i~'dese** a Icelandic ● nmf Icelander

'isola nf island. **le isole britanniche** the British Isles. **~ pedonale** traffic island. **~ spartitraffico** traffic island. **iso'lano, -a** a insular ● nmf islander

iso'lante a insulating ● nm insulator

iso'la|re vt isolate; Mech, Electr insulate; ⟨acusticamente⟩ soundproof. **~to** a isolated ● nm ⟨di appartamenti⟩ block

ispes'sir|e vt, **~si** vr thicken

ispet'rato nm inspectorate. **ispet'tore** nm inspector. **ispezio'nare** vt inspect. **ispezi'one** nf inspection

'ispido a bristly

ispi'ra|re vt inspire; suggest ⟨idea, soluzione⟩. **~rsi** vr **~rsi a** to be based on. **~to** a inspired. **~zi'one** nf inspiration; ⟨idea⟩ idea

Isra'el|e nm Israel. **i~i'ano, -a** a & nmf Israeli

is'sare vt hoist

istan'taneo, -a a instantaneous ● nf snapshot

i'stante nm instant; **all'~** instantly

i'stanza nf petition

i'sterico a hysterical. **iste'rismo** nm hysteria

isti'ga|re vt instigate; **~re qcno al male** incite sb to evil. **~tore, ~'trice** nmf instigator. **~zi'one** nf instigation

istin|tiva'mente adv instinctively. **~'tivo** a instinctive. **i'stinto** nm instinct; **d'istinto** instinctively

istitu'ire vt institute; ⟨fondare⟩ found; initiate ⟨manifestazione⟩

isti'tu|to nm institute; ⟨universitario⟩ department; Sch secondary school. **~to di bellezza** beauty salon. **~'tore, ~'trice** nmf ⟨insegnante⟩ tutor; ⟨fondatore⟩ founder

istituzio'nale a institutional. **istituzi'one** nf institution

'istmo nm isthmus

'istrice nm porcupine

istru'i|re vt instruct; ⟨addestrare⟩ train; ⟨informare⟩ inform; Jur prepare. **~to** a educated

istrut't|ivo a instructive. **~ore, ~'rice** nmf instructor; **giudice ~ore** examining magistrate. **~'oria** nf Jur investigation. **istruzi'one** nf education; ⟨indicazione⟩ instruction

I'tali|a nf Italy. **i~'ano, -a** a & nmf Italian

itine'rario nm route, itinerary

itte'rizia nf jaundice

'ittico a fishing attrib

I.V.A. nf abbr ⟨imposta sul valore aggiunto⟩ VAT

Jj

jack nm inv jack

jazz nm jazz. **jaz'zista** nmf jazz player

jeep nf inv jeep

'jolly nm inv ⟨carta da gioco⟩ joker

Jugo'slav|ia nf Yugoslavia. **j~o, -a** a & nmf Yugoslav[ian]

ju'niores nmfpl Sport juniors

Kk

ka'jal nm inv kohl

kara'oke nm inv karaoke

kara'te nm karate

kg abbr ⟨chilogrammo⟩ kg

km abbr ⟨chilometro⟩ km

LI

l' *def art mf* (*before vowel*) the; *vedi* **il**

la *def art f* the; *vedi* **il** ● *pron* (*oggetto, riferito a persona*) her; (*riferito a cosa, animale*) it; (*forma di cortesia*) you ● *nm inv Mus* (*chiave, nota*) A

là *adv* there; **di là** (*in quel luogo*) in there; (*da quella parte*) that way; **eccolo là!** there he is!; **farsi più in là** (*far largo*) make way; **là dentro** in there; **là fuori** out there; **[ma] va là** come off it!; **più in là** (*nel tempo*) later on; (*nello spazio*) further on

'labbro *nm* (*pl nf Anat* **labbra**) lip

labi'rinto *nm* labyrinth; (*di sentieri ecc*) maze

labora'torio *nm* laboratory; (*di negozio, officina ecc*) workshop

labori'oso *a* (*operoso*) industrious; (*faticoso*) laborious

labu'rista *a* Labour ● *nmf* member of the Labour Party

'lacca *nf* lacquer; (*per capelli*) hairspray, lacquer. **lac'care** *vt* lacquer

'laccio *nm* noose; (*lazo*) lasso; (*trappola*) snare; (*stringa*) lace

lace'rante *a* (*grido*) earsplitting

lace'ra|re *vt* tear; lacerate (*carne*). **~rsi** *vr* tear. **~zi'one** *nf* laceration. **'lacero** *a* torn; (*cencioso*) ragged

la'conico *a* laconic

'lacri|ma *nf* tear; (*goccia*) drop. **~'mare** *vi* weep. **~'mevole** *a* tear-jerking

lacri'mogeno *a* **gas ~** tear gas

lacri'moso *a* tearful

la'cuna *nf* gap. **lacu'noso** *a* (*preparazione, resoconto*) incomplete

la'custre *a* lake *attrib*

'ladro, -a *nmf* thief; **al ~!** stop

thief! **~'cinio** *nm* theft. **la'druncolo** *nm* petty thief

'lager *nm inv* concentration camp

laggiù *adv* down there; (*lontano*) over there

'lagna *nf* (*fam: persona*) moaning Minnie; (*film*) bore

la'gna|nza *nf* complaint. **~rsi** *vr* moan; (*protestare*) complain (**di** about). **la'gnoso** *a* (*persona*) moaning

'lago *nm* lake

la'guna *nf* lagoon

'laico, -a *a* lay; (*vita*) secular ● *nm* layman ● *nf* laywoman

'lama *nf* blade ● *nm inv* (*animale*) llama

lambic'carsi *vr* **~ il cervello** rack one's brains

lam'bire *vt* lap

lamé *nm inv* lamé

lamen'tar|e *vt* lament. **~si** *vr* moan. **~si di** (*lagnarsi*) complain about

lamen'te|la *nf* complaint. **~vole** *a* mournful; (*pietoso*) pitiful. **la'mento** *nm* moan

la'metta *nf* **~** [**da barba**] razor blade

la'miera *nf* sheet metal

'lamina *nf* foil. **~ d'oro** gold leaf

lami'na|re *vt* laminate. **~to** *a* laminated ● *nm* laminate; (*tessuto*) lamé

'lampa|da *nf* lamp. **~da abbronzante** sunlamp. **~da a pila** torch. **~'dario** *nm* chandelier. **~'dina** *nf* light bulb

lam'panto *a* clear

lampeggi'a|re *vi* flash. **~'tore** *nm* *Auto* indicator

lampi'one *nm* street lamp

'lampo *nm* flash of lightning; (*luce*) flash; **lampi** *pl* lightning *sg*. **~ di genio** stroke of genius; (*cerniera*) **~** zip [*fastener*], zipper *Am*

lam'pone *nm* raspberry

'lana *nf* wool; **di ~** woollen. **~ d'acciaio** steel wool. **~ vergine** new wool. **~ di vetro** glass wool

lan'cetta nf pointer; (di orologio) hand

'**lancia** nf (arma) spear, lance; Naut launch

lanci'ar|e vt throw; (da un aereo) drop; launch (missile, prodotto); give 〈grido〉 let out. **~e uno sguardo a** glance at. **~si** vr fling oneself; (intraprendere) launch out

lanci'nante a piercing

'**lancio** nm throwing; (da aereo) drop; (di missile, prodotto) launch. **~ del disco** discus [throwing]. **~ del giavellotto** javelin [throwing]. **~ del peso** putting the shot

'**landa** nf heath

langu'ire vi languish

langu'ore nm languor

lani'ero a wool

lani'ficio nm woollen mill

lan'terna nf lantern; (faro) light-house

la'nugine nf down

lapi'dare vt stone; fig demolish

lapi'dario a (conciso) terse

'**lapide** nf tombstone; (commemorativa) memorial tablet

'**lapis** nm inv pencil

'**lapsus** nm inv lapse, error

'**lardo** nm lard

larga'mente adv (ampiamente) widely

lar'ghezza nf width, breadth; fig liberality. **~ di vedute** broadmindedness

'**largo** a wide; (ampio) broad; 〈abito〉 loose; (liberale) liberal; (abbondante) generous; **stare alla larga** keep away; **~ di manica** fig generous; **~ di spalle/vedute** broadshouldered/-minded ● nm width; **andare al ~** Naut go out to sea; **fare ~** make room; **farsi ~** make one's way; **al ~ di** off the coast of

'**larice** nm larch

la'ringe nf larynx. **larin'gite** nf laryngitis

'**larva** nf larva; (persona emaciata) shadow

la'sagne nfpl lasagna sg

lasciapas'sare nm inv pass

lasci'ar|e vt leave; (rinunciare) give up; (rimetterci) lose; (smettere di tenere) let go [of]; (concedere) let; **~e di fare qcsa** (smettere) stop doing sth; **lascia perdere!** forget it!; **lascialo venire, lascia che venga** let him come. **~si** vr (reciproco) leave each other, split up; **~si andare** let oneself go

'**lascito** nm legacy

'**laser** a & nm inv [**raggio**] **~** laser [beam]

lassa'tivo a & nm laxative

'**lasso** nm **~ di tempo** period of time

lassù adv up there

'**lastra** nf slab; (di ghiaccio) sheet; (di metallo, Phot) plate; (radiografia) X-ray [plate]

lastri'ca|re vt pave. **~to, 'lastrico** nm pavement; **sul lastrico** on one's beam-ends

la'tente a latent

late'rale a side attrib; Med, Techn ecc lateral; **via ~** side street

late'rizi nmpl bricks

lati'fondo nm large estate

la'tino a & nm Latin

lati'tan|te a in hiding ● nmf fugitive [from justice]

lati'tudine nf latitude

'**lato** a (ampio) broad; **in senso ~** broadly speaking ● nm side; (aspetto) aspect; **a ~ di** beside; **dal ~ mio** (punto di vista) for my part; **d'altro ~** fig on the other hand

la'tra|re vi bark. **~to** nm barking

la'trina nf latrine

'**latta** nf tin, can

lat'taio, -a nm milkman ● nf milkwoman

lat'tante a breast-fed ● nmf suckling

'**latt|e** nm milk. **~e acido** sour milk. **~e condensato** condensed milk. **~e detergente** cleansing milk. **~e in polvere** powdered milk. **~e scremato** skimmed milk. **~eo** a milky. **~e'ria** nf dairy. **~i'cini** nmpl dairy products. **~i'era** nf milk jug

lat'tina nf can
lat'tuga nf lettuce
'laurea nf degree; **prendere la ~a** graduate. **~'ando, -a** nmf final-year student
laure'a|rsi vr graduate. **~to, -a** a & nmf graduate
'lauro nm laurel
'lauto a lavish; **~ guadagno** handsome profit
'lava nf lava
la'vabile a washable
la'vabo nm wash-basin
la'vaggio nm washing. **~ automatico** (per auto) carwash. **~ del cervello** brainwashing. **~ a secco** dry-cleaning
la'vagna nf slate; Sch blackboard
la'van|da nf wash; Bot lavender; **fare ~da gastrica** have one's stomach pumped. **~'daia** nf washerwoman. **~de'ria** nf laundry. **~deria automatica** launderette
lavan'dino nm sink; (hum: persona) bottomless pit
lavapi'atti nmf inv dishwasher
la'var|e vt wash; **~e i piatti** wash up. **~si** vr wash, have a wash; **~si i denti** brush one's teeth; **~si le mani** wash one's hands
lava'secco nmf inv dry-cleaner's
lavasto'viglie nf inv dishwasher
la'vata nf wash; **darsi una ~** have a wash; **~ di capo** fig scolding
lava'tivo, a nmf idler
lava'trice nf washing-machine
lavo'rante nmf worker
lavo'ra|re vi work ● vt work; knead (pasta ecc); till (la terra). **~re a maglia** knit. **~'tivo** a working. **~to** a (pietra, legno) carved; (cuoio) tooled; (metallo) wrought. **~'tore, ~'trice** nmf worker ● a working. **~zi'one** nf manufacture; (di terra) working; (artigianale) workmanship; (del terreno) cultivation. **lavo'rio** nm intense activity
la'voro nm work; (faticoso, sociale) labour; (impiego) job; Theat play; **mettersi al ~** set to work (su

on). **~ a maglia** knitting. **~ nero** moonlighting. **~ straordinario** overtime. **~ a tempo pieno** full-time job. **lavori** pl di casa housework. **lavori** pl in corso roadworks. **lavori** pl forzati hard labour. **lavori** pl stradali roadworks
le def art fpl the; vedi **il** ● pers pron (oggetto) them; (a lei) her; (forma di cortesia) you
le'al|e a loyal. **~'mente** adv loyally. **~tà** nf loyalty
'lebbra nf leprosy
'lecca 'lecca nm inv lollipop
leccapi'edi nmf inv pej bootlicker
lec'ca|re vt lick; fig suck up to. **~rsi** vr lick; (fig: agghindarsi) doll oneself up; **da ~rsi i baffi** mouth-watering. **~ta** nf lick
leccor'nia nf delicacy
'lecito a lawful; (permesso) permissible
'ledere vt damage; Med injure
'lega nf league; (di metalli) alloy; **far ~ con** qcno take up with sb
le'gaccio nm string; (delle scarpe) shoelace
le'gal|e a legal ● nm lawyer. **~ità** nf legality. **~iz'zare** vt authenticate; (rendere legale) legalize. **~'mente** adv legally
le'game nm tie; (amoroso) liaison; (connessione) link
lega'mento nm Med ligament
le'ga|re vt tie up (prigioniero); tie together (due cose); (unire, rilegare) bind; alloy (metalli); (connettere) connect; **~sela al dito** fig bear a grudge ● vi (far lega) get on well. **~si** vr bind oneself; **~si a** qcno become attached to sb
le'gato nm legacy; Relig legate
lega'tura nf tying; (di libro) binding
le'genda nf legend
'legge nf law; (parlamentare) act; **a norma di ~** by law
leg'genda nf legend; (didascalia) caption. **leggen'dario** a legendary
'leggere vt/i read

legge'r|ezza *nf* lightness; (*frivolezza*) frivolity; (*incostanza*) fickleness. **~'mente** *adv* slightly

leg'gero *a* light; (*bevanda*) weak; (*lieve*) slight; (*frivolo*) frivolous; (*incostante*) fickle; **alla leggera** frivolously

leg'gibile *a* (*scrittura*) legible; (*stile*) readable

leg'gio *nm* lectern; *Mus* music stand

legife'rare *vi* legislate

legio'nario *nm* legionary. **legi'one** *nf* legion

legisla'tivo *a* legislative. **~'tore** *nm* legislator. **~'tura** *nf* legislature. **~zi'one** *nf* legislation

legittimità *nf* legitimacy. **le'gittimo** *a* legitimate; (*giusto*) proper; **legittima difesa** self-defence

'legna *nf* firewood

le'gname *nm* timber

le'gnata *nf* blow with a stick

'legno *nm* wood; **di ~** wooden. **~ compensato** plywood. **le'gnoso** *a* woody

le'gume *nm* pod

'lei *pers pron* (*soggetto*) she; (*oggetto, con prep*) her; (*forma di cortesia*) you; **lo ha fatto ~ stessa** she did it herself

'lembo *nm* edge; (*di terra*) strip

'lemma *nm* headword

'lena *nf* vigour

le'nire *vt* soothe

lenta'mente *adv* slowly

'lente *nf* lens. **~ a contatto** contact lens. **~ d'ingrandimento** magnifying glass

len'tezza *nf* slowness

len'ticchia *nf* lentil

len'tiggine *nf* freckle

'lento *a* slow; (*allentato*) slack; (*abito*) loose

'lenza *nf* fishing-line

len'zuolo *nm* (*pl f* **lenzuola**) *nm* sheet

le'one *nm* lion; *Astr* Leo

leo'pardo *nm* leopard

'lepre *nf* hare

'lercio *a* filthy

'lesbica *nf* lesbian

lesi'nare *vt* grudge ● *vi* be stingy

lesio'nare *vt* damage. **lesi'one** *nf* lesion

'leso *pp di* **ledere** ● *a* injured

'lessare *vt* boil

'lessico *nm* vocabulary

'lesso *a* boiled ● *nm* boiled meat

'lesto *a* quick; (*mente*) sharp

le'tale *a* lethal

leta'maio *nm* dunghill; *fig* pigsty. **le'tame** *nm* dung

le'targ|ico *a* lethargic. **~o** *nm* lethargy; (*di animali*) hibernation

le'tizia *nf* joy

'lettera *nf* letter; **alla ~** literally; **~ maiuscola** capital letter; **~ minuscola** small letter; **lettere** *pl* (*letteratura*) literature *sg*; *Univ* Arts; **dottore in lettere** BA, Bachelor of Arts

lette'rale *a* literal

lette'rario *a* literary

lette'rato *a* well-read

lettera'tura *nf* literature

let'tiga *nf* stretcher

let'tino *nm* cot; *Med* couch

'letto *nm* bed. **~ a castello** bunkbed. **~ a una piazza** single bed. **~ a due piazze** double bed. **~ matrimoniale** double bed

letto'rato *nm* (*corso*) ≈ tutorial

let'tore, -'trice *nmf* reader; *Univ* language assistant ● *nm Comput* disk drive. **~ di CD-ROM** CD-Rom drive

let'tura *nf* reading

leuce'mia *nf* leukaemia

'leva *nf* lever; *Mil* call-up; **far ~** lever. **~ del cambio** gear lever

le'vante *nm* East; (*vento*) east wind

le'va|re *vt* (*alzare*) raise; (*togliere*) take away; (*rimuovere*) take off; (*estrarre*) pull out; **~re di mezzo qcsa** get sth out of the way. **~rsi** *vr* rise; (*da letto*) get up; **~rsi di mezzo, ~rsi dai piedi** get out of the way. **~ta** *nf* rising; (*di posta*) collection

leva'taccia *nf* fare una ~ get up at the crack of dawn

leva'toio *a* ponte ~ drawbridge

levi'ga|re *vt* smooth; (*con carta vetro*) rub down. **~to** *a* ⟨*superficie*⟩ polished

levri'ero *nm* greyhound

lezi'one *nf* lesson; *Univ* lecture; (*rimprovero*) rebuke

lezi'oso *a* ⟨*stile, modi*⟩ affected

li *pers pron mpl* them

lì *adv* there; **fin lì** as far as there; **giù di lì** thereabouts; **lì per lì** there and then

Li'bano *nm* Lebanon

'libbra *nf* (*peso*) pound

li'beccio *nm* south-west wind

li'bellula *nf* dragon-fly

libe'rale *a* liberal; (*generoso*) generous ● *nmf* liberal

libe'ra|re *vt* free; release (*prigioniero*); vacate (*stanza*); (*salvare*) rescue. **~rsi** *vr* (*stanza*) become vacant; *Teleph* become free; (*da impegno*) get out of it; **~rsi di** get rid of. **~tore, ~trice** *a* liberating ● *nmf* liberator. **~zi'one** *nf* liberation; **la L~zione** (*ricorrenza*) Liberation Day

'liber|o *a* free; (*strada*) clear. **~o docente** qualified university lecturer. **~o professionista** self-employed person. **~tà** *nf inv* freedom; (*di prigioniero*) release. **~tà provvisoria** *Jur* bail. **~tà** *pl* (*confidenze*) liberties

'liberty *nm & a inv* Art Nouveau

'Libia *nf* Libya. **l~co, -a** *a & nmf* Libyan

li'bidine *nf* lust. **~'noso** *a* lustful.

li'bido *nf* libido

libra'io *nm* bookseller

libre'ria *nf* (*negozio*) bookshop; (*mobile*) bookcase; (*biblioteca*) library

li'bretto *nm* booklet; *Mus* libretto. **~ degli assegni** cheque book. **~ di circolazione** logbook. **~ d'istruzioni** instruction booklet. **~ di risparmio** bankbook. **~ uni-**

versitario book held by students which records details of their exam performances

'libro *nm* book. **~ giallo** thriller. **~ paga** payroll

lice'ale *nmf* secondary-school student ● *a* secondary-school *attrib*

li'cenza *nf* licence; (*permesso*) permission; *Mil* leave; *Sch* school-leaving certificate; **essere in ~** be on leave

licenzia'mento *nm* dismissal

licenzi'a|re *vt* dismiss, sack *fam*. **~rsi** *vr* (*da un impiego*) resign; (*accomiatarsi*) take one's leave

li'ceo *nm* secondary school, high school. **~ classico** secondary school with an emphasis on humanities. **~ scientifico** secondary school with an emphasis on sciences

li'chene *nm* lichen

'lido *nm* beach

li'eto *a* glad; (*evento*) happy; **molto ~!** I pleased to meet you!

li'eve *a* light; (*debole*) faint; (*trascurabile*) slight

lievi'tare *vi* rise ● *vt* leaven. **li'evito** *nm* yeast. **lievito in polvere** baking powder

'lifting *nm inv* face-lift

'ligio *a* essere ~ **al dovere** have a sense of duty

'lilla *nf Bot* lilac ● *nm* (*colore*) lilac

'lima *nf* file

limacci'oso *a* slimy

li'mare *vt* file

'limbo *nm* limbo

li'metta *nf* nail-file

'limi'tare *nm* threshold ● *vt* limit. **~rsi** *vr* **~rsi a fare qcsa** limit oneself to doing sth; **~rsi in qcsa** cut down on sth. **~'tivo** *a* limiting. **~to** *a* limited. **~zi'one** *nf* limitation

'limite *nm* limit; (*confine*) boundary. **~ di velocità** speed limit

li'mitrofo *a* neighbouring

limo'nata *nf* (*bibita*) lemonade; (*succo*) lemon juice li'mone *nm* lemon; ⟨*albero*⟩ lemon tree

'limpido *a* clear; ⟨*occhi*⟩ limpid

'lince *nf* lynx

linci'are *vt* lynch

'lindo *a* neat; ⟨*pulito*⟩ clean

'linea *nf* line; ⟨*di autobus, aereo*⟩ route; ⟨*di metro*⟩ line; ⟨*di abito*⟩ cut; ⟨*di auto, mobile*⟩ design; ⟨*fisico*⟩ figure; **in ~ d'aria** as the crow flies; **è caduta la ~** I've been cut off; **in ~ di massima** as a rule; **a grandi linee** in outline; **mantenere la ~** keep one's figure; **in prima ~** in the front line; **mettersi in ~** line up; **nave di ~** liner; **volo di ~** scheduled flight. **~ d'arrivo** finishing line. **~ continua** unbroken line

linea'menti *nmpl* features

line'are *a* linear; ⟨*discorso*⟩ to the point; ⟨*ragionamento*⟩ consistent

line'etta *nf* ⟨*tratto lungo*⟩ dash; ⟨*d'unione*⟩ hyphen

lin'gotto *nm* ingot

'lingua *nf* tongue; ⟨*linguaggio*⟩ language. **~'accia** *nf* ⟨*persona*⟩ backbiter. **~'aggio** *nm* language. **~'etta** *nf* ⟨*di scarpa*⟩ tongue; ⟨*di strumento*⟩ reed; ⟨*di busta*⟩ flap

lingu'ist|a *nmf* linguist. **~ica** *nf* linguistics *sg*. **~ico** *a* linguistic

'lino *nm* Bot flax; ⟨*tessuto*⟩ linen

li'noleum *nm* linoleum

liofiliz'za|re *vt* freeze-dry. **~to** *a* freeze-dried

liposuzi'one *nf* liposuction

lique'far|e *vt*, **~si** *vr* liquefy; ⟨*sciogliersi*⟩ melt

liqui'da|re *vt* liquidate; settle ⟨*conto*⟩; pay off ⟨*debiti*⟩; clear ⟨*merce*⟩; ⟨*fam: uccidere*⟩ get rid of. **~zi'one** *nf* liquidation; ⟨*di conti*⟩ settling; ⟨*di merce*⟩ clearance sale

'liquido *a* & *nm* liquid

liqui'rizia *nf* liquorice

li'quore *nm* liqueur; **liquori** *pl* ⟨*bevande alcooliche*⟩ liquors

'lira *nf* lira; Mus lyre

'lirico, -a *a* lyrical; ⟨*poesia*⟩ lyric; ⟨*cantante, musica*⟩ opera *attrib* ● *nf* lyric poetry; Mus opera

'lisca *nf* fishbone; **avere la ~** ⟨*fam: nel parlare*⟩ have a lisp

lisci'are *vt* smooth; ⟨*accarezzare*⟩ stroke. **'liscio** *a* smooth; ⟨*capelli*⟩ straight; ⟨*liquore*⟩ neat; ⟨*acqua minerale*⟩ still; **passarla liscia** get away with it

'liso *a* worn [out]

'lista *nf* list; ⟨*striscia*⟩ strip. **~ di attesa** waiting list; **in ~ di attesa** Aeron stand-by. **~ elettorale** electoral register. **~ nera** blacklist. **~ di nozze** wedding list. **li'stare** *vt* edge; Comput list

li'stino *nm* list. **~ prezzi** price list

Lit. *abbr* ⟨*lire italiane*⟩ Italian lire

'lite *nf* quarrel; ⟨*baruffa*⟩ row; Jur lawsuit

liti'gare *vi* quarrel. **litigio** *nm* quarrel. **litigi'oso** *a* quarrelsome

lito'rale *a* coastal ● *nm* coast

'litro *nm* litre

li'turgico *a* liturgical

li'vella *nf* level. **~ a bolla d'aria** spirit level

livel'lar|e *vt* level. **~si** *vr* level out

li'vello *nm* level; **passaggio a ~** level crossing; **sotto/sul ~ del mare** below/above sea level

'livido *a* livid; ⟨*per il freddo*⟩ blue; ⟨*per una botta*⟩ black and blue ● *nm* bruise

Li'vorno *nf* Leghorn

'lizza *nf* lists *pl*; **essere in ~ per qcsa** be in the running for sth

lo *def art m* ⟨*before s* + *consonant, gn, ps, z*⟩ the; *vedi* **il** ● *pron* ⟨*riferito a persona*⟩ him; ⟨*riferito a cosa*⟩ it; **non lo so** I don't know

'lobo *nm* lobe

lo'cal|e *a* local ● *nm* ⟨*stanza*⟩ room; ⟨*treno*⟩ local train; **~i** *pl* ⟨*edifici*⟩ premises. **~e notturno** night-club. **~ità** *nf inv* locality

localiz'zare *vt* localize; ⟨*trovare*⟩ locate

lo'canda *nf* inn

locan'dina *nf* bill, poster

loca'tario, -a *nmf* tenant. **~'tore,**

~'trice nm landlord ● nf landlady.
~zi'one nf tenancy
locomo|'tiva nf locomotive.
~zi'one nf locomotion; **mezzi di**
~zione means of transport
'loculo nm burial niche
lo'custa nf locust
locuzi'one nf expression
lo'dare vt praise. **'lode** nf praise;
laurea con lode first-class degree
'loden m inv (cappotto) loden coat
lo'devole a praiseworthy
'lodola nf lark
'loggia nf loggia; (massonica)
lodge
loggi'one nm gallery, the gods
'logica nf logic
logica'mente adv (in modo logico)
logically; (ovviamente) of course
'logico a logical
lo'gistica nf logistics sg
logo'rante a (esperienza) wearing
logo'ra|re vt wear out; (sciupare)
waste. **~rsi** vr wear out; (persona:) wear oneself out. **logo'rio**
nm wear and tear. **'logoro** a worn-
out
lom'baggine nf lumbago
Lombar'dia nf Lombardy
lom'bata nf loin. **'lombo** nm Anat
loin
lom'brico nm earthworm
'Londra nf London
lon'gevo a long-lived
longi'lineo a tall and slim
longi'tudine nf longitude
lontana'mente adv distantly; (vagamente) vaguely; **neanche ~** not
for a moment
lonta'nanza nf distance; (separazione) separation; **in ~** in the
distance
lon'tano a far; (distante) distant;
(nel tempo) far-off, distant; (parente) distant; (vago) vague, (assente) absent; **più ~** further ● adv
far [away]; **da ~** from a distance;
tenersi ~ da keep away from
'lontra nf otter
lo'quace a talkative
'lordo a dirty; (somma, peso) gross

'loro[1] pron pl (soggetto) they;
(oggetto) them; (forma di cortesia)
you; **sta a ~** it is up to them
'loro[2] (**il ~** m, **la ~** f, **i ~** mpl, **le ~**
fpl) a their; (forma di cortesia)
your; **un ~** **amico** a friend of
theirs; (forma di cortesia) a friend
of yours ● pron theirs; (forma di
cortesia) yours; **i ~** their folk
lo'sanga nf lozenge; **a losanghe**
diamond-shaped
'losco a suspicious
'loto nm lotus
'lott|a nf fight, struggle; (contrasto)
conflict; Sport wrestling. **lot'tare**
vi fight, struggle; Sport, fig wres-
tle. **~a'tore** nm wrestler
lotte'ria nf lottery
'lotto nm [national] lottery; (porzione) lot; (di terreno) plot
lozi'one nf lotion
lubrifi'ca|nte a lubricating ● nm
lubricant. **~re** vt lubricate
luc'chetto nm padlock
lucci'ca|nte a sparkling. **~re** vi
sparkle. **lucci'chio** nm sparkle
'luccio nm pike
'lucciola nf glow-worm
'luce nf light; **far ~ su** shed light
on; **dare alla ~** give birth to. **~**
della luna moonlight. **luci** pl **di**
posizione sidelights. **~ del sole**
sunlight
lu'cen|te a shining. **~'tezza** nf
shine
lucer'nario nm skylight
lu'certola nf lizard
'lucida'labbra nm inv lip gloss
luci'da|re vt polish. **~'trice** nf
[floor-]polisher. **'lucido** a shiny;
(pavimento, scarpe) polished;
(chiaro) clear; (persona, mente)
lucid; (occhi) watery ● nm shine.
lucido [da scarpe] [shoe] polish
lucra'tivo a lucrative. **'lucro** nm
lucre
'luglio nm July
'lugubre a gloomy
lui pers pron (soggetto) he; (oggetto,
con prep) him; **lo ha fatto**
stesso he did it himself

lu'maca nf (mollusco) snail; fig slowcoach

'lume nm lamp; (luce) light; **a ~ di candela** by candlelight

luminosità nf brightness. **lumi-'noso** a luminous; (stanza, cielo ecc) bright

'luna nf moon; **chiaro di ~** moon-light; **avere la ~ storta** to be in a bad mood. **~ di miele** honeymoon

luna park nm inv fairground

lu'nare a lunar

lu'nario nm almanac; **sbarcare il ~** make both ends meet

lu'natico a moody

lunedì nm inv Monday

lu'netta nf half-moon [shape]

lun'gaggine nf slowness

lun'ghezza nf length. **~ d'onda** wavelength

'lungi adv ero [ben] **~ dall'imma-ginare che...** I never dreamt for a moment that...

lungimi'rante a far-sighted, far-seeing

'lungo a long; (diluito) weak; (lento) slow; **saperla lunga** be shrewd ● nm length; **di gran lunga** by far; **andare per le lunghe** drag on ● prep (durante) throughout; (per la lunghezza di) along

lungofi'ume nm riverside

lungo'lago nm lakeside

lungo'mare nm sea front

lungome'traggio nm feature film

lu'notto nm rear window

lu'ogo nm place; (punto preciso) spot; (passo d'autore) passage; **aver ~** take place; **dar ~ a** give rise to; **del ~** (usanze) local. **~ comune** platitude. **~ pubblico** public place

luogote'nente nm Mil lieutenant

lu'petto nm Cub [Scout]

'lupo nm wolf

'luppolo nm hop

'lurido a filthy. **luri'dume** nm filth

lu'singa nf flattery

lusin'g|are vt flatter. **~arsi** vr flat-ter oneself; (illudersi) fool oneself. **~hi'ero** a flattering

lus'sa|re vt, **~rsi** vr dislocate. **~zi'one** nf dislocation

Lussem'burgo nm Luxembourg

'lusso nm luxury; **di ~** luxury attrib

lussu'oso a luxurious

lussureggi'ante a luxuriant

lus'suria nf lust

lu'strare vt polish

lu'strino nm sequin

'lustro a shiny ● nm sheen; fig prestige; (quinquennio) five-year period

'lutt|o nm mourning; **~o stretto** deep mourning. **~u'oso** a mourn-ful

Mm

m abbr (metro) m

ma conj but; (eppure) yet; **ma!** (dub-bio) I don't know; (indignazione) really!; **ma davvero?** really?; **ma sì** why not!; (certo che sì) of course!

'macabro a macabre

macché int of course not!

macche'roni nmpl macaroni sg

macche'ronico a (italiano) bro-ken

'macchia¹ nf stain; (di diverso co-lore) spot; (piccola) speck; **senza ~** spotless

'macchia² nf (boscaglia) scrub; **darsi alla ~** take to the woods

macchi'a|re vt, **~rsi** vr stain. **~to a** (caffè) with a dash of milk; **~to di** (sporco) stained with

'macchina nf machine; (motore) engine; (automobile) car. **~ da cu-cire** sewing machine. **~ da presa** cine camera. **~ da scrivere** type-writer

macchinal'mente adv mechani-cally

macchi'nare vt plot

macchi'nario nm machinery

macchi'netta nf (per i denti) brace

macchi'nista *nm Rail* engine-driver; *Naut* engineer; *Theat* stagehand

macchi'noso *a* complicated

mace'donia *nf* fruit salad

macel'la|io *nm* butcher. **~re** *vt* slaughter, butcher. **macelle'ria** *nf* butcher's [shop]. **ma'cello** *nm* (*mattatoio*) slaughterhouse; *fig* shambles *sg*; **andare al macello** *fig* go to the slaughter; **mandare al macello** *fig* send to his/her death

mace'rar|e *vt* macerate; *fig* distress. **~si** *vr* be consumed

ma'cerie *nfpl* rubble *sg*; (*rottami*) debris *sg*

ma'cigno *nm* boulder

maci'lento *a* emaciated

'macina *nf* millstone

macinacaffè *nm inv* coffee mill

macina'pepe *nm inv* pepper mill

maci'na|re *vt* mill. **~to** *a* ground ● *nm* (*carne*) mince. **maci'nino** *nm* mill; (*hum: macchina*) old banger

maciul'lare *vt* (*stritolare*) crush

macrobiotic|a *nf* **negozio di ~a** health-food shop. **~o** *a* macrobiotic

macro'scopico *a* macroscopic

macu'lato *a* spotted

'madido *a* **~ di** moist with

Ma'donna *nf* Our Lady

mador'nale *a* gross

'madre *nf* mother. **~'lingua** *a inv* **inglese ~lingua** English native speaker. **~'patria** *nf* native land. **~'perla** *nf* mother-of-pearl

ma'drina *nf* godmother

maestà *nf* majesty

maestosità *nf* majesty. **mae'stoso** *a* majestic

mae'strale *nm* northwest wind

mae'stranza *nf* workers *pl*

mae'stria *nf* mastery

ma'estro, -a *nmf* teacher ● *nm* master; *Mus* maestro. **~ di cerimonie** master of ceremonies ● *a* (*principale*) chief; (*di grande abilità*) skilful

'mafi|a *nf* Mafia. **~'oso** *a* of the Mafia ● *nm* member of the Mafia, Mafioso

'maga *nf* sorceress

ma'gagna *nf* fault

ma'gari *adv* (*forse*) maybe ● *int* I wish! ● *conj* (*per esprimere desiderio*) if only; (*anche se*) even if

magazzini'ere *nm* storesman, warehouseman. **magaz'zino** *nm* warehouse; (*emporio*) shop; **grande magazzino** department store

'maggio *nm* May

maggio'lino *nm* May bug

maggio'rana *nf* marjoram

maggio'ranza *nf* majority

maggio'rare *vt* increase

maggior'domo *nm* butler

maggi'ore *a* (*di dimensioni, numero*) bigger, larger; (*superlativo*) biggest, largest; (*di età*) older; (*superlativo*) oldest; (*di importanza, Mus*) major; (*superlativo*) greatest; **la maggior parte** *di* most; **la maggior parte del tempo** most of the time ● *pron* (*di dimensioni*) the bigger, the larger; (*superlativo*) the biggest, the largest; (*di età*) the older; (*superlativo*) the oldest; (*di importanza*) the major; (*superlativo*) the greatest ● *nm Mil* major; *Aeron* squadron leader. **maggio'renne** *a* of age ● *nmf* adult

maggior|i'tario *a* (*sistema*) first-past-the-post *attrib*. **~'mente** *adv* (*all più*) (*più di tutto*) most

'Magi *nmpl* **i re ~** the Magi

ma'gia *nf* magic; (*trucco*) magic trick **magica'mente** *adv* magically. **'magico** *a* magic

magi'stero *nm* (*insegnamento*) teaching; (*maestria*) skill; **facoltà di ~** arts faculty

magi'strale *a* masterly; **istituto ~e** teachers' training college

magi'stra|to *nm* magistrate. **~'tura** *nf* magistrature. **la ~tura** the Bench

'magli|a *nf* stitch; (*lavoro ai ferri*) knitting; (*tessuto*) jersey; (*di rete*) mesh; (di catena) link; (indumento) vest; fare la ~a knit. ~a diritta knit. ~a rosa (ciclismo) ≈ yellow jersey. ~a rovescia purl. ~e'ria nf knitwear. ~'etta nf ~etta [a maniche corte] tee-shirt. ~'ficio nm knitwear factory. ma'glina nf (tessuto) jersey

magli'one nm sweater

'magma nm magma

ma'gnanimo a magnanimous

ma'gnate nm magnate

ma'gnesi|a nf magnesia. ~o nm magnesium

ma'gne|te nm magnet. ~tico a magnetic. ~'tismo nm magnetism

magne'tofono nm tape recorder

magnifi|ca'mente adv magnificently. ~'cenza nf magnificence; (generosità) munificence. ma'gnifico a magnificent; (generoso) munificent

ma'gnolia nf magnolia

'mago nm magician

ma'gone nm avere il ~ be down; mi è venuto il ~ I've got a lump in my throat

'magr|a nf low water. ma'grezza nf thinness. ~o a thin; (carne) lean; (scarso) meagre

'mai adv never; (inter, talvolta) ever; caso ~ if anything; caso ~ tornasse in case he comes back; come ~? why?; cosa ~? what on earth?; ~ più never again; più che ~ more than ever; quando ~? whenever?; quasi ~ hardly ever

mai'ale nm pig; (carne) pork

mai'olica nf majolica

maio'nese nf mayonnaise

'mais nm maize

mai'uscol|a nf capital [letter]. ~o a capital

mal vedi male

'mala nf la ~ sl the underworld

mala'fede nf bad faith

malaf'fare nm gente di ~ shady characters pl

mala'lingua nf backbiter

mala'mente adv (ridotto) badly

malan'dato a in bad shape; (di salute) in poor health

ma'lanimo nm ill will

ma'lanno nm misfortune; (malattia) illness; prendersi un ~ catch something

mala'pena: a ~ adv hardly

ma'laria nf malaria

mala'ticcio a sickly

ma'lato, -a a ill, sick; (pianta) diseased ●nmf sick person. ~ di mente mentally ill person. malat'tia nf disease, illness; ho preso due giorni di malattia I had two days off sick. malattia venerea venereal disease

malaugu'rato a ill-omened. malau'gurio nm bad o ill omen

mala'vita nf underworld

mala'voglia nf unwillingness; di ~ unwillingly

malcapi'tato a wretched

malce'lato a ill-concealed

mal'concio a battered

malcon'tento nm discontent

malco'stume nm immorality

mal'destro a awkward; (inesperto) inexperienced

maldi'cen|te a slanderous. ~za nf slander

maldi'sposto a ill-disposed

'male adv badly; funzionare ~ not work properly; star ~ be ill; star ~ a qcno (vestito ecc:) not suit sb; rimanerci ~ be hurt; non c'è ~! not bad at all! ●nm evil; (dolore) pain; (malattia) illness; (danno) harm. distinguere il bene dal ~ know right from wrong; andare a ~ go off; aver ~ a have a pain in; dove hai ~? where does it hurt?; far ~ a qcno (provocare dolore) hurt sb; (cibo:) be bad for sb; le cipolle mi fanno ~ onions don't agree with me; mi fa ~ la schiena my back is hurting; mal d'auto car-sickness. mal di denti toothache. mal di gola sore throat. mal di mare sea-sickness; avere il mal di mare be sea-sick. mal di pan-

cia stomach ache. **mal di testa** headache

male'detto a cursed; (*orribile*) awful

male'di|re vt curse. **~zi'one** nf curse; **~zione!** damn!

maledu|cata'mente adv rudely. **~'cato** a ill-mannered. **~cazi'one** nf rudeness

male'fatta nf misdeed

male'ficio nm witchcraft. **ma'lefico** a (*azione*) evil; (*nocivo*) harmful

maleodo'rante a foul-smelling

ma'lessere nm indisposition; fig uneasiness

ma'levolo a malevolent

malfa'mato a of ill repute

mal'fat|to a badly done; (*malformato*) ill-shaped. **~'tore** nm wrongdoer

mal'fermo a unsteady; (*salute*) poor

malfor'ma|to a misshapen. **~zi'one** nf malformation

malgo'verno nm misgovernment

mal'grado prep in spite of ● conj although

ma'lia nf spell

mali'gn|are vi malign. **~ità** nf malice; Med malignancy. **ma'ligno** a malicious; (*perfido*) evil; Med malignant

malinco'ni|a nf melancholy. **~co 'mente** adv melancholically. **malin'conico** a melancholy

malincu'ore: a ~ adv unwillingly, reluctantly

malinfor'mato a misinformed

malintenzio'nato, -a nmf miscreant

malin'teso a mistaken ● nm misunderstanding

ma'lizi|a nf malice; (*astuzia*) cunning; (*espediente*) trick. **~'oso** a malicious; (*birichino*) mischievous

malle'abile a malleable

mal'loppo nm fam loot

malme'nare vt ill-treat

mal'messo a (*vestito male*) shab-

bily dressed; (*casa*) poorly furnished; (*fig: senza soldi*) hard up

malnu'tri|to a undernourished. **~zi'one** nf malnutrition

'malo a in **~ modo** badly

ma'locchio nm evil eye

ma'lora nf ruin; **della ~** awful; **andare in ~** go to ruin

ma'lore nm illness; **essere colto da ~** be suddenly taken ill

malri'dotto a (*persona*) in a sorry state

mal'sano a unhealthy

'malta nf mortar

mal'tempo nm bad weather

'malto nm malt

maltrat|ta'mento nm ill-treatment. **~'tare** vt ill-treat

malu'more nm bad mood; **di ~ in a bad mood**

mal'vagi|o a wicked. **~tà** nf wickedness

malversazi'one nf embezzlement

mal'visto a unpopular (**da** with)

malvi'vente nm criminal

malvolenti'eri adv unwillingly

malvo'lere vt **farsi ~** make oneself unpopular

'mamma nf mummy, mum; **~ mia!** good gracious!

mam'mella nf breast

mam'mifero nm mammal

'mammola nf violet

ma'nata nf handful; (*colpo*) slap

'manca nf vedi **manco**

manca'mento nm **avere un ~** faint

man'can|te a missing. **~za** nf lack; (*assenza*) absence; (*insufficienza*) shortage, (*fallo*) fault; (*imperfezione*) defect; **in ~za d'altro** failing all else; **sento la sua ~za** I miss him

man'care vi be lacking; (*essere assente*) be missing; (*venir meno*) fail; (*morire*) pass away; **~ di** be lacking in; **~ a** fail to keep (*promessa*); **mi manca casa** I miss home; **mi manchi** I miss you; **mi è mancato il tempo** I didn't have [the] time; **mi mancano**

1000 lire I'm 1,000 lire short; **quanto manca alla partenza?** how long before we leave?; **è mancata la corrente** there was a power failure; **sentirsi ~** feel faint; **sentirsi ~ il respiro** be unable to breathe [properly] ● *vt* miss *(bersaglio)*; **è mancato poco che cadesse** he nearly fell
'manche *nf inv* heat
man'chevole *a* defective
'mancia *nf* tip
manci'ata *nf* handful
man'cino *a* left-handed
'manco, -a *a* left ● *nf* left hand ● *adv (nemmeno)* not even
man'dante *nmf (di delitto)* instigator
manda'rancio *nm* clementine
man'dare *vt* send; *(emettere)* give off; utter *(suono)*; **~ a chiamare** send for; **~ avanti la casa** run the house; **~ giù** *(ingoiare)* swallow
manda'rino *nm* Bot mandarin
man'data *nf (di consignment; (di serratura)* turn; **chiudere a doppia ~** double lock
man'dato *nm (incarico)* mandate; Jur warrant; *(di pagamento)* money order. **~ di comparizione [in giudizio]** subpoena. **~ di perquisizione** search warrant
man'dibola *nf* jaw
mando'lino *nm* mandolin
'mandorl|a *nf* almond; **a ~la** *(occhi)* almond-shaped. **~'lato** *nm* nut brittle *(type of nougat)*. **~lo** *nm* almond[-tree]
'mandria *nf* herd
maneg'gevole *a* easy to handle. **maneggi'are** *vt* handle
ma'neggio *nm* handling; *(intrigo)* plot; *(scuola di equitazione)* riding school
ma'nesco *a* quick to hit out
ma'netta *nf* hand lever; **manette** *pl* handcuffs
man'forte *nm* dare **~ a qcno** support sb
manga'nello *nm* truncheon
manga'nese *nm* manganese

mange'reccio *a* edible
mangia'dischi® *nm inv* type of portable record player
mangia'fumo *a inv* **candela ~** air-purifier in the form of a candle
mangia'nastri *nm inv* cassette player
mangi'a|re *vt/i* eat; *(consumare)* eat up; *(corrodere)* eat away; take *(scacchi, carte ecc)* ● *nm* eating; *(cibo)* food; *(pasto)* meal. **~rsi** *vr* **~rsi le parole** mumble; **~rsi le unghie** bite one's nails
mangi'ata *nf* big meal; **farsi una bella ~ di...** feast on...
mangia'toia *nf* manger
man'gime *nm* fodder
mangi'one, -a *nmf fam* glutton
mangiucchi'are *vt* nibble
'mango *nm* mango
ma'nia *nf* mania. **~ di grandezza** delusions of grandeur. **~co, -a** *a* maniacal ● *nmf* maniac
'manica *nf* sleeve; *(fam: gruppo)* band; **a maniche lunghe** long-sleeved; **essere in maniche di camicia** be in shirt sleeves; **essere di ~ larga** be free with one's money. **~ a vento** wind sock
'Manica *nf* **la ~ the** [English] Channel
manica'retto *nm* tasty dish
mani'chetta *nf* hose
mani'chino *nm (da sarto, vetrina)* dummy
'manico *nm* handle; Mus neck
mani'comio *nm* mental home; *(fam: confusione)* tip
mani'cotto *nm* muff; Mech sleeve
mani'cure *nf* manicure ● *nmf inv (persona)* manicurist
mani'e|ra *nf* manner; **in ~ra che** so that. **~'rato** *a* affected; *(stile)* mannered. **~'rismo** *nm* mannerism
manifat'tura *nf* manufacture; *(fabbrica)* factory
manife'stante *nmf* demonstrator
manife'sta|re *vt* show; *(esprimere)* express ● *vi* demonstrate. **~rsi** *vr* show oneself. **~zi'one** *nf* show;

(*espressione*) expression; (*sintomo*) manifestation; (*dimostrazione pubblica*) demonstration

mani'festo *a* evident ● *nm* poster; (*dichiarazione pubblica*) manifesto

ma'niglia *nf* handle; (*sostegno, in autobus ecc*) strap

manipo'la|re *vt* handle; (*massaggiare*) massage; (*alterare*) adulterate; *fig* manipulate. **~tore**, **~trice** *nmf* manipulator. **~zi'one** *nf* handling; (*massaggio*) massage; (*alterazione*) adulteration, *fig* manipulation

mani'scalco *nm* smith

man'naia *nf* (*scure*) axe; (*da macellaio*) cleaver

man'naro *a* **lupo ~** werewolf

'mano *nf* hand; (*strato di vernice ecc*) coat; **alla ~** informal; **fuori ~** out of the way; **man ~** little by little; **man ~ che** as; **sotto ~** to hand

mano'dopera *nf* labour

ma'nometro *nm* gauge

mano'mettere *vt* tamper with; (*violare*) violate

ma'nopola *nf* (*di apparecchio*) knob; (*guanto*) mitten; (*su pullman*) handle

mano'scritto *a* handwritten ● *nm* manuscript

mano'vale *nm* labourer

mano'vella *nf* handle; *Techn* crank

ma'no|vra *nf* manoeuvre; *Rail* shunting; **fare le ~vre** *Auto* manoeuvre. **~vrabile** *a fig* easy to manipulate. **~vrare** *vt* (*azionare*) operate; *fig* manipulate (*persona*) ● *vi* manoeuvre

manro'vescio *nm* slap

man'sarda *nf* attic

mansi'one *nf* task; (*dovere*) duty

mansu'eto *a* meek; (*animale*) docile

man'tell|a *nf* cape. **~o** *nm* cloak; (*soprabito, di animale*) coat; (*di neve*) mantle

mante'ner|e *vt* (*conservare*) keep;

(*in buono stato, sostentare*) maintain. **~si** *vr* **~si in forma** keep fit.

manteni'mento *nm* maintenance

'mantice *nm* bellows *pl*; (*di automobile*) hood

'manto *nm* cloak; (*coltre*) mantle

manto'vana *nf* (*di tende*) pelmet

manu'al|e *a & nm* manual. **~e d'uso** user manual. **~'mente** *adv* manually

ma'nubrio *nm* handle; (*di bicicletta*) handlebars *pl*; (*per ginnastica*) dumb-bell

manu'fatto *a* manufactured

manutenzi'one *nf* maintenance

'manzo *nm* steer; (*carne*) beef

'mappa *nf* map

mappa'mondo *nm* globe

mar *vedi* **mare**

ma'rasma *nm fig* decline

mara'to|na *nf* marathon. **~'neta** *nmf* marathon runner

'marca *nf* mark; *Comm* brand; (*fabbricazione*) make; (*scontrino*) ticket. **~ da bollo** revenue stamp

mar'ca|re *vt* mark; *Sport* score. **~ta'mente** *adv* markedly. **~to** *a* (*tratto, accento*) strong, marked. **~'tore** *nm* (*nel calcio*) scorer

mar'chese, -a *nm* marquis ● *nf* marchioness

marchi'are *vt* brand

'marchio *nm* brand; (*caratteristica*) mark. **~ di fabbrica** trademark. **~ registrato** registered trademark

'marcia *nf* march; *Auto* gear; *Sport* walk; **mettere in ~** put into gear; **mettersi in ~** start off. **~ funebre** funeral march. **~ indietro** reverse gear; **fare ~ indietro** reverse; *fig* back-pedal. **~ nuziale** wedding march

marciapi'ede *nm* pavement; (*di stazione*) platform

marci'a|re *vi* march; (*funzionare*) go, work. **~tore**, **~trice** *nmf* walker

'marcio *a* rotten ● *nm* rotten part; *fig* corruption. **mar'cire** *vi* go bad, rot

'**marco** _nm_ (_moneta_) mark
'**mare** _nm_ sea; (_luogo di mare_) sea-side; **sul ~** (_casa_) at the seaside; (_città_) on the sea; **in alto ~** on the high seas; **essere in alto ~** _fig_ not know which way to turn. **~ Adriatico** Adriatic Sea. **mar Io-nio** Ionian Sea. **mar Mediterra-neo** Mediterranean. **mar Tirreno** Tyrrhenian Sea
ma'rea _nf_ tide; **una ~ di** hundreds of; **alta ~** high tide; **bassa ~** low tide
mareggi'ata _nf_ [sea] storm
mare'moto _nm_ tidal wave, seaquake
maresci'allo _nm_ (_ufficiale_) mar-shal; (_sottufficiale_) warrant-officer
marga'rina _nf_ margarine
marghe'rita _nf_ marguerite. **margheri'tina** _nf_ daisy
margi'nal|e _a_ marginal. **~'mente** _adv_ marginally
'margine _nm_ margin; (_orlo_) brink; (_bordo_) border. **~ di errore** margin of error. **~ di sicurezza** safety margin
ma'rina _nf_ navy; (_costa_) seashore; (_quadro_) seascape. **~ mercantile** merchant navy. **~ militare** navy
mari'naio _nm_ sailor
mari'na|re _vt_ marinate; **~re la scuola** play truant. **~ta** _nf_ mari-nade. **~to** _a Culin_ marinated
ma'rino _a_ sea _attrib_, marine
mario'netta _nf_ puppet
ma'rito _nm_ husband
ma'rittimo _a_ maritime
mar'maglia _nf_ rabble
marmel'lata _nf_ jam; (_di agrumi_) marmalade
mar'mitta _nf_ pot; _Auto_ silencer. **~ catalitica** catalytic converter
'marmo _nm_ marble
mar'mocchio _nm fam_ brat
mar'mor|eo _a_ marble. **~iz'zato** _a_ marbled
mar'motta _nf_ marmot
Ma'rocco _nm_ Morocco
ma'roso _nm_ breaker

mar'rone _a_ brown ● _nm_ brown; (_castagna_) chestnut; **marroni** _pl_ **canditi** marrons glacés
mar'sina _nf_ tails _pl_
mar'supio _nm_ (_borsa_) bumbag
martedì _nm inv_ Tuesday. **~ grasso** Shrove Tuesday
martel'lante _a_ (_mal di testa_) pounding
martel'la|re _vt_ hammer ● _vi_ throb. **~ta** _nf_ hammer blow
martel'letto _nm_ (_di giudice_) gavel
mar'tello _nm_ hammer; (_di battente_) knocker. **~ pneumatico** pneu-matic drill
marti'netto _nm Mech_ jack
'martire _nmf_ martyr. **mar'tirio** _nm_ martyrdom
'martora _nf_ marten
martori'are _vt_ torment
mar'xis|mo _nm_ Marxism. **~ta** _a & nmf_ Marxist
marza'pane _nm_ marzipan
marzi'ale _a_ martial
marzi'ano, -a _nmf_ Martian
'marzo _nm_ March
mascal'zone _nm_ rascal
ma'scara _nm inv_ mascara
mascar'pone _nm_ full-fat cream cheese often used for desserts
ma'scella _nf_ jaw
'maschera _nf_ mask; (_costume_) fancy dress; _Cinema_, _Theat_ usher _m_, usherette _f_; (_nella commedia dell'arte_) stock character. **~a antigas** gas mask. **~a di bellezza** face pack. **~a ad ossigeno** oxy-gen mask. **~a'mento** _nm_ masking; _Mil_ camouflage. **masche'rare** _vt_ mask; _fig_ camouflage. **~arsi** _vr_ put on a mask; **~arsi da** dress up as. **~ata** _nf_ masquerade
maschi'accio _nm_ (_ragazza_) tom-boy
ma'schi|le _a_ masculine; (_sesso_) male ● _nm_ masculine [gender]. **~'lista** _a_ sexist. **'maschio** _a_ male; (_virile_) manly ● _nm_ male; (_figlio_) son. **masco'lino** _a_ masculine
ma'scotte _nf inv_ mascot

maso'chis|mo nm masochism. **~ta** a & nmf masochist

'**massa** nf mass; Electr earth, ground Am; **comunicazioni di ~** mass media

massa'cra|nte a gruelling. **~re** vt massacre. **mas'sacro** nm massacre; fig mess

massaggi'a|re vt massage. **mas'saggio** nm massage. **~'tore**, **~'trice** nm masseur ● nf masseuse

mas'saia nf housewife

masse'rizie nfpl household effects

mas'siccio a massive; (oro ecc) solid; (corporatura) heavy ● nm massif

'**massim|a** nf maxim; (temperatura) maximum. **~o** a greatest; (quantità) maximum, greatest ● nm **il ~o** the maximum; **al ~o** at [the] most, as a maximum

'**masso** nm rock

mas'sone nm [Free]mason. **~'ria** Freemasonry

ma'stello nm wooden box for the grape or olive harvest

masti'care vt chew; (borbottare) mumble

'**mastice** nm mastic; (per vetri) putty

ma'stino nm mastiff

masto'dontico a gigantic

'**mastro** nm master; **libro ~** ledger

mastur'ba|rsi vr masturbate. **~zi'one** nf masturbation

ma'tassa nf skein

mate'matic|a nf mathematics. maths. **~o**, **-a** a mathematical ● nmf mathematician

mataras'sino nm ● gonflabile air bed

mate'rasso nm mattress. **~ a molle** spring mattress

ma'teria nf matter; (materiale) material; (di studio) subject. **~ prima** raw material

materi'a|le a material; (grossolano) coarse ● nm material. **~'lismo** nm materialism. **~'lista** a materialistic ● nmf materialist.

~liz'zarsi vr materialize. **~l'mente** adv physically

maternità nf motherhood; ospedale di ~ maternity hospital

ma'terno a maternal; **lingua materna** mother tongue

ma'tita nf pencil

ma'trice nf matrix; (origini) roots pl; Comm counterfoil

ma'tricola nf (registro) register; Univ fresher

ma'trigna nf stepmother

matrimoni'ale a matrimonial; **vita ~** married life. **matri'monio** nm marriage; (cerimonia) wedding

ma'trona nf matron

'**matta** nf (nelle carte) joker

mattacchi'one, **-a** nmf rascal

matta'toio nm slaughterhouse

matte'rello nm rolling-pin

mat'ti|na nf morning; **la ~na** in the morning. **~'nata** nf morning; Theat matinée. **~ni'ero** a essere **~niero** be an early riser. **~no** nm morning

'**matto**, **-a** a mad, crazy; Med insane; (falso) false; (opaco) matt; **~ da legare** barking mad; **avere una voglia matta di** be dying for ● nmf madman; madwoman

mat'tone nm brick; (libro) bore

matto'nella nf tile

mattu'tino a morning attrib

matu'rare vt ripen. **maturità** nf maturity; Sch school-leaving certificate. **ma'turo** a mature; (frutto) ripe

mo'tusa nm old fogey

mauso'leo nm mausoleum

maxi- pref maxi+

'**mazza** nf club; (martello) hammer; (da baseball, cricket) bat. **~ da golf** golf-club. **maz'zata** nf blow

maz'zetta nf (di banconote) bundle

'**mazzo** nm bunch; (carte da gioco) pack

me pers pron me; **me lo ha dato** he gave it to me; **fai come me** do as I do; **è più veloce di me** he is faster than me o faster than I am

me'andro nm meander

M.E.C. nm abbr (Mercato Comune Europeo) EEC

mec'canica nf mechanics sg

mecca'nica'mente adv mechanically

mec'canico a mechanical ● nm mechanic. **mecca'nismo** nm mechanism

mèche [farsi] **fare le ~** have one's hair streaked

me'dagli|a nf medal. **~'one** nm medallion; (gioiello) locket

me'desimo a same

'medi|a nf average; Sch average mark; Math mean; **essere nella ~a** be in the mid-range. **~a** middle ● nm (calcio) half-back

medi'ante prep by

medi'a|re vt act as intermediary in. **~'tore**, **~'trice** nmf mediator; Comm middleman. **~zi'one** nf mediation

medica'mento nm medicine

medi'ca|re vt treat; dress (ferita). **~zi'one** nf medication; (di ferita) dressing

medi'c|ina nf medicine. **~ina legale** forensic medicine. **~i'nale** a medicinal ● nm medicine

'medico a medical ● nm doctor. **~ generico** general practitioner. **~ legale** forensic scientist. **~ di turno** duty doctor

medie'vale a medieval

'medio a average; (punto) middle; (statura) medium ● nm (dito) middle finger

medi'ocre a mediocre; (scadente) poor

medio'evo nm Middle Ages pl

medi'ta|re vt meditate; (progettare) plan; (considerare attentamente) think over ● vi meditate. **~zi'one** nf meditation

mediter'raneo a Mediterranean; **il [mar] M~** the Mediterranean [Sea]

me'dusa nf jellyfish

me'gafono nm megaphone

mega'lattico a fam gigantic

mega'lomane nmf megalomaniac

me'gera nf hag

'meglio adv better; **tanto ~, ~ così** so much the better ● a better; (superlativo) best ● nmf best ● nf **avere la ~ su** have the better of; **fare qcsa alla [bell'e] ~** do sth as best one can ● nm **fare del proprio ~** do one's best; **fare qcsa il ~ possibile** make an excellent job of sth; **al ~** to the best of one's ability; **per il ~** for the best

'mela nf apple. **~ cotogna** quince

mela'grana nf pomegranate

mela'nina nf melanin

melan'zana nf aubergine, eggplant Am

me'lassa nf molasses sg

me'lenso a (persona, film) dull

mel'lifluo a (parole) honeyed; (voce) sugary

'melma nf slime. **mel'moso** a slimy

melo nm apple[-tree]

melo'd|ia nf melody. **me'lodico** a melodic. **~'oso** a melodious

melo'dram|ma nm melodrama. **~'matico** a melodramatic

melo'grano nm pomegranate tree

me'lone nm melon

mem'brana nf membrane

'membro nm member; (pl nf membra Anat) limb

memo'rabile a memorable

'memore a mindful; (riconoscente) grateful

me'mori|a nf memory; (oggetto ricordo) souvenir. **imparare a ~a** learn by heart. **~a permanente** Comput non-volatile memory. **~a tampone** Comput buffer. **~a volatile** Comput volatile memory; **memorie** pl (biografiche) memoirs. **~'ale** nm memorial. **~z'zare** vt memorize; Comput save, store

mena'dito: a ~ adv perfectly

me'nare vt lead; (fam: picchiare) hit

mendi'ca|nte *nmf* beggar. **~re** *vt/i* beg

menefre'ghista *a* devil-may-care

me'ningi *nfpl* spremersi le ~ rack one's brains

menin'gite *nf* meningitis

me'nisco *nm* meniscus

'**meno** *adv* less; *(superlativo)* least; *(in operazioni, con temperatura)* minus; **far qcsa alla ~ peggio** do sth as best one can; **fare a ~ di qcsa** do without sth; **non posso fare a ~ di ridere** I can't help laughing; **~ male!** thank goodness!; **sempre ~** less and less; **venir ~** *(svenire)* faint; **venir ~ a qcno** *(coraggio:)* fail sb; **sono le tre ~ un quarto** it's a quarter to three; **che tu venga o ~** whether you're coming or not; **quanto ~** at least ● *a inv* less; *(con nomi plurali)* fewer ● *nm* least; *Math* minus sign; **il ~ possibile** as little as possible; **per lo ~** at least ● *prep* except [for] ● *conj* **a ~ che** unless

meno'ma|re *vt* (*incidente:*) maim. **~to** *a* disabled

meno'pausa *nf* menopause

'**mensa** *nf* table; *Mil* mess; *Sch, Univ* refectory

men'si|le *a* monthly ● *nm (stipendio)* [monthly] salary; *(rivista)* monthly. **~ità** *nf inv* monthly salary. **~'mente** *adv* monthly

'**mensola** *nf* bracket; *(scaffale)* shelf

'**menta** *nf* mint. **~ peperita** peppermint

men'ta|le *a* mental. **~ità** *nf inv* mentality

'**mente** *nf* mind; **a ~ fredda** in cold blood; **venire in ~ a qcno** occur to sb; **mi è uscito di ~** it slipped my mind

men'tina *nf* mint

men'tire *vi* lie

'**mento** *nm* chin

'**mentre** *conj (temporale)* while; *(invece)* whereas

menù *nm inv* menu. **~ fisso** set

menu. **~ a tendina** *Comput* pulldown menu

menzio'nare *vt* mention. **menzi'one** *nf* mention

men'zogna *nf* lie

mera'viglia *nf* wonder; **a ~ marvellously**; **che ~!** how wonderful!; **con mia grande ~** much to my amazement; **mi fa ~ che...** I am surprised that...

meravigli'ar|e *vt* surprise. **~si** *vr* **~si di** be surprised at

meravigli|osa'mente *adv* marvellously. **~'oso** *a* marvellous

mer'can|te *nm* merchant. **~teggi-'are** *vi* trade; *(sul prezzo)* bargain. **~'tile** *a* mercantile. **~'zia** *nf* merchandise, goods *pl* ● *nm* merchant ship

mer'cato *nm* market; *Fin* market [-place]. **a buon ~** (*comprare*) cheap[ly]; *(articolo)* cheap. **~ dei cambi** foreign exchange market. **M~ Comune [Europeo]** [European] Common Market. **~ coperto** covered market. **~ libero** free market. **~ nero** black market

'**merce** *nf* goods *pl*

mercé *nf* **alla ~ di** at the mercy of

merce'nario *a & nm* mercenary

merce'ria *nf* haberdashery; *(negozio)* haberdasher's

mercoledì *nm inv* Wednesday. **~ delle Ceneri** Ash Wednesday

mer'curio *nm* mercury

me'renda *nf* afternoon snack; **far ~** have an afternoon snack

meridi'ana *nf* sundial

meridi'ano *a* midday ● *nm* meridian

meridio'nale *a* southern ● *nmf* southerner. **meridi'one** *nm* south

me'rin|ga *nf* meringue. **~'gata** *nf* meringue pie

meri'tare *vt* deserve. **meri'tevole** *a* deserving

'**meri|to** *nm* merit; *(valore)* worth; **in ~ a** as to; **per ~ di** thanks to. **~'torio** *a* meritorious

mer'letto *nm* lace

'**merlo** nm blackbird

mer'luzzo nm cod

'**mero** a mere

meschine'ria nf meanness. **me-'schino** a wretched; (gretto) mean ● nm wretch

mesco||a'mento nm mixing. ~**lanza** nf mixture

mesco'la|re vt mix; shuffle (carte); (confondere) mix up; blend (tè, tabacco ecc). ~**rsi** vr mix; (immischiarsi) meddle. ~**ta** nf (a carte) shuffle; Culin stir

'**mese** nm month

me'setto nm un ~ about a month

'**messa**[1] nf Mass

'**messa**[2] nf (il mettere) putting. ~ **in moto** Auto starting. ~ **in piega** (di capelli) set. ~ **a punto** adjustment. ~ **in scena** production. ~ **a terra** earthing, grounding Am

messag'gero nm messenger. **mes-'saggio** nm message

mes'sale nm missal

'**messe** nf harvest

Mes'sia nm Messiah

messi'cano, -a a & nmf Mexican

'**Messico** nm Mexico

messin'scena nf staging; fig act

'**messo** pp di **mettere** ● nm messenger

mesti'ere nm trade; (lavoro) job; **essere del** ~ be an expert, know one's trade

'**mesto** a sad

'**mestola** nf (di cuoco) ladle

mestru'a|le a menstrual. ~**zi'one** nf menstruation. ~**zi'oni** pl periods

'**meta** nf destination; fig aim

metà nf inv half; (centro) middle; a ~ **strada** half-way; **fare a** ~ **con** qcno go halves with sb

metabo'lismo nm metabolism

meta'done nm methadone

meta'fisico a metaphysical

meta'fora nf metaphor. **meta-'forico** a metaphorical

me'tal|ico a metallic. ~**z'zato** a (grigio) metallic

me'tall|o nm metal. ~**ur'gia** nf metallurgy

metalmec'canico a engineering ● nm engineering worker

meta'morfosi nf metamorphosis

me'tano nm methane. ~**'dotto** nm methane pipeline

meta'nolo nm methanol

me'teora nf meteor. **meteo'rite** nm meteorite

meteoro|lo'gia nf meteorology. ~**'logico** a meteorological

me'ticcio, -a nmf half-caste

metico'loso a meticulous

me'tod|ico a methodical. '**metodo** nm method. ~**olo'gia** nf methodology

me'traggio nm length (in metres)

'**metrico, -a** a metric; (in poesia) metrical ● nf metrics sg

'**metro** nm metre; (nastro) tape measure ● nm inv (fam: metropolitana) tube Br, subway

me'tronomo nm metronome

metro'notte nmf inv night security guard

me'tropoli nf inv metropolis. ~**'tana** nf subway, underground Br. ~**'tano** a metropolitan

'**metter|e** vt put; (indossare) put on; (fam: installare) put in; ~**e al mondo** bring into the world; ~**e da parte** set aside; ~**e fiducia** inspire trust; ~**e qcsa in chiaro** make sth clear; ~**e in mostra** display; ~**e a posto** tidy up; ~**e in vendita** put up for sale; ~**e su** set up (casa, azienda); **metter su famiglia** start a family; **ci ho messo un'ora** it took me an hour; **mettiamo che...** let's suppose that... ~**si** vr (indossare) put on; (diventare) turn out; ~**si a start** to; ~**si con qcno** (fam: formare una coppia) start to go out with sb; ~**si a letto** go to bed; ~**si a sedere** sit down; ~**si in viaggio** set out

'**mezza** nf **è la** ~ it's half past twelve; **sono le quattro e** ~ it's half past four

mezza'luna nf half moon; (simbolo islamico) crescent; (coltello) two-handled chopping knife; **a ~** half-moon shaped

mezza'manica nf **a ~** ⟨maglia⟩ short-sleeved

mez'zano a middle

mezza'notte nf midnight

mezz'asta: a ~ adv at half mast

'mezzo a half; **di mezza età** middle-aged; **~ bicchiere** half a glass; **una mezza idea** a vague idea; **siamo mezzi morti** we're half dead; **sono le quattro e ~** it's half past four. **mezz'ora** nf half an hour. **mezza pensione** nf half board. **mezza stagione** nf una **giacca di mezza stagione** a spring/autumn jacket ●a (a metà) half ●nm (metà) half; (centro) middle; (per raggiungere un fine) means sg; **uno e ~** one and a half; **tre anni e ~** three and a half years; **in ~ a** in the middle of; **il giusto ~** the happy medium; **levare di ~** clear away; **per ~ di** by means of; **a ~ posta** by mail; **via di ~** fig halfway house; (soluzione) middle way. **mezzi** pl (denaro) means pl. **mezzi pubblici** public transport. **mezzi di trasporto** [means of] transport

mezzo'busto: a ~ a ⟨foto, ritratto⟩ half-length

mezzo'fondo nm middle-distance running

mezzogi'orno nm midday; (sud) South. **Il M~** Southern Italy. **~ in punto** high noon

mi pers pron me; (rifl) myself; **mi ha dato un libro** he gave me a book; **mi lavo le mani** I wash my hands; **eccomi here** I am ●nm Mus (chiave, 'nota) E

miago'lare vi miaow. **~io** nm miaowing

'mica¹ nf mica

'mica² adv fam (per caso) by any chance; **hai ~ visto Paolo?** have you seen Paul, by any chance?;

non è ~ bello it is not at all nice; **~ male** not bad

'miccia nf fuse

micidi'ale a deadly

'micio nm pussy-cat

'microbo nm microbe

micro'cosmo nm microcosm

micro'fiche nf inv microfiche

micro'film nm inv microfilm

mi'crofono nm microphone

microorga'nismo nm microorganism

microproces'sore nm microprocessor

mioro'scopi|o nm microscope. **~co** a microscopic

micro'solco nm (disco) long-playing record

mi'dollo nm (pl f **midolla**, Anat) marrow; **fino al ~** through and through. **~ osseo** bone marrow. **~ spinale** spinal cord

'mie, mi'ei vedi **mio**

mi'ele nm honey

mi'et|ere vt reap. **~i'trice** nf Mech harvester. **~i'tura** nf harvest

migli'aio nm (pl f **migliaia**) thousand. **a migliaia** in thousands

'miglio nm Bot millet; (misura: pl f **miglia**) mile

migliora'mento nm improvement

miglio'rare vt/i improve

migli'ore a better; (superlativo) the best ●nmf il/la ~ the best

'mignolo nm little finger; (del piede) little toe

mi'gra|re vi migrate. **~zi'one** nf migration

'mila vedi **mille**

Mi'lano nf Milan

miliar'dario, -a nm millionaire; (plurimiliardario) billionaire ●nf millionairess; billionairess

mili'ardo nm billion

mili'are a **pietra ~** milestone

milio'nario, -a nm millionaire ●nf millionairess

mili'one nm million

milio'nesimo a millionth

mili'tante a & nmf militant

mili'tare vi **~ in** be a member of

〈*partito ecc*〉 ●*a* military ●*nm* soldier; **fare il ~** do one's military service. **~ di leva** National Serviceman

'milite *nm* soldier. **mil'izia** *nf* militia

'mille *a* & *nm* 〈*pl* **mila**〉 a o one thousand; **due/tre mila** two/three thousand; **~ grazie!** thanks a lot!

mille'foglie *nm inv Culin* vanilla slice

mil'lennio *nm* millennium

millepi'edi *nm inv* centipede

mil'lesimo *a* & *nm* thousandth

milli'grammo *nm* milligram

mil'limetro *nm* millimetre

'milza *nf* spleen

mi'mare *vt* mimic 〈*persona*〉 ●*vi* mime

mi'metico *a* camouflage *attrib*

mimetiz'zar|e *vt* camouflage. **~si** *vr* camouflage oneself

'mim|ica *nf* mime. **~ico** *a* mimic. **~o** *nm* mime

mi'mosa *nf* mimosa

'mina *nf* mine; 〈*di matita*〉 lead

mi'naccia *nf* threat

minacci'are *vt* threaten. **~oso** *a* threatening

mi'nare *vt* mine; *fig* undermine

mina'tor|e *nm* miner. **~io** *a* threatening

mine'ra|le *a* & *nm* mineral. **~rio** *a* mining *attrib*

mi'nestra *nf* soup. **mine'strone** *nm* vegetable soup; 〈*fam*: *insieme confuso*〉 hotchpotch

mingher'lino *a* skinny

mini+ *pref* mini+

minia'tura *nf* miniature. **minia-turiz'zato** *a* miniaturized

mini'era *nf* mine

mini'golf *nm* miniature golf

mini'gonna *nf* miniskirt

minima'mente *adv* minimally

mini'market *nm inv* minimarket

minimiz'zare *vt* minimize

'minimo *a* least, slightest; 〈*il più basso*〉 lowest; 〈*salario, quantità ecc*〉 minimum ●*nm* minimum; **girare al ~** *Auto* idle

mini'stero *nm* ministry; 〈*governo*〉 government

mi'nistro *nm* minister. **M~ del Tesoro** Finance Minister, Chancellor of the Exchequer *Br*

mino'ranza *nf* minority *attrib*

mino'rato, -a *a* disabled ●*nmf* disabled person

mi'nore *a* 〈*gruppo, numero*〉 smaller; 〈*superlativo*〉 smallest; 〈*distanza*〉 shorter; 〈*superlativo*〉 shortest; 〈*prezzo*〉 lower; 〈*superlativo*〉 lowest; 〈*di età*〉 younger; 〈*superlativo*〉 youngest; 〈*di importanza*〉 minor; 〈*superlativo*〉 least important ●*nmf* younger; 〈*superlativo*〉 youngest; *Jur* minor; **il ~ dei mali** the lesser of two evils; **i minori di 14 anni** children under 14. **mino'renne** *a* under age ●*nmf* minor

minori'tario *a* minority *attrib*

minu'etto *nm* minuet

mi'nuscolo, -a *a* tiny ●*nf* small letter

mi'nuta *nf* rough copy

mi'nuto[1] *a* minute; 〈*persona*〉 delicate; 〈*ricerca*〉 detailed; 〈*pioggia, neve*〉 fine; **al ~** *Comm* retail

mi'nuto[2] *nm* 〈*di tempo*〉 minute; **spaccare il ~** be dead on time

mi'nuzi|a *nf* trifle. **~'oso** *a* detailed; 〈*persona*〉 meticulous

'mio 〈**il mio** *m*, **la mia** *f*, **i miei** *mpl*, **le mie** *fpl*〉 *a poss* my; **questa macchina è mia** this car is mine; **~ padre** my father; **un ~ amico** a friend of mine ●*poss pron* mine; **i miei** 〈*genitori ecc*〉 my folks

'miope *a* short-sighted. **mio'pia** *nf* short-sightedness

'mira *nf* aim; 〈*bersaglio*〉 target; **prendere la ~** take aim; **prendere di ~ qcno** *fig* have it in for sb

mi'racolo *nm* miracle. **~sa'mente** *adv* miraculously. **miraco'loso** *a* miraculous

mi'raggio *nm* mirage

mi'rar|e *vi* [take] aim. **~si** *vr* 〈*guardarsi*〉 look at oneself

mi'riade *nf* myriad

mi'rino *nm* sight; *Phot* view-finder

mir'tillo *nm* blueberry

mi'santropo, -a *nmf* misanthropist

mi'scela *nf* mixture; ⟨di caffè, tabacco ecc⟩ blend. **~'tore** *nm* ⟨di acqua⟩ mixer tap

miscel'lanea *nf* miscellany

'mischia *nf* scuffle; ⟨nel rugby⟩ scrum

mischi'ar|e *vt* mix; shuffle ⟨carte da gioco⟩. **~si** *vr* mix; ⟨immischiarsi⟩ interfere

misco'noscere *vt* not appreciate

mi'scuglio *nm* mixture; *fig* medley

mise'rabile *a* wretched

misera'mente *adv* ⟨finire⟩ miserably; ⟨vivere⟩ in abject poverty

mi'seria *nf* poverty; ⟨infelicità⟩ misery; **guadagnare una ~** earn a pittance; **porca ~!** hell!; **miserie** *pl* ⟨disgrazie⟩ misfortunes

miseri'cordi|a *nf* mercy. **~'oso** *a* merciful

'misero *a* ⟨miserabile⟩ wretched; ⟨povero⟩ poor; ⟨scarso⟩ paltry

mi'sfatto *nm* misdeed

mi'sogino *nm* misogynist

mis'saggio *nm* vision mixer

'missile *nm* missile

missio'nario, -a *nmf* missionary. **missi'one** *nf* mission

misteri|osa'mente *adv* mysteriously. **~'oso** *a* mysterious. **mi-'stero** *nm* mystery

'misti|ca *nf* mysticism. **~cismo** *nm* mysticism. **~co** *a* mystic[al] ● *nm* mystic

mistifi'ca|re *vt* distort ⟨verità⟩. **~zi'one** *nf* ⟨della verità⟩ distortion

'misto *a* mixed; **scuola mista** mixed *or* co-educational school ● *nm* mixture; **~ lana/cotone** wool/cotton mix

mi'sura *nf* measure; ⟨dimensione⟩ measurement; ⟨taglia⟩ size; ⟨limite⟩ limit; **su ~** ⟨abiti⟩ made to measure; ⟨mobile⟩ custom-made; **a ~** ⟨andare, calzare⟩ perfectly; **a**

~ che as. **~ di sicurezza** safety measure. **misu'rare** *vt* measure; try on ⟨indumenti⟩; ⟨limitare⟩ limit. **misu'rarsi** *vr* **misurarsi con** ⟨gareggiare⟩ compete with. **misu'rato** *a* measured. **misu'rino** *nm* measuring spoon

'mite *a* mild; ⟨prezzo⟩ moderate

'mitico *a* mythical

miti'gar|e *vt* mitigate. **~si** *vr* calm down; ⟨clima⟩ become mild

mitiz'zare *vt* mythicize

'mito *nm* myth. **~lo'gia** *nf* mythology. **~'logico** *a* mythological

mi'tomane *nmf* compulsive liar

'mitra *nf* Relig mitre ● *nm* inv Mil machine-gun

mitragli'a|re *vt* machine-gun; **~re di domande** fire questions at. **~'trice** *nf* machine-gun

mit'tente *nmf* sender

mne'monico *a* mnemonic

mo' *nm* **a ~ di** by way of ⟨esempio, consolazione⟩

'mobile¹ *a* mobile; ⟨volubile⟩ fickle; ⟨che si può muovere⟩ movable; **beni mobili** personal estate; **squadra ~** flying squad

'mobile² *nm* piece of furniture; **mobili** *pl* furniture sg. **mo'bilia** *nf* furniture. **~'li'ficio** *nm* furniture factory

mo'bilio *nm* furniture

mobilità *nf* mobility

mobili'ta|re *vt* mobilize. **~zi'one** *nf* mobilization

moca'ssino *nm* moccasin

mocci'oso, -a *nmf* brat

'moccolo *nm* ⟨di candela⟩ candle-end; ⟨moccio⟩ snot

'moda *nf* fashion; **di ~** in fashion; **alla ~** ⟨musica, vestiti⟩ up-to-date; **fuori ~** unfashionable

modalità *nf* inv formality; **~ d'uso** instruction

mo'della *nf* model. **model'lare** *vt* model

model'li|no *nm* model. **~sta** *nmf* designer

mo'dello *nm* model; ⟨stampo⟩

mould; (*di carta*) pattern; (*modulo*) form

'**modem** *nm inv* modem; **mandare per** ~ modem, send by modem

mode'ra|re *vt* moderate; (*diminuire*) reduce. ~**rsi** *vr* control oneself. ~**ta'mente** *adv* moderately ●**to** *a* moderate. ~**'tore**, ~**'trice** *nmf* (*in tavola rotonda*) moderator. ~**zi'one** *nf* moderation

modern|a'mente *adv* (*in modo moderno*) in a modern style. ~**iz'zare** *vt* modernize. **mo'derno** *a* modern

mo'dest|ia *nf* modesty. ~**o** *a* modest

'**modico** *a* reasonable

mo'difica *nf* modification

modifi'ca|re *vt* modify. ~**'one** *nf* modification

mo'dista *nf* milliner

'**modo** *nm* way; (*garbo*) manners *pl*; (*occasione*) chance; *Gram* mood; **ad ogni** ~ anyhow; **di** ~ **che** so that; **fare in** ~ **di** try to; **in che** ~ (*inter*) how; **in qualche** ~ somehow; **in questo** ~ like this; ~ **di dire** idiom; **per** ~ **di dire** so to speak

modu'la|re *vt* modulate. ~**zi'one** *nf* modulation. ~**zione di frequenza** frequency modulation. ~**'tore** *nm* ~**tore di frequenza** frequency modulator

'**modulo** *nm* form; (*lunare, di comando*) module. ~ **continuo** continuous paper

'**mogano** *nm* mahogany

'**mogio** *a* dejected

'**moglie** *nf* wife

'**mola** *nf* millstone; *Mech* grindstone

mo'lare *nm* molar

'**mole** *nf* mass; (*dimensione*) size

mo'lecola *nf* molecule

mole'stare *vt* bother; (*più forte*) molest. **mo'lestia** *nf* nuisance. **mo'lesto** *a* bothersome

'**molla** *nf* spring; **molle** *pl* tongs

mol'lare *vt* let go; (*fam: lasciare*) leave; *fam* give ⟨*ceffone*⟩; *Naut* cast

off ●*vi* cease; **mollala!** *fam* stop that!

'**molle** *a* soft; (*bagnato*) wet

mol'letta *nf* (*per capelli*) hair-grip; (*per bucato*) clothes-peg; **mollette** *pl* (*per ghiaccio ecc*) tongs

mol'lezz|a *nf* softness; ~**e** *pl fig* luxury

mol'lica *nf* crumb

mol'lusco *nm* mollusc

'**molo** *nm* pier; (*banchina*) dock

mol'teplic|e *a* manifold; (*numeroso*) numerous. ~**ità** *nf* multiplicity

moltipli'ca|re *vt*, ~**rsi** *vr* multiply. ~**'trice** *nf* calculating machine. ~**zi'one** *nf* multiplication

molti'tudine *nf* multitude

'**molto** *a* a lot of; (*con negazione e interrogazione*) much, a lot of; (*con nomi plurali*) many, a lot of; **non** ~ **tempo** not much time, not a lot of time ●*adv* very; (*con verbi*) a lot; (*con avverbi*) much; ~ **stupido** very stupid; **mangiare** ~ eat a lot; ~ **più veloce** much faster; **non mangiare** ~ not eat a lot, not eat much ●*pron* a lot; (*molto tempo*) a lot of time; (*con negazione e interrogazione*) much, a lot; (*plurale*) many; **non ne ho** ~ I don't have much, I don't have a lot; **non ne ho molti** I don't have many, I don't have a lot; **non ci metterò** ~ I won't be long; **fra non** ~ before long; **molti** (*persone*) a lot of people; **eravamo in molti** there were a lot of us

momentanea'mente *adv* momentarily; **è** ~ **assente** he's not here at the moment. **momen'taneo** *a* momentary

mo'mento *nm* moment; **a momenti** (*a volte*) sometimes; (*fra un momento*) in a moment; **dal** ~ **che** since; **per il** ~ for the time being; **da un** ~ **all'altro** ⟨*cambiare idea ecc*⟩ from one moment to the next; (*aspettare qcno ecc*) at any moment

'**monaca** *nf* nun. ~**o** *nm* monk

'**Monaco** *nm* Monaco ●*nf* (*di Baviera*) Munich

mo'narc|**a** *nm* monarch. **monar'chia** *nf* monarchy. **~hico, -a** *a* monarchic ● *nmf* monarchist

mona'stero *nm* (*di monaci*) monastery; (*di monache*) convent. **mo'nastico** *a* monastic.

monche'rino *nm* stump

'**monco** *a* maimed; (*fig: troncato*) truncated; **~ di un braccio** one-armed

mon'dano *a* worldly; **vita mon'dana** social life

mondi'ale *a* world *attrib*; **di fama ~** world-famous

'**mondo** *nm* world; **il bel ~** fashionable society; **un ~** (*molto*) a lot

mondovisi'one *nf* **in ~** transmitted worldwide

mo'nello, -a *nmf* urchin

mo'neta *nf* coin; (*denaro*) money; (*denaro spicciolo*) [small] change. **~ estera** foreign currency. **~ legale** legal tender. **~ unica** single currency. **mone'tario** *a* monetary

mongolfi'era *nf* hot air balloon

mo'nile *nm* jewel

'**monito** *nm* warning

moni'tore *nm* monitor

mo'nocolo *nm* monocle

monoco'lore *a* Pol one-party

mono'dose *a inv* individually packaged

manegra'fia *nf* monograph

mono'gramma *nm* monogram

mono'kini *nm inv* monokini

mono'lingue *a* monolingual

monolo'cale *nm* studio flat Br, studio apartment

mo'nologo *nm* monologue

mono'pattino *nm* [child's] scooter

mono'polio *nm* monopoly. **~o di Stato** state monopoly. **~z'aare** *vt* monopolize

mono'sci *nm inv* monoski

monosil'labico *a* monosyllabic.

mono'sillabo *nm* monosyllable

monoto'nia *nf* monotony. **mo'notono** *a* monotonous

---

mono'uso *a* disposable

monsi'gnore *nm* monsignor

mon'sone *nm* monsoon

monta'carichi *nm inv* hoist

mon'taggio *nm* Mech assembly; Cinema editing; **catena di ~** production line

mon'ta|gna *nf* mountain; (*zona*) mountains *pl*. **montagne** *pl* **russe** big dipper. **~'gnoso** *a* mountainous. **~'naro, -a** *nmf* highlander. **~no** *a* mountain *attrib*

mon'tante *nm* (*di finestra, porta*) upright

mon'ta|re *vt/i* mount; get on (*veicolo*); (*aumentare*) rise; Mech assemble; frame (*quadro*); Culin whip; edit (*film*); (*a cavallo*) ride; *fig* blow up; **~rsi la testa** get bigheaded. **~to, -a** *nmf* poser. **~'tura** *nf* Mech assembling; (*di occhiali*) frame; (*di gioiello*) mounting; *fig* exaggeration

'**monte** *nm anche fig* mountain; **a ~** up-stream; **andare a ~** be ruined; **mandare a ~ qcsa** ruin sth. **~ di pietà** pawnshop

monte'premi *nm inv* jackpot

mont'gomery *nm inv* duffle coat

mon'tone *nm* ram; **carne di ~** mutton

montu'oso *a* mountainous

monumen'tale *a* monumental. **monu'mento** *nm* monument

mo'quette *nf* (*tappeto*) fitted carpet

'**mora** *nf* (*del gelso*) mulberry; (*del rovo*) blackberry

mo'ral|e *a* moral ● *nf* morals *pl*; (*di storia*) moral ● *nm* morale. **mora'lista** *nmf* moralist. **~ità** *nf* morality; (*condotta*) morals *pl*. **~iz'zare** *vt/i* moralize. **~'mente** *adv* morally

morbi'dezza *nf* softness

'**morbido** *a* soft

mor'billo *nm* measles *sg*

'**morbo** *nm* disease. **~sità** *nf* (*qualità*) morbidity

mor'boso *a* morbid

mor'dace *a* cutting

mor'dente *a* biting. **'mordere** *vt* bite; *(corrodere)* bite into. **mordic-chi'are** *vt* gnaw

mor'fina *nf* morphine. **morfi-'nomane** *nmf* morphine addict

mori'bondo *a* dying; *(istituzione)* moribund

morige'rato *a* moderate

mo'rire *vi* die; *fig* die out; **fa un freddo da ~** it's freezing cold; I'm perishing; **~ di noia** be bored to death; **c'era da ~ dal ridere** it was killingly or hilariously funny

mor'mone *nmf* Mormon

mormo'r|are *vt/i* murmur; *(brontolare)* mutter. **~io** *nm* murmuring; *(lamentela)* grumbling

'moro *a* dark ● *nm* Moor

mo'roso *a* in arrears

'morsa *nf* vice; *fig* grip

'morse *a* **alfabeto ~** Morse code

mor'setto *nm* clamp

morsi'care *vt* bite. **'morso** *nm* bite; *(di cibo, briglia)* bit; **i morsi della fame** hunger pangs

morta'delia *nf* mortadella *(type of salted pork)*

mor'taio *nm* mortar

mor'tal|e *a* mortal; *(simile a morte)* deadly; **di una noia ~e** deadly. **~ità** *nf* mortality. **~'mente** *adv* *(ferito)* fatally; *(offeso)* mortally

morta'retto *nm* firecracker

'morte *nf* death

mortifi'cante *a* mortifying

mortifi'ca|re *vt* mortify. **~rsi** *vr* be mortified. **~to** *a* mortified. **~zi'one** *nf* mortification

'morto, -a *pp di* **morire** ● *a* dead; **~ di freddo** frozen to death; **stanco ~** dead tired ● *nm* dead man ● *nf* dead woman

mor'torio *nm* funeral

mo'saico *nm* mosaic

'Mosca *nf* Moscow

'mosca *nf* fly; *(barba)* goatee. **~ cieca** blindman's buff

mo'scato *a* muscat; **noce mosca-ta** nutmeg ● *nm* muscatel

mosce'rino *nm* midge; *(fam: persona)* midget

mo'schea *nf* mosque

moschi'cida *a* fly *attrib*

'moscio *a* limp; **avere l'erre moscia** not be able to say one's r's properly

mo'scone *nm* bluebottle; *(barca)* pedalo

'moss|a *nf* movement; *(passo)* move. **~o** *pp di* **muovere** ● *a* *(mare)* rough; *(capelli)* wavy; *(fotografia)* blurred

mo'starda *nf* mustard

'mostra *nf* show; *(d'arte)* exhibition; **far ~ di** pretend; **in ~** on show; **mettersi in ~** make oneself conspicuous

mo'stra|re *vt* show; *(indicare)* point out; *(spiegare)* explain. **~rsi** *vr* show oneself; *(apparire)* appear

'mostro *nm* monster; *(fig: persona)* genius; **~ sacro** *fig* sacred cow

mostru|osa'mente *adv* tremendously. **~'oso** *a* monstrous; *(incredibile)* enormous

mo'tel *nm inv* motel

moti'va|re *vt* cause; *Jur* justify. **~to** *a* *(persona)* motivated. **~zi'one** *nf* motivation; *(giustificazione)* justification

mo'tivo *nm* reason; *(movente)* motive; *(in musica, letteratura)* theme; *(disegno)* motif

'moto *nm* motion; *(esercizio)* exercise; *(gesto)* movement; *(sommossa)* rising ● *nf inv* *(motocicletta)* motor bike; **mettere in ~** start *(motore)*

moto'carro *nm* three-wheeler

motoci'c|letta *nf* motor cycle. **~ismo** *nm* motorcycling. **~ista** *nmf* motor-cyclist

moto'cros|s *nm* motocross. **~'sista** *nf* scrambler

moto'lancia *nf* motor launch

moto'nave *nf* motor vessel

mo'tore *a* motor ● *nm* motor, engine. **moto'retta** *nf* motor scooter.

moto'rino nm moped. **motorino d'avviamento** starter

motoriz'za|to a Mil motorized. **~zi'one** nf (ufficio) vehicle licensing office

moto'scafo nm motorboat

motove'detta nf patrol vessel

'**motto** nm motto; (facezia) witticism; (massima) saying

mountain bike nf inv mountain bike

mouse nm inv Comput mouse

mo'vento nm motive

movimen'ta|re vt enliven. **~to** a lively. **movi'mento** nm movement; **essere sempre in movimento** be always on the go

mozi'one nf motion

mozzafi'ato a nivo nail-biting

moz'zare vt cut off; dock (coda); **~ il fiato a qcno** take sb's breath away

mozza'rella nf mozzarella, mild, white cheese

mozzi'cone nm (di sigaretta) stub

'**mozzo** nm Mech hub; Naut ship's boy ●a (coda) truncated; (testa) severed

'**mucca** nf cow. **morbo della ~ pazza** mad cow disease

'**mucchio** nm heap, pile; **un ~ di** fig lots of

'**muco** nm mucus

'**muffa** nf mould; **fare la ~** go mouldy. **muf'fire** vi go mouldy

muf'fole nfpl mittens

mug'gi|re vi (mucca) moo, low; (toro) bellow. **~to** nm moo; bellow; (azione) mooing; bellowing

mu'ghetto nm lily of the valley

mugo'la|re vi whine; (persona) moan. **mugo'lio** nm whining

mugu'gnare vt fam mumble

mulat'ti'era nf mule track

mu'latto, -a nmf mulatto

muli'nello nm (d'acqua) whirlpool; (di vento) eddy, (giocattolo) windmill

mu'lino nm mill. **~ a vento** windmill

'**mulo** nm mule

'**multa** nf fine. **mul'tare** vt fine

multico'lore a multicoloured

multi'lingue a multilingual

multi'media mpl multimedia

multimedi'ale a multimedia attrib

multimiliar'dario, -a nmf multimillionaire

multinazio'nale nf multinational

'**multiplo** a & nm multiple

multiproprietà nf inv time-share

multi'uso a (utensile) all-purpose

'**mummia** nf mummy

'**mungere** vt milk

mungi'tura nf milking

munici'pa|le a municipal. **~ità** nf inv town council. **muni'cipio** nm town hall

mu'nifico a munificent

mu'nire vt fortify; **~ di** (provvedere) supply with

munizi'oni nfpl ammunition sg

'**munto** pp di mungere

mu'over|e vt move; (suscitare) arouse. **~si** vr move; **muoviti!** hurry up!, come on!

'**mura** nfpl (cinta di città) walls

mu'raglia nf wall

mu'rale a mural; (pittura) wall attrib

mu'ra|re vt wall up. **~'tore** nm bricklayer; (con pietre) mason; (operaio edile) builder. **~'tura** nf (di pietra) masonry, stonework; (di mattoni) brickwork

mu'rena nf moray eel

'**muro** nm wall; (di nebbia) bank; a ~ (armadio) built-in. **~ portante** load-bearing wall. **~ del suono** sound barrier

'**muschio** nm Bot moss

musco'la|re a muscular. **~'tura** nf muscles pl. '**muscolo** nm muscle

mu'seo nm museum

museru'ola nf muzzle

'**musi|ca** nf music. **~cal** nm inv musical. **~'cale** a musical. **~'cista** nmf musician

'**muso** nm muzzle; (pej: di persona) mug; (di aeroplano) nose; **fare il ~** sulk. **mu'sone, -a** nmf sulker '**mussola** *nf* muslin

'**musul'mano, -a** *nmf* Moslem

'**muta** *nf* (*cambio*) change; (*di penne*) moult; (*di cani*) pack; (*per immersione subacquea*) wetsuit

muta'mento *nm* change

mu'tan|de *nfpl* pants; (*da donna*) knickers. **~'doni** *nmpl* (*da uomo*) long johns; (*da donna*) bloomers

mu'tare *vt* change

mu'tevole *a* changeable

muti'la|re *vt* mutilate. **~to, -a** *nmf* disabled person. **~to di guerra** disabled ex-serviceman. **~zi'one** *nf* mutilation

mu'tismo *nm* dumbness; *fig* obstinate silence

'**muto** *a* dumb; (*silenzioso*) silent; (*fonetica*) mute

'**mutu|a** *nf* [**cassa** *nf*] **~** sickness benefit fund. **~'ato, -a** *nmf* ≈ NHS patient

mutuo[1] *a* mutual

mutuo[2] *nm* loan; (*per la casa*) mortgage; **fare un ~** take out a mortgage. **~ ipotecario** mortgage

....

Nn

'**nacchera** *nf* castanet

'**nafta** *nf* naphtha; (*per motori*) diesel oil

'**naia** *nf* cobra; (*sl: servizio militare*) national service

'**nailon** *nm* nylon

'**nanna** *nf* (*sl: infantile*) byebyes; **andare a ~** go byebyes; **fare la ~** sleep

'**nano, -a** *a & nmf* dwarf

napole'tano, -a *a & nmf* Neapolitan

'**Napoli** *nf* Naples

'**nappa** *nf* tassel; (*pelle*) soft leather

narci'sis|mo *nm* narcissism. **~ta** *a & nmf* narcissist

nar'ciso *nm* narcissus

nar'cotico *a & nm* narcotic

na'rice *nf* nostril

nar'ra|re *vt* tell. **~'tivo, -a** *a* narrative ● *nf* fiction. **~'tore, ~'trice** *nmf* narrator. **~zi'one** *nf* narration; (*racconto*) story

na'sale *a* nasal

'**nasc|ere** *vi* (*venire al mondo*) be born; (*germogliare*) sprout; (*sorgere*) rise; **~ere da** *fig* arise from. **~ita** *nf* birth. **~i'turo** *nm* unborn child

na'scond|ere *vt* hide. **~si** *vr* hide. **~zi'one** *nf* hiding-place. **~no** *nm* hide-and-seek. **na'scosto** *pp di* **nascondere** ● *a* hidden; **di nascosto** secretly

na'sello *nm* (*pesce*) hake

'**naso** *nm* nose

'**nastro** *nm* ribbon; (*di registratore ecc*) tape. **~ adesivo** adhesive tape. **~ isolante** insulating tape. **~ trasportatore** conveyor belt

na'tal|e *a* (*paese*) of one's birth. **N~e** *nm* Christmas; **~i** *pl* parentage. **~ità** *nf* [number of] births. **nata'lizio** *a* (*del Natale*) Christmas *attrib*; (*di nascita*) of one's birth

na'tante *a* floating ● *nm* craft

'**natica** *nf* buttock

na'tio *a* native

Nativi'tà *nf* Nativity. **na'tivo, -a** *a & nmf* native

'**nato** *pp di* **nascere** ● *a* born; **uno scrittore ~** a born writer; **nata Rossi** née Rossi

NATO *nf* Nato, NATO

na'tura *nf* nature; **pagare in ~** pay in kind. **~ morta** still life

natu'ra|le *a* natural; **al ~le** (*alimento*) plain, natural; **~lel** naturally, of course. **~'lezza** *nf* naturalness. **~liz'zare** *vt* naturalize. **~l'mente** *adv* (*ovviamente*) naturally, of course

natu'rista *nmf* naturalist

naufra'gare *vi* be wrecked; (*persona:*) be shipwrecked. **nau'fragio** *nm* shipwreck; *fig* wreck. '**nau-frago, -a** *nmf* survivor

'**nause|a** *nf* nausea; **avere la ~a**

feel sick. **~a'bondo** a nauseating. **~'ante** a nauseating. **~'are** vt nauseate

'nautic|a nf navigation. **~o** a nautical

na'vale a naval

na'vata nf (centrale) nave; (laterale) aisle

'nave nf ship. **~ cisterna** tanker. **~ da guerra** warship. **~ spaziale** spaceship

na'vetta nf shuttle

navicella nf **~ spaziale** nose cone

navi'gabile a navigabile

navi'ga|re vi sail; **~re in Internet** surf the Net. **~'tore**, **~'trice** nmf navigator. **~zi'one** nf navigation

na'viglio nm fleet; (canale) canal

nazio'na|le a national ● nf Sport national team. **~'lismo** nm nationalism. **~'lista** nmf nationalist **~lità** nf inv nationality. **~liz'zare** vt nationalize. **nazi'one** nf nation

na'zista a nmf Nazi

N.B. abbr (nota bene) N.B.

ne pers pron (di lui) about him; (di lei) about her; (di loro) about them; (di ciò) about it; (da ciò) from that; (di un insieme) of it; (di un gruppo) of them; **non ne conosco nessuno** I don't know any of them; **ne ho** I have some; **non ne ho più** I don't have any left ● adv from there; **ne vengo ora** I've just come from there; **me ne vado** I'm off

né conj **né... né...** neither... nor...; **non ne ho il tempo né la voglia** I don't have either the time or the inclination; **né tu né lo vogliamo andare** neither you nor I want to go; **né l'uno né l'altro** neither [of them/us]

ne'anche adv (neppure) not even; (senza) neppure) without even ● conj (e neppure) neither...; **non parlo inglese, e lui ~** I don't speak English, neither does he ● and he doesn't either

'nebbia nf mist; (in città, su strada) fog. **~'oso** a misty; foggy

necessaria'mente adv necessarily. **neces'sario** a necessary

necessità nf inv necessity; (bisogno) need

necessi'tare vi **~ di** need; (essere necessario) be necessary

necro'logio nm obituary

ne'cropoli nf inv necropolis

ne'fando a wicked

ne'fasto a ill-omened

ne'ga|re vt deny; (rifiutare) refuse; **essere ~to per qcsa** be no good at sth. **~'tivo**, **-a** a negative ● nf negative, **~zi'one** nf negation; (diniego) denial; Gram negative

ne'gletto a neglected

'negli = in + gli

negli'gen|te a negligent. **~za** nf negligence

negozi'abile a negotiable

negozi'ante nmf dealer; (bottegaio) shopkeeper

negozi'a|re vt negotiate ● vi **~re in** trade in. **~ti** nmpl negotiations

ne'gozio nm shop

'negro, **-a** a Negro, black ● nm Negro, black; (scrittore) ghost writer

'nei = in + i. **nel** = in + il. **'nella** = in + la. **'nelle** = in + le. **'nello** = in + lo

'nembo nm nimbus

ne'mico, **-a** a hostile ● nmf enemy

nem'meno conj not even

'nenia nf dirge; (per bambini) lullaby; (piagnucolio) wail

'neo nm mole; (applicato) beauty spot

'neo+ pref neo+

neofa'scismo nm neofascism

neo'litico a Neolithic

neolo'gismo nm neologism

'neon nm neon

neo'nato, **-a** a newborn ● nmf newborn baby

neozelan'dese a New Zealand ● nmf New Zealander

nep'pure conj not even

'nerb|o nm (forza) strength; fig backbone. **~o'ruto** a brawny

ne'retto nm Typ bold [type]

'**nero** *a* black; (*fam: arrabbiato*) fuming ● *nm* black; **mettere ● su bianco** put in writing

nerva'tura *nf* nerves *pl*; *Bot* veining; (*di libro*) band

'**nervo** *nm* nerve; *Bot* vein; **avere i nervi** be bad-tempered; **dare ai nervi a qcno** get on sb's nerves. ~'**sismo** *nm* nerviness

ner'voso *a* nervous; (*irritabile*) bad-tempered; **avere il ~** be irritable; **esaurimento** *nm* ~ nervous breakdown

'**nespol|a** *nf* medlar. ~**o** *nm* medlar[-tree]

'**nesso** *nm* link

nes'suno *a* no, not... any; (*qualche*) any; **non ho nessun problema** I don't have any problems, I have no problems; **non lo trovo da nessuna parte** I can't find it anywhere; **in nessun modo** on no account; **nessuna notizia?** any news? ● *pron* nobody, no one, not... anybody, not... anyone; (*qualcuno*) anybody, anyone; **hai delle domande?** – **nessuna** do you have any questions? – none; ~ **di voi** none of you; ~ **dei due** (*di voi due*) neither of you; **non ho visto** ~ **dei tuoi amici** I haven't seen any of your friends; **c'è** ~? is anybody there?

'**nettare** *nm* nectar

net'tare *vt* clean

net'tezza *nf* cleanliness. ~ **urbana** cleansing department

'**netto** *a* clean; (*chiaro*) clear; *Comm* net; **di** ~ just like that

nettur'bino *nm* dustman

neu'tral|e *a & nmf* neutral. ~**ità** *nf* neutrality. ~**iz'zare** *vt* neutralize.

'**neutro** *a* neutral; *Gram* neuter ● *nm Gram* neuter

neu'trone *nm* neutron

'**neve** *nf* snow

nevi'care *vi* snow; ~**ca** it is snowing. ~'**cata** *nf* snowfall. **ne'vischio** *nm* sleet. **ne'voso** *a* snowy

nevral'gia *nf* neuralgia. **ne'vralgico** *a* neuralgic

ne'vro|si *nf inv* neurosis. ~**tico** *a* neurotic

'**nibbio** *nm* kite

'**nicchia** *nf* niche

nicchi'are *vi* shilly-shally

'**nichel** *nm* nickel

nichi'lista *a & nmf* nihilist

nico'tina *nf* nicotine

nidi'ata *nf* brood. '**nido** *nm* nest; (*giardino d'infanzia*) crèche

ni'ente *pron* nothing, not... anything; (*qualcosa*) anything; **non ho fatto** ~ **di male** I didn't do anything wrong, I did nothing wrong; **grazie!** – **di** ~! thank you! – don't mention it!; **non serve a** ~ it is no use; **vuoi** ~? do you want anything?; **da** ~ (*poco importante*) minor; (*di poco valore*) worthless ● *a inv fam* **non ho** ~ **fame** I'm not the slightest bit hungry ● *adv* **non fa** ~ (*non importa*) it doesn't matter; **per** ~ at all; (*litigare*) over nothing; ~ **affatto!** no way! ● *nm* **un bel** ~ absolutely nothing

nientedi'meno, **niente'meno** *adv* ~ **che** no less than ● *int* fancy that!

'**ninfa** *nf* nymph

nin'fea *nf* water-lily

ninna'nanna *nf* lullaby

'**ninnolo** *nm* plaything; (*fronzolo*) knick-knack

ni'pote *nm* (*di zii*) nephew; (*di nonni*) grandson, grandchild ● *nf* (*di zii*) niece; (*di nonni*) granddaughter, grandchild

'**nisba** *pron* (*sl: niente*) zilch

'**nitido** *a* neat; (*chiaro*) clear

ni'trato *nm* nitrate

ni'tri|re *vi* neigh. ~**to** *nm* (*di cavallo*) neigh

n° *abbr* (**numero**) No

no *adv* no; (*con congiunzione*) not; **dire di no** say no; **credo di no** I don't think so; **perché no?** why not?; **io no** not me; **ha detto così, no?** he said so, didn't he?; **fa freddo, no?** it's cold, isn't it?

'nobil|e *a* noble ● *nm* noble, nobleman ● *nf* noble, noblewoman. **~i'are** *a* noble. **~tà** *nf* nobility

'nocca *nf* knuckle

nocci'ol|a *nf* hazelnut. **~o** *nm* (*albero*) hazel

'nocciolo *nm* stone; *fig* heart

'noce *nf* walnut ● *nm* (*albero*, *legno*) walnut. **~ moscata** nutmeg. **~'pesca** *nf* nectarine

no'civo *a* harmful

'nodo *nm* knot; *fig* lump; *Comput* node; **fare il ~ della cravatta** do up one's tie. **~ alla gola** lump in the throat. **no'doso** *a* knotty.

'nodulo *nm* nodule

'noi *pers pron* (*soggetto*) we; (*oggetto, con prep*) us; **chi è? ~ siamo** ~ who is it? – it's us

'noia *nf* boredom; (*fastidio*) bother; (*persona*) bore; **dar ~** annoy

noi'altri *pers pron* we

noi'oso *a* boring; (*fastidioso*) tiresome

noleggi'are *vt* hire; (*dare a noleggio*) hire out; charter (*nave, aereo*). **no'leggio** *nm* hire; (*di nave, aereo*) charter. **'nolo** *nm* hire; *Naut* freight; **a nolo** for hire

'nomade *a* nomadic ● *nmf* nomad

'nome *nm* name; *Gram* noun; **a ~ di** in the name of; **di ~** by name; **farsi un ~** make a name for oneself. **~ di famiglia** surname. **~ da ragazza** maiden name.

no'mea *nf* reputation

nomencla'tura *nf* nomenclature

no'mignolo *nm* nickname

'nomina *nf* appointment. **nomi'nale** *a* nominal; *Gram* noun *attrib*

nomi'na|re *vt* name; (*menzionare*) mention; (*eleggere*) appoint. **~'tivo** *a* nominative; *Comm* registered ● *nm* nominative; (*nome*) name

non *adv* not; **~ ti amo** I do not o don't love you; **~ c'è** che not at all

nonché *conj* (*tanto meno*) let alone; (*e anche*) as well as

noncu'ran|te *a* nonchalant; (*negligente*) indifferent. **~za** *nf* nonchalance; (*negligenza*) indifference

nondi'meno *conj* nevertheless

'nonna *nf* grandmother, grandma *fam*

'nonno *nm* grandfather, grandpa *fam*; **nonni** *pl* grandparents

non'nulla *nm inv* trifle

'nono *a & nm* ninth

nono'stante *prep* in spite of ● *conj* although

nontiscordardimé *nm inv* forget-me-not

nonvio'lento *a* nonviolent

nord *nm* north; **del ~** northern

nor-d-est *nm* northeast; **a ~** northeasterly

'nordico *a* northern

nordoccidenta'le *a* northwestern

nordorienta'le *a* northeastern

nor-d-ovest *nm* northwest; **a ~** northwesterly

'norma *nf* rule; (*istruzione*) instruction; **a ~ di legge** according to law; **è buona ~** it's advisable

nor'mal|e *a* normal. **~ità** *nf* normality. **~iz'zare** *vt* normalize. **~'mente** *adv* normally

norve'gese *a & nmf* Norwegian. **Nor'vegia** *nf* Norway

nossi'gnore *adv* no way

nostal'gia *nf* (*di casa, patria*) homesickness; (*del passato*) nostalgia; **aver ~** be homesick; **aver ~ di qcno** miss sb. **no'stalgico, -a** *a* nostalgic ● *nmf* reactionary

no'strano *a* local; (*fatto in casa*) home-made

'nostro (**il nostro** *m*, **la nostra** *f*, **i nostri** *mpl*, **le nostre** *fpl*) *poss a* our; **quella macchina è nostra** that car is ours; **~ padre** our father; **un ~ amico** a friend of ours ● *poss pron* ours

'nota *nf* (*segno*) sign; (*comunicazione, commento, Mus*) note; (*conto*) bill; (*lista*) list; **degno di ~** noteworthy; **prendere ~** take note. **note** *pl* **caratteristiche** distinguishing marks

no'tabile *a & nm* notable

no'taio *nm* notary

no'ta|re *vt (segnare)* mark; *(annotare)* note down; *(osservare)* notice; **far ~re qcsa** point sth out; **farsi ~re** get oneself noticed. **~zi'one** *nf* marking; *(annotazione)* notation

'notes *nm inv* notepad

no'tevole *a (degno di nota)* remarkable; *(grande)* considerable

noti'fica *nf* notification. **notifi'care** *vt* notify; *Comm* advise. **~zi'one** *nf* notification

no'tizi|a *nf* **una ~a** a piece of news, some news; *(informazione)* a piece of information, some information; **le ~e** the news *sg.* **~'ario** *nm* news *sg*

'noto *a* [well-]known; **rendere ~** *(far sapere)* announce

notorietà *nf* fame; **raggiungere la ~** become famous. **no'torio** *a* well-known; *pej* notorious

not'tambulo *nm* night-bird

not'tata *nf* night; **far ~** stay up all night

'notte *nf* night; **di ~** at night; **~ bianca** sleepless night; **peggio che andar di ~** worse than ever. **~'tempo** *adv* at night

not'turno *a* nocturnal; *(servizio ecc)* night

no'vanta *a & nm* ninety

novan't|enne *a & nmf* ninety-year-old. **~esimo** *a* ninetieth. **~ina** *nf* about ninety. **'nove** *a & nm* nine. **nove'cento** *a & nm* nine hundred. **il N~cento** the twentieth century

no'vella *nf* short story

novel'lino, -a *a* inexperienced ● *nmf* novice, beginner. **no'vello** *a* new

no'vembre *nm* November

novità *nf inv* novelty; *(notizie)* news *sg*; **l'ultima ~** *(moda)* the latest fashion

novizi'ato *nm Relig* novitiate; *(tirocinio)* apprenticeship

nozi'one *nf* notion; **nozioni** *pl* rudiments

'nozze *nfpl* marriage *sg*; *(cerimonia)* wedding *sg*. **~ d'argento** silver wedding [anniversary]. **~ d'oro** golden wedding [anniversary]

'nub|e *nf* cloud. **~e tossica** toxic cloud. **~i'fragio** *nm* cloudburst

'nubile *a* unmarried ● *nf* unmarried woman

'nuca *nf* nape

nucle'are *a* nuclear

'nucleo *nm* nucleus; *(unità)* unit

nu'di|smo *nm* nudism. **~sta** *nmf* nudist. **~tà** *nf inv* nudity, nakedness

'nudo *a* naked; *(spoglio)* bare; **a occhio ~** to the naked eye

'nugolo *nm* large number

'nulla *pron* = **niente**; **da ~** worthless

nulla'osta *nm inv* permit

nulla'nente *nm* **i nullatenenti** the have-nots

nullità *nf inv (persona)* nonentity

'nullo *a Jur* null and void

nume'ra|bile *a* countable. **~le** *a & nm* numeral

nume'ra|re *vt* number. **~zi'one** *nf* numbering. **nu'merico** *a* numerical

'numero *nm* number; *(romano, arabo)* numeral; *(di scarpe ecc)* size; **dare i numeri** be off one's head. **~ cardinale** cardinal [number]. **~ decimale** decimal. **~ ordinale** ordinal [number]. **~ di telefono** phone number. **nume'roso** *a* numerous

'nunzio *nm* nuncio

nu'ocere *vi* **~ a** harm

nu'ora *nf* daughter-in-law

nuo'ta|re *vi* swim; *fig* wallow; **~re nell'oro** be stinking rich, be rolling in it. **nu'oto** *nm* swimming. **~'tore, ~'trice** *nmf* swimmer

'nuovo *a* new ● *nm* new. **nuova** *nf (notizia)* news *sg*. **~a'mente** *adv* again. **~o** *a* new; **di ~o** again; **rimettere a ~o** give a new lease of life to

nutri'ente a nourishing. **~'mento** nm nourishment

nu'tri|re vt nourish; harbour (sentimenti). **~rsi** eat; **~rsi di** fig live on. **~'tivo** a nourishing. **~zi'one** nf nutrition

'nuvola nf cloud. **nuvo'loso** a cloudy

nuzi'ale a nuptial; (vestito, anello ecc) wedding attrib

●●●●●●●●●●●●●●●●●●●●●●●

Oo

●●●●●●●●●●●●●●●●●●●●●●●

O abbr (ovest) W

o conj or; **~ l'uno ~ l'altro** one or the other, either

'oasi nf inv oasis

obbedi'ente ecc = **ubbidiente** ecc

obbli'ga|re vt force, oblige; **~rsi** vr **~rsi a** undertake to. **~to a** obliged. **~'torio** a compulsory. **~zi'one** nf obligation; Comm bond. **'obbligo** nm obligation; (dovere) duty; **avere obblighi verso** be under an obligation to; **d'obbligo** obligatory

obbligatoria'mente adv fare qcsa **~** be obliged to do sth; **bisogna ~ farlo** you absolutely have to do it

ob'bro|brio nm disgrace. **~'brioso** a disgraceful

obe'lisco nm obelisk

obe'rare vt overburden

obesità nf obesity. **o'beso** a obese

obiet'tare vt/i object; **~ su** object to

obietti|va'mente adv objectively. **~vità** nf objectivity. **obiet'tivo** a objective ● nm objective; (scopo) object

obie'|ttore nm objector. **~ttore di coscienza** conscientious objector. **~zi'one** nf objection

obi'torio nm mortuary

o'blio nm oblivion

o'bliquo a oblique; fig underhand

oblite'rare vt obliterate

oblò nm inv porthole

'oboe nm oboe

obso'leto a obsolete

'oca nf (pl oche) goose; (donna) silly girl

occasio'nal|e a occasional. **~'mente** adv occasionally

occasi'one nf occasion; (buon affare) bargain; (motivo) cause; (opportunità) chance; **d'~** second-hand

occhi'aia nf eye socket; **occhiaie** pl shadows under the eyes

occhi'ali nmpl glasses, spectacles. **~ da sole** sunglasses. **~ da vista** glasses, spectacles

occhi'ata nf look; **dare un'~ a** have a look at

occhieggi'are vt ogle ● vi (far capolino) peep

occhi'ello nm buttonhole; (asola) eyelet

'occhio nm eye; **~!** watch out!; **a quattr'occhi** in private; **tenere d'~ qcno** keep an eye on sb; **a ~ [e croce]** roughly; **chiudere un'~** turn a blind eye; **dare nell'~** attract attention; **pagare ~ spendere un ~ [della testa]** pay an arm and a leg; **saltare agli occhi** be blindingly obvious. **~ nero** (pesto) black eye. **~ di pernice** (callo) corn. **~'lino** nm **fare l'~lino a** wink at sb

occiden'tale a western ● nmf westerner. **occi'dente** nm west

oc'clu|dere vt obstruct. **~si'one** nf occlusion

occor'ren|te a necessary ● nm the necessary. **~za** nf need; **all'~za** if need be

oc'correre vi be necessary

occulta'mento nm **~ di prove** concealment of evidence

occul'ta|re vt hide. **~ismo** nm occult. **oc'culto** a hidden; (magico) occult

occu'pante nmf occupier; (abusivo) squatter

occu'pa|re vt occupy; spend ⟨tempo⟩; take up ⟨spazio⟩; ⟨dar lavoro a⟩ employ. **~rsi** vr occupy oneself; ⟨trovare lavoro⟩ find a job; **~rsi di** ⟨badare⟩ look after. **~to a** engaged; ⟨persona⟩ busy; ⟨posto⟩ taken. **~zi'one** nf occupation; **trovarsi un~zione** ⟨interesse⟩ find oneself something to do

o'ceano nm ocean. **~ Atlantico** Atlantic [Ocean]. **~ Pacifico** Pacific [Ocean]

'ocra nf ochre

ocu'lare a ocular; ⟨testimone, bagno⟩ eye attrib

ocula'tezza nf care. **ocu'lato** a ⟨scelta⟩ wise

ocu'lista nmf optician; ⟨per malattie⟩ ophthalmologist

od conj or

'ode nf ode

odi'are vt hate

odi'erno a of today; ⟨attuale⟩ present

'odi|o nm hatred; **avere in ~o** hate. **~'oso** a hateful

odo'ra|re vt smell; ⟨profumare⟩ perfume ● vi **~re di** smell of. **~to** nm sense of smell. **o'dore** nm smell; ⟨profumo⟩ scent; **c'è odore di...** there's a smell of...; **sentire odore di** smell; **odori** pl Culin herbs. **odo'roso** a fragrant

of'fender|e vt offend; ⟨ferire⟩ injure. **~si** vr take offence

offen'siv|a nf Mil offensive. **~o** a offensive

offe'rente nf offerer; ⟨in aste⟩ bidder

of'fert|a nf offer; ⟨donazione⟩ donation; Comm supply; ⟨nelle aste⟩ bid; **in ~a speciale** on special offer. **~o** pp di **offrire**

of'fes|a nf offence. **~o** pp di **offendere** ● a offended

offi'ciare vt officiate

offi'cina nf workshop; **~ [meccanica]** garage

of'frir|e vt offer. **~si** vr offer oneself; ⟨occasione:⟩ present itself; **~si di fare qcsa** offer to do sth

offu'scar|e vt darken; fig dull ⟨memoria, bellezza⟩; blur ⟨vista⟩. **~si** vr darken; ⟨fig: memoria, bellezza:⟩ fade away; ⟨vista:⟩ become blurred

of'talmico a ophthalmic

oggettività nf objectivity. **ogget'tivo** a objective

og'getto nm object; ⟨argomento⟩ subject; **oggetti** pl **smarriti** lost property, lost and found Am

'oggi adv & nm today; ⟨al giorno d'oggi⟩ nowadays; **da ~ in poi** from today on; **~ a otto** a week today; **dall'~ al domani** overnight; **il giornale di ~** today's paper; **al giorno d'~** these days, nowadays. **~gi'orno** adv nowadays

'ogni a inv every; ⟨qualsiasi⟩ any; **~ tre giorni** every three days; **ad ~ costo** at any cost; **ad ~ modo** anyway; **~ cosa** everything; **~ tanto** now and then; **~ volta che** every time, whenever

o'gnuno pron everyone, everybody; **~ di voi** each of you

ohimè int oh dear!

'ola nf inv Mexican wave

O'lan|da nf Holland. **o~'dese** a Dutch ● nm Dutchman; ⟨lingua⟩ Dutch ● nf Dutchwoman

ole'andro nm oleander

ole'at|o a oiled; **carta ~a** greaseproof paper

oleo'dotto nm oil pipeline. **ole'oso** a oily

ol'fatto nm sense of smell

oli'are vt oil

oli'era nf cruet

olim'piadi nfpl Olympic Games. **o'limpico** a Olympic. **olim'pionico** a ⟨primato, squadra⟩ Olympic

'olio nm oil; **sott'~** in oil; **colori a ~ oils**; **quadro a ~** oil painting. **~ di mais** corn oil. **~ d'oliva** olive oil. **~ di semi** vegetable oil. **~ solare** sun-tan oil

o'liv|a nf olive. **oli'vastro** a olive. **oli'veto** nm olive grove. **~o** nm olive tree

'olmo *nm* elm

oltraggi|are *vt* offend. **ol'traggio** *nm* offence

ol'tranza *nf* **ad ~** to the bitter end

'oltre *adv* (*di luogo*) further; (*di tempo*) longer ● *prep* (*di luogo*) over; (*di tempo*) later than; (*di più*) more than; (*in aggiunta*) besides; **~ a** (*eccetto*) except, apart from; **per ~ due settimane** for more than two weeks; **una settimana e ~** a week and more. **~'mare** *adv* overseas. **~'modo** *adv* extremely

oltrepas'sare *vt* go beyond; (*eccedere*) exceed

o'maggio *nm* homage; (*dono*) gift; **in ~ con** free with; **omaggi** *pl* (*saluti*) respects

ombeli'cale *a* umbilical; **cordone ~** umbilical cord. **ombe'lico** *nm* navel

'ombr|a *nf* (*zona*) shade; (*immagine oscura*) shadow; **all'~a** in the shade. **~eggi'are** *vt* shade

om'brello *nm* umbrella. **ombrel-'lone** *nm* beach umbrella

om'bretto *nm* eye-shadow

om'broso *a* shady; (*cavallo*) skittish

ome'lette *nf inv* omelette

ome'lia *nf Relig* sermon

omeopa'tia *nf* homoeopathy. **omeo'patico** *a* homoeopathic ● *nm* homoeopath

omertà *nf* conspiracy of silence

o'messo *pp* *di* omettere

o mettere *vt* omit

omi'cid|a *a* murderous ● *nmf* murderer. **~io** *nm* murder. **~io colposo** manslaughter

omissi'one *nf* omission

omogeneiz'zato *a* homogenized. **omo'geneo** *a* homogeneous

omolo'gare *vt* approve

o'nomimo, a *nmf* namesake ● *nm* (*parola*) homonym

omosessu'al|e *a & nmf* homosexual. **~ità** *nf* homosexuality

On. *abbr* (*onorevole*) MP

'oncia *nf* ounce

'onda *nf* wave; **andare in ~** Radio

go on the air. **a ondate** in waves. **onde** *pl* **corte** short wave. **onde** *pl* **lunghe** long wave. **onde** *pl* **medie** medium wave. **on'data** *nf* wave

'onde *conj* so that ● *pron* whereby

ondeggi'are *vi* wave; (*barca:*) roll

ondula'torio *a* undulating. **~zi'o-ne** *nf* undulation; (*di capelli*) wave

'oner|e *nm* burden. **~'oso** *a* onerous

onestà *nf* honesty; (*rettitudine*) integrity. **o'nesto** *a* honest; (*giusto*) just

'onice *nf* onyx

onnipo'tente *a* omnipotent

onnipre'sente *a* ubiquitous; *Rel* omnipresent

ono'mastico *nm* name-day

ono'ra|bile *a* honourable. **~re** *vt* (*fare onore a*) be a credit to; honour (*promessa*). **~rio** *a* honorary ● *nm* fee. **~rsi** *vr* **~rsi di** be proud of

o'nore *nm* honour; **in ~ di** (*festa, ricevimento*) in honour of; **fare ~ a** do justice to (*pranzo*); **farsi ~** in excel in; **fare gli onori di casa** do the honours

ono'revole *a* honourable ● *nmf* Member of Parliament

onorifi'cenza *nf* honour; (*decorazione*) decoration. **ono'rifico** *a* honorary

'onta *nf* shame

O.N.U. *nf abbr* (**Organizzazione delle Nazioni Unite**) UN

o paco *a* opaque; (*colori ecc*) dull; (*vetro, luce*) matt

o'pale *nf* opal

'opera *nf* (*lavoro*) work; (*azione*) deed; *Mus* opera; (*teatro*) opera house; (*ente*) institution; **mettere in ~** put into effect; **mettersi all'~** get to work; **opere** *pl* **pubbliche** public works. **~ d'arte** work of art. **~ lirica** opera

ope'raio, -a *a* working ● *nmf* worker; **~ specializzato** skilled worker

ope'ra|re *vt Med* operate on; **farsi ~re** have an operation ● *vi* oper ate; ⟨*agire*⟩ work. ~**'tivo**, ~**'torio** *a* operating *attrib.* ~**'tore**, ~**'trice** *nmf* operator; *TV* cameraman. ~**tore turistico** tour operator. ~**zi'one** *nf* operation; *Comm* transaction

ope'retta *nf* operetta

ope'roso *a* industrious

opini'one *nf* opinion; **rimanere della propria** ~ still feel the same way. ~ **pubblica** public opinion, vox pop

'oppio *nm* opium

oppo'nente *a* opposing ● *nmf* opponent

op'por|re *vt* oppose; ⟨*obiettare*⟩ object; ~**re resistenza** offer resistance. ~**si** *vr* ~**si a** oppose

opportu'ni|smo *nm* expediency. ~**sta** *nmf* opportunist. ~**tà** *nf inv* opportunity; ⟨*l'essere opportuno*⟩ timeliness. **op'portuno** *a* opportune; ⟨*adeguato*⟩ appropriate; **ritenere opportuno fare qcsa** think it appropriate to do sth; **il momento opportuno** the right moment

opposi|'tore *nm* opposer. ~**zi'one** *nf* opposition; **d'~zione** ⟨*giornale, partito*⟩ opposition

op'posto *pp di* **opporre** ● *a* opposite; ⟨*opinioni*⟩ opposing ● *nm* opposite; **all'~** on the contrary

oppres|si'one *nf* oppression. ~**sivo** *a* oppressive. **op'presso** *pp di* **opprimere** ● *a* oppressed. ~**'sore** *nm* oppressor

oppri'me|nte *a* oppressive. **op'primere** *vt* oppress; ⟨*gravare*⟩ weigh down

op'pure *conj* otherwise, or [else]; **lunedì ~ martedì** Monday or Tuesday

op'tare *vi* ~ **per** opt for

opu'lento *a* opulent

o'puscolo *nm* booklet; ⟨*pubblicitario*⟩ brochure

opzio'nale *a* optional. **opzi'one** *nf* option

'ora¹ *nf* time; ⟨*unità*⟩ hour; **di buon'~** early; **che ~ è?, che ore**

sono? what time is it?; **mezz'~** half an hour; **a ore** ⟨*lavorare, pagare*⟩ by the hour; **50 km all'~** 50 km an hour; **a un'~ di macchina** one hour by car; **non vedo l'~ di vederti** I can't wait to see you; **fare le ore piccole** stay up until the small hours. ~ **d'arrivo** arrival time. **l'~ esatta** *Teleph* speaking clock. ~ **legale** daylight saving time. ~ **di punta**, **ore** *pl* **di punta** peak time; ⟨*per il traffico*⟩ rush hour

'ora² *adv* now; ⟨*tra poco*⟩ presently; ~ **come** ~ just now, at the moment; **d'~ in poi** from now on; **per** ~ for the time being, for now; **è** ~ **di finirla!** that's enough now! ● *conj* ⟨*dunque*⟩ now [then]; ~ **che ci penso,...** now that I come to think about it,...

o'racolo *nm* oracle

'orafo *nm* goldsmith

o'rale *a & nm* oral; **per via** ~ by mouth

ora'mai *adv* = **ormai**

o'rario *a* ⟨*tariffa*⟩ hourly; ⟨*segnale*⟩ time *attrib*; ⟨*velocità*⟩ per hour ● *nm* time; ⟨*tabella dell'orario*⟩ timetable, schedule *Am*; **essere in** ~ be on time; **in senso** ~ clockwise. ~ **di chiusura** closing time. ~ **flessibile** flexitime. ~ **di sportello** banking hours. ~ **d'ufficio** business hours. ~ **di visita** *Med* consulting hours

o'rata *nf* gilthead

ora'tore, -**'trice** *nmf* speaker

ora'torio, -**a** *a* oratorical ● *nm Mus* oratorio ● *nmf* oratory. **orazi'one** *nf Relig* prayer

'orbita *nf* orbit; *Anat* [eye-]socket

or'chestra *nf* orchestra; ⟨*parte del teatro*⟩ pit

orche'stra|le *a* orchestral ● *nmf* member of an/the orchestra. ~**re** *vt* orchestrate

orchi'dea *nf* orchid

'orco *nm* ogre

'orda *nf* horde

or'digno *nm* device; (*arnese*) tool. ~ esplosivo explosive device

ordi'nale *a* & *nm* ordinal

ordina'mento *nm* order; (*leggi*) rules *pl*.

ordi'nanza *nf* (*del sindaco*) bylaw; d'~ (*soldato*) on duty

ordi'na|re *vt* (*sistemare*) arrange; (*comandare*) order; (*prescrivere*) prescribe; *Relig* ordain

ordi'nario *a* ordinary; (*grossolano*) common; (*professore*) with a permanent position; di ordinaria amministrazione routine ● *nm* ordinary; *Univ* professor

ordi'nato *a* (*in ordine*) tidy

ordinazi'one *nf* order; fare un'~ place an order

'ordine *nm* order; (*di avvocati, medici*) association; mettere in ~ put in order; tidy up (*appartamento ecc*); di prim'~ first-class; di terz'~ e (*film, albergo*) third-rate; di ~ pratico/economico (*problema*) of a practical/economic nature; fino a nuovo ~ until further notice; parola d'~ password. ~ del giorno agenda. ordini sacri *pl* Holy Orders

or'dire *vt* (*tramare*) plot

orec'chino *nm* ear-ring

o'recchi|o *nm* (*pl nf* orecchie) ear; avere ~o have a good ear; mi è giunto all'~o che... I've heard that...; parlare all'~o a qcno whisper in sb's ear; suonare a ~o play by ear; ~'oni *pl Med* mumps *sg*

o'refice *nm* jeweller. ~'ria *nf* (*arte*) goldsmith's art; (*negozio*) goldsmith's [shop]

'orfano, -a *a* orphan ● *nmf* orphan. ~'trofio *nm* orphanage

orga'netto *nm* barrel-organ; (*a bocca*) mouth-organ; (*fisarmonica*) accordion

or'ganico *a* organic ● *nm* personnel

orga'nismo *nm* organism; (*corpo umano*) body

orga'nista *nmf* organist

organiz'za|re *vt* organize. ~rsi *vr* get organized. ~'tore, ~'trice *nmf* organizer. ~zi'one *nf* organization

'organo *nm* organ

or'gasmo *nm* orgasm; *fig* agitation

'orgia *nf* orgy

or'gogli|o *nm* pride. ~'oso *a* proud

orien'tale *a* eastern; (*cinese ecc*) oriental

orienta'mento *nm* orientation; perdere l'~ lose one's bearings; senso dell'~ sense of direction

orien'ta|re *vt* orientate. ~rsi *vr* find one's bearings; (*tendere*) tend

ori'ente *nm* east. l'Estremo O~ the Far East. il Medio O~ the Middle East

o'rigano *nm* oregano

origi'nale *a* original; (*eccentrico*) odd ● *nm* original. ~'lità *nf* originality. ~re *vt/i* originate. ~rio *a* (*nativo*) native

o'rigine *nf* origin; in ~ originally; aver ~ da originate from; dare ~ a give rise to

origli'are *vi* eavesdrop

o'rina *nf* urine. ori'nale *nm* chamber-pot. ori'nare *vi* urinate

ori'undo *a* native

oriz'zontale *a* horizontal

orizzon'tare *vt* = orientare. oriz'zonte *nm* horizon

or'la|re *vt* hem. ~'tura *nf* hem. 'orlo *nm* edge; (*di vestito ecc*) hem

'orma *nf* track; (*di piede*) footprint; (*impronta*) mark

or'mai *adv* by now; (*passato*) by then; (*quasi*) almost

ormeggi'are *vt* moor. or'meggio *nm* mooring

ormo'nale *a* hormonal. or'mone *nm* hormone

ornamen'tale *a* ornamental. orna'mento *nm* ornament

or'na|re *vt* decorate. ~rsi *vr* deck oneself. ~to *a* (*stile*) ornate

ornitolo'gia *nf* ornithology

'oro *nm* gold; **d'~** gold; *fig* golden; **una persona d'~** a wonderful person

orologi'aio, -a *nmf* clockmaker, watchmaker

oro'logio *nm* (*portatile*) watch; (*da tavolo, muro ecc*) clock. **~ a pendolo** grandfather clock. **~ da polso** wrist-watch. **~ a sveglia** alarm clock

o'roscopo *nm* horoscope

or'rendo *a* awful, dreadful

or'ribile *a* horrible

orripi'lante *a* horrifying

or'rore *nm* horror; **avere qcsa in ~** hate sth

orsacchi'otto *nm* teddy bear

'orso *nm* bear; (*persona scontrosa*) hermit. **~ bianco** polar bear

or'taggio *nm* vegetable

or'tensia *nf* hydrangea

or'tica *nf* nettle. **orti'caria** *nf* nettle-rash

orticol'tura *nf* horticulture. **'orto** *nm* vegetable plot

orto'dosso *a* orthodox

ortogo'nale *a* perpendicular

orto'gra'fia *nf* spelling. **~'grafico** *a* spelling *attrib*

orto'lano *nm* market gardener; (*negozio*) greengrocer's

orto'pe'dia *nf* orthopaedics *sg*. **~'pedico** *a* orthopaedic ● *nm* orthopaedist

orza'iolo *nm* sty

or'zata *nf* barley-water

osan'nato *a* praised to the skies

o'sare *vt/i* dare; (*avere audacia*) be daring

oscenità *nf inv* obscenity. **o'sceno** *a* obscene

oscil'la|re *vi* swing; (*prezzi ecc*) fluctuate; *Tech* oscillate; (*fig: essere indeciso*) vacillate. **~zi'one** *nf* swinging; (*di prezzi*) fluctuation; *Tech* oscillation

oscura'mento *nm* darkening; (*fig: di vista, mente*) dimming; (*totale*) black-out

oscu'r|are *vt* darken; *fig* obscure.

~arsi *vr* get dark. **~ità** *nf* darkness. **o'scuro** *a* dark; (*triste*) gloomy; (*incomprensibile*) obscure

ospe'dal|e *nm* hospital. **~i'ero** *a* hospital *attrib*

ospi'ta|le *a* hospitable. **~lità** *nf* hospitality. **~re** *vt* give hospitality to. **'ospite** *nm* (*chi ospita*) host; (*chi viene ospitato*) guest ● *nf* hostess; guest

o'spizio *nm* (*per vecchi*) [old people's] home

ossa'tura *nf* bone structure; (*di romanzo*) structure, framework. **'osseo** *a* bone *attrib*

ossequi'l|are *vt* pay one's respects to. **o'sequio** *nm* homage. **ossequi** *pl* respects. **~'oso** *a* obsequious

osser'van|te *a* (*cattolico*) practising. **~za** *nf* observance

osser'va|re *vt* observe; (*notare*) notice; keep (*ordine, silenzio*). **~'tore, ~'trice** *nmf* observer. **~'torio** *nm Astr* observatory; *Mil* observation post. **~zi'one** *nf* observation; (*rimprovero*) reproach

ossessio'na|nte *a* haunting; (*persona*) nagging. **~re** *vt* obsess; (*infastidire*) nag. **ossessi'one** *nf* obsession; (*assillo*) pain in the neck. **osses'sivo** *a* obsessive. **os'sesso** *a* obsessed

os'sia *conj* that is

ossi'dabile *a* liable to tarnish

ossi'dar|e *vt*, **~si** *vr* oxidize

'ossido *nm* oxide. **~ di carbonio** carbon monoxide

os'sidrico *a* **fiamma ossidrica** blowlamp

ossige'nar|e *vt* oxygenate; (*decolorare*) bleach. **~si** *vr fig* put back on its feet (*azienda*); **~si i capelli** dye one's hair blonde **os'sigeno** *nm* oxygen

'osso *nm* (*Anat: pl nf* ossa) bone; (*di frutto*) stone

osso'buco *nm* marrowbone

os'suto *a* bony

ostaco'lare *vt* hinder, obstruct.

o'stacolo nm obstacle; Sport hurdle

o'staggio nm hostage; **prendere in ~** take hostage

o'stello nm **~ della gioventù** youth hostel

osten'ta|re vt show off; **~re indifferenza** pretend to be indifferent. **~zi'one** nf ostentation

oste'ria nf inn

o'stetrico, -a a obstetric ● nmf obstetrician

'ostia nf host; (cialda) wafer

'ostico a tough

o'stil|e a hostile. **~ità** nf inv hostility

osti'na|rsi vr persist (a in). **~to** a obstinate. **~zi'one** nf obstinacy

ostra'cismo nm ostracism

'ostrica nf oyster

ostro'goto nm parlare **~** talk double Dutch

ostru'ire vt obstruct. **~zi'one** nf obstruction

otorinolaringoi'atra nmf ear, nose and throat specialist

ottago'nale a octagonal. **ot'tagono** nm octagon

ot'tan|ta a & nm eighty. **~tenne** a & nmf eighty-year-old. **~'tesimo** a eightieth. **~'tina** nf about eighty

ot'tav|a nf octave. **~o** a eighth

otte'nere vt obtain; (più comune) get; (conseguire) achieve

'ottico, -a a optic[al] ● nmf optician ● nf (scienza) optics sg; (di lenti ecc) optics nt

otti'ma|le a optimum. **~'mente** adv very well

atti'mia|me nm optimism. **la** nmf optimist. **~tico** a optimistic

'ottimo a very good ● nm optimum

'otto a & nm eight

ot'tobre nm October

otto'cento a & nm eight hundred; **l'O~** the nineteenth century

ot'tone nm brass

ottuage'nario, -a a & nmf octogenarian

ottu'ra|re vt block; fill (dente). **~rsi** vr clog. **~'tore** nm Phot shutter. **~zi'one** nf stopping; (di dente) filling

ot'tuso pp di ottundere ● a obtuse

o'vaia nf ovary

o'vale a & nm oval

o'vat|ta nf cotton wool. **~'tato** a (suono, passi) muffled

ovazi'one nf ovation

over'dose nf inv overdose

'ovest nm west

o'vi|le nm sheep-fold. **~no** a sheep attrib

ovo'via nf two-seater cable car

ovulazi'one nf ovulation

o'vunque adv = dovunque

ov'vero conj or; (cioè) that is

ovvia'mente adv obviously

ovvi'are vi a qcsa counter sth. **'ovvio** a obvious

ozi'are vi laze around. **'ozio** nm idleness; **stare in ozio** idle about. **ozi'oso** a idle; (questione) pointless

o'zono nm ozone; **buco nell'~** hole in the ozone layer

Pp

pa'ca|re vt quieten. **~to** a quiet

pac'chetto nm packet; (postale) parcel, package; (di sigarette) pack, packet, **~ software** software package

'pacchia nf (fam: situazione) bed of roses

pacchia'nata nf è una **~** it's so garish. **pacchi'ano** a garish

'pacco nm parcel; (involto) bundle. **~ regalo** gift-wrapped package

paccot'tiglia nf (roba scadente) junk, rubbish

'pace nf peace, **darsi ~** forget it, **fare ~ con qcno** make it up with sb; **lasciare in ~ qcno** leave sb in peace

pachi'derma nm (animale) pachyderm

pachi'stano, -a nm & a Pakistani

pacifi'ca|re vt reconcile; (mettere pace) pacify. **~zi'one** nf reconciliation

pa'cifico a pacific; (calmo) peaceful; **il P~** the Pacific

paci'fis|mo nm pacifism. **~ta** nmf pacifist

pacioc'cone, -a nmf fam chubbychops

pa'dano a pianura padana Po Valley

pa'del|la nf frying-pan; (per malati) bedpan. **~'lata** nf una **~lata di** a frying-panful of

padigli'one nm pavilion

'padr|e nm father; **~i** pl (antenati) forefathers. **pa'drino** nm godfather. **~e'nostro** nm il **~e-nostro** the Lord's Prayer. **~e-'terno** nm God Almighty

padro'nanza nf mastery. **~ di sé** self-control

pa'drone, -a nmf master; mistress; (datore di lavoro) boss; (proprietario) owner. **~ggi'are** vt master

pae'sag|gio nm scenery; (pittura) landscape. **~'gista** nmf landscape architect

pae'sano, -a a country ● nmf villager

pa'ese nm (nazione) country; (territorio) land; (villaggio) village; **il Bel P~** Italy; **va' a quel ~!** get lost!; **Paesi** pl **Bassi** Netherlands

paf'futo a plump

'paga nf pay, wages pl

pa'gabile a payable

pa'gaia nf paddle

paga'mento nm payment; **a ~** ⟨parcheggio⟩ which you have to pay to use. **~ anticipato** Comm advance payment. **~ alla consegna** cash on delivery, COD

paga'nesimo nm paganism

pa'gano, -a a & nmf pagan

pa'gare vt/i pay; **~ da bere a qcno**

buy sb a drink; **te la faccio ~** you'll pay for this

pa'gella nf [school] report

'pagina nf page. **Pagine** pl **Gialle** Yellow Pages. **~ web** Comput web page

'paglia nf straw

pagliac'cetto nm (per bambini) rompers pl

pagliac'ciata nf farce

pagli'accio nm clown

pagli'aio nm haystack

pagli'ericcio nm straw mattress

pagli'etta nf (cappello) boater; (per pentole) steel wool

pagli'uzza nf wisp of straw; (di metallo) particle

pa'gnotta nf [round] loaf

pail'lette nf inv sequin

'paio nm (pl inv **paia**) pair; **un ~** (circa due) a couple; **un ~ di** ⟨scarpe, forbici⟩ a pair of

Paki'stan nm Pakistan

'pala nf shovel; (di remo, elica) blade; (di ruota) paddle

pala'fitta nf pile-dwelling

pala'sport nm inv indoor sports arena

pa'late nfpl **a ~** ⟨fare soldi⟩ hand over fist

pa'lato nm palate

palaz'zetto nm **~ dello sport** indoor sports arena

palaz'zina nf villa

pa'lazzo nm palace; (edificio) building. **~ delle esposizioni** exhibition centre. **~ di giustizia** law courts pl, courthouse. **~ dello sport** indoor sports arena

'palco nm (pedana) platform; Theat box. **~['scenico]** nm stage

pale'sar|e vt disclose. **~si** vr reveal oneself. **pa'lese** a evident

Pale'sti|na nf Palestine. **~'nese** nmf Palestinian

pa'lestra nf gymnasium, gym; (ginnastica) gymnastics pl

pa'letta nf spade; (per focolare) shovel. **~ [della spazzatura]** dustpan

pa'letto nm peg

'**palio** nm (premio) prize. **il P~** horse-race held at Siena

pali'zata nf fence

'**palla** nf ball; (proiettile) bullet; (fam: bugia) porkie; **che palle!** vulg this is a pain in the arse!. **~ di neve** snowball. **~ al piede** fig millstone round one's neck

pallaca'nestro nf basketball

palla'mano nf handball

pallanu'oto nf water polo

palla'volo nf volley-ball

palleggi'are vi (calcio) practise ball control; Tennis knock up

pallia'tivo nm palliative

'**pallido** a pale; **non ne ho la più pallida idea** I don't have the faintest idea

pal'lina nf (di vetro) marble

pal'lino nm **avere il ~ del calcio** be crazy about football

pallon'cino nm balloon; (lanterna) Chinese lantern; (fam: etilometro) Breathalyzer®

pal'lone nm ball; (calcio) football; (aerostato) balloon

pal'lore nm pallor

pal'loso a sl boring

pal'lottola nf pellet; (proiettile) bullet

'**palm|a** nf Bot palm. **~o** nm Anat palm; (misura) hand's-breadth; **restare con un ~o di naso** feel disappointed

'**palo** nm pole; (di sostegno) stake; (in calcio) goalpost; **fare il ~** (ladro) keep a lookout; **~ della luce** lamppost

palom'baro nm diver

pal'pare vt feel

'palpebra nf eyelid

palpi'ta|re vi throb; (fremere) quiver. **~zi'one** nf palpitation

'**palpito** nm throb; (del cuore) beat

pa'lude nf marsh, swamp

palu'doso a marshy

pa'lustre a marshy; (piante, uccelli) marsh attrib

pam'pino nm vine leaf

pana'cea nf panacea

'**panca** nf bench; (in chiesa) pew

pancar'ré nm sliced bread

pan'cetta nf Culin bacon; (di una certa età) paunch

pan'chetto nm [foot]stool

pan'china nf garden seat; (in calcio) bench

'**pancia** nf belly, tummy fam; **mal di ~** stomach-ache; **metter su ~** develop a paunch; **a ~ in giù** lying face down. **panci'era** nf corset

panci'olle: **stare in ~** lounge about

panci'one nm (persona) pot belly

panci'otto nm waistcoat

pande'monio nm pandemonium

pan'doro nm kind of sponge cake traditionally eaten at Christmas

'**pane** nm bread; (pagnotta) loaf; (di burro) block. **~ a cassetta** sliced bread. **pan grattato** breadcrumbs pl. **~ di segale** rye bread. **pan di Spagna** sponge cake. **~ tostato** toast

panett|e'ria nf bakery; (negozio) baker's [shop]. **~i'ere, -a** nmf baker

panet'tone nf dome-shaped cake with sultanas and candied fruit eaten at Christmas

pan'filo nm yacht

pan'forte nm nougat-like spicy delicacy from Siena

'**panico** nm panic; **lasciarsi prendere dal ~** panic

pani'ere nm basket; (cesta) hamper

pani'ficio nm bakery; (negozio) baker's [shop]

pani'naro nm sl preppie

pa'nino nm [bread] roll. **~ imbottito** filled roll. **~ al prosciutto** ham roll. **~teca** nf sandwich bar

'**panna** nf cream. **~ da cucina** [single] cream. **~ montata** whipped cream

'**panne** nf Mech **in ~** broken down; **restare in ~** break down

pan'nello nm panel. **~ solare** solar panel

'**panno** nm cloth; **panni** pl (abiti)

clothes; **mettersi nei panni di qcno** *fig* put oneself in sb's shoes
pan'nocchia *nf (di granoturco)* cob
panno'lino *nm (per bambini)* nappy; *(da donna)* sanitary towel
pano'ram|a *nm* panorama; *fig* overview. **~ico** *a* panoramic
pantacol'lant *nmpl* leggings
pantalon'cini *nmpl* ~ [**corti**] shorts
panta'loni *nmpl* trousers, pants *Am*
pan'tano *nm* bog
pan'tera *nf* panther; *(auto della polizia)* high-speed police car
pan'tofo|la *nf* slipper. **~'laio, -a** *nmf fig* stay-at-home
pan'zana *nf fig*
pao'nazzo *a* purple
'papa *nm* Pope
papà *nm inv* dad[dy]
pa'pale *a* papal
papa'lina *nf* skull-cap
papa'razzo *nm* paparazzo
pa'pato *nm* papacy
pa'pavero *nm* poppy
'paper|a *nf (errore)* slip of the tongue. **~o** *nm* gosling
papil'lon *nm inv* bow tie
pa'piro *nm* papyrus
'pappa *nf (per bambini)* pap
pappa'gallo *nm* parrot
pappa'molle *nmf* wimp
'para *nf* **suole** *nfpl* **di ~** crêpe soles
pa'rabola *nf* parable; *(curva)* parabola
para'bolico *a* parabolic
para'brezza *nm inv* windscreen, windshield *Am*
paracadu'tar|e *vt* parachute. **~si** *vr* parachute
paraca'du|te *nm inv* parachute. **~'tismo** *nm* parachuting. **~'tista** *nmf* parachutist
para'carro *nm* roadside post
paradi'siaco *a* heavenly
para'diso *nm* paradise. **~ terre-stre** Eden, earthly paradise
parados'sale *a* paradoxical. **para-'dosso** *nm* paradox

para'fango *nm* mudguard
paraf'fina *nf* paraffin
parafra'sare *vt* paraphrase
para'fulmine *nm* lightning-conductor
pa'raggi *nmpl* neighbourhood *sg*
parago'na|bile *a* comparable (a to). **~re** *vt* compare. **para'gone** *nm* comparison; **a paragone di** in comparison with
pa'ragrafo *nm* paragraph
pa'ra|lisi *nf inv* paralysis. **~'litico, -a** *a* & *nmf* paralytic. **~liz'zare** *vt* paralyse. **~liz'zato** *a (dalla paura)* transfixed
paral'lel|a *nf* parallel line. **~a'mente** *adv* in parallel. **~o** *a* & *nm* parallel; **~e** *pl* parallel bars. **~o'gramma** *nm* parallelogram
para'lume *nm* lampshade
para'medico *nm* paramedic
pa'rametro *nm* parameter
para'noi|a *nf* paranoia. **~co, -a** *a* & *nmf* paranoid
paranor'male *a (fenomeno, facoltà)* paranormal
para'occhi *nmpl* blinkers. **parao'recchie** *nm* earmuffs
para'petto *nm* parapet
para'piglia *nm* turmoil
para'plegico, -a *a* & *nmf* paraplegic
pa'rar|e *vt (addobbare)* adorn; *(riparare)* shield; save *(tiro, pallone)*; ward off, parry *(schiaffo, pugno)* ● *vi (mirare)* lead up to. **~si** *vr (abbigliarsi)* dress up; *(da pioggia, pugni)* protect oneself; **~si innanzi a qcno** appear in front of sb
pa'rasole *nm inv* parasol
paras'sita *a* parasitic ● *nm* parasite
parasta'tale *a* government-controlled
pa'rata *nf* parade; *(in calcio)* save; *(in scherma, pugilato)* parry
para'urti *nm inv* Auto bumper, fender *Am*
para'vento *nm* screen
par'cella *nf* bill
parcheggi'a|re *vt* park. **par-**

'**cheggio** nm parking; (*posteggio*) carpark, parking lot Am. **~ 'tore, ~'trice** nmf parking attendant. **~tore abusivo** person who illegally earns money by looking after parked cars

par'chimetro nm parking-meter

'**parco**[1] a sparing; (*moderato*) moderate

'**parco**[2] nm park. **~ di divertimenti** fun-fair. **~ giochi** playground. **~ naturale** wildlife park. **~ nazionale** national park. **~ regionale** [regional] wildlife park

pa'recchi a a good many ● pron several

pa'recchio a quite a lot of ● pron quite a lot ● adv rather; (*parecchio tempo*) quite a time

pareggi'are vt level; (*eguagliare*) equal; Comm balance ● vi draw

pa'reggio nm Comm balance; Sport draw

paren'tado nm relatives pl; (*vincolo di sangue*) relationship

pa'rente nmf relative. **~ stretto** close relation

paren'tela nf relatives pl; (*vincolo di sangue*) relationship

pa'rentesi nf inv parenthesis; (*segno grafico*) bracket; (*fig: pausa*) break. **~ pl graffe** curly brackets. **~ quadre** square brackets. **~ tonde** round brackets

pa'reo nm (*copricostume*) sarong; **a ~** (*gonna*) wrap-around

pa'rere[1] nm opinion; **a mio ~** in my opinion

pa'rere[2] vi seem; (*pensare*) think; **che te ne pare?** what do you think of it?; **pare di sì** it seems so

pa'rete nf wall; (*in alpinismo*) face. **~ divisoria** partition wall

'**pari** a inv equal; (*numero*) even; **andare di ~ passo** keep pace; **essere ~** be even o quits; **arrivare ~** draw; **~** (*copiare, ripetere*) word for word, **fare ~ o dispari** toss a coin ● nmf inv equal, peer; **ragazza alla ~** au pair [girl]; **mettersi in ~ con qcsa** catch up

with sth ● nm (*titolo nobiliare*) peer

Pa'rigi nf Paris

pa'riglia nf pair

pari'tà nf equality; Tennis deuce. **~'tario** a parity attrib

parlamen'tare a parliamentary ● nmf Member of Parliament ● vi discuss. **parla'mento** nm Parliament. **il Parlamento europeo** the European Parliament

parlan'tina nf **avere la ~** be a chatterbox

par'la|**re** vt/i speak, talk; (*confessare*) talk; **~ bene/male di qcno** speak well/ill of somebody; **non parliamone più** let's forget about it; **non se ne parla nemmeno!** don't even mention it!. **~to** a (*lingua*) spoken. **~'torio** nm parlour; (*in prigione*) visiting room

parlot'tare vi mutter. **parlot'tio** nm muttering

parmigi'ano nm Parmesan

paro'dia nf parody

pa'rola nf word; (*facoltà*) speech; **è una ~!** it is easier said than done!; **parole** pl (*di canzone*) words, lyrics; **rivolgere la ~ a** address; **dare a qcno la propria ~** give sb one's word; **in parole povere** crudely speaking. **parole** pl **incrociate** crossword [puzzle] sg. **~ d'onore** word of honour. **~ d'ordine** password. **paro'laccia** nf swear-word

par'quet nm inv (*pavimento*) parquet flooring

par'rocchi|**a** nf parish. **~'ale** a parish attrib. **~'ano, -a** nmf parishioner. '**parr**|**oco** nm parish priest

par'rucca nf wig

parrucchi'ere, -a nmf hairdresser

parruc'chino nm toupée, hairpiece

parsi'moni|**a** nf thrift. **~'oso** a thrifty

'**parso** pp di **parere**

'**parte** nf part; (*lato*) side; (*partito*) party; (*porzione*) share; **a ~** apart from; **in ~** in part; **la maggior**

di the majority of; **d'altra ~** on the other hand; **da ~** aside; (*in disparte*) to one side; **farsi da ~** stand aside; **da ~ di** from; (*per conto di*) on behalf of; **è gentile da ~ tua** it is kind of you; **fare una brutta ~ a** qcno behave badly towards sb; **da che ~ è...?** whereabouts is...?; **da una ~..., dall'altra...** on the one hand..., on the other hand...; **dall'altra ~** di on the other side of; **da nessuna ~** nowhere; **da tutte le parti** (*essere*) everywhere; **da questa ~** (*in questa direzione*) this way; **da un anno a questa ~** for about a year now; **essere dalla ~ di** qcno be on sb's side; **prendere le parti di** qcno take sb's side; **essere ~ in causa** be involved; **fare ~** (*appartenere a*) be a member of; **rendere ~** a take part in. **~ civile** plaintiff

parteci'pante *nmf* participant

parteci'pa|re *vi* **~re a** participate in, take part in; (*condividere*) share in. **~zi'one** *nf* participation; (*annuncio*) announcement; *Fin* shareholding; (*presenza*) presence. **par'tecipe** *a* participating

parteggi'are *vi* **~ per** side with

par'tenza *nf* departure; *Sport* start; **in ~ per** leaving for

parti'cella *nf* particle

parti'cipio *nm* participle

partico'lar|e *a* particular; (*privato*) private ● *nm* detail, particular; **fin nei minimi ~** down to the smallest detail. **~eggi'ato** *a* detailed. **~ità** *nf inv* particularity; (*dettaglio*) detail

partigi'ano, -a *a* & *nmf* partisan

par'tire *vi* leave; (*aver inizio*) start; **a ~ da** [beginning] from

par'tita *nf* game; (*incontro*) match; *Comm* lot; (*contabilità*) entry. **~ di calcio** football match. **~ a carte** game of cards

par'tito *nm* party; (*scelta*) choice; (*occasione di matrimonio*) match;

per ~ preso out of sheer pig-headedness

'parto *nm* childbirth; **un ~ facile** an easy birth *o* labour; **dolori** *pl* **del ~** labour pains. **~ cesareo** Caesarian section. **~'rire** *vt* give birth to

par'venza *nf* appearance

parzi'al|e *a* partial. **~ità** *nf* partiality. **~'mente** *adv* (*non completamente*) partially; **~'mente scremato** semi-skimmed

pasco'lare *vt* graze. **'pascolo** *nm* pasture

'Pasqua *nf* Easter. **pa'squale** *a* Easter attrib

'passa: **e ~** *adv* (*e oltre*) plus

pas'sabile *a* passable

pas'saggio *nm* passage; (*traversata*) crossing; *Sport* pass; (*su veicolo*) lift; **essere di ~** be passing through. **~ a livello** level crossing, grade crossing *Am*. **~ pedonale** pedestrian crossing

passamon'tagna *nm inv* balaclava

pas'sante *nmf* passer-by ● *nm* (*di cintura*) loop ● *a* *Tennis* passing

passa'porto *nm* passport

pas'sa|re *vi* pass; (*attraversare*) pass through; (*far visita*) call; (*andare*) go; (*essere approvato*) be passed; **~re alla storia** go down in history; **mi ~ to di mente** it slipped my mind; **~re per un genio/idiota** be taken for a genius/an idiot; **farsi ~re per** qcno pass oneself off as sb ● *vt* (*far scorrere*) pass over; (*sopportare*) go through; (*al telefono*) put through; *Culin* strain; **~re di moda** go out of fashion; **le passo il signor Rossi** I'll put you through to Mr Rossi; **~rsela bene** be well off; **come te la passi?** how are you doing? **~ta** *nf* (*di vernice*) coat; (*spolverata*) dusting; (*occhiata*) look

passa'tempo *nm* pastime

pas'sato *a* past; **l'anno ~** last year; **sono le tre passate** it's past

o after three o'clock ● *nm* past; (*arte*)
Culin purée; *Gram* past tense. ~
prossimo *Gram* present perfect.
~ **remoto** *Gram* [simple] past. ~
di verdure cream of vegetable
soup

passaver'dure *nm inv* food mill

passeg'gero, -a *a* passing ● *nmf*
passenger

passeggi'a|re *vi* walk, stroll. **~ta**
nf walk, stroll; (*luogo*) public
walk; (*in bicicletta*) ride; **fare una
~ta** go for a walk

passeg'gino *nm* pushchair,
stroller *Am*

pas'seggio *nm* walk; (*luogo*)
promenade; **andare a ~** go for a
walk; **scarpe da ~** walking
shoes

passe-partout *nm inv* master-key

passe'rella *nf* gangway; *Aeron*
boarding bridge; (*per sfilate*) catwalk

'passero *nm* sparrow. **passe'rotto**
nm (*passero*) sparrow

pas'sibile *a* ~ **di** liable to

passio'nale *a* passionate. **passi'o-
ne** *nf* passion

pas'sivo *a* passive ● *nm* passive;
Comm liabilities *pl*; **in** ~ (*bilancio*) loss-making

'passo *nm* step; (*orma*) footprint;
(*andatura*) pace; (*brano*) passage;
(*valico*) pass; **a due passi da qui** a
stone's throw away; **a ~ d'uomo**
at walking pace; **di buon** ~ at
a spanking pace; **fare due passi**
go for a stroll; **di pari** ~ *fig* hand
in hand. ~ **carrabile, ~ carraio**
driveway

'past|a *nf* (*impasto per pane ecc*)
dough; (*per dolci, pasticcini*) pastry; (*pastasciutta*) pasta; (*massa
molle*) paste; *fig* nature. **~a frolla**
shortcrust pastry. **pa'stella** *nf* batter

pastasci'utta *nf* pasta

pa'stello *nm* pastel

pa'sticca *nf* pastille; (*fam: pastiglia*) pill

pasticce'ria *nf* cake shop, patisse-

rie; (*pasticcini*) pastries *pl*; (*arte*)
confectionery

pasticci'are *vi* make a mess ● *vt*
make a mess of

pasticci'ere, -a *nmf* confectioner

pastic'cino *nm* little cake

pa'sticc|o *nm Culin* pie; (*lavoro
disordinato*) mess; **mettersi nei
pasticci** get into trouble. ~**'one,
-a** *nmf* bungler ● *a* bungling

pasti'ficio *nm* pasta factory

pa'stiglia *nf Med* pill, tablet; (*di
menta*) sweet. ~ **dei freni** brake
pad

'pasto *nm* meal

pasto'rale *a* pastoral. **pa'store** *nm*
shepherd; *Relig* pastor. **pastore
tedesco** German shepherd, Alsatian

pastoriz'za|re *vt* pasteurize. ~**to** *a*
pasteurized. ~**zi'one** *nf* pasteuri-
zation

pa'stoso *a* doughy; *fig* mellow

pa'stura *nf* pasture; (*per pesci*)
bait

pa'tacca *nf* (*macchia*) stain; (*fig:
oggetto senza valore*) piece of junk

pa'tata *nf* potato. **patate fritte**
chips *Br*, French fries. **pata'tine**
nfpl [potato] crisps, chips *Am*

pata'trac *nm inv* (*crollo*) crash

pâté *nm inv* pâté

pa'tella *nf* limpet

pa'tema *nm* anxiety

pa'tente *nf* licence. ~ **di guida**
driving licence, driver's license
Am

pater'nale *nf* scolding. ~**'lista** *nm*
paternalist

paternità *nf* paternity. **pa'terno** *a*
paternal; (*affetto ecc*) fatherly

pa'tetico *a* pathetic. **'pathos** *nm*
pathos

pa'tibolo *nm* gallows *sg*

pa'tina *nf* patina; (*sulla lingua*)
coating

pa'ti|re *vt/i* suffer. ~**to, -a** *a* suffer-
ing ● *nmf* fanatic. ~**to della
musica** music lover

patolo'gia *nf* pathology. **pato-
'logico** *a* pathological

'patria *nf* native land
patri'arca *nm* patriarch
pa'trigno *nm* stepfather
patrimoni'ale *a* property *attrib.*
patri'monio *nm* estate
patri'ota *nmf* patriot. **~tico** *a* patriotic. **~tismo** *nm* patriotism
pa'trizio, -a *a & nmf* patrician
patro|ci'nare *vt* support. **~'cinio** *nm* support
patro'nato *nm* patronage. **pa'trono** *nm* Relig patron saint; Jur counsel
'patta¹ *nf (di tasca)* flap
'patta² *nf (pareggio)* draw
patteggi|a'mento *nm* bargaining. **~'are** *vt/i* negotiate
patti'naggio *nm* skating. **~ su ghiaccio** ice skating. **~ a rotelle** roller skating
patti'na|re *vi* skate; *(auto:)* skid. **~tore, ~'trice** *nmf* skater. **'pattino** *nm* skate; Aeron skid. **pattino da ghiaccio** iceskate. **pattino a rotelle** roller-skate
'patto *nm* deal; Pol pact; **a ~ che** on condition that
pat'tuglia *nf* patrol. **~ stradale** patrol car; police motorbike, highway patrol Am
pattu'ire *vt* negotiate
pattumi'era *nf* dustbin, trashcan Am
pa'ura *nf* fear; *(spavento)* fright; **aver ~** be afraid; **mettere ~ a** frighten. **pau'roso** *a (che fa paura)* frightening; *(che ha paura)* fearful; *(fam: enorme)* awesome
'pausa *nf* pause; *(nel lavoro)* break; **fare una ~** pause; *(nel lavoro)* have a break
pavimen'ta|re *vt* pave *(strada)*. **~zi'one** *nf (operazione)* paving. **pavi'mento** *nm* floor
pa'vone *nm* peacock. **~ggi'arsi** *vr* strut
pazien'tare *vi* be patient
pazi'ente *a & nmf* patient. **~'mente** *adv* patiently. **pazi'enza** *nf* patience; **pazienza!** never mind!

'pazza *nf* madwoman. **~'mente** *adv* madly
paz'z|esco *a* foolish; *(esagerato)* crazy. **~ia** *nf* madness; *(azione)* [act of] folly. **'pazzo** *a* mad; *fig* crazy ●*nm* madman; **essere pazzo di/per** be crazy about; **pazzo di gioia** mad with joy; **da pazzi** *fam* crackpot; **darsi alla pazza gioia** live it up. **paz'zoide** *a* whacky
'pecca *nf* fault; **senza ~** flawless. **peccami'noso** *a* sinful
pec'ca|re *vi* sin; **~re di** be guilty of *(ingratitudine)*. **~to** *nm* sin; **~to che...** it's a pity that...; **[che] ~to!** [what a] pity!. **~'tore, ~'trice** *nmf* sinner
'pece *nf* pitch
'peco|ra *nf* sheep. **~ra nera** black sheep. **~'raio** *nm* shepherd. **~'rella** *nf* cielo a **~relle** sky full of fluffy white clouds. **~'rino** *nm (formaggio)* sheep's milk cheese
peculi'are *a* **~ di** peculiar to. **~ità** *nf inv* peculiarity
pe'daggio *nm* toll
peda'go|gia *nf* pedagogy. **peda'gogico** *a* pedagogical
peda'lare *vi* pedal. **pe'dale** *nm* pedal. **pedalò** *nm inv* pedalo
pe'dana *nf* footrest; Sport springboard
pe'dante *a* pedantic. **~'ria** *nf* pedantry. **pedan'tesco** *a* pedantic
pe'data *nf (in calcio)* kick; *(impronta)* footprint
pede'rasta *nm* pederast
pe'destre *a* pedestrian
pedi'atra *nmf* paediatrician. **pedia'tria** *nf* paediatrics *sg*
pedi'cure *nmf inv* chiropodist, podiatrist Am ●*nm (cura dei piedi)* pedicure
pedi'gree *nm inv* pedigree
pe'dina *nf (alla dama)* piece; *fig* pawn. **~'mento** *nm* shadowing. **pedi'nare** *vt* shadow
pe'dofilo, -a *nmf* paedophile
pedo'nale *a* pedestrian. **pe'done, -a** *nmf* pedestrian

peeling *nm inv* exfoliation treatment

'peggio *adv* worse; **~ per te!** too bad!; **~ di così** any worse; **la persona ~ vestita** the worst dressed person ●*a* worse; **niente di ~** nothing worse ●*nm* **il ~ è che...** the worst of it is that...; **pensare al ~** think the worst ●*nf* **alla ~** at worst; **avere la ~** get the worst of it; **alla meno ~** as best I can

peggiora'mento *nm* worsening

peggio'ra|re *vt* make worse, worsen ●*vi* get worse, worsen. **~'tivo** *a* pejorative

peggi'ore *a* worse; (*superlativo*) worst; **nella ~ delle ipotesi** if the worst comes to the worst ●*nmf* **il/la ~** the worst

'pegno *nm* pledge; (*nei giochi di società*) forfeit; *fig* token

pelan'drone *nm* slob

pe'la|re *vt* (*spennare*) pluck; (*spellare*) skin; (*sbucciare*) peel; (*fam: spillare denaro*) fleece. **~rsi** *vr fam* lose one's hair. **~to** *a* bald. **~ti** *nmpl* (*pomodori*) peeled tomatoes

pel'lame *nm* skins *pl*

'pelle *nf* skin; (*cuoio*) leather; (*buccia*) peel; **avere la ~ d'oca** have goose-flesh

pellegri'naggio *nm* pilgrimage. **pelle'grino, -a** *nmf* pilgrim

pelle'rossa *nmf* Red Indian, Redskin

pelle'tteria *nf* leather goods *pl*

pelli'cano *nm* pelican

pellicce'ria *nf* furrier's [shop]. **pel'licc|ia** *nf* fur; (*indumento*) fur coat. **~i'aio, -a** *nmf* furrier

pel'licola *nf* Phot, Cinema film. **~ [trasparente]** cling film

'pelo *nm* hair; (*di animale*) coat; (*di lana*) pile; **per un ~** by the skin of one's teeth; **cavarsela per un ~** have a narrow escape. **pe'loso** *a* hairy

'peltro *nm* pewter

pe'luche *nm inv* **giocattolo di ~** soft toy

pe'luria *nf* down

'pelvico *a* pelvic

'pena *nf* (*punizione*) punishment; (*sofferenza*) pain; (*dispiacere*) sorrow; (*disturbo*) trouble; **a mala ~** hardly; **mi fa ~** I pity him; **vale la ~ andare** it is worth [while] going. **~ di morte** death sentence

pe'na|le *a* criminal; **diritto ~e** criminal law. **~ità** *nf inv* penalty

penaliz'za|re *vt* penalize. **~zi'one** *nf* (*penalità*) penalty

pe'nare *vi* suffer; (*faticare*) find it difficult

pen'daglio *nm* pendant

pen'dant *nm inv* **fare ~ [con]** match

pen'den|te *a* hanging; Comm outstanding ●*nm* (*ciondolo*) pendant; **~ti** *pl* drop earrings. **~za** *nf* slope; Comm outstanding account

'pendere *vi* hang; (*superficie:*) slope; (*essere inclinato*) lean

pendo'l|are *a* pendulum ●*nmf* commuter. **~ino** *nm* (*treno*) special, first class only, fast train

'pendolo *nm* pendulum

'pene *nm* penis

pene'trante *a* penetrating; (*freddo*) biting

pene'tra|re *vt/i* penetrate; (*trafiggere*) pierce ●*vt* (*odore:*) get into ●*vi* (*entrare furtivamente*) steal in. **~zi'one** *nf* penetration

penicil'lina *nf* penicillin

pe'nisola *nf* peninsula

peni'ten|te *a & nmf* penitent. **~za** *nf* penitence; (*punizione*) penance; (*in gioco*) forfeit. **~zi'ario** *nm* penitentiary

'penna *nf* (*da scrivere*) pen; (*di uccello*) feather. **~ a feltro** felttip[ped pen]. **~ a sfera** ball-point [pen]. **~ stilografica** fountain-pen

pen'nacchio *nm* plume

penna'rello *nm* felt-tip[ped pen]

pennel'la|re *vt* paint. **~ta** *nf* brushstroke. **pen'nello** *nm* brush, **a pennello** (*a perfezione*) perfectly

pen'nino *nm* nib

pen'none *nm* (*di bandiera*) flag-pole

pen'nuto *a* feathered

pe'nombra *nf* half-light

pe'noso *a* (*fam: pessimo*) painful

pen'sa|re *vi* think; **penso di sì** I think so; **~re** a think of; remember to ⟨*chiudere il gas ecc*⟩; **pensa ai fatti tuoi!** mind your own business!; **ci penso io** I'll take care of it; **~re di fare qcsa** think of doing sth; **~re tra sé e sé** think to oneself ● *vt* think. **~ta** *nf* idea

pensi'e|ro *nm* thought; (*mente*) mind; (*preoccupazione*) worry; **stare in ~ro per** be anxious about. **~roso** *a* pensive

'pensi|le *a* hanging; **giardino ~le** roof-garden ●*nm* (*mobile*) wall unit. **~lina** *nf* (*di fermata d'autobus*) bus shelter

pensio'nante *nmf* boarder; (*ospite pagante*) lodger

pensio'nato, -a *nmf* pensioner ●*nm* (*per anziani*) [old folks'] home; (*per studenti*) hostel. **pensi'one** *nf* pension; (*albergo*) boarding-house; (*vitto e alloggio*) board and lodging; **andare in pensione** retire; **mezza pensione** half board. **pensione completa** full board

pen'soso *a* pensive

pen'tagono *nm* pentagon

Pente'coste *nf* Whitsun

penti'mento *nm* repentance

pen'ti|rsi *vr* **~rsi** of repent of; (*rammaricarsi*) regret. **~'tismo** *nm* turning informant. **~to** *nm* Mafioso turned informant

'pentola *nf* saucepan; (*contenuto*) potful. **~ a pressione** pressure cooker

pe'nultimo *a* last but one, penultimate

pe'nuria *nf* shortage

penzo'l|are *vi* dangle. **~oni** *a* dangling

pe'pa|re *vt* pepper. **~to** *a* peppery

'pepe *nm* pepper; **grano di ~** peppercorn. **~ in grani** whole pepper-

corns. **~ macinato** ground pepper

pepero'n|ata *nf* peppers cooked in olive oil with onion, tomato and garlic. **~'cino** *nm* chilli pepper. **pepe'rone** *nm* pepper. **peperone verde** green pepper

pe'pita *nf* nugget

per *prep* for; (*attraverso*) through; (*stato in luogo*) in, on; (*distributivo*) per; (*mezzo, entro*) by; (*causa*) with; (*in qualità di*) as; **~ strada** on the street; **~ la fine del mese** by the end of the month; **in fila ~ due** in double file; **l'ho sentito ~ telefono** I spoke to him on the phone; **~ iscritto** in writing; **~ caso** by chance; **ho aspettato ~ ore** I've been waiting for hours; **~ tempo** in time; **~ sempre** forever; **~ scherzo** as a joke; **gridare ~ il dolore** scream with pain; **vendere ~ 10 milioni** sell for 10 million; **uno ~ volta** one at a time; **uno ~ uno** one by one; **venti ~ cento** twenty per cent; **~ fare qcsa** [in order to] do sth; **stare ~** be about to; **è troppo bello ~ essere vero** it's too good to be true

'pera *nf* pear; **farsi una ~** (*sl: di eroina*) shoot up

perbe'nis|mo *nm* prissiness. **~ta** *a inv* prissy

per'cento *adv* per cent. **percen'tuale** *nf* percentage

perce'pibile *a* perceivable; ⟨*somma*⟩ payable

perce'pi|re *vt* perceive; (*riscuotere*) cash

perce't|tibile *a* perceptible. **~zi'one** *nf* perception

perché *conj* (*in interrogazioni*) why; (*per il fatto che*) because; (*affinché*) so that; **~ non vieni?** why don't you come?; **dimmi ~** tell me why; **~ no/sì!** because!; **la ragione ~ l'ho fatto** the reason [that] I did it, the reason why I did it; **è troppo difficile ~ lo possa capire** it's too difficult for me to understand ●*nm inv* reason

[why]; **senza un** ~ without any reason

perciò *conj* so

per'correre *vt* cover ⟨*distanza*⟩; ⟨*viaggiare*⟩ travel. **per'corso** *pp di* **percorrere** ● *nm* ⟨*tragitto*⟩ course, route; ⟨*distanza*⟩ distance; ⟨*viaggio*⟩ journey

per'coss|a *nf* blow. **~o** *pp di* **percuotere**. **percu'otere** *vt* strike

percussi'o|ne *nf* percussion; **strumenti** *pl a* ~ne percussion instruments. **~'nista** *nmf* percussionist

per'dente *nmf* loser

'perder|e *vt* lose; ⟨*sprecare*⟩ waste; ⟨*non prendere*⟩ miss; ⟨*fig: vizio:*⟩ ruin; **~e tempo** waste time ● *vi* lose; ⟨*recipiente:*⟩ leak; **lascia** ~**e!** forget it!. **~si** *vr* get lost; ⟨*reciproco*⟩ lose touch

perdifi'ato: a ~ *adv* ⟨*gridare*⟩ at the top of one's voice

perdigi'orno *nmf inv* idler

'perdita *nf* loss; ⟨*spreco*⟩ waste; ⟨*falla*⟩ leak; **a** ~ **d'occhio** as far as the eye can see. ~ **di tempo** waste of time. **perdi'tempo** *nm* waste of time

perdo'nare *vt* forgive; ⟨*scusare*⟩ excuse. **per'dono** *nm* forgiveness; *Jur* pardon

perdu'rare *vi* last; ⟨*perseverare*⟩ persist

perduta'mente *adv* hopelessly. **per'duto** *pp di* **perdere** ● *a* lost; ⟨*rovinato*⟩ ruined

pe'renne *a* everlasting; *Bot* perennial; **nevi perenni** perpetual snow. **~'mente** *adv* perpetually

peren'torio *a* peremptory

per'fetto *a* perfect ● *nm Gram* perfect [tense]

perfezio'nar|e *vt* perfect; ⟨*migliorare*⟩ improve. **~si** *vr* improve oneself; ⟨*specializzarsi*⟩ specialize

perfezi'o|ne *nf* perfection; **alla** ~**ne** to perfection. **~'nismo** *nm* perfectionism. **~'nista** *nmf* perfectionist

per'fidia *nf* wickedness; ⟨*atto*⟩

wicked act. **'perfido** *a* treacherous; ⟨*malvagio*⟩ perverse

per'fino *adv* even

perfo'ra|re *vt* pierce; punch ⟨*schede*⟩; *Mech* drill. **~'tore**, **~'trice** *nmf* punch-card operator ● *nm* perforator. **~zi'one** *nf* perforation; ⟨*di schede*⟩ punching

per'formance *nf inv* performance

perga'mena *nf* parchment

perico'lante *a* precarious; ⟨*azienda*⟩ shaky

pe'rico|lo *nm* danger; ⟨*rischio*⟩ risk; **mettere in** ~**lo** endanger. ~**lo pubblico** danger to society. **~'loso** *a* dangerous

perife'ria *nf* periphery; ⟨*di città*⟩ outskirts *pl*; *fig* fringes *pl*

peri'feric|a *nf* peripheral; ⟨*strada*⟩ ring road. **~o** *a* ⟨*quartiere*⟩ outlying

pe'rifrasi *nf inv* circumlocution

pe'rimetro *nm* perimeter

peri'odico *nm* periodical ● *a* periodical; ⟨*vento, mal di testa, Math*⟩ recurring. **pe'riodo** *nm* period; *Gram* sentence. **periodo di prova** trial period

peripe'zie *nfpl* misadventures

pe'rire *vi* perish

peri'scopio *nm* periscope

pe'ri|to, -a *a* skilled ● *nmf* expert

perito'nite *nf* peritonitis

pe'rizia *nf* skill; ⟨*valutazione*⟩ survey

'perla *nf* pearl. **per'lina** *nf* bead

perlo'meno *adv* at least

perlu'stra|re *vt* patrol. **~zi'one** *nf* patrol; **andare in** ~**zione** go on patrol

perma'loso *a* touchy

perma'ne|nte *a* permanent ● *nf* perm; **farsi [fare] la** ~**nte** have a perm. **~nza** *nf* permanence; ⟨*soggiorno*⟩ stay; **in** ~**nza** permanently. **~re** *vi* remain

perme'are *vt* permeate

per'messo *pp di* **permettere** ● *nm* permission; ⟨*autorizzazione*⟩ permit; *Mil* leave; **[è]** ~**?** ⟨*posso entrare?*⟩ may I come in?; ⟨*posso* *passare?*) excuse me. ~ **di lavoro** work permit

per'mettere *vt* allow, permit; **po-tersi ~ qcsa** (*finanziariamente*) be able to afford sth; **come si permette?** how dare you?. permis'**'sivo** *a* permissive

permutazi'one *nf* exchange; *Math* permutation

per'nacchia *nf* (*sl: con la bocca*) raspberry *sl*

per'nic|e *nf* partridge. **~i'oso** *a* pernicious

'perno *nm* pivot

pernot'tare *vi* stay overnight

'pero *nm* pear-tree

però *conj* but; (*tuttavia*) however

pero'rare *vt* plead

perpendico'lare *a & nf* perpendicular

perpe'trare *vt* perpetrate

perpetu'are *vt* perpetuate. **per'petuo** *a* perpetual

perplessità *nf inv* perplexity; (*dubbio*) doubt. **per'plesso** *a* perplexed

perqui'si|re *vt* search. **~zi'one** *nf* search. **~zione domiciliare** search of the premises

persecu'|tore, -'trice *nmf* persecutor. **~zi'one** *nf* persecution

persegu'ire *vt* pursue

persegui'tare *vt* persecute

perseve'ra|nte *a* persevering. **~nza** *nf* perseverance. **~re** *vi* persevere

persi'ano, -a *a* Persian ● *nf* (*di finestra*) shutter. '**persico** *a* Persian

per'sino *adv* = **perfino**

persi'sten|te *a* persistent. **~za** *nf* persistence. **per'sistere** *vi* persist

'perso *pp di* **perdere** ● *a* lost; **a tempo ~** in one's spare time

per'sona *nf* person; (*un tale*) somebody; **di ~, in ~** in person, personally; **per ~** per person, a head; **per interposta ~** through an intermediary; **persone** *pl* people

perso'naggio *nm* (*persona di riguardo*) personality; *Theat ecc* character

perso'nal|e *a* personal ● *nm* staff. **~e di terra** ground crew. **~ità** *nf inv* personality. **~iz'zare** *vt* customize (*auto ecc*); personalize (*penna ecc*)

personifi'ca|re *vt* personify. **~zi'one** *nf* personification

perspi'cac|e *a* shrewd. **~ia** *nf* shrewdness

persua'|dere *vt* convince; impress (*critici*); **~dere qcno a fare qcsa** persuade sb to do sth. **~si'one** *nf* persuasion. **~'sivo** *a* persuasive. **persu'aso** *pp di* **persuadere**

per'tanto *conj* therefore

'pertica *nf* pole

perti'nente *a* relevant

per'tosse *nf* whooping cough

pertur'ba|re *vt* perturb. **~rsi** *vr* be perturbed. **~zi'one** *nf* disturbance. **~zione atmosferica** atmospheric disturbance

per'va|dere *vt* pervade. **~so** *pp di* **pervadere**

perve'nire *vi* reach; **far ~ qcsa a qcno** send sth to sb

perver'si|one *nf* perversion. **~ità** *nf* perversity. **per'verso** *a* perverse

perver'ti|re *vt* pervert. **~to** *a* perverted ● *nm* pervert

per'vinca *nm* (*colore*) blue with a touch of purple

p. es. *abbr* (**per esempio**) e.g.

pesa *nf* weighing; (*bilancia*) weighing machine; (*per veicoli*) weighbridge

pe'sante *a* heavy; (*stomaco*) overfull ● *adv* (*vestirsi*) warmly. **~'mente** *adv* (*cadere*) heavily. **pesan'tezza** *nf* heaviness

pe'sar|e *vt/i* weigh; **~e su** *fig* lie heavy on; **~e le parole** weigh one's words. **~si** *vr* weigh oneself

'pesca[1] *nf* (*frutto*) peach

'pesca[2] *nf* fishing; **andare a ~** go fishing. **~ subaquea** underwater fishing. **pe'scare** *vt* (*andare a pesca di*) fish for; (*prendere*) catch;

(fig: trovare) fish out. **~'tore** *nm* fisherman

'pesce *nm* fish. **~ d'aprile!** April Fool!. **~ grosso** *fig* big fish. **~ piccolo** *fig* small fry. **~ rosso** goldfish. **~ spada** swordfish. **Pesci** *Astr* Pisces

pesce'cane *nm* shark

pesche'reccio *nm* fishing boat

pesc|he'ria *nf* fishmonger's [shop]. **~hi'era** *nf* fish-pond. **~i'vendolo** *nm* fishmonger

'pesco *nm* peach-tree

pe'suo *nm* weight: **essere di ~ per qcno** be a burden to sb; **di poco ~** *(senza importanza)* not very important; **non dare ~ a qcsa** not attach any importance to sth

pessi'mis|mo *nm* pessimism. **~ta** *nmf* pessimist ● *a* pessimistic. **'pessimo** *a* very bad

pe'staggio *nm* beating-up. **pe'stare** *vt* tread on; *(schiacciare)* crush; *(picchiare)* beat; crush *(aglio, prezzemolo)*

'peste *nf* plague; *(persona)* pest

pe'stello *nm* pestle

pesti'cida *nm* pesticide. **pe'stifero** *a (fastidioso)* pestilential

pesti'len|za *nf* pestilence; *(fetore)* stench. **~zi'ale** *a (odore aria)* noxious

'pesto *a* ground; **occhio ~** black eye ● *nm* basil and garlic sauce

'petalo *nm* petal

pe'tardo *nm* banger

peti|zi'one *nf* petition; **fare una ~** draw up a petition

petro'li era *nf* [oil] tanker. **~'lifero** *a* oil-bearing. **pe'trolio** *nm* oil

pettego'lare *vi* gossip. **~'lezzo** *nm* piece of gossip; **far ~lezzi** gossip

pet'tegolo, -a *a* gossipy ● *nmf* gossip

petti'na|re *vt* comb. **~rsi** *vr* comb one's hair. **~'tura** *nf* combing; *(acconciatura)* hair-style. **'pettine** *nm* comb

'petting *nm* petting

petti'nino *nm (fermaglio)* comb

petti'rosso *nm* robin [redbreast]

'petto *nm* chest; *(seno)* breast; **a doppio ~** double-breasted

petto'rale *nm (in gare sportive)* number.. **~'rina** *nf (di salopette)* bib. **~'ruto** *a (donna)* full-breasted; *(uomo)* broad-chested

petu'lante *a* impertinent

'pezza *nf* cloth; *(toppa)* patch; *(rotolo di tessuto)* roll

pez'zente *nmf* tramp; *(avaro)* miser

'pezzo *nm* piece; *(parte)* part; **un bel ~ d'uomo** a figure of a man; **un ~** *(di tempo)* some time; *(di spazio)* a long way; **al ~** *(costare)* each; **essere a pezzi** *(stanco)* be shattered; **fare a pezzi** tear to shreds. **~ grosso** bigwig

pia'cente *a* attractive

pia'ce|re *nm* pleasure; *(favore)* favour; **a ~re** as much as one likes; **per ~re!** please!; **~re [di conoscerla]** pleased to meet you!; **con ~re** with pleasure ● *vi* **la Scozia mi piace** I like Scotland; **mi piacciono i dolci** I like sweets; **faccio come mi pare e piace** I do as I please; **ti piace?** do you like it?; **lo spettacolo è piaciuto** the show was a success. **~vole** *a* pleasant

piaci'mento *nm* **a ~** as much as you like

pia'dina *nf* unleavened focaccia bread

pi'aga *nf* sore; *fig* scourge; *(fig: persona noiosa)* pain; *(fig: ricordo doloroso)* wound

pia'gnisteo *nm* whining

piagnuco'lare *vi* whimper

pi'alla *nf* plane. **pial'lare** *vt* plane

pi'ana *nf (di pianura)* plane. **pianeg-gi'ante** *a* level

piane'rottolo *nm* landing

pia'neta *nm* planet

pi'angere *vi* cry; *(disperatamente)* weep ● *nt* *(lamentare)* lament; *(per un lutto)* mourn

pianifi'ca|re *vt* plan. **~zi'one** *nf* planning

pia'nista *nmf* *Mus* pianist

pi'ano *a* flat; (*a livello*) flush; (*regolare*) smooth; (*facile*) easy ● *adv* slowly; (*con cautela*) gently; **andarci ~** go carefully ● *nm* plain; (*di edificio*) floor; (*livello*) plane; (*progetto*) plan; *Mus* piano; **di primo ~** first-rate; **primo ~** *Phot* close-up; **in primo ~** in the foreground. **~ regolatore** town plan. **~ di studi** syllabus

piano'forte *nm* piano. **~ a coda** grand piano

piano'terra *nm inv* ground floor, first floor *Am*

pi'anta *nf* plant; (*del piede*) sole; (*disegno*) plan; **di sana ~** (*totalmente*) entirely; **in ~ stabile** permanently. **~ stradale** road map. **~gi'one** *nf* plantation

piantagran'e *nmf fam* è un/una **~** he's/she's bolshie

pian'tar|e *vt* plant; (*conficcare*) drive; (*fam: abbandonare*) dump; **piantala** *fam* stop it!. **~si** *vr* plant oneself; (*fam: lasciarsi*) leave each other

pianter'reno *nm* ground floor, first floor *Am*

pi'anto *pp di* **piangere** ● *nm* crying; (*disperato*) weeping; (*lacrime*) tears *pl*

pian|to'nare *vt* guard. **~'tone** *nm* guard

pia'nura *nf* plain

pi'astra *nf* plate; (*lastra*) slab; *Culin* griddle. **~ elettronica** circuit board. **~ madre** *Comput* motherboard

pia'strella *nf* tile

pia'strina *nf Mil* identity disc; *Med* platelet; *Comput* chip

piatta'forma *nf* platform. **~ di lancio** launch pad

piat'tino *nm* saucer

pi'atto *a* flat ● *nm* plate; (*da portata, vivanda*) dish; (*portata*) course; (*parte piatta*) flat; (*di giradischi*) turntable; **piatti** *pl Mus* cymbals; **lavare i piatti** do the dishes, do the washing-up. **~**

fondo soup plate. **~ piano** [ordinary] plate

pi'azza *nf* square; *Comm* market; **letto a una ~** single bed; **letto a due piazze** double bed; **far ~ pulita** make a clean sweep. **~'forte** *nf* stronghold. **piaz'zale** *nm* large square. **~'mento** *nm* (*in classifica*) placing

piaz'zar|e *vt* place. **~rsi** *vr Sport* be placed; **~rsi secondo** come second. **~to a** (*cavallo*) placed; **ben ~to** (*robusto*) well built

piaz'zista *nm* salesman

piaz'zuola *nf* **~ di sosta** pull-in

pic'cante *a* hot; (*pungente*) sharp; (*salace*) spicy

pic'carsi *vr* (*risentirsi*) take offence; **~ di** (*vantarsi di*) claim to

'picche *nfpl* (*in carte*) spades

picchet'tare *vt* stake; (*scioperanti*) picket. **pic'chetto** *nm* picket

picchi'a|re *vt* beat, hit ● *vi* (*bussare*) knock; *Aeron* nosedive; **~re in testa** (*motore:*) knock. **~ta** *nf* beating; *Aeron* nosedive; **scendere in ~ta** nosedive

picchiet'tare *vt* tap; (*punteggiare*) spot

picchiet'tio *nm* tapping

'picchio *nm* woodpecker

pic'cino *a* tiny; (*gretto*) mean; (*di poca importanza*) petty ● *nm* little one, child

picci'one *nm* pigeon

'picco *nm* peak; **a ~** vertically; **colare a ~** sink

'piccolo, -a *a* small, little; (*di età*) young; (*di statura*) short; (*gretto*) petty ● *nmf* child, little one; **da ~** as a child

pic'co|ne *nm* pickaxe. **~zza** *nf* ice axe

pic'nic *nm inv* picnic

pi'docchio *nm* louse

piè *nm inv* **a ~ di pagina** at the foot of the page; **saltare a ~ pari** skip

pi'ede *nm* foot; **a piedi** on foot; **andare a piedi** walk; **a piedi nudi** barefoot; **a ~ libero** free; **in piedi**

standing; **alzarsi in piedi** stand up; **in punta di piedi** on tiptoe; **ai piedi di** ⟨*montagna*⟩ at the foot of; **prendere** ~ *fig* gain ground; ⟨*moda:*⟩ catch on; **mettere in piedi** ⟨*allestire*⟩ set up; **togliti dai piedi!** get out of the way!. ~ **di porco** ⟨*strumento*⟩ jemmy

pie'dino *nm* **fare a ~ a qcno** play footsie with sb

piedi'stallo *nm* pedestal

pi'ega *nf* ⟨*piegatura*⟩ fold; ⟨*di gonna*⟩ pleat; ⟨*di pantaloni*⟩ crease; ⟨*grinza*⟩ wrinkle; ⟨*andamento*⟩ turn; **non fare una** ~ ⟨*ragionamento:*⟩ be flawless

pie'ga|re *vt* fold; ⟨*flettere*⟩ bend ● *vi* bend. **~rsi** *vr* bend. **~rsi a** *fig* yield to. ~ **'tura** *nf* folding

pieghet'ta|re *vt* pleat. **~to** *a* pleated. **pie'ghevole** *a* pliable; ⟨*tavolo*⟩ folding ● *nm* leaflet

piemon'tese *a* Piedmontese

pi'en|a *nf* ⟨*di fiume*⟩ flood; ⟨*folla*⟩ crowd. **~o** *a* full; ⟨*massiccio*⟩ solid; **in ~a estate** in the middle of summer; **a ~i voti** ⟨*diplomarsi*⟩ ≈ with A-grades, with first class honours ● *nm* ⟨*colmo*⟩ height; ⟨*carico*⟩ full load; **in ~o** ⟨*completamente*⟩ fully; **fare il ~o** ⟨*di benzina*⟩ fill up

pie'none *nm* **c'era il ~** the place was packed

pietà *nf* pity; ⟨*misericordia*⟩ mercy; **senza** ~ ⟨*persona*⟩ pitiless; ⟨*spietatamente*⟩ pitilessly; **avere** ~ **di qcno** take pity on sb; **far ~** ⟨*far pena*⟩ be pitiful

pie'tanza *nf* dish

pie'toso *a* pitiful, merciful; ⟨*fam: pessimo*⟩ terrible

pi'etr|a *nf* stone. **~a dura** semiprecious stone. **~a preziosa** precious stone. **~a dello scandalo** cause of the scandal. **pie'trame** *nm* stones pl. **~ifi'care** *vt* petrify. **pie'trina** *nf* ⟨*di accendino*⟩ flint. **pie'troso** *a* stony

'piffero *nm* fife

pig'iama *nm* pyjamas pl

'pigia 'pigia *nm inv* crowd, crush. **pigi'are** *vt* press

pigi'one *nf* rent; **dare a** ~ let, rent out; **prendere a** ~ rent

pigli'are *vt* ⟨*fam: afferrare*⟩ catch. **'piglio** *nm* air

pig'mento *nm* pigment

pig'meo, -a *a* & *nmf* pygmy

'pigna *nf* cone

pi'gnolo *a* pedantic

pigo'lare *vi* chirp. **pigo'lio** *nm* chirping

pi'grizia *nf* laziness. **'pigro** *a* lazy; ⟨*intelletto*⟩ slow

'pila *nf* pile; *Electr* battery; ⟨*fam: lampadina tascabile*⟩ torch; ⟨*vasca*⟩ basin; **a pile** battery operated, battery powered

pi'lastro *nm* pillar

'pillola *nf* pill; **prendere la** ~ be on the pill

pi'lone *nm* pylon; ⟨*di ponte*⟩ pier

pi'lota *nmf* pilot ● *nm* *Auto* driver. **pilo'tare** *vt* pilot; drive ⟨*auto*⟩

pinaco'teca *nf* art gallery

'Pinco Pallino *nm* so-and-so

pi'neta *nf* pine-wood

ping-'pong *nm* table tennis, ping-pong *fam*

'pingue *a* fat. **~'edine** *nf* fatness

pingu'ino *nm* penguin; ⟨*gelato*⟩ choc ice on a stick

'pinna *nf* fin; ⟨*per nuotare*⟩ flipper

'pino *nm* pine[-tree]. **pi'nolo** *nm* pine kernel. ~ **marittimo** cluster or maritime pine

'pinta *nf* pint

'pinza *nf* pliers pl; *Med* forceps pl

pin'za|re *vt* ⟨*con pinzatrice*⟩ staple. **~'trice** *nf* stapler

pin'zette *nfpl* tweezers pl

pinzi'monio *nm* sauce for crudités

'pio *a* pious; ⟨*benefico*⟩ charitable

pi'oggia *nf* rain; ⟨*fig: di pietre, insulti*⟩ hail, shower; **sotto la** ~ in the rain. **~ acida** acid rain

pi'olo *nm* ⟨*di scala*⟩ rung

piom'ba|re *vi* fall heavily; **~re su** fall upon ● *vt* fill ⟨*dente*⟩. **~'tura** *nf* ⟨*di dente*⟩ filling. **piom'bino** *nm* (*sigillo*) [lead] seal; (*da pesca*) sinker; (*in gonne*) weight

pi'ombo *nm* lead; (*sigillo*) [lead] seal; **a ~** plumb; **senza ~** (*benzina*) lead-free

pioni'ere, -a *nmf* pioneer

pi'oppo *nm* poplar

pio'vano *a* **acqua piovana** rainwater

pi'ov|ere *vi* rain; **~e** it's raining; **~iggi'nare** *vi* drizzle. **pio'voso** *a* rainy

'pipa *nf* pipe

pipi *nf* **fare** [**la**] **~** pee, piddle; **andare a fare** [**la**] **~** go for a pee

pipi'strello *nm* bat

pi'ramide *nf* pyramid

pi'ranha *nf inv* piranha

pi'rat|a *nm* pirate. **~ a della strada** road-hog ● *a inv* pirate. **~e'ria** *nf* piracy

piro'etta *nf* pirouette

pi'rofil|a *nf* (*tegame*) oven-proof dish. **~o** *a* heat-resistant

pi'romane *nmf* pyromaniac

pi'roscafo *nm* steamer. **~ di linea** liner

pisci'are *vi* *vulg* piss

pi'scina *nf* swimming pool. **~ coperta** indoor swimming pool. **~ scoperta** outdoor swimming pool

pi'sello *nm* pea; (*fam: pene*) willie

piso'lino *nm* nap; **fare un ~** have a nap

'pista *nf* track; Aeron runway; (*orma*) footprint; (*sci*) slope, piste. **~ d'atterraggio** airstrip. **~ da ballo** dance floor. **~ ciclabile** cycle track

pi'stacchio *nm* pistachio

pi'stola *nf* pistol; (*per spruzzare*) spray-gun. **~ a spruzzo** paint spray

pi'stone *nm* piston

pi'tone *nm* python

pit'to|re, -'trice *nmf* painter. **~'resco** *a* picturesque. **pit'torico** *a* pictorial

pit'tu|ra *nf* painting. **~'rare** *vt* paint

più *adv* more; (*superlativo*) most;

Math plus; **~ importante** more important; **il ~ importante** the most important; **~ caro** dearer; **il ~ caro** the dearest; **di ~** more; **una coperta in ~** an extra blanket; **non ho ~ soldi** I don't have any more money; **non vive ~ a Milano** he no longer lives in Milan, he doesn't live in Milan any longer; **o meno** more or less; **il ~ lentamente possibile** as slow as possible; **per di ~** what's more; **mai ~!** I never again!; **~ di** more than; **sempre ~** more and more ● *a* more; (*superlativo*) most; **~ tempo** more time; **la classe con ~ alunni** the class with most pupils; **~ volte** several times ● *nm* most; Math plus sign; **il ~ è fatto** the worst is over; **parlare del ~ e del meno** make small talk; **I ~** the majority

piucche'per'fetto *nm* pluperfect

pi'uma *nf* feather. **piu'maggio** *nm* plumage. **piu'mino** *nm* (*di cigni*) down; (*copriletto*) eiderdown; (*per cipria*) powder-puff; (*per spolverare*) feather duster; (*giacca*) down jacket. **piu'mone®** *nm* duvet, continental quilt

piut'tosto *adv* rather; (*invece*) instead

pi'vello *nm fam* greenhorn

'pizza *nf* pizza; Cinema reel.

pizzai'ola *nf* slices of beef in tomato sauce, oregano and anchovies

pizze'ria *nf* pizza restaurant, pizzeria

pizzi'c|are *vt* pinch; (*pungere*) sting; (*di sapore*) taste sharp; (*fam: sorprendere*) catch; Mus pluck ● *vi* scratch; (*cibo:*) be spicy

'pizzico *nm*, **~otto** *nm* pinch

'pizzo *nm* lace; (*di montagna*) peak

pla'car|e *vt* placate; assuage (*fame, dolore*). **~si** *vr* calm down

'placca *nf* plate; (*commemorativa, dentale*) plaque; Med patch

plac'ca|re *vt* plate. **~to a d'argento** silver-plated. **~to d'oro** gold-plated. **~'tura** *nf* plating

197

pla'centa *nf* placenta
'placido *a* placid
plagi'are *vt* plagiarize; pressure (*persona*). **'plagio** *nm* plagiarism
plaid *nm inv* tartan rug
pla'nare *vi* glide
'plancia *nf Naut* bridge; (*passerella*) gangplank
plane'tario *a* planetary ● *nm* planetarium
pla'smare *vt* mould
'plastic|a *nf* (*arte*) plastic art; *Med* plastic surgery; (*materia*) plastic. **~o** *a* plastic ● *nm* plastic model
'platano *nm* plane[-tree]
pla'tea *nf* stalls *pl*; (*pubblico*) audience
'platino *nm* platinum
pla'tonico *a* platonic
plau'sibil|e *a* plausible. **~ità** *nf* plausibility
ple'baglia *nf pej* mob
pleni'lunio *nm* full moon
'plettro *nm* plectrum
pleu'rite *nf* pleurisy
'plico *nm* packet; **in ~ a parte** under separate cover
plissé *a inv* plissé; (*gonna*) accordeon-pleated
plo'tone *nm* platoon; (*di ciclisti*) group. **~ d'esecuzione** firing-squad
'plumbeo *a* leaden
plu'ral|e *a & nm* plural; **al ~e** in the plural. **~ità** *nf* (*maggioranza*) majority
pluridiscipli'nare *a* multidisciplinary
plurien'nale *a* **~ esperienza** many years' experience
pluripar'titico *a Pol* multi-party
plu'tonio *nm* plutonium
pluvi'ale *a* rain *attrib*
pneu'matico *a* pneumatic ● *nm* tyre
pneu'monia *nf* pneumonia
po' *vedi* poco
po'chette *nf inv* clutch bag
po'chino *nm* **un ~** a little bit
'poco *a* little; (*tempo*) short; (*con nomi plurali*) few ● *pron* little;

(*poco tempo*) a short time; (*plurale*) few ● *nm* little; **un po'** a little [bit]; **un po' di** a little, some; (*con nomi plurali*) some; **a ~ a ~** little by little; **fra ~** soon; **per ~** (*a poco prezzo*) cheap; (*quasi*) nearly; **~ fa** a little while ago; **sono arrivato da ~** I have just arrived; **un bel po'** quite a lot; **un ~ di buono** a shady character ● *adv* (*con verbi*) not much; (*con avverbi*) not very; **parla ~** he doesn't speak much; **lo conosco ~** I don't know him very well; **~ spesso** not very often
po'dere *nm* farm
pode'roso *a* powerful
'podio *nm* dais; *Mus* podium
po'dis|mo *nm* walking. **~ta** *nmf* walker
po'e|ma *nm* poem. **~sia** *nf* poetry; (*componimento*) poem. **~ta** *nm* poet. **~'tessa** *nf* poetess. **~tico** *a* poetic
poggiapi'edi *nm inv* footrest
poggi'a|re *vt* lean; (*posare*) place ● *vi* **~re su** be based on. **~'testa** *nm inv* head-rest
'poggio *nm* hillock
poggi'olo *nm* balcony
'poi *adv* (*dopo*) then; (*più tardi*) later [on]; (*finalmente*) finally. **d'ora in ~** from now on; **questa ~!** well!
poiché *conj* since
pois *nm inv* **a ~** polka-dot
'poker *nm* poker
po'lacco, -a *a* Polish ● *nmf* Pole ● *nm* (*lingua*) Polish
pu'lar|e *a* polar. **~iz'zare** *vt* polarize
'polca *nf* polka
po'lemic|a *nf* controversy. **~mente** *adv* controversially. **~co** *a* controversial. **~z'zare** *vi* engage in controversy
po'lenta *nf* cornmeal porridge
poli'clinico *nm* general hospital
poli'estere *nm* polyester
poliga'mia *nf* polygamy. **po'ligamo** *a* polygamous
polio[mie'lite] *nf* polio[myelitis]

'polipo nm polyp
poli'sti'rolo nm polystyrene
poli'tecnico nm polytechnic
po'litic|a nf politics sg; (linea di condotta) policy; fare ~a be in politics. ~iz'zare vt politicize. ~o, -a a political ● nmf politician
poliva'lente a catch-all
poli'zi|a nf police. ~a giudiziaria ≈ Criminal Investigation Department, CID. ~a stradale traffic police. ~'esco a police attrib; ⟨romanzo, film⟩ detective attrib. ~'otto nm policeman
'polizza nf policy
pol'la|io nm chicken run; (fam: luogo chiassoso) mad house. ~me nm poultry. ~'strello nm spring chicken. ~stro nm cockerel
'pollice nm thumb; (unità di misura) inch
'polline nm pollen; allergia al ~ hay fever
polli'vendolo, -a nmf poulterer
'pollo nm chicken; (fam: sempli-cione) simpleton. ~ arrosto roast chicken
polmo'nare a pulmonary. pol'mo-ne nm lung. polmone d'acciaio iron lung. ~'nite nf pneumonia
'polo nm pole; Sport polo; (maglietta) polo top. ~ nord North Pole. ~ sud South Pole
Po'lonia nf Poland
'polpa nf pulp
pol'paccio nm calf
polpa'strello nm fingertip
pol'pet|ta nf meatball. ~'tone nm meat loaf
'polpo nm octopus
pol'poso a fleshy
pol'sino nm cuff
'polso nm pulse; Anat wrist; fig authority; avere ~ be strict
pol'tiglia nf mush
pol'trire vi lie around
pol'tron|a nf armchair; Theat seat in the stalls. ~e a lazy
'polve|re nf dust; (sostanza polve-rizzata) powder; in ~re powdered; sapone in ~re soap powder. ~re

da sparo gun powder. ~'rina nf (medicina) powder. ~riz'zare vt pulverize; (nebulizzare) atomize. ~'rone nm cloud of dust. ~'roso a dusty
po'mata nf ointment, cream
po'mello nm knob; (guancia) cheek
pomeridi'ano a afternoon attrib; alle tre pomeridiane at three in the afternoon, at three p.m. pome'riggio nm afternoon
'pomice nf pumice
'pomo nm (oggetto) knob. ~ d'Adamo Adam's apple
pomo'doro nm tomato
'pompa nf pump; (sfarzo) pomp. pompe pl funebri (funzione) funeral. pom'pare vt pump; (gonfia-re d'aria) pump up; (fig: esagera-re) exaggerate; pompare fuori pump out
pom'pelmo nm grapefruit
pompi'ere nm fireman; i pompieri the fire brigade
pom'pon nm inv pompom
pom'poso a pompous
ponde'rare vt ponder
po'nente nm west
'ponte nm bridge; Naut deck; (impalcatura) scaffolding; fare il ~ fig make a long weekend of it
pon'tefice nm pontiff
pontifi'ca|re vi pontificate. ~to nm pontificate
ponti'ficio a papal
pon'tile nm jetty
popò nf inv fam pooh
popo'lano a of the [common] people
popo'la|re a popular; (comune) common ● vt populate. ~rsi vr get crowded. ~rità nf popularity. ~zi'one nf population. 'popolo nm people. popo'loso a populous
'poppa nf Naut stern; (mammella) breast; a ~ astern
pop'pa|re vt suck. ~ta nf (pasto) feed. ~'toio nm [feeding-]bottle
popu'lista nmf populist

por'cata *nf* load of rubbish; **porcate** *pl* (*fam: cibo*) junk food

porcel'lana *nf* porcelain, china

porcel'lino *nm* piglet. ~ **d'India** guinea-pig

porche'ria *nf* dirt; (*fig: cosa orrenda*) piece of filth; (*fam: robaccia*) rubbish

por'ci|le *nm* pigsty. ~**no** *a* pig *attrib* ● **nm** (*fungo*) edible mushroom. '**porco** pig; (*curne*) pork

porco'spino *nm* porcupine

'**porgere** *vt* give; (*offrire*) offer; **porgo distinti saluti** (*in lettera*) I remain, yours sincerely

porno|gra'fia *nf* pornography. ~'**grafico** *a* pornographic

'**poro** *nm* pore. **po'roso** *a* porous

'**porpora** *nf* purple

'**por|re** *vt* put; (*collocare*) place; (*supporre*) suppose; ask (*domanda*); present (*candidatura*); **poniamo il caso che...** let us suppose that...; ~**re fine** *o* **termine** *a* put an end to. ~**si** *vr* put oneself; ~**si a sedere** sit down; ~**si in cammino** set out

'**porro** *nm* Bot leek; (*verruca*) wart

'**porta** *nf* door; Sport goal; (*di città*) gate; Comput port. ~ **a** ~ door-to-door; **mettere alla** ~ show sb the door. ~ **di servizio** tradesmen's entrance

portaba'gagli *nm inv* (*facchino*) porter; (*di treno ecc*) luggage rack; Auto boot, trunk Am; (*sul tetto di un'auto*) roof rack

portabot'tiglie *nm inv* bottle rack, wine rack

porta'cenere *nm inv* ashtray

portachi'avi *nm inv* keyring

porta'cipria *nm inv* compact

portadocu'menti *nm inv* document wallet

porta'erei *nf inv* aircraft carrier

portafi'nestra *nf* French window

porta'foglio *nm* wallet; (*per documenti*) portfolio; (*ministero*) ministry

portafor'tuna *nm inv* lucky charm ● *a inv* lucky

portagi'oie *nm inv* jewellery box

por'tale *nm* door

portama'tite *nm inv* pencil case

porta'mento *nm* carriage; (*condotta*) behaviour

porta'mina *nm inv* propelling pencil

porta'monete *nm inv* purse

por'tante *a* bearing *attrib*

portaom'brelli *nm inv* umbrella stand

porta'pacchi *nm inv* roof rack; (*su bicicletta*) luggage rack

porta'penne *nm inv* pencil case

por'ta|re *vt* (*verso chi parla*) bring; (*lontano da chi parla*) take; (*sorreggere*, Math) carry; (*condurre*) lead; (*indossare*) wear; (*avere*) bear. ~**rsi** *vr* (*trasferirsi*) move; (*comportarsi*) behave; ~**rsi bene/male gli anni** look young/old for one's age

portari'viste *nm inv* magazine rack

porta'sci *nm inv* ski rack

portasiga'rette *nm inv* cigarette-case

porta'spilli *nm inv* pin-cushion

por'ta|ta *nf* (*di pranzo*) course; Auto carrying capacity; (*di arma*) range; (*fig: abilità*) capability; **a ~ta di mano** within reach; **alla ~ta di tutti** accessible to all; (*finanziariamente*) within everybody's reach. **por'tatile** *a* & *nm* portable. ~**to** *a* (*indumento*) worn; (*dotato*) gifted; **essere ~to per qcsa** have a gift for sth; **essere ~to a** (*tendere a*) be inclined to. ~'**tore**, ~'**trice** *nmf* bearer; **al ~tore** to the bearer. ~**tore di handicap** disabled person

portatova'gliolo *nm* napkin ring

portau'ovo *nm inv* egg-cup

porta'voce *nm inv* spokesman ● *nf inv* spokeswoman

por'tento *nm* marvel; (*persona dotata*) prodigy

'**portico** *nm* portico

porti'er|a *nf* door; (*tendaggio*)

door curtain. **~e** nm porter, doorman; *Sport* goalkeeper. **~e di notte** night porter

porti'n|aio, -a nmf caretaker, concierge. **~e'ria** nf concierge's room; (di ospedale) porter's lodge

'**porto** pp di **porgere** ●nm harbour; (complesso) port; (vino) port [wine]; (spesa di trasporto) carriage; **andare in ~** succeed. **~ d'armi** gun licence

Porto'gallo nm Portugal. **p~hese** a & nmf Portuguese

por'tone nm main door

portu'ale nm dockworker, docker

porzi'one nf portion

'**posa** nf laying; (riposo) rest; *Phot* exposure; (atteggiamento) pose; **mettersi in ~** pose

po'sa|re vt put; (giù) put [down] ●vi (poggiare) rest; (per un ritratto) pose. **~rsi** vr alight; (sostare) rest; Aeron land. **~te** pl piece of cutlery; **~te** pl cutlery sg. **~to a sedate** sedate

po'scritto nm postscript

posi'tivo a positive

posizio'nare vt position

posizi'one nf position; **farsi una ~** get ahead

posolo'gia nf dosage

po'spo|rre vt place after; (posticipare) postpone. **~sto** pp di **posporre**

posse'd|ere vt possess, own. **~i'mento** nm possession

posses'sivo a possessive. **pos'sesso** nm ownership; (bene) possession. **~'sore** nm owner

pos'sibil|e a possible; **il più presto ~e** as soon as possible ●nm **fare [tutto] il ~e** do one's best. **~ità** nf inv possibility; (occasione) chance ●nfpl (mezzi) means

possi'dente nmf land-owner

'**posta** nf post, mail; (ufficio postale) post office; (al gioco) stake; **spese di ~** postage; **per ~** by post, by mail; **la ~ in gioco è...** fig what's at stake is...; **a bella ~** on purpose; **Poste e Telecomunica-** zioni pl [Italian] Post Office. **~ elettronica** electronic mail, e-mail. **~ elettronica vocale** voicemail.

posta'giro nm postal giro

po'stale a postal

postazi'one nf position

postda'tare vt postdate (assegno)

posteggi'a|re vt/i park. **~'tore, ~'trice** nmf parking attendant. **po'steggio** nm car-park, parking lot Am; (di taxi) taxi-rank

'**posteri** nmpl descendants. **~'ore** a rear; (nel tempo) later ●nm fam posterior, behind. **~tà** nf posterity

po'sticcio a artificial; (baffi, barba) false ●nm hair-piece

postici'pare vt postpone

po'stilla nf note; Jur rider

po'stino nm postman, mailman Am

'**posto** pp di **porre** ●nm place; (spazio) room; (impiego) job; Mil post; (sedile) seat; **a/fuori ~** in/out of place; **prendere ~** take up room; **sul ~** on-site; **essere a ~** ⟨casa, libri⟩ be tidy; **mettere a ~** tidy ⟨stanza⟩; **fare ~** make room for; **al ~ di** (invece di) in place of, instead of. **~ di blocco** checkpoint. **~ di guida** driving seat. **~ di lavoro** workstation. **posti** pl **in piedi** standing room. **~ di polizia** police station. **posti** pl **a sedere** seating

post-partum a post-natal

'**postumo** a posthumous ●nm after-effect

po'tabile a drinkable; **acqua ~** drinking water

po'tare vt prune

po'tassio nm potassium

po'ten|te a powerful; (efficace) potent. **~za** nf power; (efficacia) potency. **~zi'ale** a & nm potential

po'tere nm power; **al ~** in power ●vi can, be able to; **posso entrare?** can I come in?; (formale) may I come in?; **posso fare qualche cosa?** can I do something?; **che tu possa essere felice!** may you be happy!; **non ne posso più** (*sono stanco*) I can't go on; (*sono stufo*) I can't take any more; **può darsi** perhaps; **può darsi che sia vero** perhaps it's true; **potrebbe aver ragione** he could be right; he might be right; **avresti potuto telefonare** you could have phoned, you might have phoned; **spero di poter venire** I hope to be able to come; **senza poter telefonare** without being able to phone

potestà *nf inv* power

'pover|o, -a *a* poor; (*semplice*) plain ●*nm* poor man ●*nf* poor woman; **i ~i** the poor. **~tà** *nf* poverty

'pozza *nf* pool. **poz'zanghera** *nf* puddle

'pozzo *nm* well; (*minerario*) pit. ~ **petrolifero** oil-well

PP.TT. *abbr* (**Poste e Telegrafi**) [Italian] Post Office

prag'matico *a* pragmatic

prali'nato *a* (*mandorla, gelato*) praline-coated

pram'matica *nf* **essere di** ~ **be** customary

pran'zare *vi* dine; (*a mezzogiorno*) lunch. **'pranzo** *nm* dinner; (*a mezzogiorno*) lunch. **pranzo di nozze** wedding breakfast

'prassi *nf* standard procedure

prate'ria *nf* grassland

'prati|ca *nf* practice; (*esperienza*) experience; (*documentazione*) file; **avere ~ca di qcsa** be familiar with sth, far ~ca a gain experience; **fare le pratiche per** gather the necessary papers for. **~'cabile** *a* practicable; (*strada*) passable. **~ca'mente** *adv* practically. **~'cante** *nmf* apprentice; *Relig* [regular] church-goer

prati'care *vt* practise; (*frequentare*) associate with; (*fare*) make

praticità *nf* practicality. **'pratico** *a* practical; (*esperto*) experienced; **essere pratico di qcsa** know about sth

'prato *nm* meadow; (*di giardino*) lawn

pre'ambolo *nm* preamble

preannunci'are *vt* give advance notice of

preavvi'sare *vt* forewarn. **preav-'viso** *nm* warning

pre'cario *a* precarious

precauzi'one *nf* precaution; (*cautela*) care

prece'den|te *a* previous ●*nm* precedent. **~te'mente** *adv* previously. **~za** *nf* precedence; (*di veicoli*) right of way; **dare la ~za** give way. **pre'cedere** *vt* precede

pre'cetto *nm* precept

precipi'ta|re *vt* **~re le cose** precipitate events; **~re qcno nella disperazione** cast sb into a state of despair ●*vi* fall headlong; (*situazione, eventi:*) come to a head. **~rsi** *vr* (*gettarsi*) throw oneself; (*affrettarsi*) rush; **~rsi a fare qcsa** rush to do sth. **~zi'one** *nf* (*fretta*) haste; (*atmosferica*) precipitation. **precipi'toso** *a* hasty; (*avventato*) reckless; (*caduta*) headlong

preci'pizio *nm* precipice; **a ~** headlong

precisa'mente *adv* precisely

preci'sare *vt* specify; (*spiegare*) clarify. **~zi'one** *nf* clarification

precisi'one *nf* precision. **pre'ciso** *a* precise; (*ore*) sharp; (*identico*) identical

pre'clud|ere *vt* preclude. **~so** *pp di precludere*

pre'coce *a* precocious; (*prematuro*) premature. **~ità** *nf* precociousness

precon'cetto *a* preconceived ●*nm* prejudice

pre'correre *vt* **~ere i tempi** be ahead of one's time

precur'sore *nm* forerunner, precursor

'preda *nf* prey; (*bottino*) booty; **essere in ~ al panico** be panicstricken; **in ~ alle fiamme** engulfed in flames. **pre'dare** vt plunder. **~'tore** nm predator

predeces'sore nmf predecessor

pre'del|la nf platform. **~'lino** nm step

predesti'na|re vt predestine. **~to** a Relig predestined, preordained

predetermi'nato a predetermined, preordained

pre'detto pp di predire

'**predica** nf sermon; fig lecture

predi'ca|re vt preach. **~to** nm predicate

predi'le|tto, -a pp di **prediligere** ● a favourite ● nmf pet. **~zi'one** nf predilection. **predi'ligere** vt prefer

pre'di|re vt foretell

predi'spo|rre vt arrange. **~rsi** vr **~rsi** a prepare oneself for. **~sizi'one** nf predisposition; (al disegno ecc) bent a (for). **~sto** pp di predisporre

predizi'one nf prediction

predomi'na|nte a predominant. **~re** vi predominate. **predo'minio** nm predominance

pre'done nm robber

prefabbri'cato a prefabricated ● nm prefabricated building

prefazi'one nf preface

prefe'ren|za nf preference; **di ~a** preferably. **~i'ale** a preferential; **corsia ~iale** bus and taxi lane

prefe'ribil|e a preferable. **~'mente** adv preferably

prefe'ri|re vt prefer. **~to, -a** a **~** nmf favourite

pre'fet|to nm prefect. **~'tura** nf prefecture

pre'figgersi vr be determined

pre'fisso pp di prefiggere ● nm prefix; Teleph [dialling] code

pre'ga|re vt/i pray; (supplicare) beg; **farsi ~** need persuading

pre'gevole a valuable

preghi'era nf prayer; (richiesta) request

pregi'ato a esteemed; (prezioso) valuable. '**pregio** nm esteem; (va-

lore) value; (di persona) good point; **di pregio** valuable

pregiudi'ca|re vt prejudice; (danneggiare) harm. **~to** a prejudiced ● nm Jur previous offender

pregiu'dizio nm prejudice; (danno) detriment

'**prego** int (non c'è di che) don't mention it!; (per favore) please; **~?** I beg your pardon?

pregu'stare vt look forward to

prei'storia nf prehistory. **prei-'storica** a prehistoric

pre'lato nm prelate

prela'vaggio nm prewash

preleva'mento nm withdrawal. **prele'vare** vt withdraw (denaro); collect (merci); Med take. **preli'evo** nm (di soldi) withdrawal. **prelievo di sangue** blood sample

prelimi'nare a preliminary ● nm **preliminari** pl preliminaries

pre'ludio nm prelude

prema'man nm inv maternity dress ● a maternity attrib

prematrimoni'ale a premarital

prema'turo, -a a premature ● nmf premature baby

premedi'ta|re vt premeditate. **~zi'one** nf premeditation

'premere vt press; Comput hit (tasto) ● vi **~** a (importare) matter to; **mi preme sapere** I need to know; **~ su** press on; push (pulsante)

pre'messa nf introduction

pre'messo pp di premettere. **~sso che** bearing in mind that. **~ttere** vt put forward; (mettere prima) put before.

premi'a|re vt give a prize to; (ricompensare) reward. **~zi'one** nf prize giving

premi'nente a pre-eminent

'**premio** nm prize; (ricompensa) reward; Comm premium. **~ di consolazione** booby prize

premoni'tore a (sogno, segno) premonitory. **~zi'one** nf premonition

premu'nir|e vt fortify. **~si** vr take

protective measures; **~si di provide** oneself with; **~si contro** protect oneself against

pre'mu|ra *nf* (*fretta*) hurry; (*cura*) care. **~'roso** *a* thoughtful

prena'tale *a* antenatal

'prender|e *vt* take; (*afferrare*) seize; catch 〈*treno, malattia, ladro, pesce*〉; have 〈*cibo, bevanda*〉; (*far pagare*) charge; (*assumere*) take on; (*ottenere*) get; (*occupare*) take up; **~e informazioni** make inquiries; **~e a calci/pugni** kick/ punch; **che ti prende?** what's got into you?; **quanto prende?** what do you charge?; **~e una persona per un'altra** mistake a person for someone else ● *vi* (*voltare*) turn; (*attecchire*) take root; (*rapprendersi*) set; **~e a destra/sinistra** turn right/left; **~e a fare qcsa** start doing sth. **~si** *vr* 〈*mani:*〉 take; **~si a pugni** come to blows; **~si cura di** take care of 〈*ammalato*〉; **~sela** take it to heart

prendi'sole *nm* sundress

preno'ta|re *vt* book, reserve. **~to** *a* booked, reserved **~zi'one** *nf* booking, reservation

'prensile *a* prehensile

preoccu'pante *a* alarming

preoccu'pa|re *vt* worry. **~rsi** *vr* **~rsi** worry (**di** about); **~rsi di fare qcsa** take the trouble to do sth. **~to** *a* (*ansioso*) worried. **~zi'one** *nf* worry; (*apprensione*) concern

prepa'ra|re *vt* prepare. **~rsi** *vr* get ready. **~'tivi** *mpl* preparations. **~to** *nm* (*prodotto*) preparation. **~'torio** *a* preparatory. **~zi'one** *nf* preparation

prepensiona'mento *nm* early retirement

preponde'ran|te *a* predominant. **~za** *nf* prevalence

pre'porre *vt* place before

preposizi'one *nf* preposition

pre'posto *pp di* **preporre** ● *a* ~ *a* (*addetto a*) in charge of

prepo'ten|te *a* overbearing

● *nmf* bully. **~za** *nf* high-handedness

preroga'tiva *nf* prerogative

'presa *nf* taking; (*conquista*) capture; (*stretta*) hold; (*di cemento ecc*) setting; *Electr* socket; (*pizzico*) pinch; **essere alle prese con** be struggling o grappling with; **a ~ rapida** 〈*cemento, colla*〉 quick-setting; **fare ~ su qcno** influence sb. **~ d'aria** air vent. **~ in giro** leg-pull. **~ multipla** adaptor

pre'sagio *nm* omen. **presa'gire** *vt* foretell

'presbite *a* long-sighted

presbiteri'ano, -a *a & nmf* Presbyterian. **presbi'terio** *nm* presbytery

pre'scelto *a* selected

pre'scindere *vi* ~ **da** leave aside; **a ~ da** apart from

presco'lare *a* **in età** ~ pre-school

pre'scri|tto *pp di* **prescrivere**

pre'scri|vere *vt* prescribe. **~zi-'one** *nf* prescription; (*norma*) rule

preselezi'one *nf* **chiamare qcno in ~** call sb via the operator

presen'ta|re *vt* present; (*far conoscere*) introduce; show 〈*documento*〉; (*inoltrare*) submit. **~rsi** *vr* present oneself; (*farsi conoscere*) introduce oneself; (*a ufficio*) attend; (*alla polizia ecc*) report; (*come candidato*) stand, run; (*occasione:*) occur; **~rsi bene/ male** 〈*persona:*〉 make a good/bad impression; (*situazione:*) look good/bad. **~'tore, ~'trice** *nmf* presenter; (*di notizie*) announcer. **~zi'one** *nf* presentation; (*per conoscersi*) introduction

presenti'mento *nm* foreboding

pre'sente *a* present; (*attuale*) current; (*questo*) this; **aver ~** remember ● *nm* present; **i presenti** those present ● *nf* **allegato alla ~** (*in lettera*) enclosed

pre'senza *nf* presence; (*aspetto*) appearance; **in ~ di, alla ~ di** in the presence of; **di bella ~ per-**

sonable. ~ **di spirito** presence of mind

presenzi'are *vi* ~ a attend

pre'sepe *nm*, **pre'sepio** *nm* crib

preser'va|re *vt* preserve; (*proteggere*) protect (**da** from). ~**'tivo** *nm* condom. ~**zi'one** *nf* preservation

'**preside** *nm* headmaster; *Univ* dean ●*nf* headmistress; *Univ* dean

presi'den|te *nm* chairman; *Pol* president ●*nf* chairwoman; *Pol* president. ~ **del consiglio** [**dei ministri**] Prime Minister. ~ **della repubblica** President of the Republic. ~**za** *nf* presidency; (*di assemblea*) chairmanship. ~**zi'ale** *a* presidential

presidi'are *vt* garrison. **pre'sidio** *nm* garrison

presi'edere *vt* preside over

'**preso** *pp di* **prendere**

'**pressa** *nf Mech* press

pres'sante *a* urgent

pressap'poco *adv* about

pres'sare *vt* press

pressi'one *nf* pressure; **far** ~ **su** put pressure on. ~ **del sangue** blood pressure

'**presso** *prep* near; (*a casa di*) with; (*negli indirizzi*) care of, c/o; (*lavorare*) for ●**pressi** *nmpl*: **nei pressi di...** in the neighbourhood o vicinity of...

pressoché *adv* almost

pressuriz'za|re *vt* pressurize. ~**to** *a* pressurized

prestabi'li|re *vt* arrange in advance. ~**to** *a* agreed

prestam'pato *a* printed ●*nm* (*modulo*) form

pre'stante *a* good-looking

pre'star|e *vt* lend; ~**e attenzione** pay attention; ~**e aiuto** lend a hand; **farsi** ~**e** borrow (**da** from). ~**si** *vr* (*frase:*) lend itself; (*persona:*) offer

prestazi'one *nf* performance; **prestazioni** *pl* (*servizi*) services

prestigia'tore, **-'trice** *nmf* conjurer

pre'stigi|o *nm* prestige; **gioco di** ~**o** conjuring trick. ~**'oso** *nm* prestigious

pre'stito *nm* loan; **dare in** ~ lend; **prendere in** ~ borrow

'**presto** *adv* soon; (*di buon'ora*) early; (*in fretta*) quickly; **a** ~ see you soon; **al più** ~ as soon as possible; ~ **o tardi** sooner or later; **far** ~ be quick

pre'sumere *vt* presume; (*credere*) think

presu'mibile *a* è ~ **che...** presumably,...

pre'sunto *a* (*colpevole*) presumed

presun|tu'oso *a* presumptuous ●*nm* presumptuous person. ~**zi'one** *nf* presumption

presup'po|rre *vt* suppose; (*richiedere*) presuppose. ~**sizi'one** *nf* presupposition. ~**sto** *nm* essential requirement

'**prete** *nm* priest

preten'dente *nmf* pretender ●*nm* (*corteggiatore*) suitor

pre'ten|dere *vt* (*sostenere*) claim; (*esigere*) demand ●*vi* ~**dere a** claim to; ~**dere di** (*esigere*) demand to. ~**si'one** *nf* pretension. ~**zi'osa** *a* pretentious

pre'tes|a *nf* pretension; (*esigenza*) claim; **senza** ~**e** unpretentious. ~**o** *pp di* **pretendere**

pre'testo *nm* pretext

pre'tore *nm* magistrate

pretta'mente *adv* decidedly

pre'tura *nf* magistrate's court

preva'le|nte *a* prevalent. ~**nte-'mente** *adv* primarily. ~**nza** *nf* prevalence. ~**re** *vi* prevail

pre'valso *pp di* **prevalere**

preve'dere *vt* foresee; forecast (*tempo*); (*legge ecc:*) provide for

preve'nire *vt* precede; (*evitare*) prevent; (*avvertire*) forewarn

preven|ti'vare *vt* estimate; (*aspettarsi*) expect. ~**'tivo** *a* preventive ●*nm Comm* estimate

preve'n|uto *a* forewarned; (*mal disposto*) prejudiced. ~**zi'one** *nf* prevention; (*preconcetto*) prejudice

previ'den|te *a* provident. ~za *nf* foresight. ~za sociale social security, welfare *Am*. ~zi'ale *a* provident '

'previo *a* ~ pagamento on payment

previsi'one *nf* forecast; in ~ di in anticipation of

pre'visto *pp di* prevedere ● *a* foreseen ● *nm* più/meno/prima del ~ more/less/earlier than expected

prezi'oso *a* precious

prez'zemolo *nm* parsley

'prezzo *nm* price. ~ di fabbrica factory price. ~ all'ingrosso wholesale price. [a] metà ~ half price

prigi'on|e *nf* prison; (*pena*) imprisonment. prigio'nia *nf* imprisonment. ~i'ero, -a *a* imprisoned ● *nmf* prisoner

'prima *adv* before; (*più presto*) earlier; (*in primo luogo*) first; ~, finiamo questo let's finish this first; puoi venire ~? (*di giorni*) can't you come any sooner?; (*di ore*) can't you come any earlier?; ~ o poi sooner or later; quanto ~ as soon as possible ● *prep* ~ di before; ~ d'ora before now ● *conj* ~ che before ● *nf* first class; *Theat* first night; *Auto* first [gear]

pri'mario *a* primary; (*principale*) principal

pri'mat|e *nm* primate. ~o *nm* supremacy; *Sport* record

prima've|ra *nf* spring. ~'rile *a* spring *attrib*

primeggi'are *vi* excel

primi'tivo *a* primitive; (*originario*) original

pri'mizie *nfpl* early produce *sg*

'primo *a* first; (*fondamentale*) principal; (*precedente di due*) former; (*iniziale*) early; (*migliore*) best ● *nm* first; primi *pl* (*di primi giorni*) the beginning; in un ~ tempo at first. prima copia master copy

primo'genito, -a *a* & *nmf* first-born

primordi'ale *a* primordial

'primula *nf* primrose

princi'pale *a* main ● *nm* head, boss *fam*

princi'pato *nm* principality. 'principe *nm* prince. principe ereditario crown prince. ~'pesco *a* princely. ~'pessa *nf* princess

prinoipi'ante *nmf* beginner

prin'cipio *nm* beginning; (*concetto*) principle; (*causa*) cause; per ~ on principle

pri'ore *nm* prior

priori'tà *nf inv* priority. ~'tario *a* having priority

'prisma *nm* prism

pri'va|re *vt* deprive. ~rsi *vr* deprive oneself

privatizzazi'one *nf* privatization.

pri'vato, -a *a* private ● *nmf* private citizen

privazi'one *nf* deprivation

privilegi'are *vt* privilege; (*considerare più importante*) favour. privi'legio *nm* privilege

'privo *a* ~ di devoid of; (*mancante*) lacking in

pro *prep* for ● *nm* advantage; a che ~? what's the point?; il ~ e il contro the pros and cons

pro'babil|e *a* probable. ~ità *nf inv* probability. ~'mente *adv* probably

pro'ble|ma *nm* problem. ~'matico *a* problematic

pro'boscide *nf* trunk

procacci'ar|e *vt*, ~si *vr* obtain

pro'cace *a* (*ragazza*) provocative

pro'ced|ere *vi* proceed; (*iniziare*) start; ~ere contro *Jur* start legal proceedings against. ~i'mento *nm* process; *Jur* proceedings *pl*.

pro'cedura *nf* procedure

proces'sare *vt* *Jur* try

processi'one *nf* procession

pro'cesso *nm* process; *Jur* trial

proces'sore *nm* *Comput* processor

processu'ale *a* trial

pro'cinto *nm* **essere in ~ di** be about to

pro'clama *nm* proclamation

procla'ma|re *vt* proclaim. **~zi'one** *nf* proclamation

procrasti'na|re *vt liter* postpone

procreazi'one *nf* procreation

pro'cura *nf* power of attorney; **per ~** by proxy

procu'ra|re *vt/i* procure; *(causare)* cause; *(cercare)* try. **~'tore** *nm* attorney. **P~tore Generale** Attorney General. **~tore legale** lawyer. **~tore della repubblica** public prosecutor

'**prode** *a* brave. **pro'dezza** *nf* bravery

prodi'gar|e *vt* lavish. **~si** *vr* do one's best

pro'digi|o *nm* prodigy. **~'oso** *a* prodigious

pro'dotto *pp di* **produrre** ● *nm* product. **prodotti agricoli** farm produce *sg*. **~ derivato** by-product. **~ interno lordo** gross domestic product. **~ nazionale lordo** gross national product

pro'du|rre *vt* produce. **~rsi** *vr* *(attore)* play; *(accadere)* happen. **~ttività** *nf* productivity. **~t'tivo** *a* productive. **~t'tore, ~'trice** *nmf* producer. **~zi'one** *nf* production

profa'na|re *vt* desecrate. **~zi'one** *nf* desecration. **pro'fano** *a* profane

profe'rire *vt* utter

Prof.essa *abbr* (**Professoressa**) Prof.

profes'sare *vt* profess; practise *(professione)*

professio'nale *a* professional

professi'o|ne *nf* profession; **libera ~ne** profession. **~'nismo** *nm* professionalism. **~'nista** *nmf* professional

profes'sor|e, -'essa *nmf* *Sch* teacher; *Univ* lecturer; *(titolare di cattedra)* professor

pro'fe|ta *nm* prophet. **~'tico** *a* prophetic. **~tiz'zare** *vt* prophesy. **~'zia** *nf* prophecy

pro'ficuo *a* profitable

profi'lar|e *vt* outline; *(ornare)* border; *Aeron* streamline. **~si** *vr* stand out

profi'lattico *a* prophylactic ● *nm* condom

pro'filo *nm* profile; *(breve studio)* outline; **di ~** in profile

profit'tare *vi* **~ di** *(avvantaggiarsi)* profit by; *(approfittare)* take advantage of. **pro'fitto** *nm* profit; *(vantaggio)* advantage

profonda'mente *adv* deeply, profoundly. **~ità** *nf inv* depth

pro'fondo *a* deep; *fig* profound; *(cultura)* great

'**profugo, -a** *nmf* refugee

profu'mar|e *vt* perfume. **~si** *vr* put on perfume

profumata'mente *adv* **pagare ~** pay through the nose

profu'mato *a* *(fiore)* fragrant; *(fazzoletto ecc)* scented

profume'ria *nf* perfumery. **pro'fumo** *nm* perfume, scent

profusi'one *nf* profusion; **a ~** in profusion. **pro'fuso** *pp di* **profondere** ● *a* profuse

proget'tare *vt* plan. **~'tista** *nmf* designer. **pro'getto** *nm* plan; *(di lavoro importante)* project. **progetto di legge** bill

pro'gnosi *nf inv* prognosis; **in ~ riservata** on the danger list

pro'gramma *nm* programme; *Comput* program. **~ scolastico** syllabus

program'ma|re *vt* programme; *Comput* program. **~'tore, ~'trice** *nmf* [computer] programmer. **~zi'one** *nf* programming

progre'dire *vi* [make] progress

progres'sione *nf* progression. **~'sivo** *a* progressive. **pro'gresso** *nm* progress

proi'bi|re *vt* forbid. **~'tivo** *a* prohibitive. **~to a** forbidden. **~zi'one** *nf* prohibition

proiet'tare *vt* project; show *(film)*. **~'tore** *nm* projector; *Auto* headlight

proi'ettile *nm* bullet

proiezi'one *nf* projection

'prole *nf* offspring. **proletari'ato** *nm* proletariat. **prole'tario** *a* & *nm* proletarian

prolife'rare *vi* proliferate. **pro'lifico** *a* prolific

pro'lisso *a* verbose, prolix

'prologo *nm* prologue

pro'lunga *nf Electr* extension

prolun'gar|e *vt* prolong; *(allungare)* lengthen; extend *(contratto, scadenza)*. **~si** *vr* continue; **~si su** *(dilungarsi)* dwell upon

prome'moria *nm* memo; *(per se stessi)* reminder, note; *(formale)* memorandum

pro'me|ssa *nf* promise. **~sso** *pp di* **promettere**. **~ttere** *vt/i* promise

promet'tente *a* promising

promi'nente *a* prominent

promiscuità *nf* promiscuity. **pro'miscuo** *a* promiscuous

promon'torio *nm* promontory

pro'mo|sso *pp di* **promuovere** ● *a Sch* who has gone up a year; *Univ* who has passed an exam. **~tore**, **~'trice** *nmf* promoter

promozio'nale *a* promotional. **promozi'one** *nf* promotion

promul'gare *vt* promulgate

promu'overe *vt* promote; *Sch* move up a class

proni'pote *nm (di bisnonno)* great-grandson; *(di prozio)* great-nephew ● *nf (di bisnonno)* great-granddaughter; *(di prozio)* great-niece

pro'nome *nm* pronoun

pronosti'care *vt* forecast, predict. **pro'nostico** *nm* forecast

pron'tezza *nf* readiness; *(rapidità)* quickness

'pronto *a* ready; *(rapido)* quick; **~!** *Teleph* hallo!; **tenersi ~** be ready *(per* for); **pronti, via!** *(in gare)* ready! steady! go!. **~ soccorso** first aid; *(in ospedale)* accident and emergency

prontu'ario *nm* handbook

pro'nuncia *nf* pronunciation

pronunci'a|re *vt* pronounce; *(dire)*

utter; deliver *(discorso)*. **~rsi** *vr (su un argomento)* give one's opinion. **~to** *a* pronounced; *(prominente)* prominent

pro'nunzia ecc = **pronuncia** ecc

propa'ganda *nf* propaganda

propa'ga|re *vt* propagate. **~rsi** *vr* spread. **~zi'one** *nf* propagation

prope'deutico *a* introductory

pro'pen|dere *vi* **~dere per** be in favour of. **~si'one** *nf* inclination, propensity. **~so** *pp di* **propendere** ● *a essere* **~so a fare qcsa** be inclined to do sth

propi'nare *vt* administer

pro'pizio *a* favourable

proponi'mento *nm* resolution

pro'por|re *vt* propose; *(suggerire)* suggest. **~si** *vr* set oneself *(obiettivo, meta)*; **~si di** intend to

proporzio'na|le *a* proportional. **~re** *vt* proportion. **~to** *a* proportioned. **proporzi'one** *nf* proportion

pro'posito *nm* purpose; **a ~** by the way; **a ~ di** with regard to; **di ~** *(apposta)* on purpose; **capitare a ~**, **giungere a ~** come at just the right time

proposizi'one *nf* clause; *(frase)* sentence

pro'post|a *nf* proposal. **~o** *pp di* **proporre**

proprietà *nf inv* property; *(diritto)* ownership; *(correttezza)* propriety. **~ immobiliare** property. **~ privata** private property. **proprie'taria** *nf* owner; *(di casa affittata)* landlady. **proprie'tario** *nm* owner; *(di casa affittata)* landlord

'proprio *a* one's [own]; *(caratteristico)* typical; *(appropriato)* proper ● *adv* just; *(veramente)* really; **non ~** not really, not exactly; *(affatto)* not... at all ● *pron* one's own ● *nm* one's [own]; **lavorare in ~** be one's own boss; **mettersi in ~** set up on one's own

propul'si|one *nf* propulsion. **~'sore** *nm* propeller

pro'roga *nf* extension

proro'ga|bile *a* extendable. **~re** *vt* extend

pro'rompere *vi* burst out

'prosa *nf* prose. **pro'saico** *a* prosaic

pro'scio|gliere *vt* release; *Jur* acquit. **~lto** *pp di* prosciogliere

prosciu'gar|e *vt* dry up; *(bonificare)* reclaim. **~si** *vr* dry up

prosci'utto *nm* ham. **~ cotto** cooked ham. **~ crudo** type of dry-cured ham, Parma ham

pro'scri|tto, -a *pp di* proscrivere ● *nmf* exile

prosecuzi'one *nf* continuation

prosegui'mento *nm* continuation; **buon ~!** *(viaggio)* have a good journey!; *(festa)* enjoy the rest of the party!

prosegu'ire *vt* continue ● *vi* go on, continue

prospe'r|are *vi* prosper. **~ità** *nf* prosperity. **'prospero** *a* prosperous; *(favorevole)* favourable. **~oso** *a* flourishing; *(ragazza)* buxom

prospet'tar|e *vt* show. **~si** *vr* seem

prospet'tiva *nf* perspective; *(panorama)* view; *fig* prospect. **pro'spetto** *nm* *(vista)* view; *(facciata)* façade; *(tabella)* table

prospici'ente *a* facing

prossima'mente *adv* soon

prossimità *nf* proximity

'prossimo, -a *a* near; *(seguente)* next; *(molto vicino)* close; **l'anno ~** next year ● *nmf* neighbour

prosti'tu|ta *nf* prostitute. **~zi'one** *nf* prostitution

pro'stra|re *vt* prostrate. **~rsi** *vr* prostrate oneself. **~to** *a* prostrate

protago'nista *nmf* protagonist

pro'te|ggere *vt* protect; *(favorire)* favour

prote'ina *nf* protein

pro'tendere *vt* stretch out. **~si** *vr (in avanti)* lean out. **pro'teso** *pp di* protendere

pro'te|sta *nf* protest; *(dichiarazione)* protestation. **~'stante** *a & nmf* Protestant. **~'stare** *vt/i* protest

prote|t'tivo *a* protective. **~tto** *pp*

di proteggere. **~t'tore, ~t'trice** *nmf* protector; *(sostenitore)* patron ● *nm (di prostituta)* pimp. **~zi'one** *nf* protection

protocol'lare *a (visita)* protocol ● *vt* register

proto'collo *nm* protocol; *(registro)* register; **carta ~** official stamped paper

pro'totipo *nm* prototype

pro'tra|rre *vt* protract; *(differire)* postpone. **~rsi** *vr* go on, continue. **~tto** *pp di* protrarre

protube'ran|te *a* protuberant. **~za** *nf* protuberance

'prova *nf* test; *(dimostrazione)* proof; *(tentativo)* try; *(di abito)* fitting; *Sport* heat; *Theat* rehearsal; *(bozza)* proof; **fino a ~ contraria** until I'm told otherwise; **in ~** *(assumere)* for a trial period; **mettere alla ~** put to the test. **~ generale** dress rehearsal

pro'var|e *vt* test; *(dimostrare)* prove; *(tentare)* try; try on *(abiti ecc)*; *(sentire)* feel; *Theat* rehearse. **~si** *vr* try

proveni'enza *nf* origin. **prove'nire** *vi* **provenire da** come from

pro'vento *nm* proceeds *pl*

prove'nuto *pp di* provenire

pro'verbio *nm* proverb

pro'vetta *nf* test-tube; **bambino in ~** test-tube baby

pro'vetto *a* skilled

pro'vinc|ia *nf* province; *(strada)* B road, secondary road. **~'ale** *a* provincial; **strada ~ale** B road, secondary road

pro'vino *nm* specimen; *Cinema* screen test

provo'ca|nte *a* provocative. **~re** *vt* provoke; *(causare)* cause. **~'tore, ~'trice** *nmf* trouble-maker. **~'torio** *a* provocative. **~zi'one** *nf* provocation

provve'd|ere *vi* **~ere a** provide for. **~'mento** *nm* measure; *(previdenza)* precaution

provvi'denz|a *nf* providence. **~i'ale** *a* providential

provvigi'one nf Comm commission

provvi'sorio a provisional

prov'vista nf supply

pro'zio, -a nm great-uncle ● nf great-aunt

'prua nf prow

pru'den|te a prudent. **~za** nf prudence; **per ~za** as a precaution

'prudere vi itch

'prugn|a nf plum. **~a secca** prune. **~o** nm plum[-tree]

prurigi'noso a itchy. **pru'rito** nm itch

pseu'donimo nm pseudonym

psica'na|lisi nf psychoanalysis. **~'lista** nmf psychoanalyst. **~liz'zare** vt psychoanalyse

'psiche nf psyche

psichi'a|tra nmf psychiatrist. **~'tria** nf psychiatry. **~trico** a psychiatric

'psichico a mental

psico|lo'gia nf psychology. **~'lo-gico** a psychological. **psi'co-logo, -a** nmf psychologist

psico'patico, -a a psychopathic ● nmf psychopath

PT abbr (Posta e Telecomunicazioni) PO

pubbli'ca|re vt publish. **~zi'one** nf publication. **~zioni** pl (di matrimonio) banns

pubbli'cista nmf Journ correspondent

pubblici'tà nf inv publicity, advertising; (annuncio) advertisement advert; **fare ~ a qcsa** advertise sth, **piccola ~** small advertisements. **pubblici'tario** a advertising

'pubblico a public; **scuola pubblica** state school ● nm public; (spettatori) audience; **grande ~** general public. **Pubblica Sicurezza** Police. **~ ufficiale** civil servant

'pube nm pubis

puber'tà nf puberty

pu'dico a modest. **pu'dore** nm modesty

pue'rile a children's; pej childish

pugi'lato nm boxing. **'pugile** nm boxer

pugna'la|re vt stab. **~ta** nf stab. **pu'gnale** nm dagger

'pugno nm fist; (colpo) punch; (manciata) fistful; (fig: numero limitato) handful; **dare un ~ a** punch

'pulce nf flea; (microfono) bug

pul'cino nm chick; (nel calcio) junior

pu'ledra nf filly

pu'ledro nm colt

pu'li|re vt clean. **~re a secco** dry-clean. **~to a** clean. **~'tura** nf cleaning. **~'zia** nf (il pulire) cleanness; (l'essere pulito) cleanliness; **~zie** pl housework; **fare le ~zie** do the cleaning

'pullman nm inv bus, coach; (urbano) bus

pul'mino nm minibus

'pulpito nm pulpit

pul'sante nm button; Electr [push-]button. **~ di accensione** on/off switch

pul'sa|re vi pulsate. **~zi'one** nf pulsation

pul'viscolo nm dust

'puma nm inv puma

pun'gente a prickly; (insetto) stinging; (odore ecc) sharp

'pungere vt prick; (insetto) sting. **~si** vr **~si un dito** prick one's finger

pungigli'one nm sting

pu'ni|re vt punish. **~'tivo** a punitive. **~zi'one** nf punishment; Sport free kick

'punta nf point; (estremità) tip; (di monte) peak; (un po') pinch; Sport forward; **doppie punte** (di capelli) split ends

pun'tare vt point; (spingere con forza) push; (scommettere) bet; (fam: appuntare) fasten ● vi **~ su** fig rely on; **~ verso** (dirigersi) head for; **~ a** aspire to

punta'spilli nm inv pincushion

pun'tat|a nf (di una storia) instalment; (televisiva) episode; (al gioco) stake, bet; (breve visita) flying visit; **a ~e** serialized, in, instalments; **fare una ~a a/in** pop over to ‹luogo›

punteggia'tura nf punctuation

pun'teggio nm score

puntel'lare vt prop. **pun'tello** nm prop

pun'tigli|o nm spite; (ostinazione) obstinacy. **~'oso** a punctilious, pernickety pej

pun'tin|a nf (da disegno) drawing pin, thumb tack Am; (di giradischi) stylus. **~o** nm dot; **a ~o** perfectly; ‹cotto› to a T

'punto nm point; (in cucito, Med) stitch; (in punteggiatura) full stop; **in che ~?** where, exactly?; **di ~ in bianco** all of a sudden; **due punti** colon; **in ~** sharp; **mettere a ~** put right; fig fine tune; tune up ‹motore›; **essere sul ~ di fare qcsa** be about to do sth, be on the point of doing sth. **punti pl cardinali** points of the compass. **~ debole** blind spot. **~ esclamativo** exclamation mark. **~ interrogativo** question mark. **~ nero** Med blackhead. **~ di riferimento** landmark; (per la qualità) benchmark. **~ di vendita** point of sale. **~ e virgola** semicolon. **~ di vista** point of view

puntu'al|e a punctual. **~ità** nf punctuality. **~'mente** adv punctually, on time

pun'tura nf (di insetto) sting; (di ago ecc) prick; Med puncture; (iniezione) injection; (fitta) stabbing pain

punzecchi'are vt prick; fig tease

'pupa nf doll. **pu'pazzo** nm puppet. **pupazzo di neve** snowman

pu'pilla nf Anat pupil

pu'pillo, -a nmf (di professore) favourite

purché conj provided

'pure adv too, also; (concessivo) **fate ~!** please do! ● conj (tuttavia)

yet; (anche se) even if; **pur di** just to

purè nm inv purée. **~ di patate** mashed potatoes, creamed potatoes

pu'rezza nf purity

'purga nf purge. **pur'gante** nm laxative. **pur'gare** vt purge

purga'torio nm purgatory

purifi'care vt purify

puri'tano, -a a & nmf Puritan

'puro a pure; (vero ecc) undiluted; **per ~ caso** by sheer chance, purely by chance

puro'sangue a & nm thoroughbred

pur'troppo adv unfortunately

pus nm pus. **'pustola** nf pimple

puti'ferio nm uproar

putre'far|e vi, **~si** vr putrefy

'putrido a putrid

put'tana nf vulg whore

'puzza nf = puzzo

puz'zare vi stink; **~ di bruciato** fig smell fishy

'puzzo nm stink, bad smell. **~la** nf polecat. **~'lente** a stinking

p.zza abbr (piazza) Sq.

Qq

qua adv here; **da un anno in ~** for the last year; **da quando in ~?** since when?; **di ~** this way; **di ~ di** on this side of; **~ dentro** in here; **~ sotto** under here; **~ vicino** near here; **~ e là** here and there

qua'derno nm exercise book; (per appunti) notebook

quadrango'lare a (forma) quadrangular. **qua'drangolo** nm quadrangle

qua'drante nm quadrant; (di orologio) dial

qua'dra|re vt square; (contabilità) balance ● vi fit in. **~to** a square; (equilibrato) level-headed ● nm square; (*pugilato*) ring; **al ~to** squared

quadret'tato *a* squared; (*carta*) graph *attrib.* **qua'dretto** *nm* square; (*piccolo quadro*) small picture; **a quadretti** (*tessuto*) check

quadricro'mia *nf* four-colour printing

quadrien'nale *a* (*che dura quattro anni*) four-year

quadri'foglio *nm* four-leaf clover

quadri'latero *nm* quadrilateral

quadri'mestre *nm* four-month period

'**quadro** *nm* picture, painting; (*quadrato*) square; (*fig: scena*) sight; (*tabella*) table; *Theat* scene; *Comm* executive **quadri** *pl* (*carte*) diamonds; **a quadri** (*tessuto, giacca, motivo*) check. **quadri** *pl direttivi* senior management

qua'drupede *nm* quadruped

quaggiù *adv* down here

'**quaglia** *nf* quail

'**qualche** *a* (*alcuni*) a few, some; (*un certo*) some; (*in interrogazioni*) any; **ho ~ problema** I have a few problems, I have some problems; **~ tempo fa** some time ago; **hai ~ libro italiano?** have you any Italian books?; **posso prendere ~ libro?** can I take some books?; **in ~ modo** somehow; **in ~ posto** somewhere; **~ volta** sometimes; **~ cosa = qualcosa**

qual'cosa *pron* something; (*in interrogazioni*) anything; **~'altro** something else; **vuoi ~'altro?** would you like anything else?; **~a di strano** something strange; **vuoi ~a da mangiare?** would you like something to eat?

qual'cuno *pron* someone, somebody; (*in interrogazioni*) anyone, anybody; (*alcuni*) some; (*in interrogazioni*) any; **c'è ~?** is anybody in?; **qualcun altro** someone else, somebody else; **c'è qualcun altro che aspetta?** is anybody else waiting?; **ho letto ~ dei suoi libri** I've read some of his books; **cono-**

sci ~ dei suoi amici? do you know any of his friends?

'**quale** *a* which; (*indeterminato*) what; (*come*) as, like; **~ macchina è la tua?** which car is yours?; **~ motivo avrà di parlare così?** what reason would he have to speak like that?; **~ onore!** what an honour!; **città quali Venezia** towns like Venice; **~ che sia la tua opinione** whatever you may think ● *pron inter* which [one]; **~ preferisci?** which [one] do you prefer? ● *pron rel* **il/la ~** (*persona*) who; (*animale, cosa*) that, which; (*oggetto: con prep*) whom; (*animale, cosa*) which; **ho incontrato tua madre, la ~ mi ha detto...** I met your mother, who told me...; **l'ufficio nel ~ lavoro** the office in which I work; **l'uomo con il ~ parlavo** the man to whom I was speaking ● *avv* (*come*) as

qua'lifica *nf* qualification; (*titolo*) title

qualifi'ca|re *vt* qualify; (*definire*) define. **~rsi** *vr* be placed. **~'tivo** *a* qualifying. **~to** *a* (*operaio*) semiskilled. **~zi'one** *nf* qualification

qualità *nf inv* quality; (*specie*) kind; **in ~ di** in one's capacity as. **~tiva'mente** *adv* qualitatively. **~'tivo** *a* qualitative

qua'lora *conj* in case

qual'siasi, qua'lunque *a* any; (*non importa quale*) whatever; (*ordinario*) ordinary; **dammi una penna ~** give me any pen [whatsoever]; **farei ~ cosa** I would do anything; **~ cosa io faccia** whatever I do; **~ persona** anyone; **in ~ caso** in any case; **uno ~** any one, whichever; **l'uomo qualunque** the man in the street; **vivo in una casa ~** I live in an ordinary house

qualunqu'ismo *nm* lack of political views

'**quando** *conj & adv* when; **da ~ ti ho visto** since I saw you; **da ~ esci con lui?** how long have you been going out with him?; **da ~ in qua?** since when?; **~...~... ~...** sometimes..., sometimes...

quantifi'care *vt* quantify

quantità *nf inv* quantity; **una ~ di (gran numero)** a great deal of. **~tiva'mente** *adv* quantitatively. **~'tivo** *nm* amount ● *a* quantitative

'**quanto** *a inter* how much; (*con nomi plurali*) how many; (*in esclamazione*) what a lot of; **~ tempo?** how long?; **quanti anni hai?** how old are you? ● *a rel* as much... as; (*con nomi plurali*) as many... as; **prendi ~ denaro ti serve** take as much money as you need; **prendi quanti libri vuoi** take as many books as you like ● *pron inter* how much; (*quanto tempo*) how long; (*plurale*) how many; **quanti ne abbiamo oggi?** what date is it today?, what's the date today? ● *pron rel* as much as; (*quanto tempo*) as long as; (*plurale*) as many as; **prendine ~/quanti ne vuoi** take as much/as many as you like; **stai ~ vuoi** stay as long as you like; **questo è ~** that's it ● *adv inter* how much; (*quanto tempo*) how long; **~ sei alto?** how tall are you?; **~ hai aspettato?** how long did you wait for?; **~ costa?** how much is it?; **~ mi dispiace!** I'm so sorry!; **~ è bello!** how nice! ● *adv rel* as much as; **lavoro ~ posso** I work as much as I can; **è tanto intelligente ~ bello** he's as intelligent as he's good-looking; **in ~** (*in qualità di*) as; (*poiché*) since; **in ~ a me** as far as I'm concerned; **per ~** however; **per ~ ne sappia** as far as I know; **per mi riguarda** as far as I'm concerned; **per ~ mi sia simpatico** much as I like him; **~ a** so far; **~ prima** (*al più presto*) as soon as possible

quan'tunque *conj* although

qua'ranta *a & nm* forty

quaran'tena *nf* quarantine

quaran'tenn|e *a* forty-year-old. **~io** *nm* period of forty years

quaran't|esimo *a* fortieth. **~ina** *nf* **una ~ina** about forty

qua'resima *nf* Lent

quar'tetto *nm* quartet

quarti'ere *nm* district; *Mil* quarters *pl*. **~ generale** headquarters

quarto *a* a fourth ● *nm* fourth; (*quarta parte*) quarter; **le sette e un ~** a quarter past seven. **quarti pl di finale** quarterfinals. **~ d'ora** quarter of an hour. **quar'tultimo**, *-a nm/f* fourth from the end, fourth last

'**quarzo** *nm* quartz

'**quasi** *adv* almost, nearly; **~ mai** hardly ever ● *conj* (*come se*) as if; **~ ~ sto a casa** I'm tempted to stay home

quassù *adv* up here

'**quatto** *a* crouching; (*silenzioso*) silent; **starsene ~** keep very quiet

quat'tordici *a & nm* fourteen

quat'trini *nmpl* money *sg*, dosh *sg fam*

quattro *a & nm* four; **dirne ~ a** qcno give sb a piece of one's mind; **farsi in ~ (per** qcno/per fare qcsa) go to a lot of trouble (for sb/ to do sth); **in ~ e quat'tr'otto** in a flash. **~ per ~** *nm inv Auto* four-wheel drive [vehicle]

quat'trocchi: a ~ *adv* in private

quattro'cento *a & nm* four hundred; **il ~cento** the fifteenth century

quattro'mila *a & nm* four thousand

'**quell|o** *a* that (*pl* those); **quell'albero** that tree; **quegli alberi** those trees; **quel cane** that dog; **quei cani** those dogs ● *pron* that [one] (*pl* those [ones]); **~o lì** that one over there; **~o che** the one that; (*ciò che*) what; **quelli che** the ones that, those that; **~o a destra** the one on the right

'**quercia** *nf* oak

que'rela *nf* [legal] action

que're'lare *vt* bring an action against

que'sito *nm* question

questio'nario *nm* questionnaire

quest'ione *nf* question; (*faccenda*) matter; (*litigio*) quarrel; **in ~** in doubt; **è fuori ~** it's out of the question; **è ~ di vita o di morte** it's a matter of life and death

'questo |*o*| *a* this (*pl* these) ● *pron* this [one] (*pl* these [ones]); **~o qui, ~o qua** this one here; **~o è quello che a detto** that's what he said; **per ~o** for this or that reason. **quest'oggi** today

que'store *nm* chief of police

que'stura *nf* police headquarters *pl*

qui *adv* here; **da ~ in poi** from now on; **fin ~** (*di tempo*) up till now, until now; **~ dentro** in here; **~ sotto** under here; **~ vicino** *adv* near here ● *nm* **~ pro quo** misunderstanding

quie'scienza *nf* **trattamento di ~** retirement package

quie'tanza *nf* receipt

quie'tar|e *vt* calm. **~si** *vr* quieten down

qui'et|e *nf* quiet; **disturbo della ~e pubblica** breach of the peace. **~o** *a* quiet

'quindi *adv* then ● *conj* therefore

'quindi|ci *a & nm* fifteen. **~'cina** *nf* **una ~cina** about fifteen; **una ~cina di giorni** a fortnight *Br*, two weeks *pl*

quinquen'nale *a* (*che dura cinque anni*) five-year. **quin'quennio** *nm* [period of] five years

quin'tale *nm* a hundred kilograms

'quinte *nfpl Theat* wings

quin'tetto *nm* quintet

'quinto *a* fifth

quin'tuplo *a* quintuple

qui'squiglia *nf* **perdersi in quisquiglie** get bogged down in details

'quota *nf* quota; (*rata*) instalment; (*altitudine*) height; *Aeron* altitude, height; (*ippica*) odds *pl*; **per-**

dere ~ lose altitude; **prendere ~** gain altitude. **~ di iscrizione** entry fee

quo'ta|re *vt Comm* quote. **~to a** quoted; **essere ~to in Borsa** be quoted on the Stock Exchange. **~zi'one** *nf* quotation

quotidi|ana'mente *adv* daily. **~'ano** *a* daily; (*ordinario*) everyday ● *nm* daily [paper]

quozi'ente *nm* quotient. **~ d'intelligenza** intelligence quotient, IQ

Rr

ra'barbaro *nm* rhubarb

'rabbia *nf* rage; (*ira*) anger; *Med* rabies *sg*; **che ~!** what a nuisance!; **mi fa ~** it makes me angry

rab'bino *nm* rabbi

rabbiosa'mente *adv* furiously. **rabbi'oso** *a* hot-tempered; *Med* rabid; (*violento*) violent

rabbo'nir|e *vt* pacify. **~si** *vr* calm down

rabbrivi'dire *vi* shudder; (*di freddo*) shiver

rabbui'arsi *vr* become dark

raccapez'zar|e *vt* put together. **~si** *vr* see one's way ahead

raccapricci'ante *a* horrifying

raccatta'palle *nm inv* ball boy ● *nf inv* ball girl

raccat'tare *vt* pick up

rac'chetta *nf* racket. **~ da ping pong** table-tennis bat. **~ da sci** ski stick, ski pole. **~ da tennis** tennis racket

'racchio *a fam* ugly

racchi'udere *vt* contain

rac'cogl|iere *vt* pick; (*da terra*) pick up, (*mietere*) harvest; (*collezionare*) collect; (*radunare*) gather; win (*voti*); (*dare asilo a*) take in. **~ersi** *vr* gather; (*concentrarsi*) collect one's thoughts. **~'mento** *nm* concentration.

~'tore, ~'trice nmf collector
●nm (cartella) ring-binder

rac'colto, -a pp di raccogliere
●a (rannicchiato) hunched; (intimo) cosy; (concentrato) engrossed
●nm (mietitura) harvest ●nf
collection; (di scritti) compilation;
(del grano ecc) harvesting; (aduna-
ta) gathering

raccoman'dabile a recommend-
able; poco ~ (persona) shady
raccoman'da|re vt recommend;
(affidare) entrust. ~rsi vr (implorare) beg. ~ta nf registered letter;
~ta con ricevuta di ritorno re-
corded delivery. ~espresso nf
guaranteed next-day delivery of re-
corded items. ~zi'one nf recom-
mendation
raccon'tare vt tell. rac'conto nm
story
raccorci'are vt shorten
raccor'dare vt join. rac'cordo nm
connection; (stradale) feeder. raccordo anulare ring road. raccordo ferroviario siding
ra'chitico a rickety; (poco svilup-
pato) stunted
racimo'lare vt scrape together
'racket nm inv racket
'radar nm radar
raddol'cir|e vt sweeten; fig soften.
~si vr become milder; (carattere:)
mellow
raddoppi'are vt double. rad'doppio nm doubling
raddriz'zare vt straighten
'rader|e vt shave; graze (muro); ~e
al suolo raze [to the ground]. ~si
vr shave
radi'are vt strike off; ~ dall'albo
strike off
radia'tore nm radiator. ~zi'one
nf radiation
'radica nf briar
radi'cale a radical ●nm Gram
root; Pol radical
ra'dicchio nm chicory
ra'dice nf root; mettere [le] radici
fig put down roots. ~ quadrata
square root

'radio nf inv radio; via ~ by radio.
~ a transistor transistor radio
●nm Chem radium.
radioama'tore, -'trice nmf [ra-
dio] ham
radioascolta'tore, -'trice nmf listener
radioat'tività nf radioactivity.
~'tivo a radioactive
radio'cro|naca nf radio commen-
tary; fare la ~naca di
commentate on. ~'nista nmf radio reporter
radiodiffusi'one nf broadcasting
radiogra'fare vt X-ray. ~'fia nf
X-ray [photograph]; (radiologia)
radiography; fare una ~fia
(paziente:) have an X-ray; (dottore:) take an X-ray
radio'fonico a radio attrib
radio'lina nf transistor
radi'ologo, -a nmf radiologist
radi'oso a radiant
radio'sveglia nf radio alarm
radio'taxi nm inv radio taxi
radiote'lefono nm radiotele-
phone; (privato) cordless [phone]
radiotelevi'sivo a broadcasting
attrib
'rado a sparse; (non frequente)
rare; di ~ seldom
radu'nar|e vt, ~si vr gather [to-
gether]. ra'duno nm meeting;
Sport rally
ra'dura nf clearing
'rafano nm horseradish
raffazzo'nato a (discorso, lavoro)
botched
raf'fermo a stale
'raffica nf gust; (di armi da fuoco)
burst; (di domande) barrage
raffigu'ra|re vt represent. ~zi'one
nf representation
raffi'na|re vt refine. ~ta'mente
adv elegantly. ~'tezza nf refinement. ~to a refined. raffine'ria nf
refinery
rafforza|'mento nm reinforce-
ment; (di muscolatura) strength-
ening. ~re vt reinforce. ~'tivo a
Gram intensifier

raffredda'mento *nm* (*processo*) cooling

raffred'd|are *vt* cool. **~arsi** *vr* get cold; (*prendere un raffreddore*) catch a cold. **~ore** *nm* cold. **~ore da fieno** hay fever

raf'fronto *nm* comparison

'rafia *nf* raffia

Rag. *abbr* **ragioniere**

ra'gaz|za *nf* girl; (*fidanzata*) girlfriend. **~za alla pari** au pâir [girl]. **~'zata** *nf* prank. **~zo** *nm* boy; (*fidanzato*) boyfriend; **da ~zo** (*da giovane*) as a boy

ragge'lar|e *vt fig* freeze. **~si** *vr fig* turn to ice

raggi'ante *a* radiant; **~ di successo** flushed with success

raggi'era *nf* **a ~** with a pattern like spokes radiating from a centre

'raggio *nm* ray; *Math* radius; (*di ruota*) spoke; **~ d'azione** range. **~ laser** laser beam

raggi'rare *vt* trick. **rag'giro** *nm* trick

raggi'un|gere *vt* reach; (*conseguire*) achieve. **~'gibile** *a* (*luogo*) within reach

raggomito'lar|e *vt* wind. **~si** *vr* curl up

raggranel'lare *vt* scrape together

raggrin'zir|e *vt*, **~si** *vr* wrinkle

raggrup|pa'mento *nm* (*gruppo*) group; (*azione*) grouping. **~'pare** *vt* group together

ragguagli'are *vt* compare; (*informare*) inform. **raggu'aglio** *nm* comparison; (*informazione*) information

ragguar'devole *a* considerable

'ragia *nf* resin; **acqua ~** turpentine

ragiona'mento *nm* reasoning; (*discussione*) discussion. **ragio'nare** *vi* reason; (*discutere*) discuss

ragi'one *nf* reason; (*ciò che è giusto*) right; **a ~ o a torto** rightly or wrongly; **aver ~** be right; **perdere la ~** go out of one's mind;

a ragion veduta after due consideration

ragione'ria *nf* accountancy

ragio'nevol|e *a* reasonable. **~'mente** *adv* reasonably

ragioni'ere, -a *nmf* accountant

ragli'are *vi* bray

ragna'tela *nf* cobweb. **'ragno** *nm* spider

ragù *nm inv* meat sauce

RAI *nf abbr* (**Radio Audizioni Italiane**) *Italian public broadcasting company*

ralle'gra|re *vt* gladden. **~rsi** *vr* rejoice; **~rsi con qcno** congratulate sb. **~'menti** *nmpl* congratulations

rallenta'mento *nm* slowing down

rallen'ta|re *vt/i* slow down; (*allentare*) slacken. **~rsi** *vr* slow down. **~'tore** *nm* (*su strada*) speed bump; **al ~tore** in slow motion

raman'zina *nf* reprimand

ra'marro *nm* type of lizard

ra'mato *a* (*capelli*) copper[-coloured]

'rame *nm* copper

ramifi'ca|re *vi*, **~rsi** *vr* branch out; (*strada:*) branch. **~zi'one** *nf* ramification

rammari'carsi *vr* **~ di** regret; (*lamentarsi*) complain (**di** about). **ram'marico** *nm* regret

rammen'dare *vt* darn. **ram'mendo** *nm* darning

rammen'tar|e *vt* remember; **~e qcsa a qcno** (*richiamare alla memoria*) remind sb of sth. **~si** *vr* remember

rammol'li|re *vt* soften. **~rsi** *vr* go soft. **~to, -a** *nmf* wimp

'ramo *nm* branch. **~'scello** *nm* twig

'rampa *nf* (*di scale*) flight. **~ d'accesso** slip road. **~ di lancio** launch[ing] pad

ram'pante *a* **giovane ~** yuppie

rampi'cante *a* climbing ● *nm Bot* creeper

ram'pollo *nm hum* brat; (*discendente*) descendant

ram'pone nm harpoon; (per scarpe) crampon

'rana nf frog; (nel nuoto) breaststroke; **uomo ~** frogman

'rancido a rancid

ran'core nm resentment

ran'dagio a stray

'rango nm rank

rannicchi'arsi vr huddle up

rannuvola'mento nm clouding over. **rannuvo'larsi** vr cloud over

ra'nocchio nm frog

ranto'lare vi wheeze. **'rantolo** nm wheeze; (di moribondo) death-rattle

'rapa nf turnip

ra'pace a rapacious; (uccello) predatory

ra'pare vt crop

'rapida nf rapids pl. **~'mente** adv rapidly

rapidità nf speed

'rapido a swift ● nm (treno) express [train]

rapi'mento nm (crimine) kidnapping

ra'pina nf robbery; **~ a mano armata** armed robbery. **~ in banca** bank robbery. **rapi'nare** vt rob. **~'tore** nm robber

ra'pire vt abduct; (a scopo di riscatto) kidnap; (estasiare) ravish. **~'tore**, **~'trice** nmf kidnapper

rappacifi'care vt pacify. **~rsi** vr be reconciled, make it up. **~zi'one** nf reconciliation

rappor'tare vt reproduce (disegno); (confrontare) compare

rap'porto nm report; (connessione) relation; (legame) relationship; Math, Techn ratio; **rapporti** pl relationship; **essere in buoni rapporti** be on good terms. **~ di amicizia** friendship. **~ di lavoro** working relationship. **rapporti** pl **sessuali** sexual intercourse

rap'prendersi vr set; (latte:) curdle

rappre'saglia nf reprisal

rappresen'tan|te nmf representa-

tive. **~te di classe** class representative. **~te di commercio** sales representative, [sales] rep fam. **~za** nf delegation; Comm agency; **spese** pl **di ~za** entertainment expenses; **di ~za** (appartamento ecc) company

rappresen'ta|re vt represent; Theat perform. **~'tivo** a representative. **~zi'one** nf representation; (spettacolo) performance

rap'preso pp di **rapprendersi**

rapso'dia nf rhapsody

'raptus nm inv fit of madness

rara'mente adv rarely, seldom

rare'fa|re vt, **~rsi** vr rarefy. **~tto** a rarefied

rarità nf inv rarity. **'raro** a rare

ra'sare vt shave; trim (siepe ecc). **~si** vr shave

raschia'mento nm Med curettage

raschi'are vt scrape; (togliere) scrape off

rasen'tare vt go close to. **ra'sente** prep very close to

'raso pp di **radere** ● a smooth; (colmo) full to the brim; (barba) close-cropped; **~ terra** close to the ground; **un cucchiaio ~** a level spoonful ● nm satin

ra'soio nm razor

ras'segna nf review; (mostra) exhibition; (musicale, cinematografica) festival; **passare in ~** review; Mil inspect

rasse'gna|re vt present. **~rsi** vr resign oneself. **~to** a (persona, aria, tono) resigned. **~zi'one** nf resignation

rassere'nar|e vt clear; fig cheer up. **~si** vr become clear; fig cheer up

rasset'tare vt tidy up; (riparare) mend

rassicu'ra|nte a (persona, parole, presenza) reassuring. **~re** vt reassure. **~zi'one** nf reassurance

rasso'dare vt harden; fig strengthen

rassomigli'a|nza *nf* resemblance. **~re** *vi* **~re a** resemble

rastrella'mento *nm* (*di fieno*) raking; (*perlustrazione*) combing. **rastrel'lare** *vt* rake; (*perlustrare*) comb

rastrelli'era *nf* rack; (*per biciclette*) bicycle rack; (*scolapiatti*) [plate] rack. **ra'strello** *nm* rake

'rata *nf* instalment; **pagare a rate** pay by instalments; **comprare qcsa a rate** buy sth on hire purchase, buy sth on the installment plan *Am.* **rate'ale** *a* by instalments; **pagamento rateale** payment by instalments

rate'are, **rateiz'zare** *vt* divide into instalments

ra'tifica *nf Jur* ratification

ratifi'care *vt Jur* ratify

'ratto *nm* (*roditore*) rat

rattop'pare *vt* patch. **rat'toppo** *nm* patch

rattrap'pir|e *vt* make stiff. **~si** *vr* become stiff

rattri'star|e *vt* sadden. **~si** *vr* become sad

rau'cedine *nf* hoarseness. **'rauco** *a* hoarse

rava'nello *nm* radish

ravi'oli *nmpl* ravioli *sg*

ravve'dersi *vr* mend one's ways

ravvicina'mento *nm* (*tra persone*) reconciliation; *Pol* rapprochement

ravvi'nar|e *vt* bring closer; (*riconciliare*) reconcile. **~si** *vr* be reconciled

ravvi'sare *vt* recognize

ravvi'var|e *vt* revive, *fig* brighten up. **~si** *vr* revive

'rayon *nm* rayon

razio'cinio *nm* rational thought; (*buon senso*) common sense

razio'nal|e *a* rational. **~ità** *nf* (*raziocinio*) rationality; (*di ambiente*) functional nature. **~iz'zare** *vt* rationalize (*programmi, metodi, spazio*). **~'mente** *adv* (*con raziocinio*) rationally

razio'nare *vt* ration. **razi'one** *nf* ration

'razza *nf* race; (*di cani ecc*) breed; (*genere*) kind; **che ~ di idiota!** *fam* what an idiot!

raz'zia *nf* raid

razzi'ale *a* racial

raz'zis|mo *nm* racism. **~ta** *a* e *nmf* racist

'razzo *nm* rocket. **~ da segnalazione** flare

razzo'lare *vi* (*polli*:) scratch about

re *nm inv* king; *Mus* (*chiave, nota*) D

rea'giro *vi* react

re'ale *a* real; (*di re*) royal

rea'lis|mo *nm* realism. **~ta** *nmf* realist; (*fautore del re*) royalist

realistica'mente *adv* realistically. **rea'listico** *a* realistic

realiz'zabile *a* (*programma*) feasible

realizza|re *vt* (*attuare*) carry out, realize; *Comm* make; score (*gol, canestro*); (*rendersi conto di*) realize. **~rsi** *vr* come true; (*nel lavoro ecc*) fulfil oneself. **~zi'one** *nf* realization; (*di sogno, persona*) fulfilment. **~zione scenica** production

rea'lizzo *nm* (*vendita*) proceeds *pl*; (*riscossione*) yield

real'mente *adv* really

realtà *nf inv* reality. **~ virtuale** virtual reality

re'ato *nm* crime, criminal offence

reat'tivo *a* reactive

reat'tore *nm* reactor; *Aeron* jet [aircraft]

reazio'nario, -a *a* e *nmf* reactionary

reazi'one *nf* reaction. **~ a catena** chain reaction

'rebus *nm inv* rebus; (*enigma*) puzzle

recapi'tare *vt* deliver. **re'capito** *nm* address; (*consegna*) delivery. **recapito a domicilio** home delivery. **recapito telefonico** contact telephone number

re'car|e vt bear; (produrre) cause. **~si** vr go

re'cedere vi recede; fig give up

recensi'one nf review

recen'sire vt review. **~ore** nm reviewer

re'cente a recent; **di ~** recently. **~'mente** adv recently

recessi'one nf recession

reces'sivo a Biol recessive

re'cesso nm recess

re'cidere vt cut off

reci'divo, **-a** a Med recurrent ● nmf repeat offender

recin'tare vt close off. **re'cinto** nm enclosure; (per animali) pen; (per bambini) play-pen. **~zi'one** nf (muro) wall; (rete) wire fence; (cancellata) railings pl

recipi'ente nm container

re'ciproco a reciprocal

re'ciso pp di recidere

'recita nf performance. **reci'tare** vt recite; Theat act; play (ruolo). **~zi'one** nf recitation; Theat acting

recla'mare vi protest ● vt claim

ré'clame nf inv advertising; (avviso pubblicitario) advertisement

re'clamo nm complaint; **ufficio reclami** complaints department or office

recli'na|bile a reclining; **sedile ~bile** reclining seat. **~re** vt tilt (sedile); lean (capo)

reclusi'one nf imprisonment. **re'cluso**, **-a** a secluded ● nmf prisoner

'recluta nf recruit

reclu|ta'mento nm recruitment. **~'tare** vt recruit

'record nm inv record ● a inv (cifra) record attrib

recrimi'na|re vi recriminate. **~zi'one** nf recrimination

recupe'rare vt recover. **re'cupero** nm recovery; **corso di recupero** additional classes; **minuti di recupero** Sport injury time

redargu'ire vt rebuke

re'datto pp di redigere

redat'tore, **-'trice** nmf editor; (di testo) writer

redazi'one nf (ufficio) editorial office; (di testi) editing

red'dizio a profitable

'reddito nm income. **~ imponibile** taxable income

re'den|to pp di redimere. **~'tore** nm redeemer. **~zi'one** nf redemption

re'digere vt write; draw up (documento)

re'dimer|e vt redeem. **~si** vr redeem oneself

'redini nfpl reins

'reduce a **~ da** back from ● nmf survivor

refe'rendum nm inv referendum

refe'renza nf reference

refet'torio nm refectory

refrat'tario a refractory; **essere ~ a** have no aptitude for

refrige'ra|re vt refrigerate. **~zi'o-ne** nf refrigeration

refur'tiva nf stolen goods pl

re'gale a regal

re'galo nm present, gift

re'gata nf regatta

reg'gen|te nmf regent. **~za** nf regency

'regger|e vt (sorreggere) bear; (tenere in mano) hold; (dirigere) run; (governare) govern; Gram take ● vi (resistere) hold out; (durare) last; fig stand. **~si** vr stand

'reggia nf royal palace

reggi'calze nm inv suspender belt

reggi'mento nm regiment; (fig: molte persone) army

reggi'petto, **reggi'seno** nm bra

re'gia nf Cinema direction; Theat production

re'gime nm regime; (dieta) diet; Mech speed. **~ militare** military regime

re'gina nf queen

'regio a royal

regio'na|le a regional. **~'lismo** nm (parola) regionalism

regi'one nf region

re'gista *nmf Cinema* director; *Theat, TV* producer

regi'stra|re *vt* register; *Comm* enter; (*incidere su nastro*) tape, record; (*su disco*) record. ~'tore *nm* recorder; (*magnetofono*) tape-recorder. ~'tore di cassa cash register. ~zi'one *nf* registration; *Comm* entry; (*di programma*) recording

re'gistro *nm* register; (*ufficio*) registry. ~ di cassa ledger

re'gnare *vi* reign

'regno *nm* kingdom; (*sovranità*) reign. R~ Unito United Kingdom

'regola *nf* rule; essere in ~ be in order; (*persona*:) have one's papers in order. rego'labile *a* (*meccanismo*) adjustable. ~'mento *nm* regulation; *Comm* settlement. ~mento di conti settling of scores

rego'la|re *a* regular ● *vt* regulate; (*ridurre, moderare*) limit; (*sistemare*) settle. ~si *vr* (*agire*) act; (*moderarsi*) control oneself. ~ità *nf inv* regularity. ~iz'zare *vt* settle (*debito*)

rego'la|ta *nf* darsi una ~ta pull oneself together. ~'tore, ~'trice *nmf* (*in una conferenza*) speaker

re'lax *nm* relaxation

relazi'one *nf* relation[ship]; (*rapporto amoroso*) [love] affair; (*resoconto*) report; pubbliche relazioni *pl* public relations

rele'gare *vt* relegate

religi'o|ne *nf* religion. ~so, -a *a* religious ● *nm* monk ● *nf* nun

re'liqui|a *nf* relic. ~'ario *nm* reliquary

re'litto *nm* wreck

re'ma|re *vi* row. ~'tore, ~'trice *nmf* rower

remini'scenza *nf* reminiscence

remissi'one *nf* remission; (*sottomissione*) submissiveness. remis'sivo *a* submissive

'remo *nm* oar

'remora *nf* senza remore without hesitation

re'moto *a* remote

remune'ra|re *vt* remunerate. ~'tivo *a* remunerative. ~zi'one *nf* remuneration

'render|e *vt* (*restituire*) return; (*esprimere*) render; (*fruttare*) yield; (*far diventare*) make. ~si *vi* become; ~si conto di qcsa realize sth; ~si utile make oneself useful

rendi'conto *nm* report

rendi'mento *nm* rendering; (*produzione*) yield

'rendita *nf* income; (*dello Stato*) revenue; vivere di ~ *fig* rest on one's laurels

'rene *nm* kidney. ~ artificiale kidney machine

'reni *nfpl* (*schiena*) back

reni'tente *a* essere ~ a (*consigli di qcno*) be unwilling to accept

'renna *nf* reindeer (*pl inv*); (*pelle*) buckskin

'Reno *nm* Rhine

'reo, -a *a* guilty ● *nmf* offender

re'parto *nm* department; *Mil* unit

repel'lente *a* repulsive

repen'taglio *nm* mettere a ~ risk

repen'tino *a* sudden

repe'ribile *a* available; non è ~ (*perduto*) it's not to be found

repe'rire *vt* trace (*fondi*)

re'perto *nm* ~ archeologico find

reper'torio *nm* repertory; (*elenco*)

index; **immagini** *pl* **di ~** archive footage

'replica *nf* reply; (*obiezione*) objection; (*copia*) replica; *Theat* repeat performance. **repli'care** *vt* reply; *Theat* repeat

repor'tage *nm inv* report

repres|si'one *nf* repression. **~'si-vo** *a* repressive. **re'presso** *pp di* **reprimere. re'primere** *vt* repress

re'pubbli|ca *nf* republic. **~'cano, -a** *a a & nmf* republican

repu'tare *vt* consider

reputazi'one *nf* reputation

requi'si|re *vt* requisition. **~to** *nm* requirement

requisi'toria *nf* (*arringa*) closing speech

requisizi'one *nf* requisition

'resa *nf* surrender; *Comm* rendering. **~ dei conti** rendering of accounts

'residence *nm inv* residential hotel

resi'den|te *a & nmf* resident. **~za** *nf* residence; (*soggiorno*) stay. **~zi'ale** *a* residential; **zona ~ziale** residential district

re'siduo *a* residual ●*nm* remainder

'resina *nf* resin

resi'sten|te *a* resistant; **~te all'acqua** water-resistant. **~za** *nf* resistance; (*fisica*) stamina; *Electr* resistor; **la R~za** the Resistance

re'sistere *vi* ~ [a] resist; (*a colpi, scosse*) stand up to; **~ alla pioggia/al vento** be rain-/wind-resistant

'reso *pp di* **rendere**

reso'conto *nm* report

respin'gente *nm* *Rail* buffer

re'spin|gere *vt* repel; (*rifiutare*) reject; (*bocciare*) fail. **~to** *pp di* **respingere**

respi'ra|re *vt/i* breathe. **~'tore** *nm* respirator; **~'tore [a tubo]** snorkel **~'torio** *a* respiratory. **~zi'one** *nf* breathing; *Med* respiration. **~zione bocca a bocca** mouth-to-mouth rescuscitation; kiss of life.

re'spiro *nm* breath; (*il respirare*) breathing; *fig* respite

respon'sabil|e *a* responsible (**di** for); *Jur* liable ●*nmf* person responsible. **~e della produzione** production manager. **~ità** *nf inv* responsibility; *Jur* liability. **~iz'zare** *vt* give responsibility to

re'sponso *nm* response

'ressa *nf* crowd

re'stante *a* remaining ●*nm* remainder

re'stare *vi* = **rimanere**

restau'ra|re *vt* restore. **~'tore, ~'trice** *nmf* restorer. **~zi'one** *nf* restoration. **re'stauro** (*riparazione*) repair

re'stio *a* restive; **~ a** reluctant to

restitu'|ire *vt* return; (*reintegrare*) restore. **~zi'one** *nf* return; *Jur* restitution

'resto *nm* remainder; (*saldo*) balance; (*denaro*) change; **resti** *pl* (*avanzi*) remains; **del ~** besides

re'strin|gere *vt* contract; take in (*vestiti*); (*limitare*) restrict; shrink (*stoffa*). **~si** *vr* contract; (*farsi più vicini*) close up; (*stoffa:*) shrink. **restringi'mento** *nm* (*di tessuto*) shrinkage

restrit'tivo *a* (*legge, clausola*) restrictive. **~zi'one** *nf* restriction

resurrezi'one *nf* resurrection

resusci'tare *vt/i* revive

re'tata *nf* round-up

'rete *nf* net; (*sistema*) network; (*televisiva*) channel; (*in calcio, hockey*) goal; *fig* trap; (*per la spesa*) string bag. **~ locale** *Comput* local [area] network, LAN. **~ stradale** road network. **~ televisiva** television channel

reti'cen|te *a* reticent. **~za** *nf* reticence

retico'lato *nm* grid; (*rete metallica*) wire netting. **re'ticolo** *nm* network

re'tina *nf* retina

re'tina *nf* (*per capelli*) hair net

re'torico, -a *a* rhetorical; **domanda retorica** rhetorical question ●*nf* rhetoric

retribu'ire vt remunerate. **~zi'one** nf remuneration

'retro adv behind; **vedi ~** see over ● nm inv back. **~ di copertina** outside back cover

retroat'tivo a retroactive

retro'ce|dere vi retreat ● vt Mil demote; Sport relegate. **~ssi'one** nf Sport relegation

retro'datare vt backdate

re'trogrado a retrograde; fig old-fashioned; Pol reactionary

retrogu'ardia nf Mil rearguard

retro'marcia nf reverse [gear]

retro'scena nm inv Theat backstage; fig background details pl

retrospet'tivo a retrospective

retro'stante a **il palazzo ~** the building behind

retrovi'sore nm rear-view mirror

'retta[1] nf Math straight line; (di collegio, pensionato) fee

'retta[2] nf **dar ~ a qcno** take sb's advice

rettango'lare a rectangular. **ret'tangolo** a right-angled ● nm rectangle

ret'tifica nf rectification. **~'care** vt rectify

'rettile nm reptile

retti'lineo a rectilinear; (retto) upright ● nm Sport back straight

retti'tudine nf rectitude

'retto pp di reggere ● a straight; fig upright; (giusto) correct; **angolo ~** right angle

ret'tore nm Relig rector; Univ chancellor

reu'matico a rheumatic

reuma'tismi nmpl rheumatism

reve'rendo a reverend

rever'sibile a reversible

revisio'nare vt revise; Comm audit; Auto overhaul. **revisi'one** nf revision; Comm audit; Auto overhaul. **revi'sore** nm (di conti) auditor; (di bozze) proof-reader; (di traduzioni) reviser

re'vival nm inv revival

'revoca nf repeal. **revo'care** vt repeal

riabili'ta|re vt rehabilitate. **~zi'one** nf rehabilitation

riabitu'ar|e vt reaccustom. **~si** vr reaccustom oneself

riac'cender|e vt rekindle ⟨fuoco⟩. **~si** vr ⟨luce.⟩ come back on

riacqui'stare vt buy back; regain ⟨libertà, prestigio⟩; recover ⟨vista, udito⟩

riagganci'are vt replace ⟨ricevitore⟩; **~ la cornetta** hang up ● vi hang up

riallac'ciare vt refasten; reconnect ⟨corrente⟩, renew ⟨amicizia⟩

rial'zare vt raise ● vi rise. **ri'alzo** nm rise

riani'mar|e vt Med resuscitate; (ridare forza a) revive; ⟨ridare coraggio a⟩ cheer up. **~si** vr regain consciousness; (riprendere forza) revive; (riprendere coraggio) cheer up

riaper'tura nf reopening

ria'prir|e vt, **~si** vr reopen

ri'armo nm rearmament

rias'sumere vt (ricapitolare) resume

riassun'tivo a summarizing. **rias'sunto** pp di riassumere ● nm summary

ria'ver|e vt get back; regain ⟨salute, vista⟩. **~si** vr recover

riavvicina'mento nm (tra persone) reconciliation

riavvici'nar|e vt reconcile ⟨paesi, persone⟩. **~si** vr ⟨riconciliarsi⟩ reconciled, make it up

riba'dire vt (confermare) reaffirm

ri'balta nf flap; Theat footlights pl; fig limelight

ribal'tabile a tip-up

ribal'tar|e vt/i. **~si** vr tip over; Naut capsize

ribas'sare vt lower ● vi fall. **ri'basso** nm fall; (sconto) discount

ri'battere vt (a macchina) retype; (controbattere) deny ● vi answer back

ribell|arsi vr rebel. **ri'belle** a rebellious ● nmf rebel. **~'ione** nf rebellion

'ribes *nm inv* (*rosso*) redcurrant; (*nero*) blackcurrant

ribol'lire *vi* (*fermentare*) ferment; *fig* seethe

ri'brezzo *nm* disgust; **far ~ a** disgust

rica'dere *vi* fall back; (*nel peccato ecc*) lapse; (*pendere*) hang [down]; **~ su** (*riversarsi*) fall on. **rica'duta** *nf* relapse

rical'care *vt* trace

ricalci'trante *a* recalcitrant

rica'ma|re *vt* embroider. **~to a em-**broidered

ri'cambi *nmpl* spare parts

ricambi'are *vt* return; reciprocate (*sentimento*); **~ qcsa a qcno** repay sb for sth. **ri'cambio** *nm* replacement; *Biol* metabolism; **pezzo di ricambio** *Mech* spare [part]

ri'camo *nm* embroidery

ricapito'la|re *vt* sum up. **~zi'one** *nf* summary, recap *fam*

ri'carica *nf* (*di cellulari*) rewinding

ricari'care *vt* reload (*macchina fotografica, fucile, camion*); recharge (*batteria*); *Comput* reboot

ricat'ta|re *vt* blackmail. **~'tore,** **~'trice** *nmf* blackmailer. **ri'catto** *nm* blackmail

rica'va|re *vt* get; (*ottenere*) obtain; (*dedurre*) draw. **~to** *nm* proceeds *pl*. **ri'cavo** *nm* proceeds *pl*

'ricca *nf* rich woman. **~'mente** *adv* lavishly

ric'chezza *nf* wealth; *fig* richness; **ricchezze** *pl* riches

'riccio *a* curly ● *nm* curl; (*animale*) hedgehog. **~ di mare** sea-urchin. **~lo** *nm* curl. **~'luto** *a* curly. **ricci'uto** *a* (*barba*) curly

'ricco *a* rich ● *nm* rich man

ri'cerca *nf* search; (*indagine*) investigation; (*scientifica*) research; *Sch* project

ricer'ca|re *vt* search for; (*fare ricerche su*) research. **~ta** *nf* wanted woman. **~'tezza** *nf* refinement. **~to** *a* sought-after; (*raffina-*

to) refined; (*affettato*) affected ● *nm* (*polizia*) wanted man

ricetrasmit'tente *nf* transceiver

ri'cetta *nf Med* prescription; *Culin* recipe

ricet'tacolo *nm* receptacle

ricet'tario *nm* (*di cucina*) recipe book

ricetta|'tore, -'trice *nmf* fence, receiver of stolen goods. **~zi'one** *nf* receiving [stolen goods]

rice'vente *a* (*apparecchio, stazione*) receiving ● *nmf* receiver

ri'cev|ere *vt* receive; (*dare il benvenuto*) welcome; (*di albergo*) accommodate. **~i'mento** *nm* receiving; (*accoglienza*) welcome; (*trattenimento*) reception

ricevi'tor|e *nm* receiver. **~'ia** *nf* **~ia del lotto** *agency authorized to sell lottery tickets*

rice'vuta *nf* receipt. **~ fiscale** tax receipt

ricezi'one *nf Radio, TV* reception

richia'mare *vt* (*al telefono*) call back; (*far tornare*) recall; (*rimproverare*) rebuke; (*attirare*) draw; **~ alla mente** call to mind. **richi'amo** *nm* recall; (*attrazione*) call

richi'edere *vt* ask for; (*di nuovo*) ask again for; **~ a qcno di fare qcsa** ask *o* request sb to do sth. **richi'esta** *nf* request; *Comm* demand

ri'chiuder|e *vt* shut again, close again. **~si** *vr* (*ferita*) heal

ri'ciclaggio *nm* recycling

rici'clar|e *vt* recycle. **~si** *vr* retrain; (*cambiare lavoro*) change one's line of work

ri'cino *nm* **olio di ~** castor oil

ricogni'zi'one *nf Mil* reconnaissance

ri'colmo *a* full

ricomin'ciare *vt/i* start again

ricompa'rire *vi* reappear

ricom'pen|sa *nf* reward. **~'sare** *vt* reward

ricom'por|re *vt* (*riscrivere*) rewrite; (*ricostruire*) reform; *Typ* reset. **~si** *vr* regain one's composure

riconcilia|re *vt* reconcile. **~rsi** *vr* be reconciled. **~zi'one** *nf* reconciliation

ricono'scen|te *a* grateful. **~za** *nf* gratitude

rico'nosc|ere *vt* recognize; (*ammettere*) acknowledge. **~i'mento** *nm* recognition; (*ammissione*) acknowledgement; (*per la polizia*) identification. **~i'uto** *a* recognized

riconqui'stare *vt* Mil retake, reconquer

riconside'rare *vt* rethink

rico'prire *vt* re-cover; (*rivestire*) coat; (*di insulti*) shower (**di** with); hold ⟨*carica*⟩

ricor'dar|e *vt* remember; (*richiamare alla memoria*) recall; (*far ricordare*) remind; (*rassomigliare*) look like. **~si** *vr* **~si** [**di**] remember. **ri'cordo** *nm* memory; ⟨*oggetto*⟩ memento; (*di viaggio*) souvenir; **ricordi** *pl* (*memorie*) memoirs

ricor'ren|te *a* recurrent. **~za** *nf* recurrence; (*anniversario*) anniversary

ri'correre *vi* recur; (*accadere*) occur; ⟨*data:*⟩ fall; **~ a** have recourse to; (*rivolgersi a*) turn to.

ri'corso *pp* **di ricorrere ●** *nm* recourse; *Jur* appeal

ricostitu'ente *nm* tonic

ricostitu'ire *vt* re-establish

ricostru'ire *vt* reconstruct. **~zi'one** *nf* reconstruction

ricove'ra|re *vt* give shelter to; **~re in ospedale** admit to hospital, hospitalize. **~to, -a** *nmf* hospital patient. **ri'covero** *nm* shelter; (*ospizio*) home

ricre'a|re *vt* re-create; (*ristorare*) restore. **~rsi** *vr* amuse oneself **~tivo** *a* recreational. **~zi'one** *nf* recreation; *Sch* break

ri'credersi *vr* change one's mind

ricupe'rare *vt* recover; rehabilitate ⟨*tossicodipendente*⟩; **~ il tem-**

po perduto make up for lost time.

ri'cupero *nm* recovery; (*di tossicodipendente*) rehabilitation; (*salvataggio*) rescue; [**minuti** *nmpl* **di**] **ricupero** injury time

ri'curvo *a* bent

ridacchi'are *vi* giggle

ri'dare *vt* give back, return

ri'dente *a* (*piacevole*) pleasant

'ridere *vi* laugh; **~ di** (*deridere*) laugh at

ri'detto *pp* **di ridire**

ridicoliz'zare *vt* ridicule. **ri'dicolo** *a* ridiculous

ridimensio'nare *vt* reshape; *fig* see in the right perspective

ri'dire *vt* repeat; (*criticare*) find fault with; **trova sempre da ~** he's always finding fault

ridon'dante *a* redundant

ri'dotto *pp* **di ridurre ●** *nm* Theat foyer **●** *a* reduced

ri'du|rre *vt* reduce. **~rsi** *vr* diminish. **~rsi a** be reduced to. **~tivo** *a* reductive. **~zi'one** *nf* reduction; (*per cinema, teatro*) adaptation

rieducazi'one *nf* (*di malato*) rehabilitation

riem'pire *vt* fill [up]; fill in ⟨*moduli ecc.*⟩. **~rsi** *vr* fill [up]. **~tivo** *a* filling **●** *nm* filler

rien'tranza *nf* recess

rien'trare *vi* go/come back in; (*tornare*) return; (*piegare indentro*) recede; **~ in** (*far parte*) fall within. **ri'entro** *nm* return; (*di astronave*) re-entry

riepilo'gare *vt* recapitulate. **rie'pilogo** *nm* roundup

riesami'nare *vt* reappraise

ri'essere *vi* **ci risiamo!** here we go again!

riesu'mare *vt* exhume

rievo'ca|re *vt* (*commemorare*) commemorate. **~zi'one** *nf* (*commemorazione*) commemoration

rifaci'mento *nm* remake

ri'fa|re *vt* do again; (*creare*) make again; (*riparare*) repair; (*imitare*) imitate; make ⟨*letto*⟩. **~rsi** *vr* (*rimettersi*) recover; (*vendicarsi*) get even; **~rsi una vita/carriera** make a new life/career for oneself; **~rsi il trucco** touch up one's makeup; **~rsi di** make up for. **~tto** pp di **rifare**

riferi'mento nm reference

rife'rir|e vt report; **~e a** attribute to ● vi make a report. **~si** vr **~si a** refer to

rifi'lare vt (tagliare a filo) trim; (fam: affibbiare) saddle

rifi'ni|re vt finish off. **~'tura** nf finish

rifio'rire vi blossom again; fig flourish again

rifiu'tare vt refuse. **rifi'uto** nm refusal; **rifiuti** pl (immondizie) rubbish sg. **rifiuti** pl **urbani** urban waste sg

riflessi'one nf reflection; (osservazione) remark. **rifles'sivo** a thoughtful; Gram reflexive

ri'flesso pp di **riflettere** ● nm (luce) reflection; Med reflex; **per ~** indirectly

ri'fletter|e vt reflect ● vi think. **~si** vr be reflected

riflet'tore nm reflector; (proiettore) searchlight

ri'flusso nm ebb

rifocil'lar|e vt restore. **~si** vr liter, hum take some refreshment

ri'fondere vt (rimborsare) refund

ri'forma nf reform; Relig reformation; Mil exemption on medical grounds

rifor'ma|re vt re-form; (migliorare) reform; Mil declare unfit for military service. **~to a** ⟨chiesa⟩ Reformed. **~tore, ~'trice** nmf reformer. **~'torio** nm reformatory. **rifor'mista** a reformist

riforni'mento nm supply; (scorta) stock; (di combustibile) refuelling; **stazione** nf **di ~** petrol station

rifor'nir|e vt **~e di** provide with. **~si** vr restock, stock up (**di with**)

ri'fra|ngere vt refract. **~tto** pp di **rifrangere**. **~zi'one** nf refraction

rifug'gire vi **~ da** fig shun

rifugi'a|rsi vr take refuge. **~to, -a** nmf refugee

ri'fugio nm shelter; (nascondiglio) hideaway

'riga nf line; (fila) row; (striscia) stripe; (scriminatura) parting; (regolo) rule; **a righe** (stoffa) striped; (quaderno) ruled; **mettersi in ~** line up

ri'gagnolo nm rivulet

ri'gare vt rule (foglio) ● vi **~ dritto** behave well

rigatti'ere nm junk dealer

rigene'rare vt regenerate

riget'tare vt (gettare indietro) throw back; (respingere) reject; (vomitare) throw up. **ri'getto** nm rejection

ri'ghello nm ruler

rigid|a'mente adv rigidly. **~ità** nf rigidity; (di clima) severity; (severità) strictness. **'rigido** a rigid; (freddo) severe; (severo) strict

rigi'rar|e vt turn again; (ripercorrere) go round; fig twist (argomentazione) ● vi walk about. **~si** vr turn round; (nel letto) turn over. **ri'giro** nm (imbroglio) trick

'rigo nm line; Mus staff

ri'goglio nm bloom. **~'oso** a luxuriant

ri'gonfio a swollen

ri'gore nm rigours pl; **a ~** strictly speaking; **calcio di ~** penalty [kick]; **area di ~** penalty area; **essere di ~** be compulsory

rigo|rosa'mente adv (giudicare) severely. **~'roso** a (severo) strict; (scrupoloso) rigorous

riguada'gnare vt regain ⟨quota, velocità⟩

riguar'dar|e vt look at again; (considerare) regard; (concernere) concern; **per quanto riguarda** with regard to. **~si** vr take care of oneself. **rigu'ardo** nm care; (considerazione) consideration; **nei riguardi di** towards; **riguardo a** with regard to

ri'gurgito nm regurgitation

rilanci'are vt throw back (palla);

(di nuovo) throw again; increase *(offerta)* revive *(moda)*; relaunch *(prodotto)* ● *vi (a carte)* raise the stakes

rilasci'ar|e *vt (concedere)* grant; *(liberare)* release; issue *(documento)*. **~si** *vr* relax. **ri'lascio** *nm* release; *(di documento)* issue

rilassa'mento *nm (relax)* relaxation

rilas'sa|re *vt*, **~rsi** *vr* relax. **~to** *a (ambiente)* relaxed

rile'ga|re *vt* bind *(libro)*. **~to** *a* bound. **~'tura** *nf* binding

ri'leggere *vt* reread

ri'lento: a ~ *adv* slowly

rileva'mento *nm* survey, Comm buyout

rile'vante *a* considerable

rile'va|re *vt (trarre)* get; *(mettere in evidenza)* point out; *(notare)* notice; *(topografia)* survey; Comm take over; Mil relieve. **~zi'one** *nf (statistica)* survey

rili'evo *nm* relief; Geog elevation; *(topografia)* survey; *(importanza)* importance; *(osservazione)* remark; **mettere in ~** *qcsa* point sth out

rilut'tan|te *a* reluctant. **~za** *nf* reluctance

'rima *nf* rhyme; **far ~ con** *qcsa* rhyme with sth

riman'dare *vt (posporre)* postpone; *(mandare indietro)* send back; *(mandare di nuovo)* send again; *(far ridare un esame)* make resit an examination. **ri'mando** *nm* return; *(in un libro)* cross-reference

rima'nen|te *a* remaining ● *nm* remainder. **~za** *nf* remainder; **~ze** *pl* remnants

rima'no|re *vi* stay, remain; *(essere d'avanzo)* be left; *(venirsi a trovare)* be; *(restare stupito)* be astonished; *(restare d'accordo)* agree

rimar'chevole *a* remarkable

ri'mare *vt/i* rhyme

rimargi'nar|e *vt*, **~si** *vr* heal

ri'masto *pp di* **rimanere**

rima'sugli *nmpl (di cibo)* leftovers

rimbal'zar|e *vi* rebound; *(proiettile:)* ricochet; **far ~** bounce. **rim'balzo** *nm* rebound; *(di proiettile)* ricochet

rimbam'bi|re *vi* be in one's dotage ● *vt* stun. **~to** *a* in one's dotage

rimboc'care *vt* turn up; roll up *(maniche)*; tuck in *(coperte)*

rimbom'bare *vi* resound

rimbor'sare *vt* reimburse, repay. **rim'borso** *nm* reimbursement, repayment. **rimborso spese** reimbursement of expenses

rime'di|are *vi* **~a** a remedy; make up for *(errore)*; *(procurare)* scrape up. **ri'medio** *nm* remedy

rimesco'lare *vt* mix [up]; shuffle *(carte)*; *(rivangare)* rake up

ri'messa *nf (locale per veicoli)* garage; *(per aerei)* hangar; *(per autobus)* depot; *(di denaro)* remittance; *(di merci)* consignment

ri'messo *pp di* **rimettere**

ri'metter|e *vt (a posto)* put back; *(restituire)* return; *(affidare)* entrust; *(perdonare)* remit; *(rimandare)* put off; *(vomitare)* bring up; **~ci** *(fam: perdere)* lose [out]. **~si** *vr (ristabilirsi)* recover; *(tempo:)* clear up; **~si a** start again

'rimmel® *nm inv* mascara

rimoder'nare *vt* modernize

rimon'tare *vt (risalire)* go up; Mech reassemble ● *vi* remount; **~** *a (risalire)* go back to

rimorchi'are *vt* tow; *fam* pick up *(ragazza)*. **~ tore** *nm* tug[boat]. **ri'morchio** *nm* tow; *(veicolo)* trailer

ri'morso *nm* remorse

rimo'stranza *nf* complaint

rimozi'one *nf* removal; *(da un incarico)* dismissal. **~ forzata** *illegally parked vehicles removed at owner's expense*

rim'pasto *nm* Pol reshuffle

rimpatri'are *vt/i* repatriate. **rim'patrio** *nm* repatriation

rimpi'an|gere *vt* regret. **~to** *pp di* **rimpiangere** ● *nm* regret

rimpiat'tino *nm* hide-and-seek
rimpiaz'zare *vt* replace
rimpiccio'lire *vi* become smaller
rimpinz'ar|e *vt* ~e **di** stuff with.
~**si** *vr* stuff oneself
rimprove'rare *vt* reproach; ~
qcsa a qcno reproach sb for sth.
rim'provero *nm* reproach
rimugi'nare *vt* rummage; *fig* ~ **su**
brood over
rimune'ra|re *vt* remunerate.
~**tivo** *a* remunerative. ~**zi'one** *nf*
remuneration
ri'muovere *vt* remove
ri'nascere *vi* be reborn, be born
again
rinascimen'tale *a* Renaissance.
Rinasci'mento *nm* Renaissance
ri'nascita *nf* rebirth
rincal'zare *vt* (*sostenere*) support;
(*rimboccare*) tuck in. **rin'calzo** *nm*
support; **rincalzi** *pl Mil* reserves
rincantucci'arsi *vr* hide oneself
away in a corner
rinca'rare *vt* increase the price of
● *vi* become more expensive.
rin'caro *nm* price increase
rinca'sare *vi* return home
rinchi'uder|e *vt* shut up. ~**si** *vr*
shut oneself up
rin'correre *vt* run after
rin'cors|a *nf* run-up. ~**o** *pp di*
rincorrere
rin'cresc|ere *vi* **mi rincresce di
non...** I'm sorry *o* I regret that I
can't...; **non ti** ~**e** if you don't
mind. ~**i'mento** *nm* regret. ~**i'uto**
pp di **rincrescere**
rincreti'nire *vi* be stupid
rincu'lare *vi* (*arma:*) recoil;
(*cavallo:*) shy. **rin'culo** *nm* recoil
rincuo'rar|e *vt* encourage. ~**si** *vr*
take heart
rinfacci'are *vt* ~ **qcsa a qcno**
throw sth in sb's face
rinfor'zare *vt* strengthen; (*rendere
più saldo*) reinforce. ~**si** *vr* become stronger. **rin'forzo** *nm* rein-
forcement; *fig* support
rinfran'care *vt* reassure
rinfre'scante *a* cooling

rinfre'scar|e *vt* cool; (*rinnovare*)
freshen up ● *vi* get cooler. ~**si** *vr*
freshen [oneself] up. **rin'fresco**
nm light refreshment; (*ricevimento*) party
rin'fusa *nf* **alla** ~ at random
ringhi'are *vi* snarl
ringhi'era *nf* railing; (*di scala*)
banisters *pl*
ringiova'nire *vt* rejuvenate (*pelle,
persona*); (*vestito:*) make look
younger ● *vi* become young again;
(*sembrare*) look young again
ringrazi|a'mento *nm* thanks *pl.*
~**'are** *vt* thank
rinne'ga|re *vt* disown. ~**to, -a** *nmf*
renegade
rinnova'mento *nm* renewal; (*di
edifici*) renovation
rinno'var|e *vt* renew; renovate
(*edifici*). ~**si** *vr* be renewed;
(*ripetersi*) recur, happen again.
rin'novo *nm* renewal
rino'ceronte *nm* rhinoceros
rino'mato *a* renowned
rinsal'dare *vt* consolidate
rinsa'vire *vi* come to one's senses
rinsec'chi|re *vi* shrivel up. ~**to** *a*
shrivelled up
rinta'narsi *vr* hide oneself away;
(*animale:*) retreat into its den
rintoc'care *vi* (*campana:*) toll;
(*orologio:*) strike. **rin'tocco** *nm*
toll; (*di orologio*) stroke
rinton'ti|re *vt* **anche** *fig* stun. ~**to** *a*
(*stordito*) dazed
rintracci'are *vt* trace
rintro'nare *vt* stun ● *vi* boom
ri'nuncia *nf* renunciation
rinunci'a|re *vi* ~**re a** renounce,
give up. ~**tario** *a* defeatist
ri'nunzia, rinunzi'are = **rinuncia,
rinunciare**
rinveni'mento *nm* (*di reperti*) discovery; (*di refurtiva*) recovery.
rinve'nire *vt* find ● *vi* (*riprendere i
sensi*) come round; (*ridiventare
fresco*) revive
rinvi'are *vt* put off; (*mandare
indietro*) return; (*in libro*) refer; ~
a giudizio indict

rin'vio nm Sport goal kick; (in libro) cross-reference; (di appuntamento) postponement; (di merce) return

rio'nale a local. **ri'one** nm district

riordi'nare vt tidy [up]; (ordinare di nuovo) reorder; (riorganizzare) reorganize

riorganiz'zare vt reorganize

ripa'gare vt repay

ripa'ra|re vt (proteggere) shelter, protect; (aggiustare) repair; (porre rimedio) remedy ● vi ~**re a** make up for. ~**rsi** vr take shelter. ~to a (luogo) sheltered. ~**zi'one** nf repair; fig reparation. **ri'paro** nm shelter; (rimedio) remedy

ripar'ti|re vt (dividere) divide ● vi leave again. ~**zi'one** nf division

ripas'sa|re vt recross; (rivedere) revise ● vi pass again. ~**ta** nf (di vernice) second coat. **ri'passo** nm (di lezione) revision

ripensa'mento nm second thoughts pl

ripen'sare vi (cambiare idea) change one's mind; ~ **a** think of; **ripensaci!** think again!

riper'correre vt (con la memoria) go back over

riper'cosso pp di **ripercuotere**

ripercu'oter|e vt strike again. ~**si** vr (suono:) reverberate; ~**si su** (fig: avere conseguenze) impact on. **ripercussi'one** nf repercussion

ripe'scare vt fish out (oggetti)

ripe'tente nmf student repeating a year

ripe'te|re vt repeat. ~**rsi** vr (evento:) recur. ~**zi'one** nf repetition; (di lezione) revision; (lezione privata) private lesson. ~**uta-'mente** adv repeatedly

ri'piano nm (di scaffale) shelf; (terreno pianeggiante) table

ri'picc|a nf fare qcsa per ~ **a** do sth out of spite. ~**o** nm spite

'ripido a steep

ripie'ga|re vt refold; (abbassare) lower ● vi (indietreggiare) retreat.

~**si** vr bend; (sedile:) fold. **ripi'ego** nm expedient; (via d'uscita) way out

ripi'eno a full; Culin stuffed ● nm filling; Culin stuffing

ripopo'lar|e vt repopulate. ~**si** vr be repopulated

ri'porre vt put back; (mettere da parte) put away; (collocare) place; repeat (domanda)

ripor'ta|re vt (restituire) bring/ take back; (riferire) report; (subire) suffer; Math carry; win (vittoria); transfer (disegno). ~**si** vr go back, (riferirsi) refer. **ri'porto** nm **cane da riporto** gun dog

ripo'sante a (colore) restful, soothing

ripo'sa|re vi rest ● vt put back. ~**rsi** vr rest. ~**to** a (mente) fresh. **ri'poso** nm rest; **andare a riposo** retire; **riposo!** Mil at ease!; **giorno di riposo** day off

ripo'stiglio nm cupboard

ri'posto pp di **riporre**

ri'prender|e vt take again; (prendere indietro) take back; (riconquistare) recapture; (ricuperare) recover; (ricominciare) resume; (rimproverare) reprimand; take in (cucitura); Cinema shoot. ~**si** vr recover; (correggersi) correct oneself

ri'presa nf resumption; (ricupero) recovery; Theat revival; Cinema shot; Auto acceleration; Mus repeat. ~ **aerea** bird's-eye view

ripresen'ta|re vt resubmit (domanda, certificato). ~**rsi** vr (a ufficio) go/come back again; (come candidato) stand o run again; (occasione:) arise again

ri'preso pp di **riprendere**

ripristi'nare vt restore

ripro'dotto pp di **riprodurre**

ripro'du|rre vt, ~**rsi** vr reproduce. ~**t'tivo** a reproductive. ~**zi'one** nf reproduction

ripro'mettersi vr (intendere) intend

ri'prova nf confirmation

ripudi'are *vt* repudiate

ripu'gnan|te *a* repugnant. **~za** *nf* disgust. **ripu'gnare** *vi* **ripugnare a** disgust

ripu'li|re *vt* clean [up]; *fig* polish. **~ta** *nf* darsi una **~ta** have a wash and brushup

ripuls|i'one *nf* repulsion. **~'ivo** *a* a repulsive

ri'quadro *nm* square; (*pannello*) panel

ri'sacca *nf* undertow

ri'saia *nf* rice field, paddy field

risa'lire *vt* go back up ● *vi* ~ **a** (*nel tempo*) go back to; (*essere datato a*) date back to, go back to

risal'tare *vi* (*emergere*) stand out. **ri'salto** *nm* prominence; (*rilievo*) relief

risa'nare *vt* heal; (*bonificare*) reclaim

risa'puto *a* well-known

risarci'mento *nm* compensation. **risar'cire** *vt* indemnify

ri'sata *nf* laugh

riscalda'mento *nm* heating. ~ **autonomo** central heating (*for one flat*)

riscal'dar|e *vt* heat; warm (*persona*). **~si** *vr* warm up

riscat'tar|e *vt* ransom. **~si** *vr* redeem oneself. **ri'scatto** *nm* ransom; (*morale*) redemption

rischia'rar|e *vt* light up; brighten (*colore*). **~si** *vr* light up; (*cielo:*) clear up

rischi'are *vt* risk ● *vi* run the risk. **'rischio** *nm* risk. **~'oso** *a* risky

risciac'quare *vt* rinse. **risci'acquo** *nm* rinse

riscon'trare *vt* (*confrontare*) compare; (*verificare*) check; (*rilevare*) find. **ri'scontro** *nm* comparison; check; (*Comm: risposta*) reply

ri'scossa *nf* revolt; (*riconquista*) recovery

riscossi'one *nf* collection

ri'scosso *pp di* **riscuotere**

riscu'oter|e *vt* shake; (*percepire*)

draw; (*ottenere*) gain; cash (*assegno*). **~si** *vr* rouse oneself

risen'ti|re *vt* hear again; (*provare*) feel ● *vi* **~re di** feel the effect of. **~rsi** *vr* (*offendersi*) take offence. **~to** *a* resentful

ri'serbo *nm* reserve; **mantenere il ~** remain tight-lipped

ri'serva *nf* reserve; (*di caccia, pesca*) preserve; *Sport* substitute, reserve. **~ di caccia** game reserve. **~ indiana** Indian reservation. **~ naturale** wildlife reserve

riser'va|re *vt* reserve; (*prenotare*) book; (*per occasione*) keep. **~rsi** *vr* (*ripromettersi*) plan for oneself (*cambiamento*). **~'tezza** *nf* reserve. **~to** *a* reserved

ri'siedere *vi* **~ a** a reside in

'riso[1] *pp di* **ridere** ● *nm* (*pl nf* **risa**) laughter; (*singolo*) laugh. **~'lino** *nm* giggle

'riso[2] *nm* (*cereale*) rice

ri'solto *pp di* **risolvere**

risolu|'tezza *nf* determination. **riso'luto** *a* resolute, determined. **~zi'one** *nf* resolution

ri'solver|e *vt* resolve; *Math* solve. **~si** *vr* (*decidersi*) decide; **~si in** turn into

riso'na|nza *nf* resonance; **aver ~nza** *fig* arouse great interest. **~re** *vi* resound; (*rimbombare*) echo

ri'sorgere *vi* rise again

risorgi'mento *nm* revival; (*storico*) Risorgimento

ri'sorsa *nf* resource; (*espediente*) resort

ri'sorto *pp di* **risorgere**

ri'sotto *nm* risotto

ri'sparmi *nmpl* (*soldi*) savings

risparmi'a|re *vt* save; (*salvare*) spare. **~'tore, ~'trice** *nmf* saver

ri'sparmio *nm* saving

rispecchi'are *vt* reflect

rispet'tabile *a* respectable. **~ità** *nf* respectability

rispet'tare *vt* respect; **farsi ~** command respect

rispet'tivo *a* respective

ri'spetto *nm* respect; **~ a** as regards; (*in paragone a*) compared to

rispet/tosa'mente *adv* respectfully. **~toso** *a* respectful

risplen'dente *a* shining. **ri'splendere** *vi* shine

rispon'den|te *a* **~te a** in keeping with. **~za** *nf* correspondence

ri'spondere *vt* answer; (*rimbeccare*) answer back; (*obbedire*) respond; **~ a** a reply to; **~ di** (*rendersi responsabile*) answer for

ri'spost|a *nf* answer, reply, (*reazione*) response. **~o** *pp di* **rispondere**

'rissa *nf* brawl. **ris'soso** *a* pugnacious

ristabi'lir|e *vt* re-establish. **~si** *vr* (*in salute*) recover

rista'gnare *vi* stagnate; (*sangue:*) coagulate. **ri'stagno** *nm* stagnation

ri'stampa *nf* reprint; (*azione*) reprinting. **ristam'pare** *vt* reprint

risto'rante *nm* restaurant

risto'ra|re *vt* refresh. **~rsi** *vr* liter take some refreshment; (*riposarsi*) take a rest. **~'tore, ~'trice** *nmf* (*proprietario di ristorante*) restaurateur; (*fornitore*) caterer ● *a* refreshing. **ri'storo** *nm* refreshment; (*sollievo*) relief

ristret'tezza *nf* narrowness; (*povertà*) poverty; **vivere in ristrettezze** live in straitened circumstances

ri'stretto *pp di* **restringere** ● *a* narrow; (*condensato*) condensed; (*limitato*) restricted; **di idee ristrette** narrow-minded

ristruttu'rare *vt* restructure, reorganize (*ditta*); refurbish (*casa*)

risucchi'are *vt* suck in. **ri'succhio** *nm* whirlpool; (*di corrente*) undertow

risul'ta|re *vi* result; (*riuscire*) turn out. **~to** *nm* result

risuo'nare *vi* (*grida, parola:*) echo; *Phys* resonate

risurrezi'one *nf* resurrection

risusci'tare *vt* resuscitate; *fig* revive ● *vi* return to life

risvegli'ar|e *vt* reawaken (*interesse*). **~si** *vr* wake up; (*natura:*) awake; (*desiderio:*) be aroused.

ri'sveglio *nm* waking up; (*dell'interessa*) revival; (*del desiderio*) arousal

ri'svolto *nm* (*di giacca*) lapel; (*di pantaloni*) turn-up, cuff *Am*; (*di manica*) cuff; (*di tasca*) flap; (*di libro*) inside flap

ritagli'are *vt* cut out. **ri'taglio** *nm* cutting; (*di stoffa*) scrap

ritar'da|re *vi* be late; (*orologio:*) be slow ● *vt* delay; slow down (*progresso*); (*differire*) postpone. **~'tario, -a** *nmf* late-comer. **~to** *a Psych* retarded

ri'tardo *nm* delay; **essere in ~** be late; (*volo:*) be delayed

ri'tegno *nm* reserve

rite'n|ere *vt* retain; deduct (*somma*); (*credere*) believe. **~uta** *nf* (*sul salario*) deduction

riti'ra|re *vt* throw back (*palla*); (*prelevare*) withdraw; (*riscuotere*) draw; collect (*pacco*). **~rsi** *vr* withdraw; (*stoffa:*) shrink; (*da attività*) retire; (*marea:*) recede. **~ta** *nf* retreat; (*WC*) toilet. **ri'tiro** *nm* withdrawal; *Relig* retreat; (*da attività*) retirement. **ritiro bagagli** baggage reclaim

'ritmo *nm* rhythm

'rito *nm* rite; **di ~** customary

ritoc'care *vt* (*correggere*) touch up. **ri'tocco** *nm* retouch

ritor'nare *vi* return; (*andare/venire indietro*) go/come back; (*ricorrere*) recur; (*ridiventare*) become again

ritor'nello *nm* refrain

ri'torno *nm* return

ritorsi'one *nf* retaliation

ri'trarre *vt* (*ritirare*) withdraw; (*distogliere*) turn away; (*rappresentare*) portray

ritrat'ta|re *vt* deal with again; retract (*dichiarazione*). **~zi'one** *nf* withdrawal, retraction

ritrat'tista *nmf* portrait painter.
ri'tratto *pp di* **ritrarre** ● *nm* portrait

ritro'sia *nf* shyness. **ri'troso** *a*
backward; *(timido)* shy; **a ritroso**
backwards; **ritroso a** reluctant to

ritrova'mento *nm (azione)* finding

ritro'va|re *vt* find [again]; regain
(salute). **~rsi** *vr* meet; *(di nuovo)*
meet again; *(capitare)* find oneself; *(raccapezzarsi)* see one's way.
~to *nm* discovery. **ri'trovo** *nm*
meeting-place; *(notturno)* nightclub

'ritto *a* upright; *(diritto)* straight

ritu'ale *a & nm* ritual

riunifi'ca|re *vt* reunify. **~rsi** *vr* be
reunited. **~zi'one** *nf* reunification

riuni'one *nf* meeting; *(fra amici)*
reunion

riu'nir|e *vt (unire)* join together;
(radunare) gather. **~si** *vr* be reunited; *(adunarsi)* meet

riu'sc'i|re *vi (aver successo)* succeed; *(in matematica ecc)* be good
(in at); *(aver esito)* turn out; **le è
riuscito simpatico** she found him
likeable. **~ta** *nf (esito)* result;
(successo) success

'riva *nf (di mare, lago)* shore; *(di
fiume)* bank

ri'val|e *nmf* rival. **~ità** *nf inv* rivalry

rivalutazi'one *nf* revaluation

rivan'gare *vt* dig up again

rive'dere *vt* see again; revise
(lezione); (verificare) check

rive'la|re *vt* reveal. **~rsi** *vr
(dimostrarsi)* turn out. **~'tore** *a*
a revealing ● *nm* *Techn* detector.
~zi'one *nf* revelation

ri'vendere *vt* resell

rivendi'ca|re *vt* claim. **~zi'one** *nf*
claim

ri'vendi|ta *nf (negozio)* shop.
~'tore, **~'trice** *nmf* retailer.
~'tore autorizzato authorized
dealer

ri'verbero *nm* reverberation; *(bagliore)* glare

rive'renza *nf* reverence; *(inchino)*
curtsy; *(di uomo)* bow

rive'rire *vt* respect; *(ossequiare)*
pay one's respects to

river'sar|e *vt* pour. **~si** *vr (fiume:)*
flow

river'sibile *a* reversible

rivesti'mento *nm* covering

rive'sti|re *vt (rifornire di abiti)*
clothe; *(ricoprire)* cover; *(internamente)* line; hold *(carica).* **~rsi** *vr*
get dressed again; *(per una festa)*
dress up

rivi'era *nf* coast; **la ~ ligure** the
Italian Riviera

ri'vincita *nf Sport* return match;
(vendetta) revenge

rivis'suto *pp di* **rivivere**

ri'vista *nf* review; *(pubblicazione)*
magazine; *Theat* revue; **passare
in ~** review

ri'vivere *vi* come to life again;
(riprendere le forze) revive ● *vt* relive

ri'volger|e *vt* turn; *(indirizzare)*
address; **~e da** *(distogliere)* turn
away from. **~si** *vr* turn round; **~si
a** *(indirizzarsi)* turn to

ri'volta *nf* revolt

rivol'tante *a* disgusting

rivol'tar|e *vt* turn [over]; *(mettendo
l'interno verso l'esterno)* turn inside out; *(sconvolgere)* upset. **~si**
vr (ribellarsi) revolt

rivol'tella *nf* revolver

rivoluzio'nar|e *vt* revolutionize.
~io, -a *a & nmf* revolutionary.
rivoluzi'one *nf* revolution; *(fig:
disordine)* chaos

riz'zar|e *vt* raise; *(innalzare)* erect;
prick up *(orecchie).* **~si** *vr* stand
up; *(capelli:)* stand on end;
(orecchie:) prick up

'roba *nf (personale)* belongings *pl*, stuff; *(faccenda)* thing; *(sl:
droga)* drugs *pl*; **~ da mattil** absolute madness!. **~ da mangiare**
food, things to eat

ro'baccia *nf* rubbish

robot | rotto

ro'bot *nm inv* robot. ~iz'zato *a* robotic

robu'stezza *nf* sturdiness, robustness; (*forza*) strength. ro'busto *a* sturdy, robust; (*forte*) strong

'rocca *nf* fortress. ~'forte *nf* stronghold

roc'chetto *nm* reel

'roccia *nf* rock

ro'daggio *nm* running in. ~re *vt* run in

'roder|e *vt* gnaw; (*corrodere*) corrode. ~si *vr* ~si da (*logorarsi*) be consumed with. rodi'tore *nm* rodent

rodo'dendro *nm* rhododendron

'rogna *nf* scabies *sg*; *fig* nuisance

ro'gnone *nm* Culin kidney

'rogo *nm* (*supplizio*) stake; (*per cadaveri*) pyre

'Roma *nf* Rome

Roma'nia *nf* Romania

ro'manico *a* Romanesque

ro'mano, -a *a & nmf* Roman

romanti'cismo *nm* romanticism.

ro'mantico *a* romantic

ro'man|za *nf* romance. ~'zato *a* romanticized. ~'zesco *a* fictional; (*stravagante*) wild, unrealistic. ~zi'ere *nm* novelist

ro'manzo *a* Romance ● *nm* novel. ~ d'appendice serial story. ~ giallo thriller

'rombo *nm* rumble; Math rhombus; (*pesce*) turbot

'romper|e *vt* break; break off (*relazione*); non ~e [le scatole]! (*fam: seccare*) don't be a pain [in the neck]!. ~si *vr* break; ~si una gamba break one's leg

rompi'capo *nm* nuisance, (*indovinello*) puzzle

rompi'collo *nm* daredevil; a ~ at breakneck speed

rompighi'accio *nm* ice-breaker

rompi'scatole *nmf inv fam* pain

'ronda *nf* rounds pl

ron'della *nf* Mech washer

ron'dine *nf* swallow

ron'done *nm* swift

ron'fare *vi* (*russare*) snore

ron'zare *vi* buzz; ~ attorno a qcno *fig* hang about sb

ron'zino *nm* jade

ron'zio *nm* buzz

'rosa *nf* rose. ~ dei venti wind rose ● *a & nm* (*colore*) pink. ro'saio *nm* rose-bush

ro'sario *nm* rosary

ro'sato *a* rosy ● *nm* (*vino*) rosé

'roseo *a* pink

ro'seto *nm* rose garden

rosicchi'are *vt* nibble; (*rodere*) gnaw

rosma'rino *nm* rosemary

'roso *pp di* rodere

roso'lare *vt* brown

roso'lia *nf* German measles

ro'sone *nm* rosette; (*apertura*) rose-window

'rospo *nm* toad

ros'setto *nm* (*per labbra*) lipstick

'rosso *a & nm* red; passare con il ~ jump a red light. ~ d'uovo yolk. ros'sore *nm* redness; (*della pelle*) flush

rosticce'ria *nf* shop selling cooked meat and other prepared food

ro'tabile *a* strada ~ carriageway

ro'taia *nf* rail; (*solco*) rut

ro'ta|re *vt/i* rotate. ~zi'one *nf* rotation

rote'are *vt/i* roll

ro'tella *nf* small wheel; (*di mobile*) castor

roto'lar|e *vt/i* roll. ~si *vr* roll [about]. 'rotolo *nm* roll; andare a rotoli go to rack and ruin

rotondità *nf* (*qualità*) roundness; ~ pl (*curve femminili*) curves. ro'tondo, -a *a* round ● *nf* (*spiazzo*) terrace

ro'tore *nm* rotor

'rotta[1] *nf* Naut, Aeron course; far ~ per make course for; fuori ~ off course

'rotta[2] *nf* a ~ di collo at breakneck speed; essere in ~ con be on bad terms with

rot'tame *nm* scrap; *fig* wreck

'rotto *pp di* rompere ● *a* broken; (*stracciato*) torn

rot'tura nf break; **che ~ di scatole!** fam what a pain!

'**rotula** nf kneecap

rou'lette nf inv roulette

rou'lotte nf inv caravan, trailer Am

rou'tine nf inv routine; **di ~** ⟨operazioni, controlli⟩ routine

ro'vente a scorching

'**rovere** nm ⟨legno⟩ oak

rovesci'ar|e vt ⟨buttare a terra⟩ knock over; ⟨sottosopra⟩ turn upside down; ⟨rivoltare⟩ turn inside out; spill ⟨liquido⟩; overthrow ⟨governo⟩; reverse ⟨situazione⟩. **~si** vr ⟨capovolgersi⟩ overturn; ⟨riversarsi⟩ pour. **ro'vescio** a ⟨contrario⟩ reverse; **alla rovescia** ⟨capovolto⟩ upside down; ⟨con l'interno all'esterno⟩ inside out ● nm reverse; ⟨nella maglia⟩ purl; ⟨di pioggia⟩ downpour; Tennis backhand

ro'vina nf ruin; ⟨crollo⟩ collapse

rovi'na|re vt ruin; ⟨guastare⟩ spoil ● vi crash. **~rsi** vr be ruined. **~to** a ⟨oggetto⟩ ruined. **rovi'noso** a ruinous

rovi'stare vt ransack

'**rovo** nm bramble

'**rozzo** a rough

R.R. abbr ⟨ricevuta di ritorno⟩ return receipt for registered mail

'**ruba** nf **andare a ~** sell like hot cakes

ru'bare vt steal

rubi'netto nm tap, faucet Am

ru'bino nm ruby

ru'brica nf ⟨in giornale⟩ column; ⟨in programma televisivo⟩ TV report; ⟨quaderno con indice⟩ address book. **~ telefonica** telephone and address book

'**rude** a rough

'**rudere** nm ruin

rudimen'tale a rudimentary. **rudi'menti** nmpl rudiments

ruffi'an|a nf procuress. **~o** nm pimp; ⟨adulatore⟩ bootlicker

'**ruga** nf wrinkle

'**ruggine** nf rust; **fare la ~** go rusty

rug'gi|re vi roar. **~to** nm roar

rugi'ada nf dew

ru'goso a wrinkled

rul'lare vi roll; Aeron taxi

rul'lino nm film

rul'lio nm rolling; Aeron taxiing

'**rullo** nm roll; Techn roller

rum nm inv rum

ru'meno, -a a & nmf Romanian

rumi'nare vt ruminate

ru'mor|e nm noise; fig rumour. **~eggi'are** vi rumble. **rumo'roso** a noisy; ⟨sonoro⟩ loud

ru'olo nm role; Theat role; **di ~** on the staff

ru'ota nf wheel; **andare a ~ libera** free-wheel. **~ di scorta** spare wheel

'**rupe** nf cliff

ru'rale a rural

ru'scello nm stream

'**ruspa** nf bulldozer

rus'sare vi snore

'**Russ|ia** nf Russia. **r~o, -a** a & nmf Russian; ⟨lingua⟩ Russian

'**rustico** a rural; ⟨carattere⟩ rough

rut'tare vi belch. '**rutto** nm belch

ru'vido a coarse

ruzzo'l|are vi tumble down. **~one** nm tumble; **cadere ruzzoloni** tumble down

Ss

'**sabato** nm Saturday

'**sabbi|a** nf sand. **~e** pl mobili quicksand. **~'oso** a sandy

sabo'ta|ggio nm sabotage. **~re** vt sabotage. **~'tore, ~'trice** nmf saboteur

'**sacca** nf bag. **~ da viaggio** travelling-bag

sacca'rina nf saccharin

sac'cente a pretentious ● nmf know-all

sacchegi'a|re vt sack; hum raid

⟨frigo⟩. ~'tore, ~'trice nmf plunderer. sac'cheggio nm sack

sac'chetto nm bag

'sacco nm sack; Anat sac; mettere nel ~ fig swindle; un ~ ⟨moltissimo⟩ a lot; un ~ di ⟨gran quantità⟩ lots of. ~ a pelo sleeping-bag

sacer'do|te nm priest. ~zio nm priesthood

sacra'mento nm sacrament

sacrifi'ca|re vt sacrifice. ~rsi vr sacrifice oneself. ~to a ⟨non valorizzato⟩ wasted. sacri'ficio nm sacrifice

sacri'legio nm sacrilege. sa'crilego a sacrilegious

'sacro a sacred ● nm Anat sacrum

sacro'santo a sacrosanct

'sadico, -a a sadistic ● nmf sadist. sa'dismo nm sadism

sa'etta nf arrow

sa'fari nm inv safari

'saga nf saga

sa'gace a shrewd

sag'gezza nf wisdom

saggi'are vt test

'saggio[1] nm ⟨scritto⟩ essay; ⟨prova⟩ proof; ⟨di metallo⟩ assay; ⟨campione⟩ sample; ⟨esempio⟩ example

'saggio[2] a wise ● nm ⟨persona⟩ sage

sag'gistica nf non-fiction

Sagit'tario nm Astr Sagittarius

'sagoma nf shape; ⟨profilo⟩ outline; che ~! fam what a character!. sago'mato a shaped

'sagra nf festival

sagre'stano nm sacristan. ~'stia nf sacristy

'sala nf hall, ⟨stanza⟩ room; ⟨salotto⟩ living room. ~ d'attesa waiting room. ~ da ballo ballroom. ~ d'imbarco departure lounge. ~ macchine engine room. ~ operatoria operating theatre Br, operating room Am. ~ parto delivery room. ~ da pranzo dining room

sa'lame nm salami

sala'moia nf brine

sa'lare vt salt

sa'lario nm wages pl

sa'lasso nm essere un ~ fig cost a fortune

sa'latini nmpl savouries ⟨eaten with aperitifs⟩

sa'lato a salty; ⟨costoso⟩ dear

sal'ciccia nf = salsiccia

sal'da|re vt weld; set ⟨osso⟩; pay off ⟨debito⟩; settle ⟨conto⟩; ~e a stagno solder. ~si vr ⟨Med: osso⟩ knit

salda'trice nf welder; ⟨a stagno⟩ soldering iron

salda'tura nf weld; ⟨azione⟩ welding; ⟨di osso⟩ knitting

'saldo a firm; ⟨resistente⟩ strong ● nm ⟨di conto⟩ settlement; ⟨svendita⟩ sale; Comm balance

'sale nm salt; restare di ~ be struck dumb [with astonishment]. ~ fine table salt. ~ grosso cooking salt. sali pl e tabacchi tobacconist's shop

'salice nm willow. ~ piangente weeping willow

sali'ente a outstanding; i punti salienti di un discorso the main points of a speech

sali'era nf salt-cellar

sa'lina nf salt-works sg

sa'li|re vi go/come up; ⟨levarsi⟩ rise; ⟨su treno⟩ get on; ⟨in macchina⟩ get in ● vt go/come up ⟨scale⟩. ~ta nf climb; ⟨aumento⟩ rise; in ~ta uphill

sa'liva nf saliva

'salma nf corpse

'salmo nm psalm

sal'mone nm & a inv salmon

sa'lone nm hall; ⟨salotto⟩ living room; ⟨di parrucchiere⟩ salon. ~ di bellezza beauty parlour

salo'pette nf inv dungarees pl

salot'tino nm bower

sa'lotto nm drawing room; ⟨soggiorno⟩ sitting room; ⟨mobili⟩ [three piece] suite; fare ~ chat

sal'pare vt/i sail; ~ l'ancora weigh anchor

'salsa nf sauce. ~ di pomodoro tomato sauce

sal'sedine nf saltiness

sal'siccia *nf* sausage
salsi'era *nf* sauce-boat
sal'ta|re *vi* jump; (*venir via*) come off; (*balzare*) leap; (*esplodere*) blow up; **~r fuori** spring from nowhere; (*oggetto cercato:*) turn up; **è ~to fuori che...** it emerged that...; **~re fuori con...** come out with...; **~re in aria** blow up; **~re in mente** spring to mind ●*vt* jump [over]; skip (*pasti, lezioni*); **Culin** sauté. **~to a Culin** sautéed
saltel'lare *vi* hop; (*di gioia*) skip
saltim'banco *nm* acrobat
'salto *nm* jump; (*balzo*) leap; (*dislivello*) drop; (*fig: omissione, lacuna*) gap; **fare un ~** (*a visitare*) drop in on; **in un ~** *fig* in a jiffy. **~ in alto** high jump. **~ con l'asta** pole-vault. **~ in lungo** long jump. **~ pagina** Comput page down
saltuaria'mente *adv* occasionally. **saltu'ario** *a* desultory; **lavoro saltuario** casual work
sa'lubre *a* healthy
salume'ria *nf* delicatessen. **sa'lumi** *nmpl* cold cuts
salu'tare *vt* greet; (*congedandosi*) say goodbye to; (*portare i saluti a*) give one's regards to; **Mil** salute ●*a* healthy
sa'lute *nf* health; **~!** (*dopo uno starnuto*) bless you!; (*a un brindisi*) cheers!
sa'luto *nm* greeting; (*di addio*) goodbye; **Mil** salute; **saluti** *pl* (*ossequi*) regards
'salva *nf* salvo; **sparare a salve** fire blanks
salvada'naio *nm* money box
salva'gente *nm* lifebelt; (*a giubbotto*) life-jacket; (*ciambella*) rubber ring; (*spartitraffico*) traffic island
salvaguar'dare *vt* safeguard. **salvagu'ardia** *nf* safeguard
sal'var|e *vt* save; (*proteggere*) protect. **~si** *vr* save oneself
salva'slip *nm inv* panty-liner
salva|'taggio *nm* rescue; Naut salvage; Comput saving; **battello di**

~taggio lifeboat. **~'tore, ~'trice** *nmf* saviour
sal'vezza *nf* safety; Relig salvation
'salvia *nf* sage
salvi'etta *nf* serviette
'salvo *a* safe ●*prep* except [for] ●*conj* ~ **che** (*a meno che*) unless; (*eccetto che*) except that
samari'tano, -a *a* & *nmf* Samaritan
sam'buco *nm* elder
san *nm* **S~ Francesco** Saint Francis
sa'nare *vt* heal
sana'torio *nm* sanatorium
san'cire *vt* sanction
'sandalo *nm* sandal; Bot sandalwood
'sangu|e *nm* blood; **al ~e** (*carne*) rare; **farsi cattivo ~e per** worry about; **occhi iniettati di ~e** bloodshot eyes. **~e freddo** composure; **a ~e freddo** in cold blood. **~'igno** *a* blood
sangui'naccio *nm* Culin black pudding
sangui'nante *a* bleeding
sangui'nar|e *vi* bleed. **~io** *a* bloodthirsty
sangui'noso *a* bloody
sangui'suga *nf* leech
sanità *nf* soundness; (*salute*) health. **~ mentale** sanity, mental health
sani'tario *a* sanitary; **Servizio S~** National Health Service
'sano *a* sound; (*salutare*) healthy; **~ di mente** sane; **~ come un pesce** as fit as a fiddle
San Sil'vestro *nm* New Year's Eve
santifi'care *vt* sanctify
'santo *a* holy; (*con nome proprio*) saint ●*nm* saint. **san'tone** *nm* guru. **santu'ario** *nm* sanctuary
sanzi'one *nf* sanction
sa'pere *vt* know; (*essere capace di*) be able to; (*venire a sapere*) hear; **saperla lunga** know a thing or two ●*vi* ~ **di** know about; (*aver sapore di*) taste of; (*aver odore di*)

smell of; **saperci fare** have the know-how ●*nm* knowledge

sapi'en|te *a* wise; (*esperto*) expert ●*nm* (*uomo colto*) sage. **~za** *nf* wisdom

sa'pone *nm* soap. **~ da bucato** washing soap. **sapo'netta** *nf* bar of soap

sa'pore *nm* taste. **saporita'mente** *adv* (*dormire*) soundly. **sapo'rito** *a* tasty

saputello, -a *a* & *nm sl* know-all, know-it-all *Am*

saraci'nesca *nf* roller shutter

sar'casmo *nm* sarcasm. **~tico** *a* sarcastic

Sar'degna *nf* Sardinia

sar'dina *nf* sardine

'sardo, -a *a* & *nmf* Sardinian

sar'donico *a* sardonic

'sarto, -a *nm* tailor ●*nf* dressmaker. **~'ria** *nf* tailor's; dressmaker's; (*arte*) couture

sas'sata *nf* blow with a stone; **prendere a sassate** stone. **'sasso** *nm* stone; (*ciottolo*) pebble

sassofo'nista *nmf* saxophonist. **sas'sofono** *nm* saxophone

sas'soso *a* stony

'Satana *nf* Satan. **sa'tanico** *a* satanic

sa'tellite *a inv* & *nm* satellite

sati'nato *a* glossy

'satira *nf* satire. **sa'tirico** *a* satirical

satu'ra|re *vt* saturate. **~zi'one** *nf* saturation. **'saturo** *a* saturated; (*pieno*) full

'sauna *nf* sauna

savoi'ardo *nm* (*biscotto*) sponge finger

sazi'a|re *vt* satiate. **~si** *vr* **~si di** *fig* grow tired of

sazietà *nf* **mangiare a ~** eat one's fill. **'sazio** *a* satiated

sbaciucchi'a|re *vt* smother with kisses. **~si** *vr* kiss and cuddle

sbada'ta|ggine *nf* carelessness; **è stata una ~ggine** it was careless. **~'mente** *adv* carelessly. **sba'dato** *a* careless

sbadigli'are *vi* yawn. **sba'diglio** *nm* yawn

sba'fa|re *vt* sponge. **~ta** *nf sl* nosh

'sbafo *nm* sponging; **a ~** (*gratis*) without paying

sbagli'a|re *vi* make a mistake; (*aver torto*) be wrong ●*vt* make a mistake in; **~e strada** go the wrong way; **~e numero** get the number wrong; *Teleph* dial a wrong number. **~si** *vr* make a mistake. **'sbaglio** *nm* mistake; **per sbaglio** by mistake

sbal'la|re *vt* unpack; *fam* screw up (*conti*) ●*vi fam* go crazy. **~ato** *a* (*squilibrato*) unbalanced. **'sballo** *nm fam* scream; (*per droga*) trip; **da sballo** *sl* terrific

sballot'tare *vt* toss about

sbalor'di|re *vt* stun ●*vi* be stunned. **~'tivo** *a* amazing. **~to** *a* stunned

sbal'za|re *vt* throw; (*da una carica*) dismiss ●*vi* bounce; (*saltare*) leap. **'sbalzo** *nm* bounce; (*sussulto*) jolt; (*di temperatura*) sudden change; **a sbalzi** in spurts; **a sbalzo** (*lavoro a rilievo*) embossed

sban'care *vt* bankrupt; **~ il banco** break the bank

sbanda'mento *nm* *Auto* skid; *Naut* list; *fig* going off the rails

sban'da|re *vi* *Auto* skid; *Naut* list. **~rsi** *vr* (*disperdersi*) disperse. **~ta** *nf* skid; *Naut* list; **prendere una ~ta per** get a crush on. **~to, -a** *a* mixed-up ●*nmf* mixed-up person

sbandie'rare *vt* wave; *fig* display

sbarac'care *vt/i* clear up

sbaragli'are *vt* rout. **sba'raglio** *nm* rout; **mettere allo sbaraglio** rout

sbaraz'zar|e *vt* clear. **~si** *vr* **~si di** get rid of

sbaraz'zino, -a *a* mischievous ●*nmf* scamp

sbar'ba|re *vt*, **~si** *vr* shave

sbar'care *vt/i* disembark; **~ il lunario** make ends meet. **'sbarco** *nm* landing; (*di merci*) unloading

'sbarra *nf* bar; (*di passaggio a li-*

vello) barrier. ~'**mento** nm barricade. **sbar'rare** vt bar; (*ostruire*) block; cross (*assegno*); (*spalancare*) open wide

sbatacchi'are vt/i sl bang, slam

'**sbatter|e** vt bang; slam, bang (*porta:*); (*urtare*) knock; Culin beat; flap (*ali*); shake (*tappeto*) ● vi bang; (*porta:*) slam, bang. ~**si** vr sl rush around; ~**sene di qcsa** not give a damn about sth. **sbat'tuto** a tossed; Culin beaten; fig run down

sba'va|re vi dribble; (*colore:*) smear. ~'**tura** nf smear; **senza** ~**ture** fig faultless

sbelli'carsi vr ~ **dalle risa** split one's sides [with laughter]

'**sberla** nf slap

sbia'di|re vt/i, ~**rsi** vr fade. ~**to** a faded; fig colourless

sbian'ca|re vt/i, ~**si** vr whiten

sbi'eco a slanting; **di** ~ on the slant; (*guardare*) sidelong; **guardare qcno di** ~ look askance at sb; **tagliare di** ~ cut on the bias

sbigot'ti|re vt dismay ● vi, ~**rsi** vr be dismayed. ~**to** a dismayed

sbilanci'ar|e vt unbalance ● vi (*perdere l'equilibrio*) overbalance. ~**si** vr lose one's balance

sbirci'a|re vt cast sidelong glances at. ~'**ta** nf furtive glance. ~'**tina** nf **dare una** ~ a sneak a glance at

sbizzar'rirsi vr satisfy one's whims

sbloc'care vt unblock; Mech release; decontrol (*prezzi*)

sboc'care vi ~ **in** (*fiume:*) flow into; (*strada:*) lead to; (*folla:*) pour into

sboc'cato a foul-mouthed

sbocci'are vi blossom

'**sbocco** nm flowing; (*foce*) mouth; Comm outlet

sbolo'gnare vt fam get rid of

'**sbornia** nf **prendere una** ~ get drunk

sbor'sare vt pay out

sbot'tare vi burst out

sbotto'nar|e vt unbutton. ~**si** vr (*fam: confidarsi*) open up; ~**si la camicia** unbutton one's shirt

sbra'carsi vr put on something more comfortable; ~ **dalle risate** fam split one's sides laughing

sbracci'a|rsi vr wave one's arms. ~**to** a bare-armed; (*abito*) sleeveless

sbrai'tare vi bawl

sbra'nare vt tear to pieces

sbricio'lar|e vt, ~**si** vr crumble

sbri'ga|re vt expedite; (*occuparsi di*) attend to. ~**rsi** vr be quick. ~'**tivo** a quick

sbrindel'la|re vt tear to shreds. ~**to** a in rags

sbro'do|lare vt stain. ~**one** nm messy eater, dribbler

'**sbronza** nf **prendersi una** ~**a** get tight. **sbron'zarsi** vr get tight. ~**o** a (*ubriaco*) tight

sbruffo'nata nf boast. **sbruf'fone, -a** nmf boaster

sbu'care vi come out

sbucci'ar|e vt peel; shell (*piselli*). ~**si** vr graze oneself

sbuf'fare vi snort; (*per impazienza*) fume. '**sbuffo** nm puff

'**scabbia** nf scabies sg

sca'broso a rough; fig difficult; (*scena*) indecent

scacci'are vt chase away

'**scacco** nm check; ~**hi** pl (*gioco*) chess; (*pezzi*) chessmen; **dare** ~**o matto** a checkmate; **a** ~**hi** (*tessuto*) checked. ~**hi'era** nf chess-board

sca'dente a shoddy

sca'de|nza nf (*di contratto*) expiry; Comm maturity; (*di progetto*) deadline; **a breve/lunga** ~**nza** short-/long-term. ~**re** vi expire; (*valore:*) decline; (*debito:*) be due. **sca'duto** a (*biglietto*) out-of-date

sca'fandro nm diving suit; (*di astronauta*) spacesuit

scaf'fale nm shelf; (*libreria*) bookshelf

'**scafo** nm hull

scagion'are vt exonerate

'**scaglia** *nf* scale; (*di sapone*) flake; (*scheggia*) chip

scagli'ar|e *vt* fling. **~si** *vr* fling oneself; **~si contro** *fig* rail against

scagli|o'nare *vt* space out. **~'one** *nm* group; **a ~oni** in groups. **~one di reddito** tax bracket

'**scala** *nf* staircase; (*portatile*) ladder; (*Mus, misura, fig*) scale; **scale** *pl* stairs. **~ mobile** escalator; (*dei salari*) cost of living index

sca'la|re *vt* climb; layer (*capelli*); (*detrarre*) deduct. **~ta** *nf* climb; (*dell'Everest ecc*) ascent; **fare delle ~te** go climbing. **~'tore, ~'trice** *nmf* climber

scalca'gnato *a* down at heel

scalci'are *vi* kick

scalci'nato *a* shabby

scalda'bagno *nm* water heater

scalda'muscoli *nm inv* leg-warmer

scal'dar|e *vt* heat. **~si** *vr* warm up; (*eccitarsi*) get excited

scal'fi|re *vt* scratch. **~t'tura** *nf* scratch

scalli'nata *nf* flight of steps. **sca'lino** *nm* step; (*di scala a pioli*) rung

scalma'narsi *vr* get worked up

'**scalo** *nm* slipway; Aeron, Naut port of call; **fare ~** a call at; Aeron land at

sca'lo|gna *nf* bad luck. **~'gnato** *a* unlucky

scalo'ppina *nf* escalope

scal'pello *nm* chisel

scalpi'tare *vi* paw the ground, *fig* champ at the bit

'**scalpo** *nm* scalp

scal'pore *nm* noise; **far ~** *fig* cause a sensation

scal'trezza *nf* shrewdness. **scal'trirsi** *vr* get shrewder. '**scaltro** *a* shrewd

scal'zare *vt* bare the roots of (*albero*); *fig* undermine; (*da una carica*) oust

'**scalzo** *a & adv* barefoot

scambi'are *vt* exchange; **~are qcno per qualcun altro** mistake sb for somebody else. **~'evole** *a* reciprocal

'**scambio** *nm* exchange; Comm trade; **libero ~** free trade

scamosci'ato *a* suede

scampa'gnata *nf* trip to the country

scampa'nato *a* (*gonna*) flared

scampanel'lata *nf* [loud] ring

soam'pare *vt* save; (*evitare*) escape; **scamparla bella** have a lucky escape. '**scampo** *nm* escape

'**scampolo** *nm* remnant

scanala'tura *nf* groove

scanda'listico *a* sensational

scandaliz'zare *vt* scandalize. **~iz'zarsi** *vr* be scandalized

'**scandalo** *nm* scandal. **~'loso** *a* (*somma ecc*) scandalous; (*fortuna*) outrageous

Scandi'navia *nf* Scandinavia.
scandi'navo, -a *a & nmf* Scandinavian

scan'dire *vt* scan (*verso*); pronounce clearly (*parole*)

scan'nare *vt* slaughter

scanneriz'zare *vt* Comput scan

scansafa'tiche *nmf inv* lazybones

scan'sar|e *vt* shift; (*evitare*) avoid. **~si** *vr* get out of the way

scansi'one *nf* Comput scanning

'**scanso** *nm* **a ~ di** in order to avoid; **a ~ di equivoci** to avoid any misunderstanding

scanti'nato *nm* basement

scanto'nare *vi* turn the corner; (*svignarsela*) sneak off

scanzo'nato *a* easy-going

scapacci'one *nm* smack

scape'strato *a* dissolute

'**scapito** *nm* loss. **a ~ di** to the detriment of

'**scapola** *nf* shoulder-blade

'**scapolo** *nm* bachelor

scappa'mento *nm Auto* exhaust

scap'pare *vi* escape; (*andarsene*) dash [off]; (*sfuggire*) slip; **mi ~ da ridere!** I want to burst out laughing; **mi ~ la pipì** I'm bursting; I need a pee. **~ta** *nf* short visit. **~'tella** *nf* escapade; (*infedeltà*) fling. **~'toia** *nf* way out

scappel'lotto *nm* cuff

scara'bocchio *nm* scribble

scara'faggio *nm* cockroach

scara'mantico *a* (*gesto*) to ward off the evil eye

scara'muccia *nf* skirmish

scarabocchi'are *vt* scribble

scaraven'tare *vt* hurl

scarce'rare *vt* release [from prison]

scardi'nare *vt* unhinge

'scarica *nf* discharge; (*di arma da fuoco*) volley; *fig* shower

scari'ca|re *vt* discharge; unload (*arma, merci*); (*di orologio, batteria:*) flow; (*orologio, batteria:*) run-down; *fig* unwind. **~rsi** *vr* (*fiume:*) flow; (*orologio, batteria:*) flow; *fig* unwind. **~'tore** *nm* loader; (*di porto*) docker. **'scarico** *a* unloaded; (*vuoto*) empty; (*orologio*) run-down; (*batteria*) flat; *fig* untroubled ● *nm* unloading; (*di rifiuti*) dumping; (*di acqua*) draining; (*di sostanze inquinanti*) discharge; (*luogo rubbish*) dump; *Auto* exhaust; (*idraulico*) drain; (*tubo*) waste pipe

scarlat'tina *nf* scarlet fever

scar'latto *a* scarlet

'scarno *a* thin; (*fig: stile*) bare

sca'ro|gna *nf fam* bad luck. **~'gnato** *a fam* unlucky

'scarpa *nf* shoe; (*fam: persona*) dead loss. **scarpe** *pl* **da ginnastica** trainers, gym shoes

scar'pata *nf* slope; (*burrone*) escarpment

scarpi'nare *vi* hike

scar'pone *nm* boot. **scarponi** *pl* **da sci** ski boot. **scarponi** *pl* **da trekking** walking boots

scarroz'zare *vt/i* drive around

scarseggi'are *vi* be scarce; (*mancare*) be short of

scar'sezza *nf* scarcity, shortage. **scarsità** *nf* shortage. **'scarso** *a* scarce; (*manchevole*) short

scarta'mento *nm Rail* gauge. **~ ridotto** narrow gauge

scar'tare *vt* discard; unwrap (*pacco*); (*respingere*) reject ● *vi* (*deviare*) swerve. **'scarto** *nm* scrap; (*in carte*) discard; (*deviazione*) swerve; (*distacco*) gap

scar'toffie *nfpl* bumf, bumph

scas'sa|re *vt* break. **~to** *a fam* clapped out

scassi'nare *vt* force open

scassina'tore, -'trice *nmf* burglar. **'scasso** *nm* (*furto*) house-breaking

scate'na|re *vt fig* stir up. **~rsi** *vr* break out; (*fig: temporale:*) break; (*fam: infiammarsi*) get excited. **~to** *a* crazy

'scatola *nf* box; (*di latta*) can, tin *Br*; **in ~** (*cibo*) canned, tinned *Br*; **rompere le scatole a qcno** *fam* get on sb's nerves

scat'tare *vi* go off; (*balzare*) spring up; (*adirarsi*) lose one's temper; take (*foto*). **'scatto** *nm* (*balzo*) spring; (*d'ira*) outburst; (*di telefono*) unit; (*dispositivo*) release; **a scatti** jerkily; **di scatto** suddenly

scatu'rire *vi* spring

scaval'care *vt* jump over (*muretto*); climb over (*muro*); (*fig: superare*) overtake

sca'vare *vt* dig (*buca*); dig up (*tesoro*); excavate (*città sepolta*). **'scavo** *nm* excavation

scazzot'tata *nf fam* punch-up

'scegliere *vt* choose, select

scelle'rato *a* wicked

'scel|ta *nf* choice; (*di articoli*) range; **...a ~a** (*in menù*) choice of...; **prendine uno a ~a** take your choice o pick; **di prima ~a** top-grade, choice. **~o** *pp* *di* **scegliere** ● *a* select; (*merce ecc*) choice

sce'mare *vt/i* diminish

sce'menza *nf* silliness; (*azione*) silly thing to do/say. **'scemo** *a* silly

'scempio *nm* havoc; (*fig: di pae-*

saggio) ruination; **fare ~ di** play havoc with

'scena *nf* scene; (*palcoscenico*) stage; **entrare in ~** go/come on; *fig* enter the scene; **fare ~** put on an act; **fare una ~** make a scene; **andare in ~** *Theat* be staged, be put on. **sce'nario** *nm* scenery

sce'nata *nf* row, scene

'scendere *vi* go/come down; (*da treno, autobus*) get off; (*da macchina*) get out; (*strada:*) slope; (*notte, prezzin foll* ● *vt* go/come down (*scale*)

sceneggi'are *vt* dramatize. **~to** *nm* television serial. **~'tura** *nf* screenplay

'scenico *a* scenic

scervel'larsi *vr* rack one's brains. **~to** *a* brainless

'sceso *pp di* **scendere**

scetti'cismo *nm* scepticism. **'scettico, -a** *a* sceptical ● *nmf* sceptic

'scettro *nm* sceptre

'scheda *nf* card. **~ elettorale** ballot-paper. **~ di espansione** *Comput* expansion card. **~ perforata** punch card. **~ telefonica** phonecard. **sche'dare** *vt* file. **sche'dario** *nm* file; (*mobile*) filing cabinet

'schedina *nf* ≈ pools coupon; **giocare la ~** do the pools

'scheggia *nf* fragment; (*di legno*) splinter. **~'arsi** *vr* chip; (*legno:*) splinter

'scheletro *nm* skeleton

'schema *nm* diagram; (*abbozzo*) outline. **sche'matico** *a* schematic. **~tiz'zare** *vt* schematize

'scherma *nf* fencing

scher'mirsi *vr* protect oneself

'schermo *nm* screen; **grande ~** big screen

scher'nire *vt* mock. **'scherno** *nm* mockery

scher'zare *vi* joke; (*giocare*) play

'scherzo *nm* joke; (*trucco*) trick; (*effetto*) play; *Mus* scherzo; **fare uno ~ a** qcno play a joke on sb;

per ~ for fun; **stare allo ~** take a joke. **scher'zoso** *a* playful

schiaccia'noci *nm inv* nutcrackers *pl*

schiacci'ante *a* damning

schiacci'are *vt* crush; *Sport* smash; press (*pulsante*); crack (*noce*); **~ un pisolino** grab forty winks

schiaffeggi'are *vt* slap. **schi'affo** *nm* slap; **dare uno schiaffo a** slap

schiamaz'zare *vi* make a racket; (*galline:*) cackle

schian'tare *vt* break. **~si** *vr* crash ● **mi schianta dalla fatica** I'm wiped out. **'schianto** *nm* crash; *fam* knock-out; (*divertente*) scream

schia'rire *vt* clear; (*sbiadire*) fade ● *vi*, **~si** *vr* brighten up; **~si la gola** clear one's throat

schiavitù *nf* slavery. **schi'avo, -a** *nmf* slave

schi'ena *nf* back; **mal di ~** backache. **schi'nale** *nm* (*di sedia*) back

schi'er|a *nf Mil* rank; (*moltitudine*) crowd. **~'amento** *nm* lining up

schie'rare *vt* draw up. **~si** *vr* draw up; **~si con** (*parteggiare*) side with

schi'ettezza *nf* frankness. **schi'etto** *a* frank; (*puro*) pure

schi'fezza *nf* **una ~** rubbish. **schifil'toso** *a* fussy. **'schifo** *nm* disgust; **mi fa schifo** it makes me sick. **schi'foso** *a* disgusting; (*di cattiva qualità*) rubbishy

schioc'care *vt* crack; snap (*dita*). **schi'occo** *nm* (*di frusta*) crack; (*di bacio*) smack; (*di dita, lingua*) click

schi'oppo *nm* **ad un tiro di ~** a stone's throw away

schi'uder|e *vt*, **~si** *vr* open

schi'um|a *nf* foam; (*di sapone*) lather; (*feccia*) scum. **~ma da barba** shaving foam. **~'mare** *vt* skim ● *vi* foam

schi'uso *pp di* **schiudere** ●

schi'vare vt avoid. **'schivo** a bashful

schizo'frenico a schizophrenic

schiz'zare vt squirt; (inzaccherare) splash; (abbozzare) sketch ● vi spurt; **~ via** scurry away

schiz'zato, -a a & nmf sl loony

schizzi'noso a squeamish

'schizzo nm squirt; (di fango) splash; (abbozzo) sketch

sci nm inv ski; (sport) skiing. **~ d'acqua** water-skiing

'scia nf wake; (di fumo ecc) trail

sci'abola nf sabre

sciabor'dare vt/i lap

scia'callo nm jackal; fig profiteer

sciac'quare vt rinse. **~si** vr rinse oneself. **sciac'quo** nm mouthwash

scia'gura nf disaster. **~'rato** a unfortunate; (scellerato) wicked

scialac'quare vt squander

scia'lare vi spend money like water

sci'albo a pale; fig dull

sci'alle nm shawl

scia'luppa nf dinghy. **~ di salvataggio** lifeboat

sci'ame nm swarm

sci'ampo nm shampoo

scian'cato a lame

sci'are vi ski

sci'arpa nf scarf

sci'atica nf Med sciatica

scia'tore, -'trice nmf skier

sci'atto a slovenly; (stile) careless. **sciat'tone, -a** nmf slovenly person

scienti'fico a scientific

sci'enza nf science; (sapere) knowledge. **~i'ato, -a** nmf scientist

'scimmi|a nf monkey. **~ot'tare** vt ape

scimpanzé nm inv chimpanzee, chimp

scimu'nito a idiotic

'scinder|e vt, **~si** vr split

scin'tilla nf spark. **scintil'lante** a sparkling. **scintil'lare** vi sparkle

scioc'ca|nte a shocking. **~re** vt shock

scioc'chezza nf foolishness; (assurdità) nonsense. **sci'occo** a foolish

sci'oglier|e vt untie; undo, untie (nodo); (liberare) release; (liquefare) melt; dissolve (contratto, qcsa nell'acqua); loosen up (muscoli). **~si** vr release oneself; (liquefarsi) melt; (contratto:) be dissolved; (pastiglia:) dissolve

sciogli'lingua nm inv tonguetwister

scio'lina nf wax

sciol'tezza nf agility; (disinvoltura) ease

sci'olto pp di **sciogliere** ● a loose; (agile) agile; (disinvolto) easy; **versi sciolti** blank verse sg

sciope'ra|nte nmf striker. **~re** vi go on strike, strike. **sci'opero** nm strike. **sciopero a singhiozzo** onoff strike

sciori'nare vt fig show off

sci'pito a insipid

scip'pa|re vt fam snatch. **~'tore, ~'trice** nmf bag snatcher. **'scippo** nm bag-snatching

sci'rocco nm sirocco

sciropp'ato a (frutta) in syrup. **sci'roppo** nm syrup

'scisma nm schism

scissi'one nf division

'scisso pp di **scindere**

sciu'par|e vt spoil; (sperperare) waste. **~si** vr get spoiled; (deperire) wear oneself out. **sciu'pio** nm waste

scivo'l|are vi slide; (involontariamente) slip. **'scivolo** nm slide; Techn chute. **~oso** a slippery

scle'rosi nf sclerosis

scoc'care vt shoot ● vi (scintilla:) shoot out; (ora:) strike

scocci'a|re vt (dare noia a) bother. **~rsi** vr be bothered. **~to** a fam narked. **~'tore, ~'trice** nmf bore. **~'tura** nf nuisance

sco'della nf bowl

scodinzo'lare vi wag its tail

scogli'era nf cliff; (a fior d'acqua)

reef. **'scoglio** nm rock; (fig: ostacolo) stumbling block

scoi'attolo nm squirrel

scola'pasta nm inv colander.
~**pi'atti** nm inv dish drainer

sco'lara nf schoolgirl

sco'lare vt drain; strain (pasta, verdura) ● vi drip

sco'la|ro nm schoolboy. ~**'resca** nf pupils pl. ~**stico** a school attrib

scoli'osi nf curvature of the spine

scol'la|re vt cut away the neck of (abito); (staccare) unstick. ~**to** a (abito); (staccare) low-necked. ~**'tura** nf neckline

'scolo nm drainage

scolo'ri|re vt, ~**rsi** vr fade. ~**to** a faded

scol'pire vt carve; (imprimere) engrave

scombi'nare vt upset

scombus'so|lare vt muddle up

scom'mess|a nf bet. ~**o** pp di **scommettere**. **scom'mettere** vt bet

scomo'dar|e vt, ~**si** vr trouble.
scomodità nf discomfort. **'scomodo** a uncomfortable ● nm **essere di scomodo a qcno** be a trouble to sb

scompa'rire vi disappear; (morire) pass on. **scom'parsa** nf disappearance; (morte) passing, death. **scom'parso, -a** pp di **scomparire** ● nmf departed

scompar'ti|mento nm compartment. **scom'parto** nm compartment

scom'penso nm imbalance

scompigli'are vt disarrange. **scom'piglio** nm confusion

scom'po|rre vt take to pieces; (fig: turbare) upset. ~**rsi** vr get flustered, lose one's composure. ~**sto** pp di **scomporre** ● a (sguaiato) unseemly; (disordinato) untidy

sco'muni|ca nf excommunication. ~**'care** vt excommunicate

sconcer'tare vt disconcert; (rendere perplesso) bewilder. ~**to** a disconcerted; bewildered

scon'cezza nf obscenity. **'sconcio** a (osceno) dirty ● nm **è uno sconcio che...** it's a disgrace that...

conclusio'nato a incoherent

scon'dito a unseasoned; (insalata) with no dressing

sconfes'sare vt disown

scon'figgere vt defeat

sconfi'na|re vi cross the border; (in proprietà privata) trespass. ~**to** a unlimited

scon'fitt|a nf defeat. ~**o** pp di **sconfiggere**

scon'forto nm dejection

sconge'lare vt thaw out (cibo), defrost

scongiu'rare vt beseech; (evitare) avert. **scon'giuro** nm **fare gli scongiuri** touch wood, knock on wood Am

scon'nesso pp di **sconnettere** ● a fig incoherent. **scon'nettere** vt disconnect

sconosci'uto, -a a unknown ● nmf stranger

sconquas'sare vt smash; (sconvolgere) upset

conside'rato a inconsiderate

sconsigli'a|bile a not advisable. ~**re** vt advise against

sconso'lato a disconsolate

scon'ta|re vt discount; (dedurre) deduct; (pagare) pay off; serve (pena). ~**to** a discount; (ovvio) expected; ~**to del 10%** with 10% discount; **dare qcsa per ~to** take sth for granted

scon'tento a displeased ● nm discontent

'sconto nm discount; **fare uno ~** give a discount

scon'trarsi vr clash; (urtare) collide

scon'trino nm ticket; (di cassa) receipt

'scontro nm clash; (urto) collision

scon'troso a unsociable

sconveni'ente a unprofitable; (scorretto) unseemly

sconvol'gente a mind-blowing

scon'vol|gere vt upset; (mettere in disordine) disarrange. ~**gi'mento**

nm upheaval. **~to** *pp di* **sconvolgere ● a** distraught

'scopa *nf* broom. **sco'pare** *vt* sweep; *vulg* shag, screw

scoperchi'are *vt* take the lid off *(pentola)*; take the roof off *(casa)*

sco'pert|a *nf* discovery. **~o** *pp di* **scoprire ● a** uncovered; *(senza riparo)* exposed; *(conto)* overdrawn; *(spoglio)* bare

'scopo *nm* aim; **allo ~ di** in order to

scoppi'are *vi* burst; *fig* break out. **scoppiet'tare** *vi* crackle. **'scoppio** *nm* burst; *(di guerra)* outbreak; *(esplosione)* explosion

sco'prire *vt* discover; *(togliere la copertura a)* uncover

scoraggi'ante *a* discouraging

scoraggi'a|re *vt* discourage. **~rsi** *vr* lose heart

scor'butico *a* peevish

scorcia'toia *nf* short cut

'scorcio *nm (di epoca)* end; *(di cielo)* patch; *(in arte)* foreshortening; **di ~** *(vedere)* from an angle. **~ panoramico** panoramic view

scor'da|re *vt*, **~rsi** *vr* forget. **~to a** *Mus* out of tune

sco'reggi|a *nf fam* fart. **~'are** *vi fam* fart

'scorgere *vt* make out; *(notare)* notice

scoria *nf* waste; *(di metallo, carbone)* slag; **scorie** *pl* **radioattive** radioactive waste

scor'nato *a fig* hangdog. **'scorno** *nm* humiliation

scorpacci'ata *nf* bellyful; **fare una ~ di** stuff oneself with

scorpi'one *nm* scorpion; *Astr* Scorpio

scorraz'zare *vi* run about

'scorrere *vt (dare un'occhiata)* glance through ● *vi* run; *(scivolare)* slide; *(fluire)* flow; *Comput* scroll. **scor'revole a porta scorrevole** sliding door

scorre'ria *nf* raid

scorret'tezza *nf (mancanza di educazione)* bad manners *pl*. **scor-**

'retto *a* incorrect; *(sconveniente)* improper

scorri'banda *nf* raid; *fig* excursion

'scors|a *nf* glance. **~o** *pp di* **scorrere ● a** last

scor'solo a nodo ~ noose

'scor|ta *nf* escort; *(provvista)* supply. **~'tare** *vt* escort

scor'te|se *a* discourteous. **~'sia** *nf* discourtesy

scorti'ca|re *vt* skin. **~'tura** *nf* graze

'scorto *pp di* **scorgere**

'scorza *nf* peel; *(crosta)* crust; *(corteccia)* bark

sco'sceso *a* steep

'scossa *nf* shake; *Electr, fig* shock; **prendere la ~** get an electric shock. **~ elettrica** electric shock. **~ sismica** earth tremor

'scosso *pp di* **scuotere ● a** shaken; *(sconvolto)* upset

sco'stante *a* off-putting

sco'sta|re *vt* push away. **~rsi** *vr* stand aside

scostu'mato *a* dissolute; *(maleducato)* ill-mannered

scot'tante *a (argomento)* dangerous

scot'ta|re *vt* scald ● *vi* burn; *(bevanda:)* be too hot; *(sole, pentola:)* be very hot. **~rsi** *vr* burn oneself; *(al sole)* get sunburnt; *fig* get one's fingers burnt. **~'tura** *nf* burn; *(da liquido)* scald; **~'tura solare** sunburn; *fig* painful experience

'scotto *a* overcooked

sco'vare *vt (scoprire)* discover

'Scoz|ia *nf* Scotland. **~'zese** *a* Scottish ● *nmf* Scot

scredi'tare *vt* discredit

scre'mare *vt* skim

screpo'la|re *vt*, **~rsi** *vr* crack. **~to** *a (labbra)* chapped. **~'tura** *nf* crack

screzi'ato *a* speckled

'screzio *nm* disagreement

scribac|chi'are *vt* scribble. **~'chino, -a** *nmf* scribbler; *(impiegato)* penpusher

scricchio'l|are vi creak. **~io** nm creaking

'scricciolo nm wren

'scrigno nm casket

scrimina'tura nf parting

'scrit|ta nf writing; (su muro) graffiti. **~to** pp di **scrivere ●a** written **●**nm writing; (lettera) letter. **~'toio** nm writing-desk. **~'tore, ~'trice** nmf writer. **~'tura** nf writing; Relig scripture

scrittu'rare vt engage

scriva'nia nf desk

'scrivere vt write; (descrivere) write about; **~ a macchina** type

scroc'c|are vi **~are** a sponge of life. **'scrocco** nm **a scrocco** fam without paying; **vivere a scrocco** sponge off other people. **~one, ~a** nmf sponger

'scrofa nf sow

scrol'lar|e vt shake; **~e le spalle** shrug one's shoulders. **~si** vr shake oneself; **~si qcsa di dosso** shake sth off

scrosci'are vi roar; (pioggia:) pelt down. **'scroscio** nm roar; (di pioggia) pelting; **uno scroscio di applausi** thunderous applause

scro'star|e vt scrape. **~si** vr peel off

'scrupolo nm scruple; (diligenza) care; **senza scrupoli** unscrupulous, without scruples. **~'loso** a scrupulous

scru'ta|re vt scan; (indagare) search. **~'tore** nm (alle elezioni) returning officer

scruti'nare vt scrutinize. **scru'tinio** nm (di voti alle elezioni) poll; Sch assessment of progress

scu'cire vt unstitch. **scuci i soldi!** fam cough up [the money]!

scude'ria nf stable

scu'detto nm Sport championship shield

'scudo nm shield

sculacci'a|re vt spank. **~'ata** nf spanking. **~'one** nm spanking

sculet'tare vi wiggle one's hips

scul'tore, -'trice nm sculptor **●**nf sculptress. **~'tura** nf sculpture

scu'ola nf school. **~ elementare** primary school. **~ guida** driving school. **~ materna** day nursery. **~ media** secondary school. **~ media [inferiore]** secondary school (10-13). **~ [media] superiore** secondary school (13-18). **~ dell'obbligo** compulsory education

scu'oter|e vt shake. **~si** vr (destarsi) rouse oneself; **~si di dosso** shake off

'scure nf axe

scu'reggia nf fam fart. **scureggi'are** vi fam fart

scu'rire vt/i darken

'scuro a dark **●**nm darkness; (imposta) shutter

scur'rile a scurrilous

'scusa nf excuse; (giustificazione) apology; **chiedere ~** apologize; **chiedo ~!** I'm sorry!

scu'sar|e vt excuse. **~si** vr **~si apologize (di for); [mi] scusi!** excuse me!; (chiedendo perdono) [I'm] sorry!

sdebi'tarsi vr (disobbligarsi) repay a kindness

sde'gna|re vt despise. **~rsi** vr get angry. **~to** a indignant. **'sdegno** nm disdain. **sde'gnoso** a disdainful

sden'tato a toothless

sdolci'nato a sentimental, schmaltzy

sdoppi'are vt halve

sdrai'arsi vr lie down. **'sdraio** nm [sedia a] sdraio deckchair

sdrammatiz'zare ni provide some comic relief

sdruccio'l|are vi slither. **~evole** a slippery

se conj if; (interrogativo) whether, if; **se mai** (caso mai) if need be; **se mai telefonasse,...** should he call,..., if he calls,..., be otherwise, or else; **se non altro** at least, if nothing else; **se pure** (sebbene) even though; (anche se) even if; **non so se sia vero** I don't know whether it's true, I don't know if it's true; **come se as if; se lo avessi saputo prima!** if only I had known before!; **e se andassimo fuori a cena?** how about going out for dinner? ● *nm inv* if

sé *pers pron* oneself; (*lui*) himself; (*lei*) herself; (*esso, essa*) itself; (*loro*) themselves; **l'ha fatto da sé** he did it himself; **ha preso i soldi con sé** he took the money with him; **si sono tenuti le notizie per sé** they kept the news to themselves

seb'bene *conj* although

'secca *nf* shallows *pl*; **in ~** (*nave*) aground

sec'cante *a* annoying

sec'ca|re *vt* dry; (*importunare*) annoy ● *vi* dry up. **~rsi** *vr* dry up; (*irritarsi*) get annoyed; (*annoiarsi*) get bored. **~'tore, ~'trice** *nmf* nuisance. **~'tura** *nf* bother

secchi'ello *nm* pail

'secchio *nm* bucket. **~ della spazzatura** rubbish bin, trash can *Am*

'secco, -a *a* dry; (*disseccato*) dried; (*magro*) thin; (*brusco*) curt; (*preciso*) sharp; **restare a ~** be left penniless; **restarci ~** (*fam: morire di colpo*) be killed on the spot ● *nm* (*siccità*) drought; **lavare a ~** dry-clean

secessi'one *nf* secession

seco'lare *a* age-old; (*laico*) secular. **'secolo** *nm* century; (*epoca*) age; **è un secolo che non lo vedo** *fam* I haven't seen him for ages o yonks

se'cond|a *nf* *Sch, Rail* second class; *Auto* second [gear]. **~o a** *a* second ● *nm* second; (*secondo piatto*) main course ● *prep* according to; **~o me** in my opinion

secondo'genito, -a *a & nm* second-born

secrezi'one *nf* secretion

'sedano *nm* celery

seda'tivo *a & nm* sedative

'sede *nf* seat; (*centro*) centre; *Relig* see; *Comm* head office. **~ sociale** registered office

seden'tario *a* sedentary

se'der|e *vi* sit. **~si** *vr* sit down ● *nm* (*deretano*) bottom

'sedia *nf* chair. **~ a dondolo** rocking chair. **~ a rotelle** wheelchair

sedi'cente *a* self-styled

'sedici *a & nm* sixteen

se'dile *nm* seat

sedizi'o|ne *nf* sedition. **~so a** seditious

se'dotto *pp di* **sedurre**

sedu'cente *a* seductive; (*allettante*) enticing

se'durre *vt* seduce

se'duta *nf* session; (*di posa*) sitting. **~ stante** *adv* here and now

seduzi'one *nf* seduction

'sega *nf* saw; *vulg* wank

se'gale *nf* rye

se'gare *vt* saw

sega'tura *nf* sawdust

'seggio *nm* seat. **~ elettorale** polling station

seg'gio|la *nf* chair. **~'lino** *nm* seat; (*da bambino*) child's seat. **~'lone** *nm* (*per bambini*) high chair

seggio'via *nf* chair lift

seghe'ria *nf* sawmill

se'ghetto *nm* hacksaw

seg'mento *nm* segment

segna'la|re *vt* signal; (*annunciare*) announce; (*indicare*) point out. **~si** *vr* distinguish oneself

se'gnale *nm* signal; (*stradale*) sign. **~le acustico** beep. **~le orario** time signal. **~letica** *nf* signals *pl*. **~letica stradale** road signs *pl*

segna'libro *nm* bookmark

se'gnar|e *vt* mark; (*prendere nota*) note; (*indicare*) indicate; *Sport* score. **~si** *vr* cross oneself. **'segno** *nm* sign; (*traccia, limite*) mark; (*bersaglio*) target; **far segno** (*col capo*) nod; (*con la mano*) beckon. **segno zodiacale** birth sign

segre'ga|re *vt* segregate. **~zi'one** *nf* segregation

segretari'ato *nm* secretariat

segre'tario, -a *nmf* secretary. **~ comunale** town clerk

segre'ria nf (uffico) [administrative] office; (segretariato) secretariat. **~ telefonica** answering machine, answerphone

segre'tezza nf secrecy

se'greto a & nm secret; **in ~** in secret

segu'ace nmf follower

segu'ente a following, next

se'gugio nm bloodhound

segu'ire vt/i follow; (continuare) continue

segui'tare vt/i continue

'seguito nm (ritinuo) (sequela) series; (continuazione) continuation; **di ~** in succession; **in ~** later on; **in ~ a** following; **al ~** in his/her wake; (a causa di) owing to; **fare ~ a** Comm follow up

'sei a & nm six. **sei'cento** a & nm six hundred; **il Seicento** the seventeenth century. **sei'mila** a & nm six thousand

sel'ciato nm paving

selet'tivo a selective. **selezio'nare** vt select. **selezi'one** nf selection

'sella nf saddle. **sel'lare** vt saddle

seltz nm soda water

'selva nf forest

selvag'gina nf game

sel'vaggio, -a a wild; (primitivo) savage ● nmf savage

sel'vatico a wild

se'maforo nm traffic lights pl

se'mantica nf semantics sg

sem'brare vi seem; **che te ne sembra?** what do you think?; **mi sembra che...** I think...

'seme nm seed; (di mela) pip; (di carte) suit; (sperma) semen

se'mestre nm half-year

semi'cerchio nm semicircle

semifi'nale nf semifinal

semi'freddo nm ice cream and sponge dessert

'semina nf sowing

semi'nare vt sow; fam shake off (inseguitori)

semi'nario nm seminar; Relig seminary

seminter'rato nm basement

se'mitico a Semitic

sem'mai conj in case ● adv **è lui, ~, che...** if anyone, it's him who...

'semola nf bran. **semo'lino** nm semolina

'semplice a simple; **in parole semplici** in plain words. **~cemente** adv simply. **~ci'otto, -a** a nmf simpleton. **~cistico** a simplistic. **~cità** nf simplicity. **~fi'care** vt simplify

'sempre adv always; (ancora) still; **per ~** for ever

sempre'verde a & nm evergreen

'senape nf mustard

se'nato nm senate. **sena'tore** nm senator

se'nile a senile. **~ità** nf senility

'senno nm sense

'seno nm (petto) breast; Math sine; **in ~ a** in the bosom of

sen'sato a sensible

sensazio'nale a sensational. **~o'ne** nf sensation

sen'sibile a sensitive; (percepibile) perceptible; (notevole) considerable. **~ità** nf sensitivity. **~iz'zare** vt make more aware (a of)

sen'sitivo, -a a sensory ● nmf sensitive person; (medium) medium

'senso nm sense; (significato) meaning; (direzione) direction; **far ~ a qcno** make sb shudder; **non ha ~** it doesn't make sense; **senza ~** meaningless; **perdere i sensi** lose consciousness. **~ dell'umorismo** sense of humour. **~ unico** (strada) one-way. **~ vietato** no entry

sensu'ale a sensual. **~ità** nf sensuality

sen'tenza nf sentence; (massima) saying. **~i'are** vi Jur pass judgment

senti'ero nm path

sentimen'tale a sentimental. **senti'mento** nm feeling

senti'nella nf sentry

sen'tire vt feel; (udire) hear; (ascoltare) listen to, (gustare) taste;

(*odorare*) smell ● *vi* feel; (*udire*) hear; ~**re caldo/freddo** feel hot/cold. ~**rsi** *vr* feel; ~**rsi di fare qcsa** feel like doing sth; ~**rsi bene** feel well; ~**rsi poco bene** feel unwell; ~**rsela di fare qcsa** feel up to doing sth. ~**to** *a* (*sincero*) sincere; **per** ~**to dire** by hearsay

sen'tore *nm* inkling

'**senza** *prep* without; ~ **correre** without running; **senz'altro** certainly; ~ **ombrello** without an umbrella

senza'tetto *nm inv* i ~ the homeless

sepa'ra|re *vt* separate. ~**rsi** *vr* separate; (*amici:*) part; ~**rsi da** be separated from. ~**ta'mente** *adv* separately. ~**zi'one** *nf* separation

se'pol|cro *nm* sepulchre. ~**to** *pp di* **seppellire**. ~'**tura** *nf* burial

seppel'lire *vt* bury

'**seppia** *nf* cuttle fish; **nero di** ~ sepia

sep'pure *conj* even if

se'quenza *nf* sequence

seque'strare *vt* (*rapire*) kidnap; *Jur* impound; (*confiscare*) confiscate. **se'questro** *nm* *Jur* impounding; (*di persona*) kidnap[ping]

'**sera** *nf* evening; **di** ~ in the evening. **se'rale** *a* evening. **se'rata** *nf* evening; (*ricevimento*) party

ser'bare *vt* keep; harbour (*odio*); cherish (*speranza*)

serba'toio *nm* tank. ~ **d'acqua** water tank; (*per una città*) reservoir

'**serbo, -a** *a* & *nmf* Serbian ● *nm* (*lingua*) Serbian; **mettere in** ~ put aside

sere'nata *nf* serenade

sereni'tà *nf* serenity. **se'reno** *a* serene; (*cielo*) clear

ser'gente *nm* sergeant

seria'mente *adv* seriously

'**serie** *nf inv* series; (*complesso*) set; *Sport* division; **fuori** ~ custom-

built; **produzione in** ~ mass production; **di** ~ **B** second-rate

serietà *nf* seriousness. '**serio** *a* serious; (*degno di fiducia*) reliable; **sul serio** seriously; (*davvero*) really

ser'mone *nm* sermon

'**serpe** *nf liter* viper. ~**ggi'are** *vi* meander; (*diffondersi*) spread

ser'pente *nm* snake. ~ **a sonagli** rattlesnake

'**serra** *nf* greenhouse; **effetto** ~ greenhouse effect

ser'randa *nf* shutter

ser'ra|re *vt* shut; (*stringere*) tighten; (*incalzare*) press on. ~'**tura** *nf* lock

ser'vir|e *vt* serve; (*al ristorante*) wait on ● *vi* serve; (*essere utile*) be of use; **non serve** it's no good. ~**si** *vr* (*di cibo*) help oneself; ~**si da** buy from; ~**si di** use

servitù *nf inv* servitude; (*personale di servizio*) servants *pl*

servizi'evole *a* obliging

ser'vizio *nm* service; (*da caffè ecc*) set; (*di cronaca, sportivo*) report; **servizi** *pl* bathroom; **essere di** ~ be on duty; **fare** ~ ⟨*autobus ecc:*⟩ run; **fuori** ~ ⟨*bus*⟩ not in service; (*ascensore*) out of order; ~ **compreso** service charge included. ~ **in camera** room service. ~ **civile** civilian duties done instead of national service. ~ **militare** military service. ~ **pubblico** utility company. ~ **al tavolo** waiter service

'**servo, -a** *nmf* servant

servo'sterzo *nm* power steering

ses'san|ta *a* & *nm* sixty. ~'**tina** *nf* **una** ~**tina** about sixty

sessi'one *nf* session

'**sesso** *nm* sex

sessu'al|e *a* sexual. ~**ità** *nf* sexuality

'**sesto**[1] *a* a sixth

'**sesto**[2] *nm* (*ordine*) order

'**seta** *nf* silk

setacci'are *vt* sieve. **se'taccio** *nm* sieve

'**sete** *nf* thirst; **avere** ~ be thirsty

'setola nf bristle

'setta nf sect

set'tan|ta a & nm seventy. ~'**tina** nf una ~**tina** about seventy

'sette a & nm seven. ~'**cento** a & nm seven hundred; **il S~cento** the eighteenth century

set'tembre nm September

settentri|o'nale a northern ● nmf northerner. ~'**one** nm north

setti'mana nf week. ~'**nale** a & nm weekly

'settimo a seventh

set'tore nm sector

severità nf severity. **se'vero** a severe; (rigoroso) strict

se'vizi|a nf torture; **se'vizie** pl torture sg. ~'**are** vt torture

sezio'nare vt divide; Med dissect. **sezi'one** nf section; (reparto) department; Med dissection

sfaccen'dato a idle

sfacchi'na|re vi toil. ~**ta** nf drudgery

sfacci|a'taggine nf cheek, insolence. ~'**ato** a cheeky, fresh Am

sfa'celo nm ruin; **in** ~ in ruins

sfal'darsi vr flake off

sfa'mar|e vt feed. ~**si** vr satisfy one's hunger, eat one's fill

'sfar|zo nm pomp. ~'**zoso** a sumptuous

sfa'sato a fam confused; (motore) which needs tuning

sfasci|'are vt unbandage; (fracassare) smash. ~**rsi** vr fall to pieces. ~**to** a beat-up

sfa'tare vt explode

sfati'cato a lazy

sfavil'la|nte a sparkling. ~**re** vi sparkle

sfavo'revole a unfavourable

sfavo'rire vt disadvantage, put at a disadvantage

'sfer|a nf sphere. ~**ico** a spherical

sfer'rare vt unshoe (cavallo); (scagliare) land

sfer'zare vt lash

sfian'carsi vr wear oneself out

sfi'bra|re vt exhaust. ~**to** a exhausted

'sfida nf challenge. **sfi'dare** vt challenge

sfi'duci|a nf mistrust. ~'**ato** a discouraged

'sfiga nf vulg bloody bad luck

sfigu'rare vt disfigure ● vi (far cattiva figura) look out of place

sfilacci'ar|e vt, ~**si** vr fray

sfi'la|re vt unthread; (togliere di dosso) take off ● vi (truppe:) march past; (in parata) parade. ~**rsi** vr come unthreaded; (collant:) ladder; take off (pantaloni). ~**ta** nf parade; (sfilza) series. ~**ta** di moda fashion show

'sfilza nf (di errori, domande) string

'sfinge nf sphinx

sfi'nito a worn out

sfio'rare vt skim; touch on (argomento)

sfio'rire vi wither; (bellezza:) fade

'sfitto a vacant

'sfizio nm whim, fancy; **togliersi uno** ~ satisfy a whim

sfo'cato a out of focus

sfoci'are vi flow into

sfode'ra|re vt draw (pistola, spada). ~**to** a unlined

sfo'gar|e vt vent. ~**si** vr give vent to one's feelings

sfoggi'are vt/i show off. **'sfoggio** nm show, display; **fare sfoggio di** show off

'sfoglia nf sheet of pastry; **pasta** ~ puff pastry

sfogli'are vt leaf through

'sfogo nm outlet; fig outburst; Med rash; **dare** ~ **a** give vent to

sfol'lare vt clear ● vt Mil be evacuated

sfol'tire vt thin [out]

sfon'dare vt break down ● vi (aver successo) make a name for oneself

'sfondo nm background

sfor'ma|re vt pull out of shape (tasche); ~**rsi** vr lose its shape; (persona:) lose one's figure. ~**to** nm Culin flan

sfor'nito a ~ **di** (negozio) out of

sfor'tuna nf bad luck. ~**ta'mente** adv unfortunately. **sfortu'nato** a unlucky

sfor'zar|e vt force. ~**si** vr try hard. **'sforzo** nm effort; (tensione) strain

'sfottere vt sl tease

sfracel'larsi vr smash

sfrat'tare vt evict. **'sfratto** nm eviction

sfrecci'are vi flash past

sfregi'a|re vt slash. ~**to** a scarred **'sfregio** nm slash

sfre'na|rsi vr run wild. ~**to** a wild

sfron'tato a shameless

sfrutta'mento nm exploitation. **sfrut'tare** vt exploit

sfug'gente a elusive; (mento) receding

sfug'gi|re vi escape; ~**re** a escape [from]; **mi sfugge** it escapes me; **mi è sfuggito di mano** I lost hold of it ● vt avoid. ~**ta** nf **di** ~**ta** in passing

sfu'ma|re vi (svanire) vanish; (colore:) shade off ● vt soften (colore). ~**tura** nf shade

sfuri'ata nf outburst [of anger]

sga'bello nm stool

sgabuz'zino nm cupboard

sgam'bato a (costume da bagno) high-cut

sgambet'tare vi kick one's legs; (camminare) trot. **sgam'betto** nm **fare lo sgambetto a qcno** trip sb up

sganasci'arsi vr ~ **dalle risa** roar with laughter

sganci'ar|e vt unhook; Rail uncouple; drop (bombe); fam cough up (denaro). ~**si** vr become unhooked; fig get away

sanghe'rato a ramshackle

sgar'bato a rude. **'sgarbo** nm discourtesy; **fare uno sgarbo a** qcno be rude

sgargi'ante a garish

sgar'rare vi be wrong; (da regola) stray from the straight and narrow. **'sgarro** nm mistake, slip

sgattaio'lare vi sneak away; ~ **via** decamp

sghignaz'zare vi laugh scornfully, sneer

sgob'b|are vi slog; (fam: studente:) swot. ~**one, -a** nmf slogger; (fam: studente) swot

sgoccio'lare vi drip

sgo'larsi vr shout oneself hoarse

sgomb|e]'rare vt clear [out]. **'sgombro** a clear ● nm (trasloco) removal; (pesce) mackerel

sgomen'tar|e vt dismay. ~**si** vr be dismayed. **sgo'mento** nm dismay

sgomi'nare vt defeat

sgom'mata nf screech of tyres

sgonfi'ar|e vt deflate. ~**si** vr go down. **'sgonfio** a flat

'sgorbio nm scrawl; (fig: vista sgradevole) sight

sgor'gare vi gush [out] ● vt flush out, unblock (lavandino)

sgoz'zare vt ~ **qcno** cut sb's throat

sgra'd|evole a disagreeable. ~**ito** a unwelcome

sgrammati'cato a ungrammatical

sgra'nare vt shell (piselli); open wide (occhi)

sgran'chir|e vt, ~**si** vr stretch

sgranocchi'are vt munch

sgras'sare vt remove the grease from

sgrazi'ato a ungainly

sgreto'lar|e vt, ~**si** vr crumble

sgri'da|re vt scold. ~**ta** nf scolding

sgros'sare vt rough-hew (marmo); fig polish

sgua'ia|to a coarse

sgual'cire vt crumple

sgual'drina nf slut

sgu'ardo nm look; (breve) glance

'sguattero, -a nmf skivvy

guaz'zare vi splash; (nel fango) wallow

sguinzagli'are vt unleash

sgusci'are vt shell ● vi (sfuggire) slip away; ~ **fuori** slip out

shake'rare vt shake

si pers pron (riflessivo) oneself; (lui)

himself; (*lei*) herself; (*esso, essa*) itself; (*loro*) themselves; (*reciproco*) each other; (*tra più di due*) one another; (*impersonale*) you, one; **lavarsi** wash [oneself]; **si è lavata** she washed [herself]; **lavarsi le mani** wash one's hands; **si è lavata le mani** she washed her hands; **si è mangiato un pollo intero** he ate an entire chicken by himself; **incontrarsi** meet each other; **la gente si aiuta a vicenda** people help one another; **non si sa mai** you never know, one never knows *fml*; **queste cose si dimenticano facilmente** these things are easily forgotten ● *nm* (*chiave, nota*) B

sì *adv* yes

'sia' *vedi* **essere**

'sia² *conj* ~...~... (*entrambi*) both...and...; (*o l'uno o l'altro*) either...or...~ **che venga, ~ che non venga** whether he comes or not; **scegli ~ questo ~ quello** choose either this one or that one; **voglio ~ questo che quello** I want both this one and that one

sia'mese *a* Siamese

sibi'lare *vi* hiss. **'sibilo** *nm* hiss

si'cario *nm* hired killer

sicché *conj* (*perciò*) so [that]; (*allora*) then

siccità *nf* drought

sic'come *conj* as

Si'cilia *nf* Sicily. **s~ano, -a** *a & nmf* Sicilian

si'cura *nf* safety catch; (*di portiera*) child-proof lock. **~'mente** *adv* definitely

sicu'rezza *nf* (*certezza*) certainty; (*salvezza*) safety; **uscita di ~** emergency exit

si'curo *a* (*non pericoloso*) safe; (*certo*) sure; (*saldo*) steady; *Comm* sound ● *adv* certainly ● *nm* safety; **al ~** safe; **andare sul ~** play [it] safe; **di ~** definitely; **di ~, sarà arrivato** he must have arrived

siderur'gia *nf* iron and steel in-

dustry. **side'rurgico** *a* iron and steel *attrib*

'sidro *nm* cider

si'epe *nf* hedge

si'ero *nm* serum

sieroposi'tivo *a* HIV positive

si'esta *nf* afternoon nap, siesta

si'fone *nm* siphon

Sig. *abbr* (*signore*) Mr

Sig.a *abbr* (*signora*) Mrs, Ms

siga'retta *nf* cigarette; **pantaloni a ~** drainpipes

'sigaro *nm* cigar

Sigg. *abbr* (*signori*) Messrs

sigil'lare *vt* seal. **si'gillo** *nm* seal

'sigla *nf* initials pl. **~ musicale** signature tune. **si'glare** *vt* initial

Sig.na *abbr* (*signorina*) Miss, Ms

signifi'ca|re *vt* mean. **~'tivo** *a* significant. **~to** *nm* meaning

si'gnora *nf* lady; (*davanti a nome proprio*) Mrs; (*non sposata*) Miss; (*in lettere ufficiali*) Dear Madam; **il signor Vené e ~** Mr and Mrs Vené

si'gnore *nm* gentleman; *Relig* lord; (*davanti a nome proprio*) Mr; (*in lettere ufficiali*) Dear Sir. **signo'rile** *a* gentlemanly; (*di lusso*) luxury

signo'rina *nf* young lady; (*seguito da nome proprio*) Miss

silenzia'tore *nm* silencer

si'lenzi|o *nm* silence. **~'oso** *a* silent

silhou'ette *nf* silhouette, outline

si'licio *nm* **piastrina di ~** silicon chip

sili'cone *nm* silicone

'sillaba *nf* syllable

sil'lurare *vt* torpedo. **si'luro** *nm* torpedo

simboleggi'are *vt* symbolize

sim'bolico *a* symbolic[al]

'simbolo *nm* symbol

similarità *nf* *inv* similarity

'simil|e *a* similar; (*tale*) such; **~e a** like ● *nm* (*il prossimo*) fellow man. **~'mente** *adv* similarly. **~'pelle** *nf* Leatherette®

simme'tria *nf* symmetry. **sim'metrico** *a* symmetric[al]

simpa'ti|a *nf* liking; *(compenetrazione)* sympathy; **prendere qcno in ~a** take a liking to sb. **sim'patico** *a* nice. **~iz'zante** *nmf* well-wisher. **~iz'zare** *vi* **~izzare con** take a liking to; **~izzare per qcsa/qcno** lean towards sth/sb

sim'posio *nm* symposium

simu'la|re *vt* simulate; feign *(amicizia, interesse)*. **~zi'one** *nf* simulation

simul'tane|a *nf* **in ~a** simultaneously. **~o** *a* simultaneous

sina'goga *nf* synagogue

sincerità *nf* sincerity. **sin'cero** *a* sincere

'sincope *nf* syncopation; *Med* fainting fit

sincron'ia *nf* synchronization; **in ~** with synchronized timing

sincroniz'za|re *vt* synchronize. **~zi'one** *nf* synchronization

sinda'ca|le *a* [trade] union, [labor] union *Am.* **~'lista** *nmf* trade unionist, labor union member *Am.* **~re** *vt* inspect. **~to** *nm* [trade] union, [labor] union *Am*; *(associazione)* syndicate

'sindaco *nm* mayor

'sindrome *nf* syndrome

sinfo'nia *nf* symphony. **sin'fonico** *a* symphonic

singhi|oz'zare *vi* *(di pianto)* sob. **~'ozzo** *nm* hiccup; *(di pianto)* sob; **avere il ~ozzo** have the hiccups

singo'lar|e *a* singular ● *nm* singular. **~'mente** *adv* individually; *(stranamente)* peculiarly

'singolo *a* single ● *nm* individual; *Tennis* singles *pl*

si'nistra *nf* left; **a ~** on the left; **girare a ~** turn to the left; **con la guida a ~** *(auto)* with left-hand drive

sini'strato *a* injured

si'nistr|o, -a *a* left[-hand]; *(avverso)* sinister ● *nm* accident ● *nf* left [hand]; *Pol* left [wing]

'sino *prep* = **fino**

si'nonimo *a* synonymous ● *nm* synonym

sin'ta|ssi *nf* syntax. **~ttico** *a* syntactic[al]

'sintesi *nf* synthesis; *(riassunto)* summary

sin'teti|co *a* synthetic; *(conciso)* summary. **~z'zare** *vt* summarize

sintetizza'tore *nm* synthesizer

sinto'matico *a* symptomatic.

'sintomo *nm* symptom

sinto'nia *nf* tuning; **in ~** on the same wavelength

sinu'oso *a* *(strada)* winding

sinu'site *nf* sinusitis

si'pario *nm* curtain

si'rena *nf* siren

'Siri|a *nf* Syria. **s~'ano, -a** *a* & *nmf* Syrian

si'ringa *nf* syringe

'sismico *a* seismic

si'stem|a *nm* system. **S~a Monetario Europeo** European Monetary System. **~a operativo** *Comput* operating system

siste'ma|re *vt* *(mettere)* put; tidy up *(casa, camera)*; *(risolvere)* sort out; *(procurare lavoro a)* fix up with a job; *(trovare alloggio a)* find accommodation for; *(sposare)* marry off; *(fam: punire)* sort out. **~rsi** *vr* settle down; *(trovare un lavoro)* find a job; *(trovare alloggio)* find accommodation; *(sposarsi)* marry. **~tico** *a* systematic. **~zi'one** *nf* arrangement; *(di questione)* settlement; *(lavoro)* job; *(alloggio)* accommodation; *(matrimonio)* marriage

'sito *nm* site. **~ web** *Comput* web site

situ'are *vt* place

situazi'one *nf* situation

ski-'lift *nm* ski tow

slacci'are *vt* unfasten

slanci'a|rsi *vr* hurl oneself. **~to** *a* slender. **'slancio** *nm* impetus; *(impulso)* impulse

sla'vato *a* *(carnagione, capelli)* fair

'slavo *a* Slav[onic]

sle'al|e *a* disloyal. **~tà** *nf* disloyalty

sle'gare *vt* untie

'slitta *nf* sledge, sleigh. **~'mento**

nm (di macchina) skid; *(fig: di riunione)* postponement

slit'ta|re *vi Auto* skid; *(riunione:)* be put off. **~ta** *nf* skid

slit'tino *nm* toboggan

'slogan *nm inv* slogan

slo'ga|re *vt* dislocate. **~rsi** *vr* **~rsi una caviglia** sprain one's ankle. **~'tura** *nf* dislocation

sloggi'are *vt* dislodge ● *vi* move out

Slo'vacchia *nf* Slovakia

Slo'venia *nf* Slovenia

smacchi'a|re *vt* clean. **~'tore** *nm* stain remover

'smacco *nm* humiliating defeat

smagli'ante *a* dazzling

smagli|a'rsi *vr (calza:)* ladder *Br*, run. **~'tura** *nf* ladder *Br*, run

smalizi'ato *a* cunning

smal'ta|re *vt* enamel; glaze *(ceramica)*; varnish *(unghie)*. **~to a** enamelled

smalti'mento *nm* disposal; *(di merce)* selling off. **~ rifiuti** waste disposal; *(di grassi)* burning off

smal'tire *vt* burn off; *(merce)* sell off; *fig* get through *(corrispondenza)*; **~ la sbornia** sober up

'smalto *nm* enamel; *(di ceramica)* glaze; *(per le unghie)* nail varnish

'smani|a *nf* fidgets *pl*; *(desiderio)* longing. **~'are** *vi* have the fidgets; **~are per** long for. **~'oso** *a* restless

smantel|la'mento *nm* dismantling. **~'lare** *vt* dismantle

smarri'mento *nm* loss; *(psicologico)* bewilderment

smar'ri|re *vt* lose; *(temporaneamente)* mislay. **~rsi** *vr* get lost; *(turbarsi)* be bewildered

smasche'ra|re *vt* unmask. **~rsi** *vr (tradirsi)* give oneself away

SME *nm abbr* **(Sistema Monetario Europeo)** EMS

smemo'rato, -a *a* forgetful ● *nmf* scatterbrain

smen'ti|re *vt* deny. **~ta** *nf* denial

sme'raldo *nm & a* emerald

smerci'are *vt* sell off

smerigli'ato *a* emery; **vetro ~** frosted glass. **sme'riglio** *nm* emery

'smesso *pp di* **smettere** ● *a (abiti)* cast-off

'smett|ere *vt* stop; stop wearing *(abiti)*. **~!la!** stop it!

smidol'lato *a* spineless

sminu'ir|e *vt* diminish. **~si** *vr fig* belittle oneself

sminuz'zare *vt* crumble; *(fig: analizzare)* analyse in detail

smista'mento *nm* clearing; *(postale)* sorting. **smi'stare** *vt* sort; *Mil* post

smisu'rato *a* boundless; *(esorbitante)* excessive

smobili'ta|re *vt* demobilize. **~zi'one** *nf* demobilization

smo'dato *a* immoderate

smog *nm* smog

'smoking *nm inv* dinner jacket, tuxedo *Am*

smon'tabile *a* jointed

smon'ta|re *vt* take to pieces; *(scoraggiare)* dishearten ● *vi (da veicolo)* get off; *(da cavallo)* dismount; *(dal servizio)* go off duty. **~si** *vr* lose heart

smorfi|a *nf* grimace; *(moina)* simper; **fare ~e** make faces. **~'oso** *a* affected

smorto *a* pale; *(colore)* dull

smor'zare *vt* dim *(luce)*; tone down *(colori)*; deaden *(suoni)*; quench *(sete)*

'smosso *pp di* **smuovere**

smotta'mento *nm* landslide

smunto *a* emaciated

smu'over|e *vt* shift; *(commuovere)* move. **~si** *vr* move; *(commuoversi)* be moved

smus'sar|e *vt* round off; *(fig: attenuare)* tone down. **~si** *vr* go blunt

snatu'rato *a* inhuman

snel'li|re *vt* slim down. **~si** *vr* slim [down]. **'snello** *a* slim

sner'vante *a* enervating

sner'va|re *vt* enervate. **~rsi** *vr* get exhausted

snidare | solare

252

sni'dare vt drive out

snif'fare vt snort

snob'bare vt snub. **sno'bismo** nm snobbery

snoccio'lare vt stone; fig blurt out

sno'da|re vt untie; (sciogliere) loosen. **~rsi** vr come untied; (strada:) wind. **~to** a (persona) double-jointed; (dita) flexible

so'ave a gentle

sobbal'zare vi jerk; (trasalire) start. **sob'balzo** nm jerk; (trasalimento) start

sobbar'carsi vr ~ a undertake

sobil'la|re vt stir up

'sobrio a sober

soc'chiu|dere vt half-close. **~so** pp di **socchiudere** ● a (occhi) half-closed; (porta) ajar

soc'combere vi succumb

soc'cor|rere vt assist. **~so** pp di **soccorrere** ● nm assistance; **soccorsi** pl rescuers; (dopo disastro) relief workers. **~so stradale** breakdown service

socialdemo'cra|tico, -a a Social Democratic ● nmf Social Democrat. **~zia** nf Social Democracy

soci'ale a social

socia'li|smo nm Socialism. **~sta** a & nmf Socialist. **~z'zare** vi socialize

società nf inv society; Comm company. **~ per azioni** plc. **~ a responsabilità limitata** limited liability company

soci'evole a sociable

'socio, -a nmf member; Comm partner

sociolo'gia nf sociology. **socio-'logico** a sociological

'soda nf soda

soddisfa'cente a satisfactory

soddi'sfa|re vt/i satisfy; meet (richiesta); make amends for (offesa). **~tto** pp di **soddisfare** ● a satisfied. **~zi'one** nf satisfaction

'sodo a hard; fig firm; (uovo) hard-boiled ● adv hard; **dormire ~**

sleep soundly ● nm **venire al ~** get to the point

sofà nm inv sofa

soffe'ren|te a (malato) ill. **~za** nf suffering

soffer'marsi vr pause; **~ su** dwell on

sof'ferto pp di **soffrire**

soffi'a|re vt blow; reveal (segreto); (rubare) pinch fam ● vi blow. **~ta** nf fig sl tip-off

'soffice a soft

'soffio nm puff; Med murmur

sof'fitt|a nf attic. **~o** nm ceiling

soffo'ca|mento nm suffocation

soffo'ca|nte a suffocating. **~re** vt/i suffocate; (con cibo) choke; fig stifle

sof'friggere vt fry lightly

sof'frire vt/i suffer; (sopportare) bear; **~ di** suffer from

sof'fritto pp di **soffriggere**

sof'fuso a (luce) soft

sofisti'ca|re vt (adulterare) adulterate ● vi (sottilizzare) quibble. **~to** a sophisticated

sogget'tiva'mente adv subjectively. **~'tivo** a subjective

sog'getto nm subject ● a subject; **essere ~ a** be subject to

soggezi'one nf subjection; (rispetto) awe

sogghi'gnare vi sneer. **sog'ghigno** nm sneer

soggio'gare vt subdue

soggior'nare vi stay. **soggi'orno** nm stay; (stanza) living room

soggi'ungere vt add

'soglia nf threshold

'sogliola nf sole

so'gna|re vt/i dream; **~re a occhi aperti** daydream. **~'tore, -'trice** nmf dreamer. **'sogno** nm dream; **fare un sogno** have a dream; **neanche per sogno!** not at all!

'soia nf soya

sol nm Mus (chiave, nota) G

so'laio nm attic

sola'mente adv only

so'lar|e a (energia, raggi) solar;

⟨*crema*⟩ sun *attrib*. **~ium** *nm inv* solarium

sol'care *vt* plough. '**solco** *nm* furrow; ⟨*di ruota*⟩ track; ⟨*di nave*⟩ wake; ⟨*di disco*⟩ groove

sol'dato *nm* soldier

'soldo *nm* **non ha un ~** he hasn't got a penny to his name; **senza un ~** penniless; **soldi** *pl* ⟨*denaro*⟩ money *sg*

'**sole** *nm* sun; ⟨*luce del sole*⟩ sun[light]; **al ~** in the sun; **prendere il ~** sunbathe

soleggi'ato *a* sunny

so'lenn|e *a* solemn. **~ità** *nf* solemnity

so'lere *vi* be in the habit of; **come si suol dire** as they say

sol'fato *nm* sulphate

soli'dale *a* in agreement. **~rietà** *nf* solidarity

solidifi'car|e *vt/i*, **~si** *vr* solidify

solidità *nf* solidity; ⟨*di colori*⟩ fastness. '**solido** *a* solid; ⟨*robusto*⟩ sturdy; ⟨*colore*⟩ fast ● *nm* solid

soli'loquio *nm* soliloquy

so'lista *a* solo ● *nmf* soloist

solita'mente *adv* usually

soli'tario *a* solitary; ⟨*isolato*⟩ lonely ● *nm* ⟨*brillante*⟩ solitaire; ⟨*gioco di carte*⟩ patience, solitaire

'solito *a* usual; **essere ~ fare qcsa** be in the habit of doing sth ● *nm* usual; **di ~** usually

soli'tudine *nf* solitude

solleci'tare *vt* speed up; urge ⟨*persona*⟩. **~zi'one** *nf* ⟨*richiesta*⟩ request; ⟨*preghiera*⟩ entreaty

sol'lecito *a* prompt ● *nm* reminder. **~'tudine** *nf* promptness; ⟨*interessamento*⟩ concern

solle'one *nm* noonday sun; ⟨*periodo*⟩ dog days of summer

solleti'care *vt* tickle. **sol'letico** *nm* ticking; **fare il solletico a qeno** tickle sb; **soffrire il solletico** be ticklish

solleva'mento *nm* **~ pesi** weightlifting

solle'var|e *vt* lift; ⟨*elevare*⟩ raise;

⟨*confortare*⟩ comfort. **~si** *vr* rise; ⟨*riaversi*⟩ recover

solli'evo *nm* relief

'**solo**, **-a** *a* alone; ⟨*isolato*⟩ lonely; ⟨*unico*⟩ only; *Mus* solo; **da ~** by myself/yourself/himself etc ● *nmf* **il ~, la sola** the only one ● *nm Mus* solo ● *adv* only

sol'stizio *nm* solstice

sol'tanto *adv* only

so'lubile *a* soluble; ⟨*caffè*⟩ instant

soluzi'one *nf* solution; *Comm* payment

sol'vente *a* & *nm* solvent; **~ per unghie** nail polish remover

'**soma** *nf* **bestia da ~** beast of burden

so'maro *nm* ass; *Sch* dunce

so'matico *a* somatic

somigli'an|te *a* similar. **~za** *nf* resemblance

somigli'ar|e *vi* **~e a** resemble. **~si** *vr* be alike

'**somma** *nf* sum; *Math* addition

som'mare *vt* add; ⟨*totalizzare*⟩ add up

som'mario *a* & *nm* summary

som'mato *a* **tutto ~** all things considered

sommeli'er *nm inv* wine waiter

som'merg|ere *vt* submerge. **~'gibile** *nm* submarine. **~so** *pp di* **sommergere**

som'messo *a* soft

sommini'stra|re *vt* administer. **~zi'one** *nf* administration

sommità *nf inv* summit

'**sommo** *a* highest; *fig* supreme ● *nm* summit

som'mossa *nf* rising

sommozza'tore *nm* frogman

so'naglio *nm* bell

so'nata *nf* sonata; *fig fam* beating

'**sonda** *nf Mech* drill; ⟨*spaziale*, *Med*⟩ probe. **son'daggio** *nm* drilling; ⟨*spaziale*, *Med*⟩ probe; ⟨*indagine*⟩ survey. **sondaggio d'opinioni** opinion poll. **son'dare** *vt* sound; ⟨*investigare*⟩ probe

so'netto *nm* sonnet

sonnambu'lismo *nm* sleepwalking. **son'nambulo, -a** *nmf* sleep-walker

sonnecchi'are *vi* doze

son'nifero *nm* sleeping-pill

'**sonno** *nm* sleep; **aver ~** be sleepy. **~'lenza** *nf* sleepiness

so'noro *a* resonant; *(rumoroso)* loud; *(onde, scheda)* sound *attrib*

sontu'oso *a* sumptuous

sopo'rifero *a* soporific

sop'palco *nm* platform

soppe'rire *vi* **~ a qcsa** provide for sth

soppe'sare *vt* weigh up *(situazione)*

soppi'atto: di ~ *adv* furtively

soppor'ta|re *vt* support; *(tollerare)* stand; bear *(dolore)*

soppressi'one *nf* removal; *(di legge)* abolition; *(di diritti, pubblicazione)* suppression; *(annullamento)* cancellation. **sop'presso** *pp di* **sopprimere**

sop'primere *vt* get rid of; abolish *(legge)*; suppress *(diritti, pubblicazione)*; *(annullare)* cancel

'**sopra** *adv* on top; *(più in alto)* higher [up]; *(al piano superiore)* upstairs; *(in testo)* above; **mettilo lì ~** put it up there; **di ~** upstairs; **dormirci ~** *fig* sleep on it; **pensarci ~** think about it; **vedi ~** see above ● *prep* ~ **[a]** on; *(senza contatto, oltre)* over; *(riguardo a)* about; **è ~ al tavolo, è ~ il tavolo** it's on the table; **il quadro è appeso ~ al camino** the picture is hanging over the fireplace; **il ponte passa ~ all'autostrada** the bridge crosses over the motorway; **è caduto ~ il tetto** it fell on the roof; **l'uno ~ l'altro** one on top of the other; *(senza contatto)* one above the other; **abita ~ di me** he lives upstairs from me; **i bambini ~ i dieci anni** children over ten; **20' ~ lo zero** 20' above zero; **~ il livello del mare** above sea level; **rifletti ~ quello che è successo** think about what happened; **non ha nessuno ~ di sé** he has no-

body above him; **al di ~ di** over ● *nm* **il [di] ~** the top

so'prabito *nm* overcoat

soprac'ciglio *nm* *(pl* **sopracciglia***)* eyebrow

sopracco'per|ta *nf* *(di letto)* bedspread; *(di libro)* [dust-]jacket. **~'tina** *nf* book jacket

soprad'detto *a* above-mentioned

sopraele'vata *nf* elevated railway

sopraf'fa|re *vt* overwhelm. **~tto** *pp di* **sopraffare**. **~zi'one** *nf* abuse of power

sopraf'fino *a* excellent; *(gusto, udito)* highly refined

sopraggi'ungere *vi* *(persona:)* turn up; *(accadere)* happen

soprallu'ogo *nm* inspection

sopram'mobile *nm* ornament

soprannatu'rale *a* & *nm* supernatural

sopran'nome *nm* nickname. **~i'nare** *vt* nickname

so'prano *nmf* soprano

soprappensi'ero *adv* lost in thought

sopras'salto: nm di ~ with a start

soprasse'dere *vi* **~ a** postpone

soprat'tutto *adv* above all

sopravvalu'tare *vt* overvalue

soprav've'nire *vi* turn up; *(accadere)* happen. **~'vento** *nm* *fig* upper hand

sopravvi'suto *pp di* **sopravvivere**. **~'venza** *nf* survival. **soprav'vivere** *vi* survive; **sopravvivere a** outlive *(persona)*

soprinten'den|te *nmf* supervisor; *(di museo ecc)* keeper. **~za** *nf* supervision; *(ente)* board

so'pruso *nm* abuse of power

soq'quadro *nm* **mettere a ~** turn upside down

sor'betto *nm* sorbet

sor'bire *vt* sip; *fig* put up with

'**sordido** *a* sordid; *(avaro)* stingy

sor'dina *nf* mute; **in ~** *fig* on the quiet

sordità *nf* deafness. '**sordo, -a** *a* deaf; *(rumore, dolore)* dull ● *nmf*

deaf person. **sordo'muto, -a** *a*
deaf-and-dumb ● *nmf* deaf mute
so'rel|la *nf* sister. **~'lastra** *nf* step-
sister
sor'gente *nf* spring; (*fonte*) source
'sorgere *vi* rise; *fig* arise
sormon'tare *vt* surmount
sorni'one *a* sly
sorpas'sa|re *vt* surpass; (*eccedere*)
exceed; overtake, pass *Am* (*veicolo*). **~to** *a* old-fashioned. **sor'passo** *nm* overtaking, passing *Am*
sorpren'dente *a* surprising;
(*straordinario*) remarkable
sor'prendere *vt* surprise; (*cogliere
in flagrante*) catch
sor'pres|a *nf* surprise; **di ~a** by
surprise. **~o** *pp di* **sorprendere**
sor're|ggere *vt* support; (*tenere*)
hold up. **~ggersi** *vr* support oneself. **~tto** *pp di* **sorreggere**
sorri'dente *a* smiling
sor'ri|dere *vi* smile. **~so** *pp di*
sorridere ● *nm* smile
sorseggi'are *vt* sip. **'sorso** *nm* sip;
(*piccola quantità*) drop
'sorta *nf* sort; **di ~** whatever; **ogni
~ di** all sorts of
'sorte *nf* fate; (*caso imprevisto*)
chance; **tirare a ~** draw lots.
~ggi'are *vt* draw lots for.
sor'teggio *nm* draw
sorti'legio *nm* witchcraft
sor'ti|re *vi* come out. **~ta** *nf Mil*
sortie; (*battuta*) witticism
sorto *pp di* **sorgere**
sorvegli'an|te *nmf* keeper; (*con-
trollore*) overseer. **~za** *nf* watch;
Mil etc surveillance
sorvegli'are *vt* watch over;
(*controllare*) oversee; (*polizia*:)
watch, keep under surveillance
sorvo'lare *vt* fly over; *fig* skip
'sosia *nm inv* double
so'spen|dere *vt* hang, (*interrom-
pere*) stop; (*privare di una carica*)
suspend. **~si'one** *nf* suspension
so'speso *pp di* **sospendere** ● *a*
(*impiegato, alunno*) suspended; **~**
a hanging from; **~ a un filo** *fig*

hanging by a thread ● *nm* **in ~**
pending; (*emozionato*) in suspense
sospet'tare *vt* suspect. **so'spetto**
a suspicious; **persona sospet-
ta** suspicious person ● *nm* suspicion; (*persona*) suspect. **~'toso** *a*
suspicious
so'spin|gere *vt* drive. **~to** *pp di*
sospingere
sospi'rare *vi* sigh ● *vt* long for.
so'spiro *nm* sigh
'sosta *nf* stop; (*pausa*) pause; **senza ~** non-stop; **"divieto di ~"** "no
parking"
sostan'tivo *nm* noun
so'stanz|a *nf* substance; **~e** *pl*
(*patrimonio*) property *sg*; **in ~a** to
sum up. **~i'oso** *a* substantial;
(*cibo*) nourishing
so'stare *vi* stop; (*fare una pausa*)
pause
so'stegno *nm* support
soste'ner|e *vt* support; (*sopporta-
re*) bear; (*resistere*) withstand;
(*affermare*) maintain; (*nutrire*)
sustain; sit (*esame*); **~e le spese**
meet the costs. **~si** *vr* support
oneself
sosteni'tore, -'trice *nmf* supporter
sosteni'mento *nm* maintenance
soste'nuto *a* (*stile*) formal; (*prezzi, velocità*) high
sostitu'ir|e *vt* substitute (a for),
replace (*con* with). **~si** *vr* **~si a**
replace
sosti'tuto, -a *nm* replacement,
stand in ● *nm* (*surrogato*) substitute. **~zi'one** *nf* substitution
sotta'ceto *a* pickled; **sottaceti** *pl*
pickles
sot'tana *nf* petticoat; (*di prete*) cas-
sock
sotter'fugio *nm* subterfuge; **di ~**
secretly
sotter'raneo *a* underground ● *nm*
cellar
sotter'rare *vt* bury
sottigli'ezza *nf* slimness; *fig*
subtlety
sot'til|e *a* thin; (*udito, odorato*)

keen; (osservazione, distinzione) subtle. ~iz'zare vi split hairs
sottin'te|ndere vt imply. ~so pp di sottintendere ●nm allusion; senza ~si openly ●a implied

'sotto adv below; (più in basso) lower [down]; (al di sotto) underneath; (al piano di sotto) downstairs; è lì ~ it's underneath; ~ ~ deep down; (di nascosto) on the quiet; di ~ downstairs; mettersi ~ fig get down to it; mettere ~ (fam: investire) knock down; fatti ~! fam get stuck in! ●prep ~ [a] under; (al di sotto di) under[neath]; abita ~ di me he lives downstairs from me; i bambini ~ i dieci anni children under ten; 20° ~ zero 20° below zero; ~ il livello del mare below sea level; ~ la pioggia in the rain; ~ Elisabetta I under Elizabeth I; ~ calmante under sedation; ~ condizione che... on condition that...; ~ giuramento under oath; ~ sorveglianza under surveillance; ~ Natale/gli esami around Christmas/exam time; al di ~ di under; andare ~ i 50 all'ora do less than 50km an hour ●nm il [di] ~ the bottom
sotto'banco adv under the counter
sottobicchi'ere nm coaster
sotto'bosco nm undergrowth
sotto'braccio adv arm in arm
sotto'fondo nm background
sottoline'are vt underline; fig stress
sot'tolio adv in oil
sotto'mano adv within reach
sotto'marino a & nm submarine
sotto'messo pp di sottomettere ●a (remissivo) submissive
sotto'mettere vt submit; subdue (popolo). ~si vr submit. sottomissi'one nf submission
sottopa'gare vt underpay
sottopas'saggio nm underpass; (pedonale) subway
sotto'por|re vt submit; (costringe-

re) subject. ~si vr submit oneself; ~si a undergo. sotto'posto pp di sottoporre
sotto'scala nm cupboard under the stairs
sotto'scritto pp di sottoscrivere ●nm undersigned
sotto'scri|vere vt sign; (approvare) sanction, subscribe to. ~zi'one nf (petizione) petition; (approvazione) sanction; (raccolta di denaro) appeal
sottosegre'tario nm undersecretary
sotto'sopra adv upside down
sotto'stante a la strada ~ the road below
sottosu'olo nm subsoil
sottosvi'lup'pato a underdeveloped. ~'luppo nm underdevelopment
sotto'terra adv underground
sotto'titolo nm subtitle
sottovalu'tare vt underestimate
sotto'veste nf slip
sotto'voce adv in a low voice
sottovu'oto a vacuum-packed
sot'tra|rre vt remove; embezzle (fondi); Math subtract. ~rsi vr ~rsi a escape from; avoid (responsabilità). ~tto pp di sottrarre. ~zi'one nf removal; (di fondi) embezzlement; Math subtraction
sottuffici'ale nm non-commissioned officer; Naut petty officer
sou'brette nf inv showgirl
so'vietico, -a a & nmf Soviet
sovraccari'care vt overload. sovrac'carico a overloaded (di with) ●nm overload
sovraffati'carsi vr overexert oneself
sovrannatu'rale a & nm = soprannaturale
so'vrano, -a a sovereign; fig supreme ●nmf sovereign
sovrap'por|re vt superimpose. ~si vr overlap. sovrapposizi'one nf superimposition
sovra'stare vt dominate; (fig: pericolo:) hang over

sovrinten'den|te, **~za** = **soprin-tendente, soprintendenza**

sovru'mano *a* superhuman

sovvenzi'one *nf* subsidy

sovver'sivo *a* subversive

'sozzo *a* filthy

S.p.A. *abbr* (**società per azioni**) plc

spac'ca|re *vt* split; chop ‹legna›. **~rsi** *vr* split. **~tura** *nf* split

spacci'a|re *vt* deal in, push ‹droga›; **~re qcsa per qcsa** pass sth off as sth; **essere ~to** to be done for, be a goner. **~rsi** *vr* **~rsi per** pass oneself off as. **~'tore**, **~'trice** *nmf* (di droga) pusher; (di denaro falso) distributor of forged bank notes. **'spaccio** *nm* (di droga) dealer, pusher; (negozio) shop

'spacco *nm* split

spac'cone, -a *nmf* boaster

'spada *nf* sword. **~c'cino** *nm* swordsman

spadroneggi'are *vi* act the boss

spae'sato *a* disorientated

spa'ghetti *nmpl* spaghetti *sg*

spa'ghetto *nm* (fam: spavento) fright

'Spagna *nf* Spain

spa'gnolo, -a *a* Spanish ●*nmf* Spaniard ●*nm* (lingua) Spanish

'spago *nm* string; **dare ~ a** qcno encourage sb

spal'ato *a* odd

spalan'ca|re *vt*, **~rsi** *vr* open wide. **~to** *a* wide open

spa'lare *vt* shovel

'spalla *nf* shoulder; (di comico) straight man; **~ a ~** (di schiena) back; **alle ~e di** qcno (ridere) behind sb's back. **~eggi'are** *vt* back up

spal'letta *nf* parapet

spalli'era *nf* back; (di letto) head-board; (ginnastica) wall bars *pl*

spal'lina *nf* strap; (imbottitura) shoulder pad

spal'mare *vt* spread

'spande|re *vt* spread; (versare) spill. **~si** *vr* spread

spappo'lare *vt* crush

spa'ra|re *vt/i* shoot; **~rle grosse** talk big. **~ta** *nf fam* tall story. **~'toria** *nf* shooting

sparecchi'are *vt* clear

spa'reggio *nm Comm* deficit; *Sport* play-off

'sparg|ere *vt* scatter; (diffondere) spread; shed ‹lacrime, sangue›. **~ersi** *vr* spread. **~i'mento** *nm* scattering; (di lacrime, sangue) shedding; **~imento di sangue** bloodshed

spa'ri|re *vi* disappear; **~scll** get lost!. **~zi'one** *nf* disappearance

spar'lare *vi* **~ di** run down

'sparo *nm* shot

sparpagli'a|re *vt*, **~si** *vr* scatter

'sparso *pp di* **spargere** ●*a* scattered; (sciolto) loose

spar'tire *vt* share out; (separare) separate

sparti'traffico *nm inv* traffic island; (di autostrada) central reservation, median strip *Am*

spartizi'one *nf* division

spa'ruto *a* gaunt; (gruppo) small; (peli, capelli) sparse

sparvi'ero *nm* sparrow-hawk

spasi'ma|nte *nm* admirer. **~re** *vi* suffer agonies

'spasimo *nm* spasm

spa'smodico *a* spasmodic

spas'sar|si *vr* amuse oneself; **~sela** have a good time

spassio'nato *a* ‹osservatore› dispassionate, impartial

'spasso *nm* fun; **essere uno ~** be hilarious; **andare a ~** go for a walk. **spas'soso** *a* hilarious

'spatola *nf* spatula

spau'racchio *nm* scarecrow; *fig* bugbear. **spau'rire** *vt* frighten

spa'valdo *a* defiant

spaventa'passeri *nm inv* scarecrow

spaven'ta|re *vt* frighten, scare. **~si** *vr* be frightened, be scared. **spa'vento** *nm* fright. **spaven'toso** *a* frightening; (fam: enorme) incredible

spazi'ale *a* spatial; *(cosmico)* space *attrib*

spazi'are *vt* space out ● *vi* range

spazien'tirsi *vr* lose [one's] patience

'**spazi|o** *nm* space. **~'oso** *a* spacious

spazzaca'mino *nm* chimney sweep

spaz'z|are *vt* sweep; **~are via** sweep away; *(fam: mangiare)* devour. **~a'tura** *vf (immondizia)* rubbish. **~ino** *nm* road sweeper; *(netturbino)* dustman

'**spazzo|la** *nf* brush; *(di tergicristallo)* blade. **~'lare** *vt* brush. **~'lino** *nm* small brush. **~lino da denti** toothbrush. **~'lone** *nm* scrubbing brush

specchi'arsi *vr* look at oneself in a/the mirror; *(riflettersi)* be mirrored; **~ in qcno** model oneself on sb

specchi'etto *nm* **~ retrovisore** driving mirror

'**specchio** *nm* mirror

speci'a|le *a* special ● *nm* TV special [programme]. **~'lista** *nmf* specialist. **~lità** *nf inv* speciality, specialty *Am*

specializ'za|re *vt*, **~rsi** *vr* specialize. **~to** *a (operaio)* skilled

special'mente *adv* especially

'**specie** *nf inv (scientifico)* species; *(tipo)* kind; **fare ~ a** surprise

specifi'care *vt* specify. **spe'cifico** *a* specific

specu'lare¹ *vi* speculate; **~ su** *(indagare)* speculate on; *Fin* speculate in

specu'lare² *a* mirror *attrib*

specula'tore, -'trice *nmf* speculator. **~zi'one** *nf* speculation

spe'di|re *vt* send. **~to** *pp di* **spedire** ● *a* quick; *(parlata)* fluent. **~zi'one** *nf (di lettere ecc)* dispatch; *Comm* consignment; *(scientifica)* expedition

'**spegner|e** *vt* put out; turn off *(gas, luce)*; switch off *(motore)*;

slake *(sete)*. **~si** *vr* go out; *(morire)* pass away

spelacchi'ato *a (tappeto)* threadbare; *(cane)* mangy

spe'lar|e *vt* skin *(coniglio)*. **~si** *vr (cane)* moult

speleolo'gia *nf* potholing, speleology

spel'lar|e *vt* skin; *fig* fleece. **~si** *vr* peel off

spe'lonca *nf* cave; *fig* dingy hole

spendacci'one, -a *nmf* spendthrift

'**spendere** *vt* spend; **~ fiato** waste one's breath

spen'nare *vt* pluck; *fam* fleece *(cliente)*

spennel'lare *vt* brush

spensie|ra'tezza *nf* lightheartedness. **~'rato** *a* carefree

'**spento** *pp di* **spegnere** ● *a* off; *(gas)* out; *(smorto)* dull

spe'ranza *nf* hope; **pieno di ~** hopeful; **senza ~** hopeless

spe'rare *vt* hope for; *(aspettarsi)* expect ● *vi* **~ in** trust in; **spero di sì** I hope so

'**sper|dersi** *vr* get lost. **~'duto** *a* lost; *(isolato)* secluded

spergi'uro, -a *nmf* perjurer ● *nm* perjury

sperico'lato *a* swashbuckling

sperimen'ta|le *a* experimental. **~re** *vt* experiment with; test *(resistenza, capacità, teoria)*. **~zi'one** *nf* experimentation

'**sperma** *nm* sperm

spe'rone *nm* spur

sperpe'rare *vt* squander. 'sperpero *nm* waste

'**spes|a** *nf* expense; *(acquisto)* purchase; **andare a far ~e** go shopping; **fare la ~a** do the shopping; **fare le ~e di** pay for. **~e** *pl* **bancarie** bank charges. **~e a carico del destinatario** carriage forward. **~e di spedizione** shipping costs. **~e sostenute** all-expenses-paid. **~o** *pp di* **spendere**

'**spesso¹** *a* thick

'**spesso²** *adv* often

spes'sore nm thickness; (fig: consistenza) substance

spet'tabile a (Comm abbr **Spett.**) **S~ ditta Rossi** Messrs Rossi

spettaco'lare a spectacular. **spet'tacolo** nm spectacle; (rappresentazione) show. **~'loso** a spectacular

spet'tare vi ~ **a** be up to; (diritto:) be due to

spetta'tore, -'trice nmf spectator; **spettatori** pl (di cinema ecc) audience sg

spette'golare vi gossip

spetti'nar|e vt **~e qcno** ruffle sb's hair. **~si** vr ruffle one's hair

spet'trale a ghostly. **spettro** nm ghost; Phys spectrum

'spezie nfpl spices

spez'zar|e vt, **~si** vr break

spezza'tino nm stew

spez'zato nm coordinated jacket and trousers

spezzet'tare vt break into small pieces

'spia nf spy; (della polizia) informer; (di porta) peep-hole; **fare la ~** sneak. **~ [luminosa]** light. **~ dell'olio** oil [warning] light

spiacci'care vt squash

spia'ce|nte a sorry. **~vole** a unpleasant

spi'aggia nf beach

spia'nare vt level; (rendere liscio) smooth; roll out (pasta); raze to the ground (edificio)

spi'ano nm **a tutto ~** flat out

spian'tato a fig penniless

spi'are vt spy on; wait for (occasione ecc)

spiattel'lare vt blurt out; shove (oggetto)

spiaz'zare vt wrong-foot

spi'azzo nm (radura) clearing

spic'ca|re vt **~re un salto** jump; **~re il volo** take flight ● vi stand out. **~to** a marked

'spicchio nm (di agrumi) segment; (di aglio) clove

spicci'a|rsi vr hurry up. **~'tivo** a speedy

'spicciolo a (comune) banal; (denaro, 10 000 lire) in change. **spiccioli** pl change sg

'spicco nm relief; **fare ~** stand out

'spider nmf inv open-top sports car

spie'dino nm kebab. **spi'edo** nm spit; **allo spiedo** on a spit, spit-roasted

spie'ga|re vt explain; open out (cartina); unfurl (vele). **~rsi** vr explain oneself; (vele, bandiere:) unfurl. **~zi'one** nf explanation

spiega'zzato a crumpled

spie'tato a ruthless

spiff'erare vt blurt out ● vi (vento:) whistle. **'spiffero** nm (corrente d'aria) draught

'spiga nf spike; Bot ear

spigli'ato a self-possessed

'spigolo nm edge; (angolo) corner

'spilla nf (gioiello) brooch. **~ da balia** safety pin. **~ di sicurezza** safety pin

spil'lare vt tap

'spillo nm pin. **~ di sicurezza** safety pin; (in arma) safety catch

spil'orcio a stingy

spilun'gone, -a nmf beanpole

'spina nf thorn; (di pesce) bone; Electr plug. **~ dorsale** spine

spi'naci nmpl spinach

spi'nale a spinal

spi'nato a (filo) barbed; (pianta) thorny

spi'nello nm fam joint

'spinger|e vt push; fig drive. **~si** vr (andare) proceed

spi'noso a thorny

'spinta nf push; (violenta) thrust; fig spur. **~o** pp di **spingere**

spio'naggio nm espionage, spying

spio'vente a (tetto) sloping

spi'overe vi liter stop raining; (ricadere) fall; (scorrere) flow down

'spira nf coil

spi'raglio nm small opening; (soffio d'aria) breath of air; (raggio di luce) gleam of light

spi'rale a spiral ● nf spiral; (negli

orologi) hairspring; (*anticoncezionale*) coil

spi'rare *vi* (*soffiare*) blow; (*morire*) pass away

spirit'|ato *a* possessed; (*espressione*) wild. ~ismo *nm* spiritualism. 'spirito *nm* spirit; (*arguzia*) wit; (*intelletto*) mind; fare dello spirito be witty; sotto spirito in brandy. ~o'saggine *nf* witticism. spiri'toso *a* witty

spiritu'ale *a* spiritual

splen'dente *a* shining

splen|dere *vi* shine. ~dido *a* splendid. ~dore *nm* splendour

spode'stare *vt* dispossess; depose (*re*)

'spoglia *nf* (*di animale*) skin; spoglie *pl* (*salma*) mortal remains; (*bottino*) spoils

spogli|a|re *vt* strip; (*svestire*) undress; (*fare lo spoglio di*) go through. ~'rello *nm* strip-tease. ~rsi *vr* strip, undress. ~'toio *nm* dressing room; *Sport* changing room; (*guardaroba*) cloakroom, checkroom *Am*. 'spoglio *a* undressed; (*albero, muro*) bare ● *nm* (*scrutinio*) perusal

'spola *nf* shuttle; fare la ~ shuttle

spol'pare *vt* take the flesh off; *fig* fleece

spolve'rare *vt* dust; *fam* devour (*cibo*)

'sponda *nf* (*di mare, lago*) shore; (*di fiume*) bank; (*bordo*) edge

sponsoriz'zare *vt* sponsor

spon'taneo *a* spontaneous

spopo'lar|e *vt* depopulate ● *vi* (*avere successo*) draw the crowds. ~si *vr* become depopulated

sporadica'mente *adv* sporadically. spo'radico *a* sporadic

sporcacci'one, -a *a* dirty pig

spor'c|are *vt* dirty; (*macchiare*) soil. ~arsi *vr* get dirty. ~izia *nf* dirt. 'sporco *a* dirty; avere la coscienza sporca have a guilty conscience ● *nm* dirt

spor'gen|te *a* jutting. ~za *nf* projection

'sporger|e *vt* stretch out; ~e querela contro take legal action against ● *vi* jut out. ~si *vr* lean out

sport *nm inv* sport

'sporta *nf* shopping basket

spor'tello *nm* door; (*di banca ecc*) window. ~ automatico cash dispenser

spor'tivo, -a *a* sports *attrib*; (*persona*) sporty ● *nm* sportsman ● *nf* sportswoman

'sporto *pp di* sporgere

'sposa *nf* bride. ~'lizio *nm* wedding

spo'sa|re *vt* marry; *fig* espouse. ~rsi *vr* get married; (*vino:*) go (con with). ~to *a* married. 'sposo *nm* bridegroom; sposi *pl* [novelli] newlyweds

spossa'tezza *nf* exhaustion. spos'sato *a* exhausted, worn out

spo'sta|re *vt* move; (*differire*) postpone; (*cambiare*) change. ~rsi *vr* move. ~to, -a *a* ill-adjusted ● *nmf* (*disadattato*) misfit

'spranga *nf* bar. spran'gare *vt* bar

'sprazzo *nm* (*di colore*) splash; (*di luce*) flash; *fig* glimmer

spre'care *vt* waste. 'spreco *nm* waste

spre'g|evole *a* despicable. ~ia'tivo *a* pejorative. 'spregio *nm* contempt

spregiudi'cato *a* unscrupulous

'spremer|e *vt* squeeze. ~si *vr* ~si le meningi rack one's brains

spremia'grumi *nm* lemon squeezer

spre'muta *nf* juice. ~ d'arancia fresh orange [juice]

sprez'zante *a* contemptuous

sprigio'nar|e *vt* emit. ~si *vr* burst out

spriz'zare *vt/i* spurt; be bursting with (*salute, gioia*)

sprofon'dar|e *vi* sink; (*crollare*) collapse. ~si *vr* ~si in sink into; *fig* be engrossed in

spro'nare *vt* spur on. 'sprone *nm* spur; (*sartoria*) yoke

sproporzio'nato *a* disproportionate. **~'one** *nf* disproportion

sproposi'tato *a* full of blunders; (*enorme*) huge. **spro'posito** *nm* blunder; (*eccesso*) excessive amount; **a sproposito** inopportunely

sprovve'duto *a* unprepared; **~ di** lacking in

sprov'visto *a* **~ di** out of; lacking in (*fantasia, pazienza*); **alla sprovvista** unexpectedly

spruz'za|re *vt* sprinkle; (*vaporizzare*) spray; (*inzaccherare*) spatter. **~tore** *nm* spray; **'spruzzo** *nm* spray; (*di fango*) splash

spudo'ratezza *nf* shamelessness. **~'rato** *a* shameless

'spugna *nf* sponge; (*tessuto*) towelling. **spu'gnoso** *a* spongy

'spuma *nf* foam; (*schiuma*) froth; *Culin* mousse. **spu'mante** *nm* sparkling wine, spumante. **spumeggi'are** *vi* foam

spun'ta|re *vt* (*rompere la punta di*) break the point of; trim (*capelli*); **~rla** *fig* win ● *vi* (*pianta:*) sprout; (*capelli:*) begin to grow; (*sorgere*) rise; (*apparire*) appear. **~rsi** *vr* get blunt. **~ta** *nf* trim

spun'tino *nm* snack

'spunto *nm* cue; *fig* starting point; **dare ~ a** give rise to

spur'gar|e *vt* purge. **~si** *vr Med* expectorate

spu'tare *vt/i* spit; **~ sentenze** pass judgment. **'sputo** *nm* spit

'squadra *nf* (*gruppo*) team, squad; (*di polizia etc*) squad; (*da disegno*) square. **squa'drare** *vt* square; (*guardare*) look up and down

squa'driglia *nf*, **~'one** *nm* squadron

squagli'ar|e *vt*, **~si** *vr* melt; **~sela** (*fam: svignarsela*) steal out

squa'lifi|ca *nf* disqualification. **~'care** *vt* disqualify

squal'lido *a* squalid. **squal'lore** *nm* squalor

'squalo *nm* shark

'squama *nf* scale; (*di pelle*) flake

squa'm|are *vt* scale. **~arsi** *vr* (*pelle:*) flake off. **~'moso** *a* scaly; (*pelle*) flaky

squarcia'gola: a ~ *adv* at the top of one's voice

squarci'are *vt* rip. **'squarcio** *nm* rip; (*di ferita, in nave*) gash; (*di cielo*) patch

squar'tare *vt* quarter; dismember (*animale*)

squattri'nato *a* penniless

squili'bra|re *vt* unbalance. **~to, -a** *a* unbalanced ● *nmf* lunatic. **squi'librio** *nm* imbalance

squil'la|nte *a* shrill. **~re** *vi* (*campana:*) peal; (*tromba:*) blare; (*telefono:*) ring. **'squillo** *nm* blare; *Teleph* ring; (*ragazza*) call girl

squi'sito *a* exquisite

squit'tire *vi* (*pappagallo, fig:*) squawk; (*topo:*) squeak

sradi'care *vt* uproot; eradicate (*vizio, male*)

sragio'nare *vi* rave

srego'latezza *nf* dissipation. **~'lato** *a* inordinate; (*dissoluto*) dissolute

s.r.l. *abbr* (**società a responsabilità limitata**) Ltd

sroto'lare *vt* uncoil

SS *abbr* (**strada statale**) national road

'stabile *a* stable; (*permanente*) lasting; (*saldo*) steady; **compagnia ~** *Theat* repertory company ● *nm* (*edificio*) building

stabili'mento *nm* factory; (*industriale*) plant; (*edificio*) establishment. **~ balneare** lido

stabi'li|re *vt* establish; (*decidere*) decide. **~rsi** *vr* settle. **~tà** *nf* stability

stabiliz'za|re *vt* stabilize. **~rsi** *vr* stabilize. **~'tore** *nm* stabilizer

stac'car|e *vt* detach; pronounce clearly (*parole*); (*separare*) separate, turn off (*corrente*); **~ gli occhi da** take one's eyes off ● *vi* (*fam: finire di lavorare*) knock off. **~si** *vr* come off; **~si da** break away from (*partito, famiglia*)

staccio'nata nf fence
'**stacco** nm gap
'**stadio** nm stadium
'**staffa** nf stirrup
staf'fetta nf dispatch rider
stagio'nale a seasonal
stagio'na|re vt season ⟨legno⟩;
  mature ⟨formaggio⟩. **~to** a ⟨legno⟩
  seasoned; ⟨formaggio⟩ matured
stagi'one nf season; **alta/bassa ~**
  high/low season
stagli'arsi vr stand out
sta'gna|nte a stagnant. **~re** vt
  ⟨saldare⟩ solder; ⟨chiudere ermeti-
  camente⟩ seal ● vi ⟨acqua:⟩ stagnate. '**stagno** a ⟨a tenuta d'acqua⟩
  watertight ● nm ⟨acqua ferma⟩
  pond; ⟨metallo⟩ tin
sta'gnola nf tinfoil
stalag'mite nf stalagmite
stalat'tite nf stalactite
'**stall|a** nf stable; ⟨per buoi⟩ cow-
  shed. **~i'ere** nm groom
stal'lone nm stallion
sta'mani, stamat'tina adv this
  morning
stam'becco nm ibex
stam'berga nf hovel
'**stampa** nf Typ printing; ⟨giornali,
  giornalisti⟩ press; ⟨riproduzione⟩
  print
stam'pa|nte nf printer. **~nte ad
  aghi** dot matrix printer. **~nte laser** laser printer. **~re** vt print.
  ~'tello nm block letters pl
stam'pella nf crutch
'**stampo** nm mould; **di vecchio ~**
  ⟨persona⟩ of the old school
sta'nare vt drive out
stan'car|e vt tire; ⟨annoiare⟩ bore.
  ~si vr get tired
stan'chezza nf tiredness. '**stanco**
  a tired. **stanco di** ⟨stufo⟩ fed up
  with. **stanco morto** dead tired,
  knackered fam
'**standard** a & nm inv standard.
  ~iz'zare vt standardize
'**stan|ga** nf bar; ⟨persona⟩ bean-
  pole. **~'gata** nf fig blow; ⟨fam: nel
  calcio⟩ big kick; **prendere una
  ~gata** ⟨fam: agli esami, economi-

ca⟩ come a cropper. **stan'ghetta** nf
  ⟨di occhiali⟩ leg
sta'notte nf tonight; ⟨la notte scor-
  sa⟩ last night
'**stante** prep on account of; **a sé ~**
  separate
stan'tio a stale
stan'tuffo nm piston
'**stanza** nf room; ⟨metrica⟩ stanza
stanzi'are vt allocate
stap'pare vt uncork
'**stare** vi ⟨rimanere⟩ stay; ⟨abitare⟩
  live; ⟨con gerundio⟩ be; **sto solo
  cinque minuti** I'll stay only five
  minutes; **sto in piazza Peyron** I
  live in Peyron Square; **sta dor-
  mendo** he's sleeping; **~** a ⟨attener-
  si⟩ keep to; ⟨spettare⟩ be up to; **~
  bene** ⟨economicamente⟩ be well
  off; ⟨di salute⟩ be well; ⟨addirsi⟩
  suit; **~ dietro a** ⟨seguire⟩ follow;
  ⟨sorvegliare⟩ keep an eye on; ⟨cor-
  teggiare⟩ run after; **~ in piedi**
  stand; **~ per** be about to; **ben ti
  sta** it serves you right!; **come
  stai/sta?** how are you?; **lasciar ~**
  leave alone; **starci** ⟨essere conten-
  to⟩ go into; ⟨essere d'accordo⟩
  agree; **in 3 ci sta 12 ci sta 4 volte** 3
  into 12 goes 4; **non sa ~ agli
  scherzi** he can't take a joke; **~ su**
  ⟨con la schiena⟩ sit up straight; **~
  sulle proprie** keep oneself to oneself. **starsene** vr ⟨rimanere⟩ stay
starnu'tire vi sneeze. **star'nuto**
  nm sneeze
sta'sera adv this evening, tonight
sta'tale a state attrib ● nmf state
  employee ● nf ⟨strada⟩ main road,
  trunk road
'**statico** a static
sta'tista nm statesman
sta'tistic|a nf statistics sg. **~o** a
  statistical
'**stato** pp di **essere, stare** ● nm
  state; ⟨posizione sociale⟩ position;
  Jur status. **~ d'animo** frame of
  mind. **~ civile** marital status. **S~
  Maggiore** Mil General Staff. **Stati
  pl Uniti [d'America]** United States
  [of America]

'statua *nf* statue

statuni'tense *a* United States attrib, US attrib ● *nmf* citizen of the United States, US citizen

sta'tura *nf* height; di alta ~ tall; di bassa ~ short

sta'tuto *nm* statute

stazio'nario *a* stationary

stazi'one *nf* station; (città) resort. ~ balneare seaside resort. ~ ferroviaria railway station Br, train station. ~ di servizio petrol station Br, service station. ~ termale spa

'stecca *nf* stick; (di ombrello) rib; (da biliardo) cue; (di sigarette) carton; (di reggiseno) stiffener

stec'cato *nm* fence

stec'chito *a* skinny; (rigido) stiff; (morto) stone cold dead

'stella *nf* star; stelle alle stelle ⟨prezzi⟩ rise sky-high. ~ alpina edelweiss. ~ cadente shooting star. ~ filante streamer. ~ di mare starfish

stel'la|re *a* star attrib; ⟨grandezza⟩ stellar. ~to *a* starry

'stelo *nm* stem; lampada *nf* a ~ standard lamp

'stemma *nm* coat of arms

stempi'ato *a* bald at the temples

sten'dardo *nm* standard

'stender|e *vt* spread out; (appendere) hang out; (distendere) stretch [out]; (scrivere) write down. ~rsi *vr* stretch out

stendibianche'ria *nm inv*, sten-di'toio *nm* clothes horse

stenodattilogra'fia *nf* shorthand typing. ~'lografo, -a *nmf* shorthand typist

stenogra'f|are *vt* take down in shorthand. ~ia *nf* shorthand

sten'ta|re *vi* ~re a find it hard to. ~to *a* laboured. 'stento *nm* (fatica) a stento with difficulty; stenti *pl* hardships, privations

'sterco *nm* dung

'stereo'fonico *a* stereo[phonic]

stereoti'pato *a* stereotyped; ⟨sorriso⟩ insincere. stere'otipo *nm* stereotype

'steril|e *a* sterile; ⟨terreno⟩ barren. ~ità *nf* sterility. ~iz'zare *vt* sterilize. ~izzazi'one *nf* sterilization

ster'lina *nf* pound; lira ~ [pound] sterling

stermi'nare *vt* exterminate

stermi'nato *a* immense

ster'minio *nm* extermination

'sterno *nm* breastbone

ste'roide *nm* steroid

ster'zare *vi* steer. 'sterzo *nm* steering

'steso *pp di* stendere

'stesso *a* same; io ~ myself; tu ~ yourself; me ~ myself; se ~ himself; in quel momento ~ at that very moment; dalla stessa regina (in persona) by the Queen herself; tuo fratello ~ dice che hai torto even your brother says you're wrong; coi miei stessi occhi with my own eyes ● *pron* lo ~ the same one; (la stessa cosa) the same; fa lo ~ it's all the same; ci vado lo ~ I'll go just the same

ste'sura *nf* drawing up; (documento) draft

stick *nm* colla a ~ glue stick; deodorante a ~ stick deodorant

'stigma *nm* stigma. ~te *nfpl* stigmata

sti'lare *vt* draw up

'stile *nm* style. ~e libero (nel nuoto) freestyle, crawl. sti'lista *nmf* stylist. ~iz'zato *a* stylized

stil'lare *vi* ooze

stilo'graf|ica *nf* fountain pen. ~o *a* penna ~a fountain pen

'stima *nf* esteem; (valutazione) estimate. sti'mare *vt* esteem; (valutare) estimate; (ritenere) consider

stimo'la|nte *a* stimulating ● *nm* stimulant. ~re *vt* stimulate; (incitare) incite

'stimolo *nm* stimulus; (fitta) pang

'stinco *nm* shin

'stinger|e *vt/i* fade. ~si *vr* fade. 'stinto *pp di* stingere

sti'par|e vt cram. **~si** vr crowd together

stipendi'ato a salaried ● nm salaried worker. **sti'pendio** nm salary

'stipite nm doorpost

stipu'la|re vt stipulate. **~zi'one** nf stipulation; ⟨accordo⟩ agreement

stira'mento nm sprain

sti'ra|re vt iron; ⟨distendere⟩ stretch. **~rsi** vr ⟨distendersi⟩ stretch; pull ⟨muscolo⟩. **~tura** nf ironing. **'stiro** nm **ferro da stiro** iron

'stirpe nf stock

stiti'chezza nf constipation. **'stitico** a constipated

'stiva nf Naut hold

sti'vale nm boot. **stivali** pl **di gomma** Wellington boots, Wellingtons

'stizza nf anger

stiz'zi|re vt irritate. **~rsi** vr become irritated. **~to** a irritated. **stiz'zoso** a peevish

stocca'fisso nm stockfish

stoc'cata nf stab; ⟨battuta pungente⟩ gibe

'stoffa nf material; fig stuff

'stola nf stole

'stolto a foolish

stoma'chevole a revolting

'stomaco nm stomach; **mal di ~** stomach-ache

sto'na|re vt/i sing/play out of tune ● vi ⟨non intonarsi⟩ clash. **~to** a out of tune; ⟨discordante⟩ clashing; ⟨confuso⟩ bewildered. **~tura** nf false note; ⟨discordanza⟩ clash

'stoppia nf stubble

stop'pino nm wick

stop'poso a tough

'storcer|e vt, **~si** vr twist

stor'di|re vt stun; ⟨intontire⟩ daze. **~rsi** vr dull one's senses. **~to** a stunned; ⟨intontito⟩ dazed; ⟨sventato⟩ heedless

'storia nf history; ⟨racconto, bugia⟩ story; ⟨pretesto⟩ excuse; **senza storie** no fuss!; **fare [delle] storie** make a fuss

'storico, -a a historical; ⟨di impor-

tanza storica⟩ historic ● nmf historian

stori'one nm sturgeon

'stormo nm flock

'storno nm starling

storpi'a|re vt cripple; mangle ⟨parole⟩. **~'tura** nf deformation. **'storpio, -a** a crippled ● nmf cripple

'stort|a nf ⟨distorsione⟩ sprain; **prendere una ~a alla caviglia** sprain one's ankle. **~o** pp di **storcere** ● a crooked; ⟨ritorto⟩ twisted; ⟨gambe⟩ bandy; fig wrong

sto'viglie nfpl crockery sg

'strabico a cross-eyed; **essere ~** be cross-eyed, have a squint.

strabili'ante a astonishing

stra'bismo nm squint

strabboc'care vi overflow

stra'carico a overloaded

stracci'a|re vt tear; ⟨fam: vincere⟩ thrash. **~'ato** a torn; ⟨persona⟩ in rags; ⟨prezzi⟩ slashed; **a un prezzo ~ato** dirt cheap. **'straccio** a torn ● nm rag; ⟨strofinaccio⟩ cloth **~'one** nm tramp

stra'cotto a overdone; ⟨fam: innamorato⟩ head over heels ● nm stew

'strada nf road; ⟨di città⟩ street; ⟨fig: cammino⟩ way; **essere fuori ~** be on the wrong track; **fare ~** lead the way; **farsi ~** make one's way. **~ maestra** main road. **~ a senso unico** one-way street. **~ senza uscita** blind alley. **stra'dale** a road attrib

strafalci'one nm blunder

stra'fare vi overdo it, overdo things

stra'foro: di ~ adv on the sly

strafot'ten|te a arrogant. **~za** nf arrogance

'strage nf slaughter

'stralcio nm ⟨parte⟩ extract

stralu'na|re vt **~re gli occhi** open one's eyes wide. **~to** a ⟨occhi⟩ staring; ⟨persona⟩ distraught

stramaz'zare vi fall heavily

strambe'ria *nf* oddity. **'strambo** *a* strange

strampa'lato *a* odd

stra'nezza *nf* strangeness

strango'lare *vt* strangle

strani'ero, -a *a* foreign ● *nmf* foreigner

'strano *a* strange

straordi|naria'mente *adv* extraordinarily. **~'nario** *a* extraordinary; *(notevole)* remarkable; *(edizione)* special; **lavoro ~nario** overtime; **treno ~nario** special train

strapaz'zar|e *vt* ill-treat; scramble *(uova)*. **~si** *vr* tire oneself out. **stra'pazzo** *nm* strain; **da strapazzo** *fig* worthless

strapi'eno *a* overflowing

strapi'ombo *nm* projection; **a ~** sheer

strap'par|e *vt* tear; *(per distruggere)* tear up; pull out *(dente, capelli)*; *(sradicare)* pull up; *(estorcere)* wring. **~si** *vr* get torn; *(allontanarsi)* tear oneself away. **'strappo** *nm* tear; *(strattone)* jerk; *(fam: passaggio)* lift; **fare uno strappo alla regola** make an exception to the rule. **~ muscolare** muscle strain

strapun'tino *nm* folding seat

strari'pare *vi* flood

strasci'c|are *vt* trail; shuffle *(piedi)*; drawl *(parole)*. **'strascico** *nm* train; *fig* after-effect

strass *nm inv* rhinestone

strata'gemma *nm* stratagem

strate'gia *nf* strategy. **stra'tegico** *a* strategic

'strato *nm* layer; *(di vernice ecc)* coat, layer; *(roccioso, sociale)* stratum. **~'sfera** *nf* stratosphere. **~'sferico** *a* stratospheric; *fig* sky-high

stravac'ca|rsi *vr fam* slouch. **~to** *a fam* slouching

strava'gan|te *a* extravagant; *(eccentrico)* eccentric. **~za** *nf* extravagance; *(eccentricità)* eccentricity

stra'vecchio *a* ancient

strave'dere *vt* **~ per** worship

stravizi'are *vi* indulge oneself. **stra'vizio** *nm* excess

stra'volg|ere *vt* twist; *(turbare)* upset. **~i'mento** *nm* twisting. **stra'volto** *a* distraught; *(fam: stanco)* done in

strazi'a|nte *a* heartrending; *(dolore)* agonizing. **~re** *vt* grate on *(orecchie)*; break *(cuore)*. **'strazio** *nm* agony; **essere uno strazio** be agony; **che strazio!** *fam* it's awful!

'strega *nf* witch. **stre'gare** *vt* bewitch. **stre'gone** *nm* wizard

'stregua *nf* **alla ~ di** like

stre'ma|re *vt* exhaust. **~to** *a* exhausted

'stremo *nm* **ridotto allo ~** at the end of one's tether

'strenuo *a* strenuous

strepi|'tare *vi* make a noise. **'strepito** *nm* noise. **~'toso** *a* noisy; *fig* resounding

stres'sa|nte *a* *(lavoro, situazione)* stressful. **~to** *a* stressed [out]

'stretta *nf* grasp; *(dolore)* pang; **essere alle strette** be in dire straits; **mettere alle strette qcno** have sb's back up against the wall. **~ di mano** handshake

stret'tezza *nf* narrowness; **stret'tezze** *pl* *(difficoltà finanziarie)* financial difficulties

'stret|to *pp di* **stringere** ● *a* narrow; *(serrato)* tight; *(vicino)* close; *(dialetto)* broad; *(rigoroso)* strict; **lo ~to necessario** the bare minimum ● *nm* Geog strait. **~'toia** *nf* bottleneck; *(fam: difficoltà)* tight spot

stri'a|to *a* striped. **~'tura** *nf* streak

stri'dente *a* strident

'stridere *vi* squeak; *fig* clash. **'stridore** *nm* screech

'stridulo *a* shrill

strigli'a|re *vt* groom. **~'ta** *nf* grooming, *fig* dressing down

stril'l|are *vi/t* scream. **'strillo** *nm* scream

strimin'zito a skimpy; (magro) skinny

strimpel'lare vt strum

'strin|ga nf lace; Comput string. **~'gato** a fig terse

'stringer|e vt press; (serrare) squeeze; (tenere stretto) hold tight; take in (abito); (comprimere) be tight; (restringere) tighten; **~e la mano** a shake hands with ●vi (premere) press. **~si** vr (accostarsi) draw close (**a** to); (avvicinarsi) squeeze up

'striscia nf strip; (riga) stripe. **strisce** pl [**pedonali**] zebra crossing sg

strisci'ar|e vi crawl; (sfiorare) graze ●vt drag (piedi). **~si** vr **~si a** rub against. **'striscio** nm graze; Med smear; **colpire di striscio** graze

strisci'one nm banner

strito'lare vt grind

striz'zare vt squeeze; (torcere) wring [out]; **~ l'occhio** wink

'strofa nf strophe

strofi'naccio nm cloth; (per spolverare) duster. **~ da cucina** tea towel

strofi'nare vt rub

stromboz'zare vt boast about ●vi hoot

strombaz'zata nf (di clacson) hoot

stron'care vt cut off; (reprimere) crush; (criticare) tear to shreds

'stronzo nm vulg shit

stropicci'are vt rub; crumple (vestito)

stroz'zar|e vt strangle. **~'tura** nf strangling; (di strada) narrowing

strozzi'naggio nm loan-sharking

stroz'zino nm pej usurer; (truffatore) shark

strug'gente a all-consuming

'struggersi vr liter pine [away]

strumen'tale a instrumental

strumentaliz'zare vt make use of

strumentazi'one nf instrumentation

stru'mento nm instrument; (arnese) tool. **~ a corda** string instrument. **~ musicale** musical instrument

strusci'are vt rub

'strutto nm lard

strut'tura nf structure. **struttu'rale** a structural

struttu'rare vt structure

strutturazi'one nf structuring

'struzzo nm ostrich

stuc'care vt stucco

stuc'chevole a nauseating

'stucco nm stucco

stu'den|te, -'essa nmf student; (di scuola) schoolboy; schoolgirl. **~'tesco** a student; (di scolaro) school attrib

studi'are vt study. **~si** vr **~si di** try to

'studi|o nm studying; (stanza, ricerca) study; (di artista, TV ecc) studio; (di professionista) office. **~'oso, -a** a studious ●nmf scholar

'stufa nf stove. **~ elettrica** electric fire

stu'far|e vt Culin stew; (dare fastidio) bore. **~rsi** vr get bored. **~to** nm stew

'stufo a bored; **essere ~ di** be fed up with

stu'oia nf mat

stupefa'cente a amazing ●nm drug

stu'pendo a stupendous

stupi'd|aggine nf (azione) stupid thing; (cosa di poco) nothing. **~ata** nf stupid thing. **~ità** nf stupidity. **'stupido** a stupid

stu'pir|e vt astonish ●vi, **~si** vr be astonished. **stu'pore** nm amazement

stu'pra|re vt rape. **~'tore** nm rapist. **'stupro** nm rape

sturalavan'dini nm inv plunger

stu'rare vt uncork; unblock (lavandino)

stuzzica'denti nm inv toothpick

stuzzi'care vt prod [at]; pick (denti); poke (fuoco); (molestare) tease; whet (appetito)

stuzzi'chino nm Culin appetizer

su *prep* on; (*senza contatto*) over; (*riguardo a*) about; (*circa, intorno a*) about, around; **le chiavi sono sul tavolo** the keys are on the table; **il quadro è appeso sul camino** the picture is hanging over the fireplace; **un libro sull'antico Egitto** a book on *o* about Ancient Egypt; **costa sulle 50 000 lire** it costs about 50,000 lire; **decidere sul momento** decide at the time; **su commissione** on commission; **su due piedi** on the spot; **uno su dieci** one out of ten; ~ *adv* (*sopra*) up; (*al piano di sopra*) upstairs; (*addosso*) on; **ho su il cappotto** I've got my coat on; **in su** (*guardare*) up; **dalla vita in su** from the waist up; **su!** come on!

su'bacqueo *a* underwater
subaffit'tare *vt* sublet. **subaf'fitto** *nm* sublet
subal'terno *a* & *nm* subordinate
sub'buglio *nm* turmoil
sub'conscio *a* & *nm* subconscious
subdola'mente *adv* deviously.
'subdolo *a* devious, underhand
suben'trare *vi* (*circostanze:*) come up; ~ **a** take the place of
su'bire *vt* undergo; (*patire*) suffer
subis'sare *vt* fig ~ **di** overwhelm with
'subito *adv* at once; ~ **dopo** straight after
sub'lime *a* sublime
subodo'rare *vt* suspect
subordi'nato, -a *a* & *nmf* subordinate
subur'bano *a* suburban
suc'cedere *vi* (*accadere*) happen; ~**e a** succeed; (*venire dopo*) follow; ~**e al trono** succeed to the throne. ~**si** *vr* happen one after the other
successi'one *nf* succession; **in** ~ in succession
succes'siva'mente *adv* subsequently. ~'**sivo** *a* successive
suc'ces|so *pp di* **succedere** ● *nm* success; (*esito*) outcome; (*disco ecc*) hit. ~'**sone** *nm* huge success

succes'sore *nm* successor
succhi'are *vt* suck [up]
suc'cinto *a* (*conciso*) concise; (*abito*) scanty
'succo *nm* juice; *fig* essence; ~ **di frutta** fruit juice. **suc'coso** *a* juicy
succube *nm* **essere** ~ **di qcno** be totally dominated by sb
succu'lento *a* succulent
succur'sale *nf* branch [office]
sud *nm* south; **del** ~ southern
su'dare *vi* sweat, perspire; (*faticare*) sweat blood; ~**re freddo** be in a cold sweat. ~**ta** *nf* anche fig sweat. ~'**ticcio** *a* sweaty. ~**to a** sweaty
sud'detto *a* above-mentioned
'suddito, -a *nmf* subject
suddi'videre *vt* subdivide. ~**si'one** *nf* subdivision
su'd-est *nm* southeast
'sudicio *a* dirty, filthy. ~'**ume** *nm* dirt, filth
sudorazi'one *nf* perspiring. **su'dore** *nm* sweat, perspiration; *fig* sweat
su'd-ovest *nm* southwest
suffici'en|te *a* sufficient; (*presuntuoso*) conceited ● *nm* bare essentials *pl*; *Sch* pass mark. ~**za** *nf* sufficiency; (*presunzione*) conceit; *Sch* pass; **a** ~**za** enough
suf'fisso *nm* suffix
suf'fragio *nm* (*voto*) vote. ~ **universale** universal suffrage
suggeri'mento *nm* suggestion
sugge'ri|re *vt* suggest; *Theat* prompt. ~'**tore, -'trice** *nmf Theat* prompter
suggestiona'bile *a* suggestible
suggestio'na|re *vt* influence, ~**to** *a* influenced. **suggesti'one** *nf* influence
sugge'stivo *a* suggestive; (*musica ecc*) evocative
'sughero *nm* cork
'sugli = **su + gli**
'sugo *nm* (*di frutta*) juice; (*di carne*) gravy; (*salsa*) sauce; (*sostanza*) substance
'sui = **su + i**

sui'cid|a *a* suicidal ● *nmf* suicide. **suici'darsi** *vr* commit suicide. **~io** *nm* suicide

su'ino *a* **carne suina** pork ● *nm* swine

sul = **su** + **il**. **'sullo** = **su** + **lo**. **'sulla** = **su** + **la**. **'sulle** = **su** + **le**

sul'ta|na *nf* sultana. **~'nina** *a* **uva ~nina** sultana. **~no** *nm* sultan

'sunto *nm* summary

'suo, -a *poss a* **il ~, i suoi** his; (*di cosa, animale*) its; (*forma di cortesia*) your; **la sua, le sue** her; (*di cosa, animale*) its; (*forma di cortesia*) your; **questa macchina è sua** this car is his/hers; **~ padre** his/her/your father; **un ~ amico** a friend of his/hers/yours ● *poss pron* **il ~, i suoi** his; (*di cosa, animale*) its; (*forma di cortesia*) yours; **la sua, le sue** hers; (*di cosa, animale*) its; (*forma di cortesia*) yours; **i suoi** his/her folk

su'ocera *nf* mother-in-law

su'ocero *nm* father-in-law

su'ola *nf* sole

su'olo *nm* ground; (*terreno*) soil

suo'na|re *vt/i Mus* play; ring (*campanello*); sound (*allarme, clacson*); (*orologio:*) strike. **~'tore, ~'trice** *nmf* player. **suone'ria** *nf* alarm. **su'ono** *nm* sound

su'ora *nf* nun; **Suor Maria** Sister Maria

superal'colico *nm* spirit ● *a* **bevande** *pl* **superalcoliche** spirits

supera'mento *nm* (*di timidezza*) overcoming; (*di esame*) success (**di** in)

supe'rare *vt* surpass; (*eccedere*) exceed; (*vincere*) overcome; overtake, pass *Am* (*veicolo*); pass (*esame*)

su'perbia *nf* haughtiness. **~o** *a* haughty; (*magnifico*) proud

super'donna *nf* superwoman

super'dotato *a* highly gifted

superfici'al|e *a* superficial ● *nmf* superficial person. **~ità** *nf* superficiality. **super'ficie** *nf* surface; (*area*) area

su'perfluo *a* superfluous

superi'or|e *a* superior; (*di grado*) senior; (*più elevato*) higher; (*sovrastante*) upper; (*al di sopra*) above ● *nmf* superior. **~ità** *nf* superiority

superla'tivo *a* & *nm* superlative

supermer'cato *nm* supermarket

super'sonico *a* supersonic

su'perstite *a* surviving ● *nmf* survivor

superstizi'o|ne *nf* superstition. **~so** *a* superstitious

super'strada *nf* toll-free motorway

supervi|si'one *nf* supervision. **~'sore** *nm* supervisor

su'pino *a* supine

suppel'lettili *nfpl* furnishings

suppergiù *adv* about

supplemen'tare *a* additional, supplementary

supple'mento *nm* supplement; **~ rapido** express train supplement

sup'plen|te *a* temporary ● *nmf Sch* supply teacher. **~za** *nf* temporary post

'suppli|ca *nf* plea; (*domanda*) petition. **~'care** *vt* beg. **~'chevole** *a* imploring

sup'plire *vt* replace ● *vi* **~ a** (*compensare*) make up for

sup'plizio *nm* torture

sup'porre *vt* suppose

sup'porto *nm* support

supposizi'one *nf* supposition

sup'posta *nf* suppository

sup'posto *pp di* **supporre**

supre'mazia *nf* supremacy. **su'premo** *a* supreme

sur'fare *vi* **~ in Internet** surf the Net

surge'la|re *vt* deep-freeze. **~ti** *nmpl* frozen food *sg*. **~to** *a* frozen

surrea'lis|mo *nm* surrealism. **~ta** *nmf* surrealist

surrisca'ldare *vt* overheat

surro'gato *nm* substitute

suscet'tibil|e *a* touchy. **~ità** *nf* touchiness

susci'tare *vt* stir up; arouse ⟨*ammirazione ecc*⟩

su'sina *nf* plum. **~o** *nm* plumtree

su'spense *nf* suspense

susse'guire *a* subsequent. **~'irsi** *vr* follow one after the other

sussidi'are *vt* subsidize. **~io** *a* subsidiary. **sus'sidio** *nm* subsidy; ⟨*aiuto*⟩ aid. **sussidio di disoccupazione** unemployment benefit

sus'siego *nm* haughtiness

sussi'stenza *nf* subsistence. **sus'sistere** *vi* subsist; ⟨*essere valido*⟩ hold good

sussul'tare *vi* start. **sus'sulto** *nm* start

sussur'rare *vt* whisper. **sus'surro** *nm* whisper

su'tura *nf* suture. **~'rare** *vt* suture

sva'gare *vt* amuse. **~si** *vr* amuse oneself. **'svago** *nm* relaxation; ⟨*divertimento*⟩ amusement

svaligi'are *vt* rob, burgle ⟨*casa*⟩

svalu'tare *vt* devalue; *fig* underestimate. **~rsi** *vr* lose value. **~zi'one** *nf* devaluation

svam'pito *a* absent-minded

sva'nire *vi* vanish

svantaggi'ato *a* at a disadvantage; ⟨*bambino, paese*⟩ disadvantaged. **svan'taggio** *nm* disadvantage; **essere in svantaggio** *Sport* be losing; **in svantaggio di tre punti** three points down; **~'oso** *a* disadvantageous

svapo'rare *vi* evaporate

svari'ato *a* varied

sva'sato *a* flared

sva'stica *nf* swastika

sve'dese *a & nm* ⟨*lingua*⟩ Swedish ● *nmf* Swede

'sveglia *nf* ⟨*orologio*⟩ alarm [clock]; **~! get up!; mettere la ~** set the alarm [clock]

svegli'are *vt* wake up; *fig* awaken, **~si** *vr* wake up. **'sveglio** *a* awake; ⟨*di mente*⟩ quick-witted

sve'lare *vt* reveal

svel'tezza *nf* speed; *fig* quickwittedness

svel'tire *vt* quicken. **~si** *vr* ⟨*per-*

sona:⟩ liven up. **'svelto** *a* quick; ⟨*slanciato*⟩ svelte; **alla svelta** quickly

'svendere *vt* undersell. **~ita** *nf* [clearance] sale

sveni'mento *nm* fainting fit. **sve'nire** *vi* faint

sven'tare *vt* foil. **~to** *a* thoughtless ● *nmf* thoughtless person

'sventola *nf* slap; **orecchie** *nfpl* a **~** protruding ears

svento'lare *vt/i* wave

sven'trare *vt* disembowel; *fig* demolish ⟨*edificio*⟩

sven'tura *nf* misfortune. **sventu'rato** *a* unfortunate

sve'nuto *pp di* **svenire**

svergo'gnato *a* shameless

sver'nare *vi* winter

sve'stire *vt* undress. **~si** *vr* undress, get undressed

'Svezia *nf* Sweden

svezza'mento *nm* weaning. **svez'zare** *vt* wean

svi'are *vt* divert; ⟨*corrompere*⟩ lead astray. **~si** *vr* *fig* go astray

svico'lare *vi* turn down a side street; ⟨*fig: dalla questione ecc*⟩ evade the issue; ⟨*fig: da una persona*⟩ dodge out of the way

svi'gnarsela *vr* slip away

svi'lire *vt* debase

svilup'pare *vt*, **~si** *vr* develop. **svi'luppo** *nm* development; **paese in via di sviluppo** developing country

svinco'lare *vt* release; clear ⟨*merce*⟩, **~si** *vr* free oneself. **'svincolo** *nm* clearance; ⟨*di autostrada*⟩ exit

svi'scerare *vt* gut; *fig* dissect. **~to** *a* ⟨*amore*⟩ passionate; ⟨*ossequioso*⟩ obsequious

'svista *nf* oversight

svi'tare *vt* unscrew. **~to** *a* ⟨*fam: matto*⟩ cracked, nutty

'Svizzera *nf* Switzerland. **s~o, -a** *a & nmf* Swiss

svogli'atezza *nf* half-heartedness. **~'ato** *a* lazy

svolaz'zante *a* ⟨*capelli*⟩ windswept. **~re** *vi* flutter 'svolger|e *vt* unwind; unwrap ⟨*pacco*⟩; ⟨*risolvere*⟩ solve; ⟨*portare a termine*⟩ carry out; ⟨*sviluppare*⟩ develop. ~**si** *vr* ⟨*accadere*⟩ take place. **svolgi'mento** *nm* course; ⟨*sviluppo*⟩ development

'svolta *nf* turning; *fig* turning-point. svol'tare *vi* turn

'svolto *pp* di svolgere

svuo'tare *vt* empty [out]

Tt

tabac'c|aio, -a *nmf* tobacconist. ~he'ria *nf* tobacconist's ⟨*which also sells stamps, postcards etc*⟩. ta'bacco *nm* tobacco

ta'bel|la *nf* table; ⟨*lista*⟩ list. ~**la dei prezzi** price list. ~**lina** *nf* Math multiplication table. ~**lone** *nm* wall chart. ~**lone del canestro** backboard

taber'nacolo *nm* tabernacle

tabù *à* & *nm inv* taboo

tabu'lato *nm* Comput [data] printout

'tacca *nf* notch; **di mezza** ~ ⟨*attore, giornalista*⟩ second-rate

tac'cagno *a fam* stingy

tac'cheggio *nm* shoplifting

tac'chetto *nm* Sport stud

tac'chino *nm* turkey

tacci'are *vt* ~ **qcno di qcsa** accuse sb of sth

'tacco *nm* heel; **alzare i tacchi** take to one's heels; **scarpe senza** ~ flat shoes. **tacchi** *pl* **a spillo** stiletto heels

taccu'ino *nm* notebook

ta'cere *vi* be silent ● *vt* say nothing about; **mettere a** ~ **qcsa** ⟨*scandalo*⟩ hush sth up; **mettere a** ~ **qcno** silence sb

ta'chimetro *nm* speedometer

'tacito *a* silent; ⟨*inespresso*⟩ tacit. **taci'turno** *a* taciturn

ta'fano *nm* horsefly

taffe'ruglio *nm* scuffle

'taglia *nf* ⟨*riscatto*⟩ ransom; ⟨*ricompensa*⟩ reward; ⟨*statura*⟩ height; ⟨*misura*⟩ size. ~ **unica** one size

taglia'carte *nm inv* paperknife

taglia'erba *nm inv* lawn-mower

tagliafu'oco *a inv* **porta** ~ fire door; **striscia** ~ fire break

tagli'ando *nm* coupon; **fare il** ~ ≈ put one's car in for its MOT

tagli'ar|e *vt* cut; ⟨*attraversare*⟩ cut across; ⟨*interrompere*⟩ cut off; ⟨*togliere*⟩ cut out; carve ⟨*carne*⟩; mow ⟨*erba*⟩; **farsi** ~ **e i capelli** have a haircut ● *vi* cut. ~**si** *vr* cut oneself; ~**si i capelli** have a haircut

taglia'telle *nfpl* tagliatelle *sg*, thin, flat strips of egg pasta

taglieggi'are *vt* extort money from

tagli'e|nte *a* sharp ● *nm* cutting edge. ~**re** *nm* chopping board

'taglio *nm* cut; ⟨*il tagliare*⟩ cutting; ⟨*di stoffa*⟩ length; ⟨*parte tagliente*⟩ edge; **a doppio** ~ double-edged. ~ **cesareo** Caesarean section

tagli'ola *nf* trap

tagli'one *nm* **legge del** ~ an eye for an eye and a tooth for a tooth

tagliuz'zare *vt* cut into small pieces

tail'leur *nm inv* [lady's] suit

talassotera'pia *nf* thalassotherapy

'talco *nm* talcum powder

'tale *a* ⟨*con nomi plurali*⟩ such; **c'è un** ~ **disordine** there is such a mess; **non accetto tali scuse** I won't accept such excuses; **il rumore era** ~ **che non si sentiva nulla** there was so much noise you couldn't hear yourself think; **il** ~ **giorno** on such and such a day; **quel tal signore** that gentleman; ~ **quale** just like ● *pron un* ~ someone; **quel** ~ that man; **il tal dei tali** such and such a person

ta'lento *nm* talent

tali'smano *nm* talisman

tallo'nare *vt* be hot on the heels of

tallon'cino *nm* coupon

tal'lone *nm* heel

tal'mente *adv* so

ta'lora *adv* = **talvolta**

'talpa *nf* mole

tal'volta *adv* sometimes

tamburel'lare *vi* (con le dita) drum; (pioggia:) beat, drum. **tambu'rello** *nm* tambourine. **tambu'rino** *nm* drummer. **tam'buro** *nm* drum

Ta'migi *nm* Thames

tampona'mento *nm* Auto collision; (di ferita) dressing; (di falla) plugging. ~ **a catena** pile-up.

tampo'nare *vt* (urtare) crash into; (otturare) plug. **tam'pone** *nm* swab; (per timbri) pad; (per mestruazioni) tampon; (per treni, Comput) buffer

'tana *nf* den

'tanfo *nm* stench

'tanga *nm inv* tanga

tan'gente *a* tangent ● *nf* tangent; (somma) bribe. **~'topoli** *nf* widespread corruption in Italy in the early 90s. **~zi'ale** *nf* orbital road

tan'gibile *a* tangible

'tango *nm* tango

tan'tino: un ~ *adv* a little [bit]

'tanto *a* [so] much; (con nomi plurali) [so] many, [such] a lot of; ~ **tempo** [such] a long time; **non ha tanta pazienza** he doesn't have much patience; ~ **tempo quanto ti serve** as much time as you need; **non è ~ intelligente quanto suo padre** he's not as intelligent as his father; **tanti amici quanti parenti** as many friends as relatives ● *pron* much; (plurale) many; (tanto tempo) a long time; **è un uomo come tanti** he's just an ordinary man; **tanti** (molte persone) many people; **non ci vuole così ~** it doesn't take that long; ~ **quanto** as much as; **tanti quanti** as many as ● *conj* (comunque) anyway, in any case ● *adv* (così) so; (con verbi) so much; ~ **debole**

so weak; ~ **ingenuo da crederle** he's naive enough to believe her; **di ~ in ~** every now and then; ~ **l'uno come l'altro** both; ~ **quanto** as much as; **tre volte** ~ three times as much; **una volta** ~ once in a while; ~ **meglio così** so much the better! **tant'è** so much so; ~ **per cambiare** for a change

'tappa *nf* stop; (parte di viaggio) stage

tappa'buchi *nm inv* stopgap

tap'pare *vt* plug; cork (bottiglia); ~**e la bocca a qcno** *fam* shut sb up. **~si** *vr* **~si gli occhi** cover one's eyes; **~si il naso** hold one's nose; **~si le orecchie** put one's fingers in one's ears

tappa'rella *nf fam* roller blind

tappe'tino *nm* mat; Comput mouse mat. ~ **antiscivolo** safety bathmat

tap'peto *nm* carpet; (piccolo) rug; **andare al** ~ (pugilato:) hit the canvas; **mandare qcno al** ~ knock sb down

tappez'zare *vt* paper (pareti); (rivestire) cover. **~e'ria** *nf* tapestry; (di carta) wallpaper; (arte) upholstery. **~i'ere** *nm* upholsterer; (imbianchino) decorator

'tappo *nm* plug; (di sughero) cork; (di metallo, per penna) top; (fam: persona piccola) dwarf. ~ **di sughero** cork

'tara *nf* (difetto) flaw; (ereditaria) hereditary defect; (peso) tare

la'rantola *nf* tarantula

ta'rare *vt* calibrate (strumento). **~to** *a* Comm discounted; Techn calibrated; Med with a hereditary defect; *fam* crazy

tarchi'ato *a* stocky

tar'dare *vi* be late ● *vt* delay

'tardi *adv* late; **al più ~i** at the latest; **più ~i** later [on]; **sul ~i** late in the day; **far ~i** (essere in ritardo) be late; (con gli amici) stay up late; **a più ~i** see you later **tar'divo** *a* late; (bambino) retarded. **~o** *a* slow, (tempo) late

'targa nf plate; *Auto* numberplate. **~a di circolazione** numberplate. **tar'gato** a **un'auto targata...** a car with the registration number... **~'hetta** nf (*su porta*) nameplate; (*sulla valigia*) name tag

ta'riffa nf rate, tariff. **~'fario** nm price list

tar'larsi vr get wormeaten. **'tarlo** nm woodworm

'tarma nf moth. **tar'marsi** vr get moth-eaten

ta'rocco nm tarot; **ta'rocchi** pl tarot

tartagli'are vi stutter

'tartaro a & nm tartar

tarta'ruga nf tortoise; (*di mare*) turtle; (*per pettine ecc*) tortoise-shell

tartas'sare vt (*angariare*) harass

tar'tina nf canapé

tar'tufo nm truffle

'tasca nf pocket; (*in borsa*) compartment; **da ~** pocket *attrib*; **avere le tasche piene di qcsa** *fam* have had a bellyful of sth. **~ pasticciere** icing bag

ta'scabile a pocket *attrib* ● nm paperback

tasca'pane nm inv haversack

ta'schino nm breast pocket

'tassa nf tax; (*discrizione ecc*) fee; (*doganale*) duty. **~ di circolazione** road tax. **~ d'iscrizione** registration fee

tas'sametro nm taximeter

tas'sare vt tax

tassa|tiva'mente adv without question. **~'tivo** a peremptory

tassazi'one nf taxation

tas'sello nm wedge; (*di stoffa*) gusset

tassì nm inv taxi. **tas'sista** nmf taxi driver

'tasso[1] nm *Bot* yew; (*animale*) badger

'tasso[2] nm *Comm* rate. **~ di cambio** exchange rate. **~ di interesse** interest rate

ta'stare vt feel; (*sondare*) sound; **~**

il terreno *fig* test the water *or* the ground

tasti'e|ra nf keyboard. **~'rista** nmf keyboarder

'tasto nm key; (*tatto*) touch. **~ delicato** *fig* touchy subject. **~ funzione** *Comput* function key. **~ tabulatore** tab key

ta'stoni: a ~ adv gropingly

'tattica nf tactics pl

'tattico a tactical

'tatto nm (*senso*) touch; (*accortezza*) tact; **aver ~** be tactful

tatu'aggio nm tattoo. **~re** vt tattoo

'tavola nf table; (*illustrazione*) plate; (*asse*) plank. **~ calda** snackbar

tavo'lato nm boarding; (*pavimento*) wood floor

tavo'letta nf bar; (*medicinale*) tablet; **andare a ~** *Auto* drive flat out

tavo'lino nm small table

'tavolo nm table. **~ operatorio** *Med* operating table

tavo'lozza nf palette

'tazza nf cup; (*del water*) bowl. **~ da caffè/tè** coffee-cup/teacup

taz'zina nf **~ da caffè** espresso coffee cup

T.C.I. abbr (**Touring Club Italiano**) Italian Touring Club

te pers pron you; **te l'ho dato** I gave it to you

tè nm inv tea

tea'trale a theatrical

te'atro nm theatre. **~ all'aperto** open-air theatre. **~ di posa** *Cinema* set. **~ tenda** marquee for theatre performances

'tecnico, -a a technical ● nmf technician **~** nf technique

tec'nigrafo nm drawing board

tecno'lo'gia nf technology. **~'logico** a technological

te'desco, -a a & nmf German

'tedio nm tedium. **~'oso** a tedious

te'game nm saucepan

'teglia nf baking tin

'tegola nf tile; *fig* blow

tei'era nf teapot

tek *nm* teak

'tela *nf* cloth; (*per quadri, vele*) canvas; *Theat* curtain. **~ cerata** oilcloth. **~ di lino** linen

te'laio *nm* (*di bicicletta, finestra*) frame; *Auto* chassis; (*per tessere*) loom

tele'camera *nf* television camera

teleco|man'dato *a* remote-controlled, remote control *attrib*. **~'mando** *nm* remote control

Telecom Italia *nf* Italian State telephone company

telecomunicazi'oni *nfpl* telecommunications

tele'cro|naca *nf* [television] commentary. **~naca diretta** live [television] coverage. **~naca registrata** recording. **~'nista** *nmf* television commentator

tele'ferica *nf* cableway

telefo'na|re *vt/i* [tele]phone, ring. **~ta** *nf* call. **~ta interurbana** long-distance call

telefonica'mente *adv* by [tele]phone

tele'fo|nico *a* [tele]phone *attrib*. **~'nino** *nm* mobile [phone]. **~'nista** *nmf* operator

te'lefono *nm* [tele]phone. **~ senza filo** cordless [phone]. **~ a gettoni** pay phone, coin-box. **~ interno** internal telephone. **~ a schede** cardphone

telegior'nale *nm* television news *sg*

telegra'fare *vt* telegraph. **tele-'grafico** *a* telegraphic; (*risposta*) monosyllabic; **sii telegrafico** keep it brief

tele'gramma *nm* telegram

tele'matica *nf* data communications, telematics

tulouo'vela *nf* soap opera

teleobiet'tivo *nm* telephoto lens

telepa'tia *nf* telepathy

tele'romanzo *nm* television serial

tele'schermo *nm* television screen

tele'scopio *nm* telescope

teleselezi'one *nf* subscriber

trunk dialling, STD; **chiamare in ~ dial** direct

telespetta'tore, **-'trice** *nmf* viewer

tele'text® *nm* Teletext®

tele'video *nm* videophone

televisi'one *nf* television; **guardare la ~** watch television

televi'sivo *a* television *attrib*; **operatore ~** television cameraman; **apparecchio ~** television set

televi'sore *nm* television [set]

'tema *nm* theme; *Sch* essay. **te'matica** *nf* main theme

teme'rario *a* reckless

te'mere *vt* be afraid of, fear ● *vi* be afraid, fear

tem'paccio *nm* filthy weather

temperama'tite *nm inv* pencil-sharpener

tempera'mento *nm* temperament

tempe'ra|re *vt* temper; sharpen (*matita*). **~to** *a* temperate. **~'tura** *nf* temperature. **~'tura ambiente** room temperature

tempe'rino *nm* penknife

tem'pe|sta *nf* storm. **~sta di neve** snowstorm. **~sta di sabbia** sandstorm

tempe|stiva'mente *adv* quickly. **~'stivo** *a* timely. **~'stoso** *a* stormy

'tempia *nf Anat* temple

'tempio *nm Relig* temple

tem'pismo *nm* timing

'tempo *nm* time; (*atmosferico*) weather; *Mus* tempo; (*Gram*) tense; (*di film*) part; (*di partita*) half; **a suo ~** in due course; **~ fa** some time ago; **un ~** once; **ha fatto il suo ~** it's superannuated. **~ supplementare** *Sport* extra time, overtime *Am*. **~'rale** *a* temporal ● *nm* [thunder]storm. **~ranea-'mente** *adv* temporarily. **~'raneo** *a* temporary. **~reggi'are** *vi* play for time

tem'prare *vt* temper

te'nac|e *a* tenacious. **~ia** *nf* tenacity

te'naglia *nf* pincers *pl*

'**tenda** *nf* curtain; (*per campeggio*) tent; (*tendone*) awning. ~ **a ossi'geno** oxygen tent

ten'denz|a *nf* tendency. ~**ial'mente** *adv* by nature. ~**i'oso** *a* tendentious

'**tendere** *vt* (*allargare*) stretch [out]; (*tirare*) tighten; (*porgere*) hold out; *fig* lay (*trappola*) ● *vi* ~ **a** aim at; (*essere portato a*) tend to

'tendine *nm* tendon

ten'do|ne *nm* awning; (*di circo*) tent. ~**poli** *nf inv* tent city

'**tenebre** *nfpl* darkness. **tene'broso** *a* gloomy

te'nente *nm* lieutenant

tenera'mente *adv* tenderly

te'ner|e *vt* hold; (*mantenere*) keep; (*gestire*) run; (*prendere*) take; (*seguire*) follow; (*considerare*) consider ● *vi* hold; ~**ci a,** ~**e a** be keen on; ~**e per** support (*squadra*). ~**si** *vr* hold on (**a** to); (*in una condizione*) keep oneself; (*seguire*) stick to; ~**si indietro** stand back

tene'rezza *nf* tenderness. '**tenero** *a* tender

'**tenia** *nf* tapeworm

'**tennis** *nm* tennis. ~ **da tavolo** table tennis. **ten'nista** *nmf* tennis player

te'nore *nm* standard; *Mus* tenor; **a** ~ **di legge** by law. ~ **di vita** standard of living

tensi'one *nf* tension; *Electr* voltage; **alta** ~ high voltage

ten'tacolo *nm* tentacle

ten'ta|re *vt* attempt; (*sperimentare*) try; (*indurre in tentazione*) tempt. ~**tivo** *nm* attempt. ~**zi'one** *nf* temptation

tenten|na'mento *nm* wavering. ~**'nare** *vi* waver

'**tenue** *a* fine; (*debole*) weak; (*esiguo*) small; (*leggero*) slight

te'nuta *nf* (*capacità*) capacity; (*Sport: resistenza*) stamina; (*possedimento*) estate; (*divisa*) uniform; (*abbigliamento*) clothes *pl*; **a**

~ **d'aria** airtight. ~ **di strada** road holding

teolo'gia *nf* theology. **teo'logico** *a* theological. **te'ologo** *nm* theologian

teo'rema *nm* theorem

teo'ria *nf* theory

teorica'mente *adv* theoretically. **te'orico** *a* theoretical

te'pore *nm* warmth

'**teppa** *nf* mob. **tep'pismo** *nm* hooliganism. **tep'pista** *nm* hooligan

tera'peutico *a* therapeutic. **tera'pia** *nf* therapy

tergicri'stallo *nm* windscreen wiper, windshield wiper *Am*

tergilu'notto *nm* rear windscreen wiper

tergiver'sare *vi* hesitate

'**tergo** *nm* **a** ~ behind; **segue a** ~ please turn over, PTO

ter'male *a* thermal; **stazione** ~ spa. **'terme** *nfpl* thermal baths

'**termico** *a* thermal

termi'na|le *a* & *nm* terminal; **malato** ~ **le** terminally ill person. ~**re** *vt/i* finish, end. '**termine** *nm* (*limite*) limit; (*fine*) end; (*condizione, espressione*) term

terminolo'gia *nf* terminology

'termite *nf* termite

termoco'perta *nf* electric blanket

ter'mometro *nm* thermometer

'**termos** *nm inv* '**termos**®

termosi'fone *nm* radiator; (*sistema*) central heating

ter'mostato *nm* thermostat

'**terra** *nf* earth; (*regione*) land; (*terreno*) ground; (*argilla*) clay; (*cosmetico*) dark face powder (*which gives the impression of a tan*); **a** ~ (*sulla costa*) ashore; (*installazioni*) onshore; **per** ~ on the ground; **sotto** ~ underground. ~'**cotta** *nf* terracotta; **vasellame di** ~'**cotta** earthenware. ~'**ferma** *nf* dry land. ~**pi'eno** *nm* embankment

ter'razza *nf* balcony

terremo'tato, -a *a* (*zona*) affected by an earthquake ● *nmf* earthquake victim. **terre'moto** nm earthquake

ter'reno a earthly ● nm ground; (suolo) soil; (proprietà terriera) land; **perdere/guadagnare ~** lose/gain ground. **~ di gioco** playing field

ter'restre a terrestrial; **esercito ~** land forces pl

ter'ribil|e a terrible. **~'mente** adv terribly

ter'riccio nm potting compost

terri'ficante a terrifying

territori'ale a territorial. **terri'to-rio** nm territory

ter'rore nm terror

terro'ris|mo nm terrorism. **~ta** nmf terrorist

terroriz'zare vt terrorize

terso a clear

ter'zetto nm trio

terzi'ario a tertiary

terzo a third; **di terz'ordine** (locale, servizio) third-rate; **fare il ~ grado a qn** give sb the third degree; **la terza età** the third age ● nm third; **terzi** pl Jur third party sg. **ter'zultimo, -a** a & nmf third from last

tesa nf brim

teschio nm skull

tesi nf inv thesis

teso pp di **tendere** ● a taut; fig tense

tesor'e'ria nf treasury. **~i'ere** nm treasurer

te'soro nm treasure; (tesoreria) treasury

tessera nf card; (abbonamento all'autobus) season ticket

tossere vt weave; hatch (complotto)

tesse'rino nm travel card

tessile a textile. **tessili** nmpl textiles; (operai) textile workers

tessi|'tore, -'trice nmf weaver. **~'tura** nf weaving

tes'suto nm fabric; Anat tissue

testa nf head; (cervello) brain; **essere in ~ a** be ahead of; **in ~** Sport in the lead; **~ o croce?**

heads or tails?; **fare ~ o croce** have a toss-up to decide

'testa-'coda nm inv **fare un ~** spin right round

testa'mento nm will; **T~** Relig Testament

testar'daggine nf stubbornness. **te'stardo** a stubborn

te'stata nf head; (intestazione) heading; (colpo) butt

'teste nmf witness

te'sticolo nm testicle

testi'mon|e nmf witness. **~e oculare** eye witness

testi'monial nmf inv celebrity who promotes a brand of cosmetics

testimoni'anza nf testimony; **falsa ~anza** Jur perjury. **~are** vt testify to ● vi testify, give evidence

'testo nm text; **far ~** be an authority

te'stone, -a nmf blockhead

testu'ale a textual

'tetano nm tetanus

'tetro a gloomy

tetta'rella nf teat

'tetto nm roof. **~ apribile** (di auto) sunshine roof. **tet'toia** nf roofing. **tet'tuccio** nm **tettuccio apribile** sun-roof

'Tevere nm Tiber

ti pers pron you; (riflessivo) yourself; **ti ha dato un libro** he gave you a book; **lavati le mani** wash your hands; **eccoti!** here you are!; **sbrigati!** hurry up!

ti'ara nf tiara

tic nm inv tic

ticchet't|are vi tick. **~io** nm ticking

'ticchio nm tic; (ghiribizzo) whim

'ticket nm inv (per farmaco, esame) amount paid by National Health patients

tiepida'mente adv half-heartedly. **ti'epido** a anche fig lukewarm

ti'fare vi ~ **per** shout for. **'tifo** nm Med typhus; **fare il tifo per** fig be a fan of

tifol'dea nf typhoid

ti'fone nm typhoon

ti'foso, -a *nmf* fan

'tiglio *nm* lime

ti'grato *a* **gatto ~** tabby [cat]

'tigre *nf* tiger

'tilde *nmf* tilde

tim'ballo *nm* Culin pie

tim'brare *vt* stamp; **~ il cartellino** clock in/out

'timbro *nm* stamp; *(di voce)* tone

timida'mente *adv* timidly, shyly. **timi'dezza** *nf* timidity, shyness. **'timido** *a* timid, shy

'timo *nm* thyme

ti'mone *nm* rudder. **~i'ere** *nm* helmsman

ti'more *nm* fear; *(soggezione)* awe. **timo'roso** *a* timorous

'timpano *nm* eardrum; *Mus* kettledrum

ti'nello *nm* dining-room

'tingere *vt* dye; *(macchiare)* stain. **~si** *vi* ⟨viso, cielo:⟩ be tinged (di with); **~si i capelli** have one's hair dyed; *(da solo)* dye one's hair

'tino *nm* dyed, **ti'nozza** *nf* tub

'tint|a *nf* dye; *(colore)* colour; **in ~a unita** plain. **~a'rella** *nf fam* suntan

tintin'nare *vi* tinkle

'tinto *pp* **di tingere**. **~'ria** *nf* *(negozio)* cleaner's. **tin'tura** *nf* dyeing; *(colorante)* dye.

'tipico *a* typical

'tipo *nm* type; *(fam: individuo)* chap, guy

tipogra'fia *nf* printery; *(arte)* typography. **tipo'grafico** *a* typographic[al]. **ti'pografo** *nm* printer

tip tap *nm* tap dancing

ti'raggio *nm* draught

tiramisù *nm inv* dessert made of coffee-soaked sponge, eggs, Marsala, cream and cocoa powder

tiran|neggi'are *vt* tyrannize. **~'nia** *nf* tyranny. **ti'ranno, -a** *a* tyrannical ●*nmf* tyrant

tirapi'edi *nm inv pej* hanger-on

ti'rar|e *vt* pull; *(gettare)* throw; kick *(palla)*; *(sparare)* fire; *(tracciare)* draw; *(stampare)* print ●*vi* pull; ⟨vento:⟩ blow; ⟨abito:⟩ be

tight; *(sparare)* fire; **~e avanti** get by; **~e su** *(crescere)* bring up; *(da terra)* pick up; **tirar su col naso** sniffle. **~si** *vr* **~si indietro** *fig* back out, pull out

tiras'segno *nm* target shooting; *(alla fiera)* rifle range

ti'rata *nf* *(strattone)* pull, tug; **in una ~** in one go

tira'tore *nm* shot. **~ scelto** marksman

tira'tura *nf* printing; *(di giornali)* circulation; *(di libri)* [print] run

tirchie'ria *nf* meanness. **'tirchio** *a* mean

tiri'tera *nf* spiel

'tiro *nm* *(traino)* draught; *(lancio)* throw; *(sparo)* shot; *(scherzo)* trick. **~ con l'arco** archery. **~ alla fune** tug-of-war. **~ a segno** rifle-range

tiro'cinio *nm* apprenticeship

ti'roide *nf* thyroid

Tir'reno *nm* **il** [**mar**] **~** the Tyrrhenian Sea

ti'sana *nf* herb[al] tea

tito'lare *a* regular ●*nmf* principal; *(proprietario)* owner; *(calcio)* regular player

'titolo *nm* title; *(accademico)* qualification; *Comm* security; **a ~ di** as; **a ~ di favore** as a favour. **titoli** *pl* **di studio** qualifications

titu'ba|nte *a* hesitant. **~nza** *nf* hesitation. **~re** *vi* hesitate

tivù *nf inv fam* TV, telly

'tizio *nm* fellow

tiz'zone *nm* brand

toc'cante *a* touching

toc'ca|re *vt* touch; touch on ⟨argomento⟩; *(tastare)* feel; *(riguardare)* concern ●*vi* **~re a** *(capitare)* happen to; **mi tocca aspettare** I'll have to wait; **tocca a te** it's your turn; *(da pagare da bere)* it's your round

tocca'sana *nm inv* cure-all

'tocco *nm* touch; *(di pennello, orologio)* stroke; *(di pane ecc)* chunk ●*a fam* crazy, touched '**toga** nf toga; (*accademica, di magi-strato*) gown

'**toglier|e** vt take off (*coperta*); take away (*bambino da scuola, sete, Math*); take out, remove (*dente*); **~e cqsa di mano a qcno** take sth away from sb; **~e qcno dei guai** get sb out of. trouble; **ciò non toglie che...** nevertheless... **~si** vr take off (*abito*); **~si la vita** take one's [own] life; **togliti dai piedi!** get out of here!

toilette nf inv, **to'letta** nf toilet; (*mobile*) dressing table

tolle'ra|nte a tolerant. **~nza** nf tolerance. **~re** vt tolerate

'**tolto** pp di **togliere**

to'maia nf upper

'**tomba** nf grave, tomb

tom'bino nm manhole cover

'**tombola** nf bingo; (*caduta*) tumble

'**tomo** nm tome

tonaca nf habit

tonalità nf inv Mus tonality

'**tondo** a round ● nm circle

'**tonfo** nm thud; (*in acqua*) splash

'**tonico** a & nm tonic

tonifi'care vt brace

tonnel'la|ggio nm tonnage. **~ta** nf ton

'**tonno** nm tuna [fish]

'**tono** nm tone

ton'sil|la nf tonsil. **~'lite** nf tonsillitis

'**tonto** a fam thick

top nm inv (*indumento*) sun-top

to'pazio nm topaz

'**topless** nm inv **in ~** topless

'**topo** nm mouse. **~ di biblioteca** fig bookworm

topogra'fia nf topography. **topo-'grafico** a topographic[al]

to'ponimo nm place name

'**toppa** nf (*rattoppo*) patch; (*serratura*) keyhole

to'race nm chest. **to'racico** a thoracic; **gabbia toracica** rib cage

'**torba** nf peat

'**torbido** a cloudy; fig troubled

'**torcer|e** vt twist; wring [out] (*biancheria*). **~si** vr twist

'**torchio** nm press

'**torcia** nf torch

torci'collo nm stiff neck

'**tordo** nm thrush

to'rero nm bullfighter

To'rino nf Turin

tor'menta nf snowstorm

tormen'tare vt torment. **tor'mento** nm torment

torna'conto nm benefit

tor'nado nm tornado

tor'nante nm hairpin bend

tor'nare vi return, go/come back; (*ridiventare*) become again; (*conto*) add up; **~ a sorridere** become happy again

tor'neo nm tournament

'tornio nm lathe

'**torno** nm **togliersi di ~** get out of the way

'**toro** nm bull; Astr Taurus

tor'pedin|e nf torpedo. **~'i'era** nf torpedo boat

tor'pore nm torpor

'**torre** nf tower; (*scacchi*) castle. **~ di controllo** control tower

torrefazi'one nf roasting

tor'ren|te nm torrent, mountain stream; (*fig: di lacrime*) flood. **~zi'ale** a torrential

tor'retta nf turret

'**torrido** a torrid

torri'one nm keep

tor'rone nm nougat

'**torso** nm torso; (*di mela, pera*) core; **a ~ nudo** bare-chested

'**torsolo** nm core

'**torta** nf cake; (*crostata*) tart

tortel'lini nmpl tortellini, small packets of pasta stuffed with pork, ham, Parmesan and nutmeg

torti'era nf baking tin

tor'tino nm pie

'**torto** pp di **torcere** ● a twisted ● nm wrong; (*colpa*) fault; **aver ~** be wrong; **a ~** wrongly

'tortora nf turtle-dove

tortu'oso a winding, (*ambiguo*) tortuous

tor'tu|ra *nf* torture. **~'rare** *vt* torture

'torvo *a* grim

to'sare *vt* shear

tosa'tura *nf* shearing

To'scana *nf* Tuscany

'tosse *nf* cough

'tossico *a* toxic ● *nm* poison. **tossi'comane** *nmf* drug addict, drug user

tos'sire *vi* cough

tosta'pane *nm inv* toaster

to'stare *vt* toast ⟨*pane*⟩; roast ⟨*caffè*⟩

'tosto *adv* ⟨*subito*⟩ soon ● *a fam* cool

tot *a inv* **una cifra ~** such and such a figure ● *nm un* **~** so much

to'tal|e *a* & *nm* total. **~ità** *nf* entirety; **la ~ità dei presenti** all those present

totali'tario *a* totalitarian

totaliz'zare *vt* total; score ⟨*punti*⟩

total'mente *adv* totally

'totano *nm* squid

toto'calcio *nm* ≈ [football] pools *pl*

tournée *nf inv* tour

to'vaglia *nf* tablecloth. **~'etta** *nf* **~etta [all'americana]** place mat. **~'olo** *nm* napkin

'tozzo *a* squat ● *nm* **~ di pane** stale piece of bread

tra = fra

trabal'la|nte *a* staggering; ⟨*sedia*⟩ rickety, wonky. **~re** *vi* stagger; ⟨*veicolo*⟩ jolt

tra'biccolo *nm fam* contraption; ⟨*auto*⟩ jalopy

traboc'care *vi* overflow

trabocchetto *nm* trap

tracan'nare *vt* gulp down

'traccia *nf* track; ⟨*orma*⟩ footstep; ⟨*striscia*⟩ trail; ⟨*residuo*⟩ trace; *fig* sign. **~'are** *vt* trace; sketch out ⟨*schema*⟩; draw ⟨*linea*⟩. **~'ato** *nm* ⟨*schema*⟩ layout

tra'chea *nf* windpipe

tra'colla *nf* shoulder-strap; **borsa a ~** shoulder-bag

tra'collo *nm* collapse

tradi'mento *nm* betrayal; *Pol* treason

tra'di|re *vt* betray; be unfaithful to ⟨*moglie, marito*⟩. **~'tore**, **~'trice** *nmf* traitor

tradizio'na|le *a* traditional. **~'lista** *nmf* traditionalist. **~l'mente** *adv* traditionally. **tradizi'one** *nf* tradition

tra'dotto *pp di* tradurre

tra'du|rre *vt* translate. **~t'tore**, **~t'trice** *nmf* translator. **~ttore elettronico** electronic phrasebook. **~zi'one** *nf* translation

tra'ente *nmf Comm* drawer

trafe'lato *a* breathless

traffi'ca|nte *nmf* dealer. **~nte di droga** [drug] pusher. **~re** *vi* ⟨*affaccendarsi*⟩ busy oneself; **~re in** *pej* traffic in. **'traffico** *nm* traffic; *Comm* trade

tra'figgere *vt* stab; ⟨*straziare*⟩ pierce

tra'fila *nf fig* rigmarole

trafo'rare *vt* bore, drill. **tra'foro** *nm* boring; ⟨*galleria*⟩ tunnel

trafu'gare *vt* steal

tra'gedia *nf* tragedy

traghet'tare *vt* ferry. **tra'ghetto** *nm* ferrying; ⟨*nave*⟩ ferry

tragica'mente *adv* tragically. **'tragico** *a* tragic ● *nm* ⟨*autore*⟩ tragedian

tra'gitto *nm* journey; ⟨*per mare*⟩ crossing

tragu'ardo *nm* finishing post; ⟨*meta*⟩ goal

traiet'toria *nf* trajectory

trai'nare *vt* drag; ⟨*rimorchiare*⟩ tow

tralasci'are *vt* interrupt; ⟨*omettere*⟩ leave out

'tralcio *nm Bot* shoot

tra'liccio *nm* ⟨*graticcio*⟩ trellis

tram *nm inv* tram, streetcar *Am*

'trama *nf* weft; ⟨*di film ecc*⟩ plot

traman'dare *vt* hand down

tra'mare *vt* weave; ⟨*macchinare*⟩ plot

tram'busto *nm* turmoil, hullabaloo

trame'stio *nm* bustle
tramez'zino *nm* sandwich
tra'mezzo *nm* partition
'tramite *prep* through ● *nm* link;
fare da ~ act as go-between
tramon'tana *nf* north wind
tramon'tare *vi* set; *(declinare)* decline. **tra'monto** *nm* sunset; *(declino)* decline
tramor'tire *vt* stun ● *vi* faint
trampo'lino *nm* springboard; *(per lo sci)* ski-jump
'trampolo *nm* stilt
tramu'tare *vt* transform
trancia *nf* shears *pl*; *(fetta)* slice
tra'nello *nm* trap
trangugi'are *vt* gulp down, gobble up
'tranne *prep* except
tranquilla'mente *adv* peacefully
tranquil'lante *nm* tranquillizer
tranquil'lità *nf* calm; *(di spirito)* tranquillity. **~z'zare** *vt* reassure.
tran'quillo *a* quiet; *(pacifico)* peaceful; *(coscienza)* easy
transat'lantico *a* transatlantic ● *nm* ocean liner
tran'sa|tto *pp di* **transigere**.
~zi'one *nf Comm* transaction
tran'senna *nf (barriera)* barrier
tran'sigere *vi* reach an agreement; *(cedere)* yield
transi'ta|bile *a* passable. **~re** *vi* pass
transi'tivo *a* transitive
'transi|to *nm* transit; **diritto di ~** right of way; **"divieto di ~to"** "no thoroughfare". **~'torio** *a* transitory. **~zi'one** *nf* transition
tran'tran *nm fam* routine
tranvi'ere *nm* tram driver, streetcar driver *Am*
'trapano *nm* drill
trapas'sare *vt* go [right] through ● *vi (morire)* pass away
tra'passo *nm* passage
trape'lare *vi (liquido, fig:)* leak out
tra'pezio *nm* trapeze; *Math* trapezium
trapi|an'tare *vt* transplant. **~'anto** *nm* transplant

'trappola *nf* trap
tra'punta *nf* quilt
'trarre *vt* draw; *(ricavare)* obtain;
~ in inganno deceive
trasa'lire *vi* start
trasan'dato *a* shabby
trasbor'dare *vt* transfer; *Naut* tran[s]ship ● *vi* change. **tra'sbordo** *nm* trans[s]hipment
tra'scendere *vt* transcend ● *vi (eccedere)* go too far
trasci'na|re *vt* drag; *(fig: entusiasmo:)* carry away. **~si** *vr* drag oneself
tra'scorrere *vt* spend ● *vi* pass
tra'scri|tto *pp di* **trascrivere**.
~vere *vt* transcribe. **~zl'one** *nf* transcription
trascu'ra|bile *a* negligible. **~re** *vt* neglect; *(non tenere conto di)* disregard. **~'tezza** *nf* negligence.
~to *a* negligent; *(curato male)* neglected; *(nel vestire)* slovenly
traseco'lato *a* amazed
trasferi'mento *nm* transfer; *(trasloco)* move
trasfe'ri|re *vt* transfer. **~rsi** *vr* move
tra'sferta *nf* transfer; *(indennità)* subsistence allowance; *Sport* away match; **in ~** *(impiegato)* on secondment; **giocare in ~** play away
trasfigu'rare *vt* transfigure
trasfor'ma|re *vt* transform; *(in rugby)* convert. **~'tore** *nm* transformer. **~zi'one** *nf* transformation; *(in rugby)* conversion
trasfor'mista *nmf (artista)* quick-change artist
trasfusi'one *nf* transfusion
trasgre'dire *vt* disobey; *Jur* infringe
trasgredi'trice *nf* transgressor
trasgres|si'one *nf* infringement.
~sivo *a* intended to shock.
~sore *nm* transgressor
tra'slato *a* metaphorical
traslo'car|e *vt* move ● *vi*, **~si** *vr* move house. **tra'sloco** *nm* removal

tra'smesso *pp di* **trasmettere**

tra'smett|ere *vt* pass on; *TV, Radio* broadcast; *Techn, Med* transmit. **~i'tore** *nm* transmitter

trasmis'si|bile *a* transmissible. **~'one** *nf* transmission; *TV, Radio* programme

trasmit'tente *nm* transmitter ● *nf* broadcasting station

traso'gna|re *vi* day-dream. **~to** *a* dreamy

traspa'ren|te *a* transparent. **~za** *nf* transparency; **in ~za** against the light. **traspa'rire** *vi* show [through]

traspi'ra|re *vi* perspire; *fig* transpire. **~zi'one** *nf* perspiration

tra'sporre *vt* transpose

traspor'tare *vt* transport; **lasciarsi ~ da** get carried away by. **tra'sporto** *nm* transport; *(passione)* passion

trastul'lar|e *vt* amuse. **~si** *vr* amuse oneself

trasu'dare *vi* ooze with ● *vi* sweat

trasver'sale *a* transverse

trasvo'la|re *vt* fly over ● *vi* **~re su** *fig* skim over. **~ta** *nf* crossing [by air]

'tratta *nf* *(traffico illegale)* trade; *Comm* draft

trat'tabile *a* or nearest offer, o.n.o.

tratta'mento *nm* treatment. **~ di riguardo** special treatment

trat'ta|re *vt* treat; *(commerciare in)* deal in; *(negoziare)* negotiate ● *vi* **~re di** deal with. **~rsi** *vr* **di che si tratta?** what is it about?; **si tratta di...** it's about... **~'tive** *nfpl* negotiations. **~to** *nm* treaty; *(opera scritta)* treatise

tratteggi'are *vt* outline; *(descrivere)* sketch

tratte'ner|e *vt* *(far restare)* keep; hold *(respiro, in questura)*; hold back *(lacrime, riso)*; *(frenare)* restrain; *(da paga)* withhold; **sono stato trattenuto** *(ritardato)* I was o got held up. **~si** *vr* restrain oneself; *(fermarsi)* stay; **~si su** *(indugiare)* dwell on. **tratteni'mento**

nm entertainment; *(ricevimento)* party

tratte'nuta *nf* deduction

trat'tino *nm* dash; *(in parole composte)* hyphen

'tratto *pp di* **trarre** ● *nm* *(di spazio, tempo)* stretch; *(di penna)* stroke; *(linea)* line; *(brano)* passage; **tratti** *pl* *(lineamenti)* features; **a tratti** at intervals; **ad un ~** suddenly

trat'tore *nm* tractor

tratto'ria *nf* restaurant

'trauma *nm* trauma. **trau'matico** *a* traumatic. **~tiz'zare** *vt* traumatize

tra'vaglio *nm* labour; *(angoscia)* anguish

trava'sare *vt* decant

'trave *nf* beam

tra'veggole *nfpl* **avere le ~** be seeing things

tra'versa *nf* crossbar; **è una ~ di Via Roma** it's off Via Roma, it crosses via Roma

traver'sa|re *vt* cross. **~ta** *nf* crossing

traver'sie *nfpl* misfortunes

traver'sina *nf* *Rail* sleeper

tra'verso *a* crosswise ● *adv* **di ~o** crossways; **andare di ~o** *(cibo:)* go down the wrong way; **camminare di ~o** not walk in a straight line; **guardare qcno di ~o** look askance at sb. **~one** *nm* *(in calcio)* cross

travesti'mento *nm* disguise

trave'sti|re *vt* disguise. **~rsi** *vr* disguise oneself. **~to** *a* disguised ● *nm* transvestite

travi'are *vt* lead astray

travi'sare *vt* distort

travol'gente *a* overwhelming

tra'vol|gere *vt* sweep away; *(sopraffare)* overwhelm. **~to** *pp di* **travolgere**

trazi'one *nf* traction. **~ anteriore/posteriore** front-/rear-wheel drive

tre *a & nm* three

trebbi'a|re *vt* thresh

'treccia *nf* plait, braid

tre'cento *a & nm* three hundred; **il T~** the fourteenth century

tredi'cesima *nf extra month's salary paid as a Christmas bonus*

'tredici *a & nm* thirteen

'tregua *nf* truce; *fig* respite

tre'mare *vi* tremble; *(di freddo)* shiver. **trema'rella** *nf fam* jitters *pl*

tremenda'mente *adv* terribly. **tre'mendo** *a* terrible; **ho una fame tremenda** I'm terribly hungry

tremen'tina *nf* turpentine

tre'mila *a & nm* three thousand

'tremito *nm* tremble

tremo'lare *vi* shake; *(luce:)* flicker. **tre'more** *nm* trembling

tre'nino *nm* miniature railway

'treno *nm* train

'tren|ta *a & nm* thirty; **~ta e lode** top marks. **~tatré** *qui nm* LP. **~'tenne** *a & nmf* thirty-year-old. **~'tesimo** *a & nm* thirtieth. **~'tina** *nf* **una ~tina di** about thirty

trepi'dare *vi* be anxious. **'trepido** *a* anxious

'treppiede *nm* tripod

'tresca *nf* intrigue; *(amorosa)* affair

'trespolo *nm* perch

triango'lare *a* triangular. **tri'angolo** *nm* triangle

tribo'la|re *vi (soffrire)* suffer; *(fare fatica)* go through all kinds of trials and tribulations. **~zi'one** *nf* tribulation

tribù *nf inv* tribe

tri'buna *nf* tribune; *(per uditori)* gallery; *Sport* stand. **~ coperta** stand

tribu'nale *nm* court

tribu'tare *vt* bestow

tribu'tario *a* tax *attrib.* **tri'buto** *nm* tribute; *(tassa)* tax

tri'checo *nm* walrus

tri'ciclo *nm* tricycle

trico'lore *a* three-coloured ● *nm (bandiera)* tricolour

tri'dente *nm* trident

trien'nale *a (ogni tre anni)* three-yearly; *(lungo tre anni)* three-year.

tri'ennio *nm* three-year period

tri'foglio *nm* clover

trifo'lato *a* sliced thinly and cooked with olive oil, parsley and garlic

'triglia *nf* mullet

trigonome'tria *nf* trigonometry

tril'lare *vi* trill

tril'lo *nm* trill

trilo'gia *nf* trilogy

tri'mestre *nm* quarter; *Sch* term

'trina *nf* lace

trin'cea *nf* trench. **~'rare** *vt* entrench

trincia'pollo *nm inv* poultry shears *pl*

trinci'are *vt* cut up

Trinità *nf* Trinity

'trio *nm* trio

trion'fa|le *a* triumphal. **~nte** *a* triumphant. **~re** *vi* triumph; **~re su** triumph over. **tri'onfo** *nm* triumph

tripli'care *vt* triple. **'triplice** *a* triple; **in triplice [copia]** in triplicate. **'triplo** *a* treble ● *nm* **il triplo (di)** three times as much (as)

'trippa *nf* tripe; *(fam: pancia)* belly

'tristo *a* sad; *(lungo)* gloomy. **tri'stezza** *nf* sadness. **~o** *a* wicked; *(meschino)* miserable

trita'carne *nm inv* mincer. **~ghi'accio** *nm inv* ice-crusher

tri'ta|re *vt* mince. **'trito** *a* **trito e ritrito** well-worn, trite

'trittico *nm* triptych

tritu'rare *vt* chop finely

triumvi'rato *nm* triumvirate

tri'vella *nf* drill. **trivel'lare** *vt* drill

trivi'ale *a* vulgar

tro'feo *nm* trophy

'trogolo *nm (per maiali)* trough

'troia *nf* sow; *vulg* bitch; *(sessuale)* whore

'tromba *nf* trumpet; *Auto* horn; *(delle scale)* well. **~ d'aria** whirlwind

trom'bare *vt vulg* screw; *(fam: in esame)* fail

trom'b|etta *nm* toy trumpet. **~one** *nm* trombone

trom'bosi *nf* thrombosis

tron'care *vt* sever; truncate ⟨*parola*⟩

'tronco *a* truncated; **licenziare in ~** fire on the spot ● *nm* trunk; ⟨*di strada*⟩ section. **tron'cone** *nm* stump

troneggi'are *vi* **~ su** tower over

'trono *nm* throne

tropi'cale *a* tropical. **'tropico** *nm* tropic

'troppo *a* too much; ⟨*con nomi plurali*⟩ too many ● *pron* too much; ⟨*plurale*⟩ too many; ⟨*troppo tempo*⟩ too long; **troppi** ⟨*troppa gente*⟩ too many people ● *adv* too; ⟨*con verbi*⟩ too much; **~ stanco** too tired; **ho mangiato ~** I ate too much; **hai fame? – non ~** are you hungry? - not very; **sentirsi di ~** feel unwanted

'trota *nf* trout

trot'tare *vi* trot. **trotterel'lare** *vi* trot along; ⟨*bimbo:*⟩ toddle

'trotto *nm* trot; **andare al ~** trot

'trottola *nf* [spinning] top; ⟨*movimento*⟩ spin

troupe *nf inv* **~ televisiva** camera crew

tro'va|re *vt* find; ⟨*scoprire*⟩ find out; ⟨*incontrare*⟩ meet; ⟨*ritenere*⟩ think; **andare a ~re** go and see. **~rsi** *vr* find oneself; ⟨*luogo:*⟩ be; ⟨*sentirsi*⟩ feel. **~ta** *nf* bright idea. **~ta pubblicitaria** advertising gimmick

truc'ca|re *vt* make up; ⟨*falsificare*⟩ fix *sl*. **~rsi** *vr* make up. **~tore, ~'trice** *nmf* make-up artist

'trucco *nm* ⟨*cosmetico*⟩ make-up; ⟨*imbroglio*⟩ trick

'truce *a* fierce; ⟨*delitto*⟩ appalling

truci'dare *vt* slay

truci'olo *nm* shaving

trucu'lento *a* truculent

'truffa *nf* fraud. **truf'fare** *vt* swindle. **~tore, ~trice** *nmf* swindler

'truppa *nf* troops *pl*; ⟨*gruppo*⟩ group

tu *pers pron* you; **sei tu?** is that you?; **l'hai fatto tu?** did you do it

yourself?; **a tu per tu** in private; **darsi del tu** *use the familiar* **tu**

'tuba *nf* Mus tuba; ⟨*cappello*⟩ top hat

tu'bare *vi* coo

tuba'tura, tubazi'one *nf* piping

tubazi'oni *nfpl* piping *sg*, pipes

tuberco'losi *nf* tuberculosis

tu'betto *nm* tube

tu'bino *nm* ⟨*vestito*⟩ shift

'tubo *nm* pipe; *Anat* canal; **non ho capito un ~** *fam* I understood zilch. **~ di scappamento** exhaust [pipe]

tubo'lare *a* tubular

tuffa|re *vt* plunge. **~rsi** *vr* dive. **~'tore, ~'trice** *nmf* diver

'tuffo *nm* dive; ⟨*bagno*⟩ dip; **ho avuto un ~ al cuore** my heart missed a beat. **~ di testa** dive

'tufo *nm* tufa

tu'gurio *nm* hovel

tuli'pano *nm* tulip

'tulle *nm* tulle

tume'fatto *a* swollen. **~zi'one** *nf* swelling. **'tumido** *a* swollen

tu'more *nm* tumour

tumulazi'one *nf* burial

tu'multo *nm* turmoil; ⟨*sommossa*⟩ riot. **~u'oso** *a* uproarious

'tunica *nf* tunic

Tuni'sia *nf* Tunisia

'tunnel *nm inv* tunnel

'tuo (*il* **~** *m*, **la tua** *f*, **i ~i** *mpl*, **le tue** *fpl*) *poss a* your; **è tua questa macchina?** is this car yours?; **un ~ amico** a friend of yours; **~ padre** your father ● *poss pron* yours; **i tuoi** your folks

tuo'nare *vi* thunder. **tu'ono** *nm* thunder

tu'orlo *nm* yolk

tu'racciolo *nm* stopper; ⟨*di sughero*⟩ cork

tu'rar|e *vt* stop; cork ⟨*bottiglia*⟩. **~si** *vr* become blocked; **~si le orecchie** stick one's fingers in one's ears; **~si il naso** hold one's nose

turba'mento *nm* disturbance; ⟨*sconvolgimento*⟩ upsetting. **~ del-**

la quiete pubblica breach of the peace

tur'bante *nm* turban

turba|re *vt* upset. **~rsi** *vr* get upset. **~to** *a* upset

tur'bina *nf* turbine

turbi'nare *vi* whirl. **'turbine** *nm* whirl. **turbine di vento** whirlwind

turbo'len|to *a* turbulent. **~za** *nf* turbulence

turboreat'tore *nm* turbo-jet

tur'chese *a* & *nmf* turquoise

Tur'chia *nf* Turkey

tur'chino *a* & *nm* deep blue

turco, -a *a* Turkish ● *nmf* Turk ● *nm* (*lingua*) Turkish; *fig* double Dutch; **fumare come un ~** smoke like a chimney; **bestemmiare come un ~** swear like a trooper

tu'ris|mo *nm* tourism. **~ta** *nmf* tourist. **~tico** *a* tourist *attrib*

'turno *nm* turn; **a ~** in turn; **di ~** on duty; **fare a ~** take turns. **~ di notte** night shift

'turp|e *a* base. **~i'loquio** *nm* foul language

'tuta *nf* overalls *pl*; *Sport* tracksuit. **~ da ginnastica** tracksuit. **~ da lavoro** overalls *pl*. **~ mimetica** camouflage. **~ spaziale** spacesuit. **~ subacquea** wetsuit

tu'tela *nf* *Jur* guardianship; (*protezione*) protection. **tutelare** *vt* protect

tu'tina *nf* sleepsuit; (*da danza*) leotard

tu'tore, -'trice *nmf* guardian

'tutta *nf* mettercela **~ per fare qcsa** go flat out for sth

tutta'via *conj* nevertheless, still

'tutto *a* whole; (*con nomi plurali*) all; (*ogni*) every; **tutta la classe** the whole class, all the class; **tutti gli alunni** all the pupils; **a tutta velocità** at full speed; **ho aspettato ~ il giorno** I waited all day [long]; **in ~ il mondo** all over the world, **noi tutti** all of us; **era tutta contenta** she was delighted; **tutti e due** both; **tutti e tre** all three ● *pron* all; (*tutta la gente*)

everybody; (*tutte le cose*) everything; (*qualunque cosa*) anything; **l'ho mangiato ~** I ate it all; **le ho lavate tutte** I washed them all; **raccontami ~** tell me everything; **lo sanno tutti** everybody knows; **è capace di ~** he's capable of anything; **~ compreso** all in; **del ~ ~** quite; **in ~** altogether ● *adv* completely; **tutt'a un tratto** all at once; **tutt'altro** not at all; **tutt'altro che** anything but ● *nm* whole; **tentare il ~ per ~** go for broke. **~fare** *a inv* & *nmf* **[impiegato] ~** general handyman; **donna ~** general maid

tut'tora *adv* still

tutù *nm inv* tutu, ballet dress

tv *nf inv* TV

Uu

ubbidi'en|te *a* obedient. **~za** *nf* obedience. **ubbi'dire** *vi* **~ (a)** obey

ubi'ca|to *a* located. **~zi'one** *nf* location

ubria'car|e *vt* get drunk. **~si** *vr* get drunk; **~si di** *fig* become intoxicated with

ubria'chezza *nf* drunkenness; **in stato di ~** inebriated

ubri'aco, -a *a* drunk; **~ fradicio** dead o blind drunk ● *nmf* drunk

ubria'cone *nm* drunkard

uccelli'era *nf* aviary. **uc'cello** *nm* bird; (*vulg: pene*) cock

uc'cider|e *vt* kill. **~si** *vr* kill oneself

ucci'si|one *nf* killing. **uc'ciso** *pp di* uccidere. **~sore** *nm* killer

u'dente *a* **i non udenti** the hearing-impaired

u'dibile *a* audible

udi'enza *nf* audience; (*colloquio*) interview; *Jur* hearing

u'dire *vt* hear. **~'tivo** *a* auditory. **~to** *nm* hearing. **~'tore, ~'trice**

nmf listener; *Sch* unregistered student *(allowed to sit in on lectures)*. ~'torio *nm* audience

'uffa *int* (con *impazienza*) come on!; (con *tono seccato*) damn!

uffici'al|e *a* official ● *nm* officer; (*funzionario*) official; **pubblico** ~e public official. ~e **giudiziario** clerk of the court. ~iz'zare *vt* make official, officialize

uf'ficio *nm* office; (*dovere*) duty. ~ **di collocamento** employment office. ~ **informazioni** information office. ~ **del personale** personnel department. ~sa'mente *adv* unofficially

uffici'oso *a* unofficial

'ufo[1] *nm inv* UFO

'ufo[2]: **a** ~ *adv* without paying

uggi'oso *a* boring

uguagli'a|nza *nf* equality. ~re *vt* make equal; (*essere uguale*) equal; (*livellare*) level. ~rsi *vr* ~rsi *a* compare oneself to

ugu'al|e *a* equal; (*lo stesso*) the same; (*simile*) like. ~'mente *adv* equally; (*malgrado tutto*) all the same

'ulcera *nf* ulcer

uli'veto *nm* olive grove

ulteri'or|e *a* further. ~'mente *adv* further

ultima'mente *adv* lately

ulti'ma|re *vt* complete. ~tum *nm inv* ultimatum

ulti'missime *nfpl Journ* stop press, latest news *sg*

'ultimo *a* last; (*notizie ecc*) latest; (*più lontano*) farthest; *fig* ultimate ● *nm* last; **fino all'**~ to the last; **per** ~ at the end; **l'**~ **piano** the top floor

ultrà *nmf inv Sport* fanatical supporter

ultramo'derno *a* ultramodern

ultra'rapido *a* extra-fast

ultrasen'sibile *a* ultrasensitive

ultra's|onico *a* ultrasonic. ~'u'ono *nm* ultrasound

ultrater'reno *a* (*vita*) after death

ultravio'letto *a* ultraviolet

ulu'la|re *vi* howl. ~to *nm* howling; **gli** ~ti the howls, the howling

umana'mente *adv* (*trattare*) humanely; ~ **impossibile** not humanly possible

uma'nesimo *nm* humanism

umani|tà *nf* humanity. ~'tario *a* humanitarian. u'mano *a* human; (*benevolo*) humane

umidifica'tore *nm* humidifier

umidi|tà *nf* dampness; (*di clima*) humidity. 'umido *a* damp; (*clima*) humid; (*mani, occhi*) moist ● *nm* dampness; **in umido** *Culin* stewed

'umile *a* humble

umili'a|nte *a* humiliating. ~re *vt* humiliate. ~rsi *vr* humble oneself. ~zi'one *nf* humiliation. umil|tà *nf* humility. umil'mente *adv* humbly

u'more *nm* humour; (*stato d'animo*) mood; **di cattivo/buon** ~ in a bad/good mood

umo'ris|mo *nm* humour. ~ta *nmf* humorist. ~tico *a* humorous

un *indef art a*; (*davanti a vocale o h muta*) an; *vedi* uno

una *indef art f a*; *vedi* un

u'nanim|e *a* unanimous. ~e'mente *adv* unanimously. ~ità *nf* unanimity; **all'**~ità unanimously

unci'nato *a* hooked; (*parentesi*) angle

unci'netto *nm* crochet hook

un'cino *nm* hook

'undici *a & nm* eleven

unger|e *vt* grease; (*sporcare*) get greasy; *Relig* anoint; (*blandire*) flatter. ~si *vr* (con *olio solare*) oil oneself; ~si **le mani** get one's hands greasy

unghe'rese *a & nmf* Hungarian. Unghe'ria *nf* Hungary; (*lingua*) Hungarian

'unghi|a *nf* nail; (*di animale*) claw. ~'ata *nf* (*graffio*) scratch

ungu'ento *nm* ointment

unica'mente *adv* only. 'unico *a* only; (*singolo*) single; (*incomparabile*) unique

unifi·ca|re vt unify. **~zi'one** nf unification

unifor·ma|re vt level. **~si** vr conform (**a** to)

uni·for|me a & nf uniform. **~ità** nf uniformity

unilate·ra'le a unilateral

uni'one nf union; (armonia) unity. **U~ Europea** European Union. **U~ Monetaria Europea** European Monetary Union. **~ sindacale** trade union; labor union Am. **U~ Sovietica** Soviet Union

u'ni|re vt unite; (collegare) join; blend (colori ecc.). **~rsi** vr unite; (collegarsi) join

'unisex a inv unisex

unità nf inv unity; Math, Mil unit; Comput drive. **~ di misura** unit of measurement. **~rio** a unitary

u'nito a united; (tinta) plain

univer·sa'le a universal. **~iz'zare** vt universalize. **~'mente** adv universally

università nf inv university. **~rio, -a** a university attrib ● nmf (insegnante) university lecturer; (studente) undergraduate

uni'verso nm universe

uno, -a indef art (before s + consonant, gn, ps, z) ● pron one; **a ~ a ~** one by one; **l'~ e l'altro** both [of them]; **né l'~ né l'altro** neither [of them]; **~ di noi** one of us; **~ fa quello che può** you do what you can ● a a, one ● nm (numerale) one; (un tale) some man ● nf some woman

'unt|o pp di ungere ● a greasy ● nm grease. **~u'oso** a greasy.

unzi'one nf l'Estrema Unzione Extreme Unction

u'omo nm (pl uomini) man. **~ d'affari** business man. **~ di fiducia** right-hand man. **~ di Stato** statesman

u'ovo nm (pl nf uova) egg. **~ in camicia** poached egg. **~ alla coque** boiled egg. **~ di Pasqua** Easter egg. **~ sodo** hard-boiled egg. **~ strapazzato** scrambled egg

ura'gano nm hurricane

u'ranio nm uranium

urba·niz·mo nm urbanization. **~ista** nmf town planner. **~istica** nf town planning. **~istico** a urban. **urbaniz·za·zi'one** nf urbanization. **ur·ba·no** a urban; (cortese) urbane

ur·gen·te a urgent. **~te'mente** adv urgently. **~za** nf urgency; in caso d'**~za** in an emergency; d'**~za** (misura, chiamata) emergency

'urgere vi be urgent

u·ri·na nf urine. **uri'nare** vi urinate

ur·la·re vi shout, yell; (cane, vento:) howl. **'urlo** nm (pl nm urli, nf urla) shout; (di cane, vento) howling

'urna nf urn; (elettorale) ballot box; andare alle urne go to the polls

urrà int hurrah!

U.R.S.S. nf abbr (Unione delle Repubbliche Socialiste Sovietiche) USSR

ur·ta·re vt knock against; (scontrarsi) bump into; fig irritate. **~si** vr collide; fig clash

'urto nm knock; (scontro) crash; (contrasto) conflict; fig clash; d'**~** (misure, terapia) shock

usa e getta a inv (rasoio, siringa) throw-away, disposable

u'sanza nf custom; (moda) fashion

u·sa·re vt use; (impiegare) employ; (esercitare) exercise; **~re fare qcsa** be in the habit of doing sth ● vi (essere di moda) be fashionable; **non si usa più** it is out of fashion; (attrezzatura, espressione:) it's not used any more. **~to** a used; (non nuovo) second-hand

U.S.A. nmpl abbr US[A] sg

u'scente a (presidente) outgoing

usci'ere nm usher. **'uscio** nm door

u'sci|re vi come out; (andare fuori) go out; (sfuggire) get out; (essere sorteggiato) come up; (giornale:) come out; **~re da** Comput exit from, quit; **~re di strada** leave the road. **~ta** nf exit, way out; (spesa) outlay; (di autostrada) junction; (battuta) witty remark; essere in libera ~ta be off duty. ~ta di servizio back door. ~ta di sicurezza emergency exit

usi'gnolo nm nightingale

'uso nm use; (abitudine) custom; (usanza) usage; fuori ~ out of use; per ~ esterno (medicina) for external use only

U.S.S.L. nf abbr (Unità Socio-Sanitaria Locale) local health centre

ustio'na|rsi vr burn oneself. ~to, -a nmf burns case ●a burnt.

usti'one nf burn

usu'ale a usual

usufru'ire vi ~ di take advantage of

u'sura nf usury. **usu'raio** nm usurer

usur'pare vt usurp

u'tensile nm tool; Culin utensil; cassetta degli utensili tool box

u'tente nmf user. ~ finale end user

u'tenza nf use; (utenti) users pl. ~ finale end users

ute'rino a uterine. **'utero** nm womb

'util|e a useful ●nm Comm profit. ~ità nf usefulness, utility; Comput utility. ~i'taria nf Auto small car. ~i'tario a utilitarian

utiliz'za|re vt utilize. ~zi'one nf utilization. **uti'lizzo** nm (utilizzazione) use

uto'pistico a Utopian

'uva nf grapes pl; chicco d'~ grape. ~ passa raisins pl. ~ sultanina currants pl

. . . .

Vv

. . . .

va'cante a vacant

va'canza nf holiday; (posto vacante) vacancy. essere in ~ be on holiday

'vacca nf cow. ~ da latte dairy cow

vacc|i'nare vt vaccinate. ~inazi'one nf vaccination. **vac'cino** nm vaccine

vacil'la|nte a tottering; (oggetto) wobbly; (luce) flickering; fig wavering. ~re vi totter; (oggetto:) wobble; (luce:) flicker; fig waver

'vacuo a (vano) vain; fig empty ●nm vacuum

vagabon'dare vi wander. **vaga-'bondo, -a** a (cane) stray; gente vagabonda tramps pl ●nmf tramp

va'gare vi wander

vagheggi'are vt long for

va'gi|na nf vagina. ~'nale a vaginal

va'gi|re vi whimper. ~'to nm whimper

'vaglia nm inv money order. ~ bancario bank draft. ~ postale postal order

vagli'are vt sift; fig weigh

'vago a vague

vagon'cino nm (di funivia) car

va'gone nm (per passeggeri) carriage; (per merci) wagon. ~ letto sleeper. ~ ristorante restaurant car

vai'olo nm smallpox

va'langa nf avalanche

va'lente a skilful

va'ler|e vi be worth; (contare) count; (regola:) apply (per to); (essere valido) be valid; far ~e i propri diritti assert one's rights; farsi ~ assert oneself; non vale that's not fair!; tanto vale che me ne vada I might as well go ●vt ~re qcsa a qcno (procurare) earn sb sth; ~ne la pena be worth it; vale la pena di vederlo it's worth seeing; ~si di avail oneself of

valeri'ana nf valerian

va'levole a valid

vali'care vt cross. **'valico** nm pass

validità nf validity; con ~ illimitata valid indefinitely

'valido a valid; (efficace) efficient; (contributo) valuable

valige'ria nf (fabbrica) leather factory; (negozio) leather goods shop

va'ligia nf suitcase; **fare le valigie** pack; fig pack one's bags. ~ **diplomatica** diplomatic bag

val'lata nf valley. **valle** nf valley; **a valle** downstream

val'letta nf TV assistant. ~**o** nm valet; TV assistant

val'lone nm (valle) deep valley

va'lore nm value, worth; (merito) merit; (coraggio) valour; ~**i** pl Comm securities; **di** ~ (oggetto) valuable; **oggetti** pl **di** ~ valuables; **senza** ~**e** worthless. ~**iz'zare** vt (mettere in valore) use to advantage; (aumentare di valore) increase the value of; (migliorare l'aspetto di) enhance

valo'roso a courageous

'valso pp di **valere**

va'luta nf currency. ~ **estera** foreign currency

valu'ta|re vt value; weigh up (situazione). ~**rio** a (mercato, norme) currency. ~**zi'one** nf valuation

'valva nf valve. **'valvola** nf valve; Electr fuse

'valzer nm inv waltz

vam'pata nf blaze; (di calore) blast; (al viso) flush

vam'piro nm vampire; fig bloodsucker

vana'mente adv (inutilmente) in vain

van'da|lico a atto ~**lico** act of vandalism. ~**lismo** nm vandalism. **'vandale** nm vandal

vaneggi'are vi rave

'vanga nf spade. **van'gare** vt dig

van'gelo nm Gospel; (fam: verità) gospel [truth]

vanifi'care vt nullify

va'niglia nf vanilla. ~**'ato** a (zucchero) vanilla attrib

vanil'lina nf vanillin

vanità nf vanity. **vani'toso** a vain

'vano a vain ● nm (stanza) room; (spazio vuoto) hollow

van'taggio nm advantage; Sport lead; Tennis advantage; **trarre** ~ **da qcsa** derive benefit from sth. ~**'oso** a advantageous

van't|are vt praise; (possedere) boast. ~**arsi** vr boast. ~**e'ria** nf boasting. **'vanto** nm boast

'vanvera nf **a** ~ at random; **parlare a** ~ talk nonsense

va'po|re nm steam; (di benzina, cascata) vapour; **a** ~**e** steam attrib; **al** ~**e** Culin steamed. ~**e acqueo** steam, water vapour; **battello a** ~**e** steamboat. **vapo'retto** nm ferry. ~**i'era** nf steam engine

vaporiz'za|re vt vaporize. ~**'tore** nm spray

vapo'roso a (vestito) filmy; **capelli vaporosi** big hair sg

va'rare vt launch

var'care vt cross. **'varco** nm passage; **aspettare al varco** lie in wait

vari'abi|le a changeable, variable ● nf variable. ~**ità** nf changeableness, variability

vari'a|nte nf variant. ~**re** vt/i vary; ~**re di umore** change one's mood. ~**zi'one** nf variation

va'rice nf varicose vein

vari'cella nf chickenpox

vari'coso a varicose

varie'gato a variegated

varietà nf inv variety ● nm inv variety show

'vario a varied; (al pl, parecchi) various; **vari** pl (molti) several; **varie ed eventuali** any other business

vario'pinto a multicoloured

'varo nm launch

va'salo nm potter

'vasca nf tub; (piscina) pool; (lunghezza) length. ~ **da bagno** bath

va'scello nm vessel

va'schetta nf tub

vase'lina nf Vaseline®

vasel'lame nm china. ~ **d'oro/d'argento** gold/silver plate

'vaso nm pot; (da fiori) vase; Anat vessel; (per cibi) jar. ~ **da notte** chamber pot

vas'soio nm tray

vastità *nf* vastness. '**vasto** *a* vast; **di vaste vedute** broad-minded

Vati'cano *nm* Vatican

vattela'pesca *adv fam* God knows!

ve *pers pron* you; **ve l'ho dato I** gave it to you

vecchia *nf* old woman. **vecchi'aia** *nf* old age. '**vecchio** *a* old ●*nmf* old man; **i vecchi** old people

'**vece** *nf* **in ~ di** in place of; **fare le veci di** qcno take sb's place

ve'**dente** *a* **i non vedenti** the visually handicapped

ve'**der|e** *vt/i* see; **far ~e** show; **farsi ~e** show one's face; **non vedo l'ora di...** I can't wait to.... **~si** *vr* see oneself; (*reciproco*) see each other

ve'**detta** *nf* (*luogo*) lookout; *Naut* patrol vessel

'**vedovo, -a** *nm* widower ●*nf* widow

ve'**duta** *nf* view

vee'**mente** *a* vehement

vege'**ta|le** *a & nm* vegetable. **~li'ano** *a & nmf* vegan. **~re** *vi* vegetate. **~ri'ano, -a** *a & nmf* vegetarian. **~zi'one** *nf* vegetation

'**vegeto** *a vedi* **vivo**

veg'**gente** *nmf* clairvoyant

'**veglia** *nf* watch; **fare la ~** keep watch. **~ funebre** vigil

vegli'**ar|e** *vi* be awake; **~are su** watch over. **New Year's Eve celebration

ve'**icolo** *nm* vehicle

'**vela** *nf* sail; *Sport* sailing; **far ~** set sail

ve'**la|re** *vt* veil; (*fig: nascondere*) hide. **~rsi** *vr* (*vista:*) mist over; (*voce:*) go husky. **~ta'mente** *adv* indirectly. **~to** *a* veiled; (*occhi*) misty; (*collant*) sheer

'**velcro®** *nm* velcro®

veleggi'**are** *vi* sail

ve'**leno** *nm* poison. **vele'noso** *a* poisonous

veli'**ero** *nm* sailing ship

ve'**lina** *nf* (**carta**) **~** tissue paper; (*copia*) carbon copy

ve'**lista** *nm* yachtsman ●*nf* yachtswoman

ve'**livolo** *nm* aircraft

velle|i'**tà** *nf inv* foolish ambition. **~tario** *a* unrealistic

'**vello** *nm* fleece

vellu'**tato** *a* velvety. **vel'luto** *nm* velvet. **velluto a coste** corduroy

'**velo** *nm* veil; (*di zucchero, cipria*) dusting; (*tessuto*) voile

ve'**loc|e** *a* fast. **~e'mente** *adv* quickly. **velo'cista** *nmf* Sport sprinter. **~ità** *nf inv* speed; (*Auto: marcia*) gear. **~ità di crociera** cruising speed. **~iz'zare** *vt* speed up

ve'**lodromo** *nm* cycle track

'**vena** *nf* vein; **essere in ~ di** be in the mood for

ve'**nale** *a* venal; (*persona*) mercenary, venal

ve'**nato** *a* grainy

vena'**torio** *a* hunting *attrib*

vena'**tura** *nf* (*di legno*) grain; (*di foglia, marmo*) vein

ven'**demmia** *nf* grape harvest. **~'are** *vt* harvest

'**vender|e** *vt* sell. **~si** *vr* sell oneself; **vendesi** for sale

ven'**detta** *nf* revenge

vendi'**ca|re** *vt* avenge. **~rsi** *vr* get one's revenge. **~tivo** *a* vindictive

'**vendi|ta** *nf* sale; **in ~ta** on sale. **~ta all'asta** sale by auction. **~ta al dettaglio** retailing. **~ta all'ingrosso** wholesaling. **~ta al minuto** retailing. **~ta porta a porta** door-to-door selling. **~tore, -'trice** *nmf* seller. **~tore ambulante** hawker, pedlar

vene'**ra|bile, ~ndo** *a* venerable

vene'**ra|re** *vt* revere

vener'**dì** *nm inv* Friday. **V~ Santo** Good Friday

'**Venere** *nf* Venus. **ve'nereo** *a* venereal

Ve'**nezia** *nf* Venice. **v~'ano, -a** *a & nmf* Venetian ●*nf* (*persiana*) Venetian blind; *Culin* sweet bun

veni·ale *a* venial

ve·nire *vi* come; (*riuscire*) turn out; (*costare*) cost; (*in passivi*) be; **~ a sapere** learn; **~ in mente** occur; **~ meno** (*svenire*) faint; **~ meno a un contratto** go back on a contract; **~ via** come away; (*staccarsi*) come off; **mi viene da piangere** I feel like crying; **vieni a prendermi** come and pick me up

ven·taglio *nm* fan

ven·tata *nf* gust [of wind]; *fig* breath

ven·te|nne *a & nmf* twenty-year-old. **~simo** *a & nm* twentieth. **'venti** *a & nm* twenty

venti·la|re *vt* air. **~·tore** *nm* fan. **~·zi·one** *nf* ventilation

ven·tina *nf* una **~** (*circa venti*) about twenty

ventiquat·trore *nf inv* (*valigia*) overnight case

'vento *nm* wind; **farsi ~** fan oneself

ven·tosa *nf* sucker

ven·toso *a* windy

'ventre *nm* stomach. **ven·triloquo** *nm* ventriloquist

ven·tura *nf* fortune; **andare alla ~** trust to luck

ven·turo *a* next

ve·nuta *nf* coming

vera·mente *adv* really

ve·randa *nf* veranda

ver·ba|le *a* verbal ●*nm* (*di riunione*) minutes *pl.* **~·mente** *adv* verbally

'verbo *nm* verb. **~ ausiliare** auxiliary [verb]

'verde *a* green ●*nm* green; (*vegetazione*) greenery; (*semaforo*) green light; **essere al ~** be broke. **~ oliva** olive green. **~ pisello** pea green. **~·rame** *nm* verdigris

ver·detto *nm* verdict

ver·dura *nf* vegetables *pl*, **una ~** a vegetable

'verga *nf* rod

vergi·n|ale *a* virginal. **'vergine** *nf* virgin; *Astr* Virgo ●*a* virgin; (*cassetta*) blank. **~·ità** *nf* virginity

ver·gogna *nf* shame; (*timidezza*) shyness

vergo·gn|arsi *vr* feel ashamed; (*essere timido*) feel shy. **~·oso** *a* ashamed; (*timido*) shy; (*disonorevole*) shameful

ve·rifica *nf* check. **verifi·cabile** *a* verifiable

verifi·car|e *vt* check. **~·si** *vr* come true

ve·rismo *nm* realism

ve·rità *nf* truth. **~·l'ero** *a* truthful

'verme *nm* worm. **~ solitario** tapeworm

ver·miglio *a & nm* vermilion

ver·mut *nm inv* vermouth

ver·nacolo *nm* vernacular

ver·nic|e *nf* paint; (*trasparente*) varnish; (*pelle*) patent leather; *fig* veneer; **"vernice fresca"** "wet paint". **~·i·are** *vt* paint; (*con vernice trasparente*) varnish. **~·ia·tura** *nf* painting; (*strato*) paintwork; *fig* veneer

'vero *a* true; (*autentico*) real; (*perfetto*) perfect; **è ~?** is that so?; **~ e proprio** full-blown; **sei stanca, ~?** you're tired, aren't you ●*nm* truth; (*realtà*) life

verosimigli·anza *nf* probability. **vero·simile** *a* probable

ver·ruca *nf* wart; (*sotto la pianta del piede*) verruca

versa·mento *nm* (*pagamento*) payment; (*in banca*) deposit

ver·sante *nm* slope

ver·sa|re *vt* pour; (*spargere*) shed; (*rovesciare*) spill; pay (*denaro*). **~·rsi** *vr* spill; (*fiume*) flow

ver·satile *a* versatile. **~·ità** *nf* versatility

ver·setto *nm* verse

versi·one *nf* version; (*traduzione*) translation; **"~ integrale"** "unabridged version"; **"~ ridotta"** "abridged version"

'verso¹ *nm* verse; (*grido*) cry; (*gesto*) gesture; (*senso*) direction; (*modo*) manner; **fare il ~ a qcno** ape sb; **non c'è ~ di** there is no way of

'verso² prep towards; (nei pressi di) round about; ~ **dove?** which way?

'vertebra nf vertebra

'vertere vi ~ **su** focus on

verti'cal|e a vertical; (in parole crociate) down ● nm vertical ● nf handstand. ~'mente adv vertically

'vertice nm summit; Math vertex; **conferenza al** ~ summit conference

ver'tigine nf dizziness; Med vertigo. **vertigini** pl giddy spells; **aver le vertigini** feel dizzy

vertigi|nosa'mente adv dizzily. ~'noso a dizzy; (velocità) breakneck; (prezzi) sky-high; (scollatura) plunging

ve'scica nf bladder; (sulla pelle) blister

'vescovo nm bishop

'vespa nf wasp

vespasi'ano nm urinal

'vespro nm vespers pl

ves'sillo nm standard

ve'staglia nf dressing gown

'vest|e nf dress; (rivestimento) covering; **in** ~**e di** in the capacity of; **in** ~**e ufficiale** in an official capacity. ~**i'ario** nm clothing

ve'stibolo nm hall

ve'stigio nm (pl nm **vestigi**, pl nf **vestigia**) trace

ve'st|ire vt dress. ~**rsi** vr get dressed. ~**ti** pl clothes. ~**to** a dressed ● nm (da uomo) suit; (da donna) dress

vete'rano, -a a e nmf veteran

veteri'naria nf veterinary science

veteri'nario a veterinary ● nm veterinary surgeon

'veto nm inv veto

ve'tra|io nm glazier. ~**ta** nf big window; (in chiesa) stained-glass window; (porta) glass door. ~**to** a glazed. **vetre'ria** nf glass works

ve'trina nf [shop-]window; (mobile) display cabinet. ~**'nista** nmf window dresser

vetri'olo nm vitriol

'vetro nm glass; (di finestra, porta) pane. ~**'resina** nf fibreglass

'vetta nf peak

vet'tore nm vector

vetto'vaglie nfpl provisions

vet'tura nf coach; (ferroviaria) carriage; Auto car. **vettu'rino** nm coachman

vezzeggia'|re vt fondle. ~**'tivo** nm pet name. **'vezzo** nm habit; (attrattiva) charm; **vezzi** pl (moine) affectation sg. **vez'zoso** a charming; pej affected

vi pers pron you; (riflessivo) yourselves; (reciproco) each other; (tra più persone) one another; **vi ho dato un libro** I gave you a book; **lavatevi le mani** wash your hands; **eccovi** here you are!
● adv = **ci**

'via¹ nf street, road; fig way; Anat tract; **in** ~ **di** in the course of; **per** ~ **di** on account of; ~ **che** as; **per** ~ **aerea** by airmail

'via² adv away; (fuori) out; **andar** ~ go away; **e così** ~ and so on; **e** ~ **dicendo** and whatnot ● int ~! go away!; Sport go!; (andiamo) come on! ● nm starting signal

viabilità nf road conditions pl; (rete) road network; (norme) road and traffic laws pl

via'card nf inv motorway card

via'dotto nm viaduct

viaggi'a|re vi travel. ~**'tore**, ~**'trice** nmf traveller

vi'aggio nm journey; (breve) trip; **buon** ~! safe journey!, have a good trip!; **fare un** ~ go on a journey. ~ **di nozze** honeymoon

vi'ale nm avenue; (privato) drive

via'vai nm coming and going

vi'bra|nte a vibrant. ~**re** vi vibrate; (fremere) quiver. ~**zi'one** nf vibration

vi'cario nm vicar

'vice+ pref vice+

'vice nmf deputy. ~**diret'tore** nm assistant manager

vi'cenda nf event; **a** ~ (fra due) each other; (a turno) in turn[s]

vice'versa *adv* vice versa

vici'na|nza *nf* nearness; **~nze** *pl* (*paraggi*) neighbourhood. **~to** *nm* neighbourhood; (*vicini*) neighbours *pl*

vi'cino, -a *a* near; (*accanto*) next ● *adv* near, close. **~ a** *prep* near [to] ● *nmf* neighbour. **~ di casa** nextdoor neighbour

vicissi'tudine *nf* vicissitude

'vicolo *nm* alley

'video *nm* video. **~'camera** *nf* camcorder. **~cas'setta** *nf* video cassette

videoci'tofono *nm* video entry phone

video'clip *nm inv* video clip

videogi'oco *nm* video game

videoregistra'tore *nm* video-recorder

video'teca *nf* video library

video'tel® *nm* ≈ Videotex®

videotermi'nale *nm* visual display unit, VDU

vidi'mare *vt* authenticate

vie'ta|re *vt* forbid; **sosta ~ta** no parking; **~to fumare** no smoking; **~to ai minori di 18 anni** prohibited to children under the age of 18

vi'gente *a* in force. **'vigere** *vi* be in force

vigi'la|nte *a* vigilant **~nza** *nf* vigilance. **~re** *vt* keep an eye on ● *vi* keep watch

'vigile *a* watchful ● *nm* ≈ [urbano] policeman. **~ del fuoco** fireman

vi'gilia *nf* eve

vigliacche'ria *nf* cowardice. **vi-gli'acco, -a** *a* cowardly ● *nmf* coward

'vigna *nf*, **vi'gneto** *nm* vineyard

vi'gnetta *nf* cartoon

vi'gore *nm* vigour; **entrare in ~** come into force. **vigo'roso** *a* vigorous

'vile *a* cowardly; (*abietto*) vile

'villa *nf* villa

vil'laggio *nm* village. **~ turistico** holiday village

vil'lano *a* rude ● *nm* boor; (*contadino*) peasant

villeggi'a|nte *nmf* holiday-maker. **~re** *vi* spend one's holidays. **~'tura** *nf* holiday[s] [*pl*], vacation *Am*

vil'letta *nf* small detached house. **~ino** *nm* detached house

viltà *nf* cowardice

'vimine *nm* wicker

'vinc|ere *vt* win; (*sconfiggere*) beat; (*superare*) overcome. **~ita** *nf* win; (*somma vinta*) winnings *pl*. **~i'tore, ~i'trice** *nmf* winner

vinco'la|nte *a* binding. **~re** *vt* bind; *Comm* tie up. **'vincolo** *nm* bond

vi'nicolo *a* wine attrib

vinil'polle® *nm* Leatherette®

'vino *nm* wine. **~ spumante** sparkling wine. **~ da taglio** blending wine. **~ da tavola** table wine

'vinto *pp di* **vincere**

vi'ola *nf Bot* violet; *Mus* viola. **vio'laceo** *a* purplish; (*labbra*) blue

vio'la|re *vt* violate. **~zi'one** *nf* violation. **~zione di domicilio** breaking and entering

violen'tare *vt* rape

violente'mente *adv* violently

vio'len|to *a* violent. **~za** *nf* violence. **~za carnale** rape

vio'letta *nf* violet

vio'letto *a & nm* (*colore*) violet

violi'nista *nmf* violinist. **vio'lino** *nm* violin. **violon'cello** *nm* cello

vi'ottolo *nm* path

'vipera *nf* viper

vi'ra|ggio *nm Phot* toning; *Naut, Aeron* turn. **~re** *vi* turn; **~re di bordo** veer

'virgola *nf* comma. **~ette** *nfpl* inverted commas

vi'ri|le *a* virile; (*da uomo*) manly. **~ità** *nf* virility; manliness

virtù *nf inv* virtue; **in ~ di** (*legge*) under. **~'ale** *a* virtual. **~'oso** *a* virtuous ● *nm* virtuoso

viru'lento *a* virulent

'virus *nm inv* virus

visa'gista *nmf* beautician

visce'rale *a* visceral; ⟨*odio*⟩ deep-seated; ⟨*reazione*⟩ gut

'viscere *nm* internal organ ● *nfpl* guts

'vischi|o *nm* mistletoe. **~'oso** *a* ⟨*viscous*⟩; ⟨*appiccicoso*⟩ sticky

'viscido *a* slimy

vi'scont|e *nm* viscount. **~'essa** *nf* viscountess

vi'scoso *a* viscous

vi'sibile *a* visible

visi'bilio *nm* profusion; **andare in ~** go into ecstasies

visibilità *nf* visibility

visi'era *nf* ⟨*di elmo*⟩ visor; ⟨*di berretto*⟩ peak

visio'nare *vt* examine; *Cinema* screen. **visi'one** *nf* vision; **prima visione** *Cinema* first showing

'visit|a *nf* visit; ⟨*breve*⟩ call; *Med* examination; **fare ~a a qcno** pay sb a visit. **~a di controllo** *Med* checkup. **visi'tare** *vt* visit; ⟨*brevemente*⟩ call on; *Med* examine; **~a'tore, ~a'trice** *nmf* visitor

vi'sivo *a* visual

'viso *nm* face

vi'sone *nm* mink

'vispo *a* lively

vis'suto *pp di* **vivere** ● *a* experienced

'vist|a *nf* sight; ⟨*veduta*⟩ view; **a ~a d'occhio** ⟨*crescere*⟩ visibly; ⟨*estendersi*⟩ as far as the eye can see; **in ~a di** in view of; **perdere di ~a qcno** lose sight of sb; *fig* lose touch with sb. **~o** *pp di* **vedere** ● *nm* visa. **vi'stoso** *a* showy; ⟨*notevole*⟩ considerable

visu'alle *a* visual. **~izza'tore** *nm* *Comput* display, VDU. **~izzazi'one** *nf* *Comput* display

'vit|a *nf* life; ⟨*durata della vita*⟩ lifetime; *Anat* waist; **a ~ for life**; **essere in fin di ~** at death's door; **essere in ~** be alive

vi'tal|e *a* vital. **~ità** *nf* vitality

vita'lizio *a* life *attrib* ● *nm* [life] annuity

vita'min|a *nf* vitamin. **~iz'zato** *a* vitamin-enriched

'vite *nf* *Mech* screw; *Bot* vine

vi'tello *nm* calf; *Culin* veal; ⟨*pelle*⟩ calfskin

vi'ticcio *nm* tendril

viticol'tor|e *nm* wine grower. **~ura** *nf* wine growing

'vitreo *a* vitreous; ⟨*sguardo*⟩ glassy

'vittima *nf* victim

'vitto *nm* food; ⟨*pasti*⟩ board. **~ e alloggio** board and lodging

vit'toria *nf* victory

vittori'ano *a* Victorian

vittori'oso *a* victorious

vi'uzza *nf* narrow lane

'viva *int* hurrah!; **~ la Regina!** long live the Queen!

vi'vac|e *a* vivacious; ⟨*mente*⟩ lively; ⟨*colore*⟩ bright. **~ità** *nf* vivacity; ⟨*di mente*⟩ liveliness; ⟨*di colore*⟩ brightness. **~iz'zare** *vt* liven up

vi'vaio *nm* nursery; ⟨*per pesci*⟩ pond; *fig* breeding ground

viva'mente *adv* ⟨*ringraziare*⟩ warmly

vi'vanda *nf* food; ⟨*piatto*⟩ dish

vi'vente *a* living ● *nmpl* **i viventi** the living

'vivere *vi* live; **~ di** live on ● *vt* ⟨*passare*⟩ go through ● *nm* life

'viveri *nmpl* provisions

'vivido *a* vivid

vivisezi'one *nf* vivisection

'vivo *a* alive; ⟨*vivente*⟩ living; ⟨*vivace*⟩ lively; ⟨*colore*⟩ bright; **~ e vegeto** alive and kicking; **farsi ~** keep in touch; ⟨*arrivare*⟩ turn up ● *nm* **colpire qcno sul ~** cut sb to the quick; **dal ~** ⟨*trasmissione*⟩ live; ⟨*disegnare*⟩ from life; **i vivi** the living

vizi'are *vt* spoil ⟨*bambino ecc*⟩; ⟨*guastare*⟩ vitiate. **~'ato** *a* spoilt; ⟨*aria*⟩ stale. **'vizio** *nm* vice; ⟨*cattiva abitudine*⟩ bad habit; ⟨*difetto*⟩ flaw. **~'oso** *a* dissolute; ⟨*difettoso*⟩ faulty; **circolo ~oso** vicious circle

vocabo'lario *nm* dictionary;

(*lessico*) vocabulary. **vo'cabolo** *nm* word

vo'cale *a* vocal ● *nf* vowel. **vo-'calico** *a* ⟨*corde*⟩ vocal; ⟨*suono*⟩ vowel *attrib*

vocazi'one *nf* vocation

'voce *nf* voice; ⟨*diceria*⟩ rumour; ⟨*di bilancio, dizionario*⟩ entry

voci'are *vi* ⟨*spettegolare*⟩ gossip ● *nm* buzz of conversation

vocife'rare *vi* shout; **si vocifera che...** it is rumoured that...

'voga *nf* rowing; ⟨*lena*⟩ enthusiasm; ⟨*moda*⟩ vogue; **essere in ~a** be in fashion. **vo'gare** *vi* row. **~a'tore** *nm* oarsman; ⟨*attrezzo*⟩ rowing machine

'voglia *nf* desire; ⟨*volontà*⟩ will; ⟨*della pelle*⟩ birthmark; **aver ~a di fare qcsa** feel like doing sth. **~'oso** *a* ⟨*occhi, persona*⟩ covetous

'voi *pers pron* you; **siete ~?** is that you?; **l'avete fatto ~?** did you do it yourself?. **~ 'altri** *pers pron* you

vo'lano *nm* shuttlecock; *Mech* flywheel

vo'lante *a* flying; ⟨*foglio*⟩ loose ● *nm* steering-wheel

volan'tino *nm* leaflet

vo'lare *vi* fly. **~ta** *nf* *Sport* final sprint; **di ~ta** in a rush

vo'latile *a* ⟨*liquido*⟩ volatile ● *nm* bird

volée *nf inv* *Tennis* volley

vo'lente *a* **o nolente** whether you like it or not

volente'roso *a* willing

volenti'eri *adv* willingly; **~!** with pleasure!

vo'lere *vt* want; ⟨*chiedere di*⟩ ask for; ⟨*aver bisogno di*⟩ need, **vuole che lo faccia io** he wants me to do it; **fai come vuoi** do as you like; **se tuo padre vuole, ti porto al cinema** if your father agrees, I'll take you to the cinema; **vorrei un caffè** I'd like a coffee; **la leggenda vuole che...** legend has it that...; **la vuoi smettere?** will you stop that!; **senza ~** without meaning to; **voler bene/male a qcno** love/

have something against sb; **voler dire** mean; **ci vuole il latte** we need milk; **ci vuole tempo/pazienza** it takes time/patience; **volerne a** have a grudge against; **vuoi...vuoi...** either...or... ● *nm* will; **voleri** *pl* wishes

vol'gar|e *a* vulgar; ⟨*popolare*⟩ common. **~ità** *nf inv* vulgarity. **~iz'zare** *vt* popularize. **~'mente** *adv* ⟨*grossolanamente*⟩ vulgarly, coarsely; ⟨*comunemente*⟩ commonly

'volger|e *vt/i* turn. **~si** *vr* turn [round]; **~si a** ⟨*dedicarsi*⟩ take up

voli'era *nf* aviary

voli'tivo *a* strong-minded

'volo *nm* flight; **al ~** ⟨*fare qcsa*⟩ quickly; ⟨*prendere qcsa*⟩ in midair; **alzarsi in ~** ⟨*uccello*⟩ take off; **in ~** airborne. **● di linea** scheduled flight. **~ nazionale** domestic flight. **~ a vela** gliding.

volontà *nf inv* will; ⟨*desiderio*⟩ wish; **a ~** ⟨*mangiare*⟩ as much as you like. **~ria'mente** *adv* voluntarily. **volon'tario** *a* voluntary ● *nm* volunteer

volonte'roso *a* willing

'volpe *nf* fox

volt *nm inv* volt

'volta *nf* time; ⟨*turno*⟩ turn; ⟨*curva*⟩ bend; *Archit* vault; **4 volte 4** 4 times 4; **a volte** sometimes; **c'era una ~...** once upon a time, there was...; **una ~** once; **due volte** twice; **tre/quattro volte** three/four times; **una ~ per tutte** once and for all; **uno per ~** one at a time; **uno alla ~** one at a time; **alla ~ di** in the direction of

volta'faccia *nm inv* volte-face

vol'taggio *nm* voltage

vol'ta|re *vt/i* turn; ⟨*rigirare*⟩ turn round; ⟨*rivoltare*⟩ turn over; **~re pagina** *fig* forget the past. **~rsi** *vr* turn [round]

volta'stomaco *nm* nausea; *fig* disgust

volteggi'are *vi* circle; ⟨*ginnastica*⟩ vault

'**volto** pp di **volgere** ● nm face; **mi ha mostrato il suo vero ~** he revealed his true colours

vo'**lubile** a fickle

vo'**lum|e** nm volume. **~i'noso** a voluminous

volu'**tamente** adv deliberately

voluttu|o**sità** nf voluptuousness. **~'oso** a voluptuous

vomi'**tare** vt vomit, be sick. vomi'**tevole** a nauseating. '**vomito** nm vomit.

'**vongola** nf clam

vo'**race** a voracious. **~'mente** adv voraciously

vo'**ragine** f abyss

'**vortice** nm whirl; (gorgo) whirlpool; (di vento) whirlwind

'**vostro** (**il ~ m**, **la vostra** f, **i vostri** mpl, **le vostre** fpl) poss a your; **è vostra questa macchina?** is this car yours?; **un ~ amico** a friend of yours; **~ padre** your father ● poss pron yours; **i vostri** your folks

vo'**ta|nte** nmf voter. **~re** vi vote. **~zi'one** nf voting; Sch marks pl. '**voto** nm vote; Sch mark; Relig vow

vs. abbr Comm (**vostro**) yours

vul'**canico** a volcanic. vul'**cano** nm volcano

vulne'**rabil|e** a vulnerable. **~ità** nf vulnerability

vuo'**tare** vt, **vuo'tarsi** vr empty

vu'**oto** a empty; (non occupato) vacant; **~ di** (sprovvisto) devoid of ● nm empty space; Phys vacuum; fig void; **assegno a ~** dud cheque; **sotto ~** (prodotto) vacuum-packed; **~ a perdere** no deposit. **~ d'aria** air pocket

Ww

W abbr (**viva**) long live

'**wafer** nm inv (biscotto) wafer

walkie-'**talkie** nm inv walkie-talkie

watt nm inv watt

WC nm inv WC

'**western** a inv cowboy attrib ● nm Cinema western

Xx

X, x a raggi pl **X** X-rays; **il giorno X** D-day

xenofo'**bia** nf xenophobia. xe'**nofobo**, **-a** a xenophobic ● nmf xenophobe

xe'**res** nm inv sherry

xi'**lofono** nm xylophone

Yy

yacht nm inv yacht

yen nm inv Fin yen

'**yoga** nm yoga; (praticante) yogi

'**yogurt** nm inv yoghurt. **~i'era** nf yoghurt-maker

Zz

zaba[gl]i'**one** nm zabaglione (dessert made from eggs, wine or marsala and sugar)

zaf'**fata** nf whiff; (di fumo) cloud

zaffe'**rano** nm saffron

zaf'**firo** nm sapphire

'**zaino** nm rucksack

'zampa *nf* leg; **a quattro zampe** ⟨*animale*⟩ four-legged; ⟨*carponi*⟩ on all fours. **zampe** *pl* **di gallina** crow's feet

zampil'la|nte *a* spurting. **~re** *vi* spurt. **zam'pillo** *nm* spurt

zam'pogna *nf* bagpipe

zam'pone *nfpl* stuffed pig's trotter *with lentils*

'zanna *nf* fang; ⟨*di elefante*⟩ tusk

zan'zar|a *nf* mosquito. **~i'era** *nf* ⟨*velo*⟩ mosquito net; ⟨*su finestra*⟩ insect screen

'zappa *nf* hoe. **zap'pare** *vt* hoe

'zattera *nf* raft

zatte'roni *nmpl* ⟨*scarpe*⟩ wedge shoes

za'vorra *nf* ballast; *fig* dead wood

'zazzera *nf* mop of hair

'zebra *nf* zebra; **zebre** *pl* ⟨*passaggio pedonale*⟩ zebra crossing

'zecca¹ *nf* mint; **nuovo di ~** brand-new

'zecca² *nf* ⟨*parassita*⟩ tick

zec'chino *nm* sequin; **oro ~** pure gold

ze'lante *a* zealous. **'zelo** *nm* zeal

'zenit *nm* zenith

'zenzero *nm* ginger

'zeppa *nf* wedge

'zeppo *a* packed full; **pieno ~** crammed *o* packed with

zer'bino *nm* doormat

'zero *nm* zero, nought; ⟨*in calcio*⟩ nil; *Tennis* love; **due a ~** ⟨*in partite*⟩ two nil; **ricominciare da ~** *fig* start again from scratch

'zeta *nf* zed, zee *Am*

'zia *nf* aunt

zibel'lino *nm* sable

'zigomo *nm* cheek-bone

zig'zag *nm inv* zigzag; **andare a ~** zigzag

zim'bello *nm* decoy; ⟨*oggetto di scherno*⟩ laughing-stock

'zinco *nm* zinc

'zingaro, -a *nmf* gypsy

'zio *nm* uncle

zi'tel|la *nf* spinster; *pej* old maid. **~'lona** *nf pej* old maid

zit'tire *vi* fall silent ● *vt* silence.

'zitto *a* silent; **sta' zitto!** keep quiet!

ziz'zania *nf* ⟨*discordia*⟩ discord; **seminare ~** cause trouble

'zoccolo *nm* clog; ⟨*di cavallo*⟩ hoof; ⟨*di terra*⟩ clump; ⟨*di parete*⟩ skirting board, baseboard *Am*; ⟨*di colonna*⟩ base

zodia'cale *a* of the zodiac. **zo'diaco** *nm* zodiac

'zolfo *nm* sulphur

'zolla *nf* clod; ⟨*di zucchero*⟩ lump

zol'letta *nf* sugar cube, sugar lump

'zombi *nmf inv fig* zombi

'zona *nf* zone; ⟨*area*⟩ area. **~ di depressione** area of low pressure. **~ disco** area for parking discs only. **~ pedonale** pedestrian precinct. **~ verde** green belt

'zonzo *adv* **andare a ~** stroll about

zoo *nm inv* zoo

zoolo'gia *nf* zoology. **zoo'logico** *a* zoological. **zo'ologo, -a** *nmf* zoologist

zoo sa'fari *nm inv* safari park

zoppi'ca|nte *a* limping, *fig* shaky. **~re** *vi* limp; ⟨*essere debole*⟩ be shaky. **'zoppo, -a** *a* lame ● *nmf* cripple

zoti'cone *nm* boor

'zucca *nf* marrow; ⟨*fam: testa*⟩ head; ⟨*fam: persona*⟩ thickie

zucche'r|are *vt* sugar. **~i'era** *nf* sugar bowl. **~i'ficio** *nm* sugar refinery. **zucche'rino** *a* sugary ● *nm* sugar cube, sugar lump

'zucchero *nm* sugar. **~ di canna** cane sugar. **~ a vaniglia** vanilla sugar. **~ a velo** icing sugar. **zucche'roso** *a fig* honeyed

zuc'chin|a *nf*, **~o** *nm* courgette, zucchini *Am*

zuc'cone *nm* blockhead

'zuffa *nf* scuffle

zufo'lare *vt* whistle

zu'mare *vi* zoom

'zuppa *nf* soup. **~ inglese** *fig* trifle

zup'petta *nf* **fare ~** ⟨*con*⟩ dunk

zuppi'era *nf* soup tureen

'zuppo *a* soaked

Numbers/Numeri

Cardinal numbers/ Numeri cardinali

0	zero	zero
1	one	uno
2	two	due
3	three	tre
4	four	quattro
5	five	cinque
6	six	sei
7	seven	sette
8	eight	otto
9	nine	nove
10	ten	dieci
11	eleven	undici
12	twelve	dodici
13	thirteen	tredici
14	fourteen	quattordici
15	fifteen	quindici
16	sixteen	sedici
17	seventeen	diciassette
18	eighteen	diciotto
19	nineteen	diciannove
20	twenty	venti
21	twenty-one	ventuno
22	twenty-two	ventidue
30	thirty	trenta
40	forty	quaranta
50	fifty	cinquanta
60	sixty	sessanta
70	seventy	settanta
80	eighty	ottanta
90	ninety	novanta
100	a hundred	cento
101	a hundred and one	centouno
110	a hundred and ten	centodieci
200	two hundred	duecento
1,000	a thousand **mille**	
10,000	ten thousand **diecimila**	
100,000	a hundred thousand **centomila**	
1,000,000	a million **un milione**	

Ordinal numbers/ Numeri ordinali

1st	first	primo
2nd	second	secondo
3rd	third	terzo
4th	fourth	quarto
5th	fifth	quinto
6th	sixth	sesto
7th	seventh	settimo
8th	eighth	ottavo
9th	ninth	nono
10th	tenth	decimo
11th	eleventh	undicesimo
20th	twentieth	ventesimo
21st	twenty-first **ventunesimo**	
30th	thirtieth **trentesimo**	
40th	fortieth **quarantesimo**	
50th	fiftieth **cinquantesimo**	
100th	hundredth **centesimo**	
1,000th	thousandth **millesimo**	

Phrasefinder/Trovafrasi

Useful phrases | ## Frasi utili

yes, please — sì, grazie
no, thank you — no, grazie
sorry — scusa
excuse me — mi scusi
you're welcome — prego
I'm sorry, I don't understand — scusi, non capisco

Meeting people | ### Incontri

hello/goodbye — ciao/arrivederci
how do you do? — come sta?
how are you? — come stai?
nice to meet you — piacere

Asking questions | ### Fare domande

do you speak English/Italian? — parli inglese/italiano?
what's your name? — come ti chiami?
where are you from? — di dove sei?
where is...? — dov'è...?
can I have...? — posso avere...?
would you like...? — vuoi...?
do you mind if...? — le dispiace se...?

Statements about yourself | ### Presentarsi

my name is... — mi chiamo...
I'm English/Italian — sono inglese/italiano
I don't speak Italian/English — non parlo molto bene
very well — l'italiano/l'inglese
I'm here on holiday — sono qui in vacanza
I live near York/Pisa — abito vicino a York/Pisa

Emergencies | ### Emergenze

can you help me, please? — mi può aiutare, per favore?
I'm lost — mi sono perso
I'm ill — sto male
call an ambulance/the Police — chiami un'ambulanza/la polizia
watch out! — attenzione!

❶ Going Places

On the road | Sulla strada

where's the nearest garage/petrol station (US filling station)?
dov'è la stazione di servizio più vicina?

what's the best way to get there?
qual è la strada migliore per arrivarci?

I've got a puncture
ho bucato

I'd like to hire a bike/car
vorrei noleggiare una bicicletta/una macchina

I'm looking for somewhere to park
sto cercando parcheggio

there's been an accident
c'è stato un incidente

my car's broken down
ho la macchina in panne

the car won't start
la macchina non parte

By rail | In treno

where can I buy a ticket?
dove si fanno i biglietti?

what time is the next train to York/Milan?
a che ora è il prossimo treno per York/Milano?

do I have to change?
devo cambiare?

can I take my bike on the train?
posso portare la bicicletta sul treno?

which platform for the train to Bath/Florence?
da quale binario parte il treno per Bath/Firenze?

there's a train to London at 10 o'clock
c'è un treno per Londra alle 10

a single/return to Birmingham/Turin, please
un biglietto di sola andata/di andata e ritorno per Birmingham/Torino, per favore

I'd like a cheap day-return/an all-day ticket
vorrei un biglietto giornaliero di andata e ritorno a tariffa ridotta

I'd like to reserve a seat
vorrei prenotare un posto

At the airport | All'aeroporto

when's the next flight to Paris/Rome?	quand'è il prossimo volo per Parigi/Roma?
what time do I have to check in?	a che ora si fa il check-in?
where do I check in?	dov'è il check-in?
I'd like to confirm my flight	vorrei confermare il mio volo
I'd like a window seat/an aisle seat	vorrei un posto accanto al finestrino/di corridoio
I want to change/cancel my reservation	voglio cambiare/annullare la mia prenotazione

Getting there | Chiedere e dare indicazioni

could you tell me the way to the castle?	può indicarmi la strada per il castello?
how long will it take to get there?	quanto ci vuole per arrivarci?
how far is it from here?	quanto dista da qui?
which bus do I take for the cathedral?	quale autobus devo prendere per andare al duomo?
can you tell me where to get off?	può dirmi dove devo scendere?
how much is the fare to the town centre (US center)?	quant'è la tariffa per il centro?
what time is the last bus?	a che ora è l'ultimo autobus?
how do I get to the airport?	come si arriva all'aeroporto?
where's the nearest underground (US subway) station?	dov'è la metropolitana più vicina?
can you call me a taxi, please?	può chiamarmi un taxi, per favore?
take the first turning right	prenda la prima svolta a destra
turn left at the traffic lights/ just past the church	al semaforo giri a sinistra/ appena dopo la chiesa
I'll take a taxi	prenderò un taxi

❷ Keeping in touch

On the phone	Al telefono
where can I buy a phone card?	dove si comprano le schede telefoniche?
may I use your phone?	posso usare il telefono?
do you have a mobile?	ha il telefonino?
what is the code for Venice/Sheffield?	qual è il prefisso di Venezia/Sheffield?
I want to make a phone call	vorrei fare una telefonata
I'd like to reverse the charges (US call collect)	vorrei fare una telefonata a carico del destinatario
the line's engaged (US busy)	è occupato
there's no answer	non risponde nessuno
hello, this is Natalie	pronto, sono Natalie
is Richard there, please?	c'è Richard, per favore?
who's calling?	chi parla?
sorry, wrong number	ha sbagliato numero
just a moment, please	un attimo, prego
would you like to hold?	vuole attendere in linea?
please tell him/her I called	gli/le dica che ho chiamato, per favore
I'd like to leave a message for him/her	vorrei lasciare un messaggio
I'll try again later	riproverò più tardi
please tell her that Clare called	le dica che ha chiamato Clare
can he/she ring me back?	mi può richiamare?
my home number is…	il mio numero è…
my business number is…	il mio numero al lavoro è…
my fax number is…	il mio numero di fax è…
we were cut off	è caduta la linea

Writing	Corrispondenza
what's your address?	qual è il tuo indirizzo?
here's my business card	questo è il mio biglietto da visita
where is the nearest post office?	dov'è l'ufficio postale più vicino?
could I have a stamp for the UK/Italy, please?	mi dà un francobollo per la Gran Bretagna/l'Italia, per favore?
I'd like stamps for two postcards to the USA, please	vorrei due francobolli per cartolina per gli Stati Uniti, per favore
I'd like to send a parcel/a telegram	vorrei spedire un pacco/mandare un telegramma

On line	Internet
are you on the Internet?	sei su Internet?
what's your e-mail address?	qual è il tuo indirizzo di posta elettronica?
we could send it by e-mail	possiamo spedirlo con la posta elettronica
I'll e-mail it to you on Thursday	te lo mando per posta elettronica giovedì
I looked it up on the Internet	l'ho cercato su Internet
the information is on their website	le informazioni si trovano sul sito web

Meeting up	Appuntamenti
what shall we do this evening?	cosa facciamo stasera?
where shall we meet?	dove ci diamo appuntamento?
I'll see you outside the café at 6 o'clock	ci vediamo davanti al bar alle 6
see you later	a più tardi
I can't today, I'm busy	oggi non posso, sono impegnato

❸ Food and drink

Booking a restaurant | Prenotare un ristorante

can you recommend a good restaurant?	può consigliarmi un buon ristorante?
I'd like to reserve a table for four	vorrei prenotare un tavolo per quattro
a reservation for tomorrow evening at eight o'clock	una prenotazione per domani sera alle otto
I booked a table for two	ho prenotato un tavolo per due

Ordering | Ordinare

could we see the menu/wine list, please?	possiamo avere il menù/la carta dei vini, per favore?
do you have a vegetarian/children's menu?	avete un menù vegetariano/per bambini?
could we have some more bread/wine?	possiamo avere dell'altro pane/vino?
could I have the bill (US check)?	il conto, per favore
a bottle of mineral water, please	una bottiglia d'acqua minerale, per favore
as a starter ... and to follow ...	come antipasto ... e poi ...
a black/white coffee	un caffè/un caffè macchiato
we'd like to pay separately	conti separati, per favore

Reading a menu | Leggere il menù

cover charge	coperto
starters	antipasti
soups/first courses	minestre/primi piatti
main courses	secondi piatti
dish/soup of the day	piatto/minestra del giorno
salads/choice of vegetables	insalate/verdure a scelta
meat/game and poultry	carne/selvaggina e pollame
side dishes	contorni
desserts	dolci
drinks	bevande

Any complaints?

there's a mistake in the bill (US check)

the meat isn't cooked/ is overdone

that's not what I ordered

we are waiting to be served

we are still waiting for our drinks

my coffee is cold

the wine is not chilled

Lamentele?

c'è un errore nel conto

la carne è poco/troppo cotta

non avevo ordinato questo

stiamo aspettando che ci servano

stiamo ancora aspettando da bere

il caffè è freddo

il vino non è fresco

Food shopping

where is the nearest super-market?

is there a baker's/butcher's near here?

can I have a carrier bag

how much is it?

I'll have that one/this one

Fare la spesa

dov'è il supermercato più vicino?

c'è una panetteria/macelleria qui vicino?

mi dà un sacchetto di plastica

quant'è?

prendo quello/questo

On the shopping list

I'd like some bread

that's all, thank you

a bit more/less, please

that's enough, thank you

100 grams of salami/cheese

half a kilo of tomatoes

a packet of tea

a carton/litre of milk

a can/bottle of beer

La lista della spesa

vorrei del pane

nient'altro, grazie

un po' di più/meno, grazie

basta così, grazie

un etto di salame/formaggio

mezzo chilo di pomodori

un pacchetto di tè

un cartone/litro di latte

una lattina/bottiglia di birra

❹ Places to stay

Camping

can we pitch our tent here?	possiamo montare la tenda qui?
can we park our caravan here?	possiamo parcheggiare la roulotte qui?
what are the facilities like?	che attrezzature ci sono?
how much is it per night?	quant'è a notte?
where do we park the car?	dov'è il parcheggio?
we're looking for a campsite	stiamo cercando un campeggio
this is a list of local campsites	questo è l'elenco dei campeggi della zona
we go on a camping holiday every year	andiamo in campeggio tutti gli anni

In campeggio

At the hotel

I'd like a double/single room with bath	vorrei una camera doppia/singola con bagno
we have a reservation in the name of Morris	abbiamo prenotato a nome Morris
we'll be staying three nights, from Friday to Sunday	ci fermiamo tre notti, da venerdì a domenica
how much does the room cost?	quant'è la camera?
I'd like to see the room, please	vorrei vedere la camera, per favore
what time is breakfast?	a che ora è la colazione?
can I leave this in your safe?	posso lasciare questo nella cassaforte?
bed and breakfast	camera e prima colazione
we'd like to stay another night	vorremmo fermarci un'altra notte
please call me at 7:30	mi chiami alle 7:30, per favore
are there any messages for me?	ci sono messaggi per me?

In albergo

Hostels | Ostelli

could you tell me where the youth hostel is? — mi sa dire dov'è l'ostello della gioventù?

what time does the hostel close? — a che ora chiude l'ostello?

I'm staying in a hostel — alloggio in un ostello

the hostel we're staying in is great value — l'ostello in cui alloggiamo è molto conveniente

I know a really good hostel in Dublin — conosco un ottimo ostello a Dublino

I'd like to go backpacking in Australia — mi piacerebbe girare l'Australia con zaino e sacco a pelo

Rooms to let | In affitto

I'm looking for a room with a reasonable rent — vorrei affittare una camera a prezzo modico

I'd like to rent an apartment for a few weeks — vorrei affittare un appartamento per qualche settimana

where do I find out about rooms to let? — dove posso informarmi su camere in affitto?

what's the weekly rent? — quant'è l'affitto alla settimana?

I'm staying with friends at the moment — al momento alloggio presso amici

I rent an apartment on the outskirts of town — affitto un appartamento in periferia

the room's fine—I'll take it — la camera mi piace, la prendo

the deposit is one month's rent in advance — la caparra è di un mese d'affitto

❺ Shopping and money

At the bank | In banca

I'd like to change some money	vorrei cambiare dei soldi
I want to change some lire into pounds	vorrei cambiare delle lire in sterline
do you take Eurocheques?	accettate Eurochèque?
what's the exchange rate today?	quant'è il tasso di cambio oggi?
I prefer traveller's cheques (US traveler's checks) to cash	preferisco i traveller's cheque al contante
I'd like to transfer some money from my account	vorrei fare un bonifico
I'll get some money from the cash machine	prenderò dei soldi dal bancomat®
I'm with another bank	ho il conto in un'altra banca

Finding the right shop | Il negozio giusto

where's the main shopping district?	dov'è la zona commerciale principale?
where's a good place to buy sunglasses/shoes?	qual è il posto migliore per comprare occhiali da sole/scarpe?
where can I buy batteries/postcards?	dove posso comprare pile/cartoline?
where's the nearest chemist/bookshop?	dov'è la farmacia/libreria più vicina?
is there a good food shop around here?	c'è un buon negozio di generi alimentari qui vicino?
what time do the shops open/close?	a che ora aprono/chiudono i negozi?
where can I hire a car?	dove posso noleggiare una macchina?
where did you get those?	dove le/li hai comprati?
I'm looking for presents for my family	sto cercando dei regalini per la mia famiglia
we'll do all our shopping on Saturday	faremo la spesa sabato
I love shopping	adoro fare spese

Are you being served?

how much does that cost?	quanto costa quello?
can I try it on?	posso provarlo?
can you keep it for me?	me lo mette da parte?
could you wrap it for me, please?	me lo incarta, per favore?
can I pay by credit card/cheque (US check)?	posso pagare con la carta di credito/un assegno?
do you have this in another colour (US color)?	c'è in altri colori?
could I have a bag, please?	mi dà un sacchetto, per favore?
I'm just looking	sto solo dando un'occhiata
I'll think about it	ci devo pensare
I'd like a receipt, please	mi dà lo scontrino, per favore?
I need a bigger/smaller size	mi serve la taglia più grande/piccola
I take a size 10/a medium	porto la 42/la media
it doesn't suit me	non mi sta bene
I'm sorry, I don't have any change/anything smaller	mi dispiace, non ho spiccioli/biglietti più piccoli
that's all, thank you	nient'altro, grazie

Nei negozi

Changing things

can I have a refund?	rimborsate i soldi?
can you mend it for me?	può ripararlo?
can I speak to the manager?	posso parlare con il direttore?
it doesn't work	non funziona
I'd like to change it, please	vorrei cambiarlo, per favore
I bought this here yesterday	l'ho comprato qui ieri

Cambiare un acquisto

❻ Sport and leisure

Keeping fit

where can we play football/squash?

where is the local sports centre (US center)?

what's the charge per day?

is there a reduction for children/a student discount?

I'm looking for a swimming pool/tennis court

you have to be a member

I play tennis on Mondays

I would like to go fishing/riding

I want to do aerobics

I love swimming/rollerblading

we want to hire skis/ snowboards

Tenersi in forma

dove possiamo giocare a calcio/squash?

dov'è il centro sportivo della zona?

quant'è la tariffa giornaliera?

c'è uno sconto per bambini/ studenti?

sto cercando una piscina/ un campo da tennis

bisogna essere soci

gioco a tennis di lunedì

vorrei andare a pescare/ a cavallo

vorrei fare aerobica

mi piace nuotare/pattinare

vorremmo noleggiare degli sci/snowboard

Watching sport

is there a football match on Sunday?

which teams are playing?

where can I get tickets?

I'd like to see a rugby/football match

my favourite (US favorite) team is…

let's watch the match on TV

Assistere a un incontro sportivo

c'è una partita di calcio domenica?

quali squadre giocano?

dove si comprano i biglietti?

mi piacerebbe vedere una partita di rugby/calcio

la mia squadra preferita è…

guardiamo la partita in TV

Going to the cinema/ theatre/club

what's on?

Andare al cinema/a teatro/ in discoteca

cosa danno?

when does the box office open/close?	a che ora apre/chiude il botteghino?
what time does the concert/performance start?	a che ora inizia il concerto/lo spettacolo?
when does it finish?	a che ora finisce?
are there any seats left for tonight?	ci sono dei posti per stasera?
how much are the tickets?	quanto costano i biglietti?
where can I get a programme (US program)?	dove si comprano i programmi?
I want to book tickets for tonight's performance	vorrei prenotare dei biglietti per lo spettacolo di stasera
I'll book seats in the circle	prenoterò dei posti in galleria
I'd rather have seats in the stalls	preferirei dei posti in platea
somewhere in the middle, but not too far back	dei posti al centro, ma non troppo distanti
four, please	quattro, per favore
for Saturday	per sabato
we'd like to go to a club	vorremmo andare in discoteca
I go clubbing every weekend	vado in discoteca tutti i fine settimana

Hobbies | ## Hobby

do you have any hobbies?	che hobby hai?
what do you do at the weekend?	cosa fai il fine settimana?
I like yoga/listening to music	mi piace lo yoga/ascoltare musica
I spend a lot of time surfing the Net	passo molto tempo a navigare in Internet
I read a lot	leggo molto
I collect comic books	faccio collezione di fumetti

❼ Good timing

Telling the time

could you tell me the time?
what time is it?
it's 2 o'clock
at about 8 o'clock
at 9 o'clock tomorrow
from 10 o'clock onwards
at 8 a.m./p.m.
at 5 o'clock in the morning/
afternoon
it's five past/quarter past/half
past one
it's twenty-five to/quarter to/five
to one
a quarter /three quarters of an
hour

Dire l'ora

mi dice che ore sono?
che ora è?
sono le due
verso le otto
domani mattina alle nove
dalle dieci in poi
alle otto di mattina/di sera
alle cinque del mattino/di sera

è l'una e cinque/e un quarto/
e mezza
è l'una meno venticinque/
meno un quarto/meno cinque
un quarto/tre quarti d'ora

Days and dates

Sunday, Monday, Tuesday,
Wednesday, Thursday, Friday,
Saturday

January, February, March,
April, May, June, July,
August, September, October,
November, December

what's the date?
it's the second of June
we meet up every Monday
she comes on Tuesdays
we're going away in August
it was the first of April
on November 8th

Giorni, mesi e date

domenica, lunedì, martedì,
mercoledì, giovedì, venerdì,
sabato

gennaio, febbraio, marzo,
aprile, maggio, giugno, luglio,
agosto, settembre, ottobre,
novembre, dicembre

quanti ne abbiamo oggi?
è il due giugno
ci incontriamo ogni lunedì
viene di martedì
saremo via ad agosto
era il primo aprile
l'otto novembre

Public holidays and special days	Festività
Bank holiday	festa civile
Bank holiday Monday	festa civile che cade di lunedì
long weekend	ponte
New Year's Day (Jan 1)	Capodanno (1 gennaio)
Epiphany (Jan 6)	Epifania (la Befana: 6 gennaio)
St Valentine's Day (Feb 14)	San Valentino (14 febbraio)
Shrove Tuesday/Pancake Day	martedì grasso
Ash Wednesday	mercoledì delle Ceneri
St Joseph's Day (Mar 19)	San Giuseppe (19 marzo)
Mother's Day	Festa della mamma
Palm Sunday	domenica delle Palme
Maundy Thursday	giovedì grasso
Good Friday	venerdì santo
Easter Day	Pasqua
Easter Monday	lunedì dell'Angelo (pasquetta)
Anniversary of the liberation of Italy in 1945	anniversario della Liberazione (25 aprile)
May Day (May 1)	Festa del lavoro (1 maggio)
Father's Day	Festa del papà
Independence Day (Jul 4)	anniversario dell'Indipendenza (4 luglio)
Assumption (Aug 15)	Assunzione (ferragosto: 15 agosto)
Halloween (Oct 31)	vigilia d'Ognissanti
All Saints' Day (Nov 1)	Ognissanti (1 novembre)
Thanksgiving	giorno del Ringraziamento
Christmas Eve (Dec 24)	vigilia di Natale (24 dicembre)
Christmas Day (Dec 25)	Natale (25 dicembre)
Boxing Day (Dec 26)	Santo Stefano (26 dicembre)
New Year's Eve (Dec 31)	San Silvestro (31 dicembre)

❽ Conversion charts/Tabelle di conversione

Length/Lunghezze

inches/pollici	0.39	3.9	7.8	11.7	15.6	19.7	39
cm/centimetri	1	10	20	30	40	50	100

Distance/Distanze

miles/miglia	0.62	6.2	12.4	18.6	24.9	31	62
km/kilometri	1	10	20	30	40	50	100

Weight/Pesi

pounds/libbre	2.2	22	44	66	88	110	220
kg/kilogrammi	1	10	20	30	40	50	100

Capacity/Capacità

gallons/galloni	0.22	2.2	4.4	6.6	8.8	11	22
litres/litri	1	10	20	30	40	50	100

Temperature/Temperature

°C	0	5	10	15	20	25	30	37	38	40
°F	32	41	50	59	68	77	86	98.4	100	104

Clothing and shoe sizes/Taglie e numeri di scarpe

Women's clothing sizes/Abbigliamento femminile

UK	8	10	12	14	16	18
US	6	8	10	12	14	16
Italy	40	42	44	46	48	50

Men's clothing sizes/Abbigliamento maschile

UK/US	36	38	40	42	44	46
Italy	46	48	50	52	54	56

Men's and women's shoes/Scarpe da uomo e da donna

UK women	3	4	5	6	7	7.5	8			
UK men					6	7	8	9	10	
US		5.5	6.5	7.5	8.5	9.5	10.5	11.5	12.5	13.5
Italy	36	37	38	39	40	41	42	43	44	

Aa

A /eɪ/ n Mus la m inv

a /ə/, accentato /eɪ/ (davanti a una vocale **an**) indef art un m, una f; (before s + consonant, gn, ps and z) uno; (before feminine noun starting with a vowel) un'; (each) a; **I am a lawyer** sono avvocato; **a tiger is a feline** la tigre è un felino; **a knife and fork** un coltello e una forchetta; **a Mr Smith is looking for you** un certo signor Smith ti sta cercando; **£2 a kilo/a head** due sterline al chilo/a testa

aback /ə'bæk/ adv **be taken ~** essere preso in contropiede

abandon /ə'bændən/ vt abbandonare; (give up) rinunciare a ● n abbandono m. **~ed** a abbandonato

abashed /ə'bæʃt/ a imbarazzato

abate /ə'beɪt/ vi calmarsi

abattoir /'æbətwɑː(r)/ n mattatoio m

abbey /'æbɪ/ n abbazia f

abbreviat|e /ə'briːvɪeɪt/ vt abbreviare. **~ion** /-'eɪʃn/ n abbreviazione f

abdicat|e /'æbdɪkeɪt/ vi abdicare ● vt rinunciare a. **~ion** /-'keɪʃn/ n abdicazione f

abdom|en /'æbdəmən/ n addome m. **~inal** /-'dɒmɪnl/ a addominale

abduct /əb'dʌkt/ vt rapire. **~ion** /-ʌkʃn/ n rapimento m

aberration /æbə'reɪʃn/ n aberrazione f

abet /ə'bet/ vt (pt/pp **abetted**) **aid and ~** Jur essere complice di

abeyance /ə'beɪəns/ n **in ~** in sospeso; **fall into ~** cadere in disuso

abhor /əb'hɔː(r)/ vt (pt/pp **abhorred**) aborrire. **~rence** /-'hɒrəns/ n orrore m

abid|e /ə'baɪd/ vt (pt/pp **abided**) (tolerate) sopportare ● **abide by** vi rispettare. **~ing** a perpetuo

ability /ə'bɪlətɪ/ n capacità f inv

abject /'æbdʒekt/ a (poverty) degradante; (apology) umile; (coward) abietto

ablaze /ə'bleɪz/ a in fiamme; **be ~ with light** risplendere di luci

able /'eɪbl/ a capace, abile; **be ~ to do sth** poter fare qcsa; **were you ~ to...?** sei riuscito a...? **~-bodied** a robusto; Mil abile

ably /'eɪblɪ/ adv abilmente

abnormal /æb'nɔːml/ a anormale. **~ity** /-'mælɪtɪ/ n anormalità f inv. **~ly** adv in modo anormale

aboard /ə'bɔːd/ adv & prep a bordo

abolish /ə'bɒlɪʃ/ vt abolire. **~ition** /æbə'lɪʃn/ n abolizione f

abominable /ə'bɒmɪnəbl/ a abominevole

Aborigine /æbə'rɪdʒənɪ/ n aborigeno, -a mf d'Australia

abort /ə'bɔːt/ vt fare abortire; fig annullare. **~ion** /-'ɔːʃn/ n aborto m; **have an ~ion** abortire. **~ive** /-tɪv/ a (attempt) infruttuoso

abound /ə'baʊnd/ vi abbondare; **~ in** abbondare di

about /ə'baʊt/ adv (here and there) [di] qua e [di] là; (approximately) circa; **be ~** (illness, tourists:) essere in giro; **be up and ~** essere alzato; **leave sth lying ~** lasciare in giro qcsa ● prep (concerning) su; (in the region of) intorno a; (here and there in) per; **what is the book/the film ~?** di cosa parla il libro/il film?; **he wants to see you - what ~?** ti vuole vedere - a che proposito?; **talk/know ~** parlare/sapere di; **I know nothing ~ it** non ne so niente; **~ 5 o'clock** intorno alle 5; **travel ~ the world**

viaggiare per il mondo; **be ~ to do sth** stare per fare qcsa; **how ~ going to the cinema?** e se andassimo al cinema?

about: ~·'**face** n, ~·'**turn** n dietro front m inv

above /ə'bʌv/ adv & prep sopra; **~ all** soprattutto

above: ~·'**board** a onesto. ~·'**mentioned** a suddetto

abrasive /ə'breɪsɪv/ a abrasivo; (remark) caustico ● n abrasivo m

abreast /ə'brest/ adv fianco a fianco; **come ~ of** allinearsi con; **keep ~ of** tenersi al corrente di

abridged /ə'brɪdʒd/ a ridotto

abroad /ə'brɔːd/ adv all'estero

abrupt /ə'brʌpt/ a brusco

abscess /'æbsɪs/ n ascesso m

abscond /əb'skɒnd/ vi fuggire

absence /'æbsəns/ n assenza f; (lack) mancanza f

absent[1] /'æbsənt/ a assente

absent[2] /æb'sent/ vt ~ **oneself** essere assente

absentee /æbsən'tiː/ n assente mf

absent-minded /æbsənt'maɪndɪd/ a distratto

absolute /'æbsəluːt/ a assoluto; **an ~ idiot** un perfetto idiota. ~**ly** adv assolutamente; (fam: indicating agreement) esattamente

absolution /æbsə'luːʃn/ n assoluzione f

absolve /əb'zɒlv/ vt assolvere

absorb /əb'sɔːb/ vt assorbire; ~**ed in** assorto in. ~**ent** /-ənt/ a assorbente

absorption /əb'sɔːpʃn/ n assorbimento m; (in activity) concentrazione f

abstain /əb'steɪn/ vi astenersi (from da)

abstemious /əb'stiːmɪəs/ a moderato

abstention /əb'stenʃn/ n Pol astensione f

abstinence /'æbstɪnəns/ n astinenza f

abstract /'æbstrækt/ a astratto

● n astratto m; (summary) estratto m

absurd /əb'sɜːd/ a assurdo. ~**ity** n assurdità f inv

abundan|ce /ə'bʌndəns/ n abbondanza f. ~**t** a abbondante

abuse[1] /ə'bjuːz/ vt (misuse) abusare di; (insult) insultare; (ill-treat) maltrattare

abuse[2] /ə'bjuːs/ n abuso m; (verbal) insulti mpl; (ill-treatment) maltrattamento m. ~**ive** /-ɪv/ a offensivo

abut /ə'bʌt/ vi (pt/pp **abutted**) confinare (**onto** con)

abysmal /ə'bɪzml/ a fam pessimo; (ignorance) abissale

abyss /ə'bɪs/ n abisso m

academic /ækə'demɪk/ a teorico; (qualifications, system) scolastico; **be ~** (person:) avere predisposizione allo studio ● n docente mf universitario, -a

academy /ə'kædəmɪ/ n accademia f; (of music) conservatorio m

accede /ək'siːd/ vi ~ **to** accedere a (request); salire (throne)

accelerat|e /ək'seləreɪt/ vt/i accelerare. ~**ion** /-'reɪʃn/ n accelerazione f. ~**or** n Auto acceleratore m

accent /'æksənt/ n accento m

accentuate /ək'sentjʊeɪt/ vt accentuare

accept /ək'sept/ vt accettare. ~**able** /-əbl/ a accettabile. ~**ance** n accettazione f

access /'æksəs/ n accesso m. ~**ible** /ək'sesɪbl/ a accessibile

accession /ək'seʃn/ n (to throne) ascesa f al trono

accessory /ək'sesərɪ/ n accessorio m; Jur complice mf

accident /'æksɪdənt/ n incidente m; (chance) caso m; **by ~** per caso; (unintentionally) senza volere; **I'm sorry, it was an ~** mi dispiace, non l'ho fatto apposta. ~**al** /-'dentl/ a (meeting) casuale; (death) incidentale; (unintentional) involontario. ~**ally** adv

caso; (*unintentionally*) inavvertitamente
acclaim /ə'kleɪm/ n acclamazione
f ● vt acclamare (**as come**)
acclimatize /ə'klaɪmətaɪz/ vt become ~**d** acclimatarsi
accolade /'ækəleɪd/ n riconoscimento m
accommodat|e /ə'kɒmədeɪt/ vt
ospitare; (*oblige*) favorire. ~**ing**
a accomodante. ~**ion** /-'deɪʃn/ n
(*place to stay*) sistemazione f
accompan|iment /ə'kʌmpəni-
mənt/ n accompagnamento m.
~**ist** n Mus accompagnatore,
-trice mf
accompany /ə'kʌmpəni/ vt (*pt/pp*
-**ied**) accompagnare
accomplice /ə'kʌmplɪs/ n complice mf
accomplish /ə'kʌmplɪʃ/ vt
(*achieve*) concludere; realizzare
(*aim*). ~**ed** a dotato; (*fact*) compiuto. ~**ment** n realizzazione f;
(*achievement*) risultato m; (*talent*)
talento m
accord /ə'kɔːd/ n (*treaty*) accordo
m; **with one** ~ tutti d'accordo; **of
his own** ~ di sua spontanea volontà. ~**ance** n **in** ~**ance with** in
conformità di o a
according /ə'kɔːdɪŋ/ adv ~ **to** secondo. ~**ly** adv di conseguenza
accordion /ə'kɔːdɪən/ n fisarmonica f
accost /ə'kɒst/ vt abbordare
account /ə'kaʊnt/ n conto m;
(*report*) descrizione f; (*of eye-
witness*) resoconto m; ~**s** pl Comm
conti mpl; **on** ~ of a causa di. **on
no** ~ per nessun motivo; **on this**
~ per questo motivo; **on my** ~ per
causa mia; **on** ~ di nessuna importanza; **take into** ~ tener conto
di. ● **account for** vt (*explain*) spiegare; (*person*) render conto di;
(*constitute*) costituire. ~**ability** n
responsabilità f inv. ~**able** a responsabile (**for** di)
accountant /ə'kaʊntənt/ n (*book-*

keeper) contabile mf; (*consultant*)
commercialista mf
accredited /ə'kredɪtɪd/ a accredi-
tato
accrue /ə'kruː/ vi (*interest:*) maturare
accumulat|e /ə'kjuːmjʊleɪt/ vt ac-
cumulare ● vi accumularsi. ~**ion**
/-'leɪʃn/ n accumulazione f
accura|cy /'ækʊrəsɪ/ n precisione
f. ~**te** /-rət/ a preciso. ~**tely** adv
con precisione
accusation /ækjʊ'zeɪʃn/ n accusa f
accusative /ə'kjuːzətɪv/ a & n ~
[**case**] Gram accusativo m
accuse /ə'kjuːz/ vt accusare; ~ **sb
of doing sth** accusare qcno di fare
qcsa. ~**d** n **the** ~**d** l'accusato m,
l'accusata f
accustom /ə'kʌstəm/ vt abituare
(**to** a); **grow** or **get** ~**ed to** abituarsi a. ~**ed** a abituato
ace /eɪs/ n Cards asso m; (*tennis*)
ace m inv
ache /eɪk/ n dolore m ● vi dolere,
far male; ~ **all over** essere tutto
indolenzito
achieve /ə'tʃiːv/ vt ottenere (*success*); realizzare (*goal, ambition*).
~**ment** n (*feat*) successo m
acid /'æsɪd/ a & n acido m ● n acido m.
~**ity** /ə'sɪdətɪ/ n acidità f. ~ **'rain** n
pioggia f acida
acknowledge /ək'nɒlɪdʒ/ vt riconoscere; rispondere a (*greeting*);
far cenno di aver notato (*sb's
presence*); ~ **receipt of** accusare
ricevuta di. ~**ment** n riconoscimento m; **send an** ~**ment of a
letter** confermare il ricevimento
di una lettera
acne /'æknɪ/ n acne f
acorn /'eɪkɔːn/ n ghianda f
acoustic /ə'kuːstɪk/ a acustico. ~**s**
npl acustica fsg
acquaint /ə'kweɪnt/ vt ~ **sb with**
metter qcno al corrente di; **be**
~**ed with** conoscere (*person*); essere a conoscenza di (*fact*). ~**ance**
n (*person*) conoscente mf; **make**

acquiesce /ˌækwɪˈes/ *vi* acconsentire (**to, in** a). **~nce** *n* acquiescenza *f*

acquire /əˈkwaɪə(r)/ *vt* acquisire

acquisit|ion /ˌækwɪˈzɪʃn/ *n* acquisizione *f*. **~ive** /əˈkwɪzətɪv/ *a* avido

acquit /əˈkwɪt/ *vt* (*pt/pp* **acquitted**) assolvere; **~ oneself well** cavarsela bene. **~tal** *n* assoluzione *f*

acre /ˈeɪkə(r)/ *n* acro *m* (= 4 047 *m²*)

acrid /ˈækrɪd/ *a* acre

acrimon|ious /ˌækrɪˈməʊnɪəs/ *a* aspro. **~y** /ˈækrɪmənɪ/ *n* asprezza *f*

acrobat /ˈækrəbæt/ *n* acrobata *mf*. **~ic** /-ˈbætɪk/ *a* acrobatico

across /əˈkrɒs/ *adv* dall'altra parte; (*wide*) in larghezza; (*not lengthwise*) attraverso; (*in crossword*) orizzontale; **come ~ sth** imbattersi in qcsa; **go ~** attraversare su; (*on the other side of*) dall'altra parte di

act /ækt/ *n* atto *m*; (*in variety show*) numero *m*; **put on an ~** *fam* fare scena ● *vi* agire; (*behave*) comportarsi; *Theat* recitare; (*pretend*) fingere; **~ as** fare da ● *vt* recitare (*role*). **~ing** *a* (*deputy*) provvisorio ● *n* *Theat* recitazione *f*; (*profession*) teatro *m*. **~ing profession** *n* professione *f* dell'attore

action /ˈækʃn/ *n* azione *f*; *Mil* combattimento *m*; *Jur* azione *f* legale; **out of ~** (*machine:*) fuori uso; **take ~** agire. **~ 'replay** *n* replay *m* *inv*

activ|e /ˈæktɪv/ *a* attivo. **~ely** *adv* attivamente. **~ity** /-ˈtɪvətɪ/ *n* attività *f* *inv*

act|or /ˈæktə(r)/ *n* attore *m*. **~ress** *n* attrice *f*

actual /ˈæktʃʊəl/ *a* (*real*) reale. **~ly** *adv* in realtà

acumen /ˈækjʊmən/ *n* acume *m*

acupuncture /ˈækjʊ-/ *n* agopuntura *f*

acute /əˈkjuːt/ *a* acuto; (*shortage, hardship*) estremo

AD *abbr* (**Anno Domini**) d.C.

ad /æd/ *n* *fam* pubblicità *f* *inv*

adamant /ˈædəmənt/ *a* categorico (**that** sul fatto che)

adapt /əˈdæpt/ *vt* adattare (*play*) ● *vi* adattarsi. **~ability** /-əˈbɪlətɪ/ *n* adattabilità *f*. **~able** /-əbl/ *a* adattabile

adaptation /ˌædæpˈteɪʃn/ *n Theat* adattamento *m*

adapter, adaptor /əˈdæptə(r)/ *n* adattatore *m*; (*two-way*) presa *f* multipla

add /æd/ *vt* aggiungere; *Math* addizionare ● *vi* addizionare; **~ to** (*fig: increase*) aggravare. **add up** *vt* addizionare (*figures*) ● *vi* addizionare; **~ up to** ammontare a; **it doesn't ~ up** *fig* non quadra

adder /ˈædə(r)/ *n* vipera *f*

addict /ˈædɪkt/ *n* tossicodipendente *mf*; *fig* fanatico, -a *mf*

addict|ed /əˈdɪktɪd/ *a* assuefatto (**to** a); **~ed to drugs** tossicodipendente; **he's ~ed to television** è videodipendente. **~ion** /-ɪkʃn/ *n* dipendenza *f*; (*to drugs*) tossicodipendenza *f*. **~ive** /-ɪv/ *a* **be ~ive** dare assuefazione

addition /əˈdɪʃn/ *n Math* addizione *f*; (*thing added*) aggiunta *f*; **in ~** in aggiunta. **~al** *a* supplementare. **~ally** *adv* in più

additive /ˈædɪtɪv/ *n* additivo *m*

address /əˈdres/ *n* indirizzo *m*; (*speech*) discorso *m*; **form of ~** formula *f* di cortesia ● *vt* indirizzare; (*speak to*) rivolgersi a (*person*); tenere un discorso a (*meeting*). **~ee** /ædreˈsiː/ *n* destinatario, -a *mf*

adenoids /ˈædənɔɪdz/ *npl* adenoidi *fpl*

adept /ˈædept/ *a & n* esperto, -a *mf* (**at** in)

adequate /ˈædɪkwət/ *a* adeguato. **~ly** *adv* adeguatamente

adhere /ədˈhɪə(r)/ *vi* aderire; **~ to** attenersi a (*principles, rules*)

adhesive /əd'hiːsɪv/ *a* adesivo ● *n* adesivo *m*

adjacent /ə'dʒeɪsənt/ *a* adiacente

adjective /'ædʒɪktɪv/ *n* aggettivo *m*

adjoin /ə'dʒɔɪn/ *vt* essere adiacente a. **~ing** *a* adiacente

adjourn /ə'dʒɜːn/ *vt/i* aggiornare ⟨until a⟩. **~ment** *n* aggiornamento *m*

adjudicate /ə'dʒuːdɪkeɪt/ *vi* decidere; ⟨in competition⟩ giudicare

adjust /ə'dʒʌst/ *vt* modificare; regolare ⟨focus, sound etc⟩ ● *vi* adattarsi. **~able** /-əbl/ *a* regolabile. **~ment** *n* adattamento *m*; Techn regolamento *m*

ad lib /æd'lɪb/ *a* improvvisato ● *adv* a piacere ● *vi* ⟨pt/pp libbed⟩ *fam* improvvisare

administer /əd'mɪnɪstə(r)/ *vt* amministrare; somministrare ⟨medicine⟩

administrat|ion /ədmɪnɪ'streɪʃn/ *n* amministrazione *f*; Pol governo *m*. **~or** /əd'mɪnɪstreɪtə(r)/ *n* amministratore, -trice *mf*

admirable /'ædmərəbl/ *a* ammirevole

admiral /'ædmərəl/ *n* ammiraglio *m*

admiration /ædmə'reɪʃn/ *n* ammirazione *f*

admire /əd'maɪə(r)/ *vt* ammirare. **~r** *n* ammiratore, -trice *mf*

admissible /əd'mɪsəbl/ *a* ammissibile

admission /əd'mɪʃn/ *n* ammissione *f*; ⟨to hospital⟩ ricovero *m*; ⟨entry⟩ ingresso *m*

admit /əd'mɪt/ *vt* ⟨pt/pp admitted⟩ ⟨let in⟩ far entrare; ⟨to hospital⟩ ricoverare; ⟨acknowledge⟩ ammettere ● *vi* **~ to sth** ammettere qcsa. **~tance** *n* ammissione *f*; 'no **~tance**' 'vietato l'ingresso'. **~tedly** *adv* bisogna riconoscerlo

admonish /əd'mɒnɪʃ/ *vt* ammonire

ado /ə'duː/ *n* **without more ~** senza ulteriori indugi

adolescen|ce /ædə'lesns/ *n* adolescenza *f*. **~t** *a* & *n* adolescente *mf*

adopt /ə'dɒpt/ *vt* adottare; Pol scegliere ⟨candidate⟩. **~ion** /-ɒpʃn/ *n* adozione *f*. **~ive** /-ɪv/ *a* adottivo *m*

ador|able /ə'dɔːrəbl/ *a* adorabile. **~ation** /ædə'reɪʃn/ *n* adorazione *f*

adore /ə'dɔː(r)/ *vt* adorare

adrenalin /ə'drenəlɪn/ *n* adrenalina *f*

Adriatic /eɪdrɪ'ætɪk/ *a* & *n* **the ~** [Sea] il mare Adriatico, l'Adriatico *m*

adrift /ə'drɪft/ *a* alla deriva; **be ~** andare alla deriva; **come ~** staccarsi

adroit /ə'drɔɪt/ *a* abile

adulation /ædjʊ'leɪʃn/ *n* adulazione *f*

adult /'ædʌlt/ *n* adulto, -a *mf*

adulterate /ə'dʌltəreɪt/ *vt* adulterare ⟨wine⟩

adultery /ə'dʌltərɪ/ *n* adulterio *m*

advance /əd'vɑːns/ *n* avanzamento *m*; Mil avanzata *f*; ⟨payment⟩ anticipo *m*; **in ~** in anticipo ● *vi* avanzare; ⟨make progress⟩ fare progressi ● *vt* avanzare ⟨theory⟩; promuovere ⟨cause⟩; anticipare ⟨money⟩. **~ booking** *n* prenotazione *f* [in anticipo]. **~d** *a* avanzato *f*. **~ment** *n* promozione *f*

advantage /əd'vɑːntɪdʒ/ *n* vantaggio *m*; **take ~ of** approfittare di. **~ous** /ædvən'teɪdʒəs/ *a* vantaggioso

advent /'ædvent/ *n* avvento *m*

adventur|e /əd'ventʃə(r)/ *n* avventura *f*. **~ous** /-rəs/ *a* avventuroso

adverb /'ædvɜːb/ *n* avverbio *m*

adversary /'ædvəsərɪ/ *n* avversario, -a *m*

advers|e /'ædvɜːs/ *a* avverso. **~ity** /əd'vɜːsətɪ/ *n* avversità *f*

advert /'ædvɜːt/ *n* *fam* = **advertisement**

advertise /'ædvətaɪz/ *vt* reclamizzare; mettere un annuncio per ⟨job, flat⟩ ● *vi* fare pubblicità; ⟨for job, flat⟩ mettere un annuncio

advertisement /əd'vɜ:tɪsmənt/ n pubblicità f inv; (in paper) inserzione f, annuncio m

advertis|er /'ædvətaɪzə(r)/ n (in newspaper) inserzionista mf. **~ing** n pubblicità f ● attrib pubblicitario

advice /əd'vaɪs/ n consigli mpl; **piece of ~** consiglio m

advisable /əd'vaɪzəbl/ a consigliabile

advise /əd'vaɪz/ vt consigliare; (inform) avvisare; **~ sb to do sth** consigliare a qcno di fare qcsa; **~ sb against sth** sconsigliare qcsa a qcno. **~er** n consulente mf. **~ory** a consultivo

advocate[1] /'ædvəkət/ n (supporter) sostenitore, -trice mf

advocate[2] /'ædvəkeɪt/ vt propugnare

aerial /'eərɪəl/ a aereo ● n antenna f

aerobics /eə'rəʊbɪks/ n aerobica fsg

aero|drome /'eərədrəʊm/ n aerodromo m. **~plane** n aeroplano m

aerosol /'eərəsɒl/ n bomboletta f spray

aesthetic /i:s'θetɪk/ a estetico

afar /ə'fɑ:(r)/ adv **from ~** da lontano

affable /'æfəbl/ a affabile

affair /ə'feə(r)/ n affare m; (scandal) caso m; (sexual) relazione f

affect /ə'fekt/ vt influire su; (emotionally) colpire; (concern) riguardare. **~ation** /æfek'teɪʃn/ n affettazione f. **~ed** a affettato

affection /ə'fekʃn/ n affetto m. **~ate** /-ət/ a affettuoso

affiliated /ə'fɪlɪeɪtɪd/ a affiliato

affinity /ə'fɪnətɪ/ n affinità f inv

affirm /ə'fɜ:m/ vt affermare; Jur dichiarare solennemente

affirmative /ə'fɜ:mətɪv/ a affermativo ● n **in the ~** affermativamente

afflict /ə'flɪkt/ vt affliggere. **~ion** /-ɪkʃn/ n afflizione f

affluen|ce /'æfluəns/ n agiatezza f. **~t** a agiato

afford /ə'fɔ:d/ vt **be able to ~ sth** potersi permettere qcsa. **~able** /-əbl/ a abbordabile

affray /ə'freɪ/ n rissa f

affront /ə'frʌnt/ n affronto m

afield /ə'fi:ld/ adv **further ~** più lontano

afloat /ə'fləʊt/ a a galla

afoot /ə'fʊt/ a **there's something ~** si sta preparando qualcosa

aforesaid /ə'fɔ:sed/ a Jur suddetto

afraid /ə'freɪd/ a **~** aver paura; **I'm ~ not** purtroppo no; **I'm ~ so** temo di sì; **I'm ~ I can't help you** mi dispiace, ma non posso esserle d'aiuto

afresh /ə'freʃ/ adv da capo

Africa /'æfrɪkə/ n Africa f. **~n** a & n africano, -a mf

after /'ɑ:ftə(r)/ adv dopo; **the day ~** il giorno dopo; **be ~** cercare ● prep dopo; **~ all** dopotutto; **the day ~ tomorrow** dopodomani ● conj dopo che

after: **~-effect** n conseguenza f. **~math** /-mɑ:θ/ n conseguenze fpl; **the ~math of war** il dopoguerra; **in the ~math of** nel periodo successivo a. **~'noon** n pomeriggio m; **good ~noon!** buon giorno! **~-sales service** n servizio m assistenza clienti. **~shave** n [lozione f] dopobarba m inv. **~thought** n added as an **~thought** aggiunto in un secondo momento. **~wards** adv in seguito

again /ə'gem/ adv di nuovo; [then] **~** (besides) inoltre; (on the other hand) d'altra parte; **~ and ~** continuamente

against /ə'gemst/ prep contro

age /eɪdʒ/ n età f inv; (era) era f; **~s** fam secoli; **what ~ are you?** quanti anni hai?; **be under ~** non avere l'età richiesta; **he's two years of ~** ha due anni ● vt/i (pres p ageing) invecchiare

aged[1] /eɪdʒd/ a **~ two** di due

aged² /'eɪdʒɪd/ a anziano ● the ~ pl gli anziani

ageless /'eɪdʒlɪs/ a senza età

agency /'eɪdʒənsɪ/ n agenzia f; **have the ~ for** essere un concessionario di

agenda /ə'dʒendə/ n ordine m del giorno; **on the ~** all'ordine del giorno; fig in programma

agent /'eɪdʒənt/ n agente mf

aggravat|e /'ægrəveɪt/ vt aggravare; (annoy) esasperare. **~ion** /-'veɪʃn/ n aggravamento m; (annoyance) esasperazione f

aggregate /'ægrɪgət/ a totale ● n totale m; **on ~** nel complesso

aggress|ion /ə'greʃn/ n aggressione f. **~ive** /-sɪv/ a aggressivo. **~iveness** n aggressività f. **~or** n aggressore m

aggro /'ægrəʊ/ n fam aggressività f; (problems) grane fpl

aghast /ə'gɑːst/ a inorridito

agil|e /'ædʒaɪl/ a agile. **~ity** /ə'dʒɪlətɪ/ n agilità f

agitat|e /'ædʒɪteɪt/ vt mettere in agitazione; (shake) agitare ● vi fig **~e for** creare delle agitazioni per. **~ed** a agitato. **~ion** /-'teɪʃn/ n agitazione f. **~or** n agitatore, -trice mf

agnostic /æg'nɒstɪk/ n agnostico, -a mf

ago /ə'gəʊ/ adv fa; **a long time ~** molto tempo fa; **a month ~** un mese fa

agog /ə'gɒg/ a eccitato

agoniz|e /'ægənaɪz/ vi angosciarsi (over per). **~ing** a angosciante

agony /'ægənɪ/ n agonia f; (mental) angoscia f; **be in ~** avere dei dolori atroci

agree /ə'griː/ vt accordarsi su; **~ to do sth** accettare di fare qcsa; **~ that** essere d'accordo [sul fatto] che ● vi essere d'accordo; (figures:) concordare; (reach agreement) mettersi d'accordo; (get on) andare d'accordo; (consent) acconsentire (to a); **it doesn't ~ with me** mi fa male; **~ with sth** (approve of) approvare qcsa

agreeable /ə'griːəbl/ a gradevole; (willing) d'accordo

agreed /ə'griːd/ a convenuto

agreement /ə'griːmənt/ n accordo m; **in ~** d'accordo

agricultur|al /ægrɪ'kʌltʃərəl/ a agricolo. **~e** /'ægrɪkʌltʃə(r)/ n agricoltura f

aground /ə'graʊnd/ adv **run ~** (ship:) arenarsi

ahead /ə'hed/ adv avanti; **be ~ of** essere davanti a; fig essere avanti rispetto a; **draw ~** passare davanti (of a); **get ~** (in life) riuscire; **go ~!** fai pure!; **look ~** pensare all'avvenire; **plan ~** fare progetti per l'avvenire

aid /eɪd/ n aiuto m; **in ~ of** a favore di ● vt aiutare

aide /eɪd/ n assistente mf

Aids /eɪdz/ n AIDS m

ail|ing /'eɪlɪŋ/ a malato. **~ment** n disturbo m

aim /eɪm/ n mira f; fig scopo m; **take ~** prendere la mira ● vt puntare (gun) (at contro) ● vi mirare; **~ to do sth** aspirare a fare qcsa. **~less**, **~lessly** adv senza scopo

air /eə(r)/ n aria f; **be on the ~** (programme:) essere in onda; **put on ~s** darsi delle arie; **by ~** in aereo; (airmail) per via aerea ● vt arieggiare; far conoscere (views)

air: **~-bed** n materassino m [gonfiabile]. **~-conditioned** a con aria condizionata. **~-conditioning** n aria f condizionata. **~craft** n aereo m. **~craft carrier** n portaerei f inv. **~fare** n tariffa f aerea. **~field** n campo m d'aviazione. **~ force** n aviazione f. **~ freshener** n deodorante m per l'ambiente. **~gun** n fucile m pneumatico. **~ hostess** n hostess f inv. **~ letter** n aerogramma m. **~line** n compagnia f aerea. **~lock** n bolla f d'aria. **~mail** n posta f aerea. **~plane** n Am aereo m. **~ pocket** n vuoto m d'aria. **~port** n aeroporto m. **~-raid** n incursione f aerea. **~-raid shelter** n rifugio m an-

tiaereo. **~ship** *n* dirigibile *m*.
~tight *a* ermetico. **~ traffic** *n*
traffico *m* aereo. **~traffic con-
troller** *n* controllore *m* di volo.
~worthy *a* idoneo al volo

airy /'eərɪ/ *a* (**-ier, -iest**) arieggiato;
⟨*manner*⟩ noncurante

aisle /aɪl/ *n* corridoio *m*. (*in
supermarket*) corsia *f*; (*in church*)
navata *f*

ajar /ə'dʒɑ:(r)/ *a* socchiuso

akin /ə'kɪn/ *a* **~ to** simile a

alacrity /ə'lækrətɪ/ *n* alacrità *f inv*

alarm /ə'lɑ:m/ *n* allarme *m*; **set
the ~** (*of alarm clock*) mettere la
sveglia ● *vt* allarmare. **~ clock** *n*
sveglia *f*

alas /ə'læs/ *int* ahimè

album /'ælbəm/ *n* album *m inv*

alcohol /'ælkəhɒl/ *n* alcol *m*. **~ic**
/-'hɒlɪk/ *a* alcolico ● *n* alcolizzato,
-a *mf*. **~ism** *n* alcolismo *m*

alcove /'ælkəʊv/ *n* alcova *f*

alert /ə'lɜ:t/ *a* sveglio; (*watchful*)
vigile ● *n* segnale *m* d'allarme;
be on the ~ stare allerta ● *vt*
allertare

algae /'ældʒi:/ *npl* alghe *fpl*

algebra /'ældʒɪbrə/ *n* algebra *f*

Algeria /æl'dʒɪərɪə/ *n* Algeria *f*.
~n *a* & *n* algerino, -a *mf*

alias /'eɪlɪəs/ *n* pseudonimo *m*
● *adv* alias *p*

alibi /'ælɪbaɪ/ *n* alibi *m inv*

alien /'eɪlɪən/ *a* straniero; *fig* estraneo ● *n* straniero, -a *mf*; (*from
space*) alieno, -a *mf*

alienat|e /'eɪlɪəneɪt/ *vt* alienare.
~ion /-'neɪʃn/ *n* alienazione *f*

alight¹ /ə'laɪt/ *vi* scendere; ⟨*bird*:⟩
posarsi

alight² *a* **be ~** essere in fiamme;
set ~ dar fuoco a

align /ə'laɪn/ *vt* allineare. **~ment** *n*
allineamento *m*; **out of ~ment**
non allineato

alike /ə'laɪk/ *a* simile; **be ~** rassomigliarsi ● *adv* in modo simile;
look ~ rassomigliarsi; **summer
and winter ~** sia d'estate che d'inverno

alimony /'ælɪmənɪ/ *n* alimenti *mpl*

alive /ə'laɪv/ *a* vivo; **~ with** bruli-
cante di; **~ to** sensibile a; **~ and
kicking** vivo e vegeto

alkali /'ælkəlaɪ/ *n* alcali *m*

all /ɔ:l/ *a* tutto; **~ the children, ~
children** tutti i bambini; **~ day**
tutto il giorno; **he refused ~ help**
ha rifiutato qualsiasi aiuto; **for ~
that** (*nevertheless*) ciononostante;
in ~ sincerity in tutta sincerità;
be ~ for essere favorevole a
● *pron* tutto; **~ of you/them** tutti
voi/loro; **~ of it** tutto; **~ of the
town** tutta la città; **in ~** in tutto;
in ~ tutto sommato; **most of ~**
più di ogni altra cosa; **once and
for ~** una volta per tutte ● *adv*
completamente; **~ but** quasi; **~ at
once** (*at the same time*) tutto in
una volta; **~ at once, ~ of a
sudden** all'improvviso; **~ too
soon** troppo presto; **~ the same**
(*nevertheless*) ciononostante; **~
the better** meglio ancora; **she's
not ~ that good an actress** non è
poi così brava come attrice; **~ in**
in tutto; *fam* esausto; **thirty/three
~** (*in sport*) trenta/tre pari; **~
over** (*finished*) tutto finito; (*everywhere*) dappertutto; **it's ~ right** (*I
don't mind*) non ha niente; **I'm ~
right** (*not hurt*) non ho niente; **~
right!** va bene!

allay /ə'leɪ/ *vt* placare ⟨*suspicions,
anger*⟩

allegation /ælɪ'geɪʃn/ *n* accusa *f*

allege /ə'ledʒ/ *vt* dichiarare. **~d**
a presunto. **~dly** /-ɪdlɪ/ *adv* a quanto si dice

allegiance /ə'li:dʒəns/ *n* fedeltà *f*

allegor|ical /ælɪ'gɒrɪkl/ *a* allegori-
co. **~y** /'ælɪgərɪ/ *n* allegoria *f*

allergic /ə'lɜ:dʒɪk/ *a* allergico. **~y**
/'ælədʒɪ/ *n* allergia *f*

alleviate /ə'li:vɪeɪt/ *vt* alleviare

alley /'ælɪ/ *n* vicolo *m*; (*for
bowling*) corsia *f*

alliance /ə'laɪəns/ *n* alleanza *f*

allied /'ælaɪd/ *a* alleato; (*fig:
related*) connesso (**to** a)

alligator /'ælɪgeɪtə(r)/ n alligatore m

allocat|e /'æləkeɪt/ vt assegnare; distribuire ⟨resources⟩. **~ion** /-'keɪʃn/ n assegnazione f; ⟨of resources⟩ distribuzione f

allot /ə'lɒt/ vt ⟨pt/pp **allotted**⟩ distribuire. **~ment** n distribuzione f; ⟨share⟩ parto f; ⟨land⟩ piccolo lotto m di terreno

allow /ə'laʊ/ vt permettere; ⟨grant⟩ accordare; ⟨reckon on⟩ contare; ⟨agree⟩ ammettere; **~ for** tener conto di; **~ sb to do sth** permettere a qcno di fare qcsa; **you are not ~ed to...** è vietato...

allowance /ə'laʊəns/ n sussidio m; ⟨Am: pocket money⟩ paghetta f; ⟨for petrol etc⟩ indennità f inv; ⟨of luggage, duty free⟩ limite m; **make ~s for** essere indulgente verso ⟨sb⟩; tener conto di ⟨sth⟩

alloy /'ælɔɪ/ n lega f

allude /ə'luːd/ vi alludere

allusion /ə'luːʒn/ n allusione f

ally¹ /'ælaɪ/ n alleato, -a mf

ally² /ə'laɪ/ vt ⟨pt/pp **-ied**⟩ alleare; **~ oneself** with allearsi con

almighty /ɔːl'maɪtɪ/ a ⟨fam: big⟩ mega inv ● **the A~** l'Onnipotente m

almond /'ɑːmənd/ n mandorla f; ⟨tree⟩ mandorlo m

almost /'ɔːlməʊst/ adv quasi

alone /ə'ləʊn/ a solo; **leave me ~!** lasciami in pace!; **let ~** ⟨not to mention⟩ figurarsi ● adv da solo

along /ə'lɒŋ/ prep lungo ● adv **~ with** assieme a; **all ~** tutto il tempo; **come ~!** ⟨hurry up⟩ vieni qui!; **I'll be ~ in a minute** arrivo tra un attimo; **move ~** spostarsi; **move ~!** circolare!

along'side adv lungo bordo ● prep lungo; **work ~ sb** lavorare fianco a fianco con qcno

aloof /ə'luːf/ a distante

aloud /ə'laʊd/ adv ad alta voce

alphabet /'ælfəbet/ n alfabeto m. **~ical** /-'betɪkl/ a alfabetico

alpine /'ælpaɪn/ a alpino

Alps /ælps/ npl Alpi fpl

already /ɔːl'redɪ/ adv già

Alsatian /æl'seɪʃn/ n ⟨dog⟩ pastore m tedesco

also /'ɔːlsəʊ/ adv anche; **~, I need...** e inoltre, ho bisogno di...

altar /'ɔːltə(r)/ n altare m

alter /'ɔːltə(r)/ vt cambiare; aggiustare ⟨clothes⟩ ● vi cambiare. **~ation** /-'reɪʃn/ n modifica f

alternate¹ /'ɔːltəneɪt/ vi alternarsi ● vt alternare

alternate² /ɔːl'tɜːnət/ a alterno; **on ~ days** a giorni alterni

'alternating current n corrente f alternata

alternative /ɔːl'tɜːnətɪv/ a alternativo ● n alternativa f. **~ly** adv alternativamente

although /ɔːl'ðəʊ/ conj benché, sebbene

altitude /'æltɪtjuːd/ n altitudine f

altogether /ɔːltə'geðə(r)/ adv ⟨in all⟩ in tutto; ⟨completely⟩ completamente; **I'm not ~ sure** non sono del tutto sicuro

altruistic /æltrʊ'ɪstɪk/ a altruistico

aluminium /æljʊ'mɪnɪəm/ n, Am **aluminum** /ə'luːmɪnəm/ n alluminio m

always /'ɔːlweɪz/ adv sempre

am /æm/ see be

a.m. abbr ⟨ante meridiem⟩ del mattino

amalgamate /ə'mælgəmeɪt/ vt fondere ● vi fondersi

amass /ə'mæs/ vt accumulare

amateur /'æmətə(r)/ n non professionista mf; pej dilettante mf ● attrib dilettante; **~dramatics** filodrammatica f. **~ish** a dilettantesco

amaze /ə'meɪz/ vt stupire. **~d** a stupito. **~ment** n stupore m

amazing /ə'meɪzɪŋ/ a incredibile

ambassador /æm'bæsədə(r)/ n ambasciatore, -trice mf

amber /'æmbə(r)/ n ambra f ● a ⟨colour⟩ ambra inv

ambidextrous /ˌæmbɪˈdekstrəs/ a ambidestro

ambience /ˈæmbɪəns/ n atmosfera f

ambigu|ity /ˌæmbɪˈgjuːətɪ/ n ambiguità f inv. **~ous** /-ˈbɪgjʊəs/ a ambiguo

ambiti|on /æmˈbɪʃn/ n ambizione f; (aim) aspirazione f. **~ous** /-ʃəs/ a ambizioso

ambivalent /æmˈbɪvələnt/ a ambivalente

amble /ˈæmbl/ vi camminare senza fretta

ambulance /ˈæmbjʊləns/ n ambulanza f

ambush /ˈæmbʊʃ/ n imboscata f ● vt tendere un'imboscata a

amenable /əˈmiːnəbl/ a conciliante; **~ to** sensibile a

amend /əˈmend/ vt modificare. **~ment** n modifica f. **~s** npl **make ~s** fare ammenda (**for** di, per)

amenities /əˈmiːnətɪz/ npl comodità fpl

America /əˈmerɪkə/ n America f. **~n** a & n americano, -a m

amiable /ˈeɪmɪəbl/ a amabile

amicable /ˈæmɪkəbl/ a amichevole

amiss /əˈmɪs/ a there's something **~** c'è qualcosa che non va ● adv **take sth ~** prendersela [a male]; **it won't come ~** non sarebbe sgradito

ammonia /əˈməʊnɪə/ n ammoniaca f

ammunition /ˌæmjʊˈnɪʃn/ n munizioni fpl

amnesia /æmˈniːzɪə/ n amnesia f

amnesty /ˈæmnəstɪ/ n amnistia f

among[st] /əˈmʌŋ[st]/ prep tra, fra

amoral /eɪˈmɒrəl/ a amorale

amorous /ˈæmərəs/ a amoroso

amount /əˈmaʊnt/ n quantità f inv; (sum of money) importo m ● vi **to** ammontare a; fig equivalere a

amp /æmp/ n ampère m inv

amphibi|an /æmˈfɪbɪən/ n anfibio m. **~ous** /-ɪəs/ a anfibio

amphitheatre /ˈæmfɪ-/ n anfiteatro m

ampl|e /ˈæmpl/ a (large) grande; (proportions) ampio; (enough) largamente sufficiente

amplif|ier /ˈæmplɪfaɪə(r)/ n amplificatore m. **~y** /-faɪ/ vt (pt/pp -**ied**) amplificare (sound)

amputat|e /ˈæmpjʊteɪt/ vt amputare. **~ion** /-ˈteɪʃn/ n amputazione f

amuse /əˈmjuːz/ vt divertire. **~ment** n divertimento m. **~ment arcade** n sala f giochi

amusing /əˈmjuːzɪŋ/ a divertente

an /ən/, accentato /æn/ see **a**

anaem|ia /əˈniːmɪə/ n anemia f. **~ic** a anemico

anaesthetic /ˈænəsˈθetɪk/ n anestesia f

anaesthet|ist /əˈniːsθətɪst/ n anestesista mf

analog[ue] /ˈænəlɒg/ a analogico

analogy /əˈnælədʒɪ/ n analogia f

analyse /ˈænəlaɪz/ vt analizzare

analysis /əˈnæləsɪs/ n analisi f inv

analyst /ˈænəlɪst/ n analista mf

analytical /ænəˈlɪtɪk/ a analitico

anarch|ist /ˈænəkɪst/ n anarchico, -a mf. **~y** n anarchia f

anatom|ical /ænəˈtɒmɪkl/ a anatomico. **~ically** adv anatomicamente. **~y** /əˈnætəmɪ/ n anatomia f

ancestor /ˈænsestə(r)/ n antenato, -a mf. **~ry** n antenati mpl

anchor /ˈæŋkə(r)/ n ancora f ● vi gettar l'ancora ● vt ancorare

anchovy /ˈæntʃəvɪ/ n acciuga f

ancient /ˈeɪnʃnt/ a antico; fam vecchio

ancillary /ænˈsɪlərɪ/ a ausiliario

and /ənd/, accentato /ænd/ conj e; **two ~ two** due più due; **six hundred ~ two** seicentodue; **more ~ more** sempre più; **warm ~ warm** bello caldo; **try ~ come** cerca di venire; **go ~ get** vai a prendere

anecdote /ˈænɪkdəʊt/ n aneddoto m

anew /ə'nju:/ adv di nuovo

angel /'eɪndʒl/ n angelo m. **~ic** /æn'dʒelɪk/ a angelico

anger /'æŋgə(r)/ n rabbia f ● vt far arrabbiare

angle¹ /'æŋgl/ n angolo m; fig angolazione f; **at an ~** storto

angle² vi pescare con la lenza; **~ for** fig cercare di ottenere. **~r** n pescatore, -trice mf

Anglican /'æŋglɪkən/ a & n anglicano, -a mf

Anglo-Saxon /æŋgləʊ'sæksn/ a & n anglo-sassone m

angr|y /'æŋgrɪ/ a (**-ier, -iest**) arrabbiato; **get ~y** arrabbiarsi; **~y with** or **at sb** arrabbiato con qcno; **~y at** or **about sth** arrabbiato per qcsa. **~ily** adv rabbiosamente

anguish /'æŋgwɪʃ/ n angoscia f

angular /'æŋgjʊlə(r)/ a angolare

animal /'ænɪml/ a & n animale m

animate¹ /'ænɪmət/ a animato

animat|e² /'ænɪmeɪt/ vt animare. **~ed** a animato; (person) vivace. **~ion** /-'meɪʃn/ n animazione f

animosity /ænɪ'mosətɪ/ n animosità f inv

ankle /'æŋkl/ n caviglia f

annex /ə'neks/ vt annettere

annex[e] /'æneks/ n annesso m

annihilat|e /ə'naɪəleɪt/ vt annientare. **~ion** /-'leɪʃn/ n annientamento m

anniversary /ænɪ'vɜːsərɪ/ n anniversario m

announce /ə'naʊns/ vt annunciare. **~ment** n annuncio m. **~r** n annunciatore, -trice mf

annoy /ə'nɔɪ/ vt dare fastidio a; **get ~ed** essere infastidito. **~ance** n seccatura f; (anger) irritazione f. **~ing** a fastidioso

annual /'ænjʊəl/ a annuale; (income) annuo ● n Bot pianta f annua; (children's book) almanacco m

annuity /ə'nju:ətɪ/ n annualità f inv

annul /ə'nʌl/ vt (pt/pp **annulled**) annullare

anomaly /ə'nɒməlɪ/ n anomalia f

anonymous /ə'nɒnɪməs/ a anonimo

anorak /'ænəræk/ n giacca f a vento

anorex|ia /ænə'reksɪə/ n anoressia f. **~ic** a anoressico

another /ə'nʌðə(r)/ a & pron; **[one]** un altro, un'altra; **in ~ way** diversamente; **one ~** l'un l'altro

answer /'ɑːnsə(r)/ n risposta f; (solution) soluzione f ● vt rispondere a (person, question, letter); esaudire (prayer); **~ the door** aprire la porta; **~ the telephone** rispondere al telefono ● vi rispondere; **~ back** ribattere; **~ for** rispondere di. **~able** /-əbl/ a responsabile; **be ~able to sb** rispondere a qcno. **~ing machine** n Teleph segreteria f telefonica

ant /ænt/ n formica f

antagonis|m /æn'tægənɪzm/ n antagonismo m. **~tic** /-'nɪstɪk/ a antagonistico

antagonize /æn'tægənaɪz/ vt provocare l'ostilità di

Antarctic /æn'tɑːktɪk/ n Antartico m ● a antartico

antenatal /æntɪ'neɪtl/ a prenatale

antenna /æn'tenə/ n antenna f

anthem /'ænθəm/ n inno m

anthology /æn'θɒlədʒɪ/ n antologia f

anthropology /ænθrə'pɒlədʒɪ/ n antropologia f

anti-aircraft /æntɪ-/ a antiaereo

antibiotic /æntɪbaɪ'ɒtɪk/ n antibiotico m

'antibody n anticorpo m

anticipat|e /æn'tɪsɪpeɪt/ vt prevedere; (forestall) anticipare. **~ion** /-'peɪʃn/ n anticipo m; (excitement) attesa f

anti'climax n delusione f

anti'clockwise a & adv in senso antiorario

antics /'æntɪks/ npl gesti mpl buffi

anti'cyclone n anticiclone m

antidote /'æntɪdəʊt/ n antidoto m

'antifreeze n antigelo m

antipathy /æn'tɪpəθɪ/ n antipatia f

antiquated /'æntɪkweɪtɪd/ a antiquato

antique /æn'tiːk/ a antico ● n antichità f inv. ~ **dealer** n antiquario, -a mf

antiquity /æn'tɪkwətɪ/ n antichità f

anti-Semitic /æntɪsɪ'mɪtɪk/ a antisemita

anti'septic a & n antisettico m

anti'social a ⟨behaviour⟩ antisociale; ⟨person⟩ asociale

anti'virus program n Comput programma m di antivirus

antlers /'æntləz/ npl corna fpl

anus /'eɪnəs/ n ano m

anxiety /æŋ'zaɪətɪ/ n ansia f

anxious /'æŋkʃəs/ a ansioso. **~ly** adv con ansia

any /'enɪ/ a ⟨no matter which⟩ qualsiasi, qualunque; **have we ~ wine/biscuits?** abbiamo del vino/ dei biscotti?; **have we ~ jam/ apples?** abbiamo della marmellata/delle mele?; **~ colour/number you like** qualsiasi colore/numero ti piaccia; **we don't have ~ wine/biscuits** non abbiamo vino/ biscotti; **I don't have ~ reason to lie** non ho nessun motivo per mentire; **for ~ reason** per qualsiasi ragione ● pron ⟨some⟩ ne; ⟨no matter which⟩ uno qualsiasi; **I don't want ~ [of it]** non ne voglio [nessuno]; **there aren't ~** non ce ne sono; **have we ~?** ne abbiamo?; **have you read ~ of her books?** hai letto qualcuno dei suoi libri? ● adv **I can't go ~ quicker** non posso andare più in fretta; **is it ~ better?** va un po' meglio?; **would you like ~ more?** ne vuoi ancora?; **I can't eat ~ more** non posso mangiare più niente

'anybody pron ⟨after negative⟩ nessuno; **I haven't seen ~** non ho visto nessuno

'anyhow adv ad ogni modo, co-munque; ⟨badly⟩ non importa come

'anyone pron = anybody

'anything pron qualche cosa, qualcosa; ⟨no matter what⟩ qualsiasi cosa; ⟨after negative⟩ niente; **take/ buy ~ you like** prendi/compra quello che vuoi; **I don't remember ~** non mi ricordo niente; **he's ~ but stupid** è tutto, ma non stupido; **I'll do ~ but that** farò qualsiasi cosa, tranne quello

'anyway adv ad ogni modo, co-munque

'anywhere adv dovunque; ⟨after negative⟩ da nessuna parte; **put it ~** mettilo dove vuoi; **I can't find it ~** non lo trovo da nessuna parte; **~ else** da qualch'altra parte; ⟨after negative⟩ da nessun'altra parte; **I don't want to go ~ else** non voglio andare da nessun'altra parte

apart /ə'pɑːt/ adv lontano; **live ~** vivere separati; **100 miles ~** lontani 100 miglia; **~ from** a parte; **you can't tell them ~** non si possono distinguere; **joking ~** scherzi a parte

apartment /ə'pɑːtmənt/ n ⟨Am: flat⟩ appartamento m; **in my ~** a casa mia

apathy /'æpəθɪ/ n apatia f

ape /eɪp/ n scimmia f ● vt scimmiottare

aperitif /ə'perətiːf/ n aperitivo m

aperture /'æpətʃə(r)/ n apertura f

apex /'eɪpeks/ n vertice m

apiece /ə'piːs/ adv ciascuno

apologetic /əpɒlə'dʒetɪk/ a ⟨air, remark⟩ di scusa; **be ~** essere spiacente

apologize /ə'pɒlədʒaɪz/ vi scusarsi (**for** per)

apology /ə'pɒlədʒɪ/ n scusa f; fig **an ~ for a dinner** una sottospecie di cena

apostle /ə'pɒsl/ n apostolo m

apostrophe /ə'pɒstrəfɪ/ n apostrofo m

appal /ə'pɔ:l/ vt (pt/pp **appalled**) sconvolgere. **~ling** a sconvolgente

apparatus /æpə'reɪtəs/ n apparato m

apparent /ə'pærənt/ a evidente; (seeming) apparente. **~ly** adv apparentemente

apparition /æpə'rɪʃn/ n apparizione f

appeal /ə'pi:l/ n appello m; (attraction) attrattiva f ● vi fare appello; **~ to** ⟨be attractive to⟩ attrarre. **~ing** a attraente

appear /ə'pɪə(r)/ vi apparire; (seem) sembrare; ⟨publication⟩ uscire; Theat esibirsi. **~ance** n apparizione f; ⟨look⟩ aspetto m; **to all ~ances** a giudicare dalle apparenze; **keep up ~ances** salvare le apparenze

appease /ə'pi:z/ vt placare

appendicitis /əpendɪ'saɪtɪs/ n appendicite f

appendix /ə'pendɪks/ n (pl **-ices** /-ɪsi:z/) ⟨of book⟩ appendice f; (pl **-es**) Anat appendice f

appetite /'æpɪtaɪt/ n appetito m

appetizer /'æpɪtaɪzə(r)/ n stuzzichino m. **~ing** a appetitoso

applaud /ə'plɔ:d/ vt/i applaudire. **~se** n applauso m

apple /'æpl/ n mela f. **~-tree** n melo m

appliance /ə'plaɪəns/ n attrezzo m; [electrical] ~ elettrodomestico m

applicable /'æplɪkəbl/ a **be ~ to** essere valido per; **not ~** ⟨on form⟩ non applicabile

applicant /'æplɪkənt/ n candidato, -a mf

application /æplɪ'keɪʃn/ n applicazione f; ⟨request⟩ domanda f; ⟨for job⟩ candidatura f. **~ form** n modulo m di domanda

applied /ə'plaɪd/ a applicato

apply /ə'plaɪ/ vt (pt/pp **-ied**) applicare; **~ oneself** applicarsi ● vi applicarsi; ⟨law⟩ essere applicabile; **~ to** ⟨ask⟩ rivolgersi a; **~ for** fare domanda per ⟨job etc⟩

appoint /ə'pɔɪnt/ vt nominare; fissare ⟨time⟩. **~ment** n appuntamento m; ⟨to job⟩ nomina f; ⟨job⟩ posto m

appraisal /ə'preɪz(ə)l/ n valutazione f

appreciable /ə'pri:ʃəbl/ a sensibile

appreciate /ə'pri:ʃieɪt/ vt apprezzare; (understand) comprendere ● vi (increase in value) aumentare di valore. **~ion** /-'eɪʃn/ n (gratitude) riconoscenza f; (enjoyment) apprezzamento m; (understanding) comprensione f; (in value) aumento m. **~ive** /-ətɪv/ a riconoscente

apprehend /æprɪ'hend/ vt arrestare

apprehension /æprɪ'henʃn/ n arresto m; (fear) apprensione f. **~ive** /-sɪv/ a apprensivo

apprentice /ə'prentɪs/ n apprendista mf. **~ship** n apprendistato m

approach /ə'prəʊtʃ/ n avvicinamento m; ⟨to problem⟩ approccio m; ⟨access⟩ accesso m; **make ~es to** fare degli approcci con ● vi avvicinarsi ● vt avvicinarsi a; ⟨with request⟩ rivolgersi a; affrontare ⟨problem⟩. **~able** /-əbl/ a accessibile

appropriate[1] /ə'prəʊprɪət/ a appropriato

appropriate[2] /ə'prəʊprɪeɪt/ vt appropriarsi di

approval /ə'pru:vl/ n approvazione f; **on ~** in prova

approve /ə'pru:v/ vt approvare ● vi **~e of** approvare ⟨sth⟩; avere una buona opinione di ⟨sb⟩. **~ing** a (smile, nod) d'approvazione

approximate[1] /ə'prɒksɪmət/ a approssimativo. **~ly** adv approssimativamente

approximation /əprɒksɪ'meɪʃn/ n approssimazione f

apricot /'eɪprɪkɒt/ n albicocca f

April /'eɪprəl/ n aprile m. **~ Fool's Day** il primo d'aprile

apron /'eɪprən/ n grembiule m

apt /æpt/ *a* appropriato; **be ~ to do sth** avere tendenza a fare qcsa

aptitude /'æptɪtjuːd/ *n* disposizione *f*. **~ test** *n* test *m inv* attitudinale

aqualung /'ækwəlʌŋ/ *n* autorespiratore *m*

aquarium /ə'kweərɪəm/ *n* acquario *m*

Aquarius /ə'kweərɪəs/ *n Astr* Acquario *m*

aquatic /ə'kwætɪk/ *a* acquatico

Arab /'ærəb/ *a & n* arabo, -a *mf*. **~ian** /ə'reɪbɪən/ *a* arabo

Arabic /'ærəbɪk/ *a* arabo; **~ numerals** numeri *mpl* arabici ● *n* arabo *m*

arable /'ærəbl/ *a* coltivabile

arbitrary /'ɑːbɪtrərɪ/ *a* arbitrario

arbitrat|e /'ɑːbɪtreɪt/ *vi* arbitrare. **~ion** /-'treɪʃn/ *n* arbitraggio *m*

arc /ɑːk/ *n* arco *m*

arcade /ɑː'keɪd/ *n* portico *m*; *(shops)* galleria *f*

arch /ɑːtʃ/ *n* arco *m*; *(of foot)* dorso *m* del piede

archaeological /ɑːkɪə'lɒdʒɪkl/ *a* archeologico

archaeolog|ist /ɑːkɪ'ɒlədʒɪst/ *n* archeologo, -a *mf*. **~y** *n* archeologia *f*

archaic /ɑː'keɪɪk/ *a* arcaico

arch'bishop /ɑːtʃ-/ *n* arcivescovo *m*

arch-'enemy *n* acerrimo nemico *m*

architect /'ɑːkɪtekt/ *n* architetto *m*. **~ural** /ɑː'kɪtektʃərəl/ *a* architettonico

architecture /'ɑːkɪtektʃə(r)/ *n* architettura *f*

archives /'ɑːkaɪvz/ *npl* archivi *mpl*

archiving /'ɑːkaɪvɪŋ/ *n Comput* archiviazione *f*

archway /'ɑːtʃweɪ/ *n* arco *m*

Arctic /'ɑːktɪk/ *a* artico ● *n* the ~ l'Artico

ardent /'ɑːdənt/ *a* ardente

arduous /'ɑːdjʊəs/ *a* arduo

are /ɑː(r)/ *see* be

area /'eərɪə/ *n* area *f*; *(region)* zona

f; *(fig: field)* campo *m*. **~ code** *n* prefisso *m* [telefonico]

arena /ə'riːnə/ *n* arena *f*

aren't /ɑːnt/ = **are not** *see* be

Argentina /ɑːdʒən'tiːnə/ *n* Argentina *f*

Argentinian /-'tɪnɪən/ *a & n* argentino, -a *mf*

argue /'ɑːgjuː/ *vi* litigare (**about** su); *(debate)* dibattere; **don't ~!** non discutere! ● *vt (debate)* dibattere; *(reason)* **~ that** sostenere che

argument /'ɑːgjʊmənt/ *n* argomento *m*; *(reasoning)* ragionamento *m*; **have an ~** litigare. **~ative** /-'mentətɪv/ *a* polemico

aria /'ɑːrɪə/ *n* aria *f*

arid /'ærɪd/ *a* arido

Aries /'eəriːz/ *n Astr* Ariete *m*

arise /ə'raɪz/ *vi* (*pt* **arose**, *pp* **arisen**) *(opportunity, need, problem:)* presentarsi; *(result)* derivare

aristocracy /ærɪ'stɒkrəsɪ/ *n* aristocrazia *f*

aristocrat /'ærɪstəkræt/ *n* aristocratico, -a *mf*. **~ic** /-'krætɪk/ *a* aristocratico

arithmetic /ə'rɪθmətɪk/ *n* aritmetica *f*

arm /ɑːm/ *n* braccio *m*; *(of chair)* bracciolo *m*; **~s** *pl (weapons)* armi *fpl*; **~ in ~** a braccetto; **up in ~s** *fam* furioso **(about** per**)** ● *vt* armare

armaments /'ɑːməmənts/ *npl* armamenti *mpl*

'armchair *n* poltrona *f*

armed /ɑːmd/ *a* armato; **~ forces** forze *fpl* armate; **~ robbery** rapina *f* a mano armata

armistice /'ɑːmɪstɪs/ *n* armistizio *m*

armour /'ɑːmə(r)/ *n* armatura *f*. **~ed** *a (vehicle)* blindato

armpit *n* ascella *f*

army /'ɑːmɪ/ *n* esercito *m*; **join the ~** arruolarsi

aroma /ə'rəʊmə/ *n* aroma *f*. **~tic** /ærə'mætɪk/ *a* aromatico

arose /ə'rəʊz/ *see* arise

around /əˈraʊnd/ *adv* intorno; **all ~** tutt'intorno; **I'm not from ~ here** non sono di qui; **he's not ~** non c'è ● *prep* intorno a; in giro per ‹*room, shops, world*›

arouse /əˈraʊz/ *vt* svegliare; (*sexually*) eccitare

arrange /əˈreɪndʒ/ *vt* sistemare ‹*furniture, books*›; organizzare ‹*meeting*›; fissare ‹*date, time*›; **~ to do sth** combinare di fare qcsa. **~ment** *n* (*of furniture*) sistemazione *f*; *Mus* arrangiamento *m*; (*agreement*) accordo *m*; (*of flowers*) composizione *f*; **make ~ments** prendere disposizioni

arrears /əˈrɪəz/ *npl* arretrati *mpl*; **be in ~** essere in arretrato; **paid in ~** pagato a lavoro eseguito

arrest /əˈrest/ *n* arresto *m*; **under ~** in stato d'arresto ● *vt* arrestare

arrival /əˈraɪvl/ *n* arrivo *m*; **new ~s** *pl* nuovi arrivati *mpl*

arrive /əˈraɪv/ *vi* arrivare; **~ at** *fig* raggiungere

arrogan|ce /ˈærəgəns/ *n* arroganza *f*. **~t** *a* arrogante

arrow /ˈærəʊ/ *n* freccia *f*

arse /ɑːs/ *n vulg* culo *m*

arsenic /ˈɑːsənɪk/ *n* arsenico *m*

arson /ˈɑːsn/ *n* incendio *m* doloso. **~ist** /-sənɪst/ *n* incendiario, -a *mf*

art /ɑːt/ *n* arte *f*. **~s and crafts** *pl* artigianato *m*; **the A~s** *pl* l'arte *f*; **A~s degree** *Univ* laurea *f* in Lettere

artery /ˈɑːtərɪ/ *n* arteria *f*

artful /ˈɑːtfl/ *a* scaltro

'art gallery *n* galleria *f* d'arte

arthritis /ɑːˈθraɪtɪs/ *n* artrite *f*

artichoke /ˈɑːtɪtʃəʊk/ *n* carciofo *m*

article /ˈɑːtɪkl/ *n* articolo *m*; **~ of clothing** capo *m* d'abbigliamento

articulate¹ /ɑːˈtɪkjʊlət/ *a* ‹*speech*› chiaro; **be ~** esprimersi bene

articulate² /ɑːˈtɪkjʊleɪt/ *vt* scandire ‹*words*›. **~d lorry** *n* autotreno *m*

artifice /ˈɑːtɪfɪs/ *n* artificio *m*

artificial /ɑːtɪˈfɪʃl/ *a* artificiale.

~ly *adv* artificialmente; (*smile*) artificiosamente

artillery /ɑːˈtɪlərɪ/ *n* artiglieria *f*

artist /ˈɑːtɪst/ *n* artista *mf*

artiste /ɑːˈtiːst/ *n* *Theat* artista *mf*

artistic /ɑːˈtɪstɪk/ *a* artistico

as /æz/ *conj* come; (*since*) siccome; (*while*) mentre; **as you get older** diventando vecchio; **as you get to know her** conoscendola meglio; **young as she is** per quanto sia giovane ● *prep* come; **as a friend** come amico; **as a child** da bambino; **as a foreigner** in quanto straniero; **disguised as** travestito da ● *adv* as well (*also*) anche; **as soon as I get home** [non] appena arrivo a casa; **as quick as you can** più veloce che puoi; **as quick as you** veloce quanto te; **as far as** (*distance*) fino a; **as far as I'm concerned** per quanto mi riguarda; **as long as** finché; (*provided that*) purché

asbestos /æzˈbestɒs/ *n* amianto *m*

ascend /əˈsend/ *vi* salire ● *vt* salire a ‹*throne*›

Ascension /əˈsenʃn/ *n* *Relig* Ascensione *f*

ascent /əˈsent/ *n* ascesa *f*

ascertain /æsəˈteɪn/ *vt* accertare

ascribe /əˈskraɪb/ *vt* attribuire

ash¹ /æʃ/ *n* (*tree*) frassino *m*

ash² *n* cenere *f*

ashamed /əˈʃeɪmd/ *a* **be/feel ~** vergognarsi

ashore /əˈʃɔː(r)/ *adv* a terra; **go ~** sbarcare

ash; ~tray *n* portacenere *m*. **A~ Wednesday** *n* mercoledì *m* *inv* delle Ceneri

Asia /ˈeɪʒə/ *n* Asia *f*. **~n** *a* & *n* asiatico, -a *mf*. **~tic** /eɪʒɪˈætɪk/ *a* asiatico

aside /əˈsaɪd/ *adv* **take sb ~** prendere qcno a parte; **put sth ~** mettere qcsa da parte; **~ from you** *Am* a parte te

ask /ɑːsk/ *vt* fare ‹*question*›; (*invite*) invitare; **~ sb sth** domandare *or* chiedere qcsa a qcno; **~ sb**

to do sth domandare or chiedere a qcno di fare qcsa ● *vi* ~ **about sth** informarsi su qcsa; ~ **after** chiedere [notizie] di; ~ **for** chiedere ⟨*sth*⟩; chiedere di ⟨*sb*⟩; ~ **for trouble** *fam* andare in cerca di guai. **ask in** *vt* ~ **sb** in invitare qcno ad entrare. **ask out** *vt* ~ **sb out** chiedere a qcno di uscire

askance /əˈskɑːns/ *adv* **look** ~ **at sb/sth** guardare qcno/qcsa di traverso

askew /əˈskjuː/ *a & adv* di traverso

asleep /əˈsliːp/ *a* **be** ~ dormire; **fall** ~ addormentarsi

asparagus /əˈspærəgəs/ *n* asparagi *mpl*

aspect /ˈæspekt/ *n* aspetto *m*

aspersions /əˈspɜːʃnz/ *npl* **cast** ~ **on** diffamare

asphalt /ˈæsfælt/ *n* asfalto *m*

asphyxia /əsˈfɪksɪə/ *n* asfissia *f*. ~**te** /əsˈfɪksɪeɪt/ *vt* asfissiare. ~**tion** /-ˈeɪʃn/ *n* asfissia *f*

aspirations /æspəˈreɪʃnz/ *npl* aspirazioni *fpl*

aspire /əˈspaɪə(r)/ *vi* ~ **to** aspirare a

ass /æs/ *n* asino *m*

assailant /əˈseɪlənt/ *n* assalitore, -trice *mf*

assassin /əˈsæsɪn/ *n* assassino, -a *mf*. ~**ate** *vt* assassinare. ~**ation** /-ˈneɪʃn/ *n* assassinio *m*

assault /əˈsɔːlt/ *n Mil* assalto *m*; *Jur* aggressione *f* ● *vt* aggredire

assemble /əˈsembl/ *vi* radunarsi ● *vt* radunare; *Techn* montare

assembly /əˈsembli/ *n* assemblea *f*; *Sch* assemblea *f* giornaliera di alunni e professori di una scuola; *Techn* montaggio *m*. ~ **line** *n* catena *f* di montaggio

assent /əˈsent/ *n* assenso *m* ● *vi* acconsentire

assert /əˈsɜːt/ *vt* asserire; far valere ⟨*one's rights*⟩; ~ **oneself** farsi valere. ~**ion** /-ɜːn/ *n* asserzione *f*. ~**ive** /-tɪv/ *a* **be** ~**ive** farsi valere

assess /əˈses/ *vt* valutare; ⟨*for tax purposes*⟩ stabilire l'imponibile

di. ~**ment** *n* valutazione *f*; ⟨*of tax*⟩ accertamento *m*

asset /ˈæset/ *n* ⟨*advantage*⟩ vantaggio *m*; ⟨*person*⟩ elemento *m* prezioso. ~**s** *pl* beni *mpl*; ⟨*on balance sheet*⟩ attivo *msg*

assign /əˈsaɪn/ *vt* assegnare. ~**ment** *n* ⟨*task*⟩ incarico *m*

assimilate /əˈsɪmɪleɪt/ *vt* assimilare; integrare ⟨*person*⟩

assist /əˈsɪst/ *vt/i* assistere; ~ **sb to do sth** assistere qcno nel fare qcsa. ~**ance** *n* assistenza *f*. ~**ant** *a* ~**ant manager** vicedirettore, -trice *mf* ● *n* assistente *mf*; ⟨*in shop*⟩ commesso, -a *mf*

associat|e¹ /əˈsəʊʃɪeɪt/ *vt* associare (with a); **be** ~**ed with sth** ⟨*involved in*⟩ essere coinvolto in qcsa ● *vi* ~**e with** frequentare. ~**ion** /-ˈeɪʃn/ *n* associazione *f*. **A~ion** 'Football' [gioco *m* del] calcio *m*

associate² /əˈsəʊʃɪət/ *a* associato ● *n* collega *mf*; ⟨*member*⟩ socio, -a *mf*

assort|ed /əˈsɔːtɪd/ *a* assortito. ~**ment** *n* assortimento *m*

assum|e /əˈsjuːm/ *vt* presumere; assumere ⟨*control*⟩; ~**e** office entrare in carica; ~**ing that you're right,...** ammettendo che tu abbia ragione,...

assumption /əˈsʌmpʃn/ *n* supposizione *f*; **on the** ~ **that** partendo dal presupposto che; **the A~** *Relig* l'Assunzione *f*

assurance /əˈʃʊərəns/ *n* assicurazione *f*; ⟨*confidence*⟩ sicurezza *f*

assure /əˈʃʊə(r)/ *vt* assicurare. ~**d** *a* sicuro

asterisk /ˈæstərɪsk/ *n* asterisco *m*

astern /əˈstɜːn/ *adv* a poppa

asthma /ˈæsmə/ *n* asma *f*. ~**tic** /-ˈmætɪk/ *a* asmatico

astonish /əˈstɒnɪʃ/ *vt* stupire. ~**ing** *a* stupefacente. ~**ment** *n* stupore *m*

astound /əˈstaʊnd/ *vt* stupire

astray /əˈstreɪ/ *adv* **go** ~ smarrir-

si; (*morally*) uscire dalla retta via;
lead ~ traviare

astride /ə'straɪd/ *adv* [a] cavalcioni ● *prep* a cavalcioni di

astrolog|er /ə'strɒlədʒə(r)/ *n* astrologo, -a *mf*. **~y** *n* astrologia *f*

astronaut /'æstrənɔ:t/ *n* astronauta *mf*

astronom|er /ə'strɒnəmə(r)/ *n* astronomo, -a *mf*. **~ical** /æstrə-'nɒmɪkl/ *a* astronomico. **~y** *n* astronomia *f*

astute /ə'stju:t/ *a* astuto

asylum /ə'saɪləm/ *n* [political] ~ asilo *m* politico; [lunatic] ~ manicomio *m*

at /ət/, accentato /æt/ *prep* a; **at the station/the market** alla stazione/al mercato; **at the office/the bank** in ufficio/banca; **at the beginning** all'inizio; **at John's** da John; **at the hairdresser's** dal parrucchiere; **at home** a casa; **at work** al lavoro; **at school** a scuola; **at a party/wedding** a una festa/un matrimonio; **at 1 o'clock** all'una; **at 50 km an hour** a 50 all'ora; **at Christmas/Easter** a Natale/Pasqua; **at times** talvolta; **two at a time** due alla volta; **good at languages** bravo nelle lingue; **at sb's request** su richiesta di qcno; **are you at all worried?** sei preoccupato?

ate /et/ *see* **eat**

atheist /'eɪθɪɪst/ *n* ateo, -a *mf*

athlet|e /'æθli:t/ *n* atleta *mf*. **~ic** /-'letɪk/ *a* atletico. **~ics** /-'letɪks/ *n* atletica *fsg*

Atlantic /ət'læntɪk/ *a & n* **the** ~ [**Ocean**] l'[Oceano *m*] Atlantico *m*

atlas /'ætləs/ *n* atlante *m*

atmosphere /'ætməsfɪə(r)/ *n* atmosfera *f*. **~ic** /-'ferɪk/ *a* atmosferico

atom /'ætəm/ *n* atomo *m*. ~ **bomb** *n* bomba *f* atomica

atomic /ə'tɒmɪk/ *a* atomico

atone /ə'təʊn/ *vi* ~ **for** pagare per. **~ment** *n* espiazione *f*

atrocious /ə'trəʊʃəs/ *a* atroce; (*fam: meal, weather*) abominevole

atrocity /ə'trɒsəti/ *n* atrocità *f inv*

attach /ə'tætʃ/ *vt* attaccare; attribuire ⟨importance⟩; **be ~ed to** *fig* essere attaccato a

attaché /ə'tæʃeɪ/ *n* addetto *m*. ~ **case** *n* ventiquattrore *f inv*

attachment /ə'tætʃmənt/ *n* (*affection*) attaccamento *m*; (*accessory*) accessorio *m*

attack /ə'tæk/ *n* attacco *m*; (*physical*) aggressione *f* ● *vt* attaccare; (*physically*) aggredire. **~er** *n* assalitore, -trice *mf*; (*critic*) detrattore, -trice *mf*

attain /ə'teɪn/ *vt* realizzare ⟨ambition⟩; raggiungere ⟨success, age, goal⟩

attempt /ə'tempt/ *n* tentativo *m*
● *vt* tentare

attend /ə'tend/ *vt* essere presente a; (*go regularly to*) frequentare; ⟨doctor:⟩ avere in cura ● *vi* essere presente; (*pay attention*) prestare attenzione. **attend to** *vt* occuparsi di; (*in shop*) servire. **~ance** *n* presenza *f*. **~ant** *n* guardiano, -a *mf*

attention /ə'tenʃn/ *n* attenzione *f*; ~! *Mil* attenti!; **pay** ~ prestare attenzione; **need** ~ aver bisogno di attenzioni; ⟨skin, hair, plant:⟩ dover essere curato; ⟨car, tyres:⟩ dover essere riparato; **for the** ~ **of** all'attenzione di

attentive /ə'tentɪv/ *a* ⟨pupil, audience⟩ attento

attest /ə'test/ *vt/i* attestare

attic /'ætɪk/ *n* soffitta *f*

attitude /'ætɪtju:d/ *n* atteggiamento *m*

attorney /ə'tɜ:nɪ/ *n* (*Am: lawyer*) avvocato *m*; **power of** ~ delega *f*

attract /ə'trækt/ *vt* attirare. **~ion** /-ækʃn/ *n* attrazione *f*; (*feature*) attrattiva *f*. **~ive** /-tɪv/ *a* ⟨person⟩ attraente; ⟨proposal, price⟩ allettante

attribute[1] /'ætrɪbju:t/ *n* attributo *m*

attribut|e[2] /ə'trɪbju:t/ *vt* attribuire

attrition /ə'trɪʃn/ *n* war of ~ guerra *f* di logoramento

aubergine /'əubəʒi:n/ *n* melanzana *f*

auburn /'ɔ:bən/ *a* castano ramato

auction /'ɔ:kʃn/ *n* asta *f* ● *vt* vendere all'asta. **~eer** /-ʃə'nɪə(r)/ *n* banditore *m*

audacious /ɔ:'deɪʃəs/ *a* sfacciato; (*daring*) audace. **~ty** /-'dæsətɪ/ *n* sfacciataggine *f*; (*daring*) audacia *f*

audible /'ɔ:dəbl/ *a* udibile

audience /'ɔ:dɪəns/ *n* Theat pubblico *m*; TV telespettatori *mpl*; Radio ascoltatori *mpl*; (*meeting*) udienza *f*

audio /'ɔ:dɪəu/: **~tape** *n* audiocassetta *f*. **~ typist** *n* dattilografo, -a *mf* (*che trascrive registrazioni*). **~'visual** *a* audiovisivo

audit /'ɔ:dɪt/ *n* verifica *f* del bilancio ● *vt* verificare

audition /ɔ:'dɪʃn/ *n* audizione *f* ● *vi* fare un'audizione

auditor /'ɔ:dɪtə(r)/ *n* revisore *m* di conti

auditorium /ɔ:dɪ'tɔ:rɪəm/ *n* sala *f*

augment /ɔ:g'ment/ *vt* aumentare

augur /'ɔ:gə(r)/ *vi* ~ **well/ill** essere di buon/cattivo augurio

August /'ɔ:gəst/ *n* agosto *m*.

aunt /ɑ:nt/ *n* zia *f*

au pair /əu'peə(r)/ *n* ~ **[girl]** ragazza *f* alla pari

aura /'ɔ:rə/ *n* aura *f*

auspices /'ɔ:spɪsɪz/ *npl* **under the** ~ **of** sotto l'egida di

auspicious /ɔ:'spɪʃəs/ *a* di buon augurio

austere /ɒ'stɪə(r)/ *a* austero. **~ity** /-'terətɪ/ *n* austerità *f*

Australia /ɒ'streɪlɪə/ *n* Australia *f*. **~n** *a & n* australiano, -a *mf*

Austria /'ɒstrɪə/ *n* Austria *f*. **~n** *a & n* austriaco, -a *mf*

authentic /ɔ:'θentɪk/ *a* autentico. **~ate** *vt* autenticare. **~ity** /-'tɪsetɪ/ *n* autenticità *f*

author /'ɔ:θə(r)/ *n* autore *m*

authoritarian /ɔ:θɒrɪ'teərɪən/ *a* autoritario

authoritative /ɔ:'θɒrɪtətɪv/ *a* autorevole; (*manner*) autoritario

authority /ɔ:'θɒrətɪ/ *n* autorità *f*; (*permission*) autorizzazione *f*; **be in** ~ **over** avere autorità su

authorization /ɔ:θəraɪ'zeɪʃn/ *n* autorizzazione *f*

authorize /'ɔ:θəraɪz/ *vt* autorizzare

autobi'ography /ɔ:tə-/ *n* autobiografia *f*

autocratic /ɔ:tə'krætɪk/ *a* autocratico

autograph /'ɔ:tə-/ *n* autografo *m*

automate /'ɔ:təmeɪt/ *vt* automatizzare

automatic /ɔ:tə'mætɪk/ *a* automatico ● *n* (*car*) macchina *f* col cambio automatico; (*washing machine*) lavatrice *f* automatica. **~ally** *adv* automaticamente

automation /ɔ:tə'meɪʃn/ *n* automazione *f*

automobile /'ɔ:təməbi:l/ *n* automobile *f*

autonomous /ɔ:'tɒnəməs/ *a* autonomo. **~y** *n* autonomia *f*

autopsy /'ɒtpsɪ/ *n* autopsia *f*

autumn /'ɔ:təm/ *n* autunno *m*. **~al** /-'tʌmnl/ *a* autunnale

auxiliary /ɔ:g'zɪlɪərɪ/ *a* ausiliario ● *n* ausiliare *m*

avail /ə'veɪl/ *n* **to no** ~ invano ● *vi* ~ **oneself of** approfittare di

available /ə'veɪləbl/ *a* disponibile; (*book, record etc*) in vendita

avalanche /'ævəlɑ:nʃ/ *n* valanga *f*

avarice /'ævərɪs/ *n* avidità *f*

avenge /ə'vendʒ/ *vt* vendicare

avenue /'ævənju:/ *n* viale *m*; fig strada *f*

average /'ævərɪdʒ/ *a* medio; (*mediocre*) mediocre ● *n* media *f*; **on** ~ in media ● *vt* (*sales, attendance etc*) raggiungere una media di.

average out at *vt* risultare in media

averse /ə'vɜ:s/ *a* **not be ~e to sth**

non essere contro qcsa. **~ion** /-ɜ:ʃn/ n avversione f **(to** per)

avert /ə'vɜ:t/ vt evitare ⟨crisis⟩; distogliere ⟨eyes⟩

aviary /'eɪvɪərɪ/ n uccelliera f

aviation /eɪvɪ'eɪʃn/ n aviazione f

avid /'ævɪd/ a avido **(for** di); ⟨reader⟩ appassionato

avocado /ævə'kɑ:dəʊ/ n avocado m

avoid /ə'vɔɪd/ vt evitare. **~able** /-əbl/ a evitabile

await /ə'weɪt/ vt attendere

awake /ə'weɪk/ a sveglio; **wide ~** completamente sveglio ● vi ⟨pt awoke, pp awoken⟩ svegliarsi

awaken /ə'weɪkn/ vt svegliare. **~ing** n risveglio m

award /ə'wɔ:d/ n premio m; ⟨medal⟩ riconoscimento m; ⟨of prize⟩ assegnazione f ● vt assegnare; ⟨hand over⟩ consegnare

aware /ə'weə(r)/ a **be ~ of** ⟨sense⟩ percepire; ⟨know⟩ essere conscio di; **become ~ of** accorgersi di; ⟨learn⟩ venire a sapere di; **be ~ that** rendersi conto che. **~ness** n percezione f; ⟨knowledge⟩ consapevolezza f

awash /ə'wɒʃ/ a inondato **(with** di)

away /ə'weɪ/ adv via; **go/stay ~** andare/stare via; **he's ~ from his desk/the office** non è alla sua scrivania/in ufficio; **far ~** lontano; **four kilometres ~** a quattro chilometri; **play ~** Sport giocare fuori casa; **~ game** n partita f fuori casa

awe /ɔ:/ n soggezione f

awful /'ɔ:fl/ a terribile. **~ly** adv /'ɔ:f(ʊ)lɪ/ terribilmente; ⟨pretty⟩ estremamente

awhile /ə'waɪl/ adv per un po'

awkward /'ɔ:kwəd/ a ⟨movement⟩ goffo; ⟨moment, situation⟩ imbarazzante; ⟨time⟩ scomodo. **~ly** adv ⟨move⟩ goffamente; ⟨say⟩ con imbarazzo

awning /'ɔ:nɪŋ/ n tendone m

awoke(n) /ə'wəʊk(ən)/ see **awake**

awry /ə'raɪ/ adv storto

axe /æks/ n scure f ● vt ⟨pres p axing⟩ fare dei tagli a ⟨budget⟩; sopprimere ⟨jobs⟩; annullare ⟨project⟩

axis /'æksɪs/ n ⟨pl **axes** /-si:z/⟩ asse m

axle /'æksl/ n Techn asse m

ay[e] /aɪ/ adv sì ● n sì m invar

Bb

B /bi:/ n Mus si m inv

BA n abbr **Bachelor of Arts**

babble /'bæbl/ vi farfugliare; ⟨stream:⟩ gorgogliare

baby /'beɪbɪ/ n bambino, -a mf; ⟨fam: darling⟩ tesoro m

baby: **~ carriage** n Am carrozzina f. **~ish** a bambinesco. **~-sit** vi fare da baby-sitter. **~-sitter** n baby-sitter mf

bachelor /'bætʃələ(r)/ n scapolo m; **B~ of Arts/Science** laureato, -a mf in lettere/in scienze

back /bæk/ n schiena f; ⟨of horse, hand⟩ dorso m; ⟨of chair⟩ schienale m; ⟨of house, cheque, page⟩ retro m; ⟨in football⟩ difesa f; **at the ~** in fondo; **in the ~** Auto dietro; **~ to front** ⟨sweater⟩ il davanti di dietro; **at the ~ of beyond** in un posto sperduto ● a posteriore; ⟨taxes, payments⟩ arretrato ● adv indietro; ⟨returned⟩ di ritorno; **turn/move ~** tornare/spostarsi indietro; **put it ~ here/there** rimettilo qui/là; **~ at home** di ritorno a casa; **I'll be ~ in five minutes** torno fra cinque minuti; **I'm just ~** sono appena tornato; **when do you want the book ~?** quando rivuoi il libro? ● vt ⟨support⟩ sostenere; ⟨with money⟩ finanziare; puntare su ⟨horse⟩; ⟨cover the back of⟩ rivestire il retro

di ●*vi* Auto fare retromarcia.
back down *vi* battere in ritirata.
back in *vi* Auto entrare in retromarcia; ⟨*person:*⟩ entrare camminando all'indietro. **back out** *vi* Auto uscire camminando all'indietro; ⟨*person:*⟩ uscire camminando all'indietro; *fig* tirarsi indietro (**of** da). **back up** *vt* sostenere; confermare ⟨*person's alibi*⟩; Comput fare una copia di salvataggio di; be ~**ed up** ⟨*traffic:*⟩ essere congestionato ● *vi* Auto fare retromarcia.
back: ~**ache** *n* mal *m* di schiena. ~**bencher** *n* parlamentare *m* ordinario, -a. ~**biting** *n* maldicenza *f*. ~**bone** *n* spina *f* dorsale. ~**chat** *n* risposta *f* impertinente. ~**date** *vt* retrodatare ⟨*cheque*⟩; ~**dated to** valido a partire da. ~ '**door** *n* porta *f* di servizio
backer /'bækə(r)/ *n* sostenitore, -trice *mf*; ⟨*with money*⟩ finanzia- 'tore, -trice *mf*
back: ~'**fire** *vi* Auto avere un ritorno di fiamma; ⟨*fig: plan*⟩ fallire. ~**ground** *n* sfondo *m*; ⟨*environment*⟩ ambiente m. ~**hand** *n* ⟨*tennis*⟩ rovescio *m*. ~'**handed** *a* ⟨*compliment*⟩ implicito. ~'**hander** *n* ⟨*fam: bribe*⟩ bustarella *f*
backing /'bækɪŋ/ *n* ⟨*support*⟩ supporto *m*; ⟨*material*⟩ riserva *f*, Mus accompagnamento *m*; ~ **group** gruppo *m* d'accompagnamento
back: ~**lash** *n* fig reazione *f* opposta. ~**log** *n* ~**log of work** lavoro *m* arretrato. ~ '**seat** *n* sedile *m* posteriore. ~**side** *n* fam fondoschiena *m* inv. ~**slash** *n* Typ barra *f* retroversa. ~**stage** *a* & *adv* dietro le quinte. ~**stroke** *n* dorso *m*. ~**up** *n* rinforzi *mpl*; Comput riserva *f*. ~**up copy** *n* Comput copia *f* di riserva
backward /'bækwəd/ *a* ⟨*step*⟩ indietro; ⟨*child*⟩ lento nell'apprendimento; ⟨*country*⟩ arretrato ● *adv* ~**s** ⟨*also Am:* ~⟩ indietro; ⟨*fall, walk*⟩ all'indietro; ~**s and forwards** avanti e indietro

back: ~**water** *n* fig luogo *m* allo scarto. ~ '**yard** *n* cortile *m*
bacon /'beɪkn/ *n* ≈ pancetta *f*
bacteria /bæk'tɪərɪə/ *npl* batteri *mpl*
bad /bæd/ *a* ⟨**worse, worst**⟩ cattivo; ⟨*weather, habit, news, accident*⟩ brutto; ⟨*apple etc*⟩ marcio; **the light is** ~ non c'è una buona luce; **use** ~ **language** dire delle parolacce; **feel** ~ sentirsi male; ⟨*feel guilty*⟩ sentirsi in colpa; **have a** ~ **back** avere dei problemi alla schiena; **smoking is** ~ **for you** fumare fa male; **go** ~ andare a male; **that's just too** ~! pazienza!; **not** ~ niente male
bade /bæd/ *see* bid
badge /bædʒ/ *n* distintivo *m*
badger /'bædʒə(r)/ *n* tasso *m* ● *vt* tormentare
badly /'bædlɪ/ *adv* male; ⟨*hurt*⟩ gravemente; ~ **off** povero; ~ **behaved** maleducato; **need** ~ aver estremamente bisogno di
bad-'mannered *a* maleducato
badminton /'bædmɪntən/ *n* badminton *m*
bad-'tempered *a* irascibile
baffle /'bæfl/ *vt* confondere
bag /bæg/ *n* borsa *f*; ⟨*of paper*⟩ sacchetto *m*; **old** ~ *sl* megera *f*; ~**s under the eyes** occhiaie *fpl*; ~**s of** *fam* un sacco di
baggage /'bægɪdʒ/ *n* bagagli *mpl*
baggy /'bægɪ/ *a* ⟨*clothes*⟩ ampio
'bagpipes *npl* cornamusa *f*
Bahamas /bə'hɑːməz/ *npl* **the** ~ le Bahamas
bail /beɪl/ *n* cauzione *f*; **on** ~ su cauzione ● **bail out** *vt* Naut aggottare; ~ **sb out** Jur pagare la cauzione per qcno ● *vi* Aeron paracadutarsi
bait /beɪt/ *n* esca *f* ● *vt* innescare; ⟨*fig: torment*⟩ tormentare
bake /beɪk/ *vt* cuocere al forno; ⟨*make*⟩ fare ● *vi* cuocersi al forno
baker /'beɪkə(r)/ *n* fornaio, -a *mf*, panettiere, -a *mf*; ~**'s** ⟨**shop**⟩ pa-

netteria *f.* **~y** *n* panificio *m*, forno *m*

baking /'beɪkɪŋ/ *n* cottura *f* al forno. **~-powder** *n* lievito *m* in polvere. **~-tin** *n* teglia *f*

balance /'bæləns/ *n* equilibrio *m*; *Comm* bilancio *m*; (outstanding sum) saldo *m*; **(bank)** ~ saldo *m*; **be** *or* **hang in the** ~ *fig* essere in sospeso ● *vt* bilanciare; (budget) *Comm* fare il bilancio di (books) ● *vi* bilanciarsi; *Comm* essere in pareggio. **~d** *a* equilibrato. ~ **sheet** *n* bilancio *m* [d'esercizio]

balcony /'bælkənɪ/ *n* balcone *m*

bald /bɔːld/ *a* (person) calvo; (tyre) liscio; (statement) nudo e crudo; **go** ~ perdere i capelli

bald|ing /'bɔːldɪŋ/ *a* **be ~ing** stare perdendo i capelli. **~ness** *n* calvizie *f*

bale /beɪl/ *n* balla *f*

baleful /'beɪlfl/ *a* malvagio; (sad) triste

balk /bɔːk/ *vt* ostacolare ● *vi* ~ **at** (horse) impennarsi davanti a; *fig* tirarsi indietro davanti a

Balkans /'bɔːlknz/ *mpl* Balcani *mpl*

ball¹ /bɔːl/ *n* palla *f*; (football) pallone *m*; (of yarn) gomitolo *m*; **on the** ~ *fam* sveglio

ball² *n* (dance) ballo *m*

ballad /'bæləd/ *n* ballata *f*

ballast /'bæləst/ *n* zavorra *f*

ball-bearing *n* cuscinetto *m* a sfera

ballerina /bælə'riːnə/ *n* ballerina *f* [classica]

ballet /'bæleɪ/ *n* balletto *m*; (art form) danza *f*; ~ **dancer** *n* ballerino, -a *mf* [classico, -a]

ballistic /bə'lɪstɪk/ *a* balistico. **~s** *n* balistica *fsg*

balloon /bə'luːn/ *n* pallone *m*; *Aeron* mongolfiera *f*

ballot /'bælət/ *n* votazione *f*. **~-box** *n* urna *f*. **~-paper** *n* scheda *f* di votazione

ball: ~-point ['pen] *n* penna *f* a sfera. **~-room** *n* sala *f* da ballo

balm /bɑːm/ *n* balsamo *m*

balmy /'bɑːmɪ/ *a* (-ier, -iest) mite; (fam: crazy) strampalato

Baltic /'bɔːltɪk/ *a* & *n* **the** ~ [Sea] il [mar] Baltico

bamboo /bæm'buː/ *n* bambù *m inv*

bamboozle /bæm'buːzl/ *vt* (fam: mystify) confondere

ban /bæn/ *n* proibizione *f* ● *vt* (pt/pp **banned**) proibire; ~ **from** espellere da (club); **she was ~ned from driving** le hanno ritirato la patente

banal /bə'nɑːl/ *a* banale. **~ity** /-'nælətɪ/ *n* banalità *f inv*

banana /bə'nɑːnə/ *n* banana *f*

band /bænd/ *n* banda *f*; (stripe) nastro *m*; (Mus: pop group) complesso *m*; (Mus: brass ~) banda *f*; *Mil* fanfara *f* ● **band together** *vi* riunirsi

bandage /'bændɪdʒ/ *n* benda *f* ● *vt* fasciare (limb)

b. & b. *abbr* **bed and breakfast**

bandit /'bændɪt/ *n* bandito *m*

band: ~stand *n* palco *m* coperto [dell'orchestra]. **~wagon** *n* **jump on the ~wagon** *fig* seguire la corrente

bandy¹ /'bændɪ/ *vt* (pt/pp **-ied**) scambiarsi (words). **bandy about** *vt* far circolare

bandy² *a* (-ier, -iest) **be ~** avere le gambe storte

bang /bæŋ/ *n* (noise) fragore *m*; (of gun, firework) scoppio *m*; (blow) colpo *m* ● *adv* ~ **in the middle of** *fam* proprio nel mezzo di; **go** ~ (gun:) sparare; (balloon:) esplodere ● *int* bum! ● *vt* battere (fist); battere su (table), sbattere (door, head) ● *vi* scoppiare; (door:) sbattere

banger /'bæŋə(r)/ *n* (firework) petardo *m*; (fam: sausage) salsiccia *f, sdo* ~ (fam: car) macinino *m*

bangle /'bæŋgl/ *n* braccialetto *m*

banish /'bænɪʃ/ *vt* bandire

banisters /'bænɪstəz/ *npl* ringhiera *fsg*

bank¹ /bæŋk/ *n* (of river) sponda *f*

(*slope*) scarpata *f* ● *vi* Aeron inclinarsi in virata

bank² *n* banca *f* ● *vt* depositare in banca ● *vi* ~ **with** avere un conto [bancario] presso. **bank on** *vt* contare su

'**bank account** *n* conto *m* in banca

'**bank card** *n* carta *f* assegno

banker /'bæŋkə(r)/ *n* banchiere *m*

bank: ~ '**holiday** *n* giorno *m* festivo. ~**ing** *n* bancario *m*. ~ **manager** *n* direttore, -trice *mf* di banca. ~**note** *n* banconota *f*

bankrupt /'bæŋkrʌpt/ *a* fallito; **go** ~ **fallire** ● *n* persona *f* che ha fatto fallimento ● *vt* far fallire. ~**cy** *n* bancarotta *f*

banner /'bænə(r)/ *n* stendardo *m*; (*of demonstrators*) striscione *m*

banns /bænz/ *npl* Relig pubblicazioni *fpl* [di matrimonio]

banquet /'bæŋkwɪt/ *n* banchetto *m*

banter /'bæntə(r)/ *n* battute *fpl* di spirito

baptism /'bæptɪzm/ *n* battesimo *m*

Baptist /'bæptɪst/ *a & n* battista *mf*

baptize /bæp'taɪz/ *vt* battezzare

bar /bɑ:(r)/ *n* sbarra *f*; *Jur* cancello *m*; (*of chocolate*) tavoletta *f*; (*café*) bar *m* inv; (*counter*) banco *m*; *Mus* battuta *f*; (*fig: obstacle*) ostacolo *m*; ~ **of soap/gold** saponetta *f*/lingotto *m*; **behind** ~**s** *fam* dietro le sbarre ● *vt* (*pt/pp* **barred**) sbarrare (*way*); sprangare (*door*); escludere (*person*) ● *prep* tranne; ~ **none** in assoluto

barbarian /bɑ:'beərɪən/ *n* barbaro, -a *mf*

barbar|ic /bɑ:'bærɪk/ *a* barbarico. ~**ity** *n* barbarie *f* inv. ~**ous** /'bɑ:bərəs/ *a* barbaro

barbecue /'bɑ:bɪkju:/ *n* barbecue *m* inv; (*party*) grigliata *f*, barbecue *m* inv ● *vt* arrostire sul barbecue

barbed /bɑ:bd/ *a* ~ **wire** filo *m* spinato

barber /'bɑ:bə(r)/ *n* barbiere *m*

barbiturate /bɑ:'bɪtjʊrət/ *n* barbiturico *m*

'**bar code** *n* codice *m* a barre

bare /beə(r)/ *a* nudo; (*tree, room*) spoglio; (*floor*) senza moquette ● *vt* scoprire; mostrare (*teeth*)

bare: ~**back** *adv* senza sella. ~**faced** *a* sfacciato. ~**foot** *adv* scalzo. ~'**headed** *a* a capo scoperto

barely /'beəlɪ/ *adv* appena

bargain /'bɑ:gɪn/ *n* (*agreement*) patto *m*; (*good buy*) affare *m*; **into the** ~ per di più ● *vi* contrattare; (*haggle*) trattare. **bargain for** *vt* (*expect*) aspettarsi

barge /bɑ:dʒ/ *n* barcone *m* ● **barge in** *fam* (*to room*) piombare dentro; (*into conversation*) interrompere bruscamente. ~ **into** *vt* piombare dentro a (*room*); venire addosso a (*person*)

baritone /'bærɪtəʊn/ *n* baritono *m*

bark¹ /bɑ:k/ *n* (*of tree*) corteccia *f*

bark² *n* abbaiamento *m* ● *vi* abbaiare

barley /'bɑ:lɪ/ *n* orzo *m*

bar: ~**maid** *n* barista *f*. ~**man** *n* barista *m*

barmy /'bɑ:mɪ/ *a fam* strampalato

barn /bɑ:n/ *n* granaio *m*

barometer /bə'rɒmɪtə(r)/ *n* barometro *m*

baron /'bærn/ *n* barone *m*. ~**ess** *n* baronessa *f*

baroque /bə'rɒk/ *a & n* barocco *m*

barracks /'bærəks/ *npl* caserma *fsg*

barrage /'bærɑ:ʒ/ *n* Mil sbarramento *m*; (*fig: of criticism*) sfilza *f*

barrel /'bærl/ *n* barile *m*, botte *f*; (*of gun*) canna *f*. ~-**organ** *n* organetto *m* (a cilindro)

barren /'bærən/ *a* sterile; (*landscape*) brullo

barricade /bærɪ'keɪd/ *n* barricata *f* ● *vt* barricare

barrier /'bærɪə(r)/ *n* barriera *f*; *Rail* cancello *m*; *fig* ostacolo *m*

barring /'bɑ:rɪŋ/ *prep* ~ **accidents** tranne imprevisti

barrister /'bærɪstə(r)/ n avvocato m

barrow /'bærəʊ/ n carretto m; (wheel~) carriola f

barter /'bɑːtə(r)/ vi barattare (for con)

base /beɪs/ n base f ● a vile ● vt basare; **be ~d on** basarsi su

base: **~ball** n baseball m. **~less** a infondato. **~ment** n seminterrato m. **~ment flat** n appartamento m nel seminterrato

bash /bæʃ/ n colpo m [violento] ● vt colpire [violentemente]; (dent) ammaccare; **~ed in** ammaccato

bashful /'bæʃfl/ a timido

basic /'beɪsɪk/ a di base; (condition, requirement) basilare; (living conditions) povero; **my Italian is pretty ~** il mio italiano è abbastanza rudimentale; **the ~s** (of language, science) i rudimenti; (essentials) l'essenziale m. **~ally** adv fondamentalmente

basil /'bæzɪl/ n basilico m

basilica /bə'zɪlɪkə/ n basilica f

basin /'beɪsn/ n bacinella f; (washhand ~) lavabo m; (for food) recipiente m; Geog bacino m

basis /'beɪsɪs/ n (pl -ses /-siːz/) base f

bask /bɑːsk/ vi crogiolarsi

basket /'bɑːskɪt/ n cestino m. **~ball** n pallacanestro f

Basle /bɑːl/ n Basilea f

bass /beɪs/ a basso; **~ voice** voce f di basso ● n basso m

bastard /'bɑːstəd/ n (illegitimate child) bastardo, -a mf; sl figlio m di puttana

bastion /'bæstɪən/ n bastione m

bat¹ /bæt/ n mazza f; (for table tennis) racchetta f; **off one's own ~** fam tutto da solo ● vt (pt/pp batted) battere; **she didn't ~ an eyelid** fig non ha battuto ciglio

bat² n Zool pipistrello m

batch /bætʃ/ n gruppo m; (of goods) partita f; (of bread) infornata f

bated /'beɪtɪd/ a **with ~ breath** col fiato sospeso

bath /bɑːθ/ n (pl ~s /bɑːðz/) bagno m; (tub) vasca f da bagno; **~s** pl piscina f; **have a ~** fare un bagno ● vt fare il bagno a

bathe /beɪð/ n bagno m ● vi fare il bagno ● vt lavare (wound). **~r** n bagnante mf

bathing /'beɪðɪŋ/ n bagni mpl. **~-cap** n cuffia f. **~-costume** n costume m da bagno

bath: **~-mat** n tappetino m da bagno. **~-robe** n accappatoio m. **~room** n bagno m. **~-towel** n asciugamano m da bagno

baton /'bætn/ n Mus bacchetta f

battalion /bə'tælɪən/ n battaglione m

batter /'bætə(r)/ n Culin pastella f; **~ed** a (car) malandato; (wife, baby) maltrattato

battery /'bætərɪ/ n batteria f; (of torch, radio) pila f

battle /'bætl/ n battaglia f; fig lotta f ● vi fig lottare

battle: **~field** n campo m di battaglia. **~ship** n corazzata f

bawdy /'bɔːdɪ/ a (-ier, -iest) piccante

bawl /bɔːl/ vt/i urlare

bay¹ /beɪ/ n Geog baia f

bay² n **keep at ~** tenere a bada

bay³ n Bot alloro m. **~-leaf** n foglia f d'alloro

bayonet /'beɪənɪt/ n baionetta f

bay 'window n bay window f inv (grande finestra sporgente)

bazaar /bə'zɑː(r)/ n bazar m inv

BC abbr (before Christ) a.C.

be /biː/ vi (pres am, are, is, are; pt was, were; pp been) essere; **he is a teacher** è insegnante, fa l'insegnante; **what do you want to be?** cosa vuoi fare?; **be quiet!** sta' zitto!; **I am cold/hot** ho freddo/caldo; **it's cold/hot, isn't it?** fa freddo/caldo, vero?; **how are you?** come stai?; **I am well** sto bene; **there is** c'è; **there are** ci sono; **I have been to** Venice sono stato a

Venezia; **has the postman been?** è passato il postino?; **you're coming too, aren't you?** vieni anche tu, no?; **it's yours, is it?** è tuo, vero?; **was John there? - yes, he was** c'era John? - sì; **John wasn't there - yes he was!** John non c'era - sì che c'era!; **three and three are six** tre più tre fanno sei; **he is five** ha cinque anni; **that will be £10, please** fanno 10 sterline, per favore; **how much is it?** quanto costa?; **that's £5 you owe me** mi devi 5 sterline ● *v aux* **I am coming/reading** sto venendo/leggendo; **I'm staying** (*not leaving*) resto; **I am being lazy** sono pigro; **I was thinking of you** stavo pensando a te; **you are not to tell him** non devi dirglielo; **you are to do that immediately** devi farlo subito ● *passive* essere; **I have been robbed** sono stato derubato

beach /biːtʃ/ *n* spiaggia *f*. **~wear** *n* abbigliamento *m* da spiaggia

bead /biːd/ *n* perlina *f*

beak /biːk/ *n* becco *m*

beaker /'biːkə(r)/ *n* coppa *f*

beam /biːm/ *n* trave *f*; (*of light*) raggio *m* ● *vi* irradiare; (*person:*) essere raggiante. **~ing** *a* raggiante

bean /biːn/ *n* fagiolo *m*; (*of coffee*) chicco *m*

bear¹ /beə(r)/ *n* orso *m*

bear² *v* (*pt* bore, *pp* borne) ● *vt* (*endure*) sopportare; mettere al mondo (*child*); (*carry*) portare; **~ in mind** tenere presente ● *vi* **~ left/right** andare a sinistra/a destra. **bear with** *vt* aver pazienza con. **~able** /-əbl/ *a* sopportabile

beard /biəd/ *n* barba *f*. **~ed** *a* barbuto

bearer /'beərə(r)/ *n* portatore, -trice *mf*; (*of passport*) titolare *mf*

bearing /'beərɪŋ/ *n* portamento *m*; Techn cuscinetto *m* [a sfera]; **have a ~ on** avere attinenza con; **get one's ~s** orientarsi

beast /biːst/ *n* bestia *f*; (*fam: person*) animale *m*

beat /biːt/ *n* battito *m*; (*rhythm*) battuta *f*; (*of policeman*) giro *m* d'ispezione ● *v* (*pt* beat, *pp* beaten) *vt* battere; picchiare (*person*); **~ it!** *fam* darsela a gambe!; **it ~s me why...** *fam* non capisco proprio perché... **beat up** *vt* picchiare

beat|en /'biːtn/ *a* **off the ~en track** fuori mano. **~ing** *n* bastonata *f*; **get a ~ing** (*with fists*) essere preso a pugni; (*team, player:*) prendere una batosta

beautician /bjuː'tɪʃn/ *n* estetista *mf*

beauti|ful /'bjuːtɪfl/ *a* bello. **~fully** *adv* splendidamente

beauty /'bjuːtɪ/ *n* bellezza *f*. **~ parlour** *n* istituto *m* di bellezza. **~ spot** *n* neo *m*; (*place*) luogo *m* pittoresco

beaver /'biːvə(r)/ *n* castoro *m*

became /bɪ'keɪm/ *see* **become**

because /bɪ'kɒz/ *conj* perché; **you didn't tell me, I...** poiché non me lo hai detto,... ● *adv* **~ of** a causa di

beck /bek/ *n* **at the ~ and call of** a completa disposizione di

beckon /'bekn/ *vt/i* **[to]** chiamare con un cenno

become /bɪ'kʌm/ *v* (*pt* became, *pp* become) ● *vt* diventare ● *vi* diventare; **what has ~ of her?** che ne è di lei? **~ing** *a* (*clothes*) bello

bed /bed/ *n* letto *m*; (*of sea, lake*) fondo *m*; (*layer*) strato *m*; (*of flowers*) aiuola *f*; **in ~** a letto; **go to ~** andare a letto; **~ and breakfast** pensione *f* familiare in cui il prezzo della camera comprende la prima colazione. **~clothes** *npl* lenzuola *fpl* e coperte *fpl*. **~ding** *n* biancheria *f* per il letto, materasso e guanciali

bedlam /'bedləm/ *n* baraonda *f*

bedraggled /bɪ'dræɡld/ *a* inzaccherato

bedridden | belt

bed: ~ridden *a* costretto a letto.
~room *n* camera *f* da letto
'**bedside** *n* at his ~ al suo capezzale. ~ '**lamp** *n* abat-jour *m inv*. ~
'**table** *n* comodino *m*

bed: ~'sit *n*, ~'sitter *n*,
~-'sitting-room *n* = camera *f* ammobiliata fornita di cucina.
~spread *n* copriletto *m*. ~time *n*
l'ora *f* di andare a letto

bee /biː/ *n* ape *f*

beech /biːtʃ/ *n* faggio *m*

beef /biːf/ *n* manzo *m*. ~burger *n*
hamburger *m inv*

bee: ~hive *n* alveare *m*. ~-line *n*
make a ~line for *fam* precipitarsi
verso

been /biːn/ *see* **be**

beer /bɪə(r)/ *n* birra *f*

beetle /'biːtl/ *n* scarafaggio *m*

beetroot /'biːtruːt/ *n* barbabietola *f*

before /bɪ'fɔː(r)/ *prep* prima di; the
day ~ yesterday ieri l'altro; the
long fra poco ● *adv* prima; never
~ have I seen... non ho mai visto
prima...; ~ that prima; ~ going
prima di andare ● *conj* (*time*) prima; che; ~ you go prima che tu
vada. ~hand *adv* in anticipo

befriend /bɪ'frend/ *vt* trattare da
amico

beg /beg/ *v* (*pt/pp* begged) ● *vi*
mendicare ● *vt* pregare; chiedere
(*favour, forgiveness*)

began /bɪ'gæn/ *see* **begin**

beggar /'begə(r)/ *n* mendicante *mf*;
poor ~! povero cristo!

begin /bɪ'gɪn/ *vt/i* (*pt* began, *pp*
begun, *pres p* beginning) cominciare. ~ner *n* principiante *mf*.
~ning *n* principio *m*

begonia /bɪ'gəʊnɪə/ *n* begonia *f*

begrudge /bɪ'grʌdʒ/ *vt* (*envy*) essere invidioso di; dare malvolentieri
(*money*)

begun /bɪ'gʌn/ *see* **begin**

behalf /bɪ'hɑːf/ *n* on ~ of a nome
di; on my ~ a nome mio

behave /bɪ'heɪv/ *vi* comportarsi; ~
[oneself] comportarsi bene

behaviour /bɪ'heɪvjə(r)/ *n* comportamento *m*; (*of prisoner, soldier*)
condotta *f*

behead /bɪ'hed/ *vt* decapitare

behind /bɪ'haɪnd/ *prep* dietro; be
~ sth *fig* stare dietro qcsa ● *adv*
dietro, indietro; (*late*) in ritardo; a
long way ~ molto indietro ● *n*
fam didietro *m*. ~hand *adv* indietro

beholden /bɪ'həʊldn/ *a* obbligato
(to *verso*)

beige /beɪʒ/ *a & n* beige *m inv*

being /'biːɪŋ/ *n* essere *m*; come
into ~ nascere

belated /bɪ'leɪtɪd/ *a* tardivo

belch /beltʃ/ *vi* ruttare ● *vt* ~
[out] eruttare (*smoke*)

belfry /'belfrɪ/ *n* campanile *m*

Belgian /'beldʒən/ *a & n* belga *mf*

Belgium /'beldʒəm/ *n* Belgio *m*

belief /bɪ'liːf/ *n* fede *f*; (*opinion*)
convinzione *f*

believable /bɪ'liːvəbl/ *a* credibile

believe /bɪ'liːv/ *vt/i* credere. ~r *n*
Relig credente *mf*; be a great ~r
in credere fermamente in

belittle /bɪ'lɪtl/ *vt* sminuire
(*person, achievements*)

bell /bel/ *n* campana *f*; (*on door*)
campanello *m*

belligerent /bɪ'lɪdʒərənt/ *a* belligerante; (*aggressive*) bellicoso

bellow /'beləʊ/ *vi* gridare a squarciagola; (*animal:*) muggire

bellows /'beləʊz/ *npl* (*for fire*)
soffietto *msg*

belly /'belɪ/ *n* pancia *f*

belong /bɪ'lɒŋ/ *vi* appartenere (to
a); (*be member*) essere socio (to
di). ~ings *npl* cose *fpl*

beloved /bɪ'lʌvɪd/ *a & n* amato, -a
mf

below /bɪ'ləʊ/ *prep* sotto; (*with
numbers*) al di sotto di ● *adv* sotto,
di sotto; *Naut* sotto coperta; see ~
guardare qui di seguito

belt /belt/ *n* cintura *f*; (*area*) zona *f*;
Techn cinghia *f* ● *vi* ~ along
(*fam: rush*) filare velocemente
● *vt* (*fam: hit*) picchiare

bemused /bɪ'mju:zd/ *a* confuso

bench /bentʃ/ *n* panchina *f*; (*work*~) piano *m* da lavoro; **the B~** *Jur* la magistratura

bend /bend/ *n* curva *f*; (*of river*) ansa *f* ● *v* (*pt/pp* **bent**) ● *vt* piegare ● *vi* piegarsi; (*road:*) curvare; ~ **[down]** chinarsi. **bend over** *vi* inchinarsi

beneath /bɪ'ni:θ/ *prep* sotto, al di sotto di; **he thinks it's ~ him** *fig* pensa che sia sotto al suo livello ● *adv* giù

benediction /benɪ'dɪkʃn/ *n* *Relig* benedizione *f*

benefactor /'benɪfæktə(r)/ *n* benefattore, -trice *mf*

beneficial /benɪ'fɪʃl/ *a* benefico

beneficiary /benɪ'fɪʃərɪ/ *n* beneficiario, -a *mf*

benefit /'benɪfɪt/ *n* vantaggio *m*; (*allowance*) indennità *f inv* ● *v* (*pt/pp* **-fited**, *pres p* **-fiting**) ● *vt* giovare a ● *vi* trarre vantaggio (**from** da)

benevolen|ce /bɪ'nevələns/ *n* benevolenza *f*. ~**t** *a* benevolo

benign /bɪ'nam/ *a* benevolo; *Med* benigno

bent /bent/ *see* **bend** ● *a* (*person*) ricurvo; (*distorted*) curvato; (*fam: dishonest*) corrotto; **be ~ on doing sth** essere ben deciso a fare qcsa ● *n* predisposizione *f*

be|queath /bɪ'kwi:ð/ *vt* lasciare in eredità. ~**quest** /-'kwest/ *n* lascito *m*

bereave|d /bɪ'ri:vd/ *n* **the ~d** *pl* i familiari del defunto. ~**ment** *n* lutto *m*

bereft /bɪ'reft/ *a* ~ **of** privo di

beret /'bereɪ/ *n* berretto *m*

berry /'berɪ/ *n* bacca *f*

berserk /bə'sɜ:k/ *a* **go ~** diventare una belva

berth /bɜ:θ/ *n* (*bed*) cuccetta *f*; (*anchorage*) ormeggio *m* ● *vi* ormeggiare

beseech /bɪ'si:tʃ/ *vt* (*pt/pp* **beseeched** *or* **besought**) supplicare

beside /bɪ'saɪd/ *prep* accanto a; ~ **oneself** fuori di sé

besides /bɪ'saɪdz/ *prep* oltre a ● *adv* inoltre

besiege /bɪ'si:dʒ/ *vt* assediare

besought /bɪ'sɔ:t/ *see* **beseech**

best /best/ *a* migliore; **the ~ part of a year** la maggior parte dell'anno; ~ **before** *Comm* preferibilmente prima di ● *n* **the ~** il meglio; (*person*) il/la migliore *mf*; **at ~** tutt'al più; **all the ~!** tanti auguri!; **do one's ~** fare del proprio meglio; **to the ~ of my knowledge** per quel che ne so; **make the ~ of it** cogliere il lato buono della cosa ● *adv* meglio; nel modo migliore; **as ~ I could** meglio che potevo. ~ **'man** *n* testimone *m*

bestow /bɪ'stəʊ/ *vt* conferire (**on** a)

best'seller *n* bestseller *m inv*

bet /bet/ *n* scommessa *f* ● *vt/i* (*pt/pp* **bet** *or* **betted**) scommettere

betray /bɪ'treɪ/ *vt* tradire. ~**al** *n* tradimento *m*

better /'betə(r)/ *a* migliore; meglio; **get ~** migliorare; (*after illness*) rimettersi ● *adv* meglio; ~ **off** meglio; (*wealthier*) più ricco; **all the ~** tanto meglio; **the sooner the ~** prima è, meglio è; **I've thought ~ of it** ci ho ripensato; **you'd ~ stay** faresti meglio a restare; **I'd ~ not** è meglio che non lo faccia ● *vt* migliorare; ~ **oneself** migliorare le proprie condizioni

'betting shop *n* ricevitoria *f* (*dell'allibratore*)

between /bɪ'twi:n/ *prep* fra, tra; ~ **you and me** detto fra di noi; ~ **us** (*together*) tra me e te ● *adv* **[in]** ~ in mezzo; (*time*) frattempo

beverage /'bevərɪdʒ/ *n* bevanda *f*

beware /bɪ'weə(r)/ *vi* guardarsi (**of** da); ~ **of the dog!** attenti al cane!

bewilder /bɪ'wɪldə(r)/ *vt* disorientare; ~**ed** perplesso. ~**ment** *n* perplessità *f*

beyond /bɪ'jɒnd/ *prep* oltre; ~

reach irraggiungibile; **~ doubt** senza alcun dubbio; **~ belief** da non credere; **it's ~ me** *fam* non riesco proprio a capire ● *adv* più in là

bias /'baɪəs/ *n* (preference) preferenza *f*; *pej* pregiudizio *m* ● *vt* (*pt/pp* biased) (influence) influenzare. **~ed** *a* parziale

bib /bɪb/ *n* bavaglino *m*

Bible /'baɪbl/ *n* Bibbia *f*

biblical /'bɪblɪkl/ *a* biblico

bicarbonate /baɪ'kɑ:bənɪt/ *n* **~ of soda** bicarbonato *m* di sodio

biceps /'baɪseps/ *n* bicipite *m*

bicker /'bɪkə(r)/ *vi* litigare

bicycle /'baɪsɪkl/ *n* bicicletta *f* ● *vi* andare in bicicletta

bid[1] /bɪd/ *n* offerta *f*; (attempt) tentativo *m* ● *vt/i* (*pt/pp* bid, *pres p* bidding) offrire; (in cards) dichiarare

bid[2] *vt* (*pt* bade *or* bid, *pp* bidden *or* bid, *pres p* bidding) liter (command) comandare; **~ sb welcome** dare il benvenuto a qcno

bidder /'bɪdə(r)/ *n* offerente *mf*

bide /baɪd/ *vt* **~ one's time** aspettare il momento buono

biennial /baɪ'enɪəl/ *a* biennale

bifocals /baɪ'fəʊklz/ *npl* occhiali *mpl* bifocali

big /bɪg/ *a* (**bigger, biggest**) grande; (brother, sister) più grande; (fam: generous) generoso ● *adv* **talk ~** *fam* sparare grosso

bigam|ist /'bɪgəmɪst/ *n* bigamo, -a *mf*. **~y** *n* bigamia *f*

'big-head *n fam* gasato, -a *mf*

big-'headed *a fam* gasato

bigot /'bɪgət/ *n* fanatico, -a *mf*. **~ed** *a* di mentalità ristretta

'bigwig *n fam* pezzo *m* grosso

bike /baɪk/ *n fam* bici *f inv*

bikini /bɪ'ki:nɪ/ *n* bikini *m inv*

bile /baɪl/ *n* bile *f*

bilingual /baɪ'lɪŋgwəl/ *a* bilingue

bill[1] /bɪl/ *n* fattura *f*; (in restaurant etc) conto *m*; (poster) manifesto *m*; Pol progetto *m* di legge; (Am: note) biglietto *m* di banca ● *vt* fatturare

bill[2] *n* (beak) becco *m*

'billfold *n Am* portafoglio *m*

billiards /'bɪljədz/ *n* biliardo *m*

billion /'bɪljən/ *n* (thousand million) miliardo *m*; (old-fashioned Br: million million) mille miliardi *mpl*

billy-goat /'bɪlɪ-/ *n* caprone *m*

bin /bɪn/ *n* bidone *m*

bind /baɪnd/ *vt* (*pt/pp* bound) legare (to a); (bandage) fasciare; Jur obbligare. **~ing** *a* (promise, contract) vincolante ● *n* (of book) rilegatura *f*; (on ski) attacco *m* [di sicurezza]

binge /bɪndʒ/ *n fam* **have a ~** fare baldoria; (eat a lot) abbuffarsi ● *vi* abbuffarsi (on di)

binoculars /bɪ'nɒkjʊləz/ *npl* [**pair of**] ~ binocolo *msg*

bio'**chemist** /baɪəʊ-/ *n* biochimico, -a *mf*. **~ry** *n* biochimica *f*

biodegradable /-dɪ'greɪdəbl/ *a* biodegradabile

biograph|er /baɪ'ɒgrəfə(r)/ *n* biografo, -a *mf*. **~y** *n* biografia *f*

biological /baɪə'lɒdʒɪkl/ *a* biologico

biolog|ist /baɪ'ɒlədʒɪst/ *n* biologo, -a *mf*. **~y** *n* biologia *f*

birch /bɜ:tʃ/ *n* (tree) betulla *f*

bird /bɜ:d/ *n* uccello *m*; (fam: girl) ragazza *f*

Biro® /'baɪrəʊ/ *n* biro *f inv*

birth /bɜ:θ/ *n* nascita *f*

birth: ~ certificate *n* certificato *m* di nascita. **~-control** *n* controllo *m* delle nascite. **~day** *n* compleanno *m*. **~mark** *n* voglia *f*. **~-rate** *n* natalità *f*

biscuit /'bɪskɪt/ *n* biscotto *m*

bisect /baɪ'sekt/ *vt* dividere in due [parti]

bishop /'bɪʃəp/ *n* vescovo *m*; (in chess) alfiere *m*

bit[1] /bɪt/ *n* pezzo *m*; (smaller) pezzetto *m*; (for horse) morso *m*; Comput bit *m inv*; **a ~ of** pezzo di (cheese, paper); un po' di (time, rain, silence); **~ by ~** poco a poco, **do one's ~** fare la propria parte

bit² *see* bite

bitch /bɪtʃ/ *n* cagna *f*; *sl* stronza *f*. **~y** *a* velenoso

bit|e /baɪt/ *n* morso *m*; (*insect* ~) puntura *f*; (*mouthful*) boccone *m* ● *vt* (*pt* **bit**, *pp* **bitten**) mordere; (*insect:*) pungere; **~e one's nails** mangiarsi le unghie ● *vi* mordere; (*insect:*) pungere. **~ing** *a* (*wind, criticism*) pungente; (*remark*) mordace

bitter /'bɪtə(r)/ *a* amaro ● *n Br* birra *f* amara. **~ly** *adv* amaramente; **it's ~ly cold** c'è un freddo pungente. **~ness** *n* amarezza *f*

bitty /'bɪtɪ/ *a Br fam* frammentario

bizarre /bɪ'zɑ:(r)/ *a* bizzarro

blab /blæb/ *vi* (*pt/pp* **blabbed**) spifferare

black /blæk/ *a* nero; **be ~ and blue** essere pieno di lividi ● *n* negro, -a *mf* ● *vt* boicottare (*goods*). **black out** *vt* cancellare ● *vi* (*lose consciousness*) perdere coscienza

black: **~berry** *n* mora *f*. **~bird** *n* merlo *m*. **~board** *n Sch* lavagna *f*. **~'currant** *n* ribes *m* inv nero; **~'eye** *n* occhio *m* nero. **~'ice** *n* ghiaccio *m* (*sulla strada*). **~leg** *n Br* crumiro *m*. **~list** *vt* mettere sulla lista nera. **~mail** *n* ricatto *m* ● *vt* ricattare. **~mailer** *n* ricattatore, -trice *mf*. **~'market** *n* mercato *m* nero. **~out** *n* blackout *m* inv; **have a ~out** *Med* perdere coscienza. **~smith** *n* fabbro *m*

bladder /'blædə(r)/ *n Anat* vescica *f*

blade /bleɪd/ *n* lama *f*; (*of grass*) filo *m*

blame /bleɪm/ *n* colpa *f* ● *vt* dare la colpa a; **~ sb for doing sth** dare la colpa a qcno per aver fatto qcsa; **no one is to ~** non è colpa di nessuno. **~less** *a* innocente

blanch /blɑ:ntʃ/ *vi* sbiancare ● *vt Culin* sbollentare

blancmange /blə'mɒnʒ/ *n* biancomangiare *m* inv

bland /blænd/ *a* (*food*) insipido; (*person*) insulso

blank /blæŋk/ *a* bianco; (*look*) vuoto ● *n* spazio *m* vuoto; (*cartridge*) a salve. **~ 'cheque** *n* assegno *m* in bianco

blanket /'blæŋkɪt/ *n* coperta *f*

blank 'verse *n* versi *mpl* sciolti

blare /bleə(r)/ *vi* suonare a tutto volume. **blare out** *vt* far risuonare ● *vi* (*music, radio:*) strillare

blasé /bla:zeɪ/ *a* vissuto, blasé *inv*

blaspheme /blæs'fi:m/ *vi* bestemmiare

blasphem|ous /'blæsfəməs/ *a* blasfemo. **~y** *n* bestemmia *f*

blast /bla:st/ *n* (*gust*) raffica *f*; (*sound*) scoppio *m* ● *vt* (*with explosive*) far saltare ● *int sl* maledizione!. **~ed** *a sl* maledetto

blast: **~furnace** *n* altoforno *m*. **~off** *n* (*of missile*) lancio *m*

blatant /'bleɪtənt/ *a* sfacciato

blaze /bleɪz/ *n* incendio *m*; **a ~ of colour** un'esplosione *f* di colori ● *vi* ardere

blazer /'bleɪzə(r)/ *n* blazer *m* inv

bleach /bli:tʃ/ *n* decolorante *m*; (*for cleaning*) candeggina *f* ● *vt* sbiancare; (*hair*) ossigenare

bleak /bli:k/ *a* desolato; (*fig: prospects, future*) tetro

bleary-eyed /'blɪərɪaɪd/ *a* **look ~** avere gli occhi assonnati

bleat /bli:t/ *vi* belare ● *n* belato *m*

bleed /bli:d/ *v* (*pt/pp* **bled**) ● *vi* sanguinare ● *vt* spurgare (*brakes, radiator*)

bleep /bli:p/ *n* bip *m* ● *vi* suonare ● *vt* chiamare (*col cercapersone*) (*doctor*). **~er** *n* cercapersone *m* inv

blemish /'blemɪʃ/ *n* macchia *f*

blend /blend/ *n* (*of tea, coffee, whisky*) miscela *f*; (*of colours*) insieme *m* ● *vt* mescolare ● *vi* (*colours, sounds:*) fondersi (*with* con). **~er** *n Culin* frullatore *m*

bless /bles/ *vt* benedire. **~ed** /'blesɪd/ *a also sl* benedetto. **~ing** *n* benedizione *f*

blew /blu:/ *see* **blow²**

blight /blaɪt/ *n Bot* ruggine *f* ● *vt* far avvizzire ⟨*plants*⟩

blind¹ /blaɪnd/ *a* cieco; **the ~** *npl* i ciechi *mpl*; **~ man/woman** cieco/cieca ● *vt* accecare

blind² *n* [roller] **~** avvolgibile *m*; [**Venetian**] **~** veneziana *f*

blind: **~ 'alley** *n* vicolo *m* cieco. **~fold** *a* be **~fold** avere gli occhi bendati ● *n* benda *f* ● *vt* bendare gli occhi a. **~ly** *adv* ciecamente. **~ness** *n* cecità *f*

blink /blɪŋk/ *vi* sbattere le palpebre; ⟨*light:*⟩ tremolare

blinkered /'blɪŋkəd/ *adj fig* be **~** avere i paraocchi

blinkers /'blɪŋkəz/ *npl* paraocchi *mpl*

bliss /blɪs/ *n Rel* beatitudine *f*; ⟨*happiness*⟩ felicità *f*. **~ful** *a* beato; ⟨*happy*⟩ meraviglioso

blister /'blɪstə(r)/ *n Med* vescica *f*; ⟨*in paint*⟩ bolla *f* ● *vi* ⟨*paint:*⟩ formare una bolla/delle bolle

blitz /blɪts/ *n* bombardamento *m* aereo; **have a ~ on sth** *fig* darci sotto con qcsa

blizzard /'blɪzəd/ *n* tormenta *f*

bloated /'bləʊtɪd/ *a* gonfio

blob /blɒb/ *n* goccia *f*

bloc /blɒk/ *n Pol* blocco *m*

block /blɒk/ *n* blocco *m*; ⟨*building*⟩ isolato *m*; ⟨*building ~*⟩ cubo *m* ⟨*or*⟩ ⟨*of blocks of construction*⟩; **~ of flats** palazzo *m* ● *vt* bloccare **block up** *vt* bloccare

blockade /blɒˈkeɪd/ *n* blocco *m* ● *vt* bloccare

blockage /'blɒkɪdʒ/ *n* ostruzione *f*

block: **~head** *n* fam testa *f* di mf. **~ 'letters** *npl* stampatello *m*

bloke /bləʊk/ *n fam* tizio *m*

blonde /blɒnd/ *a* biondo ● *n* bionda *f*

blood /blʌd/ *n* sangue *m*

blood: **~ bath** *n* bagno *m* di sangue. **~ count** *n* esame *m* emocromocitometrico. **~ donor** *n* donatore *m* di sangue. **~ group** *n* gruppo *m* sanguigno. **~hound** *n* segugio *m*. **~poisoning** *n* setti-

cemia *f*. **~ pressure** *n* pressione *f* del sangue. **~shed** *n* spargimento *m* di sangue. **~shot** *a* iniettato di sangue. **~ sports** *npl* sport *mpl* cruenti. **~stained** *a* macchiato di sangue. **~stream** *n* sangue *m*. **~ test** *n* analisi *f* del sangue. **~thirsty** *a* assetato di sangue. **~ transfusion** *n* trasfusione *f* del sangue

bloody /'blʌdɪ/ *a* (**-ier**, **-iest**) insanguinato; *sl* maledetto ● *adv sl* **~ easy/difficult** facile/difficile da matti. **~-'minded** *a* scorbutico

bloom /bluːm/ *n* fiore *m*; **in ~** ⟨*flower:*⟩ sbocciato; ⟨*tree:*⟩ in fiore ● *vi* fiorire; *fig* essere in forma smagliante

bloomer /'bluːmə(r)/ *n fam* papera *f*. **~ing** *a fam* maledetto. **~ers** *npl* mutandoni *mpl* (*da donna*)

blossom /'blɒsəm/ *n* fiori *mpl* (*d'albero*); ⟨*single one*⟩ fiore *m* ● *vi* sbocciare

blot /blɒt/ *n* also *fig* macchia *f* ● **blot out** *vt* (*pt/pp* **blotted**) *fig* cancellare

blotch /blɒtʃ/ *n* macchia *f*. **~y** *a* chiazzato

'blotting-paper *n* carta *f* assorbente

blouse /blaʊz/ *n* camicetta *f*

blow¹ /bləʊ/ *n* colpo *m*

blow² *v* (*pt* **blew**, *pp* **blown**) ● *vi* ⟨*wind:*⟩ soffiare; ⟨*fuse:*⟩ saltare ● *vt* ⟨*fam: squander*⟩ sperperare; **~ one's nose** soffiarsi il naso.

blow away *vt* far volar via ⟨*papers*⟩ ● *vi* ⟨*papers:*⟩ volare via.

blow down *vt* abbattere ● *vi* abbattersi al suolo. **blow out** *vt* ⟨*extinguish*⟩ spegnere. **blow over** *vi* ⟨*storm:*⟩ passare; ⟨*fuss, trouble:*⟩ dissiparsi. **blow up** *vt* ⟨*inflate*⟩ gonfiare; ⟨*enlarge*⟩ ingrandire ⟨*photograph*⟩; ⟨*by explosion*⟩ far esplodere ● *vi* esplodere

blow: **~-dry** *vt* asciugare col fon. **~lamp** *n* fiamma *f* ossidrica

blown /bləʊn/ *see* **blow²**

blowtorch *n* fiamma *f* ossidrica

blowy /'bləʊɪ/ *a* ventoso

blue /bluː/ *a* (*pale*) celeste; (*navy*) blu *inv*; (*royal*) azzurro; **~ with cold** livido per il freddo ●*n* blu *m inv*; **have the ~s** essere giù [di tono]; **out of the ~** inaspettatamente

blue: **~bell** *n* giacinto *m* di bosco. **~berry** *n* mirtillo *m*. **~bottle** *n* moscone *m*. **~film** *n* film *m inv* a luci rosse. **~print** *n fig* riferimento *m*

bluff /blʌf/ *n* bluff *m inv* ●*vi* bluffare

blunder /'blʌndə(r)/ *n* gaffe *f inv* ●*vi* fare una/delle gaffe

blunt /blʌnt/ *a* spuntato; (*person*) reciso. **~ly** *adv* schiettamente

blur /blɜː/ *n* **it's all a ~** *fig* è tutto un insieme confuso ●*vt* (*pt/pp* **blurred**) rendere confuso. **~red** *a* (*vision, photo*) sfocato

blurb /blɜːb/ *n* soffietto *m* editoriale

blurt /blɜːt/ *vt* **~ out** spifferare

blush /blʌʃ/ *n* rossore *m* ●*vi* arrossire

blusher /'blʌʃə(r)/ *n* fard *m*

bluster /'blʌstə(r)/ *n* sbruffonata *f*. **~y** *a* (*wind*) furioso; (*day, weather*) molto ventoso

boar /bɔː(r)/ *n* cinghiale *m*

board /bɔːd/ *n* tavola *f*; (*for notices*) tabellone *m*; (*committee*) assemblea *f*; (*of directors*) consiglio *m*; **full ~** *Br* pensione *f* completa; **half ~** *Br* mezza pensione *f*; **~ and lodging** vitto e alloggio *m*; **go by the ~** *fam* andare a monte ●*vt Naut, Aviat* salire a bordo di ●*vi* (*passengers:*) salire a bordo. **board up** *vt* sbarrare con delle assi. **board with** *vt* stare a pensione da.

boarder /'bɔːdə(r)/ *n* pensionante *mf*; *Sch* convittore, -trice *mf*

board: **~-game** *n* gioco *m* da tavolo. **~ing-house** *n* pensione *f*. **~ing-school** *n* collegio *m*

boast /bəʊst/ *vi* vantarsi (**about** di). **~ful** *a* vanaglorioso

boat /bəʊt/ *n* barca *f*; (*ship*) nave *f*. **~er** *n* (*hat*) paglietta *f*

bob /bɒb/ *n* (*hairstyle*) caschetto *m* ●*vi* (*pt/pp* **bobbed**) (*also* **~ up and down**) andare su e giù

'bob-sleigh *n* bob *m*

bode /bəʊd/ *vi* **~ well/ill** essere di buono/cattivo augurio

bodily /'bɒdɪlɪ/ *a* fisico ●*adv* (*forcibly*) fisicamente

body /'bɒdɪ/ *n* corpo *m*; (*organization*) ente *m*; (*amount: of poems etc*) quantità *f*. **~guard** *n* guardia *f* del corpo. **~work** *n Auto* carrozzeria *f*

bog /bɒg/ *n* palude *f* ●*vt* (*pt/pp* **bogged**) **get ~ged down** impantanarsi

boggle /'bɒgl/ *vi* **the mind ~s** non posso neanche immaginarlo

bogus /'bəʊgəs/ *a* falso

boil[1] /bɔɪl/ *n Med* foruncolo *m*

boil[2] *n* **bring/come to the ~** portare/arrivare ad ebollizione ●*vt* [far] bollire ●*vi* bollire; (*fig: with anger*) ribollire; **the water** *or* **kettle's ~ing** l'acqua bolle. **boil down to** *vt fig* ridursi a. **boil over** *vi* straboccare (*bollendo*). **boil up** *vt* far bollire

boiler /'bɔɪlə(r)/ *n* caldaia *f*. **~suit** *n* tuta *f*

'boiling point *n* punto *m* di ebollizione

boisterous /'bɔɪstərəs/ *a* chiassoso

bold /bəʊld/ *a* audace ●*n Typ* neretto *m*. **~ness** *n* audacia *f*

bollard /'bɒləd/ *n* colonnina *f* di sbarramento al traffico

bolster /'bəʊlstə(r)/ *n* cuscino *m* (*lungo e rotondo*) ●*vt* **~ [up]** sostenere

bolt /bəʊlt/ *n* (*for door*) catenaccio *m*; (*for fixing*) bullone *m* ●*vt* fissare (*con i bulloni*) (**to** a); chiudere col chiavistello (*door*); ingurgitare (*food*) ●*vi* svignarsela; (*horse:*) scappar via ●*adv* **~ upright** diritto come un fuso

bomb /bɒm/ n bomba f ● vt bombardare

bombard /bɒm'bɑːd/ vt also fig bombardare

bombastic /bɒm'bæstɪk/ a ampolloso

bomb|er /'bɒmə(r)/ n Aviat bombardiere m; (person) dinamitardo m. **~er jacket** giubbotto m, bomber m inv. **~shell** n (fig: news) bomba f

bond /bɒnd/ n fig legame m; Comm obbligazione f ● vt (glue:) attaccare

bondage /'bɒndɪdʒ/ n schiavitù f

bone /bəʊn/ n osso m; (of fish) spina f ● vt disossare (meat); togliere le spine da (fish). **~'dry** a secco

bonfire /'bɒn-/ n falò m inv. **~ night** festa celebrata la notte del 5 novembre con fuochi d'artificio e falò

bonnet /'bɒnɪt/ n cuffia f; (of car) cofano m

bonus /'bəʊnəs/ n (individual) gratifica f; (production ~) premio m; (life insurance) dividendo m; **a ~** fig qualcosa in più

bony /'bəʊnɪ/ a (-ier, -iest) ossuto; (fish) pieno di spine

boo /buː/ interj to surprise or frighten/ hu! vt/i fischiare

boob /buːb/ n (fam: mistake) gaffe f inv; (breast) tetta f ● vi fam fare una gaffe

book /bʊk/ n libro m; (of tickets) blocchetto m; **keep the ~s** Comm tenere la contabilità; **be in s.o.'s bad/good ~s** essere nel libro nero/nelle grazie di qcno ● vt (reserve) prenotare; (for offence) multare ● vi (reserve) prenotare

book: ~case n libreria f. **~-ends** npl reggilibri mpl. **~ing-office** n biglietteria f. **~keeping** n contabilità f. **~let** n opuscolo m. **~maker** n allibratore m. **~mark** n segnalibro m. **~seller** n libraio, -a mf. **~shop** n libreria f. **~worm** n topo m di biblioteca

boom /buːm/ n Comm boom m inv;

(upturn) impennata f; (of thunder, gun) rimbombo m ● vi (thunder, gun:) rimbombare; fig prosperare

boon /buːn/ n benedizione f

boor /bʊə(r)/ n zoticone m. **~ish** a maleducato

boost /buːst/ n spinta f ● vt stimolare (sales); sollevare (morale); far crescere (hopes). **~er** n Med dose f supplementare

boot /buːt/ n stivale m; (up to ankle) stivaletto m; (football) scarpetta f; (climbing) scarpone m; Auto portabagagli m inv ● vt Comput inizializzare

booth /buːð/ n (Teleph, voting) cabina f; (at market) bancarella f

'boot-up n Comput boot m inv

booty /'buːtɪ/ n bottino m

booze /buːz/ fam n alcolici mpl. **~-up** n bella bevuta f

border /'bɔːdə(r)/ n bordo m; (frontier) frontiera f; (in garden) bordura f ● vi. **~ on** confinare con; fig essere ai confini di (madness). **~line** n linea f di demarcazione; **~line case** caso m dubbio

bore[1] /bɔː(r)/ see **bear**[2]

bore[2] vt Techn forare

bore[3] n (of gun) calibro m; (person) seccatore, -trice mf; (thing) seccatura f ● vt annoiare. **~dom** n noia f. **be ~ed** (to tears or to death) annoiarsi (da morire). **~ing** a noioso

born /bɔːn/ pp **be ~** nascere; **I was ~ in 1966** sono nato nel 1966 ● a nato; **a ~ liar/actor** un bugiardo/attore nato

borne /bɔːn/ see **bear**[2]

borough /'bʌrə/ n municipalità f inv

borrow /'bɒrəʊ/ vt prendere a prestito (from da); **can I ~ your pen?** mi presti la tua penna?

bosom /'bʊzm/ n seno m

boss /bɒs/ n direttore, -trice mf ● vt (also **~ about**) comandare a bacchetta. **~y** a autoritario

botanical /bə'tænɪkl/ a botanico

botan|ist /'bɒtənɪst/ n botanico, -a mf. **~y** n botanica f

botch /bɒtʃ/ vt fare un pasticcio con

both /bəʊθ/ adj & pron tutti e due, entrambi ● adv **~ men and women** entrambi uomini e donne; **~ [of] the children** tutti e due i bambini; **they are ~ dead** sono morti entrambi; **~ of them** tutti e due

bother /'bɒðə(r)/ n preoccupazione f; (minor trouble) fastidio m; **it's no ~** non c'è problema ● int fam che seccatura! ● vt (annoy) dare fastidio a; (disturb) disturbare ● vi preoccuparsi (about di); **don't ~** lascia perdere

bottle /'bɒtl/ n bottiglia f; (baby's) biberon m inv ● vt imbottigliare. **bottle up** vt fig reprimere

bottle: ~ bank n contenitore m per la raccolta del vetro. **~-neck** n fig ingorgo m. **~-opener** n apribottiglie m inv

bottom /'bɒtm/ a ultimo; **the ~ shelf** l'ultimo scaffale in basso ● n (of container) fondo m; (of river) fondale m; (of hill) piedi mpl; (buttocks) sedere m; **at the ~ of the page** in fondo alla pagina; **get to the ~ of** fig vedere cosa c'è sotto. **~less** a senza fondo

bough /baʊ/ n ramoscello m

bought /bɔ:t/ see **buy**

boulder /'bəʊldə(r)/ n masso m

bounce /baʊns/ vi rimbalzare; ⟨fam: cheque⟩ essere respinto ● vt far rimbalzare ⟨ball⟩

bouncer /'baʊnsə(r)/ n fam buttafuori m inv

bound¹ /baʊnd/ n balzo m ● vi balzare

bound² see **bind** ● a **~ for** ⟨ship⟩ diretto a; **be ~ to do** (likely) dovere fare per forza; (obliged) essere costretto a fare

boundary /'baʊndərɪ/ n limite m

'boundless a illimitato

bounds /baʊndz/ npl fig limiti mpl; **out of ~** fuori dai limiti

bouquet /bʊ'keɪ/ n mazzo m di fiori; (of wine) bouquet m

bourgeois /'bʊəʒwɑː/ a pej borghese

bout /baʊt/ n Med attacco m; Sport incontro m

bow¹ /bəʊ/ n (weapon) arco m; Mus archetto m; (knot) nodo m

bow² /baʊ/ n inchino m ● vi inchinarsi ● vt piegare ⟨head⟩

bow³ /baʊ/ n Naut prua f

bowel /'baʊəl/ n intestino m; **~s** pl intestini mpl

bowl¹ /bəʊl/ n (for soup, cereal) scodella f; (of pipe) fornello m

bowl² n (ball) boccia f ● vt lanciare ● vi Cricket servire; (in bowls) lanciare. **bowl over** vt buttar giù; (fig: leave speechless) lasciar senza parole

bow-legged /bəʊ'legd/ a dalle gambe storte

bowler¹ /'bəʊlə(r)/ n Cricket lanciatore m; Bowls giocatore m di bocce

bowler² n **~ [hat]** bombetta f

bowling /'bəʊlɪŋ/ n gioco m delle bocce. **~-alley** n pista f da bowling

bowls /bəʊlz/ n gioco m delle bocce

bow-tie /bəʊ-/ n cravatta f a farfalla

box¹ /bɒks/ n scatola f; Theat palco m

box² vi Sport fare il pugile ● vt **~ sb's ears** dare uno scappaccione a qcno

box|er /'bɒksə(r)/ n pugile m. **~ing** n pugilato m. **B~ing Day** n [giorno m di] Santo Stefano m

box: ~-office n Theat botteghino m. **~-room** n Br sgabuzzino m

boy /bɔɪ/ n ragazzo m; (younger) bambino m

boycott /'bɔɪkɒt/ n boicottaggio m ● vt boicottare

boy: ~friend n ragazzo m. **~ish** a da ragazzino

bra /brɑː/ n reggiseno m

brace /breɪs/ n sostegno m; (dental) apparecchio m; **~s** npl bretelle *fpl* ● *vt* ~ **oneself** *fig* farsi forza (**for** per affrontare)

bracelet /'breɪslɪt/ *n* braccialetto *m*

bracing /'breɪsɪŋ/ *a* tonificante

bracken /'brækn/ *n* felce *f*

bracket /'brækɪt/ *n* mensola *f*; (*group*) categoria *f*; *Typ* parentesi *f inv* ● *vt* mettere fra parentesi

brag /bræg/ *vi* (*pt/pp* **bragged**) vantarsi (**about** di)

braid /breɪd/ *n* (*edging*) passamano *m*

braille /breɪl/ *n* braille *m*

brain /breɪn/ *n* cervello *m*; **~s** *pl fig* testa *fsg*

brain: **~child** *n* invenzione *f* personale. **~ dead** *a Med* celebralmente morto; *fig* fam senza cervello. **~less** *a* senza cervello. **~wash** *vt* fare il lavaggio del cervello a. **~wave** *n* lampo *m* di genio

brainy /'breɪnɪ/ *a* (**-ier, -iest**) intelligente

braise /breɪz/ *vt* brasare

brake /breɪk/ *n* freno *m* ● *vi* frenare. **~light** *n* stop *m inv*

bramble /'bræmbl/ *n* rovo *m*; (*fruit*) mora *f*

bran /bræn/ *n* crusca *f*

branch /brɑːntʃ/ *n* also *fig* ramo *m*; *Comm* succursale *f* ● *vi* (*road*) biforcarsi. **branch off** *vi* biforcarsi. **branch out** *vi* ~ **out into** allargare le proprie attività nel ramo di

brand /brænd/ *n* marca *f* (*on animal*) marchio *m* ● *vt* marcare (*animal*), *fig* tacciare (**as** di)

brandish /'brændɪʃ/ *vt* brandire

brand-new *a* nuovo fiammante

brandy /'brændɪ/ *n* brandy *m inv*

brash /bræʃ/ *a* sfrontato

brass /brɑːs/ *n* ottone *m*, **the ~** *Mus* gli ottoni *mpl*; **top ~** *fam* pezzi *mpl* grossi. **~ band** *n* banda *f* (*di soli ottoni*)

brassiere /'bræzɪə(r)/ *n fml, Am* reggipetto *m*

brat /bræt/ *n pej* marmocchio, -a *mf*

bravado /brə'vɑːdəʊ/ *n* bravata *f*

brave /breɪv/ *a* coraggioso ● *vt* affrontare. **~ry** /-ərɪ/ *n* coraggio *m*

brawl /brɔːl/ *n* rissa *f* ● *vi* azzuffarsi

brawn /brɔːn/ *n Culin* ≈ soppressata *f*

brawny /'brɔːnɪ/ *a* muscoloso

brazen /'breɪzn/ *a* sfrontato

brazier /'breɪzɪə(r)/ *n* braciere *m*

Brazil /brə'zɪl/ *n* Brasile *m*. **~ian** *a & n* brasiliano, -a *mf*. **~ nut** *n* noce *f* del Brasile

breach /briːtʃ/ *n* (*of law*) violazione *f*; (*gap*) breccia *f*; (*fig: in party*) frattura *f*; **~ of contract** inadempienza *f* di contratto; **~ of the peace** violazione *f* della quiete pubblica ● *vt* recedere (*contract*)

bread /bred/ *n* pane *m*; **a slice of ~ and butter** una fetta di pane imburrato

bread: **~ bin** *n* cassetta *f* portapane *inv*. **~crumbs** *npl* briciole *fpl*; *Culin* pangrattato *m*. **~line** *n* **be on the ~line** essere povero in canna

breadth /bredθ/ *n* larghezza *f*

'bread-winner *n* quello, -a *mf* che porta i soldi a casa

break /breɪk/ *n* rottura *f*; (*interval*) intervallo *m*; (*interruption*) interruzione *f*; (*fam: chance*) opportunità *f inv* ● *vt* (*pt* **broke**, *pp* **broken**) ● *vt* rompere; (*interrupt*) interrompere; **~ one's arm** rompersi un braccio ● *vi* rompersi; (*day:*) spuntare; (*storm:*) scoppiare; (*news:*) diffondersi; (*boy's voice:*) cambiare. **break away** *vi* scappare, *fig* chiudere (**from** con). **break down** *vi* (*machine, car:*) guastarsi; (*emotionally*) cedere (psicologicamente) ● *vt* sfondare (*door*); ripartire (*figures*). **break into** *vt* introdursi con (*la forza*) in, forzare (*car*). **break off** *vt* rompere (*engagement*) ● *vi* (*part of whole:*) rompersi. **break out** *vi* (*fight, war:*) scoppiare. **break up** *vt* far cessare (*fight*); disperdere

break|able /'breɪkəbl/ a fragile.
~age /-ɪdʒ/ n rottura f. **~down** n
(of car, machine) guasto m; Med
esaurimento m nervoso; (of
figures) analisi f inv. **~er** n (wave)
frangente m

breakfast /'brekfəst/ n [prima] colazione f

break: **~through** n scoperta f.
~water n frangiflutti m inv

breast /brest/ n seno m. **~feed** vt
allattare [al seno]. **~stroke** n
nuoto m a rana

breath /breθ/ n respiro m, fiato m;
out of **~** senza fiato

breathalyse /'breθəlaɪz/ vt sottoporre alla prova [etilica] del palloncino. **~r®** n Br alcoltest m inv

breathe /briːð/ vt/i respirare.
breathe in vi inspirare. **~** respirare (scent, air). **breathe out** vt/i
espirare

breath|er /'briːðə(r)/ n pausa f.
~ing n respirazione f

breath /breθ/: **~less** a senza fiato.
~taking a mozzafiato. **~ test** n
prova [etilica] f del palloncino

bred /bred/ see **breed**

breed /briːd/ n razza f ● v (pt/pp
bred) ● vt allevare; (give rise to)
generare ● vi riprodursi. **~er** n
allevatore, -trice mf. **~ing** n allevamento m; fig educazione f

breez|e /briːz/ n brezza f. **~y** a ven-
toso

brew /bruː/ n infuso m ● vt mettere in infusione (tea); produrre
(beer) ● vi fig (trouble:) essere
nell'aria. **~er** n birraio m. **~ery** n
fabbrica f di birra

bribe /braɪb/ n (money) bustarella
f; (large sum of money) tangente f
● vt corrompere. **~ry** /-ərɪ/ n corruzione f

brick /brɪk/ n mattone m. **~layer**
n muratore m ● **brick up** vt murare

bridal /'braɪdl/ a nuziale

bride /braɪd/ n sposa f. **~groom** n
sposo m. **~smaid** n damigella f
d'onore

bridge¹ /brɪdʒ/ n ponte m; (of nose)
setto m nasale; (of spectacles)
ponticello m ● vt fig colmare
(gap)

bridge² n Cards bridge m

bridle /'braɪdl/ n briglia f

brief¹ /briːf/ a breve

brief² n istruzioni fpl; (Jur: case)
causa f ● vt dare istruzioni a; Jur
affidare la causa a. **~case** n cartella f

brief|ing /'briːfɪŋ/ n briefing m inv.
~ly adv brevemente. **~ly,...** in breve,... **~ness** n brevità f

briefs /briːfs/ npl slip m inv

brigade /brɪ'geɪd/ n brigata f.
~ier /-ə'dɪə(r)/ n generale m di
brigata

bright /braɪt/ a (metal, idea) brillante; (day, room, future) luminoso; (clever) intelligente; **~ red** rosso m acceso

bright|en /'braɪtn/ v **~en [up]** ● vt
ravvivare; rallegrare (person)
● vi (weather:) schiarirsi; (face:)
illuminarsi; (person:) rallegrarsi.
~ly adv (shine) intensamente;
(smile) allegramente. **~ness** n luminosità f; (intelligence) intelligenza f

brilliance /'brɪljəns/ n luminosità
f; (of person) genialità f

brilliant /'brɪljənt/ a (very good) eccezionale; (very intelligent) brillante; (sunshine) splendente

brim /brɪm/ n bordo m; (of hat) tesa
f ● **brim over** vi (pt/pp brimmed)
traboccare

brine /braɪn/ n salamoia f

bring /brɪŋ/ vt (pt/pp brought)
portare (person, object). **bring
about** vt causare. **bring along** vt
portare [con sé]. **bring back** vt
restituire (sth borrowed); reintro-
durre (hanging); fare ritornare in
mente (memories). **bring down** vt
portare giù; fare cadere (government); fare abbassare (price).

bring off vt ~ sth off riuscire a fare qcsa. **bring on** vt (cause) provocare. **bring out** vt (emphasize) mettere in evidenza; pubblicare ⟨book⟩. **bring round** vt portare; (persuade) convincere; far rinvenire ⟨unconscious person⟩. **bring up** vt (vomit) rimettere; allevare ⟨children⟩; tirare fuori ⟨question, subject⟩

brink /brɪŋk/ n orlo m

brisk /brɪsk/ a svelto; ⟨person⟩ sbrigativo; ⟨trade, business⟩ reddic tizio; ⟨walk⟩ a passo spedito

bristl|e /'brɪsl/ n setola f ● vi ~ling with pieno di. ~ly a ⟨chin⟩ ispido

Brit|ain /'brɪtn/ n Gran Bretagna f. ~ish a britannico; ⟨ambassador⟩ della Gran Bretagna ● npl the ~ish il popolo britannico. ~on n cittadino, -a britannico, -a mf

brittle /'brɪtl/ a fragile

broach /brəʊtʃ/ vt toccare ⟨subject⟩

broad /brɔ:d/ a ampio; ⟨hint⟩ chiaro; ⟨accent⟩ marcato. **two metres ~** largo due metri; in ~ daylight in pieno giorno. **~ beans** npl fave fpl

'broadcast n trasmissione f ● vt/i (pt/pp -cast) trasmettere. ~er n giornalista mf radiotelevisivo, -a. ~ing n diffusione f radiotelevisiva; **be in ~ing** lavorare per la televisione/radio

broaden /'brɔ:dn/ vt allargare ● vi allargarsi

broadly /'brɔ:dlɪ/ adv largamente; ~ [speaking] generalmente

broad'minded a di larghe vedute

broccoli /'brɒkəlɪ/ n inv broccoli mpl

brochure /'brəʊʃə(r)/ n opuscolo m; (travel ~) dépliant m inv

broke /brəʊk/ see **break** ● a fam al verde

broken /'brəʊkn/ see **break** ● a rotto; ⟨fig: marriage⟩ fallito. ~ **English** inglese m stentato. **~-hearted** a affranto

broker /'brəʊkə(r)/ n broker m inv

brolly /'brɒlɪ/ n fam ombrello m

bronchitis /brɒŋ'kaɪtɪs/ n bronchite f

bronze /brɒnz/ n bronzo m ● attrib di bronzo

brooch /brəʊtʃ/ n spilla f

brood /bru:d/ n covata f; (hum: children) prole f ● vi fig rimuginare

brook /brʊk/ n ruscello m

broom /bru:m/ n scopa f. **~ stick** n manico m di scopa

broth /brɒθ/ n brodo m

brothel /'brɒθl/ n bordello m

brother /'brʌðə(r)/ n fratello m

brother: ~-in-law n (pl **~s-in-law**) cognato m. **~ly** a fraterno

brought /brɔ:t/ see **bring**

brow /braʊ/ n fronte f; (of hill) cima f

'browbeat vt (pt **-beat**, pp **-beaten**) intimidire

brown /braʊn/ a marrone; castano ⟨hair⟩ ● n marrone m ● vt rosolare ⟨meat⟩ ● vi ⟨meat⟩ rosolarsi. **~ 'paper** n carta f da pacchi

Brownie /'braʊnɪ/ n coccinella f (negli scout)

browse /braʊz/ vi (read) leggicchiare; (in shop) curiosare

bruise /bru:z/ n livido m; (on fruit) ammaccatura f ● vt ammaccare ⟨fruit⟩; ~ **one's arm** farsi un livido sul braccio. **~d** a contuso

brunette /bru:'net/ n bruna f

brunt /brʌnt/ n **bear the ~ of sth** subire maggiormente qcsa

brush /brʌʃ/ n spazzola f; (with long handle) spazzolone m (for paint) pennello m; (bushes) boscaglia f; (fig: conflict) breve scontro m ● vt spazzolare ⟨hair⟩; lavarsi ⟨teeth⟩; scopare ⟨stairs, floor⟩. **brush against** vt sfiorare. **brush aside** vt fig ignorare. **brush off** vt spazzolare; (with hands) togliere; ignorare ⟨criticism⟩. **brush up** vt/i fig ~ **up [on]** rinfrescare

brusque /brʊsk/ a brusco

Brussels /'brʌslz/ n Bruxelles f. ~

sprouts npl cavoletti mpl di Bruxelles

brutal /'bruːtl/ a brutale. **~ity** /-'tæləti/ n brutalità f inv

brute /bruːt/ n bruto m. **~ force** n forza f bruta

BSc n abbr **Bachelor of Science**

BSE n abbr (**bovine spongiform encephalitis**) encefalite f bovina spongiforme

bubble /'bʌbl/ n bolla f; (in drink) bollicina f

buck¹ /bʌk/ n maschio m del cervo; (rabbit) maschio m del coniglio ●vi ⟨horse:⟩ saltare a quattro zampe. **buck up** vi fam tirarsi su; (hurry) sbrigarsi

buck² n Am fam dollaro m

buck³ n **pass the ~** scaricare la responsabilità

bucket /'bʌkɪt/ n secchio m

buckle /'bʌkl/ n fibbia f ●vt allacciare ●vi ⟨shelf:⟩ piegarsi; ⟨wheel:⟩ storcersi

bud /bʌd/ n bocciolo m

Buddhi|sm /'bʊdɪzm/ n buddismo m. **~t** a a n buddista mf

buddy /'bʌdɪ/ n fam amico, -a mf

budge /bʌdʒ/ vt spostare ●vi spostarsi

budgerigar /'bʌdʒərɪgɑː(r)/ n cocorita f

budget /'bʌdʒɪt/ n bilancio m; (allotted to specific activity) budget m inv ●vi (pt/pp **budgeted**) prevedere le spese; **~ for sth** includere qcsa nelle spese previste

buff /bʌf/ a ⟨colour:⟩ ⟨colour⟩ camoscio ●n fam fanatico, -a mf

buffalo /'bʌfələʊ/ n (inv or pl **-es**) bufalo m

buffer /'bʌfə(r)/ n Rail respingente m; **old ~** fam vecchio bacucco m. **~ zone** n zona f cuscinetto

buffet¹ /'bʊfeɪ/ n buffet m inv

buffet² /'bʌfɪt/ vt (pt/pp **buffeted**) sferzare

buffoon /bə'fuːn/ n buffone, -a mf

bug /bʌg/ n (insect) insetto m; Comput bug m inv; (fam: device) cimice f ●vt (pt/pp **bugged**)

fam installare le microspie in ⟨room⟩; mettere sotto controllo ⟨telephone⟩; (fam: annoy) scocciare

buggy /'bʌgɪ/ n ⟨baby⟩ **~** passeggino m

bugle /'bjuːgl/ n tromba f

build /bɪld/ n (of person) corporatura f ●vt/i (pt/pp **built**) costruire. **build on** vt aggiungere ⟨extra storey⟩; sviluppare ⟨previous work⟩. **build up** vt **~ up one's strength** rimettersi in forza ●vi ⟨pressure, traffic:⟩ aumentare; ⟨excitement, tension:⟩ crescere

builder /'bɪldə(r)/ n (company) costruttore m; (worker) muratore m

building /'bɪldɪŋ/ n edificio m. **~ site** n cantiere m [di costruzione]. **~ society** n istituto m di credito immobiliare

build-up n (of gas etc) accumulo m; fig battage m inv pubblicitario

built /bɪlt/ see **build**. **~-in** a ⟨unit⟩ a muro; ⟨fig: feature⟩ incorporato. **~-up area** n Auto centro m abitato

bulb /bʌlb/ n bulbo m; Electr lampadina f

bulge /bʌldʒ/ n rigonfiamento m ●vi esser gonfio (with di); ⟨stomach, wall:⟩ sporgere; ⟨eyes, with surprise:⟩ uscire dalle orbite. **~ing** a gonfio; ⟨eyes⟩ sporgente

bulk /bʌlk/ n volume m; (greater part) grosso m; **in ~** in grande quantità; (loose) sfuso. **~y** a voluminoso

bull /bʊl/ n toro m

bulldog /bʊl/ n bulldog m inv

bulldozer /'bʊldəʊzə(r)/ n bulldozer m inv

bullet /'bʊlɪt/ n pallottola f

bulletin /'bʊlɪtɪn/ n bollettino m. **~ board** n Comput bacheca f elettronica

bullet-proof a antiproiettile inv; ⟨vehicle⟩ blindato

bullfight n corrida f. **~er** n torero m

bullion /'bʊlɪən/ n **gold** ~ oro m in lingotti

bullock /'bʊlək/ n manzo m

bull: ~**ring** /'bʊl-/ n arena f. ~**'s-eye** n centro m del bersaglio; **score a** ~**'s-eye** fare centro

bully /'bʊlɪ/ n prepotente mf ● vt fare il/la prepotente con. ~**ing** n prepotenze fpl

bum¹ /bʌm/ n Am fam sedere m

bum² n Am fam vagabondo, -a mf ● **bum around** vi fam vagabondare

bumble-bee /'bʌmbl-/ n calabrone m

bump /bʌmp/ n botta f; (swelling) bozzo m, gonfiore m; (in road) protuberanza f ● vt sbattere. **bump into** vt sbattere contro; (meet) imbattersi in. **bump off** vt fam far fuori

bumper /'bʌmpə(r)/ n Auto paraurti m inv ● a abbondante

bumpkin /'bʌmpkɪn/ n **country** ~ zoticone, -a mf

bumptious /'bʌmpʃəs/ a presuntuoso

bumpy /'bʌmpɪ/ a (road) accidentato; (flight) turbolento

bun /bʌn/ n focaccina f (dolce); (hair) chignon m inv

bunch /bʌntʃ/ n (of flowers, keys) mazzo m; (of bananas) casco m; (of people) gruppo m; ~ **of grapes** grappolo m d'uva

bundle /'bʌndl/ n fascio m; (of money) mazzetta f; **a** ~ **of nerves** fam un fascio di nervi ● vt ~ [**up**] affastellare

bung /bʌŋ/ vt fam (throw) buttare. **bung up** vt (block) otturare

bungalow /'bʌŋgələʊ/ n bungalow m inv

bungle /'bʌŋgl/ vt fare un pasticcio di

bunion /'bʌnjən/ n Med callo m all'alluce

bunk /bʌŋk/ n cuccetta f. ~**-beds** npl letti mpl a castello

bunny /'bʌnɪ/ n fam coniglietto m

buoy /bɔɪ/ n boa f

buoyan|cy /'bɔɪənsɪ/ n galleggiabilità f. ~**t** a (boat) galleggiante; (water) che aiuta a galleggiare

burden /'bɜːdn/ n carico m ● vt caricare. ~**some** /-səm/ a gravoso

bureau /'bjʊərəʊ/ n (pl -**x** /-əʊz/ or ~**s**) (desk) scrivania f; (office) ufficio m

bureaucracy /bjʊə'rɒkrəsɪ/ n burocrazia f

bureaucrat /'bjʊərəkræt/ n burocrate mf. ~**ic** /-'krætɪk/ a burocratico

burger /'bɜːgə(r)/ n hamburger m inv

burglar /'bɜːglə(r)/ n svaligiatore, -trice mf. ~ **alarm** n antifurto m inv

burglar|ize /'bɜːgləraɪz/ vt Am svaligiare. ~**y** n furto m con scasso

burgle /'bɜːgl/ vt svaligiare

Burgundy /'bɜːgəndɪ/ n Borgogna f

burial /'berɪəl/ n sepoltura f. ~ **ground** cimitero m

burlesque /bɜː'lesk/ n parodia f

burly /'bɜːlɪ/ a (-**ier**, -**iest**) corpulento

Burm|a /'bɜːmə/ n Birmania f. ~**ese** /-'miːz/ a & n birmano, -a mf

burn /bɜːn/ n bruciatura f ● v (pt/pp **burnt** or **burned**) ● vt bruciare ● vi bruciare. **burn down** vt/i bruciare. **burn out** vi fig esaurirsi. ~**er** n (on stove) bruciatore m

burnish /'bɜːnɪʃ/ vt lucidare

burnt /bɜːnt/ see **burn**

burp /bɜːp/ n fam rutto m ● vi fam ruttare

burrow /'bʌrəʊ/ n tana f ● vt scavare (hole)

bursar /'bɜːsə(r)/ n economo, -a mf. ~**y** n borsa f di studio

burst /bɜːst/ n (of gunfire, energy, laughter) scoppio m; (of speed) scatto m ● v (pt/pp **burst**) ● vt far scoppiare ● vi scoppiare; ~ **into tears** scoppiare in lacrime; **she** ~ **into the room** fig fatto irruzione nella stanza **burst out** vi ~ **out laughing/crying** scoppiare a ridere/piangere

bury /'berɪ/ vt (pt/pp **-ied**) seppellire; (hide) nascondere

bus /bʌs/ n autobus m inv, pullman m inv; (long distance) pullman m inv, corriera f

bush /bʊʃ/ n cespuglio m; (land) boscaglia f. **~y** a (**-ier, -iest**) folto

busily /'bɪzɪlɪ/ adv con grande impegno

business /'bɪznɪs/ n affare m; Comm affari mpl; (establishment) attività f di commercio; **on ~** per affari; **he has no ~ to** non ha alcun diritto di; **mind one's own ~** farsi gli affari propri; **that's none of your ~** non sono affari tuoi. **~-like** a efficiente. **~man** n uomo m d'affari. **~woman** n donna f d'affari

busker /'bʌskə(r)/ n suonatore, -trice mf ambulante

'bus station n stazione f degli autobus

'bus-stop n fermata f d'autobus

bust[1] /bʌst/ n busto m; (chest) petto m

bust[2] a fam rotto; **go ~** fallire ● vt (pt/pp **busted** or **bust**) fam ● vt far scoppiare ● vi scoppiare

bustl|e /'bʌsl/ n (activity) trambusto m ● **bustle about** vi affannarsi. **~ing** a animato

'bust-up n fam lite f

busy /'bɪzɪ/ a (**-ier, -iest**) occupato; (day, time) intenso; (street) affollato; (with traffic) pieno di traffico; **be ~ doing** essere occupato a fare ● vt **~ oneself** darsi da fare

'busybody n ficcanaso mf inv

but /bʌt/, atono /bət/ conj ma ● prep eccetto, tranne; **nobody ~ you** nessuno tranne te; **~ for** (without) se non fosse stato per; **the last ~ one** il penultimo; **the next ~ one** il secondo ● adv (only) soltanto; **there were ~ two** ce n'erano soltanto due

butcher /'bʊtʃə(r)/ n macellaio m; **~'s [shop]** macelleria f ● vt macellare; fig massacrare

butler /'bʌtlə(r)/ n maggiordomo m

butt /bʌt/ n (of gun) calcio m; (of cigarette) mozzicone m; (for water) barile m; (fig: target) bersaglio m ● vt dare una testata a; (goat:) dare una cornata a. **butt in** vi interrompere

butter /'bʌtə(r)/ n burro m ● vt imburrare. **butter up** vt fam arruffianarsi

butter-: ~cup n ranuncolo m. **~fingers** nsg fam be a **~fingers** avere le mani di pasta frolla. **~fly** n farfalla f

buttocks /'bʌtəks/ npl natiche fpl

button /'bʌtn/ n bottone m ● vt [up] abbottonare ● vi abbottonarsi. **~hole** n occhiello m, asola f

buttress /'bʌtrɪs/ n contrafforte m

buxom /'bʌksəm/ a formosa

buy /baɪ/ n **good/bad ~** buon/cattivo acquisto m ● vt (pt/pp **bought**) comprare; **~ sb a drink** pagare da bere a qcno ● fig **~ this one** (drink) questo, lo offro io. **I'll ~ this** (drink) questo, lo offro io. **~er** n compratore, -trice mf

buzz /bʌz/ n ronzio m; **give sb a ~** fam (on phone) dare un colpo di telefono a qcno ● (excite) mettere in fermento qcno ● vi ronzare ● vt **~ sb** chiamare qcno col cicalino. **buzz off** vi fam levarsi di torno

buzzer /'bʌzə(r)/ n cicalino m

by /baɪ/ prep (near, next to) vicino a; (at the latest) per; **by Mozart** di Mozart; **he was run over by a bus** è stato investito da un autobus; **by oneself** da solo; **by the sea** al mare; **by sea** via mare; **by car/bus** in macchina/autobus; **by day/night** di giorno/notte; **by the hour/metre** a ore/metri; **six metres by four** sei metri per quattro; **he won by six metres** ha vinto di sei metri; **I missed the train by a minute** ho perso il treno per un minuto; **I'll be home by six** sarò a casa per le sei; **by this time next week** a quest'ora tra una settimana; **he rushed by me** mi è passato accanto di corsa ● *adv* **she'll be here by and by** sarà qui fra poco; **by and large** in complesso

bye[-bye] /baɪ['baɪ]/ *int fam* ciao

by: **~-election** *n* elezione *f* straordinaria indetta per coprire una carica rimasta vacante in Parlamento. **~gone** *a* passato. **~-law** *n* legge *f* locale. **~pass** *n* circonvallazione *f*; *Med* by-pass *m inv* ● *vt* evitare. **~-product** *n* sottoprodotto *m*. **~stander** *n* spettatore, -trice *mf*. **~word** *n* be a **~word for** essere sinonimo di

Cc

cab /kæb/ *n* taxi *m inv*; *(of lorry, train)* cabina *f*

cabaret /'kæbəreɪ/ *n* cabaret *m inv*

cabbage /'kæbɪdʒ/ *n* cavolo *m*

cabin /'kæbɪn/ *n (of plane, ship)* cabina *f*; *(hut)* capanna *f*

cabinet /'kæbɪnɪt/ *n* armadietto *m*; **[display]** **~** vetrina *f*; C**~** *Pol* consiglio *m* dei ministri. **~-maker** *n* ebanista *mf*

cable /'keɪbl/ *n* cavo *m*. **~ 'railway** *n* funicolare *f*. **~ 'television** *n* televisione *f* via cavo

cache /kæʃ/ *n* nascondiglio *m*. **~ of arms** deposito *m* segreto di armi

cackle /'kækl/ *vi* ridacchiare

cactus /'kæktəs/ *n (pl* **-ti** /-taɪ/ *-tuses)* cactus *m inv*

caddie /'kædɪ/ *n* portabastoni *m inv*

caddy /'kædɪ/ *n* **[tea-]** ~ barattolo *m* del tè

cadet /kə'det/ *n* cadetto *m*

cadge /kædʒ/ *vt/i fam* scroccare

Caesarean /sɪ'zeərɪən/ *n* parto *m* cesareo

café /'kæfeɪ/ *n* caffè *m inv*

cafeteria /kæfə'tɪərɪə/ *n* tavola *f* calda

caffeine /'kæfiːn/ *n* caffeina *f*

cage /keɪdʒ/ *n* gabbia *f*

cagey /'keɪdʒɪ/ *a fam* riservato **(about** su)

cajole /kə'dʒəʊl/ *vt* persuadere con le lusinghe

cake /keɪk/ *n* torta *f*; *(small)* pasticcino *m*. **~d** *a* incrostato **(with** di)

calamity /kə'læmətɪ/ *n* calamità *f*

calcium /'kælsɪəm/ *n* calcio *m*

calculate /'kælkjʊleɪt/ *vt* calcolare. **~ing** *a fig* calcolatore. **~ion** /-'leɪʃn/ *n* calcolo *m*. **~or** *n* calcolatrice *f*

calendar /'kælɪndə(r)/ *n* calendario *m*

calf¹ /kɑːf/ *n (pl* **calves)** vitello *m*

calf² /kɑːf/ *n (pl* **calves)** *Anat* polpaccio *m*

calibre /'kælɪbə(r)/ *n* calibro *m*

call /kɔːl/ *n* grido *m*; *Teleph* telefonata *f*; *(visit)* visita *f*; **be on ~** *(doctor:)* essere di guardia ● *vt* chiamare; indire *(strike)*; **be ~ed** chiamarsi ● *vi* chiamare. **~ [in or round]** passare. **call back** *vt/i* richiamare. **call for** *vt (ask for)* chiedere; *(require)* richiedere; *(fetch)* passare a prendere. **call off** *vt* richiamare *(dog)*; disdire *(meeting)*; revocare *(strike)*. **call on** *vt* chiamare; *(appeal to)* fare un appello a; *(visit)* visitare. **call out** *vt* chiamare ad alta voce *(names)* ● *vi* chiamare ad alta voce. **call together** *vt* riunire. **call up** *vt Mil* chiamare alle armi; *Teleph* chiamare

call: **~-box** *n* cabina *f* telefonica. **~er** *n* visitatore, -trice *mf*; *Teleph* persona *f* che telefona. **~ing** *n* vocazione *f*

callous /'kæləs/ *a* insensibile

'call-up *n Mil* chiamata *f* alle armi

calm /kɑːm/ *a* calmo ● *n* calma *f*. **calm down** *vt* calmare ● *vi* calmarsi. **~ly** *adv* con calma

calorie /'kælərɪ/ n caloria f

calves /kɑːvz/ npl see **calf¹** & **²**

camber /'kæmbə(r)/ n curvatura f

Cambodia /kæm'bəʊdɪə/ n Cambogia f. **~n** a & n cambogiano, -a mf

camcorder /'kæmkɔːdə(r)/ n videocamera f

came /keɪm/ see **come**

camel /'kæml/ n cammello m

camera /'kæmərə/ n macchina f fotografica; TV telecamera f. **~man** n operatore m [televisivo], cameraman m inv

camouflage /'kæməflɑːʒ/ n mimetizzazione f ● vt mimetizzare

camp /kæmp/ n campeggio f; Mil campo m ● vi campeggiare; Mil accamparsi

campaign /kæm'peɪn/ n campagna f ● vi fare una campagna

camp: **~-bed** n letto m da campo. **~er** n campeggiatore, -trice mf; Auto camper m inv. **~ing** n campeggio m. **~site** n campeggio m

campus /'kæmpəs/ n (pl **-puses**) Univ città f universitaria, campus m inv

can¹ /kæn/ n (for petrol) latta f; (tin) scatola f. **~ of beer** lattina f di birra ● vt mettere in scatola

can² /kæn/, atono /kən/ v aux (pres **can**; pt **could**) (be able to) potere; (know how to) sapere; **I cannot** or **can't go** non posso andare; **he could not** or **couldn't go** non poteva andare; **she can't swim** non sa nuotare; **I ~ smell something burning** sento odor di bruciato

Canada /'kænədə/ n Canada m. **~ian** /kə'neɪdɪən/ a & n canadese mf

canal /kə'næl/ n canale m

Canaries /kə'neərɪz/ npl Canarie fpl

canary /kə'neərɪ/ n canarino m

cancel /'kænsl/ v (pt/pp **cancelled**) ● vt disdire ‹meeting, newspaper›; revocare ‹contract, order›; annullare ‹reservation, appointment, stamp›. **~lation** /-ə'leɪʃn/ n (of meeting, contract) revoca f; (in hotel, restaurant, for flight) cancellazione f

cancer /'kænsə(r)/ n cancro m; **C~** Astr Cancro m. **~ous** /-rəs/ a canceroso

candelabra /kændə'lɑːbrə/ n candelabro m

candid /'kændɪd/ a franco

candidate /'kændɪdət/ n candidato, -a mf

candle /'kændl/ n candela f. **~stick** n portacandele m inv

candour /'kændə(r)/ n franchezza f

candy /'kændɪ/ n Am caramella f; **a [piece of] ~** una caramella. **~floss** /-flɒs/ n zucchero m filato

cane /keɪn/ n (stick) bastone m; Sch bacchetta f ● vt prendere a bacchettate ‹pupil›

canine /'keɪnaɪn/ a canino. **~ tooth** n canino m

canister /'kænɪstə(r)/ n barattolo m (di metallo)

cannabis /'kænəbɪs/ n cannabis f

canned /kænd/ a in scatola; **~ music** fam musica f registrata

cannibal /'kænɪbl/ n cannibale mf. **~ism** n cannibalismo m

cannon /'kænən/ n inv cannone m. **~-ball** n palla f di cannone

cannot /'kænɒt/ see **can²**

canny /'kænɪ/ a astuto

canoe /kə'nuː/ n canoa f ● vi andare in canoa

'can-opener n apriscatole m inv

canopy /'kænəpɪ/ n baldacchino f; (of parachute) calotta f

can't /kɑːnt/ **= cannot** see **can²**

cantankerous /kæn'tæŋkərəs/ a stizzoso

canteen /kæn'tiːn/ n mensa f; **~ of cutlery** servizio m di posate

canter /'kæntə(r)/ vi andare a piccolo galoppo

canvas /'kænvəs/ n tela f; (painting) dipinto m su tela

canvass /'kænvəs/ vi Pol fare propaganda elettorale. **~ing** n sollecitazione f di voti

canyon /'kænjən/ n canyon m inv

cap /kæp/ n berretto m; (nurse's) cuffia f; (top, lid) tappo m (of (pt/pp **capped**) (fig: do better than) superare

capability /keɪpə'bɪlətɪ/ n capacità f

capable /'keɪpəbl/ a capace; (skilful) abile; **be ~e of doing sth** essere capace di fare qcsa. **~y** adv con abilità

capacity /kə'pæsətɪ/ n capacità f; (function) qualità f; **in my ~ as** in qualità di

cape[1] /keɪp/ n (cloak) cappa f

cape[2] n Geog capo m

caper[1] /'keɪpə(r)/ vi saltellare ● n fam birichinata f

caper[2] n Culin cappero m

capital /'kæpɪtl/ n (town) capitale f; (money) capitale m; (letter) lettera f maiuscola. **~ city** n capitale f

capital|ism /'kæpɪtəlɪzm/ n capitalismo m. **~ist** /-ɪst/ a & n capitalista mf. **~ize** /-aɪz/ vi **~ize on** fig trarre vantaggio da. **~ letter** n lettera f maiuscola. **~ 'punishment** n pena f capitale

capitul|ate /kə'pɪtjuleɪt/ vi capitolare. **~ion** /-'leɪʃn/ n capitolazione f

capricious /kə'prɪʃəs/ a capriccioso

Capricorn /'kæprɪkɔːn/ n Astr Capricorno m

capsize /kæp'saɪz/ vi capovolgersi ● vt capovolgere

capsule /'kæpsjuːl/ n capsula f

captain /'kæptɪn/ n capitano m ● vt comandare (team)

caption /'kæpʃn/ n intestazione f; (of illustration) didascalia f

captivate /'kæptɪveɪt/ vt incantare

captiv|e /'kæptɪv/ a prigioniero; **hold/take ~e** tenere/fare prigioniero ● n prigioniero a mf. **~ity** /-'tɪvətɪ/ n prigionia f; (animals) cattività f

capture /'kæptʃə(r)/ n cattura f ● vt catturare; attirare (attention)

car /kɑː(r)/ n macchina f; **by ~** in macchina

carafe /kə'ræf/ n caraffa f

caramel /'kærəmel/ n (sweet) caramella f al mou; Culin caramello m

carat /'kærət/ n carato m

caravan /'kærəvæn/ n roulotte f inv; (horse-drawn) carovana f

carbohydrate /kɑːbə'haɪdreɪt/ n carboidrato m

carbon /'kɑːbən/ n carbonio m

carbon: **~ copy** n copia f in carta carbone; (fig: person) ritratto m. **~ di'oxide** n anidride f carbonica. **~ paper** n carta f carbone

carburettor /kɑːbjʊ'retə(r)/ n carburatore m

carcass /'kɑːkəs/ n carcassa f

card /kɑːd/ n (for birthday, Christmas etc) biglietto m di auguri; (playing) carta f [da gioco]; (membership ~) tessera f; (business ~) biglietto m da visita; (credit ~) carta f di credito; Comput scheda f

'cardboard n cartone m. **~ 'box** n scatola f di cartone; (large) scatolone m

'card-game n gioco m di carte

cardiac /'kɑːdɪæk/ a cardiaco

cardigan /'kɑːdɪgən/ n cardigan m inv

cardinal /'kɑːdɪnl/ a cardinale; **~ number** numero m cardinale ● n Relig cardinale m

card 'index n schedario m

care /keə(r)/ n cura f; (caution) attenzione f; (worry) preoccupazione f; **~ of** (on letter abbr c/o) presso; **take ~** (be cautious) fare attenzione; **bye, take ~** ciao, stammi bene; **take ~** of occuparsi di; **be taken into ~** essere preso in custodia da un ente assistenziale ● vi **~ about** interessarsi di; **~ for** (feel affection for) volere bene a; (look after) aver cura di; **I don't ~** **for chocolate** non mi piace il cioccolato; **I don't ~** non me ne importa; **who ~s?** chi se ne frega?

career /kə'rɪə(r)/ n carriera f

(*profession*) professione *f* ● *vi* andare a tutta velocità

care: ~free *a* spensierato. **~ful** *a* attento; ⟨*driver*⟩ prudente. **~fully** *adv* con attenzione. **~less** *a* irresponsabile; ⟨*in work*⟩ trascurato; ⟨*work*⟩ fatto con poca cura; ⟨*driver*⟩ distratto. **~lessly** *adv* negligentemente. **~lessness** *n* trascuratezza *f*. **~r** *n* persona *f* che accudisce a un anziano o a un malato

caress /kə'res/ *n* carezza *f* ● *vt* accarezzare

'**caretaker** *n* custode *mf*; ⟨*in school*⟩ bidello *m*

'**car ferry** *n* traghetto *m* ⟨*per il trasporto di auto*⟩

cargo /'kɑːgəʊ/ *n* (*pl* **-es**) carico *m*

Caribbean /kærɪ'biːən/ *n* the ~ ⟨*sea*⟩ il Mar dei Caraibi ● *a* caraibico

caricature /'kærɪkətjʊə(r)/ *n* caricatura *f*

caring /'keərɪŋ/ *a* ⟨*parent*⟩ premuroso; ⟨*attitude*⟩ altruista; the ~ **professions** le attività assistenziali

carnage /'kɑːnɪdʒ/ *n* carneficina *f*

carnal /'kɑːnl/ *a* carnale

carnation /kɑː'neɪʃn/ *n* garofano *m*

carnival /'kɑːnɪvl/ *n* carnevale *m*

carnivorous /kɑː'nɪvərəs/ *a* carnivoro

carol /'kærəl/ *n* [Christmas] ~ canzone *f* natalizia

carp[1] /kɑːp/ *n inv* carpa *f*

carp[2] *vi* ~ **at** trovare da ridire su

'**car park** *n* parcheggio *m*

carpent|er /'kɑːpɪntə(r)/ *n* falegname *m*. **~ry** *n* falegnameria *f*

carpet /'kɑːpɪt/ *n* tappeto *m*; ⟨*wall-to-wall*⟩ moquette *f inv* ● *vt* mettere la moquette in ⟨*room*⟩

'**car phone** *n* telefono *m* in macchina

carriage /'kærɪdʒ/ *n* carrozza *f*; ⟨*of goods*⟩ trasporto *m*; ⟨*cost*⟩ spese *fpl* di trasporto; ⟨*bearing*⟩ portamento *m*; **~way** *n* strada *f* carroz-

zabile; **north-bound** **~way** carreggiata *f* nord

carrier /'kærɪə(r)/ *n* ⟨*company*⟩ impresa *f* di trasporti; *Aeron* compagnia *f* di trasporto aereo; ⟨*of disease*⟩ portatore *m*. ~ [**bag**] *n* borsa *f* [per la spesa]

carrot /'kærət/ *n* carota *f*

carry /'kærɪ/ *v* (*pt/pp* **-ied**) ● *vt* portare; ⟨*transport*⟩ trasportare; **get carried away** *fam* lasciarsi prender la mano ● *vi* ⟨*sound*⟩ trasmettersi. **carry off** *vt* portare via; vincere ⟨*prize*⟩. **carry on** *vi* continuare; ⟨*fam: make scene*⟩ fare delle storie; ~ **on with sth** continuare qcsa; ~ **on with sb** *fam* intendersela con qcno ● *vt* mantenere ⟨*business*⟩. **carry out** *vt* portare fuori; eseguire ⟨*instructions, task*⟩; mettere in atto ⟨*threat*⟩; effettuare ⟨*experiment, survey*⟩

'**carry-cot** *n* porte-enfant *m inv*

cart /kɑːt/ *n* carretto *m* ● *vt* ⟨*fam: carry*⟩ portare

cartilage /'kɑːtɪlɪdʒ/ *n* Anat cartilagine *f*

carton /'kɑːtn/ *n* scatola *f* di cartone; ⟨*for drink*⟩ cartone *m*; ⟨*of cream, yoghurt*⟩ vasetto *m*; ⟨*of cigarettes*⟩ stecca *f*

cartoon /kɑː'tuːn/ *n* vignetta *f*; ⟨*strip*⟩ vignette *fpl*; ⟨*film*⟩ cartone *m* animato; ⟨*in art*⟩ bozzetto *m*. **~ist** *n* vignettista *mf*; ⟨*for films*⟩ disegnatore, -trice *mf* di cartoni animati

cartridge /'kɑːtrɪdʒ/ *n* cartuccia *f*; ⟨*for film*⟩ bobina *f*; ⟨*of record player*⟩ testina *f*

carve /kɑːv/ *vt* scolpire; tagliare ⟨*meat*⟩

carving /'kɑːvɪŋ/ *n* scultura *f*. **~-knife** *n* trinciante *m*

'**car wash** *n* autolavaggio *m inv*

case[1] /keɪs/ *n* caso *m*; **in any** ~ in ogni caso; **in that** ~ in questo caso; **just in** ~ per sicurezza; **in** ~ **he comes** nel caso in cui venisse

case[2] *n* ⟨*container*⟩ scatola *f*;

(crate) cassa *f*; *(for spectacles)* astuccio *m*; *(suitcase)* valigia *f*; *(for display)* vetrina *f*

cash /kæʃ/ *n* denaro *m* contante; *(fam: money)* contanti *npl*; **pay [in]** ~ pagare in contanti; ~ **on delivery** pagamento alla consegna ● *vt* incassare *(cheque)*. ~ **desk** *n* cassa *f*

cashier /kæˈʃɪə(r)/ *n* cassiere, -a *mf*

'cash register *n* registratore *m* di cassa

casino /kəˈsiːnəʊ/ *n* casinò *m inv*

casket /ˈkɑːskɪt/ *n* scrigno *m*; *(Am: coffin)* bara *f*

casserole /ˈkæsərəʊl/ *n* casseruola *f*; *(stew)* stufato *m*

cassette /kəˈset/ *n* cassetta *f*. ~ **recorder** *n* registratore *m* *(a cassette)*

cast /kɑːst/ *n* *(mould)* forma *f*; *Theat* cast *m inv*; *(plaster)* Med ingessatura *f* ● *vt* *(pt/pp* **cast)** dare *(votes)*; *Theat* assegnare le parti di *(play)*; fondere *(metal)*; *(throw)* gettare; ~ **an actor as** dare ad un attore il ruolo di; ~ **a glance at** lanciare uno sguardo a. **cast off** *vi Naut* sganciare gli ormeggi ● *vi* *(in knitting)* diminuire. **cast on** *vi* *(in knitting)* avviare

castaway /ˈkɑːstəweɪ/ *n* naufrago, -a *mf*

caste /kɑːst/ *n* casta *f*

caster /ˈkɑːstə(r)/ *n* *(wheel)* rotella *f*. ~ **sugar** *n* zucchero *m* raffinato

cast iron *n* ghisa *f*

cast-iron *a* ghisa *f*; *fig* solido

castle /ˈkɑːsl/ *n* castello *m*; *(in chess)* torre *f*

'cast-offs *npl* abiti *mpl smessi*

castor /ˈkɑːstə(r)/ *n* *(wheel)* rotella *f*. ~ **oil** *n* olio *m* di ricino. ~ **sugar** *n* zucchero *m* raffinato

castrat|e /kæˈstreɪt/ *vt* castrare. ~**ion** /-eɪʃn/ *n* castrazione *f*

casual /ˈkæʒʊəl/ *a* *(chance)* casuale; *(remark)* senza importanza; *(glance)* di sfuggita; *(attitude, approach)* disinvolto; *(chat)* infor-

male; *(clothes)* casual *inv*; *(work)* saltuario; ~ **wear** abbigliamento *m* casual. ~**ly** *adv* *(dress)* casual; *(meet)* casualmente

casualty /ˈkæʒʊəltɪ/ *n* *(injured person)* ferito *m*; *(killed)* vittima *f*. ~ **[department]** *n* pronto soccorso *m*

cat /kæt/ *n* gatto *m*; *pej* arpia *f*

catalogue /ˈkætəlɒg/ *n* catalogo *m* ● *vt* catalogare

catalyst /ˈkætəlɪst/ *n* Chem & fig catalizzatore *m*

catalytic /kætəˈlɪtɪk/ *a* ~ **converter** *Auto* marmitta *f* catalitica

catapult /ˈkætəpʌlt/ *n* catapulta *f*; *(child's)* fionda *f* ● *vt fig* catapultare

cataract /ˈkætərækt/ *n* Med cataratta *f*

catarrh /kəˈtɑː(r)/ *n* catarro *m*

catastroph|e /kəˈtæstrəfɪ/ *n* catastrofe *f*. ~**ic** /kætəˈstrɒfɪk/ *a* catastrofico

catch /kætʃ/ *n* *(of fish)* pesca *f*; *(fastener)* fermaglio *m*; *(on door)* fermo *m*; *(on window)* gancio *m*; *(fam: snag)* tranello *m* ● *v* *(pt/pp* **caught)** ● *vt* acchiappare *(ball)*; *(grab)* afferrare; prendere *(illness, fugitive, train)*; ~ **a cold** prendersi un raffreddore; ~ **sight of** scorgere; **I caught him stealing** l'ho sorpreso mentre rubava; ~ **one's finger in the door** chiudersi il dito nella porta; ~ **sb's eye** or **attention** attirare l'attenzione di qcno ● *vi* *(fire)* prendere; *(get stuck)* impigliarsi. **catch on** *vi fam* *(understand)* afferrare; *(become popular)* diventare popolare. **catch up** *vt* raggiungere ● *vi* recuperare; *(runner:)* riguadagnare terreno; ~ **up with** raggiungere *(sb)*; mettersi in pari con *(work)*

catching /ˈkætʃɪŋ/ *a* contagioso

catch: ~**-phrase** *n* tormentone *m*. ~**word** *n* slogan *m inv*

catchy /ˈkætʃɪ/ *a* (**-ier, -iest)** orecchiabile

categor|ical /kætɪˈɡɒrɪkl/ a categorico. **~y** /ˈkætɪɡərɪ/ n categoria f

cater /ˈkeɪtə(r)/ vi **~ for** provvedere a ⟨needs⟩; fig venire incontro alle esigenze di. **~ing** n ⟨trade⟩ ristorazione f; ⟨food⟩ rinfresco m

caterpillar /ˈkætəpɪlə(r)/ n bruco m

cathedral /kəˈθiːdrl/ n cattedrale f

Catholic /ˈkæθəlɪk/ a & n cattolico, -a mf. **~ism** /kəˈθɒlɪsɪzm/ n cattolicesimo m

cat's eyes npl catarifrangente msg ⟨inserito nell'asfalto⟩

cattle /ˈkætl/ npl bestiame msg

catty /ˈkætɪ/ a (-ier, -iest) dispettoso

catwalk /ˈkætwɔːk/ n passerella f

caught /kɔːt/ see catch

cauliflower /ˈkɒlɪ-/ n cavolfiore m

cause /kɔːz/ n causa f ● vt causare; **~ sb to do sth** far fare qcsa a qcno

'causeway /ˈkɔːz-/ n strada f sopraelevata

caustic /ˈkɔːstɪk/ a caustico

caution /ˈkɔːʃn/ n cautela f; ⟨warning⟩ ammonizione f ● vt mettere in guardia; Jur ammonire

cautious /ˈkɔːʃəs/ a cauto

cavalry /ˈkævəlrɪ/ n cavalleria f

cave /keɪv/ n caverna f ● **cave in** vi ⟨roof:⟩ crollare; ⟨fig: give in⟩ capitolare

cavern /ˈkævən/ n caverna f

caviare /ˈkævɪɑː(r)/ n caviale m

caving /ˈkeɪvɪŋ/ n speleologia f

cavity /ˈkævətɪ/ n cavità f inv; ⟨in tooth⟩ carie f inv

cavort /kəˈvɔːt/ vi saltellare

CD n CD m inv. **~ player** n lettore m [di] compact

CD-Rom /siːdiːˈrɒm/ n CD-Rom m inv. **~ drive** n lettore m [di] CD-Rom

cease /siːs/ n without **~** incessantemente ● vt/i cessare. **~-fire** n cessate il fuoco m inv. **~less** a incessante

cedar /ˈsiːdə(r)/ n cedro m

cede /siːd/ vt cedere

ceiling /ˈsiːlɪŋ/ n soffitto m; fig tetto m ⟨massimo⟩

celebrat|e /ˈselɪbreɪt/ vt festeggiare ⟨birthday, victory⟩ ● vi far festa. **~ed** a celebre (**for** per). **~ion** /-ˈbreɪʃn/ n celebrazione f

celebrity /sɪˈlebrətɪ/ n celebrità f inv

celery /ˈselərɪ/ n sedano m

celiba|cy /ˈselɪbəsɪ/ n celibato m. **~te** a ⟨man⟩ celibe; ⟨woman⟩ nubile

cell /sel/ n cella f; Biol cellula f

cellar /ˈselə(r)/ n scantinato m; ⟨for wine⟩ cantina f

cellist /ˈtʃelɪst/ n violoncellista mf

cello /ˈtʃeləʊ/ n violoncello m

Cellophane® /ˈseləfeɪn/ n cellofan m inv

cellular phone /seljʊləˈfəʊn/ n [telefono m] cellulare m

celluloid /ˈseljʊlɔɪd/ n celluloide f

Celsius /ˈselsɪəs/ a Celsius

Celt /kelt/ n celta mf. **~ic** a celtico

cement /sɪˈment/ n cemento m; ⟨adhesive⟩ mastice m ● vt cementare; fig consolidare

cemetery /ˈsemətrɪ/ n cimitero m

censor /ˈsensə(r)/ n censore m ● vt censurare. **~ship** n censura f

censure /ˈsenʃə(r)/ vt biasimare

census /ˈsensəs/ n censimento m

cent /sent/ n ⟨coin⟩ centesimo m

centenary /senˈtiːnərɪ/ n, Am **centennial** /senˈtenɪəl/ n centenario m

center /ˈsentə(r)/ n Am = **centre**

centi|grade /ˈsentɪ-/ a centigrado. **~metre** n centimetro m. **~pede** /-piːd/ n centopiedi m inv

central /ˈsentrl/ a centrale. **~ 'heating** n riscaldamento m autonomo. **~ize** vt centralizzare. **~ly** adv al centro; **~ly heated** con riscaldamento autonomo. **~ reser'vation** n Auto banchina f spartitraffico

centre /ˈsentə(r)/ n centro m ● v (pt/pp **centred**) ● vt centrare ● vi **~ on** fig incentrarsi su. **~-'forward** n centravanti m inv

centrifugal /sentrɪ'fju:gl/ *n* ~ **force** forza *f* centrifuga

century /'sentʃərɪ/ *n* secolo *m*

ceramic /sɪ'ræmɪk/ *a* ceramico. **~s** *n* (*art*) ceramica *fsg*; (*objects*) ceramiche *fpl*

cereal /'stərɪəl/ *n* cereale *m*

cerebral /'serɪbrl/ *a* cerebrale

ceremon|ial /serɪ'məʊnɪəl/ *a* cerimonia ●*n* cerimoniale *m*. **~ious** /-ɪəs/ *a* cerimonioso

ceremony /'serɪmənɪ/ *n* cerimonia *f*

certain /'sɜ:tn/ *a* certo; **for ~** di sicuro; **make ~** accertarsi; **he is ~ to win** è certo di vincere; **it's not ~ whether he'll come** non è sicuro che venga. **~ly** *adv* certamente; **~ly not!** no di certo! **~ty** *n* certezza *f*; **it's a ~ty** è una cosa certa

certificate /sə'tɪfɪkət/ *n* certificato *m*

certify /'sɜ:tɪfaɪ/ *vt* (*pt/pp* -**ied**) certificare; (*declare insane*) dichiarare malato di mente

cessation /se'seɪʃn/ *n* cessazione *f*

cesspool /'ses-/ *n* pozzo *m* nero

cf *abbr* (*compare*) cf, cfr

chafe /tʃeɪf/ *vt* irritare

chain /tʃeɪn/ *n* catena *f* ●*vt* incatenare (*prisoner*); attaccare con la catena (*dog*) (**to** a). **chain up** *vt* legare alla catena (*dog*)

chain: ~ **reaction** *n* reazione *f* a catena. **~-smoke** *vi* fumare una sigaretta dopo l'altra. **~-smoker** *n* fumatore, -trice *mf* accanito, -a. **~ store** *n* negozio *m* appartenente a una catena

chair /tʃeə(r)/ *n* sedia *f*; *Univ* cattedra *f* ●*vt* presiedere. **~-lift** *n* seggiovia *f*. **~man** *n* presidente *m*

chalet /'ʃæleɪ/ *n* chalet *m inv*; (*in holiday camp*) bungalow *m inv*

chalice /'tʃælɪs/ *n Relig* calice *m*

chalk /tʃɔ:k/ *n* gesso *m*. **~y** *a* gessoso

challeng|e /'tʃælɪndʒ/ *n* sfida *f*; *Mil* intimazione *f* ●*vt* sfidare; *Mil* intimare il chi va la a; *fig* mettere in dubbio (*statement*). **~er** *n* sfi-

dante *mf*. **~ing** *a* (*job*) impegnativo

chamber /'tʃeɪmbə(r)/ *n* **C~ of Commerce** camera *f* di commercio

chamber: **~maid** *n* cameriera *f* [d'albergo]. **~ music** *n* musica *f* da camera

chamois[1] /'ʃæmwɑ:/ *n inv* (*animal*) camoscio *m*

chamois[2] /'ʃæmɪ/ *n* ~ [*leather*] [pelle *f* di] camoscio *m*

champagne /ʃæm'peɪn/ *n* champagne *m inv*

champion /'tʃæmpɪən/ *n Sport* campione *m*; (*of cause*) difensore, difenditrice *mf* ●*vt* (*defend*) difendere; (*fight for*) lottare per. **~ship** *n Sport* campionato *m*

chance /tʃɑ:ns/ *n* caso *m*; (*possibility*) possibilità *f inv*; (*opportunity*) occasione *f*; **by ~** per caso; **take a ~** provarci; **give sb a second ~** dare un'altra possibilità a qcno ●*attrib* fortuito ●*vt* **I'll ~ it** *fam* corro il rischio

chancellor /'tʃɑ:nsələ(r)/ *n* cancelliere *m*; *Univ* rettore *m*; **C~ of the Exchequer** ≈ ministro *m* del tesoro

chancy /'tʃɑ:nsɪ/ *a* rischioso

chandelier /ʃændə'lɪə(r)/ *n* lampadario *m*

change /tʃeɪndʒ/ *n* cambiamento *m*; (*money*) resto *m*; (*small coins*) spiccioli *mpl*; **for a ~** tanto per cambiare; **a ~ of clothes** un cambio di vestiti; **the ~ [of life]** la menopausa ●*vt* cambiare; (*substitute*) scambiare (**for** con); **~ one's clothes** cambiarsi i vestiti; **~ trains** cambiare treno ●*vi* cambiare; (**~ clothes**) cambiarsi; **all ~!** stazione terminale!

changeable /'tʃeɪndʒəbl/ *a* mutevole; (*weather*) variabile

changing-room *n* camerino *m* (*for sports*) spogliatoio *m*

channel /'tʃænl/ *n* canale *m*; **the [English] C~** la Manica; **the C~ Islands** le Isole del Canale ●*vt*

(*pt/pp* **channelled**) ~ **one's**
energies into sth convogliare le
proprie energie in qcsa

chant /tʃɑːnt/ *n* cantilena *f*; (*of
demonstrators*) slogan *m inv* di
protesta ● *vt* cantare; (*demonstrators:*) gridare

chao|s /'keɪɒs/ *n* caos *m*. ~**tic**
/-'ɒtɪk/ *a* caotico

chap /tʃæp/ *n fam* tipo *m*

chapel /'tʃæpl/ *n* cappella *f*

chaperon /'ʃæpərəʊn/ *n* chaperon
f inv ● *vt* fare da chaperon a (*sb*)

chaplain /'tʃæplɪn/ *n* cappella-
no *m*

chapped /tʃæpt/ *a* (*skin, lips*)
screpolato

chapter /'tʃæptə(r)/ *n* capitolo *m*

char¹ /tʃɑː(r)/ *n fam* donna *f* delle
pulizie

char² *vt* (*pt/pp* **charred**) (*burn*)
carbonizzare

character /'kærɪktə(r)/ *n* carattere *m*; (*in novel, play*) personaggio
m; **quite a ~** *fam* un tipo particolare

characteristic /kærɪktə'rɪstɪk/ *a*
caratteristico ● *n* caratteristica *f*.
~**ally** *adv* tipicamente

characterize /'kærɪktəraɪz/ *vt* ca-
ratterizzare

charade /ʃə'rɑːd/ *n* farsa *f*

charcoal /'tʃɑː-/ *n* carbonella *f*

charge /tʃɑːdʒ/ *n* (*cost*) prezzo *m*;
Electr, Mil carica *f*; *Jur* accusa *f*;
free of ~ gratuito; **be in ~** essere
responsabile (**of** di); **take ~** assu-
mersi la responsabilità; **take ~ of**
occuparsi di ● *vt* far pagare (*fee*);
far pagare a (*person*); *Electr, Mil*
caricare; *Jur* accusare (**with** di); ~
sb for sth far pagare qcsa a qcno;
~ **it to my account** lo addebiti sul
mio conto ● *vi* (*attack*) caricare

chariot /'tʃærɪət/ *n* cocchio *m*

charisma /kə'rɪzmə/ *n* carisma *m*.
~**tic** /kærɪz'mætɪk/ *a* carismatico

charitable /'tʃærɪtəbl/ *a* caritate-
vole; (*kind*) indulgente

charity /'tʃærətɪ/ *n* carità *f*; (*organization*) associazione *f* di bene-

ficenza; **concert given for** ~ concerto *m* di beneficenza; **live on** ~
vivere di elemosina

charm /tʃɑːm/ *n* fascino *m*; (*object*)
ciondolo *m* ● *vt* affascinare. ~**ing**
a affascinante

chart /tʃɑːt/ *n* carta *f* nautica;
(*table*) tabella *f*

charter /'tʃɑːtə(r)/ *n* ~ **[flight]**
[volo *m*] charter *m inv* ● *vt* noleggiare. ~**ed accountant** *n* commercialista *mf*

charwoman /'tʃɑː-/ *n* donna *f* delle
pulizie

chase /tʃeɪs/ *n* inseguimento *m*
● *vt* inseguire. **chase away** *or* **off**
vt cacciare via

chasm /'kæz(ə)m/ *n* abisso *m*

chassis /'ʃæsɪ/ *n* (*pl* **chassis**
/-sɪz/) telaio *m*

chaste /tʃeɪst/ *a* casto

chastity /'tʃæstətɪ/ *n* castità *f*

chat /tʃæt/ *n* chiacchierata *f*; **have**
a ~ with fare quattro chiacchiere
con ● *vi* (*pt/pp* **chatted**) chiacchierare. ~ **show** *n* talk show *m
inv*

chatter /'tʃætə(r)/ *n* chiacchiere
fpl ● *vi* chiacchierare; (*teeth:*) battere. ~**box** *n fam* chiacchierone, -a
mf

chatty /'tʃætɪ/ *a* (-**ier, -iest**) chiacchierone; (*style*) familiare

chauffeur /'ʃəʊfə(r)/ *n* autista *mf*

chauvin|ism /'ʃəʊvɪnɪzm/ *n*
sciovinismo *m*. ~**ist** *n* sciovinista
mf. **male** ~**ist** *n fam* maschili-
sta *m*

cheap /tʃiːp/ *a* a buon mercato;
(*rate*) economico; (*vulgar*) grossolano; (*of poor quality*) scadente
● *adv* a buon mercato. ~**ly** *adv* a
buon mercato

cheat /tʃiːt/ *n* imbroglione, -a *mf*;
(*at cards*) baro *m* ● *vt* imbrogliare; ~ **sb out of sth** sottrarre qcsa
a qcno con l'inganno ● *vi* imbrogliare; (*at cards*) barare. **cheat on**
vt fam tradire (*wife*)

check¹ /tʃek/ *a* (*pattern*) a quadri
● *n* disegno *m* a quadri

check² n verifica f; (of tickets) controllo m; (in chess) scacco m; (Am: bill) conto m; (Am: cheque) assegno m; (Am: tick) segnetto m; **keep a ~ on** controllare; **keep in ~** tenere sotto controllo ● vt riservare; controllare (tickets); (restrain) contenere; (stop) bloccare ● vi controllare; **~ on sth** controllare qcsa. **check in** vi registrarsi all'arrivo (in albergo); Aeron fare il check-in ● vt registrare all'arrivo (in albergo). **check out** vi (of hotel) saldare il conto ● vt (fam: investigate) controllare. **check up** vi accertarsi; **~ up on** prendere informazioni su

check|ed /tʃekt/ a a quadri. **~ers** n Am dama f

check: **~-in** n (in airport: place) banco m accettazione, check-in m inv; **~-in time** check-in m inv. **~mark** n Am segnetto m. **~mate** int scacco matto! **~-out** n (in supermarket) cassa f. **~-room** n Am deposito m bagagli. **~-up** n Med visita f di controllo, check-up m inv

cheek /tʃiːk/ n guancia f; (impudence) sfacciataggine f. **~y** a sfacciato

cheep /tʃiːp/ vi pigolare

cheer /tʃɪə(r)/ n evviva m inv; **three ~s** tre urrà; **~s!** salute!; (goodbye) arrivederci!; (thanks) grazie! ● vt/i acclamare. **~ up** vt tirare su [di morale] ● vi tirarsi su [di morale]; **~ up!** su con la vita!. **~ful** a allegro. **~fulness** n allegria f. **~ing** n acclamazione f

cheerio /tʃɪərɪˈəʊ/ int fam arrivederci

'cheerless a triste, tetro

cheese /tʃiːz/ n formaggio m. **~cake** n dolce m al formaggio

chef /ʃef/ n cuoco, -a mf, chef mf inv

chemical /ˈkemɪkl/ a chimico ● n prodotto m chimico

chemist /ˈkemɪst/ n (pharmacist) farmacista mf; (scientist) chimico, -a mf; **~'s** [shop] farmacia f. **~ry** n chimica f

cheque /tʃek/ n assegno m. **~-book** n libretto m degli assegni. **~ card** n carta f assegni

cherish /ˈtʃerɪʃ/ vt curare teneramente; (love) avere caro; nutrire (hope)

cherry /ˈtʃerɪ/ n ciliegia f; (tree) ciliegio m

cherub /ˈtʃerəb/ n cherubino m

chess /tʃes/ n scacchi mpl

chess: **~-board** n scacchiera f. **~-man** n pezzo m degli scacchi. **~-player** n scacchista mf

chest /tʃest/ n petto m; (box) cassapanca f

chestnut /ˈtʃesnʌt/ n castagna f; (tree) castagno m

chest of 'drawers n cassettone m

chew /tʃuː/ vt masticare. **~ing-gum** n gomma f da masticare

chic /ʃiːk/ a chic inv

chick /tʃɪk/ n pulcino m; (fam: girl) ragazza f

chicken /ˈtʃɪkn/ n pollo m ● attrib (soup, casserole) di pollo ● a fam fifone ● **chicken out** vi fam he **~ed out** gli è venuta fifa. **~pox** n varicella f

chicory /ˈtʃɪkərɪ/ n cicoria f

chief /tʃiːf/ a principale ● n capo m. **~ly** adv principalmente

chilblain /ˈtʃɪlbleɪn/ n gelone m

child /tʃaɪld/ n (pl **~ren**) bambino, -a mf; (son/daughter) figlio, -a mf

child 'birth n parto m. **~hood** n infanzia f. **~ish** a infantile. **~ishness** n puerilità f. **~less** a senza figli. **~like** a ingenuo. **~-minder** n baby-sitter mf inv

children /ˈtʃɪldrən/ see **child**

Chile /ˈtʃɪlɪ/ n Cile m. **~an** a & n cileno, -a mf

chill /tʃɪl/ n freddo m; (illness) infreddatura f ● vt raffreddare

chilli /ˈtʃɪlɪ/ n (pl **-es**) [pepper] peperoncino m

chilly /ˈtʃɪlɪ/ a freddo

chime /tʃaɪm/ vi suonare

chimney /ˈtʃɪmnɪ/ n camino m.

~-pot n comignolo m. **~-sweep** n spazzacamino m

chimpanzee /tʃɪmpæn'zi:/ n scimpanzé m inv

chin /tʃɪn/ n mento m

china /'tʃaɪnə/ n porcellana f

China n Cina f. **~ese** /-'niːz/ a & n cinese mf; (language) cinese m; **the ~ese** pl i cinesi

chink[1] /tʃɪŋk/ n (slit) fessura f

chink[2] n (noise) tintinnio m

chip /tʃɪp/ n (fragment) scheggia f; (in china, paintwork) scheggiatura f; Comput chip m inv; (in gambling) fiche f. **~s** pl Br Culin patatine fpl fritte; Am Culin patatine fpl ●vt (pt/pp **chipped**) (damage) scheggiare. **chip in** vi fam intromettersi; (with money) contribuire. **~ped** a (damaged) scheggiato

chiropod|ist /kɪ'rʊpədɪst/ n podiatra mf inv. **~y** n podiatria f

chirp /tʃɜːp/ vi cinguettare; (cricket:) fare cri cri. **~y** a fam pimpante

chisel /'tʃɪzl/ n scalpello m

chival|rous /'ʃɪvlrəs/ a cavalleresco. **~ry** n cavalleria f

chives /tʃaɪvz/ npl erba f cipollina

chlorine /'klɔːriːn/ n cloro m

chloroform /'klɒrəfɔːm/ n cloroformio m

chock-a-block /tʃɒkə'blɒk/, **chock-full** /tʃɒk'fʊl/ a pieno zeppo

chocolate /'tʃɒkələt/ n cioccolato m; (drink) cioccolata f; **a** ~ un cioccolatino

choice /tʃɔɪs/ n scelta f ●a scelto

choir /'kwaɪə(r)/ n coro m. **~boy** n corista m

choke /tʃəʊk/ n Auto aria f ●vt/i soffocare

cholera /'kɒlərə/ n colera m

cholesterol /kə'lestərʊl/ n colesterolo m

choose /tʃuːz/ vt/i (pt **chose**, pp **chosen**) scegliere; **as you** ~ come vuoi

choos[e]y /'tʃuːzɪ/ a fam difficile

chop /tʃɒp/ n (blow) colpo m (d'ascia); Culin costata f. ●vt (pt/pp **chopped**) tagliare. **chop down** vt abbattere (tree). **chop off** vt spaccare

chop|per /tʃɒpə(r)/ n accetta f; fam elicottero m. **~py** a increspato

'chopsticks npl bastoncini mpl cinesi

choral /'kɔːrəl/ a corale

chord /kɔːd/ n Mus corda f

chore /tʃɔː(r)/ n corvé f inv; [household] **~s** faccende fpl domestiche

choreograph|er /kɒrɪ'ɒɡrəfə(r)/ n coreografo, -a mf. **~y** /-ɪ/ n coreografia f

chortle /'tʃɔːtl/ vi ridacchiare

chorus /'kɔːrəs/ n coro m; (of song) ritornello m

chose, chosen /tʃəʊz, 'tʃəʊzn/ see **choose**

Christ /kraɪst/ n Cristo m

christen /'krɪsn/ vt battezzare. **~ing** n battesimo m

Christian /'krɪstʃən/ a & n cristiano, -a mf. **~ity** /-stɪ'ænətɪ/ n cristianesimo m. ~ **name** n nome m di battesimo

Christmas /'krɪsməs/ n Natale m ●attrib di Natale. **'~ card** n biglietto m d'auguri di Natale. **~ Day** n il giorno di Natale. **~ Eve** n la vigilia di Natale. **~ present** n regalo m di Natale. **~ 'pudding** dolce m natalizio a base di frutta candita e liquore. **'~ tree** n albero m di Natale

chrome /krəʊm/ n, **chromium** /'krəʊmɪəm/ n cromo m

chromosome /'krəʊməsəʊm/ n cromosoma m

chronic /'krɒnɪk/ a cronico

chronicle /'krɒnɪkl/ n cronaca f

chronological /krɒnə'lɒdʒɪkl/ a cronologico. **~ly** adv (ordered) in ordine cronologico

chrysanthemum /krɪ'sænθəməm/ n crisantemo m

chubby /'tʃʌbɪ/ *a* (**-ier, -iest**) paffuto

chuck /tʃʌk/ *vt fam* buttare. **chuck out** *vt fam* buttare via ‹*object*›; buttare fuori ‹*person*›

chuckle /'tʃʌkl/ *vi* ridacchiare

chug /tʃʌg/ *vi* (*pt/pp* chugged) **the train ~ged out of the station** il treno è uscito dalla stazione sbuffando

chum /tʃʌm/ *n* amico, -a *mf*. **~my** *a fam* **be ~my with** essere amico di

chunk /tʃʌŋk/ *n* grosso pezzo *m*

church /tʃɜːtʃ/ *n* chiesa *f* **~yard** *n* cimitero *m*

churlish /'tʃɜːlɪʃ/ *a* sgarbato

churn /tʃɜːn/ *vt* churn out sfornare

chute /ʃuːt/ *n* scivolo *m*; (*for rubbish*) canale *m* di scarico

CID *n abbr* (**Criminal Investigation Department**) polizia *f* giudiziaria

cider /'saɪdə(r)/ *n* sidro *m*

cigar /sɪ'gɑː(r)/ *n* sigaro *m*

cigarette /sɪgə'ret/ *n* sigaretta *f*

cine-camera /'sɪnɪ-/ *n* cinepresa *f*

cinema /'sɪnɪmə/ *n* cinema *m inv*

cinnamon /'sɪnəmən/ *n* cannella *f*

circle /'sɜːkl/ *n* cerchio *m*; *Theat* galleria *f*; **in a ~** in cerchio ●*vt* girare intorno a; cerchiare (*mistake*) ●*vi* descrivere dei cerchi

circuit /'sɜːkɪt/ *n* circuito *m*; (*lap*) giro *m*; **~ board** *n* circuito *m* stampato. **~ous** /sə'kjuːɪtəs/ *a* **~ous route** percorso *m* lungo e indiretto

circular /'sɜːkjʊlə(r)/ *a* circolare ●*n* circolare *f*

circulat|e /'sɜːkjʊleɪt/ *vt* far circolare ●*vi* circolare. **~ion** /-'leɪʃn/ *n* circolazione *f*; (*of newspaper*) tiratura *f*

circumcis|e /'sɜːkəmsaɪz/ *vt* circoncidere. **~ion** /-'sɪʒn/ *n* circoncisione *f*

circumference /sə'kʌmfərəns/ *n* conconferenza *f*

circumstance /'sɜːkəmstəns/ *n*

circostanza *f*; **~s** *pl* (*financial*) condizioni *fpl* finanziarie

circus /'sɜːkəs/ *n* circo *m*

CIS *n abbr* (**Commonwealth of Independent States**) CSI *f*

cistern /'sɪstən/ *n* (*tank*) cisterna *f*; (*of WC*) serbatoio *m*

cite /saɪt/ *vt* citare

citizen /'sɪtɪzn/ *n* cittadino, -a *mf*; (*of town*) abitante *mf*. **~ship** *n* cittadinanza *f*

citrus /'sɪtrəs/ *n* ~ [**fruit**] agrume *m*

city /'sɪtɪ/ *n* città *f inv*; **the C~** la City (*di Londra*)

civic /'sɪvɪk/ *a* civico

civil /'sɪvl/ *a* civile

civilian /sɪ'vɪljən/ *a* civile; **in ~ clothes** in borghese ●*n* civile *mf*

civiliz|ation /sɪvɪlaɪ'zeɪʃn/ *n* civiltà *f inv*. **~e** /'sɪvɪlaɪz/ *vt* civilizzare

civil: **~ 'servant** *n* impiegato, -a *mf* statale. **C~ 'Service** *n* pubblica amministrazione *f*

clad /klæd/ *a* vestito (**in** di)

claim /kleɪm/ *n* richiesta *f*; (*right*) diritto *m*; (*assertion*) dichiarazione *f*; **lay ~ to sth** rivendicare qcsa ●*vt* richiedere; reclamare ‹*lost property*›; rivendicare ‹*ownership*›; **~ that** sostenere che. **~ant** *n* richiedente *mf*

clairvoyant /kleə'vɔɪənt/ *n* chiaroveggente *mf*

clam /klæm/ *n* Culin vongola *f* ●**clam up** *vi* (*pt/pp* clammed) zittirsi

clamber /'klæmbə(r)/ *vi* arrampicarsi

clammy /'klæmɪ/ *a* (**-ier, -iest**) appiccicaticcio

clamour /'klæmə(r)/ *n* (*protest*) *n* mostranza *f* ●*vi* **~ for** chiedere a gran voce

clamp /klæmp/ *n* morsa *f*; *Auto* mettere i ceppi bloccaruote a. **clamp down** *vi fam* essere duro; **~ down on** reprimere

clan /klæn/ *n* clan *m inv*

clandestine /klæn'destɪn/ a clandestino

clang /klæŋ/ n suono m metallico. **~er** n fam gaffe f inv

clank /klæŋk/ n rumore m metallico

clap /klæp/ n **give sb a ~** applaudire qcno; **~ of thunder** tuono m ● vt/i (pt/pp **clapped**) applaudire; **~ one's hands** applaudire. **~ping** n applausi mpl

clarif|ication /klærɪfɪ'keɪʃn/ n chiarimento m. **~fy** /'klærɪfaɪ/ vt/i (pt/pp **-ied**) chiarire

clarinet /klærɪ'net/ n clarinetto m

clarity /'klærɪtɪ/ n chiarezza f

clash /klæʃ/ n scontro m; (noise) fragore m ● vi scontrarsi; (colours:) stonare; (events:) coincidere

clasp /klɑːsp/ n chiusura f ● vt agganciare; (hold) stringere

class /klɑːs/ n classe f; (lesson) corso m ● vt classificare

classic /'klæsɪk/ a classico ● n classico m; **~s** pl Univ lettere fpl classiche. **~al** a classico

classif|ication /klæsɪfɪ'keɪʃn/ n classificazione f. **~fy** /'klæsɪfaɪ/ vt (pt/pp **-ied**) classificare

classroom n aula f

classy /'klɑːsɪ/ a (**-ier**, **-iest**) fam d'alta classe

clatter /'klætə(r)/ n fracasso m ● vi far fracasso

clause /klɔːz/ n clausola f; Gram proposizione f

claustrophob|ia /klɔːstrə'fəʊbɪə/ n claustrofobia f

claw /klɔː/ n artiglio m; (of crab, lobster & Techn) tenaglia f ● vt (cat:) graffiare

clay /kleɪ/ n argilla f

clean /kliːn/ a pulito, lindo ● adv completamente ● vt pulire (shoes, windows); **~ one's teeth** lavarsi i denti; **have a coat ~ed** portare un cappotto in lavanderia. **clean up** vt pulire ● vi far pulizia

cleaner /'kliːnə(r)/ n uomo m/donna f delle pulizie; (substance) detersivo m; [dry] **~'s** lavanderia f, tintoria f

cleanliness /'klenlɪnɪs/ n pulizia f

cleanse /klenz/ vt pulire. **~r** n detergente m

clean-shaven a sbarbato

cleansing cream /'klenz-/ n latte m detergente

clear /klɪə(r)/ a chiaro; (conscience) pulito; (road) libero; (profit, advantage, majority) netto; (sky) sereno; (water) limpido; (glass) trasparente; **make sth ~** mettere qcsa in chiaro; **have I made myself ~?** mi sono fatto capire?; **five ~ days** cinque giorni buoni ● adv **stand ~ of** allontanarsi da; **keep ~ of** tenersi alla larga da ● vt sgombrare (room, street); sparecchiare (table); (acquit) scagionare; (authorize) autorizzare; scavalcare senza toccare (fence, wall); guadagnare (sum of money); passare (Customs); **~ one's throat** schiarirsi la gola ● vi (face, sky:) rasserenarsi; (fog:) dissiparsi. **clear away** vt mettere via. **clear off** vi fam filar via. **clear out** vt sgombrare ● vi fam filar via. **clear up** vt (tidy) mettere a posto; chiarire (mystery) ● vi (weather:) schiarirsi

clearance /'klɪərəns/ n (space) spazio m libero; (authorization) autorizzazione f; (Customs) sdoganamento m. **~ sale** n liquidazione f

clear|ing /'klɪərɪŋ/ n radura f. **~ly** adv chiaramente. **~ way** n Auto strada f con divieto di sosta

cleavage /'kliːvɪdʒ/ n (woman's) décolleté m inv

cleft /kleft/ n fenditura f

clench /klentʃ/ vt serrare

clergy /'klɜːdʒɪ/ npl clero m. **~man** n ecclesiastico m

cleric /'klerɪk/ n ecclesiastico m. **~al** a impiegatizio; Relig clericale

clerk /klɑːk, Am /klɜːk/ n impiegato, -a *mf*; (*Am: shop assistant*) commesso, -a *mf*

clever /'klevə(r)/ *a* intelligente; (*skilful*) abile

cliché /'kli:ʃeɪ/ *n* cliché *m inv*

click /klɪk/ *vi* scattare ● *n* Comput click *m*. **click on** *vt* Comput cliccare su

client /'klaɪənt/ *n* cliente *mf*

clientele /kli:ɒn'tel/ *n* clientela *f*

cliff /klɪf/ *n* scogliera *f*

climat|e /'klaɪmət/ *n* clima *f*. **~ic** /-'mætɪk/ *a* climatico

climax /'klaɪmæks/ *n* punto *m* culminante

climb /klaɪm/ *n* salita *f* ● *vt* scalare (*mountain*); arrampicarsi su (*ladder, tree*) ● *vi* arrampicarsi; (*rise*) salire; (*road:*) salire. **climb down** *vi* scendere; (*from ladder, tree*) scendere; *fig* tornare sui propri passi

climber /'klaɪmə(r)/ *n* alpinista *mf*; (*plant*) rampicante *m*

clinch /klɪntʃ/ *vt fam* concludere (*deal*) ● *n* (*in boxing*) clinch *m inv*

cling /klɪŋ/ *vi* (*pt/pp* clung) aggrapparsi; (*stick*) aderire. **~ film** *n* pellicola *f* trasparente

clinic /'klɪnɪk/ *n* ambulatorio *m*. **~al** *a* clinico

clink /klɪŋk/ *n* tintinnio *m*; (*fam: prison*) galera *f* ● *vi* tintinnare

clip[1] /klɪp/ *n* fermaglio *m*; (*jewellery*) spilla *f* ● *vt* (*pt/pp* clipped) attaccare

clip[2] *n* (*extract*) taglio *m* ● *vt* obliterare (*ticket*). **~board** *n* fermablocco *m inv*. **~pers** *npl* (*for hair*) rasoio *m*; (*for hedge*) tosasiepi *m inv*; (*for nails*) tronchesina *f*. **~ping** *n* (*from newspaper*) ritaglio *m*

clique /kli:k/ *n* cricca *f*

cloak /kləʊk/ *n* mantello *m*. **~room** *n* guardaroba *m inv*; (*toilet*) bagno *m*

clock /klɒk/ *n* orologio *m*; (*fam: speedometer*) tachimetro *m* ● **clock in** *vi* attaccare. **clock out** *vi* staccare

clock: **~ tower** *n* torre *f* dell'orologio. **~wise** *a* & *adv* in senso orario. **~work** *n* meccanismo *m*

clod /klɒd/ *n* zolla *f*

clog /klɒg/ *n* zoccolo *m* ● *vt* (*pt/pp* clogged) **~ [up]** intasare (*drain*); inceppare (*mechanism*) ● *vi* (*drain:*) intasarsi

cloister /'klɔɪstə(r)/ *n* chiostro *m*

clone /kləʊn/ *n* clone *m*

close[1] /kləʊs/ *a* vicino; (*friend*) intimo; (*weather*) afoso; **have a ~ shave** *fam* scamparla bella; **be ~ to sb** essere unito a qcno ● *adv* vicino, by vicino; **it's ~ on five o'clock** sono quasi le cinque

close[2] /kləʊz/ *n* fine *f* ● *vt* chiudere ● *vi* chiudersi; (*shop:*) chiudere. **close down** *vt* chiudere ● *vi* (*TV station:*) interrompere la trasmissione; (*factory:*) chiudere

closely /'kləʊslɪ/ *adv* da vicino; (*watch, listen*) attentamente

closet /'klɒzɪt/ *n Am* armadio *m*

close-up /'kləʊs-/ *n* primo piano *m*

closure /'kləʊʒə(r)/ *n* chiusura *f*

clot /klɒt/ *n* grumo *m*; (*fam: idiot*) tonto, -a *mf* ● *vi* (*pt/pp* clotted) (*blood:*) coagularsi

cloth /klɒθ/ *n* (*fabric*) tessuto *m*; (*duster etc*) straccio *m*

clothe /kləʊð/ *vt* vestire

clothes /kləʊðz/ *npl* vestiti *mpl*, abiti *mpl*. **~-brush** *n* spazzola *f* per abiti. **~-line** *n* corda *f* stendibiancheria

clothing /'kləʊðɪŋ/ *n* abbigliamento *m*

cloud /klaʊd/ *n* nuvola *f* ● **cloud over** *vi* rannuvolarsi. **~burst** *n* acquazzone *m*

cloudy /'klaʊdɪ/ *a* (*-ier, -iest*) nuvoloso; (*liquid*) torbido

clout /klaʊt/ *n fam* colpo *m*; (*influence*) impatto *m* (**with** su) ● *vt fam* colpire

clove /kləʊv/ *n* chiodo *m* di garofano; **~ of garlic** spicchio *m* d'aglio

clover /'kləʊvə(r)/ *n* trifoglio *m*

clown /klaʊn/ *n* pagliaccio *m* ● *vi* **~ [about]** fare il pagliaccio

club /klʌb/ n club m inv; (weapon) clava f; Sport mazza f; ~s pl (Cards) fiori mpl ●v (pt/pp **clubbed**) ●vt bastonare. **club together** vi unirsi

cluck /klʌk/ vi chiocciare

clue /klu:/ n indizio m; (in crossword) definizione f; **I haven't a ~** fam non ne ho idea

clump /klʌmp/ n gruppo m

clumsiness /'klʌmzɪnɪs/ n goffaggine f

clumsy /'klʌmzɪ/ a (-ier, -iest) maldestro; ⟨tool⟩ scomodo; ⟨remark⟩ senza tatto

clung /klʌŋ/ see **cling**

cluster /'klʌstə(r)/ n gruppo m ●vi raggrupparsi (**round** intorno a)

clutch /klʌtʃ/ n stretta f; Auto frizione f; **be in sb's ~es** essere in balia di qcno ●vt stringere; (grab) afferrare ●vi ~ **at** afferrare

clutter /'klʌtə(r)/ n caos m ●vt ~ [**up**] ingombrare

c/o abbr (care of) c/o, presso

coach /kəʊtʃ/ n pullman m inv; Rail vagone m; (horse-drawn) carrozza f; Sport allenatore, -trice mf ●vt fare esercitare; Sport allenare

coagulate /kəʊ'ægjʊleɪt/ vi coagularsi

coal /kəʊl/ n carbone m

coalition /kəʊə'lɪʃn/ n coalizione f

'coal-mine n miniera f di carbone

coarse /kɔ:s/ a grossolano; ⟨joke⟩ spinto

coast /kəʊst/ n costa f ●vi (freewheel) scendere a ruota libera; Auto scendere in folle. **~al** a costiero. **~er** n (mat) sottobicchiere m inv

coast: **~guard** n guardia f costiera. **~line** n litorale m

coat /kəʊt/ n cappotto m; (of animal) manto m; (of paint) mano f; **~ of arms** stemma f ●vt coprire; (with paint) ricoprire. **~-hanger** n gruccia f. **~-hook** n gancio m [appendiabiti]

coating /'kəʊtɪŋ/ n rivestimento m; (of paint) stato m

coax /kəʊks/ vt convincere con le moine

cob /kɒb/ n (of corn) pannocchia f

cobble /'kɒbl/ vt ~ **together** raffazzonare. **~ r** n ciabattino m

'cobblestones npl ciottolato msg

cobweb /'kɒb-/ n ragnatela f

cocaine /kə'keɪn/ n cocaina f

cock /kɒk/ n gallo m; (any male bird) maschio m ●vt sollevare il grilletto di (gun); **its ears** ⟨animal:⟩ drizzare le orecchie

cockerel /'kɒkərəl/ n galletto m

cock-'eyed a fam storto; (absurd) assurdo

cockle /'kɒkl/ n cardio m

cockney /'kɒknɪ/ n (dialect) dialetto m londinese; (person) abitante mf dell'est di Londra

cock: **~pit** n Aeron cabina f. **~roach** /-rəʊtʃ/ n scarafaggio m. **~tail** n cocktail m inv. **~-up** n sl **make a ~-up** fare un casino (**of** con)

cocky /'kɒkɪ/ a (-ier, -iest) fam presuntuoso

cocoa /'kəʊkəʊ/ n cacao m

coconut /'kəʊkənʌt/ n noce f di cocco

cocoon /kə'ku:n/ n bozzolo m

COD abbr (cash on delivery) pagamento m alla consegna

cod /kɒd/ n inv merluzzo m

code /kəʊd/ n codice m. **~d** a codificato

coedu'cational /kəʊ-/ a misto

coerce /kəʊ'ɜ:s/ vt costringere. **~ion** /-'ɜ:ʃn/ n coercizione f

coe'xist vi coesistere. **~ence** n coesistenza f

coffee /'kɒfɪ/ n caffè m inv

coffee: **~-grinder** n macinacaffè m inv. **~-pot** n caffettiera f. **~-table** n tavolino m

coffin /'kɒfɪn/ n bara f

cog /kɒg/ n Techn dente m (di ruota)

cogent /'kəʊdʒənt/ a convincente

cog-wheel n ruota f dentata

cohabit /kəʊ'hæbɪt/ vi Jur convivere

coherent /kəʊ'hɪərənt/ a coerente; (when speaking) logico

coil /kɔɪl/ n rotolo m; Electr bobina f; ~s pl spire fpl ● vt ~ [up] avvolgere

coin /kɔɪn/ n moneta f ● vt coniare (word)

coincide /kəʊɪn'saɪd/ vi coincidere

coinciden|ce /kəʊ'ɪnsɪdəns/ n coincidenza f. ~tal /-'dentl/ a casuale. ~tally adv casualmente

Coke® n Coca[-cola]® f

coke /kəʊk/ n [carbone m] coke m

cold /kəʊld/ a freddo; **I'm** ~ ho freddo ● n freddo m; Med raffreddore m

cold: ~-'blooded a spietato. ~-'hearted a insensibile. ~ly adv fig freddamente. ~ meat n salumi mpl. ~ness n freddezza f

coleslaw /'kəʊlslɔ:/ n insalata f di cavolo crudo, cipolle e carote in maionese

colic /'kɒlɪk/ n colica f

collaborat|e /kə'læbəreɪt/ vi collaborare; ~e on sth collaborare in qcsa. ~ion /-'reɪʃn/ n collaborazione f; (with enemy) collaborazionismo m. ~or n collaboratore, -trice mf; (with enemy) collaborazionista mf

collapse /kə'læps/ n crollo m ● vi (person) svenire; (roof, building) crollare. ~ible a pieghevole

collar /'kɒlə(r)/ n colletto m; (for animal) collare m. ~-bone n clavicola f

colleague /'kɒli:g/ n collega mf

collect /kə'lekt/ vt andare a prendere (person); ritirare (parcel, tickets); riscuotere (taxes); raccogliere (rubbish); (as hobby) collezionare ● vi riunirsi ● adv **call** ~ Am telefonare a carico del destinatario. ~ed /-ɪd/ a controllato

collection /kə'lekʃn/ n collezione f; (in church) questua f; (of

rubbish) raccolta f; (of post) levata f

collective /kə'lektɪv/ a collettivo

collector /kə'lektə(r)/ n (of stamps etc) collezionista mf

college /'kɒlɪdʒ/ n istituto m parauniversitario; **C~ of** ... Scuola f di...

collide /kə'laɪd/ vi scontrarsi

colliery /'kɒlɪəri/ n miniera f di carbone

collision /kə'lɪʒn/ n scontro m

colloquial /kə'ləʊkwɪəl/ a colloquiale. ~ism n espressione f colloquiale

cologne /kə'ləʊn/ n colonia f

colon /'kəʊlən/ n due punti mpl; Anat colon m inv

colonel /'kɜːnl/ n colonnello m

colonial /kə'ləʊnɪəl/ a coloniale

colon|ize /'kɒlənaɪz/ vt colonizzare. ~y n colonia f

colossal /kə'lɒsl/ a colossale

colour /'kʌlə(r)/ n colore m; (complexion) colorito m; ~s pl (flag) bandiera fsg; **off** ~ fam giù di tono ● vt colorare; ~ [in] colorare ● vi (blush) arrossire

colour: ~ **bar** n discriminazione f razziale. ~-**blind** a daltonico. ~**ed** a colorato; (person) di colore ● n (person) persona f di colore. ~-**fast** a dai colori resistenti. ~-**ful** a pieno di colore. ~-**less** a incolore. ~ **television** n televisione f a colori

colt /kəʊlt/ n puledro m

column /'kɒləm/ n colonna f. ~**ist** /-nɪst/ n giornalista mf che cura una rubrica

coma /'kəʊmə/ n coma m inv

comb /kəʊm/ n pettine m; (for wearing) pettinino m ● vt pettinare; (fig: search) setacciare; ~ **one's hair** pettinarsi i capelli

combat /'kɒmbæt/ n combattimento m ● vt (pt/pp **combated**) combattere

combination /kɒmbɪ'neɪʃn/ n combinazione f

combine¹ /kəm'baɪn/ vt unire; **~ a job with being a mother** conciliare il lavoro con il ruolo di madre ● vi ⟨chemical elements:⟩ combinarsi

combine² /'kɒmbaɪn/ n Comm associazione f. **~ [harvester]** n mietitrebbia f

combustion /kəm'bʌstʃn/ n combustione f

come /kʌm/ vi ⟨pt came, pp come⟩ venire; **where do you ~ from?** da dove vieni?; **~ to** ⟨reach⟩ arrivare a; **that ~s to £10** fanno 10 sterline; **~ into money** ricevere dei soldi; **~ true** ⟨prophesy⟩ verificarsi; aprirsi; **~ first** arrivare primo; ⟨fig⟩ venire prima di tutto; **in two sizes** esistere in due misure; **the years to ~** gli anni a venire; **how ~?** fam come mai? **come about** vi succedere. **come across** vi ~ **across as being** fam dare l'impressione di essere ● vt ⟨find⟩ imbattersi in. **come along** vi venire; ⟨job, opportunity:⟩ presentarsi; ⟨progress⟩ andare bene. **come apart** vi smontarsi; ⟨break⟩ rompersi. **come away** vi venir via; ⟨button, fastener:⟩ staccarsi. **come back** vi ritornare. **come by** vi passare ● vt ⟨obtain⟩ avere. **come down** vi scendere; **~ down to** ⟨reach⟩ arrivare a. **come in** vi entrare; ⟨in race⟩ arrivare; ⟨tide:⟩ salire. **come in for** vt ~ **in for criticism** essere criticato. **come off** vi staccarsi; ⟨take place⟩ esserci; ⟨succeed⟩ riuscire. **come on** vi ⟨make progress⟩ migliorare; **~ on!** ⟨hurry⟩ dai!; ⟨indicating disbelief⟩ ma va là!. **come out** vi venir fuori; ⟨book, sun:⟩ uscire; ⟨stain:⟩ andar via. **come over** vi venire. **come round** vi venire; ⟨after fainting⟩ riaversi; ⟨change one's mind⟩ farsi convincere. **come to** vi ⟨after fainting⟩ riaversi. **come up** vi salire; ⟨sun:⟩ sorgere; ⟨plant:⟩ crescere; **something came up** ⟨I was

prevented⟩ ho avuto un imprevisto. **come up with** vt tirar fuori

'come-back n ritorno m

comedian /kə'miːdɪən/ n comico m

'come-down n passo m indietro

comedy /'kɒmədɪ/ n commedia f

comet /'kɒmɪt/ n cometa f

come-uppance /kʌm'ʌpəns/ n **get one's ~** fam avere quel che si merita

comfort /'kʌmfət/ n benessere m; ⟨consolation⟩ conforto m ● vt confortare

comfortable /'kʌmfətəbl/ a comodo; **be ~e** ⟨person:⟩ stare comodo; ⟨fig: in situation⟩ essere a proprio agio; ⟨financially⟩ star bene. **~y** adv comodamente

'comfort station n Am bagno m pubblico

comfy /'kʌmfɪ/ a fam comodo

comic /'kɒmɪk/ a comico ● n comico, -a mf; ⟨periodical⟩ fumetto m. **~al** a comico. **~ strip** n striscia f di fumetti

coming /'kʌmɪŋ/ n venuta f; **~s and goings** viavai m

comma /'kɒmə/ n virgola f

command /kə'mɑːnd/ n comando m; ⟨order⟩ ordine m; ⟨mastery⟩ padronanza f ● vt ordinare; comandare ⟨army⟩

commandeer /kɒmən'dɪə(r)/ vt requisire

command|er /kə'mɑːndə(r)/ n comandante m. **~ing** a ⟨view⟩ imponente; ⟨lead⟩ dominante. **~ing officer** n comandante m. **~ment** n comandamento m

commemorat|e /kə'meməreɪt/ vt commemorare. **~ion** /-'reɪʃn/ n commemorazione f. **~ive** /-ətɪv/ a commemorativo

commence /kə'mens/ vt/i cominciare. **~ment** n inizio m

commend /kə'mend/ vt complimentarsi con ⟨on per⟩; ⟨recommend⟩ raccomandare ⟨to a⟩. **~able** /-əbl/ a lodevole

commensurate /kə'menʃərət/ a proporzionato (**with** a)

comment /'kɒment/ n commento m ● vi fare commenti (**on** su)

commentary /'kɒməntri/ n commento m; [**running**] ~ (on radio, TV) cronaca f diretta

commentat|e /'kɒmənteɪt/ vt ~ **on** TV, Radio fare la cronaca di. ~**or** n cronista mf

commerce /'kɒmɜːs/ n commercio m

commercial /kə'mɜːʃl/ a commerciale ● n TV pubblicità f inv. ~**ize** vt commercializzare

commiserate /kə'mɪzəreɪt/ vi esprimere il proprio rincrescimento (**with** a)

commission /kə'mɪʃn/ n commissione f; receive one's ~ Mil essere promosso ufficiale; out of ~ fuori uso ● vt commissionare

commissionaire /kəmɪʃə'neə(r)/ n portiere m

commissioner /kə'mɪʃənə(r)/ n commissario m

commit /kə'mɪt/ vt (pt/pp committed) (to prison, hospital) affidare (**to** a); impegnare (funds); ~ **oneself** impegnarsi. ~**ment** n impegno m; (involvement) compromissione f. ~**ted** a impegnato

committee /kə'mɪtɪ/ n comitato m

commodity /kə'mɒdətɪ/ n prodotto m

common /'kɒmən/ a comune, (vulgar) volgare ● n prato m pubblico; have in ~ avere in comune; House of C~s Camera f dei Comuni. ~**er** n persona f non nobile

common: ~**law** n diritto m consuetudinario. ~**ly** adv comunemente. C~ '**Market** m Mercato m Comune. ~**place** a banale. ~**room** n sala f dei professori/degli studenti. ~'**sense** n buon senso m

commotion /kə'məʊʃn/ n confusione f

communal /'kɒmjʊnl/ a comune

communicate /kə'mjuːnɪkeɪt/ vt/i comunicare

communication /kəmjuːnɪ'keɪʃn/ n comunicazione f; (of disease) trasmissione f; be in ~ with sb essere in contatto con qcno; ~**s** pl (technology) telecomunicazioni fpl. ~ **cord** n fermata f d'emergenza

communicative /kə'mjuːnɪkətɪv/ a comunicativo

Communion /kə'mjuːnɪən/ n [Holy] ~ comunione f

communiqué /kə'mjuːnɪkeɪ/ n comunicato m stampa

Commun|ism /'kɒmjʊnɪzm/ n comunismo m. ~**t** /-ɪst/ a & n comunista mf

community /kə'mjuːnətɪ/ n comunità f. ~ **centre** n centro m sociale

commute /kə'mjuːt/ vi fare il pendolare ● vt Jur commutare. ~**r** n pendolare mf

compact[1] /kəm'pækt/ a compatto

compact[2] /'kɒmpækt/ n portacipria m inv. ~ **disc** n compact disc m inv

companion /kəm'pænjən/ n compagno, a mf. ~**ship** n compagnia f

company /'kʌmpənɪ/ n compagnia f; (guests) ospiti mpl. ~ **car** n macchina f della ditta

comparable /'kɒmpərəbl/ a paragonabile

comparative /kəm'pærətɪv/ a comparativo; (relative) relativo ● n Gram comparativo m. ~**ly** adv relativamente

compare /kəm'peə(r)/ vt paragonare (**with/to** a) ● vi essere paragonato

comparison /kəm'pærɪsn/ n paragone m

compartment /kəm'pɑːtmənt/ n compartimento m; Rail scompartimento m

compass /'kʌmpəs/ n bussola f. ~**es** npl, pair of ~**es** compasso msg

compassion /kəm'pæʃn/ n compassione f. ~ate /-fənət/ a compassionevole

compatible /kəm'pætəbl/ a compatibile

compatriot /kəm'pætrɪət/ n compatriota mf

compel /kəm'pel/ vt (pt/pp compelled) costringere. ~ling a (reason) inconfutabile

compensat|e /'kɒmpənseɪt/ vt risarcire ● vi ~e for fig compensare di. ~ion /-'seɪʃn/ n risarcimento m; (fig: comfort) consolazione f

compère /'kɒmpeə(r)/ n presentatore, -trice mf

compete /kəm'pi:t/ vi competere; (take part) gareggiare

competen|ce /'kɒmpɪtəns/ n competenza f. ~t a competente

competition /kɒmpə'tɪʃn/ n concorrenza f; (contest) gara f

competitive /kəm'petɪtɪv/ a competitivo; ~ prices prezzi mpl concorrenziali

competitor /kəm'petɪtə(r)/ n concorrente mf

complacen|cy /kəm'pleɪsənsɪ/ n compiacimento m. ~t a compiaciuto

complain /kəm'pleɪn/ vi lamentarsi (about di); (formally) reclamare; ~ of Med accusare. ~t n lamentela f; (formal) reclamo m; Med disturbo m

complement¹ /'kɒmplɪmənt/ n complemento m

complement² /'kɒmplɪmənt/ vt complementare; ~ each other complementarsi a vicenda. ~ary /-'mentərɪ/ a complementare

complete /kəm'pli:t/ a completo; (utter) finito ● vt completare; compilare (form). ~ly adv completamente

completion /kəm'pli:ʃn/ n fine f

complex /'kɒmpleks/ a complesso ● n complesso m

complexion /kəm'plekʃn/ n carnagione f

complexity /kəm'pleksətɪ/ n complessità f inv

compliance /kəm'plaɪəns/ n accettazione f; (with rules) osservanza f; in ~ with in osservanza a (law); conformemente a (request)

complicat|e /'kɒmplɪkeɪt/ vt complicare. ~ed a complicato. ~ion /-'keɪʃn/ n complicazione f

compliment /'kɒmplɪmənt/ n complimento m; ~s pl omaggi mpl ● vt complimentare. ~ary /-'mentərɪ/ a complimentoso; (given free) in omaggio

comply /kəm'plaɪ/ vi (pt/pp -ied) ~ with conformarsi a

component /kəm'pəʊnənt/ a & n ~ [part] componente m

compose /kəm'pəʊz/ vt comporre; ~ oneself ricomporsi; be ~d of essere composto da. ~d a (calm) composto. ~r n compositore, -trice mf

composition /kɒmpə'zɪʃn/ n composizione f; (essay) tema m

compost /'kɒmpɒst/ n composta f

composure /kəm'pəʊʒə(r)/ n calma f

compound /'kɒmpaʊnd/ a composto. ~ fracture n frattura f esposta. ~ 'interest n interesse m composto ● n Chem composto m; Gram parola f composta; (enclosure) recinto m

comprehen|d /kɒmprɪ'hend/ vt comprendere. ~sible /-'hensəbl/ a comprensibile. ~sion /-'henʃn/ n comprensione f

comprehensive /kɒmprɪ'hensɪv/ a & n comprensivo; ~ [school] scuola f media in cui gli allievi hanno capacità d'apprendimento diverse. ~ insurance n Auto polizza f casco

compress¹ /'kɒmpres/ n compressa f

compress² /kəm'pres/ vt comprimere; ~ed air aria f compressa

comprise /kəm'praɪz/ vt comprendere; (form) costituire

compromise /'kɒmprəmaɪz/ n compromesso m ● vt compromettere ● vi fare un compromesso

compuls|ion /kəm'pʌlʃn/ *n* desiderio *m* irresistibile. **~ive** /-sɪv/ *a* Psych patologico. **~ive eating** voglia *f* ossessiva di mangiare. **~ory** /-sərɪ/ *a* obbligatorio

comput|er /kəm'pju:tə(r)/ *n* computer *m* *inv*. **~erize** *vt* computerizzare. **~ing** *n* informatica *f*

comrade /'kɒmreɪd/ *n* camerata *m*; *Pol* compagno, -a *mf*. **~ship** *n* cameratismo *m*

con[1] /kɒn/ *see* **pro**

con[2] *n fam* fregatura *f* ● *vt* /*pt/pp* **conned**/ *fam* fregare

concave /'kɒnkeɪv/ *a* concavo

conceal /kən'si:l/ *vt* nascondere

concede /kən'si:d/ *vt* (*admit*) ammettere; (*give up*) rinunciare a; lasciar fare (*goal*)

conceit /kən'si:t/ *n* presunzione *f*. **~ed** *a* presuntuoso

conceivable /kən'si:vəbl/ *a* concepibile

conceive /kən'si:v/ *vt* *Biol* concepire ● *vi* aver figli. **conceive of** *vt* *fig* concepire

concentrat|e /'kɒnsəntreɪt/ *vt* concentrare ● *vi* concentrarsi. **~ion** /-'treɪʃn/ *n* concentrazione *f*. **~ion camp** *n* campo *m* di concentramento

concept /'kɒnsept/ *n* concetto *m*. **~ion** /kən'sepʃn/ *n* concezione *f*; (*idea*) idea *f*

concern /kən'sɜ:n/ *n* preoccupazione *f*; *Comm* attività *f inv* ● *vt* (*be about*, *affect*) riguardare; (*worry*) preoccupare; **be ~ed about** essere preoccupato per; **~ oneself with** preoccuparsi di; **as far as I am ~ed** per quanto mi riguarda. **~ing** *prep* riguardo a

concert /'kɒnsət/ *n* concerto *m*. **~ed** /kən'sɜ:tɪd/ *a* collettivo

concertina /kɒnsə'ti:nə/ *n* piccola fisarmonica *f*

'concertmaster *n Am* primo violino *m*

concerto /kən'tʃeətəʊ/ *n* concerto *m*

concession /kən'seʃn/ *n* conces-

sione *f*; (*reduction*) sconto *m*. **~ary** *a* (*reduced*) scontato

conciliation /kənsɪlɪ'eɪʃn/ *n* conciliazione *f*

concise /kən'saɪs/ *a* conciso

conclu|de /kən'klu:d/ *vt* concludere ● *vi* concludersi. **~ding** *a* finale

conclusion /kən'klu:ʒn/ *n* conclusione *f*; **in ~** per concludere

conclusive /kən'klu:sɪv/ *a* definitivo. **~ly** *adv* in modo definitivo

concoct /kən'kɒkt/ *vt* confezionare; *fig* inventare. **~ion** /-ɒkʃn/ *n* mistura *f*; (*drink*) intruglio *m*

concourse /'kɒnkɔ:s/ *n* atrio *m*

concrete /'kɒŋkri:t/ *a* concreto ● *n* calcestruzzo *m*

concur /kən'kɜ:(r)/ *vi* (*pt/pp* **concurred**) essere d'accordo

concurrently /kən'kʌrəntlɪ/ *adv* contemporaneamente

concussion /kən'kʌʃn/ *n* commozione *f* cerebrale

condemn /kən'dem/ *vt* condannare; dichiarare inagibile (*building*). **~ation** /kɒndem'neɪʃn/ *n* condanna *f*

condensation /kɒnden'seɪʃn/ *n* condensazione *f*

condense /kən'dens/ *vt* condensare; *Phys* condensare ● *vi* condensarsi. **~d milk** *n* latte *m* condensato

condescend /kɒndɪ'send/ *vi* degnarsi. **~ing** *a* condiscendente

condition /kən'dɪʃn/ *n* condizione *f*; **on ~ that** a condizione che ● *vt* *Psych* condizionare. **~al** *a* (*acceptance*) condizionato; *Gram* condizionale ● *n Gram* condizionale *m*. **~er** *n* balsamo *m*; (*for fabrics*) ammorbidente *m*

condolences /kən'dəʊlənsɪz/ *npl* condoglianze *fpl*

condom /'kɒndəm/ *n* preservativo *m*

condo[minium /'kɒndə('mɪnɪəm)/ *n Am* condominio *m*

condone /kən'dəʊn/ *vt* passare sopra a

conducive /kən'dju:sɪv/ *a* be ~ to contribuire a

conduct¹ /'kɒndʌkt/ *n* condotta *f*

conduct² /kən'dʌkt/ *vt* condurre; dirigere ⟨*orchestra*⟩. ~or *n* direttore *m* d'orchestra; *(of bus)* bigliettaio *m*; *Phys* conduttore *m*. ~ress *n* bigliettaia *f*

cone /kəʊn/ *n* cono *m*; *Bot* pigna *f*; *Auto* birillo *m* ● **cone off** *vt* be ~d **off** *Auto* essere chiuso da birilli

confectioner /kən'fekʃənə(r)/ *n* pasticciere, -a *mf*. ~y *n* pasticceria *f*

confederation /kənfedə'reɪʃn/ *n* confederazione *f*

confer /kən'fɜ:(r)/ *v* *(pt/pp* **conferred)** ● *vt* conferire (**on a**) ● *vi* *(discuss)* conferire

conference /'kɒnfərəns/ *n* conferenza *f*

confess /kən'fes/ *vt* confessare ● *vi* confessare; *Relig* confessarsi. ~ion /-eʃn/ *n* confessione *f*. ~ional /-eʃənəl/ *n* confessionale *m*. ~or *n* confessore *m*

confetti /kən'fetɪ/ *n* coriandoli *mpl*

confide /kən'faɪd/ *vt* confidare. **confide in** *vt* ~ **in sb** fidarsi di qcno

confidence /'kɒnfɪdəns/ *n* *(trust)* fiducia *f*; *(self-assurance)* sicurezza *f* di sé; *(secret)* confidenza *f*; **in** ~ in confidenza. ~ **trick** *n* truffa *f*

confident /'kɒnfɪdənt/ *a* fiducioso; *(self-assured)* sicuro di sé. ~**ly** *adv* con aria fiduciosa

confidential /kɒnfɪ'denʃl/ *a* confidenziale

confine /kən'faɪn/ *vt* rinchiudere; *(limit)* limitare; **be** ~**d to bed** essere confinato a letto. ~**d** *a* ⟨*space*⟩ limitato. ~**ment** *n* detenzione *f*; *Med* parto *m*

confines /'kɒnfaɪnz/ *npl* confini *mpl*

confirm /kən'fɜ:m/ *vt* confermare; *Relig* cresimare. ~**ation** /kɒnfə'meɪʃn/ *n* conferma *f*; *Relig*

cresima *f*. ~**ed** *a* incallito; ~**ed bachelor** scapolo *m* impenitente

confiscate /'kɒnfɪskeɪt/ *vt* confiscare. ~**ion** /-'keɪʃn/ *n* confisca *f*

conflict¹ /'kɒnflɪkt/ *n* conflitto *m*

conflict² /kən'flɪkt/ *vi* essere in contraddizione. ~**ing** *a* contraddittorio

conform /kən'fɔ:m/ *vi* ⟨*person:*⟩ conformarsi; ⟨*thing:*⟩ essere conforme (**to a**). ~**ist** *n* conformista *mf*

confounded /kən'faʊndɪd/ *a* fam maledetto

confront /kən'frʌnt/ *vt* affrontare; **the problems ~ing us** i problemi che dobbiamo affrontare. ~**ation** /kɒnfrʌn'teɪʃn/ *n* confronto *m*

confuse /kən'fju:z/ *vt* confondere. ~**ing** *a* che confonde. ~**ion** /-ju:ʒn/ *n* confusione *f*

congeal /kən'dʒi:l/ *vi* ⟨*blood:*⟩ coagularsi

congenial /kən'dʒi:nɪəl/ *a* congeniale

congenital /kən'dʒenɪtl/ *a* congenito

congest|ed /kən'dʒestɪd/ *a* congestionato. ~**ion** /-estʃn/ *n* congestione *f*

congratulat|e /kən'grætjʊleɪt/ *vt* congratularsi con (**on per**). ~**ions** /-'eɪʃnz/ *npl* congratulazioni *fpl*

congregat|e /'kɒŋgrɪgeɪt/ *vi* radunarsi. ~**ion** /-'geɪʃn/ *n* Relig assemblea *f*

congress /'kɒŋgres/ *n* congresso *m*. ~**man** *n* Am Pol membro *m* del congresso

conical /'kɒnɪkl/ *a* conico

conifer /'kɒnɪfə(r)/ *n* conifera *f*

conjecture /kən'dʒektʃə(r)/ *n* congettura *f*

conjugal /'kɒndʒʊgl/ *a* coniugale

conjugat|e /'kɒndʒʊgeɪt/ *vt* coniugare. ~**ion** /-'geɪʃn/ *n* coniugazione *f*

conjunction /kən'dʒʌŋkʃn/ *n* congiunzione *f*; **in** ~ **with** insieme a

conjunctivitis /kəndʒʌŋktɪ'vaɪtɪs/ *n* congiuntivite *f*

conjur|e /ˈkʌndʒə(r)/ vi ~ing tricks npl giochi mpl di prestigio. ~or n prestigiatore, -trice mf.
conjure up vt evocare ⟨image⟩; tirar fuori dal nulla ⟨meal⟩

conk /kɒŋk/ vi ~ out fam ⟨machine:⟩ guastarsi; ⟨person:⟩ crollare

'con-man n fam truffatore m

connect /kəˈnekt/ vt collegare; **be ~ed with** avere legami con; (be related to) essere imparentato con; **be well ~ed** aver conoscenze influenti ● vi essere collegato (with a.); ⟨train:⟩ fare coincidenza

connection /kəˈnekʃn/ n (between ideas) nesso m; (in travel) coincidenza f; Electr collegamento m; **in ~ with** con riferimento a. ~s pl (people) conoscenze fpl

connoisseur /kɒnəˈsɜː(r)/ n intenditore, -trice mf

conquer /ˈkɒŋkə(r)/ vt conquistare; fig superare ⟨fear⟩. ~or n conquistatore m

conquest /ˈkɒŋkwest/ n conquista f

conscience /ˈkɒnʃəns/ n coscienza f

conscientious /kɒnʃiˈenʃəs/ a coscienzioso. ~ **objector** n obiettore m di coscienza

conscious /ˈkɒnʃəs/ a conscio; ⟨decision⟩ meditato; [fully] ~ cosciente; **be/become ~ of** rendersi conto di qcsa. ~**ly** adv consapevolmente. ~**ness** n consapevolezza f; Med conoscenza f

conscript¹ /ˈkɒnskrɪpt/ n coscritto m

conscript² /kənˈskrɪpt/ vt Mil chiamare alle armi. ~**ion** /-ɪpʃn/ n coscrizione f, leva f

consecrat|e /ˈkɒnsɪkreɪt/ vt consacrare. ~**ion** /-ˈkreɪʃn/ n consacrazione f

consecutive /kənˈsekjʊtɪv/ a consecutivo

consensus /kənˈsensəs/ n consenso m

consent /kənˈsent/ n consenso m ● vi acconsentire

consequen|ce /ˈkɒnsɪkwəns/ n conseguenza f; (importance) importanza f. ~**t** a conseguente. ~**tly** adv di conseguenza

conservation /kɒnsəˈveɪʃn/ n conservazione f. ~**ist** n fautore, -trice mf della tutela ambientale

conservative /kənˈsɜːvətɪv/ a conservativo; ⟨estimate⟩ ottimistico. **C~** Pol a conservatore ● n conservatore, -trice mf

conservatory /kənˈsɜːvətrɪ/ n spazio m chiuso da vetrate adiacente alla casa

conserve /kənˈsɜːv/ vt conservare

consider /kənˈsɪdə(r)/ vt considerare; ~ **doing sth** considerare la possibilità di fare qcsa. ~**able** /-əbl/ a considerevole. ~**ably** adv considerevolmente

consider|ate /kənˈsɪdərət/ a pieno di riguardo. ~**ately** adv con riguardo. ~**ation** /-ˈreɪʃn/ n considerazione f; (thoughtfulness) attenzione f; (respect) riguardo m; (payment) compenso m; **take sth into ~ation** prendere qcsa in considerazione. ~**ing** prep considerando

consign /kənˈsaɪn/ vt affidare. ~**ment** n consegna f

consist /kənˈsɪst/ vi ~ **of** consistere di

consisten|cy /kənˈsɪstənsɪ/ n coerenza f; (density) consistenza f. ~**t** a coerente; (loyalty) costante. ~**tly** adv coerentemente; (late, loyal) costantemente

consolation /kɒnsəˈleɪʃn/ n consolazione f. ~ **prize** n premio m di consolazione

console /kənˈsəʊl/ vt consolare

consolidate /kənˈsɒlɪdeɪt/ vt consolidare

consonant /ˈkɒnsənənt/ n consonante f

consort /kənˈsɔːt/ vi ~ **with** frequentare

consortium /kən'sɔ:tɪəm/ n consorzio m

conspicuous /kən'spɪkjʊəs/ a facilmente distinguibile

conspiracy /kən'spɪrəsɪ/ n cospirazione f

conspire /kən'spaɪə(r)/ vi cospirare

constable /'kʌnstəbl/ n agente m [di polizia]

constant /'kɒnstənt/ a costante. **~ly** adv costantemente

constellation /kɒnstə'leɪʃn/ n stellazione f

consternation /kɒnstə'neɪʃn/ n costernazione f

constipat|ed /'kɒnstɪpeɪtɪd/ a stitico. **~ion** /-'peɪʃn/ n stitichezza f

constituency /kən'stɪtjʊənsɪ/ n area f elettorale di un deputato nel Regno Unito

constituent /kən'stɪtjʊənt/ n costituente m; Pol elettore, -trice mf

constitut|e /'kɒnstɪtjuːt/ vt costituire. **~ion** /-'tjuːʃn/ n costituzione f. **~ional** /-'tjuːʃənl/ a costituzionale

constrain /kən'streɪn/ vt costringere. **~t** n costrizione f; (restriction) restrizione f; (strained manner) disagio m

construct /kən'strʌkt/ vt costruire. **~ion** /-ʌkʃn/ n costruzione f; **under ~ion** in costruzione. **~ive** /-ɪv/ a costruttivo

construe /kən'struː/ vt interpretare

consul /'kɒnsl/ n console m. **~ar** /'kɒnsjʊlə(r)/ a consolare. **~ate** /'kɒnsjʊlət/ n consolato m

consult /kən'sʌlt/ vt consultare. **~ant** n consulente mf; Med specialista mf. **~ation** /kɒnsl'teɪʃn/ n consultazione f; Med consulto m

consume /kən'sjuːm/ vt consumare. **~r** n consumatore, -trice mf. **~r goods** npl beni mpl di consumo. **~r organization** n organizzazione f per la tutela dei consumatori

consumerism /kən'sjuːmərɪzm/ n consumismo m

consummate /'kɒnsəmeɪt/ vt consumare

consumption /kən'sʌmpʃn/ n consumo m

contact /'kɒntækt/ n contatto m; (person) conoscenza f ● vt mettersi in contatto con. **~ 'lenses** npl lenti fpl a contatto

contagious /kən'teɪdʒəs/ a contagioso

contain /kən'teɪn/ vt contenere; **~ oneself** controllarsi. **~er** n recipiente m; (for transport) container m inv

contaminat|e /kən'tæmɪneɪt/ vt contaminare. **~ion** /-'neɪʃn/ n contaminazione f

contemplat|e /'kɒntəmpleɪt/ vt contemplare; (consider) considerare; **~e doing sth** considerare di fare qcsa. **~ion** /-'pleɪʃn/ n contemplazione f

contemporary /kən'tempərərɪ/ a & n contemporaneo, -a mf

contempt /kən'tempt/ n disprezzo m; **beneath ~** più che vergognoso; **~ of court** oltraggio m alla Corte. **~ible** /-əbl/ a spregevole. **~uous** /-tjʊəs/ a sprezzante

contend /kən'tend/ vi **~ with** occuparsi di ● vt (assert) sostenere. **~er** n concorrente mf

content¹ /'kɒntent/ n contenuto m

content² /kən'tent/ a soddisfatto ● vt **~ oneself** accontentarsi (with di). **~ed** a soddisfatto. **~edly** adv con aria soddisfatta

contention /kən'tenʃn/ n (assertion) opinione f

contentment /kən'tentmənt/ n soddisfazione f

contents /'kɒntents/ npl contenuto m

contest¹ /'kɒntest/ n gara f

contest² /kən'test/ vt contestare (statement); impugnare (will); Pol (candidates) contendersi; (one candidate) aspirare a. **~ant** n concorrente mf

context /'kɒntekst/ n contesto m

continent /'kɒntɪnənt/ n continente m; **the C~** l'Europa f continentale

continental /kɒntɪ'nentl/ a continentale. **~ breakfast** n prima colazione f a base di pane, burro, marmellata, croissant, ecc. **~ quilt** n piumone m

contingency /kən'tɪndʒənsɪ/ n eventualità f tnv

continual /kən'tɪnjʊəl/ a continuo

continuation /kəntɪnjʊ'eɪʃn/ n continuazione f

continue /kən'tɪnju:/ vt continuare; **~ doing** or **to do sth** continuare a fare qcsa; **to be ~d** continua ● vi continuare. **~d** a continuo

continuity /kɒntɪ'nju:ətɪ/ n continuità f

continuous /kən'tɪnjʊəs/ a continuo

contort /kən'tɔ:t/ vt contorcere **~ion** /-ɔ:ʃn/ n contorsione f. **~ionist** n contorsionista mf

contour /'kɒntʊə(r)/ n contorno m; (line) curva f di livello

contraband /'kɒntrəbænd/ n contrabbando m

contraception /kɒntrə'sepʃn/ n contraccezione f. **~tive** /-tɪv/ n contraccettivo m

contract¹ /'kɒntrækt/ n contratto m

contract² /kən'trækt/ vi (get smaller) contrarsi ● vt contrarre (illness). **~ion** /-ækʃn/ n contrazione f. **~or** n imprenditore, -trice mf

contradict /kɒntrə'dɪkt/ vt contraddire. **~ion** /-ɪkʃn/ n contraddizione f. **~ory** a contraddittorio

contra-flow /'kɒntrəfləʊ/ n utilizzazione f di una corsia nei due sensi di marcia durante lavori stradali

contralto /kən'træltəʊ/ n contralto m

contraption /kən'træpʃn/ n fam aggeggio m

contrary¹ /'kɒntrərɪ/ a contrario

● adv **~ to** contrariamente a ● n contrario m; **on the ~** al contrario

contrary² /kən'treərɪ/ a disobbediente

contrast¹ /'kɒntrɑ:st/ n contrasto m

contrast² /kən'trɑ:st/ vt confrontare ● vi contrastare. **~ing** a contrastante

contravene /kɒntrə'vi:n/ vt trasgredire. **~tion** /-'venʃn/ n trasgressione f

contribut|e /kən'trɪbju:t/ vt/i contribuire. **~ion** /kɒntrɪ'bju:ʃn/ n contribuzione f; (what is contributed) contributo m. **~or** n contributore, -trice mf

contrive /kən'traɪv/ vt escogitare; **to do sth** riuscire a fare qcsa

control /kən'trəʊl/ n controllo m; **~s** pl (of car, plane) comandi mpl; **get out of ~** sfuggire al controllo ● vt (pt/pp **controlled**) controllare; **~ oneself** controllarsi

controversi|al /kɒntrə'vɜ:ʃl/ a controverso. **~y** /'kɒntrəvɜ:sɪ/ n controversia f

conurbation /kɒnɜ:'beɪʃn/ n conurbazione f

convalesce /kɒnvə'les/ vi essere in convalescenza

convalescent /kɒnvə'lesənt/ a convalescente. **~ home** n convalescenziario m

convector /kən'vektə(r)/ n ~ [heater] convettore m

convene /kən'vi:n/ vt convocare ● vi riunirsi

convenience /kən'vi:nɪəns/ n convenienza f; [public] **~s** gabinetti mpl pubblici; **with all modern ~s** con tutti i comfort

convenient /kən'vi:nɪənt/ a comodo; **be ~ for sb** andar bene per qcno; **if it is ~ [for you]** se ti va bene. **~ly** adv comodamente; **~ly located** in una posizione comoda

convent /'kɒnvənt/ n convento m

convention /kən'venʃn/ n convenzione f; (assembly) convegno m. ~al a convenzionale

converge /kən'vɜːdʒ/ vi convergere

conversant /kən'vɜːsənt/ a ~ with pratico di

conversation /kɒnvə'seɪʃn/ n conversazione f. ~al a di conversazione. ~alist n conversatore, -trice mf

converse¹ /kən'vɜːs/ vi conversare

converse² /'kɒnvɜːs/ n inverso m. ~ly adv viceversa

conversion /kən'vɜːʃn/ n conversione f

convert¹ /'kɒnvɜːt/ n convertito, a mf

convert² /kən'vɜːt/ vt convertire (into in); sconsacrare ⟨church⟩. ~ible /-əbl/ a convertibile ● n Auto macchina f decappottabile

convex /kɒnveks/ a convesso

convey /kən'veɪ/ vt portare; trasmettere ⟨idea, message⟩. ~or belt n nastro m trasportatore

convict¹ /'kɒnvɪkt/ n condannato, -a mf

convict² /kən'vɜːt/ vt giudicare colpevole. ~ion /-ɪkʃn/ n condanna f; (belief) convinzione f. previ-ous ~ion precedente m penale

convinc|e /kən'vɪns/ vt convincere. ~ing a convincente

convivial /kən'vɪvɪəl/ a conviviale

convoluted /'kɒnvəluːtɪd/ a contorto

convoy /'kɒnvɔɪ/ n convoglio m

convuls|e /kən'vʌls/ vt sconvolgere; be ~ed with laughter contorcersi dalle risa. ~ion /-ʌlʃn/ n convulsione f

coo /kuː/ vi tubare

cook /kʊk/ n cuoco, -a mf ● vt cucinare; is it ~ed? è cotto?; ~ the books fam truccare i libri contabili ● vi ⟨food:⟩ cuocere; ⟨person:⟩ cucinare. ~book n libro m di cucina

cooker /'kʊkə(r)/ n cucina f; (apple) mela f da cuocere. ~y cu-

cina f. ~y book n libro m di cucina

cookie /'kʊkɪ/ n Am biscotto m

cool /kuːl/ a fresco; (calm) calmo; (unfriendly) freddo ● n fresco m ● vt rinfrescare ● vi rinfrescarsi. ~-box n borsa f termica. ~ness n freddezza f

coop /kuːp/ n stia f ● vt ~ up rinchiudere

co-operat|e /kəʊ'ɒpəreɪt/ vi cooperare. ~ion /-'reɪʃn/ n cooperazione f

co-operative /kəʊ'ɒpərətɪv/ a cooperativo ● n cooperativa f

co-opt /kəʊ'ɒpt/ vt eleggere

co-ordinat|e /kəʊ'ɔːdɪneɪt/ vt coordinare. ~ion /-'neɪʃn/ n coordinazione f

cop /kɒp/ n fam poliziotto m

cope /kəʊp/ vi fam farcela; can she ~ by herself? ce la fa da sola?; ~ with farcela con

copious /'kəʊpɪəs/ a abbondante

copper¹ /'kɒpə(r)/ n rame m; ~s pl monete fpl da uno o due pence ● attrib di rame

copper² n fam poliziotto m

coppice /'kɒpɪs/ n, **copse** /kɒps/ n boschetto m

copulat|e /'kɒpjuleɪt/ vi accoppiarsi. ~ion /-'leɪʃn/ n copulazione f

copy /'kɒpɪ/ n copia f ● vt (pt/pp -ied) copiare

copy: ~right n diritti mpl d'autore. ~writer n copywriter mf inv

coral /'kɒrəl/ n corallo m

cord /kɔːd/ n corda f; (thinner) cordoncino m; (fabric) velluto m a coste; ~s pl pantaloni mpl di velluto a coste

cordial /'kɔːdɪəl/ a cordiale ● n analcolico m

cordon /'kɔːdn/ n cordone m (di persone) ● **cordon off** vt mettere un cordone (di persone) intorno a

corduroy /'kɔːdərɔɪ/ n velluto m a coste

core /kɔː(r)/ n (of apple, pear) tor-

solo *m*; (*fig: of organization*) cuore *m*; (*of problem, theory*) nocciolo *m*

cork /kɔːk/ *n* sughero *m*; (*for bottle*) turacciolo *m*. **~screw** *n* cavatappi *m inv*

corn[1] /kɔːn/ *n* grano *m*; (*Am: maize*) granturco *m*

corn[2] *n Med* callo *m*

cornea /'kɔːnɪə/ *n* cornea *f*

corned beef /kɔːnd'biːf/ *n* manzo *m* sotto sale

corner /'kɔːnə(r)/ *n* angolo *m*; (*football*) calcio *m* d'angolo, corner *m inv* ● *vt fig* bloccare; *Comm* accaparrarsi (*market*)

cornet /'kɔːnɪt/ *n Mus* cornetta *f*; (*for ice-cream*) cono *m*

corn: **~flour**, *Am* **~starch** *n* farina *f* di granturco

corny /'kɔːnɪ/ *a* (**-ier, -iest**) (*fam: joke, film*) scontato; (*person*) banale; (*sentimental*) sdolcinato

coronary /'kɔrənərɪ/ *a* coronario ● *n* **~** [**thrombosis**] trombosi *f* coronarica

coronation /kɒrə'neɪʃn/ *n* incoronazione *f*

coroner /'kɒrənə(r)/ *n* coroner *m inv* (*nel diritto britannico, ufficiale incaricato delle indagini su morti sospette*)

corporal[1] /'kɔːpərəl/ *n Mil* caporale *m*

corporal[2] *a* corporale; **~ punishment** punizione *f* corporale

corporate /'kɔːpərət/ *a* (*decision, policy, image*) aziendale; **~** **life** la vita in un'azienda

corporation /kɔːpə'reɪʃn/ *n* ente *m*; (*of town*) consiglio *m* comunale

corps /kɔː(r)/ *n* (*pl* **corps** /kɔːz/) corpo *m*

corpse /kɔːps/ *n* cadavere *m*

corpulent /'kɔːpjʊlənt/ *a* corpulento

corpuscle /'kɔːpʌsl/ *n* globulo *m*

correct /kə'rekt/ *a* corretto; **be ~** (*person:*) aver ragione; **~!** esatto! ● *vt* correggere. **~ion** /-ekʃn/ *n* correzione *f*. **~ly** *adv* correttamente

correlation /kɒrə'leɪʃn/ *n* correlazione *f*

correspond /kɒrɪ'spɒnd/ *vi* corrispondere (**to** a); (*two things:*) corrispondere; (*write*) scriversi. **~ence** *n* corrispondenza *f*. **~ent** *n* corrispondente *mf*. **~ing** *a* corrispondente. **~ingly** *adv* in modo corrispondente

corridor /'kɒrɪdɔː(r)/ *n* corridoio *m*

corroborate /kə'rɒbəreɪt/ *vt* corroborare

corro|de /kə'rəʊd/ *vt* corrodere ● *vi* corrodersi. **~sion** /-'rəʊʒn/ *n* corrosione *f*

corrugated /'kɒrəgeɪtɪd/ *a* ondulato. **~ iron** *n* lamiera *f* ondulata

corrupt /kə'rʌpt/ *a* corrotto ● *vt* corrompere. **~ion** /-ʌpʃn/ *n* corruzione *f*

corset /'kɔːsɪt/ *n & -s* *pl* busto *m*

Corsica /'kɔːsɪkə/ *n* Corsica *f*. **~n** *a & n* corso, -a *mf*

cortège /kɔː'teɪʒ/ *n* [**funeral**] **~** corteo *m* funebre

cosh /kɒʃ/ *n* randello *m*

cosmetic /kɒz'metɪk/ *a* cosmetico ● *n* **~s** *pl* cosmetici *mpl*

cosmic /'kɒzmɪk/ *a* cosmico

cosmonaut /'kɒzmənɔːt/ *n* cosmonauta *mf*

cosmopolitan /kɒzmə'pɒlɪtən/ *a* cosmopolita

cosmos /'kɒzmɒs/ *n* cosmo *m*

cosset /'kɒsɪt/ *vt* coccolare

cost /kɒst/ *n* costo *m*; **~s** *pl Jur* spese *fpl* processuali; **at all ~s** a tutti i costi; **I learnt to my ~** ho imparato a mie spese ● *vt/i* (*pt/pp* **cost**) costare; **it ~ me £20** mi è costato 20 sterline ● *vt* (*pt/pp* **costed**) **~** [**out**] stabilire il prezzo di

costly /'kɒstlɪ/ *a* (**-ier, -iest**) costoso

cost: **~ of 'living** *n* costo *m* della vita. **~ price** *n* prezzo *m* di costo

costume /'kɒstjuːm/ *n* costume *m*. **~ jewellery** *n* bigiotteria *f*

cosy /'kəʊzɪ/ *a* (**-ier, -iest**) (*pub,*

chat⟩ intimo; **it's nice and ~ in here** si sta bene qui

cot /kɒt/ *n* lettino *m*; (*Am: camp-bed*) branda *f*

cottage /'kɒtɪdʒ/ *n* casetta *f*. **~ 'cheese** *n* fiocchi *mpl* di latte

cotton /'kɒtn/ *n* cotone *m* ● *attrib* di cotone ● **cotton on** *vi fam* capire

cotton 'wool *n* cotone *m* idrofilo

couch /kautʃ/ *n* divano *m*. **~ pota-to** *n* pantofolaio, -a *mf*

couchette /ku:'ʃet/ *n* cuccetta *f*

cough /kɒf/ *n* tosse *f* ● *vi* tossire.

cough up *vt/i* sputare; (*fam: pay*) sborsare

'cough mixture *n* sciroppo *m* per la tosse

could /kʊd/, *atono* /kəd/ *v aux* (*see also* **can²**) **~ I have a glass of water?** potrei avere un bicchier d'acqua?; **I ~n't do it even if I wanted to** non potrei farlo nemmeno se lo volessi; **I ~n't care less** non potrebbe importarmene di meno; **he ~n't have done it without help** non avrebbe potuto farlo senza aiuto; **you ~ have phoned** avresti potuto telefonare

council /'kaʊnsl/ *n* consiglio *m*. **~ house** *n* casa *f* popolare

councillor /'kaʊnsələ(r)/ *n* consigliere, -a *mf*

'council tax *n* imposta *f* locale sugli immobili

counsel /'kaʊnsl/ *n* consigli *mpl*; *Jur* avvocato *m* ● *vt* (*pt/pp* **counselled**) consigliare a ⟨*person*⟩. **~lor** *n* consigliere, -a *mf*

count¹ /kaʊnt/ *n* (*nobleman*) conte *m*

count² *n* conto *m*; **keep ~** tenere il conto ● *vt/i* contare. **count on** *vt* contare su

countdown /'kaʊntdaʊn/ *n* conto *m* alla rovescia

countenance /'kaʊntənəns/ *n* espressione *f* ● *vt* approvare

counter¹ /'kaʊntə(r)/ *n* banco *m*; (*in games*) gettone *m*

counter² *adv* **~ to** contro, in con-trasto a; **go ~ to sth** andare contro qcsa ● *vt/i* opporre (*measure, effect*); parare ⟨*blow*⟩

counter'act *vt* neutralizzare

'counter-attack *n* contrattacco *m*

counter-'espionage *n* contro-spionaggio *m*

'counterfeit /-fɪt/ *a* contraffatto ● *n* contraffazione *f* ● *vt* contraffare

'counterfoil *n* matrice *f*

'counterpart *n* equivalente *mf*

counter-pro'ductive *a* contro-produttivo

'countersign *vt* controfirmare

countess /'kaʊntɪs/ *n* contessa *f*

countless /'kaʊntlɪs/ *a* innumerevole

country /'kʌntrɪ/ *n* nazione *f*, paese *m*; (*native land*) patria *f*; (*countryside*) campagna *f*; **in the ~** in campagna; **go to the ~** andare in campagna; *Pol* indire le elezioni politiche. **~man** *n* uomo *m* di campagna; (*fellow ~man*) compatriota *m*. **~side** *n* campagna *f*

county /'kaʊntɪ/ *n* contea *f* (*unità amministrativa britannica*)

coup /ku:/ *n Pol* colpo *m* di stato

couple /'kʌpl/ *n* coppia *f*; **a ~ of** un paio di

coupon /'ku:pɒn/ *n* tagliando *m*; (*for discount*) buono *m* sconto

courage /'kʌrɪdʒ/ *n* coraggio *m*. **~ous** /kə'reɪdʒəs/ *a* coraggioso

courgette /kʊə'ʒet/ *n* zucchino *m*

courier /'kʊrɪə(r)/ *n* corriere *m*; (*for tourists*) guida *f*

course /kɔ:s/ *n Sch* corso *m*; *Naut* rotta *f*; *Culin* piatto *m*; (*for golf*) campo *m*; **~ of treatment** *Med* serie *f inv* di cure; **of ~** naturalmente; **in the ~ of** durante; **in due ~** a tempo debito

court /kɔ:t/ *n* tribunale *m*; *Sport* campo *m*; **take sb to ~** citare qcno in giudizio ● *vt* fare la corte a ⟨*woman*⟩; sfidare ⟨*danger*⟩; **~ing couples** coppiette *fpl*

courteous /'kɜ:tɪəs/ *a* cortese

courtesy /'kɜ:təsɪ/ *n* cortesia *f*

court: ~ 'martial n (pl ~s martial) corte f marziale ● ~-martial vt (pt ~-martialled) portare davanti alla corte marziale; ~yard n cortile m

cousin /'kʌzn/ n cugino, -a mf

cove /kəʊv/ n insenatura f

cover /'kʌvə(r)/ n copertura f; (of cushion, to protect sth) fodera f; (of book, magazine) copertina f; **take ~** mettersi al riparo; **under separate ~** a parte ● vt coprire; foderare ⟨cushion⟩; Journ fare un servizio su. **cover up** vt coprire; fig soffocare ⟨scandal⟩

coverage /'kʌvərɪdʒ/ n Journ **it got a lot of ~** i media gli hanno dedicato molto spazio

cover: ~ **charge** n coperto m. ~**ing** n copertura f; (for floor) rivestimento m; ~**ing letter** lettera f d'accompagnamento. ~**-up** n messa f a tacere

covet /'kʌvɪt/ vt bramare

cow /kaʊ/ n vacca f, mucca f

coward /'kaʊəd/ n vigliacco, -a mf. ~**ice** /-ɪs/ n vigliaccheria f. ~**ly** a da vigliacco

'cowboy n cowboy m inv; fam buffone m

cower /'kaʊə(r)/ vi acquattarsi

'cowshed n stalla f

cox /kɒks/ n, **coxswain** /'kɒksn/ n timoniere, -a mf

coy /kɔɪ/ a falsamente timido; (flirtatiously) civettuolo; **be ~ about sth** essere evasivo su qcsa

crab /kræb/ n granchio m

crack /kræk/ n (in wall) crepa f; (in china, glass, bone) incrinatura f; (noise) scoppio m; (fam: joke) battuta f; **have a ~** (try) fare un tentativo ● a (fam: best) di prim'ordine ● vt incrinare ⟨china, glass⟩; schiacciare ⟨nut⟩; decifrare ⟨code⟩; fam risolvere ⟨problem⟩; ~ **a joke** fam fare una battuta ● vi ⟨china, glass⟩ incrinarsi; ⟨whip⟩ schioccare. **crack down** vt fam prendere seri provvedimenti.

crack down on vt fam prendere seri provvedimenti contro

cracked /krækt/ a ⟨plaster⟩ crepato; ⟨skin⟩ screpolato; ⟨rib⟩ incrinato; (fam: crazy) svitato

cracker /'krækə(r)/ n (biscuit) cracker m inv; (firework) petardo m; [**Christmas**] ~ tubo m di cartone colorato contenente una sorpresa

crackers /'krækəz/ a fam matto

crackle /'krækl/ vi crepitare

cradle /'kreɪdl/ n culla f

craft[1] /krɑːft/ n inv (boat) imbarcazione f

craft[2] n mestiere m; (technique) arte f. ~**sman** n artigiano m

crafty /'krɑːftɪ/ a (-ier, -iest) astuto

crag /kræg/ n rupe f. ~**gy** a scosceso; ⟨face⟩ dai lineamenti marcati

cram /kræm/ v (pt/pp crammed) ● vt stipare (**into** in) ● vi (for exams) sgobbare

cramp /kræmp/ n crampo m. ~**ed** a ⟨room⟩ stretto; ⟨handwriting⟩ appiccicato

crampon /'kræmpən/ n rampone m

cranberry /'krænbərɪ/ n Culin mirtillo m rosso

crane /kreɪn/ n (at docks, bird) gru f inv ● vt ~ **one's neck** allungare il collo

crank[1] /kræŋk/ n tipo, -a mf strampalato, -a

crank[2] n Techn manovella f. ~**shaft** n albero m a gomiti

cranky /'kræŋkɪ/ a strampalato; (Am: irritable) irritabile

cranny /'krænɪ/ n fessura f

crash /kræʃ/ n (noise) fragore m; Auto, Aeron incidente m; Comm crollo m ● vi schiantarsi (**into** contro); ⟨plane⟩ precipitare ● vt schiantare ⟨car⟩

crash: ~ **course** n corso m intensivo. ~**-helmet** n casco m. ~**-landing** n atterraggio m di fortuna

crate /kreɪt/ n (for packing) cassa f

crater /'kreɪtə(r)/ n cratere m

crav|le /kreɪv/ vt morire dalla voglia di. **~ing** n voglia f smodata

crawl /krɔːl/ n (swimming) stile m libero; **do the** ~ nuotare a stile libero; **at a** ~ a passo di lumaca ●vi andare carponi; ~ **with** brulicare di. **~er lane** n Auto corsia f riservata al traffico lento

crayon /'kreɪən/ n pastello m a cera; (pencil) matita f colorata

craze /kreɪz/ n mania f

crazy /'kreɪzɪ/ a (-ier, -iest) matto; **be** ~ **about** andar matto per

creak /kriːk/ n scricchiolio m ●vi scricchiolare

cream /kriːm/ n crema f; (fresh) panna f ●a (colour) [bianco] panna inv ●vt Culin sbattere. ~ '**cheese** n formaggio m cremoso. ~**y** a cremoso

crease /kriːs/ n piega f ●vt stropicciare ●vi stropicciarsi. ~**-resistant** a che non si stropiccia

creat|e /kriː'eɪt/ vt creare. **~ion** /-'eɪʃn/ n creazione f. **~ive** /-tɪv/ a creativo. **~or** n creatore, -trice mf

creature /'kriːtʃə(r)/ n creatura f

crèche /kreʃ/ n asilo m nido

credentials /krɪ'denʃlz/ npl credenziali fpl

credibility /kredə'bɪlətɪ/ n credibilità f

credible /'kredəbl/ a credibile

credit /'kredɪt/ n credito m; (honour) merito m; **take the** ~ **for** prendersi il merito di ●vt (pt/pp **credited**) accreditare; ~ **sb with sth** Comm accreditare qcsa a qcno; fig attribuire qcsa a qcno. **~able** /-əbl/ a lodevole

credit: ~ **card** n carta f di credito. **~or** n creditore, -trice mf

creed /kriːd/ n credo m inv

creek /kriːk/ n insenatura f; (Am: stream) torrente m

creep /kriːp/ vi (pt/pp **crept**) muoversi furtivamente ●n fam tipo m

viscido. **~er** n pianta f rampicante. **~y** a che fa venire i brividi

cremat|e /krɪ'meɪt/ vt cremare. **~ion** /-eɪʃn/ n cremazione f

crematorium /kremə'tɔːrɪəm/ n crematorio m

crêpe /kreɪp/ n (fabric) crespo m

crept /krept/ see **creep**

crescent /'kresənt/ n mezzaluna f

cress /kres/ n crescione m

crest /krest/ n cresta f; (coat of arms) cimiero m

Crete /kriːt/ n Creta f

crevasse /krɪ'væs/ n crepaccio m

crevice /'krevɪs/ n crepa f

crew /kruː/ n equipaggio m; (gang) équipe f inv. ~ **cut** n capelli mpl a spazzola. ~ **neck** n girocollo m

crib¹ /krɪb/ n (for baby) culla f

crib² /krɪb/ vt/i (pt/pp **cribbed**) fam copiare

crick /krɪk/ n. ~ **in the neck** torcicollo m

cricket¹ /'krɪkɪt/ n (insect) grillo m

cricket² n cricket m. **~er** n giocatore m di cricket

crime /kraɪm/ n crimine m; (criminality) criminalità f

criminal /'krɪmɪnl/ a criminale; (law, court) penale ●n criminale mf

crimson /'krɪmzn/ a cremisi inv

cringe /krɪndʒ/ vi (cower) acquattarsi; (at bad joke etc) fare una smorfia

crinkle /'krɪŋkl/ vt spiegazzare ●vi spiegazzarsi

cripple /'krɪpl/ n storpio, -a mf ●vt storpiare; fig danneggiare. **~d** a (person) storpio; (ship) danneggiato

crisis /'kraɪsɪs/ n (pl **-ses** /-siːz/) crisi f inv

crisp /krɪsp/ a croccante; (air) frizzante; (style) incisivo. **~bread** n crostini mpl di pane. **~s** npl patatine fpl

criterion /kraɪ'tɪərɪən/ n (pl **-ria** /-rɪə/) criterio m

critic /'krɪtɪk/ n critico, -a mf. **~al**

a critico. **~ally** *adv* in modo critico; **~ally ill** gravemente malato

criticism /'krɪtɪsɪzm/ *n* critica *f*, **he doesn't like ~** non ama le critiche

criticize /'krɪtɪsaɪz/ *vt* criticare

croak /krəʊk/ *vi* gracchiare; ⟨*frog:*⟩ gracidare

crochet /'krəʊʃeɪ/ *n* lavoro *m* all'uncinetto ● *vt* fare all'uncinetto. **~-hook** *n* uncinetto *m*

crock /krɒk/ *n fam* **old ~** ⟨*person*⟩ rudere *m*; ⟨*car*⟩ macinino *m*

crockery /'krɒkərɪ/ *n* terrecotte *fpl*

crocodile /'krɒkədaɪl/ *n* coccodrillo *m*. **~ tears** lacrime *fpl* di coccodrillo

crocus /'krəʊkəs/ *n* (*pl* **-es**) croco *m*

crony /'krəʊnɪ/ *n* compare *m*

crook /krʊk/ *n* ⟨*fam: criminal*⟩ truffatore, -trice *mf*

crooked /'krʊkɪd/ *a* storto; ⟨*limb*⟩ storpiato; ⟨*fam: dishonest*⟩ disonesto

crop /krɒp/ *n* raccolto *m*; *fig* quantità *f inv* ● *v* (*pt/pp* **cropped**) *vt* coltivare. **crop up** *vi fam* presentarsi

croquet /'krəʊkeɪ/ *n* croquet *m*

croquette /krəʊ'ket/ *n* crocchetta *f*

cross /krɒs/ *a* (*annoyed*) arrabbiato; **talk at ~ purposes** fraintendersi ● *n* croce *f*; *Bot, Zool* incrocio *m* ● *vt* sbarrare ⟨*cheque*⟩; incrociare ⟨*road, animals*⟩; **~ oneself** farsi il segno della croce; **~ one's arms** incrociare le braccia; **~ one's legs** accavallare le gambe; **keep one's fingers ~ed for sb** tenere le dita incrociate per qcno; **it ~ed my mind** mi è venuto in mente ● *vi* (*go across*) attraversare; ⟨*lines:*⟩ incrociarsi. **cross out** *vt* depennare

cross: ~bar *n* (*of goal*) traversa *f*; (*of bicycle*) canna *f*. **~-country** *n Sport* corsa *f* campestre. **~-ex·amine** *vt* sottoporre a contro-interrogatorio. **~-exami'nation** *n* controinterrogatorio *m*. **~-'eyed** *a* strabico. **~-fire** *n* fuoco *m* incrociato. **~ing** *n* (*for pedestrians*) passaggio *m* pedonale; (*sea journey*) traversata *f*. **~-'reference** *n* rimando *m*. **~roads** *n* incrocio *m*. **~-'section** *n* sezione *f*; (*of community*) campione *m*. **~-wise** *adv* in diagonale. **~word** [**puzzle**] parole *fpl* crociate

crotchet /'krɒtʃɪt/ *n Mus* semiminima *f*

crotchety /'krɒtʃɪtɪ/ *a* irritabile

crouch /kraʊtʃ/ *vi* accovacciarsi

crow /krəʊ/ *n* corvo *m*; **as the ~ flies** in linea d'aria ● *vi* cantare. **~bar** *n* piede *m* di porco

crowd /kraʊd/ *n* folla *f* ● *vt* affollare ● *vi* affollarsi. **~ed** /'kraʊdɪd/ *a* affollato

crown /kraʊn/ *n* corona *f* ● *vt* incoronare; incapsulare ⟨*tooth*⟩

crucial /'kru:ʃl/ *a* cruciale

crucifix /'kru:sɪfɪks/ *n* crocifisso *m*

cruci'fixion /kru:sɪ'fɪkʃn/ *n* crocifissione *f*. **~y** /'kru:sɪfaɪ/ *vt* (*pt/pp* **-ied**) crocifiggere

crude /kru:d/ *a* ⟨*oil*⟩ greggio; ⟨*language*⟩ crudo; ⟨*person*⟩ rozzo

cruel /kru:əl/ *a* (**crueller, cruellest**) crudele (*to* verso); **~ly** *adv* con crudeltà. **~ty** *n* crudeltà *f*

cruise /kru:z/ *n* crociera *f* ● *vi* fare una crociera; ⟨*car:*⟩ andare a velocità di crociera. **~r** *n Mil* incrociatore *m*; (*motor boat*) motoscafo *m*. **~ing speed** *n* velocità *f inv* di crociera

crumb /krʌm/ *n* briciola *f*

crumble /'krʌmbl/ *vt* sbriciolare ● *vi* sbriciolarsi; ⟨*building, society:*⟩ sgretolarsi. **~ly** *a* friabile

crumple /'krʌmpl/ *vt* spiegazzare ● *vi* spiegazzarsi

crunch /krʌntʃ/ *n fam* **when it comes to the ~** quando si viene al dunque ● *vt* sgranocchiare ● *vi* ⟨*snow:*⟩ scricchiolare

crusade /kruːˈseɪd/ n crociata f. **~r** n crociato m

crush /krʌʃ/ n (crowd) calca f. **have a ~ on sb** essersi preso una cotta per qcno ●vt schiacciare; sgualcire ⟨clothes⟩

crust /krʌst/ n crosta f

crutch /krʌtʃ/ n gruccia f; Anat inforcatura f

crux /krʌks/ n fig punto m cruciale

cry /kraɪ/ n grido m; **have a ~** farsi un pianto; **a far ~ from** fig tutta un'altra cosa rispetto a ●vi ⟨pt/pp **cried**⟩ (weep) piangere; (call) gridare

crypt /krɪpt/ n cripta f. **~ic** a criptico

crystal /ˈkrɪstl/ n cristallo m; (glassware) cristalli mpl. **~lize** vi (become clear) concretizzarsi

cub /kʌb/ n (animal) cucciolo m; **C~** [Scout] lupetto m

Cuba /ˈkjuːbə/ n Cuba f

cubby-hole /ˈkʌbɪ-/ n (compartment) scomparto m; (room) ripostiglio m

cub|e /kjuːb/ n cubo m. **~ic** a cubico

cubicle /ˈkjuːbɪkl/ n cabina f

cuckoo /ˈkʊkuː/ n cuculo m. **~ clock** n orologio m a cucù

cucumber /ˈkjuːkʌmbə(r)/ n cetriolo m

cuddl|e /ˈkʌdl/ vt coccolare ●vi **~e up to** starsene accoccolato insieme a ●n **have a ~e** ⟨child:⟩ farsi coccolare; ⟨lovers:⟩ abbracciarsi. **~y** a tenerone; (wanting cuddles) coccolone. **~y 'toy** n peluche m inv

cudgel /ˈkʌdʒl/ n randello m

cue¹ /kjuː/ n segnale m; Theat battuta f d'entrata

cue² /kjuː/ n (in billiards) stecca f. **~ ball** n pallino m

cuff /kʌf/ n polsino m; (Am: turnup) orlo m; (blow) scapaccione m. **off the ~** improvvisando ●vt dare una pacca a. **~-link** n gemello m

cul-de-sac /ˈkʌldəsæk/ n vicolo m cieco

culinary /ˈkʌlɪnərɪ/ a culinario

cull /kʌl/ vt scegliere ⟨flowers⟩; (kill) selezionare e uccidere

culminat|e /ˈkʌlmɪneɪt/ vi culminare. **~ion** /-ˈneɪʃn/ n culmine m

culottes /kjuːˈlɒts/ npl gonna fsg pantalone

culprit /ˈkʌlprɪt/ n colpevole mf

cult /kʌlt/ n culto m

cultivate /ˈkʌltɪveɪt/ vt coltivare; fig coltivarsi ⟨person⟩

cultural /ˈkʌltʃərəl/ a culturale

culture /ˈkʌltʃə(r)/ n cultura f. **~d** a colto

cumbersome /ˈkʌmbəsəm/ a ingombrante

cumulative /ˈkjuːmjʊlətɪv/ a cumulativo

cunning /ˈkʌnɪŋ/ a astuto ●n astuzia f

cup /kʌp/ n tazza f; (prize, of bra) coppa f

cupboard /ˈkʌbəd/ n armadio m. **~ love** fam amore m interessato

Cup 'Final n finale f di coppa

Cupid /ˈkjuːpɪd/ n Cupido m

curable /ˈkjʊərəbl/ a curabile

curate /ˈkjʊərət/ n curato m

curator /kjʊəˈreɪtə(r)/ n direttore, -trice mf (di museo)

curb /kɜːb/ vt tenere a freno

curdle /ˈkɜːdl/ vi coagularsi

cure /kjʊə(r)/ n cura f ●vt curare; (salt) mettere sotto sale; (smoke) affumicare

curfew /ˈkɜːfjuː/ n coprifuoco m

curio /ˈkjʊərɪəʊ/ n curiosità f inv

curiosity /kjʊərɪˈɒsɪtɪ/ n curiosità f

curious /ˈkjʊərɪəs/ a curioso. **~ly** adv (strangely) curiosamente

curl /kɜːl/ n ricciolo m ●vt arricciare ●vi arricciarsi. **curl up** vi raggomitolarsi

curler /ˈkɜːlə(r)/ n bigodino m

curly /ˈkɜːlɪ/ a (-ier, -iest) riccio

currant /ˈkʌrənt/ n (dried) uvetta f

currency /ˈkʌrənsɪ/ n valuta f; (of

word) ricorrenza *f*; **foreign** ~ valuta *f* estera

current /'kʌrənt/ *a* corrente ● *n* corrente *f*. ~ **affairs** *or* **events** *npl* attualità *fsg*. ~**ly** *adv* attualmente

curriculum /kə'rikjuləm/ *n* programma *m* di studi. ~ **vitae** /'vi:taɪ/ *n* curriculum vitae *m inv*

curry /'kʌrɪ/ *n* curry *m inv*; (*meal*) piatto *m* cucinato nel curry ● *vt* (*pt/pp* -**ied**) ~ **favour with sb** cercare d'ingraziarsi qcno

curse /kɜːs/ *n* maledizione *f*; (*oath*) imprecazione *f* ● *vt* maledire ● *vi* imprecare

cursor /'kɜːsə(r)/ *n* cursore *m*

cursory /'kɜːsərɪ/ *a* sbrigativo

curt /kɜːt/ *a* brusco

curtail /kɜːˈteɪl/ *vt* ridurre

curtain /'kɜːtn/ *n* tenda *f*; *Theat* sipario *m*

curtsy /'kɜːtsɪ/ *n* inchino *m* ● *vi* (*pt/pp* -**ied**) fare l'inchino

curve /kɜːv/ *n* curva *f* ● *vi* curvare; ~ **to the right/left** curvare a destra/sinistra. ~**d** *a* curvo

cushion /'kʊʃn/ *n* cuscino *m* ● *vt* attutire; (*protect*) proteggere

cushy /'kʊʃɪ/ *a* (-**ier**, -**iest**) *fam* facile

custard /'kʌstəd/ *n* (*liquid*) crema *f* pasticciera

custodian /kʌˈstəʊdɪən/ *n* custode *m*

custody /'kʌstədɪ/ *n* (*of child*) custodia *f*; (*imprisonment*) detenzione *f* preventiva

custom /'kʌstəm/ *n* usanza *f*; *Jur* consuetudine *f*; *Comm* clientela *f*. ~**ary** *a* (*habitual*) abituale; **it's** ~ **to**... è consuetudine.... ~**er** *n* cliente *mf*

customs /'kʌstəmz/ *npl* dogana *f*. ~ **officer** *n* doganiere *m*

cut /kʌt/ *n* (*with knife etc, of clothes*) taglio *m*; (*reduction*) riduzione *f*; (*in public spending*) taglio *m* ● *vt/i* (*pt/pp* **cut**, *pres p* **cutting**) tagliare; (*reduce*) ridurre; ~ **one's finger** tagliarsi il dito; ~ **sb's hair**

tagliare i capelli a qcno ● *vi* (*with cards*) alzare. **cut back** *vt* tagliare (*hair*); potare (*hedge*); (*reduce*) ridurre. **cut down** *vt* abbattere (*tree*); (*reduce*) ridurre. **cut off** *vt* tagliar via; (*disconnect*) interrompere; *fig* isolare; **I was** ~ **off** *Teleph* la linea è caduta. **cut out** *vt* ritagliare; (*delete*) eliminare; **be** ~ **out for** *fam* essere tagliato per; ~ **it out!** *fam* dacci un taglio!. **cut up** *vt* (*slice*) tagliare a pezzi

'**cut-back** *n* riduzione *f*; (*in government spending*) taglio *m*

cute /kjuːt/ *a fam* (*in appearance*) carino; (*clever*) acuto

cuticle /'kjuːtɪkl/ *n* cuticola *f*

cutlery /'kʌtlərɪ/ *n* posate *fpl*

cutlet /'kʌtlɪt/ *n* cotoletta *f*

'**cut-price** *a* a prezzo ridotto; (*shop*) che fa prezzi ridotti

'**cut-throat** *a* spietato

cutting /'kʌtɪŋ/ *a* (*remark*) tagliente ● *n* (*from newspaper*) ritaglio *m*; (*of plant*) talea *f*

CV *n abbr* curriculum vitae

cyanide /'saɪənaɪd/ *n* cianuro *m*

cybernetics /saɪbə'netɪks/ *n* cibernetica *f*

cycle /'saɪkl/ *n* ciclo *m*; (*bicycle*) bicicletta *f*, bici *f inv fam* ● *vi* andare in bicicletta. ~**ing** *n* ciclismo *m*. ~**ist** *n* ciclista *mf*

cyclone /'saɪkləʊn/ *n* ciclone *m*

cylinder /'sɪlɪndə(r)/ *n* cilindro *m*. ~**rical** /-'lɪndrɪkl/ *a* cilindrico

cymbals /'sɪmblz/ *npl Mus* piatti *mpl*

cynic /'sɪnɪk/ *n* cinico. ~**al** *a* cinico. ~**ism** /-sɪzm/ *n* cinismo *m*

cypress /'saɪprəs/ *n* cipresso *m*

Cypriot /'sɪprɪət/ *n* cipriota *mf*

Cyprus /'saɪprəs/ *n* Cipro *m*

cyst /sɪst/ *n* ciste *f*. ~**itis** /-'staɪtɪs/ *n* cistite *f*

Czech /tʃek/ *a* ceco; ~ **Republic** Repubblica *f* Ceca ● *n* ceco, -a *mf*

Czechoslovak /tʃekə'sləʊvæk/ *a* cecoslovacco. ~**ia** /-'vækɪə/ *n* Cecoslovacchia *f*

Dd

dab /dæb/ n colpetto m; **a ~ of** un pochino di ● vt (pt/pp **dabbed**) toccare leggermente (eyes). **dab on** vt mettere un po' di (paint etc)

dabble /'dæbl/ vi **~ in sth** fig occuparsi di qcsa a tempo perso

dachshund /'dækshʊnd/ n bassotto m

dad[dy] /'dæd[ɪ]/ n fam papà m inv, babbo m

daddy-'long-legs n zanzarone m [dei boschi]; (Am: spider) ragno m

daffodil /'dæfədɪl/ n giunchiglia f

daft /dɑ:ft/ a sciocco

dagger /'dægə(r)/ n stiletto m

dahlia /'deɪlɪə/ n dalia f

daily /'deɪlɪ/ a giornaliero ● adv giornalmente ● n (newspaper) quotidiano m; (fam: cleaner) donna f delle pulizie

dainty /'deɪntɪ/ a (-ier, -iest) grazioso; (movement) delicato

dairy /'deərɪ/ n caseificio m; (shop) latteria f. **~ cow** n mucca f da latte. **~ products** npl latticini mpl

dais /'deɪɪs/ n pedana f

daisy /'deɪzɪ/ n margheritina f; (larger) margherita f

dale /deɪl/ n liter valle f

dam /dæm/ n diga f ● vt (pt/pp **dammed**) costruire una diga su

damage /'dæmɪdʒ/ n danno m (**to** a); **~es** pl Jur risarcimento msg ● vt danneggiare; fig nuocere a. **~ing** a dannoso

dame /deɪm/ n liter dama f; Am sl donna f

damn /dæm/ a fam maledetto ● adv (lucky, late) maledettamente ● n **I don't care** or **give a ~** fam non me ne frega un accidente ● vt dannare. **~ation** /-'neɪʃn/ n dannazione f ● int fam accidenti!

damp /dæmp/ a umido ● n umidità f ● vt = **dampen**

damp|en /'dæmpən/ vt inumidire; fig raffreddare (enthusiasm). **~ness** n umidità f

dance /dɑ:ns/ n ballo m ● vt/i ballare. **~-hall** n sala f da ballo. **~ music** n musica f da ballo

dancer /'dɑ:nsə(r)/ n ballerino, -a mf

dandelion /'dændɪlaɪən/ n dente m di leone

dandruff /'dændrʌf/ n forfora f

Dane /deɪn/ n danese m; **Great ~** danese m

danger /'deɪndʒə(r)/ n pericolo m; **in/out of ~** in/fuori pericolo. **~ous** /-rəs/ a pericoloso. **~ously** adv pericolosamente; **~ously ill** in pericolo di vita

dangle /'dæŋgl/ vi penzolare ● vt far penzolare

Danish /'deɪnɪʃ/ a & n danese m. **~ 'pastry** n dolce m a base di pasta sfoglia contenente pasta di mandorle, mele ecc

dank /dæŋk/ a umido e freddo

Danube /'dænju:b/ n Danubio m

dare /deə(r)/ vt/i osare; (challenge) sfidare (**to** a); **~ [to] do sth** osare fare qcsa; **I ~ say!** molto probabilmente! ● n sfida f. **~devil** a spericolato, -a mf

daring /'deərɪŋ/ a audace ● n audacia f

dark /dɑ:k/ a buio; **~ blue/brown** blu/marrone scuro; **it's getting ~** sta cominciando a fare buio; **~ horse** fig (in race, contest) vincitore m imprevisto; (not much known about) misterioso m; **keep sth ~** fig tenere qcsa nascosto ● n **after ~** col buio; **in the ~** al buio; **keep sb in the ~** fig tenere qcno all'oscuro

dark|en /'dɑ:kn/ vt oscurare ● vi oscurarsi. **~ness** n buio m

'dark-room n camera f oscura

darling /'dɑ:lɪŋ/ a adorabile; **my ~ Joan** carissima Joan ● n tesoro m

darn /dɑ:n/ vt rammendare. **~ing-needle** n ago m da rammendo

dart /dɑːt/ n dardo m; (in sewing) pince f inv; ~s sg (game) freccette fpl ● vi lanciarsi

dartboard /ˈdɑːtbɔːd/ n bersaglio m [per freccette]

dash /dæʃ/ n Typ trattino m; (in Morse) linea f; a ~ of milk un goccio di latte; make a ~ for lanciarsi verso ● vi I must ~ devo scappare ● vt far svanire ‹hopes›. **dash off** vi scappar via ● vt ‹write quickly› buttare giù. **dash out** vi uscire di corsa

'dashboard n cruscotto m

dashing /ˈdæʃɪŋ/ a ‹bold› ardito; (in appearance) affascinante

data /ˈdeɪtə/ npl & sg dati mpl. ~**base** n base [di] dati f, database m inv. ~**comms** /ˈkɒmz/ n telematica f. ~ **processing** n elaborazione f [di] dati

date[1] /deɪt/ n (fruit) dattero m

date[2] /deɪt/ n data f; (meeting) appuntamento m; to ~ fino ad oggi; out of ~ (not fashionable) fuori moda; (expired) scaduto; (information) non aggiornato; **make a ~ with sb** dare un appuntamento a qcno; **be up to ~** essere aggiornato ● vt/i datare; (go out with) uscire con. **date back to** vi risalire a

dated /ˈdeɪtɪd/ a fuori moda; (language) antiquato

'date-line n linea f [del cambiamento] di data

daub /dɔːb/ vt imbrattare (walls)

daughter /ˈdɔːtə(r)/ n figlia f. ~**-in-law** n (pl ~s-in-law) nuora f

daunt /dɔːnt/ vt scoraggiare; **nothing ~ed** per niente scoraggiato. ~**less** a intrepido

dawdle /ˈdɔːdl/ vi bighellonare; (over work) cincischiarsi

dawn /dɔːn/ n alba f; at ~ all'alba ● vi albeggiare; **it ~ed on me** fig mi è apparso chiaro

day /deɪ/ n giorno m; (whole day) giornata f; (period) epoca f; **these ~s** oggigiorno; **in those ~s** a quei tempi; **it's had its ~** fam ha fatto il suo tempo

day: ~**break** n at ~ all'alba allo spuntar del giorno. ~**dream** n sogno m ad occhi aperti ● vi sognare ad occhi aperti. ~**light** n luce f del giorno. ~ **re'turn** n (ticket) biglietto m di andata e ritorno con validità giornaliera. ~**time** n giorno m; **in the ~time** di giorno

daze /deɪz/ n in a ~ stordito; fig sbalordito. ~**d** a stordito; fig sbalordito

dazzle /ˈdæzl/ vt abbagliare

deacon /ˈdiːkn/ n diacono m

dead /ded/ a morto; (numb) intorpidito; ~ **body** morto m; ~ **centre** pieno centro m ● adv ~ **tired** stanco morto; ~ **slow/easy** lentissimo/facilissimo; **you're ~ right** hai perfettamente ragione; **stop ~** fermarsi di colpo; **be ~ on time** essere in perfetto orario ● n the ~ pl i morti; **in the ~ of night** nel cuore della notte

deaden /ˈdedn/ vt attutire (sound); calmare (pain)

dead: ~ **'end** n vicolo m cieco. ~ **'heat** n it was a ~ **heat** è finita a pari merito. ~**line** n scadenza f. ~**lock** n reach ~**lock** fig giungere a un punto morto

deadly /ˈdedlɪ/ a (-ier, -iest) mortale; (fam: dreary) barboso; ~ **sins** peccati mpl capitali

deadpan /ˈdedpæn/ a impassibile; (humour) all'inglese

deaf /def/ a sordo; ~ **and dumb** sordomuto. ~**-aid** n apparecchio m acustico

deafen /ˈdefn/ vt assordare; (permanently) rendere sordo. ~**ening** a assordante. ~**ness** n sordità f

deal /diːl/ n (agreement) patto m; (in business) accordo m; **whose ~?** (in cards) a chi tocca dare le carte?; **a good or great ~** molto; **get a raw ~** fam ricevere un trattamento ingiusto ● vt (pt/pp dealt /delt/) (in cards) dare; ~ **sb a blow** dare un colpo a qcno. **deal in** vt trattare in. **deal out** vt (hand

out) distribuire. **deal with** vt
(*handle*) occuparsi di; trattare con
⟨*company*⟩; (*be about*) trattare di;
that's been ~t with è stato risolto

deal|er /ˈdiːlə(r)/ n commerciante
mf; (*in drugs*) spacciatore, -trice
mf. **~ings** npl **have ~ings with**
avere a che fare con

dean /diːn/ n decano m; Univ ≈
preside mf di facoltà

dear /dɪə(r)/ a caro; (*in letter*)
Caro; (*formal*) Gentile ● n caro, -a
mf ● int **oh ~!** Dio mio!. **~ly** adv
⟨*love*⟩ profondamente; ⟨*pay*⟩ pro-
fumatamente

dearth /dɜːθ/ n penuria f

death /deθ/ n morte f. **~ certificate** n certificato m di morte. **~
duty** n tassa f di successione

deathly /ˈdeθlɪ/ a **~ silence** silenzio m di tomba ● adv **~ pale** di un
pallore cadaverico

death: **~ penalty** n pena f di morte. **~trap** n trappola f mortale

debar /dɪˈbɑː(r)/ vt (*pt/pp* de-
barred) escludere

debase /dɪˈbeɪs/ vt degradare

debatable /dɪˈbeɪtəbl/ a discutibile

debate /dɪˈbeɪt/ n dibattito m ● vt
discutere; (*in formal debate*) dibattere ● vi **~ whether to...** considerare se...

debauchery /dɪˈbɔːtʃərɪ/ n disso-
lutezza f

debility /dɪˈbɪlɪtɪ/ n debilitazione f

debit /ˈdebɪt/ n debito m ● vt
(*pt/pp* debited) Comm addebitare
⟨*sum*⟩

debris /ˈdebriː/ n macerie fpl

debt /det/ n debito m; **be in ~** avere dei debiti. **~or** n debitore, -trice
mf

début /ˈdeɪbuː/ n debutto m

decade /ˈdekeɪd/ n decennio m

decaden|ce /ˈdekədəns/ n deca-
denza f. **~t** a decadente

decaffeinated /diːˈkæfɪneɪtɪd/ a
decaffeinato

decant /dɪˈkænt/ vt travasare. **~er**
n caraffa f (*di cristallo*)

decapitate /dɪˈkæpɪteɪt/ vt decapitare

decay /dɪˈkeɪ/ n (*also fig*) decaden-
za f; (*rot*) decomposizione f; (*of
tooth*) carie f inv ● vi imputridire;
(*rot*) decomporsi; ⟨*tooth*⟩ cariarsi

deceased /dɪˈsiːst/ a defunto ● n
the ~d il defunto; la defunta

deceit /dɪˈsiːt/ n inganno m. **~ful** a
falso

deceive /dɪˈsiːv/ vt ingannare

December /dɪˈsembə(r)/ n dicembre m

decency /ˈdiːsənsɪ/ n decenza f

decent /ˈdiːsənt/ a decente;
(*respectable*) rispettabile; **very ~
of you** molto gentile da parte tua.
~ly adv decentemente; (*kindly*)
gentilmente

decentralize /diːˈsentrəlaɪz/ vt
decentrare

decept|ion /dɪˈsepʃn/ n inganno
m. **~ive** /-tɪv/ a ingannevole.
~ively adv ingannevolmente; **it
looks ~ively easy** sembra facile,
ma non lo è

decibel /ˈdesɪbel/ n decibel m inv

decide /dɪˈsaɪd/ vt decidere ● vi
decidere (**on** di)

decided /dɪˈsaɪdɪd/ a risoluto.
~ly adv risolutamente; (*without
doubt*) senza dubbio

deciduous /dɪˈsɪdjʊəs/ a a foglie
decidue

decimal /ˈdesɪml/ a decimale ● n
numero m decimale. **~ point** n
virgola f

decimate /ˈdesɪmeɪt/ vt decimare

decipher /dɪˈsaɪfə(r)/ vt decifrare

decision /dɪˈsɪʒn/ n decisione f

decisive /dɪˈsaɪsɪv/ a decisivo

deck¹ /dek/ vt abbigliare

deck² n Naut ponte m; **on ~** in coperta; **top ~** (*of bus*) piano m di sopra; **~ of cards** mazzo m. **~-chair**
n [sedia f a] sdraio f inv

declaration /deklə'reɪʃn/ n dichiarazione f

declare /dɪˈkleə(r)/ vt dichiarare;
anything to ~? niente da dichiarare?

declension /dɪˈklenʃn/ n declinazione f

decline /dɪˈklaɪn/ n declino m ● vt also Gram declinare ● vi (decrease) diminuire; ⟨health:⟩ deperire; (say no) rifiutare

decode /diːˈkəʊd/ vt decifrare; Comput decodificare

decompose /diːkəmˈpəʊz/ vi decomporsi

décor /ˈdeɪkɔː(r)/ n decorazione f; (including furniture) arredamento m

decorat|e /ˈdekəreɪt/ vt decorare; (paint) pitturare; (wallpaper) tappezzare. ~ion /-ˈreɪʃn/ n decorazione f. ~ive /-rətɪv/ a decorativo. ~or n painter and ~or imbianchino m

decorum /dɪˈkɔːrəm/ n decoro m

decoy[1] /ˈdiːkɔɪ/ n esca f

decoy[2] /dɪˈkɔɪ/ vt adescare

decrease[1] /ˈdiːkriːs/ n diminuzione f

decrease[2] /dɪˈkriːs/ vt/i diminuire

decree /dɪˈkriː/ n decreto m ● vt (pt/pp decreed) decretare

decrepit /dɪˈkrepɪt/ a decrepito

dedicat|e /ˈdedɪkeɪt/ vt dedicare. ~ed a (person) scrupoloso. ~ion /-ˈkeɪʃn/ n dedizione f; (in book) dedica f

deduce /dɪˈdjuːs/ vt dedurre (from da)

deduct /dɪˈdʌkt/ vt dedurre

deduction /dɪˈdʌkʃn/ n deduzione f

deed /diːd/ n azione f; Jur atto m di proprietà

deem /diːm/ vt ritenere

deep /diːp/ a profondo; **go off the ~** end fam arrabbiarsi

deepen /ˈdiːpn/ vt approfondire; scavare più profondamente (trench) ● vi approfondirsi; ⟨fig: mystery:⟩ infittirsi

deep-freeze /ˈdiːpˈfriːz/ n congelatore m

deeply /ˈdiːplɪ/ adv profondamente

deer /dɪə(r)/ n inv cervo m

deface /dɪˈfeɪs/ vt sfigurare (picture); deturpare (monument)

defamat|ion /defəˈmeɪʃn/ n diffamazione f. **~ory** /dɪˈfæmətərɪ/ a diffamatorio

default /dɪˈfɔːlt/ n (Jur: nonpayment) morosità f; (failure to appear) contumacia f; **win by ~** Sport vincere per abbandono dell'avversario; **in ~ of** per mancanza di ● a **~ drive** Comput lettore m di default ● vi (not pay) venir meno a un pagamento

defeat /dɪˈfiːt/ n sconfitta f ● vt sconfiggere; (frustrate) vanificare (attempts); **that ~s the object** questo fa fallire l'obiettivo

defect[1] /dɪˈfekt/ vi Pol fare defezione

defect[2] /ˈdiːfekt/ n difetto m. **~ive** /dɪˈfektɪv/ a difettoso

defence /dɪˈfens/ n difesa f. **~less** a indifeso

defend /dɪˈfend/ vt difendere; (justify) giustificare. **~ant** n Jur imputato, -a mf

defensive /dɪˈfensɪv/ a difensivo ● n difensiva f; **on the ~** sulla difensiva

defer /dɪˈfɜː(r)/ v (pt/pp deferred) ● vt (postpone) rinviare ● vi **to ~ to sb** rimettersi a qcno

deferen|ce /ˈdefərəns/ n deferenza f. **~tial** /-ˈrenʃl/ a deferente

defian|ce /dɪˈfaɪəns/ n sfida f; **in ~ce of** sfidando. **~t a** (person) ribelle; (gesture, attitude) di sfida. **~tly** adv con aria di sfida

deficiency /dɪˈfɪʃənsɪ/ n insufficienza f. **~t a** insufficiente; **be ~t in** mancare di

deficit /ˈdefɪsɪt/ n deficit m inv

defile /dɪˈfaɪl/ vt fig contaminare

define /dɪˈfaɪn/ vt definire

definite /ˈdefɪnɪt/ a definito; (certain) ⟨answer, yes⟩ definitivo; (improvement, difference) netto; **he was ~ about it** è stato chiaro in proposito. **~ly** adv sicuramente

definition /defɪˈnɪʃn/ n definizione f

definitive /dɪˈfɪnɪtɪv/ a definitivo

deflat|e /dɪˈfleɪt/ vt sgonfiare. **~ion** /-eɪʃn/ n Comm deflazione f

deflect /dɪˈflekt/ vt deflettere

deform|ed /dɪˈfɔːmd/ a deforme. **~ity** n deformità f inv

defraud /dɪˈfrɔːd/ vt defraudare

defrost /diːˈfrɒst/ vt sbrinare ⟨fridge⟩; scongelare ⟨food⟩

deft /deft/ a abile

defunct /dɪˈfʌŋkt/ a morto e sepolto; ⟨law⟩ caduto in disuso

defuse /diːˈfjuːz/ vt disinnescare; calmare ⟨situation⟩

defy /dɪˈfaɪ/ vt ⟨pt/pp -ied⟩ ⟨challenge⟩ sfidare; resistere a ⟨attempt⟩; ⟨not obey⟩ disobbedire a

degenerate[1] /dɪˈdʒenəreɪt/ vi degenerare; **~ into** fig degenerare in

degenerate[2] /dɪˈdʒenərət/ a degenerato

degrading /dɪˈɡreɪdɪŋ/ a degradante

degree /dɪˈɡriː/ n grado m; Univ laurea f; **20 ~s** 20 gradi; **not to the same ~** non allo stesso livello

dehydrate /diːˈhaɪdreɪt/ vt disidratare. **~d** /-ɪd/ a disidratato

de-ice /diːˈaɪs/ vt togliere il ghiaccio da

deign /deɪn/ vi **~ to do sth** degnarsi di fare qcsa

deity /ˈdiːɪtɪ/ n divinità f inv

dejected /dɪˈdʒektɪd/ a demoralizzato

delay /dɪˈleɪ/ n ritardo m; **without ~** senza indugio • vt ritardare; **be ~ed** ⟨person:⟩ essere trattenuto; ⟨train, aircraft:⟩ essere in ritardo • vi indugiare

delegate[1] /ˈdelɪɡət/ n delegato, -a mf

delegat|e[2] /ˈdelɪɡeɪt/ vt delegare. **~ion** /-ˈɡeɪʃn/ n delegazione f

delet|e /dɪˈliːt/ vt cancellare. **~ion** /-iːʃn/ n cancellatura f

deliberate[1] /dɪˈlɪbərət/ a deliberato; ⟨slow⟩ posato. **~ly** adv deliberatamente; ⟨slowly⟩ in modo posato

deliberat|e[2] /dɪˈlɪbəreɪt/ vt/i deli-

berare. **~ion** /-ˈreɪʃn/ n deliberazione f

delicacy /ˈdelɪkəsɪ/ n delicatezza f; ⟨food⟩ prelibatezza f

delicate /ˈdelɪkət/ a delicato

delicatessen /delɪkəˈtesn/ n negozio m di specialità gastronomiche

delicious /dɪˈlɪʃəs/ a delizioso

delight /dɪˈlaɪt/ n piacere m • vt deliziare • vi **~ in** dilettarsi con. **~ed** a lieto. **~ful** a delizioso

delinquen|cy /dɪˈlɪŋkwənsɪ/ n delinquenza f. **~t** a delinquente • n delinquente mf

deli|rious /dɪˈlɪrɪəs/ a **be ~rious** delirare; ⟨fig: very happy⟩ essere pazzo di gioia. **~rium** /-rɪəm/ n delirio m

deliver /dɪˈlɪvə(r)/ vt consegnare; recapitare ⟨post, newspaper⟩; tenere ⟨speech⟩; dare ⟨message⟩; tirare ⟨blow⟩; ⟨set free⟩ liberare; **~ a baby** far nascere un bambino. **~ance** n liberazione f. **~y** n consegna f; ⟨of post⟩ distribuzione f; Med parto m; **cash on ~y** pagamento m alla consegna

delude /dɪˈluːd/ vt ingannare; **~ oneself** illudersi

deluge /ˈdeljuːdʒ/ n diluvio m • vt ⟨fig: with requests etc⟩ inondare

delusion /dɪˈluːʒn/ n illusione f

de luxe /dəˈlʌks/ a di lusso

delve /delv/ vi **~ into** ⟨into pocket etc⟩ frugare in; ⟨into notes, the past⟩ fare ricerche in

demand /dɪˈmɑːnd/ n richiesta f; Comm domanda f; **in ~** richiesto; **on ~** a richiesta • vt esigere ⟨of/from da⟩. **~ing** a esigente

demarcation /diːmɑːˈkeɪʃn/ n demarcazione f

demean /dɪˈmiːn/ vt **~ oneself** abbassarsi ⟨to a⟩

demeanour /dɪˈmiːnə(r)/ n comportamento m

demented /dɪˈmentɪd/ a demente

demise /dɪˈmaɪz/ n decesso m

demister /diːˈmɪstə(r)/ n Auto sbrinatore m

demo /ˈdeməʊ/ n ⟨pl **~s**⟩ fam manifestazione f; ~ **disk** Comput demodisk m inv

democracy /dɪˈmɒkrəsɪ/ n democrazia f

democrat /ˈdeməkræt/ n democratico, -a mf. ~**ic** /-ˈkrætɪk/ a democratico

demo|lish /dɪˈmɒlɪʃ/ vt demolire. ~**lition** /demɑˈlɪʃn/ n demolizione f

demon /ˈdiːmən/ n demonio m

demonstrat|e /ˈdemənstreɪt/ vt dimostrare; fare una dimostrazione sull'uso di (appliance) ● vi Pol manifestare. ~**ion** /-ˈstreɪʃn/ n dimostrazione f; Pol manifestazione f

demonstrative /dɪˈmɒnstrətɪv/ a Gram dimostrativo; **be** ~ essere espansivo

demonstrator /ˈdemənstreɪtə(r)/ n Pol manifestante mf; (for product) dimostratore, -trice mf

demoralize /dɪˈmɒrəlaɪz/ vt demoralizzare

demote /dɪˈməʊt/ vt retrocedere di grado; Mil degradare

demure /dɪˈmjʊə(r)/ a schivo

den /den/ n tana f; (room) rifugio m

denial /dɪˈnaɪəl/ n smentita f

denim /ˈdenɪm/ n [tessuto m] jeans m; ~**s** pl [blue]jeans mpl

Denmark /ˈdenmɑːk/ n Danimarca f

denomination /dɪnɒmɪˈneɪʃn/ n Relig confessione f, (money) valore f

denounce /dɪˈnaʊns/ vt denunciare

dens|e /dens/ a (denso; (crowd, forest) fitto; (stupid) ottuso. ~**ely** adv (populated) densamente; ~**ely wooded** fittamente ricoperto di alberi. ~**ity** n densità f inv; (of forest) fittezza f

dent /dent/ n ammaccatura f ● vt ammaccare; ~**ed** a ammaccato

dental /ˈdentl/ a dei denti; (treatment) dentistico; (hygiene) dentale. ~ **surgeon** n odontoiatra mf, medico m dentista

dentist /ˈdentɪst/ n dentista mf. ~**ry** n odontoiatria f

dentures /ˈdentʃəz/ npl dentiera fsg

denunciation /dɪnʌnsɪˈeɪʃn/ n denuncia f

deny /dɪˈnaɪ/ vt (pt/pp -**ied**) negare; (officially) smentire; ~ **sb sth** negare qcsa a qcno

deodorant /diːˈəʊdərənt/ n deodorante m

depart /dɪˈpɑːt/ vi (plane, train:) partire; (liter: person) andare via; (deviate) allontanarsi (**from** da)

department /dɪˈpɑːtmənt/ n reparto m; Pol ministero m; (of company) sezione f; Univ dipartimento m. ~ **store** n grande magazzino m

departure /dɪˈpɑːtʃə(r)/ n partenza f; (from rule) allontanamento m; **new** ~ svolta f

depend /dɪˈpend/ vi dipendere (**on** da); (rely) contare (**on** su); **it all** ~**s** dipende; ~**ing on what he says** a seconda di quello che dice. ~**able** /-əbl/ a fidato. ~**ant** n persona f a carico. ~**ence** n dipendenza f. ~**ent** a dipendente (**on** da)

depict /dɪˈpɪkt/ vt (in writing) dipingere; (with picture) rappresentare

depilatory /dɪˈpɪlətərɪ/ n (cream) crema f depilatoria

deplete /dɪˈpliːt/ vt ridurre; **totally** ~**d** completamente esaurito

deplor|able /dɪˈplɔːrəbl/ a deplorevole. ~**e** vt deplorare

deploy /dɪˈplɔɪ/ vt Mil spiegare ● vi schierarsi

deport /dɪˈpɔːt/ vt deportare. ~**ation** /diːpɔːˈteɪʃn/ n deportazione f

depose /dɪˈpəʊz/ vt deporre

deposit /dɪˈpɒzɪt/ n deposito m; (against damage) cauzione f; (first instalment) acconto m ● vt (pt/pp **deposited**) depositare. ~ **account** n libretto m di risparmio;

(without instant access) conto *m* vincolato

depot /'depəʊ/ *n* deposito *m*; *Am Rail* stazione *f* ferroviaria

deprav|e /dɪ'preɪv/ *vt* depravare. **~ed** *a* depravato. **~ity** /-'prævəti/ *n* depravazione *f*

depreciat|e /dɪ'priːʃieɪt/ *vi* deprezzarsi. **~ion** /-'eɪʃn/ *n* deprezzamento *m*

depress /dɪ'pres/ *vt* deprimere; *(press down)* premere. **~ed** *a* depresso; **~ed area** zona *f* depressa. **~ing** *a* deprimente. **~ion** /-eʃn/ *n* depressione *f*

deprivation /deprɪ'veɪʃn/ *n* privazione *f*

deprive /dɪ'praɪv/ *vt* **~ sb of sth** privare qcno di qcsa. **~d** *a* *(area, childhood)* disagiato

depth /depθ/ *n* profondità *f* inv; **in ~** *(study, analyse)* in modo approfondito; **in the ~s of winter** in pieno inverno; **be out of one's ~** *(in water)* non toccare il fondo; *fig* sentirsi in alto mare

deputation /depjʊ'teɪʃn/ *n* deputazione *f*

deputize /'depjʊtaɪz/ *vi* **~ for** fare le veci di

deputy /'depjʊti/ *n* vice *mf*; *(temporary)* sostituto. *a* *mf* **● attrib ~ leader** ≈ vicesegretario. **~ a** *mf*; **~ chairman** vicepresidente *mf*

derail /dɪ'reɪl/ *vt* **be ~ed** *(train:)* essere deragliato. **~ment** *n* deragliamento *m*

deranged /dɪ'reɪndʒd/ *a* squilibrato

derelict /'derəlɪkt/ *a* abbandonato

deri|de /dɪ'raɪd/ *vt* deridere. **~sion** /-'rɪʒn/ *n* derisione *f*

derisory /dɪ'raɪsəri/ *a* *(laughter)* derisorio; *(offer)* irrisorio

derivation /derɪ'veɪʃn/ *n* derivazione *f*

derivative /dɪ'rɪvətɪv/ *a* derivato **● n** derivato *m*

derive /dɪ'raɪv/ *vt* *(obtain)* derivare; **be ~d from** *(word:)* derivare da

dermatologist /dɜːmə'tɒlədʒɪst/ *n* dermatologo, -a *mf*

derogatory /dɪ'rɒgətrɪ/ *a* *(comments)* peggiorativo

descend /dɪ'send/ *vi* scendere **● vt** scendere da; **be ~ed from** discendere da. **~ant** *n* discendente *mf*

descent /dɪ'sent/ *n* discesa *f*; *(lineage)* origine *f*

describe /dɪ'skraɪb/ *vt* descrivere

descrip|tion /dɪ'skrɪpʃn/ *n* descrizione *f*; **they had no help of any ~tion** non hanno avuto proprio nessun aiuto. **~tive** /-tɪv/ *a* descrittivo; *(vivid)* vivido

desecrat|e /'desɪkreɪt/ *vt* profanare. **~ion** /-'kreɪʃn/ *n* profanazione *f*

desert¹ /'dezət/ *n* deserto **● a** deserto; **~ island** isola *f* deserta

desert² /dɪ'zɜːt/ *vt* abbandonare **● vi** disertare. **~ed** *a* deserto. **~er** *n* *Mil* disertore *m*. **~ion** /-'zɜːʃn/ *n* *Mil* diserzione *f*; *(of family)* abbandono *m*

deserts /dɪ'zɜːts/ *npl* **get one's just ~** ottenere ciò che ci si merita

deserv|e /dɪ'zɜːv/ *vt* meritare. **~ing** *a* meritevole; **~ing cause** opera *f* meritoria

design /dɪ'zaɪn/ *n* progettazione *f*; *(fashion ~, appearance)* design *m* inv; *(pattern)* modello *m*; *(aim)* proposito *m* **● vt** progettare; disegnare *(clothes, furniture, model)*; **be ~ed for** essere fatto per

designat|e /'dezɪgneɪt/ *vt* designare. **~ion** /-'neɪʃn/ *n* designazione *f*

designer /dɪ'zaɪnə(r)/ *n* progettista *mf*; *(of clothes)* stilista *mf*; *(Theat: of set)* scenografo, -a *mf*

desirable /dɪ'zaɪərəbl/ *a* desiderabile

desire /dɪ'zaɪə(r)/ *n* desiderio *m* **● vt** desiderare

desk /desk/ *n* scrivania *f*; *(in school)* banco *m*; *(in hotel)* reception *f* inv; *(cash ~)* cassa *f*. **~top 'publishing** *n* desktop publishing *m*, editoria *f* da tavolo

desolate /'desələt/ a desolato.
~ion /-'leɪʃn/ n desolazione f

despair /dɪ'speə(r)/ n disperazione
f; **in ~** disperato; ⟨say⟩ per disperazione ● vi **I ~ of that boy** quel
ragazzo mi fa disperare

desperat|e /'despərət/ a dispera-
to; **be ~o** ⟨criminal:⟩ essere un disperato; **be ~e for** sth morire dalla voglia di. **~ely** adv disperatamente; **he said ~ely** ha detto, disperato. **~ion** /-'reɪʃn/ n disperazione f; **in ~ion** per disperazione

despicable /dɪ'spɪkəbl/ a disprez-
zevole

despise /dɪ'spaɪz/ vt disprezzare

despite /dɪ'spaɪt/ prep malgrado

despondent /dɪ'spɒndənt/ a abbattuto

despot /'despɒt/ n despota m

dessert /dɪ'zɜ:t/ n dolce m. **~
spoon** n cucchiaio m da dolce

destination /destɪ'neɪʃn/ n desti-
nazione f

destine /'destɪn/ vt destinare; **be
~d for** sth essere destinato a qcsa

destiny /'destɪnɪ/ n destino m

destitute /'destɪtju:t/ a bisognoso

destroy /dɪ'strɔɪ/ vt distruggere.
~er n Naut cacciatorpediniere m

destruct|ion /dɪ'strʌkʃn/ n distru-
zione f. **~tive** /-ɪv/ a distruttivo;
⟨fig: criticism⟩ negativo

detach /dɪ'tætʃ/ vt staccare. **~able**
/-əbl/ a separabile. **~ed** a fig di-
staccato; **~ed house** villetta f

detachment /dɪ'tætʃmənt/ n distacco m; Mil distaccamento m

detail /'di:teɪl/ n particolare m,
dettaglio m; **in ~** particolareggia-
tamente ● vt esporre con tutti i
particolari; Mil assegnare. **~ed** a
particolareggiato, dettagliato

detain /dɪ'teɪn/ vt ⟨police:⟩ trattenere; ⟨delay⟩ far ritardare. **~ee**
/-ti:'ni:/ n detenuto, -a mf

detect /dɪ'tekt/ vt individuare,
⟨perceive⟩ percepire. **~ion** /-əkʃn/
n scoperta f

detective /dɪ'tektɪv/ n investiga-

re, -trice mf. **~ story** n racconto m
poliziesco

detector /dɪ'tektə(r)/ n ⟨for metal⟩
metal detector m inv

detention /dɪ'tenʃn/ n detenzione
f; Sch punizione f

deter /dɪ'tɜ:(r)/ vt ⟨pt/pp **deterred**⟩
impedire; **~ sb from doing** sth
impedire a qcno di fare qcsa

detergent /dɪ'tɜ:dʒənt/ n detersivo m

deteriorat|e /dɪ'tɪərɪəreɪt/ vi dete-
riorarsi. **~ion** /-'reɪʃn/ n deterio-
ramento m

determination /dɪtɜ:mɪ'neɪʃn/ n
determinazione f

determine /dɪ'tɜ:mɪn/ vt ⟨ascer-
tain⟩ determinare; **~ to** ⟨resolve⟩
decidere di. **~d** a deciso

deterrent /dɪ'terənt/ n deterren-
te m

detest /dɪ'test/ vt detestare. **~able**
/-əbl/ a detestabile

detonat|e /'detəneɪt/ vt far detona-
re ● vi detonare. **~or** n detonatore m

detour /'di:tʊə(r)/ n deviazione f

detract /dɪ'trækt/ vi **~ from** sminuire ⟨merit⟩; rovinare ⟨pleasure,
beauty⟩

detriment /'detrɪmənt/ n **to the ~
of** a danno di. **~al** /-'mentl/ a dannoso

deuce /dju:s/ n Tennis deuce m inv

devaluation /di:væljʊ'eɪʃn/ n sva-
lutazione f

de'value vt svalutare ⟨currency⟩

devastat|e /'devəsteɪt/ vt devasta-
re. **~ed** a fam sconvolto. **ing** a
devastante; ⟨news⟩ sconvolgente.
~ion /-'steɪʃn/ n devastazione f

develop /dɪ'veləp/ vt sviluppare;
contrarre ⟨illness⟩; ⟨add to value
of⟩ valorizzare ⟨area⟩ ● vi svilupparsi; **~ into** divenire. **~er** n
⟨property⟩ **~er** imprenditore,
-trice mf edile

de'veloping country n paese m
in via di sviluppo

development /dɪ'veləpmənt/

sviluppo *m*; (*of vaccine etc*) messa *f* a punto

deviant /'di:vɪənt/ *a* deviato

deviate /'di:vɪeɪt/ *vi* deviare. **~ion** /-'eɪʃn/ *n* deviazione *f*

device /dɪ'vaɪs/ *n* dispositivo *m*

devil /'devl/ *n* diavolo *m*

devious /'di:vɪəs/ *a* ⟨person⟩ subdolo; ⟨route⟩ tortuoso

devise /dɪ'vaɪz/ *vt* escogitare

devoid /dɪ'vɔɪd/ *a* ~ **of** privo di

devolution /di:və'lu:ʃn/ *n* (*of power*) decentramento *m*

devote /dɪ'vəʊt/ *vt* dedicare. **~ed** *a* ⟨daughter etc⟩ affezionato; **be ~ed to sth** consacrarsi a qcsa. **~ee** /devə'ti:/ *n* appassionato, -a *mf*

devotion /dɪ'vəʊʃn/ *n* dedizione *f*; **~s** *pl Relig* devozione *fsg*

devour /dɪ'vaʊə(r)/ *vt* divorare

devout /dɪ'vaʊt/ *a* devoto

dew /dju:/ *n* rugiada *f*

dexterity /dek'sterɪtɪ/ *n* destrezza *f*

diabet|es /daɪə'bi:ti:z/ *n* diabete *m*. **~ic** /-'betɪk/ *a* diabetico ● *n* diabetico, -a *mf*

diabolical /daɪə'bɒlɪkl/ *a* diabolico

diagnose /daɪəg'nəʊz/ *vt* diagnosticare

diagnosis /daɪəg'nəʊsɪs/ *n* (*pl* -oses /-si:z/) diagnosi *f inv*

diagonal /daɪ'ægənl/ *a* diagonale ● *n* diagonale *f*

diagram /'daɪəgræm/ *n* diagramma *m*

dial /'daɪəl/ *n* (*of clock, machine*) quadrante *m*; *Teleph* disco *m* combinatore ● *v* (*pt/pp* dialled) ● *vi Teleph* fare il numero; **~ direct** chiamare in teleselezione ● *vt* fare ⟨number⟩

dialect /'daɪəlekt/ *n* dialetto *m*

dialling /'daɪəlɪŋ/ ~ **code** *n* prefisso *m*. ~ **tone** *n* segnale *m* di linea libera

dialogue /'daɪəlɒg/ *n* dialogo *m*

'dial tone *n Am Teleph* segnale *m* di linea libera

diameter /daɪ'æmɪtə(r)/ *n* diametro *m*

diametrically /daɪə'metrɪklɪ/ *adv* ~ **opposed** diametralmente opposto

diamond /'daɪəmənd/ *n* diamante *m*, brillante *m*; (*shape*) losanga *f*; **~s** *pl* (*in cards*) quadri *mpl*

diaper /'daɪəpə(r)/ *n Am* pannolino *m*

diaphragm /'daɪəfræm/ *n* diaframma *m*

diarrhoea /daɪə'rɪə/ *n* diarrea *f*

diary /'daɪərɪ/ *n* (*for appointments*) agenda *f*; (*for writing in*) diario *m*

dice /daɪs/ *n inv* dadi *mpl* ● *vt Culin* tagliare a dadini

dicey /'daɪsɪ/ *a fam* rischioso

dictate /dɪk'teɪt/ *vt/i* dettare. **~ion** /-eɪʃn/ *n* dettato *m*

dictator /dɪk'teɪtə(r)/ *n* dittatore *m*. **~ial** /-tə'tɔ:rɪəl/ *a* dittatoriale. **~ship** *n* dittatura *f*

dictionary /'dɪkʃənrɪ/ *n* dizionario *m*

did /dɪd/ *see* **do**

didactic /dɪ'dæktɪk/ *a* didattico

diddle /'dɪdl/ *vt fam* gabbare

didn't /'dɪdnt/ = **did not**

die /daɪ/ *vi* (*pres p* dying) morire (*of* di); **be dying to do sth** *fam* morire dalla voglia di fare qcsa. **die down** *vi* calmarsi; ⟨fire, flames⟩ spegnersi. **die out** *vi* estinguersi; ⟨custom⟩ morire

diesel /'di:zl/ *n* diesel *m*

diet /'daɪət/ *n* regime *m* alimentare; (*restricted*) dieta *f*; **be on a ~** essere a dieta ● *vi* essere a dieta

differ /'dɪfə(r)/ *vi* differire; (*disagree*) non essere d'accordo

difference /'dɪfrəns/ *n* differenza *f*; (*disagreement*) divergenza *f*

different /'dɪfrənt/ *a* diverso, differente; (*various*) diversi; **be ~ from** essere diverso da

differential /dɪfə'renʃl/ *a* differenziale ● *n* differenziale *m*

differentiate /dɪfə'renʃɪeɪt/ *vt* distinguere (**between** fra); (*dis-*

criminate) discriminare **(between** fra); *(make differ)* differenziare

differently /ˈdɪfrəntlɪ/ *adv* in modo diverso; ~ **from** diversamente da

difficult /ˈdɪfɪkəlt/ *a* difficile. ~**y** *n* difficoltà *f inv*; **with** ~**y** con difficoltà

diffuse¹ /dɪˈfjuːs/ *a* diffuso; *(wordy)* prolisso

diffuse² /dɪˈfjuːz/ *vt* Phys diffondere

dig /dɪg/ *n (poke)* spinta *f*; *(remark)* frecciata *f*, Archaeol scavo *m*; ~**s** *pl fam* camera *fsg* ammobiliata ●*vt/i (pt/pp* dug, *pres p* digging) scavare *(hole)*; vangare *(garden)*; *(thrust)* conficcare; ~ **sb in the ribs** dare una gomitata a qcno. **dig out** *vt fig* tirar fuori. **dig up** *vt* scavare *(garden, street, object)*; sradicare *(plant)*; *(fig: find)* scovare

digest¹ /ˈdaɪdʒest/ *n* compendio *m*

digest² /daɪˈdʒest/ *vt* digerire. ~**ible** *a* digeribile. ~**ion** /-estʃn/ *n* digestione *f*

digger /ˈdɪgə(r)/ *n* Techn scavatrice *f*

digit /ˈdɪdʒɪt/ *n* cifra *f*; *(finger)* dito *m*

digital /ˈdɪdʒɪtl/ *a* digitale; ~ **clock** orologio *m* digitale

dignified /ˈdɪgnɪfaɪd/ *a* dignitoso

dignitary /ˈdɪgnɪtərɪ/ *n* dignitario *m*

dignity /ˈdɪgnɪtɪ/ *n* dignità *f*

digress /daɪˈgres/ *vi* divagare. ~**ion** /-eʃn/ *n* digressione *f*

dike /daɪk/ *n* diga *f*

dilapidated /dɪˈlæpɪdeɪtɪd/ *a* cadente

dilate /daɪˈleɪt/ *vi* dilatarsi

dilemma /dɪˈlemə/ *n* dilemma *m*

dilettante /dɪlɪˈtæntɪ/ *n* dilettante *mf*

dilly-dally /ˈdɪlɪdælɪ/ *vi (pt/pp -ied)* fam tentennare

dilute /daɪˈluːt/ *vt* diluire

dim /dɪm/ *a (dimmer, dimmest)* debole *(light)*; *(dark)* scuro; *(prospect, chance)* scarso; *(indis-*

tinct) impreciso; *(fam: stupid)* tonto ●*vt/i (pt/pp* dimmed) affievolire. ~**ly** *adv (see, remember)* indistintamente; *(shine)* debolmente

dime /daɪm/ *n Am* moneta *f* da dieci centesimi

dimension /daɪˈmenʃn/ *n* dimensione *f*

diminish /dɪˈmɪnɪʃ/ *vt/i* diminuire

diminutive /dɪˈmɪnjʊtɪv/ *a* minuscolo ●*n* diminutivo *m*

dimple /ˈdɪmpl/ *n* fossetta *f*

din /dɪn/ *n* baccano *m*

dine /daɪn/ *vi* pranzare. ~**r** *n (Am: restaurant)* tavola *f* calda; **the last** ~**r in the restaurant** l'ultimo cliente nel ristorante

dinghy /ˈdɪŋgɪ/ *n* dinghy *m*; *(inflatable)* canotto *m* pneumatico

dingy /ˈdɪndʒɪ/ *a (-ier, -iest)* squallido e tetro

dining /ˈdaɪnɪŋ/ ~**car** *n* carrozza *f* ristorante. ~**-room** *n* sala *f* da pranzo. ~**-table** *n* tavolo *m* da pranzo

dinner /ˈdɪnə(r)/ *n* cena *f*; *(at midday)* pranzo *m*. ~**-jacket** *n* smoking *m inv*

dinosaur /ˈdaɪnəsɔː(r)/ *n* dinosauro *m*

dint /dɪnt/ *n* **by** ~ **of** a forza di

diocese /ˈdaɪəsɪs/ *n* diocesi *f inv*

dip /dɪp/ *n (in ground)* inclinazione *f*; Culin salsina *f*; **go for a** ~ andare a fare una nuotata ●*v (pt/pp* dipped) ●*vt (in liquid)* immergere; abbassare *(head, headlights)* ●*vi (land:)* formare un avvallamento. **dip into** *vt* scorrere *(book)*

diphtheria /dɪfˈθɪərɪə/ *n* difterite *f*

diphthong /ˈdɪfθɒŋ/ *n* dittongo *m*

diploma /dɪˈpləʊmə/ *n* diploma *m*

diplomacy /dɪˈpləʊməsɪ/ *n* diplomazia *f*

diplomat /ˈdɪpləmæt/ *n* diplomatico, -a *mf*. ~**ic** /-ˈmætɪk/ *a* diplomatico. ~**ically** *adv* con diplomazia

dip-stick *n* Auto astina *f* dell'olio

dire /ˈdaɪə(r)/ *a (situation, consequences)* terribile

direct /dɪˈrekt/ a diretto ● adv direttamente ● vt (aim) rivolgere ⟨attention, criticism⟩; (control) dirigere; fare la regia di ⟨film, play⟩; ~ **sb** ⟨show the way⟩ indicare la strada a qcno; ~ **sb to do sth** ordinare a qcno di fare qcsa. ~ 'current n corrente m continua

direction /dɪˈrekʃn/ n direzione f; ⟨of play, film⟩ regia f; ~s pl indicazioni fpl

directly /dɪˈrektlɪ/ adv direttamente; ⟨at once⟩ immediatamente ● conj [non] appena

director /dɪˈrektə(r)/ n Comm direttore, -trice mf; ⟨of play, film⟩ regista mf

directory /dɪˈrektərɪ/ n elenco m; Teleph elenco m [telefonico]; ⟨of streets⟩ stradario m

dirt /dɜːt/ n sporco m; ~ **cheap** fam a [un] prezzo stracciato

dirty /'dɜːtɪ/ a (-ier, -iest) sporco; ~ **trick** brutto scherzo m; ~ **word** parolaccia f ● vt (pt/pp -ied) sporcare

dis|a'bility /dɪs-/ n infermità f inv. ~**abled** /d'seɪbld/ a invalido

disad'van|tage n svantaggio m; **at a** ~**tage** in una posizione di svantaggio. ~**taged** a svantaggiato. ~'**tageous** a svantaggioso

disa'gree vi non essere d'accordo; ~ **with** ⟨food:⟩ far male a

disa'greeable a sgradevole

disa'greement n disaccordo m; ⟨quarrel⟩ dissidio m

disal'low vt annullare ⟨goal⟩

disap'pear vi scomparire. ~**ance** n scomparsa f

disap'point vt deludere; **I'm** ~**ed** sono deluso. ~**ing** a deludente. ~**ment** n delusione f

disap'proval n disapprovazione f

disap'prove vi disapprovare; ~ **of sb/sth** disapprovare qcno/qcsa

dis'arm vt disarmare ● vi Mil disarmarsi. ~**ament** n disarmo m. ~**ing** a ⟨frankness etc⟩ disarmante

disar'ray n **in** ~ in disordine

disast|er /dɪˈzɑːstə(r)/ n disastro m. ~**rous** /-rəs/ a disastroso

dis'band vt sciogliere; smobilitare ⟨troops⟩ ● vi sciogliersi; ⟨regiment:⟩ essere smobilitato

disbe'lief n incredulità f; **in** ~ con incredulità

disc /dɪsk/ n disco m; ⟨CD⟩ compact disc m inv

discard /dɪˈskɑːd/ vt scartare; ⟨throw away⟩ eliminare; scaricare ⟨boyfriend⟩

discern /dɪˈsɜːn/ vt discernere. ~**ible** a discernibile. ~**ing** a perspicace

'**discharge**[1] n Electr scarica f; ⟨dismissal⟩ licenziamento m; Mil congedo m; ⟨Med: of blood⟩ emissione f; ⟨of cargo⟩ scarico m

dis'charge[2] vt scaricare ⟨battery, cargo⟩; ⟨dismiss⟩ licenziare; Mil congedare; Jur assolvere ⟨accused⟩; dimettere ⟨patient⟩ ● vi Electr scaricarsi

disciple /dɪˈsaɪpl/ n discepolo m

disciplinary /'dɪsɪplɪnərɪ/ a disciplinare

discipline /'dɪsɪplɪn/ n disciplina f ● vt disciplinare; ⟨punish⟩ punire

'**disc jockey** n disc jockey m inv

dis'claim vt disconoscere. ~**er** n rifiuto m

dis'clos|e vt svelare. ~**ure** n rivelazione f

disco /'dɪskəʊ/ n discoteca f

dis'colour vt scolorire ● vi scolorirsi

dis'comfort n scomodità f; fig disagio m

disconcert /dɪskənˈsɜːt/ vt sconcertare

discon'nect vt disconnettere

disconsolate /dɪsˈkɒnsələt/ a sconsolato

discon'tent n scontentezza f. ~**ed** a scontento

discon'tinue vt cessare, smettere; Comm sospendere la produzione di; ~**d line** fine f serie

'**discord** n discordia f; Mus dissonanza *f*. **~ant** /ˈdɪˈskɔːdənt/ *a* **~ant note** nota *f* discordante

discothèque /ˈdɪskətek/ *n* discoteca *f*

'discount¹ *n* sconto *m*

dis'count² *vt* (*not believe*) non credere a, (*leave out of consideration*) non tener conto di

dis'courage *vt* scoraggiare; (*dissuade*) dissuadere

'discourse *n* discorso *m*

dis'courteous *a* scortese

discover /dɪsˈkʌvə(r)/ *vt* scoprire. **~y** *n* scoperta *f*

dis'credit *n* discredito *m* • *vt* (*pt/pp* **discredited**) screditare

discreet /dɪˈskriːt/ *a* discreto

discrepancy /dɪˈskrepənsɪ/ *n* screpanza *f*

discretion /dɪˈskreʃn/ *n* discrezione *f*

discriminat|e /dɪˈskrɪmɪneɪt/ *vi* discriminare (**against** contro); **~e between** distinguere tra. **~ing** *a* esigente. **~ion** /-ˈneɪʃn/ *n* discriminazione *f*; (*quality*) discernimento *m*

discus /ˈdɪskəs/ *n* disco *m*

discuss /dɪˈskʌs/ *vt* discutere; (*examine critically*) esaminare. **~ion** /-ʌʃn/ *n* discussione *f*

disdain /dɪsˈdeɪn/ *n* sdegno *m* • *vt* sdegnare. **~ful** *a* sdegnoso

disease /dɪˈziːz/ *n* malattia *f*. **~d** *a* malato

disem'bark *vi* sbarcare

disen'chant *vt* disincantare. **~ment** *n* disincanto *m*

disen'gage *vt* disimpegnare; disinnestare (*clutch*)

disen'tangle *vt* districare

dis'favour *n* sfavore *m*

dis'figure *vt* deformare

dis'grace *n* vergogna *f*; **I am in ~** sono caduto in disgrazia; **it's a ~** è una vergogna • *vt* disonorare. **~ful** *a* vergognoso

disgruntled /dɪsˈɡrʌntld/ *a* malcontento

disguise /dɪsˈɡaɪz/ *n* travestimento *m*; **in ~** travestito • *vt* contraffare (*voice*); dissimulare (*emotions*); **~d as** travestito da

disgust /dɪsˈɡʌst/ *n* disgusto *m*; **in ~** con aria disgustata • *vt* disgustare. **~ing** *a* disgustoso

dish /dɪʃ/ *n* piatto *m*; **do the ~es** lavare i piatti • **dish out** *vt* (*serve*) servire; (*distribute*) distribuire. **dish up** *vt* servire

'dishcloth *n* strofinaccio *m*

dis'hearten *vt* scoraggiare

dishevelled /dɪˈʃevld/ *a* scompigliato

dis'honest *a* disonesto. **~y** *n* disonestà *f*

dis'honour *n* disonore *m* • *vt* disonorare (*family*); non onorare (*cheque*). **~able** *a* disonorevole. **~ably** *adv* in modo disonorevole

'dishwasher *n* lavapiatti *f inv*

disil'lusion *vt* disilludere. **~ment** *n* disillusione *f*

disin'fect *vt* disinfettare. **~ant** *n* disinfettante *m*

disin'herit *vt* diseredare

disin'tegrate *vi* disintegrarsi

disin'terested *a* disinteressato

disin'jointed *a* sconnesso

disk /dɪsk/ *n* Comput disco *m*; (*diskette*) dischetto *m*

dis'like *n* avversione *f*; **your likes and ~s** i tuoi gusti • *vt* **I ~ him/it** non mi piace; **I don't ~ him/it** non mi dispiace

dislocate /ˈdɪsləkeɪt/ *vt* slogare; **~ one's shoulder** slogarsi una spalla

dis'lodge *vt* sloggiare

dis'loyal *a* sleale. **~ty** *n* slealtà *f*

dismal /ˈdɪzməl/ *a* (*person*) abbacchiato; (*news, weather*) deprimente; (*performance*) mediocre

dismantle /dɪsˈmæntl/ *vt* smontare (*tent, machine*); *fig* smantellare

dis'may *n* sgomento *m*. **~ed** *a* sgomento

dis'miss *vt* licenziare (*employee*); (*reject*) scartare (*idea, suggestion*). **~al** *n* licenziamento *m*

dis'mount *vi* smontare

diso'bedien|ce *n* disubbidienza *f*. **~t** *a* disubbidiente

diso'bey *vt* disubbidire a ⟨*rule*⟩ ● *vi* disubbidire

dis'order *n* disordine *m*; *Med* disturbo *m*. **~ly** *a* disordinato; ⟨*crowd*⟩ turbolento; **~ly conduct** turbamento *m* della quiete pubblica

dis'organized *a* disorganizzato

dis'orientate *vt* disorientare

dis'own *vt* disconoscere

disparaging /dɪ'spærɪdʒɪŋ/ *a* sprezzante

disparity /dɪ'spærətɪ/ *n* disparità *f* *inv*

dispassionate /dɪ'spæʃənət/ *a* spassionato

dispatch /dɪ'spætʃ/ *n Comm* spedizione *f*; ⟨*Mil, report*⟩ dispaccio *m*; **with ~** con prontezza ● *vt* spedire; ⟨*kill*⟩ spedire al creatore

dispel /dɪ'spel/ *vt* (*pt*/*pp* **dispelled**) dissipare

dispensable /dɪ'spensəbl/ *a* dispensabile

dispensary /dɪ'spensərɪ/ *n* farmacia *f*

dispense /dɪ'spens/ *vt* distribuire; **~ with** fare a meno di; **dispensing chemist** farmacista *mf*; ⟨*shop*⟩ farmacia *f*. **~r** *n* ⟨*device*⟩ distributore *m*

dispersal /dɪ'spɜːsl/ *n* dispersione *f*. **~e** /dɪ'spɜːs/ *vt* disperdere ● *vi* disperdersi

dispirited /dɪ'spɪrɪtɪd/ *a* scoraggiato

dis'place *vt* spostare; **~d person** profugo, -a *mf*

display /dɪ'spleɪ/ *n* mostra *f*; *Comm* esposizione *f*; ⟨*of feelings*⟩ manifestazione *f*; *pej* ostentazione *f*; *Comput* display *m* *inv* ● *vt* mostrare; esporre ⟨*goods*⟩; manifestare ⟨*feeling*⟩; *Comput* visualizzare

dis'please *vt* non piacere a; **be ~d with** essere scontento di

dis'pleasure *n* malcontento *m*

disposable /dɪ'spəʊzəbl/ *a* ⟨*throwaway*⟩ usa e getta; ⟨*income*⟩ disponibile

disposal /dɪ'spəʊzl/ *n* ⟨*getting rid of*⟩ eliminazione *f*; **be at sb's ~** essere a disposizione di qcno

dispose /dɪ'spəʊz/ *vi* **~ of** ⟨*get rid of*⟩ disfarsi di; **be well ~d** essere ben disposto (**to** verso)

disposition /dɪspə'zɪʃn/ *n* disposizione *f*; ⟨*nature*⟩ indole *f*

disproportionate /dɪsprə'pɔːʃənət/ *a* sproporzionato

dis'prove *vt* confutare

dispute /dɪ'spjuːt/ *n* disputa *f*; ⟨*industrial*⟩ contestazione *f* ● *vt* contestare ⟨*statement*⟩

disquali'fication *n* squalifica *f*; ⟨*from driving*⟩ ritiro *m* della patente

dis'qualify *vt* (*pt*/*pp* **-ied**) escludere; *Sport* squalificare; **~ sb from driving** ritirare la patente a qcno

disquieting /dɪs'kwaɪətɪŋ/ *a* allarmante

disre'gard *n* mancanza *f* di considerazione ● *vt* ignorare

disre'pair *n* **fall into ~** deteriorarsi; **in a state of ~** in cattivo stato

dis'reputable *a* malfamato

disre'pute *n* discredito *m*; **bring sb into ~** rovinare la reputazione a qcno

disre'spect *n* mancanza *f* di rispetto. **~ful** *a* irrispettoso

disrupt /dɪs'rʌpt/ *vt* creare scompiglio in; sconvolgere ⟨*plans*⟩. **~ion** /-ʌpʃn/ *n* scompiglio *m*; ⟨*of plans*⟩ sconvolgimento *m*. **~ive** /-tɪv/ *a* ⟨*person, behaviour*⟩ indisciplinato

dissatis'faction *n* malcontento *m*

dis'satisfied *a* scontento

dissect /dɪ'sekt/ *vt* sezionare. **~ion** /-ekʃn/ *n* dissezione *f*

dissent /dɪ'sent/ *n* dissenso *m* ● *vi* dissentire

dissertation /dɪsə'teɪʃn/ *n* tesi *f* *inv*

dis'service *n* **do sb/oneself a ~** rendere un cattivo servizio a qcno/se stesso

dissident /ˈdɪsɪdənt/ n dissidente mf

dis'similar a dissimile (**to** da)

dissociate /dɪˈsəʊʃɪeɪt/ vt dissociare; ~ **oneself from** dissociarsi da

dissolute /ˈdɪsəluːt/ a dissoluto

dissolution /dɪsəˈluːʃn/ n scioglimento m

dissolve /dɪˈzɒlv/ vt dissolvere ● vi dissolversi

dissuade /dɪˈsweɪd/ vt dissuadere

distance /ˈdɪstəns/ n distanza f; **it's a short ~ from here to the station** la stazione non è lontana da qui; **in the ~** in lontananza; **from a ~** da lontano

distant /ˈdɪstənt/ a distante; (relative) lontano

dis'taste n avversione f; ~**ful** a spiacevole

distil /dɪˈstɪl/ vt (pt/pp **distilled**) distillare. ~**lation** /-ˈleɪʃn/ n distillazione f. ~**lery** /-ˈorɪ/ n distilleria f

distinct /dɪˈstɪŋkt/ a chiaro; (different) distinto. ~**ion** /-ɪŋkʃn/ n distinzione f; Sch massimo m dei voti. ~**ive** /-tɪv/ a caratteristico. ~**ly** adv chiaramente

distinguish /dɪˈstɪŋgwɪʃ/ vt/i distinguere; ~ **oneself** distinguersi. ~**ed** a rinomato; (appearance) distinto; (career) brillante

distort /dɪˈstɔːt/ vt distorcere. ~**ion** /-ˈɔːʃn/ n distorsione f

distract /dɪˈstrækt/ vt distrarre. ~**ed** /-ɪd/ a assente; (fam: worried) preoccupato. ~**ing** a che distoglie. ~**ion** /-ækʃn/ n distrazione f; (despair) disperazione f; **drive sb to** ~ portare qcno alla disperazione

distraught /dɪˈstrɔːt/ a sconvolto

distress /dɪˈstres/ n angoscia f; (pain) sofferenza f; (danger) difficoltà f ● vt sconvolgere; (sadden) affliggere. ~**ing** a penoso; (shocking) sconvolgente. ~ **signal** n segnale m di richiesta di soccorso

distribut|e /dɪˈstrɪbjuːt/ vt distri-

buire. ~**ion** /-ˈbjuːʃn/ n distribuzione f. ~**or** n distributore m

district /ˈdɪstrɪkt/ n regione f; Admin distretto m. ~ **nurse** n infermiere, -a mf che fa visite a domicilio

dis'trust n sfiducia f ● vt non fidarsi di. ~**ful** a diffidente

disturb /dɪˈstɜːb/ vt disturbare; (emotionally) turbare; spostare (papers). ~**ance** n disturbo m; ~**ances** (pl: rioting etc) disordini mpl. ~**ed** a turbato; [mentally] ~**ed** malato di mente. ~**ing** a inquietante

dis'used a non utilizzato

ditch /dɪtʃ/ n fosso m ● vt (fam: abandon) abbandonare (plan, car); piantare (lover)

dither /ˈdɪðə(r)/ vi titubare

divan /dɪˈvæn/ n divano m

dive /daɪv/ n tuffo m; Aeron picchiata f; (fam: place) bettola f ● vi tuffarsi; (when in water) immergersi; Aeron scendere in picchiata; (fam: rush) precipitarsi

diver /ˈdaɪvə(r)/ n (from board) tuffatore, -trice mf; (scuba) sommozzatore, -trice mf; (deep sea) palombaro m

diverge /daɪˈvɜːdʒ/ vi divergere. ~**gent** /-ənt/ a divergente

diverse /daɪˈvɜːs/ a vario

diversify /daɪˈvɜːsɪfaɪ/ vt/i (pt/pp -**ied**) diversificare

diversion /daɪˈvɜːʃn/ n deviazione f; (distraction) diversivo m

diversity /daɪˈvɜːsətɪ/ n varietà f

divert /daɪˈvɜːt/ vt deviare (traffic); distogliere (attention)

divest /daɪˈvest/ vt privare (**of** di)

divide /dɪˈvaɪd/ vt dividere (**by** per); **six ~d by two** sei diviso due ● vi dividersi

dividend /ˈdɪvɪdend/ n dividendo m; **pay ~s** fig ripagare

divine /dɪˈvaɪn/ a divino

diving /ˈdaɪvɪŋ/ n (from board) tuffi mpl; (scuba) immersione f. ~**-board** n trampolino m. ~ **mask**

n maschera *f* [subacquea]. **~-suit** *n* muta *f*; ⟨deep sea⟩ scafandro *m*

divinity /dɪˈvɪnətɪ/ *n* divinità *f inv*; ⟨subject⟩ teologia *f*; ⟨at school⟩ religione *f*

divisible /dɪˈvɪzɪbl/ *a* divisibile (**by** per)

division /dɪˈvɪʒn/ *n* divisione *f*; ⟨in sports league⟩ serie *f*

divorce /dɪˈvɔːs/ *n* divorzio *m* ● *vt* divorziare da. **~d** *a* divorziato; **get ~d** divorziare

divorcee /dɪvɔːˈsiː/ *n* divorziato, -a *mf*

divulge /daɪˈvʌldʒ/ *vt* rendere pubblico

DIY *n abbr* **do-it-yourself**

dizziness /ˈdɪzɪnɪs/ *n* giramenti *mpl* di testa

dizzy /ˈdɪzɪ/ *a* (**-ier, -iest**) vertiginoso; **I feel ~** mi gira la testa

do /duː/ *n* (*pl* **dos** *or* **do's**) *fam* festa *f* ● *v* (*3 sg pres tense* **does**; *pt* **did**; *pp* **done**) ● *vt* fare; ⟨c*: cheat⟩ fregare; **be done** Culin essere cotto; **well done** bravo; Culin ben cotto; **do the flowers** sistemare i fiori; **do the washing up** lavare i piatti; **do one's hair** farsi i capelli ● *vi* (*be suitable*) andare; (*be enough*) bastare; **this will do** questo va bene; **that will do!** basta così!; **do well/badly** cavarsela bene/male; **how is he doing?** come sta? ● *v aux* **do you speak Italian?** parli italiano?; **you don't like him, do you?** non ti piace, vero?; (*expressing astonishment*) non dirmi che ti piace!; **yes, I do** sì; (*emphatic*) invece sì; **no, I don't** no, I don't; **I don't smoke** non fumo; **don't you/doesn't he?** vero?; **so do I** anch'io; **do come in, John** entra, John; **how do you do?** piacere. **do away with** *vt* abolire ⟨rule⟩. **do for** *vt* **done for** *fam* rovinato. **do in** *vt* (*fam: kill*) uccidere; **farsi male a** ⟨back⟩; **done in** *fam* esausto. **do up** *vt* (*fasten*) abbottonare; (*renovate*) rimettere a nuovo; (*wrap*) avvolgere. **do with** *vt* **I**

could do with a spanner mi ci vorrebbe una chiave inglese. **do without** *vt* fare a meno di

docile /ˈdəʊsaɪl/ *a* docile

dock¹ /dɒk/ *n* Jur banco *m* degli imputati

dock² *n* Naut bacino *m* ● *vi* entrare in porto; ⟨spaceship:⟩ congiungersi. **~er** *n* portuale *m*. **~s** *npl* porto *m*. **~yard** *n* cantiere *m* navale

doctor /ˈdɒktə(r)/ *n* dottore *m*, dottoressa *f* ● *vt* alterare ⟨drink⟩; castrare ⟨cat⟩. **~ate** /-ət/ *n* dottorato *m*

doctrine /ˈdɒktrɪn/ *n* dottrina *f*

document /ˈdɒkjʊmənt/ *n* documento *m*. **~ary** /-ˈmentərɪ/ *a* documentario ● *n* documentario *m*

doddery /ˈdɒdərɪ/ *a fam* barcollante

dodge /dɒdʒ/ *n fam* trucco *m* ● *vt* schivare ⟨blow⟩; evitare ⟨person⟩ ● *vi* scansarsi; **~ out of the way** scansarsi

dodgems /ˈdɒdʒəmz/ *npl* autoscontro *msg*

dodgy /ˈdɒdʒɪ/ *a* (**-ier, -iest**) (*fam: dubious*) sospetto

doe /dəʊ/ *n* femmina *f* (di daino, renna, lepre); ⟨rabbit⟩ coniglia *f*

does /dʌz/ *see* **do**

doesn't /ˈdʌznt/ = **does not**

dog /dɒg/ *n* cane *m* ● *vt* (*pt/pp* **dogged**) ⟨illness, bad luck:⟩ perseguitare

dog: ~-biscuit *n* biscotto *m* per cani. **~-collar** *n* collare *m* (*per cani*); Relig fam collare *m* del prete. **~-eared** *a* con le orecchie

dogged /ˈdɒgɪd/ *a* ostinato

'dog house *n* **in the ~** *fam* in disgrazia

dogma /ˈdɒgmə/ *n* dogma *m*. **~tic** /-ˈmætɪk/ *a* dogmatico

'dogsbody *n fam* tirapiedi *mf inv*

doily /ˈdɔɪlɪ/ *n* centrino *m*

do-it-yourself /ˈduːɪtjəˈself/ *n* fai da te *m*, bricolage *m*. **~ shop** *n* negozio *m* di bricolage

doldrums /ˈdɒldrəmz/ *npl* be in

the ~ essere giù di corda; ⟨business:⟩ essere in fase di stasi

dole /dəʊl/ n sussidio m di disoccupazione; **be on the** ~ essere disoccupato ● **dole out** vt distribuire

doleful /'dəʊlfl/ a triste

doll /dɒl/ n bambola f ● **doll oneself up** vt fam mettersi in ghingheri

dollar /'dɒlə(r)/ n dollaro m

dollop /'dɒləp/ n fam cucchiaiata f

dolphin /'dɒlfɪn/ n delfino m

dome /dəʊm/ n cupola f

domestic /də'mestɪk/ a domestico; Pol interno; Comm nazionale. ~ **animal** n animale m domestico

domesticated /də'mestɪkeɪtɪd/ a ⟨animal⟩ addomesticato

domestic: flight n volo m nazionale. ~ '**servant** n domestico, -a mf

dominant /'dɒmɪnənt/ a dominante

dominate /'dɒmɪneɪt/ vt/i dominare. ~**ion** /-'neɪʃn/ n dominio m

domineering /dɒmɪ'nɪərɪŋ/ a autoritario

dominion /də'mɪnjən/ n Br Pol dominion m inv

domino /'dɒmɪnəʊ/ n (pl -es) tessera f del domino; ~**es** sg ⟨game⟩ domino m

don¹ /dɒn/ vt (pt/pp **donned**) liter indossare

don² n docente mf universitario, -a

donate /dəʊ'neɪt/ vt donare. ~**ion** /-eɪʃn/ n donazione f

done /dʌn/ see **do**

donkey /'dɒŋkɪ/ n asino m; ~'s **years** fam secoli mpl. ~**-work** n sgobbata f

donor /'dəʊnə(r)/ n donatore, -trice mf

don't /dəʊnt/ = **do not**

doodle /'duːdl/ vi scarabocchiare

doom /duːm/ n fato m; ⟨ruin⟩ rovina f ● vt **be ~ed** [**to failure**] essere destinato al fallimento; ~**ed** ⟨ship⟩ destinato ad affondare

door /dɔː(r)/ n porta f; ⟨of car⟩ portiera f; **out of** ~**s** all'aperto

door: ~man n portiere m. ~**mat** n zerbino m. ~**step** n gradino m della porta. ~**way** n vano m della porta

dope /dəʊp/ n fam ⟨drug⟩ droga f leggera; ⟨information⟩ indiscrezioni fpl; ⟨idiot⟩ idiota m ● vt drogare; Sport dopare

dopey /'dəʊpɪ/ a fam addormentato

dormant /'dɔːmənt/ a latente; ⟨volcano⟩ inattivo

dormer /'dɔːmə(r)/ n ~ [**window**] abbaino m

dormitory /'dɔːmɪtərɪ/ n dormitorio m

dormouse /'dɔː-/ n ghiro m

dosage /'dəʊsɪdʒ/ n dosaggio m

dose /dəʊs/ n dose f

doss /dɒs/ vi sl accamparsi. ~**er** n barbone, -a mf. ~**-house** n dormitorio m pubblico

dot /dɒt/ n punto m; **at 8 o'clock on the** ~ alle 8 in punto

dote /dəʊt/ vi ~ **on** stravedere per

dotted /'dɒtɪd/ a ~ **line** linea f punteggiata; **be** ~ **with** essere punteggiato di

dotty /'dɒtɪ/ a (-**ier**, -**iest**) fam tocco; ⟨idea⟩ folle

double /'dʌbl/ a doppio ● adv cost ~ costare il doppio; **see** ~ vedere doppio; ~ **the amount** la quantità doppia ● n doppio m; ⟨person⟩ sosia m inv; ~**s** pl Tennis doppio m; **at the** ~ di corsa ● vt raddoppiare; ⟨fold⟩ piegare in due ● vi raddoppiare. **double back** vi ⟨go back⟩ fare dietro front. **double up** vi ⟨bend⟩ piegarsi in due ⟨**with** per⟩; ⟨share⟩ dividere una stanza

double: ~'bass n contrabbasso m. ~ **bed** n letto m matrimoniale. ~-**breasted** a a doppio petto. ~ '**chin** n doppio mento m. ~-'**cross** vt ingannare. ~-'**decker** n autobus m inv a due piani. ~ '**Dutch** n fam ostrogoto m. ~ '**glazing** n doppiovetro m. ~ '**room** n camera f doppia

doubly /'dʌblɪ/ adv doppiamente

doubt /daʊt/ n dubbio m ● vt dubitare di. **~ful** a dubbio; (having doubts) in dubbio. **~fully** adv con aria dubbiosa. **~less** adv indubbiamente

dough /dəʊ/ n pasta f; (for bread) impasto m; (fam: money) quattrini mpl. **~nut** n bombolone m, krapfen m inv

douse /daʊs/ vt spegnere

dove /dʌv/ n colomba f. **~tail** n Techn incastro m a coda di rondine

dowdy /'daʊdɪ/ a (-ier, -iest) trasandato

down[1] /daʊn/ n (feathers) piumino m

down[2] adv giù; go/come ~ scendere; **~ there** laggiù; **sales are ~** le vendite sono diminuite; **£50 ~** 50 sterline d'acconto; **~ 10%** ridotto del 10%; **~ with...!** abbasso...! ● prep walk ~ the road camminare per strada; **~ the stairs** giù per le scale; **fall ~ the stairs** cadere giù dalle scale; **get that ~ you!** fam butta giù!; **be ~ the pub** fam essere al pub ● vt bere tutto d'un fiato (drink)

down: ~-and-'out n spiantato, -a mf. **~cast** a abbattuto. **~fall** n caduta f; (of person) rovina f. **~'grade** vt (in seniority) degradare. **~-'hearted** a scoraggiato. **~hill** adv in discesa; **go ~hill** fig essere in declino. **~ payment** n deposito m. **~pour** n acquazzone m. **~right** a (absolute) totale; (lie) bell'e buono; (idiot) perfetto ● adv (completely) completamente. **~'stairs** adv al piano di sotto ● a /'-/ del piano di sotto. **~'stream** adv a valle. **~-to-'earth** a (person) con i piedi per terra. **~town** adv Am in centro. **~trodden** a oppresso. **~ward[s]** a verso il basso; (slope) in discesa ● adv verso il basso

dowry /'daʊrɪ/ n dote f

doze /dəʊz/ n sonnellino m ● vi

sonnecchiare. **doze off** vi assopirsi

dozen /'dʌzn/ n dozzina f; **~s of books** libri a dozzine

Dr abbr **doctor**

drab /dræb/ a spento

draft[1] /drɑːft/ n abbozzo m; Comm cambiale f; Am Mil leva f ● vt abbozzare; Am Mil arruolare

draft[2] n Am = **draught**

drag /dræg/ n fam scocciatura f; **in ~** fam (man) travestito da donna ● vt (pt/pp dragged) trascinare; dragare (river). **drag on** vi (time, meeting:) trascinarsi

dragon /'drægən/ n drago m. **~-fly** n libellula f

drain /dreɪn/ n tubo m di scarico; (grid) tombino m; **the ~s** pl le fognature; **be a ~ on sb's finances** prosciugare le finanze di qcno ● vt drenare (land, wound); scolare (liquid, vegetables); svuotare (tank, glass, person) ● vi ~ [away] andar via

drain|age /'dreɪnɪdʒ/ n (system) drenaggio m; (of land) scolo m. **~ing board** n scolapiatti m inv. **~pipe** n tubo m di scarico

drake /dreɪk/ n maschio m dell'anatra

drama /'drɑːmə/ n arte f drammatica; (play) opera f teatrale; (event) dramma m

dramatic /drə'mætɪk/ a drammatico

dramat|ist /'dræmətɪst/ n drammaturgo, -a mf. **~ize** vt adattare per il teatro; fig drammatizzare

drank /dræŋk/ see **drink**

drape /dreɪp/ n Am tenda f ● vt appoggiare (over su)

drastic /'dræstɪk/ a drastico; **~ally** adv drasticamente

draught /drɑːft/ n corrente f [d'aria]; **~s** sg (game) [gioco m della] dama f/pl

draught: ~ beer n birra f alla spina. **~sman** n disegnatore, -trice mf

draughty /'drɔːftɪ/ *a* pieno di correnti d'aria; **it's ~ c'è corrente

draw /drɔː/ *n* (*attraction*) attrazione *f*; *Sport* pareggio *m*; (*in lottery*) sorteggio *m* ● *v* (*pt* drew, *pp* drawn) ● *vt* tirare; (*attract*) attirare; disegnare (*picture*); tracciare (*line*); ritirare (*money*); ~ **lots** tirare a sorte ● *vi* (*tea:*) essere in infusione; *Sport* pareggiare; ~ **near** avvicinarsi. **draw back** *vt* tirare indietro; ritirare (*hand*); tirare (*curtains*) ● *vi* (*recoil*) tirarsi indietro. **draw in** *vt* ritrarre (*claws etc*) ● *vi* (*train:*) arrivare; (*days:*) accorciarsi. **draw out** *vt* (*pull out*) tirar fuori; ritirare (*money*) ● *vi* (*train:*) partire; (*days:*) allungarsi. **draw up** *vt* redigere (*document*); accostare (*chair*); ~ **oneself up to one's full height** farsi grande ● *vi* (*stop*) fermarsi

draw: ~**back** *n* inconveniente *m*. ~**bridge** *n* ponte *m* levatoio

drawer /drɔː(r)/ *n* cassetto *m*

drawing /'drɔːɪŋ/ *n* disegno *m*

drawing: ~**-board** *n* tavolo *m* da disegno; *fig* **go back to the** ~**-board** ricominciare da capo. ~**-pin** *n* puntina *f*. ~**-room** *n* salotto *m*

drawl /drɔːl/ *n* pronuncia *f* strascicata

drawn /drɔːn/ *see* **draw**

dread /dred/ *n* terrore *m* ● *vt* aver il terrore di

dreadful /'dredful/ *a* terribile. ~**ly** *adv* terribilmente

dream /driːm/ *n* sogno *m* ● *attrib* di sogno ● *vt/i* (*pt/pp* dreamt /dremt/ *or* dreamed) sognare (**about/of** di)

dreary /'drɪərɪ/ *a* (-**ier**, -**iest**) tetro; (*boring*) monotono

dredge /dredʒ/ *vt/i* dragare

dregs /dregz/ *npl* feccia *fsg*

drench /drentʃ/ *vt* **get** ~**ed** inzupparsi; ~**ed** zuppo

dress /dres/ *n* (*woman's*) vestito *m*; (*clothing*) abbigliamento *m* ● *vt*

vestire; (*decorate*) adornare; *Culin* condire; *Med* fasciare; ~ **oneself, get** ~**ed** vestirsi ● *vi* vestirsi. **dress up** *vi* mettersi elegante; (*in disguise*) travestirsi (**as** da)

dress: ~ **circle** *n* *Theat* prima galleria *f*. ~**er** *n* (*furniture*) credenza *f*; (*Am: dressing-table*) toilette *f inv*

dressing /'dresɪŋ/ *n* *Culin* condimento *m*; *Med* fasciatura *f*

dressing: ~**-gown** *n* vestaglia *f*. ~**-room** *n* (*in gym*) spogliatoio *m*; *Theat* camerino *m*. ~**-table** *n* toilette *f inv*

dress: ~**maker** *n* sarta *f*. ~ **rehearsal** *n* prova *f* generale

dressy /'dresɪ/ *a* (-**ier**, -**iest**) elegante

drew /druː/ *see* **draw**

dribble /'drɪbl/ *vi* gocciolare; (*baby:*) sbavare; *Sport* dribblare

dribs and drabs /drɪbzən'dræbz/ *npl* **in** ~ alla spicciolata

dried /draɪd/ *a* (*food*) essiccato

drier /'draɪə(r)/ *n* asciugabiancheria *m inv*

drift /drɪft/ *n* movimento *m* lento; (*of snow*) cumulo *m*; (*meaning*) senso *m* ● *vi* (*off course*) andare alla deriva; (*snow:*) accumularsi; (*fig: person:*) procedere senza meta. **drift apart** *vi* (*people:*) allontanarsi l'uno dall'altro

drill /drɪl/ *n* trapano *m*; *Mil* esercitazione *f* ● *vt* trapanare; *Mil* fare esercitare ● *vi* *Mil* esercitarsi; ~ **for oil** trivellare in cerca di petrolio

drily /'draɪlɪ/ *adv* seccamente

drink /drɪŋk/ *n* bevanda *f*; (*alcoholic*) bicchierino *m*; **have a** ~ bere qualcosa; **a** ~ **of water** un po' d'acqua ● *vt/i* (*pt* drank, *pp* drunk) bere. **drink up** *vt* finire ● *vi* finire il bicchiere

drink|able /'drɪŋkəbl/ *a* potabile. ~**er** *n* bevitore, -trice *mf*

drinking-water *n* acqua *f* potabile

drip /drɪp/ *n* gocciolamento *m*; (*drop*) goccia *f*; *Med* flebo *f inv*;

(*fam: person*) mollaccione, -a *mf* ● *vi* (*pt/pp* **dripped**) gocciolare. **~·'dry** *a* che non si stira. **~ping** *n* (*from meat*) grasso *m* d'arrosto ● *a* **~ping** [**wet**] fradicio

drive /draɪv/ *n* (*in car*) giro *m*; (*entrance*) viale *m*; (*energy*) grinta *f*; *Psych* pulsione *f*; (*organized effort*) operazione *f*; *Techn* motore *m*; *Comput* lettore *m* ● *v* (*pt* **drove**, *pp* **driven**) ● *vt* portare (*person by car*); guidare (*car*); (*Sport: hit*) mandare; *Techn* far funzionare; **~ sb mad** far diventare matto qcno ● *vi* guidare. **drive at** *vt* **what are you driving at?** dove vuoi arrivare? **drive away** *vt* portare via in macchina; (*chase*) cacciare ● *vi* andare via in macchina. **drive in** *vt* piantare (*nail*) ● *vi* arrivare [in macchina]. **drive off** *vt* portare via in macchina; (*chase*) cacciare ● *vi* andare via in macchina. **drive on** *vi* proseguire (*in macchina*). **drive up** *vi* arrivare (*in macchina*)

drivel /'drɪvl/ *n* *fam* sciocchezze *fpl*

driven /'drɪvn/ *see* **drive**

driver /'draɪvə(r)/ *n* guidatore, -trice *mf*; (*of train*) conducente *mf*

driving /'draɪvɪŋ/ *a* (*rain*) violento; (*force*) motore ● *n* guida *f*

driving: **~ lesson** *n* lezione *f* di guida. **~ licence** *n* patente *f* di guida. **~ school** *n* scuola *f* guida. **~ test** *n* esame *m* di guida

drizzle /'drɪzl/ *n* pioggerella *f* ● *vi* piovigginare

drone /drəʊn/ *n* (*bee*) fuco *m*; (*sound*) ronzio *m*

droop /druːp/ *vi* abbassarsi; (*flowers:*) afflosciarsi

drop /drɒp/ *n* (*of liquid*) goccia *f*; (*fall*) caduta *f*; (*in price, temperature*) calo *m* ● *v* (*pt/pp* **dropped**) ● *vt* far cadere; sganciare (*bomb*); (*omit*) omettere; (*give up*) abbandonare ● *vi* cadere; (*price, temperature, wind:*) calare; (*ground:*) essere in pendenza. **drop in** *vi* passare. **drop off** *vt* depositare (*person*) ● *vi* cadere; (*fall asleep*)

assopirsi. **drop out** *vi* cadere; (*of race, society*) ritirarsi; **~ out of school** lasciare la scuola

'drop-out *n* persona *f* contro il sistema sociale

droppings /'drɒpɪŋz/ *npl* sterco *m*

drought /draʊt/ *n* siccità *f*

drove /drəʊv/ *see* **drive**

droves /drəʊvz/ *npl* **in ~** in massa

drown /draʊn/ *vi* annegare ● *vt* annegare; coprire (*noise*); **he was ~ed** è annegato

drowsy /'draʊzɪ/ *a* sonnolento

drudgery /'drʌdʒərɪ/ *n* lavoro *m* pesante e noioso

drug /drʌg/ *n* droga *f*; *Med* farmaco *m*; **take ~s** drogarsi ● *vt* (*pt/pp* **drugged**) drogare

drug: **~ addict** *n* tossicomane, -a *mf*. **~ dealer** *n* spacciatore, -trice *mf* [di droga]. **~gist** *n* *Am* farmacista *mf*. **~store** *n* *Am* negozio *m* di generi vari, inclusi medicinali, che funge anche da bar; (*dispensing*) farmacia *f*

drum /drʌm/ *n* tamburo *m*; (*for oil*) bidone *m*; **~s** (*pl: in pop-group*) batteria *f* ● *v* (*pt/pp* **drummed**) ● *vi* suonare il tamburo; (*in pop-group*) suonare la batteria ● *vt* **~ sth into sb** ripetere qcsa a qcno cento volte. **~mer** *n* percussionista *mf*; (*in pop-group*) batterista *mf*. **~stick** *n* bacchetta *f*; (*of chicken, turkey*) coscia *f*

drunk /drʌŋk/ *see* **drink** ● *a* ubriaco; **get ~** ubriacarsi ● *n* ubriaco, -a *mf*

drunk|**ard** /'drʌŋkəd/ *n* ubriacone, -a *mf*. **~en** *a* ubriaco; **~en driving** guida *f* in stato di ebbrezza

dry /draɪ/ *a* (**drier**, **driest**) asciutto; (*climate, country*) secco ● *vt/i* (*pt/pp* **dried**) asciugare; **~ one's eyes** asciugarsi le lacrime. **dry up** *vi* seccarsi; (*fig: source:*) prosciugarsi; (*fam: be quiet*) stare zitto; (*do dishes*) asciugare i piatti

dry: **~·'clean** *vt* pulire a secco. **~·'cleaner's** *n* (*shop*) tintoria *f*. **~ness** *n* secchezza *f*

DTP n abbr (**desktop publishing**) desktop publishing m

dual /'dju:əl/ a doppio

dual: ~ **'carriageway** n strada f a due carreggiate. ~-'**purpose** a a doppio uso

dub /dʌb/ vt (pt/pp **dubbed**) doppiare ⟨film⟩; ⟨name⟩ soprannominare

dubious /'dju:bɪəs/ a dubbio; **be ~ about** avere dei dubbi riguardo

duchess /'dʌtʃɪs/ n duchessa f

duck /dʌk/ n anatra f ● vt ⟨in water⟩ immergere; ~ **one's head** abbassare la testa ● vi abbassarsi. **~ling** n anatroccolo m

duct /dʌkt/ n condotto m; Anat dotto m

dud /dʌd/ fam a Mil disattivato; ⟨coin⟩ falso; ⟨cheque⟩ a vuoto ● n ⟨banknote⟩ banconota f falsa

due /dju:/ a dovuto; **be ~** ⟨train⟩ essere previsto; **the baby is ~ next week** il bambino dovrebbe nascere la settimana prossima; ~ **to** ⟨owing to⟩ a causa di; **be ~ to** ⟨causally⟩ essere dovuto a; **I'm ~ to...** dovrei...; **in ~ course** a tempo debito ● adv ~ **north** direttamente a nord

duel /'dju:əl/ n duello m

dues /dju:z/ npl quota f [di iscrizione]

duet /dju:'et/ n duetto m

dug /dʌg/ see **dig**

duke /dju:k/ n duca m

dull /dʌl/ a ⟨overcast, not bright⟩ cupo; ⟨not shiny⟩ opaco; ⟨sound⟩ soffocato; ⟨boring⟩ monotono; ⟨stupid⟩ ottuso ● vt intorpidire ⟨mind⟩; attenuare ⟨pain⟩

duly /'dju:lɪ/ adv debitamente

dumb /dʌm/ a muto; ⟨fam: stupid⟩ ottuso. **~founded** /dʌm'faʊndɪd/ a sbigottito

dummy /'dʌmɪ/ n ⟨tailor's⟩ manichino m; ⟨for baby⟩ succhiotto m; ⟨model⟩ riproduzione f

dump /dʌmp/ n ⟨for refuse⟩ scarico m; ⟨fam: town⟩ mortorio m; **be down in the ~s** fam essere depresso ● vt scaricare; ⟨fam: put down⟩ lasciare; ⟨fam: get rid of⟩ liberarsi di

dumpling /'dʌmplɪŋ/ n gnocco m

dunce /dʌns/ n zuccone, -a mf

dune /dju:n/ n duna f

dung /dʌŋ/ n sterco m

dungarees /dʌŋgə'ri:z/ npl tuta fsg

dungeon /'dʌndʒən/ n prigione f sotterranea

duo /'dju:əʊ/ n duo m inv; Mus duetto m

duplicate[1] /'dju:plɪkət/ a doppio ● n duplicato m; ⟨document⟩ copia f; **in ~** in duplicato

duplicate[2] /'dju:plɪkeɪt/ vt fare un duplicato di; ⟨research:⟩ essere una ripetizione di ⟨work⟩

durable /'djʊərəbl/ a resistente; durevole ⟨basis, institution⟩

duration /djʊə'reɪʃn/ n durata f

duress /djʊə'res/ n costrizione f; **under ~** sotto minaccia

during /'djʊərɪŋ/ prep durante

dusk /dʌsk/ n crepuscolo m

dust /dʌst/ n polvere f ● vt spolverare; ⟨sprinkle⟩ cospargere ⟨cake⟩ ⟨with di⟩ ● vi spolverare

dust: ~**bin** n pattumiera f. ~-**cart** n camion m della nettezza urbana. ~**er** n strofinaccio m. ~-**jacket** n sopraccoperta f. ~**man** n spazzino m. ~**pan** n paletta f per la spazzatura

dusty /'dʌstɪ/ a (-**ier**, -**iest**) polveroso

Dutch /dʌtʃ/ a olandese; **go ~** fam fare alla romana ● n ⟨language⟩ olandese m; **the ~** pl gli olandesi. ~**man** n olandese m

dutiable /'dju:tɪəbl/ a soggetto a imposta

dutiful /'dju:tɪfl/ a rispettoso

duty /'dju:tɪ/ n dovere m; ⟨task⟩ compito m; ⟨tax⟩ dogana f; **be on ~** essere di servizio. ~-**free** a esente da dogana

duvet /'du:veɪ/ n piumone m

dwarf /dwɔ:f/ n (pl -**s** or **dwarves**) nano, -a mf ● vt rimpicciolire

dwell /dwel/ *vi* (*pt/pp* **dwelt**) *liter* dimorare. **dwell on** *vt fig* soffermarsi su. **~ing** *n* abitazione *f*

dwindle /'dwindl/ *vi* diminuire

dye /daɪ/ *n* tintura *f* ● *vt* (*pres p* **dyeing**) tingere

dying /'daɪɪŋ/ *see* **die²**

dynamic /daɪ'næmɪk/ *a* dinamico

dynamite /'daɪnəmaɪt/ *n* dinamite *f*

dynamo /'daɪnəməʊ/ *n* dinamo *f inv*

dynasty /'dɪnəstɪ/ *n* dinastia *f*

dysentery /'dɪsəntrɪ/ *n* dissenteria *f*

dyslex|ia /dɪs'leksɪə/ *n* dislessia *f*. **~ic** *a* dislessico

Ee

each /iːtʃ/ *a* ogni ● *pron* ognuno; **£1 ~** una sterlina ciascuno; **they love/hate ~ other** si amano/odiano; **we lend ~ other money** ci prestiamo i soldi

eager /'iːgə(r)/ *a* ansioso (**to do** *of* fare); ⟨*pupil*⟩ avido di sapere. **~ly** *adv* ⟨*wait*⟩ ansiosamente; ⟨*offer*⟩ premurosamente. **~ness** *n* premura *f*

eagle /'iːgl/ *n* aquila *f*

ear¹ /ɪə(r)/ *n* (*of corn*) spiga *f*

ear² *n* orecchio *m*. **~ache** *n* mal *m* d'orecchi. **~drum** *n* timpano *m*

earl /ɜːl/ *n* conte *m*

early /'ɜːlɪ/ *a* (**-ier, -iest**) (*before expected time*) in anticipo; ⟨*spring*⟩ prematuro; ⟨*reply*⟩ pronto; ⟨*works, writings*⟩ primo; **be here ~!** sii puntuale!; **you're ~!** sei in anticipo!; **~ morning walk** passeggiata *f* mattutina; **in the morning** la mattina presto; **in the ~ spring** all'inizio della primavera; **~ retirement** prepensionamento *m* ● *adv* presto; (*ahead of*

time) in anticipo; **~ in the morning** la mattina presto

earmark *vt* riservare (**for** a)

earn /ɜːn/ *vt* guadagnare; (*deserve*) meritare

earnest /'ɜːnɪst/ *a* serio ● *n* **in ~** sul serio. **~ly** *adv* con aria seria

earnings /'ɜːnɪŋz/ *npl* guadagni *mpl*; (*salary*) stipendio *m*

ear: **~phones** *npl* cuffia *fsg*. **~ring** *n* orecchino *m*. **~shot** *n* **within ~shot** a portata d'orecchio; **he is out of ~shot** non può sentire

earth /ɜːθ/ *n* terra *f* **where/what on ~?** dove/che diavolo? ● *vt Electr* mettere a terra

earthenware /'ɜːθən-/ *n* terraglia *f*

earthly /'ɜːθlɪ/ *a* terrestre; **be no ~ use** *fam* essere semplicemente inutile

earthquake *n* terremoto *m*

earthy /'ɜːθɪ/ *a* terroso; (*coarse*) grossolano

earwig /'ɪəwɪg/ *n* forbicina *f*

ease /iːz/ *n* at **~** a proprio agio; **at ~!** *Mil* riposo!; **ill at ~** a disagio; **with ~** con facilità ● *vt* calmare ⟨*pain*⟩; alleviare ⟨*tension, shortage*⟩; (*slow down*) rallentare; (*loosen*) allentare ● *vi* ⟨*pain, situation, wind*⟩ calmarsi

easel /'iːzl/ *n* cavalletto *m*

easily /'iːzɪlɪ/ *adv* con facilità; **the best** certamente il meglio

east /iːst/ *n* est *m*; **to the ~ of** a est di ● *a* dell'est ● *adv* verso est

Easter /'iːstə(r)/ *n* Pasqua *f*. **~ egg** *n* uovo *m* di Pasqua

east|**erly** /'iːstəlɪ/ *a* da levante. **~ern** *a* orientale. **~ward[s]** /-wəd[z]/ *adv* verso est

easy /'iːzɪ/ *a* (**-ier, -iest**) facile; **take it** *or* **things ~** prendersela con calma; **take it ~!** (*don't get excited*) calma!; **go ~ with** andarci piano con

easy: **~ chair** *n* poltrona *f*. **~going** *a* conciliante; **too ~going** troppo accomodante

eat /iːt/ *vt/i* (*pt* **ate**, *pp* **eaten**) mangiare. **eat into** vt intaccare. **eat up** vt mangiare tutto ⟨food⟩; fig inghiottire ⟨profits⟩

eat|able /'i:təbl/ a mangiabile. **~er** n ⟨apple⟩ mela f da tavola; **be a big ~er** ⟨person:⟩ essere una buona forchetta

eau-de-Cologne /əʊdəkə'ləʊn/ n acqua f di Colonia

eaves /i:vz/ npl cornicione msg. **~drop** vi ⟨pt/pp **~dropped**⟩ origliare; **~drop on** ascoltare di nascosto

ebb /eb/ n ⟨tide⟩ riflusso m; **at a low ~** fig a terra ● vi rifluire; fig declinare

ebony /'ebənɪ/ n ebano m

EC n abbr (European Community) CE f

eccentric /ɪk'sentrɪk/ a & n eccentrico, -a mf

ecclesiastical /ɪklɪːzɪ'æstɪkl/ a ecclesiastico

echo /'ekəʊ/ n (pl **-es**) eco f or m ● v (pt/pp **echoed**, pres p **echoing**) ● vt echeggiare; ripetere ⟨words⟩ ● vi risuonare (**with** di)

eclipse /ɪ'klɪps/ n Astr eclissi f inv ● vt fig eclissare

ecolog|ical /iːkə'lɒdʒɪkl/ a ecologico. **~y** /ɪ'kɒlədʒɪ/ n ecologia f

economic /iːkə'nɒmɪk/ a economico. **~al** a economico. **~ally** adv economicamente; (thriftily) in economia. ● n economia f

economist /ɪ'kɒnəmɪst/ n economista mf

economize /ɪ'kɒnəmaɪz/ vi economizzare (**on** su)

economy /ɪ'kɒnəmɪ/ n economia f

ecstasy /'ekstəsɪ/ n estasi f inv; (drug) ecstasy f

ecstatic /ɪk'stætɪk/ a estatico

ecu /'eɪkju:/ n ecu m inv

eczema /'eksɪmə/ n eczema m

edge /edʒ/ n bordo m; ⟨of knife⟩ filo m; ⟨of road⟩ ciglio m; **on ~** con i nervi tesi; **have the ~ on** fam avere un vantaggio su ● vt bordare. **edge forward** vi avanzare lentamente

edgeways /'edʒweɪz/ adv di fianco; **I couldn't get a word in ~** non ho potuto infilare neanche mezza parola nel discorso

edging /'edʒɪŋ/ n bordo m

edgy /'edʒɪ/ a nervoso

edible /'edɪbl/ a commestibile; **this pizza's not ~** questa pizza è immangiabile

edict /'i:dɪkt/ n editto m

edifice /'edɪfɪs/ n ⟨pt/pp **-ied**⟩ edificare. **~ing** a edificante

edit /'edɪt/ vt (pt/pp **edited**) far la revisione di ⟨text⟩; curare l'edizione di ⟨anthology, dictionary⟩; dirigere ⟨newspaper⟩; montare ⟨film⟩; editare ⟨tape⟩; **~ed by** ⟨book⟩ a cura di

edition /ɪ'dɪʃn/ n edizione f

editor /'edɪtə(r)/ n ⟨of anthology, dictionary⟩ curatore, -trice mf; ⟨of newspaper⟩ redattore, -trice mf; ⟨of film⟩ responsabile mf del montaggio

editorial /edɪ'tɔːrɪəl/ a redazionale ● n Journ editoriale m

educate /'edjʊkeɪt/ vt istruire; educare ⟨public, mind⟩; **be ~d at Eton** essere educato a Eton. **~d** a istruito

education /edjʊ'keɪʃn/ n istruzione f; ⟨culture⟩ cultura f, educazione f. **~al** a istruttivo; ⟨visit⟩ educativo; ⟨publishing⟩ didattico

eel /i:l/ n anguilla f

eerie /'ɪərɪ/ a (**-ier, -iest**) inquietante

effect /ɪ'fekt/ n effetto m; **in ~** in effetti; **take ~** ⟨law:⟩ entrare in vigore, ⟨medicine:⟩ fare effetto ● vt effettuare

effective /ɪ'fektɪv/ a efficace; ⟨striking⟩ che colpisce; ⟨actual⟩ di fatto; **~ from** in vigore a partire da. **~ly** adv efficacemente; ⟨actually⟩ di fatto. **~ness** n efficacia f

effeminate /ɪ'femɪnət/ a effeminato

effervescent /efə'vesnt/ a effervescente

efficiency /ɪ'fɪʃənsɪ/ n efficienza f; (of machine) rendimento m

efficient /ɪ'fɪʃənt/ a efficiente. ~ly adv efficientemente

effort /'efət/ n sforzo m; **make an ~** sforzarsi. ~less a facile. ~lessly adv con facilità

effrontery /ɪ'frʌntərɪ/ n sfrontatezza f

effusive /ɪ'fju:sɪv/ a espansivo; (speech) caloroso

e.g. abbr (exempli gratia) per es.

egalitarian /ɪgælɪ'teərɪən/ a egalitario

egg¹ /eg/ vt **~ on** fam incitare

egg² n uovo m. **~-cup** n portauovo m inv. **~head** n fam intellettuale mf. **~shell** n guscio m d'uovo. **~timer** n clessidra f per misurare il tempo di cottura delle uova

ego /'i:gəʊ/ n ego m. **~centric** /-'sentrɪk/ a egocentrico. **~ism** n egoismo m. **~ist** n egoista mf. **~tism** n egotismo m. **~tist** n egotista mf

Egypt /'i:dʒɪpt/ n Egitto m. **~ian** /ɪ'dʒɪpʃn/ a & n egiziano, -a m

eiderdown /'aɪdə-/ n (quilt) piumino m

eight /eɪt/ a otto ● n otto m. **~'teen** a diciotto. **~'teenth** a diciottesimo

eighth /eɪtθ/ a ottavo ● n ottavo m

eightieth /'eɪtɪɪθ/ a ottantesimo

eighty /'eɪtɪ/ a ottanta

either /'aɪðə(r)/ a & pron ~ [of them] l'uno o l'altro; I don't like ~ [of them] non mi piace né l'uno né l'altro; **on ~ side** da tutte e due le parti ● adv I don't ~ nemmeno io; I don't like John or his brother ~ non mi piace John e nemmeno suo fratello ● conj ~ John or his brother will be there ci saranno o John o suo fratello; I don't like ~ John or his brother non mi piacciono né John né suo fratello; ~ you go to bed or [else]... o vai a letto o [altrimenti]...

eject /ɪ'dʒekt/ vt eiettare (pilot); espellere (tape, drunk)

eke /i:k/ vt **~ out** far bastare; (increase) arrotondare; **~ out a living** arrangiarsi

elaborate¹ /ɪ'læbərət/ a elaborato

elaborate² /ɪ'læbəreɪt/ vi entrare nei particolari (on di)

elapse /ɪ'læps/ vi trascorrere

elastic /ɪ'læstɪk/ a elastico ● n elastico m. **~ 'band** n elastico m

elasticity /ɪlæ'stɪsətɪ/ n elasticità f

elated /ɪ'leɪtɪd/ a esultante

elbow /'elbəʊ/ n gomito m

elder¹ /'eldə(r)/ n (tree) sambuco m

eld|er² a maggiore ● the ~ il/la maggiore. **~erly** a anziano. **~est** a maggiore ● the ~est il/la maggiore

elect /ɪ'lekt/ a **the president ~** il futuro presidente ● vt eleggere; **~ to do sth** decidere di fare qcsa. **~ion** /-ekʃn/ n elezione f

elector /ɪ'lektə(r)/ n elettore, -trice mf. **~al** a elettorale; **~al roll** liste fpl elettorali. **~ate** /-rət/ n elettorato m

electric /ɪ'lektrɪk/ a elettrico

electrical /ɪ'lektrɪkl/ a elettrico; **~ engineering** elettrotecnica f

electric: **~ 'blanket** n termocoperta f. **~ 'fire** n stufa f elettrica

electrician /ɪlek'trɪʃn/ n elettricista m

electricity /ɪlek'trɪsətɪ/ n elettricità f

electrify /ɪ'lektrɪfaɪ/ vt (pt/pp -ied) elettrificare; fig elettrizzare. **~ing** a fig elettrizzante

electrocute /ɪ'lektrəkju:t/ vt fulminare; (execute) giustiziare sulla sedia elettrica

electrode /ɪ'lektrəʊd/ n elettrodo m

electron /ɪ'lektrɒn/ n elettrone m

electronic /ɪlek'trɒnɪk/ a elettronico. **~ mail** n posta f elettronica. **~s** n elettronica f

elegance /'elɪgəns/ n eleganza f

elegant /'elɪgənt/ a elegante

elegy /'elɪdʒɪ/ n elegia f

element /'elɪmənt/ n elemento m. **~ary** /-'mentərɪ/ a elementare

elephant /'elɪfənt/ n elefante m

elevat|e /'elɪveɪt/ vt elevare. **~ion** /-'veɪʃn/ n elevazione f; (height) altitudine f; (angle) alzo m

elevator /'elɪveɪtə(r)/ n Am ascensore m

eleven /ɪ'levn/ a undici ● n undici m. **~th** a undicesimo; **at the ~th hour** fam all'ultimo momento

elf /elf/ n (pl **elves**) elfo m

elicit /ɪ'lɪsɪt/ vt ottenere

eligible /'elɪdʒəbl/ a eleggibile; **~ young man** buon partito; **be ~ for** aver diritto a

eliminate /ɪ'lɪmɪneɪt/ vt eliminare

élite /eɪ'liːt/ n fior fiore m

ellip|se /ɪ'lɪps/ n ellisse f. **~tical** a ellittico

elm /elm/ n olmo m

elocution /elə'kjuːʃn/ n elocuzione f

elope /ɪ'ləʊp/ vi fuggire [per sposarsi]

eloquen|ce /'eləkwəns/ n eloquenza f. **~t** a eloquente. **~tly** adv con eloquenza

else /els/ adv altro; **who ~?** e chi altro?, **he did of course, who ~?** l'ha fatto lui o chi, se no?; **nothing ~** nient'altro; **or ~** altrimenti; **someone ~** qualcun altro; **somewhere ~** da qualche altra parte; **anyone ~** chiunque altro; (as question) nessun'altro?; **anything ~** qualunque altra cosa; (as question) altro?. **~where** adv altrove

elucidate /ɪ'luːsɪdeɪt/ vt delucidare

elude /ɪ'luːd/ vt eludere; (avoid) evitare, **the name ~s me** il nome mi sfugge

elusive /ɪ'luːsɪv/ a elusivo

emaciated /ɪ'meɪsɪeɪtɪd/ a emaciato

e-mail /'iːmeɪl/ n posta f elettronica ● vt spedire via posta elettronica

emanate /'eməneɪt/ vi emanare

emancipat|ed /ɪ'mænsɪpeɪtɪd/ a emancipato. **~ion** /-'peɪʃn/ n emancipazione f; (of slaves) liberazione f

embankment /ɪm'bæŋkmənt/ n argine m; Rail massicciata f

embargo /em'bɑːgəʊ/ n (pl **-es**) embargo m

embark /ɪm'bɑːk/ vi imbarcarsi; **~ on** intraprendere. **~ation** /emba'keɪʃn/ n imbarco m

embarrass /em'bærəs/ vt imbarazzare. **~ed** a imbarazzato. **~ing** a imbarazzante. **~ment** n imbarazzo m

embassy /'embəsɪ/ n ambasciata f

embedded /ɪm'bedɪd/ a (in concrete) cementato; (traditions, feelings) radicato

embellish /ɪm'belɪʃ/ vt abbellire

embers /'embəz/ npl braci fpl

embezzle /ɪm'bezl/ vt appropriarsi indebitamente di. **~ment** n appropriazione f indebita

embitter /ɪm'bɪtə(r)/ vt amareggiare

emblem /'embləm/ n emblema m

embody /ɪm'bɒdɪ/ vt (pt/pp **-ied**) incorporare; **~ what is best in...** rappresentare quanto c'è di meglio di...

emboss /ɪm'bɒs/ vt sbalzare (metal); stampare in rilievo (paper). **~ed** a in rilievo

embrace /ɪm'breɪs/ n abbraccio m ● vt abbracciare ● vi abbracciarsi

embroider /ɪm'brɔɪdə(r)/ vt ricamare (design); fig abbellire. **~y** n ricamo m

embryo /'embrɪəʊ/ n embrione m

emerald /'emərəld/ n smeraldo m

emerge /ɪ'mɜːdʒ/ vi emergere; (come into being: nation) nascere; (sun, flowers) spuntare fuori. **~gence** /-əns/ n emergere m; (of new country) nascita f

emergency /ɪ'mɜːdʒənsɪ/ n emergenza f; in an ~ in caso di emergenza. **~ exit** n uscita f di sicurezza

emery /'emərɪ/: **~ board** n limetta f [per le unghie]

emigrant /'emɪɡrənt/ n emigrante mf

emigrat|e /'emɪɡreɪt/ vi emigrare. **~ion** /-'ɡreɪʃn/ n emigrazione f

eminent /'emɪnənt/ a eminente. **~ly** adv eminentemente

emission /ɪ'mɪʃn/ n emissione f; (of fumes) esalazione f

emit /ɪ'mɪt/ vt (pt/pp **emitted**) emettere; esalare (fumes)

emotion /ɪ'məʊʃn/ n emozione f. **~al** a denso di emozione; (person, reaction) emotivo; **become ~al** avere una reazione emotiva

emotive /ɪ'məʊtɪv/ a emotivo

empathize /'empəθaɪz/ vi ~ **with sb** immedesimarsi nei problemi di qcno

emperor /'empərə(r)/ n imperatore m

emphasis /'emfəsɪs/ n enfasi f; **put the ~ on sth** accentuare qcsa

emphasize /'emfəsaɪz/ vt accentuare (word, syllable); sottolineare (need)

emphatic /ɪm'fætɪk/ a categorico

empire /'empaɪə(r)/ n impero m

empirical /em'pɪrɪkl/ a empirico

employ /em'plɔɪ/ vt impiegare; fig usare (tact). **~ee** /emplɔɪ'iː/ n impiegato, -a mf. **~er** n datore di lavoro. **~ment** n occupazione f. **~ment agency** n ufficio m di collocamento

empower /ɪm'paʊə(r)/ vt autorizzare; (enable) mettere in grado di

empress /'emprɪs/ n imperatrice f

empties /'emptɪz/ npl vuoti mpl

emptiness /'emptɪnɪs/ n vuoto m

empty /'emptɪ/ a vuoto; (promise, threat) vano ● v (pt/pp -ied) ● vt vuotare (con-tainer) ● vi vuotarsi

emulate /'emjʊleɪt/ vt emulare

emulsion /ɪ'mʌlʃn/ n emulsione f

enable /ɪ'neɪbl/ vt ~ **sb to** mettere qcno in grado di

enact /ɪn'ækt/ vt Theat rappresentare; decretare (law)

enamel /ɪ'næml/ n smalto m ● vt (pt/pp **enamelled**) smaltare

enchant /ɪn'tʃɑːnt/ vt incantare.

~ing a incantevole. **~ment** n incanto m

encircle /ɪn'sɜːkl/ vt circondare

enclave /'enkleɪv/ n enclave f inv; fig territorio m

enclos|e /ɪn'kləʊz/ vt circondare (land); (in letter) allegare (with a). **~ed** a (space) chiuso; (in letter) allegato. **~ure** /-ʒə(r)/ n (at zoo) recinto m; (in letter) allegato m

encompass /ɪn'kʌmpəs/ vt (include) comprendere

encore /'ɒŋkɔː(r)/ n & int bis m inv

encounter /ɪn'kaʊntə(r)/ n incontro m; (battle) scontro m ● vt incontrare

encourag|e /ɪn'kʌrɪdʒ/ vt incoraggiare; promuovere (the arts, independence). **~ement** n incoraggiamento m; (of the arts) promozione f. **~ing** a incoraggiante; (smile) di incoraggiamento

encroach /ɪn'krəʊtʃ/ vt ~ **on** invadere (land, privacy); abusare di (time); interferire con (rights)

encumb|er /ɪn'kʌmbə(r)/ vt **~ered with** essere carico di (children, suitcases); ingombro di (furniture). **~rance** /-rəns/ n peso m

encyclop[a]ed|ia /ɪnsaɪklə'piːdiə/ n enciclopedia f. **~ic** a enciclopedico

end /end/ n fine f; (of box, table, piece of string) estremità f; (of town, room) parte f; (purpose) fine m; **in the ~** alla fine; **at the ~ of May** alla fine di maggio; **at the ~ of the street/garden** in fondo alla strada/al giardino; **on ~** (upright) in piedi; **for days on ~** per giorni e giorni; **for six days on ~** per sei giorni di fila; **put an ~ to sth** mettere fine a qcsa; **make ~s meet** fam sbarcare il lunario; **no ~ of** fam un sacco di ● vt/i finire. **end up** vi finire. **~ up doing sth** finire col fare qcsa

endanger /ɪn'deɪndʒə(r)/ vt rischiare (one's life); mettere a repentaglio (sb else, success of sth)

endear|ing /ɪn'dɪərɪŋ/ a accattivante. **~ment** n term of ~ment vezzeggiativo m

endeavour /ɪn'devə(r)/ n tentativo m ● vi sforzarsi (**to** di)

ending /'endɪŋ/ n fine f; Gram desinenza f

endive /'endaɪv/ n indivia f

endless /'endlɪs/ a interminabile; (patience) infinito. **~ly** adv continuamente; (patient) infinitamente

endorse /ɪn'dɔːs/ vt girare (cheque); (sports personality:) fare pubblicità a (product); approvare (plan). **~ment** n (of cheque) girata f; (of plan) conferma f; (on driving licence) registrazione f su patente di un'infrazione

endow /ɪn'daʊ/ vt dotare

endur|able /ɪn'djʊərəbl/ a sopportabile. **~ance** /-rəns/ n resistenza f; **it is beyond ~ance** è insopportabile

endur|e /ɪn'djʊə(r)/ vt sopportare ● vi durare. **~ing** a duraturo

'end user n utente m finale

enemy /'enəmɪ/ n nemico, -a m ● attrib nemico

energetic /enə'dʒetɪk/ a energico

energy /'enədʒɪ/ n energia f

enforce /ɪn'fɔːs/ vt far rispettare (law). **~d** a forzato

engage /ɪn'geɪdʒ/ vt assumere (staff); Theat ingaggiare; Auto ingranare (gear) ● vi Techn ingranare; **~ in** impegnarsi in. **~d** a (in use, busy) occupato; (person) impegnato; (to be married) fidanzato; **get ~d** fidanzarsi (**to** con). **~d tone** Teleph segnale m di occupato. **~ment** n fidanzamento m; (appointment) appuntamento m; Mil combattimento m; **~ment ring** anello m di fidanzamento

engaging /ɪn'geɪdʒɪŋ/ a attraente

engender /ɪn'dʒendə(r)/ vt fig generare

engine /'endʒɪn/ n motore m; Rail locomotrice f. **~-driver** n macchinista m

engineer /endʒɪ'nɪə(r)/ n ingegne-

re m; (service, installation) tecnico m; Naut, Am Rail macchinista m ● vt fig architettare. **~ing** n ingegneria f

England /'ɪŋglənd/ n Inghilterra f

English /'ɪŋglɪʃ/ a inglese; **the ~ Channel** la Manica ● n (language) inglese m; **the ~** pl gli inglesi. **~man** n inglese m. **~woman** n inglese f

engrav|e /ɪn'greɪv/ vt incidere. **~ing** n incisione f

engross /ɪn'grəʊs/ vt **~ed in** assorto in

engulf /ɪn'gʌlf/ vt (fire, waves:) inghiottire

enhance /ɪn'hɑːns/ vt accrescere (beauty, reputation); migliorare (performance)

enigma /ɪ'nɪgmə/ n enigma m. **~tic** /enɪg'mætɪk/ a enigmatico

enjoy /ɪn'dʒɔɪ/ vt godere di (good health); **~ oneself** divertirsi; **I ~ cooking/painting** mi piace cucinare/dipingere; **~ your meal** buon appetito. **~able** /-əbl/ a piacevole. **~ment** n piacere m

enlarge /ɪn'lɑːdʒ/ vt ingrandire ● vi **~ upon** dilungarsi su. **~ment** n ingrandimento m

enlighten /ɪn'laɪtn/ vt illuminare. **~ed** a progressista. **~ment** n **The E~ment** l'Illuminismo m

enlist /ɪn'lɪst/ vt Mil reclutare; **~ sb's help** farsi aiutare da qcno ● vi Mil arruolarsi

enliven /ɪn'laɪvn/ vt animare

enmity /'enmɪtɪ/ n inimicizia f

enormity /ɪ'nɔːmətɪ/ n enormità f

enormous /ɪ'nɔːməs/ a enorme. **~ly** adv estremamente; (grateful) infinitamente

enough /ɪ'nʌf/ a & n abbastanza; **I didn't bring ~ clothes** non ho portato abbastanza vestiti; **have you had ~?** (to eat/drink) hai mangiato/bevuto abbastanza?; **I've had ~ of ...** sono stufo di ...; **is that ~?** basta?; **that's ~** basta così!; **£50 isn't ~** 50 sterline non sono sufficienti ● adv abbastanza,

you're not working fast ~
non lavori abbastanza in fretta;
funnily ~ stranamente

enquir|e /ɪnˈkwaɪə(r)/ vi domandare; **~e about** chiedere informazioni su. **~y** n domanda f; (investigation) inchiesta f

enrage /ɪnˈreɪdʒ/ vt fare arrabbiare

enrich /ɪnˈrɪtʃ/ vt arricchire; (improve) migliorare (vocabulary)

enrol /ɪnˈrəʊl/ vi (pt/pp -rolled) (for exam, in club) iscriversi (for, in a). **~ment** n iscrizione f

ensemble /ɒnˈsɒmbl/ n (clothing & Mus) complesso m

enslave /ɪnˈsleɪv/ vt render schiavo

ensu|e /ɪnˈsjuː/ vi seguire; **the ~ing discussion** la discussione che ne è seguita

ensure /ɪnˈʃʊə(r)/ vt assicurare; **~ that** (person:) assicurarsi che; (measure:) garantire che

entail /ɪnˈteɪl/ vt comportare; **what does it ~?** in che cosa consiste?

entangle /ɪnˈtæŋgl/ vt **get ~d in** rimanere impigliato in; fig rimanere coinvolto in

enter /ˈentə(r)/ vt entrare in; iscrivere (horse, runner in race); cominciare (university); partecipare a (competition); Comput immettere (data); (write down) scrivere ● vi entrare; Theat entrare in scena; (register as competitor) iscriversi; (take part) partecipare (in a)

enterpris|e /ˈentəpraɪz/ n impresa f; (quality) iniziativa f. **~ing** a intraprendente

entertain /entəˈteɪn/ vt intrattenere; (invite) ricevere; nutrire (ideas, hopes); prendere in considerazione (possibility) ● vi intrattenersi; (have guests) ricevere. **~er** n artista mf. **~ing** a (person) di gradevole compagnia; (evening, film, play) divertente. **~ment** n (amusement) intrattenimento m

enthral /ɪnˈθrɔːl/ vt (pt/pp enthralled) **be ~led** essere affascinato (by da)

enthusias|m /ɪnˈθjuːzɪæzm/ n entusiasmo m. **~t** n entusiasta mf. **~tic** /-ˈæstɪk/ a entusiastico

entice /ɪnˈtaɪs/ vt attirare. **~ment** n (incentive) incentivo m

entire /ɪnˈtaɪə(r)/ a intero. **~ly** adv del tutto; **I'm not ~ly satisfied** non sono completamente soddisfatto. **~ty** /-rəti/ n **in its ~ty** nell'insieme

entitled /ɪnˈtaɪtld/ a (book) intitolato; **be ~ to sth** aver diritto a qcsa

entitlement /ɪnˈtaɪtlmənt/ n diritto m

entity /ˈentəti/ n entità f

entrance[1] /ˈentrəns/ n entrata f; Theat entrata f in scena; (right to enter) ammissione f; **'no ~'** ingresso vietato'. **~ examination** n esame m di ammissione. **~ fee** n how much is the **~ fee?** quanto costa il biglietto di ingresso?

entrance[2] /ɪnˈtrɑːns/ vt estasiare

entrant /ˈentrənt/ n concorrente mf

entreat /ɪnˈtriːt/ vt supplicare

entrenched /ɪnˈtrentʃt/ a (ideas, views) radicato

entrust /ɪnˈtrʌst/ vt **~ sb with sth, ~ sth to sb** affidare qcsa a qcno

entry /ˈentrɪ/ n ingresso m; (way in) entrata f; (in directory etc) voce f; (in appointment diary) appuntamento m; **no ~** ingresso vietato; Auto accesso vietato. **~ form** n modulo m di ammissione. **~ visa** n visto m di ingresso

enumerate /ɪˈnjuːməreɪt/ vt enumerare

enunciate /ɪˈnʌnsɪeɪt/ vt enunciare

envelop /ɪnˈveləp/ vt (pt/pp enveloped) avviluppare

envelope /ˈenvələʊp/ n busta f

enviable /ˈenvɪəbl/ a invidiabile

envious /ˈenvɪəs/ a invidioso. **~ly** adv con invidia

environment /ɪn'vaɪrənmənt/ n ambiente m

environmental /ˌnvaɪrən'mentl/ a ambientale. **~ist** n ambientalista mf. **~ly** adv **~ly friendly** che rispetta l'ambiente

envisage /ɪn'vɪzɪdʒ/ vt prevedere

envoy /'envɔɪ/ n inviato, -a m f

envy /'envɪ/ n invidia ● vt (pt/pp **-ied**) **~ sb sth** invidiare qcno per qcsa

enzyme /'enzaɪm/ n enzima m

epic /'epɪk/ a epico ● n epopea f

epidemic /epɪ'demɪk/ n epidemia f

epilep|sy /'epɪlepsɪ/ n epilessia f. **~tic** /-'leptɪk/ a & n epilettico, -a m f

epilogue /'epɪlɒg/ n epilogo m

episode /'epɪsəʊd/ n episodio m

epitaph /'epɪtɑːf/ n epitaffio m

epithet /'epɪθet/ n epiteto m

epitom|e /ɪ'pɪtəmɪ/ n epitome f. **~ize** vt essere il classico esempio di

epoch /'iːpɒk/ n epoca f

equal /'iːkwl/ a ⟨parts, amounts⟩ uguale; **of ~ height** della stessa altezza; **be ~ to the task** essere a l'altezza del compito ● n pari m inv ● vt (pt/pp **equalled**) ⟨be same in quantity as⟩ essere pari a; ⟨rival⟩ uguagliare; **5 plus 5 ~s 10** 5 più 5 [è] uguale a 10. **~ity** /ɪ'kwɒlətɪ/ n uguaglianza f

equalize /'iːkwəlaɪz/ vt/i Sport pareggiare. **~r** n Sport pareggio m

equally /'iːkwəlɪ/ adv ⟨divide⟩ in parti uguali; **~ intelligent** della stessa intelligenza; **~,...** allo stesso tempo...

equanimity /ekwə'nɪmətɪ/ n equanimità f

equate /ɪ'kweɪt/ vt **~ sth with sth** equiparare qcsa a qcsa. **~ion** /-eɪʒn/ n Math equazione f

equator /ɪ'kweɪtə(r)/ n equatore m

equestrian /ɪ'kwestrɪən/ a equestre

equilibrium /iːkwɪ'lɪbrɪəm/ n equilibrio m

equinox /'iːkwɪnɒks/ n equinozio m

equip /ɪ'kwɪp/ vt (pt/pp **equipped**) equipaggiare; attrezzare ⟨kitchen, office⟩. **~ment** n attrezzatura f

equitable /'ekwɪtəbl/ a giusto

equity /'ekwɪtɪ/ n ⟨justness⟩ equità f; Comm azioni fpl

equivalent /ɪ'kwɪvələnt/ a equivalente; **be ~ to** equivalere a ● n equivalente m

equivocal /ɪ'kwɪvəkl/ a equivoco

era /'ɪərə/ n età f; ⟨geological⟩ era f

eradicate /ɪ'rædɪkeɪt/ vt eradicare

erase /ɪ'reɪz/ vt cancellare. **~r** n gomma f [da cancellare]; ⟨for blackboard⟩ cancellino m

erect /ɪ'rekt/ a eretto ● vt erigere. **~ion** /-ekʃn/ n erezione f

ero|de /ɪ'rəʊd/ vt ⟨water:⟩ erodere; ⟨acid:⟩ corrodere. **~sion** /-əʊʒn/ n erosione f; ⟨by acid⟩ corrosione f

erotic /ɪ'rɒtɪk/ a erotico. **~ism** /-tɪsɪzm/ n erotismo m

err /ɜː(r)/ vi errare; ⟨sin⟩ peccare

errand /'erənd/ n commissione f

erratic /ɪ'rætɪk/ a irregolare; ⟨person, moods⟩ imprevedibile; ⟨exchange rate⟩ incostante

erroneous /ɪ'rəʊnɪəs/ a erroneo

error /'erə(r)/ n errore m; **in ~** per errore

erudite /'erʊdaɪt/ a erudito. **~ion** /-'dɪʃn/ n erudizione f

erupt /ɪ'rʌpt/ vi eruttare; ⟨spots:⟩ spuntare; (fig: in anger) dare in escandescenze. **~ion** /-ʌpʃn/ n eruzione f; fig scoppio m

escalat|e /'eskəleɪt/ vi intensificarsi ● vt intensificare. **~ion** /-'eɪʃn/ n escalation f inv. **~or** n scala f mobile

escapade /'eskəpeɪd/ n scappatella f

escape /ɪ'skeɪp/ n fuga f; ⟨from prison⟩ evasione f; **have a narrow ~** cavarsela per un pelo ● vi ⟨prisoner:⟩ evadere (from da); sfuggire (from sb alla sorveglianza di qcno); ⟨animal:⟩ scappare; ⟨gas:⟩ fuoriuscire ● vt **~ notice**

passare inosservato; **the name ~s me** mi sfugge il nome

escapism /ɪ'skeɪpɪzm/ n evasione f [dalla realtà]

escort¹ /'eskɔːt/ n (of person) accompagnatore, -trice mf; Mil etc scorta f

escort² /ɪ'skɔːt/ vt accompagnare; Mil etc scortare

Eskimo /'eskɪməʊ/ n esquimese mf

esoteric /esə'terɪk/ a esoterico

especial /ɪ'speʃl/ a speciale. **~ly** adv specialmente; ⟨kind⟩ particolarmente

espionage /'espɪənɑːʒ/ n spionaggio m

essay /'eseɪ/ n saggio m; Sch tema f

essence /'esns/ n essenza f; **in ~** in sostanza

essential /ɪ'senʃl/ a essenziale ● npl the **~s** l'essenziale m. **~ly** adv essenzialmente

establish /ɪ'stæblɪʃ/ vt stabilire ⟨contact, lead⟩; fondare ⟨firm⟩; ⟨prove⟩ accertare; **~ oneself as** affermarsi come. **~ment** n ⟨firm⟩ azienda f; **the E~ment** l'ordine m costituito

estate /ɪ'steɪt/ n tenuta f; ⟨possessions⟩ patrimonio m; ⟨housing⟩ quartiere m residenziale. **~ agent** n agente m immobiliare. **~ car** n giardiniera f

esteem /ɪ'stiːm/ n stima f ● vt stimare; ⟨consider⟩ giudicare

estimate¹ /'estɪmət/ n valutazione f; Comm preventivo m; **at a rough ~** a occhio e croce

estimate² /'estɪmeɪt/ vt stimare. **~ion** /-'meɪʃn/ n ⟨esteem⟩ stima f; **in my ~ion** ⟨judgement⟩ a mio giudizio

estuary /'estjʊərɪ/ n estuario m

etc /et'setərə/ abbr (et cetera) ecc

etching /'etʃɪŋ/ n acquaforte f

eternal /ɪ'tɜːnl/ a eterno

eternity /ɪ'tɜːnətɪ/ n eternità f

ethic /'eθɪk/ n etica f. **~al** a etico. **~s** n etica f

Ethiopia /iːθɪ'əʊpɪə/ n Etiopia f

ethnic /'eθnɪk/ a etnico

etiquette /'etɪket/ n etichetta f

EU n abbr (**European Union**) UE f

eucalyptus /juːkə'lɪptəs/ n eucalipto m

eulogy /'juːlədʒɪ/ n elogio m

euphemis|m /'juːfəmɪzm/ n eufemismo m. **~tic** /-'mɪstɪk/ a eufemistico

euphoria /juː'fɔːrɪə/ n euforia f

Euro- /'jʊərəʊ-/ pref **~cheque** n eurochèque m inv. **~dollar** n eurodollaro m

Europe /'jʊərəp/ n Europa f

European /jʊərə'pɪən/ a europeo; **~ Community** Comunità f Europea; **~ Union** Unione f Europea ● n europeo, -a mf

evacuate /ɪ'vækjʊeɪt/ vt evacuare ⟨building, area⟩. **~ion** /-'eɪʃn/ n evacuazione f

evade /ɪ'veɪd/ vt evadere ⟨taxes⟩; evitare ⟨the enemy, authorities⟩; **~ the issue** evitare l'argomento

evaluate /ɪ'væljʊeɪt/ vt valutare

evange|lical /iːvæn'dʒelɪkl/ a evangelico. **~list** /ɪ'vændʒəlɪst/ n evangelista m

evaporat|e /ɪ'væpəreɪt/ vi evaporare; fig svanire. **~ion** /-'reɪʃn/ n evaporazione f

evasion /ɪ'veɪʒn/ n evasione f

evasive /ɪ'veɪsɪv/ a evasivo

eve /iːv/ n liter vigilia f

even /'iːvn/ a ⟨level⟩ piatto; ⟨same, equal⟩ uguale; ⟨regular⟩ regolare; ⟨number⟩ pari; **get ~ with** vendicarsi di; **now we're ~** adesso siamo pari ● adv anche, ancora; **~ if** anche se; **~ so** con tutto ciò; **not ~** nemmeno; **~ bigger/hotter** ancora più grande/caldo ● vt **~ the score** Sport pareggiare. **even out** vi livellarsi. **even up** vt livellare

evening /'iːvnɪŋ/ n sera f; ⟨whole evening⟩ serata f; **this ~** stasera; **in the ~** la sera. **~ class** n corso m serale. **~ dress** n ⟨man's⟩ abito m scuro; ⟨woman's⟩ abito m da sera

evenly /'iːvnlɪ/ adv ⟨distributed⟩ uniformemente; ⟨breathe⟩ regolarmente; ⟨*divided*⟩ in uguali parti

event /ɪ'vent/ *n* avvenimento *m*; ⟨*function*⟩ manifestazione *f*; *Sport* gara *f*; **in the ~ of** nell'eventualità di; **in the ~** alla fine. **~ful** *a* movimentato

eventual /ɪ'ventjʊəl/ *a* **the ~ winner was...** alla fine il vincitore è stato... **~ity** /-'ælətɪ/ *n* eventualità *f*. **~ly** *adv* alla fine; **~ly!** finalmente!

ever /'evə(r)/ *adv* mai; **I haven't ~...** non ho mai...; **for ~** per sempre; **hardly ~** quasi mai; **~ since** da quando; ⟨*since that time*⟩ da allora; **~ so** *fam* veramente

'evergreen *n* sempreverde *m*

ever'lasting *a* eterno

every /'evrɪ/ *a* ogni; **~ one** ciascuno; **~ other day** un giorno sì un giorno no

every: **~body** *pron* tutti *pl*. **~day** *a* quotidiano, di ogni giorno. **~one** *pron* tutti *pl*; **~one else** tutti gli altri. **~thing** *pron* tutto; **~thing else** tutto il resto. **~where** *adv* dappertutto; ⟨*wherever*⟩ dovunque

evict /ɪ'vɪkt/ *vt* sfrattare. **~ion** /-ɪkʃn/ *n* sfratto *m*

eviden|ce /'evɪdəns/ *n* evidenza *f*; *Jur* testimonianza *f*; **give ~ce** testimoniare. **~t** *a* evidente. **~tly** *adv* evidentemente

evil /'iːvl/ *a* cattivo ● *n* male *m*

evocative /ɪ'vɒkətɪv/ *a* evocativo; **be ~ of** evocare

evoke /ɪ'vəʊk/ *vt* evocare

evolution /iːvə'luːʃn/ *n* evoluzione *f*

evolve /ɪ'vɒlv/ *vt* evolvere ● *vi* evolversi

ewe /juː/ *n* pecora *f*

exacerbate /ɪg'zæsəbeɪt/ *vt* esacerbare ⟨*situation*⟩

exact /ɪg'zækt/ *a* esatto ● *vt* esigere. **~ing** *a* esigente. **~itude** /-ɪtjuːd/ *n* esattezza *f*. **~ly** *adv* esattamente; **not ~ly** non proprio. **~ness** *n* precisione *f*

exaggerat|e /ɪg'zædʒəreɪt/ *vt/i* esagerare. **~ion** /-'reɪʃn/ *n* esagerazione *f*

exam /ɪg'zæm/ *n* esame *m*

examination /ɪgzæmɪ'neɪʃn/ *n* esame *m*; ⟨*of patient*⟩ visita *f*

examine /ɪg'zæmɪn/ *vt* esaminare; visitare ⟨*patient*⟩. **~r** *n* *Sch* esaminatore, -trice *mf*

example /ɪg'zɑːmpl/ *n* esempio *m*; **for ~** per esempio; **make an ~ of sb** punire qcno per dare un esempio; **be an ~ to sb** dare il buon esempio a qcno

exasperat|e /ɪg'zæspəreɪt/ *vt* esasperare. **~ion** /-'reɪʃn/ *n* esasperazione *f*

excavat|e /'ekskəveɪt/ *vt* scavare; *Archaeol* fare gli scavi di. **~ion** /-'veɪʃn/ *n* scavo *m*

exceed /ɪk'siːd/ *vt* eccedere. **~ingly** *adv* estremamente

excel /ɪk'sel/ *v* (*pt/pp* **excelled**) ● *vi* eccellere ● *vt* **~ oneself** superare se stessi

excellen|ce /'eksələns/ *n* eccellenza *f*. **E~cy** *n* ⟨*title*⟩ Eccellenza *f*. **~t** *a* eccellente

except /ɪk'sept/ *prep* eccetto, tranne; **~ for** eccetto, tranne; **~ that...** eccetto che... ● *vt* eccettuare. **~ing** *prep* eccetto, tranne

exception /ɪk'sepʃn/ *n* eccezione *f*; **take ~** to fare obiezioni a. **~al** *a* eccezionale. **~ally** *adv* eccezionalmente

excerpt /'eksɜːpt/ *n* estratto *m*

excess /ɪk'ses/ *n* eccesso *m*; **in ~ of** oltre. **~ baggage** *n* bagaglio *m* in eccedenza. **~ fare** *n* supplemento *m*

excessive /ɪk'sesɪv/ *a* eccessivo. **~ly** *adv* eccessivamente

exchange /ɪks'tʃeɪndʒ/ *n* scambio *m*; *Teleph* centrale *f*; *Comm* cambio *m*; [**stock**] **~** Borsa *f* Valori; **in ~** in cambio (**for** di) ● *vt* scambiare (**for** con); cambiare ⟨*money*⟩. **~ rate** *n* tasso *m* di cambio

exchequer /ɪks'tʃekə(r)/ *n* *Pol* tesoro *m*

excise¹ /'eksaɪz/ n dazio m; ~ **duty** dazio m

excise² /ek'saɪz/ vt recidere

excitable /ɪk'saɪtəbl/ a eccitabile

excit|e /ɪk'saɪt/ vt eccitare. ~**ed** a eccitato; **get** ~**ed** eccitarsi. ~**edly** adv tutto eccitato. ~**ement** n eccitazione f. ~**ing** a eccitante; ⟨story, film⟩ appassionante; ⟨holiday⟩ entusiasmante

exclaim /ɪk'skleɪm/ vt/i esclamare

exclamation /eksklə'meɪʃn/ n esclamazione f. ~ **mark** n, Am ~ **point** n punto m esclamativo

exclu|de /ɪk'sklu:d/ vt escludere. ~**ding** pron escluso. ~**sion** /-ʒn/ n esclusione f

exclusive /ɪk'sklu:sɪv/ a ⟨rights, club⟩ esclusivo; ⟨interview⟩ in esclusiva; ~ **of...** ...escluso. ~**ly** adv esclusivamente

excommunicate /ekskə'mju:nɪkeɪt/ vt scomunicare

excrement /'ekskrɪmənt/ n escremento m

excruciating /ɪk'skru:ʃɪeɪtɪŋ/ a atroce ⟨pain⟩; ⟨fam: very bad⟩ spaventoso

excursion /ɪk'skɜ:ʃn/ n escursione f

excusable /ɪk'skju:zəbl/ a perdonabile

excuse¹ /ɪk'skju:s/ n scusa f

excuse² /ɪk'skju:z/ vt scusare; ~ **from** esonerare da; ~ **me!** ⟨to get attention⟩ scusi!; ⟨to get past⟩ permesso!, scusi!; ⟨indignant⟩ come ha detto?

ex-di'rectory a be ~ non figurare sull'elenco telefonico

execute /'eksɪkju:t/ vt eseguire; ⟨put to death⟩ giustiziare; attuare ⟨plan⟩

execution /eksɪ'kju:ʃn/ n esecuzione f; ⟨of plan⟩ attuazione f. ~**er** n boia m inv

executive /ɪg'zekjʊtɪv/ a esecutivo ● n dirigente mf; Pol esecutivo m

executor /ɪg'zekjʊtə(r)/ n Jur esecutore, -trice mf

exemplary /ɪg'zemplərɪ/ a esemplare

exemplify /ɪg'zemplɪfaɪ/ vt ⟨pt/pp -ied⟩ esemplificare

exempt /ɪg'zempt/ a esente ● vt esentare ⟨from da⟩. ~**ion** /-empʃn/ n esenzione f

exercise /'eksəsaɪz/ n esercizio m; Mil esercitazione f; **physical** ~**s** ginnastica f; **take** ~ fare del moto ● vt esercitare ⟨muscles, horse⟩; portare a spasso ⟨dog⟩; mettere in pratica ⟨skills⟩ ● vi esercitarsi. ~ **book** n quaderno m

exert /ɪg'zɜ:t/ vt esercitare; ~ **oneself** sforzarsi. ~**ion** /-ɜ:ʃn/ n sforzo m

exhale /eks'heɪl/ vt/i esalare

exhaust /ɪg'zɔ:st/ n Auto scappamento m; ⟨pipe⟩ tubo m di scappamento; ~ **fumes** fumi mpl di scarico m ● vt esaurire. ~**ed** a esausto. ~**ing** a estenuante; ⟨climate, person⟩ sfibrante. ~**ion** /-ɔ:stʃn/ n esaurimento m. ~**ive** /-ɪv/ a fig esauriente

exhibit /ɪg'zɪbɪt/ n oggetto m esposto; Jur reperto m ● vt esporre; fig dimostrare

exhibition /eksɪ'bɪʃn/ n mostra f; ⟨of strength, skill⟩ dimostrazione f. ~**ist** n esibizionista mf

exhibitor /ɪg'zɪbɪtə(r)/ n espositore, -trice mf

exhilarat|ed /ɪg'zɪləreɪtɪd/ a rallegrato. ~**ing** a stimolante; ⟨mountain air⟩ tonificante. ~**ion** /-'reɪʃn/ n allegria f

exhort /ɪg'zɔ:t/ vt esortare

exhume /eks'zju:m/ vt esumare

exile /'eksaɪl/ n esilio m; ⟨person⟩ esule m ● vt esiliare

exist /ɪg'zɪst/ vi esistere. ~**ence** /-əns/ n esistenza f; **in** ~ esistente; **be in** ~**ence** esistere. ~**ing** a attuale

exit /'eksɪt/ n uscita f; Theat uscita f di scena ● vi Theat uscire di scena; Comput uscire

exonerate /ɪg'zɒnəreɪt/ vt esonerare

exorbitant /ɪgˈzɔːbɪtənt/ a esorbitante

exorcize /ˈeksɔːsaɪz/ vt esorcizzare

exotic /ɪgˈzɒtɪk/ a esotico

expand /ɪkˈspænd/ vt espandere ●vi espandersi; Comm sviluparsi; (metal:) dilatarsi; ~ **on** (fig: explain better) approfondire

expanse /ɪkˈspæns/ n estensione f. **~ion** /-ænʃn/ n espansione f; Comm sviluppo m; (of metal) dilatazione f. **~ive** /-ɪv/ a espansivo

expatriate /eksˈpætrɪət/ n espatriato, -a mf

expect /ɪkˈspekt/ vt aspettare (letter, baby); (suppose) pensare; (demand) esigere; **I ~ so** penso di sì; **be ~ing** essere in stato interessante

expectan|cy /ɪkˈspektənsɪ/ n aspettativa f. **~t** a in attesa; **~t mother** donna f incinta. **~tly** adv con impazienza

expectation /ekspekˈteɪʃn/ n aspettativa f, speranza f

expedient /ɪkˈspiːdɪənt/ a conveniente ●n espediente m

expedition /ekspɪˈdɪʃn/ n spedizione f. **~ary** a Mil di spedizione

expel /ɪkˈspel/ vt (pt/pp expelled) espellere

expend /ɪkˈspend/ vt consumare. **~able** /-əbl/ a sacrificabile

expenditure /ɪkˈspendɪtʃə(r)/ n spesa f

expense /ɪkˈspens/ n spesa f; **business ~s** pl spese fpl; **at my ~** a mie spese; **at the ~ of** fig a spese di

expensive /ɪkˈspensɪv/ a caro, costoso. **~ly** adv costosamente

experience /ɪkˈspɪərɪəns/ n esperienza f ●vt provare (sensation); avere (problem). **~d** a esperto

experiment /ɪkˈsperɪmənt/ n esperimento ●/-ment/ vi sperimentare. **~al** /-ˈmentl/ a sperimentale

expert /ˈekspɜːt/ a & n esperto, -a mf. **~ly** adv abilmente

expertise /ekspɜːˈtiːz/ n competenza f

expire /ɪkˈspaɪə(r)/ vi scadere

expiry /ɪkˈspaɪərɪ/ n scadenza f. **~ date** n data f di scadenza

explain /ɪkˈspleɪn/ vt spiegare

explana|tion /ekspləˈneɪʃn/ n spiegazione f. **~tory** /ɪkˈsplænətərɪ/ a esplicativo

expletive /ɪkˈspliːtɪv/ n imprecazione f

explicit /ɪkˈsplɪsɪt/ a esplicito. **~ly** adv esplicitamente

explode /ɪkˈspləʊd/ vi esplodere ●vt fare esplodere

exploit¹ /ˈeksplɔɪt/ n impresa f

exploit² /ɪkˈsplɔɪt/ vt sfruttare. **~ation** /eksplɔɪˈteɪʃn/ n sfruttamento m

explora|tion /ekspləˈreɪʃn/ n esplorazione f. **~tory** /ɪkˈsplɒrətərɪ/ a esplorativo

explore /ɪkˈsplɔː(r)/ vt esplorare; fig studiare (implications). **~r** n esploratore, -trice mf

explos|ion /ɪkˈspləʊʒn/ n esplosione f. **~ive** /-sɪv/ a & n esplosivo m

exponent /ɪkˈspəʊnənt/ n esponente mf

export /ˈekspɔːt/ n esportazione f ●/-ˈspɔːt/ esportare. **~er** n esportatore, -trice mf

expose /ɪkˈspəʊz/ vt esporre; (reveal) svelare; smascherare (traitor etc). **~ure** /-ʒə(r)/ n esposizione f; Med esposizione f prolungata al freddo/caldo; (of crimes) smascheramento m; **24 ~ures** Phot 24 pose

expound /ɪkˈspaʊnd/ vt esporre

express /ɪkˈspres/ a espresso ●adv (send) per espresso ●n (train) espresso m ●vt esprimere; **~ oneself** esprimersi. **~ion** /-ʃn/ n espressione f. **~ive** /-ɪv/ a espressivo. **~ly** adv espressamente

expulsion /ɪkˈspʌlʃn/ n espulsione f

exquisite /ekˈskwɪzɪt/ a squisito

ex-'serviceman n ex-combattente m

extend /ɪkˈstend/ vt prolungare

⟨visit, road⟩; prorogare ⟨visa, contract⟩; ampliare ⟨building, knowledge⟩; ⟨stretch out⟩ allungare; tendere ⟨hand⟩ ● *vi* ⟨garden, knowledge:⟩ estendersi

extension /ɪk'stenʃn/ *n* prolungamento *m*; ⟨of visa, contract⟩ proroga *f*; ⟨of treaty⟩ ampliamento *m*; ⟨part of building⟩ annesso *m*; ⟨length of cable⟩ prolunga *f*; Teleph interno *m*; **~ 226** interno 226

extensive /ɪk'stensɪv/ *a* ampio, vasto. **~ly** *adv* ampiamente

extent /ɪk'stent/ *n* ⟨scope⟩ portata *f*; **to a certain ~** fino a un certo punto; **to such an ~ that...** fino al punto che...

extenuating /ɪk'stenjuetɪŋ/ *a* **~ circumstances** attenuanti *fpl*

exterior /ɪk'stɪərɪə(r)/ *a & n* esterno *m*

exterminat|e /ɪk'stɜːmɪneɪt/ *vt* sterminare. **~ion** /-'neɪʃn/ *n* sterminio *m*

external /ɪk'stɜːnl/ *a* esterno; **for ~ use only** Med per uso esterno. **~ly** *adv* esternamente

extinct /ɪk'stɪŋkt/ *a* estinto. **~ion** /-ɪŋkʃn/ *n* estinzione *f*

extinguish /ɪk'stɪŋgwɪʃ/ *vt* estinguere. **~er** *n* estintore *m*

extort /ɪk'stɔːt/ *vt* estorcere. **~ion** /-ɔːʃn/ *n* estorsione *f*

extortionate /ɪk'stɔːʃənət/ *a* esorbitante

extra /'ekstrə/ *a* in più; ⟨train⟩ straordinario; **an ~ £10** 10 sterline extra, 10 sterline in più ● *adv* in più; ⟨especially⟩ più; **pay ~** pagare in più, pagare extra; **~ strong/busy** fortissimo/occupatissimo ● *n* Theat comparsa *f*; **~s** *pl* extra *mpl*

extract¹ /'ekstrækt/ *n* estratto *m*

extract² /ɪk'strækt/ *vt* estrarre ⟨tooth, oil⟩; strappare ⟨secret⟩; ricavare ⟨truth⟩. **~or** [fan] *n* aspiratore *m*

extradit|e /'ekstrədaɪt/ Jur *vt* estradare. **~ion** /-'dɪʃn/ *n* estradizione *f*

extra·marital *a* extraconiugale
extraordinar|y /ɪk'strɔːdmərɪ/ *a* straordinario. **~ily** /-ɪlɪ/ *adv* straordinariamente
extravagan|ce /ɪk'strævəgəns/ *n* ⟨with money⟩ prodigalità *f*; ⟨of behaviour⟩ stravaganza *f*. **~t** *a* spendaccione; ⟨bizarre⟩ stravagante; ⟨claim⟩ esagerato
extrem|e /ɪk'striːm/ *a* estremo ● *n* estremo *m*; **in the ~e** al massimo. **~ely** *adv* estremamente. **~ist** *n* estremista *mf*
extremity /ɪk'stremətɪ/ *n* ⟨end⟩ estremità *f inv*
extricate /'ekstrɪkeɪt/ *vt* districare
extrovert /'ekstrəvɜːt/ *n* estroverso, -a *mf*
exuberant /ɪg'zjuːbərənt/ *a* esuberante
exude /ɪg'zjuːd/ *vt also fig* trasudare
exult /ɪg'zʌlt/ *vi* esultare
eye /aɪ/ *n* occhio *m*; ⟨of needle⟩ cruna *f*; **keep an ~ on** tener d'occhio; **see ● to ~** aver le stesse idee ● *vt* (*pt/pp* **eyed**, *pres p* **ey[e]ing**) guardare
eye: **~ball** *n* bulbo *m* oculare. **~brow** *n* sopracciglio *m* (*pl* sopracciglia *f*). **~lash** *n* ciglio *m* (*pl* ciglia *f*). **~lid** *n* palpebra *f*. **~opener** *n* rivelazione *f*. **~shadow** *n* ombretto *m*. **~sight** *n* vista *f*. **~sore** *n fam* pugno *m* nell'occhio. **~witness** *n* testimone *mf* oculare

• • • • • • • • • • • • • • • • • • • •

Ff

fable /'feɪbl/ *n* favola *f*
fabric /'fæbrɪk/ *n also fig* tessuto *m*
fabrication /fæbrɪ'keɪʃn/ *n* invenzione *f*; ⟨manufacture⟩ fabbricazione *f*
fabulous /'fæbjuləs/ *a fam* favoloso

façade /fə'sɑːd/ n (of building, person) facciata f

face /feɪs/ n faccia f, viso m; (grimace) smorfia f; (surface) faccia f; (of clock) quadrante m; **~s** far boccacce; **in the ~ of** di fronte a; **on the ~ of it** in apparenza ● vt essere di fronta a; (confront) affrontare; **~ north** (house:) dare a nord; **~ the fact that** arrendersi al fatto che. **face up to** vt accettare (facts); affrontare (person)

face: **~-flannel** n ≈ guanto m di spugna. **~less** a anonimo. **~-lift** n plastica f facciale

facet /'fæsɪt/ n sfaccettatura f; fig aspetto m

facetious /fə'siːʃəs/ a spiritoso. **~ remarks** spiritosaggini mpl

face value n (of money) valore m nominale; **take sb/sth at ~** fermarsi alle apparenze

facial /'feɪʃl/ a facciale ● n trattamento m di bellezza al viso

facile /'fæsaɪl/ a semplicistico

facilitate /fə'sɪlɪteɪt/ vt rendere possibile; (make easier) facilitare

facility /fə'sɪlətɪ/ n facilità f; **~ies** pl (of area, in hotel etc) attrezzature fpl

facing /'feɪsɪŋ/ prep **~ the sea** (house) che dà sul mare; **the person ~ me** la persona di fronte a me

facsimile /fæk'sɪmɪlɪ/ n facsimile m

fact /fækt/ n fatto m; **in ~** infatti

faction /'fækʃn/ n fazione f

factor /'fæktə(r)/ n fattore m

factory /'fæktərɪ/ n fabbrica f

factual /'fæktʃʊəl/ a ~ **be ~** attenersi ai fatti. **~ly** adv (inaccurate) dal punto di vista dei fatti

faculty /'fækəltɪ/ n facoltà f inv

fad /fæd/ n capriccio m

fade /feɪd/ vi sbiadire; (sound, light:) affievolirsi; (flower:) appassire. **fade in** vt cominciare in dissolvenza (picture). **fade out** vt finire in dissolvenza (picture)

fag /fæg/ n (chore) fatica f; (fam: cigarette) sigaretta f; (Am sl: homosexual) frocio m. **~ end** n fam cicca f

fagged /fægd/ a **~ out** fam stanco morto

Fahrenheit /'færənhaɪt/ a Fahrenheit

fail /feɪl/ n **without ~** senz'altro ● vi (attempt:) fallire; (eyesight, memory:) indebolirsi; (engine, machine:) guastarsi; (marriage:) andare a rotoli; (in exam) essere bocciato; **~ to do sth** non fare qcsa; **I tried but I ~ed** ho provato ma non ci sono riuscito ● vt non superare (exam); bocciare (candidate); (disappoint) deludere; **words ~ me** mi mancano le parole

failing /'feɪlɪŋ/ n difetto m ● prep **~ that** altrimenti

failure /'feɪljə(r)/ n fallimento m; (mechanical) guasto m; (person) incapace mf

faint /feɪnt/ a leggero; (memory) vago; **feel ~** sentirsi mancare ● n svenimento m ● vi svenire

faint: **~-'hearted** a timido. **~ly** adv (slightly) leggermente. **~ness** n (physical) debolezza f

fair¹ /feə(r)/ n fiera f

fair² a (hair, person) biondo; (skin) chiaro; (weather) bello; (just) giusto; (quite good) discreto; Sch abbastanza bene; **a ~ amount** abbastanza ● adv fare un gioco pulito. **~ly** adv con giustizia; (rather) discretamente, abbastanza. **~ness** n giustizia f. **~ play** n fair play m inv

fairy /'feərɪ/ n fata f. **~ story**, **~-tale** n fiaba f

faith /feɪθ/ n fede f; (trust) fiducia f; **in good/bad ~** in buona/mala fede

faithful /'feɪθfʊl/ a fedele. **~ly** adv fedelmente; **yours ~ly** distinti saluti. **~ness** n fedeltà f

'faith-healer n guaritore, -trice mf

fake /feɪk/ a falso ● n falsificazione f; (person) impostore m ● vt falsificare; (pretend) fingere

falcon /ˈfɔːlkən/ n falcone m

fall /fɔːl/ n caduta f; (in prices) ribasso m; (Am: autumn) autunno m; have a ~ fare una caduta ● vi (pt fell, pp fallen) cadere; (night:) scendere; ~ in love innamorarsi.
fall about vi (with laughter) morire dal ridere. **fall back on** vt ritornare su. **fall for** vt fam innamorarsi di (person); cascarci (sth, trick).
fall down vi cadere; (building:) crollare. **fall for** vt caderci dentro; (collapse) crollare; Mil mettersi in riga; ~ **in with** concordare con (suggestion, plan). **fall off** vi cadere; (diminish) diminuire. **fall out** vi (quarrel) litigare; **his hair is** ~ing out perde i capelli. **fall over** vi cadere. **fall through** vi (plan:) andare a monte

fallacy /ˈfæləsɪ/ n errore m

fallible /ˈfæləbl/ a fallibile

'fall-out n pioggia f radioattiva

false /fɔːls/ a falso; ~ **bottom** doppio fondo m; ~ **start** Sport falsa partenza f. ~**hood** n menzogna f. ~**ness** n falsità f

false 'teeth npl dentiera f

falsify /ˈfɔːlsɪfaɪ/ vt (pt/pp -ied) falsificare

falter /ˈfɔːltə(r)/ vi vacillare; (making speech) esitare

fame /feɪm/ n fama f

familiar /fəˈmɪljə(r)/ a familiare; **be** ~ **with** (know) conoscere. ~**ity** /-lɪˈærɪtɪ/ n familiarità f. ~**ize** vt familiarizzare; ~**ize oneself with** familiarizzarsi con

family /ˈfæmɪlɪ/ n famiglia f

family: ~ **al'lowance** n assegni mpl familiari. ~ **'doctor** n medico m di famiglia. ~ **'life** n vita f familiare. ~ **'planning** n pianificazione f familiare. ~ **'tree** n albero m genealogico

amine /ˈfæmɪn/ n carestia f

amished /ˈfæmɪʃt/ a **be** ~ **that** avere una fame da lupo

famous /ˈfeɪməs/ a famoso

fan¹ /fæn/ n ventilatore m; (handheld) ventaglio m ● vt (pt/pp fanned) far vento a; ~ **oneself** sventagliarsi; fig ~ **the flames** soffiare sul fuoco. **fan out** vi spiegarsi a ventaglio

fan² n (admirer) ammiratore, -trice mf; Sport tifoso m; (of Verdi etc) appassionato, -a mf

fanatic /fəˈnætɪk/ n fanatico, -a mf. ~**al** a fanatico. ~**ism** /-sɪzm/ n fanatismo m

'fan belt n cinghia f per ventilatore

fanciful /ˈfænsɪfl/ a fantasioso

fancy /ˈfænsɪ/ n fantasia f; **I've taken a real** ~ **to him** mi è molto simpatico; **as the** ~ **takes you** come ti pare ● a [a] fantasia ● vt (pt/pp -ied) (believe) credere; (fam: want) aver voglia di; **he fancies you** fam gli piaci; ~ **that!** ma guarda un po'! ~ **'dress** n costume m (per maschera)

fanfare /ˈfænfeə(r)/ n fanfara f

fang /fæŋ/ n zanna f; (of snake) dente m

fan: ~ **heater** n termoventilatore m. ~**light** n lunetta f

fantasize /ˈfæntəsaɪz/ vi fantasticare. ~**tic** /-ˈtæstɪk/ a fantastico. ~**y** n fantasia f

far /fɑː(r)/ adv lontano; (much) molto; **by** ~ di gran lunga; ~ **away** lontano; **as** ~ **as the church** fino alla chiesa; **how** ~ **is it from here?** quanto dista da qui?; **as** ~ **as I know** per quanto io sappia ● a (end, side) altro; **the** F~ **East** l'Estremo Oriente m

farce /fɑːs/ n farsa f. ~**ical** a ridicolo

fare /feə(r)/ n tariffa f; (food) vitto m. ~**-dodger** /-dɒdʒə(r)/ n passeggero, -a mf senza biglietto

farewell /feəˈwel/ int liter addio! ● n addio m

far-'fetched a improbabile

farm /fɑːm/ n fattoria f ● vi fare

l'agricoltore ● *vt* coltivare ⟨*land*⟩. ~er *n* agricoltore *m*

farm: ~**house** *n* casa *f* colonica. ~**ing** *n* agricoltura *f*. ~**yard** *n* aia *f*

far: ~'**reaching** *a* di larga portata. ~'**sighted** *a fig* prudente. (*Am: long-sighted*) presbite

fart /fɑːt/ *fam* *n* scoreggia *f* ● *vi* scoreggiare

farther /ˈfɑːðə(r)/ *adv* più lontano ● *a* at the ~ **end of** all'altra estremità di

fascinat|e /ˈfæsɪneɪt/ *vt* affascinare. ~**ing** *a* affascinante. ~**ion** /-ˈneɪʃn/ *n* fascino *m*

fascis|m /ˈfæʃɪzm/ *n* fascismo *m*. ~**t** *n* fascista *mf* ● *a* fascista

fashion /ˈfæʃn/ *n* moda *f*; (*manner*) maniera *f* ● *vt* modellare. ~**able** /-əbl/ *a* di moda; be ~**able** essere alla moda. ~**ably** *adv* alla moda

fast[1] /fɑːst/ *a* veloce; ⟨*colour*⟩ indelebile; be ~ ⟨*clock*⟩ andare avanti ● *adv* velocemente; ⟨*firmly*⟩ saldamente; ~**er!** più in fretta!; be ~ **asleep** dormire profondamente

fast[2] *n* digiuno *m* ● *vi* digiunare

fasten /ˈfɑːsn/ *vt* allacciare; chiudere ⟨*window*⟩; ⟨*stop flapping*⟩ mettere un fermo a ● *vi* allacciarsi. ~**er** *n*, ~**ing** *n* chiusura *f*

fastidious /fæˈstɪdɪəs/ *a* esigente

fat /fæt/ *a* (**fatter, fattest**) ⟨*person, cheque*⟩ grasso ● *n* grasso *m*

fatal /ˈfeɪtl/ *a* mortale; ⟨*error*⟩ fatale. ~**ism** /-təlɪzm/ *n* fatalismo *m*. ~**ist** /- təlɪst/ *n* fatalista *mf*. ~**ity** /fəˈtælətɪ/ *n* morte *f*. ~**ly** *adv* mortalmente

fate /feɪt/ *n* destino *m*. ~**ful** *a* fatidico

'fat-head *n fam* zuccone. *a mf*

father /ˈfɑːðə(r)/ *n* padre *m*; F~ **Christmas** Babbo *m* Natale ● *vt* generare ⟨*child*⟩

father: ~**hood** *n* paternità *f*. ~**-in-law** *n* (*pl* ~**s-in-law**) suocero *m*. ~**ly** *a* paterno

fathom /ˈfæðəm/ *n Naut* braccio *m* ● *vt* ~ [**out**] comprendere

fatigue /fəˈtiːg/ *n* fatica *f*.

fatten /ˈfætn/ *vt* ingrassare ⟨*animal*⟩. ~**ing** *a* cream is ~**ing** la panna fa ingrassare

fatty /ˈfætɪ/ *a* grasso ● *n fam* ciccione, *a mf*

fatuous /ˈfætjʊəs/ *a* fatuo

faucet /ˈfɔːsɪt/ *n Am* rubinetto *m*

fault /fɔːlt/ *n* difetto *m*; *Geol* faglia *f*; *Tennis* fallo *m*; be at ~ avere torto; **find** ~ **with** trovare da ridire su; **it's your** ~ è colpa tua ● *vt* criticare. ~**less** *a* impeccabile

faulty /ˈfɔːltɪ/ *a* difettoso

fauna /ˈfɔːnə/ *n* fauna *f*

favour /ˈfeɪvə(r)/ *n* favore *m*; **be in** ~ **of** sth essere a favore di qcsa; **do sb a** ~ fare un piacere a qcno ● *vt* (*prefer*) preferire. ~**able** /-əbl/ *a* favorevole

favourite /ˈfeɪvərɪt/ *a* preferito ● *n* preferito, *a mf*; *Sport* favorito, *a mf*. ~**ism** *n* favoritismo *m*

fawn /fɔːn/ *a* fulvo ● *n* ⟨*animal*⟩ cerbiatto *m*

fax /fæks/ *n* ⟨*document, machine*⟩ fax *m inv*; **by** ~ per fax ● *vt* faxare. ~ **machine** *n* fax *m inv*. ~-**modem** *n* modem-fax *m inv*, fax-modem *m inv*

fear /fɪə(r)/ *n* paura *f*; **no** ~! *fam* vai tranquillo! ● *vt* temere ● *vi* ~ **for** sth temere per qcsa

fear|ful /ˈfɪəfl/ *a* pauroso; ⟨*awful*⟩ terribile. ~**less** *a* impavido. ~**some** /-səm/ *a* spaventoso

feas|ibility /fiːzɪˈbɪlɪtɪ/ *n* praticabilità *f*. ~**ible** *a* fattibile; (*possible*) probabile

feast /fiːst/ *n* festa *f*; (*banquet*) banchetto *m* ● *vi* banchettare; ~ **on** godersi

feat /fiːt/ *n* impresa *f*

feather /ˈfeðə(r)/ *n* piuma *f*

feature /ˈfiːtʃə(r)/ *n* (*quality*) caratteristica *f*; *Journ* articolo *m*; ~**s** (*of face*) lineamenti *mpl* ● *vt* ⟨*film*⟩ avere come protagonista ● *vi* (*in a list etc*) comparire. ~ **film** *n* lungometraggio *m*

February /ˈfebruərɪ/ *n* febbraio *m*

fed /fed/ *see* **feed** ● *a* **be ~ up** *fam* essere stufo (**with** di)

federal /'fed(ə)rəl/ *a* federale

federation /fedə'reɪʃn/ *n* federazione *f*

fee /fi:/ *n* tariffa *f*; (*lawyer's, doctor's*) onorario *m*; (*for membership, school*) quota *f*

feeble /'fi:bl/ *a* debole; (*excuse*) fiacco

feed /fi:d/ *n* mangiare *m*; (*for baby*) pappa *f* ● *v* (*pt/pp* **fed**) ● *vt* dar da mangiare a (*animal*); (*support*) nutrire; **~ sth into sth** inserire qcsa in qcsa ● *vi* mangiare

'feedback *n* controreazione *f*; (*of information*) reazione *f*, feedback *m*

feel /fi:l/ *v* (*pt/pp* **felt**) ● *vt* sentire; (*experience*) provare; (*think*) pensare; (*touch: searching*) tastare; (*touch: for texture*) toccare ● *vi* **~ soft/hard** essere duro/morbido al tatto; **~ hot/hungry** aver caldo/fame; **~ ill** sentirsi male; **I don't ~ like it** non ne ho voglia; **how do you ~ about it?** (*opinion*) che te ne pare?; **it doesn't ~ right** non mi sembra giusto. **~er** *n* (*of animal*) antenna *f*; **put out ~ers** *fig* tastare il terreno. **~ing** *n* sentimento *m*; (*awareness*) sensazione *f*

feet /fi:t/ *see* **foot**

feign /feɪn/ *vt* simulare

feline /'fi:laɪn/ *a* felino

fell¹ /fel/ *vt* (*knock down*) abbattere

fell² *see* **fall**

fellow /'feləʊ/ *n* (*of society*) socio *m*; (*fam: man*) tipo *m*

fellow: **~'countryman** *n* compatriota *m*. **~men** *npl* prossimi *mpl*. **~ship** *n* cameratismo *m*; (*group*) associazione *f*; *Univ* incarico *m* di ricercatore, -trice

felony /'feləʊni/ *n* delitto *m*

felt¹ /felt/ *see* **feel**

felt² *n* feltro *m*. **~[-tipped] 'pen** /-[tɪpt]/ *n* pennarello *m*

female /'fi:meɪl/ *a* femminile; **the**

~ antelope l'antilope femmina ● *n* femmina *f*

femin|ine /'femɪnɪn/ *a* femminile ● *n* *Gram* femminile *m*. **~inity** /-'nɪnəti/ *n* femminilità *f*. **~ist** *a* & *n* femminista *mf*

fenc|e /fens/ *n* recinto *m*; (*fam: person*) ricettatore *m* ● *vi* *Sport* tirar di scherma. **fence in** *vt* chiudere in un recinto. **~er** *n* schermidore *m*. **~ing** *n* steccato *m*; *Sport* scherma *f*

fend /fend/ *vi* **~ for oneself** badare a se stesso. **fend off** *vt* parare; difendersi da (*criticisms*)

fender /'fendə(r)/ *n* parafuoco *m* *inv*; (*Am: on car*) parafango *m*

fennel /'fenl/ *n* finocchio *m*

ferment¹ /'fɜ:ment/ *n* fermento *m*

ferment² /fə'ment/ *vi* fermentare ● *vt* far fermentare. **~ation** /fɜ:men'teɪʃn/ *n* fermentazione *f*

fern /fɜ:n/ *n* felce *f*

feroc|ious /fə'rəʊʃəs/ *a* feroce. **~ity** /-'rɒsəti/ *n* ferocia *f*

ferret /'ferɪt/ *n* furetto *m* ● **ferret out** *vt* scovare

ferry /'feri/ *n* traghetto *m* ● *vt* traghettare

fertil|e /'fɜ:taɪl/ *a* fertile. **~ity** /fə'tɪləti/ *n* fertilità *f*

fertilize /'fɜ:tɪlaɪz/ *vt* fertilizzare (*land, ovum*). **~r** *n* fertilizzante *m*

fervent /'fɜ:vənt/ *a* fervente

fervour /'fɜ:və(r)/ *n* fervore *m*

fester /'festə(r)/ *vi* suppurare

festival /'festɪvl/ *n* *Mus, Theat* festival *m*; *Relig* festa *f*

festiv|e /'festɪv/ *a* festivo; **~e season** periodo *m* delle feste natalizie. **~ities** /fe'stɪvətɪz/ *npl* festeggiamenti *mpl*

festoon /fe'stu:n/ *vt* **~ with** ornare di

fetch /fetʃ/ *vt* andare/venire a prendere; (*be sold for*) raggiungere [il prezzo di]

fetching /'fetʃɪŋ/ *a* attraente

fête /feɪt/ *n* festa *f* ● *vt* festeggiare

fetish /'fetɪʃ/ *n* feticcio *m*

fetter /'fetə(r)/ *vt* incatenare

fettle /'fetl/ n in fine ~ in buona forma

foud /fju:d/ n faida f

feudal /'fju:dl/ a feudale

fever /'fi:və(r)/ n febbre f. **~ish** a febbricitante; fig febbrile

few /fju:/ a pochi; **every ~ days** ogni due o tre giorni; **a ~ people** alcuni; **~er reservations** meno prenotazioni; **the ~est number** il numero più basso **●** pron pochi; **~ of us** pochi di noi; **a ~** alcuni; **quite a ~** parecchi; **~er than last year** meno dell'anno scorso

fiancé /fr'ɒnser/ n fidanzato m. **~e** n fidanzata f

fiasco /fr'æskəʊ/ n fiasco m

fib /fɪb/ n storia f; **tell a ~** raccontare una storia

fibre /'faɪbə(r)/ n fibra f. **~glass** n fibra f di vetro

fickle /'fɪkl/ a incostante

fiction /'fɪkʃn/ n [**works of**] ~ narrativa f; (fabrication) finzione f. **~al** a immaginario

fictitious /fɪk'tɪʃəs/ a fittizio

fiddle /'fɪdl/ n fam violino m; (cheating) imbroglio m **●** vi gingillarsi (with sth) **●** vt fam truccare (accounts)

fiddly /'fɪdlɪ/ a intricato

fidelity /fr'delətɪ/ n fedeltà f

fidget /'fɪdʒɪt/ vi agitarsi. **~y** a agitato

field /fi:ld/ n campo m

field: **~ events** npl atletica fsg leggera. **~glasses** npl binocolo msg. F**~ 'Marshal** n feldmarescialo m. **~work** n ricerche fpl sul terreno

fiend /fi:nd/ n demonio m

fierce /fɪəs/ a feroce. **~ness** n ferocia f

fiery /'faɪərɪ/ a (-ier, -iest) focoso

fifteen /fɪf'ti:n/ a & n quindici m. **~th** a quindicesimo

fifth /fɪfθ/ a quinto

fiftieth /'fɪftɪθ/ a cinquantesimo

fifty /'fɪftɪ/ a cinquanta

fig /fɪg/ n fico m

fight /faɪt/ n lotta f; (brawl) zuffa f;

(argument) litigio m; (boxing) incontro m **●** v (pt/pp fought) **●** vt also fig combattere **●** vi combattere; (brawl) azzuffarsi; (argue) litigare. **~er** n combattente mf; Aeron caccia m inv. **~ing** n combattimento m

figment /'fɪgmənt/ n **it's a ~ of your imagination** questo è tutta una tua invenzione

figurative /'fɪgjərətɪv/ a (sense) figurato; (art) figurativo

figure /'fɪgə(r)/ n (digit) cifra f; (carving, sculpture, illustration, form) figura f; (body shape) linea f; **~ of speech** modo m di dire **●** vi (appear) figurare **●** vt (Am: think) pensare. **figure out** vt dedurre; capire (person)

figure: **~head** n figura f simbolica. **~ skating** n pattinaggio m artistico

filament /'fɪləmənt/ n filamento m

filch /fɪltʃ/ vt fam grattare

file¹ /faɪl/ n scheda f; (set of documents) incartamento m; (folder) cartellina f, Comput file m inv **●** vt archiviare (documents)

file² n (line) fila f; **in single ~** in fila

file³ n Techn lima f **●** vt limare

filing cabinet /'faɪlɪŋkæbɪnət/ n schedario m, classificatore m

filings /'faɪlɪŋz/ npl limatura fsg

fill /fɪl/ n **eat one's ~** mangiare a sazietà **●** vt riempire; otturare (tooth) **●** vi riempirsi. **fill in** vt compilare (form). **fill out** vt compilare (form). **fill up** vi riempirsi; Auto far il pieno **●** vt riempire

fillet /'fɪlɪt/ n filetto m **●** vt (pt/pp filleted) disossare

filling /'fɪlɪŋ/ n Culin ripieno m; (of tooth) piombatura f. **~ station** n stazione f di rifornimento

filly /'fɪlɪ/ n puledra f

film /fɪlm/ n Cinema film m inv; Phot pellicola f; [**cling**] ~ pellicola f per alimenti **●** vt/i filmare. **~ star** n star f inv, divo, -a mf

filter /'fɪltə(r)/ n filtro m **●** vt filtrare. **filter through** vi ⟨news:⟩ trapelare. ~ **tip** n filtro m; ⟨cigarette⟩ sigaretta f col filtro

filth /filθ/ n sudiciume m. ~**y** a (-ier, -iest) sudicio; ⟨word⟩ sconcio

fin /fin/ n pinna f

final /'faml/ a finale; ⟨conclusive⟩ decisivo ● n Sport finale f; ~**s** pl Univ esami mpl finali

finale /fr'nɑ:lı/ n finale m

final|ist /'faməlıst/ n finalista mf. ~**ity** /-'næletı/ n finalità f

final|ize /'faməlaız/ vt mettere a punto ⟨text⟩; definire ⟨agreement⟩. ~**ly** adv ⟨at last⟩ finalmente; ⟨at the end⟩ alla fine; ⟨to conclude⟩ per finire

finance /'faınæns/ n finanza f ● vt finanziare

financial /far'nænʃl/ a finanziario

finch /fintʃ/ n fringuello m

find /faınd/ n scoperta f ● vt ⟨pt/pp found⟩ trovare; ⟨establish⟩ scoprire; ~ **sb guilty** Jur dichiarare qcno colpevole. **find out** vt scoprire ● vi ⟨enquire⟩ informarsi

findings /'faındıŋz/ npl conclusioni fpl

fine[1] /faın/ n ⟨penalty⟩ multa f ● vt multare

fine[2] a bello; ⟨slender⟩ fine; **he's ~** ⟨in health⟩ sta bene. ~ **arts** npl belle arti fpl. ● adv bene; **that's cutting it ~** non ci lascia molto tempo ● int [va] bene. ~**ly** adv ⟨cut⟩ finemente

finery /'faınərı/ n splendore m

finesse /fı'nes/ n finezza f

finger /'fıŋgə(r)/ n dito m ⟨pl dita f⟩ ● vt tastare

finger: ~**-mark** n ditata f. ~**-nail** n unghia f. ~**-print** n impronta f digitale. ~**-tip** n punta f del dito; **have sth at one's ~-tips** sapere qcsa a menadito; ⟨close at hand⟩ avere qcsa a portata di mano

finicky /'fınıkı/ a ⟨person⟩ pignolo; ⟨task⟩ intricato

finish /'fınıʃ/ n fine f; ⟨finishing line⟩ traguardo m; ⟨of product⟩ finitura f; **have a good ~** ⟨runner:⟩

avere un buon finale ● vt finire; ~ **reading** finire di leggere ● vi finire

finite /'faınaıt/ a limitato

Finland /'fınlənd/ n Finlandia f

Finn /fın/ n finlandese mf. ~**ish** a finlandese ● n ⟨language⟩ finnico m

fiord /fjɔ:d/ n fiordo m

fir /fɜ:(r)/ n abete m

fire /'faıə(r)/ n fuoco m; ⟨forest, house⟩ incendio m; **be on ~** bruciare; **catch ~** prendere fuoco; **set ~ to** dar fuoco a; **under ~** sotto il fuoco ● vt cuocere ⟨pottery⟩; sparare ⟨shot⟩; tirare ⟨gun⟩; ⟨fam: dismiss⟩ buttar fuori ● vi sparare ⟨at a⟩

fire: ~ **alarm** n allarme m antincendio. ~**arm** n arma f da fuoco. ~ **brigade** n vigili mpl del fuoco. ~**-engine** n autopompa f. ~**-escape** n uscita f di sicurezza. ~ **extinguisher** n estintore m. ~**man** n pompiere m, vigile m del fuoco. ~**-place** n caminetto m. ~**side** n by or **at the ~side** accanto al fuoco. ~ **station** n caserma f dei pompieri. ~**-wood** n legna f ⟨da ardere⟩. ~**work** n fuoco m d'artificio; ~**works** pl ⟨display⟩ fuochi mpl d'artificio

'firing squad n plotone m d'esecuzione

firm[1] /fɜ:m/ n ditta f, azienda f

firm[2] a fermo; ⟨soil⟩ compatto; ⟨stable, properly fixed⟩ solido; ⟨resolute⟩ risoluto. ~**ly** adv ⟨hold⟩ stretto; ⟨say⟩ con fermezza

first /fɜ:st/ a & n primo, -a mf; **at ~** all'inizio; **who's ~?** chi è il primo?; **from the ~** ⟨fin⟩ dall'inizio ● adv ⟨arrive, leave⟩ per primo; ⟨beforehand⟩ prima; ⟨in listing⟩ prima di tutto, innanzitutto

first: ~ **'aid** n pronto soccorso m. ~**-'aid kit** n cassetta f di pronto soccorso. ~**-class** a di prim'ordine; Rail di prima classe ● adv ⟨travel⟩ in prima classe. ~ **'floor** n primo piano m; ⟨Am: ground floor⟩

pianterreno m. **~ly** adv in primo luogo. **~name** n nome m di battesimo. **~rate** a ottimo

fish /fɪʃ/ n pesce m ● vt/i pescare. **fish out** vt tirar fuori

fish: ~bone n lisca f. **~erman** n pescatore m. **~farm** n vivaio m. **~ 'finger** n bastoncino m di pesce

fishing /'fɪʃɪŋ/ n pesca f. **~ boat** n peschereccio m. **~rod** n canna f da pesca

fish: ~monger /-mʌŋgə(r)/ n pescivendolo m. **~slice** n paletta f per fritti. **~y** a (fam: suspicious) sospetto

fission /'fɪʃn/ n Phys fissione f

fist /fɪst/ n pugno m

fit¹ /fɪt/ n (attack) attacco m; (of rage) accesso m; (of generosity) slancio m

fit² a (fitter, fittest) (suitable) adatto; (healthy) in buona salute; Sport in forma; **be ~ to do sth** essere in grado di fare qcsa; **~ to eat** buono da mangiare; **keep ~** tenersi in forma

fit³ n (of clothes) taglio m; **it's a good ~** (coat etc.) ti/le sta bene ● vt (pt/pp fitted) ● vi (be the right size) andare bene a; **it won't ~** (no room) non ci sta ● vt (fix) applicare (to a); (install) installare; **it doesn't ~ me** (coat etc.) non mi va bene; **~ with** fornire di. **fit in** (person:) adattarsi; **it won't ~ in** (no room) non ci sta ● vt (in schedule, vehicle) trovare un buon posto per

fit/ful /'fɪtfl/ a irregolare. **~fully** adv (sleep) a sprazzi. **~ments** npl (in house) impianti mpl fissi. **~ness** n (suitability) capacità f, [**physical**] **~ness** forma f, fitness m

fitted: ~'carpet n moquette f inv. **~ 'cupboard** n armadio m a muro; (smaller) armadietto m a muro. **~ 'kitchen** n cucina f componibile. **~ 'sheet** n lenzuolo m con angoli

fitter /'fɪtə(r)/ n installatore, -trice mf

fitting /'fɪtɪŋ/ a appropriato ● n (of clothes) prova f; Techn montaggio m; **~s** pl accessori mpl. **~ room** n camerino m

five /faɪv/ a & n cinque m. **~r** n fam biglietto m da cinque sterline

fix /fɪks/ n (sl: drugs) pera f; **be in a ~** fam essere nei guai ● vt fissare; (repair) aggiustare; preparare (meal). **fix up** vt fissare (meeting)

fixation /fɪk'seɪʃn/ n fissazione f

fixed /fɪkst/ a fisso

fixture /'fɪkstʃə(r)/ n Sport incontro m; **~s and fittings** impianti mpl fissi

fizz /fɪz/ vi frizzare

fizzle /'fɪzl/ vi **~ out** finire in nulla

fizzy /'fɪzɪ/ a gassoso. **~ drink** n bibita f gassata

flabbergasted /'flæbəgɑːstɪd/ a **be ~** rimanere a bocca aperta

flabby /'flæbɪ/ a floscio

flag¹ /flæg/ n bandiera f ● **flag down** vt (pt/pp flagged) far segno di fermarsi a (taxi)

flag² vi (pt/pp flagged) cedere

flag-pole n asta f della bandiera

flagrant /'fleɪgrənt/ a flagrante

flagship n Naut nave f ammiraglia; fig fiore m all'occhiello

flagstone n pietra f da lastricare

flair /fleə(r)/ n (skill) talento m; (style) stile m

flake /fleɪk/ n fiocco m ● vi **~ [off]** cadere in fiocchi

flaky /'fleɪkɪ/ a scaglie. **~ pastry** n pasta f sfoglia

flamboyant /flæm'bɔɪənt/ n (personality) brillante; (tie) sgargiante

flame /fleɪm/ n fiamma f

flammable /'flæməbl/ a infiammabile

flan /flæn/ n (fruit) ~ crostata f

flank /flæŋk/ n fianco m ● vt fiancheggiare

flannel /'flæn(ə)l/ n flanella f, (for washing) ≈ guanto m di spugna *(trousers)* pantaloni *mpl* di flanella

flannelette /flænə'let/ *n* flanella *f* di cotone

flap /flæp/ *n* *(of pocket, envelope)* risvolto *m*; *(of table)* ribalta *f*; in a ~ *fam* in grande agitazione ●*v* *(pt/pp* **flapped)** ●*vi* sbattere; *fam* agitarsi ●*vt* ~ **its wings** battere le ali

flare /fleə(r)/ *n* fiammata *f*; *(device)* razzo *m* ●**flare up** *vi* *(rash:)* venire fuori; *(fire:)* fare una fiammata; *(person, situation:)* esplodere. **~d** *a* *(garment)* svasato

flash /flæʃ/ *n* lampo *m*; **in a ~** *fam* in un attimo ●*vi* lampeggiare; **~ past** passare come un bolide ●*vt* lanciare *(smile)*; ~ **one's head-lights** lampeggiare; ~ **a torch** at puntare una torcia su

flash: **~back** *n* scena *f* retrospettiva. **~bulb** *n* Phot flash *m* *inv*. **~er** *n* Auto lampeggiatore *m*. **~light** *n* Phot flash *m* *inv*; *(Am: torch)* torcia *f* [elettrica]. **~y** *a* vistoso

flask /flɑːsk/ *n* fiasco *m*; *(vacuum* ~ termos *m* *inv*

flat /flæt/ *a* **(flatter, flattest)** piatto; *(refusal)* reciso; *(beer)* sgasato; *(battery)* scarico; *(tyre)* a terra; **A** ~ *Mus* la bemolle ●*n* appartamento *m*; *Mus* bemolle *m*; *(puncture)* gomma *f* a terra

flat: ~ **feet** *npl* piedi *mpl* piatti. **~-fish** *n* pesce *m* piatto. **~ly** *adv* *(refuse)* categoricamente. ~ **rate** *n* tariffa *f* unica

flatten /'flætn/ *vt* appiattire

flatter /'flætə(r)/ *vt* adulare. **~ing** *a* *(comments)* lusinghiero; *(colour, dress)* che fa sembrare più bello. **~y** *n* adulazione *f*

flat 'tyre *n* gomma *f* a terra

flaunt /flɔːnt/ *vt* ostentare

flautist /'flɔːtɪst/ *n* flautista *mf*

flavour /'fleɪvə(r)/ *n* sapore *m* ●*vt* condire; **chocolate ~ed** al sapore di cioccolato. **~ing** *n* condimento *m*

flaw /flɔː/ *n* difetto *m*. **~less** *a* perfetto

flax /flæks/ *n* lino *m*. **~en** *a* *(hair)* biondo platino

flea /fliː/ *n* pulce *m*. ~ **market** *n* mercato *m* delle pulci

fleck /flek/ *n* macchiolina *f*

fled /fled/ *see* **flee**

flee /fliː/ *vt/i* *(pt/pp* **fled)** fuggire **(from** da)

fleece /fliːs/ *n* pelliccia *f* ●*vt* *fam* spennare. **~y** *a* *(lining)* felpato

fleet /fliːt/ *n* flotta *f*; *(of cars)* parco *m*

fleeting /'fliːtɪŋ/ *a* **catch a ~ glance of sth** intravedere qcsa; **for a ~ moment** per un attimo

flesh /fleʃ/ *n* carne *f*; **in the ~** in persona. **~y** *a* carnoso

flew /fluː/ *see* **fly²**

flex¹ /fleks/ *vt* flettere *(muscle)*

flex² *n* Electr filo *m*

flexibility /fleksɪ'bɪlətɪ/ *n* flessibilità *f*. **~le** *a* flessibile

flexitime /'fleksɪ-/ *n* orario *m* flessibile

flick /flɪk/ *vt* dare un buffetto a; ~ **sth off sth** togliere qcsa da qcsa con un colpetto. **flick through** *vt* sfogliare

flicker /'flɪkə(r)/ *vi* tremolare

flier /'flaɪə(r)/ *n* = **flyer**

flight¹ /flaɪt/ *n* *(fleeing)* fuga *f*; **take ~** darsi alla fuga

flight² *n* *(flying)* volo *m*; ~ **of stairs** rampa *f*

flight: ~ **path** *n* traiettoria *f* di volo. ~ **recorder** *n* registratore *m* di volo

flighty /'flaɪtɪ/ *a* **(-ier, -iest)** frivolo

flimsy /'flɪmzɪ/ *a* **(-ier, -iest)** *(material)* leggero; *(shelves)* poco robusto; *(excuse)* debole

flinch /flɪntʃ/ *vi* *(wince)* sussultare; *(draw back)* ritirarsi; ~ **from a task** *fig* sottrarsi a un compito

fling /flɪŋ/ *n* **have a ~** *(fam: affair)* aver un'avventura ●*vt* *(pt/pp* **flung)** gettare

flint /flɪnt/ *n* pietra *f* focaia; *(for lighter)* pietrina *f*

flip /flɪp/ v (pt/pp flipped) ● vt dare un colpetto a; buttare in aria ⟨coin⟩ ● vi fam uscire dai gangheri; ⟨go mad⟩ impazzire. **flip through** vt sfogliare

flippant /'flɪpənt/ a irriverente

flipper /'flɪpə(r)/ n pinna f

flirt /flɜːt/ n civetta f ● vi flirtare

flirtation /flɜː'teɪʃn/ n flirt m inv. **~ious** /-ʃəs/ a civettuolo

flit /flɪt/ vi (pt/pp flitted) volteggiare

float /fləʊt/ n galleggiante m; (in procession) carro m; (money) riserva f di cassa ● vi galleggiare; Fin fluttuare

flock /flɒk/ n gregge m; (of birds) stormo m ● vi affollarsi

flog /flɒg/ vt (pt/pp flogged) bastonare; (fam: sell) vendere

flood /flʌd/ n alluvione f; (fig: of replies, letters, tears) diluvio m; **be in ~** ⟨river:⟩ essere straripato ● vt allagare ● vi ⟨river:⟩ straripare

floodlight n riflettore m ● vt (pt/pp floodlit) illuminare con riflettori

floor /flɔː(r)/ n pavimento m; (storey) piano m; (for dancing) pista f ● vt (baffle) confondere; (knock down) atterrare ⟨person⟩

floor: **~ board** n asse f del pavimento. **~-polish** n cera f per il pavimento. **~ show** n spettacolo m di varietà

flop /flɒp/ n fam (failure) tonfo m; Theat fiasco m ● vi (pt/pp flopped) (fam: fail) far fiasco. **flop down** vi accasciarsi

floppy /'flɒpɪ/ a floscio. **~ disk** n floppy disk m inv. **~ [disk] drive** n lettore di floppy m

flora /'flɔːrə/ n flora f

floral /'flɔːrəl/ a floreale

Florence /'florəns/ n Firenze f

florid /'florɪd/ a ⟨complexion⟩ florido; ⟨style⟩ troppo ricercato

florist /'florɪst/ n fioraio, -a mf

flounce /flaʊns/ n balza f ● vi **~ out** uscire con aria melodrammatica

flounder¹ /'flaʊndə(r)/ vi dibattersi; ⟨speaker:⟩ impappinarsi

flounder² n (fish) passera f di mare

flour /'flaʊə(r)/ n farina f

flourish /'flʌrɪʃ/ n gesto m drammatico; (scroll) ghirigoro m ● vi prosperare ● vt brandire

floury /'flaʊərɪ/ a farinoso

flout /flaʊt/ vt fregarsene di ⟨rules⟩

flow /fləʊ/ n flusso m ● vi scorrere; (hang loosely) ricadere

flower /'flaʊə(r)/ n fiore m ● vi fiorire

flower: **~-bed** n aiuola f. **~ed** a a fiori. **~pot** n vaso m [per i fiori]. **~y** a fiorito

flown /fləʊn/ see **fly²**

flu /fluː/ n influenza f

fluctuate /'flʌktjʊeɪt/ vi fluttuare. **~ion** /-'eɪʃn/ n fluttuazione f

fluent /'fluːənt/ a spedito; **speak ~ Italian** parlare correntemente l'italiano. **~ly** adv speditamente

fluff /flʌf/ n peluria f. **~y** a (-ier, -iest) vaporoso; ⟨toy⟩ di peluche

fluid /'fluːɪd/ a fluido ● n fluido m

fluke /fluːk/ n colpo m di fortuna

flung /flʌŋ/ see **fling**

flunk /flʌŋk/ vt Am fam essere bocciato in

fluorescent /flʊə'resnt/ a fluorescente

fluoride /'flʊəraɪd/ n fluoruro m

flurry /'flʌrɪ/ n (snow) raffica f; fig agitazione f

flush /flʌʃ/ n (blush) [vampata f di] rossore m ● vi arrossire ● vt lavare con un getto d'acqua; **~ the toilet** tirare l'acqua ● a a livello (with di); (fam: affluent) a soldi

flustered /'flʌstəd/ a in agitazione; **get ~** mettersi in agitazione

flute /fluːt/ n flauto m

flutter /'flʌtə(r)/ n battito m ● vi svolazzare

flux /flʌks/ n **In a state of ~** in uno stato di flusso

fly¹ /flaɪ/ n (pl flies) mosca f

fly² v (pt flew, pp flown) ● vi volare; ⟨*go by plane*⟩ andare in aereo; ⟨*flag:*⟩ sventolare; ⟨*rush*⟩ precipitarsi; ~ **open** spalancarsi ● *vt* pilotare ⟨*plane*⟩; trasportare [in aereo] ⟨*troops, supplies*⟩; volare con ⟨*Alitalia etc*⟩

fly[3] *n* & **flies** *pl* (on trousers) patta *f*

flyer /'flaɪə(r)/ *n* aviatore *m*; (*leaflet*) volantino *m*

flying /'flaɪɪŋ/: ~ **'buttress** *n* arco *m* rampante. ~ **'colours: with ~ colours** a pieni voti. ~ **'saucer** *n* disco *m* volante. ~ **'start** *n* **get off to a** ~ **start** fare un'ottima partenza. ~ **'visit** *n* visita *f* lampo

fly: ~ **leaf** *n* risguardo *m*. ~**over** *n* cavalcavia *m inv*

foal /fəʊl/ *n* puledro *m*

foam /fəʊm/ *n* schiuma *f*; (*synthetic*) gommapiuma® *f* ● *vi* spumare; ~ **at the mouth** far la bava alla bocca. ~ **'rubber** *n* gommapiuma® *f*

fob /fɒb/ *vt* (*pt/pp* **fobbed**) ~ **sth off** affibbiare qcsa (**on sb** a qcno); ~ **sb off** liquidare qcno

focal /'fəʊkl/ *a* focale

focus /'fəʊkəs/ *n* fuoco *m*; **in** ~ a fuoco; **out of** ~ sfocato ● *v* (*pt/pp* **focused** *or* **focussed**) ● *vt* fig concentrare (**on** su) ● *vi* Phot ~ **on** mettere a fuoco; fig concentrarsi (**on** su)

fodder /'fɒdə(r)/ *n* foraggio *m*

foe /fəʊ/ *n* nemico, -a *mf*

foetus /'fi:təs/ *n* (*pl* -**tuses**) feto *m*

fog /fɒg/ *n* nebbia *f*

fogey /'fəʊgɪ/ *n* **old** ~ persona *f* antiquata

foggy /'fɒgɪ/ *a* (**foggier, foggiest**) nebbioso; **it's** ~ c'è nebbia

'fog-horn *n* sirena *f* da nebbia

foil[1] /fɔɪl/ *n* lamina *f* di metallo

foil[2] *vt* (*thwart*) frustrare

foil[3] *n* (*sword*) fioretto *m*

foist /fɔɪst/ *vt* appioppare (**on sb** a qcno)

fold[1] /fəʊld/ *n* (*for sheep*) ovile *m*

fold[2] *n* piega *f* ● *vt* piegare; ~ **one's arms** incrociare le braccia ● *vi* piegarsi; (*fail*) crollare. **fold up** *vt*

ripiegare ⟨*chair*⟩ ● *vi* essere pieghevole; ⟨*fam: business:*⟩ collassare

fold|er /'fəʊldə(r)/ *n* cartella *f*. ~**ing** *a* pieghevole

foliage /'fəʊlɪɪdʒ/ *n* fogliame *m*

folk /fəʊk/ *npl* gente *f*; **my** ~**s** (*family*) i miei; **hello there** ~**s** ciao a tutti

folk: ~**dance** *n* danza *f* popolare. ~**lore** *n* folclore *m*. ~**song** *n* canto *m* popolare

follow /'fɒləʊ/ *vt/i* seguire; **it doesn't** ~ non è necessariamente così; ~ **suit** *fig* fare lo stesso; **as** ~**s** come segue. **follow up** *vt* fare seguito a ⟨*letter*⟩

follow|er /'fɒləʊə(r)/ *n* seguace *mf*. ~**ing** *a* seguente ● *n* seguito *m*; (*supporters*) seguaci *mpl* ● *prep* in seguito a

folly /'fɒlɪ/ *n* follia *f*

fond /fɒnd/ *a* affezionato; ⟨*hope*⟩ vivo; **be** ~ **of** essere appassionato di ⟨*music*⟩; **I'm** ~ **of...** ⟨*food, person*⟩ mi piace moltissimo...

fondle /'fɒndl/ *vt* coccolare

fondness /'fɒndnɪs/ *n* affetto *m*; (*for things*) amore *m*

font /fɒnt/ *n* fonte *f* battesimale; *Typ* carattere *m* di stampa

food /fu:d/ *n* cibo *m*; (*for animals, groceries*) mangiare *m*; **let's buy some** ~ compriamo qualcosa da mangiare

food: ~ **mixer** *n* frullatore *m*. ~ **poisoning** *n* intossicazione *f* alimentare. ~ **processor** *n* tritatutto *m inv* elettrico

fool[1] /fu:l/ *n* sciocco, -a *mf*; **she's no** ~ non è una stupida; **make a** ~ **of oneself** rendersi ridicolo ● *vt* prendere in giro ● *vi* ~ **around** giocare; ⟨*husband, wife:*⟩ avere l'amante

fool[2] *n* Culin crema *f*

'fool|hardy *a* temerario. ~**ish** *a* stolto. ~**ishly** *adv* scioccamente. ~**ishness** *n* sciocchezza *f*. ~**proof** *a* facilissimo

foot /fʊt/ *n* (*pl* **feet**) piede *m*; (*of*

animal) zampa *f*; (*measure*) piede *m* (= 30,48 cm); on ~ a piedi; on one's feet in piedi; put one's ~ in it *fam* fare una gaffe

foot: **~-and-'mouth disease** *n* afta *f* epizootica. **~ball** *n* calcio *m*; (*ball*) pallone *m*. **~baller** *n* giocatore *m* di calcio. **~ball pools** *npl* totocalcio *m*. **~brake** *n* freno *m* a pedale. **~bridge** *n* passerella *f*. **~hills** *npl* colline *fpl* pedemontane. **~hold** *n* punto *m* d'appoggio. **~ing** *n* lose one's ~ing perdere l'appiglio; on an equal ~ing in condizioni di parità. **~man** *n* valletto *m*. **~note** *n* nota *f* a piè di pagina. **~path** *n* sentiero *m*. **~print** *n* orma *f*. **~step** *n* passo *m*; follow in sb's ~steps *fig* seguire l'esempio di qcno. **~stool** *n* sgabello *m*. **~wear** *n* calzature *fpl*

for /fə(r)/, *accentato* /fɔː(r)/ *prep* per; **~ this reason** per questa ragione; **I have lived here ~ ten years** vivo qui da dieci anni; **~ supper** per cena; **~ all** that nonostante questo; **what ~?** a che scopo?; **send ~ a doctor** chiamare un dottore; **fight ~ a cause** lottare per una causa; **go ~ a walk** andare a fare una passeggiata; **there's no need ~** you to say non c'è bisogno che tu veda; **it's not ~ me to say** non sta a me dirlo; **now you're ~ it** ora sei nei pasticci ● *conj* poiché, perché

forage /ˈfɒrɪdʒ/ *n* foraggio *m* ● *vt* ~ **for** cercare

forbade /fəˈbæd/ *see* forbid

forbear|ance /fɔːˈbeərəns/ *n* pazienza *f*. **~ing** *a* tollerante

forbid /fəˈbɪd/ *vt* (*pt* forbade, *pp* forbidden) proibire. ~thing a (*prospect*) che spaventa, (*stern*) severo

force /fɔːs/ *n* forza *f*; in ~ in vigore; (*in large numbers*) in massa; come into ~ entrare in vigore; the [armed] ~s *pl* le forze armate ● *vt* forzare; ~ **sth on** sb (*decision*) imporre qcsa a qcno;

(*drink*) costringere qcno a fare qcsa

forced /fɔːst/ *a* forzato

force: **~'feed** *vt* (*pt/pp* -fed) nutrire a forza. **~ful** *a* energico. **~fully** *adv* (*say*, *argue*) con forza

forceps /ˈfɔːseps/ *npl* forcipe *m*

forcible /ˈfɔːsɪbl/ *a* forzato

ford /fɔːd/ *n* guado *m* ● *vt* guadare

fore /fɔː(r)/ *n* to the ~ in vista; come to the ~ salire alla ribalta

fore: **~arm** *n* avambraccio *m*. **~boding** /-ˈbəʊdɪŋ/ *n* presentimento *m*. **~cast** *n* previsione *f* ● *vt* (*pt/pp* ~cast) prevedere. **~court** *n* cortile *m* anteriore. **~fathers** *npl* antenati *mpl*. **~finger** *n* [dito *m*] indice *m*. **~front** *n* be in the **~front** essere all'avanguardia. **~gone** *a* be a **~gone conclusion** essere una cosa scontata. **~ground** *n* primo piano *m*. **~head** /ˈfɔːhed, ˈfɒrɪd/ *n* fronte *f*. **~hand** *n Tennis* diritto *m*

foreign /ˈfɒrən/ *a* straniero; (*trade*) estero; (*not belonging*) estraneo; **he is ~** è uno straniero. **~ currency** *n* valuta *f* estera. **~er** *n* straniero, -a *mf*. **~ language** *n* lingua *f* straniera

Foreign: **~ Office** *n* ministero *m* degli [affari] esteri. **~ 'Secretary** *n* ministro *m* degli esteri

fore: **~man** *n* caporeparto *m*. **~most** *a* principale ● *adv* first and **~most** in primo luogo. **~name** *n* nome *m* di battesimo

forensic /fəˈrensɪk/ *a* ~ medicine medicina *f* legale

'forerunner *n* precursore *m*

fore'see *vt* (*pt* -saw, *pp* -seen) prevedere. **~able** /-əbl/ *a* in the **~able future** in futuro per quanto si possa prevedere

'foresight *n* previdenza *f*

forest /ˈfɒrɪst/ *n* foresta *f*. **~er** *n* guardia *f* forestale

fore'stall *vt* prevenire

forestry /ˈfɒrɪstrɪ/ *n* silvicoltura *f*

'foretaste *n* pregustazione *f*

fore'tell *vt* (*pt/pp* -told) predire

forever /fə'revə(r)/ *adv* per sempre; **he's ~ complaining** si lamenta sempre

fore'warn *vt* avvertire

foreword /'fɔːwɜːd/ *n* prefazione *f*

forfeit /'fɔːfɪt/ *n* (*in game*) pegno *m*; *Jur* penalità *f* ● *vt* perdere

forgave /fə'geɪv/ *see* **forgive**

forge[1] /fɔːdʒ/ *vi* **~ ahead** ⟨*runner:*⟩ lasciarsi indietro gli altri; *fig* farsi strada

forge[2] *n* fucina *f* ● *vt* fucinare; (*counterfeit*) contraffare. **~r** *n* contraffattore *m*. **~ry** *n* contraffazione *f*

forget /fə'get/ *vt/i* (*pt* **-got**, *pp* **-gotten**, *pres p* **-getting**) dimenticare; dimenticarsi di ⟨*language, skill*⟩. **~ful** *a* smemorato. **~fulness** *n* smemoratezza *f*. **~-me-not** *n* non-ti-scordar-di-mé *m inv*. **~table** /-əbl/ *a* ⟨*day, film*⟩ da dimenticare

forgive /fə'gɪv/ *vt* (*pt* **-gave**, *pp* **-given**) **~ sb for sth** perdonare qcno per qcsa. **~ness** *n* perdono *m*

forgo /fɔː'gəʊ/ *vt* (*pt* **-went**, *pp* **-gone**) rinunciare a

forgot(ten) /fə'gɒt(n)/ *see* **forget**

fork /fɔːk/ *n* forchetta *f*; (*for digging*) forca *f*; (*in road*) bivio *m* ● *vi* ⟨*road:*⟩ biforcarsi. **~ right** prendere a destra. **fork out** *vt fam* sborsare

fork-lift 'truck *n* elevatore *m*

forlorn /fə'lɔːn/ *a* ⟨*look*⟩ perduto; (*place*) derelitto; **~ hope** speranza *f* vana

form /fɔːm/ *n* forma *f*; (*document*) modulo *m*; *Sch* classe *f* ● *vt* formare; formulare ⟨*opinion*⟩ ● *vi* formarsi

formal /'fɔːml/ *a* formale. **~ity** /-'mælɪtɪ/ *n* formalità *f inv*. **~ly** *adv* in modo formale; (*officially*) ufficialmente

format /'fɔːmæt/ *n* formato *m* ● *vt* formattare ⟨*disk, page*⟩

formation /fɔː'meɪʃn/ *n* formazione *f*

formative /'fɔːmətɪv/ *a* **~ years** anni *mpl* formativi

former /'fɔːmə(r)/ *a* precedente; ⟨*PM, colleague*⟩ ex; **the ~, the latter** il primo, l'ultimo. **~ly** *adv* precedentemente; (*in olden times*) in altri tempi

formidable /'fɔːmɪdəbl/ *a* formidabile

formula /'fɔːmjʊlə/ *n* (*pl* **-ae** /-liː/ *or* **-s**) formula *f*

formulate /'fɔːmjʊleɪt/ *vt* formulare

forsake /fə'seɪk/ *vt* (*pt* **-sook** /-sʊk/, *pp* **-saken**) abbandonare

fort /fɔːt/ *n Mil* forte *m*

forte /'fɔːteɪ/ *n* [pezzo *m*] forte *m*

forth /fɔːθ/ *adv* **back and ~** avanti e indietro; **and so ~** e così via

forth: **~'coming** *a* prossimo; (*communicative*) communicativo; **no response was ~** non arrivava nessuna risposta. **~right** *a* schietto. **~with** *adv* immediatamente

fortieth /'fɔːtɪɪθ/ *a* quarantesimo

fortification /fɔːtɪfɪ'keɪʃn/ *n* fortificazione *f*

fortify /'fɔːtɪfaɪ/ *vt* (*pt/pp* **-ied**) fortificare; *fig* rendere forte

fortnight /'fɔːtnaɪt/ *n Br* quindicina *f*. **~ly** *a* bimensile ● *adv* ogni due settimane

fortress /'fɔːtrɪs/ *n* fortezza *f*

fortuitous /fɔː'tjuːɪtəs/ *a* fortuito

fortunate /'fɔːtʃənət/ *a* fortunato; **that's ~!** meno male!. **~ly** *adv* fortunatamente

fortune /'fɔːtʃuːn/ *n* fortuna *f*. **~-teller** *n* indovino, -a *mf*

forty /'fɔːtɪ/ *a & n* quaranta *m*

forum /'fɔːrəm/ *n* foro *m*

forward /'fɔːwəd/ *adv* avanti; (*towards the front*) in avanti ● *a* in avanti; (*presumptuous*) sfacciato ● *n Sport* attaccante *m* ● *vt* inoltrare ⟨*letter*⟩; spedire ⟨*goods*⟩. **~s** *adv* avanti

fossil /'fɒsl/ *n* fossile *m*. **~ized** *a* fossile; ⟨*ideas*⟩ fossilizzato

foster /'fɒstə(r)/ *vt* allevare ⟨*child*⟩

~-**child** n figlio, -a mf in affidamento. ~-**mother** n madre f affidataria

fought /fɔ:t/ see **fight**

foul /faul/ a ⟨smell, taste⟩ cattivo; ⟨air⟩ viziato; ⟨language⟩ osceno; ⟨mood, weather⟩ orrendo; ~ **play** Jur delitto m ● n Sport fallo m ● vt inquinare ⟨water⟩; Sport commettere un fallo contro; ⟨nets, rope⟩ impigliarsi in. ~-**smelling** a puzzo

found[1] /faund/ see **find**

found[2] vt fondare

foundation /faun'deɪʃn/ n ⟨basis⟩ fondamento m; ⟨charitable⟩ fondazione f; ~s pl ⟨of building⟩ fondamenta fpl; **lay the** ~-**stone** porre la prima pietra

founder[1] /'faundə(r)/ n fondatore, -trice mf

founder[2] vi ⟨ship:⟩ affondare

foundry /'faundri/ n fonderia f

fountain /'fauntɪn/ n fontana f. ~-**pen** n penna f stilografica

four /fɔ:(r)/ a & n quattro m

four: ~-**poster** n letto m a baldacchino. ~-**some** /'fɔ:səm/ n quartetto m. ~-**teen** a & n quattordici m. ~-**teenth** a quattordicesimo

fourth /fɔ:θ/ a quarto

fowl /faul/ n pollame m

fox /fɒks/ n volpe f ● vt ⟨puzzle⟩ ingannare

foyer /'fɔɪeɪ/ n Theat ridotto m; ⟨in hotel⟩ salone m d'ingresso

fraction /'frækʃn/ n frazione f

fracture /'fræktʃə(r)/ n frattura f ● vt fratturare ● vi fratturarsi

fragile /'frædʒaɪl/ a fragile

fragment /'frægmənt/ n frammento m. ~**ary** a frammentario

fragran|ce /'freɪgrəns/ n fragranza f. ~**t** a fragrante

frail /freɪl/ a gracile

frame /freɪm/ n ⟨of picture, door, window⟩ cornice f; ⟨of spectacles⟩ montatura f; Anat ossatura f; ⟨structure, of bike⟩ telaio m; ~ **of mind** stato m d'animo ● vt incorniciare ⟨picture⟩; fig formulare;

⟨sl: incriminate⟩ montare. ~**work** n struttura f

franc /fræŋk/ n franco m

France /frɑ:ns/ n Francia f

franchise /'fræntʃaɪz/ n Pol diritto m di voto; Comm franchigia f

frank[1] /fræŋk/ vt affrancare ⟨letter⟩

frank[2] a franco. ~**ly** adv francamente

frankfurter /'fræŋkfə:tə(r)/ n würstel m inv

frantic /'fræntɪk/ a frenetico; **be** ~ **with worry** essere agitatissimo. ~**ally** adv freneticamente

fraternal /frə'tɜ:nl/ a fraterno

fraud /frɔ:d/ n frode f; ⟨person⟩ impostore m. ~**ulent** /-julənt/ a fraudolento

fraught /frɔ:t/ a ~ **with** pieno di

fray[1] /freɪ/ n mischia f

fray[2] vi sfilacciarsi

frayed /freɪd/ a ⟨cuffs⟩ sfilacciato; ⟨nerves⟩ a pezzi

freak /fri:k/ n fenomeno m; ⟨person⟩ scherzo m di natura; ⟨fam: weird person⟩ tipo m strambo ● a anormale. ~**ish** a strambo

freckle /'frekl/ n lentiggine f. ~**d** a lentigginoso

free /fri:/ a (**freer, freest**) libero m; ⟨ticket, copy⟩ gratuito; ⟨lavish⟩ generoso; ~ **of charge** gratuito; **set** ~ liberare ● vt ⟨pt/pp **freed**⟩ liberare

free: ~**dom** n libertà f. ~**hand** adv a mano libera. ~**hold** n proprietà f ⟨fondiaria⟩ assoluta. ~ '**kick** n calcio m di punizione. ~**lance** a & adv indipendente. ~**ly** adv liberamente; ⟨generously⟩ generosamente; **I** ~**ly admit that...** devo ammettere che... **F**~**mason** n massone m. ~**-range** a ~**-range egg** uovo m di gallina ruspante. ~**sample** n campione m gratuito. ~**style** n stile m. ~**way** n Am autostrada f. ~'**wheel** vi ⟨car:⟩ ⟨in neutral⟩ andare in folle; ⟨with engine switched off⟩ andare a motore spento; ⟨bicycle:⟩ andare a ruota libera

freez|e /friːz/ vt (pt **froze**, pp **frozen**⟩ gelare; bloccare ⟨wages⟩ ● vi (water:⟩ gelare; **it's ~ing** si gela; **my hands are ~ing** ho le mani congelate

freezer /ˈfriːzə(r)/ n freezer m inv, congelatore m. **~ing** a gelido ● n **below ~ing** sotto zero

freight /freɪt/ n carico m. **~er** n nave f da carico. **~ train** n Am treno m merci

French /frentʃ/ a francese ● n ⟨language⟩ francese m; **the ~** pl i francesi mpl

French: **~ beans** npl fagiolini mpl ⟨verdi⟩. **~ bread** n filone m ⟨di pane⟩. **~ fries** npl patate fpl fritte. **~man** n francese m. **~ window** n porta-finestra f. **~woman** n francese f

frenzied /ˈfrenzɪd/ a frenetico

frenzy /ˈfrenzɪ/ n frenesia f

frequency /ˈfriːkwənsɪ/ n frequenza f

frequent¹ /ˈfriːkwənt/ a frequente. **~ly** adv frequentemente

frequent² /frɪˈkwent/ vt frequentare

fresco /ˈfreskəʊ/ n affresco m

fresh /freʃ/ a fresco; ⟨new⟩ nuovo; ⟨Am: cheeky⟩ sfacciato. **~ly** adv di recente

freshen /ˈfreʃn/ vi ⟨wind:⟩ rinfrescare. **freshen up** vi fare una rinfrescata a ● vi rinfrescarsi

freshness /ˈfreʃnɪs/ n freschezza f

freshwater a di acqua dolce

fret /fret/ vi (pt/pp **fretted**) inquietarsi. **~ful** a irritabile

fretsaw n seghetto m da traforo

friar /ˈfraɪə(r)/ n frate m

friction /ˈfrɪkʃn/ n frizione f

Friday /ˈfraɪdeɪ/ n venerdì m inv

fridge /frɪdʒ/ n frigo m

fried /fraɪd/ see **fry** ● a fritto; **~ egg** uovo m fritto

friend /frend/ n amico, -a mf. **~ly** a (-ier, -iest) ⟨relations, meeting, match⟩ amichevole; ⟨neighbour-

hood, smile⟩ piacevole; ⟨software⟩ di facile uso; **be ~ly with** essere amico di. **~ship** n amicizia f

frieze /friːz/ n fregio m

fright /fraɪt/ n paura f; **take ~** spaventarsi

frighten /ˈfraɪtn/ vt spaventare. **~ed** a spaventato; **be ~ed** aver paura ⟨of di⟩. **~ing** a spaventoso

frightful /ˈfraɪtfl/ a terribile

frigid /ˈfrɪdʒɪd/ a frigido. **~ity** /-ˈdʒɪdətɪ/ n freddezza f, Psych frigidità f

frill /frɪl/ n volant m inv. **~y** a ⟨dress⟩ con tanti volant

fringe /frɪndʒ/ n frangia f; ⟨of hair⟩ frangetta f; ⟨fig: edge⟩ margine m. **~ benefits** npl benefici mpl supplementari

frisk /frɪsk/ vt ⟨search⟩ perquisire

frisky /ˈfrɪskɪ/ a (-ier, -iest) vispo

fritter /ˈfrɪtə(r)/ n frittella f ● **fritter away** vt sprecare

frivol|ity /frɪˈvɒlətɪ/ n frivolezza f. **~ous** /ˈfrɪvələs/ a frivolo

frizzy /ˈfrɪzɪ/ a crespo

fro /frəʊ/ see **to**

frock /frɒk/ n abito m

frog /frɒg/ n rana f. **~man** n uomo m rana

frolic /ˈfrɒlɪk/ vi (pt/pp **frolicked**) ⟨lambs:⟩ sgambettare; ⟨people:⟩ folleggiare

from /frɒm/ prep da; **~ Monday** da lunedì; **~ that day** da quel giorno; **he's ~ London** è di Londra; **this is a letter ~ my brother** questa è una lettera di mio fratello; **documents ~ the 16th century** documenti del XVI secolo; **made ~** fatto con; **she felt ill ~ fatigue** si sentiva male dalla stanchezza; **~ now on** d'ora in poi

front /frʌnt/ n parte f anteriore; ⟨fig: organization etc⟩ facciata f; ⟨of garment⟩ davanti m; ⟨sea⟩ lungomare m; Mil, Pol, Meteorol fronte m; **in ~** davanti a; **in or at the ~** davanti; **to the ~** avanti ● a davanti; ⟨page, row, wheel⟩ anteriore

frontal /ˈfrʌntl/ a frontale

front: ~ **'door** n porta f d'entrata. ~ **'garden** n giardino m d'avanti

frontier /'frʌntɪə(r)/ n frontiera f

front-wheel '**drive** n trazione f anteriore

frost /frɒst/ n gelo m, (hoar~) brina f. ~**bite** n congelamento m. ~**bitten** a congelato

frost|ed /'frɒstɪd/ a ~**ed glass** vetro m smerigliato. ~**ily** adv gelidamente. ~**ing** n Am Culin glassa f. ~**y** a also fig gelido

froth /frɒθ/ n schiuma f ●vi far schiuma. ~**y** a schiumoso

frown /fraʊn/ n cipiglio m ●vi aggrottare le sopracciglia. **frown on** vt disapprovare

froze /frəʊz/ see **freeze**

frozen /'frəʊzn/ see **freeze** ●a (corpse, hand) congelato; (wastes) gelido; Culin surgelato; **I'm** ~ sono gelato. ~ **food** n surgelati mpl

frugal /'fru:ɡl/ a frugale

fruit /fru:t/ n frutto m; (collectively) frutta f; **eat more** ~ mangia più frutta. ~ **cake** n dolce m con frutta candita

fruit|erer /'fru:tərə(r)/ n fruttivendolo, -a mf. ~**ful** a fig fruttuoso

fruition /fru:'ɪʃn/ n **come to** ~ dare dei frutti

fruit: ~ **juice** n succo m di frutta. ~**less** a infruttuoso. ~ **machine** n macchinetta f mangiasoldi. ~ '**salad** n macedonia f [di frutta]

frumpy /'frʌmpɪ/ a scialbo

frustrat|e /frʌ'streɪt/ vt frustrare; rovinare (plans). ~**ing** a frustrante. ~**ion** /-eɪʃn/ n frustrazione f

fry[1] /fraɪ/ vt/i (pt/pp **fried**) friggere

fry[2] /fraɪ/ n inv **small** ~ fig pesce m piccolo

frying pan n padella f

fuck /fʌk/ vulg vt/i scopare ●int cazzo. ~**ing** a del cazzo

fuddy-duddy /'fʌdɪdʌdɪ/ n fam matusa mf inv

fudge /fʌdʒ/ n caramella f a base di zucchero, burro e latte

fuel /'fju:əl/ n carburante m; fig nutrimento m ●vt fig alimentare

fugitive /'fju:dʒɪtɪv/ n fuggiasco, -a mf

fugue /fju:ɡ/ n Mus fuga f

fulfil /fʊl'fɪl/ vt (pt/pp **-filled**) soddisfare (conditions, need); realizzare (dream, desire); ~ **oneself** realizzarsi. ~**ling** a soddisfacente. ~**ment** n senso of ~**ment** senso m di appagamento

full /fʊl/ a pieno (**of** di); (detailed) esauriente; (bus, hotel) completo; (skirt) ampio; **at** ~ **speed** a tutta velocità; **in** ~ **swing** in pieno fervore ●n **in** ~ per intero

full: ~ '**moon** n luna f piena. ~**-scale** a (model) in scala reale; (alert) di massima gravità. ~ '**stop** n punto m. ~**-time** a & adv a tempo pieno

fully /'fʊlɪ/ adv completamente; (in detail) dettagliatamente; ~ **booked** (hotel, restaurant) tutto prenotato

fumble /'fʌmbl/ vi ~ **in** rovistare in; ~ **with** armeggiare con; ~ **for one's keys** rovistare alla ricerca delle chiavi

fume /fju:m/ vi (be angry) essere furioso

fumes /fju:mz/ npl fumi mpl; (from car) gas mpl di scarico

fumigate /'fju:mɪɡeɪt/ vt suffumicare

fun /fʌn/ n divertimento m; **for** ~ per ridere; **make** ~ **of** prendere in giro; **have** ~ divertirsi

function /'fʌŋkʃn/ n funzione f; (event) cerimonia f ●vi funzionare; ~ **as** (serve as) funzionare da ~**al** a funzionale

fund /fʌnd/ n fondo m; fig pozzo m; ~**s** pl fondi mpl ●vt finanziare

fundamental /fʌndə'mentl/ a fondamentale

funeral /'fju:nərəl/ n funerale m

funeral: ~ **directors** n impresa f di pompe funebri. ~ **home** Am, ~ **parlour** n camera f ardente. ~

march n marcia f funebre. **~ service** n rito m funebre

'funfair n luna park m inv

fungus /ˈfʌŋgəs/ n (pl -gi /-gaɪ/) fungo m

funicular /fjuːˈnɪkjʊlə(r)/ n funicolare f

funnel /ˈfʌnl/ n imbuto m; (on ship) ciminiera f

funnily /ˈfʌnɪlɪ/ adv comicamente; (oddly) stranamente; **~ enough** strano a dirsi

funny /ˈfʌnɪ/ a (-ier, -iest) buffo; (odd) strano. **~ business** n affare m losco

fur /fɜː(r)/ n pelo m; (for clothing) pelliccia f; (in kettle) deposito m. **~ 'coat** n pelliccia f

furious /ˈfjʊərɪəs/ a furioso

furnace /ˈfɜːnɪs/ n fornace f

furnish /ˈfɜːnɪʃ/ vt ammobiliare (flat); fornire (supplies). **~ed** a **~ed room** stanza f ammobiliata. **~ings** npl mobili mpl

furniture /ˈfɜːnɪtʃə(r)/ n mobili mpl

furred /fɜːd/ a (tongue) impastato

furrow /ˈfʌrəʊ/ n solco m

furry /ˈfɜːrɪ/ a (animal) peloso; (toy) di peluche

further /ˈfɜːðə(r)/ a (additional) ulteriore; **at the ~ end** all'altra estremità; **until ~ notice** fino a nuovo avviso ● adv più lontano; **~,...** inoltre,...; **~ off** più lontano ● vt promuovere

further: **~ edu'cation** n ≈ formazione f parauniversitaria. **~'more** adv per di più

furthest /ˈfɜːðɪst/ a più lontano ● adv più lontano

furtive /ˈfɜːtɪv/ a furtivo

fury /ˈfjʊərɪ/ n furore m

fuse¹ /fjuːz/ n (of bomb) detonatore m; (cord) miccia f

fuse² n Electr fusibile m ● vt fondere; Electr far saltare ● vi fondersi; Electr saltare; **the lights have ~d** sono saltate le luci. **~-box** n scatola f dei fusibili

fuselage /ˈfjuːzəlɑːʒ/ n Aeron fusoliera f

fusion /ˈfjuːʒn/ n fusione f

fuss /fʌs/ n storie fpl; **make a ~** fare storie; **make a ~ of** colmare di attenzioni ● vi fare storie

fussy /ˈfʌsɪ/ a (-ier, -iest) (person) difficile da accontentare; (clothes etc) pieno di fronzoli

fusty /ˈfʌstɪ/ a che odora di stantio; (smell) di stantio

futile /ˈfjuːtaɪl/ a inutile. **~ity** /-ˈtɪlətɪ/ n futilità f

future /ˈfjuːtʃə(r)/ a & n futuro; **in ~** in futuro. **~ perfect** futuro anteriore

futuristic /fjuːtʃəˈrɪstɪk/ a futuristico

fuzz /fʌz/ n **the ~** (sl: police) la pula

fuzzy /ˈfʌzɪ/ a (-ier, -iest) (hair) crespo; (photo) sfuocato

Gg

gab /gæb/ n fam **have the gift of the ~** avere la parlantina

gabble /ˈgæb(ə)l/ vi parlare troppo in fretta

gad /gæd/ vi (pt/pp gadded) **~ about** andarsene in giro

gadget /ˈgædʒɪt/ n aggeggio m

Gaelic /ˈgeɪlɪk/ a & n gaelico m

gaffe /gæf/ n gaffe f inv

gag /gæg/ n bavaglio m; (joke) battuta f ● vt (pt/pp gagged) imbavagliare

gaily /ˈgeɪlɪ/ adv allegramente

gain /geɪn/ n guadagno m; (increase) aumento m ● vt acquisire; **~ weight** aumentare di peso; **~ access** accedere ● vi (clock:) andare avanti. **~ful** a **~ful employment** lavoro m remunerativo

gait /geɪt/ n andatura f

gala /ˈgɑːlə/ n gala f; **swimming ~** manifestazione f di nuoto ● attrib di gala

415								**galaxy | gasoline**

galaxy /'gæləksɪ/ n galassia f
gale /geɪl/ n bufera f
gall /gɔːl/ n (impudence) impudenza f
gallant /'gælənt/ a coraggioso; (chivalrous) galante. **~ry** n coraggio m
'gall-bladder n cistifellea f
gallery /'gælərɪ/ n galleria f
galley /'gælɪ/ n (ship's kitchen) cambusa f; **~** [proof] bozza f in colonna
gallivant /'gælɪvænt/ vi fam andare in giro
gallon /'gælən/ n gallone m (= 4,5 l; Am = 3,7 l)
gallop /'gæləp/ n galoppo m ●vi galoppare
gallows /'gæləʊz/ n forca f
'gallstone n calcolo m biliare
galore /gə'lɔː(r)/ adv a bizzeffe
galvanize /'gælvənaɪz/ vt Techn galvanizzare; fig stimolare (**into** a)
gambit /'gæmbɪt/ n prima mossa f
gamble /'gæmbl/ n (risk) azzardo m ●vi giocare; (on Stock Exchange) speculare; **~e on** (rely) contare su. **~er** n giocatore, -trice mf [d'azzardo]. **~ing** n gioco m [d'azzardo]
game /geɪm/ n gioco m; (match) partita f; (animals, birds) selvaggina f; **~s** Sch ≈ ginnastica f ●a (brave) coraggioso; **are you ~?** ti va?; **be ~ for** essere pronto per
~keeper n guardacaccia m inv
gammon /'gæmən/ n coscia f di maiale
gamut /'gæmət/ n fig gamma f
gander /'gændə(r)/ n oca f maschio
gang /gæŋ/ n banda f; (of workmen) squadra f ●**gang up** vi far comunella (**on** contro)
gangling /'gæŋglɪŋ/ a spilungone
gangrene /'gæŋgriːn/ n cancrena f
gangster /'gæŋstə(r)/ n gangster m inv
gangway /'gæŋweɪ/ n passaggio m; Naut, Aeron passerella f

gaol /dʒeɪl/ n carcere m ●vt incarcerare. **~er** n carceriere m
gap /gæp/ n spazio m; (in ages, between teeth) scarto m; (in memory) vuoto m; (in story) punto m oscuro
gape /geɪp/ vi stare a bocca aperta; (be wide open) spalancarsi; **~e at** guardare a bocca aperta. **~ing** a aperto
garage /'gærɑːʒ/ n garage m inv; (for repairs) meccanico m; (for petrol) stazione f di servizio
garbage /'gɑːbɪdʒ/ n immondizia f; (nonsense) idiozie fpl. **~ can** n Am bidone m dell'immondizia
garbled /'gɑːbld/ a confuso
garden /'gɑːdn/ n giardino m; [public] **~s** pl giardini mpl pubblici ●vi fare giardinaggio. **~ centre** n negozio m di piante e articoli da giardinaggio. **~er** n giardiniere, -a mf. **~ing** n giardinaggio m
gargle /'gɑːgl/ n gargarismo m ●vi fare gargarismi
gargoyle /'gɑːgɔɪl/ n gargouille f
garish /'geərɪʃ/ a sgargiante
garland /'gɑːlənd/ n ghirlanda f
garlic /'gɑːlɪk/ n aglio m. **~ bread** n pane m condito con aglio
garment /'gɑːmənt/ n indumento m
garnish /'gɑːnɪʃ/ n guarnizione f ●vt guarnire
garrison /'gærɪsn/ n guarnigione f
garter /'gɑːtə(r)/ n giarrettiera f; (Am: for man's socks) reggicalze m inv da uomo
gas /gæs/ n gas m inv; (Am fam: petrol) benzina f ●v (pt/pp **gassed**) ●vt assfissiare ●vi fam blaterare. **~ cooker** n cucina f a gas. **~ fire** n stufa f a gas
gash /gæʃ/ n taglio m ●vt tagliare
gasket /'gæskɪt/ n Techn guarnizione f
gas: ~ mask n maschera f antigas. **~-meter** n contatore m del gas
gasoline /'gæsəliːn/ n Am benzina f

gasp /gɑ:sp/ vi avere il fiato mozzato

'gas station n Am distributore m di benzina

gastric /'gæstrɪk/ a gastrico. ~ 'flu n influenza f gastro-intestinale. ~ 'ulcer n ulcera f gastrica

gastronomy /gæ'strɒnəmɪ/ n gastronomia f

gate /geɪt/ n cancello m; (at airport) uscita f

gâteau /'gætəʊ/ n torta f

gate: ~crash vt entrare senza invito a. ~crasher n intruso, -a mf. ~way n ingresso m

gather /'gæðə(r)/ vt raccogliere; (conclude) dedurre; (in sewing) arricciare; ~ speed acquistare velocità; ~ together radunare ⟨people, belongings⟩; (obtain gradually) acquistare ● vi ⟨people⟩ radunarsi. ~ing n family ~ing ritrovo m di famiglia

gaudy /'gɔ:dɪ/ a (-ier, -iest) pacchiano

gauge /geɪdʒ/ n calibro m; Rail scartamento m; (device) indicatore m ● vt misurare; fig stimare

gaunt /gɔ:nt/ a (thin) smunto

gauze /gɔ:z/ n garza f

gave /geɪv/ see give

gawky /'gɔ:kɪ/ a (-ier, -iest) sgraziato

gawp /gɔ:p/ vi ~ [at] fam guardare con aria da ebete

gay /geɪ/ a gaio; (homosexual) omosessuale; ⟨bar, club⟩ gay

gaze /geɪz/ n sguardo m fisso ● vi guardare; ~ at fissare

GB abbr (Great Britain) GB

gear /gɪə(r)/ n equipaggiamento m; Techn ingranaggio m; Auto marcia f; in ~ con la marcia innestata; change ~ cambiare marcia ● vt finalizzare (to a)

gear: ~box n Auto scatola f del cambio. ~-lever, Am ~-shift n leva f del cambio

geese /gi:s/ see goose

geezer /'gi:zə(r)/ n sl tipo m

gel /dʒel/ n gel m inv

gelatine /'dʒelətɪn/ n gelatina f

gelignite /'dʒelɪgnaɪt/ n gelatina esplosiva f

gem /dʒem/ n gemma f

Gemini /'dʒemɪnaɪ/ n Astr Gemelli mpl

gender /'dʒendə(r)/ n Gram genere m

gene /dʒi:n/ n gene m

genealogy /dʒi:nɪ'ælədʒɪ/ n genealogia f

general /'dʒenrəl/ a generale ● n generale m; in ~ in generale. ~ e'lection n elezioni fpl politiche

generaliz|ation /dʒenrəlaɪ'zeɪʃn/ n generalizzazione f. ~e /'dʒenrəlaɪz/ vi generalizzare

generally /'dʒenrəlɪ/ adv generalmente

general prac'titioner n medico m generico

generate /'dʒenəreɪt/ vt generare

generation /dʒenə'reɪʃn/ n generazione f

generator /'dʒenəreɪtə(r)/ n generatore m

generic /dʒɪ'nerɪk/ a ~ term termine m generico

generosity /dʒenə'rɒsɪtɪ/ n generosità f

generous /'dʒenərəs/ a generoso. ~ly adv generosamente

genetic /dʒɪ'netɪk/ a genetico. ~ engineering n ingegneria f genetica. ~s n genetica f

Geneva /dʒɪ'ni:və/ n Ginevra f

genial /'dʒi:nɪəl/ a gioviale

genitals /'dʒenɪtlz/ npl genitali mpl

genitive /'dʒenɪtɪv/ a & n [case] genitivo m

genius /'dʒi:nɪəs/ n (pl -uses) genio m

genocide /'dʒenəsaɪd/ n genocidio m

genre /'ʒãrə/ n genere m [letterario]

gent /dʒent/ n fam signore m; the ~s sg il bagno per uomini

genteel /dʒen'ti:l/ a raffinato

gentle /ˈdʒentl/ a delicato; ⟨breeze, tap, slope⟩ leggero

gentleman /ˈdʒentlmən/ n signore m; ⟨well-mannered⟩ gentiluomo m

gent|leness /ˈdʒentlnɪs/ n delicatezza f. **~ly** adv delicatamente

genuine /ˈdʒenjuɪn/ a genuino. **~ly** adv ⟨sorry⟩ sinceramente

geograph|ical /dʒɪəˈɡræfɪk/ a geografico. **~y** /dʒɪˈɒɡrəfɪ/ n geografia f

geological /dʒɪəˈlɒdʒɪk/ a geologico

geolog|ist /dʒɪˈɒlədʒɪst/ n geologo. **~y** /dʒɪˈɒlədʒɪst/ n geologia f

geometr|ic(al) /dʒɪəˈmetrɪk(l)/ a geometrico. **~y** /dʒɪˈɒmɪtrɪ/ n geometria f

geranium /dʒəˈreɪnɪəm/ n geranio m

geriatric /dʒerɪˈætrɪk/ a geriatrico; **~ ward** n reparto m geriatria. **~s** n geriatria f

germ /dʒɜːm/ n germe m; **~s** pl microbi mpl

German /ˈdʒɜːmən/ a e a tedesco, -a mf; ⟨language⟩ tedesco m

Germanic /dʒəˈmænɪk/ a germanico

German: **~ 'measles** n rosolia f. **~ 'shepherd** n pastore m tedesco

Germany /ˈdʒɜːmənɪ/ n Germania f

germinate /ˈdʒɜːmɪneɪt/ vi germogliare

gesticulate /dʒeˈstɪkjuleɪt/ vi gesticolare

gesture /ˈdʒestʃə(r)/ n gesto m

get /dʒet/ v ⟨pt/pp got, pp Am also gotten, pres p getting⟩ ● vt ⟨receive⟩ ricevere; ⟨obtain⟩ ottenere; trovare ⟨job⟩; ⟨buy, catch, fetch⟩ prendere; ⟨transport, deliver to airport etc⟩ portare; ⟨reach on telephone⟩ trovare; ⟨fam: understand⟩ comprendere; preparare ⟨meal⟩; **~ sb to do sth** far fare qcsa a qcno ● vi ⟨become⟩ tired/bored/angry stancarsi/annoiarsi/arrabbiarsi; **I'm ~ting hungry** mi sta venendo fame; **~**

dressed/married vestirsi/sposarsi; **~ sth ready** preparare qcsa; **~ nowhere** non concludere nulla; **this is ~ting us nowhere** questo non ci è di nessun aiuto; **~ to** ⟨reach⟩ arrivare a. **get at** vi ⟨criticize⟩ criticare; **I see what you're ~ting at** ho capito cosa vuoi dire; **what are you ~ting at?** dove vuoi andare a parare?. **get away** vi ⟨leave⟩ andarsene; ⟨escape⟩ scappare. **get back** vi tornare ● vt ⟨recover⟩ riavere; **one's own back** rifarsi. **get by** vi passare; ⟨manage⟩ cavarsela. **get down** vi scendere; **~ down to work** mettersi al lavoro ● vt ⟨depress⟩ buttare giù. **get in** vi entrare ● vt mettere dentro ⟨washing⟩; far venire ⟨plumber⟩. **get off** vi scendere; ⟨from work⟩ andarsene; Jur essere assolto; **~ off the bus/one's bike** scendere dal pullman/dalla bici ● vt ⟨remove⟩ togliere. **get on** vi salire; ⟨be on good terms⟩ andare d'accordo; ⟨make progress⟩ andare avanti; ⟨in life⟩ riuscire; **~ on the bus/one's bike** salire sul pullman/sulla bici; **how are you ~ting on?** come va?. **get out** vi uscire; ⟨of car⟩ scendere; **~ out!** fuori!; **~ out of** ⟨avoid doing⟩ evitare ● vt togliere ⟨cork, stain⟩. **get over** vi andare al di là ● vt fig riprendersi da ⟨illness⟩. **get round** vt aggirare ⟨rule⟩; rigirare ⟨person⟩ ● vi **I never ~ round to it** non mi sono mai deciso a farlo. **get through** vi ⟨on telephone⟩ prendere la linea. **get up** vi alzarsi; ⟨climb⟩ salire; **~ up a hill** salire su una collina

get: **~away** n fuga f. **~-up** n tenuta f

geyser /ˈɡiːzə(r)/ n scaldabagno m; Geol geyser m inv

ghastly /ˈɡɑːstlɪ/ a ⟨-ier, -iest⟩ terribile; **feel ~** sentirsi da cani

gherkin /ˈɡɜːkɪn/ n cetriolino m

ghetto /ˈɡetəʊ/ n ghetto m

ghost /gəʊst/ n fantasma m. **~ly** a spettrale

ghoulish /'guːlɪʃ/ a macabro

giant /'dʒaɪənt/ n gigante m ● a gigante

gibberish /'dʒɪbərɪʃ/ n stupidaggini fpl

gibe /dʒaɪb/ n malignità f inv

giblets /'dʒɪblɪts/ npl frattaglie fpl

giddiness /'gɪdnɪs/ n vertigini fpl

giddy /'gɪdɪ/ a (-ier, -iest) vertiginoso; **feel ~** avere le vertigini

gift /gɪft/ n dono m; (to charity) donazione f. **~ed** /-ɪd/ a dotato. **~-wrap** vt impacchettare in carta da regalo

gig /gɪg/ n Mus fam concerto m

gigantic /dʒaɪˈgæntɪk/ a gigantesco

giggle /'gɪgl/ n risatina f ● vi ridacchiare

gild /gɪld/ vt dorare

gills /gɪlz/ npl branchia fsg

gilt /gɪlt/ a dorato ● n doratura f. **~-edged stock** n investimento m sicuro

gimmick /'gɪmɪk/ n trovata f

gin /dʒɪn/ n gin m inv

ginger /'dʒɪndʒə(r)/ a rosso fuoco inv; (cat) rosso ● n zenzero m. **~ ale** n, **~ beer** n bibita f allo zenzero. **~bread** n panpepato m

gingerly /'dʒɪndʒəlɪ/ adv con precauzione

gipsy /'dʒɪpsɪ/ n = **gypsy**

giraffe /dʒɪˈrɑːf/ n giraffa f

girder /'gɜːdə(r)/ n Techn trave f

girl /gɜːl/ n ragazza f; (female child) femmina f. **~friend** n amica f; (of boy) ragazza f. **~ish** a da ragazza

giro /'dʒaɪərəʊ/ n bancogiro m; (cheque) sussidio m di disoccupazione

girth /gɜːθ/ n circonferenza f

gist /dʒɪst/ n **the ~** la sostanza

give /gɪv/ n elasticità f ● v (pt gave, pp given) ● vt dare; (as present) regalare (to a); fare (lecture, present, shriek); donare (blood); **~ birth** partorire ● vi (to charity) fare delle donazioni; (yield) cedere. **give away** vt dar via; (betray) tradire; (distribute) assegnare; **~ away the bride** portare la sposa all'altare. **give back** vt restituire. **give in** vt consegnare ● vi (yield) arrendersi. **give off** vt emanare. **give over** vi **~ over!** piantala!. **give up** vt rinunciare a; **~ oneself up** arrendersi ● vi rinunciare. **give way** vi cedere; Auto dare la precedenza; (collapse) crollare

given /'gɪvn/ see **give** ● a **~ name** nome m di battesimo

glacier /'glæsɪə(r)/ n ghiacciaio m

glad /glæd/ a contento (**of** di). **~den** /'glædn/ vt rallegrare

glade /gleɪd/ n radura f

gladly /'glædlɪ/ adv volentieri

glamorize /'glæməraɪz/ vt rendere affascinante. **~ous** a affascinante

glamour /'glæmə(r)/ n fascino m

glance /glɑːns/ n sguardo m ● vi **~ at** dare un'occhiata a. **glance up** vi alzare gli occhi

gland /glænd/ n glandola f

glandular /'glændjʊlə(r)/ a ghiandolare. **~ fever** n Med mononucleosi f

glare /gleə(r)/ n bagliore m; (look) occhiataccia f ● vi **~ at** dare un'occhiataccia

glaring /'gleərɪŋ/ a sfolgorante; (mistake) madornale

glass /glɑːs/ n vetro m; (for drinking) bicchiere m; **~es** (pl: spectacles) occhiali mpl. **~y** a vitreo

glaze /gleɪz/ n smalto m ● vt mettere i vetri a (door, window); smaltare (pottery); Culin spennellare. **~d** a (eyes) vitreo

glazier /'gleɪzɪə(r)/ n vetraio m

gleam /gliːm/ n luccichio m ● vi luccicare

glean /gliːn/ vt racimolare (information)

glee /gliː/ n gioia f. **~ful** a gioioso

glen /glen/ n vallone m

glib /glɪb/ a pej insincero

glid|e /glaɪd/ vi scorrere; (through the air) planare. **~er** n aliante m

glimmer /'glɪmə(r)/ n barlume m ● vi emettere un barlume

glimpse /glɪmps/ n occhiata f; **catch a ~ of** intravedere ● vt intravedere

glint /glɪnt/ n luccichio m ● vi luccicare

glisten /'glɪsn/ vi luccicare

glitter /'glɪtə(r)/ vi brillare

gloat /gləʊt/ vi gongolare (over su)

global /'gləʊbl/ a mondiale

globe /gləʊb/ n globo m; (map) mappamondo m

gloom /gluːm/ n oscurità f; (sadness) tristezza f. **~ily** adv (sadly) con aria cupa

gloomy /'gluːmɪ/ a (-ier, -iest) cupo

glorif|y /'glɔːrɪfaɪ/ vt (pt/pp -ied) glorificare; **a ~ied waitress** niente più che una cameriera

glorious /'glɔːrɪəs/ a splendido; (deed, hero) glorioso

glory /'glɔːrɪ/ n gloria f; (splendour) splendore m; (cause for pride) vanto m ● vi (pt/pp -ied) ~ **in** vantarsi di

gloss /glɒs/ n lucentezza f. **~ paint** n vernice f lucida ● **gloss over** vt sorvolare su

glossary /'glɒsərɪ/ n glossario m

glossy /'glɒsɪ/ a (-ier, -iest) lucido; **~ [magazine]** rivista f femminile

glove /glʌv/ n guanto m. **~ compartment** n Auto cruscotto m

glow /gləʊ/ n splendore m; (in cheeks) rossore m; (of candle) luce f soffusa ● vi risplendere; (candle:) brillare; (person:) avvampare. **~ing** a ardente; (account) entusiastico

glow-worm n lucciola f

glucose /'gluːkəʊs/ n glucosio m

glue /gluː/ n colla f ● vt (pres p gluing)

glum /glʌm/ a (glummer, glummest) tetro

glut /glʌt/ n eccesso m

glutton /'glʌtən/ n ghiottone, -a

mf. **~ous** /-əs/ a ghiotto. **~y** n ghiottoneria f

gnarled /nɑːld/ a nodoso

gnash /næʃ/ vt ~ **one's teeth** digrignare i denti

gnat /næt/ n moscerino m

gnaw /nɔː/ vt rosicchiare

gnome /nəʊm/ n gnomo m

go /gəʊ/ n (pl goes) energia f; (attempt) tentativo m; **on the go** in movimento; **at one go** in una sola volta; **it's your go** tocca a te; **make a go of it** riuscire ● vi (pt went, pp gone) andare; (leave) andar via; (vanish) sparire; (become) diventare; (be sold) vendersi; **go and see** andare a vedere; **go swimming/shopping** andare a nuotare/fare spese; **where's the time gone?** come ha fatto il tempo a volare così?; **it's all gone** è finito; **be going to do** stare per fare; **I'm not going to** non ne ho nessuna intenzione; **go** (Am: hamburgers etc) da asporto; **a coffee to go** un caffè da portar via. **go about** vi andare in giro. **go away** vi andarsene. **go back** vi ritornare. **go by** vi passare. **go down** vi scendere; (sun:) tramontare; (ship:) affondare; (swelling:) diminuire. **go for** vt andare a prendere; andare a cercare (doctor); (choose) optare per; (fam: attack) aggredire; **he's not the kind I go for** non è il genere che mi attira. **go in** vi entrare. **go in for** vt partecipare a (competition); darsi a (tennis). **go off** vi andarsene; (alarm:) scattare; (gun, bomb:) esplodere; (food, milk:) andare a male; **go off well** riuscire. **go on** vi andare avanti; **what's going on?** cosa succede? **go on at** vt fam scocciare. **go out** vi uscire; (light, fire:) spegnersi. **go over** vi andare ● vt (check) controllare. **go round** vi andare in giro; (visit) andare; (turn) girare; **Is there enough to go round?** ce n'è abbastanza per tutti? **go through** vi (bill, proposal:) passare ● vt (suffer) subire; ⟨check⟩ controllare; ⟨read⟩ leggere. **go under** vi passare sotto; ⟨ship, curtain:⟩ andare sott'acqua; ⟨fail⟩ fallire. **go up** vi salire; ⟨Theat: curtain:⟩ aprirsi. **go with** vt accompagnare. **go without** vt fare a meno di ⟨supper, sleep⟩ ● vi fare senza

goad /gəʊd/ vt spingere (**into** a); ⟨taunt⟩ spronare

'go-ahead a ⟨person, company⟩ intraprendente ● n okay m

goal /gəʊl/ n ⟨in sport⟩, ⟨point scored⟩ gol m inv; ⟨in life⟩ obiettivo m; **score a ~** segnare. **~ie** fam, **~keeper** n portiere m. **~post** n palo m

goat /gəʊt/ n capra f

gobble /'gɒbl/ vt ~ [**down, up**] tranguiare

'go-between n intermediario, -a mf

God, god /gɒd/ n Dio m, dio m

god: **~child** n figlioccio, -a mf. **~daughter** n figlioccia f. **~dess** n dea f. **~father** n padrino m. **~fearing** a timorato di Dio. **~forsaken** a dimenticato da Dio. **~mother** n madrina f. **~parents** npl padrino e madrina f. **~send** n manna f. **~son** n figlioccio m

go-getter /'gəʊgetə(r)/ n ambizioso, -a mf

goggle /'gɒgl/ vi fam ~ **at** fissare con gli occhi sgranati. **~s** npl occhiali mpl; ⟨of swimmer⟩ occhialini mpl [da piscina]; ⟨of worker⟩ occhiali mpl protettivi

going /'gəʊɪŋ/ a ⟨price, rate⟩ corrente; ~ **concern** azienda f florida ● n it's hard ~ è una faticaccia; **while the ~ is good** finché si può. **~s-'on** npl avvenimenti mpl

gold /gəʊld/ n oro m ● a d'oro

golden /'gəʊldn/ a dorato. ~ **'handshake** n buonuscita f ⟨al termine di un rapporto di lavoro⟩. **~ mean** n giusto mezzo m. ~ **'wedding** n nozze fpl d'oro

gold: **~fish** n inv pesce m rosso. **~mine** n miniera f d'oro.

~plated a placcato d'oro. **~smith** n orefice m

golf /gɒlf/ n golf m

golf: **~club** n circolo m di golf; ⟨implement⟩ mazza f da golf. **~course** n campo m di golf. **~er** n giocatore, -trice mf di golf

gondola /'gɒndələ/ n gondola f. **~lier** /-'lɪə(r)/ n gondoliere m

gone /gɒn/ see **go**

gong /gɒŋ/ n gong m inv

good /gʊd/ a (**better, best**) buono; ⟨child, footballer, singer⟩ bravo; ⟨holiday, film⟩ bello; ~ **at** bravo in; **a ~ deal of anger** molta rabbia; **as ~ as** (almost) quasi; ~ **morning,** ~ **afternoon** buon giorno; ~ **evening** buona sera; ~ **night** buonanotte; **have a ~ time** divertirsi ● n bene m; **for ~** per sempre; **a ~ deal** far del bene; **do ~** far bene a qcno; **it's no ~** è inutile; **be up to no ~** combinare qualcosa

goodbye /gʊd'baɪ/ int arrivederci

good: **~-for-nothing** a buono, -a mf a nulla. **G~ 'Friday** n Venerdì m Santo

good: **~-'looking** a bello. **~-'natured** a be **~-natured** avere un buon carattere

goodness /'gʊdnɪs/ n bontà f; **my** ~! santo cielo!; **thank** ~! grazie al cielo!

goods /gʊdz/ npl prodotti mpl. **~ train** n treno m merci

good'will n buona volontà f; Comm avviamento m

goody /'gʊdɪ/ n ⟨fam: person⟩ buono m. **~-goody** n santarellino, -a mf

gooey /gu:f/ a fam appiccicaticcio; fig sdolcinato

goof /gu:f/ vi fam cannare

goose /gu:s/ n (pl **geese**) oca f

gooseberry /'gʊzbərɪ/ n uva f spina

goose /gu:s/: **~-flesh** n, **~-pimples** npl pelle fsg d'oca

gore¹ /gɔ:(r)/ n sangue m

gore² vt incornare

gorge /gɔːdʒ/ n Geog gola f ● vt ~ oneself ingozzarsi

gorgeous /'gɔːdʒəs/ a stupendo

gorilla /gə'rɪlə/ n gorilla m inv

gormless /'gɔːmlɪs/ a fam stupido

gorse /gɔːs/ n ginestrone m

gory /'gɔːrɪ/ a (-ier, -iest) cruento

gosh /gɒʃ/ int fam caspita

gospel /'gɒspl/ n vangelo m. ~ truth n sacrosanta verità f

gossip /'gɒsɪp/ n pettegolezzi mpl; (person) pettegolo, -a mf ● vi pettegolare. ~y a pettegolo

got /gɒt/ see get; **have ~** avere; **have ~ to do sth** dover fare qcsa

Gothic /'gɒθɪk/ a gotico

gotten /'gɒtn/ Am see get

gouge /gaʊdʒ/ vt ~ **out** cavare

gourmet /'gʊəmeɪ/ n buongustaio, -a mf

gout /gaʊt/ n gotta f

govern /'gʌv(ə)n/ vt/i governare; (determine) determinare

government /'gʌvnmənt/ n governo m. ~al /-'mentl/ a governativo

governor /'gʌvənə(r)/ n governatore m; (of school) membro m de consiglio di istituto; (of prison) direttore, -trice mf; (fam: boss) capo m

gown /gaʊn/ n vestito m; Univ, Jur toga f

GP n abbr general practitioner

grab /græb/ vt (pt/pp grabbed) ~ **[hold of]** afferrare

grace /greɪs/ n grazia f; (before meal) benedicite m inv; **with good ~** volentieri; **three days' ~** giorni di proroga; **~ful** a aggraziato. **~fully** adv con grazia

gracious /'greɪʃəs/ a cortese; (elegant) lussuoso

grade /greɪd/ n livello m; Comm qualità f; Sch voto m; (Am Sch: class) classe f; Am = **gradient** ● vt Comm classificare; Sch dare il voto a. **~ crossing** n Am passaggio m a livello

gradient /'greɪdɪənt/ n pendenza f

gradual /'grædʒʊəl/ a graduale. **~ly** adv gradualmente

graduate[1] /'grædʒʊət/ n laureato, -a mf

graduate[2] /'grædʒʊeɪt/ vi Univ laurearsi

graduation /grædʒʊ'eɪʃn/ n laurea f

graffiti /grə'fiːtɪ/ npl graffiti mpl

graft /grɑːft/ n (Bot, Med) innesto m; (Med: organ) trapianto m; (fam: hard work) duro lavoro m; (fam: corruption) corruzione f ● vt innestare; trapiantare ⟨organ⟩

grain /greɪn/ n (of sand, salt) granello m; (of rice) chicco m; (cereals) cereali mpl; (in wood) venatura f; **it goes against the ~** fig è contro la mia/sua natura

gram /græm/ n grammo m

grammar /'græmə(r)/ n grammatica f. **~ school** n ≈ liceo m

grammatical /grə'mætɪkl/ a grammaticale

granary /'grænərɪ/ n granaio m

grand /grænd/ a grandioso; fam eccellente

grandad /'grændæd/ n fam nonno m

grandchild n nipote m/f

granddaughter n nipote f

grandeur /'grændʒə(r)/ n grandiosità f

grandfather n nonno m. **~ clock** n pendolo m (che poggia a terra)

grandiose /'grændɪəʊs/ a grandioso

grand: ~mother n nonna f. **~parents** npl nonni mpl. **~ piano** n pianoforte m a coda. **~son** n nipote m; **~stand** n tribuna f

granite /'grænɪt/ n granito m

granny /'grænɪ/ n fam nonna f

grant /grɑːnt/ n (money) sussidio m; Univ borsa f di studio ● vt accordare; (admit) ammettere; **take sth for ~ed** dare per scontato qcsa

granulated /'grænjʊleɪtɪd/ a ~ **sugar** zucchero m semolato

granule /'grænjuːl/ n granello m

grape /greɪp/ n acino m; ~s pl uva f sg

grapefruit /'greɪp-/ n inv pompelmo m

graph /grɑːf/ n grafico m

graphic /'græfɪk/ a grafico; (vivid) vivido. ~s n grafica f

'graph paper n carta f millimetrata

grapple /'græpl/ vi ~ with also fig essere alle prese con

grasp /grɑːsp/ n stretta f; (understanding) comprensione f ●vt afferrare. ~ing a avido

grass /grɑːs/ n erba f; at the ~ roots alla base. ~hopper n cavalletta f. ~land n prateria f

grassy /'grɑːsɪ/ a erboso

grate¹ /greɪt/ n grata f

grate² vt Culin grattugiare ●vi stridere

grateful /'greɪtfl/ a grato. ~ly adv con gratitudine

grater /'greɪtə(r)/ n Culin grattugia f

gratify /'grætɪfaɪ/ vt (pt/pp -ied) appagare. ~ied a appagato. ~ying a appagante

grating /'greɪtɪŋ/ n grata f

gratis /'grɑːtɪs/ adv gratis

gratitude /'grætɪtjuːd/ n gratitudine f

gratuitous /grə'tjuːɪtəs/ a gratuito

gratuity /grə'tjuːɪtɪ/ n gratifica f

grave¹ /greɪv/ a grave

grave² n tomba f

gravel /'grævl/ n ghiaia f

grave: ~stone n lapide f. ~yard n cimitero m

gravitate /'grævɪteɪt/ vi gravitare

gravity /'grævɪtɪ/ n gravità f

gravy /'greɪvɪ/ n sugo m della carne

gray /greɪ/ a Am = grey

graze¹ /greɪz/ vi (animal:) pascolare

graze² /greɪz/ n escoriazione f ●vt (touch lightly) sfiorare; (scrape) escoriare; sbucciarsi (knee)

grease /griːs/ n grasso m ●vt un-

gere. ~-proof 'paper n carta f oleata

greasy /'griːsɪ/ a (-ier, -iest) untuoso; (hair, skin) grasso

great /greɪt/ a grande; (fam: marvellous) eccezionale

great: ~-'aunt n prozia f. G~ 'Britain n Gran Bretagna f. ~-'grandchildren npl pronipoti mpl. ~-'grandfather n bisnonno m. ~-'grandmother n bisnonna f

great|ly /'greɪtlɪ/ adv enormemente. ~ness n grandezza f

great-'uncle n prozio m

Greece /griːs/ n Grecia f

greed /griːd/ n avidità f; (for food) ingordigia f

greedily /'griːdɪlɪ/ adv avidamente; (eat) con ingordigia

greedy /'griːdɪ/ a (-ier, -iest) avido; (for food) ingordo

Greek /griːk/ a & n greco, -a mf; (language) greco m

green /griːn/ a verde; (fig: inexperienced) immaturo ●n verde m; ~s pl verdura f; the G~s pl Pol i verdi. ~ belt n zona f verde intorno a una città. ~ card n Auto carta f verde

greenery /'griːnərɪ/ n verde m

green fingers npl have ~ ~ avere il pollice verde

'greenfly n afide m

green: ~grocer n fruttivendolo, -a mf. ~house n serra f. ~house effect n effetto m serra. ~ light n fam verde m

greet /griːt/ vt salutare; (welcome) accogliere. ~ing n saluto m; (welcome) accoglienza f. ~ings card n biglietto m d'auguri

gregarious /grɪ'geərɪəs/ a gregario; (person) socievole

grenade /grɪ'neɪd/ n granata f

grew /gruː/ see grow

grey /greɪ/ a grigio; (hair) bianco ●n grigio m. ~hound n levriero m

grid /grɪd/ n griglia f; (on map) reticolato m; Electr rete f

grief /griːf/ n dolore m; **come to ~** ⟨plans:⟩ naufragare

grievance /'griːvəns/ n lamentela f

grieve /griːv/ vt addolorare ● vi essere addolorato

grill /grɪl/ n graticola f; (for grilling) griglia f; **mixed ~** griglia f mista ● vt/i cuocere alla griglia; ⟨interrogate⟩ sottoporre al terzo grado

grille /grɪl/ n grata f

grim /grɪm/ a (grimmer, grimmest) arcigno; ⟨determination⟩ accanito

grimace /grɪˈmeɪs/ n smorfia f ● vi fare una smorfia

grime /graɪm/ n sudiciume m

grimy /'graɪmɪ/ a (-ier, -iest) sudicio

grin /grɪn/ n sorriso m ● vi (pt/pp grinned) fare un gran sorriso

grind /graɪnd/ n (fam: hard work) sfacchinata f ● vt (pt/pp ground) macinare; affilare ⟨knife⟩; (Am: mince) tritare; **~ one's teeth** digrignare i denti

grip /grɪp/ n presa f, fig controllo m; (bag) borsone m; **get a ~ of oneself** controllarsi ● vt (pt/pp gripped) afferrare ⟨tyres:⟩ far presa su; tenere avvinto ⟨attention⟩

gripe /graɪp/ vi (fam: grumble) lagnarsi

gripping /'grɪpɪŋ/ a avvincente

grisly /'grɪzlɪ/ a (-ier, -iest) raccapricciante

gristle /grɪsl/ n cartilagine f

grit /grɪt/ n graniglia f; (for roads) sabbia f; ⟨courage⟩ coraggio m ● vt (pt/pp gritted) spargere sabbia su ⟨road⟩; **~ one's teeth** serrare i denti

grizzle /grɪzl/ vi piagnucolare

groan /grəʊn/ n gemito m ● vi gemere

grocer /'grəʊsə(r)/ n droghiere, -a m/f; **~'s** [shop] drogheria f. **~ies** npl generi mpl alimentari

groggy /'grɒgɪ/ a (-ier, -iest) stordito; (unsteady) barcollante

groin /grɔɪn/ n Anat inguine m

groom /gruːm/ n sposo m; (for horse) stalliere m ● vt strigliare ⟨horse⟩; fig preparare; **well-~ed** ben curato

groove /gruːv/ n scanalatura f

grope /grəʊp/ vi brancolare; **~ for** cercare a tastoni

gross /grəʊs/ a obeso; (coarse) volgare; ⟨glaring⟩ grossolano; ⟨salary, weight⟩ lordo ● n inv grossa f. **~ly** adv (very) enormemente

grotesque /grəʊˈtesk/ a grottesco

grotto /'grɒtəʊ/ n (pl -es) grotta f

grotty /'grɒtɪ/ a (-ier, -iest) (fam: flat, street) squallido

ground¹ /graʊnd/ see **grind**

ground² n terra f; Sport terreno m; (reason) ragione f. **~s** pl (park) giardini mpl; (of coffee) fondi mpl ● vi ⟨ship:⟩ arenarsi ● vt bloccare a terra ⟨aircraft⟩; Am Electr mettere a terra

ground: ~ floor n pianterreno m. **~ing** n base f. **~less** a infondato. **~sheet** n telone m impermeabile. **~work** n lavoro m di preparazione

group /gruːp/ n gruppo m ● vt raggruppare ● vi raggrupparsi

grouse¹ /graʊs/ n inv gallo m cedrone

grouse² vi fam brontolare

grovel /'grɒvl/ vi (pt/pp grovelled) strisciare. **~ling** a leccapiedi inv

grow /grəʊ/ v (pt grew, pp grown) ● vi crescere; (become) diventare; ⟨unemployment, fear:⟩ aumentare; ⟨town:⟩ ingrandirsi ● vt coltivare; **~ one's hair** farsi crescere i capelli. **grow up** vi crescere; ⟨town:⟩ svilupparsi

growl /graʊl/ n grugnito m ● vi ringhiare

grown /grəʊn/ see **grow** ● a adulto. **~-up** a & n adulto, -a mf

growth /grəʊθ/ n crescita f; (increase) aumento m; Med tumore m

grub /grʌb/ n larva f; (fam: food) mangiare m

grubby /'grʌbɪ/ a (-ier, -iest) sporco

grudg|e /grʌdʒ/ n rancore m; **bear sb a ~**e portare rancore a qcno ●vt dare a malincuore. **~ing** a reluttante. **~ingly** adv a malincuore

gruelling /'gru:əlɪŋ/ a estenuante

gruesome /'gru:səm/ a macabro

gruff /grʌf/ a burbero

grumble /'grʌmbl/ vi brontolare (at contro)

grumpy /'grʌmpɪ/ a (-ier, -iest) scorbutico

grunt /grʌnt/ n grugnito m ●vi fare un grugnito

guarant|ee /gærən'ti:/ n garanzia f ●vt garantire. **~or** n garante mf

guard /gɑ:d/ n guardia f; (security) guardiano m; (on train) capotreno m; Techn schermo m protettivo; **be on ~** essere di guardia ●vt sorvegliare; (protect) proteggere. **guard against** vt guardarsi da. **~-dog** n cane m da guardia

guarded /'gɑ:dɪd/ a guardingo

guardian /'gɑ:dɪən/ n (of minor) tutore, -trice mf

guerrilla /gə'rɪlə/ n guerrigliero, -a mf. **~ warfare** n guerriglia f

guess /ges/ n supposizione f ●vt indovinare ●vi indovinare; (Am: suppose) supporre. **~work** n supposizione f

guest /gest/ n ospite mf; (in hotel) cliente mf. **~-house** n pensione f

guffaw /gʌ'fɔ:/ n sghignazzata f ●vi sghignazzare

guidance /'gaɪdns/ n guida f; (advice) consigli mpl

guide /gaɪd/ n guida f; [Girl] G~ giovane esploratrice f ●vt guidare. **~book** n guida f turistica

guided /'gaɪdɪd/ a **~ missile** missile m teleguidato; **~ tour** giro m guidato

guide: ~-dog n cane m per ciechi. **~-lines** npl direttive fpl

guild /gɪld/ n corporazione f

guile /gaɪl/ n astuzia f

guillotine /'gɪləti:n/ n ghigliottina f; (for paper) taglierina f

guilt /gɪlt/ n colpa f. **~ily** adv con aria colpevole

guilty /'gɪltɪ/ a (-ier, -iest) colpevole; **have a ~ conscience** avere la coscienza sporca

guinea-pig /'gɪnɪ-/ n porcellino m d'India; (fig: used for experiments) cavia f

guise /gaɪz/ n **in the ~ of** sotto le spoglie di

guitar /gɪ'tɑ:(r)/ n chitarra f. **~ist** n chitarrista mf

gulf /gʌlf/ n Geog golfo m; fig abisso m

gull /gʌl/ n gabbiano m

gullet /'gʌlɪt/ n esofago m; (throat) gola f

gullible /'gʌlɪbl/ a credulone

gully /'gʌlɪ/ n burrone m; (drain) canale m di scolo

gulp /gʌlp/ n azione f di deglutire; (of food) boccone m; (of liquid) sorso m ●vi deglutire. **gulp down** vt tranguiare (food); scolarsi (liquid)

gum[1] /gʌm/ n Anat gengiva f

gum[2] /gʌm/ n gomma f; (chewing-gum) gomma f da masticare, chewing-gum m inv ●vt (pt/pp **gummed**) ingommare (**to** a)

gummed /gʌmd/ see **gum**[2] ●a (label) adesivo

gumption /'gʌmpʃn/ n fam buon senso m

gun /gʌn/ n pistola f; (rifle) fucile m; (cannon) cannone m. **gun down** vt (pt/pp **gunned**) freddare

gun: ~fire n spari mpl; (of cannon) colpi mpl [di cannone]. **~man** uomo m armato

gun: ~powder n polvere f da sparo. **~shot** n colpo m [di pistola]

gurgle /'gɜ:gl/ vi gorgogliare; (baby:) fare degli urletti

gush /gʌʃ/ vi sgorgare; (enthuse) parlare con troppo entusiasmo (over di). **gush out** vi sgorgare

~ing a eccessivamente entusiastico

gust /gʌst/ n (of wind) raffica f

gusto /'gʌstəʊ/ n with ~ con trasporto

gusty /'gʌstɪ/ a ventoso

gut /gʌt/ n intestino m; **~s** pl pancia f; (fam: courage) fegato m ●vt (pt/pp **gutted**) Culin svuotare delle interiora; **~ted by fire** sventrato da un incendio

gutter /'gʌtə(r)/ n canale m di scolo; (on roof) grondaia f; fig bassifondi mpl

guttural /'gʌtərəl/ a gutturale

guy /gaɪ/ n fam tipo m, tizio m

guzzle /'gʌzl/ vt ingozzarsi con (food); **he's ~d the lot** si è sbafato tutto

gym /dʒɪm/ n fam palestra f; (gymnastics) ginnastica f

gymnasium /dʒɪm'neɪzɪəm/ n palestra f

gymnast /'dʒɪmnæst/ n ginnasta mf. **~ics** /-'næstɪks/ n ginnastica f

gym: ~ **shoes** npl scarpe fpl da ginnastica. **~-slip** n Sch grembiule m (da bambina)

gynaecolog|ist /gaɪnə'kɒlədʒɪst/ n ginecologo, -a mf. **~y** n ginecologia f

gypsy /'dʒɪpsɪ/ n zingaro, -a mf

gyrate /dʒaɪ'reɪt/ vi roteare

Hh

haberdashery /hæbə'dæʃərɪ/ n merceria f; Am negozio m d'abbigliamento da uomo

habit /'hæbɪt/ n abitudine f; (Relig: costume) tonaca f; **be in the ~ of doing sth** avere l'abitudine di fare qcsa

habitable /'hæbɪtəbl/ a abitabile

habitat /'hæbɪtæt/ n habitat m inv

habitation /hæbɪ'teɪʃn/ n **unfit for human ~** inagibile

habitual /hə'bɪtjʊəl/ a abituale; (smoker, liar) inveterato. **~ly** adv regolarmente

hack¹ /hæk/ n (writer) scribacchino, -a mf

hack² vt tagliare; **~ to pieces** tagliare a pezzi

hackneyed /'hæknɪd/ a trito [e ritrito]

'hacksaw n seghetto m

had /hæd/ see **have**

haddock /'hædək/ n inv eglefino m

haemorrhage /'hemərɪdʒ/ n emorragia f

haemorrhoids /'hemərɔɪdz/ npl emorroidi fpl

hag /hæg/ n **old ~** vecchia befana f

haggard /'hægəd/ a sfatto

haggle /'hægl/ vi contrattare (**over** per)

hail¹ /heɪl/ vt salutare; far segno a (taxi) ●vi **~ from** provenire da

hail² n grandine f ●vi grandinare. **~stone** n chicco m di grandine. **~storm** n grandinata f

hair /heə(r)/ n capelli mpl; (on body, of animal) pelo m

hair: **~brush** n spazzola f per capelli. **~cut** n taglio m di capelli; **have a ~cut** farsi tagliare i capelli. **~do** n fam pettinatura f. **~dresser** n parrucchiere, -a mf. **~dryer** n fon m inv; (with hood) casco m [asciugacapelli]. **~grip** n molletta f. **~pin** n forcina f. **~pin 'bend** n tornante m, curva f a gomito. **~raising** a terrificante. **~style** n acconciatura f

hairy /'heərɪ/ a (-ier, -iest) peloso; (fam: frightening) spaventoso

hale /heɪl/ a **~ and hearty** in piena forma

half /hɑːf/ n pl (halves) metà f inv; **cut in ~** tagliare a metà; **one and a ~** uno e mezzo; **~ a dozen** mezza dozzina; **~ an hour** mezz'ora ● a mezzo; [at] **~ price** [a] metà prezzo ● adv a metà; **~ past two** le due e mezza

half: **~-board** n mezza pensione f. **~-'hearted** a esitante. **~'hourly** a

& adv ogni mezz'ora. ~ 'mast n at
~ mast a mezz'asta. ~ measures
npl mezze misure fpl. '~-open a
socchiuso. ~-'term n vacanza f di
metà trimestre. '~-time n Sport
intervallo m. ~'way a the ~way
mark/stage il livello intermedio
● adv a metà strada; get ~way fig
arrivare a metà. ~wit n idiota mf
hall /hɔ:l/ n (entrance) ingresso m;
(room) sala f; (mansion) residenza
f di campagna; ~ of residence
Univ casa f dello studente
'**hallmark** n marchio m di garanzia; fig marchio m
hallo /hə'ləʊ/ int ciao!; (on telephone) pronto!; say ~ to salutare
Hallowe'en /hæləʊ'i:n/ n vigilia f
d'Ognissanti e notte delle streghe,
celebrata soprattutto dai bambini
hallucination /həlu:sɪ'neɪʃn/ n allucinazione f
halo /'heɪləʊ/ n (pl -es) aureola f;
Astr alone m
halt /hɔ:lt/ n alt m inv; come to a
~ fermarsi; (traffic:) bloccarsi
● vi fermarsi; ~! alt! ● vt fermare.
~ing a esitante
halve /hɑ:v/ n dividere a metà; (reduce) dimezzare
ham /hæm/ n prosciutto m; Theat
attore, -trice mf da strapazzo
hamburger /'hæmbɜ:gə(r)/ n hamburger m inv
hamlet /'hæmlɪt/ n paesino m
hammer /'hæmə(r)/ n martello m
● vt martellare ● vi ~ at/on picchiare a
hammock /'hæmək/ n amaca f
hamper[1] /'hæmpə(r)/ n cesto m;
[gift] cestino m
hamper[2] vt ostacolare
hamster /'hæmstə(r)/ n criceto m
hand /hænd/ n mano f; (of clock)
lancetta f; (writing) scrittura f;
(worker) manovale m; at ~, to ~ a
portata di mano; on the one ~ da
un lato; on the other ~ d'altra
parte; out of ~ incontrollabile;
(summarily) su due piedi; give sb
a ~ dare una mano a qcno ● vt

porgere. hand down vt tramandare. hand in vt consegnare. hand
out vt distribuire. hand over vt
passare; (to police) consegnare
hand: ~bag n borsa f (da signora).
~book n manuale m. ~brake n
freno m a mano. ~cuffs npl manette fpl. ~ful n manciata f; be
[quite] a ~ful fam essere difficile
da tenere a freno
handicap /'hændɪkæp/ n handicap
m inv. ~ped a mentally/physically ~ped mentalmente/fisicamente handicappato
handicraft /'hændɪkrɑ:ft/ n artigianato m. ~work n opera f
handkerchief /'hæŋkətʃɪf/ n (pl
~s & -chieves) fazzoletto m
handle /'hændl/ n manico m; (of
door) maniglia f; fly off the ~ fam
perdere le staffe ● vt maneggiare;
occuparsi di (problem, customer);
prendere (difficult person); trattare (subject). ~bars npl manubrio m
hand: ~luggage n bagaglio m a
mano. ~made a fatto a mano.
~out n (at lecture) foglio m informativo; (fam: money) elemosina f.
~rail n corrimano m. ~shake n
stretta f di mano
handsome /'hænsəm/ a bello; (fig:
generous) generoso
hand: ~stand n verticale f.
~writing n calligrafia f.
~-'written a scritto a mano
handy /'hændɪ/ a (-ier, -iest) utile;
(person) abile; have/keep ~ avere/tenere a portata di mano.
~man n tuttofare m inv

hang /hæŋ/ vt (pt/pp hung) appendere (picture); (pt/pp hanged) impiccare (criminal); ~ oneself impiccarsi ● vi (pt/pp hung) pendere; (hair:) scendere ● n get the ~
of it fam afferrare. hang about vi
gironzolare. hang on vi tenersi
stretto; (fam: wait) aspettare;
Teleph restare in linea. hang on
to vt tenersi stretto a; (keep) tenere. hang out vi spuntare; where

does he usually ~ out? *fam* dove bazzica di solito? ● *vt* stendere ⟨*washing*⟩. **hang up** *vt* appendere; *Teleph* riattaccare ● *vi* essere appeso; *Teleph* riattaccare

hangar /'hæŋə(r)/ *n* Aeron hangar *m inv*

hanger /'hæŋə(r)/ *n* gruccia *f*. **~-on** *n* leccapiedi *mf*

hang: ~-glider *n* deltaplano *m*. **~-gliding** *n* deltaplano *m*. **~man** *n* boia *m*. **~over** *n* fam postumi *mpl* da sbornia. **~-up** *n fam* complesso *m*

hanker /'hæŋkə(r)/ *vi* ~ **after sth** smaniare per qcsa

hanky /'hæŋkɪ/ *n fam* fazzoletto *m*

hanky-panky /hæŋkɪ'pæŋkɪ/ *n fam* qualcosa *m* di losco

haphazard /hæp'hæzəd/ *a* a casaccio

happen /'hæpn/ *vi* capitare, succedere; **as it ~s** per caso; **I ~ed to meet him** mi è capitato di incontrarlo; **what has ~ed to him?** cosa gli è capitato?; ⟨*become of*⟩ che fine ha fatto? **~ing** *n* avvenimento *m*

happily /'hæpɪlɪ/ *adv* felicemente; ⟨*fortunately*⟩ fortunatamente. **~ness** *n* felicità *f*

happy /'hæpɪ/ *a* (-ier, -iest) contento, felice. **~-go-lucky** *a* spensierato

harass /'hærəs/ *vt* perseguitare. **~ed** *a* stressato. **~ment** *n* persecuzione *f*; **sexual ~ment** molestie *fpl* sessuali

harbour /'hɑːbə(r)/ *n* porto *m* ● *vt* dare asilo a; nutrire ⟨*grudge*⟩

hard /hɑːd/ *a* duro; ⟨*question, problem*⟩ difficile; **~ of hearing** duro d'orecchi; **be ~ on sb** ⟨*person*⟩ essere duro con qcno ● *adv* ⟨*work*⟩ duramente; ⟨*pull, hit, rain, snow*⟩ forte; **~ hit by unemployment** duramente colpito dalla disoccupazione; **take sth ~** non accettare qcsa; **think ~!** pensaci bene!; **try ~** mettercela tutta, **try ~er** metterci più impe-

gno; **~ done by** *fam* trattato ingiustamente

hard: ~back *n* edizione *f* rilegata. **~-boiled** *a* ⟨*egg*⟩ sodo. **~ copy** *n* copia *f* stampata. **~ disk** *n* hard disk *m inv*, disco *m* rigido

harden /'hɑːdn/ *vi* indurirsi

hard: ~-headed *a* ⟨*businessman*⟩ dal sangue freddo. **~-hearted** *a* dal cuore duro. **~ line** *n* linea *f* dura; **~ lines!** che sfortuna!. **~line** *a* duro. **~liner** *n* fautore, -trice *mf* della linea dura. **~ luck** *n* sfortuna *f*

hardly /'hɑːdlɪ/ *adv* appena; **~ly ever** quasi mai. **~ness** *n* durezza *f*. **~ship** *n* avversità *f inv*

hard: ~ 'shoulder *n* Auto corsia *f* d'emergenza. **~ up** *a* fam a corto di soldi; **~ up for sth** *a* corto di qcsa. **~ware** *n* ferramenta *fpl*; Comput hardware *m inv*. **~-'wearing** *a* resistente. **~-'working** *a* be **~working** essere un gran lavoratore

hardy /'hɑːdɪ/ *a* (-ier, -iest) dal fisico resistente; ⟨*plant*⟩ che sopporta il gelo

hare /heə(r)/ *n* lepre *f*. **~-brained** *a* fam ⟨*scheme*⟩ da scervellati

hark /hɑːk/ *vi* ~ **back to** *fig* ritornare su

harm /hɑːm/ *n* male *m*; ⟨*damage*⟩ danni *mpl*; **out of ~'s way** in un posto sicuro; **it won't do any ~** non farà certo male ● *vt* far male a; ⟨*damage*⟩ danneggiare. **~ful** *a* dannoso. **~less** *a* innocuo

harmonica /hɑː'mɒnɪkə/ *n* armonica *f* [a bocca]

harmonious /hɑː'məʊnɪəs/ *a* armonioso. **~ly** *adv* in armonia

harmonize /'hɑːmənaɪz/ *vi fig* armonizzare. **~y** *n* armonia *f*

harness /'hɑːnɪs/ *n* finimenti *mpl*; ⟨*of parachute*⟩ imbracatura *f* ● *vt* bardare ⟨*horse*⟩; sfruttare ⟨*resources*⟩

harp /hɑːp/ *n* arpa *f* ● **harp on** *vi* fam insistere ⟨*about* su⟩. **~ist** *n* arpista *mf*

harpoon /hɑːˈpuːn/ *n* arpione *m*

harpsichord /ˈhɑːpsɪkɔːd/ *n* clavicembalo *m*

harrowing /ˈhærəʊɪŋ/ *a* straziante

harsh /hɑːʃ/ *a* duro; ⟨light⟩ abbagliante. **~ness** *n* durezza *f*

harvest /ˈhɑːvɪst/ *n* raccolta *f*; (of grapes) vendemmia *f*; (crop) raccolto *m* ● *vt* raccogliere

has /hæz/ *see* **have**

hash /hæʃ/ *n* **make a ~ of** *fam* fare un casino con

hashish /ˈhæʃɪʃ/ *n* hascish *m*

hassle /ˈhæsl/ *n fam* rottura *f* ● *vt* rompere le scatole a

haste /heɪst/ *n* fretta *f*

hast|y /ˈheɪstɪ/ *a* (-ier, -iest) frettoloso; ⟨decision⟩ affrettato. **~ily** *adv* frettolosamente

hat /hæt/ *n* cappello *m*

hatch¹ /hætʃ/ *n* (for food) sportello *m* passavivande; *Naut* boccaporto *m*

hatch² *vi* ~[out] rompere il guscio; ⟨egg:⟩ schiudersi ● *vt* covare; tramare ⟨plot⟩

'hatchback *n* tre/cinque porte *m inv*; ⟨door⟩ porta *f* del bagagliaio

hatchet /ˈhætʃɪt/ *n* ascia *f*

hate /heɪt/ *n* odio *m* ● *vt* odiare. **~ful** *a* odioso

hatred /ˈheɪtrɪd/ *n* odio *m*

haught|y /ˈhɔːtɪ/ *a* (-ier, -iest) altezzoso. **~ily** *adv* altezzosamente

haul /hɔːl/ *n* (fish) pescata *f*; (loot) bottino *m*; (pull) tirata *f* ● *vt* tirare; trasportare ⟨goods⟩ ● *vi* ~ **on** tirare. **~age** /-ɪdʒ/ *n* trasporto *m*. **~ier** /-ɪə(r)/ *n* autotrasportatore *m*

haunt /hɔːnt/ *n* ritrovo *m* ● *vt* frequentare; (linger in the mind) perseguitare; **this house is ~ed** questa casa è abitata da fantasmi

have /hæv/ *vt* (3 sg pres tense **has**; *pt/pp* **had**) avere; fare ⟨breakfast, bath, walk etc⟩; ~ **a drink** bere qualcosa; ~ **lunch/dinner** pranzare/cenare; ~ **a rest** riposarsi; **I had my hair cut** mi sono tagliata i capelli; **we had the house painted** abbiamo fatto tinteggiare

la casa; **I had it made** l'ho fatto fare; ~ **to do sth** dover fare qcsa; ~ **him telephone me tomorrow** digli di telefonarmi domani; **he has** *or* **he's got two houses** ha due case; **you've got the money, ~n't you?** hai i soldi, no? ● *v aux* avere; (with verbs of motion & some others) essere; **I ~ seen him** l'ho visto; **he has never been there** non ci è mai stato. **have on** *vt* (be wearing) portare; (dupe) prendere in giro; **I've got something on tonight** ho un impegno stasera. **have out** *vt* ~ **it out with sb** chiarire le cose con qcno ● *npl* **the ~s and the ~-nots** i ricchi e i poveri

haven /ˈheɪvn/ *n fig* rifugio *m*

haversack /ˈhævə-/ *n* zaino *m*

havoc /ˈhævək/ *n* strage *f*; **play ~ with** *fig* scombussolare

haw /hɔː/ *see* **hum**

hawk /hɔːk/ *n* falco *m*

hay /heɪ/ *n* fieno *m*. ~ **fever** *n* raffreddore *m* da fieno. **~stack** *n* pagliaio *m*

'haywire *a fam* **go ~** dare i numeri; ⟨plans:⟩ andare all'aria

hazard /ˈhæzəd/ *n* (risk) rischio *m* ● *vt* rischiare; ~ **a guess** azzardare un'ipotesi. **~ous** /-əs/ *a* rischioso. **~ [warning] lights** *npl* Auto luci *fpl* d'emergenza

haze /heɪz/ *n* foschia *f*

hazel /ˈheɪz(ə)l/ *n* nocciolo *m*; (colour) [color *m*] nocciola *m*. **~-nut** *n* nocciola *f*

haz|y /ˈheɪzɪ/ *a* (-ier, -iest) nebbioso; ⟨fig: person⟩ confuso; (memories) vago

he /hiː/ *pron* lui; **he's tired** è stanco; **I'm going but he's not** io vengo, ma lui no

head /hed/ *n* testa *f*; (of firm) capo *m*; (of primary school) direttore, -trice *mf*; (of secondary school) preside *mf*; (on beer) schiuma *f*; **be off one's ~** essere fuori di testa; **have a good ~ for business** avere il senso degli affari; **have a good ~**

for heights non soffrire di vertigini; **10 pounds a ~** 10 sterline a testa; **20 ~ of cattle** 20 capi di bestiame; **~ first** a capofitto; **~ over heels in love** innamorato pazzo; **~s or tails?** testa o croce? ● vt essere a capo di; essere in testa a (*list*); colpire la testa (*ball*) ● vi **for** dirigersi verso.

head: **~ache** n mal m di testa. **~-dress** n acconciatura f. **~er** /'hedə(r)/ n rinvio m di testa; (*dive*) tuffo m di testa. **~hunter** n cacciatore, -trice mf di teste. **~lamp** n Auto fanale m. **~land** n promontorio m. **~light** n Auto fanale m. **~line** n titolo m. **~long** a & adv a capofitto. **~'master** n (*of primary school*) direttore m; (*of secondary school*) preside m. **~'mistress** n (*of primary school*) direttrice f; (*of secondary school*) preside f. **~office** n sede f centrale. **~-on** a (*collision*) frontale ● adv frontalmente. **~phones** npl cuffie fpl. **~quarters** npl sede fsg, Mil quartier m generale msg. **~-rest** n poggiatesta m inv. **~room** n sottotetto m; (*of bridge*) altezza f libera di passaggio. **~scarf** n foulard m inv, fazzoletto m. **~strong** a testardo. **~ waiter** n capocameriere m. **~ way** n progresso m. **~wind** n vento m di prua

heady /'hedɪ/ a che dà alla testa

heal /hiːl/ vt/i guarire

health /helθ/ n salute f

health: **~ farm** n centro m di rimessa in forma. **~ foods** npl alimenti mpl macrobiotici. **~-food shop** n negozio m di macrobiotica. **~ insurance** n assicurazione f contro malattie

healthy /'helθɪ/ a (**-ier, -iest**) sano. **~ly** adv in modo sano

heap /hiːp/ n mucchio m; **~s of** fam un sacco di ● vt ~ [**up**] ammucchiare; **~ed teaspoon** un cucchiaino abbondante

hear /hɪə(r)/ vt/i (pt/pp **heard**) sentire; **~, ~!** bravo! **~ from** vi aver notizie di. **hear of** vi sentir parlare di; **he would not ~ of it** non ne ha voluto sentir parlare

hearing /'hɪərɪŋ/ n udito m; Jur udienza f. **~-aid** n apparecchio m acustico

'hearsay n **from ~** per sentito dire

hearse /hɜːs/ n carro m funebre

heart /hɑːt/ n cuore m; **~s** pl (*in cards*) cuori mpl; **by ~** a memoria

heart: **~ache** n pena f. **~ attack** n infarto m. **~beat** n battito m cardiaco. **~break** n afflizione f. **~breaking** a straziante. **~broken** a **be ~broken** avere il cuore spezzato. **~burn** n mal m di stomaco. **~en** vt rincuorare. **~felt** a di cuore

hearth /hɑːθ/ n focolare m

heart|ily /'hɑːtɪlɪ/ adv di cuore; (*eat*) con appetito; **be ~ily sick of sth** non poterne più di qcsa. **~less** a spietato. **~-searching** n esame m di coscienza. **~-to-~** n conversazione f a cuore aperto ● a a cuore aperto. **~y** a caloroso; (*meal*) copioso; (*person*) gioviale

heat /hiːt/ n calore m, Sport prova f eliminatoria ● vt scaldare ● vi scaldarsi. **~ed** a (*swimming-pool*) riscaldato; (*discussion*) animato. **~er** n (*for room*) stufa f; (*for water*) boiler m inv; Auto riscaldamento m

heath /hiːθ/ n brughiera f

heathen /'hiːðn/ a & n pagano, -a mf

heather /'heðə(r)/ n erica f

heating /'hiːtɪŋ/ n riscaldamento m

heat: **~stroke** n colpo m di sole. **~wave** n ondata f di calore

heave /hiːv/ vt tirare; (*lift*) tirare su; (fam: *throw*) gettare; emettere (*sigh*) ● vi tirare

heaven /'hev(ə)n/ n paradiso m; **~ help you !...** Dio ti scampi se...; **H~s!** santo cielo!. **~ly** a celeste; fam delizioso

heav|y /'hevɪ/ a (**-ier, -iest**) pesante; ⟨traffic⟩ intenso; ⟨rain, cold⟩ forte; **be a ~y smoker/drinker** essere un gran fumatore/bevitore. **~ily** adv pesantemente; ⟨smoke, drink etc⟩ molto. **~yweight** n peso m massimo

Hebrew /'hi:bru:/ a ebreo

heckle /'hekl/ vt interrompere di continuo. **~r** n disturbatore, -trice mf

hectic /'hektɪk/ a frenetico

hedge /hedʒ/ n siepe f ● vi fig essere evasivo. **~hog** n riccio m

heed /hi:d/ n **pay ~ to** prestare ascolto a ● vt prestare ascolto a. **~less** a noncurante

heel[1] /hi:l/ n tallone m; (of shoe) tacco m; **take to one's ~s** fam darsela a gambe

heel[2] vi **~ over** Naut inclinarsi

hefty /'heftɪ/ a (**-ier, -iest**) massiccio

heifer /'hefə(r)/ n giovenca f

height /haɪt/ n altezza f; (of plane) altitudine f; (of season, fame) culmine m. **~en** vt fig accrescere

heir /eə(r)/ n erede mf. **~ess** n ereditiera f. **~loom** n cimelio m di famiglia

held /held/ see **hold**[2]

helicopter /'helɪkɒptə(r)/ n elicottero m

hell /hel/ n inferno m; **go to ~!** sl va' al diavolo! ● int porca miseria!

hello /hə'ləʊ/ int & n = **hallo**

helm /helm/ n timone m; **at the ~** fig al timone

helmet /'helmɪt/ n casco m

help /help/ n aiuto m; (employee) aiuto m domestico; **that's no ~** non è d'aiuto ● vt aiutare; **~ oneself to sth** servirsi di qcsa; **~ yourself** (at table) serviti pure; **I could not ~ laughing** non ho potuto trattenermi dal ridere; **it cannot be ~ed** non c'è niente da fare; **I can't ~ it** non ci posso far niente ● vi aiutare

help|er /'helpə(r)/ n aiutante mf. **~ful** a (person) di aiuto; (advice)

utile. **~ing** n porzione f. **~less** a (unable to manage) incapace; (powerless) impotente

helter-skelter /heltə'skeltə(r)/ adv in fretta e furia ● n scivolo m a spirale nei luna park

hem /hem/ n orlo m ● vt (pt/pp **hemmed**) orlare. **hem in** vt intrappolare

hemisphere /'hemɪ-/ n emisfero m

hemp /hemp/ n canapa f

hen /hen/ n gallina f; (any female bird) femmina f

hence /hens/ adv (for this reason) quindi. **~forth** adv d'ora innanzi

henchman /'hentʃmən/ n pej tirapiedi m

'hen-**party** n fam festa f di addio al celibato per sole donne. **~pecked** a tiranneggiato dalla moglie

her /hɜ:(r)/ poss a il suo m, la sua f, i suoi mpl, le sue fpl; **~ mother/father** sua madre/suo padre ● pers pron (direct object) la; (indirect object) le; (after prep) lei; **I know ~** la conosco; **give ~ the money** dalle i soldi; **give it to ~** daglielo; **I came with ~** sono venuto con lei; **it's ~** è lei; **I've seen ~** l'ho vista; **I've seen ~, but not him** ho visto lei, ma non lui

herald /'herəld/ vt annunciare

herb /hɜ:b/ n erba f

herbal /'hɜ:b(ə)l/ a alle erbe; **~ tea** tisana f

herbs /hɜ:bz/ npl (for cooking) aromi mpl (da cucina); (medicinal) erbe fpl

herd /hɜ:d/ n gregge m ● vt (tend) sorvegliare; (drive) far muovere; fig ammassare

here /hɪə(r)/ adv qui, qua; **in ~** qui dentro; **come/bring ~** vieni/porta qui; **~ is..., ~ are...** ecco...; **~ you are!** ecco qua!. **~'after** adv in futuro. **~'by** adv con la presente

heredit|ary /hɪ'redɪtərɪ/ a ereditario. **~y** n eredità f

heres|y /'herəsɪ/ n eresia f. **~tic** n eretico, -a mf

here'with *adv Comm* con la presente

heritage /'hɛrɪtɪdʒ/ *n* eredità *f*

hermetic /hɜ:'metɪk/ *a* ermetico. **~ally** *adv* ermeticamente

hermit /'hɜ:mɪt/ *n* eremita *mf*

hernia /'hɜ:nɪə/ *n* ernia *f*

hero /'hɪərəʊ/ *n* (*pl* -es) eroe *m*

heroic /hɪ'rəʊɪk/ *a* eroico

heroin /'herəʊɪn/ *n* eroina *f* (*droga*)

hero|ine /'herəʊɪn/ *n* eroina *f*. **~ism** *n* eroismo *m*

heron /'herən/ *n* airone *m*

herring /'herɪŋ/ *n* aringa *f*

hers /hɜ:z/ *poss pron* il suo *m*, la sua *f*, i suoi *mpl*, le sue *fpl*; **a friend of ~** un suo amico; **friends of ~** dei suoi amici; **that is ~** quello è suo; (*as opposed to mine*) quello è il suo

her'self *pers pron* (*reflexive*) si; (*emphatic*) lei stessa; (*after prep*) sé, se stessa; **she poured ~ a drink** si è versata da bere; **she told me so ~** me lo ha detto lei stessa; **she's proud of ~** è fiera di sé; **by ~** da sola

hesitant /'hezɪtənt/ *a* esitante. **~ly** *adv* con esitazione

hesitat|e /'hezɪteɪt/ *vi* esitare. **~ion** /-'teɪʃn/ *n* esitazione *f*

het /het/ *a* **~ up** *fam* agitato

hetero'sexual /hetərəʊ-/ *a* eterosessuale

hexagon /'heksəgən/ *n* esagono *m*. **~al** /hek'sægənl/ *a* esagonale

hey /heɪ/ *int* ehi

heyday /'heɪ-/ *n* tempi *mpl* d'oro

hi /haɪ/ *int* ciao!

hiatus /haɪ'eɪtəs/ *n* (*pl* -tuses) iato *m*

hibernat|e /'haɪbəneɪt/ *vi* andare in letargo. **~ion** /-'neɪʃn/ *n* letargo *m*

hiccup /'hɪkʌp/ *n* singhiozzo *m*; (*fam*: *hitch*) intoppo *m* ● *vi* fare un singhiozzo

hid /hɪd/, **hidden** /'hɪdn/ *see* **hide²**

hide¹ /haɪd/ *n* (*leather*) pelle *f* (*di animale*)

hide² *vt* (*pt* **hid**, *pp* **hidden**)

nascondere ● *vi* nascondersi. **~-and-'seek** *n* play **~-and-seek** giocare a nascondino

hideous /'hɪdɪəs/ *a* orribile

'hide-out *n* nascondiglio *m*

hiding¹ /'haɪdɪŋ/ *n* (*fam*: *beating*) bastonata *f*; (*defeat*) batosta *f*

hiding² *n* **go into ~** sparire dalla circolazione

hierarchy /'haɪərɑ:kɪ/ *n* gerarchia *f*

hieroglyphics /haɪərə'glɪfɪks/ *npl* geroglifici *mpl*

hi-fi /'haɪfaɪ/ *n fam* stereo *m*, hi-fi *m inv* ● *a fam* ad alta fedeltà

higgledy-piggledy /hɪgldɪ'pɪgldɪ/ *adv* alla rinfusa

high /haɪ/ *a* alto; (*meat*) che comincia ad andare a male; (*wind*) forte; (*on drugs*) fatto; **it's ~ time we did something about it** è ora di fare qualcosa in proposito ● *adv* in alto; **~ and low** in lungo e in largo ● *n* massimo *m*; (*temperature*) massima *f*; **be on a ~** *fam* essere fatto

high: **~brow** *a* **n** intellettuale *mf*. **~ chair** *n* seggiolone *m*. **~er education** *n* formazione *f* universitaria. **~'handed** *a* dispotico. **~'heeled** *a* coi tacchi alti. **~ heels** *npl* tacchi *mpl* alti. **~ jump** *n* salto *m* in alto

highlight /'haɪlaɪt/ *n fig* momento *m* clou; **~s** *pl* (*in hair*) mèche *fpl* ● *vt* (*emphasize*) evidenziare. **~er** *n* (*marker*) evidenziatore *m*

highly /'haɪlɪ/ *adv* molto; **speak ~ of** lodare; **think ~ of** avere un'alta opinione di. **~-strung** *a* nervoso

Highness /'haɪnɪs/ *n* altezza *f*; **Your ~** Sua Altezza

high: **~-rise** *a* (*building*) molto alto ● *n* edificio *m* molto alto. **~ school** *n* ≈ scuola *f* superiore. **~ season** *n* alta stagione *f*. **~ street** *n* strada *f* principale. **~ tea** *n* pasto *m* pomeridiano servito insieme al tè. **~ tide** *n* alta marea *f*. **~way code** *n* codice *m* stradale

hijack /'haɪdʒæk/ *vt* dirottare ● *n*

dirottamento *m*. **~er** *n* dirottatore, **~trice** *mf*

hike /haɪk/ *n* escursione *f* a piedi ● *vi* fare un'escursione a piedi. **~r** *n* escursionista *mf*

hilarious /hɪˈleərɪəs/ *a* esilarante

hill /hɪl/ *n* collina *f*; (*mound*) collinetta *f*; (*slope*) altura *f*

hill: **~side** *n* pendio *m*. **~y** *a* collinoso

hilt /hɪlt/ *n* impugnatura *f*; **to the ~** (*fam: support*) fino in fondo; (*mortgaged*) fino al collo

him /hɪm/ *pers pron* (*direct object*) lo; (*indirect object*) gli; (*with prep*) lui; **I know ~** lo conosco; **give ~ the money** dagli i soldi; **give it to ~** daglielo; **I spoke to ~** gli ho parlato; **it's ~** è lui; **she loves ~** lo ama; **she loves ~, not you** ama lui, non te. **~self** *pers pron* (*reflexive*) si; (*emphatic*) lui stesso; (*after prep*) sé, se stesso; **he poured ~ a drink** si è versato da bere; **he told me so ~self** me lo ha detto lui stesso; **he's proud of ~self** è fiero di sé; **by ~self** da solo

hind /haɪnd/ *a* posteriore

hind|er /ˈhɪndə(r)/ *vt* intralciare. **~rance** /-rəns/ *n* intralcio *m*

hindsight /ˈhaɪnd-/ *n* **with ~** con il senno del poi

Hindu /ˈhɪnduː/ *n* indù *mf* *inv* ● *a* indù. **~ism** *n* induismo *m*

hinge /hɪndʒ/ *n* cardine *m* ● *vi* **~ on** *fig* dipendere da

hint /hɪnt/ *n* (*clue*) accenno *m*; (*advice*) suggerimento *m*; (*indirect suggestion*) allusione *f*; (*trace*) tocco *m* ● *vt* **~ that...** far capire che... ● *vi* **~ at** alludere a

hip /hɪp/ *n* fianco *m*

hippie /ˈhɪpɪ/ *n* hippy *mf inv*

hippo /ˈhɪpəʊ/ *n* ippopotamo *m*

hip 'pocket *n* tasca *f* posteriore

hippopotamus /hɪpəˈpɒtəməs/ *n* (*pl* **-muses** *or* **-mi** /-maɪ/) ippopotamo *m*

hire /ˈhaɪə(r)/ *vt* affittare; assumere (*person*); **~ [out]** affittare ● *n* noleggio *m*; **'for ~'** 'affittasi'. **~**

car *n* macchina *f* a noleggio. **~ purchase** *n* acquisto *m* rateale

his /hɪz/ *poss a* il suo *m*, la sua *f*, i suoi *mpl*, le sue *fpl*; **~ mother/father** sua madre/suo padre ● *poss pron* il suo *m*, la sua *f*, i suoi *mpl*, le sue *fpl*; **a friend of ~** un suo amico; **friends of ~** dei suoi amici; **that is ~** questo è suo; (*as opposed to mine*) questo è il suo

hiss /hɪs/ *n* sibilo *m*; (*of disapproval*) fischio *m* ● *vt* fischiare; (*in disapproval*) sibilare; (*in disapproval*) fischiare

historian /hɪˈstɔːrɪən/ *n* storico, -a *mf*

historic /hɪˈstɒrɪk/ *a* storico. **~al** *a* storico. **~ally** *adv* storicamente

history /ˈhɪstərɪ/ *n* storia *f*; **make ~** passare alla storia

hit /hɪt/ *n* (*blow*) colpo *m*; (*fam: success*) successo *m*; **score a direct ~** (*missile:*) colpire in pieno ● *vt/i* (*pt/pp* **hit**, *pres p* **hitting**) colpire; **~ one's head on the table** battere la testa contro il tavolo; **the car ~ the wall** la macchina ha sbattuto contro il muro; **~ the roof** *fam* perdere le staffe. **hit off** *vt* **it off** andare d'accordo. **hit on** *vt fig* trovare

hitch /hɪtʃ/ *n* intoppo *m*; **technical ~** problema *m* tecnico ● *vt* attaccare; **~ a lift** chiedere un passaggio. **hitch up** *vt* tirarsi su (*trousers*). **~-hike** *vi* fare l'autostop. **~-hiker** *n* autostoppista *mf*

hit-or-'miss *a* **on a very ~ basis** all'improvvisata

hither /ˈhɪðə(r)/ *adv* **~ and thither** di qua e di là. **~'to** *adv* finora

hive /haɪv/ *n* alveare *m*; **~ of industry** fucina *f* di lavoro ● **hive off** *vt Comm* separare

hoard /hɔːd/ *n* provvista *f*; (*of money*) gruzzolo *m* ● *vt* accumulare

hoarding /ˈhɔːdɪŋ/ *n* palizzata *f*; (*with advertisements*) tabellone *m* per manifesti pubblicitari

hoarse /hɔːs/ a rauco. **~ly** adv con voce rauca. **~ness** n raucedine f

hoax /həʊks/ n scherzo m; (false alarm) falso allarme m. **~er** n burlone, -a mf

hob /hɒb/ n piano m di cottura

hobble /'hɒbl/ vi zoppicare

hobby /'hɒbɪ/ n hobby m inv. **~-horse** n fig fissazione f

hockey /'hɒkɪ/ n hockey m

hoe /həʊ/ n zappa f

hog /hɒg/ n maiale m. ● vt (pt/pp **hogged**) fam monopolizzare

hoist /hɔɪst/ n montacarichi m inv; (fam: push) spinta f in su ● vt sollevare; innalzare ⟨flag⟩; levare ⟨anchor⟩

hold[1] /həʊld/ n Naut, Aeron stiva f

hold[2] n presa f; (fig: influence) ascendente m; **get ~ of** trovare; procurarsi ⟨information⟩ ● v (pt/pp **held**) ● vt tenere; (contain:) contenere; essere titolare di ⟨licence, passport⟩; trattenere ⟨breath, suspect⟩; mantenere vivo ⟨interest⟩; civil servant etc.) occupare ⟨position⟩; (retain) mantenere; **~ sb's hand** tenere qcno per mano; **~ one's tongue** tenere la bocca chiusa; **~ sb responsible** considerare qcno responsabile; **~ that** (believe) ritenere che ● vi tenere; ⟨weather, luck:⟩ durare; ⟨offer:⟩ essere valido; Teleph restare in linea; **I don't ~ with the idea that** fam non sono d'accordo sul fatto che. **hold back** vt rallentare ● vi esitare. **hold down** vt tenere a bada ⟨sb⟩. **hold on** vi (wait) attendere; Teleph restare in linea. **hold on to** vt aggrapparsi a; (keep) tenersi. **hold out** vt porgere ⟨hand⟩; fig offrire ⟨possibility⟩ ● vi (resist) resistere. **hold up** vt tenere su; (delay) rallentare; (rob) assalire; **~ one's head up** fig tenere la testa alta

'hold-: **~all** n borsone m. **~er** n titolare mf; (of record) dotentore, -trice mf; (container) astuccio m. **~ing** n (land) terreno m in affitto;

Comm azioni fpl. **~-up** n ritardo m; (attack) rapina f a mano armata

hole /həʊl/ n buco m

holiday /'hɒlɪdeɪ/ n vacanza f; (public) giorno m festivo; (day off) giorno m di ferie; **go on ~** andare in vacanza ● vi andare in vacanza. **~-maker** n vacanziere mf

holiness /'həʊlɪnɪs/ n santità f; **Your H~** Sua Santità

Holland /'hɒlənd/ n Olanda f

hollow /'hɒləʊ/ a cavo; ⟨promise⟩ a vuoto; ⟨voice⟩ assente; ⟨cheeks⟩ infossato ● n cavità f inv; (in ground) affossamento m

holly /'hɒlɪ/ n agrifoglio m

holocaust /'hɒləkɔːst/ n olocausto m

hologram /'hɒləgræm/ n ologramma m

holster /'həʊlstə(r)/ n fondina f

holy /'həʊlɪ/ a (-ier, -est) santo; ⟨water⟩ benedetto. **H~ Ghost** or **Spirit** n Spirito m Santo. **H~ Scriptures** npl sacre scritture fpl. **H~ Week** n settimana f santa

homage /'hɒmɪdʒ/ n omaggio m; **pay ~** to rendere omaggio a

home /həʊm/ n casa f; (for children) istituto m; (for old people) casa f di riposo; (native land) patria f ● adv at ~ a casa; (football) in casa; **feel at ~** sentirsi a casa propria; **come/go ~** venire/andare a casa; **drive a nail ~** piantare un chiodo a fondo ● a domestico; ⟨movie, video⟩ casalingo; ⟨team⟩ ospitante; Pol nazionale

home-: **~ ad'dress** n indirizzo m di casa. **~ com'puter** n computer m inv da casa. **H~ Counties** npl contee fpl intorno a Londra. **~ game** n gioco m in casa. **~ help** n aiuto m domestico (per persone non autosufficienti). **~land** n patria f. **~less** a senza tetto

homely /'həʊmlɪ/ a (-ier, -lest) semplice; ⟨atmosphere⟩ familiare; (Am: ugly) bruttino

home: ~-'**made** a fatto in casa. **H**~ **Office** n Br ministero m degli interni. **H**~ '**Secretary** n Br ministro m degli interni. ~**sick** a be ~**sick** avere nostalgia (for di). ~**sickness** n nostalgia f di casa. ~'**town** n città f inv natia. ~**ward** a di ritorno ● adv verso casa. ~**work** n Sch compiti mpl

homicide /'hɒmɪsaɪd/ n (crime) omicidio m

homoeopath|ic /həʊmɪə'pæθɪk/ a omeopatico. ~**y** /-'ɒpəθɪ/ n omeopatia f

homogeneous /hɒmə'dʒiːnɪəs/ a omogeneo

homo'sexual a & n omosessuale mf

honest /'ɒnɪst/ a onesto; ⟨frank⟩ sincero. ~**ly** adv onestamente; ⟨frankly⟩ sinceramente; ~**ly!** ma insomma!. ~**y** n onestà f; ⟨frankness⟩ sincerità f

honey /'hʌnɪ/ n miele m; (fam: darling) tesoro m

honey: ~**comb** n favo m. ~**moon** n luna f di miele. ~**suckle** n caprifoglio m

honk /hɒŋk/ vi Auto clacsonare

honorary /'ɒnərərɪ/ a onorario

honour /'ɒnə(r)/ n onore m ● vt onorare. ~**able** /-əbl/ a onorevole. ~**ably** adv con onore. ~**s degree** n ≈ diploma m di laurea

hood /hʊd/ n cappuccio m; (of pram) tettuccio m; (over cooker) cappa f; Am Auto cofano m

hoodlum /'huːdləm/ n teppista m

'hoodwink vt fam infinocchiare

hoof /huːf/ n (pl ~**s** o **hooves**) zoccolo m

hook /hʊk/ n gancio m; (for fishing) amo m; (off the ~ Teleph staccato; fig fuori pericolo ● vt agganciare ● vi agganciarsi

hook|ed /hʊkt/ a ⟨nose⟩ adunco ~**ed on** (fam: drugs) dedito a; be ~**ed on skiing** essere un fanatico dello sci. ~**er** n Am sl battona f

hookey /'hʊkɪ/ n **play** ~ Am fam marinare la scuola

hooligan /'huːlɪgən/ n teppista mf. ~**ism** n teppismo m

hoop /huːp/ n cerchio m

hooray /hʊ'reɪ/ int & n = **hurrah**

hoot /huːt/ n colpo m di clacson; (of siren) ululato m; (of owl) grido m ● vi ⟨owl:⟩ gridare; ⟨car:⟩ clacsonare; ⟨siren:⟩ ululare; ⟨jeer⟩ fischiare. ~**er** n (of factory) sirena f; Auto clacson m inv

hoover® /'huːvə(r)/ n aspirapolvere m inv ● vt passare l'aspirapolvere su ⟨carpet⟩; passare l'aspirapolvere in ⟨room⟩

hop /hɒp/ n saltello m ● vi (pt/pp **hopped**) saltellare; ~ **it!** fam tela!. **hop in** vi fam saltar su

hope /həʊp/ n speranza f ● vi sperare (for in); **I** ~ **so/not** spero di sì/no ● vt ~ **that** sperare che

hope|ful /'həʊpfl/ a pieno di speranza; (promising) promettente; **be** ~**ful that** avere buone speranze che. ~**fully** adv con speranza; (it is hoped) se tutto va bene. ~**less** a senza speranze; (useless) impossibile; (incompetent) incapace. ~**lessly** adv disperatamente; (inefficient, lost) completamente. ~**lessness** n disperazione f

horde /hɔːd/ n orda f

horizon /hə'raɪzn/ n orizzonte m

horizontal /hɒrɪ'zɒntl/ a orizzontale

hormone /'hɔːməʊn/ n ormone m

horn /hɔːn/ n corno m; Auto clacson m inv

horny /'hɔːnɪ/ a calloso; fam arrapato

horoscope /'hɒrəskəʊp/ n oroscopo m

horrib|le /'hɒrɪbl/ a orribile. ~**y** adv spaventosamente

horrid /'hɒrɪd/ a orrendo

horrific /hə'rɪfɪk/ a raccapricciante; (fam: accident, prices, story) terrificante

horrify /'hɒrɪfaɪ/ vt (pt/pp -**ied**) far inorridire; **I was horrified** ero sconvolto. ~**ing** a terrificante

horror /'hɒrə(r)/ n orrore m. **~ film** n film m dell'orrore

hors-d'œuvre /ɔ:'dɜ:vr/ n antipasto m

horse /hɔ:s/ n cavallo m

horse: **~back** n on **~back** a cavallo. **~man** n cavaliere m. **~play** n gioco m pesante. **~power** n cavallo m [vapore]. **~-racing** n corse fpl di cavalli. **~shoe** n ferro m di cavallo

horti'cultural /hɔ:tɪ/ a di orticoltura

'horticulture n orticoltura f

hose /həʊz/ n (pipe) manichetta f ● **hose down** vt lavare con la manichetta

hospice /'hɒspɪs/ n (for the terminally ill) ospedale m per i malati in fase terminale

hospitable /hɒ'spɪtəbl/ a ospitale. **~y** adv con ospitalità

hospital /'hɒspɪtl/ n ospedale m

hospitality /hɒspɪ'tælətɪ/ n ospitalità f

host[1] /həʊst/ n **a ~ of** una moltitudine di

host[2] n ospite m

host[3] n Relig ostia f

hostage /'hɒstɪdʒ/ n ostaggio m; **hold sb ~** tenere qcno in ostaggio

hostel /'hɒstl/ n ostello m

hostess /'həʊstɪs/ n padrona f di casa; Aeron hostess f inv

hostile /'hɒstaɪl/ a ostile

hostility /hɒ'stɪlətɪ/ n ostilità f, **~ies** pl ostilità fpl

hot /hɒt/ a (hotter, hottest) caldo; (spicy) piccante; **I am** o **feel ~** ho caldo; **it is ~** fa caldo

'hotbed n fig focolaio m

hotchpotch /'hɒtʃpɒtʃ/ n miscuglio m

'hot-dog n hot dog m inv

hotel /həʊ'tel/ n albergo m. **~ier** /-ɪə(r)/ n albergatore, -trice mf

hot: **~head** n persona f impetuosa. **~house** n serra f. **~ly** adv fig accanitamente. **~plate** n piastra f riscaldante. **~ tap** n rubinetto m dell'acqua calda. **~-tempered** a ira-

scibile. **~'water bottle** n borsa f dell'acqua calda

hound /haʊnd/ n cane m da caccia ● vt fig perseguire

hour /'aʊə(r)/ n ora f. **~ly** a ad ogni ora; (pay, rate) ● adv ogni ora

house[1] /haʊs/ n casa f; Pol camera f; Theat sala f; **at my ~** a casa mia, da me

house[2] /haʊz/ vt alloggiare (person)

house /haʊs/: **~boat** n casa f galleggiante. **~breaking** n furto m con scasso. **~hold** n casa f, famiglia f. **~holder** n capo m di famiglia. **~keeper** n governante f di casa. **~keeping** n governo m della casa; (money) soldi mpl per le spese di casa. **~plant** n pianta f da appartamento. **~-trained** a che non sporca in casa. **~-warming [party]** n festa f di inaugurazione della nuova casa. **~wife** n casalinga f. **~work** n lavoro m domestico

housing /'haʊzɪŋ/ n alloggio m. **~ estate** n zona f residenziale

hovel /'hɒvl/ n tugurio m

hover /'hɒvə(r)/ vi librarsi; (linger) indugiare. **~craft** n hovercraft m inv

how /haʊ/ adv come; **~ are you?** come stai?; **~ about a coffee/ going on holiday?** che ne diresti di un caffè/di andare in vacanza?; **~ do you do?** molto lieto!; **~ old are you?** quanti anni hai?; **~ long** quanto tempo?; **~ many** quanti; **~ much** quanto; **~ often** ogni quanto; **and ~!** eccome!; **~ odd!** che strano!

how'ever adv (nevertheless) comunque; **~ small** per quanto piccolo

howl /haʊl/ n ululato m ● vi ululare; (cry, with laughter) singhiozzare. **~er** n fam strafalcione m

HP n abbr hire purchase; n abbr (horse power) C.V.

hub /hʌb/ n mozzo m; fig centro m

hubbub /'hʌbʌb/ n baccano m

'hub-cap n coprimozzo m

huddle /'hʌdl/ vi ~ **together** rannicchiarsi

hue[1] /hju:/ n colore m

hue[2] n ~ **and cry** clamore m

huff /hʌf/ n **be in/go into a** ~ fare il broncio

hug /hʌg/ n abbraccio m ● vt (pt/pp **hugged**) abbracciare; (keep close to) tenersi vicino a

huge /hju:dʒ/ a enorme

hulking /'hʌlkɪŋ/ a fam grosso

hull /hʌl/ n Naut scafo m

hullo /hə'ləʊ/ int = **hallo**

hum /hʌm/ n ronzio m ● v (pt/pp **hummed**) ● vt canticchiare ● vi (motor:) ronzare; fig fervere (di attività); ~ **and haw** esitare

human /'hju:mən/ a umano. ~ **being** n essere m umano. ~ '**being** n essere m umano

humane /hju:'meɪn/ a umano

humanitarian /hju:mænɪ'teərɪən/ a & n umanitario, -a mf

humanit|y /hju:'mænətɪ/ n umanità f; ~**ies** pl Univ dottrine fpl umanistiche

humble /'hʌmbl/ a umile ● vt umiliare

'**humdrum** a noioso

humid /'hju:mɪd/ a umido. ~**ifier** /-'mɪdɪfaɪə(r)/ n umidificatore m. ~**ity** /-'mɪdətɪ/ n umidità f

humiliat|e /hju:'mɪlɪeɪt/ vt umiliare. ~**ion** /-'eɪʃn/ n umiliazione f

humility /hju:'mɪlətɪ/ n umiltà f

humorous /'hju:mərəs/ a umoristico. ~**ly** adv con spirito

humour /'hju:mə(r)/ n umorismo m; (mood) umore m; **have a sense of** ~ avere il senso dell'umorismo ● vt compiacere

hump /hʌmp/ n protuberanza f; (of camel, hunchback) gobba f

hunch /hʌntʃ/ n (idea) intuizione f

'**hunch|back** n gobbo, -a mf. ~**ed** a ~**ed up** incurvato

hundred /'hʌndrəd/ a **one/a** ~ cento m cento m; ~**s of** centinaia di. ~**th** a centesimo ● n centesimo m. ~**weight** n cinquanta chili m

hung /hʌŋ/ see **hang**

Hungarian /hʌŋ'geərɪən/ n & a ungherese mf; (language) ungherese m

Hungary /'hʌŋgərɪ/ n Ungheria f

hunger /'hʌŋgə(r)/ n fame f. ~**-strike** n sciopero m della fame m

hungr|y /'hʌŋgrɪ/ a (-ier, -iest) affamato; **be** ~**y** aver fame. ~**ily** adv con appetito

hunk /hʌŋk/ n [grosso] pezzo m

hunt /hʌnt/ n caccia f ● vt andare a caccia di (animal); dare la caccia a (criminal) ● vi andare a caccia; ~ **for** cercare. ~**er** n cacciatore m. ~**ing** n caccia f

hurdle /'hɜ:dl/ n Sport & fig ostacolo m. ~**r** n ostacolista mf

hurl /hɜ:l/ vt scagliare

hurrah /hʊ'rɑ:/, **hurray** /hʊ'reɪ/ int urrà! ● n urrà m

hurricane /'hʌrɪkən/ n uragano m

hurried /'hʌrɪd/ a affrettato; (job) fatto in fretta. ~**ly** adv in fretta

hurry /'hʌrɪ/ n fretta f; **be in a** ~ aver fretta ● vi (pt/pp **-ied**) affrettarsi. **hurry up** vi sbrigarsi ● vt fare sbrigare (person); accelerare (things)

hurt /hɜ:t/ v (pt/pp **hurt**) ● vt far male a; (offend) ferire ● vi far male; **my leg** ~**s** mi fa male la gamba. ~**ful** a fig offensivo

hurtle /'hɜ:tl/ vi ~ **along** andare a tutta velocità

husband /'hʌzbənd/ n marito m

hush /hʌʃ/ n silenzio m ● **hush up** vt mettere a tacere. ~**ed** a (voice) sommesso. ~**-'hush** a fam segretissimo

husky /'hʌskɪ/ a (-ier, -iest) (voice) rauco

hustle /'hʌsl/ vt affrettare ● n attività f incessante; ~ **and bustle** trambusto m

hut /hʌt/ n capanna f

hybrid /'haɪbrɪd/ a ibrido ● n ibrido m

hydrant /'haɪdrənt/ n [fire] ~ idrante m

hydraulic /haɪ'drɔ:lɪk/ a idraulico

hydroe'lectric /haɪdrəʊ-/ a idroelettrico

hydrofoil /'haɪdrə-/ n aliscafo m

hydrogen /'haɪdrədʒən/ n idrogeno m

hyena /har'i:nə/ n iena f

hygien|e /'haɪdʒi:n/ n igiene m. **~ic** /har'dʒi:nɪk/ a igienico

hymn /hɪm/ n inno m. **~-book** n libro m dei canti

hypermarket /'haɪpəmɑ:kɪt/ n ipermercato m

hyphen /'haɪfn/ n lineetta f. **~ate** vt unire con lineetta

hypno|sis /hɪp'nəʊsɪs/ n ipnosi f. **~tic** /-'nɒtɪk/ a ipnotico

hypno|tism /'hɪpnətɪzm/ n ipnotismo m. **~tist** /-tɪst/ n ipnotizzatore, -trice mf. **~tize** vt ipnotizzare

hypochondriac /haɪpə'kɒndriæk/ a ipocondriaco ● n ipocondriaco, -a mf

hypocrisy /hɪ'pɒkrəsɪ/ n ipocrisia f

hypocrit|e /'hɪpəkrɪt/ n ipocrita mf. **~ical** /-'krɪtɪkl/ a ipocrita

hypodermic /haɪpə'dɜ:mɪk/ a & n **~ [syringe]** siringa f ipodermica

hypothe|sis /haɪ'pɒθəsɪs/ n ipotesi f inv. **~tical** /-ə'θetɪkl/ a ipotetico. **~tically** adv in teoria; (speak) per ipotesi

hysteri|a /hɪ'stɪərɪə/ n isterismo m. **~cal** /-'sterɪkl/ a isterico. **~cally** adv istericamente; **~cally funny** da morir dal ridere. **~ics** /hɪ'sterɪks/ npl attacco m isterico

Ii

I /aɪ/ pron io; **I'm tired** sono stanco; **he's going, but I'm not** lui va, ma io no

ice /aɪs/ n ghiaccio m ● vt glassare (cake). **ice over/up** vi ghiacciarsi

ice: ~ age n era f glaciale. **~-axe** n piccozza f per il ghiaccio. **~berg** /-bɜ:g/ n iceberg m inv. **~box** n Am frigorifero m. **~'cream** n gelato m. **~'cream parlour** n gelateria f. **~-cube** n cubetto m di ghiaccio. **~ hockey** n hockey m su ghiaccio

Iceland /'aɪslənd/ n Islanda f. **~er** n islandese mf; **~ic** /-'lændɪk/ a & n islandese m

ice: ~lolly n ghiacciolo m. **~ rink** n pista f di pattinaggio. **~ skater** pattinatore, -trice mf sul ghiaccio. **~ skating** pattinaggio m su ghiaccio

icicle /'aɪsɪkl/ n ghiacciolo m

icing /'aɪsɪŋ/ n glassa f. **~ sugar** n zucchero m a velo

icon /'aɪkɒn/ n icona f

icy /'aɪsɪ/ a (-ier, -iest) ghiacciato; fig gelido. **~ily** adv gelidamente

idea /aɪ'dɪə/ n idea f; **I've no ~!** non ne ho idea!

ideal /aɪ'dɪəl/ a ideale ● n ideale m. **~ism** n idealismo m. **~ist** n idealista mf. **~istic** /-'lɪstɪk/ a idealistico. **~ize** vt idealizzare. **~ly** adv idealmente

identical /aɪ'dentɪkl/ a identico

identi|fication /aɪdentɪfɪ'keɪʃn/ n identificazione f; (proof of identity) documento m di riconoscimento. **~fy** /aɪ'dentɪfaɪ/ vt (pt/pp -ied) identificare

identikit® /aɪ'dentɪkɪt/ n identikit m inv

identity /aɪ'dentətɪ/ n identità f inv. **~ card** n carta f d'identità

ideolog|ical /aɪdɪə'lɒdʒɪkl/ a ideologico. **~y** /aɪdɪ'ɒlədʒɪ/ n ideologia f

idiom /'ɪdɪəm/ n idioma f. **~atic** /-'mætɪk/ a idiomatico

idiosyncrasy /ɪdɪə'sɪŋkrəsɪ/ n idiosincrasia f

idiot /'ɪdɪət/ n idiota mf. **~ic** /-'ɒtɪk/ a idiota

idle /'aɪd(ə)l/ a (lazy) pigro, ozioso; (empty) vano; (machine) fermo ● vi oziare; (engine:) girare a vuoto to. **~eness** n ozio m. **~y** adv oziosamente

idol /'aɪdl/ n idolo m. **~ize** /'aɪdəlaɪz/ vt idolatrare

idyllic /ɪ'dɪlɪk/ a idillico

i.e. abbr (**id est**) cioè

if /ɪf/ conj se; **as if** come se

ignite /ɪg'naɪt/ vt dar fuoco a ● vi prender fuoco

ignition /ɪg'nɪʃn/ n Auto accensione f. **~ key** n chiave f d'accensione

ignoramus /ɪgnə'reɪməs/ n ignorante mf

ignoran|ce /'ɪgnərəns/ n ignoranza f. **~t** a (lacking knowledge) ignaro; (rude) ignorante

ignore /ɪg'nɔ:(r)/ vt ignorare

ill /ɪl/ a ammalato; **feel ~ at ease** sentirsi a disagio ● adv male ● n male m. **~-advised** a avventato. **~-bred** a maleducato

illegal /ɪ'li:gl/ a illegale

illegib|le /ɪ'ledʒɪbl/ a illeggibile

illegitima|cy /ɪlɪ'dʒɪtɪməsɪ/ n illegittimità f. **~te** /-mət/ a illegittimo

illicit /ɪ'lɪsɪt/ a illecito

illitera|cy /ɪ'lɪtərəsɪ/ n analfabetismo m. **~te** /-rət/ a n analfabeta mf

illness /'ɪlnɪs/ n malattia f

illogical /ɪ'lɒdʒɪkl/ a illogico

ill-treat /ɪl'tri:t/ vt maltrattare. **~ment** n maltrattamento

illuminat|e /ɪ'lu:mɪneɪt/ vt illuminare. **~ing** a chiarificatore. **~ion** /-'neɪʃn/ n illuminazione f

illusion /ɪ'lu:ʒn/ n illusione f; **be under the ~ that** avere l'illusione che

illusory /ɪ'lu:sərɪ/ a illusorio

illustrat|e /'ɪləstreɪt/ vt illustrare. **~ion** /-'streɪʃn/ n illustrazione f. **~or** n illustratore, -trice mf

illustrious /ɪ'lʌstrɪəs/ a illustre

ill 'will n malanimo m

image /'ɪmɪdʒ/ n immagine f; (exact likeness) ritratto m

imagin|able /ɪ'mædʒɪnəbl/ a immaginabile. **~ary** /-ərɪ/ a immaginario

imaginat|ion /ɪmædʒɪ'neɪʃn/ n immaginazione f, fantasia f; **it's your ~ion** è solo una tua idea. **~ive** /ɪ'mædʒɪnətɪv/ a fantasioso. **~ively** adv con fantasia or immaginazione

imagine /ɪ'mædʒɪn/ vt immaginare; (wrongly) inventare

im'balance n squilibrio m

imbecile /'ɪmbəsi:l/ n imbecille mf

imbibe /ɪm'baɪb/ vt ingerire

imbue /ɪm'bju:/ vt **~d with** impregnato di

imitat|e /'ɪmɪteɪt/ vt imitare. **~ion** /-'teɪʃn/ n imitazione f. **~or** n imitatore, -trice mf

immaculate /ɪ'mækjʊlət/ a immacolato. **~ly** adv immacolatamente

imma'terial a (unimportant) irrilevante

imma'ture a immaturo

immediate /ɪ'mi:dɪət/ a immediato; (relative) stretto; **in the ~ vicinity** nelle immediate vicinanze. **~ly** adv immediatamente; **~ly next to** subito accanto a ● conj [non] appena

immemorial /ɪmɪ'mɔ:rɪəl/ a **from time ~** da tempo immemorabile

immense /ɪ'mens/ a immenso

immers|e /ɪ'mɜ:s/ vt immergere; **be ~ed in** fig essere immerso in. **~ion** /-ʒn/ n immersione f. **~ion heater** n scaldabagno m elettrico

immigrant /'ɪmɪgrənt/ n immigrante mf

immigrat|e /'ɪmɪgreɪt/ vi immigrare. **~ion** /-'greɪʃn/ n immigrazione f

imminent /'ɪmɪnənt/ a imminente

immobil|e /ɪ'məʊbaɪl/ a immobile. **~ize** /-bɪlaɪz/ vt immobilizzare

immoderate /ɪ'mɒdərət/ a smodato

immodest /ɪ'mɒdɪst/ a immodesto

immoral /ɪ'mɒrəl/ a immorale. **~ity** /ɪmə'rælətɪ/ n immoralità f

immortal /ɪ'mɔ:tl/ a immortale. **~ity** /-'tælətɪ/ n immortalità f. **~ize** vt immortalare

immovable /ɪˈmuːvəbl/ a fig irremovibile

immune /ɪˈmjuːn/ a immune (**to/from** da). **~ system** n sistema m immunitario

immunity /ɪˈmjuːnətɪ/ n immunità f

immuniz|e /ˈɪmjonaɪz/ vt immunizzare

imp /ɪmp/ n diavoletto m

impact /ˈɪmpækt/ n impatto m

impair /ɪmˈpeə(r)/ vt danneggiare

impale /ɪmˈpeɪl/ vt impalare

impart /ɪmˈpɑːt/ vt impartire

im'parti|al a imparziale. **~'ality** n imparzialità f

im'passable a impraticabile

impasse /æmˈpɑːs/ n fig impasse f inv

impassioned /ɪmˈpæʃnd/ a appassionato

im'passive a impassibile

im'patien|ce n impazienza f. **~t** a impaziente. **~tly** adv impazientemente

impeccabl|e /ɪmˈpekəbl/ a impeccabile. **~y** adv in modo impeccabile

impede /ɪmˈpiːd/ vt impedire

impediment /ɪmˈpedɪmənt/ n impedimento m; (in speech) difetto m

impel /ɪmˈpel/ vt (pt/pp **impelled**) costringere; **feel ~led to** sentire l'obbligo di

impending /ɪmˈpendɪŋ/ a imminente

impenetrable /ɪmˈpenɪtrəbl/ a impenetrabile

imperative /ɪmˈperətɪv/ a imperativo ● n Gram imperativo m

imper'ceptible a impercettibile

im'perfect a imperfetto; (faulty) difettoso ● n Gram imperfetto m. **~ion** /-ˈfekʃn/ n imperfezione f

imperial /ɪmˈpɪərɪəl/ a imperiale. **~ism** n imperialismo m. **~ist** n imperialista mf

imperious /ɪmˈpɪərɪəs/ a imperioso

im'personal a impersonale

impersonat|e /ɪmˈpɜːsəneɪt/ vt impersonare. **~or** n imitatore, -trice mf

impertinen|ce /ɪmˈpɜːtɪnəns/ n impertinenza f. **~t** a impertinente

imperturbable /ɪmpəˈtɜːbəbl/ a imperturbabile

impervious /ɪmˈpɜːvɪəs/ a **~ to** fig indifferente a

impetuous /ɪmˈpetjʊəs/ a impetuoso. **~ly** adv impetuosamente

impetus /ˈɪmpɪtəs/ n impeto m

implacable /ɪmˈplækəbl/ a implacabile

im'plant[1] vt trapiantare; fig inculcare

'implant[2] n trapianto m

implement[1] /ˈɪmplɪmənt/ n attrezzo m

implement[2] /ˈɪmplɪment/ vt mettere in atto

implicat|e /ˈɪmplɪkeɪt/ vt implicare. **~ion** /-ˈkeɪʃn/ n implicazione f; **by ~ion** implicitamente

implicit /ɪmˈplɪsɪt/ a implicito; (absolute) assoluto

implore /ɪmˈplɔː(r)/ vt implorare

imply /ɪmˈplaɪ/ vt (pt/pp **-ied**) implicare; **what are you ~ing?** che cosa vorresti insinuare?

impo'lite a sgarbato

import[1] /ˈɪmpɔːt/ n Comm importazione f

import[2] /ɪmˈpɔːt/ vt importare

importan|ce /ɪmˈpɔːtəns/ n importanza f. **~t** a importante

importer /ɪmˈpɔːtə(r)/ n importatore, -trice mf

impos|e /ɪmˈpəʊz/ vt imporre (**on** a) ● vi imporsi. **~e on** abusare di. **~ing** a imponente. **~ition** /ɪmpəˈzɪʃn/ n imposizione f

impossi'bility n impossibilità f

im'possibl|e a impossibile

impostor /ɪmˈpɒstə(r)/ n impostore, -trice mf

impoten|ce /ˈɪmpətəns/ n impotenza f. **~t** a impotente

impound /ɪmˈpaʊnd/ vt confiscare

impoverished /ɪmˈpɒvərɪʃt/ a impoverito

im'practicable *a* impraticabile

im'practical *a* non pratico

impre'cise *a* impreciso

impregnable /ɪmˈpregnəbl/ *a* imprendibile

impregnate /ˈɪmpregneɪt/ *vt* impregnare (**with** di); *Biol* fecondare

im'press *vt* imprimere; *fig* colpire (*positivamente*); ~ **sth [up]on sb** fare capire qcsa a qcno

impression /ɪmˈpreʃn/ *n* impressione *f*; (*imitation*) imitazione *f*. ~**able** *a* (*child, mind*) influenzabile. ~**ism** *n* impressionismo *m*. ~**ist** *n* imitatore, -trice *mf*; (*artist*) impressionista *mf*

impressive /ɪmˈpresɪv/ *a* imponente

'imprint¹ *n* impressione *f*

im'print² *vt* imprimere; ~**ed on my mind** impresso nella mia memoria

im'prison *vt* incarcerare. ~**ment** *n* reclusione *f*

im'probable *a* improbabile

impromptu /ɪmˈprɒmptjuː/ *a* improvvisato

im'proper *a* (*use*) improprio; (*behaviour*) scorretto. ~**ly** *adv* scorrettamente

impro'priety *n* scorrettezza *f*

improve /ɪmˈpruːv/ *vt/i* migliorare. **improve** [**up**]**on** *vt* perfezionare. ~**ment** /-mənt/ *n* miglioramento *m*

improvise /ˈɪmprəvaɪz/ *vt/i* improvvisare

im'prudent *a* imprudente

impuden|ce /ˈɪmpjʊdəns/ *n* sfrontatezza *f*. ~**t** *a* sfrontato

impuls|e /ˈɪmpʌls/ *n* impulso *m*; **on** [**an**] ~**e** impulsivamente. ~**ive** /-ˈpʌlsɪv/ *a* impulsivo

impunity /ɪmˈpjuːnətɪ/ *n* **with** ~ impunemente

im'pur|e *a* impuro. ~**ity** *n* impurità *f inv*; ~**ities** *pl* impurità *fpl*

impute /ɪmˈpjuːt/ *vt* imputare (**to** a)

in /ɪn/ *prep* in; (*with names of towns*) a; **in the garden** in giardi-

no; **in the street** in *or* per strada; **in bed/hospital** a letto/all'ospedale; **in the world** nel mondo; **in the rain** sotto la pioggia; **in the sun** al sole; **in this heat** con questo caldo; **in summer/winter** in estate/inverno; **in 1995** nel 1995; **in the evening** la sera; **he's arriving in two hours time** arriva fra due ore; **deaf in one ear** sordo da un orecchio; **in the army** nell'esercito; **in English/Italian** in inglese/italiano; **in ink/pencil** a penna/matita; **in red** (*dressed, circled*) di rosso; **the man in the raincoat** l'uomo con l'impermeabile; **in a soft/loud voice** a voce bassa/alta; **one in ten people** una persona su dieci; **in doing this, he...** nel far questo,...; **in itself** in sé; **in that** in quanto in; (*at home*) a casa; (*indoors*) dentro; **he's not in yet** non è ancora arrivato; **in there/here** lì/qui dentro; **ten in all** dieci in tutto; **day in, day out** giorno dopo giorno; **have it in for sb** *fam* avercela con qcno; **send him in** in fallo entrare; **come** in entrare; **bring in the washing** portare dentro i panni ● *a* (*fam: in fashion*) di moda ● *n* **the ins and outs** i dettagli

ina'bility *n* incapacità *f*

inac'cessible *a* inaccessibile

in'accura|cy *n* inesattezza *f*. ~**te** *a* inesatto

in'ac|tive *a* inattivo. ~'**tivity** *n* inattività *f*

in'adequate *a* inadeguato. ~**ly** *adv* inadeguatamente

inad'missible *a* inammissibile

inad'vertently /ɪnədˈvɜːtntlɪ/ *adv* inavvertitamente

inad'visable *a* sconsigliabile

inane /ɪˈneɪn/ *a* stupido

in'animate *a* esanime

in'applicable *a* inapplicabile

inap'propriate *a* inadatto

inar'ticulate *a* inarticolato

inat'tentive *a* disattento

in'audible *a* impercettibile

inaugural /ɪˈnɔːgjʊərəl/ *a* inaugurale

inaugur|ate /ɪˈnɔːgjʊəreɪt/ *vt* inaugurare. **~ion** /-ˈreɪʃn/ *n* inaugurazione *f*

inau'spicious *a* infausto

inborn /ˈɪnbɔːn/ *a* innato

inbred /ɪnˈbred/ *a* congenito

incalculable /ɪnˈkælkjʊləbl/ *a* incalcolabile

in'capable *a* incapace

incapacitate /ɪnkəˈpæsɪteɪt/ *vt* rendere incapace

incarnat|e /ɪnˈkɑːnət/ *a* **the devil ~e** il diavolo in carne e ossa

incendiary /ɪnˈsendɪərɪ/ *a* incendiario

incense¹ /ˈɪnsens/ *n* incenso

incense² /ɪnˈsens/ *vt* esasperare

incentive /ɪnˈsentɪv/ *n* incentivo *m*

incessant /ɪnˈsesənt/ *a* incessante

incest /ˈɪnsest/ *n* incesto *m*

inch /ɪntʃ/ *n* pollice *m* (= 2.54 cm) ● *vi* **~ forward** avanzare gradatamente

inciden|ce /ˈɪnsɪdəns/ *n* incidenza *f*. **~t** *n* incidente *m*

incidental /ɪnsɪˈdentl/ *a* incidentale; **~ expenses** spese *fpl* accessorie. **~ly** *adv* incidentalmente; *(by the way)* a proposito

incinerat|e /ɪnˈsɪnəreɪt/ *vt* incenerire. **~or** *n* inceneritore *m*

incision /ɪnˈsɪʒn/ *n* incisione *f*

incisive /ɪnˈsaɪsɪv/ *a* incisivo

incisor /ɪnˈsaɪzə(r)/ *n* incisivo *m*

incite /ɪnˈsaɪt/ *vt* incitare. **~ment** *n* incitamento *m*

inclination /ɪnklɪˈneɪʃn/ *n* inclinazione *f*

incline¹ /ɪnˈklaɪn/ *vt* inclinare; **be ~d to** do sth essere propenso a fare qcsa

incline² /ˈɪnklaɪn/ *n* pendio *m*

inclu|de /ɪnˈkluːd/ *vt* includere. **~ding** *prep* incluso. **~sion** /-uːʒn/ *n* inclusione *f*

inclusive /ɪnˈkluːsɪv/ *a* incluso; **~ of** comprendente; **be ~ of** comprendere ● *adv* incluso

incognito /ɪnkɒgˈniːtəʊ/ *adv* incognito

inco'herent *a* incoerente; *(because drunk etc)* incomprensibile

income /ˈɪnkʌm/ *n* reddito *m*. **~tax** *n* imposta *f* sul reddito

'incoming *a* in arrivo. **~ tide** *n* marea *f* montante

in'comparable *a* incomparabile

incompati'bility *n* incompatibilità *f*

incom'patible *a* incompatibile

incom'peten|ce *n* incompetenza *f*. **~t** *a* incompetente

incom'plete *a* incompleto

incompre'hensible *a* incomprensibile

incon'ceivable *a* inconcepibile

incon'clusive *a* inconcludente

incongruous /ɪnˈkɒngrʊəs/ *a* contrastante

inconsequential /ɪnkɒnsɪˈkwenʃl/ *a* senza importanza

incon'siderate *a* trascurabile

incon'sistency *n* incoerenza *f*

incon'sistent *a* incoerente; **be ~ with** non essere coerente con. **~ly** *adv* in modo incoerente

incon'solable /ɪnkənˈsəʊləbl/ *a* inconsolabile

incon'spicuous *a* non appariscente. **~ly** *adv* modestamente

inconti'nen|ce /ɪnˈkɒntɪnəns/ *n* incontinenza *f*. **~t** *a* incontinente

incon'venien|ce *n* scomodità *f*; *(drawback)* inconveniente *m*; **put sb to ~e** dare disturbo a qcno. **~t** *a* scomodo; *(time, place)* inopportuno. **~tly** *adv* in modo inopportuno

incorporate /ɪnˈkɔːpəreɪt/ *vt* incorporare; *(contain)* comprendere

incor'rect *a* incorretto. **~ly** *adv* scorrettamente

incorrigible /ɪnˈkɒrɪdʒəbl/ *a* incorreggibile

incorruptible /ɪnkəˈrʌptəbl/ *a* incorruttibile

increase¹ /ˈɪnkriːs/ *n* aumento *m*; **on the ~** in aumento

increas|e² /ɪnˈkriːs/ *vt/i* aumentare. **~ing** *a* ⟨*impatience etc*⟩ crescente; ⟨*numbers*⟩ in aumento. **~ingly** *adv* sempre più

in'credible *a* incredibile

incredulous /ɪn'kredjʊləs/ *a* incredulo

increment /'ɪnkrɪmənt/ *n* incremento *m*

incriminate /ɪn'krɪmɪneɪt/ *vt Jur* incriminare

incubat|e /'ɪŋkjʊbeɪt/ *vt* incubare. **~ion** /-'beɪʃn/ *n* incubazione *f*. **~ion period** *n Med* periodo *m* di incubazione. **~or** *n* (*for baby*) incubatrice *f*

incumbent /ɪn'kʌmbənt/ *a* **be ~ on sb** incombere a qcno

incur /ɪn'kɜ:(r)/ *vt* (*pt/pp* incurred) incorrere; contrarre ⟨*debts*⟩

in'curable *a* incurabile

incursion /ɪn'kɜ:ʃn/ *n* incursione *f*

indebted /ɪn'detɪd/ *a* obbligato (**to** verso)

in'decent *a* indecente

inde'cision *n* indecisione *f*

inde'cisive *a* indeciso. **~ness** *n* indecisione *f*

indeed /ɪn'di:d/ *adv* (*in fact*) difatti; **yes ~!** sì, certamente!; **I am/do** veramente!; **very much ~** moltissimo; **thank you very much ~** grazie infinite; **~?** davvero?

indefatigable /ɪndɪ'fætɪgəbl/ *a* instancabile

inde'finable *a* indefinibile

in'definite *a* indefinito. **~ly** *adv* indefinitamente; ⟨*postpone*⟩ a tempo indeterminato

indelible /ɪn'delɪbl/ *a* indelebile

indemnity /ɪn'demnɪtɪ/ *n* indennità *f inv*

indent[1] /'ɪndent/ *n Typ* rientranza *f* dal margine

indent[2] /ɪn'dent/ *vt Typ* fare rientrare dal margine. **~ation** /-'teɪʃn/ *n* (*notch*) intaccatura *f*

inde'penden|ce *n* indipendenza *f*. **~t** *a* indipendente. **~tly** *adv* indipendentemente

indescribable /ɪndɪ'skraɪbəbl/ *a* indescrivibile

indestructible /ɪndɪ'strʌktəbl/ *a* indistruttibile

indeterminate /ɪndɪ'tɜ:mɪnət/ *a* indeterminato

index /'ɪndeks/ *n* indice *m*

index: ~ card *n* scheda *f*. **~ finger** *n* dito *m* indice. **~-'linked** *a* ⟨*pension*⟩ legato al costo della vita

India /'ɪndɪə/ *n* India *f*. **~n** *a* indiano; (*American*) indiano [d'America] ●*n* indiano, -a *mf*; (*American*) indiano, -a *mf* [d'America], pellerossa *mf inv*

indicat|e /'ɪndɪkeɪt/ *vt* indicare; (*register*) segnare ●*vi Auto* mettere la freccia. **~ion** /-'keɪʃn/ *n* indicazione *f*

indicative /ɪn'dɪkətɪv/ *a* **be ~ of** essere indicativo di ●*n Gram* indicativo *m*

indicator /'ɪndɪkeɪtə(r)/ *n Auto* freccia *f*

indict /ɪn'daɪt/ *vt* accusare. **~ment** *n* accusa *f*

in'differen|ce *n* indifferenza *f*. **~t** *a* indifferente; (*not good*) mediocre

indigenous /ɪn'dɪdʒɪnəs/ *a* indigeno

indi'gest|ible *a* indigesto. **~ion** *n* indigestione *f*

indignant /ɪn'dɪgnənt/ *a* indignato. **~ntly** *adv* con indignazione. **~tion** /-'neɪʃn/ *n* indignazione *f*

in'dignity *n* umiliazione *f*

indi'rect *a* indiretto. **~ly** *adv* indirettamente

indi'screet *a* indiscreto

indi'scretion *n* indiscrezione *f*

indiscriminate /ɪndɪ'skrɪmɪnət/ *a* indiscriminato. **~ly** *adv* senza distinzione

indi'spensable *a* indispensabile

indisposed /ɪndɪ'spəʊzd/ *a* indisposto

indisputable /ɪndɪ'spju:təbl/ *a* indisputabile

indi'stinct *a* indistinto

indistinguishable /ɪndɪ'stɪŋgwɪʃ-əbl/ a indistinguibile

individual /ɪndɪ'vɪdjʊəl/ a individuale ● n individuo m. **~ity** /-'ælɪtɪ/ n individualità f

indi'visible a indivisibile

indoctrinate /ɪn'dɒktrɪneɪt/ vt indottrinare

indomitable /ɪn'dɒmɪtəbl/ a indomito

indoor /'ɪndɔː(r)/ a interno; (shoes) per casa; (plant) da appartamento; (swimming pool etc) coperto. **~s** /-'dɔːz/ adv dentro

induce /ɪn'djuːs/ vt indurre (to a); (produce) causare. **~ment** /-(e)ntivo/ n (incentive) incentivo m

indulge /ɪn'dʌldʒ/ vt soddisfare; viziare (child) ● vi **~ in** concedersi. **~nce** /-(e)ns/ n lusso m; (leniency) indulgenza f. **~nt** a indulgente

industrial /ɪn'dʌstrɪəl/ a industriale; **take ~ action** scioperare. **~ist** n industriale mf. **~ized** a industrializzato

industr|ious /ɪn'dʌstrɪəs/ a industrioso. **~y** /'ɪndəstrɪ/ n industria f; (zeal) operosità f

inebriated /ɪ'niːbrɪeɪtɪd/ a ebbro

in'edible a immangiabile

ineffective /ɪnɪ'fektɪv/ a inefficace

ineffectual /ɪnɪ'fektʃʊəl/ a inutile; (person) inconcludente

inef'ficien|cy n inefficienza f. **~t** a inefficiente

in'eligible a inadatto

inept /ɪ'nept/ a inetto

ine'quality n ineguaglianza f

inert /ɪ'nɜːt/ a inerte. **~ia** /ɪ'nɜːʃə/ n inerzia f

inescapable /ɪnɪ'skeɪpəbl/ a inevitabile

inestimable /ɪn'estɪməbl/ a inestimabile

inevitab|le /ɪn'evɪtəbl/ a inevitabile. **~y** adv inevitabilmente

ine'xact a inesatto

inex'cusable a imperdonabile

inexhaustible /ɪnɪg'zɔːstəbl/ a inesauribile

inexorable /ɪn'eksərəbl/ a inesorabile

inex'pensive a poco costoso

inex'perience n inesperienza f. **~d** a inesperto

inexplicable /ɪnɪk'splɪkəbl/ a inesplicabile

in'fallible a infallibile

infam|ous /'ɪnfəməs/ a infame; (person) famigerato. **~y** n infamia f

infan|cy /'ɪnfənsɪ/ n infanzia f; **in its ~cy** fig agli inizi. **~t** n bambino, -a mf piccolo, -a. **~tile** a infantile

infantry /'ɪnfəntrɪ/ n fanteria f

infatuated /ɪn'fætʃʊeɪtɪd/ a infatuato (with di). **~ion** n infatuazione f

infect /ɪn'fekt/ vt infettare; **become ~ed** (wound) infettarsi. **~ion** /-'fekʃn/ infezione f. **~ious** /-'fekʃəs/ a infettivo

infer /ɪn'fɜː(r)/ vt (pt/pp inferred) dedurre (from da); (imply) implicare. **~ence** /'ɪnfərəns/ n deduzione f

inferior /ɪn'fɪərɪə(r)/ a inferiore; (goods) scadente; (in rank) subalterno ● n inferiore mf; (in rank) subalterno, -a mf

inferiority /ɪnfɪərɪ'ɒrɪtɪ/ n inferiorità f. **~ complex** n complesso m di inferiorità

infern|al /ɪn'fɜːnl/ a infernale. **~o** n inferno m

in'fertile a sterile. **~'tility** n sterilità f

infest /ɪn'fest/ vt **be ~ed with** essere infestato da

in'fidelity n infedeltà f

infighting /'ɪnfaɪtɪŋ/ n fig lotta f per il potere

infiltrate /'ɪnfɪltreɪt/ vt infiltrare; Pol infiltrarsi in

infinite /'ɪnfɪnət/ a infinito

infinitive /ɪn'fɪnətɪv/ n Gram infinito m

infinity /ɪn'fɪnətɪ/ n infinità f

infirm /ɪn'fɜːm/ a debole. **~ary** n infermeria f. **~ity** n debolezza f

inflame /ɪnˈfleɪm/ vt infiammare. **~d** a infiammato; **become ~d** infiammarsi

in'flammable a infiammabile

inflammation /ɪnfləˈmeɪʃn/ n infiammazione f

inflammatory /ɪnˈflæmətrɪ/ a incendiario

inflatable /ɪnˈfleɪtəbl/ a gonfiabile

inflat|e /ɪnˈfleɪt/ vt gonfiare. **~ion** /-eɪʃn/ n inflazione f. **~ionary** /-eɪʃənərɪ/ a inflazionario

in'flexible a inflessibile

inflexion /ɪnˈflekʃn/ n inflessione f

inflict /ɪnˈflɪkt/ vt infliggere (**on** a)

influen|ce /ˈɪnfluəns/ n influenza f ● vt influenzare. **~tial** /-ˈenʃl/ a influente

influenza /ɪnfluˈenzə/ n influenza f

influx /ˈɪnflʌks/ n afflusso f

inform /ɪnˈfɔːm/ vt informare; **keep sb ~ed** tenere qcno al corrente ● vi **~ against** denunziare

in'formal a informale; ⟨agreement⟩ ufficioso. **~ally** adv in modo informale. **~'mality** n informalità f inv

informant /ɪnˈfɔːmənt/ n informatore, -trice mf

informat|ion /ɪnfəˈmeɪʃn/ n informazioni fpl; **a piece of ~ion** un'informazione f. **~ion highway** n autostrada f telematica. **~ion technology** n informatica f. **~ive** /ɪnˈfɔːmətɪv/ a informativo; ⟨film, book⟩ istruttivo

informer /ɪnˈfɔːmə(r)/ n informatore, -trice mf; Pol delatore, -trice mf

infra-'red /ɪnfrə-/ a infrarosso

infrastructure /ˈɪnfrəstrʌktʃə(r)/ n infrastruttura f

infringe /ɪnˈfrɪndʒ/ vt **~ on** usurpare. **~ment** n violazione f

infuriate /ɪnˈfjʊərɪeɪt/ vt infuriare. **~ing** a esasperante

infusion /ɪnˈfjuːʒn/ n ⟨drink⟩ infusione f; ⟨of capital, new blood⟩ afflusso m

ingenious /ɪnˈdʒiːnɪəs/ a ingegnoso

ingenuity /ɪndʒɪˈnjuːətɪ/ n ingegnosità f

ingenuous /ɪnˈdʒenjʊəs/ a ingenuo

ingot /ˈɪŋgət/ n lingotto m

ingrained /ɪnˈgreɪnd/ a (in person) radicato; ⟨dirt⟩ incrostato

ingratiate /ɪnˈgreɪʃɪeɪt/ vt **~ oneself with sb** ingraziarsi qcno

in'gratitude n ingratitudine f

ingredient /ɪnˈgriːdɪənt/ n ingrediente m

ingrowing /ˈɪngrəʊɪŋ/ a (nail) incarnito

inhabit /ɪnˈhæbɪt/ vt abitare. **~ant** n abitante mf

inhale /ɪnˈheɪl/ vt aspirare; Med inalare ● vi inspirare; (when smoking) aspirare. **~r** n (device) inalatore m

inherent /ɪnˈhɪərənt/ a inerente

inherit /ɪnˈherɪt/ vt ereditare. **~ance** /-əns/ n eredità f inv

inhibit /ɪnˈhɪbɪt/ vt inibire. **~ed** a inibito. **~ion** /-ˈbɪʃn/ n inibizione f

inho'spitable a inospitale

in'human a disumano

initial /ɪˈnɪʃl/ a iniziale ● n iniziale f ● vt (pt/pp **initialled**) siglare. **~ly** adv all'inizio

initiat|e /ɪˈnɪʃɪeɪt/ vt iniziare. **~ion** /-ˈeɪʃn/ n iniziazione f

initiative /ɪˈnɪʃətɪv/ n iniziativa f

inject /ɪnˈdʒekt/ vt iniettare. **~ion** /-ekʃn/ n iniezione f

injur|e /ˈɪndʒə(r)/ vt ferire; (wrong) nuocere. **~y** n ferita f; (wrong) torto m

in'justice n ingiustizia f; **do sb an ~** giudicare qcno in modo sbagliato

ink /ɪŋk/ n inchiostro m

inkling /ˈɪŋklɪŋ/ n sentore m

inlaid /ɪnˈleɪd/ a intarsiato

inland /ˈɪnlənd/ a interno ● adv all'interno. **I~ Revenue** n fisco m

in-laws /ˈɪnlɔːz/ npl fam parenti mpl acquisiti

inlay /ˈɪnleɪ/ n intarsio m

inlet /ˈɪnlet/ n insenatura f; Techn entrata f

inmate /'ınmeıt/ n (of hospital) degente mf; (of prison) carcerato, -a mf

inn /ın/ n locanda f

innate /ı'neıt/ a innato

inner /'ınə(r)/ a interno. **~most** a il più profondo. **~ tube** camera f d'aria

'innkeeper n locandiere, -a mf

innocen|ce /'ınəsəns/ n innocenza f. **~t** a innocente

innocuous /ı'nɒkjʊəs/ a innocuo

innovat|e /'ınəveıt/ vi innovare. **~ion** /-'veıʃn/ n innovazione f. **~ive** /'ınəvətıv/ a innovativo. **~or** /'ınəveıtə(r)/ n innovatore, -trice mf

innuendo /ınjʊ'endəʊ/ n (pl -es) insinuazione f

innumerable /ı'njuːmərəbl/ a innumerevole

inoculat|e /ı'nɒkjʊleıt/ vt vaccinare. **~ion** /-'leıʃn/ n vaccinazione f

inof'fensive a inoffensivo

in'operable a inoperabile

in'opportune a inopportuno

inordinate /ı'nɔːdınət/ a smodato

inor'ganic a inorganico

'in-patient n degente mf

input /'ınpʊt/ n input m inv, ingresso m

inquest /'ınkwest/ n inchiesta f

inquir|e /ın'kwaıə(r)/ vi informarsi (about su); **~e into** far indagini su • vt domandare. **~y** n domanda f; (investigation) inchiesta f

inquisitive /ın'kwızıtıv/ a curioso

inroad /'ınrəʊd/ n **make ~s into** intaccare (savings); cominciare a risolvere (problem)

in'sane a pazzo; fig insensato

in'sanitary a malsano

in'sanity n pazzia f

insatiable /ın'seıʃəbl/ a insaziabile

inscri|be /ın'skraıb/ vt iscrivere. **~ption** /-'skrıpʃn/ n iscrizione f

inscrutable /ın'skruːtəbl/ a impenetrabile

insect /'ınsekt/ n insetto m.

~icide /-'sektısaıd/ n insetticida m

inse'cur|e a malsicuro; (fig: person) insicuro. **~ity** n mancanza f di sicurezza

insemination /ınsemı'neıʃn/ n inseminazione f

in'sensitive a insensibile

in'separable a inseparabile

insert¹ /'ınsɜːt/ n inserto m

insert² /ın'sɜːt/ vt inserire. **~ion** /-ɜːʃn/ n inserzione f

inside /ın'saıd/ n interno m. **~s** npl fam pancia f • attrib Aut **~ lane** n corsia f interna • adv dentro; **~ out** a rovescio; (thoroughly) a fondo • prep dentro; (of time) entro

insidious /ın'sıdıəs/ a insidioso

insight /'ınsaıt/ n intuito m (into per); **an ~ into** un quadro di

insignia /ın'sıgnıə/ npl insegne fpl

insig'nificant a insignificante

insin'cer|e a poco sincero. **~ity** /-'serıtı/ n mancanza f di sincerità

insinuat|e /ın'sınjʊeıt/ vt insinuare. **~ion** /-'eıʃn/ n insinuazione f

insipid /ın'sıpıd/ a insipido

insist /ın'sıst/ vi insistere (on per) • vt **~ that** insistere che. **~ence** n insistenza f. **~ent** a insistente

insole n soletta f

insolen|ce /'ınsələns/ n insolenza f. **~t** a insolente

in'soluble a insolubile

in'solven|cy n insolvenza f. **~t** a insolvente

insomnia /ın'sɒmnıə/ n insonnia f

inspect /ın'spekt/ vt ispezionare; controllare (ticket). **~ion** /-ekʃn/ n ispezione f; (of ticket) controllo m. **~or** n ispettore, -trice mf; (of tickets) controllore m

inspiration /ınspə'reıʃn/ n ispirazione f

inspire /ın'spaıə(r)/ vt ispirare

insta'bility n instabilità f

install /ın'stɔːl/ vt installare. **~ation** /-stə'leıʃn/ n installazione f

instalment /ın'stɔːlmənt/ n Comm

rata f; (of serial) puntata f; (of publication) fascicolo m

instance /'ɪnstəns/ n (case) caso m; (example) esempio m; **in the first ~** in primo luogo; **for ~** per esempio

instant /'ɪnstənt/ a immediato; Culin espresso ● n istante m. **~aneous** /-'teɪnɪəs/ a istantaneo

instant 'coffee n caffè m inv solubile

instantly /'ɪnstəntlɪ/ adv immediatamente

instead /ɪn'sted/ adv invece; **~ of doing** anziché fare; **~ of me** al mio posto; **~ of going** invece di andare

instep n collo m del piede

instigat|e /'ɪnstɪɡeɪt/ vt istigare. **~ion** /-'ɡeɪʃn/ n istigazione f; **at his ~ion** dietro suo suggerimento. **~or** n istigatore, -trice mf

instil /ɪn'stɪl/ vt (pt/pp **instilled**) inculcare (**into** in)

instinct /'ɪnstɪŋkt/ n istinto m. **~ive** /ɪn'stɪŋktɪv/ a istintivo

institut|e /'ɪnstɪtjuːt/ n istituto m ● vt istituire (scheme); iniziare (search); intentare (legal action). **~ion** /-'tjuːʃn/ n istituzione f; (home for elderly) istituto m per anziani; (for mentally ill) istituto m per malati di mente

instruct /ɪn'strʌkt/ vt istruire; (order) ordinare. **~ion** /-ʃn/ n istruzione f; **~s** (orders) ordini mpl. **~ive** /-ɪv/ a istruttivo. **~or** n istruttore, -trice mf

instrument /'ɪnstrəmənt/ n strumento m. **~al** /-'mentl/ a strumentale; **be ~al in** contribuire a. **~alist** n strumentista mf

insu'bordi|nate a insubordinato. **~nation** /-'neɪʃn/ n insubordinazione f

in'sufferable a insopportabile

insuf'ficient a insufficiente

insular /'ɪnsjʊlə(r)/ a fig gretto

insulat|e /'ɪnsjʊleɪt/ vt isolare. **~ing tape** n nastro m isolante. **~ion** /-'leɪʃn/ n isolamento m

insulin /'ɪnsjʊlɪn/ n insulina f

insult¹ /'ɪnsʌlt/ n insulto m

insult² /ɪn'sʌlt/ vt insultare

insuperable /ɪn'suːpərəbl/ a insuperabile

insur|ance /ɪn'ʃʊərəns/ n assicurazione f. **~e** vt assicurare

insurrection /ɪnsə'rekʃn/ n insurrezione f

intact /ɪn'tækt/ a intatto

'intake n immissione f; (of food) consumo m

in'tangible a intangibile

integral /'ɪntɪɡrəl/ a integrale

integrat|e /'ɪntɪɡreɪt/ vt integrare ● vi integrarsi. **~ion** /-'ɡreɪʃn/ n integrazione f

integrity /ɪn'teɡrətɪ/ n integrità f

intellect /'ɪntəlekt/ n intelletto m. **~ual** /-'lektjʊəl/ a & n intellettuale mf

intellig|ence /ɪn'telɪdʒəns/ n intelligenza f; Mil informazioni fpl. **~t** a intelligente

intelligentsia /ɪntelɪ'dʒentsɪə/ n intellighenzia f

intelligible /ɪn'telɪdʒəbl/ a intelligibile

intend /ɪn'tend/ vt destinare; (have in mind) aver intenzione di; **be ~ed for** essere destinato a. **~ed** a (effect) voluto ● n my **~ed** fam il mio/la mia fidanzata, -a

intense /ɪn'tens/ a intenso; (person) dai sentimenti intensi. **~ly** adv intensamente; (very) estremamente

intensi|fication /ɪntensɪfɪ'keɪʃn/ n intensificazione f. **~fy** /-'tensɪfaɪ/ v (pt/pp -ied) ● vt intensificare ● vi intensificarsi

intensity /ɪn'tensətɪ/ n intensità f

intensive /ɪn'tensɪv/ a intensivo. **~ care** (for people in coma) rianimazione f; **~ care [unit]** terapia f intensiva

intent /ɪn'tent/ a intento; **~ on** (absorbed in) preso da; **be ~ on doing sth** essere intento a fare qcsa ● n intenzione f; **to all ~s**

and purposes a tutti gli effetti. **~ly** adv attentamente

intention /ɪnˈtenʃn/ n intenzione f. **~al** a intenzionale. **~ally** adv intenzionalmente

inter'acti|on n cooperazione f. **~ve** a interattivo

intercede /ɪntəˈsiːd/ vi intercedere (**on behalf of** a favore di)

intercept /ɪntəˈsept/ vt intercettare

'interchange n scambio m; Auto raccordo m [autostradale]

inter'changeable a interscambiabile

intercom /ˈɪntəkɒm/ n citofono m

'intercourse n (sexual) rapporti mpl [sessuali]

interest /ˈɪntrəst/ n interesse m; **have an ~ in** Comm essere cointeressato in; **be of ~** essere interessante; **~ rate** n tasso m di interesse ● vt interessare. **~ed** a interessato. **~ing** a interessante

interface /ˈɪntəfeɪs/ n interfaccia f ● vt interfacciare ● vi interfacciarsi

interfere /ɪntəˈfɪə(r)/ vi interferire; **~ with** interferire con. **~nce** /-əns/ n interferenza f

interim /ˈɪntərɪm/ a temporaneo; **~ payment** acconto m ● n **in the ~** nel frattempo

interior /ɪnˈtɪərɪə(r)/ a interiore ● n interno m. **~ designer** n arredatore, -trice mf

interject /ɪntəˈdʒekt/ vt intervenire. **~ion** /-ekʃn/ n Gram interiezione f; (remark) intervento m

interloper /ˈɪntələʊpə(r)/ n intruso, -a mf

interlude /ˈɪntəluːd/ n intervallo m

inter'marry vi sposarsi tra parenti; (different groups:) contrarre matrimoni misti

intermediary /ɪntəˈmiːdɪərɪ/ n intermediario, -a mf

intermediate /ɪntəˈmiːdɪət/ a intermedio

interminable /ɪnˈtɜːmɪnəbl/ a interminabile

intermission /ɪntəˈmɪʃn/ n intervallo m

intermittent /ɪntəˈmɪtənt/ a intermittente

intern /ɪnˈtɜːn/ vt internare

internal /ɪnˈtɜːnl/ a interno. **~ly** adv internamente; (deal with) all'interno

inter'national a internazionale ● n (game) incontro m internazionale; (player) competitore, -trice mf in gare internazionali. **~ly** adv internazionalmente

Internet /ˈɪntənet/ n Internet m

internist /ɪnˈtɜːnɪst/ n Am internista mf

internment /ɪnˈtɜːnmənt/ n internamento m

'interplay n azione f reciproca

interpret /ɪnˈtɜːprɪt/ vt interpretare ● vi fare l'interprete. **~ation** /-ˈteɪʃn/ n interpretazione f. **~er** n interprete mf

inter'related a (facts) in correlazione

interrogat|e /ɪnˈterəgeɪt/ vt interrogare. **~ion** /-ˈgeɪʃn/ n interrogazione f; (by police) interrogatorio m

interrogative /ɪntəˈrɒgətɪv/ a & n **~ [pronoun]** interrogativo m

interrupt /ɪntəˈrʌpt/ vt/i interrompere. **~ion** /-ʌpʃn/ n interruzione f

intersect /ɪntəˈsekt/ vi intersecarsi ● vt intersecare. **~ion** /-ekʃn/ n intersezione f; (of street) incrocio m

interspersed /ɪntəˈspɜːst/ a **~ with** inframmezzato di

inter'twine vi attorcigliarsi

interval /ˈɪntəvl/ n intervallo m; **bright ~s** pl schiarite fpl

interven|e /ɪntəˈviːn/ vi intervenire. **~tion** /-ˈvenʃn/ n intervento m

interview /ˈɪntəvjuː/ n intervista f; (for job) colloquio m [di lavoro] ● vt intervistare. **~er** n intervistatore, -trice mf

intestin|e /ɪn'testɪn/ n intestino m.
~al a intestinale

intimacy /'ɪntɪməsɪ/ n intimità f

intimate[1] /'ɪntɪmət/ a intimo. **~ly**
adv intimamente

intimate[2] /'ɪntɪmeɪt/ vt far capire;
(imply) suggerire

intimidat|e /ɪn'tɪmɪdeɪt/ vt intimi-
dire. **~ion** /-'deɪʃn/ n intimidazio-
ne f

into /'ɪntə/, di fronte a una vocale
/'ɪntʊ/ prep dentro, in; **go ~ the
house** andare dentro [casa] o in
casa; **be ~** (fam: like) essere appassionato di; **I'm not ~ that** questo non mi piace; **7 ~ 21 goes 3** il
7 nel 21 ci sta 3 volte; **translate ~
French** tradurre in francese; **get
~ trouble** mettersi nei guai

in'tolerable a intollerabile

in'toleran|ce f intolleranza f. **~t** a
intollerante

intonation /ɪntə'neɪʃn/ n intona-
zione f

intoxicat|ed /ɪn'tɒksɪkeɪtɪd/ a ine-
briato. **~ion** /-'keɪʃn/ n ebbrezza f

intractable /ɪn'træktəbl/ a intrat-
tabile; (problem) insolubile

intransigent /ɪn'trænzɪdʒənt/ a
intransigente

in'transitive a intransitivo

intravenous /ɪntrə'viːnəs/ a endo-
venoso. **~ly** adv per via endoveno-
sa

intrepid /ɪn'trepɪd/ a intrepido

intricate /'ɪntrɪkət/ a complesso

intrigu|e /ɪn'triːg/ n intrigo m ● vt
intrigare ● vi tramare. **~ing** a in-
trigante

intrinsic /ɪn'trɪnsɪk/ a intrinseco

introduce /ɪntrə'djuːs/ vt presentare; (bring in, insert) introdurre

introduct|ion /ɪntrə'dʌkʃn/ n in-
troduzione f; (to person) presentazione f; (to book) prefazione f.
~ory /-tərɪ/ a introduttivo

introspective /ɪntrə'spektɪv/ a
introspettivo

introvert /'ɪntrəvɜːt/ n introverso,
-a mf

intru|de /ɪn'truːd/ vi intrometter-

si. **~der** n intruso, -a mf. **~sion**
/-'ʒn/ n intrusione f

intuit|ion /ɪntjʊ'ɪʃn/ n intuito m.
~ive /-'tjuːɪtɪv/ a intuitivo

inundate /'ɪnʌndeɪt/ vt fig inondare (with di)

invade /ɪn'veɪd/ vt invadere. **~r** n
invasore m

invalid[1] /'ɪnvəlɪd/ n invalido, -a mf

invalid[2] /ɪn'vælɪd/ a non valido.
~ate vt invalidare

in'valuable a prezioso; (priceless)
inestimabile

in'variab|le a invariabile. **~y** adv
invariabilmente

invasion /ɪn'veɪʒn/ n invasione f

invective /ɪn'vektɪv/ n invettiva f

invent /ɪn'vent/ vt inventare. **~ion**
/-enʃn/ n invenzione f. **~ive** /-tɪv/
a inventivo. **~or** n inventore,
-trice mf

inventory /'ɪnvəntrɪ/ n inventario m

inverse /ɪn'vɜːs/ a inverso ● n inverso m

invert /ɪn'vɜːt/ vt invertire; **in ~ed
commas** tra virgolette

invest /ɪn'vest/ vt investire ● vi
fare investimenti; **~ in** (fam: buy)
comprarsi

investigat|e /ɪn'vestɪgeɪt/ vt inve-
stigare. **~ion** /-'geɪʃn/ n investiga-
zione f

invest|ment /ɪn'vestmənt/ n inve-
stimento m. **~or** n investitore,
-trice mf

inveterate /ɪn'vetərət/ a inveterato

invidious /ɪn'vɪdɪəs/ a ingiusto;
(position) antipatico

invigilat|e /ɪn'vɪdʒɪleɪt/ vi Sch sor-
vegliare lo svolgimento di un esame. **~or** n persona f che sorveglia
lo svolgimento di un esame

invigorate /ɪn'vɪgəreɪt/ vt rinvigo-
rire

invigorating /ɪn'vɪgəreɪtɪŋ/ a tonificante

invincible /ɪn'vɪnsəbl/ a invincibile

inviolable /ɪn'vaɪələbl/ a inviolabile

in'visible a invisibile

invitation /ɪnvɪ'teɪʃn/ n invito m

invit|e /ɪn'vaɪt/ vt invitare; ⟨attract⟩ attirare. **~ing** a invitante

invoice /'ɪnvɔɪs/ n fattura f ● vt ~ **sb** emettere una fattura a qcno

invoke /ɪn'vəʊk/ vt invocare

in'voluntar|y a involontario

involve /ɪn'vɒlv/ vt comportare; ⟨affect, include⟩ coinvolgere; ⟨entail⟩ implicare; **get ~d with sb** legarsi a qcno; ⟨romantically⟩ legarsi sentimentalmente a qcno. **~d** a complesso. **~ment** n coinvolgimento m

in'vulnerable a invulnerabile; ⟨position⟩ inattaccabile

inward /'ɪnwəd/ a interno; ⟨thoughts etc⟩ interiore; ~ **investment** Comm investimento m straniero. **~ly** adv interiormente. **~[s]** adv verso l'interno

iodine /'aɪədiːn/ n iodio m

iota /aɪ'əʊtə/ n briciolo m

IOU n abbr (**I owe you**) pagherò m inv

IQ n abbr (**intelligence quotient**) Q.I.

IRA n abbr (**Irish Republican Army**) I.R.A. f

Iran /ɪ'rɑːn/ n Iran m. **~ian** /ɪ'reɪnɪən/ a & n iraniano, -a mf

Iraq /ɪ'rɑːk/ n Iraq m. **~i** a & n iracheno, -a mf

irascible /ɪ'ræsəbl/ a irascibile

irate /aɪ'reɪt/ a adirato

Ireland /'aɪələnd/ n Irlanda f

iris /'aɪrɪs/ n Anat iride f; Bot giaggiolo m inv

Irish /'aɪrɪʃ/ a irlandese ● n the ~ pl gli irlandesi mpl. **~man** n irlandese m. **~woman** n irlandese f

iron /'aɪən/ a di ferro ● **Curtain** n cortina f di ferro ● n ferro m; ⟨appliance⟩ ferro m [da stiro] ● vt/i stirare. **iron out** vt eliminare stirando; fig appianare

ironic[al] /aɪ'rɒnɪk[l]/ a ironico

ironing /'aɪənɪŋ/ n stirare m;

⟨articles⟩ roba f da stirare; **do the** ~ stirare. **~-board** n asse f da stiro

ironmonger /-mʌŋɡə(r)/ n ~'s [**shop**] negozio m di ferramenta

irony /'aɪrənɪ/ n ironia f

irradiate /ɪ'reɪdɪeɪt/ vt irradiare

irrational /ɪ'ræʃənl/ a irrazionale

irreconcilable /ɪ'rekənsaɪləbl/ a irreconciliabile

irrefutable /ɪrɪ'fjuːtəbl/ a irrefutabile

irregular /ɪ'reɡjʊlə(r)/ a irregolare. **~ity** /-'lærɪtɪ/ n irregolarità f inv

irrelevant /ɪ'reləvənt/ a non pertinente

irreparab|le /ɪ'repərəbl/ a irreparabile. **~y** adv irreparabilmente

irreplaceable /ɪrɪ'pleɪsəbl/ a insostituibile

irrepressible /ɪrɪ'presəbl/ a irrefrenabile; ⟨person⟩ incontenibile

irresistible /ɪrɪ'zɪstəbl/ a irresistibile

irresolute /ɪ'rezəluːt/ a irresoluto

irrespective /ɪrɪ'spektɪv/ a ~ **of** senza riguardo per

irresponsible /ɪrɪ'spɒnsɪbl/ a irresponsabile

irreverent /ɪ'revərənt/ a irreverente

irreversible /ɪrɪ'vɜːsəbl/ a irreversibile

irrevocab|le /ɪ'revəkəbl/ a irrevocabile. **~y** adv irrevocabilmente

irrigat|e /'ɪrɪɡeɪt/ vt irrigare. **~ion** /-'ɡeɪʃn/ n irrigazione f

irritability /ɪrɪtə'bɪlɪtɪ/ n irritabilità f

irritable /'ɪrɪtəbl/ a irritabile

irritant /'ɪrɪtənt/ n sostanza f irritante

irritat|e /'ɪrɪteɪt/ vt irritare. **~ing** a irritante. **~ion** /-'teɪʃn/ n irritazione f

is /ɪz/ see **be**

Islam /'ɪzlɑːm/ n Islam m. **~ic** /-'læmɪk/ a islamico

island /'aɪlənd/ n isola f; ⟨in road⟩

isola *f* spartitraffico. **~er** *n* isolano, -a *mf*

isle /aɪl/ *n* isola *f*

isolat|**e** /ˈaɪsəleɪt/ *vt* isolare. **~ed** *a* isolato. **~ion** /-ˈleɪʃn/ *n* isolamento *m*

Israel /ˈɪzreɪl/ *n* Israele *m*. **~i** /ɪzˈreɪlɪ/ *a* & *n* israeliano, -a *mf*

issue /ˈɪʃuː/ *n* (*outcome*) risultato *m*; (*of magazine*) numero *m*; (*of stamps etc*) emissione *f*; (*off-spring*) figli *mpl*; (*matter, question*) questione *f*; **at ~** in questione; **take ~ with sb** prendere posizione contro qcno ● *vt* distribuire (*supplies*); rilasciare (*passport*); emettere (*stamps, order*); pubblicare (*book*); **be ~d with** sth ricevere qcsa ● *vi* **~ from** uscire da

isthmus /ˈɪsməs/ *n* (*pl* **-muses**) istmo *m*

it /ɪt/ *pron* (*direct object*) lo, la *f*; (*indirect object*) gli *m*, le *f*; **it's broken** è rotto/rotta; **will it be enough?** basterà?; **it's hot** fa caldo; **it's raining** piove; **it's me** sono io; **who is it?** chi è?; **it's two o'clock** sono le due; **I doubt it** ne dubito; **take it with you** prendilo con te; **give it a wipe** dagli una pulita

Italian /ɪˈtæljən/ *a* & *n* italiano, -a *mf*; (*language*) italiano *m*

italic /ɪˈtælɪk/ *a* italico. **~s** *npl* corsivo *msg*

Italy /ˈɪtəlɪ/ *n* Italia *f*

itch /ɪtʃ/ *n* prurito *m* ● *vi* avere prurito, prudere; **be ~ing to** *fam* avere una voglia matta di. **~y** *a* che prude; **my foot is ~y** ho prurito al piede

item /ˈaɪtəm/ *n* articolo *m*; (*on agenda, programme*) punto *m*; (*on invoice*) voce *f*; **~ [of news]** notizia *f*. **~ize** *vt* dettagliare (*bill*)

itinerant /aɪˈtɪnərənt/ *a* itinerante

itinerary /aɪˈtɪnərərɪ/ *n* itinerario *m*

its /ɪts/ *poss pron* suo *m*, sua *f*, suoi *mpl*, sue *fpl*. **~ mother/cage** sua madre/la sua gabbia

it's = **it is, it has**

itself /ɪtˈself/ *pron* (*reflexive*) si; (*emphatic*) essa stessa; **the baby looked at ~ in the mirror** il bambino si è guardato nello specchio; **by ~** da solo; **the machine in ~ is simple** la macchina di per sé è semplice

ITV *n* *abbr* (**Independent Television**) stazione *f* televisiva privata britannica

ivory /ˈaɪvərɪ/ *n* avorio *m*

ivy /ˈaɪvɪ/ *n* edera *f*

Jj

jab /dʒæb/ *n* colpo *m* secco; (*fam: injection*) puntura *f* ● *vt* (*pt/pp* **jabbed**) punzecchiare

jabber /ˈdʒæbə(r)/ *vi* borbottare

jack /dʒæk/ *n* *Auto* cric *m inv*; (*in cards*) fante *m*, jack *m inv* ● **jack up** *vt* *Auto* sollevare [con il cric]

jackdaw /ˈdʒækdɔː/ *n* taccola *f*

jacket /ˈdʒækɪt/ *n* giacca *f*; (*of book*) sopraccoperta *f*. **~ po'tato** *n* patata *f* cotta al forno con la buccia

jackpot /ˈdʒækpɒt/ *n* premio *m* (*di una lotteria*); **win the ~** vincere alla lotteria; **hit the ~** *fig* fare un colpo grosso

jade /dʒeɪd/ *n* giada *f* ● *attrib* di giada

jaded /ˈdʒeɪdɪd/ *a* spossato

jagged /ˈdʒægɪd/ *a* dentellato

jail /dʒeɪl/ = **gaol**

jalopy /dʒəˈlɒpɪ/ *n* *fam* vecchia carretta *f*

jam[1] /dʒæm/ *n* marmellata *f*

jam[2] /dʒæm/ *n* *Auto* ingorgo *m*; (*fam: difficulty*) guaio *m* ● *v* (*pt/pp* **jammed**) ● *vt* (*cram*) pigiare; disturbare (*broadcast*); inceppare (*mechanism, drawer etc*); **be ~med** (*roads:*) essere congestionato ●*vi* ⟨*mechanism:*⟩ incepparsi; ⟨*window, drawer:*⟩ incastrarsi

Jamaica /dʒə'meɪkə/ *n* Giamaica *f*. ~**n** a & *n* giamaicano, -a *mf*

jam-'packed *a fam* pieno zeppo

jangle /'dʒæŋgl/ *vt* far squillare ●*vi* squillare

janitor /'dʒænɪtə(r)/ *n* ⟨*caretaker*⟩ custode *m*; ⟨*in school*⟩ bidello *m*, *mf*

January /'dʒænjʊərɪ/ *n* gennaio *m*

Japan /dʒə'pæn/ *n* Giappone *m*. ~**ese** /dʒæpə'niːz/ *a & n* giapponese *mf*; ⟨*language*⟩ giapponese *m*

jar[1] /dʒɑː(r)/ *n* ⟨*glass*⟩ barattolo *m*

jar[2] *vi* ⟨*pt/pp* jarred⟩ ⟨*sound:*⟩ stridere

jargon /'dʒɑːgən/ *n* gergo *m*

jaundice /'dʒɔːndɪs/ *n* itterizia *f*. ~**d** *fig* inacidito

jaunt /dʒɔːnt/ *n* gita *f*

jaunty /'dʒɔːntɪ/ *a* (-ier, -iest) sbarazzino

javelin /'dʒævlɪn/ *n* giavellotto *m*

jaw /dʒɔː/ *n* mascella *f*; ⟨*bone*⟩ mandibola *f*

jay-walker /'dʒeɪwɔːkə(r)/ *n* pedone *m* distratto

jazz /dʒæz/ *n* jazz *m* ●**jazz up** *vt* ravvivare. ~**y** *a* vistoso

jealous /'dʒeləs/ *a* geloso. ~**y** *n* gelosia *f*

jeans /dʒiːnz/ *npl* ⟨*blue*⟩ jeans *mpl*

jeep /dʒiːp/ *n* jeep *f inv*

jeer /dʒɪə(r)/ *n* scherno *m* ●*vi* schernire; ~ **at** prendersi gioco di ●*vt* ⟨*boo*⟩ fischiare

jell /dʒel/ *vi* concretarsi

jelly /'dʒelɪ/ *n* gelatina *f*. ~**fish** *n* medusa *f*

jeopar|dize /'dʒepədaɪz/ *vt* mettere in pericolo. ~**dy** /-dɪ/ *n* in ~**dy** in pericolo

jerk /dʒɜːk/ *n* scatto *m*, scossa *f* ●*vt* scattare ●*vi* sobbalzare; ⟨*limb, muscle:*⟩ muoversi a scatti. ~**ily** *adv* a scatti. ~**y** *a* traballante

jersey /'dʒɜːzɪ/ *n* maglia *f*; *Sport* maglietta *f*; ⟨*fabric*⟩ jersey *m*

jest /dʒest/ *n* scherzo *m*; **in** ~ per scherzo ●*vi* scherzare

Jesus /'dʒiːzəs/ *n* Gesù *m*

jet[1] /dʒet/ *n* ⟨*stone*⟩ giaietto *m*

jet[2] *n* ⟨*of water*⟩ getto *m*; ⟨*nozzle*⟩ becco *m*; ⟨*plane*⟩ aeroplano *m*, jet *m inv*

jet: ~**-'black** *a* nero ebano. ~**lag** *n* scombussolamento *m* da fuso orario. ~**-pro'pelled** *a* a reazione

jettison /'dʒetɪsn/ *vt* gettare a mare; *fig* abbandonare

jetty /'dʒetɪ/ *n* molo *m*

Jew /dʒuː/ *n* ebreo *m*

jewel /'dʒuːəl/ *n* gioiello *m*. ~**ler** *n* gioielliere *m*; ~**ler's** [**shop**] gioielleria *f*. ~**lery** *n* gioielli *mpl*

Jew|ess /'dʒuːɪs/ *n* ebrea *f*. ~**ish** *a* ebreo

jiffy /'dʒɪfɪ/ *n fam* **in a** ~ in un batter d'occhio

jigsaw /'dʒɪgsɔː/ *n* ~ [**puzzle**] puzzle *m inv*

jilt /dʒɪlt/ *vt* piantare

jingle /'dʒɪŋgl/ *n* ⟨*rhyme*⟩ canzoncina *f* pubblicitaria ●*vi* tintinnare

jinx /dʒɪŋks/ *n* ⟨*person*⟩ iettatore, -trice *mf*; **it's got a** ~ **on it** è iellato

jitter|s /'dʒɪtəz/ *npl fam* **have the** ~**s** aver una gran fifa. ~**y** *a fam* in preda alla fifa

job /dʒɒb/ *n* lavoro *m*; **this is going to be quite a** ~ *fam* [questa] non sarà un'impresa facile; **it's a good** ~ **that...** meno male che.... ~ **centre** *n* ufficio *m* statale di collocamento. ~**less** *a* senza lavoro

jockey /'dʒɒkɪ/ *n* fantino *m*

jocular /'dʒɒkjʊlə(r)/ *a* scherzoso

jog /dʒɒg/ *n* colpetto *m*; **at a** ~ in un balzo; *Sport* **go for a** ~ andare a fare jogging ●*vt* ⟨*pt/pp* jogged⟩ ●*vt* ⟨*hit*⟩ urtare; ~ **sb's memory** farlo ritornare in mente a qcno ●*vi* *Sport* fare jogging. ~**ging** *n* jogging *m*

john /dʒɒn/ *n* ⟨*Am fam: toilet*⟩ gabinetto *m*

join /dʒɔɪn/ *n* giuntura *f* ●*vt* raggiungere, unire; raggiungere ⟨*person*⟩; ⟨*become member of*⟩

iscriversi a; entrare in ⟨*firm*⟩ ● vi ⟨*roads:*⟩ congiungersi. **join in** vi partecipare. **join up** vi Mil arruolarsi ● vt unire

joiner /ˈdʒɔɪnə(r)/ n falegname m

joint /dʒɔɪnt/ a comune ● n articolazione f; (*in wood, brickwork*) giuntura f; *Culin* arrosto m; (*fam: bar*) bettola f; (*sl:drug*) spinello m. **~ly** adv unitamente

joist /dʒɔɪst/ n travetto m

jok|e /dʒəʊk/ n (*trick*) scherzo m; (*funny story*) barzelletta f ● vi scherzare. **~er** n burlone, -a mf; (*in cards*) jolly m inv. **~ing** n **~ing apart** scherzi a parte. **~ingly** adv per scherzo

jolly /ˈdʒɒlɪ/ a (**-ier, -iest**) allegro ● adv fam molto

jolt /dʒəʊlt/ n scossa f, sobbalzo m ● vt far sobbalzare ● vi sobbalzare

Jordan /ˈdʒɔːdn/ n Giordania f; (*river*) Giordano m. **~ian** /-ˈdeɪmɪən/ a & n giordano, -a mf

jostle /ˈdʒɒsl/ vt spingere

jot /dʒɒt/ n nulla f ● **jot down** vt (*pt/pp* **jotted**) annotare. **~ter** n taccuino m

journal /ˈdʒɜːnl/ n giornale m; (*diary*) diario m. **~ese** /-əˈliːz/ n gergo m giornalistico. **~ism** n giornalismo m. **~ist** n giornalista mf

journey /ˈdʒɜːnɪ/ n viaggio m

jovial /ˈdʒəʊvɪəl/ a gioviale

joy /dʒɔɪ/ n gioia f. **~ful** a gioioso. **~ride** n fam giro m con una macchina rubata. **~stick** n Comput joystick m inv

jubil|ant /ˈdʒuːbɪlənt/ a giubilante. **~ation** /-ˈleɪʃn/ n giubilo m

jubilee /ˈdʒuːbɪliː/ n giubileo m

judder /ˈdʒʌdə(r)/ vi vibrare violentemente

judge /dʒʌdʒ/ n giudice m ● vt giudicare; (*estimate*) valutare; (*consider*) ritenere ● vi giudicare (by da). **~ment** n giudizio m; *Jur* sentenza f

judic|ial /dʒuːˈdɪʃl/ a giudiziario. **~iary** /-ʃərɪ/ n magistratura f. **~ious** /-ʃəs/ a giudizioso

judo /ˈdʒuːdəʊ/ n judo m

jug /dʒʌg/ n brocca f; (*small*) bricco m

juggernaut /ˈdʒʌgənɔːt/ n fam grosso autotreno m

juggle /ˈdʒʌgl/ vi fare giochi di destrezza. **~r** n giocoliere, -a mf

juice /dʒuːs/ n succo m

juicy /ˈdʒuːsɪ/ a (**-ier, -iest**) succoso; (*fam: story*) piccante

juke-box /ˈdʒuːk-/ n juke-box m inv

July /dʒuˈlaɪ/ n luglio m

jumble /ˈdʒʌmbl/ n accozzaglia f ● vt ~ [up] mischiare. **~ sale** n vendita f di beneficenza

jumbo /ˈdʒʌmbəʊ/ n ~ [jet] jumbo jet m inv

jump /dʒʌmp/ n salto m; (*in prices*) balzo m; (*in horse racing*) ostacolo m ● vi saltare; (*with fright*) sussultare; (*prices:*) salire rapidamente; ~ **to conclusions** saltare alle conclusioni ● vt saltare; **~ the gun** fig precipitarsi; ~ **the queue** non rispettare la fila. **jump at** vt fig accettare con entusiasmo ⟨*offer*⟩. **jump up** vi rizzarsi in piedi

jumper /ˈdʒʌmpə(r)/ n (*sweater*) golf m inv

jumpy /ˈdʒʌmpɪ/ a nervoso

junction /ˈdʒʌŋkʃn/ n (*of roads*) incrocio m; (*of motorway*) uscita f; *Rail* nodo m ferroviario

juncture /ˈdʒʌŋktʃə(r)/ n **at this** ~ a questo punto

June /dʒuːn/ n giugno m

jungle /ˈdʒʌŋgl/ n giungla f

junior /ˈdʒuːnɪə(r)/ a giovane; (*in rank*) subalterno; *Sport* junior inv ● n the ~**s** Sch i più giovani. **~ school** n scuola f elementare

junk /dʒʌŋk/ n cianfrusaglie fpl. **~ food** n fam cibo m poco sano, porcherie fpl. **~ mail** posta f spazzatura

junkie /ˈdʒʌŋkɪ/ n sl tossico, -a mf

'junk-shop n negozio m di rigattiere

jurisdiction /dʒʊərɪsˈdɪkʃn/ n giurisdizione f

juror /'dʒuərə(r)/ n giurato, -a mf

jury /'dʒuəri/ n giuria f

just /dʒʌst/ a giusto ● adv (barely) appena; (simply) solo; (exactly) esattamente; **~ as tall** altrettanto alto; **~ as I was leaving** proprio quando stavo andando via; **I've ~ seen her** l'ho appena vista; **it's ~ as well** meno male; **~ at that moment** proprio in quel momento; **~ listen!** ascolta!; **I'm ~ going** sto andando proprio ora

justice /'dʒʌstɪs/ n giustizia f; **do ~ to** rendere giustizia a; **J~ of the Peace** giudice m conciliatore

justifiable /'dʒʌstɪfaɪəbl/ a giustificabile

justification /dʒʌstɪfɪ'keɪʃn/ n giustificazione f ● **-fy** /'dʒʌstɪfaɪ/ vt (pt/pp **-ied**) giustificare

justly /'dʒʌstlɪ/ adv giustamente

jut /dʒʌt/ vi (pt/pp **jutted**) **~ out** sporgere

juvenile /'dʒuːvənaɪl/ a giovanile; (childish) infantile; (for the young) per i giovani ● n giovane mf. **~ delinquency** n delinquenza f giovanile

juxtapose /dʒʌkstə'pəʊz/ vt giustapporre

Kk

kangaroo /kæŋgə'ruː/ n canguro m

karate /kə'rɑːtɪ/ n karate m

kebab /kɪ'bæb/ n Culin spiedino m di carne

keel /kiːl/ n chiglia f ● **keel over** vi capovolgersi

keen /kiːn/ a (intense) acuto; (interest) vivo; (eager) entusiastico; (competition) feroce; (wind, knife) tagliente; **~ on** entusiasta di; **she's ~ on him** le piace molto; **be ~ to do sth** avere voglia di fare qcsa. **~ness** n entusiasmo m

keep /kiːp/ n (maintenance) mantenimento m; (of castle) maschio m; **for ~s** per sempre ● v (pt/pp **kept**) ● vt tenere; (not throw away) conservare; (detain) trattenere; mantenere (family, promise); avere (shop); allevare (animals); rispettare (law, rules); **~ sth hot** tenere qcsa in caldo; **~ sb from doing sth** impedire a qcno di fare qcsa; **~ sb waiting** far aspettare qcno; **~ sth to oneself** tenere qcsa per sé; **~ sth from sb** tenere nascosto qcsa a qcno ● vi (remain) rimanere; (food:) conservarsi; **~ calm** rimanere calmo; **~ left/right** tenere la destra/la sinistra; **~ [on] doing sth** continuare a fare qcsa. **keep back** vt trattenere; **~ sth back from sb** tenere nascosto qcsa a qcno ● vi tenersi indietro. **keep in with** vt mantenersi in buoni rapporti con. **keep on** vi fam assillare (**at sb** qcno). **keep up** vi stare al passo ● vt (continue) continuare

keeper /'kiːpə(r)/ n custode mf. **~-fit** n ginnastica f. **~ing** n custodia f; **be in ~ing with** essere in armonia con. **~sake** n ricordo m

keg /keg/ n barilotto m

kennel /'kenl/ n canile m; **~s** pl (boarding) canile m; (breeding) allevamento m di cani

Kenya /'kenjə/ n Kenia m. **~n** a & n keniota mf

kept /kept/ see **keep**

kerb /kɜːb/ n bordo m del marciapiede

kernel /'kɜːnl/ n nocciolo m

kerosene /'kerəsiːn/ n Am cherosene m

ketchup /'ketʃʌp/ n ketchup m

kettle /'ketl/ n bollitore m; **put the ~ on** mettere l'acqua a bollire

key /kiː/ n also Mus chiave f; (of piano, typewriter) tasto m ● vt **~ [in]** digitare (character); **could you ~ this?** puoi battere questo?

key: **~board** n Comput, Mus tastiera f. **~boarder** n tastierista mf.

~ed-up *a* (*anxious*) estremamente agitato; (*ready to act*) psicologicamente preparato. **~hole** *n* buco *m* della serratura. **~ring** *n* portachiavi *m inv*

khaki /'kɑ:kɪ/ *a* cachi *inv* ● *n* cachi *m*

kick /kɪk/ *n* calcio *m*; (*fam: thrill*) piacere *m*; **for ~s** *fam* per spasso ● *vt* dar calci a; **~ the bucket** *fam* crepare ● *vi* (*animal:*) scalciare; (*person:*) dare calci. **kick off** *vi* Sport dare il calcio d'inizio; *fam* iniziare. **kick up** *vt* **~ up a row** fare una scenata

'kickback *n* (*fam: percentage*) tangente *f*

'kick-off *n* Sport calcio *m* d'inizio

kid /kɪd/ *n* capretto *m*; (*fam: child*) ragazzino, -a *mf* ● *v* (*pt/pp* **kidded**) ● *vt fam* prendere in giro ● *vi fam* scherzare

kidnap /'kɪdnæp/ *vt* (*pt/pp* **-napped**) rapire, sequestrare. **~per** *n* sequestratore, -trice *mf*, rapitore, -trice *mf*. **~ping** *n* rapimento *m*, sequestro *m* [di persona]

kidney /'kɪdnɪ/ *n* rene *m*; *Culin* rognone *m*. **~ machine** *n* rene *m* artificiale

kill /kɪl/ *vt* uccidere; *fig* metter fine a; ammazzare (*time*). **~er** *n* assassino, -a *mf*. **~ing** *n* uccisione *f*; (*murder*) omicidio *m*; **make a ~ing** *fig* fare un colpo grosso

'killjoy *n* guastafeste *mf*

kiln /kɪln/ *n* fornace *f*

kilo /'ki:ləʊ/ *n* chilo *m*

kilo /'kɪlə/: **~byte** *n* kilobyte *m inv*. **~gram** *n* chilogrammo *m*. **~metre** /kɪ'lɒmɪtə(r)/ *n* chilometro *m*. **~watt** *n* chilowatt *m inv*

kilt /kɪlt/ *n* kilt *m inv* (*gonnellino degli scozzesi*)

kin /kɪn/ *n* congiunti *mpl*; **next of ~** parente *m* stretto; parenti *mpl* stretti

kind¹ /kaɪnd/ *n* genere *m*, specie *f*; (*brand, type*) tipo *m*; **~ of** *fam* alquanto; **two of a ~** due della stessa specie

kind² *a* gentile, buono; **~ to animals** amante degli animali; **~ regards** cordiali saluti

kindergarten /'kɪndəga:tn/ *n* asilo *m* infantile

kindle /'kɪndl/ *vt* accendere

kind|ly /'kaɪndlɪ/ *a* (**-ier, -iest**) benevolo ● *adv* gentilmente; (*if you please*) per favore. **~ness** *n* gentilezza *f*

kindred /'kɪndrɪd/ *a* **she's a ~ spirit** è la mia/sua/tua anima gemella

kinetic /kɪ'netɪk/ *a* cinetico

king /kɪŋ/ *n* re *m inv*. **~dom** *n* regno *m*

king: **~fisher** *n* martin *m inv* pescatore. **~-sized** *a* (*cigarette*) king-size *inv*, lungo; (*bed*) matrimoniale grande

kink /kɪŋk/ *n* nodo *m*. **~y** *a fam* bizzarro

kiosk /'ki:ɒsk/ *n* chiosco *m*; *Teleph* cabina *f* telefonica

kip /kɪp/ *n* fam pisolino *m*; **have a ~** schiacciare un pisolino ● *vi* (*pt/pp* **kipped**) *fam* dormire

kipper /'kɪpə(r)/ *n* aringa *f* affumicata

kiss /kɪs/ *n* bacio *m*; **~ of life** respirazione *f* bocca a bocca ● *vt* baciare ● *vi* baciarsi

kit /kɪt/ *n* equipaggiamento *m*, kit *m inv*; (*tools*) attrezzi *mpl*; (*construction*) pezzi *mpl* da montare, kit *m inv* ● **kit out** *vt* (*pt/pp* **kitted**) equipaggiare. **~bag** *n* sacco *m* a spalla

kitchen /'kɪtʃɪn/ *n* cucina *f* ● *attrib* di cucina. **~ette** *n* /kɪtʃɪ'net/ *n* cucinino *m*

kitchen: **~ 'garden** *n* orto *m*. **~ roll** *or* **towel** Scottex® *m inv*. **~'sink** *n* lavello *m*

kite /kaɪt/ *n* aquilone *m*

kitten /'kɪtn/ *n* gattino *m*

kitty /'kɪtɪ/ *n* (*money*) cassa *f* comune

kleptomaniac /kleptə'memɪæk/ *n* cleptomane *mf*

knack /næk/ *n* tecnica *f*; **have the ~ for doing sth** avere la capacità di fare qcsa

knead /ni:d/ *vt* impastare

knee /ni:/ *n* ginocchio *m*. **~cap** *n* rotula *f*

kneel /ni:l/ *vi* (*pt/pp* **knelt**) (~ [**down**]) inginocchiarsi; **be ~ing** essere inginocchiato

knelt /nelt/ *see* **kneel**

knew /nju:/ *see* **know**

knickers /'nɪkəz/ *npl* mutandine *fpl*

knick-knacks /'nɪknæks/ *npl* ninnoli *mpl*

knife /naɪf/ *n* (*pl* **knives**) coltello *m*
● *vt fam* accoltellare

knight /naɪt/ *n* cavaliere *m*; (*in chess*) cavallo *m* ● *vt* nominare cavaliere

knit /nɪt/ *vt/i* (*pt/pp* **knitted**) lavorare a maglia; **~ one, purl one** un diritto, un rovescio. **~ting** *n* lavorare *m* a maglia; (*work*) lavoro *m* a maglia. **~ting-needle** *n* ferro *m* da calza. **~wear** *n* maglieria *f*

knives /naɪvz/ *see* **knife**

knob /nɒb/ *n* pomello *m*; (*of stick*) pomo *m*; (*of butter*) noce *f*. **~bly** *a* nodoso; (*bony*) spigoloso

knock /nɒk/ *n* colpo *m*; **there was a ~ at the door** hanno bussato alla porta ● *vt* bussare a (*door*); (*fam: criticize*) denigrare; (*fam*) **a hole in sth** fare un buco in qcsa; **~ one's head** battere la testa (**on** contro) ● *vi* (*at door*) bussare. **knock about** *vt* malmenare ● *vi fam* girovagare. **knock down** *vt* far cadere; (*with fist*) stendere con un pugno; (*in car*) investire; (*demolish*) abbattere; (*fam: reduce*) ribassare (*price*). **knock off** *vt* (*fam: steal*) fregare; (*fam: complete quickly*) fare alla bell'e meglio ● *vi* (*fam: cease work*) staccare. **knock out** *vt* eliminare; (*make unconscious*) mettere K.O.; (*fam: anaesthetize*) addormenta-

re. **knock over** *vt* rovesciare; (*in car*) investire

knock: **~-down** *a* **~-down price** prezzo *m* stracciato. **~er** *n* battente *m*. **~-kneed** /-'ni:d/ *a* con gambe storte. **~-out** *n* (*in boxing*) knock-out *m inv*

knot /nɒt/ *n* nodo *m* ● *vt* (*pt/pp* **knotted**) annodare

knotty /'nɒtɪ/ *a* (**-ier, -iest**) *fam* spinoso

know /nəʊ/ *v* (*pt* **knew**, *pp* **known**)
● *vt* sapere; conoscere (*person, place*); (*recognize*) riconoscere; **get to ~ sb** conoscere qcno; **~ how to swim** sapere nuotare ● *vi* sapere; **did you ~ about this?** lo sapevi? ● *n* **in the ~** *fam* al corrente

know: **~-all** *n fam* sapientone, -a *mf*. **~-how** *n* abilità *f*; *fam* d'intesa. **~ingly** *adv* (*intentionally*) consapevolmente; (*smile etc*) con un'aria d'intesa

knowledge /'nɒlɪdʒ/ *n* conoscenza *f*. **~able** /-əbl/ *a* ben informato

known /nəʊn/ *see* **know** ● *a* noto

knuckle /'nʌkl/ *n* nocca *f*
● **knuckle down** *vi* darci sotto (**to** con). **knuckle under** *vi* sottomettersi

Koran /kə'rɑːn/ *n* Corano *m*

Korea /kə'rɪə/ *n* Corea *f*. **~n** *a & n* coreano, -a *mf*

kosher /'kəʊʃə(r)/ *a* kasher *inv*

kowtow /kaʊ'taʊ/ *vi* piegarsi

kudos /'kju:dɒs/ *n fam* gloria *f*

lab /læb/ *n fam* laboratorio *m*

label /'leɪbl/ *n* etichetta *f* ● *vt* (*pt/pp* **labelled**) mettere un'etichetta a; *fig* etichettare (*person*)

laboratory /lə'bɒrətrɪ/ *n* laboratorio *m*

laborious /lə'bɔːrɪəs/ *a* laborioso

labour /'leɪbə(r)/ n lavoro m;
(workers) manodopera f; Med doglie fpl; **be in ~** avere le doglie;
L~ Pol partito m laburista
●attrib Pol laburista ●vi lavorare ●vt ~ **the point** fig ribadire il
concetto. **~er** n manovale m

'labour-saving a che fa risparmiare lavoro e fatica

labyrinth /'læbərɪnθ/ n labirinto m

lace /leɪs/ n pizzo m; (of shoe) laccio m ●attrib di pizzo ●vt allacciare (shoes); correggere (drink)

lacerate /'læsəreɪt/ vt lacerare

lack /læk/ n mancanza f ●vt mancare di; **I ~ the time** mi manca il
tempo ●vi be ~ing mancare; **be
~ing in sth** mancare di qcsa

lackadaisical /lækə'deɪzɪkl/ a
senza entusiasmo

laconic /lə'kɒnɪk/ a laconico

lacquer /'lækə(r)/ n lacca f

lad /læd/ n ragazzo m

ladder /'lædə(r)/ n scala f; (in
tights) sfilatura f

laden /'leɪdn/ a carico (with di)

ladle /'leɪdl/ n mestolo m ●vt ~
[out] versare (col mestolo)

lady /'leɪdɪ/ n signora f; (title)
Lady; **ladies [room]** bagno m per
donne

lady: ~bird n, Am **~bug** n coccinella f. **~like** a signorile

lag¹ /læg/ vi (pt/pp **lagged**) ~
behind restare indietro

lag² vt (pt/pp **lagged**) isolare
(pipes)

lager /'lɑːgə(r)/ n birra f chiara

lagoon /lə'guːn/ n laguna f

laid /leɪd/ see **lay³**

lain /leɪn/ see **lie²**

lair /leə(r)/ n tana f

lake /leɪk/ n lago m

lamb /læm/ n agnello m

lame /leɪm/ a zoppo; fig (argument) zoppicante; (excuse) traballante

lament /lə'ment/ n lamento m ●vt
lamentare ●vi lamentarsi

lamentable /'læməntəbl/ a deplo-
revole

laminated /'læmɪneɪtɪd/ a laminato

lamp /læmp/ n lampada f; (in
street) lampione m. **~post** n lampione m. **~shade** n paralume m

lance /lɑːns/ n fiocina f ●vt Med
incidere. **~-'corporal** n appunta-
to m

land /lænd/ n terreno m; (country)
paese m; (as opposed to sea) terra
f; **plot of ~** pezzo m di terreno
●vt Naut sbarcare; (fam: obtain)
assicurarsi; **be ~ed with sth** fam
ritrovarsi fra capo e collo qcsa
●vi Aeron atterrare; (fall) cadere.
land up vi fam finire

landing /'lændɪŋ/ n Naut sbarco
m; Aeron atterraggio m; (top of
stairs) pianerottolo m. **~stage** n
pontile m da sbarco. **~ strip** n pista f d'atterraggio di fortuna

land: ~lady n proprietaria f; (of
flat) padrona f di casa. **~locked** a
privo di sbocco sul mare. **~lord** n
proprietario m; (of flat) padrone m
di casa. **~mark** n punto m di riferimento; fig pietra f miliare.
~owner n proprietario, -a mf
terriero. **~scape** /-skeɪp/ n paesaggio m. **~slide** n frana f; Pol valanga f di voti

lane /leɪn/ n sentiero m; Auto,
Sport corsia f

language /'læŋgwɪdʒ/ n lingua f;
(speech, style) linguaggio m. **~
laboratory** n laboratorio m lin-
guistico

languid /'læŋgwɪd/ a languido

languish /'læŋgwɪʃ/ vi languire

lank /læŋk/ a (hair) diritto

lanky /'læŋkɪ/ a (-ier, -iest) allam-
panato

lantern /'læntən/ n lanterna f

lap¹ /læp/ n grembo m

lap² n (of journey) tappa f; Sport
giro m ●v (pt/pp **lapped**) ●vi
(water:) ~ **against** lambire ●vt
Sport doppiare

lap³ vt (pt/pp **lapped**) ~ **up** bere
avidamente; bersi completamente

⟨lies⟩; credere ciecamente a ⟨praise⟩

lapel /lə'pel/ *n* bavero *m*

lapse /læps/ *n* sbaglio *m*; ⟨moral⟩ sbandamento *m* [morale]; ⟨of time⟩ intervallo *m* ● *vi* ⟨expire⟩ scadere; ⟨morally⟩ scivolare; ~ **into** cadere in

laptop /'læptɒp/ *n* ~ [**computer**] computer *m inv* portabile, laptop *m inv*

larceny /'lɑːsənɪ/ *n* furto *m*

lard /lɑːd/ *n* strutto *m*

larder /'lɑːdə(r)/ *n* dispensa *f*

large /lɑːdʒ/ *a* grande; ⟨number, amount⟩ grande, grosso; **by and** ~ in complesso; **at** ~ in libertà; ⟨in general⟩ ampiamente. ~**ly** *adv* ampiamente. ~**ly because of** in gran parte a causa di

lark¹ /lɑːk/ *n* ⟨bird⟩ allodola *f*

lark² *n* ⟨joke⟩ burla *f* ● **lark about** *vi* giocherellare

larva /'lɑːvə/ *n* (*pl* **-vae** /-viː/) larva *f*

laryngitis /lærɪn'dʒaɪtɪs/ *n* laringite *f*

larynx /'lærɪŋks/ *n* laringe *f*

lascivious /lə'sɪvɪəs/ *a* lascivo

laser /'leɪzə(r)/ *n* laser *m inv*. ~ [**printer**] *n* stampante *f* laser

lash /læʃ/ *n* frustata *f*; ⟨eyelash⟩ ciglio *m* ● *vt* ⟨whip⟩ frustare; ⟨tie⟩ legare fermamente. **lash out** *vi* attaccare; ⟨spend⟩ sperperare (**on** in)

lashings /'læʃɪŋz/ *npl* ~ **of** *fam* una marea di

lass /læs/ *n* ragazzina *f*

lasso /lə'suː/ *n* lazo *m*

last¹ /lɑːst/ *a* ⟨final⟩ ultimo; ⟨recent⟩ scorso; ~ **night** ieri sera; **at** ~ alla fine; **at** ~! finalmente!; **that's the** ~ **straw** *fam* questa è l'ultima goccia ● *n* ultimo, -a *mf*; **the** ~ **but one** il penultimo ● *adv* per ultimo; ⟨last time⟩ l'ultima volta ● *vi* durare. ~**ing** *a* durevole. ~**ly** *adv* infine

last² /lɑːst/ *n* forma *f*

latch /lætʃ/ *n* chiavistello *m*

latch /lætʃ/ *a* ⟨delayed⟩ in ritardo; ⟨at a late hour⟩ tardo; ⟨deceased⟩ de-

funto; **it's** ~ ⟨at night⟩ è tardi; **in** ~ **November** alla fine di Novembre ● *adv* tardi; **stay up** ~ stare alzati fino a tardi. ~**comer** *n* ritardatario, -a *mf*; ⟨to political party etc⟩ nuovo, -a arrivato, -a *mf*. ~**ly** *adv* recentemente. ~**ness** *n* ora *f* tarda; ⟨delay⟩ ritardo *m*

latent /'leɪtnt/ *a* latente

later /'leɪtə(r)/ *a* ⟨train⟩ che parte più tardi; ⟨edition⟩ più recente ● *adv* più tardi; ~ **on** più tardi, dopo

lateral /'lætərəl/ *a* laterale

latest /'leɪtɪst/ *a* ultimo; ⟨most recent⟩ più recente; **the** ~ [**news**] le ultime notizie ● *n* **six o'clock at the** ~ alle sei al più tardi

lathe /leɪð/ *n* tornio *m*

lather /'lɑːðə(r)/ *n* schiuma *f* ● *vt* insaponare ● *vi* far schiuma

Latin /'lætɪn/ *a* latino ● *n* latino *m*. ~ **America** *n* America *f* Latina. ~ **American** *a* & *n* latino-americano, -a *mf*

latitude /'lætɪtjuːd/ *n Geog* latitudine *f*; *fig* libertà *f* d'azione

latter /'lætə(r)/ *a* ultimo ● *n* **the** ~ quest'ultimo. ~**ly** *adv* ultimamente

lattice /'lætɪs/ *n* traliccio *m*

Latvia /'lætvɪə/ *n* Lettonia *f*. ~**n** *a* & *n* lettone *mf*

laudable /'lɔːdəbl/ *a* lodevole

laugh /lɑːf/ *n* risata *f* ● *vi* ridere ⟨at/about di⟩; ~ **at sb** ⟨mock⟩ prendere in giro qcno. ~**able** /-əbl/ *a* ridicolo. ~**ing-stock** *n* zimbello *m*

laughter /'lɑːftə(r)/ *n* risata *f*

launch¹ /lɔːntʃ/ *n* ⟨boat⟩ varo *m*

launch² *n* lancio *m*; ⟨of ship⟩ varo *m* ● *vt* lanciare ⟨rocket, product⟩; varare ⟨ship⟩; sferrare ⟨attack⟩

launder /'lɔːndə(r)/ *vt* lavare e stirare; ~ **money** *fig* riciclare denaro sporco. ~**ette** /-'dret/ *n* lavanderia *f* automatica

laundry /'lɔːndrɪ/ *n* lavanderia *f*; ⟨clothes⟩ bucato *m*

laurel /ˈlɒrəl/ n lauro m; fig rest
on one's ~s dormire sugli allori

lava /ˈlɑːvə/ n lava f

lavatory /ˈlævətrɪ/ n gabinetto m

lavender /ˈlævəndə(r)/ n lavanda f

lavish /ˈlævɪʃ/ a copioso; (waste-
ful) prodigo; **on a ~ scale** su
vasta scala ● vt ~ **sth on sb**
ricoprire qcno di qcsa. **~ly** adv
copiosamente

law /lɔː/ n legge f; **study ~** studiare
giurisprudenza, studiare legge; **~
and order** ordine m pubblico

law: **~-abiding** a che rispetta la
legge. **~court** il tribunale m. **~ful**
a legittimo m. **~less** a senza legge. **~ school** n facoltà f di giurisprudenza

lawn /lɔːn/ n prato m [all'inglese].
~-mower n tosaerbe m inv

'law suit n causa f

lawyer /ˈlɔːjə(r)/ n avvocato m

lax /læks/ a negligente; ⟨morals
etc⟩ lassista

laxative /ˈlæksətɪv/ n lassativo m

laxity /ˈlæksətɪ/ n lassismo m

lay[1] /leɪ/ a laico; fig profano

lay[2] see **lie**[2]

lay[3] vt ⟨pt/pp laid⟩ porre, mettere;
apparecchiare ⟨table⟩ ● vi ⟨hen⟩
fare la uova. **lay down** vt posare;
stabilire ⟨rules, conditions⟩. **lay
off** vt licenziare ⟨workers⟩ ● vi
⟨fam: stop⟩ ~ **off!** smettila! **lay
out** vt ⟨display, set forth⟩ esporre;
⟨plan⟩ pianificare ⟨garden⟩;
⟨spend⟩ sborsare; Typ impaginare

lay: **~about** n fannullone, -a mf.
~-by n corsia f di sosta

layer /ˈleɪə(r)/ n strato m

lay: **~man** n profano m. **~out** n disposizione f; Typ impaginazione f,
layout m inv

laze /leɪz/ vi ~ [**about**] oziare

laziness /ˈleɪzɪnɪs/ n pigrizia f

lazy /ˈleɪzɪ/ a ⟨-ier, -iest⟩ pigro.
~-bones n poltrone, -a mf

lb abbr ⟨pound⟩ libbra

lead[1] /led/ n piombo m; ⟨of pencil⟩
mina f

lead[2] /liːd/ n guida f; ⟨leash⟩

giunzaglio m; ⟨flex⟩ filo m; ⟨clue⟩
indizio m; Theat parte f principale; ⟨distance ahead⟩ distanza f
⟨over su⟩; **in the ~** in testa ● v
⟨pt/pp led⟩ ● vt condurre; dirigere
⟨expedition, party etc⟩; ⟨induce⟩ indurre; ~ **the way** mettersi in testa
● vi ⟨be in front⟩ condurre; ⟨in
race, competition⟩ essere in testa;
⟨at cards⟩ giocare ⟨per primo⟩.
lead away vt portar via. **lead to** vt
portare a. **lead up to** vt preludere;
what's this ~ing up to? dove porta questo?

leaded /ˈledɪd/ a con piombo

leader /ˈliːdə(r)/ n capo m; ⟨of or-
chestra⟩ primo violino m; ⟨in
newspaper⟩ articolo m di fondo.
~ship n direzione f, leadership f
inv; **show ~ship** mostrare capacità di comando

lead-'free a senza piombo

leading /ˈliːdɪŋ/ a principale; ~
lady/man attrice f/attore m principale; ~ **question** domanda f ten-
denziosa

leaf /liːf/ n ⟨pl **leaves**⟩ foglia f;
⟨of table⟩ asse f ● **leaf through**
vt sfogliare. **~let** n dépliant m
inv; ⟨advertising⟩ dépliant m inv
pubblicitario; ⟨political⟩ manife-
stino m

league /liːg/ n lega f; Sport campionato m; **be in ~ with** essere in
combutta con

leak /liːk/ n ⟨hole⟩ fessura f; Naut
falla f; ⟨of gas & fig⟩ fuga f ● vi colare; ⟨ship:⟩ fare acqua; ⟨liquid,
gas:⟩ fuoriuscire ● vt ~ **sth to sb**
fig far trapelare qcsa a qcno. **~y** a
⟨container⟩ che fa acqua

lean[1] /liːn/ a magro

lean[2] v ⟨pt/pp **leaned** or **leant**
/lent/⟩ ● vt appoggiare ⟨against/
on contro/su⟩ ● vi appoggiarsi
⟨against/on contro/su⟩; ⟨not be
straight⟩ pendere; **be ~ing
against** essere appoggiato contro;
~ **on sb** ⟨depend on⟩ appoggiarsi a
qcno; ⟨fam: exert pressure on⟩ stare alle calcagne di qcno. **lean**

back vi sporgersi indietro. **lean forward** vi piegarsi in avanti. **lean out** vi sporgersi. **lean over** vi piegarsi

leaning /'li:nɪŋ/ n tendenza f

leap /li:p/ n salto m ● vi (pt/pp **leapt** /lept/ or **leaped**) saltare; **he leapt at it** fam l'ha preso al volo. **~-frog** n cavallina f. **~ year** n anno m bisestile

learn /lɜːn/ v (pt/pp **learnt** or **learned**) ● vt imparare; **~ to swim** imparare a nuotare; **I have ~ed that...** (heard) sono venuto a sapere che... ● vi imparare

learn|ed /'lɜːnɪd/ a colto. **~er** n also Auto principiante mf. **~ing** n cultura f

lease /li:s/ n contratto m d'affitto; (rental) affitto m ● vt affittare

leash /li:ʃ/ n guinzaglio m

least /li:st/ a più piccolo; (amount) minore; **you've got ~ luggage** hai meno bagagli di tutti ● n the **~** il meno; **at ~** almeno; **not in the ~** niente affatto ● adv meno; **the ~ expensive wine** il vino meno caro

leather /'leðə(r)/ n pelle f; (of soles) cuoio m ● attrib di pelle/cuoio. **~y** a (meat, skin) duro

leave /li:v/ n (holiday) congedo m; Mil licenza f; **on ~** in congedo/licenza ● v (pt/pp **left**) ● vt lasciare; uscire da (house, office); (forget) dimenticare; **there is nothing left** non è rimasto niente ● vi andare via; (train, bus) partire. **leave behind** vt lasciare; (forget) dimenticare. **leave out** vt omettere; (not put away) lasciare fuori

leaves /li:vz/ see **leaf**

Leban|on /'lebənən/ n Libano m. **~ese** /-'niːz/ a & n libanese mf

lecherous /'letʃərəs/ a lascivo

lectern /'lektɜːn/ n leggio m

lecture /'lektʃə(r)/ n conferenza f; Univ lezione f; (reproof) ramanzi-

na f ● vi fare una conferenza (**on** su); Univ insegnare (**on sth** qcsa) ● vt ~ **sb** rimproverare qcno. **~r** n conferenziere, -a mf; Univ docente mf universitario, -a

led /led/ see **lead**[2]

ledge /ledʒ/ n cornice f; (of window) davanzale m

ledger /'ledʒə(r)/ n libro m mastro

leech /li:tʃ/ n sanguisuga f

leek /li:k/ n porro m

leer /lɪə(r)/ n sguardo m libidinoso ● vi ~ [at] guardare in modo libidinoso

leeway /'li:weɪ/ n fig libertà f di azione

left[1] /left/ see **leave**

left[2] /left/ a sinistra ● adv a sinistra ● n also Pol sinistra f; **on the ~** a sinistra;

left: **~-'handed** a mancino. **~-'luggage [office]** n deposito m bagagli. **~overs** npl rimasugli mpl. **~-'wing** a Pol di sinistra

leg /leg/ n gamba f; (of animal) zampa f; (of journey) tappa f; Culin (of chicken) coscia f; (of lamb) cosciotto m

legacy /'legəsɪ/ n lascito m

legal /'li:gl/ a legale; **take ~ action** intentare un'azione legale. **~ly** adv legalmente

legality /lɪ'gælətɪ/ n legalità f

legalize /'li:gəlaɪz/ vt legalizzare

legend /'ledʒənd/ n leggenda f. **~ary** a leggendario

legible /'ledʒəbl/ a leggibile. **~ly** adv in modo leggibile

legislate /'ledʒɪsleɪt/ vi legiferare. **~ion** /-'leɪʃn/ n legislazione f

legislat|ive /'ledʒɪslətɪv/ a legislativo. **~ure** /-lətʃə(r)/ n legislatura f

legitimate /lɪ'dʒɪtɪmət/ a legittimo; (excuse) valido

leisure /'leʒə(r)/ n tempo m libero; **at your ~** con comodo. **~ly** a senza fretta

lemon /'lemən/ n limone m. **~ade** /-'neɪd/ n limonata f

lend /lend/ vt (pt/pp **lent**) prestare;

~ a hand *fig* dare una mano. **~ing library** *n* biblioteca *f* per il prestito

length /leŋθ/ *n* lunghezza *f*; *(piece)* pezzo *m*; *(of wallpaper)* parte *f*; *(of visit)* durata *f*; **at ~** a lungo; *(at last)* alla fine

length|en /'leŋθən/ *vt* allungare ● *vi* allungarsi. **~ways** *adv* per lungo

lengthy /'leŋθɪ/ *a* (**-ier, -iest**) lungo

lenien|ce /'li:nɪəns/ *n* indulgenza *f*. **~t** *a* indulgente

lens /lenz/ *n* lente *f*; *Phot* obiettivo *m*; *(of eye)* cristallino *m*

Lent /lent/ *n* Quaresima *f*

lent /lent/ *see* **lend**

lentil /'lentl/ *n* *Bot* lenticchia *f*

Leo /'li:əʊ/ *n* *Astr* Leone *m*

leopard /'lepəd/ *n* leopardo *m*

leotard /'li:ətɑːd/ *n* body *m* *inv*

leprosy /'leprəsɪ/ *n* lebbra *f*

lesbian /'lezbɪən/ *a* lesbico ● *n* lesbica *f*

less /les/ *a* meno di; **~ and ~** sempre meno ● *adv* & *prep* meno ● *n* meno *m*

lessen /'lesn/ *vt/i* diminuire

lesser /'lesə(r)/ *a* minore

lesson /'lesn/ *n* lezione *f*

lest /lest/ *conj* *liter* per timore che

let /let/ *vt* (*pt/pp* **let**, *pres p* **letting**) lasciare, permettere; *(rent)* affittare; **~ alone** *(not to mention)* tanto meno; **'to ~'** 'affittasi'; **~ us go** andiamo; **~ sb do sth** lasciare fare qcsa a qcno, permettere a qcno di fare qcsa; **~ me know** fammi sapere; **just ~ him try!** che ci provi solamente!; **~ oneself in for sth** *fam* impelagarsi in qcsa. **let down** *vt* sciogliersi *(hair)*; *(lengthen)* allungare; *(disappoint)* deludere; **don't ~ me down** non conta su di te. **let in** *vt* far entrare. **let off** *vt* far partire; *(not punish)* perdonare; **~ sb off doing sth** abbonare qcsa a qcno. **let out** *vt* far uscire; *(make larger)* allargare; emettere

(scream, groan). **let through** *vt* far passare. **let up** *vi* *fam* diminuire

'let-down *n* delusione *f*

lethal /'li:θl/ *a* letale

letharg|ic /lɪ'θɑːdʒɪk/ *a* apatico. **~y** /'leθədʒɪ/ *n* apatia *f*

letter /'letə(r)/ *n* lettera *f*. **~-box** *n* buca *f* per le lettere. **~-head** *n* carta *f* intestata. **~ing** *n* caratteri *mpl*

lettuce /'letɪs/ *n* lattuga *f*

'let-up *n* *fam* pausa *f*

leukaemia /luː'kiːmɪə/ *n* leucemia *f*

level /'levl/ *a* piano; *(in height, competition)* allo stesso livello; *(spoonful)* raso; **draw ~ with** sb affiancare qcno ● *n* livello *m*; **on the ~** *fam* giusto ● *vt* (*pt/pp* **levelled**) livellare; *(aim)* puntare (at su)

level: **~ 'crossing** *n* passaggio *m* a livello. **~-'headed** *a* posato

lever /'liːvə(r)/ *n* leva *f* ● **lever up** *vt* sollevare *(con una leva)*. **~age** /-rɪdʒ/ *n* azione *f* di una leva; *fig* influenza *f*

levy /'levɪ/ *vt* (*pt/pp* **levied**) imporre *(tax)*

lewd /ljuːd/ *a* osceno

liability /laɪə'bɪlətɪ/ *n* responsabilità *f*; *(fam: burden)* peso *m*; **~ies** *pl* debiti *mpl*

liable /'laɪəbl/ *a* responsabile (for di); **be ~ to** *(rain, break etc)* rischiare di; *(tend to)* tendere a

liaise /lɪ'eɪz/ *vi* *fam* essere in contatto

liaison /lɪ'eɪzɒn/ *n* contatti *mpl*; *Mil* collegamento *m*; *(affair)* relazione *f*

liar /'laɪə(r)/ *n* bugiardo, -a *mf*

libel /'laɪbl/ *n* diffamazione *f* ● *vt* (*pt/pp* **libelled**) diffamare. **~lous** *a* diffamatorio

liberal /'lɪb(ə)rəl/ *a* *(tolerant)* di larghe vedute; *(generous)* generoso. **L~** *a* *Pol* liberale ● *n* liberale *mf*

liberat|e /'lɪbəreɪt/ *vt* liberare. **~ed** *a* *(woman)* emancipata. **~ion** /-'reɪʃn/ *n* liberazione *f*; *(of* *women*) emancipazione *f*. **~or** *n* liberatore, -trice *mf*

liberty /ˈlɪbətɪ/ *n* libertà *f*; **take the ~ of doing sth** prendersi la libertà di fare qcsa; **be at ~ to do sth** essere libero di fare qcsa

Libra /ˈliːbrə/ *n Astr* Bilancia *f*

librarian /laɪˈbreərɪən/ *n* bibliotecario, -a *mf*

library /ˈlaɪbrərɪ/ *n* biblioteca *f*

Libya /ˈlɪbɪə/ *n* Libia *f*. **~n** *a* & *n* libico, -a *mf*

lice /laɪs/ *see* **louse**

licence /ˈlaɪsns/ *n* licenza *f*; (*for TV*) canone *m* televisivo; (*for driving*) patente *f*; (*freedom*) sregolatezza *f*. **~-plate** *n* targa *f*

license /ˈlaɪsns/ *vt* autorizzare; **be ~d** ⟨*car:⟩* avere il bollo; ⟨*restaurant:⟩* essere autorizzato alla vendita di alcolici

licentious /laɪˈsenʃəs/ *a* licenzioso

lick /lɪk/ *n* leccata *f*; **a ~ of paint** una passata leggera di pittura ● *vt* leccare; (*fam: defeat*) battere; leccarsi ⟨*lips*⟩

lid /lɪd/ *n* coperchio *m*; (*of eye*) palpebra *f*

lie[1] /laɪ/ *n* bugia *f*; **tell a ~** mentire ● *vi* (*pt/pp* **lied**, *pres p* **lying**) mentire

lie[2] *vi* (*pt* **lay**, *pp* **lain**, *pres p* **lying**) ⟨*person:⟩* sdraiarsi; ⟨*object:⟩* stare; (*remain*) rimanere; **leave sth lying about** *or* **around** lasciare qcsa in giro. **lie down** *vi* sdraiarsi

'lie: ~-down *n* **have a ~** fare un riposino. **~-in** *n fam* **have a ~-in** restare a letto fino a tardi

lieu /ljuː/ *n* **in ~ of** in luogo di...

lieutenant /lefˈtenənt/ *n* tenente *m*

life /laɪf/ *n* (*pl* **lives**) vita *f* ●

di tutta la vita. **~-size[d]** *a* in grandezza naturale. **~time** *n* vita *f*; **the chance of a ~time** un'occasione unica

lift /lɪft/ *n* ascensore *m*; *Auto* passaggio *m* ● *vt* sollevare; revocare (*restrictions*); (*fam: steal*) rubare ● *vi* ⟨*fog:⟩* alzarsi. **lift up** *vt* sollevare

'lift-off *n* decollo *m* (*di razzo*)

ligament /ˈlɪgəmənt/ *n Anat* legamento *m*

light[1] /laɪt/ *a* (*not dark*) luminoso; **~ green** verde chiaro ● *n* luce *f*; (*lamp*) lampada *f*; **in the ~ of** alla luce di; **have you got a ~?** ha da accendere?; **come to ~** essere rivelato ● *vt* (*pt/pp* **lit** *or* **lighted**) accendere; (*illuminate*) illuminare. **light up** *vi* ⟨*face:⟩* illuminarsi

light[2] *a* (*not heavy*) leggero ● *adv* **travel ~** viaggiare con poco bagaglio

'light-bulb *n* lampadina *f*

lighten[1] /ˈlaɪtn/ *vt* illuminare

lighten[2] *vt* alleggerire (*load*)

lighter /ˈlaɪtə(r)/ *n* accendino *m*

light: ~-fingered *a* svelto di mano. **~-headed** *a* sventato. **~-hearted** *a* spensierato. **~house** *n* faro *m*. **~ing** *n* illuminazione *f*. **~ly** *adv* leggermente; (*accuse*) con leggerezza; (*without concern*) senza dare importanza alla cosa; **get off ~ly** cavarsela a buon mercato. **~ness** *n* leggerezza *f*

lightning /ˈlaɪtnɪŋ/ *n* lampo *m*, fulmine *m*. **~-conductor** *n* parafulmine *m*

light: ~weight *a* leggero ● *n* (*in boxing*) peso *m* leggero. **~ year** *n* anno *m* luce

like[1] /laɪk/ *a* simile ● *prep* come; **~ this/that** così; **what's he ~?** com'è? ● *conj* (*fam: as*) come; (*Am: as if*) come se

like[2] *vt* piacere, gradire; **I should/would ~** vorrei, gradirei; **I ~ him** mi piace; **I ~ this car** mi piace questa macchina; **I ~ dancing** mi piace ballare; **I ~ that!** *fam* questa

~-belt *n* salvagente *m*. **~-boat** *n* lancia *f* di salvataggio; (*on ship*) scialuppa *f* di salvataggio. **~-buoy** *n* salvagente *m*. **~-guard** *n* bagnino *m*. **~-insurance** *n* assicurazione *f* sulla vita. **~-jacket** *n* giubbotto *m* di salvataggio. **~less** *a* inanimato. **~-like** *a* realistico. **~-long** *a*

mi è piaciuta! ● *n* ~s and dislikes
pl gusti *mpl*

like|able /ˈlaɪkəbl/ *a* simpatico.
~lihood /-lɪhʊd/ *n* probabilità *f*.
~ly *a* (-ier, -iest) probabile ● *adv*
probabilmente; not ~ly! *fam* neanche per sogno!

like-'minded *a* con gusti affini

liken /ˈlaɪkən/ *vt* paragonare (to a)

like|ness /ˈlaɪknɪs/ *n* somiglianza
f. '~wise *adv* lo stesso

liking /ˈlaɪkɪŋ/ *n* gusto *m*; is it to
your ~? è di suo gusto?; take a ~
to sb prendere qcno in simpatia

lilac /ˈlaɪlək/ *n* lillà *m* ● *a* color lillà

lily /ˈlɪlɪ/ *n* giglio *m*. ~ of the valley
n mughetto *m*

limb /lɪm/ *n* arto *m*

limber /ˈlɪmbə(r)/ *vi* ~ up sciogliersi i muscoli

lime¹ /laɪm/ *n* (*fruit*) cedro *m*;
(*tree*) tiglio *m*

lime² *n* calce *f*. '~light *n* be in the
~light essere molto in vista.
'~stone *n* calcare *m*

limit /ˈlɪmɪt/ *n* limite *m*; that's
the ~! *fam* questo è troppo! ● *vt*
limitare (to a). ~ation /-ˈteɪʃn/ *n*
limite *m*. ~ed *a* ristretto; ~ed
company società *f* anonima

limousine /ˈlɪməziːn/ *n* limousine
f inv

limp¹ /lɪmp/ *n* andatura *f* zoppicante; have a ~ zoppicare ● *vi* zoppicare

limp² *a* floscio

line¹ /laɪn/ *n* linea *f*; (*length of rope,
cord*) filo *m*; (*of writing*) riga *f*; (*of
poem*) verso *m*; (*row*) fila *f*;
(*wrinkle*) ruga *f*; (*of business*) settore *m*; (*Am: queue*) coda *f*; in ~
with in conformità con ● *vt* segnare; fiancheggiare (*street*). line up
vi allinearsi ● *vt* allineare

line² *vt* foderare (*garment*)

linear /ˈlɪnɪə(r)/ *a* lineare

lined¹ /laɪnd/ *a* (*face*) rugoso;
(*paper*) a righe

lined² *a* (*garment*) foderato

linen /ˈlɪnɪn/ *n* lino *m*; (*articles*)
biancheria *f* ● *attrib* di lino

liner /ˈlaɪnə(r)/ *n* nave *f* di linea

linesman *n Sport* guardalinee *m
inv*

linger /ˈlɪŋɡə(r)/ *vi* indugiare

lingerie /ˈlɒʒərɪ/ *n* biancheria *f* intima (*da donna*)

linguist /ˈlɪŋɡwɪst/ *n* linguista *mf*

linguistic /lɪŋˈɡwɪstɪk/ *a* linguisti-
co. ~s *n* linguistica *fsg*

lining /ˈlaɪnɪŋ/ *n* (*of garment*) fodera *f*; (*of brakes*) guarnizione *f*

link /lɪŋk/ *n* (*of chain*) anello *m*; *fig*
legame *m* ● *vt* collegare. link up *vi*
unirsi (with a); *TV* collegarsi

lino /ˈlaɪnəʊ/ *n*,   linoleum
/lɪˈnəʊlɪəm/ *n* linoleum *m*

lint /lɪnt/ *n* garza *f*

lion /ˈlaɪən/ *n* leone *m*. ~ess *n*
leonessa *f*

lip /lɪp/ *n* labbro *m* (*pl* labbra *f*);
(*edge*) bordo *m*

lip: ~-read *vi* leggere le labbra.
~-reading *n* lettura *f* delle labbra.
~-service *n* pay ~service to approvare soltanto a parole. ~salve
n burro *m* (*f*) cacao. ~stick *n* ros-
setto *m*

liqueur /lɪˈkjʊə(r)/ *n* liquore *m*

liquid /ˈlɪkwɪd/ *n* liquido *m* ● *a* liquido

liquidat|e /ˈlɪkwɪdeɪt/ *vt* liquidare.
~ion /-ˈdeɪʃn/ *n* liquidazione *f*;
Comm go into ~ion andare in liquidazione

liquidize /ˈlɪkwɪdaɪz/ *vt* rendere liquido. ~r *n Culin* frullatore *m*

liquor /ˈlɪkə(r)/ *n* bevanda *f* alcoolica

liquorice /ˈlɪkərɪs/ *n* liquirizia *f*

liquor store *n Am* negozio *m* di alcolici

lisp /lɪsp/ *n* pronuncia *f* con la lisca
● *vi* parlare con la lisca

list¹ /lɪst/ *n* lista *f* ● *vt* elencare

list² *vi* (*ship:*) inclinarsi

listen /ˈlɪsn/ *vi* ascoltare; ~ to
ascoltare. ~er *n* ascoltatore, -trice
mf

listings /'lıstıŋz/ *npl* TV programma *m*

listless /'lıstlıs/ *a* svogliato

lit /lıt/ *see* **light¹**

literacy /'lıtərəsı/ *n* alfabetizzazione *f*

literal /'lıtərəl/ *a* letterale. **~ly** *adv* letteralmente

literary /'lıtərərı/ *a* letterario

literate /'lıtərət/ *a* **be ~** saper leggere e scrivere

literature /'lıtrətʃə(r)/ *n* letteratura *f*

Lithuania /lıθjʊ'emıə/ *n* Lituania *f*. **~n** *a* & *n* lituano, -a *mf*

litigation /lıtı'geıʃn/ *n* causa *f* [giudiziaria]

litre /'li:tə(r)/ *n* litro *m*

litter /'lıtə(r)/ *n* immondizie *fpl*; *Zool* figliata *f* ● *vt* **be ~ed with** essere ingombrato di. **~-bin** *n* bidone *m* della spazzatura

little /'lıtl/ *a* piccolo; (*not much*) poco ● *adv* & *n* poco *m*; **a ~** un po'; **a ~ water** un po' d'acqua; **a ~ better** un po' meglio; **by ~** a poco a poco

liturgy /'lıtədʒı/ *n* liturgia *f*

live¹ /laıv/ *a* vivo; (*ammunition*) carico; **~ broadcast** trasmissione *f* in diretta; **be ~** *Electr* essere sotto tensione; **~ wire** *n fig* persona *f* dinamica ● *adv* (*broadcast*) in diretta

live² /lıv/ *vi* vivere; (*reside*) abitare; **~ with** convivere con. **live down** *vt* far dimenticare. **live off** *vt* vivere alle spalle di. **live on** *vt* vivere di ● *vi* sopravvivere. **live up** *vt* **~ it up** far la bella vita. **live up to** *vt* essere all'altezza di

livelihood /'laıvlıhʊd/ *n* mezzi *mpl* di sostentamento. **~ness** *n* vivacità *f*

lively /'laıvlı/ *a* (**-ier, -iest**) vivace

liven /'laıvn/ *vt* **~ up** vivacizzare ● *vi* vivacizzarsi

liver /'lıvə(r)/ *n* fegato *m*

lives /laıvz/ *see* **life**

livestock /'laıv-/ *n* bestiame *m*

livid /'lıvıd/ *a fam* livido

living /'lıvıŋ/ *a* vivo ● *n* **earn one's ~** guadagnarsi da vivere; **the ~** *pl* i vivi. **~-room** *n* soggiorno *m*

lizard /'lızəd/ *n* lucertola *f*

load /ləʊd/ *n* carico *m*; **~s of** *fam* un sacco di ● *vt* caricare. **~ed** *a* carico; (*fam: rich*) ricchissimo

loaf¹ /ləʊf/ *n* (*pl* **loaves**) pagnotta *f*

loaf² *vi* oziare

loan /ləʊn/ *n* prestito *m*; **on ~** in prestito ● *vt* prestare

loath /ləʊθ/ *a* **be ~ to do sth** essere restio a fare qcsa

loathe /ləʊð/ *vt* detestare. **~ing** *n* disgusto *m*. **~some** *a* disgustoso

loaves /ləʊvz/ *see* **loaf**

lobby /'lɒbı/ *n* atrio *m*; *Pol* gruppo *m* di pressione, lobby *m inv*

lobster /'lɒbstə(r)/ *n* aragosta *f*

local /'ləʊkl/ *a* locale; **I'm not ~** non sono del posto ● *n* abitante *mf* del luogo; (*fam: public house*) pub *m* locale. **~ au'thority** *n* autorità *f* locale. **~ call** *n Teleph* telefonata *f* urbana. **~ government** *n* autorità *f inv* locale

locality /ləʊ'kælətı/ *n* zona *f*

localized /'ləʊkəlaızd/ *a* localizzato

locally /'ləʊkəlı/ *adv* localmente; (*live, work*) nei paraggi

local network *n Comput* rete *f* locale

locate /ləʊ'keıt/ *vt* situare; trovare (*person*); **be ~ed** essere situato. **~ion** /-'keıʃn/ *n* posizione *f*; **filmed on ~ion** girato in esterni

lock¹ /lɒk/ *n* (*hair*) ciocca *f*

lock² /lɒk/ *n* (*on door*) serratura *f*; (*on canal*) chiusa *f* ● *vt* chiudere a chiave; bloccare (*wheels*) ● *vi* chiudersi. **lock in** *vt* chiudere dentro. **lock out** *vt* chiudere fuori. **lock up** *vt* (*in prison*) mettere dentro ● *vi* chiudere

locker /'lɒkə(r)/ *n* armadietto *m*

locket /'lɒkıt/ *n* medaglione *m*

lock: **~-out** *n* serrata *f*. **~smith** *n* fabbro *m*

locomotive /ləʊkə'məʊtıv/ *n* locomotiva *f*

locum /ˈləʊkəm/ n sostituto, -a *mf*

locust /ˈləʊkəst/ n locusta *f*

lodge /lɒdʒ/ n *(porter's)* portineria *f*; *(masonic)* loggia *f* ● *vt* presentare *‹claim, complaint›*; *(with bank, solicitor)* depositare; **be ~d** essersi conficcato ● *vi* essere a pensione **(with** da); *(become fixed)* conficcarsi. **~r** *n* inquilino, -a *mf*

lodgings /ˈlɒdʒɪŋz/ *npl* camere *fpl* in affitto

loft /lɒft/ n soffitta *f*

lofty /ˈlɒftɪ/ a (**-ier, -iest**) alto; *(haughty)* altezzoso

log /lɒg/ n ceppo *m*; *Auto* libretto *m* di circolazione; *Naut* giornale *m* di bordo ● *vt (pt* **logged)** registrare. **log on to** *vt Comput* connettersi a

logarithm /ˈlɒgərɪðm/ n logaritmo *m*

'log-book n *Naut* giornale *m* di bordo; *Auto* libretto *m* di circolazione

loggerheads /ˈlɒgə-/ *npl* **be at ~** *fam* essere in totale disaccordo

logic /ˈlɒdʒɪk/ n logica *f*. **~al** a logico. **~ally** *adv* logicamente

logistics /ləˈdʒɪstɪks/ *npl* logistica *f*

logo /ˈləʊgəʊ/ n logo *m inv*

loin /lɔɪn/ n *Culin* lombata *f*

loiter /ˈlɔɪtə(r)/ *vi* gironzolare

lollipop /ˈlɒlɪpɒp/ n lecca-lecca *m inv*. **~y** n lecca-lecca *m*; *(fam: money)* quattrini *mpl*

London /ˈlʌndən/ n Londra *f* ● *attrib* londinese, di Londra. **~er** n londinese *mf*

lone /ləʊn/ a solitario. **~liness** n solitudine *f*

lonely /ˈləʊnlɪ/ a (**-ier, -iest**) solitario; *(person)* solo

loner /ˈləʊnə(r)/ n persona *f* solitaria. **~some** a solo

long¹ /lɒŋ/ a lungo; **a ~ time** molto tempo; **a ~ way** distante; **in the ~ run** a lungo andare; *(in the end)* alla fin fine ● *adv* a lungo, lungamente; **how ~ is?** quanto è lungo?; *(in time)* quanto dura?; **all**

day ~ tutto il giorno; **not ~ ago** non molto tempo fa; **before ~** fra breve; **he's no ~er here** non è più qui; **as** *or* **so ~as** finché; *(provided that)* purché; **so ~!** *fam* ciao!; **will you be ~?** [ti] ci vuole molto?

long² *vi* **~ for** desiderare ardentemente

long-'distance a a grande distanza; *Sport* di fondo; *(call)* interurbano

'longhand n **in ~** in scrittura ordinaria

longing /ˈlɒŋɪŋ/ a desideroso ● n brama *f*. **~ly** *adv* con desiderio

longitude /ˈlɒŋgɪtjuːd/ n *Geog* longitudine *f*

long: **~ jump** n salto *m* in lungo. **~-life 'milk** n latte *m* a lunga conservazione. **~-lived** /-lɪvd/ a longevo. **~-range** a *Mil, Aeron* a lunga portata; *(forecast)* a lungo termine. **~-sighted** a presbite. **~-sleeved** a a maniche lunghe. **~-suffering** a infinitamente paziente. **~-term** a a lunga scadenza. **~ wave** n onde *fpl* lunghe. **~-winded** /-ˈwɪndɪd/ a prolisso

loo /luː/ n *fam* gabinetto *m*

look /lʊk/ n occhiata *f*; *(appearance)* aspetto *m*; **[good] ~s** *pl* bellezza *f*; **have a ~** at dare un'occhiata a ● *vi* guardare; *(seem)* sembrare; **~ here!** mi ascolti bene!; **~ at** guardare; **~ for** cercare; **~** *(resemble)* assomigliare a. **look after** *vt* badare a. **look down** *vi* guardare in basso; **~ down on sb** *fig* guardare dall'alto in basso qcno. **look forward to** *vt* essere impaziente di. **look in on** *vt* passare da. **look into** *vt (examine)* esaminare. **look out** *vi* guardare fuori; *(take care)* fare attenzione; **~ out!** cercare; **~ out!** attento! **look round** *vi* girarsi; *(in shop, town etc)* dare un'occhiata. **look through** *vt* dare un'occhiata a *‹script, notes›*. **look up** *vi* guardare in alto; ~ **up to sb** *fig* rispettare qcno ● *vt* cercare [nel dizionario] (*word*); (*visit*) andare a trovare

'**look-out** *n* guardia *f*; (*prospect*) prospettiva *f*; **be on the ~ for** tenere gli occhi aperti per

loom /luːm/ *vi* apparire; *fig* profilarsi

loony /'luːnɪ/ *a & n fam* matto, -a *mf*. **~ bin** *n* manicomio *m*

loop /luːp/ *n* cappio *m*; (*on garment*) passante *m*. **~hole** *n* (*in the law*) scappatoia *f*

loose /luːs/ *a* libero; (*knot*) allentato; (*page*) staccato; (*clothes*) largo; (*morals*) dissoluto; (*inexact*) vago; **be at a ~ end** non sapere cosa fare; **come ~** (*knot*) sciogliersi; **set ~** liberare. **~ 'change** *n* spiccioli *mpl*. **~ly** *adv* scorrevolmente; (*defined*) vagamente

loosen /'luːsn/ *vt* sciogliere

loot /luːt/ *n* bottino *m* ● *vt/i* depredare. **~er** *n* predatore, -trice *mf*. **~ing** *n* saccheggio *m*

lop /lɒp/ **~ off** *vt* (*pt/pp* lopped) potare

lop'sided *a* sbilenco

lord /lɔːd/ *n* signore *m*; (*title*) Lord *m*; **House of L~s** Camera *f* dei Lords; **the L~'s Prayer** il Padrenostro; **good L~!** Dio mio!

lore /lɔː(r)/ *n* tradizioni *fpl*

lorry /'lɒrɪ/ *n* camion *m inv*; **~ driver** camionista *mf*

lose /luːz/ *v* (*pt/pp* lost) ● *vt* perdere ● *vi* perdere; (*clock*) essere indietro; **get lost** perdersi; **get lost!** *fam* va a quel paese! **~r** *n* perdente *mf*

loss /lɒs/ *n* perdita *f*; Comm **~es** perdite *fpl*; **be at a ~** essere perplesso; **be at a ~ for words** non trovare le parole

lost /lɒst/ *see* lose ● *a* perduto. **~ 'property office** *n* ufficio *m* oggetti smarriti

lot¹ /lɒt/ (*at auction*) lotto *m*; **draw ~s** tirare a sorte

lot² *n* **the ~** il tutto; **a ~ of, ~s of** molto/i; **the ~ of you** tutti voi; **it has changed a ~** è cambiato molto

lotion /'ləʊʃn/ *n* lozione *f*

lottery /'lɒtərɪ/ *n* lotteria *f*. **~ ticket** *n* biglietto *m* della lotteria

loud /laʊd/ *a* sonoro, alto; (*colours*) sgargiante ● *adv* ad alta voce. **~ 'hailer** *n* megafono *m*. **~ly** *adv* forte. **~ 'speaker** *n* altoparlante *m*

lounge /laʊndʒ/ *n* salotto *m*; (*in hotel*) salone *m* ● *vi* poltrire. **~ suit** *n* vestito *m* da uomo, completo *m* da uomo

louse /laʊs/ *n* (*pl* lice) pidocchio *m*

lousy /'laʊzɪ/ *a* (-**ier, -iest**) *fam* schifoso

lout /laʊt/ *n* zoticone *m*. **~ish** *a* rozzo

lovable /'lʌvəbl/ *a* adorabile

love /lʌv/ *n* amore *m*; Tennis zero *m*; **in ~** innamorato (**with** di) ● *vt* amare (*person, country*); **I love watching tennis** mi piace molto guardare il tennis. **~-affair** *n* relazione *f* [sentimentale]. **~ letter** *n* lettera *f* d'amore

lovely /'lʌvlɪ/ *a* (-**ier, -iest**) bello; (*in looks*) bello, attraente; (*in character*) piacevole; (*meal*) delizioso; **have a ~ time** divertirsi molto

lover /'lʌvə(r)/ *n* amante *mf*

love: **~ song** *n* canzone *f* d'amore. **~ story** *n* storia *f* d'amore

loving /'lʌvɪŋ/ *a* affettuoso

low /ləʊ/ *a* basso; (*depressed*) giù *inv* ● *adv* basso; **feel ~** sentirsi giù ● *n* minimo *m*; Meteorol depressione *f*; **at an all-time ~** (*prices etc*) al livello minimo

low: **~brow** *a* di scarsa cultura. **~-cut** (*dress*) scollato

lower /'ləʊə(r)/ *a & adv see* low ● *vt* abbassare; **~ oneself** abbassarsi

low: **~-'fat** *a* magro. **~-'grade** *a* di qualità inferiore. **~-key** *fig* moderato. **~lands** /-ləndz/ *npl* pianure *fpl*. **~ 'tide** *n* bassa marea *f*

loyal /'lɔɪəl/ *a* leale. **~ty** *n* lealtà *f*

lozenge /'lɒzɪndʒ/ n losanga f; (tablet) pastiglia f

LP n abbr **long-playing record**

Ltd abbr (**Limited**) s.r.l.

lubricant /'lu:brɪkənt/ n lubrificante m

lubricat|e /'lu:brɪkeɪt/ vt lubrificare. **~ion** /-'keɪʃn/ n lubrificazione f

lucid /'lu:sɪd/ a (explanation) chiaro; (sane) lucido. **~ity** /-'sɪdətɪ/ n lucidità f; (of explanation) chiarezza f

luck /lʌk/ n fortuna f; **bad ~** sfortuna f; **good ~!** buona fortuna! **~ily** adv fortunatamente

lucky /'lʌkɪ/ a (-ier, -iest) fortunato; **be ~** essere fortunato; (thing:) portare fortuna. **~ 'charm** n portafortuna m inv

lucrative /'lu:krətɪv/ a lucrativo

ludicrous /'lu:dɪkrəs/ a ridicolo. **~ly** adv (expensive, complex) eccessivamente

lug /lʌg/ vt (pt/pp lugged) fam trascinare

luggage /'lʌgɪdʒ/ n bagaglio m; **~-rack** n portabagagli m inv. **~-trolley** n carrello m portabagagli. **~-van** n bagagliaio m

lukewarm /'lu:k-/ a tiepido; fig poco entusiasta

lull /lʌl/ n pausa f ● vt **~ to sleep** cullare

lullaby /'lʌləbaɪ/ n ninna nanna f

lumbago /lʌm'beɪgəʊ/ n lombaggine f

lumber /'lʌmbə(r)/ n cianfrusaglie fpl; (Am: timber) legname m ● vt fam **~ sb with sth** affibbiare qcsa a qcno. **~ jack** n tagliaboschi m inv

luminous /'lu:mɪnəs/ a luminoso

lump¹ /lʌmp/ n (of sugar) zolletta f; (swelling) gonfiore m; (in breast) nodulo m; (in sauce) grumo m ● vt **~ together** ammucchiare

lump² vt **~ it** fam **you'll just have**

to ~ it che ti piaccia o no è così

lump sum n somma f globale

lumpy /'lʌmpɪ/ a (-ier, -iest) grumoso

lunacy /'lu:nəsɪ/ n follia f

lunar /'lu:nə(r)/ a lunare

lunatic /'lu:nətɪk/ n pazzo, -a mf

lunch /lʌntʃ/ n pranzo m ● vi pranzare

luncheon /'lʌntʃn/ n (formal) pranzo m. **~ meat** n carne f in scatola. **~ voucher** n buono m pasto

lunch-: ~-hour n intervallo m per il pranzo. **~-time** n ora f di pranzo

lung /lʌŋ/ n polmone m. **~ cancer** n cancro m al polmone

lunge /lʌndʒ/ vi lanciarsi (**at** su)

lurch¹ /lɜ:tʃ/ n **leave in the ~** fam lasciare nei guai

lurch² vi barcollare

lure /lʊə(r)/ n esca f; fig lusinga f ● vt adescare

lurid /'lʊərɪd/ a (gaudy) sgargiante; (sensational) sensazionalistico

lurk /lɜ:k/ vi appostarsi

luscious /'lʌʃəs/ a saporito; fig sexy inv

lush /lʌʃ/ a lussureggiante

lust /lʌst/ n lussuria f ● vi **~ after** desiderare [fortemente]. **~ful** a lussurioso

lusty /'lʌstɪ/ a (-ier, -iest) vigoroso

lute /lu:t/ n liuto m

luxuriant /lʌg'ʒʊərɪənt/ a lussureggiante

luxurious /lʌg'ʒʊərɪəs/ a lussuoso

luxury /'lʌkʃərɪ/ n lusso m ● attrib di lusso

lying /'laɪɪŋ/ see **lie¹** & **²** n mentire m

lymph gland /'lɪmf/ n linfoghiandola f

lynch /lɪntʃ/ vt linciare

lynx /lɪŋks/ n lince f

lyric /'lɪrɪk/ a lirico. **~al** a lirico; (fam: enthusiastic) entusiasta. **~s** npl parole fpl

Mm

mac /mæk/ *n fam* impermeabile *m*

macabre /məˈkɑːbr/ *a* macabro

macaroni /mækəˈrəʊnɪ/ *n* maccheroni *mpl*

mace¹ /meɪs/ *n (staff)* mazza *f*

mace² *n (spice)* macis *m o f*

machinations /mækɪˈneɪʃnz/ *npl* macchinazioni *fpl*

machine /məˈʃiːn/ *n* macchina *f* ● *vt (sew)* cucire a macchina; *Techn* lavorare a macchina. **~-gun** *n* mitragliatrice *f*

machinery /məˈʃiːnərɪ/ *n* macchinario *m*

machinist /məˈʃiːnɪst/ *n* macchinista *mf*; *(on sewing machine)* lavorante *mf* adetto alla macchina da cucire

machismo /məˈtʃɪzməʊ/ *n* machismo *m*

macho /ˈmætʃəʊ/ *a* macho *inv*

mackerel /ˈmæk(ə)l/ *n inv* sgombro *m*

mackintosh /ˈmækɪntɒʃ/ *n* impermeabile *m*

mad /mæd/ *a* (madder, maddest) pazzo, matto; *(fam: angry)* furioso (at con); like ~ *fam* come un pazzo; be ~ about sb/sth *(fam: keen on)* andare matto per qcno/qcsa

madam /ˈmædəm/ *n* signora *f*

madden /ˈmædən/ *vt (make angry)* far diventare matto

made /meɪd/ *si maku; ~ to measure* [fatto] su misura

Madeira cake /məˈdɪərə/ *n* dulce *m* di pan di Spagna

mad|ly /ˈmædlɪ/ *adv fam* follemente; **~ly in love** innamorato follemente. **~man** *n* pazzo *m*. **~ness** *n* pazzia *f*

madonna /məˈdɒnə/ *n* madonna *f*

magazine /mægəˈziːn/ *n* rivista *f*; *Mil, Phot* magazzino *m*

maggot /ˈmægət/ *n* vermo *m*

Magi /ˈmeɪdʒaɪ/ *npl* the ~ i Re *mpl* Magi

magic /ˈmædʒɪk/ *n* magia *f*; *(tricks)* giochi *mpl* di prestigio ● *a* magico; *(trick)* di prestigio. **~al** *a* magico

magician /məˈdʒɪʃn/ *n* mago *mf*; *(entertainer)* prestigiatore, -trice *mf*

magistrate /ˈmædʒɪstreɪt/ *n* magistrato *m*

magnanim|ity /mægnəˈnɪmətɪ/ *n* magnanimità *f*. **~ous** /-ˈnænɪməs/ *a* magnanimo

magnet /ˈmægnɪt/ *n* magnete *m*, calamita *f*. **~ic** /-ˈnetɪk/ *a* magnetico. **~ism** *n* magnetismo *m*

magnification /mægnɪfɪˈkeɪʃn/ *n* ingrandimento *m*

magnificen|ce /mægˈnɪfɪsəns/ *n* magnificenza *f*. **~t** *a* magnifico

magnify /ˈmægnɪfaɪ/ *vt* (pt/pp -ied) ingrandire; *(exaggerate)* ingigantire. **~ing glass** *n* lente *f* d'ingrandimento

magnitude /ˈmægnɪtjuːd/ *n* grandezza *f*; *(importance)* importanza *f*

magpie /ˈmægpaɪ/ *n* gazza *f*

mahogany /məˈhɒgənɪ/ *n* mogano *m* ● *attrib* di mogano

maid /meɪd/ *n* cameriera *f*; old ~ *pej* zitella *f*

maiden /ˈmeɪdn/ *n (liter)* fanciulla *f* ● *a (speech, voyage)* inaugurale. **~ aunt** *n* zia *f* zitella. **~ name** *n* nome *m* da ragazza

mail /meɪl/ *n* posta *f* ● *vt* impostare

mail: **~-bag** *n* sacco *m* postale. **~box** *n Am* cassetta *f* delle lettere; *(e-mail)* casella *f* di posta elettronica. **~ing list** *n* elenco *m* d'indirizzi per un mailing. **~man** *n Am* postino *m*. **~ order** *n* vendita *f* per corrispondenza. **~-order firm** *n* ditta *f* di vendita per corrispondenza

mailshot /ˈmeɪlʃɒt/ *n* mailing *m inv*

maim /meɪm/ *vt* menomare

main¹ /meɪn/ *n (water, gas, electricity)* conduttura *f* principale

main² *a* principale; the ~ thing is

to... la cosa essenziale è di... ● *n* **in the ~** in complesso

main: **~-land** /-lənd/ *n* continente *m.* **~ly** *adv* principalmente. **~stay** *n fig* pilastro *m.* **~ street** *n* via *f* principale

maintain /mem'teɪn/ *vt* mantenere; ⟨*keep in repair*⟩ curare la manutenzione di; ⟨*claim*⟩ sostenere

maintenance /'meɪntənəns/ *n* mantenimento *m*; ⟨*care*⟩ manutenzione *f*; ⟨*allowance*⟩ alimenti *mpl*

maisonette /meɪzə'net/ *n* appartamento *m* a due piani

majestic /mə'dʒestɪk/ *a* maestoso

majesty /'mædʒəstɪ/ *n* maestà *f*; **His/Her M~** Sua Maestà

major /'meɪdʒə(r)/ *a* maggiore; **~ road** strada *f* con diritto di precedenza ● *n Mil, Mus* maggiore *m* ● *vi Am* ~ **in** specializzarsi in

Majorca /mə'jɔːkə/ *n* Maiorca *f*

majority /mə'dʒɒrətɪ/ *n* maggioranza *f*; **be in the ~** avere la maggioranza

make /meɪk/ *n* ⟨*brand*⟩ marca *f* ● *v* ⟨*pt/pp* made⟩ ● *vt* fare; ⟨*earn*⟩ guadagnare; rendere ⟨*happy, clear*⟩; prendere ⟨*decision*⟩; **~ sb laugh** far ridere qcno; **~ sb do sth** far fare qcsa a qcno; **~ it** ⟨*to party, top of hill etc*⟩ farcela; **what time do you ~ it?** che ore fai? ● *vi* **~ as if to** fare per. **make do** *vi* arrangiarsi. **make for** *vt* dirigersi verso. **make off** *vi* fuggire. **make out** *vt* ⟨*distinguish*⟩ distinguere; ⟨*write out*⟩ rilasciare ⟨*cheque*⟩; compilare ⟨*list*⟩; ⟨*claim*⟩ far credere. **make over** *vt* cedere. **make up** *vt* ⟨*constitute*⟩ comporre; ⟨*complete*⟩ completare; ⟨*invent*⟩ inventare; ⟨*apply cosmetics to*⟩ truccare; fare ⟨*parcel*⟩; **~ up one's mind** decidersi; **~ it up** ⟨*after quarrel*⟩ riconciliarsi ● *vi* ⟨*after quarrel*⟩ fare la pace; **~ up for** compensare; **~ up for lost time** recuperare il tempo perso

'make-believe *n* finzione *f*

maker /'meɪkə(r)/ *n* fabbricante *mf*; **M~** Creatore *m*

make: **~ shift** *a* di fortuna *n* espediente *m.* **~-up** *n* trucco *m*; ⟨*character*⟩ natura *f*

making /'meɪkɪŋ/ *n* **have the ~s of** aver la stoffa di

maladjust|ed /mælə'dʒʌstɪd/ *a* disadattato

malaise /mə'leɪz/ *n fig* malessere *m*

malaria /mə'leərɪə/ *n* malaria *f*

Malaysia /mə'leɪzɪə/ *n* Malesia *f*

male /meɪl/ *a* maschile ● *n* maschio *m.* **~ nurse** *n* infermiere *m*

malevolen|ce /mə'levələns/ *n* malevolenza *f*. **~t** *a* malevolo

malfunction /mæl'fʌŋkʃn/ *n* funzionamento *m* imperfetto ● *vi* funzionare male

malice /'mælɪs/ *n* malignità *f*; **bear sb ~** voler del male a qcno

malicious /mə'lɪʃəs/ *a* maligno

malign /mə'laɪn/ *vt* malignare su

malignan|cy /mə'lɪgnənsɪ/ *n* malignità *f*. **~t** *a* maligno

malinger /mə'lɪŋɡə(r)/ *vi* fingersi malato. **~er** *n* scansafatiche *mf inv*

malleable /'mælɪəbl/ *a* malleabile

mallet /'mælɪt/ *n* martello *m* di legno

malnu'trition /mæl-/ *n* malnutrizione *f*

mal'practice *n* negligenza *f*

malt /mɔːlt/ *n* malto *m*

Malta /'mɔːltə/ *n* Malta *f.* **~ese** /-iːz/ *a & n* maltese *mf*

mal'treat *vt* maltrattare. **~ment** *n* maltrattamento *m*

mammal /'mæml/ *n* mammifero *m*

mammoth /'mæməθ/ *a* mastodontico ● *n* mammut *m inv*

man /mæn/ *n* ⟨*pl* men⟩ uomo *m*; ⟨*chess, draughts*⟩ pedina *f* ● *vt* ⟨*pt/pp* manned⟩ equipaggiare; essere di servizio a ⟨*counter, telephones*⟩

manage /'mænɪdʒ/ *vt* dirigere; gestire ⟨*shop, affairs*⟩; ⟨*cope with*⟩ farcela; **~ to do sth** riuscire a fare qcsa ● *vi* riuscire; (*cope*) farcela (on con). **~able** /-əbl/ *a* (*hair*) docile; (*size*) maneggevole. **~ment** /-mənt/ *n* gestione *f*; **the ~ment** la direzione

manager /'mænɪdʒə(r)/ *n* direttore *m*; (*of shop, bar*) gestore *m*; *Sport* manager *m inv.* **~ess** /-'res/ *n* direttrice *f*. **~ial** /-'dʒɪərɪəl/ *a* **~ial staff** personale *m* direttivo

managing /'mænɪdʒɪŋ/ **~ director** direttore, -trice *mf* generale

mandarin /'mændərɪn/ *n ~* [**orange**] mandarino *m*

mandat|e /'mændeɪt/ *n* mandato *m*. **~ory** /-dətrɪ/ *a* obbligatorio

mane /meɪn/ *n* criniera *f*

mangle /'mæŋgl/ *vt* (*damage*) maciullare

mango /'mæŋgəʊ/ *n* (*pl* **-es**) mango *m*

mangy /'meɪndʒɪ/ *a* (*dog*) rognoso

man: **~'handle** *vt* malmenare. **~hole** *n* botola *f*. **~hole cover** *n* tombino *m*. **~hood** *n* età *f* adulta; (*quality*) virilità *f*. **~-hour** *n* ora *f* lavorativa. **~-hunt** *n* caccia *f* all'uomo

man|ia /'meɪnɪə/ *n* mania *f*. **~iac** /-ɪæk/ *n* maniaco, -a *f*

manicure /'mænɪkjʊə(r)/ *n* manicure *f* ● *vt* fare la manicure a

manifest /'mænɪfest/ *a* manifesto ● *vt* **~ itself** manifestarsi. **~ly** *adv* palesemente

manifesto /mænɪ'festəʊ/ *n* manifesto *m*

manifold /'mænɪfəʊld/ *a* molteplice

manipulat|e /mə'nɪpjʊleɪt/ *vt* manipolare. **~ion** /-'leɪʃn/ *n* manipolazione *f*

man'kind *n* genere *m* umano

manly /'mænlɪ/ *a* virile

man-made *a* artificiale. **~ fibre** *n* fibra *f* sintetica

manner /'mænə(r)/ *n* maniera *f*; **in this ~** in questo modo; **have no ~s** avere dei pessimi modi;

good/bad ~s buone/cattive maniere *fpl*. **~ism** *n* affettazione *f*

manœuvre /mə'nu:və(r)/ *n* manovra *f* ● *vt* fare manovra con (*vehicle*); manovrare (*person*)

manor /'mænə(r)/ *n* maniero *m*

manpower *n* manodopera *f*

mansion /'mænʃn/ *n* palazzo *m*

manslaughter *n* omicidio *m* colposo

mantelpiece /'mæntl-/ *n* mensola *f* di caminetto

manual /'mænjʊəl/ *a* manuale ● *n* manuale *m*

manufactur|e /mænjʊ'fæktʃə(r)/ *vt* fabbricare ● *n* manifattura *f*. **~r** *n* fabbricante *m*

manure /mə'njʊə(r)/ *n* concime *m*

manuscript /'mænjʊskrɪpt/ *n* manoscritto *m*

many /'menɪ/ *a* & *pron* molti; **there are as ~ boys as girls** ci sono tanti ragazzi quante ragazze; **as ~ 500** ben 500; **as ~ as that** così tanti; **as ~** altrettanti; **very ~, a good/great ~** moltissimi; **~ a time** molte volte

map /mæp/ *n* carta *f* geografica; (*of town*) mappa *f* ● **map out** *vt* (*pt/pp* **mapped**) *fig* programmare

maple /'meɪpl/ *n* acero *m*

mar /mɑ:(r)/ *vt* (*pt/pp* **marred**) rovinare

marathon /'mærəθən/ *n* maratona *f*

marble /'mɑ:bl/ *n* marmo *m*; (*for game*) pallina *f* ● *attrib* di marmo

Marah /mɑ:tʃ/ *n* marzo *m*

march *n* marcia *f*; (*protest*) dimostrazione *f* ● *vi* marciare ● *vt* far marciare; **~ sb off** scortare qcno fuori

mare /meə(r)/ *n* giumenta *f*

margarine /mɑ:dʒə'ri:n/ *n* margarina *f*

margin /'mɑ:dʒɪn/ *n* margine *m*. **~al** *a* marginale. **~ally** *adv* marginalmente

marigold /'mærɪɡəʊld/ *n* calendula *f*

marijuana /mærʊ'wɑːnə/ n marijuana f

marina /mə'riːnə/ n porticciolo m

marinade /mærɪ'neɪd/ n marinata f ● vt marinare

marine /mə'riːn/ a marino ● n (sailor) soldato m di fanteria marina

marionette /mærɪə'net/ n marionetta f

marital /'mærɪtl/ a coniugale. ~ **status** stato m civile

maritime /'mærɪtaɪm/ a marittimo

mark[1] /mɑːk/ n (currency) marco m

mark[2] n (stain) macchia f; (sign, indication) segno m; Sch voto m ● vt segnare; (stain) macchiare; Sch correggere; Sport marcare; ~ **time** Mil segnare il passo; fig non far progressi; ~ **my words** ricordati quello che dico. **mark out** vt delimitare; fig designare

marked /mɑːkt/ a marcato. ~**ly** /-kɪdlɪ/ adv notevolmente

marker /'mɑːkə(r)/ n (for highlighting) evidenziatore m; Sport marcatore m; (of exam) esaminatore, -trice mf

market /'mɑːkɪt/ n mercato m ● vt vendere al mercato; (launch) commercializzare; **on the** ~ sul mercato. ~**ing** n marketing m. ~ **re'search** n ricerca f di mercato

marksman /'mɑːksmən/ n tiratore m scelto

marmalade /'mɑːməleɪd/ n marmellata f d'arance

maroon /mə'ruːn/ a marrone rossastro

marooned /mə'ruːnd/ a abbandonato

marquee /mɑː'kiː/ n tendone m

marquis /'mɑːkwɪs/ n marchese m

marriage /'mærɪdʒ/ n matrimonio m

married /'mærɪd/ a sposato; ⟨life⟩ coniugale

marrow /'mærəʊ/ n Anat midollo m; (vegetable) zucca f

marr|y /'mærɪ/ vt (pt/pp **married**) sposare; **get** ~**ied** sposarsi ● vi sposarsi

marsh /mɑːʃ/ n palude f

marshal /'mɑːʃl/ n (steward) cerimoniere m ● vt (pt/pp **marshalled**) fig organizzare (arguments)

marshy /'mɑːʃɪ/ a paludoso

marsupial /mɑː'suːpɪəl/ n marsupiale m

martial /'mɑːʃl/ a marziale

martyr /'mɑːtə(r)/ n martire mf ● vt martorizzare. ~**dom** /-dəm/ n martirio m. ~**ed** a fam da martire

marvel /'mɑːvl/ n meraviglia f ● vi (pt/pp **marvelled**) meravigliarsi (at di). ~**lous** /-vələs/ a meraviglioso

Marxis|m /'mɑːksɪzm/ n marxismo m. ~**t** a e n marxista mf

marzipan /'mɑːzɪpæn/ n marzapane m

mascara /mæ'skɑːrə/ n mascara m inv

mascot /'mæskət/ n mascotte f inv

masculin|e /'mæskjʊlm/ a maschile ● n Gram maschile m. ~**ity** /-'lmətɪ/ n mascolinità f

mash /mæʃ/ vt impastare. ~**ed potatoes** npl purè m inv di patate

mask /mɑːsk/ n maschera f ● vt mascherare

masochis|m /'mæsəkɪzm/ n masochismo m. ~**t** /-ɪst/ n masochista mf

Mason n massone m. ~**ic** /mə'sɒnɪk/ a massonico

mason /'meɪsn/ n muratore m

masonry /'meɪsnrɪ/ n massoneria f

masquerade /mæskə'reɪd/ n fig mascherata f ● vi ~ **as** ⟨pose⟩ farsi passare per

mass[1] n Relig messa f

mass[2] n massa f; ~**es of** fam un sacco di ● vi ammassarsi

massacre /'mæsəkə(r)/ n massacro m ● vt massacrare

massage /'mæsɑːʒ/ n massaggio

m ●*vt* massaggiare; *fig* manipolare ⟨statistics⟩

masseu|r /mæˈsɜː(r)/ *n* massaggiatore *m*. ~**se** /-ˈsɜːz/ *n* massaggiatrice *f*

massive /ˈmæsɪv/ *a* enorme

mass: ~ **media** *npl* mezzi *mpl* di comunicazione di massa, mass media,*mpl*. ~**pro'duce** *vt* produrre in serie. ~**pro'duction** *n* produzione *f* in serie

mast /mɑːst/ *n Naut* albero *m*; (for radio) antenna *f*

master /ˈmɑːstə(r)/ *n* maestro *m*, padrone *m*; (teacher) professore *m*; (of ship) capitano *m*; **M**~ (boy) signorino *m*

master: ~**-key** *n* passe-partout *m* inv. ~**ly** *a* magistrale. ~**-mind** *n* cervello *m* ●*vt* ideare e dirigere. ~**piece** *n* capolavoro *m*. ~**-stroke** *n* colpo *m* da maestro. ~**y** *n* (of subject) padronanza *f*

masturbat|e /ˈmæstəbeɪt/ *vi* masturbarsi. ~**ion** /-ˈbeɪʃn/ *n* masturbazione *f*

mat /mæt/ *n* stuoia *f*; (on table) sottopiatto *m*

match[1] /mætʃ/ *n Sport* partita *f*; (equal) uguale *mf*; (marriage) matrimonio *m*; (person to marry) partito *m*; **be a good** ~ ⟨colours:⟩ intonarsi bene; **be no** ~ **for** non essere dello stesso livello di ●*vt* (equal) uguagliare; (be like) andare bene con ●*vi* intonarsi

match[2] *n* fiammifero *m*. ~**box** *n* scatola *f* di fiammiferi

matching /ˈmætʃɪŋ/ *a* intonato

mate[1] /meɪt/ *n* compagno, -a *mf*; (assistant) aiuto *m*; *Naut* secondo *m*; (fam: friend) amico, -a *mf* ●*vt* accoppiarsi ●*vt* accoppiare

mate[2] *n* (in chess) scacco *m* matto

material /məˈtɪərɪəl/ *n* materiale *m*; (fabric) stoffa *f*; **raw** ~**s** materie *fpl* prime ●*a* materiale

material|**ism** /məˈtɪərɪəlɪzm/ *n* materialismo *m*. ~**istic** /-ˈlɪstɪk/ *a* materialistico. ~**ize** /-laɪz/ *vi* materializzarsi

maternal /məˈtɜːnl/ *a* materno

maternity /məˈtɜːnəti/ *n* maternità *f*. ~ **clothes** *npl* abiti *mpl* premaman. ~ **ward** *n* maternità *f* inv

matey /ˈmeɪti/ *a fam* amichevole

mathematic|**al** /mæθəˈmætɪkl/ *a* matematico. ~**ian** /-məˈtɪʃn/ *n* matematico, -a *mf*

mathematics /mæθˈmætɪks/ *n* matematica *fsg*

maths /mæθs/ *n fam* matematica *fsg*

matinée /ˈmætɪneɪ/ *n Theat* matinée *f*

mating /ˈmeɪtɪŋ/ *n* accoppiamento *m*. ~ **season** stagione *f* degli amori

matriculat|e /məˈtrɪkjʊleɪt/ *vi* immatricolarsi. ~**ion** /-ˈleɪʃn/ *n* immatricolazione *f*

matrix /ˈmeɪtrɪks/ *n* (pl matrices /-siːz/) matrice *f*

matted /ˈmætɪd/ *a* ~ **hair** capelli *mpl* tutti appiccicati tra loro

matter /ˈmætə(r)/ *n* (affair) faccenda *f*; (question) questione *f*; (pus) pus *m*; (phys: substance) materia *f*; **as a** ~ **of** **fact** a dire la verità; **what is the** ~? che cosa c'è? ●*vi* importare; ~ **to** sb essere importante per qcno; **it doesn't** ~ non importa. ~**-of-fact** *a* pratico

mattress /ˈmætrɪs/ *n* materasso *m*

matur|e /məˈtjʊə(r)/ *a* maturo; *Comm* in scadenza ●*vi* maturare ●*vt* far maturare. ~**ity** *n* maturità *f*; *Fin* maturazione *f*

Maundy /ˈmɔːndi/ *n* ~ **Thursday** giovedì *m* santo

mauve /məʊv/ *a* malva

maxim /ˈmæksɪm/ *n* massima *f*

maximum /ˈmæksɪməm/ *a* massimo; **ten minutes** ~ dieci minuti al massimo ●*n* (pl -ima) massimo *m*

May /meɪ/ *n* maggio *m*

may /meɪ/ *v aux* (solo al presente) potere; ~ **I come in?** posso entrare?; **if I** ~ **say so** se mi posso permettere; ~ **you both be very**

happy siate felici; **I ~ as well stay** potrei anche rimanere; **it ~ be true** potrebbe esser vero; **she ~ be old, but...** sarà anche vecchia, ma...

maybe /ˈmeɪbiː/ *adv* forse, può darsi

'May Day *n* il primo maggio

mayonnaise /meɪəˈneɪz/ *n* maionese *f*

mayor /ˈmeə(r)/ *n* sindaco *m*. **~ess** *n* sindaco *m*; (*wife of mayor*) moglie *f* del sindaco

maze /meɪz/ *n* labirinto *m*

me /miː/ *pron* (*object*) mi; (*with preposition*) me; **she called me, not you** ha chiamato me, non te; **give me the money** dammi i soldi; **give it to me** dammelo; **he gave it to me** me lo ha dato; **it's ~** sono io

meadow /ˈmedəʊ/ *n* prato *m*

meagre /ˈmiːɡə(r)/ *a* scarso

meal[1] /miːl/ *n* pasto *m*

meal[2] *n* (*grain*) farina *f*

mealy-mouthed /miːlɪˈmaʊðd/ *a* ambiguo

mean[1] /miːn/ *a* avaro; (*unkind*) meschino

mean[2] *a* medio ● *n* (*average*) media *f*; **Greenwich ~ time** ora *f* media di Greenwich

mean[3] *vt* (*pt/pp* **meant**) voler dire; (*signify*) significare; (*intend*) intendere; **I ~ it** lo dico seriamente; **~ well** avere buone intenzioni; **be meant for** ⟨present:⟩ essere destinato a; ⟨remark:⟩ essere riferito a

meander /mɪˈændə(r)/ *vi* vagare

meaning /ˈmiːnɪŋ/ *n* significato *m*. **~ful** *a* significativo. **~less** *a* senza senso

means /miːnz/ *n* mezzo *m*; **~ of transport** mezzo *m* di trasporto; **by ~ of** per mezzo di; **by all ~!** certamente!; **by no ~** niente affatto ● *npl* (*resources*) mezzi *mpl*

meant /ment/ *see* **mean**[3]

'meantime *n* **in the ~** nel frattempo ● *adv* intanto

'meanwhile *adv* intanto

measles /ˈmiːzlz/ *n* morbillo *m*

measly /ˈmiːzlɪ/ *a fam* misero

measurable /ˈmeʒərəbl/ *a* misurabile

measure /ˈmeʒə(r)/ *n* misura *f* ● *vt/i* misurare. **measure up to** *vt fig* essere all'altezza di. **~d** *a* misurato. **~ment** /-mənt/ *n* misura *f*

meat /miːt/ *n* carne *f*. **~ ball** *n* *Culin* polpetta *f* di carne. **~ loaf** *n* polpettone *m*

mechan|ic /mɪˈkænɪk/ *n* meccanico *m*. **~ical** *a* meccanico; **~ical engineering** ingegneria *f* meccanica. **~ically** *adv* meccanicamente. **~ics** *n* meccanica *f* ● *npl* meccanismo *msg*

mechan|ism /ˈmekənɪzm/ *n* meccanismo *m*. **~ize** *vt* meccanizzare

medal /ˈmedl/ *n* medaglia *f*

medallion /mɪˈdælɪən/ *n* medaglione *m*

medallist /ˈmedəlɪst/ *n* vincitore, -trice *mf* di una medaglia

meddle /ˈmedl/ *vi* immischiarsi (**in** di); (*tinker*) armeggiare (**with** con)

media /ˈmiːdɪə/ *see* **medium** ● *npl* **the ~** i mass media

median /ˈmiːdɪən/ *a* **~ strip** *Am* banchina *f* spartitraffico

mediat|e /ˈmiːdɪeɪt/ *vi* fare da mediatore. **~ion** /-ˈeɪʃn/ *n* mediazione *f*. **~or** *n* mediatore, -trice *f*

medical /ˈmedɪkl/ *a* medico ● *n* visita *f* medica. **~ insurance** *n* assicurazione *f* sanitaria. **~ student** *n* studente, -essa *mf* di medicina

medicat|ed /ˈmedɪkeɪtɪd/ *a* medicato. **~ion** /-ˈkeɪʃn/ *n* (*drugs*) medicinali *mpl*

medicinal /mɪˈdɪsɪnl/ *a* medicinale

medicine /ˈmedsən/ *n* medicina *f*

medieval /medɪˈiːvl/ *a* medievale

mediocr|e /miːdɪˈəʊkə(r)/ *a* mediocre. **~ity** /-ˈɒkrətɪ/ *n* mediocrità *f*

meditat|e /ˈmedɪteɪt/ *vi* meditare (**on** su). **~ion** /-ˈteɪʃn/ *n* meditazione *f*

Mediterranean /medɪtə'reɪnɪən/ n the ~ [Sea] il [mare m] Mediterraneo m ●a mediterraneo

medium /'miːdɪəm/ a medio; Culin di media cottura ●n (pl media) mezzo m; (pl -s) (person) medium mf inv

medium: ~-sized a di taglia media. ~ wave n onde fpl medie

medley /'medlɪ/ n miscuglio m; Mus miscellanea f

meek /miːk/ a mite, mansueto. ~ly adv docilmente

meet /miːt/ v (pt/pp met) ●vt incontrare; (at station, airport) andare incontro a; (for first time) fare la conoscenza di; pagare (bill); soddisfare (requirements) ●vi incontrarsi; (committee:) riunirsi; ~ with incontrare (problem); incontrarsi con (person) ●n raduno m [sportivo]

meeting /'miːtɪŋ/ n riunione f, meeting m inv; (large) assemblea f; (by chance) incontro m

megabyte /'megəbaɪt/ n megabyte m

megalomania /megələ'meɪnɪə/ n megalomania f

megaphone /'megəfəʊn/ n megafono m

melancholy /'melənkəlɪ/ a malinconico ●n malinconia f

mellow /'meləʊ/ a (wine) generoso; (sound, colour) caldo; (person) dolce ●vi (person:) addolcirsi

melodic /mɪ'lɒdɪk/ a melodico

melodrama /'melə-/ n melodramma m. ~tic /-drə'mætɪk/ a melodrammatico

melody /'melədɪ/ n melodia f

melon /'melən/ n melone m

melt /melt/ vt sciogliere ●vi sciogliersi. **melt down** vt fondere. ~ing-pot n fig crogiuolo m

member /'membə(r)/ n membro m; ~ countries paesi mpl membri; M~ of Parliament deputato, -a mf; M~ of the European Parliament eurodeputato, -a mf.

~ship n iscrizione f; (members) soci mpl

membrane /'membreɪn/ n membrana f

memo /'meməʊ/ n promemoria m inv

memoirs /'memwɑːz/ n ricordi mpl

memorable /'memərəbl/ a memorabile

memorandum /memə'rændəm/ n promemoria m inv

memorial /mɪ'mɔːrɪəl/ n monumento m. ~ service n funzione f commemorativa

memorize /'meməraɪz/ vt memorizzare

memory /'memərɪ/ n also Comput memoria f; (thing remembered) ricordo m; from ~ a memoria; in ~ of in ricordo di

men /men/ see man

menace /'menəs/ n minaccia f; (nuisance) piaga f ●vt minacciare. ~ing a minaccioso

mend /mend/ vt riparare; (darn) rammendare ●n on the ~ in via di guarigione

'menfolk n uomini mpl

menial /'miːnɪəl/ a umile

meningitis /menɪn'dʒaɪtɪs/ n meningite f

menopause /'menə-/ n menopausa f

menstruat|e /'menstrʊeɪt/ vi mestruare. ~ion /-'eɪʃn/ n mestruazione f

mental /'mentl/ a mentale; (fam: mad) pazzo. ~ a'rithmetic n calcolo m mentale. ~ illness n malattia f mentale

mentality /men'tælətɪ/ n mentalità f inv. ~ly adv mentalmente; ~ly ill malato di mente

mention /'menʃn/ n menzione f ●vt menzionare; **don't ~ it** non c'è di che

menu /'menjuː/ n menu m inv

MEP n abbr Member of the European Parliament

mercenary /'mɜːsɪnərɪ/ a mercenario ● n mercenario m

merchandise /'mɜːtʃəndaɪz/ n merce f

merchant /'mɜːtʃənt/ n commerciante mf. ~ **bank** n banca f d'affari. ~ **'navy** n marina f mercantile

merci|ful /'mɜːsɪfl/ a misericordioso. ~**fully** adv fam grazie a Dio. ~**less** a spietato

mercury /'mɜːkjʊrɪ/ n mercurio m

mercy /'mɜːsɪ/ n misericordia f; **be at sb's** ~ essere alla mercé di qcno, essere in balia di qcno

mere /mɪə(r)/ a solo. ~**ly** adv solamente

merest /'mɪərɪst/ a minimo

merge /mɜːdʒ/ vi fondersi

merger /'mɜːdʒə(r)/ n fusione f

meringue /mə'ræŋ/ n meringa f

merit /'merɪt/ n merito m; (advantage) qualità f inv ● vt meritare

mermaid /'mɜːmeɪd/ n sirena f

merri|ly /'merɪlɪ/ adv allegramente. ~**ment** /-mənt/ n baldoria f

merry /'merɪ/ a (-**ier**, -**iest**) allegro; ~ **Christmas!** Buon Natale! **merry:** ~-**go-round** n giostra f. ~-**making** n festa f

mesh /meʃ/ n maglia f

mesmerize /'mezməraɪz/ vt ipnotizzare. ~**d** a fig ipnotizzato

mess /mes/ n disordine m, casino m fam; (trouble) guaio m; (something spilt) sporco m; Mil mensa f; **make a** ~ **of** (botch) fare un pasticcio di ● **mess about** vi I perder tempo; ~ **about with** armeggiare con ● vt prendere in giro (person). **mess up** vt mettere in disordine, incasinare fam; (botch) mandare all'aria

message /'mesɪdʒ/ n messaggio m

messenger /'mesɪndʒə(r)/ n messaggero m

Messiah /mɪ'saɪə/ n Messia m

Messrs /'mesəz/ npl (on letter) ~ **Smith** Spett. ditta Smith

messy /'mesɪ/ a (-**ier**, -**iest**) disordinato; (in dress) sciatto

met /met/ see **meet**

metal /'metl/ n metallo m ● a di metallo. ~**lic** /mɪ'tælɪk/ a metallico

metamorphosis /metə'mɔːfəsɪs/ n (pl -**phoses** /-siːz/) metamorfosi f inv

metaphor /'metəfə(r)/ n metafora f. ~**ical** /-'fɒrɪkl/ a metaforico

meteor /'miːtɪə(r)/ n meteora f. ~**ic** /-'ɒrɪk/ a fig fulmineo

meteorological /miːtɪərə'lɒdʒɪkl/ a meteorologico

meteorolog|ist /miːtɪə'rɒlədʒɪst/ n meteorologo, -a mf. ~**y** n meteorologia f

meter[1] /'miːtə(r)/ n contatore m

meter[2] n Am = **metre**

method /'meθəd/ n metodo m

methodical /mɪ'θɒdɪkl/ a metodico. ~**ly** adv metodicamente

Methodist /'meθədɪst/ n metodista mf

meths /meθs/ n fam alcol m denaturato

methylated /'meθɪleɪtɪd/ a ~ **spirit[s]** alcol m denaturato

meticulous /mɪ'tɪkjʊləs/ a meticoloso. ~**ly** adv meticolosamente

metre /'miːtə(r)/ n metro m

metric /'metrɪk/ a metrico

metropolis /mɪ'trɒpəlɪs/ n metropoli f inv

metropolitan /metrə'pɒlɪtən/ a metropolitano

mew /mjuː/ n miao m ● vi miagolare

Mexican /'meksɪkən/ a & n messicano, -a mf. '**Mexico** n Messico m

miaow /mɪ'aʊ/ n miao m ● vi miagolare

mice /maɪs/ see **mouse**

mickey /'mɪkɪ/ n **take the** ~ **out of** prendere in giro

microbe /'maɪkrəʊb/ n microbo m

micro /'maɪkrəʊ/: ~**chip** n microchip m. ~**computer** n microcomputer m. ~**film** n microfilm m. ~**phone** microfono m. ~**processor** n microprocesso-

re m. **~scope** n microscopio m.
~scopic /-'skɒpɪk/ a microscopi-
co. **~wave** n microonda f; (oven)
forno m a microonde

mid /mɪd/ a ~ **May** metà maggio; **in
~ air** a mezz'aria

midday /'mɪddeɪ/ n mezzogiorno
m

middle /'mɪdl/ a di centro; **the M~
Ages** il medioevo; **the ~
class[es]** la classe media; **the M~
East** il Medio Oriente ●n mezzo
m; **in the ~ of** (room, floor etc) in
mezzo a; **in the ~ of the night** nel
pieno della notte, a notte piena

middle: ~-aged a di mezza età.
~-class a borghese. **~man** n
Comm intermediario m

middling /'mɪdlɪŋ/ a discreto

midge /mɪdʒ/ n moscerino m

midget /'mɪdʒɪt/ n nano, -a mf

Midlands /'mɪdləndz/ npl **the ~**
l'Inghilterra fsg centrale

midnight /'mɪdnaɪt/ n mezzanotte f

midriff /'mɪdrɪf/ n diaframma m

midst /mɪdst/ n **in the ~ of** in mezzo a; **in our ~** fra di noi, in mezzo
a noi

mid: ~summer n mezza estate f.
~way adv a metà strada. **~wife** n
ostetrica f. **~wifery** /-wɪfərɪ/ n ostetricia f. **~'winter** n pieno inverno m

might¹ /maɪt/ v aux **I ~** potrei; **will
you come? - I ~** vieni? - può dar-
si; **it ~ be true** potrebbe essere
vero; **I ~ as well stay** potrei anche
restare; **you ~ have drowned**
avresti potuto affogare; **you ~
have said so!** avresti potuto dirlo!

might² n potere m

mighty /'maɪtɪ/ a (-ier, -iest) potente ●adv fam molto

migraine /'miːɡreɪn/ n emicrania f

migrant /'maɪɡrənt/ a migratore
●n (bird) migratore, -trice mf;
(person: for work) emigrante mf

migrat|e /maɪ'ɡreɪt/ vi migrare.
~ion /-'ɡreɪʃn/ n migrazione f

Mike /maɪk/ n fam microfono m

Milan /mɪ'læn/ n Milano f

mild /maɪld/ a (weather) mite;
(person) dolce; (flavour) delicato;
(illness) leggero

mildew /'mɪldjuː/ n muffa f

mild|ly /'maɪldlɪ/ adv moderata-
mente; (say) dolcemente; **to put it
~ly** a dir poco, senza esagerazio-
ne. **~ness** n (of person, words) dolcezza f; (of weather) mitezza f

mile /maɪl/ n miglio m (= 1,6 km);
~s nicer fam molto più bello

mile|age /-ɪdʒ/ n chilometraggio
m. **~stone** n pietra f miliare

militant /'mɪlɪtənt/ a & n militante
mf

military /'mɪlɪtrɪ/ a militare. **~
service** n servizio m militare

militate /'mɪlɪteɪt/ vi **~ against** opporsi a

militia /mɪ'lɪʃə/ n milizia f

milk /mɪlk/ n latte m ●vt mungere

milk: ~man n lattaio m. **~ shake** n
frappé m inv

milky /'mɪlkɪ/ a (-ier, -iest) latteo;
(tea etc) con molto latte. **M~ Way**
n Astr Via f Lattea

mill /mɪl/ n mulino m; (factory)
fabbrica f; (for coffee etc) macinino
m ●vt macinare (grain). **mill
about, mill around** vi brulicare

millennium /mɪ'lenɪəm/ n millen-
nio m

miller /'mɪlə(r)/ n mugnaio m

milli|gram /'mɪlɪ-/ n milligrammo
m. **~metre** n millimetro m

million /'mɪljən/ n milione m; **a ~
pounds** un milione di sterline.
~aire /-'neə(r)/ n miliardario, -a
mf

millstone n fig peso m

mime /maɪm/ n mimo m ●vt
mimare

mimic /'mɪmɪk/ n imitatore, -trice
mf ●vt (pt/pp mimicked) imitare.
~ry n mimetismo m

mimosa /mɪ'məʊzə/ n mimosa f

mince /mɪns/ n carne f tritata ●vt
Culin tritare; **not ~ one's words**
parlare senza mezzi termini

mince: ~meat n miscuglio m di
frutta secca; **make ~meat of** fig

demolire. **~'pie** n pasticcino m a base di frutta secca

mincer /'mɪnsə(r)/ n tritacarne m inv

mind /maɪnd/ n mente f; (sanity) ragione f; **to my ~** a mio parere; **give sb a piece of one's ~** dire chiaro e tondo a qcno quello che si pensa; **make up one's ~** decidersi; **have sth in ~** avere qcosa in mente; **bear sth in ~** tenere presente qcosa; **have something on one's ~** essere preoccupato; **have a good ~** to avere una grande voglia di; **I have changed my ~** ho cambiato idea; **in two ~s** indeciso; **are you out of your ~?** sei diventato matto? ● vt (look after) occuparsi di; **I don't ~ the noise** il rumore non mi dà fastidio; **I don't ~ what we do** non mi importa quello che facciamo; **~ the step!** attenzione al gradino! ● vi **I don't ~** non mi importa; **never ~!** non importa!; **do you ~ if...?** ti dispiace se...? **mind out** vi **~ out!** [fai] attenzione!

minder /'maɪndə(r)/ n (Br: bodyguard) gorilla m; (for child) baby-sitter mf inv

mind|ful a **~ful of** attento a. **~less** a noncurante

mine¹ /maɪn/ poss pron il mio m, la mia f, i miei mpl, le mie fpl; **a friend of ~** un mio amico; **friends of ~** dei miei amici; **that is ~** questo è il mio; (as opposed to yours) questo è il mio

mine² n miniera f; (explosive) mina f ● vt estrarre; Mil minare. **~ detector** n rivelatore m di mine. **~field** n campo m minato

miner /'maɪnə(r)/ n minatore m

mineral /'mɪnərəl/ n minerale m ● a minerale. **~ water** n acqua f minerale

minesweeper /'maɪn-/ n dragamine m inv

mingle /'mɪŋgl/ vi **~ with** mescolarsi a

mini /'mɪnɪ/ n (skirt) mini f

miniature /'mɪnɪtʃə(r)/ a in miniatura ● n miniatura f

mini|bus /'mɪnɪ-/ n minibus m, pulmino m. **~cab** n taxi m inv

minim /'mɪnɪm/ n Mus minima f

minim|al /'mɪnɪml/ a minimo. **~ize** vt minimizzare. **~um** n (pl -ima) minimo m ● a minimo; **ten minutes ~um** minimo dieci minuti

mining /'maɪnɪŋ/ n estrazione f ● a estrattivo

miniskirt /'mɪnɪ-/ n minigonna f

minist|er /'mɪnɪstə(r)/ n ministro m; Relig pastore m. **~erial** /-'stɪərɪəl/ a ministeriale

ministry /'mɪnɪstrɪ/ n Pol ministero m; **the ~** Relig il ministero sacerdotale

mink /mɪŋk/ n visone m

minor /'maɪnə(r)/ a minore ● n minorenne mf

minority /maɪ'nɒrətɪ/ n minoranza f; (age) minore età f

minor road n strada f secondaria

mint¹ /mɪnt/ n fam patrimonio m ● a **in ~ condition** in condizione perfetta

mint² n (herb) menta f

minus /'maɪnəs/ prep meno; (fam: without) senza ● n **[sign]** meno m

minute¹ /'mɪnɪt/ n minuto m; **in a ~** (shortly) in un minuto; **~s** pl (of meeting) verbale msg

minute² /maɪ'njuːt/ a (very precise) minuzioso

mirac|le /'mɪrəkl/ n miracolo m. **~ulous** /-'rækjʊləs/ a miracoloso

mirage /'mɪrɑːʒ/ n miraggio m

mirror /'mɪrə(r)/ n specchio m ● vt rispecchiare

mirth /mɜːθ/ n ilarità f

misad'venture /mɪs-/ n disavventura f

misanthropist /mɪ'zænθrəpɪst/ n misantropo, -a mf

misappre'hension n malinteso m; **be under a ~** avere frainteso

misbe'have vi comportarsi male

mis'calcu|late vt/i calcolare male.
~ 'lation n calcolo m sbagliato

'miscarriage n aborto m spontaneo; **~ of justice** errore m giudiziario. **mis'carry** vi abortire

miscellaneous /mɪsə'leɪnɪəs/ a assortito

mischief /'mɪstʃɪf/ n malefatta f; (harm) danno m

mischievous /'mɪstʃɪvəs/ a (naughty) birichino; (malicious) dannoso

miscon'ception n concetto m erroneo

mis'conduct n cattiva condotta f

misde'meanour n reato m

miser /'maɪzə(r)/ n avaro m

miserabl|e /'mɪzrəbl/ a (unhappy) infelice; (wretched) miserabile; (fig: weather) deprimente. **~y** adv (live, fail) miseramente; (say) tristemente

miserly /'maɪzəlɪ/ a avaro; (amount) ridicolo

misery /'mɪzərɪ/ n miseria f; (fam: person) piagnone, -a mf

mis'fire vi (gun:) far cilecca; (plan etc:) non riuscire

misfit n disadattato, -a mf

mis'fortune n sfortuna f

mis'givings npl dubbi mpl

mis'guided a fuorviato

mishap /'mɪshæp/ n disavventura f

misin'terpret vt fraintendere

mis'judge vt giudicar male; (estimate wrongly) valutare male

mis'lay vt (pt/pp -laid) smarrire

mis'lead vt (pt/pp -led) fuorviare. **~ing** a fuorviante

mis'manage vt amministrare male. **~ment** n cattiva amministrazione f

misnomer /mɪs'nəʊmə(r)/ n termine m improprio

'misprint n errore m di stampa

mis'quote vt citare erroneamente

misrepre'sent vt rappresentare male

Miss n (pl **-es**) signorina f

miss /mɪs/ n colpo m mancato ● vt

(fail to hit or find) mancare; perdere (train, bus, class); (feel the loss of) sentire la mancanza di; **I ~ed that part** (failed to notice) mi è sfuggita quella parte ● vi **but he ~ed** (failed to hit) ma l'ha mancato. **miss out** vt saltare, omettere

misshapen /mɪs'ʃeɪpən/ a malformato

missile /'mɪsaɪl/ n missile m

missing /'mɪsɪŋ/ a mancante; (person) scomparso; Mil disperso; **be ~** essere introvabile

mission /'mɪʃn/ n missione f

missionary /'mɪʃənrɪ/ n missionario, -a mf

mis'spell vt (pt/pp **-spelled, -spelt**) sbagliare l'ortografia di

mist /mɪst/ n (fog) foschia f ● **mist up** vi appannarsi, annebbiarsi

mistake /mɪ'steɪk/ n sbaglio m; **by ~** per sbaglio ● vt (pt **mistook**, pp **mistaken**) sbagliare (road, house); fraintendere (meaning, words); **~ for** prendere per

mistaken /mɪ'steɪkən/ a sbagliato; **be ~** sbagliarsi; **~ identity** errore m di persona. **~ly** adv erroneamente

mistletoe /'mɪsltəʊ/ n vischio m

mistress /'mɪstrɪs/ n padrona f; (teacher) maestra f; (lover) amante f

mis'trust n sfiducia f ● vt non aver fiducia in

misty /'mɪstɪ/ a (**-ier, -iest**) nebbioso

misunder'stand vt (pt/pp **-stood**) fraintendere. **~ing** n malinteso m

misuse¹ /mɪs'juːz/ n cattivo uso m

misuse² /mɪs'juːs/ n cattivo uso m

mite /maɪt/ n (child) piccino, -a mf

mitigat|e /'mɪtɪgeɪt/ vt attenuare. **~ing** a attenuante

mitten /'mɪtn/ n manopola f, muffola f

mix /mɪks/ n (combination) mescolanza f; Culin miscuglio m; (readymade) preparato m ● vt mischiare ● vi mischiarsi; (person:) inserirsi; **~ with** (associate with) fre-

quentare. **mix up** vt mescolare
⟨papers⟩; ⟨confuse, mistake for⟩
confondere

mixed /'mɪkst/ a misto; ~ up
⟨person⟩ confuso

mixer /'mɪksə(r)/ n Culin frullatore m, mixer m inv; **he's a good** ~
è un tipo socievole

mixture /'mɪkstʃə(r)/ n mescolanza f; ⟨medicine⟩ sciroppo m; Culin
miscela f

'mix-up n ⟨confusion⟩ confusione f;
⟨mistake⟩ pasticcio m

moan /məʊn/ n lamento m ● vi lamentarsi; ⟨complain⟩ lagnarsi

moat /məʊt/ n fossato m

mob /mɒb/ n folla f; ⟨rabble⟩ genta-
glia f; ⟨fam: gang⟩ banda f ● vt
⟨pt/pp **mobbed**⟩ assalire

mobile /'məʊbaɪl/ a mobile ● n
composizione f mobile. ~ **'home** n
casa f roulotte. ~ **[phone]** n [tele-
fono m] cellulare m

mobility /mə'bɪlətɪ/ n mobilità f

mock /mɒk/ a finto ● vt canzona-
re. ~**ery** n derisione f

'mock-up n modello m in scala

mode /məʊd/ n modo m; Comput
modalità f

model /'mɒdl/ n modello m;
[fashion] ~ indossatore, -trice mf,
modello, -a mf ● a ⟨yacht, plane⟩
in miniatura; ⟨pupil, husband⟩
esemplare, modello ● v ⟨pt/pp
modelled⟩ ● vt indossare ⟨clothes⟩
● vi fare l'indossatore, -trice mf;
⟨for artist⟩ posare

modem /'məʊdem/ n modem m inv

moderate¹ /'mɒdəreɪt/ vt modera-
re ● vi moderarsi

moderate² /'mɒdərət/ a moderato
● n Pol moderato, -a mf. ~**ly** adv
⟨drink, speak etc⟩ moderatamente;
⟨good, bad etc⟩ relativamente

moderation /mɒdə'reɪʃn/ n moderazione f; **in** ~ con moderazione

modern /'mɒdn/ a moderno. ~**ize**
vt modernizzare

modest /'mɒdɪst/ a modesto. ~**y** n
modestia f

modicum /'mɒdɪkəm/ n **a** ~ **of** un
po' di

modif|ication /mɒdɪfɪ'keɪʃn/ n
modificazione f. ~**y** /'mɒdɪfaɪ/ vt
⟨pt/pp **-fied**⟩ modificare

module /'mɒdjuːl/ n modulo m

moist /mɔɪst/ a umido

moisten /'mɔɪsn/ vt inumidire

moistur|e /'mɔɪstʃə(r)/ n umidità
f. ~**izer** n [crema f] idratante m

molar /'məʊlə(r)/ n molare m

molasses /mə'læsɪz/ n Am melassa f

mole¹ /məʊl/ n ⟨on face etc⟩ neo m

mole² n Zool talpa f

molecule /'mɒlɪkjuːl/ n molecola f

molest /mə'lest/ vt molestare

mollycoddle /'mɒlɪkɒdl/ vt tenere
nella bambagia

molten /'məʊltən/ a fuso

mom /mɒm/ n Am fam mamma f

moment /'məʊmənt/ n momento
m; **at the** ~ in questo momento.
~**arily** adv momentaneamente.
~**ary** a momentaneo

momentous /mə'mentəs/ a molto
importante

momentum /mə'mentəm/ n impeto m

monarch /'mɒnək/ n monarca m.
~**y** n monarchia f

monast|ery /'mɒnəstrɪ/ n mona-
stero m. ~**ic** /mə'næstɪk/ a mona-
stico

Monday /'mʌndeɪ/ n lunedì m inv

monetary /'mʌnɪtrɪ/ a monetario

money /'mʌnɪ/ n denaro m

money: ~**-box** n salvadanaio m.
~**-lender** n usuraio m

mongrel /'mʌŋɡrəl/ n bastardo m

monitor /'mɒnɪtə(r)/ n Techn monitor m inv ● vt controllare

monk /mʌŋk/ n monaco m

monkey /'mʌŋkɪ/ n scimmia f.
~**-nut** n nocciolina f americana.
~**-wrench** n chiave f inglese a rul-
lino

mono /'mɒnəʊ/ n mono m

monogram /'mɒnəɡræm/ n monogramma m

monologue /'mɒnəlɒg/ n monologo m

monopol|ize /mə'nɒpəlaɪz/ vt monopolizzare. **~y** n monopolio m

monosyllabic /mɒnəsɪ'læbɪk/ a monosillabico

monotone /'mɒnətəʊn/ n speak in a **~** parlare con tono monotono

monoton|ous /mə'nɒtənəs/ a monotono. **~y** n monotonia f

monsoon /mɒn'su:n/ n monsone m

monster /'mɒnstə(r)/ n mostro m

monstrosity /mɒn'strɒsəti/ n mostruosità f

monstrous /'mɒnstrəs/ a mostruoso

month /mʌnθ/ n mese m. **~ly** a mensile ● adv mensilmente ● n (periodical) mensile m

monument /'mɒnjʊmənt/ n monumento m. **~al** /-'mentl/ a fig monumentale

moo /mu:/ n muggito m ● vi (pt/pp **mooed**) muggire

mooch /mu:tʃ/ vi **~ about** fam gironzolare (**the house** per casa)

mood /mu:d/ n umore m; **be in a good/bad ~** essere di buon/cattivo umore; **be in the ~ for** essere in vena di

moody /'mu:dɪ/ a (-ier, -iest) (variable) lunatico; (bad-tempered) di malumore

moon /mu:n/ n luna f; **over the ~** fam al settimo cielo

moon: **~light** n chiaro m di luna ● vi fam lavorare in nero. **~lit** a illuminato dalla luna

moor¹ /mʊə(r)/ n brughiera f

moor² vt Naut ormeggiare

moose /mu:s/ n (pl **moose**) alce m

moot /mu:t/ a **it's a ~ point** è un punto controverso

mop /mɒp/ n straccio m (per i pavimenti); **~ of hair** zazzera f ● vt (pt/pp **mopped**) lavare con lo straccio. **mop up** vt (dry) asciugare con lo straccio; (clean) pulire con lo straccio

mope /məʊp/ vi essere depresso

moped /'məʊped/ n ciclomotore m

moral /'mɒrəl/ a morale ● n morale f. **~ly** adv moralmente. **~s** pl moralità f

morale /mə'rɑ:l/ n morale m

morality /mə'rælətɪ/ n moralità f

morbid /'mɔ:bɪd/ a morboso

more /mɔ:(r)/ a più; **a few books** un po' più di libri; **some tea?** ancora un po' di tè?; **there's no ~ bread** non c'è più pane; **there are no ~ apples** non ci sono più mele; **one ~ word and...** ancora una parola e... ● pron di più; **would you like some ~?** ne vuoi ancora?; **no ~, thank you** non ne voglio più, grazie ● adv più; **~ interesting** più interessante; **~ [and ~] quickly** [sempre] più veloce; **~ than** più di; **I don't love him any ~** no lo amo più; **once ~** ancora una volta; **~ or less** più o meno; **the ~ I see him, the ~ I like him** più lo vedo, più mi piace

moreover /mɔ:'rəʊvə(r)/ adv inoltre

morgue /mɔ:g/ n obitorio m

moribund /'mɒrɪbʌnd/ a moribondo

morning /'mɔ:nɪŋ/ n mattino m, mattina f; **in the ~** del mattino; (tomorrow) domani mattina

Morocc|o /mə'rɒkəʊ/ n Marocco m ● a **~an** a & n marocchino, -a mf

moron /'mɔ:rɒn/ n fam deficiente mf

morose /mə'rəʊs/ a scontroso

morphine /'mɔ:fi:n/ n morfina f

Morse /mɔ:s/ n **~ [code]** [codice m] Morse m

morsel /'mɔ:sl/ n (food) boccone m

mortal /'mɔ:tl/ a & n mortale mf. **~ity** /-'tælətɪ/ n mortalità f. **~ly** adv (wounded, offended) a morte; (afraid) a morire

mortar /'mɔ:tə(r)/ n mortaio m

mortgage /'mɔ:gɪdʒ/ n mutuo m; (on property) ipoteca f ● vt ipotecare

mortuary /'mɔːtjʊəri/ n camera f mortuaria
mosaic /məʊ'zeɪik/ n mosaico m
Moscow /'mɒskəʊ/ n Mosca f
Moslem /'mʊzlim/ a & n musulmano, -a mf
mosque /mɒsk/ n moschea f
mosquito /mɒs'kiːtəʊ/ n (pl -es) zanzara f
moss /mɒs/ n muschio m. ~**y** a muschioso
most /məʊst/ a (majority) la. ~ gior parte di; **for the ~ part** per lo più ● adv più, maggiormente; (very) estremamente, molto; **the ~ interesting** la giornata più interessante; **a ~ interesting day** una giornata estremamente interessante; **the ~ beautiful woman in the world** la donna più bella del mondo; ~ **unlikely** veramente improbabile ● pron ~ of them la maggior parte di loro; **at [the] ~** al massimo; **make the ~ of** sfruttare al massimo; ~ **of the time** la maggior parte del tempo. ~**ly** adv per lo più
MOT n revisione f obbligatoria di autoveicoli
motel /məʊ'tel/ n motel m inv
moth /mɒθ/ n falena f; [clothes-] ~ tarma f
moth: ~**ball** n pallina f di naftalina. ~**-eaten** a tarmato
mother /'mʌðə(r)/ n madre f; **M~'s Day** la festa della mamma ● vt fare da madre a
mother: ~**board** n Comput scheda f madre. ~**hood** n maternità f. ~**-in-law** n (pl **~s-in-law**) suocera f. ~**ly** a materno. ~**-of-pearl** n madreperla f. ~**-to-be** n futura mamma f. ~ **tongue** n madrelingua f
mothproof /'mɒθ-/ a antitarmico
motif /məʊ'tiːf/ n motivo m
motion /'məʊʃn/ n moto m; (proposal) mozione f; (gesture) gesto m ● vt/i ~ [to] sb to enter fare segno a qcno di entrare. ~**less** a immobile. ~**lessly** adv senza alcun movimento

motivate /'məʊtiveit/ vt motivare. ~**ion** /-'veiʃn/ n motivazione f
motive /'məʊtiv/ n motivo m
motley /'mɒtli/ a disparato
motor /'məʊtə(r)/ n motore m; (car) macchina f ● a a motore; Anat motore ● vi andare in macchina
Motorail /'məʊtəreil/ n treno m per trasporto auto
motor: ~ **bike** n fam moto f inv. ~ **boat** n motoscafo m. ~**cade** /-keid/ n Am corteo m di auto. ~ **car** n automobile f. ~ **cycle** n motocicletta f. ~**-cyclist** n motociclista mf. ~**ing** n automobilismo m. ~**ist** n automobilista mf. ~ **racing** n corse fpl automobilistiche. ~ **vehicle** n autoveicolo m. ~**way** n autostrada f
mottled /'mɒtld/ a chiazzato
motto /'mɒtəʊ/ n (pl -es) motto m
mould¹ /məʊld/ n (fungus) muffa f
mould² n stampo m ● vt foggiare; fig formare. ~**ing** n Archit cornice f
mouldy /'məʊldi/ a ammuffito; (fam: worthless) ridicolo
moult /məʊlt/ vi (bird:) fare la muta; (animal:) perdere il pelo
mound /maʊnd/ n mucchio m; (hill) collinetta f
mount /maʊnt/ n (horse) cavalcatura f; (of jewel, photo, picture) montatura f ● vt montare a (horse); salire su (bicycle); incastonare (jewel); incorniciare (photo, picture) ● vi aumentare. **mount up** vi aumentare
mountain /'maʊntin/ n montagna f; ~ **bike** n mountain bike f inv
mountaineer /maʊntɪ'nɪə(r)/ n alpinista mf. ~**ing** n alpinismo m
mountainous /'maʊntinəs/ a montagnoso
mourn /mɔːn/ vt lamentare ● vi ~ **for** piangere la morte di. ~**er** n persona f che partecipa a un funerale. ~**ful** a triste. ~**ing** n in ~ in lutto
mouse /maʊs/ n (pl mice) topo m;

Comput mouse *m inv.* **~trap** *n* trappola *f* [per topi]

mousse /muːs/ *n Culin* mousse *f inv*

moustache /məˈstaːʃ/ *n* baffi *mpl*

mousy /ˈmaʊsɪ/ *a* ‹colour› grigio topo

mouth¹ /maʊð/ *vt* **~ sth** dire qcsa silenziosamente muovendo solamente le labbra

mouth² /maʊθ/ *n* bocca *f*; *(of river)* foce *f*

mouth: **~ful** *n* boccone *m*. **~-organ** *n* armonica *f* [a bocca]. **~piece** *n* imboccatura *f*; *(fig: person)* portavoce *m inv.* **~ watering** *a* che fa venire l'acquolina in bocca

movable /ˈmuːvəbl/ *a* mobile

move /muːv/ *n* mossa *f*; *(moving house)* trasloco *m*; *(in game)* mossa *f*; **on the ~** in movimento; **get a ~ on** *fam* darsi una mossa ● *vt* muovere; *(emotionally)* commuovere; spostare ‹car, furniture›; *(transfer)* trasferire; *(propose)* proporre; **~ house** traslocare ● *vi* muoversi; *(move house)* traslocare. **move along** *vi* andare avanti ● *vt* muovere in avanti. **move away** *vi* allontanarsi; *(move house)* trasferirsi ● *vt* allontanare. **move forward** *vi* avanzare ● *vt* spostare avanti. **move in** *vi* *(to a house)* trasferirsi. **move off** *vi* ‹vehicle:› muoversi. **move out** *vi* *(of house)* andare via. **move over** *vi* spostarsi ● *vt* spostare. **move up** *vi* muoversi; *(advance, increase)* avanzare

movement /ˈmuːvmənt/ *n* movimento *m*

movie /ˈmuːvɪ/ *n* film *m inv*; **go to the ~s** andare al cinema

moving /ˈmuːvɪŋ/ *a* mobile; *(touching)* commovente

mow /məʊ/ *vt* (*pt* **mowed**, *pp* **mown** *or* **mowed**) tagliare ‹lawn›. **mow down** *vt (destroy)* sterminare

mower /ˈməʊə(r)/ *n* tosaerba *m inv*

MP *n abbr* **Member of Parliament**

Mr /ˈmɪstə(r)/ *n* (*pl* **Messrs**) Signor *m*

Mrs /ˈmɪsɪz/ *n* Signora *f*

Ms /mɪz/ *n* Signora *f* ‹modo *m* formale di rivolgersi ad una donna quando non si vuole connotarla come sposata o nubile›

much /mʌtʃ/ *a, adv & pron* molto; **~ as** per quanto; **I love you just as ~ as before/him** ti amo quanto prima/lui; **as ~ as £5 million** ben cinque milioni di sterline; **as ~ as that** così tanto; **very ~** tantissimo, moltissimo; **~ the same** quasi uguale

muck /mʌk/ *n* (*dirt*) sporcizia *f*; *(farming)* letame *m*; *(fam: filth)* porcheria *f*. **muck about** *vi fam* perder tempo; **~ about with** trafficare con. **muck up** *vt fam* rovinare; *(make dirty)* sporcare

mucky /ˈmʌkɪ/ *a* (**-ier, -iest**) sudicio

mucus /ˈmjuːkəs/ *n* muco *m*

mud /mʌd/ *n* fango *m*

muddle /ˈmʌdl/ *n* disordine *m*; *(mix-up)* confusione *f* ● *vt* **~ [up]** confondere ‹dates›

muddy /ˈmʌdɪ/ *a* (**-ier, -iest**) ‹path› fangoso; ‹shoes› infangato

mudguard *n* parafango *m*

muesli /ˈmuːzlɪ/ *n* muesli *m inv*

muffle /ˈmʌfl/ *vt* smorzare ‹sound›. **muffle [up]** *vt (for warmth)* imbacuccare

muffler /ˈmʌflə(r)/ *n* sciarpa *f*; *Am Auto* marmitta *f*

mug¹ /mʌg/ *n* tazza *f*; *(for beer)* boccale *m*; *(fam: face)* muso *m*; *(fam: simpleton)* pollo *m*

mug² /mʌg/ *n* (*pt/pp* **mugged**) aggredire e derubare. **~ger** *n* assalitore, -trice *mf*. **~ging** *n* aggressione *f* per furto

muggy /ˈmʌgɪ/ *a* (**-ier, -iest**) afoso

mule /mjuːl/ *n* mulo *m*

mull /mʌl/ *vt* **~ over** rimuginare su

mulled /mʌld/ *a* **~ wine** vin brulé *m inv*

multi /ˈmʌltɪ/: **~coloured** *a* variopinto. **~lingual** /-'lɪŋgwəl/ a multilingue inv. **~'media** n multimedia mpl ● a multimediale. **~'national** a multinazionale ● n multinazionale f

multiple /'mʌltɪpl/ a multiplo

multiplication /mʌltɪplɪ'keɪʃn/ n moltiplicazione f

multiply /'mʌltɪplaɪ/ v (pt/pp -ied) ● vt moltiplicare (by per) ● vi moltiplicarsi

multi'storey a ~ car park parcheggio m a più piani

mum¹ /mʌm/ a keep ~ fam non aprire bocca

mum² n fam mamma f

mumble /'mʌmbl/ vt/i borbottare

mummy¹ /'mʌmɪ/ n fam mamma f

mummy² n Archaeol mummia f

mumps /mʌmps/ n orecchioni mpl

munch /mʌntʃ/ vt/i sgranocchiare

mundane /mʌn'deɪn/ a ⟨everyday⟩ banale

municipal /mjʊ'nɪsɪpl/ a municipale

mural /'mjʊərəl/ n dipinto m murale

murder /'mɜːdə(r)/ n assassinio m ● vt assassinare; ⟨fam: ruin⟩ massacrare. **~er** n assassino, -a m/f. **~ous** /-rəs/ a omicida

murky /'mɜːkɪ/ a (-ier, -iest) oscuro

murmur /'mɜːmə(r)/ n mormorio m ● vt/i mormorare

muscle /'mʌsl/ n muscolo m ● **muscle in** vi sl intromettersi (on in)

muscular /'mʌskjʊlə(r)/ a muscolare; ⟨strong⟩ muscoloso

muse /mjuːz/ vi meditare (on su)

museum /mjʊ'zɪəm/ n museo m

mushroom /'mʌʃrʊm/ n fungo m ● vi fig spuntare come funghi

music /'mjuːzɪk/ n musica f; ⟨written⟩ spartito m.

musical /'mjuːzɪkl/ a musicale; ⟨person⟩ dotato di senso musicale ● n commedia f musicale. **~ box** n

carillon m inv. **~ instrument** n strumento m musicale

music: ~ **box** n carillon m inv. ~ **centre** impianto m stereo; **'~-hall** n teatro m di varietà

musician /mjuː'zɪʃn/ n musicista m/f

Muslim /'mʊzlɪm/ a & n musulmano, -a m/f

mussel /'mʌsl/ n cozza f

must /mʌst/ v aux (solo al presente) dovere; **you ~ not be late** non devi essere in ritardo; **she ~ have finished by now** ⟨probability⟩ deve aver finito ormai ● n a ~ fam una cosa da non perdere

mustard /'mʌstəd/ n senape f

musty /'mʌstɪ/ a (-ier, -iest) stantio

mutation /mjuː'teɪʃn/ n Biol mutazione f

mute /mjuːt/ a muto

muted /'mjuːtɪd/ a smorzato

mutilat|e /'mjuːtɪleɪt/ vt mutilare. **~ion** /-'leɪʃn/ n mutilazione f

mutin|ous /'mjuːtɪnəs/ a ammutinato. **~y** n ammutinamento m ● vi (pt/pp -ied) ammutinarsi

mutter /'mʌtə(r)/ vt/i borbottare

mutton /'mʌtn/ n carne f di montone

mutual /'mjuːtjʊəl/ a reciproco; ⟨fam: common⟩ comune. **~ly** adv reciprocamente

muzzle /'mʌzl/ n (of animal) muso m; (of firearm) bocca f; (for dog) museruola f ● vt fig mettere il bavaglio a

my /maɪ/ a il mio m, la mia f, i miei mpl, le mie fpl; **my mother/father** mia madre/mio padre

myself /maɪ'self/ pron (reflexive) mi; (emphatic) me stesso; (after prep) me; **I've seen it** ~ l'ho visto io stesso; **by** ~ da solo; **I thought to** ~ ho pensato tra me e me; **I'm proud of** ~ sono fiero di me

mysterious /mɪ'stɪərɪəs/ a misterioso. **~ly** adv misteriosamente

mystery /'mɪstərɪ/ n mistero m; ~ [story] racconto m del mistero

483

mystic|c[al] /'mɪstɪk[l]/ *a* mistico. **~cism** /-sɪzm/ *n* misticismo *m*

mystified /'mɪstɪfaɪd/ *a* disorientato

mystify /'mɪstɪfaɪ/ *vt* (*pt/pp* **-ied**) disorientare

mystique /mɪ'stiːk/ *n* mistica *f*

myth /mɪθ/ *n* mito *m*. **~ical** *a* mitico

mythology /mɪ'θɒlədʒɪ/ *n* mitologia *f*

Nn

nab /næb/ *vt* (*pt/pp* **nabbed**) *fam* beccare

naff /næf/ *a Br fam* banale

nag¹ /næg/ *n* (*horse*) ronzino *m*

nag² /pp/pp **nagged**) *vt* assillare ● *vi* essere insistente ● *n* (*person*) brontolone, a *mf*. **~ging** *a* (*pain*) persistente

nail /neɪl/ *n* chiodo *m*; (*of finger, toe*) unghia ● **nail down** *vt* inchiodare; **~ sb down to a time/price** far fissare a qcno un'ora/un prezzo

nail: **~-brush** *n* spazzolino *m* da unghie. **~-file** *n* limetta *f* da unghie. **~ polish** *n* smalto *m* [per unghie]. **~ scissors** *npl* forbicine *fpl* da unghie. **~ varnish** *n* smalto *m* [per unghie]

naïve /naɪˈiːv/ *a* ingenuo. **~ty** /-ətɪ/ *n* ingenuità *f*

naked /'neɪkɪd/ *a* nudo; **with the ~ eye** a òcchio nudo

name /neɪm/ *n* nome *m*; **what's your ~?** come ti chiami?; **my ~ is Matthew** mi chiamo Matthew; **I know her by ~** la conosco di nome; **by the ~ of Bates** di nome Bates; **call sb ~s** *fam* insultare qcno ● *vt* (*to position*) nominare; *(identify)* citare; *(identify)* citare; *(name)* chiamare *(baby)*; **be ~d after** essere chiamato col

nome di. **~less** *a* senza nome. **~ly** *adv* cioè

name: **~-plate** *n* targhetta *f*. **~sake** *n* omonimo, -a *mf*

nanny /'nænɪ/ *n* bambinaia *f*. **~-goat** *n* capra *f*

nap /næp/ *n* pisolino *m*; **have a ~** fare un pisolino ● *vi* (*pt/pp* **napped**) **catch sb ~ping** cogliere qcno alla sprovvista

nape /neɪp/ *n* **~ [of the neck]** nuca *f*

napkin /'næpkɪn/ *n* tovagliolo *m*

Naples /'neɪplz/ *n* Napoli *f*

nappy /'næpɪ/ *n* pannolino *m*

narcotic /nɑːˈkɒtɪk/ *a* & *n* narcotico *m*

narrat|e /nəˈreɪt/ *vt* narrare. **~ion** /-eɪʃn/ *n* narrazione *f*

narrative /'nærətɪv/ *a* narrativo ● *n* narrazione *f*

narrator /nəˈreɪtə(r)/ *n* narratore, -trice *mf*

narrow /'nærəʊ/ *a* stretto; *(fig: views)* ristretto; *(margin, majority)* scarso ● *vt* restringersi. **~ly** *adv* **~ly escape death** evitare la morte per un pelo. **~-minded** *a* di idee ristrette

nasal /'neɪzl/ *a* nasale

nastily /'nɑːstɪlɪ/ *adv* (*spitefully*) con cattiveria

nasty /'nɑːstɪ/ *a* (**-ier, -iest**) *(smell, person, remark)* cattivo; *(injury, situation, weather)* brutto; **turn ~** *(person:)* diventare cattivo

nation /'neɪʃn/ *n* nazione *f*

national /'næʃənl/ *a* nazionale ● *n* cittadino, -a *mf*

national: **~** *anthem* *n* inno *m* nazionale. **N~** **'Health Service** *n Br* servizio *m* sanitario. **N~** **In'surance** *n* ≈ Previdenza *f* sociale

nationalism /'næʃənəlɪzm/ *n* nazionalismo *m*

nationality /næʃəˈnælətɪ/ *n* nazionalità *f inv*

national|ization /næʃənəlaɪˈzeɪʃn/ *n* nazionalizzazione *f*. **~ize** /'næʃənəlaɪz/ *vt* nazionalizzare.

~ly /'næʃənəli/ adv a livello nazionale

'**nation-wide** a su scala nazionale

native /'neitiv/ a nativo; (innate) innato ●n nativo, -a mf; (local inhabitant) abitante mf del posto; (outside Europe) indigeno, -a mf; she's a ~ of Venice è originaria di Venezia

native: ~ 'land n paese m nativo. ~ 'language n lingua f madre

Nativity /nə'tɪvɪtɪ/ n the ~ la Natività f. ~ play n rappresentazione f sulla nascita di Gesù

natter /'nætə(r)/ vi fam chiacchierare

natural /'nætʃrəl/ a naturale

natural: ~ 'gas n metano m. ~ 'history n storia f naturale

naturalist /'nætʃ(ə)rəlɪst/ n naturalista mf

natural|ization /nætʃ(ə)rəlaɪ'zeɪʃn/ n naturalizzazione f. ~ize /'nætʃ(ə)rəlaɪz/ vt naturalizzare

naturally /'nætʃ(ə)rəlɪ/ adv (of course) naturalmente; (by nature) per natura

nature /'neɪtʃə(r)/ n natura f; by ~ per natura. ~ reserve n riserva f naturale

naughtily /'nɔ:tɪlɪ/ adv male

naughty /'nɔ:tɪ/ a (-ier, -iest) monello; (slightly indecent) spinto

nausea /'nɔ:zɪə/ n nausea f

nause|ate /'nɔ:zɪeɪt/ vt nauseare. ~ating a nauseante. ~ous /-ɪəs/ a I feel ~ous ho la nausea

nautical /'nɔ:tɪkl/ a nautico. ~ mile n miglio m marino

naval /'neɪvl/ a navale

nave /neɪv/ n navata f centrale

navel /'neɪvl/ n ombelico m

navigable /'nævɪgəbl/ a navigabile

navigat|e /'nævɪgeɪt/ vi navigare; Auto fare da navigatore ●vt navigare su ⟨river⟩. ~ion /-'geɪʃn/ n navigazione f. ~or n navigatore m

navy /'neɪvɪ/ n marina f ●~ [blue] a blu marine inv ●n blu m inv marine

Neapolitan /nɪə'pɒlɪtən/ a & n napoletano, -a mf

near /nɪə(r)/ a vicino; ⟨future⟩ prossimo; the ~est bank (la banca più vicina ●adv vicino; draw ~ avvicinarsi; ~ at hand a portata di mano ●prep vicino a; he was ~ to tears aveva le lacrime agli occhi ●vt avvicinarsi a

near: ~'by a & adv vicino. ~ly adv quasi; it's not ~ly enough non è per niente sufficiente. ~ness n vicinanza f. ~ side n Auto ⟨wheel⟩ (left) sinistro; (right) destro. ~-sighted a Am miope

neat /ni:t/ a (tidy) ordinato; (clever) efficace; (undiluted) liscio. ~ly adv ordinatamente; (cleverly) efficacemente. ~ness n (tidiness) ordine f

necessarily /nesə'serɪlɪ/ adv necessariamente

necessary /'nesəsərɪ/ a necessario

necessit|ate /nɪ'sesɪteɪt/ vt rendere necessario. ~y n necessità f inv

neck /nek/ n collo m; (of dress) colletto m; ~ and ~ testa a testa

necklace /'neklɪs/ n collana f

neck: ~line n scollatura f. ~tie n cravatta f

neé /neɪ/ a ~ Brett nata Brett

need /ni:d/ n bisogno m; be in ~ of avere bisogno di; if ~ be se ce ne fosse bisogno; there is a ~ for c'è bisogno di; there is no ~ for that non ce n'è bisogno; there is no ~ for you to go non c'è bisogno che tu vada ●vt aver bisogno di; I ~ to know devo saperlo; it ~s to be done bisogna farlo ●v aux you ~ not go non c'è bisogno che tu vada; ~ I come? devo [proprio] venire?

needle /'ni:dl/ n ago m; (for knitting) uncinetto m; (of record player) puntina f ●vt (fam: annoy) punzecchiare

needless /'ni:dlɪs/ a inutile

'**needlework** n cucito m

needy /'niːdɪ/ a (**-ier, -iest**) bisognoso

negation /nɪ'geɪʃn/ n negazione f

negative /'negǝtɪv/ a negativo ● n negazione f; *Phot* negativo m; **in the ~** *Gram* alla forma negativa

neglect /nɪ'glekt/ n trascuratezza f; **state of ~** stato m di abbandono ● vt trascurare; **he ~ed to write** non si è curato di scrivere. **~ed** a trascurato. **~ful** a negligente; **be ~ful of** trascurare

négligée /'neglɪʒeɪ/ n négligé m inv

neglig|ence /'neglɪdʒǝns/ n negligenza f. **~t** a negligente

negligible /'neglɪdʒǝbl/ a trascurabile

negotiable /nɪ'gǝʊʃǝbl/ a (*road*) transitabile; *Comm* negoziabile; **not ~** (*cheque*) non trasferibile

negotiat|e /nɪ'gǝʊʃɪeɪt/ vt negoziare; *Auto* prendere (*bend*) ● vi negoziare. **~ion** /-'eɪʃn/ n negoziato m. **~or** n negoziatore, -trice mf

Negro /'niːgrǝʊ/ a & n (pl **-es**) negro, -a mf

neigh /neɪ/ vi nitrire

neighbour /'neɪbǝ(r)/ n vicino, -a mf. **~hood** n vicinato m; **in the ~hood of** nei dintorni di; *fig* circa. **~ing** a vicino. **~ly** a amichevole

neither /'naɪðǝ(r)/ a & pron nessuno dei due, né l'uno né l'altro ● adv **~ ... nor** né... né ● conj neppure, neanche; **~ do/did I** nemmeno io

neon /'niːɒn/ n neon m. **~ light** n luce f al neon

nephew /'nevjuː/ n nipote m

nerve /nɜːv/ n nervo m; (*fam: courage*) coraggio m; (*fam: impudence*) faccia f tosta; **lose one's ~** perdersi d'animo. **~-racking** a logorante

nervous /'nɜːvǝs/ a nervoso; **he makes me ~** mi mette in agitazione; **be a ~ wreck** avere i nervi a pezzi. **~ 'breakdown** n esaurimento m nervoso. **~ly** adv nervo-

samente. **~ness** n nervosismo m; (*before important event*) tensione f

nervy /'nɜːvɪ/ a (**-ier, -iest**) nervoso; (*Am: impudent*) sfacciato

nest /nest/ n nido m ● vi fare il nido. **~-egg** n gruzzolo m

nestle /'nesl/ vi accoccolarsi

net¹ /net/ n rete f ● vt (pt/pp **netted**) (*catch*) prendere (con la rete)

net² a netto ● vt (pt/pp **netted**) incassare un utile netto di

'netball n sport m inv femminile, simile a pallacanestro

Netherlands /'neðǝlǝndz/ npl **the ~** i Paesi mpl Bassi

netting /'netɪŋ/ n (*wire*) ~ reticolato m

nettle /'netl/ n ortica f

'network n rete f

neuralgia /njʊǝ'rældʒǝ/ n nevralgia f

neurolog|ist /njʊǝ'rɒlǝdʒɪst/ n neurologo. -a mf

neur|osis /njʊǝ'rǝʊsɪs/ n (pl **-oses** /-siːz/) nevrosi f inv. **~otic** /-'rɒtɪk/ a nevrotico

neuter /'njuːtǝ(r)/ a *Gram* neutro ● n *Gram* neutro m ● vt sterilizzare

neutral /'njuːtrǝl/ a neutro; (*country, person*) neutrale ● n **in ~** *Auto* in folle. **~ity** /-'trælǝtɪ/ n neutralità f. **~ize** vt neutralizzare

never /'nevǝ(r)/ adv [non...] mai; (*fam: expressing disbelief*) ma va; **~ again** mai più; **well I ~!** chi l'avrebbe detto!. **~-ending** a interminabile

nevertheless /nevǝðǝ'les/ adv tuttavia

new /njuː/ a nuovo

new: ~'born a neonato **~comer** n nuovo, -a arrivato, -a mf. **~fangled** /-'fæŋgld/ a pej modernizzante. **~-laid** a fresco

newly adv (*recently*) di recente; **~-built** costruito di recente. **~weds** npl sposini mpl

new: ~ 'moon n luna f nuova. **~ness** n novità f

news /njuːz/ n notizie fpl; TV telegiornale m; Radio giornale m radio; **piece of ~** notizia f

news: ~agent n giornalaio, -a mf. **~ bulletin** n notiziario m. **~caster** n giornalista mf televisivo, -a/radiofonico, -a. **~flash** n notizia f flash. **~letter** n bollettino m d'informazione. **~paper** n giornale m; (material) carta f di giornale. **~reader** n giornalista mf televisivo, -a/radiofonico, -a

new: ~ year n (next year) anno m nuovo; **N~ Year's Day** n Capodanno m. **N~ Year's 'Eve** n vigilia f di Capodanno. **N~ Zealand** /'ziːlənd/ n Nuova Zelanda f. **N~ Zealander** n neozelandese mf

next /nekst/ a prossimo, (adjoining) vicino; **who's ~?** a chi tocca?; **~ door** accanto; **~ to nothing** quasi niente; **the ~ day** il giorno dopo; **~ week** la settimana prossima; **the week after ~** fra due settimane ● adv dopo; **when will you see him ~?** quando lo rivedi la prossima volta?; **~ to** accanto a ● n seguente mf. **~ of kin** parente m prossimo

NHS n abbr **National Health Service**

nib /nɪb/ n pennino m

nibble /'nɪbl/ vt/i mordicchiare

nice /naɪs/ a (day, weather, holiday) bello; (person) gentile, simpatico; (food) buono; **it's a ~ meeting you** è stato un piacere conoscerla. **~ly** adv gentilmente; (well) bene. **~ties** /'naɪsətɪz/ npl finezze fpl

niche /niːʃ/ n nicchia f

nick /nɪk/ n tacca f; (on chin etc) taglietto m; (fam: prison) galera f; (fam: police station) centrale f [di polizia]; **in the ~ of time** fam appena in tempo ● vt intaccare; (fam: steal) fregare; (fam: arrest) beccare; **~ one's chin** farsi un taglietto nel mento

nickel /'nɪkl/ n nichel m; Am moneta f da cinque centesimi

'nickname n soprannome m ● vt soprannominare

nicotine /'nɪkətiːn/ n nicotina f

niece /niːs/ n nipote f

Nigeria /nar'dʒɪərɪə/ n Nigeria f. **~n** a & n nigeriano mf

niggling /'nɪglɪŋ/ a (detail) insignificante; (pain) fastidioso; (doubt) persistente

night /naɪt/ n notte f; (evening) sera f; **at ~** la notte, di notte; (in the evening) la sera, di sera; **Monday ~** lunedì notte/sera ● a di notte

night: ~cap n papalina f; (drink) bicchierino m bevuto prima di andare a letto. **~club** n locale m notturno, night[-club] m inv. **~dress** n camicia f da notte. **~fall** n crepuscolo m. **~gown**, fam **~ie** /'naɪtɪ/ n camicia f da notte

nightingale /'naɪtɪŋgeɪl/ n usignolo m

night: ~life n vita f notturna. **~ly** a di notte, di sera ● adv ogni notte, ogni sera. **~mare** n incubo m. **~school** n scuola f serale. **~time** n at **~time** di notte, la notte. **~'watchman** n guardiano m notturno

nil /nɪl/ n nulla m; Sport zero m

nimble /'nɪmbl/ a agile. **~y** adv agilmente

nine /naɪn/ a nove inv ● n nove m. **~teen** a diciannove inv ● n diciannove. **~teenth** a & n diciannovesimo, -a mf

ninetieth /'naɪntɪɪθ/ a & n novantesimo, -a mf

ninety /'naɪntɪ/ a novanta inv ● n novanta m

ninth /naɪnθ/ a & n nono, -a mf

nip /nɪp/ n pizzicotto m; (bite) morso m ● vt pizzicare; (bite) mordere; **~ in the bud** fig stroncare sul nascere ● vi (fam: run) fare un salto

nipple /'nɪpl/ n capezzolo m; (Am: on bottle) tettarella f

nippy /'nɪpɪ/ a (-ier, -iest) fam (cold) pungente.

nitrogen /'naɪtrədʒən/ n azoto m

nitwit /'nɪtwɪt/ n fam imbecille m

no /nəʊ/ adv no ● n (pl noes) no m inv ● a nessuno; I have no time non ho tempo; in no time in un baleno; 'no parking' 'sosta vietata'; 'no smoking' 'vietato fumare'; no one = nobody

nobility /nəʊ'bɪlətɪ/ n nobiltà f

noble /'nəʊbl/ a nobile. ~man n nobile m

nobody /'nəʊbədɪ/ pron nessuno; he knows ~ non conosce nessuno ● n he's a ~ non è nessuno

nocturnal /nɒk'tɜːnl/ a notturno

nod /nɒd/ n cenno m del capo● vi (pt/pp nodded) fare un cenno col capo; (in agreement) fare di sì col capo ● vt ~ one's head fare di sì col capo. nod off vi assopirsi

nodule /'nɒdjuːl/ n nodulo m

noise /nɔɪz/ n rumore m; (loud) rumore m, chiasso m. ~less a silenzioso. ~lessly adv silenziosamente

noisy /'nɔɪzɪ/ a (-ier, -iest) rumoroso

nomad /'nəʊmæd/ n nomade mf. ~ic /-'mædɪk/ a nomade

nominal /'nɒmɪnl/ a nominale

nominate /'nɒmɪneɪt/ vt proporre come candidato; (appoint) designare. ~ion /-'neɪʃn/ n nomina f; (person nominated) candidato, -a mf

nominative /'nɒmɪnətɪv/ a & n Gram ~ [case] nominativo m

nominee /nɒmɪ'niː/ n persona f nominata

nonchalant /'nɒnʃələnt/ a disinvolto

non-com'missioned /nɒn-/ a ~ officer sottufficiale m

non-com'mittal a che non si sbilancia

nondescript /'nɒndɪskrɪpt/ a qualunque

none /nʌn/ pron (person) nessuno; (thing) niente; ~ of us nessuno di

noi; ~ of this niente di questo; there's ~ left non ce n'è più ● adv she's ~ too pleased non è per niente soddisfatta; I'm ~ the wiser non ne so più di prima

nonentity /nɒ'nentətɪ/ n nullità f

non-event n delusione f

non-ex'istent a inesistente

non-'fiction a saggistica f

non-'iron a che non si stira

nonplussed /nɒn'plʌst/ a perplesso

nonsens|e /'nɒnsəns/ n sciocchezze fpl. ~ical /-'sensɪkl/ a assurdo

non-'smoker n non fumatore, -trice mf; (compartment) scompartimento m non fumatori

non-'stick a antiaderente

non-'stop a ~ 'flight volo m diretto ● adv senza sosta; (fly) senza scalo

non-'violent a non violento

noodles /'nuːdlz/ npl taglierini mpl

nook /nʊk/ n cantuccio m

noon /nuːn/ n mezzogiorno m; at ~ a mezzogiorno

noose /nuːs/ n nodo m scorsoio

nor /nɔː(r)/ adv & conj né; ~ do I neppure io

Nordic /'nɔːdɪk/ a nordico

norm /nɔːm/ n norma f

normal /'nɔːml/ a normale. ~ity /-'mælətɪ/ n normalità f. ~ly adv (usually) normalmente

north /nɔːθ/ n nord m; to the ~ of a nord di ● a del nord, settentrionale ● adv a nord

north: N~ A'merica n America f del Nord. ~bound a Auto in direzione nord. ~-east n nord-est, nordorientale ● n nord-est m ● adv a nord-est; (travel) verso nord-est

norther|ly /'nɔːðəlɪ/ a (direction) nord; (wind) del nord. ~n a del nord, settentrionale. N~n Ireland n Irlanda f del Nord

north: N~ 'Pole n polo m nord. N~ 'Sea n Mare m del Nord ~ward[s] /-wəd[z]/ adv verso nord. **~-west** *a* di nord-ovest, nordoccidentale ● *n* nord-ovest *m* ● *adv* a nord-ovest; ⟨*travel*⟩ verso nord-ovest

Nor|way /'nɔ:weɪ/ *n* Norvegia *f.* **~wegian** /-'wi:dʒn/ *a & n* norvegese *mf*

nose /nəʊz/ *n* naso *m*

nose: **~bleed** *n* emorragia *f* nasale. **~dive** *n* Aeron picchiata *f*

nostalg|ia /nɒ'stældʒɪə/ *n* nostalgia *f.* **~ic** *a* nostalgico

nostril /'nɒstrəl/ *n* narice *f*

nosy /'nəʊzɪ/ *a* (**-ier, -iest**) *fam* ficcanaso *inv*

not /nɒt/ *adv* non; **he is ~** Italian non è italiano; **I hope ~** spero di no; **~ all of us have been invited** non siamo stati tutti invitati; **if ~** se no; **~ at all** niente affatto; **~ a bit** per niente; **~ even** neanche; **~ yet** non ancora; **~ only... but also...** non solo... ma anche...

notab|le /'nəʊtəbl/ *a* (*remarkable*) notevole. **~y** *adv* (*in particular*) in particolare

notary /'nəʊtərɪ/ *n* notaio *m;* **~ 'public** notaio *m*

notch /nɒtʃ/ *n* tacca *f* ● **notch up** *vt* (*score*) segnare

note /nəʊt/ *n* nota *f; (short letter; banknote)* biglietto *m; (memo, written comment etc)* appunto *m;* **~ of** ⟨*person*⟩ di spicco; ⟨*comments, event*⟩ degno di nota; **make a ~ of** prendere nota di; **take ~ of** ⟨*notice*⟩ prendere nota di ● *vt* ⟨*notice*⟩ notare; ⟨*write*⟩ annotare. **note down** *vt* annotare

'notebook *n* taccuino *m;* Comput notebook *m inv*

noted /'nəʊtɪd/ *a* noto, celebre (**for** per)

note: **~paper** *n* carta *f* da lettere. **~worthy** *a* degno di nota

nothing /'nʌθɪŋ/ *pron* niente, nulla ● *adv* niente affatto. **for ~** (*free, in vain*) per niente; (*with no reason*) senza motivo; **~ but** nient'altro che; **~ much** poco o nulla; **~ interesting** niente di interes-

---

sante; **it's ~ to do with you** non ti riguarda

notice /'nəʊtɪs/ *n* (*on board*) avviso *m;* (*review*) recensione *f;* (*termination of employment*) licenziamento *m;* [*advance*] **~** preavviso *m;* **two months ~** due mesi di preavviso; **at short ~** con breve preavviso; **until further ~** fino nuovo avviso; **give [in one's] ~** ⟨*employee:*⟩ dare le dimissioni; **give an employee ~** dare il preavviso a un impiegato; **take no ~ of** non fare caso a; **take no ~!** non farci caso! ● *vt* notare. **~able** /-əbl/ *a* evidente. **~ably** *adv* sensibilmente.

~board *n* bacheca *f*

noti|fication /nəʊtɪfɪ'keɪʃn/ *n* notifica *f.* **~fy** /'nəʊtɪfaɪ/ *vt* (*pt/pp* -**ied**) notificare

notion /'nəʊʃn/ *n* idea *f,* nozione *f.* **~s** *pl* (*Am: haberdashery*) merceria *f*

notoriety /nəʊtə'raɪətɪ/ *n* notorietà *f*

notorious /nəʊ'tɔ:rɪəs/ *a* famigerato; **be ~ for** essere tristemente famoso per

notwith'standing *prep* malgrado ● *adv* nonostante

nougat /'nu:gɑ:/ *n* torrone *m*

nought /nɔ:t/ *n* zero *m*

noun /naʊn/ *n* nome *m,* sostantivo *m*

nourish /'nʌrɪʃ/ *vt* nutrire. **~ing** *a* nutriente. **~ment** *n* nutrimento *m*

novel /'nɒvl/ *a* insolito ● *n* romanzo *m.* **~ist** *n* romanziere, -a *mf.* **~ty** *n* novità *f;* **~ties** *pl* (*objects*) oggettini *mpl*

November /nəʊ'vembə(r)/ *n* novembre *m*

novice /'nɒvɪs/ *n* novizio, -a *mf*

now /naʊ/ *adv* ora, adesso; **by ~** ormai; **just ~** proprio ora; **right ~** subito; **~ and again, ~ and then** ogni tanto; **~, ~!** su! ● *conj* [**that**] ora che, adesso che

'nowadays *adv* oggigiorno

nowhere /'nəʊ-/ *adv* in nessun posto, da nessuna parte

noxious /'nɒkʃəs/ a nocivo

nozzle /'nɒzl/ n bocchetta f

nuance /'nju:ɒs/ n sfumatura f

nuclear /'nju:klɪə(r)/ a nucleare

nucleus /'nju:klɪəs/ n (pl **-lei** /-lɪaɪ/) nucleo m

nude /nju:d/ a nudo ● n nudo m; **in the ~** nudo

nudge /nʌdʒ/ n colpetto m di gomito ● vt dare un colpetto col gomito a

nudism /'nju:dɪzm/ n nudismo m

nud|ist /'nju:dɪst/ n nudista mf. **~ity** n nudità f

nugget /'nʌgɪt/ n pepita f

nuisance /'nju:sns/ n seccatura f; (person) piaga f; **what a ~!** che seccatura!

null /nʌl/ a **~ and void** nullo

numb /nʌm/ a intorpidito; **~ with cold** intirizzito dal freddo

number /'nʌmbə(r)/ n numero m; **a ~ of people** un certo numero di persone ● vt numerare; (include) annoverare. **~-plate** n targa f

numeral /'nju:mərəl/ n numero m, cifra f

numerate /'nju:mərət/ a **be ~** saper fare i calcoli

numerical /nju:'merɪkl/ a numerico; **in ~ order** in ordine numerico

numerous /'nju:mərəs/ a numeroso

nun /nʌn/ n suora f

nurse /nɜ:s/ n infermiere, -a mf; **children's ~** bambinaia f ● vt curare

nursery /'nɜ:səri/ n stanza f dei bambini; (for plants) vivaio m; **[day] ~** asilo m. **~ rhyme** n filastrocca f. **~ school** n scuola f materna

nursing /'nɜ:sɪŋ/ n professione f d'infermiere. **~ home** n casa f di cura per anziani

nurture /'nɜ:tʃə/ vt allevare; fig coltivare

nut /nʌt/ n noce f; Techn dado m; (fam: head) zucca f. **~s** npl frutta f secca; **be ~s** fam essere svitato.

~crackers npl schiaccianoci m inv. **~meg** n noce f moscata

nutrit|ion /nju:'trɪʃn/ n nutrizione f. **~ious** /-ʃəs/ a nutriente

'nutshell n **in a ~** fig in parole povere

nuzzle /'nʌzl/ vt (horse, dog:) strofinare il muso contro

nylon /'naɪlɒn/ n nailon m; **~s** pl calze fpl di nailon ● attrib di nailon

* * *

Oo

O /əʊ/ n Teleph zero m

oaf /əʊf/ n (pl **oafs**) zoticone, -a mf

oak /əʊk/ n quercia f ● attrib di quercia

OAP n abbr (old-age pensioner) pensionato, -a mf

oar /ɔ:(r)/ n remo m. **~sman** n vogatore m

oasis /əʊ'eɪsɪs/ n (pl **oases** /-si:z/) oasi f inv

oath /əʊθ/ n giuramento m; (swearword) bestemmia f

oatmeal /'əʊt-/ n farina f d'avena

oats /əʊts/ npl avena fsg; Culin **[rolled] ~** fiocchi mpl di avena

obedien|ce /ə'bi:dɪəns/ n ubbidienza f. **~t** a ubbidiente

obese /ə'bi:s/ a obeso. **~ity** n obesità f

obey /ə'beɪ/ vt ubbidire a; osservare (instructions, rules) ● vt ubbidire

obituary /ə'bɪtjʊərɪ/ n necrologio m

object[1] /'ɒbdʒɪkt/ n oggetto m; Gram complemento m oggetto; **money is no ~** i soldi non sono un problema

object[2] /əb'dʒekt/ vi (be against) opporsi (**to** a); **~ that...** obiettare che...

objection /əb'dʒekʃn/ n obiezione f, **have no ~** non avere niente in contrario. **~able** /-əbl/ a discutibile; (person) sgradevole

objective /əb'dʒektɪv/ a oggettivo ● n obiettivo m. **~ly** adv obiettivamente. **~ity** /-'tɪvəti/ n oggettività f

obligation /ɒblɪ'ɡeɪʃn/ n obbligo m; **be under an ~** avere un obbligo; **without ~** senza impegno

obligatory /ə'blɪɡətɪ/ a obbligatorio

oblige /ə'blaɪdʒ/ vt (compel) obbligare; **much ~ed** grazie mille. **~ing** a disponibile

oblique /ə'bliːk/ a obliquo; fig indiretto ● n ~ **[stroke]** barra f

obliterate /ə'blɪtəreɪt/ vt obliterare

oblivion /ə'blɪvɪən/ n oblio m

oblivious /ə'blɪvɪəs/ a essere dimentico (**of, to** di)

oblong /'ɒblɒŋ/ a oblungo ● n rettangolo m

obnoxious /əb'nɒkʃəs/ a detestabile

oboe /'əʊbəʊ/ n oboe m inv

obscene /əb'siːn/ a osceno; (profits, wealth) vergognoso. **~ity** /-'senəti/ n oscenità f inv

obscure /əb'skjʊə(r)/ a oscuro ● vt oscurare; (confuse) mettere in ombra. **~ity** n oscurità f

obsequious /əb'siːkwɪəs/ a ossequioso

observance /əb'zɜːvəns/ n (of custom) osservanza f. **~nt** a attento. **~tion** /ɒbzə'veɪʃn/ n osservazione f

observatory /əb'zɜːvətrɪ/ n osservatorio m

observe /əb'zɜːv/ vt osservare; (notice) notare; (keep, celebrate) celebrare. **~r** n osservatore, -trice mf

obsess /əb'ses/ vt **be ~ed by** essere fissato con. **~ion** /-eʃn/ n fissazione f. **~ive** /-ɪv/ a ossessivo

obsolete /'ɒbsəliːt/ a obsoleto; (word) desueto

obstacle /'ɒbstəkl/ n ostacolo m

obstetrician /ɒbstə'trɪʃn/ n

ostetrico, -a mf. **obstetrics** /əb'stetrɪks/ n ostetricia f

obstinacy /'ɒbstɪnəsi/ n ostinazione f. **~te** /-nət/ a ostinato

obstreperous /əb'strepərəs/ a turbolento

obstruct /əb'strʌkt/ vt ostruire; (hinder) ostacolare. **~ion** /-ʌkʃn/ n ostruzione f; (obstacle) ostacolo m. **~ive** /-ɪv/ a be **~ive** (person:) creare dei problemi

obtain /əb'teɪn/ vt ottenere. **~able** /-əbl/ a ottenibile

obtrusive /əb'truːsɪv/ a (object) stonato

obtuse /əb'tjuːs/ a ottuso

obvious /'ɒbvɪəs/ a ovvio. **~ly** adv ovviamente

occasion /ə'keɪʒn/ n occasione f; (event) evento m; **on ~** talvolta; **on the ~ of** in occasione di

occasional /ə'keɪʒənl/ a saltuario; **he has the ~ glass of wine** ogni tanto beve un bicchiere di vino. **~ly** adv ogni tanto

occult /ɒ'kʌlt/ a occulto

occupant /'ɒkjʊpənt/ n occupante mf; (of vehicle) persona f a bordo

occupation /ɒkjʊ'peɪʃn/ n occupazione f; (job) professione f. **~al** a professionale

occupier /'ɒkjʊpaɪə(r)/ n residente mf

occupy /'ɒkjʊpaɪ/ vt (pt/pp **occupied**) occupare; (keep busy) tenere occupato

occur /ə'kɜː(r)/ vi (pt/pp **occurred**) accadere; (exist) trovarsi; **it ~red to me that** mi è venuto in mente che. **~rence** /ə'kʌrəns/ n (event) fatto m

ocean /'əʊʃn/ n oceano m

o'clock /ə'klɒk/ adv **it's 7 ~** sono le sette; **at 7 ~** alle sette;

octave /'ɒktɪv/ n Mus ottava f

October /ɒk'təʊbə(r)/ n ottobre m

octopus /'ɒktəpəs/ n (pl **-puses**) polpo m

odd /ɒd/ a (number) dispari; (not of set) scompagnato; (strange) strano; **forty ~** quaranta e rotti;

~ **jobs** lavoretti *mpl;* **the ~ one out** l'eccezione; **at ~ moments** a tempo perso; **have the ~ glass of wine** avere un bicchiere di vino ogni tanto

odd|ity /ˈɒdɪtɪ/ *n* stranezza *f.* **~ly** *adv* stranamente; **~ly enough** stranamente. **~ment** *n (of fabric)* scampolo *m*

odds /ɒdz/ *npl (chances)* probabilità *fpl;* **at ~** in disaccordo; **~ and ends** cianfrusaglie *fpl;* **it makes no ~** non fa alcuna differenza

ode /əud/ *n* ode *f*

odour /ˈəudə(r)/ *n* odore *m.* **~less** *a* inodore

of /ɒv/, /əv/ *prep* di; **a cup of tea/coffee** una tazza di tè/caffè; **the hem of my skirt** l'orlo della mia gonna; **the summer of 1989** l'estate del 1989; **the two of us** noi due; **made of** di; **that's very kind of you** è molto gentile da parte tua; **a friend of mine** un mio amico; **a child of three** un bambino di tre anni; **the fourth of January** il quattro gennaio; **within a year of their divorce** a circa un anno dal loro divorzio; **half of it** la metà; **the whole of the room** tutta la stanza

off /ɒf/ *prep* da; *(distant from)* lontano da; **take £10 ~ the price** ridurre il prezzo di 10 sterline; **the coast** presso la costa; **a street ~ the main road** una traversa della via principale; *(near)* una strada vicino alla via principale; **get ~ the bus** uscire dall'autobus; **leave the lid ~ the saucepan** lasciare la pentola senza il coperchio ● *adv (button, handle)* staccato; *(light, machine)* spento; *(brake)* tolto; *(tap)* chiuso; **'off'** *(on appliance)* 'off'; **2 kilometres ~** a due chilometri di distanza; **a long way ~** molto distante; *(time)* lontano; **~ and on** di tanto in tanto; **with his hat/coat ~** senza il cappello/cappot-

to; **with the light ~** a luce spenta; **20% ~** 20% di sconto; **be ~** *(leave)* andar via; *Sport* essere partito; *(food:)* essere andato a male; *(all gone)* essere finito; *(wedding, engagement:)* essere cancellato; **I'm ~ alcohol** ho smesso di bere; **be ~ one's food** non avere appetito; **she's ~ today** *(on holiday)* è in ferie oggi; *(ill)* è malata oggi; **I'm ~ home** vado a casa; **you'd be better ~ doing...** faresti meglio a fare...; **have a day ~** avere un giorno di vacanza; **drive/sail ~** andare via

offal /ˈɒfl/ *n Culin* frattaglie *fpl*

'off-beat *a* insolito

'off-chance *n* possibilità *f* remota

off-'colour *a (not well)* giù di forma; *(joke, story)* sporco

offence /əˈfens/ *n (illegal act)* reato *m;* **give ~** offendere; **take ~** offendersi **(at** per)

offend /əˈfend/ *vt* offendere. **~er** *n Jur* colpevole *mf*

offensive /əˈfensɪv/ *a* offensivo ● *n* offensiva *f*

offer /ˈɒfə(r)/ *n* offerta *f* ● *vt* offrire; opporre *(resistance);* **~ sb sth** offrire qcsa a qcno; **~ to do sth** offrirsi di fare qcsa. **~ing** *n* offerta *f*

off'hand *a (casual)* spiccio ● *adv* su due piedi

office /ˈɒfɪs/ *n* ufficio *m; (post, job)* carica *f.* **~ hours** *pl* orario *m* d'ufficio

officer /ˈɒfɪsə(r)/ *n* ufficiale *m; (police)* agente *m* [di polizia]

official /əˈfɪʃl/ *a* ufficiale ● *n* funzionario, -a *mf; Sport* dirigente *m.* **~ly** *adv* ufficialmente

officiate /əˈfɪʃɪeɪt/ *vi* officiare

offing *n* **in the ~** in vista

'off-licence *n* negozio *m* per la vendita di alcolici

'off-load *vt* scaricare

'off-putting *a fam* scoraggiante

offset *vt (pt/pp* **-set***, pres p* **-setting)** controbilanciare

'offshoot *n* ramo *m; fig* diramazione *f*

'offshore a ‹wind› di terra; ‹company, investment› offshore. ~ **rig** n piattaforma f petrolifera. ~ **shore** m inv

off·side a Sport [in] fuori gioco; ‹wheel etc› (left) sinistro; (right) destro

'offspring n prole f

off'stage adv dietro le quinte

off-'white a bianco sporco

often /'ɒfn/ adv spesso; **how ~** ogni quanto; **every so ~** una volta ogni tanto

ogle /'əʊgl/ vt mangiarsi con gli occhi

oh /əʊ/ int oh!; ~ **dear** oh Dio!; ~ **yes** ma sì

oil /ɔɪl/ n olio m; ‹petroleum› petrolio m; (for heating) nafta f ● vt oliare

oil: ~**field** n giacimento m di petrolio. ~**-painting** n pittura f a olio. ~ **refinery** n raffineria f di petrolio. ~ **rig** piattaforma f per trivellazione subacquea. ~**skins** npl vestiti mpl di tela cerata. ~**-slick** n chiazza f di petrolio. ~**-tanker** n petroliera f. ~ **well** n pozzo m petrolifero

oily /'ɔɪli/ a (-ier, -iest) unto; fig untuoso

ointment /'ɔɪntmənt/ n pomata f

OK /əʊ'keɪ/ int va bene, o.k. ● a **if that's OK with you** se ti va bene; **she's OK** (well) sta bene; **is the milk still OK?** il latte è ancora buono? ● adv (well) bene ● vt (anche okay) (pt/pp okayed) dare l'o.k.

old /əʊld/ a vecchio; ‹girlfriend› ex; **how ~ is she?** quanti anni ha?; **she is ten years ~** ha dieci anni

old: ~**-age** n vecchiaia f. ~**-age 'pensioner** n pensionato, -a mf. ~ **boy** n Sch ex-allievo m. ~**-'fashioned** a antiquato. ~ **girl** n Sch ex-allieva f. ~ **'maid** n zitella f

olive /'ɒlɪv/ n (fruit, colour) oliva f; (tree) olivo m ● a d'oliva; (colour) olivastro. ~ **branch** n fig ramo-

scello m d'olivo. ~ **'oil** n olio m di oliva

Olympic /ə'lɪmpɪk/ a olimpico; ~**s,** ~ **Games** Olimpiadi fpl

omelette /'ɒmlɪt/ n omelette f inv

omen /'əʊmən/ n presagio m

ominous /'ɒmɪnəs/ a sinistro

omission /ə'mɪʃn/ n omissione f

omit /ə'mɪt/ vt (pt/pp **omitted**) omettere; ~ **to do sth** tralasciare di fare qcsa

omnipotent /ɒm'nɪpətənt/ a onnipotente

on /ɒn/ prep su; (on horizontal surface) su, sopra; **on Monday** lunedì; **on Mondays** di lunedì; **on the first of May** il primo di maggio; **on arriving** all'arrivo; **on one's finger** ‹cut› nel dito; ‹ring› al dito; **on foot** a piedi; **on the right/left** a destra/sinistra; **on the Rhine/Thames** sul Reno/Tamigi; **on the radio/television** alla radio/televisione; **on the bus/train** in autobus/treno; **go on the bus/train** andare in autobus/treno; **get on the bus/train** salire sull'autobus/sul treno; **on me** (with me) con me; **it's on me** fam tocca a me ● adv (further on) dopo; ‹switched on, brake› inserito; (in operation) in funzione; **'on'** (on machine) 'on'; **he had his hat/coat on** portava il cappello/cappotto; **without his hat/coat** senza cappello/cappotto; **with/without the lid on** con/senza coperchio; **be on** ‹film, programme, event:› esserci; **it's not on** fam non è giusto; **be on at** fam tormentare (to per); **on and on** senza sosta; **on and off** a intervalli; **and so on** e così via; **go on** continuare, drive **on** spostarsi (con la macchina); **stick on** attaccare; **sew on** cucire

once /wʌns/ adv una volta; (formerly) un tempo; **upon a time there was** c'era una volta; **at ~** subito; (at the same time) contemporaneamente; ~ **and for all** una volta per tutte ● conj (non] appena. **~over** n fam **give sb/sth the ~-over** (look, check) dare un'occhiata veloce a qcno/qcsa

'oncoming a che si avvicina dalla direzione opposta

one /wʌn/ a uno, una; **not ~ person** nemmeno una persona ● n uno m ● pron uno; (impersonal) si; **~ another** l'un l'altro; **by ~** [a] uno a uno; **~ never knows** non si sa mai

one: **~-eyed** a con un occhio solo. **~-off** a unico. **~-parent 'family** n famiglia f con un solo genitore. **~self** pron (reflexive) si; (emphatic) sé, se stesso; **by ~self** da solo; **be proud of ~self** essere fieri di sé. **~-sided** a unilaterale. **~-way** (street) a senso unico; (ticket) di sola andata

onion /'ʌnjən/ n cipolla f

'onlooker n spettatore, -trice mf

only /'əʊnlı/ a solo; **~ child** figlio, -a mf unico, -a ● adv & conj solo, solamente; **~ just** appena

on/'off switch n pulsante m di accensione

'onset (beginning) inizio m

'onslaught /'ɒnslɔːt/ n attacco m

onus /'əʊnəs/ n **the ~ is on me** spetta a me la responsabilità (**to** di)

'onward[s] /'ɒnwəd[z]/ adv in avanti; **from then ~** da allora [in poi]

ooze /uːz/ vi fluire

opal /'əʊpl/ n opale f

opaque /əʊ'peɪk/ a opaco

open /'əʊpn/ a aperto; (flower, door) aperto; (view) ampio; (not all) pubblico; (job) vacante; **in the ~ air** all'aperto ● n **in the ~** all'aperto; fig alla luce del sole ● vt aprire ● vi (door:) aprirsi; (shop:) aprire; (flower:) sbocciare. **open up** vt aprire ● vi aprirsi

open: **~-air 'swimming pool** n piscina f all'aperto. **~ day** n giorno m di apertura al pubblico

opener /'əʊpənə(r)/ n (for tins) apriscatole m inv; (for bottles) apribottiglie m inv

opening /'əʊpənıŋ/ n apertura f; (beginning) inizio m; (job) posto m libero; (job) posto m d'apertura

openly /'əʊpənlı/ adv apertamente

open: **~-'minded** a aperto; (broadminded) di vedute larghe. **~-plan** a a pianta aperta. **~ 'sandwich** n tartina f. **~ secret** segreto m di Pulcinella. **~-ticket** biglietto m aperto. **O~ University** corsi mf universitari per corrispondenza

opera /'ɒpərə/ n opera f

operable /'ɒpərəbl/ a operabile

opera: **~-glasses** npl binocolo msg da teatro. **~-house** n teatro m lirico. **~-singer** n cantante mf lirico, -a

operate /'ɒpəreɪt/ vt far funzionare (machine, lift); azionare (lever, brake); mandare avanti (business) ● vi Techn funzionare; (be in action) essere in funzione; Mil, fig operare; **~ on** Med operare

operatic /ɒpə'rætık/ a lirico, operistico

operation /ɒpə'reɪʃn/ n operazione f; Tech funzionamento m; **in ~** Techn in funzione; **come into ~** fig entrare in funzione; (law:) entrare in vigore; **have an ~** Med subire un'operazione. **~al** a operativo; (law etc) in vigore

operative /'ɒpərətɪv/ a operativo

operator /'ɒpəreɪtə(r)/ n (user) operatore, -trice mf; Teleph centralinista mf

operetta /ɒpə'retə/ n operetta f

opinion /ə'pınjən/ n opinione f; **in my ~** secondo me. **~ated** a dogmatico

opponent /ə'pəʊnənt/ n avversario, -a mf

opportune /'ɒpətjuːn/ a opportuno. **~ist** /-'tjuːnɪst/ n opportunista mf. **~istic** a opportunistico

opportunity /ɒpə'tjuːnətı/ n opportunità f inv

oppose /ə'pəʊz/ vt opporre; **be ~ed to sth** esssere contrario a qcsa; **as ~ed to** al contrario di.

~ing *a* avversario; (*opposite*) opposto

opposite /'ɒpəzɪt/ *a* opposto; ⟨*house*⟩ di fronte; ~ **number** *fig* controparte *f*; **the** ~ **sex** l'altro sesso ● *n* contrario *m* ● *adv* di fronte ● *prep* di fronte a

opposition /ɒpə'zɪʃn/ *n* opposizione *f*

oppress /ə'pres/ *vt* opprimere. ~**ion** /-eʃn/ *n* oppressione *f*. ~**ive** /-ɪv/ *a* oppressivo; ⟨*heat*⟩ opprimente. ~**or** *n* oppressore *m*

opt /ɒpt/ *vi* ~ **for** optare per; ~ **out** dissociarsi (**of** da)

optical /'ɒptɪkl/ *a* ottico; ~ **illusion** illusione *f* ottica

optician /ɒp'tɪʃn/ *n* ottico *m*

optimis|m /'ɒptɪmɪzm/ *n* ottimismo *m*. ~**t** /-mɪst/ *n* ottimista *mf*. ~**tic** /-'mɪstɪk/ *a* ottimistico

optimum /'ɒptɪməm/ *a* ottimale ● *n* (*pl* -**ima**) optimum *m*

option /'ɒpʃn/ *n* scelta *f*; *Comm* opzione *f*. ~**al** *a* facoltativo; ~**al extras** *pl* optional *m inv*

opulen|ce /'ɒpjʊləns/ *n* opulenza *f*. ~**t** *a* opulento

or /ɔ:(r)/ *conj* o, oppure; (*after negative*) né; **or** [**else**] se no; **in a year or two** fra un anno o due

oracle /'ɒrəkl/ *n* oracolo *m*

oral /'ɔ:rəl/ *a* orale ● *n fam* esame *m* orale. ~**ly** *adv* oralmente

orange /'ɒrɪndʒ/ *n* arancia *f*; (*colour*) arancione *m* ● *a* arancione. ~**ade** /-'dʒeɪd/ *n* aranciata *f*. ~ **juice** *n* succo *m* d'arancia

orator /'ɒrətə(r)/ *n* oratore, -trice *mf*

oratorio /ɒrə'tɔ:rɪəʊ/ *n* oratorio *m*

oratory /'ɒrətərɪ/ *n* oratorio *m*

orbit /'ɔ:bɪt/ *n* orbita *f* ● *vt* orbitare. ~**al** *a* ~**al road** tangenziale *f*

orchard /'ɔ:tʃəd/ *n* frutteto *m*

orchestra /'ɔ:kɪstrə/ *n* orchestra *f*. ~**tral** /-'kestrəl/ *a* orchestrale. ~**trate** *vt* orchestrare

orchid /'ɔ:kɪd/ *n* orchidea *f*

ordain /ɔ:'deɪn/ *vt* decretare; *Relig* ordinare

ordeal /ɔ:'di:l/ *n fig* terribile esperienza *f*

order /'ɔ:də(r)/ *n* ordine *m*; *Comm* ordinazione *f*; **out of** ~ ⟨*machine*⟩ fuori servizio; **in** ~ **that** affinché; **in** ~ **to** per ● *vt* ordinare

orderly /'ɔ:dəlɪ/ *a* ordinato ● *n Mil* attendente *m*; *Med* inserviente *m*

ordinary /'ɔ:dɪnərɪ/ *a* ordinario

ordination /ɔ:dɪ'neɪʃn/ *n Relig* ordinazione *f*

ore /ɔ:(r)/ *n* minerale *m* grezzo

organ /'ɔ:gən/ *n Anat, Mus* organo *m*

organic /ɔ:'gænɪk/ *a* organico; (*without chemicals*) biologico. ~**ally** *adv* organicamente; ~**ally grown** coltivato biologicamente

organism /'ɔ:gənɪzm/ *n* organismo *m*

organist /'ɔ:gənɪst/ *n* organista *mf*

organization /ɔ:gənaɪ'zeɪʃn/ *n* organizzazione *f*

organize /'ɔ:gənaɪz/ *vt* organizzare. ~**r** *n* organizzatore, -trice *mf*

orgasm /'ɔ:gæzm/ *n* orgasmo *m*

orgy /'ɔ:dʒɪ/ *n* orgia *f*

Orient /'ɔ:rɪənt/ *n* Oriente *m*. **o**~**al** /-'entl/ *a* orientale ● *n* orientale *mf*

orient|ate /'ɔ:rɪənteɪt/ *vt* ~**ate oneself** orientarsi. ~**ation** /-'teɪʃn/ *n* orientamento *m*

origin /'ɒrɪdʒɪn/ *n* origine *f*

original /ə'rɪdʒənl/ *a* originario; (*not copied, new*) originale ● *n* originale *m*; **in the** ~ in versione originale. ~**ity** /-'nælətɪ/ *n* originalità *f*. ~**ly** *adv* originariamente

originate /ə'rɪdʒɪneɪt/ *vi* ~**e in** avere origine in. ~**or** *n* ideatore, -trice *mf*

ornament /'ɔ:nəmənt/ *n* ornamento *m*; (*on mantelpiece etc*) soprammobile *m*. ~**al** /-'mentl/ *a* ornamentale. ~**ation** /-'teɪʃn/ *n* decorazione *f*

ornate /ɔ:'neɪt/ *a* ornato

orphan /'ɔ:fn/ *n* orfano, -a *mf* ● *vt*

rendere orfano; **be ~ed** rimanere
orfano. **~age** /-ɪdʒ/ n orfanotro-
fio m

orthodox /ˈɔːθədɒks/ a ortodosso

orthopaedic /ɔːθəˈpiːdɪk/ a orto-
pedico

oscillate /ˈɒsɪleɪt/ vi oscillare

ostensibl|e /ɒˈstensəbl/ a appa-
rente. **~y** adv apparentemente

ostentat|ion /ɒstenˈteɪʃn/ n osten-
tazione f. **~ious** /-ʃəs/ a ostentato

osteopath /ˈɒstɪəpæθ/ n osteopata
mf

ostracize /ˈɒstrəsaɪz/ vt bandire

ostrich /ˈɒstrɪtʃ/ n struzzo m

other /ˈʌðə(r)/ a, pron & n altro,
-a mf; **the ~ [one]** l'altro, -a mf;
the ~ two gli altri due; **two ~s**
altri due; **the ~ people** gli altri; **any
~ questions?** altre domande?;
every ~ day (alternate days) a
giorni alterni; **the ~ day** l'altro
giorno; **the ~ evening** l'altra
sera; **someone/something or ~**
qualcuno/qualcosa ● adv ~ **than**
him tranne lui; **somehow or ~** in
qualche modo; **somewhere or ~**
da qualche parte

otherwise adv altrimenti; (differently) diversamente

otter /ˈɒtə(r)/ n lontra f

ouch /aʊtʃ/ int ahi!

ought /ɔːt/ v aux I/we ~ **to stay** do-
vrei/dovremmo rimanere; **he ~
not to have done it** non avrebbe
dovuto farlo; **that ~ to be enough**
questo dovrebbe bastare

ounce /aʊns/ n oncia f (= 28, 35 g)

our /ˈaʊə(r)/ a il nostro m, la nostra
f, i nostri mpl, le nostre fpl;
mother/father nostra madre/no-
stro padre

ours /ˈaʊəz/ poss pron il nostro m,
la nostra f, i nostri mpl, le nostre
fpl; **a friend of ~** un nostro amico;
friends of ~ dei nostri amici; **that
is ~** quello è nostro; (as opposed to
yours) quello è il nostro

ourselves /aʊəˈselvz/ pron (reflexive) ci; (emphatic) noi, noi stessi;
we poured ~ a drink ci siamo

versati da bere; **we heard it ~**
l'abbiamo sentito noi stessi; **we
are proud of ~** siamo fieri di noi;
by ~ da soli

out /aʊt/ adv fuori; (not alight)
spento; **be ~** (flower:) essere sbocciato; (workers:) essere in sciopero; (calculation:) essere sbagliato;
Sport essere fuori; (unconscious)
aver perso i sensi; (fig: not feasible) fuori questione; **the sun is ~** è
uscito il sole, **~ and about** in piedi; **get ~!** fam fuori!; **you should
get ~ more** dovresti uscire più
spesso; **~ with it!** fam sputa il rospo!; ● prep ~ **of** fuori da; (~
of date) scaduto; (passport) scaduto; (passport) scaduto; **~ of order** guasto;
~ of print/stock esaurito; **be ~ of
bed/the room** fuori dal letto/dalla
stanza; **~ of breath** senza fiato;
~ of danger fuori pericolo; **~ of
work** disoccupato; **nine ~ of ten**
nove su dieci; **be ~ of sugar/bread**
rimanere senza zucchero/pane; **go
~ of the room** uscire dalla stanza

out'bid vt (pt/pp -**bid**, pres p
-**bidding**) **~ sb** rilanciare l'offerta
di qcno

outboard a ~ **motor** motore m

outbreak n (of war) scoppio m; (of
disease) insorgenza f

outbuilding n costruzione f annessa

outburst n esplosione f

outcome n risultato m

outcry n protesta f

out'dated a sorpassato

out'do vt (pt -**did**, pp -**done**) superare

outdoor a (life, sports) all'aperto;
~ clothes pl vestiti pm per uscire;
~ swimming pool piscina f scoperta

out'doors adv all'aria aperta; **go
~** uscire all'aria aperta

outer a esterno

outfit n equipaggiamento m;
(clothes) completo m; (fam: organization) organizzazione f. **~ter**
n **men's ~ter's** negozio m di
abbigliamento maschile

'**outgoing** a (president) uscente; (mail) in partenza; (sociable) estroverso. **~s** npl uscite fpl

out'grow vi (pt -**grew**, pp -**grown**) diventare troppo grande per

'**outhouse** n costruzione f annessa

outing /'aʊtɪŋ/ n gita f

outlandish /aʊt'lændɪʃ/ a stravagante

'**outlaw** n fuorilegge mf inv ● vt dichiarare illegale

'**outlay** n spesa f

'**outlet** n sbocco m; fig sfogo m; Comm punto m [di] vendita

'**outline** n contorno m; (summary) sommario m ● vt tracciare il contorno di; (describe) descrivere

out'live vt sopravvivere a

'**outlook** n vista f; (future prospect) prospettiva f; (attitude) visione f

'**outlying** a **~ areas** pl zone fpl periferiche

out'number vt superare in numero

'**out-patient** n paziente mf esterno, -a; **~s' department** ambulatorio m

'**output** n produzione f

'**outrage** n oltraggio m ● vt oltraggiare. **~ous** /-'reɪdʒəs/ a oltraggioso; (price) scandaloso

'**outright**[1] a completo; (refusal) netto

out'right[2] adv completamente; (at once) immediatamente; (frankly) francamente

'**outset** n inizio m; **from the ~** fin dall'inizio

'**outside**[1] a esterno ● n esterno m; **from the ~** dall'esterno; **at the ~** al massimo

out'side[2] adv all'esterno, fuori; (out of doors) fuori; **go ~** andare fuori ● prep fuori da; (in front of) davanti a

out'sider n estraneo, -a mf

'**outskirts** npl sobborghi mpl

out'spoken a schietto

'**outstanding** a eccezionale; (landmark) prominente; (not settled) in sospeso

out'stretched a allungato

out'strip vt (pt/pp -**stripped**) superare

out'vote vt mettere in minoranza

'**outward** /-wəd/ a esterno; (journey) di andata ● adv verso l'esterno. **~ly** adv esternamente. **~s** adv verso l'esterno

out'weigh vt aver maggior peso di

out'wit vt (pt/pp -**witted**) battere in astuzia

oval /'əʊvl/ a ovale ● n ovale m

ovary /'əʊvəri/ n Anat ovaia f

ovation /əʊ'veɪʃn/ n ovazione f

oven /'ʌvn/ n forno m. **~-ready** a pronto da mettere in forno

over /'əʊvə(r)/ prep sopra; (across) al di là di; (during) durante; (more than) più di; **~ the phone** al telefono; **~ the page** alla pagina seguente; **all ~ Italy** in tutta [l']Italia; (travel) per l'Italia ● adv Math così tanto; (ended) finito; **~ again** un'altra volta; **~ and ~** più volte; **~ and above** oltre a; **~ here/there** qui/là; **all ~** (everywhere) dappertutto; **it's all ~** è tutto finito; **I ache all ~** ho male dappertutto; **come/bring ~** venire/portare; **turn ~** girare

over- pref (too) troppo

overall[1] /'əʊvərɔːl/ n grembiule m; **~s** pl tuta fsg [da lavoro]

overall[2] /əʊvər'ɔːl/ a complessivo; (general) generale ● adv complessivamente

over'balance vi perdere l'equilibrio

over'bearing a prepotente

'**overboard** adv Naut in mare

over'cast a coperto

over'charge vt **~ sb** far pagare più del dovuto a qcno ● vi far pagare più del dovuto

'**overcoat** n cappotto m

over'come vt (pt -**came**, pp -**come**) vincere; **be ~ by** essere sopraffatto da

over'crowded a sovraffollato

over'do vt (pt -**did**, pp -**done**) esagerare; (cook too long) stracuocere; ~ it *(fam: do too much)* strafare

'**overdose** *n* overdose *f inv*

'**overdraft** *n* scoperto *m*; **have an** ~ avere il conto scoperto

over'draw *vt (pt* -drew, *pp* -drawn) ~ one's account andare allo scoperto; be ~n by *(account:)* essere [allo] scoperto di

over'due *a* in ritardo

over'estimate *vt* sopravvalutare

'overflow¹ *n (water)* acqua *f* che deborda; *(people)* pubblico *m* in eccesso; *(outlet)* scarico *m*

over'flow² *vi* debordare

over'grown *a (garden)* coperto di erbacce

over'haul¹ *n* revisione *f*

over'haul² *vt* Techn revisionare

over'head¹ *adv* in alto

'overhead² *a* aereo; *(railway)* sopraelevato; *(lights)* da soffitto. ~s *npl* spese *fpl* generali

over'hear *vt (pt/pp* -heard) sentire per caso *(conversation)*

over'heat *vi* Auto surriscaldarsi ● *vt* surriscaldare

over'joyed *a* felicissimo

'overland *a & adv* via terra; ~ route via *f* terrestre

over'lap *v (pt/pp* -lapped) ● *vi* sovrapporsi ● *vt* sovrapporre

'overleaf *adv* sul retro

over'load *vt* sovraccaricare

over'look *vt* dominare; *(fail to see, ignore)* lasciarsi sfuggire

overly /'əʊvəlɪ/ *adv* eccessivamente

over'night¹ *adv* per la notte; **stay** ~ fermarsi a dormire

'overnight² *a* notturno; ~ **bag** piccola borsa *f* da viaggio; ~ **stay** sosta *f* per la notte

'overpass *n* cavalcavia *m inv*

over'pay *vt (pt/pp* -paid) strapagare

over'populated *a* sovrappopolato

over'power *vt* sopraffare. ~ing *a* insostenibile

over'priced *a* troppo caro

overpro'duce *vt* produrre in eccesso

over'rate *vt* sopravvalutare. ~d *a* sopravvalutato

over'reach *vt* ~ oneself puntare troppo in alto

overre'act *vi* avere una reazione eccessiva. ~ion *n* reazione *f* eccessiva

over'rid|e *vt (pt* -rode, *pp* -ridden) passare sopra a. ~ing *a* prevalente

over'rule *vt* annullare *(decision)*

over'run *vt (pt* -ran, *pp* -run, *pres p* -running) invadere; oltrepassare *(time)*; be ~ with essere invaso da

over'seas¹ *adv* oltremare

over'seas² *a* d'oltremare

over'see *vt (pt* -saw, *pp* -seen) sorvegliare

over'shadow *vt* adombrare

over'shoot *vt (pt/pp* -shot) oltrepassare

'oversight *n* disattenzione *f*; an ~ una svista

over'sleep *vi (pt/pp* -slept) svegliarsi troppo tardi

over'step *vt (pt/pp* -stepped) ~ the mark oltrepassare ogni limite

overt /əʊ'vɜːt/ *a* palese

over'tak|e *vt/i (pt* -took, *pp* -taken) sorpassare. ~ing *n* sorpasso *m*; no ~ing divieto di sorpasso

over'tax *vt fig* abusare di

'overthrow¹ *n* Pol rovesciamento *m*

over'throw² *vt (pt* -threw, *pp* -thrown) Pol rovesciare

'overtime *n* lavoro *m* straordinario ● *adv* work ~ fare lo straordinario

over'tired *a* sovraffaticato

'overtone *n fig* sfumatura *f*

overture /'əʊvətjʊə(r)/ *n* Mus preludio *m*; ~s *pl fig* approccio *msg*

over'turn *vt* ribaltare ● *vi* ribaltarsi

'overweight *a* sovrappeso

over'whelm /-'welm/ *vt* sommergere (with di); *(with emotion)* confondere. **~ing** a travolgente; ⟨victory, majority⟩ schiacciante

over'work n lavoro m eccessivo ● vt far lavorare eccessivamente ● vi lavorare eccessivamente

ow|e /əʊ/ vt also fig dovere ⟨[to] sb a qcno⟩; **~e sb sth** dovere qcsa a qcno. **~ing** a be **~ing** ⟨money⟩: essere da pagare ● prep **~ing to** a causa di

owl /aʊl/ n gufo m

own[1] /əʊn/ a proprio ● pron **a car of my ~** una macchina per conto mio; **on one's ~** da solo; **hold one's ~** with tener testa a; **get one's ~ back** fam prendersi una rivincita

own[2] vt possedere; ⟨confess⟩ ammettere; **I don't ~ it** non mi appartiene. **own up** vi confessare ⟨to sth qcsa⟩

owner /'əʊnə(r)/ n proprietario, -a mf. **~ship** n proprietà f

ox /ɒks/ n (pl **oxen**) bue m (pl buoi)

oxide /'ɒksaɪd/ n ossido m

oxygen /'ɒksɪdʒən/ n ossigeno m; **~ mask** maschera f a ossigeno

oyster /'ɔɪstə(r)/ n ostrica f

ozone /'əʊzəʊn/ n ozono m. **~-'friendly** a che non danneggia l'ozono. **~ layer** n fascia f d'ozono

....

Pp

....

PA abbr (**per annum**) all'anno

pace /peɪs/ n passo m; ⟨speed⟩ ritmo m; **keep ~ with** camminare di pari passo con ● vi **~ up and down** camminare avanti e indietro. **~-maker** n Med pacemaker m; ⟨runner⟩ battistrada m

Pacific /pə'sɪfɪk/ a & n **the ~** [**Ocean**] l'oceano m Pacifico, il Pacifico

pacifier /'pæsɪfaɪə(r)/ n Am ciuccio m, succhiotto m

pacifist /'pæsɪfɪst/ n pacifista mf

pacify /'pæsɪfaɪ/ vt (pt/pp **-ied**) placare ⟨person⟩; pacificare ⟨country⟩

pack /pæk/ n ⟨of cards⟩ mazzo m; ⟨of hounds⟩ muta f; ⟨of wolves, thieves⟩ branco m; ⟨of cigarettes etc⟩ pacchetto m; **a ~ of lies** un mucchio di bugie ● vt impacchettare ⟨article⟩; fare ⟨suitcase⟩; mettere in valigia ⟨swimsuit etc⟩; ⟨press down⟩ comprimere; **~ed [out]** ⟨crowded⟩ pieno zeppo ● vi fare i bagagli; **send sb ~ing** fam mandare qcno a stendere. **pack up** vt impacchettare ● vi ⟨machine⟩ piantare in asso

package /'pækɪdʒ/ n pacco m ● vt impacchettare. **~ deal** offerta f tutto compreso. **~ holiday** n vacanza f organizzata. **~ tour** viaggio m organizzato

packaging /'pækɪdʒɪŋ/ n confezione f

packed 'lunch n pranzo m al sacco

packet /'pækɪt/ n pacchetto m; **cost a ~** fam costare un sacco

packing /'pækɪŋ/ n imballaggio m

pact /pækt/ n patto m

pad[1] /pæd/ n imbottitura f; ⟨for writing⟩ bloc-notes m, taccuino m; ⟨fam: home⟩ [piccolo] appartamento m ● vt (pt/pp **padded**) imbottire. **pad out** vt gonfiare

pad[2] vi (pt/pp **padded**) camminare con passo felpato

padded /'pædɪd/ a **~ bra** reggiseno m imbottito

padding /'pædɪŋ/ n imbottitura f; ⟨in written work⟩ fronzoli mpl

paddle[1] /'pæd(ə)l/ n pagaia f ● vt ⟨row⟩ spingere remando

paddle[2] vi ⟨wade⟩ sguazzare

paddock /'pædək/ n recinto m

padlock /'pædlɒk/ n lucchetto m ● vt chiudere con lucchetto

paediatrician /piːdɪə'trɪʃn/ n pediatra mf

paediatrics /piːdɪ'ætrɪks/ n pediatria f

page[1] /peɪdʒ/ n pagina f

page² n (boy) paggetto m; (in hotel) fattorino m ●vt far chiamare (person)

pageant /'pædʒənt/ n parata f. **~ry** n cerimoniale m

pager /'peɪdʒə(r)/ n cercapersone m inv

paid /peɪd/ see **pay** ●a ~ **employment** lavoro m remunerato; **put ~ to** mettere un termine a

pail /peɪl/ n secchio m

pain /peɪn/ n dolore m; **be in ~** soffrire; **take ~s** darsi un gran d'affare; **~ in the neck** fam spina f nel fianco

pain: **~ful** a doloroso; (laborious) penoso.. **~killer** n calmante m. **~less** a indolore

painstaking /'peɪnzteɪkɪŋ/ a minuzioso

paint /peɪnt/ n pittura f; **~s** colori mpl ●vt/i pitturare; (artist:) dipingere. **~brush** n pennello m. **~er** n pittore, -trice mf; (decorator) imbianchino m. **~ing** n pittura f; (picture) dipinto m. **~work** n pittura f

pair /peə(r)/ n paio m; (of people) coppia f; **~ of trousers** paio m di pantaloni; **~ of scissors** paio m di forbici

pajamas /pə'dʒɑːməz/ npl Am pigiama msg

Pakistan /pɑːkɪ'stɑːn/ n Pakistan m, **~i** a pakistano ●n pakistano, -a mf

pal /pæl/ n fam amico, -a mf

palace /'pælɪs/ n palazzo m

palatable /'pælətəbl/ a gradevole (al gusto)

palate /'pælət/ n palato m

palatial /pə'leɪʃl/ a sontuoso

palaver /pə'lɑːvə(r)/ n (fam: fuss) storie fpl

pale /peɪl/ a pallido

Palestin|e /'pælɪstaɪn/ n Palestina f. **~ian** /pælɪ'stɪnɪən/ a palestinese ●n palestinese mf

palette /'pælɪt/ n tavolozza f

pallid /'pælɪd/ a pallido. **~or** n pallore m

palm /pɑːm/ n palmo m; (tree) palma f. P**~ 'Sunday** n Domenica f delle Palme. **palm off** vt **~ sth off on sb** rifilare qcsa a qcno

palpable /'pælpəbl/ a palpabile; (perceptible) tangibile

palpitat|e /'pælpɪteɪt/ vi palpitare. **~ions** /-'teɪʃnz/ npl palpitazioni fpl

paltry /'pɔːltrɪ/ a (-ier, -iest) insignificante

pamper /'pæmpə(r)/ vt viziare

pamphlet /'pæmflɪt/ n opuscolo m

pan /pæn/ n tegame m, pentola f; (for frying) padella f; (of scales) piatto m ●vt (pt/pp panned) (fam: criticize) stroncare

panache /pə'næʃ/ n stile m

pancake n crêpe f inv, frittella f

pancreas /'pæŋkrɪəs/ n pancreas m inv

panda /'pændə/ n panda m inv. **~ car** n macchina f della polizia

pandemonium /pændɪ'məʊnɪəm/ n pandemonio m

pander /'pændə(r)/ vi **~ to sb** compiacere qcno

pane /peɪn/ n **~ [of glass]** vetro m

panel /'pænl/ n pannello m; (group of experts) giuria f; **~ of experts** gruppo m di esperti. **~ling** n pannelli mpl

pang /pæŋ/ n **~s of hunger** morsi mpl della fame; **~s of conscience** rimorsi mpl di coscienza

panic /'pænɪk/ n panico m ●vi (pt/pp panicked) lasciarsi prendere dal panico. **~-stricken** a in preda al panico

panoram|a /pænə'rɑːmə/ n panorama m. **~ic** /-'ræmɪk/ a panoramico

pansy /'pænzɪ/ n viola f del pensiero; (fam: effeminate man) finocchio m

pant /pænt/ vi ansimare

panther /'pænθə(r)/ n pantera f

panties /'pæntɪz/ npl mutandine fpl

pantomime /'pæntəmaɪm/ n pantomima f

pantry /'pæntrɪ/ n dispensa f

pants /pænts/ npl (underwear) mutande fpl; (woman's) mutandine fpl; (trousers) pantaloni mpl

'pantyhose n Am collant m pl

papal /'peɪpl/ a papale

paper /'peɪpə(r)/ n carta f; (wallpaper) carta f da parati; (newspaper) giornale m; (exam) esame m; (treatise) saggio m; **~s** pl (documents) documenti mpl; (for identification) documento m [d'identità]; **on ~** in teoria; **put down on ~** mettere per iscritto ● attrib di carta ● vt tappezzare

paper: **~back** n edizione f economica. **~clip** n graffetta f. **~knife** n tagliacarte m inv. **~weight** n fermacarte m inv. **~work** n lavoro m d'ufficio

par /pɑː(r)/ n (in golf) par m inv; **on a ~ with** alla pari con; **feel below ~** essere un po' giù di tono

parable /'pærəbl/ n parabola f

parachut|e /'pærəʃuːt/ n paracadute m ● vi lanciarsi col paracadute. **~ist** n paracadutista mf

parade /pə'reɪd/ n (military) parata f militare ● vi sfilare ● vt (show off) far sfoggio di

paradise /'pærədaɪs/ n paradiso m

paradox /'pærədɒks/ n paradosso m. **~ical** /-'dɒksɪkl/ a paradossale. **~ically** adv paradossalmente

paraffin /'pærəfɪn/ n paraffina f

paragon /'pærəgən/ n **~ of virtue** modello m di virtù

paragraph /'pærəgrɑːf/ n paragrafo m

parallel /'pærəlel/ a & adv parallelo. **~ bars** npl parallele fpl. **~ port** n Comput porta f parallela in Geog, fig parallelo m; (line) parallela f ● vt essere paragonabile a

paralyse /'pærəlaɪz/ vt also fig paralizzare

paralysis /pə'ræləsɪs/ n (pl **-ses** /-siːz/ paralisi f inv

parameter /pə'ræmɪtə(r)/ n parametro m

paramount /'pærəmaʊnt/ a supremo; **be ~** essere essenziale

paranoia /pærə'nɔɪə/ n paranoia f

paranoid /'pærənɔɪd/ a paranoico

paraphernalia /pærəfə'neɪlɪə/ n armamentario m

paraphrase /'pærəfreɪz/ n parafrasi f ● vt parafrasare

paraplegic /pærə'pliːdʒɪk/ a paraplegico ● n paraplegico, -a mf

parasite /'pærəsaɪt/ n parassita mf

parasol /'pærəsɒl/ n parasole m

paratrooper /'pærətruːpə(r)/ n paracadutista m

parcel /'pɑːsl/ n pacco m

parch /pɑːtʃ/ vt disseccare; **be ~ed** (person) morire dalla sete

pardon /'pɑːdn/ n perdono m; Jur grazia f; **~?** prego?; **I beg your ~?** fml chiedo scusa?; **I do beg your ~** (sorry) chiedo scusa! ● vt perdonare; Jur graziare

pare /peə(r)/ vt (peel) pelare

parent /'peərənt/ n genitore, -trice mf; **~s** pl genitori mpl. **~al** /pə'rentl/ a dei genitori

parenthesis /pə'renθəsɪs/ n (pl **-ses** /-siːz/) parentesi m inv

Paris /'pærɪs/ n Parigi f

parish /'pærɪʃ/ n parrocchia f. **~ioner** /pə'rɪʃənə(r)/ n parrocchiano, -a mf

Parisian /pə'rɪzɪən/ a & n parigino, -a mf

parity /'pærətɪ/ n parità f

park /pɑːk/ n parco m ● vt/i Auto posteggiare, parcheggiare; **~ oneself** fam installarsi

parka /'pɑːkə/ n parka m inv

parking /'pɑːkɪŋ/ n parcheggio m, posteggio m; **'no ~'** 'divieto di sosta'. **~-lot** n Am posteggio m, parcheggio m. **~-meter** n parchimetro m. **~ space** n posteggio m, parcheggio m

parliament /'pɑːləmənt/ n parlamento m. **~ary** /-'mentərɪ/ a parlamentare

parlour /'pɑːlə(r)/ n salotto m

parochial /pəˈrəʊkɪəl/ a parrocchiale; *fig* ristretto

parody /ˈpærədɪ/ n parodia f ●vt (pt/pp **-ied**) parodiare

parole /pəˈrəʊl/ n on ~ in libertà condizionale●vt mettere in libertà condizionale

parquet /ˈpɑːkeɪ/ n ~ **floor** parquet m

parrot /ˈpærət/ n pappagallo m

parry /ˈpærɪ/ vt (pt/pp **-ied**) parare ⟨*blow*⟩; (*in fencing*) eludere

parsimonious /pɑːsɪˈməʊnɪəs/ a parsimonioso

parsley /ˈpɑːslɪ/ n prezzemolo m

parsnip /ˈpɑːsnɪp/ n pastinaca f

parson /ˈpɑːsn/ n pastore m

part /pɑːt/ n parte f; (*of machine*) pezzo m; **for my** ~ per quanto mi riguarda; **on the** ~ **of** da parte di; **take sb's** ~ prendere le parti di qcno; **take** ~ **in** prendere parte a ●adv in parte ●vt ~ **one's hair** farsi la riga ●vi ⟨*people*⟩ separarsi; ~ **with** separarsi da

part-ex'change n take in ~ prendere indietro

partial /ˈpɑːʃl/ a parziale; **be** ~ **to** aver un debole per. **~ly** adv parzialmente

particip|ant /pɑːˈtɪsɪpənt/ n partecipante mf. **~ate** /-peɪt/ vi partecipare (**in** a). **~ation** /-ˈpeɪʃn/ n partecipazione f

participle /ˈpɑːtɪsɪpl/ n participio m; **present/past** ~ participio m presente/passato

particle /ˈpɑːtɪkl/ n Phys, Gram particella f

particular /pəˈtɪkjʊlə(r)/ a particolare; (*precise*) meticoloso; *pej* noioso; **in** ~ in particolare. **~ly** adv particolarmente. **~s** npl particolari mpl

parting /ˈpɑːtɪŋ/ n separazione f; (*in hair*) scriminatura f ● attrib di commiato

partisan /pɑːtɪˈzæn/ n partigiano, -a mf

partition /pɑːˈtɪʃn/ n (*wall*) pareto f divisoria; *Pol* divisione f ● vt di-

videre (*in parti*). **partition off** vt separare

partly /ˈpɑːtlɪ/ adv in parte

partner /ˈpɑːtnə(r)/ n Comm socio, -a mf; (*sport*, *in relationship*) compagno, -a mf. **~ship** n Comm società f

partridge /ˈpɑːtrɪdʒ/ n pernice f

part-'time a & adv part time; **be** or **work** ~ lavorare part time

party /ˈpɑːtɪ/ n ricevimento m, festa f; (*group*) gruppo m; *Pol* partito m; *Jur* parte f [in causa]; **be** ~ **to** essere parte attiva in

'party line[1] n Teleph duplex m inv

'party line[2] n Pol linea f del partito

pass /pɑːs/ n lasciapassare m inv; (*in mountains*) passo m; *Sport* passaggio m; *Sch* (*mark*) [voto m] sufficiente m; **make a** ~ **at** *fam* tentare le avances a ● vt passare; (*overtake*) sorpassare; (*approve*) far passare; fare ⟨*remark*⟩; *Jur* pronunciare ⟨*sentence*⟩; ~ **the time** passare il tempo ● vi passare; (*in exam*) essere promosso. **pass away** vi mancare. **pass down** vt passare; *fig* trasmettere. **pass out** vi *fam* svenire. **pass round** vt far passare. **pass through** vt attraversare. **pass up** vt passare; (*fam*: *miss*) lasciarsi scappare

passable /ˈpɑːsəbl/ a ⟨*road*⟩ praticabile; (*satisfactory*) passabile

passage /ˈpæsɪdʒ/ n passaggio m; (*corridor*) corridoio m; (*voyage*) traversata f

passenger /ˈpæsɪndʒə(r)/ n passeggero, -a mf. ~ **seat** n posto m accanto al guidatore

passer-by /pɑːsəˈbaɪ/ n (pl ~**s-by**) passante m

'passing place n piazzola f di sosta per consentire il transito dei veicoli nei due sensi

passion /ˈpæʃn/ n passione f. **~ate** /-ət/ a appassionato

passive /ˈpæsɪv/ a passivo ●n passivo m. **~ness** n passività f

'**pass-mark** *n Sch* [voto *m*] sufficiente *m*

Passover /'pɑːsəuvə(r)/ *n* Pasqua *f* ebraica

pass: ~**port** *n* passaporto *m*. ~**word** *n* parola *f* d'ordine

past /pɑːst/ *a* passato; (*former*) ex; **in the** ~ **few days** nei giorni scorsi; **that's all** ~ tutto questo è passato; **the** ~ **week** la settimana scorsa ●*n* passato *m* ●*prep* oltre; **at ten** ~ **two** alle due e dieci ●*adv* oltre; **go/come** ~ passare

pasta /'pæstə/ *n* pasta[sciutta] *f*

paste /peɪst/ *n* pasta *f*; (*dough*) impasto *m*; (*adhesive*) colla *f* ●*vt* incollare

pastel /'pæstl/ *n* pastello *m* ●*attrib* pastello

pasteurize /'pɑːstʃəraɪz/ *vt* pastorizzare

pastille /'pæstl/ *n* pastiglia *f*

pastime /'pɑːstaɪm/ *n* passatempo *m*

pastoral /'pɑːstərəl/ *a* pastorale

pastrami /pæ'strɑːmi/ *n* carne *f* di manzo affumicata

pastry /'peɪstrɪ/ *n* pasta *f*; ~**ies** pasticcini *mpl*

pasture /'pɑːstʃə(r)/ *n* pascolo *m*

pasty[1] /'pæstɪ/ *n* ≈ pasticcio *m*

pasty[2] /'peɪstɪ/ *a* smorto

pat /pæt/ *n* buffetto *m*; (*of butter*) pezzetto *m* ●*adv* **have sth off** ~ conoscere qcsa a menadito ●*vt* (*pt/pp* patted) dare un buffetto a; ~ **sb on the back** *fig* congratularsi con qcno

patch /pætʃ/ *n* toppa *f*; (*spot*) chiazza *f*; (*period*) periodo *m*; **not a** ~ **on** *fam* molto inferiore a ●*vt* mettere una toppa su. **patch up** *vt* riparare alla bell'e meglio; appianare ⟨*quarrel*⟩

patchy /'pætʃɪ/ *a* incostante

pâté /'pæteɪ/ *n* pâté *m inv*

patent /'peɪtnt/ *a* palese ●*n* brevetto *m* ●*vt* brevettare. ~ **leather shoes** *npl* scarpe *fpl* di vernice. ~**ly** *adv* in modo palese

patern|al /pə'tɜːnl/ *a* paterno. ~**ity** *n* paternità *f inv*

path /pɑːθ/ *n* (*pl* ~**s** /pɑːðz/) sentiero *m*; (*orbit*) traiettoria *m*; *fig* strada *f*

pathetic /pə'θetɪk/ *a* patetico; (*fam: very bad*) penoso

patholog|ical /pæθə'lɒdʒɪkl/ *a* patologico. ~**ist** /pə'θɒlədʒɪst/ *n* patologo, -a *mf*. ~**y** patologia *f*

pathos /'peɪθɒs/ *n* pathos *m*

patience /'peɪʃns/ *n* pazienza *f*; (*game*) solitario *m*

patient /'peɪʃnt/ *a* paziente ●*n* paziente *mf*. ~**ly** *adv* pazientemente

patio /'pætɪəʊ/ *n* terrazza *f*

patriot /'pætrɪət/ *n* patriota *mf*. ~**ic** /-'ɒtɪk/ *a* patriottico. ~**ism** *n* patriottismo *m*

patrol /pə'trəʊl/ *n* pattuglia *f* ●*vt/i* pattugliare. ~ **car** *n* autopattuglia *f*

patron /'peɪtrən/ *n* patrono *m*; (*of charity*) benefattore, -trice *mf*; (*of the arts*) mecenate *mf*; (*customer*) cliente *mf*

patroniz|e /'pætrənaɪz/ *vt* frequentare abitualmente; *fig* trattare con condiscendenza. ~**ing** *a* condiscendente. ~**ingly** *adv* con condiscendenza

patter[1] /'pætə(r)/ *n* picchiettio *m* ●*vi* picchiettare

patter[2] *n* (*of salesman*) chiacchiere *fpl*

pattern /'pætn/ *n* disegno *m* (*stampato*); (*for knitting, sewing*) modello *m*

paunch /pɔːntʃ/ *n* pancia *f*

pause /pɔːz/ *n* pausa *f* ●*vi* fare una pausa

pave /peɪv/ *vt* pavimentare; ~ **the way** preparare la strada (**for** a). ~**ment** *n* marciapiede *m*

pavilion /pə'vɪljən/ *n* padiglione *m*

paw /pɔː/ *n* zampa *f* ●*vt fam* mettere le zampe addosso a

pawn[1] /pɔːn/ *n* (*in chess*) pedone *m*; *fig* pedina *f*

pawn[2] *vt* impegnare ●*n* **in** ~ in pegno. ~**broker** *n* prestatore, -trice *mf* su pegno. **~shop** *n* monte *m* di pietà

pay /peɪ/ *n* paga *f*; **in the ~ of** al soldo di ● *v* (*pt/pp* **paid**) ● *vt* pagare; prestare ⟨*attention*⟩; **~ cash** pagare in contanti ● *vi* pagare; (*be profitable*) rendere; **it doesn't ~ to...** *fig* è fatica sprecata...; **~ for** sth pagare per qcsa. **pay back** *vt* ripagare. **pay in** *vt* versare. **pay off** *vt* saldare ⟨*debt*⟩ ● *vi fig* dare dei frutti. **pay up** *vi* pagare

payable /ˈpeɪəbl/ *a* pagabile; **make ~ to** intestare a

payee /peɪˈiː/ *n* beneficiario *m* (*di una somma*)

payment /ˈpeɪmənt/ *n* pagamento *m*

pay: ~ packet *n* busta *f* paga. **~ phone** *n* telefono *m* pubblico

PC *n abbr* (**personal computer**) PC *m inv*

pea /piː/ *n* pisello *m*

peace /piːs/ *n* pace *f*; **~ of mind** tranquillità *f*

peace|able /ˈpiːsəbl/ *a* pacifico. **~ful** *a* calmo, sereno. **~fully** *adv* in pace. **~maker** *n* mediatore, -trice *mf*

peach /piːtʃ/ *n* pesca *f*; (*tree*) pesco *m*

peacock /ˈpiːkɒk/ *n* pavone *m*

peak /piːk/ *n* picco *m*; *fig* culmine *m*. **~ed 'cap** *n* berretto *m* a punta. **~ hours** *npl* ore *fpl* di punta

peaky /ˈpiːkɪ/ *a* malaticcio

peal /piːl/ *n* ⟨*of bells*⟩ scampanio *m*; **~s of laughter** fragore *m f* di risate

'peanut *n* nocciolina *f* [americana]; **~s** *fam* miseria *f*

pear /peə(r)/ *n* pera *f*; (*tree*) pero *m*

pearl /pɜːl/ *n* perla *f*

peasant /ˈpeznt/ *n* contadino, -a *mf*

pebble /ˈpebl/ *n* ciottolo *m*

peck /pek/ *n* beccata *f*; (*kiss*) bacetto *m* ● *vt* beccare; (*kiss*) dare un bacetto a. **~ing order** *n* gerarchia *f*. **peck at** *vt* beccare

peckish /ˈpekɪʃ/ *a* **be ~** *fam* avere un languorino [allo stomaco]

peculiar /prˈkjuːlɪə(r)/ *a* strano; (*special*) particolare; **~ to** tipico di. **~ity** /-ˈærɪtɪ/ *n* stranezza *f*; (*feature*) particolarità *f inv*

pedal /ˈpedl/ *n* pedale *m* ● *vi* pedalare. **~ bin** *n* pattumiera *f* a pedale

pedantic /prˈdæntɪk/ *a* pedante

pedestal /ˈpedɪstl/ *n* piedistallo *m*

pedestrian /prˈdestrɪən/ *n* pedone *m* ● *a fig* scadente. **~ 'crossing** *n* passaggio *m* pedonale. **~ 'precinct** *n* zona *f* pedonale

pedicure /ˈpedɪkjʊə(r)/ *n* pedicure *f inv*

pedigree /ˈpedɪgriː/ *n* pedigree *m inv*; (*of person*) lignaggio *m* ● *attrib* ⟨*animal*⟩ di razza, con pedigree

pee /piː/ *vi* (*pt/pp* **peed**) *fam* fare [la] pipì

peek /piːk/ *vi fam* sbirciare

peel /piːl/ *n* buccia *f* ● *vt* sbucciare ● *vi* ⟨*nose etc.*⟩ spellarsi; ⟨*paint*⟩ staccarsi

peep /piːp/ *n* sbirciata *f* ● *vi* sbirciare

peer¹ /pɪə(r)/ *vi* **~ at** scrutare

peer² *n* nobile *m*; **his ~s** *pl* (*in rank*) i suoi pari *mpl*; (*in age*) i suoi coetanei *mpl*. **~age** *n* nobiltà *f*

peeved /piːvd/ *a fam* irritato

peg /peg/ *n* (*hook*) piolo *m*; (*for tent*) picchetto *m*; (*for clothes*) molletta *f*. **~ off the ~** *fam* prêt-à-porter

pejorative /prˈdʒɒrətɪv/ *a* peggiorativo

pelican /ˈpelɪkən/ *n* pellicano *m*

pellet /ˈpelɪt/ *n* pallottola *f*

pelt /pelt/ *vt* bombardare ● *vi* (*fam*: *run fast*) catapultarsi; **~ [down]** ⟨*rain*⟩ venir giù a fiotti

pelvis /ˈpelvɪs/ *n Anat* bacino *m*

pen¹ /pen/ *n* (*for animals*) recinto *m*

pen² *n* penna *f*; (*ball-point*) penna *f* a sfera

penal /ˈpiːnl/ *a* penale. **~ize** *vt* penalizzare

penalty /ˈpenltɪ/ *n* sanzione *f*;

(*fine*) multa *f*; (*in football*) ~
[kick] [calcio *m* di] rigore *m*; ~
area or **box** area *f* di rigore
penance /'penəns/ *n* penitenza *f*
pence /pens/ *see* **penny**
pencil /'pensl/ *n* matita *f*.
~**-sharpener** *n* temperamatite *m*
inv
pendant /'pendənt/ *n* ciondolo *m*
pending /'pendɪŋ/ *a* in sospeso
● *prep* in attesa di
pendulum /'pendjʊləm/ *n* pendolo *m*
penetrat|e /'penɪtreɪt/ *vt/i* penetrare. ~**ing** *a* acuto; (*sound, stare*)
penetrante. ~**ion** /-'treɪʃn/ *n*
penetrazione *f*
'penfriend *n* amico, -a *mf* di penna
penguin /'peŋgwɪn/ *n* pinguino *m*
penicillin /penɪ'sɪlɪn/ *n* penicillina *f*
peninsula /pɪ'nɪnsjʊlə/ *n* penisola *f*
penis /'piːnɪs/ *n* pene *m*
peniten|ce /'penɪtəns/ *n* penitenza
f. ~**t** *a* penitente ● *n* penitente *mf*
penitentiary /penɪ'tenʃərɪ/ *n* Am
penitenziario *m*
pen: ~**knife** *n* temperino *m*.
~**-name** *n* pseudonimo *m*
pennant /'penənt/ *n* bandiera *f*
penniless /'penɪlɪs/ *a* senza un soldo
penny /'penɪ/ *n* (*pl* **pence**: *single coins* **pennies**) penny *m*; Am centesimo *m*; **spend a** ~ *fam* andare in bagno
pension /'penʃn/ *n* pensione *f*. ~**er** *n* pensionato, -a *mf*
pensive /'pensɪv/ *a* pensoso
Pentecost /'pentɪkɒst/ *n* Pentecoste *f*
pent-up /'pentʌp/ *a* represso
penultimate /pɪ'nʌltɪmət/ *a* penultimo
people /'piːpl/ *npl* persone *fpl*,
gente *fsg*; (*citizens*) popolo *msg*; **a lot of** ~ una marea di gente; **the** ~ la gente; **English** ~ gli inglesi; ~ **say** si dice; **for four** ~ per quattro
● *vt* popolare

pepper /'pepə(r)/ *n* pepe *m*; (*vegetable*) peperone *m* ● *vt* (*season*) pepare
pepper: ~**corn** *n* grano *m* di pepe.
~ **mill** *n* macinapepe *m* *inv*. ~**mint** *n* menta *f* peperita; (*sweet*) caramella *f* alla menta. ~**pot** *n* pepiera *f*
per /pɜː(r)/ *prep* per; ~ **annum** all'anno; ~ **cent** percento
perceive /pə'siːv/ *vt* percepire; (*interpret*) interpretare
percentage /pə'sentɪdʒ/ *n* percentuale *f*
perceptible /pə'septəbl/ *a* percettibile; (*difference*) sensibile
perception /pə'sepʃn/ *n* percezione *f*. ~**ive** /-tɪv/ *a* perspicace
perch /pɜːtʃ/ *n* pertica *f* ● *vi* 〈*bird:*〉 appollaiarsi
percolator /'pɜːkəleɪtə(r)/ *n* caffettiera *f* a filtro
percussion /pə'kʌʃn/ *n* percussione *f*. ~ **instrument** *n* strumento *f* a percussione
peremptory /pə'remptərɪ/ *a* perentorio
perennial /pə'renɪəl/ *a* perenne
● *n* pianta *f* perenne
perfect[1] /'pɜːfɪkt/ *a* perfetto ● *n* Gram passato *m* prossimo
perfect[2] /pə'fekt/ *vt* perfezionare.
~**ion** /-ekʃn/ *n* perfezione *f*; **to** ~**ion** alla perfezione. ~**ionist** *n* perfezionista *mf*
perfectly /'pɜːfɪktlɪ/ *adv* perfettamente
perforat|e /'pɜːfəreɪt/ *vt* perforare.
~**ed** *a* perforato; (*ulcer*) perforante. ~**ion** *n* perforazione *f*
perform /pə'fɔːm/ *vt* compiere,
fare; eseguire 〈*operation, sonata*〉;
recitare 〈*role*〉; mettere in scena
〈*play*〉 ● *vi* Theat recitare; Techn
funzionare. ~**ance** *n* esecuzione *f*;
(*at theatre, cinema*) rappresentazione *f*; Techn rendimento *m*. ~**er**
n artista *mf*
perfume /'pɜːfjuːm/ *n* profumo *m*
perfunctory /pə'fʌŋktərɪ/ *a* superficiale
perhaps /pə'hæps/ *adv* forse

peril /'perɪl/ n pericolo m. **~ous** /-əs/ a pericoloso

perimeter /pə'rɪmɪtə(r)/ n perimetro m

period /'pɪərɪəd/ n periodo m; (menstruation) mestruazioni fpl; Sch ora f di lezione; (full stop) punto m fermo ● attrib ⟨costume⟩ d'epoca; ⟨furniture⟩ in stile. **~ic** /-'ɒdɪk/ a periodico. **~ical** /-'ɒdɪk/ n periodico m, rivista f

peripheral /pə'rɪfərəl/ a periferico. **~y** n periferia f

periscope /'perɪskəʊp/ n periscopio m

perish /'perɪʃ/ vi (rot) deteriorarsi; (die) perire. **~able** /-əbl/ a deteriorabile

perjur|e /'pɜːdʒə(r)/ vt **~e** oneself spergiurare. **~y** n spergiuro m

perk /pɜːk/ n fam vantaggio m

perk up vt tirare su ● vi tirarsi su

perky /'pɜːkɪ/ a allegro

perm /pɜːm/ n permanente f ● vt **~ sb's** hair fare la permanente a qno

permanent /'pɜːmənənt/ a permanente; ⟨job, address⟩ stabile. **~ly** adv stabilmente

permeate /'pɜːmɪeɪt/ vt impregnare

permissible /pə'mɪsəbl/ a ammissibile

permission /pə'mɪʃn/ n permesso m

permissive /pə'mɪsɪv/ a permissivo

permit[1] /pə'mɪt/ vt (pt/pp -mitted) permettere; **~ sb to do sth** permettere a qno di fare qcsa

permit[2] /'pɜːmɪt/ n autorizzazione f

perpendicular /pɜːpən'dɪkjʊlə(r)/ a perpendicolare ● n perpendicolare f

perpetual /pə'petjʊəl/ a perenne. **~ly** adv perennemente

perpetuate /pə'petjʊeɪt/ vt perpetuare

perplex /pə'pleks/ vt lasciare perplesso. **~ed** a perplesso. **~ity** n perplessità f inv

persecut|e /'pɜːsɪkjuːt/ vt perseguitare. **~ion** /-'kjuːʃn/ n persecuzione f

perseverance /pɜːsɪ'vɪərəns/ n perseveranza f

persever|e /pɜːsɪ'vɪə(r)/ vi perseverare. **~ing** a assiduo

Persian /'pɜːʃn/ a persiano

persist /pə'sɪst/ vi persistere; **~ in doing sth** persistere nel fare qcsa. **~ence** n persistenza f. **~ent** a persistente. **~ently** adv persistentemente

person /'pɜːsn/ n persona f; **in ~** di persona

personal /'pɜːsənl/ a personale. **~ hygiene** n igiene f personale. **~ly** adv personalmente. **~ organizer** n Comput agenda f elettronica

personality /pɜːsə'nælətɪ/ n personalità f inv; (on TV) personaggio m

personnel /pɜːsə'nel/ n personale m

perspective /pə'spektɪv/ n prospettiva f

perspiration /pɜːspɪ'reɪʃn/ n sudore m. **~ire** /-'spaɪə(r)/ vi sudare

persuade /pə'sweɪd/ vt persuadere. **~sion** /-eɪʒn/ n persuasione f; (belief) convinzione f

persuasive /pə'sweɪsɪv/ a persuasivo. **~ly** adv in modo persuasivo

pertinent /'pɜːtɪnənt/ a pertinente (to a)

perturb /pə'tɜːb/ vt perturbare

peruse /pə'ruːz/ vt leggere

pervade /pə'veɪd/ vt pervadere. **~sive** /-sɪv/ a pervasivo

pervers|e /pə'vɜːs/ a irragionevole. **~ion** /-ʒn/ n perversione f

pervert /pə'vɜːt/ n pervertito, -a mf

perverted /pə'vɜːtɪd/ a perverso

pessimis|m /'pesɪmɪzm/ n pessimismo m. **~t** /-mɪst/ n pessimista mf. **~tic** /-'mɪstɪk/ a pessimistico. **~tically** adv in modo pessimistico

pest /pest/ n piaga f; (fam: person)
peste f

pester /'pestə(r)/ vt molestare

pesticide /'pestisaid/ n pesticida m

pet /pet/ n animale m domestico;
(favourite) cocco, -a mf ● a prediletto ● v (pt/pp petted) ● vt coccolare ● vi (couple:) praticare il
petting

petal /'petl/ n petalo m

peter /'piːtə(r)/ vi ~ out finire

petite /pə'tiːt/ a minuto

petition /pə'tɪʃn/ n petizione f

pet 'name n vezzeggiativo m

petrify /'petrifai/ vt (pt/pp -ied)
pietrificare. ~ied a (frightened)
pietrificato

petrol /'petrəl/ n benzina f

petroleum /pɪ'trəʊliəm/ n petrolio m

petrol: ~-pump n pompa f di benzina. ~ station n stazione f di servizio. ~ tank n serbatoio m della
benzina

'pet shop n negozio m di animali
[domestici]

petticoat /'petikəʊt/ n sottoveste f

petty /'peti/ a (-ier, -iest) insignificante; (mean) meschino. ~ 'cash
n cassa f per piccole spese

petulant /'petjʊlənt/ a petulante

pew /pjuː/ n banco m (di chiesa)

pewter /'pjuːtə(r)/ n peltro m

phallic /'fælɪk/ a fallico

phantom /'fæntəm/ n fantasma m

pharmaceutical /fɑːmə'sjuːtɪkl/ a
farmaceutico

pharmacist /'fɑːməsɪst/ n farmacista mf. ~y n farmacia f

phase /feɪz/ n fase f ● vt phase
in/out introdurre/eliminare gradualmente

Ph.D. n abbr (Doctor of Philosophy) ≈ dottorato m di ricerca

pheasant /'feznt/ n fagiano m

phenomenal /fɪ'nɒmɪnl/ a fenomenale; (incredible) incredibile.
~ally adv incredibilmente. ~on n
(pl -na) fenomeno m

philanderer /fɪ'lændərə(r)/ n donnaiolo m

philanthropic /fɪlən'θrɒpɪk/ a filantropico. ~ist /fɪ'lænθrəpɪst/ n
filantropo, -a mf

philately /fɪ'lætəlɪ/ n filatelia f.
~ist n filatelico, -a mf

philharmonic /fɪlhɑː'mɒnɪk/ n (orchestra) orchestra f filarmonica
● a filarmonico

Philippines /'fɪlɪpiːnz/ npl Filippine fpl

philistine /'fɪlɪstam/ n filisteo, -a

philosopher /fɪ'lɒsəfə(r)/ n filosofo, -a mf. ~ical /fɪlə'sɒfɪkl/ a filosofico. ~ically adv con filosofia.
~y n filosofia f

phlegm /flem/ n Med flemma f

phlegmatic /fleg'mætɪk/ a flemmatico

phobia /'fəʊbɪə/ n fobia f

phone /fəʊn/ n telefono m; be on
the ~ avere il telefono; (be
phoning) essere al telefono ● vt telefonare a ● vi telefonare. phone
back vt/i richiamare. ~ book n
guida f del telefono. ~ box n cabina f telefonica. ~ card n scheda f
telefonica. ~ call n telefonata f.
~-in n trasmissione f con chiamate in diretta. ~ number n numero
m telefonico

phonetic /fə'netɪk/ a fonetico. ~s
n fonetica f

phoney /'fəʊnɪ/ a (-ier, -iest) fasullo

phosphorus /'fɒsfərəs/ n fosforo m

photo /'fəʊtəʊ/ n foto f; ~ album
album m inv di fotografie.
~copier n fotocopiatrice f. ~copy
n fotocopia f ● vt fotocopiare

photogenic /fəʊtəʊ'dʒenɪk/ a fotogenico

photograph /'fəʊtəgrɑːf/ n fotografia f ● vt fotografare

photographer /fə'tɒgrəfə(r)/ n fotografo, -a mf. ~ic /fəʊtə'græfɪk/ a
fotografico. ~y n fotografia f

phrase /freɪz/ n espressione f ● vt

esprimere. **~-book** n libro m di fraseologia

physical /'fɪzɪkl/ a fisico. **~ edu'cation** n educazione f fisica. **~ly** adv fisicamente

physician /fɪ'zɪʃn/ n medico m

physic|ist /'fɪzɪsɪst/ n fisico, -a mf. **~s** n fisica f

physiology /fɪzɪ'ɒlədʒɪ/ n fisiologia f

physiotherap|ist /ˌfɪzɪəʊ-/ n fisioterapista mf. **~y** n fisioterapia f

physique /fɪ'ziːk/ n fisico m

pianist /'pɪənɪst/ n pianista mf

piano /pɪ'ænəʊ/ n piano m

pick[1] /pɪk/ n (tool) piccone m

pick[2] n scelta f; **take your ~** prendi quello che vuoi ● vt (select) scegliere; cogliere (flowers); scassinare (lock); borseggiare (pockets); **~ and choose** fare il difficile; **~ one's nose** mettersi le dita nel naso; **~ a quarrel** attaccar briga; **~ holes in** fam criticare; **~ at one's food** spilluzzicare. **pick on** vt (fam: nag) assillare; **he always ~s on me** ce l'ha con me. **pick out** vt (identify) individuare. **pick up** vt sollevare; (off the ground, information) raccogliere; prendere in braccio (baby); (learn) imparare; prendersi (illness); (buy) comprare; captare (signals); (collect) andare/venire a prendere; prendere (passengers, habit); (police:) arrestare (criminal); fam rimorchiare (girl); **~ oneself up** riprendersi ● vi (improve) recuperare; (weather:) rimettersi

'pickaxe n piccone m

picket /'pɪkɪt/ n picchettista mf ● vt picchettare. **~ line** n picchetto m

pickle /'pɪkl/ n **~s** pl sottaceti mpl; **in a ~** fig nei pasticci ● vt mettere sottaceto

pick: ~pocket n borsaiolo m. **~-up** n (truck) furgone m; (on record-player) pickup m inv

picnic /'pɪknɪk/ n picnic m ● vi (pt/pp **-nicked**) fare un picnic

picture /'pɪktʃə(r)/ n (painting) quadro m; (photo) fotografia f; (drawing) disegno m; (film) film m inv; **put sb in the ~** fig mettere qcno al corrente; **~s** il cinema ● vt (imagine) immaginare

picturesque /pɪktʃə'resk/ a pittoresco

pie /paɪ/ n torta f

piece /piːs/ n pezzo m; (in game) pedina f; **a ~ of bread/paper** un pezzo di pane/carta; **a ~ of news/advice** una notizia/un consiglio; **take to ~s** smontare; **~meal** adv un po' alla volta. **~-work** n lavoro m a cottimo ● **piece together** vt montare; fig ricostruire

pier /pɪə(r)/ n molo m; (pillar) pilastro m

pierce /pɪəs/ vt perforare; **~e a hole in sth** fare un buco in qcsa. **~ing** a penetrante

pig /pɪg/ n maiale m

pigeon /'pɪdʒɪn/ n piccione m. **~-hole** n casella f

piggy /'pɪgɪ/ **~back** n **give sb a ~back** portare qcno sulle spalle. **~ bank** n salvadanaio m

pig'headed a fam cocciuto

pig: ~skin n pelle f di cinghiale. **~tail** n (plait) treccina f

pile /paɪl/ n (heap) pila f ● vt **~ sth on to** sth appilare qcsa su qcsa. **pile up** vt accatastare ● vi ammucchiarsi

piles /paɪlz/ npl emorroidi fpl

'pile-up n tamponamento a catena

pilfering /'pɪlfərɪŋ/ n piccoli furti mpl

pilgrim /'pɪlgrɪm/ n pellegrino, -a mf. **~age** /-ɪdʒ/ n pellegrinaggio m

pill /pɪl/ n pillola f

pillage /'pɪlɪdʒ/ vt saccheggiare

pillar /'pɪlə(r)/ n pilastro m. **~-box** n buca f delle lettere

pillion /'pɪljən/ n sellino m posteriore; **ride ~** viaggiare dietro

pillory /'pɪlərɪ/ vt (pt/pp **-ied**) fig mettere alla berlina

pillow /'pɪləʊ/ n guanciale m. ~**case** n federa f

pilot /'paɪlət/ n pilota mf ● vt pilotare. ~**-light** n fiamma f di sicurezza

pimp /pɪmp/ n protettore m

pimple /'pɪmpl/ n foruncolo m

pin /pɪn/ n spillo m; Electr spinotto m; Med chiodo m; **I have ~s and needles in my leg** fam mi formicola una gamba ● vt (pt/pp pinned) appuntare (**to/on** su); (sewing) fissare con gli spilli; (hold down) immobilizzare; ~ **sb down to a date** ottenere un appuntamento da qcno; ~ **sth on sb** fam addossare a qcno la colpa di qcsa. **pin up** vt appuntare; (on wall) affiggere

pinafore /'pɪnəfɔː(r)/ n grembiule m. ~ **dress** n scamiciato m

pincers /'pɪnsəz/ npl tenaglie fpl

pinch /pɪntʃ/ n pizzicotto m; (of salt) presa f; **at a ~** in caso di bisogno ● vt pizzicare; (fam: steal) fregare ● vi (shoe:) stringere

'**pincushion** n puntaspilli m inv

pine[1] /paɪn/ n (tree) pino m

pine[2] /paɪn/ vi **she is pining for you** le manchi molto. **pine away** vi deperire

pineapple /'paɪn-/ n ananas m inv

ping /pɪŋ/ n rumore m metallico

'**ping-pong** n ping-pong m

pink /pɪŋk/ a rosa m

pinnacle /'pɪnəkl/ n guglia f

PIN number n codice m segreto

pin-: ~**point** vt definire con precisione. ~**stripe** a gessato

pint /paɪnt/ n pinta f (= 0,571, Am: 0,47 l); **a ~** fam una birra media

'**pin-up** n ragazza f da copertina, pin-up f inv

pioneer /paɪə'nɪə(r)/ n pioniere, -a mf ● vt essere un pioniere di

pious /'paɪəs/ a pio

pip /pɪp/ n (seed) seme m

pipe /paɪp/ n tubo m; (for smoking) pipa f; **the ~s** Mus la cornamusa ● vt far arrivare con tubature

(water, gas etc). **pipe down** vi fam abbassare la voce

pipe: ~**-cleaner** n scovolino m. ~**-dream** n illusione f. ~**line** n conduttura f; **in the ~line** fam in cantiere

piper /'paɪpə(r)/ n suonatore m di cornamusa

piping /'paɪpɪŋ/ a ~ **hot** bollente

pirate /'paɪrət/ n pirata m

Pisces /'paɪsiːz/ n Astr Pesci mpl

piss /pɪs/ vi sl pisciare

pistol /'pɪstl/ n pistola f

piston /'pɪstn/ n Techn pistone m

pit /pɪt/ n fossa f; (mine) miniera f; (for orchestra) orchestra f ● vt (pt/pp pitted) fig opporre (**against** a)

pitch[1] /pɪtʃ/ n (tone) tono m; (level) altezza f; (in sport) campo m; (fig: degree) grado m ● vt montare (tent). **pitch in** vi fam mettersi sotto

pitch[2] n ~**-'black** a nero come la pece. ~**-'dark** a buio pesto

'**pitchfork** n forca f

piteous /'pɪtɪəs/ a pietoso

'**pitfall** n fig trabocchetto m

pith /pɪθ/ n (of lemon, orange) interno m della buccia

pithy /'pɪθɪ/ a (-ier, -iest) fig conciso

piti|ful /'pɪtɪfl/ a pietoso. ~**less** a spietato

pittance /'pɪtns/ n miseria f

pity /'pɪtɪ/ n pietà f; [**what a**] ~! che peccato!; **take** ~ **on** avere compassione di ● vt aver pietà di

pivot /'pɪvət/ n perno m; fig fulcro m ● vi imperniarsi (**on** su)

pizza /'piːtsə/ n pizza f

placard /'plækɑːd/ n cartellone m

placate /plə'keɪt/ vt placare

place /pleɪs/ n posto m; (fam: house) casa f; (in book) segno m; **feel out of** ~ sentirsi fuori posto; **take** ~ aver luogo; **all over the** ~ dappertutto ● vt collocare; (remember) identificare; ~ **an order** fare un'ordinazione; **be** ~**d** (in *race*) piazzarsi. **~-mat** n sottopiatto m

placid /'plæsɪd/ a placido

plagiar|ism /'pleɪdʒərɪzm/ n plagio m. **~ize** vt plagiare

plague /pleɪg/ n peste f

plaice /pleɪs/ n inv platessa f

plain /pleɪn/ a chiaro; (*simple*) semplice; (*not pretty*) scialbo; (*not patterned*) normale; (*chocolate*) fondente; **in ~ clothes** in borghese ● adv (*simply*) semplicemente ● n pianura f. **~ly** adv francamente; (*simply*) semplicemente; (*obviously*) chiaramente

plaintiff /'pleɪntɪf/ n Jur parte f lesa

plaintive /'pleɪntɪv/ a lamentoso

plait /plæt/ n treccia f ● vt intrecciare

plan /plæn/ n progetto m, piano m ● vt (*pt/pp* **planned**) progettare; (*intend*) prevedere

plane[1] /pleɪn/ n (*tree*) platano m

plane[2] n aeroplano m

plane[3] n (*tool*) pialla f ● vt piallare

planet /'plænɪt/ n pianeta m

plank /plæŋk/ n asse f

planning /'plænɪŋ/ n pianificazione f. **~ permission** n licenza f edilizia

plant /plɑːnt/ n pianta f; (*machinery*) impianto m; (*factory*) stabilimento m ● vt piantare. **~ation** /plæn'teɪʃn/ n piantagione f

plaque /plɑːk/ n placca f

plasma /'plæzmə/ n plasma m

plaster /'plɑːstə(r)/ n intonaco m; Med gesso m; (*sticking ~*) cerotto m; **~ of Paris** gesso m ● vt intonacare (*wall*); (*cover*) ricoprire. **~ed** a sl sbronzo. **~er** n intonacatore m

plastic /'plæstɪk/ n plastica f ● a plastico

Plasticine® /'plæstɪsiːn/ n plasticina® f

plastic: ~ **'surgeon** n chirurgo n plastico. ~ **surgery** n chirurgia f plastica

plate /pleɪt/ n piatto m; (*flat sheet*)

placca f; (*gold and silverware*) argenteria f; (*in book*) tavola f [fuori testo] ● vt (*cover with metal*) placcare

plateau /'plætəʊ/ n (*pl* ~x /-əʊz/) altopiano m

platform /'plætfɔːm/ n (*stage*) palco m; Rail marciapiede m; Pol piattaforma f; **~ 5** binario 5

platinum /'plætɪnəm/ n platino m ● attrib di platino

platitude /'plætɪtjuːd/ n luogo m comune

platonic /plə'tɒnɪk/ a platonico

platoon /plə'tuːn/ n Mil plotone m

platter /'plætə(r)/ n piatto m da portata

plausible /'plɔːzəbl/ a plausibile

play /pleɪ/ n gioco m; Theat, TV rappresentazione f; Radio sceneggiato m radiofonico; **~ on words** gioco m di parole ● vt giocare a; (*act*) recitare; suonare (*instrument*); giocare (*card*) ● vi giocare; Mus suonare; **~ safe** non prendere rischi. **play down** vt minimizzare. **play up** vi fam fare i capricci

play: **~boy** n playboy m inv. **~er** n giocatore, -trice mf. **~ful** a scherzoso. **~ground** n Sch cortile m (*per la ricreazione*). **~group** n asilo m

playing: ~**-card** n carta f da gioco. ~**-field** n campo m da gioco

play: **~mate** n compagno, -a mf di gioco. **~-pen** n box m inv. **~thing** n giocattolo m. **~wright** /-raɪt/ n drammaturgo, -a mf

plc n abbr (**public limited company**) s.r.l.

plea /pliː/ n richiesta f; **make a ~ for** fare un appello a

plead /pliːd/ vi fare appello (**for** a); **~ guilty** dichiararsi colpevole; **~ with** sb implorare qcno

pleasant /'plez(ə)nt/ a piacevole. **~ly** adv piacevolmente; (*say, smile*) cordialmente

please /pliːz/ adv per favore; **~ do** prego ● vt far contento; **~ oneself** fare il proprio comodo;

~e yourself! come vuoi!; *pej* fai come ti pare!. **~ed** a lieto; **~ed with/about** contento di. **~ing** a gradevole

pleasurable /'pleʒərəbl/ a gradevole

pleasure /'pleʒə(r)/ n piacere m; **with ~** con piacere, volentieri

pleat /pli:t/ n piega f ● vt pieghettare. **~ed 'skirt** n gonna f a pieghe

pledge /pledʒ/ n pegno m; *(promise)* promessa f ● vt impegnarsi a; *(pawn)* impegnare

plentiful /'plentɪfl/ a abbondante

plenty /'plentɪ/ n abbondanza f; **~ of money** molti soldi; **~ of people** molta gente; **I've got ~** ne ho in abbondanza

pliable /'plaɪəbl/ a flessibile

pliers /'plaɪəz/ npl pinze fpl

plight /plaɪt/ n condizione f

plimsolls /'plɪmsəlz/ npl scarpe fpl da ginnastica

plinth /plɪnθ/ n plinto m

plod /plɒd/ vi *(pt/pp* **plodded)** trascinarsi; *(work hard)* sgobbare

plonk /plɒŋk/ n *fam* vino m mediocre

plot /plɒt/ n complotto m; *(of novel)* trama f; **~ of land** appezzamento m [di terreno] ● vt/i complottare

plough /plaʊ/ n aratro m ● vt/i arare. **plough back** vt *Comm* reinvestire

ploy /plɔɪ/ n *fam* manovra f

pluck /plʌk/ n fegato m ● vt strappare; depilare *(eyebrows)*; spennare *(bird)*; cogliere *(flower)*. **pluck up ~ up courage** farsi coraggio

plucky /'plʌkɪ/ a (-ier, -iest) coraggioso

plug /plʌg/ n tappo m; *Electr* spina f; *Auto* candela f; *(fam: advertisement)* pubblicità f inv ● vt *(pt/pp* **plugged)** tappare; *(fam: advertise)* pubblicizzare con insistenza. **plug in** vt *Electr* inserire la spina di

plum /plʌm/ n prugna f; *(tree)* prugno m

plumage /'plu:mɪdʒ/ n piumaggio m

plumb /plʌm/ a verticale ● adv esattamente ● **plumb in** vt collegare

plumb|er /'plʌmə(r)/ n idraulico m. **~ing** n impianto m idraulico

'plumb-line n filo m a piombo

plume /plu:m/ n piuma f

plummet /'plʌmɪt/ vi precipitare

plump /plʌmp/ a paffuto ● **plump for** vt scegliere

plunge /plʌndʒ/ n tuffo m; **take the ~** *fam* buttarsi ● vt tuffare; *fig* sprofondare ● vi tuffarsi

plunging /'plʌndʒɪŋ/ a *(neckline)* profondo

plu'perfect /plu:-/ n trapassato m prossimo

plural /'plʊərəl/ a plurale ● n plurale m

plus /plʌs/ prep più ● a in più; **500 ~ più** di 500 ● n più m; *(advantage)* extra m inv

plush /plʌʃ/ a lussuoso

plutonium /plu:'təʊnɪəm/ n plutonio m

ply /plaɪ/ vt *(pt/pp* **plied)** **~ sb with drink** continuare a offrire da bere a qcno. **~wood** n compensato m

PM n *abbr* Prime Minister

p.m. *abbr* *(post meridiem)* del pomeriggio

pneumatic /nju:'mætɪk/ a pneumatico. **~ 'drill** n martello m pneumatico

pneumonia /nju:'məʊnɪə/ n polmonite f

P.O. *abbr* Post Office

poach /pəʊtʃ/ vt *Culin* bollire; cacciare di frodo *(deer)*; pescare di frodo *(salmon)*. **~ed egg** uovo m in camicia. **~er** n bracconiere m

pocket /'pɒkɪt/ n tasca f; **be out of ~** rimetterci ● vt intascare. **~-book** n taccuino m; *(wallet)* portafoglio m. **~-money** n denaro m per le piccole spese

pod /pɒd/ n baccello m

podgy /'pɒdʒɪ/ a (-ier, -iest) grassoccio

poem /'pəʊɪm/ n poesia f

poet /'pəʊɪt/ n poeta m. **~ic** /-'etɪk/ a poetico

poetry /'pəʊɪtrɪ/ n poesia f

poignant /'pɔɪnjənt/ a emozionante

point /pɔɪnt/ n punto m; (sharp end) punta f; (meaning, purpose) senso m; Electr presa f [di corrente]; **~s** pl Rail scambio m; **~ of view** punto m di vista; **good/bad ~s** aspetti mpl positivi/negativi; **what is the ~?** a che scopo?; **the ~ is** il fatto è; **I don't see the ~** non vedo il senso; **up to a ~** fino a un certo punto; **be on the ~ of doing sth** essere sul punto di fare qcsa ● vt puntare (at verso) ● vi (with finger) puntare il dito; **~ at/to** (person:) mostrare col dito; (indicator:) indicare. **point out** vt far notare (fact); **~ sth out to sb** far notare qcsa a qcno

point-'blank a a bruciapelo

point|ed /'pɔɪntɪd/ a appuntito; (question) diretto. **~ers** npl (advice) consigli mpl. **~less** a inutile

poise /pɔɪz/ n padronanza f. **~d** a in equilibrio; **~d** to sul punto di

poison /'pɔɪzn/ n veleno m ● vt avvelenare. **~ous** a velenoso

poke /pəʊk/ n [piccola] spinta f ● vt spingere; (fire) attizzare; (put) ficcare; **~ fun at** prendere in giro. **poke about** vi frugare

poker¹ /'pəʊkə(r)/ n attizzatoio m

poker² n (Cards) poker m

poky /'pəʊkɪ/ a (-ier, -iest) angusto

Poland /'pəʊlənd/ n Polonia f

polar /'pəʊlə(r)/ a polare. **~ bear** n orso m bianco. **~ize** vt polarizzare

Pole /pəʊl/ n polacco, -a mf

pole¹ n palo m

pole² n (Geog, Electr) polo m

'pole-star n stella f polare

'pole-vault n salto m con l'asta

police /pə'li:s/ npl polizia f ● vt pattugliare (area)

police: ~man n poliziotto m. **~ state** n. stato m militarista. **~ station** n commissariato m. **~woman** n donna f poliziotto

policy¹ /'pɒlɪsɪ/ n politica f

policy² n (insurance) polizza f

polio /'pəʊlɪəʊ/ n polio f

Polish /'pəʊlɪʃ/ a polacco ● n (language) polacco m

polish /'pɒlɪʃ/ n (shine) lucentezza f; (substance) lucido m; (for nails) smalto m; fig raffinatezza f ● vt lucidare; fig smussare. **polish off** vt fam finire in fretta; spazzolare (food)

polished /'pɒlɪʃt/ a (manner) raffinato; (performance) senza sbavature

polite /pə'laɪt/ a cortese. **~ly** adv cortesemente. **~ness** n cortesia f

politic /'pɒlɪtɪk/ a prudente

political /pə'lɪtɪkl/ a politico. **~ally** adv dal punto di vista politico. **~ian** /-'tɪʃn/ n politico m

politics /'pɒlɪtɪks/ n politica f

poll /pəʊl/ n votazione f; (election) elezioni fpl; [opinion] **~** sondaggio m d'opinione; **go to the ~s** andare alle urne ● vt ottenere (votes)

pollen /'pɒlən/ n polline m

polling /'pəʊlɪŋ/: **~-booth** n cabina f elettorale. **~-station** n seggio m elettorale

'poll tax n imposta f locale sulle persone fisiche

pollutant /pə'lu:tənt/ n sostanza f inquinante

pollute /pə'lu:t/ vt inquinare. **~ion** /-ʃn/ n inquinamento m

polo /'pəʊləʊ/ n polo m. **~-neck** n collo m alto. **~ shirt** n dolcevita f

polyester /pɒlɪ'estə(r)/ n poliestere m

polystyrene® /pɒlɪ'staɪri:n/ n polistirolo m

polytechnic /pɒlɪ'teknɪk/ n politecnico m

polythene /'pɒlɪθi:n/ n politene m. **~ bag** n sacchetto m di plastica

polyun'saturated a polinsaturo

pomegranate /'pɒmɪgrænɪt/ *n* melagrana *f*

pomp /pɒmp/ *n* pompa *f*

pompon /'pɒmpɒn/ *n* pompon *m*

pompous /'pɒmpəs/ *a* pomposo

pond /pɒnd/ *n* stagno *m*

ponder /'pɒndə(r)/ *vt/i* ponderare

pong /pɒŋ/ *n fam* puzzo *m*

pontiff /'pɒntɪf/ *n* pontefice *m*

pony /'pəʊnɪ/ *n* pony *m*. **~-tail** *n* coda *f* di cavallo. **~-trekking** *n* escursioni *fpl* col pony

poodle /'puːdl/ *n* barboncino *m*

pool¹ /puːl/ *n* (of water, blood) pozza *f*; [**swimming**] **~** piscina *f*

pool² *n* (common fund) cassa *f* comune; (in cards) piatto *m*; (game) biliardo *m* a buca. **~s** *npl* ≈ totocalcio *msg* ● *vt* mettere insieme

poor /pʊə(r)/ *a* povero; (not good) scadente; **in ~ health** in cattiva salute ● *npl* **the ~** i poveri. **~ly** *a* **be ~ly** non stare bene ● *adv* male

pop¹ /pɒp/ *n* botto *m*; (drink) bibita *f* gasata ● *v* (pt/pp **popped**) ● *vt* (fam: put) mettere; (burst) far scoppiare ● *vi* (burst) scoppiare. **pop in/out** *vi fam* fare un salto/un salto fuori

pop² *n fam* musica *f* pop ● *attrib* pop

popcorn /'pɒpkɔːn/ *n* popcorn *m inv*

pope /pəʊp/ *n* papa *m*

poplar /'pɒplə(r)/ *n* pioppo *m*

poppy /'pɒpɪ/ *n* papavero *m*

popular /'pɒpjʊlə(r)/ *a* popolare; (belief) diffuso. **~ity** /-'lærətɪ/ *n* popolarità *f inv*

populate /'pɒpjʊleɪt/ *vt* popolare. **~ion** /-'leɪʃn/ *n* popolazione *f*

porcelain /'pɔːsəlɪn/ *n* porcellana *f*

porch /pɔːtʃ/ *n* portico *m*; *Am* veranda *f*

porcupine /'pɔːkjʊpaɪn/ *n* porcospino *m*

pore¹ /pɔː(r)/ *n* poro *m*

pore² *vi* **~ over** immergersi in

pork /pɔːk/ *n* carne *f* di maiale

porn /pɔːn/ *n fam* porno *m*. **~o** *a fam* porno *inv*

pornographic /pɔːnə'græfɪk/ *a* pornografico. **~y** /-'nɒgrəfɪ/ *n* pornografia *f*

porous /'pɔːrəs/ *a* poroso

porpoise /'pɔːpəs/ *n* focena *f*

porridge /'pɒrɪdʒ/ *n* farinata *f* di fiocchi d'avena

port¹ /pɔːt/ *n* porto *m*

port² *n* (Naut: side) babordo *m*

port³ *n* (wine) porto *m*

portable /'pɔːtəbl/ *a* portatile

porter /'pɔːtə(r)/ *n* portiere *m*; (for luggage) facchino *m*

portfolio /pɔːt'fəʊlɪəʊ/ *n* cartella *f*; *Comm* portafoglio *m*

porthole /n oblò *m inv*

portion /'pɔːʃn/ *n* parte *f*; (of food) porzione *f*

portly /'pɔːtlɪ/ *a* (**-ier, -iest**) corpulento

portrait /'pɔːtrɪt/ *n* ritratto *m*

portray /pɔː'treɪ/ *vt* ritrarre; (represent) descrivere; (actor:) impersonare. **~al** *n* ritratto *m*

Portugal /'pɔːtjʊgl/ *n* Portogallo *m*. **~uese** /-'giːz/ *a* portoghese ● *n* portoghese *mf*

pose /pəʊz/ *n* posa *f* ● *vt* porre (problem, question) ● *vi* (for painter) posare; **~ as** atteggiarsi a

posh /pɒʃ/ *a fam* lussuoso; (people) danaroso

position /pə'zɪʃn/ *n* posizione *f*; (job) posto *m*; (status) ceto *m* [sociale] ● *vt* posizionare

positive /'pɒzɪtɪv/ *a* positivo; (certain) sicuro; (progress) concreto ● *n* positivo *m*. **~ly** *adv* positivamente; (decidedly) decisamente

possess /pə'zes/ *vt* possedere. **~ion** /pə'zeʃn/ *n* possesso *m*; **~ions** *pl* beni *mpl*

possessive /pə'zesɪv/ *a* possessivo. **~iveness** *n* carattere *m* possessivo. **~or** *n* possessore, -ditrice *mf*

possibility /pɒsə'bɪlətɪ/ *n* possibilità *f inv*

possible /'pɒsɪbl/ *a* possibile. **~ly** *adv* possibilmente; **I couldn't ~ly accept** non mi è possibile accettare; **he can't ~ly be right** non può possibile che abbia ragione; **could you ~ly...?** potrebbe per favore...?

post[1] /pəʊst/ n (pole) palo m ● vt affiggere ⟨notice⟩

post[2] n (place of duty) posto m ● vt appostare; (transfer) assegnare

post[3] n (mail) posta f; **by ~** per posta ● vt spedire; (put in letter-box) imbucare; (as opposed to fax) mandare per posta; **keep sb ~ed** tenere qcno al corrente

post- pref dopo

postage /'pəʊstɪdʒ/ n affrancatura f. **~ stamp** n francobollo m

postal /'pəʊstl/ a postale. **~ order** n vaglia m postale

post: **~-box** n cassetta f delle lettere. **~card** n cartolina f. **~code** n codice m postale. **~-date** vt postdatare

poster /'pəʊstə(r)/ n poster m inv; (advertising, election) cartellone m

posterior /pɒ'stɪərɪə(r)/ n fam posteriore m

posterity /pɒ'sterətɪ/ n posterità f

posthumous /'pɒstjʊməs/ a postumo. **~ly** adv dopo la morte

post: **~man** n postino m. **~mark** n timbro m postale

post-mortem /-'mɔːtəm/ n autopsia f

'post office n ufficio m postale

postpone /pəʊst'pəʊn/ vt rimandare. **~ment** n rinvio m

posture /'pɒstʃə(r)/ n posizione f

post-'war a del dopoguerra

pot /pɒt/ n vaso m; (for tea) teiera f; (for coffee) caffettiera f (for cooking) pentola f; **~s of money** fam un sacco di soldi; **go to ~** fam andare in malora

potassium /pə'tæsɪəm/ n potassio m

potato /pə'teɪtəʊ/ n (pl -es) patata f

poten|t /'pəʊtənt/ a potente. **~tate** n potentato m

potential /pə'tenʃl/ a potenziale ● n potenziale m. **~ly** adv potenzialmente

pot: **~-hole** n cavità f inv; (in road) buca f. **~-holer** n speleologo, -a mf. **~-luck** n take **~-luck** affidarsi alla sorte. **~ 'plant** n pianta f da appartamento. **~-shot** n take a **~-shot at** sparare a casaccio a

potted /'pɒtɪd/ a conservato; (shortened) condensato. **~ 'plant** n pianta f da appartamento

potter[1] /'pɒtə(r)/ vi **~ [about]** gingillarsi

potter[2] n vasaio, -a mf. **~y** n lavorazione f della ceramica; (articles) ceramiche fpl; (place) laboratorio m di ceramiche

potty /'pɒtɪ/ a (-ier, -iest) fam matto ● n vasino m

pouch /paʊtʃ/ n marsupio m

pouffe /puːf/ n pouf m inv

poultry /'pəʊltrɪ/ n pollame m

pounce /paʊns/ vi balzare; **~ on** saltare su

pound[1] /paʊnd/ n libbra f (= 0,454 kg); (money) sterlina f

pound[2] vt battere ● vi ⟨heart:⟩ battere forte; (run heavily) correre pesantemente

pour /pɔː(r)/ vt versare ● vi riversarsi; (with rain) piovere a dirotto. **pour out** vi riversarsi fuori ● vt versare ⟨drink⟩; sfogare ⟨troubles⟩

pout /paʊt/ vi fare il broncio ● n broncio m

poverty /'pɒvətɪ/ n povertà f

powder /'paʊdə(r)/ n polvere f; (cosmetic) cipria f ● vt polverizzare; (face) incipriare. **~y** a polveroso

power /'paʊə(r)/ n potere m; Electr corrente f [elettrica]; Math potenza f. **~ cut** n interruzione f di corrente. **~ed** a **~ed by electricity** dotato di corrente [elettrica]. **~ful** a potente. **~less** a impotente. **~-station** n centrale f elettrica

PR n abbr public relations

practicable /'præktɪkəbl/ a praticabile

practical /'præktɪkl/ a pratico. **~**

'joke n burla f. **~ly** adv praticamente

practice /'præktɪs/ n pratica f; (custom) usanza f; (habit) abitudine f; (exercise) esercizio m; Sport allenamento m; **in ~** (in reality) in pratica; **out of ~** fuori esercizio; **put into ~** mettere in pratica

practise /'præktɪs/ vt fare pratica in; (carry out) mettere in pratica; esercitare ‹profession› ● vi esercitarsi; ‹doctor:› praticare. **~d** a esperto

pragmatic /præg'mætɪk/ a pragmatico

praise /preɪz/ n lode f ● vt lodare. **~worthy** a lodevole

pram /præm/ n carrozzella f

prance /prɑːns/ vi saltellare

prank /præŋk/ n tiro m

prattle /'prætl/ vi parlottare

prawn /prɔːn/ n gambero m. **~ 'cocktail** n cocktail m inv di gamberetti

pray /preɪ/ vi pregare. **~er** /preə(r)/ n preghiera f

preach /priːtʃ/ vt/i predicare. **~er** n predicatore, -trice mf

preamble /priː'æmbl/ n preambolo m

pre-ar'range /priː-/ vt predisporre

precarious /prɪ'keərɪəs/ a precario. **~ly** adv in modo precario

precaution /prɪ'kɔːʃn/ n precauzione f; **as a ~** per precauzione. **~ary** a preventivo

precede /prɪ'siːd/ vt precedere

preceden|ce /'presɪdəns/ n precedenza f. **~t** n precedente m

preceding /prɪ'siːdɪŋ/ a precedente

precinct /'priːsɪŋkt/ n (traffic-free) zona f pedonale; (Am: district) circoscrizione f

precious /'preʃəs/ a prezioso; ‹style› ricercato ● adv fam **~ little** ben poco

precipice /'presɪpɪs/ n precipizio m

precipitate /prɪ'sɪpɪteɪt/ vt precipitare

précis /'preɪsiː/ n (pl précis /-siːz/) sunto m

precis|e /prɪ'saɪs/ a preciso. **~ely** adv precisamente. **~ion** /-'sɪʒn/ n precisione f

precursor /priː'kɜːsə(r)/ n precursore m

predator /'predətə(r)/ n predatore, -trice mf. **~y** a rapace

predecessor /'priːdɪsesə(r)/ n predecessore m

predicament /prɪ'dɪkəmənt/ n situazione f difficile

predicate /'predɪkət/ n Gram predicato m. **~ive** /prɪ'dɪkətɪv/ a predicativo

predict /prɪ'dɪkt/ vt predire. **~able** /-əbl/ a prevedibile. **~ion** /-'dɪkʃn/ n previsione f

pre'domin|ant /prɪ-/ a predominante. **~ate** vi predominare

pre-'eminent /prɪ-/ a preminente

preen /priːn/ vt lisciarsi; **~ oneself** fig farsi bello

pre'fab /prɪ'fæb/ n fam casa f prefabbricata. **~'fabricated** a prefabbricato

preface /'prefɪs/ n prefazione f

prefect /'priːfekt/ n Sch studente, -tessa mf della scuola superiore con responsabilità disciplinari, ecc

prefer /prɪ'fɜː(r)/ vt (pt/pp ferred) preferire

prefera|ble /'prefərəbl/ a preferibile (**to** a). **~bly** adv preferibilmente

preferen|ce /'prefərəns/ n preferenza f. **~tial** /-'renʃl/ a preferenziale

prefix /'priːfɪks/ n prefisso m

pregnan|cy /'pregnənsɪ/ n gravidanza f. **~t** a incinta

prehi'storic /priː-/ a preistorico

prejudice /'predʒʊdɪs/ n pregiudizio m ● vt influenzare (against contro); (harm) danneggiare. **~d** a prevenuto

preliminary /prɪ'lɪmɪnərɪ/ a preliminare

prelude /'preljuːd/ n preludio m

pre-'marital *a* prematrimoniale

premature /'prematjʊə(r)/ *a* prematuro

pre-'meditated /priː-/ *a* premeditato

premier /'premiə(r)/ *a* primario ● *n Pol* primo ministro *m*, premier *m inv*

première /'premieə(r)/ *n* prima *f*

premises /'premisɪz/ *npl* locali *mpl*; **on the ~** sul posto

premium /'priːmiəm/ *n* premio *m*; **be at a ~** essere una cosa rara

premonition /preməˈnɪʃn/ *n* presentimento *m*

preoccupied /priːˈɒkjʊpaɪd/ *a* preoccupato

prep /prep/ *n Sch* compiti *mpl*

preparation /prepəˈreɪʃn/ *n* preparazione *f*. **~s** preparativi *mpl*

preparatory /prɪˈpærətrɪ/ *a* preparatorio ● *adv* ~ **to** per

prepare /prɪˈpeə(r)/ *vt* preparare ● *vi* prepararsi (**for** per); **~d to** disposto a

pre'pay /priː-/ *vt* (*pt/pp* **-paid**) pagare in anticipo

preposition /prepəˈzɪʃn/ *n* preposizione *f*

prepossessing /priːpəˈzesɪŋ/ *a* attraente

preposterous /prɪˈpɒstərəs/ *a* assurdo

prerequisite /priːˈrekwɪzɪt/ *n* condizione *f* sine qua non

prescribe /prɪˈskraɪb/ *vt* prescrivere

prescription /prɪˈskrɪpʃn/ *n Med* ricetta *f*

presence /'prezns/ *n* presenza *f*; **~ of mind** presenza *f* di spirito

present¹ /'preznt/ *a* presente ● *n* presente *m*; **at ~** attualmente

present² *n* (*gift*) regalo *m*; **give sb sth as a ~** regalare qcsa a qcno

present³ /prɪˈzent/ *vt* presentare; **~ sb with an award** consegnare un premio a qcno. **~able** /-əbl/ *a* **be ~able** essere presentabile

presentation /preznˈteɪʃn/ *n* presentazione *f*

presently /'prezntlɪ/ *adv* fra poco; (*Am: now*) attualmente

preservation /prezəˈveɪʃn/ *n* conservazione *f*

preservative /prɪˈzɜːvətɪv/ *n* conservante *m*

preserve /prɪˈzɜːv/ *vt* preservare; (*maintain, Culin*) conservare ● *n* (*in hunting & fig*) riserva *f*; (*jam*) marmellata *f*

preside /prɪˈzaɪd/ *vi* presiedere (**over** a)

presidency /'prezɪdənsɪ/ *n* presidenza *f*

president /'prezɪdənt/ *n* presidente *m*. **~ial** /-'denʃl/ *a* presidenziale

press /pres/ *n* (*machine*) pressa *f*; (*newspapers*) stampa *f* ● *vt* premere; pressare (*flower*); (*iron*) stirare; (*squeeze*) stringere ● *vi* (*urge*) incalzare. **press for** *vt* fare pressione per; **be ~ed for** essere a corto di. **press on** *vi* andare avanti

press: **~ conference** *n* conferenza *f* stampa. **~ cutting** *n* ritaglio *m* di giornale. **~ing** *a* urgente. **~-stud** *n* [bottone *m*] automatico *m*. **~-up** *n* flessione *f*

pressure /'preʃə(r)/ *n* pressione *f* ● *vt* = **pressurize.** **~-cooker** *n* pentola *f* a pressione. **~ group** *n* gruppo *m* di pressione

pressurize /'preʃəraɪz/ *vt* far pressione su. **~d** *a* pressurizzato

prestige /preˈstiːʒ/ *n* prestigio *m*. **~ious** /-'stɪdʒəs/ *a* prestigioso

presumably /prɪˈzjuːməblɪ/ *adv* presumibilmente

presume /prɪˈzjuːm/ *vt* presumere; **~ to do sth** permettersi di fare

presumption /prɪˈzʌmpʃn/ *n* presunzione *f*; (*boldness*) impertinenza *f*. **~uous** /-ˈzʌmptjʊəs/ *a* impertinente

presuppose /priː-/ *vt* presupporre

pretence /prɪˈtens/ *n* finzione *f*; (*pretext*) pretesto *m*; **it's all ~** è tutta una scena

pretend /prɪ'tend/ vt fingere; (claim) pretendere ● vi fare finta

pretentious /prɪ'tenʃəs/ a pretenzioso

pretext /'priːtekst/ n pretesto m

pretty /'prɪtɪ/ a (-ier, -iest) carino ● adv (fam: fairly) abbastanza

prevail /prɪ'veɪl/ vi prevalere; ~ on sb to do sth convincere qcno a fare qcsa. ~ing a prevalente

prevalen|ce /'prevələns/ n diffusione f. ~t a diffuso

prevent /prɪ'vent/ vt impedire; ~ sb [from] doing sth impedire a qcno di fare qcsa. ~ion /-enʃn/ n prevenzione f. ~ive /-ɪv/ a preventivo

preview /'priːvjuː/ n anteprima f

previous /'priːvɪəs/ a precedente. ~ly adv precedentemente

pre-'war /priː-/ a anteguerra

prey /preɪ/ n preda f; **bird of** ~ uccello m rapace ● vi ~ **on** far preda di; ~ **on sb's mind** attanagliare qcno

price /praɪs/ n prezzo m ● vt Comm fissare il prezzo di. ~less a inestimabile; (fam: amusing) spassosissimo. ~y a fam caro

prick /prɪk/ n puntura f ● vt pungere. **prick up** vt ~ **up one's ears** rizzare le orecchie

prickl|e /'prɪkl/ n spina f; (sensation) formicolio m. ~y a pungente; (person) irritabile

pride /praɪd/ n orgoglio m ● vt ~ **oneself on** vantarsi di

priest /priːst/ n prete m

prim /prɪm/ a (primmer, primmest) perbenino

primarily /'praɪmərɪlɪ/ adv in primo luogo

primary /'praɪmərɪ/ a primario; (chief) principale. ~ **school** n scuola f elementare

prime[1] /praɪm/ a principale, primo; (first-rate) eccellente ● n **be in one's** ~ essere nel fiore degli anni

prime[2] vt preparare (surface, person)

Prime Minister n Primo m Ministro

primeval /praɪ'miːvl/ a primitivo

primitive /'prɪmɪtɪv/ a primitivo

primrose /'prɪmrəʊz/ n primula f

prince /prɪns/ n principe m

princess /prɪn'ses/ n principessa f

principal /'prɪnsəpl/ a principale ● n Sch preside m

principality /prɪnsɪ'pælətɪ/ n principato m

principally /'prɪnsəplɪ/ adv principalmente

principle /'prɪnsəpl/ n principio m; **in** ~ in teoria; **on** ~ per principio

print /prɪnt/ n (mark, trace) impronta f; Phot copia f; (picture) stampa f; **in** ~ (printed out) stampato; (book) in commercio; **out of** ~ esaurito ● vt stampare; (write in capitals) scrivere in stampatello. ~**ed matter** n stampe fpl

print|er /'prɪntə(r)/ n stampante f; Typ tipografo, -a mf. ~**er port** n Comput porta f per la stampante. ~**ing** n tipografia f

'printout n Comput stampa f

prior /'praɪə(r)/ a precedente. ~ **to** prep prima di

priority /praɪ'ɒrətɪ/ n precedenza f; (matter) priorità f inv

prise /praɪz/ vt ~ **open/up** forzare

prison /'prɪz(ə)n/ n prigione f. ~**er** n prigioniero, -a mf

privacy /'prɪvəsɪ/ n privacy f inv

private /'praɪvət/ a privato; (car, secretary, letter) personale ● n Mil soldato m semplice; **in** ~ in privato. ~**ly** adv (funded, educated) privatamente; (in secret) in segreto; (confidentially) in privato; (inwardly) interiormente

privation /praɪ'veɪʃn/ n privazione f; ~**s** npl stenti mpl

privatize /'praɪvətaɪz/ vt privatizzare

privilege /'prɪvɪlɪdʒ/ n privilegio m. ~**d** a privilegiato

privy /'prɪvɪ/ a **be** ~ **to** essere al corrente di

prize /praɪz/ n premio m ●a (idiot etc) perfetto ●vt apprezzare.
~-giving n premiazione f.
~-winner n vincitore, -trice mf.
~-winning a vincente

pro /prəʊ/ n (fam: professional) professionista mf, **the ~s and cons** il pro e il contro

probability /probə'bɪlətɪ/ n probabilità f inv

probabl|e /'probəbl/ a probabile.
~y adv probabilmente

probation /prə'beɪʃn/ n prova f; Jur libertà f vigilata. **~ary** a in prova; **~ary period** periodo m di prova

probe /prəʊb/ n sonda f; (fig: investigation) indagine f ●vt sondare; (investigate) esaminare a fondo

problem /'probləm/ n problema m ●a difficile. **~atic** /-'mætɪk/ a problematico

procedure /prə'si:dʒə(r)/ n procedimento m

proceed /prə'si:d/ vi procedere ●vt **~ to do sth** proseguire facendo qcsa

proceedings /prə'si:dɪŋz/ npl (report) atti mpl; Jur azione f sg legale

proceeds /'prəʊsi:dz/ npl ricavato msg

process /'prəʊses/ n processo m; (procedure) procedimento m; **in the ~** nel far ciò ●vt trattare; Admin occuparsi di; Phot sviluppare

procession /prə'seʃn/ n processione f

proclaim /prə'kleɪm/ vt proclamare

procure /prə'kjʊə(r)/ vt ottenere

prod /prod/ n colpetto m ●vt (pt/pp **prodded**) punzecchiare; fig incitare

prodigal /'prodɪgl/ a prodigo

prodigious /prə'dɪdʒəs/ a prodigioso

prodigy /'prodɪdʒɪ/ n [infant] **~** bambino m prodigio

produce¹ /'prodju:s/ n prodotti mpl; **~ of Italy** prodotto in Italia

produce² /prə'dju:s/ vt produrre; (bring out) tirar fuori; (cause) causare; (fam: give birth to) fare. **~r** n produttore m

product /'prodʌkt/ n prodotto m.
~ion /prə'dʌkʃn/ n produzione f; Theat spettacolo m

productiv|e /prə'dʌktɪv/ a produttivo. **~ity** /-'tɪvətɪ/ n produttività f

profan|e /prə'feɪn/ a profano; (blasphemous) blasfemo. **~ity** /-'fænətɪ/ n (oath) bestemmia f

profession /prə'feʃn/ n professione f. **~al** a professionale; (not amateur) professionista; (piece of work) da professionista; (man) di professione ●n professionista mf.
~ally adv professionalmente

professor /prə'fesə(r)/ n professore m [universitario]

proficien|cy /prə'fɪʃnsɪ/ n competenza f. **~t a be ~t** in essere competente in

profile /'prəʊfaɪl/ n profilo m

profit /'profɪt/ n profitto m ●vi **~ from** trarre profitto da. **~able** /-əbl/ a proficuo. **~ably** adv in modo proficuo

profound /prə'faʊnd/ a profondo.
~ly adv profondamente

profus|e /prə'fju:s/ a **~e apologies/flowers** una profusione di scuse/fiori. **~ion** /-ju:ʒn/ n profusione f; **in ~ion** in abbondanza

progeny /'prodʒənɪ/ n progenie f inv

prognosis /prog'nəʊsɪs/ n (pl **-oses**) prognosi f inv

program /'prəʊgræm/ n programma m ●vt (pt/pp **programmed**) programmare

programme /'prəʊgræm/ n Br programma m. **~r** n Comput programmatore, -trice mf

progress¹ /'prəʊgres/ n progresso m; **in ~** in corso; **make ~** fig fare progressi

progress² /prə'gres/ vt progredire; fig fare progressi

progressive /prə'gresɪv/ a progressivo; (*reforming*) progressista. **~ly** adv progressivamente

prohibit /prə'hɪbɪt/ vt proibire. **~ive** /-ɪv/ a proibitivo

project¹ /'prɒdʒekt/ n progetto m; *Sch* ricerca f

project² /prə'dʒekt/ vt proiettare (*film, image*) ● vi (*jut out*) sporgere

projectile /prə'dʒektaɪl/ n proiettile m

projector /prə'dʒektə(r)/ n proiettore m

prolific /prə'lɪfɪk/ a prolifico

prologue /'prəʊlɒg/ n prologo m

prolong /prə'lɒŋ/ vt prolungare

promenade /prɒmə'nɑːd/ n lungomare m inv

prominent /'prɒmɪnənt/ a prominente; (*conspicuous*) di rilievo

promiscuity /prɒmɪ'skjuːətɪ/ n promiscuità f. **~ous** /prə'mɪskjʊəs/ a promiscuo

promis|e /'prɒmɪs/ n promessa f ● vt promettere; **~ sb that** promettere a qcno che; **I ~ed to** l'ho promesso. **~ing** a promettente

promot|e /prə'məʊt/ vt promuovere; **be ~ed** *Sport* essere promosso. **~ion** /-əʊʃn/ n promozione f

prompt /prɒmpt/ a immediato; (*punctual*) puntuale ● adv in punto ● vt incitare (**to** a); *Theat* suggerire a ● vi suggerire. **~er** n suggeritore, -trice mf. **~ly** adv puntualmente

Proms /prɒmz/ npl rassegna f di concerti estivi di musica classica presso l'*Albert Hall* a Londra

prone /prəʊn/ a **be ~ to do sth** essere incline a fare qcsa

prong /prɒŋ/ n dente m (*di forchetta*)

pronoun /'prəʊnaʊn/ n pronome m

pronounce /prə'naʊns/ vt pronunciare; (*declare*) dichiarare. **~d** a (*noticeable*) pronunciato

pronunciation /prənʌnsɪ'eɪʃn/ n pronuncia f

proof /pruːf/ n prova f; *Typ* bozza f, prova f ● a **~ against** a prova di

prop¹ /prɒp/ n puntello m ● vt (*pt/pp* **propped**) **~ open** tenere aperto; **~ against** (*lean*) appoggiare a. **prop up** vt sostenere

prop² /prɒp/ n *Theat, fam* accessorio m di scena

propaganda /prɒpə'gændə/ n propaganda f

propel /prə'pel/ vt (*pt/pp* **propelled**) spingere. **~ler** n elica f

proper /'prɒpə(r)/ a corretto; (*suitable*) adatto; (*fam: real*) vero [e proprio]. **~ly** adv correttamente. **~ 'name**, **~ 'noun** n nome m proprio

property /'prɒpətɪ/ n proprietà f inv. **~ developer** n agente m immobiliare. **~ market** n mercato m immobiliare

prophecy /'prɒfəsɪ/ n profezia f

prophesy /'prɒfɪsaɪ/ vt (*pt/pp* **-ied**) profetizzare

prophet /'prɒfɪt/ n profeta m. **~ic** /prə'fetɪk/ a profetico

proportion /prə'pɔːʃn/ n proporzione f; (*share*) parte f; **~s** pl (*dimensions*) proporzioni fpl. **~al** a proporzionale. **~ally** adv in proporzione

proposal /prə'pəʊzl/ n proposta f; (*of marriage*) proposta f di matrimonio

propose /prə'pəʊz/ vt proporre; (*intend*) proporsi ● vi fare una proposta di matrimonio

proposition /prɒpə'zɪʃn/ n proposta f; (*fam: task*) impresa f

proprietor /prə'praɪətə(r)/ n proprietario, -a mf

prosaic /prə'zeɪɪk/ a prosaico

prose /prəʊz/ n prosa f

prosecut|e /'prɒsɪkjuːt/ vt intentare azione contro. **~ion** /-'kjuːʃn/ n azione f giudiziaria; **the ~ion** l'accusa f. **~or** n [**Public**] **P~or** il Pubblico Ministero m

prospect¹ /'prɒspekt/ n (*expectation*) prospettiva f

prospect² /prə'spekt/ *vi* ~ **for** cercare

prospect|ive /prə'spektɪv/ *a* (*future*) futuro; (*possible*) potenziale. **~or** *n* cercatore *m*

prospectus /prə'spektəs/ *n* prospetto *m*

prosper /'prɒspə(r)/ *vi* prosperare; ⟨*person:*⟩ stare bene finanziariamente. **~ity** /-'sperəti/ *n* prosperità *f*

prosperous /'prɒspərəs/ *a* prospero

prostitut|e /'prɒstɪtjuːt/ *n* prostituta *f*. **~ion** /-'tjuːʃn/ *n* prostituzione *f*

prostrate /'prɒstreɪt/ *a* prostrato; ~ **with grief** *fig* prostrato dal dolore

protagonist /prəʊ'tægənɪst/ *n* protagonista *mf*

protect /prə'tekt/ *vt* proteggere (**from** da). **~ion** /-ekʃn/ *n* protezione *f*. **~ive** /-ɪv/ *a* protettivo. **~or** *n* protettore, -trice *mf*

protégé /'prɒtɪʒeɪ/ *n* protetto *m*

protein /'prəʊtiːn/ *n* proteina *f*

protest¹ /'prəʊtest/ *n* protesta *f*

protest² /prə'test/ *vt/i* protestare

Protestant /'prɒtɪstənt/ *a* protestante ● *n* protestante *mf*

protester /prə'testə(r)/ *n* contestatore, -trice *mf*

protocol /'prəʊtəkɒl/ *n* protocollo *m*

prototype /'prəʊtə-/ *n* prototipo *m*

protract /prə'trækt/ *vt* protrarre

protrude /prə'truːd/ *vi* sporgere

proud /praʊd/ *a* fiero (**of** di). **~ly** *adv* fieramente

prove /pruːv/ *vt* provare ● *vi* ~ **to be a lie** rivelarsi una bugia. **~n** *a* dimostrato

proverb /'prɒvɜːb/ *n* proverbio *m*. **~ial** /prə'vɜːbɪəl/ *a* proverbiale

provide /prə'vaɪd/ *vt* fornire; ~ **sb with sth** fornire qcsa a qcno ● *vi* ~ **for** ⟨*law:*⟩ prevedere

provided /prə'vaɪdɪd/ *conj* ~ [**that**] purché

providen|ce /'prɒvɪdəns/ *n* prov-

videnza *f*. **~tial** /-'denʃl/ *a* provvidenziale

providing /prə'vaɪdɪŋ/ *conj* = **provided**

provinc|e /'prɒvɪns/ *n* provincia *f*; *fig* campo *m*. **~ial** /prə'vɪnʃl/ *a* provinciale

provision /prə'vɪʒn/ *n* (*of food, water*) approvvigionamento *m* (**of** di); (*of law*) disposizione *f*; **~s** *pl* provviste *fpl*. **~al** *a* provvisorio

proviso /prə'vaɪzəʊ/ *n* condizione *f*

provoc|ation /prɒvə'keɪʃn/ *n* provocazione *f*. **~ive** /prə'vɒkətɪv/ *a* provocatorio; (*sexually*) provocante. **~ively** *adv* in modo provocatorio

provoke /prə'vəʊk/ *vt* provocare

prow /praʊ/ *n* prua *f*

prowess /'praʊɪs/ *n* abilità *f* *inv*

prowl /praʊl/ *vi* aggirarsi ● *n* **on the** ~ in cerca di preda. **~er** *n* tipo *m* sospetto

proximity /prɒk'sɪmətɪ/ *n* prossimità *f*

proxy /'prɒksɪ/ *n* procura *f*; (*person*) persona *f* che agisce per procura

prude /pruːd/ *n* **be a** ~ essere eccessivamente pudico

pruden|ce /'pruːdəns/ *n* prudenza *f*. **~t** *a* prudente; (*wise*) oculatezza *f*

prudish /'pruːdɪʃ/ *a* eccessivamente pudico

prune¹ /pruːn/ *n* prugna *f* secca

prune² *vt* potare

pry /praɪ/ *vi* (*pt/pp* **pried**) ficcare il naso

psalm /saːm/ *n* salmo *m*

pseudonym /'sjuːdənɪm/ *n* pseudonimo *m*

psychiatric /saɪkɪ'ætrɪk/ *a* psichiatrico

psychiatr|ist /saɪ'kaɪətrɪst/ *n* psichiatra *mf*. **~y** *n* psichiatria *f*

psychic /'saɪkɪk/ *a* psichico; **I'm not** ~ non sono un indovino

psycho|analyse /saɪkəʊ-/ *vt* psicanalizzare. **~'analysis** *n* psica-

nalisi f. ~'**analyst** n psicanalista
mf

psychological /saɪkə'rɒdʒɪkl/ a
psicologico

psycholog|ist /saɪ'kɒlədʒɪst/ n
psicologo, -a mf. ~**y** n psicologia f

psychopath /'saɪkəpæθ/ n psico-
patico, -a mf

P.T.O. abbr (**please turn over**) vedi
retro

pub /pʌb/ n fam pub m inv

puberty /'pjuːbətɪ/ n pubertà f

public /'pʌblɪk/ a pubblico ●**in the
~** il pubblico; **in ~** in pubblico.
~**ly** adv pubblicamente

publican /'pʌblɪkən/ n gestore,
-trice mf/proprietario, -a mf di un
pub

publication /pʌblɪ'keɪʃn/ n pubblicazione f

public: ~ **con'venience** n gabinetti mpl pubblici. ~ **'holiday** n festa
f nazionale. ~ **'house** n pub m

publicity /pʌb'lɪsətɪ/ n pubblicità f

publicize /'pʌblɪsaɪz/ vt pubblicizzare

public: ~ **'library** n biblioteca f
pubblica. ~ **relations** fpl. ~ **'school** n scuola f
privata; Am scuola f pubblica.
~**-'spirited** a **be ~spirited** essere
dotato di senso civico. ~
'transport n mezzi mpl pubblici

publish /'pʌblɪʃ/ vt pubblicare.
~**er** n editore m; (firm) editore m,
casa f editrice. ~**ing** n editoria f

pudding /'pʊdɪŋ/ n dolce m cotto al
vapore; (course) dolce m

puddle /'pʌdl/ n pozzanghera f

pudgy /'pʌdʒɪ/ a (-ier, -iest) grassoccio

puff /pʌf/ n (of wind) soffio m; (of
smoke) tirata f; (for powder) piumino m ●vt sbuffare. **puff at** vt
tirare boccate da (pipe). **puff out**
vt lasciare senza fiato (person);
spegnere (candle). ~**ed** a (out of
breath) senza fiato. ~ **pastry** n pasta f sfoglia

puffy /'pʌfɪ/ a gonfio

pull /pʊl/ n trazione f; (fig: attrac-

tion) attrazione f; (fam: influence)
influenza f ●vt tirare; estrarre
(tooth); stirarsi (muscle); ~ **faces**
far boccace; ~ **oneself together**
cercare di controllarsi; ~ **one's
weight** mettercela tutta; ~ **sb's
leg** fam prendere in giro qcno.
pull down vt (demolish) demolire.
pull in vi Auto accostare. **pull off**
vt togliere; fam azzeccare. **pull out**
vt tirar fuori ●vi Auto spostarsi;
(of competition) ritirarsi. **pull
through** vi (recover) farcela. **pull
up** vt sradicare (plant); (reprimand) rimproverare ●vi Auto
fermarsi

pulley /'pʊlɪ/ n Techn puleggia f

pullover /'pʊləʊvə(r)/ n pullover m

pulp /pʌlp/ n poltiglia f; (of fruit)
polpa f; (for paper) pasta f

pulpit /'pʊlpɪt/ n pulpito m

pulsate /pʌl'seɪt/ vi pulsare

pulse /pʌls/ n polso m

pulses /'pʌlsɪz/ npl legumi mpl
secchi

pulverize /'pʌlvəraɪz/ vt polverizzare

pumice /'pʌmɪs/ n pomice f

pummel /'pʌml/ vt (pt/pp pum-
melled) prendere a pugni

pump /pʌmp/ n pompa f ●vt pompare; fam cercare di estorcere da.
pump up vt (inflate) gonfiare

pumpkin /'pʌmpkɪn/ n zucca f

pun /pʌn/ n gioco m di parole

punch¹ /pʌntʃ/ n pugno m; (device)
pinza f per forare ●vt dare un pugno a; forare (ticket); perforare
(hole)

punch² n (drink) ponce m inv

punch: ~ **line** n battuta f finale.
~**-up** n rissa f

punctual /'pʌŋktjʊəl/ a puntuale.
~**ity** /-'ælɪtɪ/ n puntualità f. ~**ly**
adv puntualmente

punctuat|e /'pʌŋktjʊeɪt/ vt pun-
teggiare. ~**ion** /-'eɪʃn/ n punteggiatura f. ~**ion mark** n segno m di
interpunzione

puncture /'pʌŋktʃə(r)/ n foro m;
(tyre) foratura f ●vt forare

pungent /'pʌndʒənt/ a acre

punish /'pʌnɪʃ/ vt punire. **~able** /-əbl/ a punibile. **~ment** n punizione f

punitive /'pju:nɪtɪv/ a punitivo

punk /pʌŋk/ n punk m inv

punnet /'pʌnɪt/ n cestello m (per frutta)

punt /pʌnt/ n (boat) barchino m

punter /'pʌntə(r)/ n (gambler) scommettitore, -trice mf; (client) consumatore, -trice mf

puny /'pju:nɪ/ a (-ier, -iest) striminzito

pup /pʌp/ n = **puppy**

pupil /'pju:pl/ n alluno, -a mf; (of eye) pupilla f

puppet /'pʌpɪt/ n marionetta f (glove ~, fig) burattino m

puppy /'pʌpɪ/ n cucciolo m

purchase /'pɜ:tʃəs/ n acquisto m; (leverage) presa f ● vt acquistare. **~r** n acquirente mf

pure /pjʊə(r)/ a puro. **~ly** adv puramente

purée /'pjʊəreɪ/ n purè m

purgatory /'pɜ:gətrɪ/ n purgatorio m

purge /pɜ:dʒ/ Pol n epurazione f ● vt epurare

puri|fication /pjʊərɪfɪ'keɪʃn/ n purificazione f. **~fy** /'pjʊərɪfaɪ/ vt (pt/pp -ied) purificare

puritan /'pjʊərɪtən/ n puritano, -a mf. **~ical** a puritano

purity /'pjʊərɪtɪ/ n purità f

purple /'pɜ:pl/ n viola

purpose /'pɜ:pəs/ n scopo m; (determination) fermezza f; on ~ apposta. **~-built** a costruito ad hoc. **~ful** a deciso. **~fully** adv con decisione. **~ly** adv apposta

purr /pɜ:(r)/ vi (cat:) fare le fusa

purse /pɜ:s/ n borsellino m; (Am: handbag) borsa f ● vt increspare (lips)

pursue /pə'sju:/ vt inseguire; fig proseguire. **~r** /-ə(r)/ n inseguitore, -trice mf

pursuit /pə'sju:t/ n inseguimento m; (fig: of happiness) ricerca f;

(pastime) attività f inv; in ~ all'inseguimento

pus /pʌs/ n pus m

push /pʊʃ/ n spinta f; (fig: effort) sforzo m; (drive) iniziativa f; at a ~ in caso di bisogno; get the ~ fam essere licenziato ● vt spingere; premere (button); (pressurize) far pressione su; be **~ed for time** fam non avere tempo ● vi spingere. **push aside** vt scostare. **push back** vt respingere. **push off** vt togliere ● vi (fam: leave) levarsi dai piedi. **push on** vi (continue) continuare. **push up** vt alzare (price)

push: **~-button** n pulsante m. **~-chair** n passeggino m. **~-over** n fam bazzecola f. **~-up** n flessione f

pushy /'pʊʃɪ/ a fam troppo intraprendente

puss /pʊs/ n, **pussy** /'pʊsɪ/ n micio m

put /pʊt/ vt (pt/pp put, pres p putting) mettere; ~ the cost of sth at valutare il costo di qcsa ● vi ~ to sea salpare. **put aside** vt mettere da parte. **put away** vt mettere via. **put back** vt rimettere; mettere indietro (clock). **put by** vt mettere da parte. **put down** vt mettere giù; (suppress) reprimere; (kill) sopprimere; (write) annotare; **~ one's foot down** fam essere fermo; Auto dare un'accelerata; **~ down to** (attribute) attribuire. **put forward** vt avanzare; mettere avanti (clock). **put in** vt (insert) introdurre; (submit) presentare ● vi **~ in for** far domanda di. **put off** vt spegnere (light); (postpone) rimandare; **~ sb off** tenere a bada qcno; (deter) smontare qcno; (disconcert) distrarre qcno; **~ sb off sth** (disgust) disgustare qcno di qcsa. **put on** vt mettersi (clothes); mettere (brake); Culin mettere su; accendere (light); mettere in scena (play); prendere (accent); **~ on weight** mettere su qualche chilo. **put out** vt spegnere (fire, light); tendere (hand);

⟨hand⟩; ⟨inconvenience⟩ creare degli inconvenienti a. **put through to him** glielo passo. **put up** vt alzare; erigere ⟨building⟩; montare ⟨tent⟩; aprire ⟨umbrella⟩; affiggere ⟨notice⟩; aumentare ⟨price⟩; ospitare ⟨guest⟩; **~ sb up to sth** mettere qcsa in testa a qcno ● vi ⟨at hotel⟩ stare; **~ up with** sopportare ● a **stay ~!** rimani lì!

putty /'pʌti/ n mastice m

put-up /'pʊtʌp/ a **~ job** truffa f

puzzle /'pʌzl/ n enigma m; ⟨jigsaw⟩ puzzle m inv ● vt lasciare perplesso ● vi **~ e over** scervellarsi su. **~ing** a inspiegabile

pygmy /'pɪgmɪ/ n pigmeo, -a mf

pyjamas /pə'dʒɑːməz/ npl pigiama msg

pylon /'paɪlən/ n pilone m

pyramid /'pɪrəmɪd/ n piramide f

python /'paɪθn/ n pitone m

....

Qq

quack¹ /kwæk/ n qua qua m inv ● vi fare qua qua

quack² n ⟨doctor⟩ ciarlatano m

quad /kwɒd/ n ⟨fam: court⟩ = **quadrangle**. **~s** pl = **quadruplets**

quadrangle /'kwɒdræŋgl/ n quadrangolo m; ⟨court⟩ cortile m quadrangolare

quadruped /'kwɒdrʊped/ n quadrupede m

quadruple /'kwɒdrʊpl/ a quadruplo ● vt quadruplicare ● vi quadruplicarsi. **~ts** -plɪts/ npl quattro gemelli mpl

quagmire /'kwɒgmaɪə(r)/ n pantano m

quaint /kweɪnt/ a pittoresco; ⟨odd⟩ bizzarro

quake /kweɪk/ n fam terremoto m ● vi tremare

qualification /kwɒlɪfɪ'keɪʃn/ n qualifica f. ⟨diploma⟩ titolo m qualificato; ⟨limited⟩ con riserva

qualify /'kwɒlɪfaɪ/ v ⟨pt/pp **-ied**⟩ ● vt ⟨course:⟩ dare la qualifica a ⟨as di⟩; ⟨entitle⟩ autorizzare a; ⟨limit⟩ precisare ● vi ottenere la qualifica; Sport qualificarsi

quality /'kwɒlɪtɪ/ n qualità f inv

qualm /kwɑːm/ n scrupolo m

quandary /'kwɒndərɪ/ n dilemma m

quantity /'kwɒntɪtɪ/ n quantità f inv; **in ~** in grande quantità

quarantine /'kwɒrəntiːn/ n quarantena f

quarrel /'kwɒrəl/ n lite f ● vi ⟨pt/pp **quarrelled**⟩ litigare. **~some** a litigioso

quarry¹ /'kwɒrɪ/ n ⟨prey⟩ preda f

quarry² n cava f

quart /kwɔːt/ n 1.14 litro

quarter /'kwɔːtə(r)/ n quarto m; ⟨of year⟩ trimestre m; Am 25 centesimi mpl; **~s** pl Mil quartiere msg; **at [a] ~ to six** alle sei meno un quarto ● vt dividere in quattro. **~-'final** n quarto m di finale

quarterly /'kwɔːtəlɪ/ a trimestrale ● adv trimestralmente

quartet /kwɔː'tet/ n quartetto m

quartz /kwɔːts/ n quarzo m. **~ watch** n orologio m al quarzo

quash /kwɒʃ/ vt annullare; soffocare ⟨rebellion⟩

quaver /'kweɪvə(r)/ vi tremolare

quay /kiː/ n banchina f

queasy /'kwiːzɪ/ a **I feel ~** ho la nausea

queen /kwiːn/ n regina f. **~ mother** n regina f madre

queer /kwɪə(r)/ a strano; ⟨dubious⟩ sospetto; ⟨fam: homosexual⟩ finocchio ● n fam finocchio m

quell /kwel/ vt reprimere

quench /kwentʃ/ vt **~ one's thirst** dissetarsi

query /'kwɪərɪ/ n domanda f. ⟨question mark⟩ punto m interrogativo ● vt ⟨pt/pp **-ied**⟩ interrogare; ⟨doubt⟩ mettere in dubbio

quest /kwest/ *n* ricerca *f* (**for** di)

question /'kwestʃən/ *n* domanda *f*; (*for discussion*) questione *f*; **out of the ~** fuori discussione; **without ~** senza dubbio; **in ~** in questione ● *vt* interrogare; (*doubt*) mettere in dubbio. **~able** /-əbl/ *a* discutibile. **~ mark** *n* punto *m* interrogativo

questionnaire /kwestʃə'neə(r)/ *n* questionario *m*

queue /kju:/ *n* coda *f*, fila *f* ● *vi* **~ [up]** mettersi in coda (**for** per)

quick /kwɪk/ *a* veloce; **be ~** sbrigati!; **have a ~ meal** fare uno spuntino ● *adv* in fretta ● *n* **be cut to the ~** *fig* essere punto sul vivo. **~ly** *adv* in fretta. **~-tempered** *a* collerico

quid /kwɪd/ *n inv fam* sterlina *f*

quiet /'kwaɪət/ *a* (*calm*) tranquillo; (*silent*) silenzioso; (*voice, music*) basso; **keep ~ about** *fam* non raccontare a nessuno ● *n* quiete *f*; **on the ~** di nascosto. **~ly** *adv* (*peacefully*) tranquillamente; (*say*) a bassa voce

quiet|en /'kwaɪətn/ *vt* calmare. **quieten down** *vi* calmarsi. **~ness** *n* quiete *f*

quilt /kwɪlt/ *n* piumino *m*. **~ed** *a* trapuntato

quins /kwɪnz/ *npl fam* = **quintuplets**

quintet /kwɪn'tet/ *n* quintetto *m*

quintuplets /'kwɪntjʊplɪts/ *npl* cinque gemelli *mpl*

quirk /kwɜ:k/ *n* stranezza *f*

quit /kwɪt/ *v* (*pt/pp* **quitted, quit**) ● *vt* lasciare; (*give up*) smettere (**doing** di fare) ● *vi* (*fam: resign*) andarsene; *Comput* uscire; **give sb notice to ~** ⟨*landlord:*⟩ dare a qcno il preavviso di sfratto

quite /kwaɪt/ *adv* (*fairly*) abbastanza; (*completely*) completamente; (*really*) veramente; **~ [so]!** proprio così!; **~ a few** parecchi

quits /kwɪts/ *a* pari

quiver /'kwɪvə(r)/ *vi* tremare

quiz /kwɪz/ *n* (*game*) quiz *m inv* ● *vt* (*pt/pp* **quizzed**) interrogare

quota /'kwəʊtə/ *n* quota *f*

quotation /kwəʊ'teɪʃn/ *n* citazione *f*; (*price*) preventivo *m*; (*of shares*) quota *f*. **~ marks** *npl* virgolette *fpl*

quote /kwəʊt/ *n fam* = **quotation**; **in ~s** tra virgolette ● *vt* citare; quotare (*price*)

Rr

rabbi /'ræbaɪ/ *n* rabbino *m*; (*title*) rabbi

rabbit /'ræbɪt/ *n* coniglio *m*

rabble /'ræbl/ *n* **the ~** la plebaglia

rabies /'reɪbi:z/ *n* rabbia *f*

race[1] /reɪs/ *n* (*people*) razza *f*

race[2] /reɪs/ *n* corsa *f* ● *vi* correre ● *vt* gareggiare con; fare correre (*horse*)

race: **~course** *n* ippodromo *m*. **~horse** *n* cavallo *m* da corsa. **~-track** *n* pista *f*

racial /'reɪʃl/ *a* razziale. **~ism** *n* razzismo *m*

racing /'reɪsɪŋ/ *n* corse *fpl*; (*horse-*) corse *fpl* dei cavalli. **~ car** *n* macchina *f* da corsa. **~ driver** *n* corridore *m* automobilistico

racis|m /'reɪsɪzm/ *n* razzismo *m*. **~t** /-ɪst/ *a* razzista ● *n* razzista *mf*

rack[1] /ræk/ *n* (*for bikes*) rastrelliera *f*; (*for luggage*) portabagagli *m inv*, (*for plates*) scolapiatti *m inv* ● *vt* **~ one's brains** scervellarsi

rack[2] /ræk/ *n* **go to ~ and ruin** andare in rovina

racket[1] /'rækɪt/ *n Sport* racchetta *f*

racket[2] /'rækɪt/ *n* (*din*) chiasso *m*; (*swindle*) truffa *f*; (*crime*) racket *m inv*, giro *m*

radar /'reɪdɑ:(r)/ *n* radar *m inv*

radian|ce /'reɪdɪəns/ *n* radiosità *f inv*. **~t** *a* raggiante

radiat|e /'reɪdɪeɪt/ *vt* irradiare ● *vi*

⟨heat:⟩ irradiarsi. **~ion** /-'eɪʃn/ n radiazione f

radiator /'reɪdɪeɪtə(r)/ n radiatore m

radical /'rædɪkl/ a radicale ● n radicale mf. **~ly** adv radicalmente

radio /'reɪdɪəʊ/ n radio f inv

radio'active a radioattivo. **~ac'tivity** n radioattività f

radiograph|er /reɪdɪ'ɒɡrəfə(r)/ n radiologo, -a mf. **~y** n radiografia f

radio'therapy n radioterapia f

radish /'rædɪʃ/ n ravanello m

radius /'reɪdɪəs/ n (pl **-dii** /-dɪaɪ/) raggio m

raffle /'ræfl/ n lotteria f

raft /rɑːft/ n zattera f

rafter /'rɑːftə(r)/ n trave f

rag /ræɡ/ n straccio m; ⟨pej: newspaper⟩ giornalaccio m; **in ~s** stracciato

rage /reɪdʒ/ n rabbia f; **all the ~** fam all'ultima moda ● vi infuriarsi; ⟨storm:⟩ infuriare; ⟨epidemic:⟩ imperversare

ragged /'ræɡɪd/ a logoro; ⟨edge⟩ frastagliato

raid /reɪd/ n (by thieves) rapina f, Mil incursione f, raid m inv; ⟨police⟩ irruzione f ● vt Mil fare un'incursione in; ⟨police, burglars:⟩ fare irruzione in. **~er** n (of bank) rapinatore, -trice mf

rail /reɪl/ n ringhiera f; (hand~) ringhiera f; Naut parapetto m; **by ~** per ferrovia

'railroad n Am = railway

railway n ferrovia f. **~man** n ferroviere m. **~ station** n stazione f ferroviaria

rain /reɪn/ n pioggia f ● vi piovere

rain: **~bow** n arcobaleno m. **~coat** n impermeabile m. **~fall** n precipitazione f [atmosferica]

rainy /'reɪnɪ/ a (-ier, -iest) piovoso

raise /reɪz/ n Am aumento m ● vt alzare; levarsi ⟨hat⟩; allevare ⟨children, animals⟩; sollevare ⟨question⟩; ottenere ⟨money⟩

raisin /'reɪzn/ n uva f passa

rake /reɪk/ n rastrello m ● vt rastrellare. **rake up** vt raccogliere col rastrello; fam rivangare

rally /'rælɪ/ n raduno m; Auto rally m inv; Tennis scambio m ● vt (pt/pp **-ied**) radunare ● vi radunarsi; ⟨recover strength⟩ riprendersi

RAM /ræm/ n [memoria f] RAM f

ram /ræm/ n montone m; Astr Ariete m ● vt (pt/pp **rammed**) cozzare contro

rambl|e /'ræmbl/ n escursione f ● vi gironzolare; (in speech) divagare. **~er** n escursionista mf; ⟨rose⟩ rosa f rampicante. **~ing** a (in speech) sconnesso; ⟨club⟩ escursionistico

ramp /ræmp/ n rampa f; Aeron scaletta f mobile (di aerei)

rampage /'ræmpeɪdʒ/ n be/go on the **~** scatenarsi ● vi **~ through the streets** scatenarsi per le strade

rampant /'ræmpənt/ a dilagante

rampart /'ræmpɑːt/ n bastione f

ramshackle /'ræmʃækl/ a sgangherato

ran /ræn/ see **run**

ranch /rɑːntʃ/ n ranch m

rancid /'rænsɪd/ a rancido

rancour /'ræŋkə(r)/ n rancore m

random /'rændəm/ a casuale; **~ sample** campione m a caso ● n **at ~** a casaccio

randy /'rændɪ/ a (-ier, -iest) fam eccitato

rang /ræŋ/ see **ring²**

range /reɪndʒ/ n serie f; Comm, Mus gamma f; (of mountains) catena f; (distance) raggio m; (for shooting) portata f; (stove) cucina f economica; **at a ~ of** a una distanza di ● vi estendersi; **~ from... to...** andare da... a... **~r** n guardia f forestale

rank /ræŋk/ n (row) riga f; Mil grado m; (social position) rango m; **the ~ and file** la base f; **the ~s** Mil i soldati mpl semplici ● vi (*place*) annoverare (**among** tra) ● *vi* (*be placed*) collocarsi

rankle /'ræŋkl/ *vi fig* bruciare

ransack /'rænsæk/ *vt* rovistare; (*pillage*) saccheggiare

ransom /'rænsəm/ *n* riscatto *m*; **hold sb to** ~ tenere qcno in ostaggio (*per il riscatto*)

rant /rænt/ *vi* ~ **[and rave]** inveire; **what's he** ~**ing on about?** cosa sta blaterando?

rap /ræp/ *n* colpo *m* [secco]; *Mus* rap *m* ● *v* (*pt/pp* **rapped**) ● *vt* dare colpetti a ● *vi* ~ **at** bussare a

rape¹ /reɪp/ *n* (*sexual*) stupro *m* ● *vt* violentare, stuprare

rapid /'ræpɪd/ *a* rapido. ~**ity** /rə'pɪdətɪ/ rapidità *f*. ~**ly** *adv* rapidamente

rapids /'ræpɪdz/ *npl* rapida *fsg*

rapist /'reɪpɪst/ *n* violentatore *m*

rapport /ræ'pɔː(r)/ *n* rapporto *m* di intesa

rapture /'ræptʃə(r)/ *n* estasi *f*. ~**ous** /~rəs/ *a* entusiastico

rare¹ /reə(r)/ *a* raro. ~**ly** *adv* raramente

rare² *a* Culin al sangue

rarefied /'reərɪfaɪd/ *a* rarefatto

rarity /'reərətɪ/ *n* rarità *f inv*

rascal /'rɑːskl/ *n* mascalzone *m*

rash¹ /ræʃ/ *n* Med eruzione *f*

rash² *a* avventato. ~**ly** *adv* avventatamente

rasher /'ræʃə(r)/ *n* fetta *f* di pancetta

rasp /rɑːsp/ *n* (*noise*) stridio *m*. ~**ing** a di timbro stridulo

raspberry /'rɑːzbərɪ/ *n* lampone *m*

rat /ræt/ *n* topo *m*; (*fam. person*) carogna *f*; **smell a** ~ *fam* sentire puzzo di bruciato

rate /reɪt/ *n* (*speed*) velocità *f*; (*of payment*) tariffa *f*; (*of exchange*) tasso *m*; ~**s** *pl* (*taxes*) imposte *fpl* comunali sui beni immobili; **at any** ~ in ogni caso; **at this** ~ di questo passo ● *vt* stimare; ~ **among** annoverare tra ● *vi* ~ **as** essere considerato

rather /'rɑːðə(r)/ *adv* piuttosto; ~**!** eccome!; ~ **too...** un po' troppo...

ratification /rætɪfɪ'keɪʃn/ *n* ratifica *f*. ~**fy** /'rætɪfaɪ/ *vt* (*pt/pp* **-ied**) ratificare

rating /'reɪtɪŋ/ *n*; ~**s** *pl* Radio, TV indice *m* d'ascolto, audience *f inv*

ratio /'reɪʃɪəʊ/ *n* rapporto *m*

ration /'ræʃn/ *n* razione *f* ● *vt* razionare

rational /'ræʃənl/ *a* razionale. ~**ize** /ɪz/ *vt/i* razionalizzare

'rat race *n fam* corsa *f* al successo

rattle /'rætl/ *n* tintinnìo *m*; (*toy*) sonaglio *m* ● *vi* tintinnare ● *vt* (*shake*) scuotere; *fam* innervosire. **rattle off** *vt fam* sciorinare

'rattlesnake *n* serpente *m* a sonagli

raucous /'rɔːkəs/ *a* rauco

rave /reɪv/ *vi* vaneggiare; ~ **about** andare in estasi per

raven /'reɪvn/ *n* corvo *m* imperiale

ravenous /'rævənəs/ *a* (*person*) affamato

ravine /rə'viːn/ *n* gola *f*

raving /'reɪvɪŋ/ *a* ~ **mad** *fam* matto da legare

ravishing /'rævɪʃɪŋ/ *a* incantevole

raw /rɔː/ *a* crudo; (*not processed*) grezzo; (*weather*) gelido; (*inexperienced*) inesperto; **get a** ~ **deal** *fam* farsi fregare. ~ **ma'terials** *npl* materie *fpl* prime

ray /reɪ/ *n* raggio *m*; ~ **of hope** barlume *m* di speranza

raze /reɪz/ *vt* ~ **to the ground** radere al suolo

razor /'reɪzə(r)/ *n* rasoio *m*. ~ **blade** *n* lametta *f* da barba

re /riː/ *prep* con riferimento a

reach /riːtʃ/ *n* portata *f*; **within** ~ a portata di mano; **out of** ~ of fuori dalla portata di; **within easy** ~ facilmente raggiungibile ● *vt* arrivare a (*place, decision*); (*pass*) passare; **I can't** ~ **it** non ci arrivo ● *vi* arrivare (**to** a); ~ **for** allungare la mano per prendere

re'act /rɪ-/ *vi* reagire

re'action /rɪ-/ n reazione f. ~ary a reazionario, -a mf

reactor /rɪ'æktə(r)/ n reattore m

read /riːd/ vt (pt/pp read /red/) leggere; Univ studiare ● vi leggere; (instrument:) indicare. read out vt leggere ad alta voce

readable /'riːdəbl/ a piacevole a leggersi; (legible) leggibile

reader /'riːdə(r)/ n lettore, -trice mf; (book) antologia f

readi|ly /'redɪlɪ/ adv volentieri; (easily) facilmente. ~ness n disponibilità f inv; in ~ness pronto

reading /'riːdɪŋ/ n lettura f

rea'djust /riː-/ vt regolare di nuovo ● vi riabituarsi (to a)

ready /'redɪ/ a (-ier, -iest) pronto; (quick) veloce; get ~ prepararsi

ready: ~-made a confezionato. ~ 'money n contanti mpl. ~-to-'wear a prêt-à-porter

real /rɪːl/ a vero; (increase) reale ● adv Am fam veramente. ~ esta-te n beni mpl immobili

realis|m /'rɪəlɪzm/ n realismo m. ~t /-lɪst/ n realista mf. ~tic /-'lɪstɪk/ a realistico

reality /rɪ'ælɪtɪ/ n realtà f inv

realization /rɪəlar'zeɪʃn/ n realizzazione f

realize /'rɪəlaɪz/ vt realizzare

really /'rɪəlɪ/ adv davvero

realm /relm/ n regno m

realtor /'rɪəltə(r)/ n Am agente mf immobiliare

reap /riːp/ vt mietere

reap'pear /riː-/ vi riapparire

rear¹ /rɪə(r)/ a posteriore; Auto di dietro; ~ end fam didietro m ● in the ~ (of building) il retro m ● n (of bus, plane) la parte f posteriore; from the ~ da dietro

rear² vt allevare ● vi ~ [up] (horse:) impennarsi

'rear-light n luce f posteriore

re'arm /riː-/ vt riarmare ● vi riarmarsi

rear'range /riː-/ vt cambiare la disposizione di

rear-view 'mirror n Auto specchietto m retrovisore

reason /'riːzn/ n ragione f; within ~ nei limiti del ragionevole ● vi ragionare; ~ with cercare di far ragionare. ~able /-əbl/ a ragionevole. ~ably /-əblɪ/ adv (in reasonable way, fairly) ragionevolmente

reas'sur|ance /riː-/ n rassicurazione f. ~e vt rassicurare; ~e sb of sth rassicurare qcno su qcsa. ~ing a rassicurante

rebate /'riːbeɪt/ n rimborso m; (discount) deduzione f

rebel¹ /'rebl/ n ribelle mf

rebel² /rɪ'bel/ vi (pt/pp rebelled) ribellarsi. ~lion n ribellione f. ~lious /-jəs/ a ribelle

re'bound¹ /rɪ-/ vi rimbalzare; fig ricadere

'rebound² /rɪ-/ n rimbalzo m

rebuff /rɪ'bʌf/ n rifiuto m

re'build /riː-/ vt (pt/pp -built) ricostruire

rebuke /rɪ'bjuːk/ vt rimproverare

rebuttal /rɪ'bʌtl/ n rifiuto m

re'call /riː-/ n richiamo m; beyond ~ irrevocabile ● vt richiamare; riconvocare (diplomat, parliament); (remember) rievocare

recap /'riːkæp/ vt/i fam = recapitulate ● n ricapitolazione f

recapitulate /riːkə'pɪtjuleɪt/ vt/i ricapitolare

re'capture /riː-/ vt riconquistare; ricatturare (person, animal)

recede /rɪ'siːd/ vi allontanarsi. ~ing a (forehead, chin) sfuggente; have ~ing hair essere stempiato

receipt /rɪ'siːt/ n ricevuta f; (receiving) ricezione f; ~s pl Comm entrate fpl

receive /rɪ'siːv/ vt ricevere. ~r n Teleph ricevitore m; Radio, TV apparecchio m ricevente; (of stolen goods) ricettatore, -trice mf

recent /'riːsnt/ a recente. ~ly adv recentemente

receptacle /rɪ'septəkl/ n recipiente m

reception /rɪ'sepʃn/ n ricevimento m; (welcome) accoglienza f; Radio ricezione f; ~ **[desk]** (in hotel) reception f inv. ~**ist** n persona f alla reception

receptive /rɪ'septɪv/ a ricettivo

recess /rɪ'ses/ n rientranza f; (holiday) vacanza f; Am Sch intervallo m

recession /rɪ'seʃn/ n recessione f

re'charge /riː-/ vt ricaricare

recipe /'resəpɪ/ n ricetta f

recipient /rɪ'sɪpɪənt/ n (of letter) destinatario, -a mf; (of money) beneficiario, -a mf

recipro|cal /rɪ'sɪprəkl/ a reciproco. ~**cate** /-keɪt/ vt ricambiare

recital /rɪ'saɪtl/ n recital m inv

recite /rɪ'saɪt/ vt recitare; (list) elencare

reckless /'reklɪs/ a (action, decision) sconsiderato; **be a ~ driver** guidare in modo pericoloso. ~**ly** adv in modo sconsiderato. ~**ness** n sconsideratezza f

reckon /'rekən/ vt calcolare; (consider) pensare. **reckon on/ with** vt fare i conti con

re'claim /rɪ-/ vt reclamare; bonificare (land)

recline /rɪ'klaɪn/ vi sdraiarsi. ~**ing** a (seat) reclinabile

recluse /rɪ'kluːs/ n recluso, -a mf

recognition /rekəg'nɪʃn/ n riconoscimento m; **beyond ~** irriconoscibile

recognize /'rekəgnaɪz/ vt riconoscere

re'coil /rɪ-/ vi (in fear) indietreggiare

recollect /rekə'lekt/ vt ricordare. ~**ion** /-ekʃn/ n ricordo m f

recommend /rekə'mend/ vt raccomandare. ~**ation** /-'deɪʃn/ n raccomandazione f

recompense /'rekəmpens/ n ricompensa f

reconcile /'rekənsaɪl/ vt riconciliare; conciliare (facts); ~**cile oneself to** rassegnarsi a.

~**ciliation** /-sɪlɪ'eɪʃn/ n riconciliazione f

recon'dition /riː-/ vt ripristinare. ~**ed engine** n motore m che ha subito riparazioni

reconnaissance /rɪ'kɒnɪsns/ n Mil ricognizione f

reconnoitre /rekə'nɔɪtə(r)/ vi (pres p -**tring**) fare una recognizione

recon'sider /riː-/ vt riconsiderare

recon'struct /riː-/ vt ricostruire. ~**ion** n ricostruzione f

record¹ /rɪ'kɔːd/ vt registrare; (make a note of) annotare

record² /'rekɔːd/ n (file) documentazione f; Mus disco m; Sport record m inv; ~**s** pl (files) schedario msg; **keep a ~ of** tener nota di; **off the ~** in via ufficiosa; **have a [criminal] ~** avere la fedina penale sporca

recorder /rɪ'kɔːdə(r)/ n Mus flauto m dolce

recording /rɪ'kɔːdɪŋ/ n registrazione f

'record-player n giradischi m inv

recount /rɪ'kaʊnt/ vt raccontare

re-'count¹ /rɪ-/ vt ricontare

re-'count² /'riː-/ n Pol nuovo conteggio m

recoup /rɪ'kuːp/ vt rifarsi di (losses)

recourse /rɪ'kɔːs/ n **have ~ to** ricorrere a

re-'cover /riː-/ vt rifoderare

recover /rɪ'kʌvə(r)/ vt/i recuperare. ~**y** n recupero m; (of health) guarigione m

recreation /rekrɪ'eɪʃn/ n ricreazione f. ~**al** a ricreativo

recrimination /rɪkrɪmɪ'neɪʃn/ n recriminazione f

recruit /rɪ'kruːt/ n Mil recluta f; **new ~** (member) nuovo, -a adepto, -a mf; (worker) neoassunto, -a mf ● vt assumere (staff). ~**ment** n assunzione f

rectangle /'rektæŋgl/ n rettangolo m. ~**ular** /-'tæŋgjʊlə(r)/ a rettangolare

rectify /'rektɪfaɪ/ vt (pt/pp -ied) rettificare

recuperate /rɪ'ku:pəreɪt/ vi ristabilirsi

recur /rɪ'kɜ:(r)/ vi (pt/pp recurred) ricorrere; (illness:) ripresentarsi

recurrenjce /rɪ'kʌrəns/ n ricorrenza f; (of illness) ricomparsa f. **~t** a ricorrente

recycle /ri:'saɪkl/ vt riciclare

red /red/ a (redder, reddest) rosso ● n rosso m; **in the ~** (account) scoperto. **R~ Cross** n Croce f rossa

redden /'redn/ vt arrossare ● vi arrossire. **~ish** a rossastro

re'decorate /ri:-/ vt (paint) ridipingere; (wallpaper) ritappezzare

redeem /rɪ'di:m/ vt **~ing quality** unico aspetto m positivo

redemption /rɪ'dempʃn/ n riscatto m

rede'ploy /ri:-/ vt ridistribuire

red: ~-haired a con i capelli rossi. **~-handed** a catch sb **~-handed** cogliere qcno con le mani nel sacco. **~ 'herring** n diversione f. **~-hot** a rovente

red: ~ 'light n Auto semaforo m rosso

re'double /ri:-/ vt raddoppiare

redress /rɪ'dres/ n riparazione f. ● vt ristabilire (balance)

red 'tape n fam burocrazia f

reducje /rɪ'dju:s/ vt ridurre; Culin far consumare. **~tion** /-'dʌkʃn/ n riduzione f

redundanjcy /rɪ'dʌndənsɪ/ n licenziamento m; (payment) cassa f integrazione. **~t** a superfluo; **make ~t** licenziare; **be made ~t** essere licenziato

reed /ri:d/ n Bot canna f

reef /ri:f/ n scogliera f

reek /ri:k/ vi puzzare (of di)

reel /ri:l/ n bobina f ● vi (stagger) vacillare. **reel off** vt fig snocciolare

refectory /rɪ'fektərɪ/ n refettorio m; Univ mensa f universitaria

refer /rɪ'fɜ:(r)/ v (pt/pp referred) ● vt rinviare (matter) (to a); indirizzare (person) ● vi ~ **to** fare allusione a; (consult) rivolgersi a (book)

referee /refə'ri:/ n arbitro m; (for job) garante mf ● vt/i (pt/pp refereed) arbitrare

reference /'refərəns/ n riferimento m; (in book) nota f bibliografica; (for job) referenza f; Comm 'your ~' 'riferimento'; **with ~ to** con riferimento a; **make [a] ~ to** fare riferimento a. **~ book** n libro m di consultazione. **~ number** n numero m di riferimento

referendum /refə'rendəm/ n referendum m inv

re'fill¹ /ri:-/ vt riempire di nuovo; ricaricare (pen, lighter)

refill² /'ri:fɪl/ n (for pen) ricambio m

refine /rɪ'faɪn/ vt raffinare. **~d** a raffinato. **~ment** n raffinatezza f; Techn raffinazione f. **~ry** /-ərɪ/ n raffineria f

reflect /rɪ'flekt/ vt riflettere; **be ~ed in** essere riflesso in ● vi (think) riflettere (on su); ~ **badly on sb** fig mettere in cattiva luce qcno. **~ion** /-ekʃn/ n riflessione f; (image) riflesso m; **on ~ion** dopo riflessione. **~ive** /-ɪv/ a riflessivo. **~or** n riflettore m

reflex /'ri:fleks/ n riflesso m ● attrib di riflesso

reflexive /rɪ'fleksɪv/ a riflessivo

reform /rɪ'fɔ:m/ n riforma f ● vt riformare ● vi correggersi. **R~ation** /refə'meɪʃn/ n Relig riforma f. **~er** n riformatore, -trice mf

refrain¹ /rɪ'freɪn/ n ritornello m

refrain² /rɪ'freɪn/ vi astenersi (**from** da)

refresh /rɪ'freʃ/ vt rinfrescare. **~ing** a rinfrescante. **~ments** npl rinfreschi mpl

refrigerate /rɪ'frɪdʒəreɪt/ vt conservare in frigo. **~or** n frigorifero m

re'fuel /ri:-/ v (pt/pp **-fuelled**) ● vt rifornire (di carburante) ● vi fare rifornimento

refuge /'refju:dʒ/ n rifugio m; **take ~** rifugiarsi

refugee /refjʊ'dʒi:/ n rifugiato, -a mf

'refund¹ /'ri:-/ n rimborso m

re'fund² /rɪ-/ vt rimborsare

refurbish /ri:'fɜːbɪʃ/ vt rimettere a nuovo

refusal /rɪ'fjuːzl/ n rifiuto m

refuse¹ /rɪ'fjuːz/ vt/i rifiutare; **~ to do sth** rifiutare di fare qcsa

refuse² /'refjuːs/ n rifiuti mpl. **~ collection** n raccolta f dei rifiuti

refute /rɪ'fjuːt/ vt confutare

re'gain /rɪ-/ vt riconquistare

regal /'riːgl/ a regale

regalia /rɪ'geɪlɪə/ npl insegne fpl reali

regard /rɪ'gaːd/ n (heed) riguardo m; (respect) considerazione f; **~s** pl saluti mpl; **send/give my ~s to your brother** salutami tuo fratello ● vt (consider) considerare (as come); **as ~s** riguardo a. **~ing** prep riguardo a. **~less** adv lo stesso; **~ of** senza badare a

regatta /rɪ'gætə/ n regata f

regenerate /rɪ'dʒenəreɪt/ vt rigenerare ● vi rigenerarsi

regime /reɪ'ʒiːm/ n regime m

regiment /'redʒɪmənt/ n reggimento m. **~al** /-'mentl/ a reggimentale. **~ation** /-mentɪ'teɪʃn/ n irreggimentazione f

region /'riːdʒən/ n regione f; **in the ~ of** fig approssimativamente. **~al** a regionale

register /'redʒɪstə(r)/ n registro m ● vt registrare; mandare per raccomandata (letter); assicurare (luggage); immatricolare (vehicle); mostrare (feeling) ● vi (instrument:) funzionare; (student:) iscriversi (for a); **~ with** iscriversi nella lista di (doctor)

registrar /redʒɪ'straː(r)/ n ufficiale m di stato civile

registration /redʒɪ'streɪʃn/ n (of

vehicle) immatricolazione f; (of letter) raccomandazione f; (of luggage) assicurazione f; (for course) iscrizione f. **~ number** n Auto targa f

registry office /'redʒɪstrɪ-/ n anagrafe f

regret /rɪ'gret/ n rammarico m ● vt (pt/pp **regretted**) rimpiangere; **I ~ that** mi rincresce che. **~fully** adv con rammarico

regrettab|le /rɪ'gretəbl/ a spiacevole. **~ly** adv spiacevolmente; (before adjective) deplorevolmente

regular /'regjʊlə(r)/ a regolare; (usual) abituale ● n cliente mf abituale. **~ity** /-'lærətɪ/ n regolarità f. **~ly** adv regolarmente

regulat|e /'regjʊleɪt/ vt regolare. **~ion** /-'leɪʃn/ n (rule) regolamento m

rehabilitat|e /riːhə'bɪlɪteɪt/ vt riabilitare. **~ion** /-'teɪʃn/ n riabilitazione f

rehears|al /rɪ'hɜːsl/ n Theat prova f. **~e** vt/i provare

reign /reɪn/ n regno m ● vi regnare

reimburse /riːɪm'bɜːs/ vt **~ sb for sth** rimborsare qcsa a qcno

rein /reɪn/ n redine f

reincarnation /riːɪnkɑː'neɪʃn/ n reincarnazione f

reinforce /riːɪn'fɔːs/ vt rinforzare. **~d 'concrete** n cemento m armato. **~ment** n rinforzo m

reinstate /riːɪn'steɪt/ vt reintegrare

reiterate /riː'ɪtəreɪt/ vt reiterare

reject /rɪ'dʒekt/ vt rifiutare. **~ion** /-kʃn/ n rifiuto m; Med rigetto m

rejoic|e /rɪ'dʒɔɪs/ vi liter rallegrarsi. **~ing** n gioia f

rejuvenate /rɪ'dʒuːvəneɪt/ vt ringiovanire

relapse /rɪ'læps/ n ricaduta f ● vi ricadere

relate /rɪ'leɪt/ vt (tell) riportare; (connect) collegare ● vi **~ to** riferirsi a; identificarsi con (person). **~d** a imparentato (to a); (ideas etc) affine

relation /rɪ'leɪʃn/ n rapporto m; (*person*) parente mf. **~ship** n rapporto m (*blood tie*) parentela f; (*affair*) relazione f

relative /'relətɪv/ n parente mf ● a relativo. **~ly** adv relativamente

relax /rɪ'læks/ vt rilassare; allentare (*pace, grip*) ● vi rilassarsi. **~ation** /riːlæk'seɪʃn/ n rilassamento m, relax m inv; (*recreation*) svago m. **~ing** a rilassante

relay¹ /riː'leɪ/ vt (pt/pp -laid) ritrasmettere; *Radio*, *TV* trasmettere

relay² /'riːleɪ/ n *Electr* relais m inv; **work in ~s** fare i turni. **~ [race]** n [corsa f] staffetta f

release /rɪ'liːs/ n rilascio m; (of film) distribuzione f ● vt liberare; lasciare ⟨hand⟩; togliere ⟨brake⟩; distribuire ⟨film⟩; rilasciare (*information etc*)

relegate /'relɪgeɪt/ vt relegare; be **~d** *Sport* essere retrocesso

relent /rɪ'lent/ vi cedere. **~less** a inflessibile; (*unceasing*) incessante. **~lessly** adv incessantemente

relevance /'reləvns/ n pertinenza f. **~t** a pertinente (**to** a)

reliability /rɪlaɪə'bɪlətɪ/ n affidabilità f. **~le** /-'laɪəbl/ a affidabile a. **~ly** adv in modo affidabile; be **~ly informed** sapere da fonte certa

reliance /rɪ'laɪəns/ n fiducia f (**on** in). **~t** a fiducioso (**on** in)

relic /'relɪk/ n *Relig* reliquia f; **~s** npl resti mpl

relief /rɪ'liːf/ n sollievo m; (*assistance*) soccorso m; (*distraction*) diversivo m; (*replacement*) cambio m; (*in art*) rilievo m; **in ~** in rilievo. **~ map** n carta f in rilievo. **~ train** n treno m supplementare

relieve /rɪ'liːv/ vt alleviare; (*take over from*) dare il cambio a; **~ of** liberare da ⟨burden⟩

religion /rɪ'lɪdʒən/ n religione f

religious /rɪ'lɪdʒəs/ a religioso. **~ly** adv (*conscientiously*) scrupolosamente

relinquish /rɪ'lɪŋkwɪʃ/ vt abbandonare; **~ sth to sb** rinunciare a qcsa in favore di qcno

relish /'relɪʃ/ n gusto m; *Culin* salsa f ● vt fig apprezzare

relo'cate /riː-/ vt trasferire

reluctance /rɪ'lʌktəns/ n riluttanza f. **~t** a riluttante. **~tly** adv a malincuore

rely /rɪ'laɪ/ vi (pt/pp -ied) **~ on** dipendere da; (*trust*) contare su

remain /rɪ'meɪn/ vi restare. **~der** n resto m. **~ing** a restante. **~s** npl resti mpl; (*dead body*) spoglie fpl

remand /rɪ'mɑːnd/ n **on ~** in custodia cautelare ● vt **~ in custody** rinviare con detenzione provvisoria

remark /rɪ'mɑːk/ n osservazione f ● vt osservare. **~able** /-əbl/ a notevole. **~ably** adv notevolmente

remarry /riː-/ vi risposarsi

remedial /rɪ'miːdɪəl/ a correttivo; *Med* curativo

remedy /'remədɪ/ n rimedio m (**for** contro) ● vt (pt/pp -ied) rimediare a

remember /rɪ'membə(r)/ vt ricordare, ricordarsi; **~ to do sth** ricordarsi di fare qcsa; **~ me to him** salutamelo ● vi ricordarsi

remind /rɪ'maɪnd/ vt **~ sb of sth** ricordare qcsa a qcno. **~er** n ricordo m; (*memo*) promemoria m; (*letter*) lettera f di sollecito

reminisce /remɪ'nɪs/ vi rievocare il passato. **~nces** /-ənsɪz/ npl reminiscenze fpl. **~nt** a be **~nt of** richiamare alla memoria

remiss /rɪ'mɪs/ a negligente

remission /rɪ'mɪʃn/ n remissione f; (of sentence) condono m

remit /rɪ'mɪt/ vt (pt/pp remitted) rimettere ⟨money⟩. **~tance** n rimessa f

remnant /'remnənt/ n resto m; (of material) scampolo m; (*trace*) traccia f

remonstrate /'remənstreɪt/ vi fare rimostranze; **~ with sb** fare rimostranza a qcno

remorse /rɪˈmɔːs/ n rimorso m. **~ful** a pieno di rimorso. **~less** a spietato. **~lessly** adv senza pietà

remote /rɪˈməʊt/ a remoto; (slight) minimo. **~ access** n Comput accesso m remoto. **~ con'trol** n telecomando m. **~-con'trolled** a a telecomandato. **~ly** adv lontanamente; **be not ~ly...** non essere lontanamente...

re'movable /rɪ-/ a rimovibile

removal /rɪˈmuːvl/ n rimozione f; (from house) trasloco m. **~ van** n camion m inv da trasloco

remove /rɪˈmuːv/ vt togliere; togliersi (clothes); eliminare (stain, doubts)

remuneration /rɪmjuːnəˈreɪʃn/ n rimunerazione f. **~ive** /-ˈmjuːnərətɪv/ a rimunerativo

render /ˈrendə(r)/ vt rendere (service)

rendering /ˈrend(ə)rɪŋ/ n Mus interpretazione f

renegade /ˈrenɪɡeɪd/ n rinnegato, -a mf

renew /rɪˈnjuː/ vt rinnovare (contract). **~al** n rinnovo m

renounce /rɪˈnaʊns/ vt rinunciare a

renovate /ˈrenəveɪt/ vt rinnovare. **~ion** /-ˈveɪʃn/ n rinnovo m

renown /rɪˈnaʊn/ n fama f. **~ed** a rinomato

rent /rent/ n affitto m ● vt affittare; **~ [out]** dare in affitto. **~al** n affitto m

renunciation /rɪnʌnsɪˈeɪʃn/ n rinuncia f

re'open /riː-/ vt/i riaprire

re'organize /riː-/ vt riorganizzare

rep /rep/ n Comm fam rappresentante mf; Theat ≈ teatro m stabile

repair /rɪˈpeə(r)/ n riparazione f; **in good/bad ~** in cattive/buone condizioni ● vt riparare

repatriate /riːˈpætrɪeɪt/ vt rimpatriare. **~ion** /-ˈeɪʃn/ n rimpatrio m

re'pay /riː-/ vt (pt/pp -paid) ripagare. **~ment** n rimborso m

repeal /rɪˈpiːl/ n abrogazione f ● vt abrogare

repeat /rɪˈpiːt/ n TV replica f ● vt/i ripetere; **~ oneself** ripetersi. **~ed** a ripetuto. **~edly** adv ripetutamente

repel /rɪˈpel/ vt (pt/pp repelled) respingere; fig ripugnare. **~lent** a ripulsivo

repent /rɪˈpent/ vi pentirsi. **~ance** n pentimento m. **~ant** a pentito

repercussions /riːpəˈkʌʃnz/ npl ripercussioni fpl

repertoire /ˈrepətwɑː(r)/ n repertorio m

repetition /repɪˈtɪʃn/ n ripetizione f. **~ive** /rɪˈpetɪtɪv/ a ripetitivo

re'place /rɪ-/ vt (put back) rimettere a posto; (take the place of) sostituire; **~ sth with sth** sostituire qcsa con qcsa. **~ment** n sostituzione m; (person) sostituto, -a mf. **~ment part** n pezzo m di ricambio

'replay /ˈriː-/ n Sport partita f ripetuta; [action] ~ replay m inv

replenish /rɪˈplenɪʃ/ vt rifornire (stocks); (refill) riempire di nuovo

replica /ˈreplɪkə/ n copia f

reply /rɪˈplaɪ/ n risposta f (to a) ● vt/i (pt/pp replied) rispondere

report /rɪˈpɔːt/ n rapporto m; TV, Radio servizio m; Journ cronaca f; Sch pagella f; (rumour) diceria f ● vt riportare; **~ sb to the police** denunciare qcno alla polizia ● vi riportare; (present oneself) presentarsi (to a). **~edly** adv secondo quanto si dice. **~er** n cronista mf, reporter mf inv

repose /rɪˈpəʊz/ n riposo m

repos'sess /riː-/ vt riprendere possesso di

reprehensible /reprɪˈhensəbl/ a riprovevole

represent /reprɪˈzent/ vt rappresentare

representative /reprɪˈzentətɪv/ a rappresentativo ● n rappresentante mf

repress /rɪˈpres/ vt reprimere.

~ion /-ʃn/ n repressione f. **~ive** /-ɪv/ a repressivo

reprieve /rɪ'priːv/ n commutazione f della pena capitale; (*postponement*) sospensione f della pena capitale; *fig* tregua f ● vt sospendere la sentenza a; *fig* risparmiare

reprimand /'reprɪmɑːnd/ n rimprovero m ● vt rimproverare

'reprint[1] /'riː-/ n ristampa f

re'print[2] /riː-/ vt ristampare

reprisal /rɪ'praɪzl/ n rappresaglia f; **in ~ for** per rappresaglia contro

reproach /rɪ'prəʊtʃ/ n ammonimento m ● vt ammonire. **~ful** a di rimprovero. **~fully** adv con aria di rimprovero

repro'duc|e /riː-/ vt riprodurre ● vi riprodursi. **~tion** /-'dʌkʃn/ n riproduzione f. **~tive** /-'dʌktɪv/ a riproduttivo

reprove /rɪ'pruːv/ vt rimproverare

reptile /'reptaɪl/ n rettile m

republic /rɪ'pʌblɪk/ n repubblica f. **~an** a repubblicano ● n repubblicano, -a mf

repudiate /rɪ'pjuːdɪeɪt/ vt ripudiare; respingere (*view, suggestion*)

repugnan|ce /rɪ'pʌɡnəns/ n ripugnanza f. **~t** a ripugnante

repuls|ion /rɪ'pʌlʃn/ n repulsione f. **~ive** /-ɪv/ a ripugnante

reputable /'repjʊtəbl/ a affidabile

reputation /repjʊ'teɪʃn/ n reputazione f

repute /rɪ'pjuːt/ n reputazione f. **~d** /-ɪd/ a presunto; **he is ~d** to be si presume che sia. **~dly** adv presumibilmente

request /rɪ'kwest/ n richiesta f ● vt richiedere. **~ stop** n fermata f a richiesta

require /rɪ'kwaɪə(r)/ vt (*need*) necessitare di; (*demand*) esigere. **~d** a richiesto; **I am ~d to** do si esige che io faccia. **~ment** n esigenza f; (*condition*) requisito m

requisite /'rekwɪzɪt/ a necessario ● n **toilet/travel ~s** pl articoli mpl da toilette/viaggio

re'sale /riː-/ n rivendita f

rescue /'reskjuː/ n salvataggio m ● vt salvare. **~r** n salvatore, -trice mf

research /rɪ'sɜːtʃ/ n ricerca f ● vt fare ricerche su; *Journ* fare un'inchiesta su ● vi ~ **into** fare ricerche su. **~er** n ricercatore, -trice mf

resem|blance /rɪ'zembləns/ n rassomiglianza f. **~ble** /-bl/ vt rassomigliare a

resent /rɪ'zent/ vt risentirsi per. **~ful** a pieno di risentimento. **~fully** adv con risentimento. **~ment** n risentimento m

reservation /rezə'veɪʃn/ n (*booking*) prenotazione f; (*doubt, enclosure*) riserva f

reserve /rɪ'zɜːv/ n riserva f; (*shyness*) riserbo m ● vt riservare; riservarsi (*right*). **~d** a riservato

reservoir /'rezəvwɑː(r)/ n bacino m idrico

re'shape /riː-/ vt ristrutturare

re'shuffle /riː-/ n *Pol* rimpasto m ● vt *Pol* rimpastare

reside /rɪ'zaɪd/ vi risiedere

residence /'rezɪdəns/ n residenza f; (*stay*) soggiorno m. **~ permit** n permesso m di soggiorno

resident /'rezɪdənt/ a residente ● n residente mf. **~ial** /-'denʃl/ a residenziale

residue /'rezɪdjuː/ n residuo m

resign /rɪ'zaɪn/ vt dimettersi da; **~ oneself to** rassegnarsi a ● vi dare le dimissioni. **~ation** /rezɪɡ'neɪʃn/ n rassegnazione f; (*from job*) dimissioni fpl. **~ed** a rassegnato

resilient /rɪ'zɪlɪənt/ a elastico; *fig* con buone capacità di ripresa

resin /'rezɪn/ n resina f

resist /rɪ'zɪst/ vt resistere a ● vi resistere. **~ance** n resistenza f. **~ant** a resistente

resolut|e /'rezəluːt/ a risoluto. **~ely** adv con risolutezza. **~ion** /-'luːʃn/ n risolutezza f

resolve /rɪ'zɒlv/ vt ~ **to do** decidere di fare

resonan|ce /'rezənəns/ n risonanza f. ~**t** a risonante

resort /rɪ'zɔ:t/ n (place) luogo m di villeggiatura; **as a last ~** come ultima risorsa ● vi ~ **to** ricorrere a

resound /rɪ'zaʊnd/ vi risonare (**with** di). ~**ing** a (success) risonante

resource /rɪ'sɔ:s/ n ~**s** pl risorse fpl. ~**ful** a pieno di risorse; (solution) ingegnoso. ~**fulness** n ingegnosità f inv

respect /rɪ'spekt/ n rispetto m; (aspect) aspetto m; **with ~ to** per quanto riguarda ● vt rispettare

respectability /rɪspektə'bɪlətɪ/ n rispettabilità f inv

respect|able /rɪ'spektəbl/ a rispettabile. ~**ably** adv rispettabilmente. ~**ful** a rispettoso

respective /rɪ'spektɪv/ a rispettivo. ~**ly** adv rispettivamente

respiration /respɪ'reɪʃn/ n respirazione f

respite /'respaɪt/ n respiro m

respond /rɪ'spɒnd/ vi rispondere; (react) reagire (**to** a); (patient:) rispondere (**to** a)

response /rɪ'spɒns/ n risposta f; (reaction) reazione f

responsibility /rɪspɒnsɪ'bɪlətɪ/ n responsabilità f inv

responsib|le /rɪ'spɒnsəbl/ a responsabile; (job) impegnativo

responsive /rɪ'spɒnsɪv/ a **be ~** (audience etc:) reagire; (brakes:) essere sensibile

rest[1] /rest/ n riposo m; Mus pausa f. **have a ~** riposarsi ● vt riposare; (lean) appoggiare (**on** su); (place) appoggiare ● vi riposarsi; (elbows:) appoggiarsi; (hopes:) posare

rest[2] n **the ~** il resto m; (people) gli altri mpl ● vi **it ~s with you** sta a te

restaurant /'restərɒnt/ n ristorante m. ~ **car** n vagone m ristorante

restful /'restfl/ a riposante

restive /'restɪv/ a irrequieto

restless /'restlɪs/ a nervoso

restoration /restə'reɪʃn/ n (of building) restauro m

restore /rɪ'stɔ:(r)/ vt ristabilire; restaurare (building); (give back) restituire

restrain /rɪ'streɪn/ vt trattenere; ~ **oneself** controllarsi. ~**ed** a controllato. ~**t** n restrizione f; (moderation) ritegno m

restrict /rɪ'strɪkt/ vt limitare; ~ **to** limitarsi a. ~**ion** /-ɪkʃn/ n limite m; (restraint) restrizione f. ~**ive** /-ɪv/ a limitativo

'rest room n Am toilette f inv

result /rɪ'zʌlt/ n risultato m; **as a ~** a causa (**of** di) ● vi ~ **from** risultare da; ~ **in** portare a

resume /rɪ'zju:m/ vt/i riprendere

résumé /'rezjʊmeɪ/ n riassunto m; Am curriculum vitae m inv

resumption /rɪ'zʌmpʃn/ n ripresa f

resurgence /rɪ'sɜ:dʒəns/ n rinascita f

resurrect /rezə'rekt/ vt fig risuscitare. ~**ion** /-ekʃn/ n **the R~ion** Relig la Risurrezione

resuscitat|e /rɪ'sʌsɪteɪt/ vt rianimare. ~**ion** /-'teɪʃn/ n rianimazione f

retail /'ri:teɪl/ n vendita f al minuto a & adv al minuto ● vt vendere al minuto ● vi ~ **at** essere venduto al pubblico al prezzo di. ~**er** n dettagliante mf

retain /rɪ'teɪn/ vt conservare; (hold back) trattenere

retaliat|e /rɪ'tælieɪt/ vi vendicarsi. ~**ion** /-'eɪʃn/ n rappresaglia f; **in ~ion** for per rappresaglia contro

retarded /rɪ'tɑ:dɪd/ a ritardato

retentive /rɪ'tentɪv/ a (memory) buono

rethink /ri:'θɪŋk/ vt (pt/pp rethought) ripensare

reticen|ce /'retɪsəns/ n reticenza f. ~**t** a reticente

retina /'retɪnə/ n retina f

retinue /'retɪnju:/ n seguito m

retire /rɪ'taɪə(r)/ vi andare in pensione; ⟨withdraw⟩ ritirarsi ●vt mandare in pensione ⟨employee⟩. ~**d** a in pensione. ~**ment** n pensione f; **since my ~ment** da quando sono andato in pensione

retiring /rɪ'taɪərɪŋ/ a riservato

retort /rɪ'tɔːt/ n replica f ●vt ribattere

re'touch /riː-/ vt Phot ritoccare

re'trace /rɪ-/ vt ripercorrere; ~ **one's steps** ritornare sui propri passi

retract /rɪ'trækt/ vt ritirare; ritrattare ⟨statement, evidence⟩ ●vi ritrarsi

re'train /riː-/ vt riqualificare ●vi riqualificarsi

retreat /rɪ'triːt/ n ritirata f; ⟨place⟩ ritiro m ●vi ritirarsi; Mil battere in ritirata

re'trial /riː-/ n nuovo processo m

retribution /retrɪ'bjuːʃn/ n castigo m

retrieval /rɪ'triːvəl/ n recupero m

retrieve /rɪ'triːv/ vt recuperare

retrograde /'retrəgreɪd/ a retrogrado

retrospect /'retrəspekt/ n in ~ guardando indietro. ~**ive** /-'spektɪv/ a retrospettivo; ⟨legislation⟩ retroattivo ●n retrospettiva f

return /rɪ'tɜːn/ n ritorno m; ⟨giving back⟩ restituzione f; Comm profitto m; ⟨ticket⟩ biglietto m di andata e ritorno; **by ~ [of post]** a stretto giro di posta; **in ~** in cambio ⟨for di⟩; **many happy ~s!** cento di questi giorni! ●vi ritornare ●vt ⟨give back⟩ restituire; ricambiare ⟨affection, invitation⟩; ⟨put back⟩ rimettere; ⟨send back⟩ mandare indietro; ⟨elect⟩ eleggere

return: ~ **flight** n volo m di andata e ritorno. ~ **match** n rivincita f. ~ **ticket** n biglietto m di andata e ritorno

reunion /riː'juːnjən/ n riunione f

reunite /riːjuː'naɪt/ vt riunire

re'us|able /riː-/ a riutilizzabile. ~**e** vt riutilizzare

rev /rev/ n Auto, fam giro m ⟨di motore⟩ ●v ⟨pt/pp revved⟩ ●vt ~ [up] far andare su di giri ●vi andare su di giri

reveal /rɪ'viːl/ vt rivelare; ⟨dress:⟩ scoprire. ~**ing** a rivelatore; ⟨dress⟩ osé

revel /'revl/ vi ⟨pt/pp revelled⟩ ~ **in sth** godere di qcsa

revelation /revə'leɪʃn/ n rivelazione f

revelry /'revlrɪ/ n baldoria f

revenge /rɪ'vendʒ/ n vendetta f; Sport rivincita f; **take** ~ vendicarsi ●vt vendicare

revenue /'revənjuː/ n reddito m

reverberate /rɪ'vɜːbəreɪt/ vi riverberare

revere /rɪ'vɪə(r)/ vt riverire. ~**nce** /'revərəns/ n riverenza f

Reverend /'revərənd/ a reverendo

reverent /'revərənt/ a riverente

reverse /rɪ'vɜːs/ a opposto; **in** ~ **order** in ordine inverso ●n contrario m; ⟨back⟩ rovescio m; Auto marcia m indietro ●vt invertire; ~ **the car into the garage** entrare in garage a marcia indietro; ~ **the charges** Teleph fare una telefonata a carico ●vi Auto fare marcia indietro

revert /rɪ'vɜːt/ vi ~ **to** tornare a

review /rɪ'vjuː/ n ⟨survey⟩ rassegna f; ⟨re-examination⟩ riconsiderazione f; Mil rivista f; ⟨book, play⟩ recensione f ●vt riesaminare ⟨situation⟩; Mil passare in rivista; recensire ⟨book, play⟩. ~**er** n critico, -a mf

revile /rɪ'vaɪl/ vt ingiuriare

revis|e /rɪ'vaɪz/ vt rivedere; ⟨for exam⟩ ripassare. ~**ion** /-'vɪʒn/ n revisione f; ⟨for exam⟩ ripasso m

revival /rɪ'vaɪvl/ n ritorno m; ⟨of patient⟩ recupero m; ⟨from coma⟩ risveglio m

revive /rɪ'vaɪv/ vt resuscitare; rianimare ⟨person⟩ ●vi riprendersi; ⟨person:⟩ rianimarsi

revoke /rɪ'vəʊk/ vt revocare

revolt /rɪ'vəʊlt/ n rivolta f ● vi ribellarsi ● vt rivoltare. **~ing** a rivoltante

revolution /revə'luːʃn/ n rivoluzione f, Auto **~s per minute** giri mpl al minuto. **~ary** /-ərɪ/ a & n rivoluzionario, -a mf. **~ize** vt rivoluzionare

revolve /rɪ'vɒlv/ vi ruotare; **~ around** girare intorno

revolver /rɪ'vɒlvə(r)/ n rivoltella f, revolver m inv. **~ing** a ruotante

revue /rɪ'vjuː/ n rivista f

revulsion /rɪ'vʌlʃn/ n ripulsione f

reward /rɪ'wɔːd/ n ricompensa f ● vt ricompensare. **~ing** a gratificante

re'write /riː-/ vt (pt rewrote, pp rewritten) riscrivere

rhapsody /'ræpsədɪ/ n rapsodia f

rhetoric /'retərɪk/ n retorica f. **~al** /rɪ'tɒrɪkl/ a retorico

rheumatic /ruː'mætɪk/ a reumatico. **~ism** /'ruːmətɪzm/ n reumatismo m

Rhine /raɪn/ n Reno m

rhinoceros /raɪ'nɒsərəs/ n rinoceronte m

rhubarb /'ruːbɑːb/ n rabarbaro m

rhyme /raɪm/ n rima f; (poem) filastrocca f ● vi rimare

rhythm /'rɪðm/ n ritmo m. **~ic[al]** a ritmico. **~ically** adv con ritmo

rib /rɪb/ n costola f

ribald /'rɪbld/ a spinto

ribbon /'rɪbən/ n nastro m; **in ~s** a brandelli

rice /raɪs/ n riso m

rich /rɪtʃ/ a ricco; (food) pesante ● n the **~** pl i ricchi mpl. **~es** pl ricchezze fpl. **~ly** adv riccamente; (deserve) largamente

rickety /'rɪkɪtɪ/ a malfermo

ricochet /'rɪkəʃeɪ/ vi rimbalzare ● n rimbalzo m

rid /rɪd/ vt (pt/pp rid, pres p ridding) sbarazzare (of di); **get ~ of** sbarazzarsi di

riddance /'rɪdns/ n **good ~!** che liberazione!

ridden /'rɪdn/ see ride

riddle /'rɪdl/ n enigma m

riddled /'rɪdld/ a **~ with** crivellato di

ride /raɪd/ n (on horse) cavalcata f; (in vehicle) giro m; (journey) viaggio m; **take sb for a ~** fam prendere qcno in giro ● v (pt rode, pp ridden) ● vt montare (horse); andare su (bicycle) ● vi andare a cavallo; (jockey, showjumper:) cavalcare; (cyclist:) andare in bicicletta; (in vehicle) viaggiare. **~r** n cavallerizzo, -a mf; (in race) fantino m; (on bicycle) ciclista mf; (in document) postilla f

ridge /rɪdʒ/ n spigolo m; (on roof) punta f; (of mountain) cresta f

ridicule /'rɪdɪkjuːl/ n ridicolo m ● vt mettere in ridicolo

ridiculous /rɪ'dɪkjʊləs/ a ridicolo

riding /'raɪdɪŋ/ n equitazione f ● attrib d'equitazione

rife /raɪf/ a **be ~** essere diffuso; **~ with** pieno di

riff-raff /'rɪfræf/ n marmaglia f

rifle /'raɪfl/ n fucile m; **~-range** tiro m al bersaglio ● vt **~ [through]** mettere a soqquadro

rig¹ /rɪg/ n equipaggiamento m; (at sea) piattaforma f per trivellazioni subacquee ● vt (pt/pp rigged) equipaggiare. **rig out** vt allestire

rig² vt (pt/pp rigged) manovrare (election)

right /raɪt/ a giusto; (not left) destro, **be ~** (person:) aver ragione; (clock:) essere giusto; **put ~** mettere all'ora (clock); correggere (person); rimediare a (situation); **that's ~!** proprio così! ● adv (correctly) bene; (not left) a destra; (directly) proprio; (completely) completamente ● n giusto m; (not left) destra f; (what is due) diritto m; **on/to the ~** a destra; **be in the ~** essere nel giusto; **know ~ from wrong** distinguere il bene dal

male; **by ~s** secondo giustizia;
the **R~** *Pol* la destra *f* ● *vt* raddrizzare; **~ a wrong** *fig* riparare a
un torto. **~ angle** *n* angolo *m* retto
rightful /'raɪtfl/ *a* legittimo
right: **~-'handed** *a* che usa la
mano destra. **~-hand 'man** *n* *fig*
braccio *m* destro
rightly /'raɪtlɪ/ *adv* giustamente
right: **~ of way** *n* diritto *m* di transito; (*path*) passaggio *m*; *Auto* precedenza *f*. **~-'wing** *a* *Pol* di destra
● *n* *Sport* ala *f* destra
rigid /'rɪdʒɪd/ *a* rigido. **~ity**
/-'dʒɪdətɪ/ *n* rigidità *f* inv
rigmarole /'rɪgmərəʊl/ *n* trafila *f*;
(*story*) tiritera *f*
rigorous /'rɪgərəs/ *a* rigoroso
rile /raɪl/ *vt* fam irritare
rim /rɪm/ *n* bordo *m*; (*of wheel*)
cerchione *m*
rind /raɪnd/ *n* (*on fruit*) scorza *f*;
(*on cheese*) crosta *f*; (*on bacon*) co-
tenna *f*
ring[1] /rɪŋ/ *n* (*circle*) cerchio *m*; (*on
finger*) anello *m*; (*boxing*) ring *m*
inv; (*for circus*) pista *f*; **stand in a
~** essere in cerchio
ring[2] *n* suono *m*; **give sb a ~**
Teleph dare un colpo di telefono a
qcno ● *v* (*pt* **rang**, *pp* **rung**) ● *vt*
suonare; **~ [up]** *Teleph* telefonare
a ● *vi* suonare; *Teleph* **~ [up]** telefonare. **ring back** *vt/i* *Teleph* richiamare. **ring off** *vi* *Teleph*
riattaccare
ring: **~-leader** *n* capobanda *m*. **~
road** *n* circonvallazione *f*
rink /rɪŋk/ *n* pista *f* di pattinaggio
rinse /rɪns/ *n* risciacquo *m*; (*hair
colour*) cachet *m* inv ● *vt* sciacquare
riot /'raɪət/ *n* rissa *f*; (*of colour*) accozzaglia *f*; **~s** *pl* disordini *mpl*;
run ~ impazzare ● *vi* creare disordini. **~er** *n* dimostrante *m*.
~ous /-əs/ *a* sfrenato
rip /rɪp/ *n* strappo *m* ● *v* (*pt/pp*
ripped) strappare; **~ open** aprire
con uno strappo. **rip off** *vt* fam fregare

ripe /raɪp/ *a* maturo; (*cheese*) sta-
gionato
ripen /'raɪpn/ *vi* maturare;
(*cheese:*) stagionarsi ● *vt* far maturare; stagionare (*cheese*)
ripeness /'raɪpnɪs/ *n* maturità *f*
inv
'rip-off *n* fam frode *f*
ripple /'rɪpl/ *n* increspatura *f*;
(*sound*) mormorio *m*
rise /raɪz/ *n* (*of sun*) levata *f*; (*fig: to
fame, power*) ascesa *f*; (*increase*)
aumento *m*; **give ~ to** dare adito a
● *vi* (*pt* **rose**, *pp* **risen**) alzarsi;
(*sun:*) sorgere; (*dough:*) lievitare;
(*prices, water level:*) aumentare;
(*to power, position*) arrivare (**to** a).
~r *n* **early ~r** persona *f* mattinie-
ra
rising /'raɪzɪŋ/ *a* (*sun*) levante; **~
generation** nuova generazione *f*
● *n* (*revolt*) sollevazione *f*
risk /rɪsk/ *n* rischio *m*; **at one's
own ~** a proprio rischio e pericolo ● *vt* rischiare
risky /'rɪskɪ/ *a* (**-ier, -iest**) rischioso
risqué /'rɪskeɪ/ *a* spinto
rite /raɪt/ *n* rito *m*; **last ~s** estrema
unzione *f*
ritual /'rɪtjʊəl/ *a* rituale ● *n* rituale *m*
rival /'raɪvl/ *a* rivale ● *n* rivale *mf*;
~s *pl* *Comm* concorrenti *mpl* ● *vt*
(*pt/pp* **rivalled**) rivaleggiare con.
~ry *n* rivalità *f* inv; *Comm* concorrenza *f*
river /'rɪvə(r)/ *n* fiume *m*. **~-bed** *n*
letto *m* del fiume
rivet /'rɪvɪt/ *n* rivetto *m* ● *vt*
rivettare; **~ed by** *fig* inchiodato
da
Riviera /rɪvɪ'eərə/ *n* **the Italian ~**
la riviera ligure
road /rəʊd/ *n* strada *f*, via *f*; **be on
the ~** viaggiare
road: **~-block** *n* blocco *m* stradale.
~-hog *n* fam pirata *m* della strada. **~-map** *n* carta *f* stradale. **~
safety** *n* sicurezza *f* sulle strade.
~ sense *n* prudenza *f* (*per stra*-

da). **~side** *n* bordo *m* della strada. **~-sign** cartello *m* stradale. **~way** *n* carreggiata *f*, corsia *f*. **~works** *npl* lavori *mpl* stradali. **~worthy** *a* sicuro

roam /rəʊm/ *vi* girovagare

roar /rɔ:(r)/ *n* ruggito *m*; **~s of laughter** scroscio *msg* di risa ● *vi* ruggire; ⟨*lorry, thunder:*⟩ rombare; **~ with laughter** ridere fragorosamente. **~ing** *a* **do a ~ing trade** *fam* fare affari *fpl*

roast /rəʊst/ *a* arrosto; **~ pork** arrosto *m* di maiale ● *n* arrosto *m* ● *vt* arrostire ⟨*meat*⟩ ● *vi* arrostirsi

rob /rɒb/ *vt* ⟨*pt/pp* **robbed**⟩ derubare (**of** di); svaligiare ⟨*bank*⟩. **~ber** *n* rapinatore *m*. **~bery** *n* rapina *f*

robe /rəʊb/ *n* tunica *f*; (*Am: bathrobe*) accappatoio *m*

robin /ˈrɒbɪn/ *n* pettirosso *m*

robot /ˈrəʊbɒt/ *n* robot *m inv*

robust /rəʊˈbʌst/ *a* robusto

rock[1] /rɒk/ *n* roccia *f*; (*in sea*) scoglio *m*; (*sweet*) zucchero *m* candito. **on the ~s** ⟨*ship*⟩ incagliato; ⟨*marriage*⟩ finito; ⟨*drink*⟩ con ghiaccio

rock[2] *vt* cullare ⟨*baby*⟩; (*shake*) far traballare; (*shock*) scuotere ● *vi* dondolarsi

rock[3] *n Mus* rock *m inv*

rock-'bottom *a* bassissimo ● *n* livello *m* più basso

rockery /ˈrɒkərɪ/ *n* giardino *m* roccioso

rocket /ˈrɒkɪt/ *n* razzo *m* ● *vi* salire alle stelle

rocking /ˈrɒkɪŋ/: **~-chair** *n* sedia *f* a dondolo. **~-horse** *n* cavallo *m* a dondolo

rocky /ˈrɒkɪ/ *a* (**-ier, -iest**) roccioso; *fig* traballante

rod /rɒd/ *n* bacchetta *f*; (*for fishing*) canna *f*

rode /rəʊd/ *see* **ride**

rodent /ˈrəʊdnt/ *n* roditore *m*

roe /rəʊ/ *n* (*pl* **roe** *or* **roes**) ● [**-deer**] capriolo *m*

rogue /rəʊg/ *n* farabutto *m*

role /rəʊl/ *n* ruolo *m*

roll /rəʊl/ *n* rotolo *m*; (*bread*) panino *m*; (*list*) lista *f*; (*of ship, drum*) rullio *m* ● *vi* rotolare; **be ~ing in money** *fam* nuotare nell'oro ● *vt* spianare ⟨*lawn, pastry*⟩. **roll over** *vi* rigirarsi. **roll up** *vt* arrotolare; rimboccarsi ⟨*sleeves*⟩ ● *vi fam* arrivare

'roll-call *n* appello *m*

roller /ˈrəʊlə(r)/ *n* rullo *m*; (*for hair*) bigodino *m*. **~ blind** *n* tapparella *f*. **~-coaster** *n* montagne *fpl* russe. **~-skate** *n* pattino *m* a rotelle

'rolling-pin *n* mattarello *m*

Roman /ˈrəʊmən/ *a* romano ● *n* romano, -a *mf*. **~ Catholic** *a* cattolico ● *n* cattolico, -a *mf*

romance /rəʊˈmæns/ *n* (*love-affair*) storia *f* d'amore; (*book*) romanzo *m* rosa

Romania /rəʊˈmeɪnɪə/ *n* Romania *f* ● *a* rumeno ● *n* rumeno, -a *mf*

romantic /rəʊˈmæntɪk/ *a* romantico. **~ally** *adv* romanticamente. **~ism** /-tɪsɪzm/ *n* romanticismo *m*

Rome /rəʊm/ *n* Roma *f*

romp /rɒmp/ *n* gioco *m* rumoroso ● *vi* giocare rumorosamente. **~ers** *npl* pagliaccetto *msg*

roof /ru:f/ *n* tetto *m*; (*of mouth*) palato *m* ● *vt* mettere un tetto su. **~-rack** *n* portabagagli *m inv*. **~-top** *n* tetto *m*

rook /rʊk/ *n* corvo *m*; (*in chess*) torre *f*

room /ru:m/ *n* stanza *f*; (*bedroom*) camera *f*; (*for functions*) sala *f*; (*space*) spazio *m*. **~y** *a* spazioso; ⟨*clothes*⟩ ampio

roost /ru:st/ *vi* appollaiarsi

root[1] /ru:t/ *n* radice *f*; **take ~** mettere radici ● **root out** *vt fig* scovare

root[2] *vi* **~ about** grufolare; **~ for sb** *Am fam* fare il tifo per qcno

rope /rəʊp/ *n* corda *f*; **know the ~s** *fam* conoscere i trucchi del mestiere ● **rope in** *vt fam* coinvolgere

rosary /'rəʊzərɪ/ n rosario m

rose¹ /rəʊz/ n rosa f; (of watering-can) bocchetta f

rose² see **rise**

rosé /'rəʊzeɪ/ n [vino m] rosé m inv

rosemary /'rəʊzmərɪ/ n rosmarino m

rosette /rəʊ'zet/ n coccarda f

roster /'rɒstə(r)/ n tabella f dei turni

rostrum /'rɒstrəm/ n podio m

rosy /'rəʊzɪ/ a (-ier, -iest) roseo

rot /rɒt/ n marciume m; (fam: nonsense) sciocchezze fpl ● vi (pt/pp rotted) marcire

rota /'rəʊtə/ n tabella f dei turni

rotary /'rəʊtərɪ/ a rotante

rotate /rəʊ'teɪt/ vt far ruotare; avvicendare (crops) ● vi ruotare. **~ion** /-eɪʃn/ n rotazione f, **in ~ion** a turno

rote /rəʊt/ n **by ~** meccanicamente

rotten /'rɒtn/ a marcio; fam schifoso; (person) penoso

rotund /rəʊ'tʌnd/ a paffuto

rough /rʌf/ a (not smooth) ruvido; (ground) accidentato; (behaviour) rozzo; (sport) violento; (area) malfamato; (crossing, time) brutto; (estimate) approssimativo ● adv (play) grossolanamente; **sleep ~** dormire sotto i ponti ● vt ~ **it** vivere senza confort. **rough out** vt abbozzare

roughage /'rʌfɪdʒ/ n fibre fpl

rough 'draft n abbozzo m

rough|ly /'rʌflɪ/ adv rozzamente; (more or less) pressappoco. **~ness** n ruvidità f; (of behaviour) rozzezza f

rough paper n carta f da brutta

roulette /ru:'let/ n roulette f inv

round /raʊnd/ a rotondo ● n tondo m; (slice) fetta f; (of visits, drinks) giro m; (of competition) partita f; (boxing) ripresa f, round m inv; **do one's ~s** (doctor:) fare il giro delle visite ● prep intorno a; **open ~ the clock** aperto ventiquattr'ore ● adv **all ~** tutt'intorno; **ask sb ~** invitare qcno; **go/come ~ to** (a

friend etc) andare da; **turn/look ~** girarsi; **~ about** (approximately) intorno a ● vt arrotondare; girare (corner). **round down** vt arrotondare (per difetto). **round off** vt (end) terminare. **round on** vt aggredire. **round up** vt radunare; arrotondare (prices)

roundabout /'raʊndəbaʊt/ a indiretto ● n giostra f; (for traffic) rotonda f

round: **~ 'trip** n viaggio m di andata e ritorno

rous|e /raʊz/ vt svegliare; risvegliare (suspicion, interest). **~ing** a di incoraggiamento

route /ru:t/ n itinerario m; Naut, Aeron rotta f; (of bus) percorso m

routine /ru:'ti:n/ a di routine ● n routine f inv; Theat numero m

rov|e /rəʊv/ vi girovagare. **~ing** a (reporter, ambassador) itinerante

row¹ /rəʊ/ n (line) fila f; **three years in a ~** tre anni di fila

row² vi (in boat) remare

row³ /raʊ/ n fam (quarrel) litigata f; (noise) baccano m ● vi fam litigare

rowdy /'raʊdɪ/ a (-ier, -iest) chiassoso

rowing boat /'rəʊɪŋ-/ n barca f a remi

royal /rɔɪəl/ a reale

royal|ty /'rɔɪəltɪ/ n appartenenza f alla famiglia reale; (persons) i membri mpl della famiglia reale. **~ies** npl (payments) diritti mpl d'autore

rpm abbr **revolutions per minute**

rub /rʌb/ n **give sth a ~** dare una sfregata a qcsa ● vt (pt/pp rubbed) sfregare. **rub in** vt **don't ~ it in** fam non rigirare il coltello nella piaga. **rub off** vt mandar via sfregando (stain); (from blackboard) cancellare ● vi andar via; **~ off on** essere trasmesso a. **rub out** vt cancellare

rubber /'rʌbə(r)/ n gomma f; (eraser) gomma f [da cancellare].

~ band n elastico m. **~y** a gommoso

rubbish /'rʌbɪʃ/ n immondizie fpl; (fam: nonsense) idiozie fpl; (fam: junk) robaccia f ● vt fam fare a pezzi. **~ bin** n pattumiera f. **~ dump** n discarica f; (official) discarica f comunale

rubble /'rʌbl/ n macerie fpl

ruby /'ru:bɪ/ n rubino m ● attrib di rubini; ⟨lips⟩ scarlatta

rucksack /'rʌksæk/ n zaino m

rudder /'rʌdə(r)/ n timone m

ruddy /'rʌdɪ/ a (-ier, -iest) rubicondo; fam maledetto

rude /ru:d/ a scortese; (improper) spinto. **~ly** adv scortesemente. **~ness** n scortesia f

rudiment /'ru:dɪmənt/ n ~s pl rudimenti mpl. **~ary** /-'mentərɪ/ a rudimentale

rueful /'ru:fl/ a rassegnato

ruffian /'rʌfɪən/ n farabutto m

ruffle /'rʌfl/ n gala f ● vt scompigliare ⟨hair⟩

rug /rʌg/ n tappeto m; (blanket) coperta f

rugby /'rʌgbɪ/ n ~ [football] rugby m

rugged /'rʌgɪd/ a ⟨coastline⟩ roccioso

ruin /'ru:ɪn/ n rovina f; in ~s in rovina ● vt rovinare. **~ous** /-əs/ a estremamente costoso

rule /ru:l/ n regola f; (control) ordinamento m; (for measuring) metro m; ~s regolamento msg; **as a ~** generalmente ● vt governare; dominare ⟨colony, behaviour⟩; ~ **that** stabilire che ● vi governare. **rule out** vt escludere

ruled /ru:ld/ a ⟨paper⟩ a righe

ruler /'ru:lə(r)/ n capo m di Stato; (sovereign) sovrano, -a mf; (measure) righello m, regolo m

ruling /'ru:lɪŋ/ a ⟨class⟩ dirigente; ⟨party⟩ di governo ● n decisione f

rum /rʌm/ n rum m inv

rumble /'rʌmbl/ n rombo m; (of stomach) brontolio m ● vi rombare; ⟨stomach⟩ brontolare

rummage /'rʌmɪdʒ/ vi rovistare (in/through in)

rummy /'rʌmɪ/ n ramino m

rumour /'ru:mə(r)/ n diceria f ● vt **it is ~ed that** si dice che

rump /rʌmp/ n natiche fpl. **~ steak** n bistecca f di girello

rumpus /'rʌmpəs/ n fam baccano m

run /rʌn/ n (on foot) corsa f; (distance to be covered) tragitto m; (outing) giro m; Theat rappresentazioni fpl; (in skiing) pista f; (Am: ladder) smagliatura f (in calze); **at a ~** di corsa; **~ of bad luck** periodo m sfortunato; **on the ~** in fuga; **have the ~ of** avere a disposizione; **in the long ~** a lungo termine ● v (pt ran, pp run, pres p running) ● vi correre; ⟨river:⟩ scorrere; ⟨nose, makeup:⟩ colare; ⟨bus:⟩ fare servizio; ⟨play:⟩ essere in cartellone; ⟨colours:⟩ sbiadire; (in election) presentarsi [come candidato] ● vt (manage) dirigere; tenere ⟨house⟩; (drive) dare un passaggio a; correre ⟨risk⟩; Comput lanciare; Journ pubblicare ⟨article⟩; (pass) far scorrere ⟨eyes, hand⟩; **~ a bath** far scorrere l'acqua per il bagno. **run across** vt (meet, find) imbattersi in. **run away** vi scappare [via]. **run down** vi scaricarsi; ⟨clock:⟩ scaricarsi; ⟨stocks:⟩ esaurirsi ● vt Auto investire; (reduce) esaurire; (fam: criticize) denigrare. **run in** vi entrare di corsa. **run into** vt (meet) imbattersi in; (knock against) urtare. **run off** vi andare via di corsa ● vt stampare ⟨copies⟩. **run out** vi uscire di corsa; ⟨supplies, money:⟩ esaurirsi; **~ out of** rimanere senza. **run over** vi correre; (overflow) traboccare ● vt Auto investire. **run through** vi scorrere. **run up** vi salire di corsa; (towards) arrivare di corsa ● vt accumulare ⟨debts, bill⟩; ⟨sew⟩ cucire

'runaway n fuggitivo, -a mf

run-'down a (area) in abbandono; ⟨person⟩ esaurito ●n analisi f

rung[1] /rʌŋ/ n (of ladder) piolo m

rung[2] see **ring**[2]

runner /'rʌnə(r)/ n podista mf; (in race) corridore, -trice mf; (on sledge) pattino m. **~ bean** n fagiolino m. **~-up** n secondo, -a mf classificato, -a

running /'rʌnɪŋ/ a in corsa; ⟨water⟩ corrente; **four times ~** quattro volte di seguito ●n corsa f; ⟨management⟩ direzione f; **be in the ~** essere in lizza. **~ 'commentary** n cronaca f

runny /'rʌnɪ/ a semiliquido; **~ nose** naso che cola

run: ~-of-the-'mill a ordinario. **~up** n Sport rincorsa f; **the ~up to** il periodo precedente. **~way** n pista f

rupture /'rʌptʃə(r)/ n rottura f; Med ernia f ●vt rompere; **~ oneself** farsi venire l'ernia ●vi rompersi

rural /'rʊərəl/ a rurale

ruse /ruːz/ n astuzia f

rush[1] /rʌʃ/ n Bot giunco m

rush[2] n fretta f; **in a ~** di fretta ●vi precipitarsi ●vt far premura a; **~ sb to hospital** trasportare qcno di corsa all'ospedale. **~-hour** n ora f di punta

rusk /rʌsk/ n biscotto m

Russia /'rʌʃə/ n Russia f. **~n** a & n russo, -a mf; ⟨language⟩ russo m

rust /rʌst/ n ruggine f ●vi arrugginirsi

rustic /'rʌstɪk/ a rustico

rustle /'rʌsl/ vi frusciare ●vt far frusciare; Am rubare ⟨cattle⟩. **rustle up** vt fam rimediare

'rustproof a a prova di ruggine

rusty /'rʌstɪ/ a (-ier, -iest) arrugginito

rut /rʌt/ n solco m; **in a ~** fam nella routine

ruthless /'ruːθlɪs/ a spietato. **~ness** n spietatezza f

rye /raɪ/ n segale f

Ss

sabbath /'sæbəθ/ n domenica f; (Jewish) sabato m

sabbatical /sə'bætɪkl/ n Univ anno m sabbatico

sabot|age /'sæbətɑːʒ/ n sabotaggio m ●vt sabotare. **~eur** /-'tɜː(r)/ n sabotatore, -trice mf

saccharin /'sækərɪn/ n saccarina f

sachet /'sæʃeɪ/ n bustina f; (scented) sacchetto m profumato

sack[1] /sæk/ vt (plunder) saccheggiare

sack[2] n sacco m; **get the ~** fam essere licenziato ●vt fam licenziare. **~ing** n tela f per sacchi; (fam: dismissal) licenziamento m

sacrament /'sækrəmənt/ n sacramento m

sacred /'seɪkrɪd/ a sacro

sacrifice /'sækrɪfaɪs/ n sacrificio m ●vt sacrificare

sacrilege /'sækrɪlɪdʒ/ n sacrilegio m

sad /sæd/ a (sadder, saddest) triste. **~den** vt rattristare

saddle /'sædl/ n sella f ●vt sellare; **I've been ~d with...** fig mi hanno affibbiato...

sadis|m /'seɪdɪzm/ n sadismo m. **~t** /-dɪst/ n sadico, -a mf. **~tic** /sə'dɪstɪk/ a sadico

sadly /'sædlɪ/ adv tristemente (unfortunately) sfortunatamente. **~ness** n tristezza f

safe /seɪf/ a sicuro; (out of danger salvo; ⟨object⟩ al sicuro; **~ and sound** sano e salvo ●n cassaforte f. **~guard** n protezione f ●vt proteggere. **~ly** adv in modo sicuro ⟨arrive⟩ senza incidenti; ⟨assume⟩ con certezza

safety /'seɪftɪ/ n sicurezza f. **~-belt** n cintura f di sicurezza. **~-deposit box** n cassetta f di sicurezza. **~-pin** n spilla f di sicurezza *o da balia.* ~-**valve** *n* valvola *f* di sicurezza

sag /sæg/ *vi* (*pt/pp* **sagged**) abbassarsi

saga /'sɑːgə/ *n* saga *f*

sage /seɪdʒ/ *n* (*herb*) salvia *f*

Sagittarius /sædʒɪ'teərɪəs/ *n* Sagittario *m*

said /sed/ *see* **say**

sail /seɪl/ *n* vela *f*; (*trip*) giro *m* in barca a vela ● *vi* navigare; *Sport* praticare la vela; (*leave*) salpare ● *vt* pilotare

'sailboard *n* tavola *f* del windsurf. ~-**ing** *n* windsurf *m inv*

sailing /'seɪlɪŋ/ *n* vela *f*. ~-**boat** *n* barca *f* a vela. ~-**ship** *n* veliero *m*

sailor /'seɪlə(r)/ *n* marinaio *m*

saint /seɪnt/ *n* santo, -a *mf*. ~-**ly** *a* da santo

sake /seɪk/ *n* **for the** ~ **of** per il bene di; (*peace*) per amor di; **for the** ~ **of it** per il gusto di farlo

salad /'sæləd/ *n* insalata *f*. ~ **bowl** *n* insalatiera *f*. ~ **cream** *n* salsa *f* per condire l'insalata. ~-**dressing** *n* condimento *m* per insalata

salary /'sælərɪ/ *n* stipendio *m*

sale /seɪl/ *n* vendita *f* (*at reduced prices*) svendita *f*; **for/on** ~ in vendita

sales|man /'seɪlzmən/ *n* venditore *m*; (*traveller*) rappresentante *m*. ~**woman** *n* venditrice *f*

salient /'seɪlɪənt/ *a* saliente

saliva /sə'laɪvə/ *n* saliva *f*

sallow /'sæləʊ/ *a* giallastro

salmon /'sæmən/ *n* salmone *m*

saloon /sə'luːn/ *n* *Auto* berlina *f*; (*Am: bar*) bar *m*

salt /sɔːlt/ *n* sale *m* ● *a* salato; (*fish, meat*) sotto sale ● *vt* salare; (*cure*) mettere sotto sale. ~-**cellar** *n* saliera *f*. ~ **'water** *n* acqua *f* di mare. ~**y** *a* salato

salutary /'sæljʊtərɪ/ *a* salutare

salute /sə'luːt/ *Mil n* saluto *m* ● *vt* salutare ● *vi* fare il saluto

salvage /'sælvɪdʒ/ *n* *Naut* recupero *m* ● *vt* recuperare

salvation /sæl'veɪʃn/ *n* salvezza *f*. **S**~ **'Army** *n* Esercito *m* della Salvezza

salvo /'sælvəʊ/ *n* salva *f*

same /seɪm/ *a* stesso (**as** di) ● *pron* **the** ~ lo stesso; **be all the** ~ essere tutti uguali ● *adv* **the** ~ nello stesso modo; **all the** ~ (*however*) lo stesso; **the** ~ **to you** altrettanto

sample /'sɑːmpl/ *n* campione *m* ● *vt* testare

sanatorium /sænə'tɔːrɪəm/ *n* casa *f* di cura

sanctimonious /sæŋktɪ'məʊnɪəs/ *a* moraleggiante

sanction /'sæŋkʃn/ *n* (*approval*) autorizzazione *f*; (*penalty*) sanzione *f* ● *vt* autorizzare

sanctity /'sæŋktɪtɪ/ *n* santità *f inv*

sanctuary /'sæŋktjʊərɪ/ *n* *Relig* santuario *m*; (*refuge*) asilo *m*; (*for wildlife*) riserva *f*

sand /sænd/ *n* sabbia *f* ● *vt* ~ [**down**] carteggiare

sandal /'sændl/ *n* sandalo *m*

sand: ~-**bank** *n* banco *m* di sabbia. ~-**paper** *n* carta *f* vetrata ● *vt* cartavetrare. ~-**pit** *n* recinto *m* contenente sabbia dove giocano i bambini

sandwich /'sænwɪdʒ/ *n* tramezzino *m* ● *vt* ~**ed between** schiacciato tra

sandy /'sændɪ/ *a* (-**ier**, -**iest**) (*beach, soil*) sabbioso; (*hair*) biondiccio

sane /seɪn/ *a* (*not mad*) sano di mente; (*sensible*) sensato

sang /sæŋ/ *see* **sing**

sanitary /'sænɪtərɪ/ *a* igienico; (*system*) sanitario. ~ **napkin** *n* *Am*, ~ **towel** *n* assorbente *m* igienico

sanitation /sænɪ'teɪʃn/ *n* impianti *mpl* igienici

sanity /'sænɪtɪ/ *n* sanità *f inv* di mente; (*common sense*) buon senso *m*

sank /sæŋk/ *see* **sink**

sapphire /'sæfaɪə(r)/ *n* zaffiro *m* ● *a* blu zaffiro

sarcas|m /'sɑːkæzm/ n sarcasmo m. **~tic** /-'kæstɪk/ a sarcastico
sardine /sɑː'diːn/ n sardina f
Sardinia /sɑː'dɪnɪə/ n Sardegna f. **~n** a & n sardo, -a mf
sardonic /sɑː'dɒnɪk/ a sardonico
sash /sæʃ/ n fascia f; ⟨for dress⟩ fusciacca f
sat /sæt/ see **sit**
satanic /sə'tænɪk/ a satanico
satchel /'sætʃl/ n cartella f
satellite /'sætəlaɪt/ n satellite m. **~ dish** n antenna f parabolica. **~ television** n televisione f via satellite
satin /'sætɪn/ n raso m ●attrib di raso
satire /'sætaɪə(r)/ n satira f
satirical /sə'tɪrɪkl/ a satirico
satir|ist /'sætɪrɪst/ n scrittore, -trice mf satirico, -a; ⟨comedian⟩ comico, -a mf satirico, -a. **~ize** vt satireggiare
satisfaction /sætɪs'fækʃn/ n soddisfazione f; **be to sb's ~** soddisfare qcno
satisfactor|y /sætɪs'fæktəri/ a soddisfacente. **~ily** adv in modo soddisfacente
satisf|y /'sætɪsfaɪ/ vt (pt/pp **-fied**) soddisfare; ⟨convince⟩ convincere; **be ~ied** essere soddisfatto. **~ying** a soddisfacente
saturat|e /'sætʃəreɪt/ vt inzuppare (**with** di); Chem, fig saturare (**with** di). **~ed** a saturo
Saturday /'sætədeɪ/ n sabato m.
sauce /sɔːs/ n salsa f; ⟨cheek⟩ impertinenza f. **~pan** n pentola f
saucer /'sɔːsə(r)/ n piattino m
saucy /'sɔːsɪ/ a (**-ier, -iest**) impertinente
Saudi Arabia /saʊdɪə'reɪbɪə/ n Arabia f Saudita
sauna /'sɔːnə/ n sauna f
saunter /'sɔːntə(r)/ vi andare a spasso
sausage /'sɒsɪdʒ/ n salsiccia f; ⟨dried⟩ salame m
savage /'sævɪdʒ/ a feroce; ⟨tribe, custom⟩ selvaggio ●n selvaggio,

-a mf ●vt fare a pezzi. **~ry** n ferocia f
save /seɪv/ n Sport parata f ●vt salvare (**from** da); ⟨keep, collect⟩ tenere; risparmiare ⟨time, money⟩; ⟨avoid⟩ evitare; Sport parare ⟨goal⟩; Comput salvare, memorizzare ●vi **~ [up]** risparmiare ●prep salvo
saver /'seɪvə(r)/ n risparmiatore, -trice mf
savings /'seɪvɪŋz/ npl ⟨money⟩ risparmi mpl. **~ account** n libretto m di risparmio. **~ bank** n cassa f di risparmio
saviour /'seɪvjə(r)/ n salvatore m
savour /'seɪvə(r)/ n sapore m ●vt assaporare. **~y** a salato; fig rispettabile
saw¹ /sɔː/ see **see¹**
saw² n sega f ●vt/i (pt **sawed**, pp **sawn** or **sawed**) segare. **~dust** n segatura f
saxophone /'sæksəfəʊn/ n sassofono m
say /seɪ/ n **have one's ~** dire la propria; **have a ~** avere voce in capitolo ●vt/i (pt/pp **said**) dire; **that is to ~** cioè; **that goes without ~ing** questo è ovvio; **when all is said and done** alla fine dei conti. **~ing** n proverbio m
scab /skæb/ n crosta f; pej crumiro m
scaffold /'skæfəld/ n patibolo m. **~ing** n impalcatura f
scald /skɔːld/ vt scottare; ⟨milk⟩ scaldare ●n scottatura f
scale¹ /skeɪl/ n ⟨of fish⟩ scaglia f
scale² n scala f; **on a grand ~** su vasta scale ●vt ⟨climb⟩ scalare. **scale down** vt diminuire
scales /skeɪlz/ npl ⟨for weighing⟩ bilancia fsg
scallop /'skɒləp/ n ⟨shellfish⟩ pettine m
scalp /skælp/ n cuoio m capelluto
scalpel /'skælpl/ n bisturi m inv
scam /skæm/ n fam fregatura f
scamper /'skæmpə(r)/ vi **~ away** sgattaiolare via

scampi /'skæmpɪ/ *npl* scampi *mpl*

scan /skæn/ *n Med* scanning *m inv*, scansioscintigrafia *f* ● *vt* (*pt/pp* **scanned**) scrutare; (*quickly*) dare una scorsa a; *Med* fare uno scanning di

scandal /'skændl/ *n* scandalo *m*; (*gossip*) pettegolezzi *mpl*. **~ize** /-d(ə)laɪz/ *vt* scandalizzare. **~ous** /-əs/ *a* scandaloso

Scandinavia /skændɪ'neɪvɪə/ *n* Scandinavia *f*. **~n** *a* & *n* scandinavo, -a *mf*

scanner /'skænə(r)/ *n Comput* scanner *m inv*

scant /skænt/ *a* scarso

scant|y /'skæntɪ/ *a* (**-ier, -iest**) scarso; (*clothing*) succinto. **~ily** *adv* scarsamente; (*clothed*) succintamente

scapegoat /'skeɪp-/ *n* capro *m* espiatorio

scar /skɑː(r)/ *n* cicatrice *f* ● *vt* (*pt/pp* **scarred**) lasciare una cicatrice a

scarc|e /skeəs/ *a* scarso; *fig* raro; **make oneself ~e** *fam* svignarsela. **~ely** *adv* appena; **~ely anything** quasi niente. **~ity** *n* scarsezza *f*

scare /skeə(r)/ *n* spavento *m*; (*panic*) panico *m* ● *vt* spaventare; **be ~d** aver paura (**of** di)

scarecrow /'skeəkrəʊ/ *n* spaventapasseri *m inv*

scarf /skɑːf/ *n* (*pl* **scarves**) sciarpa *f*; (*square*) foulard *m inv*

scarlet /'skɑːlət/ *a* scarlatto. **~ fever** *n* scarlattina *f*

scary /'skeərɪ/ *a* ● far paura

scathing /'skeɪðɪŋ/ *a* mordace

scatter /'skætə(r)/ *vt* spargere; (*disperse*) disperdere ● *vi* disperdersi. **~brained** *a fam* scervellato. **~ed** *a* sparso

scatty /'skætɪ/ *a* (**-ier, -iest**) *fam* svitato

scavenge /'skævɪndʒ/ *vi* frugare nella spazzatura. **~r** *n* persona *f* che fruga nella spazzatura

scenario /sɪ'nɑːrɪəʊ/ *n* scenario *m*

scene /siːn/ *n* scena *f*; (*quarrel*) scenata *f*; **behind the ~s** dietro le quinte

scenery /'siːnərɪ/ *n* scenario *m*

scenic /'siːnɪk/ *a* panoramico

scent /sent/ *n* odore *m*; (*trail*) scia *f*; (*perfume*) profumo *m*. **~ed** *a* profumato (**with** di)

sceptic|al /'skeptɪkl/ *a* scettico. **~ism** /-tɪsɪzm/ *n* scetticismo *m*

schedule /'ʃedjuːl/ *n* piano *m*, programma *m*; (*of work*) programma *m*; (*timetable*) orario *m*; **behind ~** indietro; **on ~** nei tempi previsti; **according to ~** secondo i tempi previsti ● *vt* prevedere. **~d flight** *n* volo *m* di linea

scheme /skiːm/ *n* (*plan*) piano *m*; (*plot*) macchinazione *f* ● *vi pej* macchinare

schizophren|ia /skɪtsə'friːnɪə/ *n* schizofrenia *f*. **~ic** /-'frenɪk/ *a* schizofrenico

scholar /'skɒlə(r)/ *n* studioso, -a *mf*. **~ly** *a* erudito. **~ship** *n* erudizione *f*; (*grant*) borsa *f* di studio

school /skuːl/ *n* scuola *f*; (*in university*) facoltà *f*; (*of fish*) branco *m*

school: **~boy** *n* scolaro *m*. **~girl** *n* scolara *f*. **~ing** *n* istruzione *f*. **~teacher** *n* insegnante *mf*

sciatica /saɪ'ætɪkə/ *n* sciatica *f*

scien|ce /saɪəns/ *n* scienza *f*. **~ce fiction** fantascienza *f*. **~tific** /-'tɪfɪk/ *a* scientifico. **~tist** *n* scienziato, -a *mf*

scintillating /'sɪntɪleɪtɪŋ/ *a* brillante

scissors /'sɪzəz/ *npl* forbici *fpl*

scoff¹ /skɒf/ *vi* ~ **at** schernire

scoff² *vt fam* divorare

scold /skəʊld/ *vt* sgridare. **~ing** *n* sgridata *f*

scone /skɒn/ *n* pasticcino *m da tè*

scoop /skuːp/ *n* paletta *f*; *Journ* scoop *m inv* ● *scoop out vt* svuotare. **scoop up** *vt* tirar su

scoot /skuːt/ *vi fam* filare. **~er** *n* motoretta *f*

scope /skəʊp/ n portata f; (*opportunity*) opportunità f inv

scorch /skɔːtʃ/ vt bruciare. **~er** n fam giornata f torrida. **~ing** a caldissimo

score /skɔː(r)/ n punteggio m; (*individual*) punteggio m; Mus partitura f; (*for film, play*) musica f; **a ~ [of]** (*twenty*) una ventina [di]; **keep [the] ~** tenere il punteggio; **on the ~** a questo proposito ●vt segnare (goal); (cut) incidere ●vi far punti; (*in football etc*) segnare; (*keep score*) tenere il punteggio. **~r** n segnapunti m inv; (*of goals*) giocatore, -trice mf che segna

scorn /skɔːn/ n disprezzo m ●vt disprezzare. **~ful** a sprezzante

Scorpio /ˈskɔːpɪəʊ/ n Scorpione m

scorpion /ˈskɔːpɪən/ n scorpione m

Scot /skɒt/ n scozzese mf

Scotch /skɒtʃ/ a scozzese ●n (*whisky*) whisky m [scozzese]

scotch vt far cessare

scot-'free a **get off ~** cavarsela impunemente

Scot|land /ˈskɒtlənd/ n Scozia f. **~s, ~tish** a scozzese

scoundrel /ˈskaʊndrəl/ n mascalzone m

scour[1] /ˈskaʊə(r)/ vt (*search*) perlustrare

scour[2] vt (*clean*) strofinare

scourge /skɜːdʒ/ n flagello m

Scout n [Boy] **~** [boy]scout m inv

scout /skaʊt/ n Mil esploratore m ●vi **~ for** andare in cerca di

scowl /skaʊl/ n sguardo m torvo ●vi guardare [di] storto

Scrabble® /ˈskræbl/ n Scarabeo® m

scraggy /ˈskrægɪ/ a (**-ier, -iest**) pej scarno

scram /skræm/ vi fam levarsi dai piedi

scramble /ˈskræmbl/ n (*climb*) arrampicata f ●vi (*clamber*) arrampicarsi; **~ for** azzuffarsi per ●vt

Teleph creare delle interferenze in; (*eggs*) strapazzare

scrap[1] /skræp/ n (*fam: fight*) litigio m

scrap[2] n pezzetto m; (*metal*) ferraglia f; **~s** pl (*of food*) avanzi mpl ●vt (pt/pp **scrapped**) buttare via

'scrap-book n album m inv

scrape /skreɪp/ vt raschiare; (*damage*) graffiare. **scrape through** vi passare per un pelo. **scrape together** vt racimolare

scraper /ˈskreɪpə(r)/ n raschietto m

scrappy /ˈskræpɪ/ a frammentario

'scrap-yard n deposito m di ferraglia; (*for cars*) cimitero m delle macchine

scratch /skrætʃ/ n graffio m; (*to relieve itch*) grattata f; **start from ~** partire da zero; **up to ~** (*work*) all'altezza ●vt graffiare; (*to relieve itch*) grattare ●vi grattarsi

scrawl /skrɔːl/ n scarabocchio m ●vt/i scarabocchiare

scrawny /ˈskrɔːnɪ/ a (**-ier, -iest**) pej magro

scream /skriːm/ n strillo m ●vt/i strillare

screech /skriːtʃ/ n stridore m ●vi stridere ●vt strillare

screen /skriːn/ n paravento m; Cinema, TV schermo m ●vt proteggere; (*conceal*) riparare; proiettare (film); (*candidates*) passare al setaccio; Med sottoporre a visita medica. **~ing** n Med visita f medica; (*of film*) proiezione f. **~play** n sceneggiatura f

screw /skruː/ n vite f ●vt avvitare. **screw up** vt (*crumple*) accartocciare; strizzare (eyes); stor- cere (face); (*sl: bungle*) mandare all'aria

'screwdriver n cacciavite m

screwy /ˈskruːɪ/ a (**-ier, -iest**) fam svitato

scribble /ˈskrɪbl/ n scarabocchio m ●vt/i scarabocchiare

script /skrɪpt/ n scrittura f (a mano); ⟨of film⟩ sceneggiatura f
'script-writer n sceneggiatore, -trice mf
scroll /skrəʊl/ n rotolo m (di pergamena); ⟨decoration⟩ voluta f
scrounge /skraʊndʒ/ vt/i scroccare. **~r** n scroccone, -a mf
scrub[1] /skrʌb/ n (land) boscaglia f
scrub[2] vt/i (pt/pp **scrubbed**) strofinare; ⟨fam: cancel⟩ cancellare ⟨plan⟩
scruff /skrʌf/ n by the ~ of the neck per la collottola
scruffy /'skrʌfɪ/ a (-ier, -iest) trasandato
scrum /skrʌm/ n (in rugby) mischia f
scruple /'skruːpl/ n scrupolo m
scrupulous /'skruːpjʊləs/ a scrupoloso
scrutin|ize /'skruːtɪnaɪz/ vt scrutinare. **~y** n (look) esame m minuzioso
scuffle /'skʌfl/ n tafferuglio m
sculpt /skʌlpt/ vt/i scolpire. **~or** /'skʌlptə(r)/ n scultore m. **~ure** /-tʃə(r)/ n scultura f
scum /skʌm/ n schiuma f; ⟨people⟩ feccia f
scurrilous /'skʌrɪləs/ a scurrile
scurry /'skʌrɪ/ vi (pt/pp **-ied**) affrettare il passo
scuttle /'skʌtl/ vi (hurry) ~ away correre via
sea /siː/ n mare m; at ~ in mare; fig confuso; by ~ via mare. **~board** n costiera f. **~food** n frutti mpl di mare. **~gull** n gabbiano m
seal[1] /siːl/ n Zool foca f
seal[2] n sigillo m; Techn chiusura f ermetica ● vt sigillare; Techn chiudere ermeticamente. **seal off** vt bloccare ⟨area⟩
sea-level n livello m del mare
seam /siːm/ n cucitura f; (of coal) strato m
seaman n marinaio m
seamless /'siːmlɪs/ a senza cucitura

seamy /'siːmɪ/ a sordido; ⟨area⟩ malfamato
seance /'seɪɑːns/ n seduta f spiritica
sea: **~plane** n idrovolante m. **~port** n porto m di mare
search /sɜːtʃ/ n ricerca f; ⟨official⟩ perquisizione f; in ~ of alla ricerca di ● vt frugare (for alla ricerca di); perlustrare ⟨area⟩; ⟨officially⟩ perquisire ● vi ~ for cercare. **~ing** a penetrante
search: **~light** n riflettore m. **~party** n squadra f di ricerca
sea: **~sick** a be/get ~ avere il mal di mare. **~side** n at/to the ~side al mare. **~side resort** n stazione f balneare. **~side town** città f di mare
season /'siːzn/ n stagione f ● vt ⟨flavour⟩ condire. **~able** /-əbl/ a, **~al** a stagionale. **~ing** n condimento m
'season ticket n abbonamento m
seat /siːt/ n (chair) sedia f; (in car) sedile m; (place to sit) posto m [a sedere]; (bottom) didietro m; (of government) sede f; **take a** ~ sedersi ● vt mettere a sedere; (have seats for) aver posti [a sedere] per; **remain ~ed** mantenere il proprio posto. **~-belt** n cintura f di sicurezza
sea: **~weed** n alga f marina. **~worthy** a in stato di navigare
secateurs /sekə'tɜːz/ npl cesoie fpl
seclu|ded /sɪ'kluːdɪd/ a appartato. **~sion** /-ʒn/ n isolamento m
second[1] /sɪ'kɒnd/ vt (transfer) distaccare
second[2] /'sekənd/ a secondo; on ~ thoughts ripensandoci meglio ● n secondo m; **~s** pl (goods) merce fsg di seconda scelta; **have** ~**s** (at meal) fare il bis; **John the S~** Giovanni Secondo ● adv (in race) al secondo posto ● vt assistere; appoggiare ⟨proposal⟩
secondary /'sekəndrɪ/ a secondaria. ~ **school** n ≈ scuola f media (inferiore e superiore)

second: ~-**best** a secondo dopo il migliore; **be** ~-**best** pej essere un ripiego. ~ '**class** adv ⟨travel, send⟩ in seconda classe. ~-**class** a di seconda classe

'**second hand** n ⟨on clock⟩ lancetta f dei secondi

second-'hand a & adv di seconda mano

secondly /'sekəndlı/ adv in secondo luogo

second-'rate a di second'ordine

secrecy /'si:krəsı/ n segretezza f; **in** ~ in segreto

secret /'si:krıt/ a segreto ●n segreto m

secretarial /sekrə'teərıəl/ a ⟨work, staff⟩ di segreteria

secretary /'sekrətərı/ n segretario, -a mf

secret|e /sı'kri:t/ vt secernere ⟨poison⟩. ~**ion** /-ʃn/ n secrezione f

secretive /'si:krətıv/ a riservato. ~**ness** n riserbo m

secretly /'si:krıtlı/ adv segretamente

sect /sekt/ n setta f. ~**arian** a settario

section /'sekʃn/ n sezione f

sector /'sektə(r)/ n settore m

secular /'sekjələ(r)/ a secolare; ⟨education⟩ laico

secure /sı'kjʊə(r)/ a sicuro ●vt proteggere; chiudere bene ⟨door⟩; rendere stabile ⟨ladder⟩; ⟨obtain⟩ assicurarsi. ~**ly** adv saldamente

security /sı'kjʊərətı/ n sicurezza f; ⟨for loan⟩ garanzia f. ~**ies** npl titoli mpl

sedate¹ /sı'deıt/ a posato

sedate² vt somministrare sedativi a

sedation /sı'deıʃn/ n somministrazione f di sedativi; **be under** ~ essere sotto l'effetto di sedativi

sedative /'sedətıv/ a sedativo ●n sedativo m

sedentary /'sedəntərı/ a sedentario

sediment /'sedımənt/ n sedimento m

seduce /sı'dju:s/ vt sedurre

seduct|ion /sı'dʌkʃn/ n seduzione f. ~**ive** /-tıv/ a seducente

see¹ /si:/ v ⟨pt saw, pp seen⟩ ●vt vedere; ⟨understand⟩ capire; ⟨escort⟩ accompagnare; **go and** ~ andare a vedere; ⟨visit⟩ andare a trovare; ~ **you!** ci vediamo!; ~ **you later!** a più tardi!; ~**ing that** visto che ●vi vedere; ⟨understand⟩ capire; ~ **that** ⟨make sure⟩ assicurarsi che; ~ **about** occuparsi di. **see off** vt veder partire; ⟨chase away⟩ mandar via. **see through** vi vedere attraverso; fig non farsi ingannare da ●vt portare a buon fine. **see to** vi occuparsi di

see² /si:/ n sede f

seed /si:d/ n seme m; Tennis testa f di serie; **go to** ~ fare seme; fig lasciarsi andare. ~**ed player** n Tennis testa f di serie. ~**ling** n pianticella f

seedy /'si:dı/ a ⟨-ier, -iest⟩ squallido

seek /si:k/ vt ⟨pt/pp sought⟩ cercare

seem /si:m/ vi sembrare. ~**ingly** adv apparentemente

seen /si:n/ see **see¹**

seep /si:p/ vi filtrare

see-saw /'si:sɔ:/ n altalena f

seethe /si:ð/ vi ~ **with anger** ribollire di rabbia

'**see-through** a trasparente

segment /'segmənt/ n segmento m; ⟨of orange⟩ spicchio m

segregat|e /'segrıgeıt/ vt segregare. ~**ion** /-'geıʃn/ n segregazione f

seize /si:z/ vt afferrare; Jur confiscare. **seize up** vi Techn bloccarsi

seizure /'si:ʒə(r)/ n Jur confisca f; Med colpo m ⟨apoplettico⟩

seldom /'seldəm/ adv raramente

select /sı'lekt/ a scelto; ⟨exclusive⟩ esclusivo ●vt scegliere; seleziona re ⟨team⟩. ~**ion** /-ekʃn/ n selezione f. ~**ive** /-ıv/ a selettivo. ~**or** n Sport selezionatore, -trice mf

self /self/ n io m

self: **~-ad'dressed** *a* con il proprio indirizzo. **~-ad'hesive** *a* autoadesivo. **~-as'surance** *n* sicurezza *f* di sé. **~-as'sured** *a* sicuro di sé. **~-'catering** *a* in appartamento attrezzato di cucina. **~-'centred** *a* egocentrico. **~-'confidence** *n* fiducia *f* in se stesso. **~-'confident** *a* sicuro di sé. **~-'conscious** *a* impacciato. **~-con'tained** *a* ⟨flat⟩ con ingresso indipendente. **~-con'trol** *n* autocontrollo *m*. **~-de'fence** *n* autodifesa *f*; *Jur* legittima difesa *f*. **~-de'nial** *n* abnegazione *f*. **~-determi'nation** *n* autodeterminazione *f*. **~-em'ployed** *a* che lavora in proprio. **~-e'steem** *n* stima *f* di sé. **~-'evident** *a* ovvio. **~-'governing** *a* autonomo. **~-'help** *n* iniziativa *f* personale. **~-in'dulgent** *a* indulgente con se stesso. **~-'interest** *n* interesse *m* personale

self|ish /'selfɪʃ/ *a* egoista. **~ishness** *n* egoismo *m*. **~less** *a* disinteressato

self: **~-made** *a* che si è fatto da sé. **~-pity** *n* autocommiserazione *f*. **~-'portrait** *n* autoritratto *m*. **~-pos'sessed** *a* padrone di sé. **~-preser'vation** *n* istinto *m* di conservazione. **~-re'spect** *n* amor proprio *m*. **~-'righteous** *a* presuntuoso. **~-'sacrifice** *n* abnegazione *f*. **~-'satisfied** *a* compiaciuto di sé. **~-'service** *n* self-service *m* *inv* **●** *attrib* self-service. **~-suf'ficient** *a* autosufficiente. **~-'willed** *a* ostinato

sell /sel/ *v* ⟨*pt/pp* **sold**⟩ **●** *vt* vendere; **be sold out** essere esaurito **●** *vt* vendersi. **sell off** *vt* liquidare

seller /'selə(r)/ *n* venditore, -trice *mf*

Sellotape® /'seləʊ-/ *n* nastro *m* adesivo, scotch® *m*

sell-out *n* ⟨*fam*: betrayal⟩ tradimento *m*; **be a ~** ⟨concert:⟩ fare il tutto esaurito

selves /selvz/ *pl* *of* **self**

semblance /'sembləns/ *n* parvenza *f*

semen /'si:mən/ *n Anat* liquido *m* seminale

semester /sɪ'mestə(r)/ *n Am* semestre *m*

semi /'semɪ/: **~breve** /'semɪbri:v/ *n* semibreve *f*. **~circle** /'semɪs3:k(ə)l/ *n* semicerchio *m*. **~'circular** *a* semicircolare. **~'colon** *n* punto e virgola *m*. **~de'tached** *a* gemella **●** *n* casa *f* gemella. **~'final** *n* semifinale *f*

seminar /'semɪnɑ:(r)/ *n* seminario *m*. **~y** /-nərɪ/ *n* seminario *m*

semolina /semə'li:nə/ *n* semolino *m*

senat|e /'senət/ *n* senato *m*. **~or** *n* senatore *m*

send /send/ *vt/i* ⟨*pt/pp* **sent**⟩ mandare; **~ for** mandare a chiamare ⟨person⟩; far venire ⟨thing⟩. **~er** *n* mittente *mf*. **~-off** *n* commiato *m*

senil|e /'si:naɪl/ *a* arteriosclerotico; *Med* senile. **~ity** /sɪ'nɪlətɪ/ *n* senilismo *m*

senior /'si:nɪə(r)/ *a* più vecchio; (*in* rank) superiore **●** *n* (*in* rank) superiore *mf*; (*in sport*) senior *mf*; **she's two years my ~** è più vecchia di me di due anni. **~ 'citizen** *n* anziano, -a *mf*

seniority /si:nɪ'ɒrətɪ/ *n* anzianità *f* *inv* di servizio

sensation /sen'seɪʃn/ *n* sensazione *f*. **~al** *a* sensazionale. **~ally** *adv* in modo sensazionale

sense /sens/ *n* senso *m*; (common -) buon senso *m*; **in a ~** in un certo senso; **make ~** aver senso **●** *vt* sentire. **~less** *a* insensato; (*unconscious*) privo di sensi

sensibl|e /'sensəbl/ *a* sensato; (*suitable*) appropriato. **~y** *adv* in modo appropriato

sensitiv|e /'sensɪtɪv/ *a* sensibile; (*touchy*) suscettibile. **~ely** *adv* con sensibilità. **~ity** /-'tɪvɪtɪ/ *n* sensibilità *f* *inv*

sensory /'sensərɪ/ *a* sensoriale

sensual | set

sensual /'sensjʊəl/ a sensuale.
~ity /-'ælətɪ/ n sensualità f inv

sensuous /'sensjʊəs/ a voluttuoso

sent /sent/ see **send**

sentence /'sentəns/ n frase f; Jur
sentenza f; (punishment) condanna f ● vt to condannare

sentiment /'sentɪmənt/ n sentimento m; (opinion) opinione f;
(sentimentality) sentimentalismo
m. **~al** /-'mentl/ a sentimenta-
le; pej sentimentalista. **~ality**
/-'tælətɪ/ n sentimentalità f inv

sentry /'sentrɪ/ n sentinella f

separable /'sepərəbl/ a separabile

separate¹ /'sepərət/ a separato.
~ly adv separatamente

separate² /'sepəreɪt/ vt separare
● vi separarsi. **~ion** /-'reɪʃn/ n separazione f

September /sep'tembə(r)/ n settembre m

septic /'septɪk/ a settico; **go ~** infettarsi. **~ tank** n fossa f biologica

sequel /'siːkwəl/ n seguito m

sequence /'siːkwəns/ n sequenza f

sequin /'siːkwɪn/ n lustrino m,
paillette f inv

serenade /serə'neɪd/ n serenata f
● vt fare una serenata a

serene /sɪ'riːn/ a sereno. **~ity**
/-'renətɪ/ n serenità f inv

sergeant /'sɑːdʒənt/ n sergente m

serial /'sɪərɪəl/ n racconto a puntate; TV sceneggiato m a puntate;
Radio commedia f radiofonica.
~ize vt pubblicare a puntate; Radio, TV trasmettere a puntate. **~
killer** n serial killer mf inv. **~
number** n numero m di serie. **~
port** n Comput porta f seriale

series /'sɪəriːz/ n serie f inv

serious /'sɪərɪəs/ a serio; (illness,
error) grave. **~ly** adv seriamente;
(ill) gravemente; **take ~ly** prendere sul serio. **~ness** n serietà f
inv; (of situation) gravità f inv

sermon /'sɜːmən/ n predica f

serpent /'sɜːpənt/ n serpente m

serrated /se'reɪtɪd/ a dentellato

serum /'sɪərəm/ n siero m

servant /'sɜːvənt/ n domestico, -a
mf

serve /sɜːv/ n Tennis servizio m
● vt servire; scontare (sentence);
~ its purpose servire al proprio
scopo; **it ~s you right!** ben ti sta!;
~s two per due persone ● vi prestare servizio; Tennis servire; **~
as** servire da

server /'sɜːvə(r)/ n Comput server
m inv

service /'sɜːvɪs/ n servizio m;
Relig funzione f; (maintenance) revisione f; **~s** pl forze fpl armate;
(on motorway) area f di servizio;
in the ~s sotto le armi; **of ~** too
utile a; **out of ~** (machine:)
guasto ● vt Techn revisionare.
~able /-əbl/ a utilizzabile; (hard-
wearing) resistente; (practical)
pratico

service: ~ area n area f di servizio. **~ charge** n servizio m. **~man**
n militare m. **~ provider** n
fornitore, -trice mf di servizi. **~
station** n stazione f di servizio

serviette /sɜːvɪ'et/ n tovagliolo m

servile /'sɜːvaɪl/ a servile

session /'seʃn/ n seduta f; Jur ses-
sione f; Univ anno m accademico

set /set/ n serie f, set m inv; (of
crockery, cutlery) servizio m; TV,
Radio apparecchio m; Math insieme m; Theat scenario m; Cinema,
Tennis set m inv; (of people) circolo m; (of hair) messa f in piega ● a
(ready) pronto; (rigid) fisso;
(book) in programma; **be ~ on
doing sth** essere risoluto a fare
qcsa; **be ~ in one's ways** essere
abitudinario ● v (pt/pp set, pres p
setting) vt mettere, porre; mettere (alarm clock); assegnare
(task, homework); fissare (date,
limit); chiedere (questions); montare (gem); assestare (bone); apparecchiare (table); **~ fire to** dare
fuoco a; **~ free** liberare ● vi (sun:)
tramontare; (jelly, concrete:) soli-
dificare; **~ about doing sth** mettersi a fare qcsa. **set back**

tere indietro; (*hold up*) ritardare; (*fam: cost*) costare a. **set off** *vi* partire ● *vt* avviare; mettere (*alarm*); fare esplodere (*bomb*).

set out *vi* partire; ~ **out to do sth** proporsi di fare qcsa ● *vt* disporre; (*state*) esporre. **set to** *vi* mettersi all'opera. **set up** *vt* fondare (*company*); istituire (*committee*)

'set-back *n* passo m indietro

settee /se'ti:/ *n* divano m

setting /'setɪŋ/ *n* scenario m; (*position*) posizione f; (*of sun*) tramonto m; (*of jewel*) montatura f

settle /'setl/ *vt* (*decide*) definire; risolvere (*argument*); fissare (*date*); calmare (*nerves*); saldare (*bill*) ● *vi* (*to live*) stabilirsi; (*snow, dust, bird:*) posarsi; (*subside*) assestarsi; (*sediment:*) depositarsi. **settle down** *vi* sistemarsi; (*stop making noise*) calmarsi. **settle for** *vt* accontentarsi di. **settle up** *vi* regolare i conti

settlement /'setlmənt/ *n* (*agreement*) accordo m; (*of bill*) saldo m; (*colony*) insediamento m

settler /'setlə(r)/ *n* colonizzatore, -trice mf

'set-to *n fam* zuffa f; (*verbal*) batti-becco m

'set-up *n* situazione f

seven /'sevn/ *a* sette. **~'teen** *a* diciassette. **~'teenth** *a* diciassettesimo

seventh /'sevnθ/ *a* settimo

seventieth /'sevntɪəθ/ *a* settantesimo

seventy /'sevntɪ/ *a* settanta

sever /'sevə(r)/ *vt* troncare (*relations*)

several /'sevrəl/ *a & pron* parecchi

severe /sɪ'vɪə(r)/ *a* severo; (*illness*) grave; (*winter*) rigido. **~ely** *adv* severamente; (*ill*) gravemente. **~ity** /-'verətɪ/ *n* severità f inv; (*of pain*) violenza f; (*of illness*) gravità f; (*of winter*) rigore m

sew /səʊ/ *vt/i* (*pt* sewed, *pp* sewn

or sewed) cucire. **sew up** *vt* ricucire

sewage /'su:ɪdʒ/ *n* acque *fpl* di scolo

sewer /'su:ə(r)/ *n* fogna f

sewing /'səʊɪŋ/ *n* cucito m; (*work*) lavoro m di cucito. **~ machine** *n* macchina f da cucire

sewn /səʊn/ *see* **sew**

sex /seks/ *n* sesso m; **have ~** avere rapporti sessuali. **~ist** *a* sessista. **~ offender** *n* colpevole mf di delitti a sfondo sessuale

sexual /'seksjʊəl/ *a* sessuale. **~ 'intercourse** *n* rapporti mpl sessuali. **~ity** /-'ælətɪ/ *n* sessualità f inv. **~ly** *adv* sessualmente

sexy /'seksɪ/ *a* (-**ier**, -**iest**) sexy

shabb|y /'ʃæbɪ/ *a* (-**ier**, -**iest**) scialbo; (*treatment*) meschino. **~iness** *n* trasandatezza f, (*of treatment*) meschinità f inv

shack /ʃæk/ *n* catapecchia f ● **shack up with** *vt fam* vivere con

shade /ʃeɪd/ *n* ombra f; (*of colour*) sfumatura f; (*for lamp*) paralume m; (*Am: for window*) tapparella f; **a ~ better** un tantino meglio ● *vt* riparare dalla luce; (*draw lines on*) ombreggiare. **~s** *npl fam* occhiali mpl da sole

shadow /'ʃædəʊ/ *n* ombra f; **S~ Cabinet** governo m ombra ● *vt* (*follow*) pedinare. **~y** *a* ombroso

shady /'ʃeɪdɪ/ *a* (-**ier**, -**iest**) ombroso; (*fam: disreputable*) losco

shaft /ʃɑ:ft/ *n Techn* albero m; (*of light*) raggio m; (*of lift*) vano m; (*of axle, column*) pozzo m; **~s** *pl* (*of cart*) stanghe fpl

shaggy /'ʃægɪ/ *a* (-**ier**, -**iest**) irsuto; (*animal*) dal pelo arruffato

shake /ʃeɪk/ *n* scrollata f ● *v* (*pt* shook, *pp* shaken) ● *vt* scuotere; agitare (*bottle*); far tremare (*building*); **~ hands with** stringere la mano a ● *vi* tremare. **shake off** *vt* scrollarsi di dosso. **~-up** *n Pol* rimpasto m; *Comm* ristrutturazione f

shaky /'ʃeɪkɪ/ *a* (-**ier**, -**iest**) tremante; ‹table etc› traballante; (unreliable) vacillante

shall /ʃæl/ v aux I ~ go andrò; we ~ see vedremo; what ~ I do? cosa faccio?; **I'll come too, ~ I?** vengo anch'io, no?; **thou shalt not kill** liter non uccidere

shallow /ˈʃæləʊ/ a basso, poco profondo; ‹dish› poco profondo; fig superficiale

sham /ʃæm/ a falso ● n finzione f; (person) spaccone, -a mf ● vt (pt/pp **shammed**) simulare

shambles /ˈʃæmblz/ n baraonda fsg

shame /ʃeɪm/ n vergogna f; **it's a ~ that** è un peccato che; **what a ~!** che peccato! **~-faced** a vergognoso

shame|ful /ˈʃeɪmfl/ a vergognoso. **~less** a spudorato

shampoo /ʃæmˈpuː/ n shampoo m inv ● vt fare uno shampoo a

shandy /ˈʃændɪ/ n bevanda f a base di birra e gassosa

shan't /ʃɑːnt/ = **shall not**

shanty town /ˈʃæntɪtaʊn/ n bidonville f inv, baraccopoli f inv

shape /ʃeɪp/ n forma f; (figure) ombra f; **take ~** prendere forma; **get back in ~** ritornare in forma ● vt dare forma a ‹into di› ● vi [up] mettere la testa a posto; **~ up nicely** mettersi bene. **~less** a informe

shapely /ˈʃeɪplɪ/ a (-ier, -iest) ben fatto

share /ʃeə(r)/ n porzione f; Comm azione f ● vt dividere; condividere ‹views› ● vi dividere. **~holder** n azionista mf

shark /ʃɑːk/ n squalo m, pescecane m; fig truffatore, -trice mf

sharp /ʃɑːp/ a ‹knife etc› tagliente; ‹pencil› appuntito; ‹drop› a picco; (reprimand) severo; (outline) marcato; (alert) acuto, (unscrupulous) senza scrupoli; **~ pain** fitta f ● adv in punto; Mus fuori tono; **look ~!** sbrigati! ● n Mus diesis m

inv. **~en** vt affilare ‹knife›; appuntire ‹pencil›

shatter /ˈʃætə(r)/ vt frantumare; fig mandare in frantumi; **~ed** (fam: exhausted) a pezzi ● vi frantumarsi

shav|e /ʃeɪv/ n rasatura f; **have a ~e** farsi la barba ● vt radere ● vi radersi. **~er** n rasoio m elettrico. **~ing-brush** n pennello m da barba; **~ing foam** n schiuma f da barba; **~ing soap** n sapone m da barba

shawl /ʃɔːl/ n scialle m

she /ʃiː/ pron lei

sheaf /ʃiːf/ n (pl **sheaves**) fascio m

shear /ʃɪə(r)/ vt (pt **sheared**, pp **shorn** or **sheared**) tosare

shears /ʃɪəz/ npl (for hedge) cesoie fpl

sheath /ʃiːθ/ n (pl **~s** /ˈʃiːðz/) guaina f

shed¹ /ʃed/ n baracca f; (for cattle) stalla f

shed² vt (pt/pp **shed**, pres p **shedding**) perdere; versare ‹blood, tears›; **~ light on** far luce su

sheen /ʃiːn/ n lucentezza f

sheep /ʃiːp/ n inv pecora f. **~-dog** n cane m da pastore

sheepish /ˈʃiːpɪʃ/ a imbarazzato. **~ly** adv con aria imbarazzata

'sheepskin n [pelle f di] montone m

sheer /ʃɪə(r)/ a puro; (steep) a picco; (transparent) trasparente ● adv a picco

sheet /ʃiːt/ n lenzuolo m; (of paper) foglio m; (of glass, metal) lastra f

shelf /ʃelf/ n (pl **shelves**) ripiano m; (set of shelves) scaffale m

shell /ʃel/ n conchiglia f; (of egg, snail, tortoise) guscio m; (of crab) corazza f; (of unfinished building) ossatura f; Mil granata f ● vt sgusciare ‹peas›; Mil bombardare. **shell out** vi fam sborsare

'shellfish n inv mollusco m; Culin frutti mpl di mare

shelter /ˈʃeltə(r)/ n rifugio m; (air raid) rifugio m antiaereo ● vi riparare (**from** da); *fig* mettere al riparo; (*give lodging to*) dare asilo a ● *vi* rifugiarsi. ~**ed** *a* (*spot*) riparato; (*life*) ritirato

shelve /ʃelv/ *vt* accantonare (*project*)

shelves /ʃelvz/ *see* **shelf**

shelving /ˈʃelvɪŋ/ *n* (*shelves*) ripiani *mpl*

shepherd /ˈʃepəd/ *n* pastore *m* ● *vt* guidare. ~'**s pie** *n* pasticcio *m* di carne tritata e patate

sherry /ˈʃerɪ/ *n* sherry *m*

shield /ʃiːld/ *n* scudo *m*; (*for eyes*) maschera *f*; *Techn* schermo *m* ● *vt* proteggere (**from** da)

shift /ʃɪft/ *n* cambiamento *m*; (*in position*) spostamento *m*; (*at work*) turno *m* ● *vt* spostare; (*take away*) togliere; riversare (*blame*) ● *vi* spostarsi; (*wind:*) cambiare; (*fam: move quickly*) darsi una mossa
'**shift work** *n* turni *mpl*

shifty /ˈʃɪftɪ/ *a* (**-ier, -iest**) *pej* losco; (*eyes*) sfuggente

shilly-shally /ˈʃɪlɪʃælɪ/ *vi* titubare

shimmer /ˈʃɪmə(r)/ *n* luccichio *m* ● *vi* luccicare

shin /ʃɪn/ *n* stinco *m*

shine /ʃaɪn/ *n* lucentezza *f*; **give sth a** ~ dare una lucidata a qcsa ● *v* (*pt/pp* **shone**) ● *vi* splendere; (*reflect light*) brillare; (*hair, shoes:*) essere lucido ● *vt* ~ **a light on** puntare una luce su

shingle /ˈʃɪŋgl/ *n* (*pebbles*) ghiaia *f*

shingles /ˈʃɪŋglz/ *n Med* fuochi *mpl* di Sant'Antonio

shiny /ˈʃaɪnɪ/ *a* (**-ier, -iest**) lucido

ship /ʃɪp/ *n* nave *f* ● *v* (*pt/pp* **shipped**) spedire; (*by sea*) spedire via mare

ship: ~**ment** *n* spedizione *f*; (*consignment*) carico *m*. ~**per** *n* spedizioniere *m*. ~**ping** *n* trasporto *m*; (*traffic*) imbarcazioni *fpl*. ~**shape** *a* & *adv* in perfetto ordine. ~**wreck** *n* naufragio *m*. ~**wrecked** *a* naufragato. ~**yard** *n* cantiere *m* navale

shirk /ʃɜːk/ *vt* scansare. ~**er** *n* scansafatiche *mf* inv

shirt /ʃɜːt/ *n* camicia *f*; **in** ~-**sleeves** in maniche di camicia

shit /ʃɪt/ *vulg n* & *int* merda *f* ● *vi* (*pp* **shit**) cagare

shiver /ˈʃɪvə(r)/ *n* brivido *m* ● *vi* rabbrividire

shoal /ʃəʊl/ *n* (*of fish*) banco *m*

shock /ʃɒk/ *n* (*impact*) urto *m*; *Electr* scossa *f* [elettrica]; *fig* colpo *m*, shock *m inv*; *Med* shock *m inv*; **get a** ~ *Electr* prendere la scossa ● *vt* scioccare. ~**ing** *a* scioccante; (*fam: weather, handwriting etc*) tremendo

shod /ʃɒd/ *see* **shoe**

shoddy /ˈʃɒdɪ/ *a* (**-ier, -iest**) scadente

shoe /ʃuː/ *n* scarpa *f*; (*of horse*) ferro *m* ● *vt* (*pt/pp* **shod**, *pres p* **shoeing**) ferrare (*horse*)

shoe: ~**horn** *n* calzante *m*. ~-**lace** *n* laccio *m* da scarpa. ~-**maker** *n* calzolaio *m*. ~-**shop** *n* calzoleria *f*. ~-**string** *n* **on a** ~-**string** *fam* con una miseria

shone /ʃɒn/ *see* **shine**

shoo /ʃuː/ *vt* ~ **away** cacciar via ● *int* sciò

shook /ʃʊk/ *see* **shake**

shoot /ʃuːt/ *n Bot* germoglio *m*; (*hunt*) battuta *f* di caccia ● *v* (*pt/pp* **shot**) ● *vt* sparare; girare (*film*) ● *vi* (*hunt*) andare a caccia. **shoot down** *vt* abbattere. **shoot out** *vi* (*rush*) precipitarsi fuori. **shoot up** *vi* (*grow*) crescere in fretta; (*prices:*) salire di colpo

'**shooting-range** *n* poligono *m* di tiro

shop /ʃɒp/ *n* negozio *m*; (*workshop*) officina *f*; **talk** ~ *fam* parlare di lavoro ● *vi* (*pt/pp* **shopped**) far compere; **go** ~**ping** andare a fare compere. **shop around** *vi* confrontare i prezzi

shop: ~ **assistant** *n* commesso, -a *mf*. ~**keeper** *n* negoziante *mf*. ~-**lifter** *n* taccheggiatore, -trice *mf*. **~-lifting** *n* taccheggio *m*; **~per** *n* compratore, -trice *mf*

shopping /ˈʃɒpɪŋ/ *n* compere *fpl*; *(articles)* acquisti *mpl*; **do the ~** fare la spesa. **~ bag** *n* borsa *f* per la spesa. **~ centre** *n* centro *m* commerciale. **~ trolley** *n* carrello *m*

shop: **~-steward** *n* rappresentante *mf* sindacale. **~-window** *n* vetrina *f*

shore /ʃɔː(r)/ *n* riva *f*

shorn /ʃɔːn/ *see* **shear**

short /ʃɔːt/ *a* corto; *(not lasting)* breve; *(person)* basso; *(curt)* brusco; **a ~ time ago** poco tempo fa; **be ~ of** essere a corto di; **be in ~ supply** essere scarso; *fig* essere raro; **Mick is ~ for Michael** Mick è il diminutivo di Michael ●*adv* bruscamente; **in ~** in breve; **~ of doing** a meno che di fare; **go ~** essere privato (**of**); **stop ~ of doing sth** non arrivare fino a fare qcsa; **cut ~** interrompere *(meeting, holiday)*; **to cut a long story ~** per farla breve

shortage /ˈʃɔːtɪdʒ/ *n* scarsità *f inv*

short: **~bread** *n* biscotto *m* di pasta frolla. **~ circuit** *n* corto *m* circuito. **~coming** *n* difetto *m*. **'~ cut** *n* scorciatoia *f*

shorten /ˈʃɔːtn/ *vt* abbreviare; accorciare *(garment)*

short: **~-hand** *n* stenografia *f*. **~-handed** *a* a corto di personale. **~hand 'typist** *n* stenodattilografo, -a *mf*. **~ list** *n* lista *f* dei candidati selezionati per un lavoro. **~-lived** /-lɪvd/ *a* di breve durata

shortly /ˈʃɔːtlɪ/ *adv* presto; **~ly before/after** poco prima/dopo. **~ness** *n* brevità *f inv*; *(of person)* bassa statura *f*

short-range *a* di breve portata

shorts /ʃɔːts/ *npl* calzoncini *mpl* corti

short: **~-sighted** *a* miope. **~-sleeved** *a* a maniche corte. **~-staffed** *a* a corto di personale. **~ 'story** *n* racconto *m*, novella *f*.

~-'tempered *a* irascibile. **~-term** *a* a breve termine. **~ wave** *n* onde *fpl* corte

shot /ʃɒt/ *see* **shoot** ●*n* colpo *m*; *(person)* tiratore *m*; *Phot* foto *f*; *(injection)* puntura *f*; *(fam: attempt)* prova *f*; **like a ~** *fam* come un razzo. **~gun** *n* fucile *m* da caccia

should /ʃʊd/ *v aux* **I ~ go** dovrei andare; **I ~ have seen him** avrei dovuto vederlo; **I ~ like** mi piacerebbe; **this ~ be enough** questo dovrebbe bastare; **if he ~ come** se dovesse venire

shoulder /ˈʃəʊldə(r)/ *n* spalla *f* ●*vt* mettersi in spalla; *fig* accollarsi. **~-bag** *n* borsa *f* a tracolla. **~-blade** *n* scapola *f*. **~-strap** *n* spallina *f*; *(of bag)* tracolla *f*

shout /ʃaʊt/ *n* grido *m* ●*vt/i* gridare. **shout at** *vt* alzar la voce con. **shout down** *vt* azzittire gridando

shouting /ˈʃaʊtɪŋ/ *n* grida *fpl*

shove /ʃʌv/ *n* spintone *m* ●*vt* spingere; *(fam: put)* ficcare ●*vi* spingere. **shove off** *vi fam* togliersi di torno

shovel /ˈʃʌvl/ *n* pala *f* ●*vt* *(pt/pp* **shovelled)** spalare

show /ʃəʊ/ *n (display)* manifestazione *f*; *(exhibition)* mostra *f*; *(ostentation)* ostentazione *f*; *Theat, TV* spettacolo *m*; *(programme)* programma *m*; **on ~** esposto ●*v (pt* **showed,** *pp* **shown)** ●*vt* mostrare; *(put on display)* esporre; proiettare *(film)* ●*vi (film:)* essere proiettato; **your slip is ~ing** ti si vede la sottoveste. **show in** *vt* fare accomodare. **show off** *vi fam* mettersi in mostra ●*vt* mettere in mostra. **show up** *vi* risaltare; *(fam: arrive)* farsi vedere ●*vt (fam: embarrass)* far fare una brutta figura a

'show down *n* regolamento *m* dei conti

shower /ˈʃaʊə(r)/ *n* doccia *f*; *(of rain)* acquazzone *m*; **have a ~** fare la doccia ● *vt* ~ **with** coprire di ● *vi* fare la doccia. **~proof** *a* impermeabile. **~y** *a* da acquazzoni

show-jumping *n* concorso *m* ippico

shown /ʃəʊn/ *see* **show**

show-off *n* esibizionista *mf*

showy /ʃəʊi/ *a* appariscente

shrank /ʃræŋk/ *see* **shrink**

shred /ʃred/ *n* brandello *m; fig* briciolo *m* ● *vt* (*pt/pp* **shredded**) fare a brandelli; *Culin* tagliuzzare. **~der** *n* distruttore *m* di documenti

shrewd /ʃruːd/ *a* accorto. **~ness** *n* accortezza *f*

shriek /ʃriːk/ *n* strillo *m* ● *vt/i* strillare

shrift /ʃrɪft/ *n* **give sb short ~** liquidare qcno rapidamente

shrill /ʃrɪl/ *a* penetrante

shrimp /ʃrɪmp/ *n* gamberetto *m*

shrine /ʃraɪn/ *n* (*place*) santuario *m*

shrink /ʃrɪŋk/ *vi* (*pt* **shrank**, *pp* **shrunk**) restringersi; (*draw back*) ritrarsi (**from** da)

shrivel /ʃrɪvl/ *vi* (*pt/pp* **shrivelled**) raggrinzare

shroud /ʃraʊd/ *n* sudario *m; fig* manto *m*

Shrove /ʃrəʊv/ *n* ~ **Tuesday** martedì *m* grasso

shrub /ʃrʌb/ *n* arbusto *m*

shrug /ʃrʌg/ *n* scrollata *f* di spalle ● *vt/i* (*pt/pp* **shrugged**) ~ (**one's shoulders**) scrollare le spalle

shrunk /ʃrʌŋk/ *see* **shrink**. **~en** *a* rimpicciolito

shudder /ʃʌdə(r)/ *n* fremito *m* ● *vi* fremere

shuffle /ʃʌfl/ *vi* strascicare i piedi ● *vt* mescolare (*cards*)

shun /ʃʌn/ *vt* (*pt/pp* **shunned**) rifuggire

shunt /ʃʌnt/ *vt* smistare

hush /ʃʊʃ/ *int* zitto!

shut /ʃʌt/ *vt* (*pt/pp* **shut**, *pres p* **shutting**) ● *vt* chiudere ● *vi* chiudersi; (*shop:*) chiudere. **shut down** *vt/i* chiudere. **shut up** *vt*

chiudere; *fam* far tacere ● *vi fam* stare zitto; ~ **up!** stai zitto!

'shut-down *n* chiusura *f*

shutter /ʃʌtə(r)/ *n* serranda *f; Phot* otturatore *m*

shuttle /ʃʌtl/ *n* navetta *f* ● *vi* far la spola

shuttle: ~**cock** *n* volano *m*. ~ **service** *n* servizio *m* pendolare

shy /ʃaɪ/ *a* (*timid*) timido. **~ness** *n* timidezza *f*

Siamese /saɪəˈmiːz/ *a* siamese

sibling /ˈsɪblɪŋ/ *n* (*brother*) fratello *m*; (*sister*) sorella *f*; ~**s** fratelli *mpl*

Sicily /ˈsɪsɪlɪ/ *n* Sicilia *f*. ~**ian** *a &* *n* siciliano, -a *mf*

sick /sɪk/ *a* ammalato; (*humour*) macabro; **be** ~ (*vomit*) vomitare; **be** ~ **of sth** *fam* essere stufo di qcsa; **feel** ~ aver la nausea

sicken /ˈsɪkn/ *vt* disgustare ● *vi* **be** ~**ing for something** covare qualche malanno. ~**ing** *a* disgustoso

sickly /ˈsɪklɪ/ *a* (**-ier, -iest**) malaticcio. ~**ness** *n* malattia *f*; (*vomiting*) vomitevole. ~**ness benefit** *n* indennità *f* di malattia

side /saɪd/ *n* lato *m*; (*of person, mountain*) fianco *m*; (*of road*) bordo *m*; **on the** ~ (*as sideline*) come attività secondaria; ~ **by** ~ fianco a fianco; **take** ~**s** immischiarsi; **take sb's** ~ prendere le parti di qcno; **be on the safe** ~ andare sul sicuro ● *attrib* laterale ● *vi* ~ **with** parteggiare per

side: ~**board** *n* credenza *f*. ~**burns** *npl* basette *fpl*. ~**-effect** *n* effetto *m* collaterale. ~**lights** *npl* luci *fpl* di posizione. ~**line** *n* attività *f inv* complementare. ~**-show** *n* attrazione *f*. ~**-step** *vt* schivare. ~**-track** *vt* sviare. ~**walk** *n Am* marciapiede *m*. ~**ways** *adv* obliquamente

siding /ˈsaɪdɪŋ/ *n* binario *m* di raccordo

sidle /ˈsaɪdl/ *vi* camminare furtivamente (**up to** verso)

siege /siːdʒ/ *n* assedio *m*

sieve /sɪv/ n setaccio m ● vt setacciare

sift /sɪft/ vt setacciare; ~ **[through]** fig passare al setaccio

sigh /saɪ/ n sospiro m ● vi sospirare

sight /saɪt/ n vista f; (on gun) mirino m; **the ~s** pl le cose da vedere; **at first ~** a prima vista; **be within/out of ~** essere/non essere in vista; **lose ~ of** perdere di vista; **know by ~** conoscere di vista; **have bad ~** vederci male ● vt avvistare

'sightseeing n **go ~** andare a visitare posti

sign /saɪn/ n segno m; (notice) insegna f ● vt/i firmare. **sign on** vi (as unemployed) presentarsi all'ufficio di collocamento; Mil arruolarsi

signal /'sɪgnl/ n segnale m ● v (pt/pp **signalled**) ● vt segnalare ● vi fare segnali; ~ **to sb** far segno a qcno (**to do**). ~-**box** n cabina f di segnalazione

signature /'sɪgnətʃə(r)/ n firma f. ~ **tune** n sigla f [musicale]

signet-ring /'sɪgnɪt-/ n anello m con sigillo

significan|ce /sɪg'nɪfɪkəns/ n significato m. ~**t** a significativo

signify /'sɪgnɪfaɪ/ vt (pt/pp -**ied**) indicare

sign-language n linguaggio m dei segni

signpost /'saɪn-/ n segnalazione f stradale

silence /'saɪləns/ n silenzio m ● vt far tacere. ~ **r** n (on gun) silenziatore m; Auto marmitta f

silent /'saɪlənt/ a silenzioso; (film) muto; **remain ~** rimanere in silenzio. ~**ly** adv silenziosamente

silhouette /sɪlu'et/ n sagoma f, silhouette f inv ● vt **be ~d** profilarsi

silicon /'sɪlɪkən/ n silicio m. ~ **chip** piastrina f di silicio

silk /sɪlk/ n seta f ● attrib di seta. ~**worm** n baco m da seta

silky /'sɪlkɪ/ a (-**ier**, -**iest**) come la seta

sill /sɪl/ n davanzale m

silly /'sɪlɪ/ a (-**ier**, -**iest**) sciocco

silo /'saɪləʊ/ n silo m

silt /sɪlt/ n melma f

silver /'sɪlvə(r)/ a d'argento; (paper) argentato ● n argento m; (silverware) argenteria f

silver: ~-**plated** a placcato d'argento. ~**ware** n argenteria f. ~ **'wedding** n nozze fpl d'argento

similar /'sɪmɪlə(r)/ a simile. ~**ity** /-'lærətɪ/ n somiglianza f. ~**ly** adv in modo simile

simile /'sɪmɪlɪ/ n similitudine f

simmer /'sɪmə(r)/ vi bollire lentamente ● vt far bollire lentamente. **simmer down** vi calmarsi

simple /'sɪmpl/ a semplice; (person) sempliciotto. ~-**'minded** a sempliciotto

simplicity /sɪm'plɪsətɪ/ n semplicità f inv

simpli|fication /sɪmplɪfɪ'keɪʃn/ n semplificazione f. ~**fy** /'sɪmplɪfaɪ/ vt (pt/pp -**ied**) semplificare

simply /'sɪmplɪ/ adv semplicemente

simulat|e /'sɪmjʊleɪt/ vt simulare. ~**ion** /-'leɪʃn/ n simulazione f

simultaneous /sɪml'teɪnɪəs/ a simultaneo

sin /sɪn/ n peccato m ● vi (pt/pp **sinned**) peccare

since /sɪns/ prep da ● adv da allora ● conj da quando; (because) siccome

sincere /sɪn'sɪə(r)/ a sincero. ~**ly** adv sinceramente; **Yours ~ly** distinti saluti

sincerity /sɪn'serətɪ/ n sincerità f inv

sinful /'sɪnfl/ a peccaminoso

sing /sɪŋ/ vt/i (pt **sang**, pp **sung**) cantare

singe /sɪndʒ/ vt (pres p **singeing**) bruciacchiare

singer /'sɪŋə(r)/ n cantante mf

single /'sɪŋgl/ a solo; (not double) semplice; (unmarried) celibe

⟨woman⟩ nubile; ⟨room⟩ singolo; ⟨bed⟩ a una piazza ●n ⟨ticket⟩ biglietto m di sola andata; ⟨record⟩ singolo m; ~s pl Tennis singolo m ● **single out** vt scegliere; ⟨distinguish⟩ distinguere

single: ~**-breasted** a a un petto. ~**-handed** a & adv da solo. ~**-minded** a risoluto. ~ **'parent** n genitore m che alleva il figlio da solo

singly /'sɪŋglɪ/ adv singolarmente

singular /'sɪŋgjʊlə(r)/ a Gram singolare ●n singolare m. ~**ly** adv singolarmente

sinister /'sɪnɪstə(r)/ a sinistro

sink /sɪŋk/ n lavandino m ●v ⟨pt sank, pp sunk⟩ ●vi affondare ●vt affondare ⟨ship⟩; scavare ⟨shaft⟩; investire ⟨money⟩. **sink in** vi penetrare; **it took a while to ~ in** ⟨fam: be understood⟩ c'è voluto un po' a capirlo

sinner /'sɪnə(r)/ n peccatore, -trice mf

sinus /'saɪnəs/ n seno m paranasale. ~**itis** n sinusite f

sip /sɪp/ n sorso m ●vt ⟨pt sipped⟩ sorseggiare

siphon /'saɪfn/ n ⟨bottle⟩ sifone m ● **siphon off** vt travasare ⟨con sifone⟩

sir /sɜ:(r)/ n signore m; **S~** ⟨title⟩ Sir m; **Dear S~s** Spettabile ditta

siren /'saɪrən/ n sirena f

sissy /'sɪsɪ/ n femminuccia f

sister /'sɪstə(r)/ n sorella f; ⟨nurse⟩ [infermiera f] caposala f. ~**-in-law** n ⟨pl **~-s-in-law**⟩ cognata f. ~**ly** a da sorella

sit /sɪt/ v ⟨pt/pp **sat**, pres p **sitting**⟩ ●vi essere seduto; ⟨sit down⟩ sedersi; ⟨committee:⟩ riunirsi ●vt sostenere ⟨exam⟩. **sit back** vi fig starsene con le mani in mano. **sit down** vi mettersi a sedere. **sit up** vi mettersi seduto; ⟨not slouch⟩ star seduto diritto; ⟨stay up⟩ stare alzato

site /saɪt/ n posto m; Archaeol sito

m; ⟨building ~⟩ cantiere m ●vt collocare

sit-in /'sɪtɪn/ n occupazione f ⟨di fabbrica, ecc.⟩

sitting /'sɪtɪŋ/ n seduta f; ⟨for meals⟩ turno m. ~**-room** n salotto m

situat|e /'sɪtjʊeɪt/ vt situare. ~**ed** a situato. ~**ion** /-'eɪʃn/ n situazione f; ⟨location⟩ posizione f; ⟨job⟩ posto m

six /sɪks/ a sei. ~**teen** a sedici. ~**teenth** a sedicesimo

sixth /sɪksθ/ a sesto

sixtieth /'sɪkstɪɪθ/ a sessantesimo

sixty /'sɪkstɪ/ a sessanta

size /saɪz/ n dimensioni fpl; ⟨of clothes⟩ taglia f, misura f; ⟨of shoes⟩ numero m; **what ~ is the room?** che dimensioni ha la stanza? ● **size up** vt fam valutare

sizeable /'saɪzəbl/ a piuttosto grande

sizzle /'sɪzl/ vi sfrigolare

skate¹ /skeɪt/ n inv ⟨fish⟩ razza f

skate² n pattino m ●vi pattinare

skateboard /'skeɪtbɔ:d/ n skateboard m inv

skater /'skeɪtə(r)/ n pattinatore, -trice mf

skating /'skeɪtɪŋ/ n pattinaggio m. ~**-rink** n pista f di pattinaggio

skeleton /'skelɪtn/ n scheletro m. ~ **'key** n passe-partout m inv. ~ **'staff** n personale m ridotto

sketch /sketʃ/ n schizzo m; Theat sketch m inv ●vt fare uno schizzo di

sketch|y /'sketʃɪ/ a ⟨**-ier**, **-iest**⟩ abbozzato. ~**ily** adv in modo abbozzato

skewer /'skjʊə(r)/ n spiedo m

ski /ski:/ n sci m inv ●vi ⟨pt/pp **skied**, pres p **skiing**⟩ sciare; **go ~ing** andare a sciare

skid /skɪd/ n slittata f ●vi ⟨pt/pp **skidded**⟩ slittare

skier /'ski:ə(r)/ n sciatore, -trice mf

skiing /'ski:ɪŋ/ n sci m

skilful /'skɪlfl/ a abile

'ski-lift n impianto m di risalita

skill /skɪl/ n abilità f inv. **~ed** a dotato; (worker) specializzato

skim /skɪm/ vt (pt/pp **skimmed**) schiumare; scremare (milk). **skim off** vt togliere. **skim through** vt scorrere

skimp /skɪmp/ vi **~ on** lesinare su

skimpy /ˈskɪmpɪ/ a (-ier, -iest) succinto

skin /skɪn/ n pelle f; (on fruit) buccia f ● vt (pt/pp **skinned**) spellare

skin: **~-deep** a superficiale. **~-diving** n nuoto m subacqueo

skinflint /ˈskɪnflɪnt/ n miserabile mf

skinny /ˈskɪnɪ/ a (-ier, -iest) molto magro

skip¹ /skɪp/ n (container) benna f

skip² n salto m ● v (pt/pp **skipped**) ● vi saltellare; (with rope) saltare la corda ● vt omettere

skipper /ˈskɪpə(r)/ n skipper m inv

skipping-rope /ˈskɪpɪŋrəup/n corda f per saltare

skirmish /ˈskɜːmɪʃ/ n scaramuccia f

skirt /skɜːt/ n gonna f ● vt costeggiare

skit /skɪt/ n bozzetto m comico

skittle /ˈskɪtl/ n birillo m

skive /skaɪv/ vi fam fare lo scansafatiche

skulk /skʌlk/ vi aggirarsi furtivamente

skull /skʌl/ n cranio m

skunk /skʌŋk/ n moffetta f

sky /skaɪ/ n cielo m. **~light** n lucernario m. **~scraper** n grattacielo m

slab /slæb/ n lastra f; (slice) fetta f; (of chocolate) tavoletta f

slack /slæk/ a lento; (person) fiacco ● vi fare lo scansafatiche. **slack off** vi rilassarsi

slacken /ˈslækn/ vi allentare; **~ [off]** (trade:) rallentare; (speed, rain:) diminuire ● vt allentare; (speed)

slacks /slæks/ npl pantaloni mpl sportivi

slag /slæg/ n scorie fpl ● **slag off**

vt (pt/pp **slagged**) Br fam criticare

slain /sleɪn/ see slay

slam /slæm/ v (pt/pp **slammed**) ● vt sbattere; (fam: criticize) stroncare ● vi sbattere

slander /ˈslɑːndə(r)/ n diffamazione f ● vt diffamare. **~ous** /-rəs/ a diffamatorio

slang /slæŋ/ n gergo m. **~y** a gergale

slant /slɑːnt/ n pendenza f; (point of view) angolazione f; **on the ~** in pendenza ● vt pendere; fig distorcere (report) ● vi pendere

slap /slæp/ n schiaffo m ● vt (pt/pp **slapped**) schiaffeggiare; (put) schiaffare ● adv in pieno

slap: **~dash** a fam frettoloso. **~-up** a fam di prim'ordine

slash /slæʃ/ n taglio m ● vt tagliare; ridurre drasticamente (prices)

slat /slæt/ n stecca f

slate /sleɪt/ n ardesia f ● vt fam fare a pezzi

slaughter /ˈslɔːtə(r)/ n macello m; (of people) massacro m ● vt macellare; massacrare (people). **~house** n macello m

Slav /slɑːv/ a slavo ● n slavo, -a f

slave /sleɪv/ n schiavo, -a mf ● vi **~ [away]** lavorare come un negro. **~-driver** n schiavista mf

slavery /ˈsleɪvərɪ/ n schiavitù f inv. **~ish** a servile

Slavonic /sləˈvɒnɪk/ a slavo

slay /sleɪ/ vt (pt slew, pp slain) ammazzare

sleazy /ˈsliːzɪ/ a (-ier, -iest) sordido

sledge /sledʒ/ n slitta f. **~-hammer** n martello m

sleek /sliːk/ a liscio, lucente; (well-fed) pasciuto

sleep /sliːp/ n sonno m; **go to ~** addormentarsi; **put to ~** far addormentare ● v (pt/pp **slept**) ● vi dormire ● vt **~ six** ha sei posti letto. **~er** n Rail treno m con vagoni letto; (compartment) vagone m

557

letto; **be a light/heavy ~er** avere il sonno leggero/pesante

sleeping: ~-bag n sacco m a pelo. **~-car** n vagone m letto. **~-pill** n sonnifero m

sleep: ~less a insonne. **~lessness** n insonnia f. **~-walker** n sonnambulo, -a mf. **~-walking** n sonnambulismo m

sleepy /ˈsliːpɪ/ a (-ier, -iest) assonnato; **be ~** aver sonno

sleet /sliːt/ n nevischio m ● vi **it is ~ing** nevischia

sleeve /sliːv/ n manica f; (for record) copertina f. **~less** a senza maniche

sleigh /sleɪ/ n slitta f

sleight /slaɪt/ n **~ of hand** gioco m di prestigio

slender /ˈslendə(r)/ a snello; (fingers, stem) affusolato; fig scarso; (chance) magro

slept /slept/ see **sleep**

sleuth /sluːθ/ n investigatore m, detective m inv

slew¹ /sluː/ vi girare

slew² see **slay**

slice /slaɪs/ n fetta f ● vt affettare; **~d bread** pane m a cassetta

slick /slɪk/ a liscio, (cunning) astuto ● n (of oil) chiazza f di petrolio

slide /slaɪd/ n scivolata f; (in playground) scivolo m; (for hair) fermaglio m (per capelli); Phot diapositiva f ● vi (pt/pp slid) ● vi scivolare ● vt far scivolare. **~-rule** n regolo m calcolatore. **~ing** a scorrevole; (door, seat) scorrevole; **~ing scale** scala f mobile

slight /slaɪt/ a leggero; (importance) poco; (slender) esile. **~est** a minimo; **not in the ~est** niente affatto ● vt offendere ● n offesa f. **~ly** adv leggermente

slim /slɪm/ a (slimmer, slimmest) snello; fig scarso; (chance) magro ● vi dimagrire

slime /slaɪm/ n melma f. **~y** a melmoso; fig viscido

sling /slɪŋ/ n Med benda f al collo ● vt (pt/pp slung) fam lanciare

slip /slɪp/ n scivolata f; (mistake) lieve errore m; (petticoat) sottoveste f. (for pillow) federa f; (paper) scontrino m; **give sb the ~** fam sbarazzarsi di qcno; **~ of the tongue** lapsus m inv ● vi (pt/pp slipped) ● vi scivolare; (go quickly) sgattaiolare; (decline) retrocedere ● vt **he ~ped it into his pocket** se l'è infilato in tasca; **~ sb's mind** sfuggire di mente a qcno. **slip away** vi scivolare via; (time:) sfuggire. **slip into** vi infilarsi (clothes). **slip up** vi fam sbagliare

slipped 'disc n Med ernia f del disco

slipper /ˈslɪpə(r)/ n pantofola f

slippery /ˈslɪpərɪ/ a scivoloso

slip-road n bretella f

slipshod /ˈslɪpʃɒd/ a trascurato

slip-up n fam sbaglio m

slit /slɪt/ n spacco m; (tear) strappo m; (hole) fessura f ● vt (pt/pp slit) tagliare

slither /ˈslɪðə(r)/ vi scivolare

sliver /ˈslɪvə(r)/ n scheggia f

slobber /ˈslɒbə(r)/ vi sbavare

slog /slɒg/ n [hard] ~ sgobbata f ● vi (pt/pp slogged) (work) sgobbare

slogan /ˈsləʊgən/ n slogan m inv

slop /slɒp/ v (pt/pp slopped) ● vt versare. **slop over** vi versarsi

slope /sləʊp/ n pendenza f; (ski ~) pista f ● vi essere inclinato, inclinarsi. **~ing** a in pendenza

sloppy /ˈslɒpɪ/ a (-ier, -iest) (work) trascurato; (worker) negligente, (in dress) sciatto; (sentimental) sdolcinato

slosh /slɒʃ/ vi fam (person, feet:) squazzare; (water:) scrosciare ● vt (fam: hit) colpire

sloshed /slɒʃt/ a fam sbronzo

slot /slɒt/ n fessura f; (time~) spazio m ● v (pt/pp slotted) ● vt infilare. **slot in** vi incastrarsi

'slot-machine n distributore m automatico; (for gambling) slot-machine f inv

slouch /slaʊtʃ/ *vi* (*in chair*) stare scomposto

slovenly /'slʌvnlɪ/ *a* sciatto. **~iness** *n* sciatteria *f*

slow /sləʊ/ *a* lento; **be ~** (*clock:*) essere indietro; **in ~ motion** al rallentatore ● *adv* lentamente ● **slow down/up** *vt/i* rallentare

slow: **~coach** *n fam* tartaruga *f*. **~ly** *adv* lentamente. **~ness** *n* lentezza *f*

sludge /slʌdʒ/ *n* fanghiglia *f*

slug /slʌg/ *n* lumacone *m*; (*bullet*) pallottola *f*

sluggish /'slʌgɪʃ/ *a* lento

sluice /slu:s/ *n* chiusa *f*

slum /slʌm/ *n* (*house*) tugurio *m*; **~s** *pl* bassifondi *mpl*

slumber /'slʌmbə(r)/ *vi* dormire

slump /slʌmp/ *n* crollo *m*; (*economic*) depressione *f* ● *vi* crollare

slung /slʌŋ/ *see* **sling**

slur /slɜ:(r)/ *n* (*discredit*) calunnia *f* ● *vt* (*pt/pp* **slurred**) biascicare

slurp /slɜ:p/ *vt/i* bere rumorosamente

slush /slʌʃ/ *n* pantano *m* nevoso; *fig* sdolcinatezza *f*. **~ fund** *n* fondi *mpl* neri

slushy /'slʌʃɪ/ *a* fangoso; (*sentimental*) sdolcinato

slut /slʌt/ *n* sgualdrina *f*

sly /slaɪ/ *a* (*-er, -est*) scaltro ● *n* **on the ~** di nascosto

smack¹ /smæk/ *n* (*on face*) schiaffo *m*; (*on bottom*) sculaccione *m* ● *vt* (*on face*) schiaffeggiare; (*on bottom*) sculacciare; **~ one's lips** far schioccare le labbra ● *adv* schiaffo in pieno

smack² *vi* **~ of** *fig* sapere di

small /smɔ:l/ *a* piccolo; **be out/ work/***etc* **until the ~ hours** fare le ore piccole ● *adv* **chop up ~** fare a pezzettini ● *n* **the ~ of the back** le reni *fpl*

small: **~ ads** *npl* annunci *mpl* [commerciali]. **~ 'change** *n* spiccioli *mpl*. **~-holding** *n* piccola te-

nuta *f*. **~pox** *n* vaiolo *m*. **~ talk** *n* chiacchiere *fpl*

smarmy /'smɑ:mɪ/ *a* (*-ier, -iest*) *fam* untuoso

smart /smɑ:t/ *a* elegante; (*clever*) intelligente; (*brisk*) svelto; **be ~** (*fam: cheeky*) fare il furbo ● *vi* (*hurt*) bruciare

smarten /'smɑ:tn/ *vt* **~ oneself up** farsi bello

smash /smæʃ/ *n* fragore *m*; (*collision*) scontro *m*; *Tennis* schiacciata *f* ● *vt* spaccare; *Tennis* schiacciare ● *vi* spaccarsi; (*crash*) schiantarsi (**into** contro). **~ [hit]** *n* successo *m*. **~ing** *a fam* fantastico

smattering /'smætərɪŋ/ *n* infarinatura *f*

smear /smɪə(r)/ *n* macchia *f*; *Med* striscio *m* ● *vt* imbrattare; (*coat*) spalmare (**with** di); *fig* calunniare

smell /smel/ *n* odore *m*; (*sense*) odorato *m* ● *v* (*pt/pp* **smelt** or **smelled**) ● *vt* odorare; (*sniff*) annusare ● *vi* odorare (**of** di)

smelly /'smelɪ/ *a* (*-ier, -iest*) puzzolente

smelt¹ /smelt/ *see* **smell**

smelt² *vt* fondere

smile /smaɪl/ *n* sorriso *m* ● *vi* sorridere; **~ at** sorridere a (*sb*); sorridere di (*sth*)

smirk /smɜ:k/ *n* sorriso *m* compiaciuto

smithereens /smɪðə'ri:nz/ *npl* **to/in ~** in mille pezzi

smitten /'smɪtn/ *a* **~ with** tutto preso da

smock /smɒk/ *n* grembiule *m*

smog /smɒg/ *n* smog *m inv*

smoke /sməʊk/ *n* fumo *m* ● *vt/i* fumare. **~less** *a* senza fumo; (*fuel*) che non fa fumo

smoker /'sməʊkə(r)/ *n* fumatore, -trice *mf*; *Rail* vagone *m* fumatori

'smoke-screen *n* cortina *f* di fumo

smoking /'sməʊkɪŋ/ *n* fumo *m*; **'no ~'** 'vietato fumare'

smoky /'sməʊkɪ/ *a* (*-ier, -iest*) fumoso; (*taste*) di fumo

smooth /smuːð/ a liscio; (*movement*) scorrevole; (*sea*) calmo; (*manners*) mellifluo ●*vt* lisciare. **smooth out** *vt* lisciare. **~ly** *adv* in modo scorrevole

smother /ˈsmʌðə(r)/ *vt* soffocare

smoulder /ˈsməʊldə(r)/ *vi* fumare; (*with rage*) consumarsi

smudge /smʌdʒ/ *n* macchia *f* ●*vt/i* imbrattare

smug /smʌg/ a (**smugger, smuggest**) compiaciuto. **~ly** *adv* con aria compiaciuta

smuggl|e /ˈsmʌgl/ *vt* contrabbandare. **~er** *n* contrabbandiere, a *mf*. **~ing** *n* contrabbando *m*

smut /smʌt/ *n* macchia *f* di fuliggine; *fig* sconcezza *f*

smutty /ˈsmʌti/ a (**-ier, -iest**) fuligginoso; *fig* sconcio

snack /snæk/ *n* spuntino *m*. **~-bar** *n* snack bar *m inv*

snag /snæg/ *n* (*problem*) intoppo *m*

snail /sneil/ *n* lumaca *f*; **at a ~'s pace** a passo di lumaca

snake /sneik/ *n* serpente *m*

snap /snæp/ *n* colpo *m* secco; (*photo*) istantanea *f* ●*attrib* (*decision*) istantaneo ●*v* (*pt/pp* **snapped**) ●*vi* (*break*) spezzarsi; **~ at** (*dog*:) cercare di azzannare; (*person*:) parlare seccamente a ●*vt* (*break*) spezzare; (*say*) dire seccamente; *Phot* fare un'istantanea di. **snap up** *vt* afferrare

snappy /ˈsnæpi/ a (**-ier, -iest**) scorbutico; (*smart*) elegante; **make it ~!** sbrigati!

snapshot *n* istantanea *f*

snare /sneə(r)/ *n* trappola *f*

snarl /snɑːl/ *n* ringhio *m* ●*vi* ringhiare

snatch /snætʃ/ *n* strappo *m*; (*fragment*) brano *m*; (*theft*) scippo *m*; **make a ~ at** cercare di afferrare qcsa ●*vt* strappare (di mano) (**from** a); (*steal*) scippare; rapire (*child*)

sneak /sniːk/ *n fam* spia *mf* ●*vi* (*fam: tell tales*) fare la spia ●*vt* (*take*) rubare; **~ a look at** dare

una sbirciata a. **sneak in/out** *vi* sgattaiolare dentro/fuori

sneakers /ˈsniːkəz/ *npl Am* scarpe *fpl* da ginnastica

sneaking /ˈsniːkɪŋ/ a furtivo; (*suspicion*) vago

sneaky /ˈsniːkɪ/ a sorniono

sneer /snɪə(r)/ *n* ghigno *m* ●*vi* sogghignare; (*mock*) ridere di

sneeze /sniːz/ *n* starnuto *m* ●*vi* starnutire

snide /snaid/ a *fam* insinuante

sniff /snif/ *n* (*of dog*) annusata *f* ●*vi* tirare su col naso ●*vt* odorare (*flower*); sniffare (*glue, cocaine*); (*dog*:) annusare

snigger /ˈsnigə(r)/ *n* risatina *f* soffocata ●*vi* ridacchiare

snip /snip/ *n* taglio *m*; (*fam: bargain*) affare *m* ●*vt/i* (*pt/pp* **snipped**) ~ [**at**] tagliare

snipe /snaip/ *vi* ~ **at** tirare su; *fig* sparare a zero su. **~r** *n* cecchino *m*

snippet /ˈsnipit/ *n* a ~ **of information/news** una breve notizia/informazione

snivel /ˈsnivl/ *vi* (*pt/pp* **snivelled**) piagnucolare. **~ling** a piagnucoloso

snob /snob/ *n* snob *mf*. **~bery** *n* snobismo *m*. **~bish** a da snob

snooker /ˈsnuːkə(r)/ *n* snooker *m*

snoop /snuːp/ *n* spia *f* ●*vi fam* curiosare

snooty /ˈsnuːti/ a *fam* sdegnoso

snooze /snuːz/ *n* sonnellino *m* ●*vi* fare un sonnellino

snore /snɔː(r)/ *vi* russare

snorkel /ˈsnɔːkl/ *n* respiratore *m*

snort /snɔːt/ *n* sbuffo *m* ●*vi* sbuffare

snout /snaut/ *n* grugno *m*

snow /snəʊ/ *n* neve *f* ●*vi* nevicare; **~ed under with** *fig* sommerso di

snow: ~ball *n* palla *f* di neve ●*vi* fare a palle di neve. **~-drift** *n* cumulo *m* di neve. **~-drop** *n* bucaneve *m*. **~-fall** *n* nevicata *f*. **~-flake** *n* fiocco *m* di neve. **~-man** *n* pupazzo *m* di neve. **~-plough** *n* spazzaneve *m*. ~**storm** *n* tormenta *f*. ~**y** *a* nevoso

snub /snʌb/ *n* sgarbo *m* ● *vt* (*pt/pp* **snubbed**) snobbare

'**snub-nosed** *a* dal naso all'insù

snuff /snʌf/ *n* tabacco *m* da fiuto

snug /snʌg/ *a* (**snugger,** **snuggest**) comodo; (*tight*) aderente

snuggle /snʌgl/ *vi* rannicchiarsi (**up to** accanto a)

so /səʊ/ *adv* così; *so far* finora; *so am I* anch'io; *so I see* così pare; *that is so* è così; *so much* così tanto; *so much the better* tanto meglio; *so it is proprio* così; *if so* se è così; *so as to* in modo da; *so long!* *fam* a presto! ● *pron* **I hope/think/am afraid so** spero/penso/temo di sì; **I told you so** te l'ho detto; **because I say so** perché lo dico io; **I did so!** è vero!; *so saying/doing,...* così dicendo/facendo,...; *or so* circa; *very much so* sì, molto; *and so forth* or *on* e così via ● *conj* (*therefore*) perciò; (*in order that*) così; *so that* affinché; *so there!* ecco!; *so what!* e allora?; *so where have you been?* allora, dove sei stato?

soak /səʊk/ *vt* mettere a bagno ● *vi* stare a bagno; ~ **into** (*liquid:*) penetrare. **soak up** *vt* assorbire

soaking /səʊkɪŋ/ *n* ammollo *m* ● *a & adv* ~ [**wet**] *fam* inzuppato

so-and-so /səʊənsəʊ/ *n* Tal dei Tali *mf*; (*euphemism*) specie *f* di imbecille

soap /səʊp/ *n* sapone *m*. ~ **opera** *n* telenovela *f*, soap opera *f* *inv*. ~ **powder** *n* detersivo *m* in polvere

soapy /səʊpɪ/ *a* (**-ier,** **-iest**) insaponato

soar /sɔ:(r)/ *vi* elevarsi; (*prices:*) salire alle stelle

sob /sɒb/ *n* singhiozzo *m* ● *vi* (*pt/pp* **sobbed**) singhiozzare

sober /səʊbə(r)/ *a* sobrio; (*serious*) serio ● **sober up** *vi* ritornare sobrio

'**so-called** *a* cosiddetto

soccer /sɒkə(r)/ *n* calcio *m*

sociable /səʊʃəbl/ *a* socievole

social /səʊʃl/ *a* sociale; (*sociable*) socievole

socialis|m /səʊʃəlɪzm/ *n* socialismo *m*. ~**t** /-ɪst/ *a* socialista ● *n* socialista *mf*

socialize /səʊʃəlaɪz/ *vi* socializzare

socially /səʊʃəlɪ/ *adv* socialmente; **know sb** ~ frequentare qcno

social: ~ **se'curity** *n* previdenza *f* sociale. ~ **work** *n* assistenza *f* sociale. ~ **worker** *n* assistente *mf* sociale

society /sə'saɪətɪ/ *n* società *f* *inv*

sociolog|ist /səʊsɪ'ɒlədʒɪst/ *n* sociologo, -a *mf*. ~**y** *n* sociologia *f*

sock[1] /sɒk/ *n* calzino *m*; (*kneelength*) calza *f*

sock[2] *n fam* pugno *m* ● *vt fam* dare un pugno a

socket /sɒkɪt/ *n* (*wall plug*) presa *f* [di corrente]; (*for bulb*) portalampada *m* *inv*

soda /səʊdə/ *n* soda *f*; *Am* gazzosa *f*. ~ **water** *n* seltz *m* *inv*

sodden /sɒdn/ *a* inzuppato

sodium /səʊdɪəm/ *n* sodio *m*

sofa /səʊfə/ *n* divano *m*. ~ **bed** *n* divano *m* letto

soft /sɒft/ *a* morbido, soffice; (*voice*) sommesso; (*light, colour*) tenue; (*not strict*) indulgente; (*fam: silly*) stupido; **have a** ~ **spot for sb** avere un debole per qcno. ~ **drink** *n* bibita *f* analcolica

soften /sɒfn/ *vt* ammorbidire; *fig* attenuare ● *vi* ammorbidirsi

softly /sɒftlɪ/ *adv* (*say*) sottovoce; (*treat*) con indulgenza; (*play music*) in sottofondo

soft: ~ **toy** *n* pupazzo *m* di peluche. ~ **ware** *n* software *m*

soggy /sɒgɪ/ *a* (**-ier,** **-iest**) zuppo

soil[1] /sɔɪl/ *n* suolo *m*

soil[2] *vt* sporcare

solar /səʊlə(r)/ *a* solare

sold /səʊld/ *see* **sell**

solder /səʊldə(r)/ *n* lega *f* da saldatura ● *vt* saldare

soldier /'səʊldʒə(r)/ n soldato m ● **soldier on** vi perseverare

sole¹ /səʊl/ n (of foot) pianta f; (of shoe) suola f

sole² n (fish) sogliola f

sole³ a unico, solo. ~**ly** adv unicamente

solemn /'sɒləm/ a solenne. ~**ity** /sə'lemnəti/ n solennità f inv

solicit /sə'lɪsɪt/ vt sollecitare ● vi (prostitute:) adescare

solicitor /sə'lɪsɪtə(r)/ n avvocato m

solid /'sɒlɪd/ a solido; (oak, gold) massiccio ● n (figure) solido m; ~**s** pl (food) cibi mpl solidi

solidarity /sɒlɪ'dærətɪ/ n solidarietà f inv

solidify /sə'lɪdɪfaɪ/ vi (pt/pp -**ied**) solidificarsi

soliloquy /sə'lɪləkwɪ/ n soliloquio m

solitaire /sɒlɪ'teə(r)/ n solitario m

solitary /'sɒlɪtərɪ/ a solitario; (sole) solo. ~ **con'finement** n cella f di isolamento

solitude /'sɒlɪtjuːd/ n solitudine f

solo /'səʊləʊ/ n Mus assolo m ● a (flight) in solitario ● adv in solitario. ~**ist** n solista mf

solstice /'sɒlstɪs/ n solstizio m

soluble /'sɒljʊbl/ a solubile

solution /sə'luːʃn/ n soluzione f

solve /sɒlv/ vt risolvere

solvent /'sɒlvənt/ a solvente ● n solvente m

sombre /'sɒmbə(r)/ a tetro; (clothes) scuro

some /sʌm/ a (a certain amount of) del; (a certain number of) qualche, alcuni; ~ **day** un giorno o l'altro; I **need** ~ **money/books** ho bisogno di soldi/libri; **do** ~ **shopping** fare qualche acquisto ● pron (a certain amount) un po'; (a certain number) alcuni; I **want** ~ ne voglio

some: ~**body** /-bədɪ/ pron & n qualcuno m. ~**how** adv in qualche modo; ~**how or other** in un modo o nell'altro. ~**one** pron & n = **somebody**

somersault /'sʌməsɔːlt/ n capriola f; **turn a** ~ fare una capriola

something pron qualche cosa, qualcosa; ~ **different** qualcosa di diverso; ~ **like** un po' come; (approximately) qualcosa come; **see** ~ **of sb** vedere qcno un po'

some: ~**time** adv un giorno o l'altro; ~**time** last summer durante l'estate scorsa. ~**times** adv qualche volta. ~**what** adv piuttosto. ~**where** adv da qualche parte ● pron ~**where to eat** un posto in cui mangiare

son /sʌn/ n figlio m

sonata /sə'nɑːtə/ n sonata f

song /sɒŋ/ n canzone f

sonic /'sɒnɪk/ a sonico. ~ '**boom** n bang m inv sonico

'son-in-law n (pl ~**s-in-law**) genero m

sonnet /'sɒnɪt/ n sonetto m

soon /suːn/ adv presto; (in a short time) tra poco; **as** ~ **as** [non] appena; **as** ~ **as possible** il più presto possibile; ~**er or later** prima o poi, the ~**er the better** prima è, meglio è; **no** ~**er had I arrived than**... ero appena arrivato quando...; **I would** ~**er go** preferirei andare; ~ **after** subito dopo

soot /sʊt/ n fuliggine f

soothe /suːð/ vt calmare

sooty /'sʊtɪ/ a fuligginoso

sophisticated /sə'fɪstɪkeɪtɪd/ a sofisticato

soporific /sɒpə'rɪfɪk/ a soporifero

sopping /'sɒpɪŋ/ a & adv **be** ~ [wet] essere bagnato fradicio

soppy /'sɒpɪ/ a (-**ier, -iest**) fam svenevole

soprano /sə'prɑːnəʊ/ n soprano m

sordid /'sɔːdɪd/ a sordido

sore /sɔː(r)/ a dolorante; (Am: vexed) arrabbiato; **it's** ~ fa male; **have a** ~ **throat** avere mal di gola ● n piaga f. ~**ly** adv (tempted) seriamente

sorrow /'sɒrəʊ/ n tristezza f. ~**ful** a triste

sorry /'sɒrɪ/ a (-**ier, -iest**) (sad)

spiacente; (*wretched*) pietoso;
you'll be ~! te ne pentirai!; **I am
~** mi dispiace; **be** o **feel ~ for**
provare compassione per; **~!** scusa!; (*more polite*) scusi!

sort /sɔːt/ n specie f; (*fam: person*)
tipo m; **it's a ~ of fish** è un tipo di
pesce; **be out of ~s** (*fam: unwell*)
stare poco bene ● vt classificare.
sort out vt selezionare (*papers*);
fig risolvere (*problem*); occuparsi
di (*person*)

'so-so a & adv così così

sought /sɔːt/ *see* seek

soul /soʊl/ n anima f

sound[1] /saʊnd/ a sano; (*sensible*)
saggio; (*secure*) solido; (*thrashing*) clamoroso ● adv **~ asleep**
profondamente addormentato

sound[2] n suono m; (*noise*) rumore
m; **I don't like the ~ of it** fam non
mi suona bene ● vi suonare;
(*seem*) aver l'aria ● vt (*pronounce*)
pronunciare; Med auscoltare
(*chest*). **~ barrier** n muro m del
suono. **~ card** n Comput scheda f
sonora. **~less** a silenzioso. **sound
out** vt fig sondare

soundly /'saʊndlɪ/ adv (*sleep*)
profondamente; (*defeat*) clamorosamente

'sound: ~proof a impenetrabile al
suono. **~track** n colonna f sonora

soup /suːp/ n minestra f. **~ed-up** a
fam (*engine*) truccato

soup: ~-plate n piatto m fondo.
~-spoon n cucchiaio m da minestra

sour /saʊə(r)/ a agro; (*not fresh &
fig*) acido

source /sɔːs/ n fonte f

south /saʊθ/ n sud m; **to the ~ of** a
sud di ● a del sud, meridionale
● adv verso il sud

south: ~ 'Africa n Sudafrica m.
S~ **America** n America f del Sud.
S~ **American** a & n sud-americano, -a mf. **~'east** n sud-est m

southerly /'sʌðəlɪ/ a del sud

southern /'sʌðən/ a del sud, meri-

dionale; **~ Italy** il Mezzogiorno m.
~er n meridionale mf

South 'Pole n polo m Sud

'southward[s] /-wəd[z]/ adv verso il
sud

souvenir /suːvə'nɪə(r)/ n ricordo
m, souvenir m inv

sovereign /'sɒvrɪn/ a sovrano ● n
sovrano, -a mf. **~ty** n sovranità f
inv

Soviet /'səʊvɪət/ a sovietico; ~
Union Unione f Sovietica

sow[1] /saʊ/ n scrofa f

sow[2] /səʊ/ vt (*pt* sowed, *pp* sown
or sowed) seminare

soya /'sɔɪə/ n **~ bean** soia f

spa /spɑː/ n stazione f termale

space /speɪs/ n spazio m ● a
(*research etc*) spaziale ● vt **~** [out]
distanziare

space: ~ship n astronave f. **~
shuttle** n navetta f spaziale

spacious /'speɪʃəs/ a spazioso

spade /speɪd/ n vanga f; (*for child*)
paletta f; **~s** pl (*in cards*) picche
fpl. **~work** n lavoro m preparatorio

Spain /speɪn/ n Spagna f

span[1] /spæn/ n spanna f; (*of arch*)
luce f; (*of time*) arco m; (*of wings*)
apertura f ● vt (*pt/pp* spanned)
estendersi su

span[2] *see* spick

Spaniard /'spænjəd/ n spagnolo,
-a mf. **~ish** a spagnolo ● n (*language*) spagnolo m; **the ~ish** pl gli
spagnoli

spank /spæŋk/ vt sculacciare.
~ing n sculacciata f

spanner /'spænə(r)/ n chiave f inglese

spar /spɑː(r)/ vi (*pt/pp* sparred)
(*boxing*) allenarsi; (*argue*) litigare
● adv verso il sud

spare /speə(r)/ a (*surplus*) in più;
(*additional*) di riserva ● n (*part*)
ricambio m ● vt risparmiare; (*do
without*) fare a meno di; **can you
~ five minutes?** avresti cinque
minuti?; **to ~** (*surplus*) in eccedenza. **~ part** n pezzo m di ricam-

bio. **~ time** n tempo m libero. **~ 'wheel** n ruota f di scorta

sparing /'speərɪŋ/ a parco (**with** di). **~ly** adv con parsimonia

spark /spɑ:k/ n scintilla f. **~ing-plug** n Auto candela f

sparkl|e /'spɑ:kl/ n scintillio m ● vi scintillare. **~ing** a frizzante; (wine) spumante

sparrow /'spærəʊ/ n passero m

sparse /spɑ:s/ a rado. **~ly** adv scarsamente; **~ly populated** a bassa densità di popolazione

spartan /'spɑ:tn/ a spartano

spasm /'spæzm/ n spasmo m. **~odic** /-'mɒdɪk/ a spasmodico

spastic /'spæstɪk/ a spastico ● n spastico, -a mf

spat /spæt/ see **spit¹**

spate /speɪt/ n (series) successione f; **be in full ~** essere in piena

spatial /'speɪʃl/ a spaziale

spatter /'spætə(r)/ vt schizzare

spatula /'spætjʊlə/ n spatola f

spawn /spɔ:n/ n uova fpl (di pesci, rane, ecc.) ● vi deporre le uova ● vt fig generare

spay /speɪ/ vt sterilizzare

speak /spi:k/ v (pt **spoke**, pp **spoken**) ● vi parlare (to a); **~ing!** Teleph sono io! ● vt dire; **~ one's mind** dire quello che si pensa. **speak for** vi parlare a nome di. **speak up** vi parlare più forte; **~ up for oneself** parlare a favore di

speaker /'spi:kə(r)/ n parlante mf; (in public) oratore, -trice mf; (of stereo) cassa f

spear /spɪə(r)/ n lancia f

spec /spek/ n **on ~** fam senza certezza

special /'speʃl/ a speciale. **~ist** n specialista mf. **~ity** /-ʃɪ'ælətɪ/ n specialità f inv

special|ize /'speʃəlaɪz/ vi specializzarsi. **~ly** adv specialmente; (particularly) particolarmente

species /'spi:ʃi:z/ n specie f inv

specific /spə'sɪfɪk/ a specifico. **~ally** adv in modo specifico

specifications /spesɪfɪ'keɪʃnz/ npl descrizione f

specify /'spesɪfaɪ/ vt (pt/pp **-ied**) specificare

specimen /'spesɪmən/ n campione m

speck /spek/ n macchiolina f; (particle) granello m

speckled /'spekld/ a picchiettato

specs /speks/ npl fam occhiali mpl

spectacle /'spektəkl/ n (show) spettacolo m. **~s** npl occhiali mpl

spectacular /spek'tækjʊlə(r)/ a spettacolare

spectator /spek'teɪtə(r)/ n spettatore, -trice mf

spectre /'spektə(r)/ n spettro m

spectrum /'spektrəm/ n (pl **-tra**) spettro m; fig gamma f

speculat|e /'spekjʊleɪt/ vi speculare. **~ion** /-'leɪʃn/ n speculazione f. **~ive** /-ɪv/ a speculativo. **~or** n speculatore, -trice mf

sped /sped/ see **speed**

speech /spi:tʃ/ n linguaggio m; (address) discorso m. **~less** a senza parole

speed /spi:d/ n velocità f inv; (gear) marcia f; **at ~** a tutta velocità ● vi (pt/pp **sped**) andare veloce; (pt/pp **speeded**) (go too fast) andare a velocità eccessiva. **speed up** (pt/pp **speeded up**) vt/i accelerare

speed: **~boat** n motoscafo m. **~ing** n eccesso m di velocità. **~ limit** n limite m di velocità

speedometer /spi:'dɒmɪtə(r)/ n tachimetro m

speed|y /'spi:dɪ/ a (**-ier, -iest**) rapido. **~ily** adv rapidamente

spell¹ /spel/ n (turn) turno m; (of weather) periodo m

spell² v (pt/pp **spelled, spelt**) ● vt **how do you ~...?** come si scrive...?; **could you ~ that for me?** me lo può compitare?; **~ disaster** essere disastroso ● vi **he can't ~** fa molti errori d'ortografia

spell³ n (magic) incantesimo m. **~bound** a affascinato

spelling /'spelɪŋ/ n ortografia f
spelt /spelt/ see **spell**[2]
spend /spend/ vt/i (pt/pp **spent**) spendere; passare ⟨time⟩
spent /spent/ see **spend**
sperm /spɜːm/ n spermatozoo m; ⟨semen⟩ sperma m
spew /spjuː/ vt/i vomitare
spher|e /sfɪə(r)/ n sfera f. **~ical** /'sferɪkl/ a sferico
spice /spaɪs/ n spezia f, fig pepe m
spick /spɪk/ a **~ and span** lindo
spicy /'spaɪsɪ/ a piccante
spider /'spaɪdə(r)/ n ragno m
spik|e /spark/ n punta f; Bot, Zool spina f; ⟨on shoe⟩ chiodo m. **~y** a ⟨plant⟩ pungente
spill /spɪl/ v (pt/pp **spilt** or **spilled**) ● vt versare ⟨blood⟩ ● vi rovesciarsi
spin /spɪn/ v (pt/pp **spun**, pres p **spinning**) ● vt far girare; filare ⟨wool⟩; centrifugare ⟨washing⟩ ● vi girare; ⟨washing machine:⟩ centrifugare ● n rotazione f; ⟨short drive⟩ giretto m. **spin out** vt far durare
spinach /'spɪnɪdʒ/ n spinaci mpl
spinal /'spaɪnl/ a spinale. **~ 'cord** n midollo m spinale
spindl|e /'spɪndl/ n fuso m. **~y** a affusolato
spin-'drier n centrifuga f
spine /spaɪn/ n spina f dorsale; ⟨of book⟩ dorso m; Bot, Zool spina f. **~less** a fig smidollato
spinning /'spɪnɪŋ/ n filatura f. **~-wheel** n filatoio m
'spin-off n ricaduta f
spiral /'spaɪrəl/ a a spirale ● n spirale f ● vi (pt/pp **spiralled**) formare una spirale. **~ 'staircase** n scala f a chiocciola
spire /'spaɪə(r)/ n guglia f
spirit /'spɪrɪt/ n spirito m; ⟨courage⟩ ardore m; **~s** pl ⟨alcohol⟩ liquori mpl; **in good ~s** di buon umore; **in low ~s** abbattuto
spirited /'spɪrɪtɪd/ a vivace; ⟨courageous⟩ pieno d'ardore
spirit: ~-level n livella f a bolla

d'aria. **~ stove** n fornellino m [da campeggio]
spiritual /'spɪrɪtjʊəl/ a spirituale ● n spiritual m. **~ism** /-ɪzm/ n spiritismo m. **~ist** /-ɪst/ n spiritista mf
spit[1] /spɪt/ n ⟨for roasting⟩ spiedo m
spit[2] n sputo m ● vt/i (pt/pp **spat**, pres p **spitting**) sputare; ⟨cat:⟩ soffiare; ⟨fat:⟩ sfrigolare; **it's ~ting [with rain]** piovviggina; **the ~ting image of** il ritratto spiccicato di
spite /spaɪt/ n dispetto m; **in ~ of** malgrado ● vt far dispetto a. **~ful** a indispettito
spittle /'spɪtl/ n saliva f
splash /splæʃ/ n schizzo m; ⟨of colour⟩ macchia f; ⟨fam: drop⟩ goccio m ● vt schizzare; **~ sb with sth** schizzare qcno di qcsa ● vi schizzare. **splash about** vi schizzarsi. **splash down** vi ⟨spacecraft:⟩ ammarare
spleen /spliːn/ n Anat milza f
splendid /'splendɪd/ a splendido
splendour /'splendə(r)/ n splendore m
splint /splɪnt/ n Med stecca f
splinter /'splɪntə(r)/ n scheggia f ● vi scheggiarsi
split /splɪt/ n fessura f; ⟨quarrel⟩ rottura f; ⟨division⟩ scissione f; ⟨tear⟩ strappo m ● v (pt/pp **split**, pres p **splitting**) ● vt spaccare; ⟨share, divide⟩ dividere; ⟨tear⟩ strappare ● vi spaccarsi; ⟨tear⟩ strapparsi; ⟨divide⟩ dividersi; **~ on sb** fam denunciare qcno ● a **~ second** una frazione f di secondo. **split up** vt dividersi ● vi ⟨couple:⟩ separarsi
splutter /'splʌtə(r)/ vi farfugliare
spoil /spɔɪl/ n **~s** pl bottino msg ● v (pt/pp **spoilt** or **spoiled**) ● vt rovinare; viziare ⟨person⟩ ● vi andare a male. **~sport** n guastafeste mf inv
spoke[1] /spəʊk/ n raggio m
spoke[2], **spoken** /'spəʊkn/ see **speak**

'spokesman n portavoce m inv

sponge /spʌndʒ/ n spugna f ● vt pulire (con la spugna) ● vi ~ on scroccare da. **~-cake** n pan m di Spagna

'sponger /'spʌndʒə(r)/ n scroccone, -a mf. **~y** a spugnoso

sponsor /'spɒnsə(r)/ n garante m; Radio, TV sponsor m inv; (godparent) padrino m, madrina f; (for membership) socio, -a mf garante ● vt sponsorizzare. **~ship** n sponsorizzazione f

spontaneous /spɒn'teɪnɪəs/ a spontaneo

spoof /spuːf/ n fam parodia f

spooky /'spuːkɪ/ a (-ier, -iest) fam sinistro

spool /spuːl/ n bobina f

spoon /spuːn/ n cucchiaio m ● vt mettere col cucchiaio. **~-feed** vt (pt/pp -fed) fig imboccare. **~ful** n cucchiaiata f

sporadic /spə'rædɪk/ a sporadico

sport /spɔːt/ n sport m inv ● vt sfoggiare. **~ing** a sportivo. **~ing chance** possibilità f inv

sports: **~car** n automobile f sportiva. **~coat** n, **~jacket** n giacca f sportiva. **~man** n sportivo m. **~woman** n sportiva f

sporty /'spɔːtɪ/ a (-ier, -iest) sportivo

spot /spɒt/ n macchia f; (pimple) brufolo m; (place) posto m; (in pattern) pois m inv; (of rain) goccia f; (of water) goccio m; **~s** pl (rash) sfogo msg; a **~** of fam un po' di; a **~** of bother qualche problema; **on the ~** sul luogo; (immediately) immediatamente; in a (tight) **~** fam in difficoltà ● vt (pt/pp spotted) macchiare; (fam: notice) individuare

spot: **~ 'check** n (without warning) controllo m a sorpresa; **do a ~ check** on sth dare una controllata a qcsa. **~less** a immacolato. **~light** n riflettore m

spotted /'spɒtɪd/ a (material) a pois

spotty /'spɒtɪ/ a (-ier, -iest) (pimply) brufoloso

spouse /spauz/ n consorte mf

spout /spaut/ n becco m ● vi zampillare (from da)

sprain /spreɪn/ n slogatura f ● vt slogare

sprang /spræŋ/ see **spring²**

sprawl /sprɔːl/ vi (in chair) stravaccarsi; (city etc:) estendersi; **go ~ing** (fall) cadere disteso

spray /spreɪ/ n spruzzo m; (preparation) spray m inv; (container) spruzzatore m inv ● vt spruzzare. **~gun** n pistola f a spruzzo

spread /spred/ n estensione f; (of disease) diffusione f; (paste) crema f; (fam: feast) banchetto m ● vt (pt/pp spread) ● vt spargere; spalmare (butter, jam); stendere (cloth, arms); diffondere (news, disease); dilazionare (payments); **~ sth with** spalmare qcsa di ● vi spargersi; (butter:) spalmarsi; (disease:) diffondersi. **~sheet** n Comput foglio m elettronico. **spread out** vt sparpagliare ● vi sparpagliarsi

spree /spriː/ n fam go on a ~ far baldoria; **go on a shopping ~** fare spese folli

sprig /sprɪg/ n rametto m

sprightly /'spraɪtlɪ/ a (-ier, -iest) vivace

spring¹ /sprɪŋ/ n primavera f ● attrib primaverile

spring² n (jump) balzo m; (water) sorgente f; (device) molla f; (elasticity) elasticità f inv ● v (pt sprang, pp sprung) ● vi (arise) provenire (from da) ● vt he just sprang it on me me l'ha detto a cose fatte compiuto. **spring up** balzare; fig spuntare

spring: **~board** n trampolino m. **~-'cleaning** n pulizia fpl di Pasqua. **~time** n primavera f

sprinkle /'sprɪŋkl/ vt (scatter) spruzzare (liquid); spargere (flour, cocoa); ~ sth with spruzzare qcsa di (liquid); cospargere qcsa di

⟨*flour, cocoa*⟩. **~er** n sprinkler m inv; (*for lawn*) irrigatore m. **~ing** n (*of liquid*) spruzzatina f; (*of pepper, salt*) pizzico m; (*of flour, sugar*) spolverata f; (*of knowledge*) infarinatura f; (*of people*) pugno m

sprint /sprɪnt/ n sprint m inv ● vi fare uno sprint; *Sport* sprintare. **~er** n sprinter mf inv

sprout /spraʊt/ n germoglio m; [**Brussels**] **~s** pl cavolini mpl di Bruxelles ● vi germogliare

spruce /spruːs/ a elegante ● n abete m

sprung /sprʌŋ/ see **spring²** ● a molleggiato

spud /spʌd/ n fam patata f

spun /spʌn/ see **spin**

spur /spɜː(r)/ n sperone m; (*stimulus*) stimolo m; (*road*) svincolo m, **on the ~ of the moment** su due piedi ● vt (pt/pp **spurred**) **~** [**on**] fig spronare [a]

spurious /ˈspjʊərɪəs/ a falso

spurn /spɜːn/ vt sdegnare

spurt /spɜːt/ n getto m; *Sport* scatto m; **put on a ~** fare uno scatto ● vi sprizzare; (*increase speed*) scattare

spy /spaɪ/ n spia f ● v (pt/pp **spied**) ● vi spiare ● vt (*fam: see*) spiare. **spy on** vi spiare

spying /ˈspaɪɪŋ/ n spionaggio m

squabble /ˈskwɒbl/ n bisticcio m ● vi bisticciare

squad /skwɒd/ n squadra f; *Sport* squadra

squadron /ˈskwɒdrən/ n *Mil* squadrone m; *Aeron, Naut* squadriglia f

squalid /ˈskwɒlɪd/ a squallido

squalor /ˈskwɒlə(r)/ n squallore m

squander /ˈskwɒndə(r)/ vt sprecare

square /skweə(r)/ a quadrato; ⟨*meal*⟩ sostanzioso; (*fam: old-fashioned*) vecchio stampo; **all ~** fam pari m quadrato m; (*in city*) piazza f; (*on chessboard*) riquadro m ● vt (*settle*) far quadrare; *Math*

elevare al quadrato ● vi (*agree*) armonizzare

squash /skwɒʃ/ n (*drink*) spremuta f; (*sport*) squash m; (*vegetable*) zucca f ● vt schiacciare; soffocare ⟨*rebellion*⟩

squat /skwɒt/ a tarchiato ● n fam edificio m occupato abusivamente ● vi (pt/pp **squatted**) accovacciarsi; **~** in occupare abusivamente. **~ter** n occupante mf abusivo m

squawk /skwɔːk/ n gracchio m ● vi gracchiare

squeak /skwiːk/ n squittio m; (*of hinge, brakes*) scricchiolio m ● vi squittire; ⟨*hinge, brakes:*⟩ scricchiolare

squeal /skwiːl/ n strillo m; (*of brakes*) cigolio m ● vi strillare; sl spifferare

squeamish /ˈskwiːmɪʃ/ a dallo stomaco delicato

squeeze /skwiːz/ n stretta f; (*crush*) pigia pigia m inv ● vt premere; (*to get juice*) spremere; stringere ⟨*hand*⟩; (*force*) spingere a forza; (*fam: extort*) estorcere (**out of** da). **squeeze in/out** vi sgusciare dentro/fuori. **squeeze up** vi stringersi

squelch /skweltʃ/ vi sguazzare

squid /skwɪd/ n calamaro m

squiggle /ˈskwɪɡl/ n scarabocchio m

squint /skwɪnt/ n strabismo m ● vi essere strabico

squire /skwaɪə(r)/ n signorotto m di campagna

squirm /skwɜːm/ vi contorcersi; (*feel embarrassed*) sentirsi imbarazzato

squirrel /ˈskwɪrəl/ n scoiattolo m

squirt /skwɜːt/ n spruzzo m; (*fam: person*) presuntuoso m ● vt/i spruzzare

St abbr (**Saint**) S; abbr **Street**

stab /stæb/ n pugnalata f, coltellata f; (*sensation*) fitta f; (*fam: attempt*) tentativo m ● vt (pt/pp **stabbed**) pugnalare, accoltellare

stability /stə'bɪlətɪ/ n stabilità f inv

stabilize /'steɪbɪlaɪz/ vt stabilizzare ● vi stabilizzarsi

stable[1] /'steɪbl/ a stabile

stable[2] n stalla f; (establishment) scuderia f

stack /stæk/ n catasta f; (of chimney) comignolo m; (chimney) ciminiera f; (fam: large quantity) montagna f ● vt accatastare

stadium /'steɪdɪəm/ n stadio m

staff /stɑːf/ n (stick) bastone m; (employees) personale m; (teachers) corpo m insegnante, Mil Stato m Maggiore ● vt fornire di personale. **~-room** n Sch sala f insegnanti

stag /stæg/ n cervo m

stage /steɪdʒ/ n palcoscenico m; (profession) teatro m; (in journey) tappa f; (in process) stadio m; **go on the ~** darsi al teatro; **by or in ~s** a tappe ● vt mettere in scena; (arrange) organizzare

stage: **~ door** n ingresso m degli artisti. **~ fright** n panico m da scena. **~ manager** n direttore, -trice mf di scena

stagger /'stægə(r)/ vi barcollare ● vt sbalordire; scaglionare (holidays etc); **I was ~ed** sono rimasto sbalordito ● n vacillamento m. **~ing** a sbalorditivo

stagnant /'stægnənt/ a stagnante

stagnat|e /stæg'neɪt/ vi fig [ri]stagnare. **~ion** /-'neɪʃn/ n fig inattività f

'**stag party** n addio m al celibato

staid /steɪd/ a posato

stain /steɪn/ n macchia f; (for wood) mordente m ● vt macchiare; (wood) dare il mordente a; **~ed glass** vetro m colorato; **~ed-glass window** vetrata f colorata. **~less** a senza macchia; (steel) inossidabile. **~ remover** n smacchiatore m

stair /steə(r)/ n gradino m; **~s** pl scale fpl. **~case** n scale fpl

stake /steɪk/ n palo m; (wager) po-

sta f; Comm partecipazione f; **at ~** in gioco ● vt puntellare; (wager) scommettere

stale /steɪl/ a stantio; (air) viziato; (uninteresting) trito (e ritrito). **~mate** n (in chess) stallo m; (deadlock) situazione f di stallo

stalk[1] /stɔːk/ n gambo m

stalk[2] vt inseguire ● vi camminare impettito

stall /stɔːl/ n box m inv; **~s** pl Theat platea f; (in market) bancarella f ● vi (engine) spegnersi; fig temporeggiare ● vt far spegnere (engine); tenere a bada (person)

stallion /'stæljən/ n stallone m

stalwart /'stɔːlwət/ a fedele

stamina /'stæmɪnə/ n [capacità f inv di] resistenza f

stammer /'stæmə(r)/ n balbettio m ● vt/i balbettare

stamp /stæmp/ n (postage ~) francobollo m; (instrument) timbro m; fig impronta f ● vt affrancare (letter); timbrare (bill); battere (feet). **stamp out** vt spegnere; fig soffocare

stampede /stæm'piːd/ n fuga f precipitosa; fam fuggi-fuggi m ● vi fuggire precipitosamente

stance /stɑːns/ n posizione f

stand /stænd/ n (for bikes) rastrelliera f; (at exhibition) stand m inv; (in market) bancarella f; (in stadium) gradinata f inv; fig posizione f ● vt (pt/pp **stood**) ● vi stare in piedi; (rise) alzarsi [in piedi]; (be) trovarsi; (be candidate) essere candidato (for a); (stay valid) rimanere valido; **~ still** non muoversi; **I don't know where I ~** non so qual'è la mia posizione; **~ firm** fig tener duro; **~ together** essere solidali; **~ to lose/gain** rischiare di perdere/vincere; **~ to reason** essere logico ● vt (withstand) resistere a; (endure) sopportare; (place) mettere; **~ a chance** avere una possibilità; **~ one's ground** tener duro; **~ the test of time** superare la prova del tempo; **~ sb a**

beer offrire una birra a qcno.
stand by *vi* stare a guardare; *(be ready)* essere pronto ● *vt (support)* appoggiare. **stand down** *vi (retire)* ritirarsi. **stand for** *vt (mean)* significare; *(tolerate)* tollerare. **stand in for** *vt* sostituire.
stand out *vi* spiccare. **stand up** *vi* alzarsi [in piedi]. **stand up for** *vt* prendere le difese di; **~ up for oneself** farsi valere. **stand up to** *vt* affrontare

standard /'stændəd/ *a* standard;
be ~ practice essere pratica corrente ● *n* standard *m inv*; *Techn* norma *f*; *(level)* livello *m*; *(quality)* qualità *f inv*; *(flag)* stendardo *m*;
~s *pl (morals)* valori *mpl*; **~ of living** tenore *m* di vita. **~ize** *vt* standardizzare

'**standard lamp** *n* lampada *f* a stelo

'**stand-by** *n* riserva *f*; **on ~** *(at airport)* in lista d'attesa

'**stand-in** *n* controfigura *f*

standing /'stændɪŋ/ *a (erect)* in piedi; *(permanent)* permanente
● *n* posizione *f*; *(duration)* durata *f*. **~ 'order** *n* addebitamento *m* diretto. **~-room** *n* posti *mpl* in piedi

stand: **~-offish** /stænd'ɒfɪʃ/ *a* scostante. **~point** *n* punto *m* di vista.
~still *n* **come to a ~still** fermarsi; **at a ~still** in un periodo di stasi

stank /stæŋk/ *see* **stink**

staple[1] /'steɪpl/ *n (product)* prodotto *m* principale

staple[2] *n* graffa *f* ● *vt* pinzare. **~r** *n* pinzatrice *f*, cucitrice *f*

star /stɑː(r)/ *n* stella *f*; *(asterisk)* asterisco *m*; *Theat, Cinema, Sport* divo, -a *mf*, stella *f* ● *vi (pt/pp* starred) essere l'interprete principale

starboard /'stɑːbəd/ *n* tribordo *m*

starch /stɑːtʃ/ *n* amido *m* ● *vt* inamidare. **~y** *a* ricco di amido; *fig* compito

stare /steə(r)/ *n* sguardo *m* fisso
● *vi* **it's rude to ~** è da maleducati

fissare la gente; **~ at** fissare; **~ into space** guardare nel vuoto

'**starfish** *n* stella *f* di mare

stark /stɑːk/ *a* austero; *(contrast)* forte ● *adv* completamente; **~ naked** completamente nudo

starling /'stɑːlɪŋ/ *n* storno *m*

'**starlit** *a* stellato

starry /'stɑːrɪ/ *a* stellato

start /stɑːt/ *n* inizio *m*; *(departure)* partenza *f*; *(jump)* sobbalzo *m*;
from the ~ *(fin)* dall'inizio; **for a ~** tanto per cominciare; **give sb a ~** *Sport* dare un vantaggio a qcno
● *vi* [in]cominciare; *(set out)* avviarsi; *(engine, car:)* partire;
(jump) trasalire; **to ~ with,...** tanto per cominciare... ● *vt* [in]cominciare; *(cause)* dare inizio a; *(found)* mettere su; mettere in moto *(car)*; mettere in giro *(rumour)*. **~er** *n Culin* primo *m* [piatto *m*]; *(in race: giving signal)* starter *m inv*; *(participant)* corrente *mf*; *Auto* motorino *m* d'avviamento. **~ing-point** *n* punto *m* di partenza

startle /'stɑːtl/ *vt* far trasalire; *(news:)* sconvolgere

starvation /stɑː'veɪʃn/ *n* fame *f*

starve /stɑːv/ *vi* morire di fame
● *vt* far morire di fame

stash /stæʃ/ *vt fam* **~ [away]** nascondere

state /steɪt/ *n* stato *m*; *(grand style)* pompa *f*; **~ of play** punteggio *m*;
be in a ~ *(person:)* essere agitato;
lie in ~ essere esposto ● *attrib* di Stato; *Sch* pubblico; *(with ceremony)* di gala ● *vt* dichiarare;
(specify) precisare. **~less** *a* apolide

stately /'steɪtlɪ/ *a* (-ier, -iest) maestoso. **~ 'home** *n* dimora *f* signorile

statement /'steɪtmənt/ *n* dichiarazione *f*; *Jur* deposizione *f*; *(in banking)* estratto *m* conto; *(account)* rapporto *m*

'**statesman** *n* statista *mf*

static /'stætɪk/ *a* statico

station /'steɪʃn/ n stazione f; (*police*) commissariato m ● vt appostare (*guard*); **be ~ed in** Germany essere di stanza in Germania. **~ary** /-ərɪ/ a immobile

stationer /'steɪʃənə(r)/ n ~'s [**shop**] cartoleria f. **~y** n cartoleria f

'**station-wagon** n Am familiare f

statistic|al /stə'tɪstɪkl/ a statistico. **~s** n & pl statistica f

statue /'stætjuː/ n statua f

stature /'stætʃə(r)/ n statura f

status /'steɪtəs/ n condizione f; (*high rank*) alto rango m. **~ symbol** n status symbol m inv

statut|e /'stætjuːt/ n statuto m. **~ory** a statutario

staunch /stɔːntʃ/ a fedele. **~ly** adv fedelmente

stave /steɪv/ vt ~ **off** tenere lontano

stay /steɪ/ n soggiorno m ● vi restare, rimanere; (*reside*) alloggiare; ~ **the night** passare la notte; ~ **put** non muoversi ● vt ~ **the course** resistere fino alla fine. **stay away** vi stare lontano. **stay behind** vi non andare con gli altri. **stay in** vi (*at home*) stare in casa; Sch restare a scuola dopo le lezioni. **stay up** vi stare su; (*person:*) stare alzato

stead /sted/ n **in his** ~ in sua vece; **stand sb in good** ~ tornare utile a qcno. **~fast** a fedele; (*refusal*) fermo

steadily /'stedɪlɪ/ adv (*continually*) continuamente

steady /'stedɪ/ a (-**ier**, -**iest**) saldo, fermo; (*breathing*) regolare; (*job, boyfriend*) fisso; (*dependable*) serio

steak /steɪk/ n (*for stew*) spezzatino m; (*for grilling, frying*) bistecca f

steal /stiːl/ v (*pt* **stole**, *pp* **stolen**) ● vt rubare (**from** da). **steal in/out** vi entrare/uscire furtivamente

stealth /stelθ/ n **by** ~ di nascosto. **~y** a furtivo

steam /stiːm/ n vapore m; **under one's own** ~ fam da solo ● vt Culin cucinare a vapore ● vi fumare. **steam up** vi appannarsi

'**steam-engine** n locomotiva f

steamer /'stiːmə(r)/ n piroscafo m; (*saucepan*) pentola f a vapore

'**steamroller** n rullo m compressore

steamy /'stiːmɪ/ a appannato

steel /stiːl/ n acciaio m ● vt ~ **oneself** temprarsi

steep¹ /stiːp/ vt (*soak*) lasciare a bagno

steep² a ripido; (*fam: price*) esorbitante. **~ly** adv ripidamente

steeple /'stiːpl/ n campanile m. **~chase** n corsa f ippica a ostacoli

steer /stɪə(r)/ vt/i guidare; ~ **clear of** stare alla larga da. **~ing** n Auto sterzo m. **~ing-wheel** n volante m

stem¹ /stem/ n stelo m; (*of glass*) gambo m; (*of word*) radice f ● vi (*pt/pp* **stemmed**) ~ **from** derivare da

stem² vt (*pt/pp* **stemmed**) contenere

stench /stentʃ/ n fetore m

step /step/ n passo m; (*stair*) gradino m; **~s** pl (*ladder*) scala f portatile; **in** ~ al passo; **be out of** ~ non stare al passo; **~ by** ~ un passo alla volta ● vi (*pt/pp* **stepped**) ~ **into** entrare in; ~ **out of** uscire da; ~ **out of line** sgarrare. **step down** vi fig dimettersi. **step forward** vi farsi avanti. **step in** vi fig intervenire. **step up** vt (*increase*) aumentare

step: **~brother** n fratellastro m. **~child** n figliastro, -a mf. **~daughter** n figliastra f. **~father** n patrigno m. **~ladder** n scala f portatile. **~mother** n matrigna f

'**stepping-stone** n pietra f per guadare; fig trampolino m

step: **~sister** n sorellastra f. **~son** n figliastro m

stereo /'sterɪəʊ/ n stereo m; **in** ~

in stereofonia. **~phonic** /-'fɒnɪk/ a stereofonico

stereotype /'steriətaip/ n stereotipo m. **~d** a stereotipato

steril|e /'sterail/ a sterile. **~ity** /stə'rɪləti/ n sterilità f inv

steriliz|ation /sterəlar'zeiʃn/ n sterilizzazione f. **~e** /'ster-/ vt sterilizzare

sterling /'stɜːlɪŋ/ a fig apprezzabile; **~ silver** argento m pregiato ● n sterlina f

stern[1] /stɜːn/ a severo

stern[2] n (of boat) poppa f

stethoscope /'steθəskəup/ n stetoscopio m

stew /stjuː/ n stufato m; **in a ~** fam agitato ● vt/i cuocere in umido; **~ed fruit** frutta f cotta

steward /'stjuːəd/ n (at meeting) organizzatore, -trice mf; (on ship, aicraft) steward m inv. **~ess** n hostess f inv

stick[1] /stɪk/ n bastone m; (of celery, rhubarb) gambo m; Sport mazza f

stick[2] v (pt/pp stuck) ● vt (stab) [con]ficcare; (glue) attaccare; (fam: put) mettere; (fam: endure) sopportare ● vi (adhere) attaccarsi (to a); (jam) bloccarsi; **~ to** attenersi a (facts); mantenere (story); perseverare in (task); **~ at it** fam tener duro; **~ at nothing** fam non fermarsi di fronte a niente; **be stuck** (vehicle, person:) essere bloccato; (drawer:) essere incastrato; **be stuck with sth** fam farsi incastrare con qcsa. **stick out** vi (project) sporgere; (fam: catch the eye) risaltare ● vt fam fare (tongue). **stick up for** vt fam difendere

sticker /'stɪkə(r)/ n autoadesivo m

'sticking plaster n cerotto m

stick-in-the-mud n retrogrado m

stickler /'stɪklə(r)/ n **be a ~ for** tenere molto a

sticky /'stɪkɪ/ a (-ier, -iest) appiccicoso; (adhesive) adesivo; (fig: difficult) difficile

stiff /stɪf/ a rigido; (brush, task)

duro; (person) controllato; (drink) forte; (penalty) severo; (price) alto; **bored ~** fam annoiato a morte. **~ neck** torcicollo m. **~en** vt irrigidire ● vi irrigidirsi. **~ness** n rigidità f inv

stifl|e /'staifl/ vt soffocare. **~ing** a soffocante

stigma /'stɪgmə/ n marchio m

stiletto /stɪ'letəu/ n stiletto m; **~ heels** tacchi mpl a spillo; **~s** (shoes) scarpe fpl coi tacchi a spillo

still[1] /stɪl/ n distilleria f

still[2] a (drink) non gasato; **keep/stand ~** stare fermo ● n quiete f; (photo) posa f ● adv ancora; (nevertheless) nondimeno, comunque; **I'm ~ not sure** non sono ancora sicuro

'stillborn a nato morto

still 'life n natura f morta

stilted /'stɪltɪd/ a artificioso

stilts /stɪlts/ npl trampoli mpl

stimulant /'stɪmjulənt/ n eccitante m

stimulat|e /'stɪmjuleɪt/ vt stimolare. **~ion** /-'leɪʃn/ n stimolo m

stimulus /'stɪmjuləs/ n (pl -li /-laɪ/) stimolo m

sting /stɪŋ/ n puntura f; (from nettle, jellyfish) sostanza f irritante; (organ) pungiglione m ● vt (pt/pp stung) ● vt pungere; (jellyfish:) pizzicare ● vi (insect:) pungere. **~ing nettle** n ortica f

stingy /'stɪndʒɪ/ a (-ier, -iest) tirchio

stink /stɪŋk/ n puzza f ● vi (pt stank, pp stunk) puzzare

stint /stɪnt/ n lavoro m; **do one's ~** fare la propria parte ● vt **~ on** lesinare su

stipulat|e /'stɪpjuleɪt/ vt porre come condizione. **~ion** /-'leɪʃn/ n condizione f

stir /stɜː(r)/ n mescolata f; (commotion) trambusto m ● v (pt/pp stirred) ● vt muovere; (mix) mescolare ● vi muoversi

stirrup /'stɪrəp/ n staffa f

stitch /stɪtʃ/ n punto m; (in knitting) maglia f; (pain) fitta f; **have sb in ~es** fam far ridere qcno a crepapelle ● vt cucire

stock /stɒk/ n (for use or selling) scorta f, stock m inv; (livestock) bestiame m; (lineage) stirpe f; Fin titoli mpl; Culin brodo m; **in ~** disponibile; **out of ~** esaurito; **take ~** fig fare il punto ● a solito ● vt (shop:) vendere; approvvigionare (shelves). **stock up** vi far scorta (**with** di)

stock: **~broker** n agente m di cambio. **~ cube** n dado m [da brodo]. **S~ Exchange** n Borsa f Valori

stocking /ˈstɒkɪŋ/ n calza f

stockist /ˈstɒkɪst/ n rivenditore m

stock: **~market** n mercato m azionario. **~pile** vt fare scorta di ● n riserva f. **~-still** a immobile. **~-taking** n Comm inventario m

stocky /ˈstɒkɪ/ a (-ier, -iest) tarchiato

stodgy /ˈstɒdʒɪ/ a indigesto

stoic /ˈstəʊɪk/ n stoico, -a mf. **~al** a stoico. **~ism** n -sɪzm/ stoicismo m

stoke /stəʊk/ vt alimentare

stole[1] /stəʊl/ n stola f

stole[2], **stolen** /stəʊln/ see **steal**

stolid /ˈstɒlɪd/ a apatico

stomach /ˈstʌmək/ n pancia f; Anat stomaco m ● vt fam reggere. **~-ache** n mal m di pancia

stone /stəʊn/ n pietra f; (in fruit) nocciolo m; Med calcolo m; (weight) 6,348 kg a di pietra; (wall, Age) della pietra ● vt snocciolare (fruit). **~-cold** a gelido. **~-deaf** a fam sordo come una campana

stony /ˈstəʊnɪ/ a pietroso; (glare) glaciale

stood /stʊd/ see **stand**

stool /stuːl/ n sgabello m

stoop /stuːp/ n curvatura f ● vi stare curvo; (bend down) chinarsi; fig abbassarsi

stop /stɒp/ n (break) sosta f; (for bus, train) fermata f; Gram punto m; **come to a ~** fermarsi; **put a ~**

to sth mettere fine a qcsa ● v (pt/pp **stopped**) ● vt fermare; arrestare (machine); (prevent) impedire; **~ sb doing sth** impedire a qcno di fare qcsa; **~ doing sth** smettere di fare qcsa; **~ that!** smettila! ● vi fermarsi; (rain:) smettere ● int fermo!. **stop off** vi fare una sosta. **stop up** vt otturare (sink); tappare (hole). **stop with** vi (fam: stay with) fermarsi da

stop: **~gap** n palliativo m; (person) tappabuchi m inv. **~over** n sosta f; Aeron scalo m

stoppage /ˈstɒpɪdʒ/ n ostruzione f; (strike) interruzione f; (deduction) trattenute fpl

stopper /ˈstɒpə(r)/ n tappo m

stop: **~-press** n ultimissime fpl. **~-watch** n cronometro m

storage /ˈstɔːrɪdʒ/ n deposito m; (in warehouse) immagazzinaggio m; Comput memoria f

store /stɔː(r)/ n (stock) riserva f; (shop) grande magazzino m; (depot) deposito m; **in ~** in deposito; **what the future has in ~ for me** cosa mi riserva il futuro; **set great ~ by** tenere in gran conto ● vt tenere; (in warehouse, Comput) immagazzinare. **~-room** n magazzino m

storey /ˈstɔːrɪ/ n piano m

stork /stɔːk/ n cicogna f

storm /stɔːm/ n temporale m; (with thunder) tempesta f ● vt prendere d'assalto. **~y** a tempestoso

story /ˈstɔːrɪ/ n storia f; (in newspaper) articolo m

stout /staʊt/ a (shoes) resistente; (fat) robusto; (defence) strenuo

stove /stəʊv/ n stufa f; (for cooking) cucina f [economica]

stow /stəʊ/ vt metter via. **~away** n passeggero, -a mf clandestino, -a

straddle /ˈstrædl/ vt stare a cavalcioni su; (standing) essere a cavallo su

straggl|e /ˈstrægl/ vi crescere disordinatamente; (dawdle) rimanere indietro. **~er** *n* persona *f* che rimane indietro. **~y** *a* in disordine

straight /streɪt/ *a* diritto, dritto; ⟨*answer, question, person*⟩ diretto; ⟨*tidy*⟩ in ordine; ⟨*drink, hair*⟩ liscio ● *adv* diritto, dritto; ⟨*directly*⟩ direttamente; **~ on** *or* **ahead** diritto; **~ out** *fig* apertamente; **go ~** *fam* rigare diritto; **put sth ~** mettere qcsa in ordine; **sit/stand up ~** stare diritto

straighten /streɪtn/ *vt* raddrizzare ● *vi* raddrizzarsi; **~ [up]** ⟨*person:*⟩ mettersi diritto. **straighten out** *vt fig* chiarire ⟨*situation*⟩

straight'forward *a* franco; ⟨*simple*⟩ semplice

strain¹ /streɪn/ *n* ⟨*streak*⟩ vena *f*; *Bot* varietà *f inv*; ⟨*of virus*⟩ forma *f*

strain² *n* tensione *f*; ⟨*injury*⟩ stiramento *m*; **~s** *pl* ⟨*of music*⟩ note *fpl* ● *vt* tirare; sforzare ⟨*eyes, voice*⟩; stirarsi ⟨*muscle*⟩; *Culin* scolare ● *vi* sforzarsi. **~ed** *a* ⟨*relations*⟩ teso. **~er** *n* colino *m*

strait /streɪt/ *n* stretto *m*; **in dire ~s** in serie difficoltà. **~jacket** *n* camicia *f* di forza. **~·'laced** *a* puritano

strand¹ /strænd/ *n* ⟨*of thread*⟩ gugliata *f*; ⟨*of beads*⟩ filo *m*; ⟨*of hair*⟩ capello *m*

strand² *vt* be **~ed** rimanere bloccato

strange /streɪndʒ/ *a* strano; ⟨*not known*⟩ sconosciuto; ⟨*unaccustomed*⟩ estraneo. **~ly** *adv* stranamente; **~ly enough** curiosamente. **~r** *n* estraneo, -a *mf*

strangle /stræŋgl/ *vt* strangolare; *fig* reprimere

strangulation /stræŋgjʊ'leɪʃn/ *n* strangolamento *m*

strap /stræp/ *n* cinghia *f* (*to grasp in vehicle*) maniglia *f*; ⟨*of watch*⟩ cinturino *m*; ⟨*shoulder ~*⟩ bretella *f*, spallina *f* ● *vt* (*pt/pp* **strapped**) legare; **~ in** *or* **down** assicurare

strapping /stræpɪŋ/ *a* robusto

strata /strɑːtə/ *npl see* **stratum**

stratagem /strætədʒəm/ *n* stratagemma *m*

strategic /strəˈtiːdʒɪk/ *a* strategico

strategy /strætədʒɪ/ *n* strategia *f*

stratum /strɑːtəm/ *n* (*pl* **strata**) strato *m*

straw /strɔː/ *n* paglia *f*; ⟨*single piece*⟩ fuscello *m*; ⟨*for drinking*⟩ cannuccia *f*; **the last ~** l'ultima goccia

strawberry /strɔːbərɪ/ *n* fragola *f*

stray /streɪ/ *a* ⟨*animal*⟩ randagio ● *n* randagio *m* ● *vi* andarsene per conto proprio; ⟨*deviate*⟩ deviare (**from** da)

streak /striːk/ *n* striatura *f*; ⟨*fig: trait*⟩ vena *f* ● *vi* sfrecciare. **~y** *a* striato; ⟨*bacon*⟩ grasso

stream /striːm/ *n* ruscello *m*; ⟨*current*⟩ corrente *f*; ⟨*of blood, people*⟩ flusso *m*; *Sch* classe *f* ● *vi* scorrere. **stream in/out** *vi* entrare/uscire a fiotti

streamer /striːmə(r)/ *n* ⟨*paper*⟩ stella *f* filante; ⟨*flag*⟩ pennone *m*

'streamline *vt* rendere aerodinamico; ⟨*simplify*⟩ snellire. **~d** *a* aerodinamico

street /striːt/ *n* strada *f*. **~car** *n* *Am* tram *m inv*. **~lamp** *n* lampione *m*

strength /streŋθ/ *n* forza *f*; ⟨*of wall, bridge etc*⟩ solidità *f inv*; **~s** punti *mpl* forti; **on the ~ of** grazie a. **~en** *vt* rinforzare

strenuous /strenjʊəs/ *a* faticoso; ⟨*attempt, denial*⟩ energico

stress /stres/ *n* ⟨*emphasis*⟩ insistenza *f*; *Gram* accento *m* tonico; ⟨*mental*⟩ stress *m inv*; *Mech* spinta *f* ● *vt* ⟨*emphasize*⟩ insistere su; *Gram* mettere l'accento ⟨*tonico*⟩ su. **~ed** *a* ⟨*mentally*⟩ stressato. **~ful** *a* stressante

stretch /stretʃ/ *n* stiramento *m*; ⟨*period*⟩ periodo *m* di tempo; ⟨*of road*⟩ estensione *f*; ⟨*elasticity*⟩ elasticità *f inv*; **at a ~** di fila; **have a ~** stirarsi ● *vt* tirare; allargare ⟨*shoes, arms etc*⟩; ⟨*person:*⟩ allungare ●*vi* (*become wider*) allargarsi; (*extend*) estendersi; ⟨*person*:⟩ stirarsi. **~er** *n* barella *f*

strew /struː/ *vt* (*pp* **strewn** or **strewed**) sparpagliare

stricken /ˈstrɪkn/ *a* prostrato; **~ with** affetto da ⟨*illness*⟩

strict /strɪkt/ *a* severo; (*precise*) preciso. **~ly** *adv* severamente; **~ly speaking** in senso stretto

stride /straɪd/ *n* [lungo] passo *m*; **take sth in one's ~** accettare qcsa con facilità ●*vi* (*pt* **strode**, *pp* **stridden**) andare a gran passi

strident /ˈstraɪdənt/ *a* stridente; ⟨*colour*⟩ vistoso

strife /straɪf/ *n* conflitto *m*

strike /straɪk/ *n* sciopero *m*; *Mil* attacco *m*; **on ~** in sciopero ●*v* (*pt/pp* **struck**) *vt* colpire; accendere ⟨*match*⟩; trovare ⟨*oil, gold*⟩; (*delete*) depennare; (*occur to*) venire in mente a; *Mil* attaccare ●*vi* ⟨*lightning*:⟩ cadere; ⟨*clock*:⟩ suonare; *Mil* attaccare; ⟨*workers*:⟩ scioperare; **~ lucky** azzeccarla. **strike off**, **strike out** *vt* eliminare. **strike up** *vt* fare ⟨*friendship*⟩; attaccare ⟨*conversation*⟩. **~-breaker** *n* persona *f* che non aderisce a uno sciopero

striker /ˈstraɪkə(r)/ *n* scioperante *mf*

striking /ˈstraɪkɪŋ/ *a* impressionante; (*attractive*) affascinante

string /strɪŋ/ *n* spago *m*; (*of musical instrument, racket*) corda *f*; (*of pearls*) filo *m*; (*of lies*) serie *f*; **the ~s** *Mus* gli archi, **pull ~s** *fam* usare le proprie conoscenze ●*vt* (*pt/pp* **strung**) (*thread*) infilare ⟨*beads*⟩. **~ed** *a* ⟨*instrument*⟩ a corda

stringent /ˈstrɪndʒnt/ *a* rigido

strip /strɪp/ *n* striscia *f* ●*v* (*pt/pp* **stripped**) *vt* spogliare; togliere le lenzuola da ⟨*bed*⟩; scrostare ⟨*wood, furniture*⟩; smontare ⟨*machine*⟩; (*deprive*) privare (**of** di) ●*vi* (*undress*) spogliarsi. **~ car-**

toon *n* striscia *f*. **~ club** *n* locale *m* di strip-tease

stripe /straɪp/ *n* striscia *f*; *Mil* gallone *m*. **~d** *a* a strisce

'striplight *n* tubo *m* al neon

stripper /ˈstrɪpə(r)/ *n* spogliarellista *mf*; (*solvent*) sverniciatore *m*

strip-'tease *n* spogliarello *m*, strip-tease *m inv*

strive /straɪv/ *vi* (*pt* **strove**, *pp* **striven**) sforzarsi (**to** di); **~ for** sforzarsi di ottenere

strode /strəʊd/ *see* **stride**

stroke[1] /strəʊk/ *n* colpo *m*; (*of pen*) tratto *m*, (*in swimming*) bracciata *f*; *Med* ictus *m inv*; **~ of luck** colpo *m* di fortuna; **put sb off his ~** far perdere il filo a qcno

stroke[2] *vt* accarezzare

stroll /strəʊl/ *n* passeggiata *f* ●*vi* passeggiare. **~er** *n* (*Am*: *push-chair*) passeggino *m*

strong /strɒŋ/ *a* (**-er** /-gə(r)/, **-est** /-gɪst/) forte; ⟨*argument*⟩ valido

strong: **~-box** *n* cassaforte *f*. **~-hold** *n* roccaforte *f*. **~ly** *adv* fortemente. **~-'minded** *a* risoluto. **~-room** *n* camera *f* blindata

stroppy /ˈstrɒpɪ/ *a* scorbutico

strove /strəʊv/ *see* **strive**

struck /strʌk/ *see* **strike**

structural /ˈstrʌktʃərəl/ *a* strutturale. **~ly** *adv* strutturalmente

structure /ˈstrʌktʃə(r)/ *n* struttura *f*

struggle /ˈstrʌgl/ *n* lotta *f*; **with a ~** lottare con ●*vi* lottare; **~ for breath** respirare con fatica; **~ to do sth** fare fatica a fare qcosa; **~ to one's feet** alzarsi con fatica

strum /strʌm/ *vt/i* (*pt/pp* **strummed**) strimpellare

strung /strʌŋ/ *see* **string**

strut[1] /strʌt/ *n* (*component*) puntello *m*

strut[2] *vi* (*pt/pp* **strutted**) camminare impettito

stub /stʌb/ *n* mozzicone *m*; (*counterfoil*) matrice *f* ●*vt* (*pt/pp* **stubbed**) **~ one's toe** sbattere il dito del piede (**on** contro). **stub out** vt spegnere ⟨cigarette⟩

stubb|le /'stʌbl/ n barba f ispida. **~ly** a ispido

stubborn /'stʌbən/ a testardo; ⟨refusal⟩ ostinato

stubby /'stʌbɪ/ a (**-ier, -iest**) tozzo

stucco /'stʌkəʊ/ n stucco m

stuck /stʌk/ see **stick²**. **~-up** a fam snob

stud¹ /stʌd/ n (on boot) tacchetto m; (on jacket) borchia f; (for ear) orecchino m [a bottone]

stud² n (of horses) scuderia f

student /'stju:dənt/ n studente m, studentessa f; (school child) scolaro, -a mf. **~ nurse** n studente, studentessa infermiere, -a

studied /'stʌdɪd/ a intenzionale; ⟨politeness⟩ studiato

studio /'stju:dɪəʊ/ n studio m

studious /'stju:dɪəs/ a studioso; ⟨attention⟩ studiato

study /'stʌdɪ/ n studio m ● vt/i (pt/pp **studied**) studiare

stuff /stʌf/ n materiale m; (fam: things) roba f ● vt riempire; (with padding) imbottire; Culin farcire; **~ sth into a drawer/one's pocket** ficcare qcsa alla rinfusa in un cassetto/in tasca. **~ing** n (padding) imbottitura f; Culin ripieno m

stuffy /'stʌfɪ/ a (**-ier, -iest**) che sa di chiuso; (old-fashioned) antiquato

stumbl|e /'stʌmbl/ vi inciampare; **~e across** or **on** imbattersi in. **~ing-block** n ostacolo m

stump /stʌmp/ n ceppo m; (of limb) moncone m. **~ed** a fam perplesso ● **stump up** vt/i fam sganciare

stun /stʌn/ vt (pt/pp **stunned**) stordire; (astonish) sbalordire

stung /stʌŋ/ see **sting**

stunk /stʌŋk/ see **stink**

stunning /'stʌnɪŋ/ a fam favoloso; ⟨blow, victory⟩ sbalorditivo

stunt¹ /stʌnt/ n fam trovata f pubblicitaria

stunt² vt arrestare lo sviluppo di. **~ed** a stentato

stupendous /stju:'pendəs/ a stupendo. **~ly** adv stupendamente

stupid /'stju:pɪd/ a stupido. **~ity** /-'pɪdətɪ/ n stupidità f. **~ly** adv stupidamente

stupor /'stju:pə(r)/ n torpore m

sturdy /'stɜ:dɪ/ a (**-ier, -iest**) robusto; ⟨furniture⟩ solido

stutter /'stʌtə(r)/ n balbuzie f ● vt/i balbettare

sty, stye /staɪ/ n (pl **styes**) Med orzaiolo m

style /staɪl/ n stile m; (fashion) moda f; (sort) tipo m; (hair~) pettinatura f; **in ~** in grande stile

stylish /'staɪlɪʃ/ a elegante. **~ly** adv con eleganza

stylist /'staɪlɪst/ n stilista mf; (hair~) parrucchiere, -a mf. **~ic** /-'lɪstɪk/ a stilistico

stylized /'staɪlaɪzd/ a stilizzato

stylus /'staɪləs/ n (on record player) puntina f

suave /swɑ:v/ a dai modi garbati

sub|conscious /sʌb-/ a subcosciente ● n subcosciente m. **~ly** adv in modo inconscio

subcon'tract vt subappaltare (**to** a). **~or** n subappaltatore m

'subdivi|de vt suddividere. **~sion** n suddivisione f

subdue /səb'dju:/ vt sottomettere; (make quieter) attenuare. **~d** a ⟨light⟩ attenuato; ⟨person, voice⟩ pacato

subhuman /sʌb'hju:mən/ a disumano

subject¹ /'sʌbdʒɪkt/ a **~ to** soggetto a; (depending on) subordinato a; **~ to availability** nei limiti della disponibilità ● n soggetto m; (of ruler) suddito, -a mf; Sch materia f

subject² /səb'dʒekt/ vt (to attack, abuse) sottoporre; assoggettare ⟨country⟩

subjective /səb'dʒektɪv/ a soggettivo. **~ly** adv soggettivamente

subjugate /'sʌbdʒʊgeɪt/ vt soggiogare

subjunctive /səb'dʒʌŋktɪv/ a & n congiuntivo m

sub'let vt (pt/pp -let) subaffittare

sublime /sə'blaɪm/ a sublime. **~ly** adv sublimamente

subliminal /sə'blɪmɪnl/ a subliminale

sub-ma'chine-gun n mitraglietta f

subma'rine /sʌbmə'riːn/ n sommergibile m

submerge /səb'mɜːdʒ/ vt immergere; **be ~d** essere sommerso ● vi immergersi

submiss|ion /səb'mɪʃn/ n sottomissione f. **~ive** /-sɪv/ a sottomesso

submit /səb'mɪt/ v (pt/pp -mitted, pres p -mitting) ● vt sottoporre ● vi sottomettersi

subordinate /sə'bɔːdɪneɪt/ vt subordinare **(to** a)

subordinate /sə'bɔːdɪnət/ a subordinato. **~ clause** subordinata f

subscribe /səb'skraɪb/ vi contribuire; **~ to** abbonarsi a ⟨newspaper⟩; sottoscrivere ⟨fund⟩; fig aderire a. **~r** n abbonato, -a mf

subscription /səb'skrɪpʃn/ n (to club) sottoscrizione f; (to newspaper) abbonamento m

subsequent /'sʌbsɪkwənt/ a susseguente. **~ly** adv in seguito

subservient /səb'sɜːvɪənt/ a subordinato; ⟨servile⟩ servile. **~ly** adv servilmente

subside /səb'saɪd/ vi sprofondare; ⟨ground:⟩ avvallarsi; ⟨storm:⟩ placarsi

subsidiary /səb'sɪdɪərɪ/ a secondario ● n **~ [company]** filiale f

subsid|ize /'sʌbsɪdaɪz/ vt sovvenzionare. **~y** n sovvenzione f

subsist /səb'sɪst/ vi vivere **(on** di). **~ence** n sussistenza f

substance /'sʌbstəns/ n sostanza f

sub'standard a di qualità inferiore

substantial /səb'stænʃl/ a solido; ⟨meal⟩ sostanzioso; ⟨considerable⟩ notevole. **~ly** adv notevolmente; ⟨essentially⟩ sostanzialmente

substantiate /səb'stænʃɪeɪt/ vt comprovare

substitut|e /'sʌbstɪtjuːt/ n sostituto m ● vt **~e A for B** sostituire B con A ● vi **~e for sb** sostituire qcno. **~ion** /-'tjuːʃn/ n sostituzione f

subterranean /sʌbtə'reɪnɪən/ a sotterraneo

'subtitle n sottotitolo m

subt|le /'sʌtl/ a sottile; ⟨taste, perfume⟩ delicato. **~tlety** n sottigliezza f. **~tly** adv sottilmente

subtract /səb'trækt/ vt sottrarre. **~ion** /-ækʃn/ n sottrazione f

suburb /'sʌbɜːb/ n sobborgo m; **in the ~s** in periferia. **~an** /sə'bɜːbən/ a suburbano. **~ia** /sə'bɜːbɪə/ n i sobborghi mpl

subversive /səb'vɜːsɪv/ a sovversivo

'subway n sottopassaggio m; (Am: railway) metropolitana f

succeed /sək'siːd/ vi riuscire; (follow) succedere a; **~ in doing** riuscire a fare ● vt succedere a ⟨king⟩. **~ing** a successivo

success /sək'ses/ n successo m; **be a ~** (in life) aver successo. **~ful** a riuscito; ⟨businessman, artist etc⟩ di successo. **~fully** adv con successo

succession /sək'seʃn/ n successione f; **in ~** di seguito

successive /sək'sesɪv/ a successivo. **~ly** adv successivamente

successor /sək'sesə(r)/ n successore m

succinct /sək'sɪŋkt/ a succinto

succulent /'sʌkjʊlənt/ a succulento

succumb /sə'kʌm/ vi soccombere **(to** a)

such /sʌtʃ/ a tale; **~ a tale**; **~ a book** un libro di questo genere; **~ a thing** una cosa di questo genere; **~ a long time ago** talmente tanto tempo fa; **there is no ~ thing** non esiste una cosa così; **there is no ~ person** non esiste una persona così ● pron **as ~** come tale; **~ as** chi; **and ~** e simili; **~ as it is** così com'è. **~like** *pron fam* di tal genere

suck /ʃʌk/ *vt* succhiare. **suck up** *vt* assorbire. **suck up to** *vt fam* fare il lecchino con

sucker /ˈʃʌkə(r)/ *n Bot* pollone *m*; *(fam: person)* credulone, -a *mf*

suction /ˈsʌkʃn/ *n* aspirazione *f*

sudden /ˈsʌdn/ *a* improvviso ● **all of a ~** all'improvviso. **~ly** *adv* improvvisamente

sue /suː/ *vt (pres p suing)* fare causa a *(for* per) ● *vi* fare causa

suede /sweɪd/ *n* pelle *f* scamosciata

suet /ˈsuːɪt/ *n* grasso *m* di rognone

suffer /ˈsʌfə(r)/ *vi* soffrire *(from* per) ● *vt* soffrire; subire *⟨loss etc⟩*; *(tolerate)* subire. **~ing** *n* sofferenza *f*

suffice /səˈfaɪs/ *vi* bastare

sufficient /səˈfɪʃnt/ *a* sufficiente. **~ly** *adv* sufficientemente

suffix /ˈsʌfɪks/ *n* suffisso *m*

suffocat|e /ˈsʌfəkeɪt/ *vt/i* soffocare. **~ion** /-ˈkeɪʃn/ *n* soffocamento *m*

sugar /ˈʃʊgə(r)/ *n* zucchero *m* ● *vt* zuccherare. **~ basin, ~-bowl** *n* zuccheriera *f*. **~y** *a* zuccheroso; *fig* sdolcinato

suggest /səˈdʒest/ *vt* suggerire; *(indicate, insinuate)* fare pensare a. **~ion** /-estʃən/ *n* suggerimento *m*; *(trace)* traccia *f*. **~ive** /-ɪv/ *a* allusivo. **~ively** *adv* in modo allusivo

suicidal /suːɪˈsaɪdl/ *a* suicida

suicide /ˈsuːɪsaɪd/ *n* suicidio *m*; *(person)* suicida *mf*; **commit ~** suicidarsi

suit /suːt/ *n* vestito *m*; *(woman's)* tailleur *m inv*; *(in cards)* seme *m*; *Jur* causa *f*; **follow ~** *fig* fare lo stesso ● *vt* andar bene a; *(adapt)* adattare *(to* a); *(be convenient for)* andare bene per; **be ~ed to** *or* **for** essere adatto a; **~ yourself!** fa' come vuoi!

suitabl|e /ˈsuːtəbl/ *a* adatto. **~y** *adv* convenientemente

suitcase /ˈsuːtkeɪs/ *n* valigia *f*

suite /swiːt/ *n* suite *f inv*; *(of furniture)* divano *m* e poltrone *fpl* assortiti

sulk /sʌlk/ *vi* fare il broncio. **~y** *a* imbronciato

sullen /ˈsʌlən/ *a* svogliato

sulphur /ˈsʌlfə(r)/ *n* zolfo *m*. **~ic** /-ˈfjuːrɪk/ **~ic acid** *n* acido *m* solforico

sultana /sʌlˈtɑːnə/ *n* uva *f* sultanina

sultry /ˈsʌltrɪ/ *a* (**-ier, -iest**) *(weather)* afoso; *fig* sensuale

sum /sʌm/ *n* somma *f*; *Sch* addizione *f* ● **sum up** *(pt/pp summed)* *vi* riassumere ● *vt* valutare

summar|ize /ˈsʌmaraɪz/ *vt* riassumere. **~y** *n* sommario *m* ● *a* sommario; *(dismissal)* sbrigativo

summer /ˈsʌmə(r)/ *n* estate *f*. **~-house** *n* padiglione *m*. **~time** *n* *(season)* estate *f*

summery /ˈsʌmərɪ/ *a* estivo

summit /ˈsʌmɪt/ *n* cima *f*. **~ conference** *n* vertice *m*

summon /ˈsʌmən/ *vt* convocare; *Jur* citare. **summon up** *vt* raccogliere *(strength)*; rievocare *(memory)*

summons /ˈsʌmənz/ *n Jur* citazione *f* ● *vt* citare in giudizio

sump /sʌmp/ *n Auto* coppa *f* dell'olio

sumptuous /ˈsʌmptjʊəs/ *a* sontuoso. **~ly** *adv* sontuosamente

sun /sʌn/ *n* sole *m* ● *vt* *(pt/pp sunned)* **~ oneself** prendere il sole

sun: ~bathe *vi* prendere il sole. **~bed** *n* lettino *m* solare. **~burn** *n* scottatura *f* *(solare)*. **~burnt** *a* scottato *(dal sole)*

sundae /ˈsʌndeɪ/ *n* gelato *m* guarnito

Sunday /ˈsʌndeɪ/ *n* domenica *f*

sundial *n* meridiana *f*

sundry /ˈsʌndrɪ/ *a* svariati; **all and ~** tutti quanti

sunflower *n* girasole *m*

sung /sʌŋ/ *see* sing

'**sun-glasses** *npl* occhiali *mpl* da sole

sunk /sʌŋk/ *see* **sink**

sunken /'sʌŋkn/ *a* incavato

'**sunlight** *n* luce *f* del sole *m*

sunny /'sʌnɪ/ *a* (**-ier, -iest**) assolato

sun: **~rise** *n* alba *f*. **~-roof** *n* Auto tettuccio *m* apribile. **~set** *n* tramonto *m*. **~shade** *n* parasole *m*. **~shine** *n* luce *f* del sole *m*. **~stroke** *n* insolazione *f*. **~tan** *n* abbronzatura *f*. **~tanned** *a* abbronzato. **~tan oil** *n* olio *m* solare

super /'su:pə(r)/ *a fam* fantastico

superb /su'pɜ:b/ *a* splendido

supercilious /su:pə'sɪlɪəs/ *a* altezzoso

superficial /su:pə'fɪʃl/ *a* superficiale. **~ly** *adv* superficialmente

superfluous /su:'pɜ:fluəs/ *a* superfluo

super'human *a* sovrumano

superintendent /su:pərɪn'tendənt/ *n* (*of police*) commissario *m* di polizia

superior /su:'pɪərɪə(r)/ *a* superiore ● *n* superiore, -a *mf*. **~ity** /-'ɒrəti/ *n* superiorità *f*

superlative /su:'pɜ:lətɪv/ *a* eccellente ● *n* superlativo *m*

'**superman** *n* superuomo *m*

'**supermarket** *n* supermercato *m*

'**supermodel** *n* top model *f inv*

super'natural *a* soprannaturale

'**superpower** *n* superpotenza *f*

supersede /su:pə'si:d/ *vt* rimpiazzare

super'sonic *a* supersonico

superstition /su:pə'stɪʃn/ *n* superstizione *f*. **~ious** /-'stɪʃəs/ *a* superstizioso

supervis|e /'su:pəvaɪz/ *vt* supervisionare. **~ion** /-'vɪʒn/ *n* supervisione *f*. **~or** *n* supervisore *m*

supper /'sʌpə(r)/ *n* cena *f*

supple /'sʌpl/ *a* slogato

supplement /'sʌplɪmənt/ *n* supplemento *m* ● *vt* integrare. **~ary** /-'mentarɪ/ *a* supplementare

supplier /sə'plaɪə(r)/ *n* fornitore, -trice *mf*

supply /sə'plaɪ/ *n* fornitura *f*; (*in economics*) offerta *f*; **supplies** *pl* Mil approvvigionamenti *mpl* ● *vt* (*pt/pp* **-ied**) fornire; **~ sb with sth** fornire qcsa a qcno

support /sə'pɔ:t/ *n* sostegno *m*; (*base*) supporto *m*; (*keep*) sostentamento *m* ● *vt* sostenere; mantenere (*family*); (*give money to*) mantenere finanziariamente; Sport fare il tifo per. **~er** *n* sostenitore, -trice *mf*; Sport tifoso, -a *mf*. **~ive** /-ɪv/ *a* incoraggiante

suppose /sə'pəʊz/ *vt* (*presume*) supporre; (*imagine*) pensare; **be ~d to do** dover fare; **not be ~d to** *fam* non avere il permesso di; **I ~ so** suppongo di sì. **~dly** /-ɪdlɪ/ *adv* presumibilmente

suppress /sə'pres/ *vt* sopprimere. **~ion** /-eʃn/ *n* soppressione *f*

supremacy /su:'preməsɪ/ *n* supremazia *f*

supreme /su:'pri:m/ *a* supremo

surcharge /'sɜ:tʃɑ:dʒ/ *n* supplemento *m*

sure /ʃʊə(r)/ *a* sicuro, certo; **make ~** accertarsi; **be ~ to do it** mi raccomando di farlo ● *adv* Am *fam* certamente, **~ enough** infatti. **~ly** *adv* certamente; (*Am: gladly*) volentieri

surety /'ʃʊərətɪ/ *n* garanzia *f*; **stand ~ for** garantire

surf /sɜ:f/ *n* schiuma *f* ● *vt* Comput **~ the Net** surfare in Internet

surface /'sɜ:fɪs/ *n* superficie *f*; **on the ~** *fig* in apparenza ● *vi* (*emerge*) emergere. **~ mail** *n* by **~ mail** per posta ordinaria

'**surfboard** *n* tavola *f* da surf

'**surfing** /'sɜ:fɪŋ/ *n* surf *m inv*

surge /sɜ:dʒ/ *n* (*of sea*) ondata *f*; (*of interest*) aumento *m*; (*in demand*) impennata *f*; (*of anger, pity*) impeto *m* ● *vi* riversarsi; **~ forward** buttarsi in avanti

surgeon /'sɜ:dʒən/ *n* chirurgo

surgery /'sɜ:dʒərɪ/ *n* chirurgia *f*; (*place, consulting room*) ambulatorio *m*; (*hours*) ore *fpl* di

have ~ subire un'intervento [chirurgico]

surgical /'sɜːdʒɪkl/ a chirurgico

surly /'sɜːlɪ/ a (-ier, -iest) scontroso

surmise /sə'maɪz/ vt supporre

surmount /sə'maʊnt/ vt sormontare

surname /'sɜːneɪm/ n cognome m

surpass /sə'pɑːs/ vt superare

surplus /'sɜːpləs/ a d'avanzo ● n sovrappiù m

surprise /sə'praɪz/ n sorpresa f ● vt sorprendere; **be ~ed** essere sorpreso (**at** da). **~ing** a sorprendente. **~ingly** adv sorprendentemente

surrender /sə'rendə(r)/ n resa f ● vi arrendersi ● vt cedere

surreptitious /sʌrəp'tɪʃəs/ a & adv di nascosto

surrogate /'sʌrəgət/ n surrogato m. ~ 'mother n madre f surrogata

surround /sə'raʊnd/ vt circondare. ~ing a circostante. ~ings npl dintorni mpl

surveillance /sə'veɪləns/ n sorveglianza f

survey¹ /'sɜːveɪ/ n sguardo m; (poll) sondaggio m; (investigation) indagine f; (of land) rilevamento m; (of house) perizia f

survey² /sə'veɪ/ vt esaminare; fare un rilevamento di ⟨land⟩; fare una perizia di ⟨building⟩. **~or** n perito m; (of land) topografo, -a mf

survival /sə'vaɪvl/ n sopravvivenza f; (relic) resto m

survive /sə'vaɪv/ vt sopravvivere a ● vi sopravvivere. **~or** n superstite mf; **be a ~or** fam riuscire sempre a cavarsela

susceptible /sə'septəbl/ a influenzabile; **~ to** sensibile a

suspect¹ /sə'spekt/ vt sospettare; (assume) supporre

suspect² /'sʌspekt/ a & n sospetto, -a mf

suspend /sə'spend/ vt appendere; (stop, from duty) sospendere. **~er** belt n reggicalze m inv. **~ders** npl

giarrettiere fpl; (Am: braces) bretelle mpl

suspense /sə'spens/ n tensione f; (in book etc) suspense f

suspension /sə'spenʃn/ n Auto sospensione f. **~ bridge** n ponte m sospeso

suspicion /sə'spɪʃn/ n sospetto m; (trace) pizzico m; **under ~on** sospettato. **~ous** /-ʃəs/ a sospettoso; (arousing suspicion) sospetto. **~ously** adv sospettosamente; (arousing suspicion) in modo sospetto

sustain /sə'steɪn/ vt sostenere; mantenere ⟨life⟩; subire ⟨injury⟩

sustenance /'sʌstɪnəns/ n nutrimento m

swab /swɒb/ n Med tampone m

swagger /'swægə(r)/ vi pavoneggiarsi

swallow¹ /'swɒləʊ/ vt/i inghiottire. **swallow up** vt divorare; ⟨earth, crowd:⟩ inghiottire

swallow² n (bird) rondine f

swam /swæm/ see **swim**

swamp /swɒmp/ n palude f ● vt fig sommergere. **~y** a paludoso

swan /swɒn/ n cigno m

swap /swɒp/ n fam scambio m ● vt (pt/pp **swapped**) fam scambiare (**for** con) ● vi fare cambio

swarm /swɔːm/ n sciame m ● vi sciamare; **be ~ing with** brulicare di

swarthy /'swɔːðɪ/ a (-ier, -iest) di carnagione scura

swastika /'swɒstɪkə/ n svastica f

swat /swɒt/ vt (pt/pp **swatted**) schiacciare

sway /sweɪ/ n fig influenza f ● vi oscillare; ⟨person:⟩ ondeggiare ● vt (influence) influenzare

swear /sweə(r)/ v (pt **swore**, pp **sworn**) ● vt giurare ● vi giurare; (curse) dire parolacce; **~ at sb** imprecare contro qcno; **~ by** fam credere ciecamente in. **~-word** n parolaccia f

sweat /swet/ n sudore m ● vi sudare

sweater /'sweta(r)/ *n* golf *m inv*

sweaty /'sweti/ *a* sudato

swede /swi:d/ *n* rapa *f* svedese

Swede|**e** *n* svedese *mf*. **~en** *n* Svezia *f*. **~ish** *a* svedese

sweep /swi:p/ *n* scopata *f*, spazzata *f*; (*curve*) curva *f*; (*movement*) movimento *m* ampio; **make a clean ~** *fig* fare piazza pulita ● *v* (*pt/pp* **swept**) ● *vt* scopare, spazzare; (*wind:*) spazzare ● *vi* (go *swiftly*) andare rapidamente; (*wind:*) soffiare. **sweep away** *vt fig* spazzare via. **sweep up** *vt* spazzare

sweeping /'swi:piŋ/ *a* (*gesture*) ampio; (*statement*) generico; (*changes*) radicale

sweet /swi:t/ *a* dolce; **have a ~ tooth** essere goloso ● *n* caramella *f*; (*dessert*) dolce *m*. **~ corn** *n* mais *m*

sweeten /'swi:tn/ *vt* addolcire. **~er** *n* dolcificante *m*

sweet: **~heart** *n* innamorato, -a *mf*; **hi, ~heart** ciao, tesoro. **~ness** *n* dolcezza *f*. **~ 'pea** *n* pisello *m* odoroso. **~shop** *n* negozio *m* di dolciumi

swell /swel/ ● *v* (*pt* **swelled**, *pp* **swollen** *or* **swelled**) ● *vi* gonfiarsi; (*increase*) aumentare ● *vt* gonfiare; (*increase*) far salire. **~ing** *n* gonfiore *m*

swelter /'swelta(r)/ *vi* soffocare [dal caldo]

swept /swept/ *see* **sweep**

swerve /sw3:v/ *vi* deviare bruscamente

swift /swift/ *a* rapido. **~ly** *adv* rapidamente

swig /swig/ *n fam* sorso *m* ● *vt* (*pt/pp* **swigged**) *fam* scolarsi

swill /swil/ *n* (*for pigs*) brodaglia *f* ● *vt* **~ [out]** risciacquare

swim /swim/ *n* **have a ~** fare una nuotata ● *v* (*pt* **swam**, *pp* **swum**) ● *vi* nuotare; (*room:*) girare; **my head is ~ming** mi gira la testa ● *vt* percorrere a nuoto. **~mer** *n* nuotatore, -trice *mf*

swimming /'swimiŋ/ *n* nuoto *m*.

~-baths *npl* piscina *fsg*. **~ costume** *n* costume *m* da bagno. **~-pool** *n* piscina *f*. **~ trunks** *npl* calzoncini *mpl* da bagno

'swim-suit *n* costume *m* da bagno

swindle /'swindl/ *n* truffa *f* ● *vt* truffare. **~r** *n* truffatore, -trice *mf*

swine /swain/ *n fam* porco *m*

swing /swiŋ/ *n* oscillazione *f*; (*shift*) cambiamento *m*; (*seat*) altalena *f*, *Mus* swing *m*; **in full ~** in piena attività ● *v* (*pt/pp* **swung**) ● *vi* oscillare; (on *swing, sway*) dondolare; (*dangle*) penzolare; (*turn*) girare ● *vt* oscillare; far deviare (*vote*). **~-'door** *n* porta *f* a vento

swingeing /'swindʒiŋ/ *a* (*increase*) drastico

swipe /swaip/ *n fam* botta *f* ● *vt fam* colpire; (*steal*) rubare; far passare nella macchinetta (*credit card*)

swirl /sw3:l/ *n* (*of smoke, dust*) turbine *m* ● *vi* (*water:*) fare mulinello

swish /swiʃ/ *a fam* chic ● *vi* schioccare

Swiss /swis/ *a & n* svizzero, -a *mf*; **the ~** *pl* gli svizzeri. **~ 'roll** *n* rotolo *m* di pan di Spagna ripieno di marmellata

switch /switʃ/ *n* interruttore *m*; (*change*) mutamento *m* ● *vt* cambiare; (*exchange*) scambiare ● *vi* cambiare; **~ to** passare a. **switch off** *vt* spegnere. **switch on** *vt* accendere

switch: **~back** *n* montagne *fpl* russe. **~board** *n* centralino *m*

Switzerland /'switsələnd/ *n* Svizzera *f*

swivel /'swivl/ *v* (*pt/pp* **swivelled**) ● *vt* girare ● *vi* girarsi

swollen /'swəʊlən/ *see* **swell** ● *a* gonfio. **~-headed** *a* presuntuoso

swoop /swu:p/ *n* (*by police*) incursione *f* ● *vi* **~ [down]** (*bird:*) piombare; *fig* fare un'incursione

sword /sɔ:d/ *n* spada *f*

swore /swɔː(r)/ *see* **swear**

sworn /swɔːn/ *see* **swear**

swot /swɒt/ *n fam* sgobbone, -a *f*
● *vt* (*pt/pp* **swotted**) *fam* sgobbare

swum /swʌm/ *see* **swim**

swung /swʌŋ/ *see* **swing**

syllable /ˈsɪləbl/ *n* sillaba *f*

syllabus /ˈsɪləbəs/ *n* programma *m* [dei corsi]

symbol /ˈsɪmbl/ *n* simbolo *m* (**of** di). **~ic** /-ˈbɒlɪk/ *a* simbolico. **~ism** /-ɪzm/ *n* simbolismo *m*. **~ize** *vt* simboleggiare

symmetr|ical /sɪˈmetrɪkl/ *a* simmetrico. **~y** /ˈsɪmətrɪ/ *n* simmetria *f*

sympathetic /sɪmpəˈθetɪk/ *a* (*understanding*) comprensivo; (*showing pity*) compassionevole. **~ally** *adv* con comprensione/compassione

sympathize /ˈsɪmpəθaɪz/ *vi* capire; (*in grief*) solidarizzare; **~ with sb** capire qcno/solidarizzare con qcno. **~r** *n Pol* simpatizzante *mf*

sympathy /ˈsɪmpəθɪ/ *n* comprensione *f*; (*pity*) compassione *f*; (*condolences*) condoglianze *fpl*; **in ~ with** (*strike*) per solidarietà con

symphony /ˈsɪmfənɪ/ *n* sinfonia *f*

symptom /ˈsɪmptəm/ *n* sintomo *m*. **~atic** /-ˈmætɪk/ *a* sintomatico (**of** di)

synagogue /ˈsɪnəgɒg/ *n* sinagoga *f*

synchronize /ˈsɪŋkrənaɪz/ *vt* sincronizzare

syndicate /ˈsɪndɪkət/ *n* gruppo *m*

syndrome /ˈsɪndrəʊm/ *n* sindrome *f*

synonym /ˈsɪnənɪm/ *n* sinonimo *m*. **~ous** /-ˈnɒnɪməs/ *a* sinonimo

synopsis /sɪˈnɒpsɪs/ *n* (*pl* **-opses** /-siːz/) (*of opera, ballet*) trama *f*; (*of book*) riassunto *m*

syntax /ˈsɪntæks/ *n* sintassi *f inv*

synthesize /ˈsɪnθəsaɪz/ *vt* sintetizzare. **~r** *n Mus* sintetizzatore *m*

synthetic /sɪnˈθetɪk/ *a* sintetico ● *n* fibra *f* sintetica

Syria /ˈsɪrɪə/ *n* Siria *f*. **~n** *a & n* siriano, -a *mf*

syringe /sɪˈrɪndʒ/ *n* siringa *f*

syrup /ˈsɪrəp/ *n* sciroppo *m*; *Br* tipo *m di* melassa

system /ˈsɪstəm/ *n* sistema *m*. **~atic** /-ˈmætɪk/ *a* sistematico

....

Tt

....

tab /tæb/ *n* linguetta *f*; (*with name*) etichetta *f*; **keep ~s on** *fam* sorvegliare; **pick up the ~** *fam* pagare il conto

tabby /ˈtæbɪ/ *n* gatto *m* tigrato

table /ˈteɪbl/ *n* tavolo *m*; (*list*) tavola *f*; **at [the] ~** a tavola; **~ of contents** tavola *f* delle materie ● *vt* proporre. **~-cloth** *n* tovaglia *f*. **~-spoon** *n* cucchiaio *m* da tavola. **~spoon[ful]** *n* cucchiaiata *f*

'table tennis *n* tennis *m* da tavolo; (*everyday level*) ping pong *m*

tabloid /ˈtæblɔɪd/ *n* [giornale *m* formato] tabloid *m inv*; *pej* giornale *m* scandalistico

taboo /təˈbuː/ *a* tabù *inv* ● *n* tabù *m inv*

tacit /ˈtæsɪt/ *a* tacito

taciturn /ˈtæsɪtɜːn/ *a* taciturno

tack /tæk/ *n* (*nail*) chiodino *m*; (*stitch*) imbastitura *f*; *Naut* virata *f*; *fig* linea *f* di condotta ● *vt* inchiodare; (*sew*) imbastire ● *vi Naut* virare

tackle /ˈtækl/ *n* (*equipment*) attrezzatura *f*; (*football etc*) contrasto *m*, tackle *m inv* ● *vt* affrontare

tacky /ˈtækɪ/ *a* (*paint*) non ancora asciutto; (*glue*) appiccicoso; *fig* pacchiano

tact /tækt/ *n* tatto *m*. **~ful** *a* pieno di tatto; (*remark*) delicato. **~fully** *adv* con tatto

tactic|al /ˈtæktɪkl/ *a* tattico. **~s** *npl* tattica *fsg*

tactless /ˈtæktlɪs/ *a* privo di tatto.

~ly adv senza tatto. **~ness** n mancanza f di tatto; (of remark) indelicatezza f

tadpole /'tædpəʊl/ n girino m

tag¹ /tæg/ n (label) etichetta f ● vt (pt/pp tagged) attaccare l'etichetta a. **tag along** vi seguire passo passo

tag² n (game) acchiapparello m

tail /teɪl/ n coda f; **~s** pl (tailcoat) frac m inv ● vt (fam: follow) pedinare. **tail off** vi diminuire

tail: **~back** n coda f. **~-end** n parte f finale; (of train) coda f. **~ light** n fanalino m di coda

tailor /'teɪlə(r)/ n sarto m. **~-made** a fatto su misura

'tail wind n vento m di coda

taint /teɪnt/ vt contaminare

take /teɪk/ n Cinema ripresa f ● v (pt took, pp taken) ● vt prendere; (to a place) portare ⟨person, object⟩; (contain) contenere ⟨passengers etc⟩; (endure) sopportare; (require) occorrere; (teach) insegnare; (study) studiare ⟨subject⟩; fare ⟨exam, holiday, photograph, walk, bath⟩; sentire ⟨pulse⟩; misurare ⟨sb's temperature⟩; **~** sb prisoner fare prigioniero qcno; **be ~n ill** ammalarsi; **~ sth calmly** prendere con calma qcsa ● vi ⟨plant⟩ attecchire. **take after** vt assomigliare a. **take away** vt (with one) portare via; (remove) togliere; (subtract) sottrarre; **to ~ away** 'da asporto'. **take back** vt riprendere; ritirare ⟨statement⟩; (return) riportare [indietro]. **take down** vt portare giù; (remove) tirare giù; (write down) prendere nota di. **take in** vt (bring indoors) portare dentro; (to one's home) ospitare; (understand) capire; (deceive) ingannare; riprendere ⟨garment⟩; (include) includere. **take off** vt togliersi ⟨clothes⟩; (deduct) togliere; (mimic) imitare; **~ time off prendere delle vacan**ze; **~ oneself off** andarsene ● vi Aeron decollare. **take on** vt farsi

carico di; assumere ⟨employee⟩; (as opponent) prendersela con. **take out** vt portare fuori; togliere ⟨word, stain⟩; (withdraw) ritirare ⟨money, books⟩; **~ out a subscription to sth** abbonarsi a qcsa; **~ it out on sb** fam prendersela con qcno. **take over** vt assumere il controllo di ⟨firm⟩ ● vi **~ over from sb** sostituire qcno; (permanently) succedere a qcno. **take to** vt (as a habit) darsi a; **I took to her** ⟨idea⟩ mi è piaciuta. **take up** vt portare su; accettare ⟨offer⟩; intraprendere ⟨profession⟩; dedicarsi a ⟨hobby⟩; prendere ⟨time⟩; occupare ⟨space⟩; tirare su ⟨floorboards⟩; accorciare ⟨dress⟩; **~ sth up with sb** discutere qcsa con qcno ● vi **~ up with sb** legarsi a qcno

take: **~-away** n (meal) piatto m da asporto; (restaurant) ristorante m che prepara piatti da asporto. **~-off** n Aeron decollo m. **~-over** n rilevamento m. **~-over bid** offerta f di assorbimento

takings /'teɪkɪŋz/ npl incassi mpl

talcum /'tælkəm/ n **~ [powder]** talco m

tale /teɪl/ n storia f; pej fandonia f

talent /'tælənt/ n talento m. **~ed** a [ricco] di talento

talk /tɔːk/ n conversazione f; (lecture) conferenza f; (gossip) chiacchere fpl; **make small ~** parlare del più e del meno ● vi parlare ● vt parlare di ⟨politics etc⟩; **~ sb into sth** convincere qcno di qcosa. **talk over** vt discutere

talkative /'tɔːkətɪv/ a loquace

'talking-to n sgridata f

talk show n talk show m inv

tall /tɔːl/ a alto. **~boy** n cassettone m. **~ order** n impresa f difficile. **~ 'story** n frottola f

tally /'tælɪ/ n conteggio m; **keep a ~ of** tenere il conto di ● vi coincidere

tambourine /tæmbə'riːn/ n tamburello m

tame /teɪm/ a ⟨animal⟩ domestico; ⟨dull⟩ insulso ● vt domare. **~ly** adv docilmente. **~r** n domatore, -trice mf

tamper /'tæmpə(r)/ vi ~ **with** manomettere

tampon /'tæmpɒn/ n tampone m

tan /tæn/ a marrone rossiccio ● n marrone m rossiccio; ⟨from sun⟩ abbronzatura f ● v (pt/pp **tanned**) ● vt conciare ⟨hide⟩ ● vi abbronzarsi

tang /tæŋ/ n sapore m forte; ⟨smell⟩ odore m penetrante

tangent /'tændʒənt/ n tangente f

tangible /'tændʒɪbl/ a tangibile

tangle /'tæŋgl/ n groviglio m; ⟨in hair⟩ nodo m ● vt ~[**up**] aggrovigliare ● vi aggrovigliarsi

tango /'tæŋgəʊ/ n tango m inv

tank /tæŋk/ n contenitore m; ⟨for petrol⟩ serbatoio m; ⟨fish ~⟩ acquario m; Mil carro m armato

tankard /'tæŋkəd/ n boccale m

tanker /'tæŋkə(r)/ n nave f cisterna; ⟨lorry⟩ autobotte f

tanned /tænd/ a abbronzato

tantalize /'tæntəlaɪz/ vt tormentare. **~ing** a allettante; ⟨smell⟩ stuzzicante

tantamount /'tæntəmaʊnt/ a ~ **to** equivalente a

tantrum /'tæntrəm/ n scoppio m d'ira

tap /tæp/ n rubinetto m; ⟨knock⟩ colpo m; **on** ~ a disposizione ● v (pt/pp **tapped**) ● vt dare un colpetto a; sfruttare ⟨resources⟩; mettere sotto controllo ⟨telephone⟩ ● vi picchiettare. **~-dance** n tip tap m ● vi ballare il tip tap

tape /teɪp/ n nastro m; ⟨recording⟩ cassetta f ● vt legare con nastro; ⟨record⟩ registrare

'tape: ~ backup drive n Comput unità f di backup a nastro. **~-deck** n piastra f. **~-measure** n metro m [a nastro]

taper /'teɪpə(r)/ n candela f sottile ● **taper off** vi assottigliarsi

'tape: ~ recorder n registratore m. **~ recording** n registrazione f

tapestry /'tæpɪstrɪ/ n arazzo m

'tap water n acqua f del rubinetto

tar /tɑ:(r)/ n catrame m ● vt (pt/pp **tarred**) incatramare

tardy /'tɑ:dɪ/ a (-**ier**, -**iest**) tardivo

target /'tɑ:gɪt/ n bersaglio m; fig obiettivo m

tariff /'tærɪf/ n ⟨price⟩ tariffa f; ⟨duty⟩ dazio m

Tarmac® /'tɑ:mæk/ n macadam m al catrame. **tarmac** n Aeron pista f di decollo

tarnish /'tɑ:nɪʃ/ vi ossidarsi ● vt ossidare; fig macchiare

tarpaulin /tɑ:'pɔ:lɪn/ n telone m impermeabile

tart¹ /tɑ:t/ a aspro; fig acido

tart² n crostata f; ⟨individual⟩ crostatina f; ⟨sl: prostitute⟩ donnaccia f ● **tart up** vt fam ~ **oneself up** agghindarsi

tartan /'tɑ:tn/ n tessuto m scozzese, tartan m inv ● attrib di tessuto scozzese

tartar /'tɑ:tə(r)/ n ⟨on teeth⟩ tartaro m

tartar 'sauce /tɑ:tə-/ n salsa f tartara

task /tɑ:sk/ n compito m; **take sb to** ~ riprendere qcno. **~ force** n Pol commissione f; Mil task-force f inv

tassel /'tæsl/ n nappa f

taste /teɪst/ n gusto m; ⟨sample⟩ saggio m; **get a** ~ **of sth** fig assaporare il gusto di qcsa ● vt sentire il sapore di; ⟨sample⟩ assaggiare ● vi sapere ⟨of di⟩; **it ~s lovely** è ottimo. **~ful** a di [buon] gusto. **~fully** adv con gusto. **~less** a senza gusto. **~lessly** adv con cattivo gusto

tasty /'teɪstɪ/ a (-**ier**, -**iest**) saporito

tat /tæt/ see **tit²**

tatter|ed /'tætəd/ a cencioso; ⟨pages⟩ stracciato. **~s** npl **in ~s** a brandelli

tattoo¹ /tæ'tu:/ n tatuaggio m ● vt tatuare

tattoo² n Mil parata f militare

tatty /'tætɪ/ a (-ier, -iest) ⟨clothes, person⟩ trasandato; ⟨book⟩ malandato

taught /tɔːt/ see **teach**

taunt /tɔːnt/ n scherno m ● vt schernire

Taurus /'tɔːrəs/ n Toro m

taut /tɔːt/ a teso

tawdry /'tɔːdrɪ/ a (-ier, -iest) pacchiano

tax /tæks/ n tassa f; ⟨on income⟩ imposte fpl; **before ~** ⟨price⟩ tasse escluse; ⟨salary⟩ lordo ● vt tassare; fig mettere alla prova; **~ with** accusare di. **~able** /-əbl/ a tassabile. **~ation** /'seɪʃn/ n tasse fpl. **~ evasion** n evasione f fiscale. **~-free** a esentasse. **~ haven** n paradiso m fiscale

taxi /'tæksɪ/ n taxi m inv ● vi ⟨pt/pp **taxied**, pres p **taxiing**⟩ ⟨aircraft:⟩ rullare. **~ driver** n tassista mf. **~ rank** n posteggio m per taxi

taxpayer n contribuente mf

tea /tiː/ n tè m inv. **~-bag** n bustina f di tè. **~-break** n intervallo m per il tè

teach /tiːtʃ/ vt/i ⟨pt/pp **taught**⟩ insegnare; **~ sb sth** insegnare qcsa a qcno. **~er** n insegnante mf; ⟨primary⟩ maestro, -a mf. **~ing** n insegnamento m

tea: **~-cloth** n ⟨for drying⟩ asciugapiatti m inv. **~-cup** n tazza f da tè

teak /tiːk/ n tek m

tea-leaves npl tè m inv sfuso; ⟨when infused⟩ fondi m del tè

team /tiːm/ n squadra f; fig équipe f inv ● **team up** vi unirsi

team-work n lavoro m di squadra; fig lavoro m d'équipe

teapot n teiera f

tear¹ /teə(r)/ n strappo m ● vt ⟨pt **tore**, pp **torn**⟩ ● vt strappare ● vi strappare; ⟨material:⟩ strapparsi; ⟨run:⟩ precipitarsi. **tear apart** vt ⟨fig: criticize⟩ fare a pezzi; ⟨separate⟩ dividere. **tear away** vt ~

oneself away andare via; **~ oneself away from** staccarsi da ⟨television⟩. **tear open** vt aprire strappando. **tear up** vt strappare; rompere ⟨agreement⟩

tear² /tɪə(r)/ n lacrima f. **~-ful** a ⟨person⟩ in lacrime; ⟨farewell⟩ lacrimevole. **~fully** adv in lacrime. **~-gas** n gas m lacrimogeno

tease /tiːz/ vt prendere in giro ⟨person⟩; tormentare ⟨animal⟩

tea: **~-set** n servizio m da tè. **~-shop** n sala f da tè. **~-spoon** n cucchiaino m ⟨da tè⟩. **~-spoon[ful]** n cucchiaino m

teat /tiːt/ n capezzolo m; ⟨on bottle⟩ tettarella f

tea-towel n strofinaccio m ⟨per i piatti⟩

technical /'teknɪkl/ a tecnico. **~ity** /-'kælətɪ/ n tecnicismo m; Jur cavillo m giuridico. **~ly** adv tecnicamente; ⟨strictly⟩ strettamente

technician /tek'nɪʃn/ n tecnico, -a mf

technique /tek'niːk/ n tecnica f

technological /teknə'lɒdʒɪkl/ a tecnologico

technology /tek'nɒlədʒɪ/ n tecnologia f

teddy /'tedɪ/ n **~ [bear]** orsacchiotto m

tedious /'tiːdɪəs/ a noioso

tedium /'tiːdɪəm/ n tedio m

tee /tiː/ n ⟨in golf⟩ tee m inv

teem /tiːm/ vi ⟨rain⟩ piovere a dirotto; **be ~ing with** ⟨full of⟩ pullulare di

teenage /'tiːneɪdʒ/ a per ragazzi; **~ boy/girl** adolescente mf. **~r** n adolescente mf

teens /tiːnz/ npl **the ~** l'adolescenza fsg; **be in one's ~** essere adolescente

teeny /'tiːnɪ/ a (-ier, -iest) piccolissimo

teeter /'tiːtə(r)/ vi barcollare

teeth /tiːθ/ see **tooth**

teethe /tiːð/ vi mettere i primi denti. **~ing troubles** npl fig difficoltà fpl iniziali

teetotal /ˈtiːˈtəʊtl/ a astemio. **~ler** n astemio, -a mf

telecommunications /telɪkəmjuːnɪˈkeɪʃnz/ npl telecomunicazioni fpl

telegram /ˈtelɪɡræm/ n telegramma m

telegraph /ˈtelɪɡrɑːf/ n telegrafo m. **~ic** /-ˈɡræfɪk/ a telegrafico. **~ pole** n palo m del telegrafo

telepathy /trˈlepəθɪ/ n telepatia f

telephone /ˈtelɪfəʊn/ n telefono m; **be on the ~** avere il telefono; (be telephoning) essere al telefono ● vt telefonare a ● vi telefonare

telephone: ~ book n elenco m telefonico. **~ booth** n, **~ box** n cabina f telefonica. **~ directory** n elenco m telefonico. **~ number** n numero m di telefono

telephonist /trˈlefənɪst/ n telefonista mf

'telephoto /ˈtelɪ-/ a **~ lens** teleobiettivo m

telescop|e /ˈtelɪskəʊp/ n telescopio m. **~ic** /-ˈskɒpɪk/ a telescopico

televise /ˈtelɪvaɪz/ vt trasmettere per televisione

television /ˈtelɪvɪʒn/ n televisione f; **watch ~** guardare la televisione. **~ set** n televisore m

telex /ˈteleks/ n telex m inv

tell /tel/ vt (pt/pp told) dire; raccontare (story); (distinguish) distinguere (from da); **~ sb sth** dire qcsa a qcno; **~ the time** dire l'ora; **I couldn't ~ why...** non sapevo perché... ● vi (produce an effect) avere effetto; **time will ~** il tempo ce lo dirà; **his age is beginning to ~** l'età comincia a farsi sentire [per lui]; **you mustn't ~** non devi dire niente. **tell off** vt sgridare

teller /ˈtelə(r)/ n (in bank) cassiere, -a mf

telling /ˈtelɪŋ/ a significativo; (argument) efficace

telly /ˈtelɪ/ n fam tv f inv

temerity /trˈmerətɪ/ n audacia f

temp /temp/ n fam impiegato, -a mf temporaneo, -a

temper /ˈtempə(r)/ n (disposition) carattere m; (mood) umore m; (anger) collera f; **lose one's ~** arrabbiarsi; **be in a ~** essere arrabbiato; **keep one's ~** mantenere la calma

temperament /ˈtemprəmənt/ n temperamento m. **~al** /-ˈmentl/ a (moody) capriccioso

temperate /ˈtempərət/ a (climate) temperato

temperature /ˈtemprətʃə(r)/ n temperatura f; **have a ~** avere la febbre

tempest /ˈtempɪst/ n tempesta f. **~uous** /-ˈpestjʊəs/ a tempestoso

temple¹ /ˈtempl/ n tempio m

temple² n Anat tempia f

tempo /ˈtempəʊ/ n ritmo m; Mus tempo m

temporar|y /ˈtempərərɪ/ a temporaneo; (measure, building) provvisorio. **~ily** adv temporaneamente; (introduced, erected) provvisoriamente

tempt /tempt/ vt tentare; sfidare (fate); **~ sb** to indurre qcno a; be **~ed** essere tentato (to di); **I am ~ed by the offer** l'offerta mi tenta. **~ation** /-ˈteɪʃn/ n tentazione f. **~ing** a allettante; (food, drink) invitante

ten /ten/ a dieci

tenable /ˈtenəbl/ a fig sostenibile

tenaci|ous /trˈneɪʃəs/ a tenace. **~ty** /-ˈnæsətɪ/ n tenacia f

tenant /ˈtenənt/ n inquilino, -a mf; Comm locatario, -a mf

tend¹ /tend/ vt (look after) prendersi cura di

tend² vi **~ to do sth** tendere a far qcsa

tendency /ˈtendənsɪ/ n tendenza f

tender¹ /ˈtendə(r)/ n Comm offerta f; **be legal ~** avere corso legale ● vt offrire; presentare (resignation)

tender² a (painful) dolorante. **~ly** adv teneramente. **~ness** n tenerezza f; (painfulness) dolore m

tendon /'tendən/ n tendine m

tenement /'tenəmənt/ n casamento m

tenner /'tenə(r)/ n fam biglietto m da dieci sterline

tennis /'tenıs/ n tennis m. **~-court** n campo m da tennis. **~ player** n tennista mf

tenor /'tenə(r)/ n tenore m

tense[1] /tens/ n Gram tempo m

tense[2] a teso ● vt tendere ‹muscle›. **tense up** vi tendersi

tension /'tenʃn/ n tensione f

tent /tent/ n tenda f

tentacle /'tentəkl/ n tentacolo m

tentative /'tentətıv/ a provvisorio; ‹smile, gesture› esitante. **~ly** adv timidamente; ‹accept› provvisoriamente

tenterhooks /'tentəhʊks/ npl be on **~** essere sulle spine

tenth /tenθ/ a decimo ● n decimo, -a mf

tenuous /'tenjʊəs/ a fig debole

tepid /'tepıd/ a tiepido

term /tɜ:m/ n periodo m; Sch Univ trimestre m; (expression) termine m; **~s** pl (conditions) condizioni fpl; **~ of office** carica f; **in the short/long ~** a breve/lungo termine; **be on good/bad ~s** essere in buoni/cattivi rapporti; **come to ~s with** accettare ‹past, fact›; **easy ~s** facilità f di pagamento

terminal /'tɜ:mın(ə)l/ a finale; Med terminale ● n Aeron terminal m inv; Rail stazione f di testa; (of bus) capolinea m; (on battery) morsetto m; Comput terminale m. **~ly** adv be **~ly ill** essere in fase terminale

terminat|**e** /'tɜ:mıneıt/ vt terminare; rescindere ‹contract›; interrompere ‹pregnancy› ● vi terminare; **~e in** finire in. **~ion** /-'neıʃn/ n termine m; Med interruzione f di gravidanza

terminology /tɜ:mı'nɒlədʒı/ n terminologia f

terminus /'tɜ:mınəs/ n (pl **-ni**

/-naı/) (for bus) capolinea m; (for train) stazione f di testa

terrace /'terəs/ n terrazza f; (houses) fila f di case a schiera; **the ~s** Sport le gradinate. **~d house** n casa f a schiera

terrain /te'reın/ n terreno m

terrib|**le** /'terəbl/ a terribile. **~y** adv terribilmente

terrier /'terıə(r)/ n terrier m inv

terrific /tə'rıfık/ a fam (excellent) fantastico; (huge) enorme. **~ally** adv fam terribilmente

terri|**fy** /'terıfaı/ vt (pt/pp **-ied**) atterrire; **be ~fied** essere terrorizzato. **~fying** a terrificante

territorial /terı'tɔ:rıəl/ a territoriale

territory /'terıtərı/ n territorio m

terror /'terə(r)/ n terrore m. **~ism** /-ızm/ n terrorismo m. **~ist** /-ıst/ n terrorista mf. **~ize** vt terrorizzare

terse /tɜ:s/ a conciso

test /test/ n esame m; (in laboratory) esperimento m; (of friendship, machine) prova m; (of intelligence, aptitude) test m inv; **put to the ~** mettere alla prova ● vt esaminare; provare ‹machine›

testament /'testəmənt/ n testamento m; **Old/New T~** Antico/Nuovo Testamento m

testicle /'testıkl/ n testicolo m

testify /'testıfaı/ vt/i (pt/pp **-ied**) testimoniare

testimonial /testɪ'məʊnɪəl/ n lettera f di referenze

testimony /'testɪmənɪ/ n testimonianza f

'test: **~ match** n partita f internazionale. **~-tube** n provetta f. **~-tube 'baby** n fam bambino, -a mf in provetta

tetanus /'tetənəs/ n tetano m

tether /'teðə(r)/ n be at the end of one's **~** non poterne più

text /tekst/ n testo m. **~book** n manuale m

textile /'tekstaıl/ a tessile ● n stoffa f

texture /'tekstʃə(r)/ n (of skin) gra-

na f; (of food) consistenza f; **of a smooth ~** (to the touch) soffice al tatto

Thai /taɪ/ a & n tailandese mf. **~land** n Tailandia f

Thames /temz/ n Tamigi m

than /ðən/, accentato /ðæn/ conj che; (with numbers, names) di; **older ~ me** più vecchio di me

thank /θæŋk/ vt ringraziare; **~ you** [**very much**] grazie [mille]. **~ful** a grato. **~fully** adv con gratitudine; (happily) fortunatamente. **~less** a ingrato

thanks /θæŋks/ npl ringraziamenti mpl; **~!** fam grazie!; **~ to** grazie a

that /ðæt/ a & pron (pl those) quel, quei pl; (before s + consonant, gn, ps and z) quello, quegli pl; (before vowel) quell' mf, quegli mpl, quelle fpl; **~ one** quello; **I don't like those** quelli non mi piacciono; **~ is** cioè; **is ~ you?** sei tu?; **who is ~?** chi è?; **what did you do after ~?** cosa hai fatto dopo?; **like ~** in questo modo, così; **a man like ~** un uomo così; **~ is why** ecco perché; **~'s it!** (you've understood) ecco!; (I've finished) ecco fatto!; (I've had enough) basta così!; (there's nothing more) tutto qui!; **~'s ~!** (with job) ecco fatto!; (with relationship) è tutto finito!; (with anger) **~'s ~!** punto e basta! **all ~ I know** tutto quello che so ● adv così; **it wasn't ~ good** non era poi così buono ● rel pron che; **the man ~ I spoke to** l'uomo con cui ho parlato; **the day ~ I saw him** il giorno in cui l'ho visto; **all ~ I know** tutto quello che so ● conj che; **I think ~...** penso che...

thatch /θætʃ/ n tetto m di paglia. **~ed** a coperto di paglia

thaw /θɔ:/ n disgelo m ● vt fare scongelare (food) ● vi (food): scongelarsi; **it's ~ing** sta sgelando

the /ðə/, di fronte a una vocale /ði:/ def art il, la f; i mpl, le fpl; (before s + consonant, gn, ps and z) lo, gli

mpl; (before vowel) l' mf, gli mpl, le fpl; **at ~ cinema/station** al cinema/alla stazione; **from ~ cinema/station** dal cinema/dalla stazione ● adv **~ more ~ better** più ce n'è meglio è; (with reference to pl) più ce ne sono, meglio è; **all ~ better** tanto meglio

theatre /ˈθɪətə(r)/ n teatro m; Med sala f operatoria

theatrical /θɪˈætrɪkl/ a teatrale; (showy) melodrammatico

theft /θeft/ n furto m

their /ðeə(r)/ a il loro m, la loro f, i loro mpl, le loro fpl; **~ mother/father** la loro madre/il loro padre

theirs /ðeəz/ poss pron il loro m, la loro f, i loro mpl, le loro fpl; **a friend of ~** un loro amico; **friends of ~** dei loro amici; **those are ~** quelli sono loro; (as opposed to ours) quelli sono i loro

them /ðem/ pron (direct object) li m, le f; (indirect object) gli, loro fml; (after prep: with people) loro; (after preposition: with things) essi; **we haven't seen ~** non li/le abbiamo visti/viste; **give ~ the money** dai loro or dagli i soldi; **give it to ~** daglielo; **I've spoken to ~** ho parlato con loro; **it's ~** sono loro

theme /θi:m/ n tema m. **~ song** n motivo m conduttore

them'selves pron (reflexive) si; (emphatic) se stessi; **they poured ~ a drink** si sono versati da bere; **they said so ~** lo hanno detto loro stessi; **they kept it to ~** se lo sono tenuti per sé; **by ~** da soli

then /ðen/ adv allora; (next) poi; **by ~** (in the past) ormai; (in the future) per allora; **since ~** sin da allora; **before ~** prima di allora; **from ~ on** da allora in poi; **now and ~** ogni tanto; **there and ~** all'istante ● conj allora; **~ and there** all'istante ● a di allora

theolog'ian /θɪəˈləʊdʒɪən/ n teologo, -a mf. **~y** /-ˈblədʒɪ/ n teologia f

theorem /ˈθɪərəm/ n teorema m

theoretical /θɪəˈretɪkl/ a teorico

theory /ˈθɪərɪ/ n teoria f; **in ~** in teoria

therapeutic /θerəˈpjuːtɪk/ a terapeutico

therap|ist /ˈθerəpɪst/ n terapista mf. **~y** n terapia f

there /ðeə(r)/ adv là, lì; **down/up ~** laggiù/lassù; **~ is/are** c'è/ci sono; **~ he/she is** eccolo/eccola ● int ~, ~! dai, su!

there: ~abouts adv [or] **~abouts** (roughly) all'incirca. **~'after** adv dopo di che. **~by** adv in tal modo. **~fore** /-fɔː(r)/ adv perciò

thermal /ˈθɜːm(ə)l/ a termale. **~ 'underwear** n biancheria f che mantiene la temperatura corporea

thermometer /θəˈmɒmɪtə(r)/ n termometro m

Thermos® /ˈθɜːməs/ n ~ **[flask]** termos m inv

thermostat /ˈθɜːməstæt/ n termostato m

thesaurus /θɪˈsɔːrəs/ n dizionario m dei sinonimi

these /ðiːz/ see **this**

thesis /ˈθiːsɪs/ n (pl **-ses** /-siːz/) tesi f inv

they /ðeɪ/ pron loro; **~ are tired** sono stanchi; **we're going, but ~ are not** noi andiamo, ma loro no; **~ say** (generalizing) si dice; **~ are building a new road** stanno costruendo una nuova strada

thick /θɪk/ a spesso; (forest) fitto; (liquid) denso; (hair) folto; (fam: stupid) ottuso; (fam: close) molto unito; **be 5 mm ~** essere 5 mm di spessore ● adv densamente ● n **in the ~ of** nel mezzo di. **~en** vt ispessire (sauce) ● vi ispessirsi; (fog:) infittirsi. **~ly** adv densamente; (cut) a fette spesse. **~ness** n spessore m

thick-: ~set a tozzo. **~-skinned** a fam insensibile

thief /θiːf/ n (pl **thieves**) ladro, -a mf

thieving /ˈθiːvɪŋ/ a ladro ● n furti mpl

thigh /θaɪ/ n coscia f

thimble /ˈθɪmbl/ n ditale m

thin /θɪn/ a (**thinner, thinnest**) sottile; (shoes, sweater) leggero; (liquid) liquido; (person) magro; (fig: excuse, plot) inconsistente ● adv = **thinly** ● v (pt/pp **thinned**) ● vt diluire (liquid) ● vi diradarsi. **thin out** vi diradarsi. **~ly** adv (populated) scarsamente; (disguised) leggermente; (cut) a fette sottili

thing /θɪŋ/ n cosa f; **~s** pl (belongings) roba fsg; **for one ~** in primo luogo; **the right ~** la cosa giusta; **just the ~!** proprio quel che ci vuole!; **how are ~s?** come vanno le cose?; **the latest ~** fam l'ultima cosa; **the best ~ would be** la cosa migliore sarebbe; **poor ~!** poveretto!

think /θɪŋk/ vt/i (pt/pp **thought**) pensare; (believe) credere; **I ~ so** credo di sì; **what do you ~?** (what is your opinion?) cosa ne pensi?; **~ of/about** pensare a; **what do you ~ of it?** cosa ne pensi di questo?. **think over** vt riflettere su. **think up** vt escogitare

third /θɜːd/ a & n terzo, -a mf. **~ly** adv terzo. **~-rate** a scadente

thirst /θɜːst/ n sete f. **~ily** adv con sete. **~y** a assetato; **be ~y** aver sete

thirteen /θɜːˈtiːn/ a tredici. **~th** a tredicesimo

thirtieth /ˈθɜːtɪɪθ/ a trentesimo

thirty /ˈθɜːtɪ/ a trenta

this /ðɪs/ a (pl **these**) questo; **~ man/woman** quest'uomo/questa donna; **these men/women** questi uomini/queste donne; **~ one** questo; **~ morning/evening** stamattina/stasera ● pron (pl **these**) questo; **we talked about ~ and that** abbiamo parlato del più e del meno; **like ~** così; **~ is Peter** questo è Peter; Teleph sono Peter; **who is ~?** chi è?; Teleph chi parla? ● adv così; **~ big** così grande

thistle /ˈθɪsl/ n cardo m

thorn /θɔːn/ n spina f. **~y** a spinoso

thorough /'θʌrə/ a completo; ⟨knowledge⟩ profondo; ⟨clean, search, training⟩ a fondo; ⟨person⟩ scrupoloso

thorough: **~bred** n purosangue m inv. **~fare** n via f principale; **'no ~fare'** 'strada non transitabile '

thoroughly /'θʌrəlɪ/ adv ⟨clean, search, know sth⟩ a fondo; ⟨extremely⟩ estremamente. **~ness** n completezza f

those /ðəʊz/ see **that**

though /ðəʊ/ conj sebbene; **as ~** come se ● adv fam tuttavia

thought /θɔ:t/ see **think** ● n pensiero m; ⟨idea⟩ idea f. **~ful** a pensieroso; ⟨considerate⟩ premuroso. **~fully** adv pensierosamente; ⟨considerately⟩ premurosamente. **~less** a ⟨inconsiderate⟩ sconsiderato. **~lessly** adv con noncuranza

thousand /'θaʊznd/ a **one/a ~** mille m inv ● n mille m inv; **~s of** migliaia fpl di. **~th** a millesimo ● n millesimo. -a mf

thrash /θræʃ/ vt picchiare; ⟨defeat⟩ sconfiggere. **thrash out** vt mettere a punto

thread /θred/ n filo m; ⟨of screw⟩ filetto m ● vt infilare ⟨beads⟩; **~ one's way through** farsi strada fra. **~bare** a logoro

threat /θret/ n minaccia f

threaten /'θretn/ vt minacciare ⟨to do di fare⟩ ● vi/fig incalzare. **~ing** a minaccioso; ⟨sky, atmosphere⟩ sinistro

three /θri:/ a tre. **~fold** a & adv triplo. **~some** /-səm/ n trio m

thresh /θreʃ/ vt trebbiare

threshold /'θreʃəʊld/ n soglia f

threw /θru:/ see **throw**

thrift /θrɪft/ n economia f. **~y** a parsimonioso

thrill /θrɪl/ n emozione f; ⟨of fear⟩ brivido m ● vt entusiasmare; **be ~ed with** essere entusiasta di. **~er** n ⟨book⟩ romanzo m giallo m; ⟨film⟩ film m giallo m. **~ing** a eccitante

thrive /θraɪv/ vi ⟨pt thrived or

throve, pp **thrived** or **thriven** /'θrɪvn/⟩ ⟨business⟩: prosperare; ⟨child, plant⟩: crescere bene; **I ~ on pressure** mi piace essere sotto tensione

throat /θrəʊt/ n gola f; **sore ~** mal m di gola

throb /θrɒb/ n pulsazione f; ⟨of heart⟩ battito m ● vi ⟨pt/pp throbbed⟩ ⟨vibrate⟩ pulsare; ⟨heart⟩: battere

throes /θrəʊz/ npl **in the ~ of** fig alle prese con

thrombosis /θrɒm'bəʊsɪs/ n trombosi f

throne /θrəʊn/ n trono m

throng /θrɒŋ/ n calca f

throttle /'θrɒtl/ n ⟨on motorbike⟩ manopola f di accelerazione ● vt strozzare

through /θru:/ prep attraverso; ⟨during⟩ durante; ⟨by means of⟩ tramite; ⟨thanks to⟩ grazie a; **Saturday ~ Tuesday** Am da sabato a martedì incluso ● adv attraverso; **~ and ~** fino in fondo; **wet ~** completamente bagnato; **read sth ~** dare una lettura a qcsa; **let ~** lasciar passare ⟨sb⟩ ● a ⟨train⟩ diretto; **be ~** ⟨finished⟩ aver finito; Teleph avere la comunicazione

throughout /θru:'aʊt/ prep per tutto ● adv completamente; ⟨time⟩ per tutto il tempo

throw /θrəʊ/ n tiro m ● vt ⟨pt threw, pp thrown⟩ lanciare; ⟨throw away⟩ gettare; azionare ⟨switch⟩; disarcionare ⟨rider⟩; ⟨fam: disconcert⟩ disorientare; fam dare ⟨party⟩. **throw away** vt gettare via. **throw out** vt gettare via; rigettare ⟨plan⟩; buttare fuori ⟨person⟩. **throw up** vt alzare ● vi ⟨vomit⟩ vomitare

'throw-away a ⟨remark⟩ buttato lì; ⟨paper cup⟩ usa e getta inv

thrush /θrʌʃ/ n tordo m

thrust /θrʌst/ n spinta f ● vt ⟨pt/pp thrust⟩ ⟨push⟩ spingere; ⟨insert⟩ conficcare; **~ [up]on** imporre a

thud /θʌd/ n tonfo m

thug /θʌg/ n deliquente m

thumb /θʌm/ n pollice m; **as a rule of** ~ come regola generale; **under sb's** ~ succube di qcno ● vt ~ **a lift** fare l'autostop. **~-index** n indice m a rubrica. **~tack** n Am puntina f da disegno

thump /θʌmp/ n colpo m; (noise) tonfo m ● vt battere su (table, door); battere (fist); colpire (person) ● vi battere (on su); (heart:) battere forte. **thump about** vi camminare pesantemente

thunder /ˈθʌndə(r)/ n tuono m; (loud noise) rimbombo m ● vi tuonare; (make loud noise) rimbombare. **~clap** n rombo m di tuono. **~storm** n temporale m. **~y** a temporalesco

Thursday /ˈθɜːzdeɪ/ n giovedì m inv

thus /ðʌs/ adv così

thwart /θwɔːt/ vt ostacolare

thyme /taɪm/ n timo m

Tiber /ˈtaɪbə(r)/ n Tevere m

tick /tɪk/ n (sound) ticchettìo m; (mark) segno m; (fam: instant) attimo m ● vi ticchettare. **tick off** vt spuntare; fam sgridare. **tick over** vi (engine:) andare al minimo

ticket /ˈtɪkɪt/ n biglietto m; (for item deposited, library) tagliando m; (label) cartellino m; (fine) multa f. **~-collector** n controllore m. **~-office** n biglietteria f

tickle /ˈtɪkl/ n solletico m ● vt fare il solletico a; (amuse) divertire ● vi fare prurito. **~lish** /ˈtɪklɪʃ/ a che soffre il solletico

tidal /ˈtaɪdl/ a ⟨river, harbour⟩ di marea. ~ **wave** n onda f di marea

tiddly-winks /ˈtɪdlɪwɪŋks/ n gioco m delle pulci

tide /taɪd/ n marea f; (of events) corso m; **the** ~ **is in/out** c'è alta/bassa marea ● **tide over** vt ~ **sb over** aiutare qcno a andare avanti

tidily /ˈtaɪdɪlɪ/ adv in modo ordinato

tidiness /ˈtaɪdɪnɪs/ n ordine m

tidy /ˈtaɪdɪ/ a (-ier, -iest) ordinato; (fam: amount) bello ● vt (pt/pp -ied) ~ [up] ordinare; ~ **oneself up** mettersi in ordine

tie /taɪ/ n cravatta f; (cord) legaccio m; (fig: bond) legame m; (restriction) impedimento m; Sport pareggio m ● v (pres p **tying**) ● vt legare; fare (knot); **be** ~**d** (in competition) essere in parità ● vi pareggiare. **tie in with** vi corrispondere a. **tie up** vt legare; vincolare (capital); **be** ~**d up** (busy) essere occupato

tier /tɪə(r)/ n fila f; (of cake) piano m; (in stadium) gradinata f

tiff /tɪf/ n battibecco m

tiger /ˈtaɪgə(r)/ n tigre f

tight /taɪt/ a stretto; (taut) teso; (fam: drunk) sbronzo; (fam: mean) spilorcio; ~ **corner** fam brutta situazione f ● adv strettamente; (hold) forte; (closed) bene

tighten /ˈtaɪtn/ vt stringere; avvitare (screw); intensificare (control) ● vi stringersi

tight: ~**-fisted** a tirchio. **~-fitting** a aderente. **~ly** adv strettamente; (hold) forte; (closed) bene. **~rope** n fune f (da funambulo)

tights /taɪts/ npl collant m inv

tile /taɪl/ n mattonella f; (on roof) tegola f ● vt rivestire di mattonelle (wall)

till[1] /tɪl/ prep & conj = **until**

till[2] n cassa f

tiller /ˈtɪlə(r)/ n barra f del timone

tilt /tɪlt/ n inclinazione f; **at full** ~ a tutta velocità ● vt inclinare ● vi inclinarsi

timber /ˈtɪmbə(r)/ n legname m

time /taɪm/ n tempo m; (occasion) volta f; (by clock) ora f; **two** ~**s four** due volte quattro; **at any** ~ in qualsiasi momento; **this** ~ questa volta; **at** ~**s, from** ~ **to** ~ ogni tanto; ~ **and again** cento volte; **two at a** ~ due alla volta; **on** ~ in orario; **in** ~ in tempo; (eventually) col tempo; **in no** ~ **at all** velocemente; **in a year's** ~ fra un anno;

behind ~ in ritardo; **behind the
~s** antiquato; **for the ~** being per
il momento; **what is the ~?** che
ora è?; **by the ~ we arrive** quando
arriviamo; **did you have a nice
~?** ti sei divertito?; **have a good
~!** divertiti! ● *vt* scegliere il momento per; cronometrare *(race)*;
be well ~d essere ben calcolato
time: **~ bomb** *n* bomba *f* a orologe-
ria. **~-lag** *n* intervallo *m* di tempo.
~-less *a* eterno. **~ly** *a* opportuno.
~-switch *n* interruttore *m* a tempo. **~-table** *n* orario *m*
timid /'tɪmɪd/ *a (shy)* timido;
(fearful) timoroso
timing /'taɪmɪŋ/ *n* Sport, Techn
cronometraggio *m*; **the ~ of the
election** il momento scelto per le
elezioni
tin /tɪn/ *n* stagno *m*; *(container)* barattolo *m* ● *vt (pt/pp tinned)*
inscatolare. **~ foil** *n* [carta *f*] stagnola *f*
tinge /tɪndʒ/ *n* sfumatura *f* ● *vt ~d
with fig* misto a
tingle /'tɪŋgl/ *vi* pizzicare
tinker /'tɪŋkə(r)/ *vi* armeggiare
tinkle /'tɪŋkl/ *n* tintinnio *m*; *(fam:
phone call)* colpo *m* di telefono
● *vi* tintinnare
tinned /tɪnd/ *a* in scatola
'**tin opener** *n* apriscatole *m inv*
tinsel /'tɪnsl/ *n* filo *m* d'argento
tint /tɪnt/ *n* tinta *f* ● *vt* tingersi
(hair)
tiny /'taɪnɪ/ *a* (**-ier, -iest**) minuscolo
tip¹ /tɪp/ *n* punta *f*
tip² *n (money)* mancia *f*; *(advice)*
consiglio *m*; *(for rubbish)* discarica *f* ● *v (pt/pp tipped)* ● *vt (tilt)* inclinare; *(overturn)* capovolgere;
(pour) versare; *(reward)* dare una
mancia a ● *vi* inclinarsi; *(overturn)* capovolgersi. **tip off** *vt ~ sb
off (inform)* fare una' soffiata a
qcno. **tip out** *vt* rovesciare. **tip
over** *vt* capovolgere ● *vi* capovolgersi
'**tip-off** *n* soffiata *f*

tipped /tɪpt/ *a (cigarette)* col filtro
tipsy /'tɪpsɪ/ *a fam* brillo
tiptoe /'tɪptəʊ/ *n* **on ~** in punta di
piedi
tiptop /tɪp'tɒp/ *a fam* in condizioni
perfette
tire /'taɪə(r)/ *vt* stancare ● *vi* stancarsi. **~d** *a* stanco; **~d of** stanco
di; **~d out** stanco morto. **~less** *a*
instancabile. **~some** /-səm/ *a* fastidioso
tiring /'taɪərɪŋ/ *a* stancante
tissue /'tɪʃuː/ *n* tessuto *m*;
(handkerchief) fazzolettino *m* di
carta. **~-paper** *n* carta *f* velina
tit¹ /tɪt/ *n (bird)* cincia *f*
tit² *n* **for tat** pan per focaccia
title /'taɪtl/ *n* titolo *m*. **~-deed** *n*
atto *m* di proprietà. **~-role** *n* ruolo *m* principale
tittle-tattle /'tɪtltætl/ *n* pettegolezzi *mpl*
to /tu:/, *atono* /tə/ *prep* a; *(to
countries)* in; *(towards)* verso; *(up
to, until)* fino a; **I'm going to
John's/the butcher's** vado da
John/dal macellaio; **come/go to
sb** venire/andare da qcno; **go to
Italy/Switzerland** in Italia/Sviz-
zera; **I've never been to Rome**
non sono mai stato a Roma; **go to
the market** andare al mercato; **go to
the toilet/my room** in bagno/ca-
mera mia; **to an exhibition** a una
mostra; **to university** all'università; **twenty/quarter to eight** le otto
meno venti/un quarto; **5 to 6
kilos** da 5 a 6 chili; **to the end** alla
fine; **to this day** fino a oggi; **to the
best of my recollection** per quanto mi possa ricordare; **give/say
sth to sb** dare/dire qcsa a qcno;
give it to me dammelo; **there's
nothing to it** è una cosa da niente
● *verbal constructions* **to go** andare; **learn to swim** imparare a nuotare; **I want to/have to go**
voglio/devo andare; **it's easy to
forget** è facile da dimenticare; **too
ill/tired to go** troppo malato/stan-
co per andare; **you have to** devi; **I**

don't want to non voglio; **live to be** 90 vivere fino a 90 anni; **he was the last to arrive** è stato l'ultimo ad arrivare; **to be honest,...** per essere sincero,... ● *adv* **pull to** chiudere; **to and fro** avanti e indietro

toad /təʊd/ *n* rospo *m*. **~stool** *n* fungo *m* velenoso

toast /təʊst/ *n* pane *m* tostato; (*drink*) brindisi *m* ● *vt* tostare (*bread*); (*drink a ~ to*) brindare a. **~er** *n* tostapane *m inv*

tobacco /təˈbækəʊ/ *n* tabacco *m*. **~nist's** [**shop**] *n* tabaccheria *f*

toboggan /təˈbɒgən/ *n* toboga *m* ● *vi* andare in toboga

today /təˈdeɪ/ *a & adv* oggi *m*; **a week ~** una settimana a oggi; **~'s paper** il giornale di oggi

toddler /ˈtɒdlə(r)/ *n* bambino, -a *mf* ai primi passi

to-do /təˈduː/ *n fam* baccano *m*

toe /təʊ/ *n* dito *m* del piede; (*of footwear*) punta *f*; **big ~** alluce *m* ● *vt* **~ the line** rigar diritto. **~nail** *n* unghia *f* del piede

toffee /ˈtɒfɪ/ *n* caramella *f* al mou

together /təˈgeðə(r)/ *adv* insieme; (*at the same time*) allo stesso tempo; **~ with** insieme a

toilet /ˈtɔɪlɪt/ *n* (*lavatory*) gabinetto *m*. **~ paper** *n* carta *f* igienica

toiletries /ˈtɔɪlɪtrɪz/ *npl* articoli *mpl* da toilette

toilet: ~ roll *n* rotolo *m* di carta igienica. **~ water** *n* acqua *f* di colonia

token /ˈtəʊkən/ *n* segno *m*; (*counter*) gettone *m*; (*voucher*) buono *m* ● *vattrib* simbolico

told /təʊld/ *see* **tell** ● *a* **all ~** in tutto

tolerable /ˈtɒl(ə)rəbl/ *a* tollerabile; (*not bad*) discreto. **~y** *adv* discretamente

toleran|ce /ˈtɒl(ə)r(ə)ns/ *n* tolleranza *f*. **~t** *a* tollerante. **~tly** *adv* con tolleranza

tolerate /ˈtɒləreɪt/ *vt* tollerare

toll[1] /təʊl/ *n* pedaggio *m*; **death ~** numero *m* di morti

toll[2] *vi* suonare a morto

tom /tɒm/ *n* (*cat*) gatto *m* maschio

tomato /təˈmɑːtəʊ/ *n* (*pl* **-es**) pomodoro *m*. **~ ketchup** *n* ketchup *m*. **~ purée** *n* concentrato *m* di pomodoro

tomb /tuːm/ *n* tomba *f*

tomboy /ˈtɒmbɔɪ/ *n* maschiaccio *m*

tombstone *n* pietra *f* tombale

tom-cat *n* gatto *m* maschio

tomfoolery /tɒmˈfuːlərɪ/ *n* stupidaggini *fpl*

tomorrow /təˈmɒrəʊ/ *a & adv* domani *m*; **~ morning** domani mattina; **the day after ~** dopodomani; **see you ~!** a domani!

ton /tʌn/ *n* tonnellata *f* (= *1,016 kg.*); **~s of** *fam* un sacco di

tone /təʊn/ *n* tono *m*; (*colour*) tonalità *f inv* ● **tone down** *vt* attenuare. **tone up** *vt* tonificare (*muscles*)

toner /ˈtəʊnə(r)/ *n* toner *m*

tongs /tɒŋz/ *npl* pinze *fpl*

tongue /tʌŋ/ *n* lingua *f*; **~ in cheek** *fam:* say) ironicamente. **~-twister** *n* scioglilingua *m inv*

tonic /ˈtɒnɪk/ *n* tonico *m*; (*for hair*) lozione *f* per i capelli; *fig* toccasana *m inv*; **~ [water]** acqua *f* tonica

tonight /təˈnaɪt/ *adv* stanotte; (*evening*) stasera ● *n* questa notte *f*; (*evening*) questa sera *f*

tonne /tʌn/ *n* tonnellata *f* metrica

tonsil /ˈtɒnsl/ *n Anat* tonsilla *f*. **~litis** /-əˈlaɪtɪs/ *n* tonsillite *f*

too /tuː/ *adv* troppo; (*also*) anche; **~ many** troppi; (*much* troppo; **~ little** troppo poco

took /tʊk/ *see* **take**

tool /tuːl/ *n* attrezzo *m*

toot /tuːt/ *n* colpo *m* di clacson ● *vi Auto* clacsonare

tooth /tuːθ/ *n* (*pl* **teeth**) dente *m*

tooth|ache *n* mal *m* di denti. **~brush** *n* spazzolino *m* da denti. **~less** *a* sdentato. **~paste** *n* dentifricio *m*. **~pick** *n* stuzzicadenti *m inv*

top¹ /tɒp/ n (toy) trottola f

top² n cima f; Sch primo, -a mf; (upper part or half) parte f superiore; (of page, list, street) inizio m; (upper surface) superficie f; (lid) coperchio m; (of bottle) tappo m; (garment) maglia f; (blouse) camicia f; Auto marcia f più alta; **at the ~ of** ~ fig al vertice; **at the ~ of one's voice** a squarciagola; **on ~/ on ~ of** sopra; **on ~ of that** (besides) per di più; **from ~ to bottom** da cima a fondo ● a in alto; (official, floor of building) superiore; (pupil, musician etc) migliore; (speed) massimo ● vt (pt/pp topped) essere in testa a (list); (exceed) sorpassare; **~ped with ice-cream** ricoperto di gelato. **top up** vt riempire

top: ~ **'floor** n ultimo piano m. ~ **hat** n cilindro m. ~**-heavy** a con la parte superiore sovraccarica

topic /ˈtɒpɪk/ n soggetto m; (of conversation) argomento m. ~**al** a d'attualità

top: ~**less** a & adv topless. ~**most** a più alto

topple /ˈtɒpl/ vt rovesciare ● vi rovesciarsi. **topple off** vi cadere

top-'secret a segretissimo, top secret inv

topsy-turvy /tɒpsɪˈtɜːvɪ/ a & adv sottosopra

torch /tɔːtʃ/ n torcia f [elettrica]; (flaming) fiaccola f

tore /tɔː(r)/ see **tear¹**

torment¹ /ˈtɔːment/ n tormento m

torment² /tɔːˈment/ vt tormentare

torn /tɔːn/ see **tear¹** ● a bucato

tornado /tɔːˈneɪdəʊ/ n (pl -es) tornado m inv

torpedo /tɔːˈpiːdəʊ/ n (pl -es) siluro m ● vt silurare

torrent /ˈtɒrənt/ n torrente m. ~**ial** /təˈrenʃl/ a (rain) torrenziale

torso /ˈtɔːsəʊ/ n torso m; (in art) busto m

tortoise /ˈtɔːtəs/ n tartaruga f

tortuous /ˈtɔːtʃʊəs/ a tortuoso

torture /ˈtɔːtʃə(r)/ n tortura f ● vt torturare

Tory /ˈtɔːrɪ/ a & n fam conservatore, -trice mf

toss /tɒs/ vt gettare; (into the air) lanciare in aria; (shake) scrollare; (horse:) disarcionare; mescolare (salad); rivoltare facendo saltare in aria (pancake); **~ a coin** fare testa o croce ● vi ~ **and turn** (in bed) rigirarsi; **let's ~ for it** facciamo testa o croce

tot¹ /tɒt/ n bimbetto, -a mf; (fam: of liquor) goccio m

tot² vt (pt/pp totted) **~ up** fam fare la somma di

total /ˈtəʊtl/ a totale ● n totale m ● vt (pt/pp totalled) ammontare a; (add up) sommare

totalitarian /təʊtælɪˈteərɪən/ a totalitario

totally /ˈtəʊtəlɪ/ adv totalmente

totter /ˈtɒtə(r)/ vi barcollare; (government:) vacillare

touch /tʌtʃ/ n tocco m; (sense) tatto m; (contact) contatto m; (trace) traccia f; (of irony, humour) tocco m; **get/be in ~** mettersi/essere in contatto ● vt toccare; (lightly) sfiorare; (equal) eguagliare; (fig: move) commuovere ● vi toccarsi. **touch down** vi Aeron atterrare. **touch on** vt fig accennare a. **touch up** vt ritoccare (painting)

touch|ing /ˈtʌtʃɪŋ/ a commovente. ~**y** a permaloso; (subject) delicato

tough /tʌf/ a duro; (severe, harsh) severo; (durable) resistente; (resilient) forte

toughen /ˈtʌfn/ vt rinforzare. **toughen up** vt rendere più forte (person)

tour /tʊə(r)/ n giro m; (of building, town) visita f; Theat, Sport tournée f inv; (of duty) servizio m ● vt fare un giro turistico; Theat essere in tournée

touris|m /ˈtʊərɪzm/ n turismo m. ~**t** /-rɪst/ n turista mf ● attrib turistico. ~**t office** n ufficio m turistico

tournament /'tʊənəmənt/ n torneo m

'tour operator n tour operator mf inv, operatore, -trice mf turistico

tousle /'taʊzl/ vt spettinare

tout /taʊt/ n (ticket ~) bagarino m; (horse-racing) informatore m • vi ~ **for** sollecitare

tow /təʊ/ n rimorchio m; **'on** ~' a rimorchio; **in** ~ fam al seguito • vt rimorchiare. **tow away** vt portare via col carro attrezzi

toward[s] /tə'wɔːd(z)/ prep verso (with respect to) nei riguardi di

towel /'taʊəl/ n asciugamano m. ~**ling** n spugna f

tower /'taʊə(r)/ n torre f • vi ~ **above** dominare. ~ **block** n palazzone m. ~**ing** a torreggiante; (rage) violento

town /taʊn/ n città f inv. ~ **hall** n municipio m

tow: ~**path** n strada f alzaia. ~**rope** n cavo m da rimorchio

toxic /'tɒksɪk/ a tossico

toxin /'tɒksɪn/ n tossina f

toy /tɔɪ/ n giocattolo m. ~**shop** n negozio m di giocattoli. **toy with** vt giocherellare con

trace /treɪs/ n traccia f • vt seguire le tracce di; (find) rintracciare; (draw) tracciare; (with tracing-paper) ricalcare

track /træk/ n traccia f, (path, Sport) pista f, Rail binario m; **keep** ~ **of** tenere d'occhio • vt seguire le tracce di. **track down** vt scovare

'track: ~**ball** n Comput trackball f inv. ~**suit** n tuta f da ginnastica

tractor /'træktə(r)/ n trattore m

trade /treɪd/ n commercio m; (line of business) settore m; (craft) mestiere m; **by** ~ di mestiere • vt commerciare; ~ **sth for sth** scambiare qcsa per qcsa • vi commerciare. **trade in** vt (give in part exchange) dare in pagamento parziale

'trade mark n marchio m di fabbrica

trader /'treɪdə(r)/ n commerciante mf

trade: ~**sman** n (joiner etc) operaio m. ~ **union** n sindacato m. ~ **'unionist** n sindacalista mf

trading /'treɪdɪŋ/ n commercio m. ~ **estate** n zona f industriale

tradition /trə'dɪʃn/ n tradizione f. ~**al** a tradizionale. ~**ally** adv tradizionalmente

traffic /'træfɪk/ n traffico m • vi (pt/pp **trafficked**) trafficare

traffic: ~ **circle** n Am isola f rotatoria. ~ **jam** n ingorgo m. ~ **lights** npl semaforo msg. ~ **warden** n vigile m [urbano]; (woman) vigilessa f

tragedy /'trædʒədi/ n tragedia f

tragic /'trædʒɪk/ a tragico. ~**ally** adv tragicamente

trail /treɪl/ n traccia f; (path) sentiero m • vi strisciare; (plant:) arrampicarsi; ~ **[behind]** rimanere indietro; (in competition) essere in svantaggio • vt trascinare

trailer /'treɪlə(r)/ n Auto rimorchio m; (Am: caravan) roulotte f inv; (film) presentazione f (di un film)

train /treɪn/ n treno m; ~ **of thought** filo m dei pensieri • vt formare professionalmente; Sport allenare; (aim) puntare; educare (child); addestrare (animal, soldier) • vi fare il tirocinio; Sport allenarsi. ~**ed** a (animal) addestrato (to do a rare)

trainee /treɪ'niː/ n apprendista mf

trainer /'treɪnə(r)/ n Sport allenatore, -trice mf; (in circus) domatore, -trice mf; (of dog, racehorse) addestratore, -trice mf; ~**ors** pl scarpe fpl da ginnastica. ~**ing** n tirocinio m; Sport allenamento m; (of animal, soldier) addestramento m

traipse /treɪps/ vi ~ **around** fam andare in giro

trait /treɪt/ n caratteristica f

traitor /'treɪtə(r)/ n traditore, -trice mf

tram | tray 594

tram /træm/ n tram m inv. **~-lines** npl rotaie fpl del tram

tramp /træmp/ n (hike) camminata f; (vagrant) barbone, -a mf; (of feet) calpestio m ● vi camminare con passo pesante; (hike) percorrere a piedi

trample /'træmpl/ vt/i ~ [on] calpestare

trampoline /'træmpəli:n/ n trampolino m

trance /trɑ:ns/ n trance f inv

tranquil /'træŋkwɪl/ a tranquillo. **~lity** /-'kwɪlətɪ/ n tranquillità f **~lizer** /'træŋkwɪlaɪzə(r)/ n tranquillante m

transact /træn'zækt/ vt trattare. **~ion** /-ækʃn/ n transazione f

transatlantic /trænzət'læntɪk/ a transatlantico

transcend /træn'send/ vt trascendere

transfer¹ /'trænsfɜ:(r)/ n trasferimento m; Sport cessione f; (design) decalcomania f

transfer² /træns'fɜ:(r)/ v (pt/pp transferred) ● vt trasferire; Sport cedere ● vi trasferirsi; (when travelling) cambiare. **~able** /-əbl/ a trasferibile

transform /træns'fɔ:m/ vt trasformare. **~ation** /-fə'meɪʃn/ n trasformazione f. **~er** n trasformatore m

transfusion /træns'fju:ʒn/ n trasfusione f

transient /'trænzɪənt/ a passeggero

transistor /træn'zɪstə(r)/ n transistor m inv; (radio) radiolina f a transistor

transit /'trænzɪt/ n transito m; **in** ~ (goods) in transito

transition /træn'zɪʃn/ n transizione f. **~al** /-l/ a di transizione

transitive /'trænzɪtɪv/ a transitivo

transitory /'trænzɪtərɪ/ a transitorio

translate /trænz'leɪt/ vt tradurre. **~ion** /-'leɪʃn/ n traduzione f. **~or** n traduttore, -trice mf

transmission /trænz'mɪʃn/ n trasmissione f

transmit /trænz'mɪt/ vt (pt/pp transmitted) trasmettere. **~ter** n trasmettitore m

transparen|cy /træn'spærənsɪ/ n Phot diapositiva f. **~t** a trasparente

transpire /træn'spaɪə(r)/ vi emergere; (fam: happen) accadere

transplant¹ /'trænsplɑ:nt/ n trapianto m

transplant² /træns'plɑ:nt/ vt trapiantare

transport¹ /'trænspɔ:t/ n trasporto m

transport² /træn'spɔ:t/ vt trasportare. **~ation** /-'teɪʃn/ n trasporto m

transvestite /trænz'vestaɪt/ n travestito, -a mf

trap /træp/ n trappola f; (fam: mouth) boccaccia f ● vt (pt/pp trapped) intrappolare; schiacciare (finger in door). **~'door** n botola f

trapeze /trə'pi:z/ n trapezio m

trash /træʃ/ n robaccia f; (rubbish) spazzatura f; (nonsense) sciocchezze fpl. **~can** n Am secchio m della spazzatura. **~y** a scadente

trauma /'trɔ:mə/ n trauma m. **~tic** /-'mætɪk/ a traumatico. **~tize** /-taɪz/ traumatizzare

travel /'trævl/ n viaggi mpl ● v (pt/pp travelled) ● vi viaggiare; (to work) andare ● vt percorrere (distance). **~ agency** n agenzia f di viaggi. **~ agent** n agente mf di viaggio

traveller /'trævələ(r)/ n viaggiatore, -trice mf; Comm commesso m viaggiatore; **~s** pl (gypsies) zingari mpl. **~'s cheque** n traveller's cheque m inv

trawler /'trɔ:lə(r)/ n peschereccio m

tray /treɪ/ n vassoio m; (for baking) teglia f; (for documents) vaschetta f sparticarta; (of printer, photocopier) vassoio m

treacher|ous /'tretʃərəs/ a traditore; (*weather, currents*) pericoloso. **~y** n tradimento m

treacle /'tri:kl/ n melassa f

tread /tred/ n andatura f; (*step*) gradino m; (*of tyre*) battistrada m inv ● v (pt **trod**, pp **trodden**) ● vi (*walk*) camminare. **tread on** vt calpestare (*grass*); pestare (*foot*)

treason /'tri:zn/ n tradimento m

treasure /'treʒə(r)/ n tesoro m ● vt tenere in gran conto. **~r** n tesoriere, -a mf

treasury /'treʒəri/ n the **T~** il Ministero del Tesoro

treat /tri:t/ n piacere m; (*present*) regalo m; **give sb a ~** fare una sorpresa a qcno ● vt trattare; Med curare; **~ sb to sth** offrire qcsa a qcno

treatise /'tri:tiz/ n trattato m

treatment /'tri:tmənt/ n trattamento m; Med cura f

treaty /'tri:ti/ n trattato m

treble /'trebl/ a triplo ● n Mus (*voice*) voce f bianca ● vt triplicare ● vi triplicarsi. **~ clef** n chiave f di violino

tree /tri:/ n albero m

trek /trek/ n scarpinata f; (*as holiday*) trekking m inv ● vi (pt/pp **trekked**) farsi una scarpinata; (*on holiday*) fare trekking

tremble /'trembl/ vi tremare

tremendous /trɪ'mendəs/ a (*huge*) enorme; (*fam: excellent*) formidabile. **~ly** adv (*very*) straordinariamente; (*a lot*) enormemente

tremor /'tremə(r)/ n tremito m; (*earth~*) scossa f [sismica]

trench /trentʃ/ n fosso m; Mil trincea f. **~ coat** n trench m inv

trend /trend/ n tendenza f; (*fashion*) moda f. **~y** a (-ier, -iest) fam di o alla moda

trepidation /trepɪ'deɪʃn/ n trepidazione f

trespass /'trespəs/ vi **~ on** introdursi abusivamente in; fig abusare di. **~er** n intruso, -a mf

trial /'traɪəl/ n Jur processo m;

(*test, ordeal*) prova f; **on ~** in prova; Jur in giudizio; **by ~ and error** per tentativi

triang|le /'traɪæŋgl/ n triangolo m. **~ular** /-'æŋgjʊlə(r)/ a triangolare

tribe /traɪb/ n tribù f inv

tribulation /trɪbjʊ'leɪʃn/ n tribolazione f

tribunal /traɪ'bju:nl/ n tribunale m

tributary /'trɪbjʊtəri/ n affluente m

tribute /'trɪbju:t/ n tributo m; **pay ~** rendere omaggio

trice /traɪs/ n **in a ~** in un attimo

trick /trɪk/ n trucco m; (*joke*) scherzo m; (*in cards*) presa f; **do the ~** fam funzionare; **play a ~ on** fare uno scherzo a ● vt imbrogliare

trickle /'trɪkl/ vi colare

trick|ster /'trɪkstə(r)/ n imbroglione, -a mf. **~y** a (-ier, -iest) a (*operation*) complesso; (*situation*) delicato

tricycle /'traɪsɪkl/ n triciclo m

tried /traɪd/ *see* **try**

trifle /'traɪfl/ n inezia f; Culin zuppa f inglese. **~ing** a insignificante

trigger /'trɪgə(r)/ n grilletto m ● vt **~ [off]** scatenare

trigonometry /trɪgə'nɒmɪtri/ n trigonometria f

trim /trɪm/ a (**trimmer, trimmest**) curato; (*figure*) snello ● n (*of hair, hedge*) spuntata f; (*decoration*) rifinitura f; **in good ~** in buono stato; (*person*) in forma ● vt (pt/pp **trimmed**) spuntare (*hair etc*); (*decorate*) ornare; Naut orientare. **~ming** n bordo m; **~mings** pl (*decorations*) guarnizioni fpl; **with all the ~mings** Culin guarnito

trinket /'trɪŋkɪt/ n ninnolo m

trio /'tri:əʊ/ n trio m

trip /trɪp/ n (*excursion*) gita f; (*journey*) viaggio m; (*stumble*) passo m falso ● v (pt/pp **tripped**) ● vt far inciampare ● vi inciampare (**on/over** in). **trip up** vt far inciampare

tripe /traɪp/ n trippa f; (*sl: nonsense*) fesserie fpl

triple /ˈtrɪpl/ a triplo ● vt triplicare ● vi triplicarsi

triplets /ˈtrɪplɪts/ npl tre gemelli mpl

triplicate /ˈtrɪplɪkət/ n **in** ~ in triplice copia

tripod /ˈtraɪpɒd/ n treppiede m inv

tripper /ˈtrɪpə(r)/ n gitante mf

trite /traɪt/ a banale

triumph /ˈtraɪʌmf/ n trionfo m ● vi trionfare (**over** su). ~**ant** /-ˈʌmf(ə)nt/ a trionfante. ~**antly** adv (exclaim) con tono trionfante

trivial /ˈtrɪvɪəl/ a insignificante. ~**ity** /-ˈæləti/ n banalità f inv

trod, trodden /trɒd, ˈtrɒdn/ see **tread**

trolley /ˈtrɒlɪ/ n carrello m; (Am: tram) tram m inv. ~ **bus** n filobus m inv

trombone /trɒmˈbəʊn/ n trombone m

troop /truːp/ n gruppo m; ~**s** pl truppe fpl ● vi ~ **in/out** entrare/ uscire in gruppo

trophy /ˈtrəʊfɪ/ n trofeo m

tropic /ˈtrɒpɪk/ n tropico m; ~**s** pl tropici mpl. ~**al** a tropicale

trot /trɒt/ n trotto m ● vi (pt/pp **trotted**) trottare

trouble /ˈtrʌbl/ n guaio m; (difficulties) problemi mpl; (inconvenience, Med) disturbo m; (conflict) conflitto m; **be in** ~ essere nei guai; (swimmer, climber:) essere in difficoltà; **get into** ~ finire nei guai; **get sb into** ~ mettere qcno nei guai; **take the** ~ **to do sth** darsi la pena di far qcsa ● vt (worry) preoccupare; (inconvenience) disturbare; (conscience, old wound:) tormentare ● vi **don't** ~! non ti disturbare!. ~**-maker** n be a ~-maker seminare zizzania. ~**some** /-səm/ a fastidioso

trough /trɒf/ n trogolo m; (atmospheric) depressione f

trounce /traʊns/ vt (in competition) schiacciare

troupe /truːp/ n troupe f inv

trousers /ˈtraʊzəz/ npl pantaloni mpl

trout /traʊt/ n inv trota f

trowel /ˈtraʊəl/ n (for gardening) paletta f; (for builder) cazzuola f

truant /ˈtruːənt/ n **play** ~ marinare la scuola

truce /truːs/ n tregua f

truck /trʌk/ n (lorry) camion m inv

trudge /trʌdʒ/ n camminata f faticosa ● vi arrancare

true /truː/ a vero; **come** ~ avverarsi

truffle /ˈtrʌfl/ n tartufo m

truism /ˈtruːɪzm/ n truismo m ~ distinti saluti

truly /ˈtruːlɪ/ adv veramente; **Yours** ~ distinti saluti

trump /trʌmp/ n (in cards) atout m inv

trumpet /ˈtrʌmpɪt/ n tromba f. ~**er** n trombettista m f

truncheon /ˈtrʌntʃn/ n manganello m

trunk /trʌŋk/ n (of tree, body) tronco m; (of elephant) proboscide f; (for travelling, storage) baule m; (Am: of car) bagagliaio m; ~**s** pl calzoncini mpl da bagno

truss /trʌs/ n Med cinto m erniario

trust /trʌst/ n fiducia f; (group of companies) trust m inv; (organization) associazione f; **on** ~ sulla parola ● vt fidarsi di; (hope) augurarsi ● vi ~ **in** credere in; ~ **to** affidarsi a. ~**ed** a fidato

trustee /trʌsˈtiː/ n amministratore, -trice mf fiduciario, -a

trust'ful /ˈtrʌstfl/ a fiducioso. ~**ing** a fiducioso. ~**worthy** a fidato

truth /truːθ/ n (pl -s /ˈtruːðz/) verità f inv. ~**ful** a veritiero. ~**fully** adv sinceramente

try /traɪ/ n tentativo m, prova f; (in rugby) meta f ● v (pt/pp **tried**) ● vt provare; (be a strain on) mettere a dura prova; Jur processare (person); discutere (case); ~ **to do sth** provare a fare qcsa ● vi provare. **try on** vt provarsi (garment). **try out** vt provare

trying /'traɪɪŋ/ a duro; ⟨person⟩ irritante

T-shirt /'tiː-/ n maglietta f

tub /tʌb/ n tinozza f; ⟨carton⟩ vaschetta f; ⟨bath⟩ vasca f da bagno

tuba /'tjuːbə/ n Mus tuba f

tubby /'tʌbɪ/ a (-ier, -iest) tozzo

tube /tjuːb/ n tubo m; ⟨of toothpaste⟩ tubetto m; Rail metro f

tuber /'tjuːbə(r)/ n tubero m

tuberculosis /tjuːbɜːkjʊ'ləʊsɪs/ n tubercolosi f

tubular /'tjuːbjʊlə(r)/ a tubolare

tuck /tʌk/ n piega f ● vt ⟨put⟩ infilare. **tuck in** vt rimboccare; ~ **sb in** rimboccare le coperte a qcno ● vi ⟨fam: eat⟩ mangiare con appetito. **tuck up** vt rimboccarsi ⟨sleeves⟩; ⟨in bed⟩ rimboccare le coperte a

Tuesday /'tjuːzdeɪ/ n martedì m inv

tuft /tʌft/ n ciuffo m

tug /tʌg/ n strattone m; Naut rimorchiatore m ● v (pt/pp **tugged**) ● vt tirare ● vi dare uno strattone. ~ **of war** n tiro m alla fune

tuition /tjuː'ɪʃn/ n lezioni fpl

tulip /'tjuːlɪp/ n tulipano m

tumble /'tʌmbl/ n ruzzolone m ● vi ruzzolare. ~**down** a cadente. ~**drier** n asciugabiancheria f

tumbler /'tʌmblə(r)/ n bicchiere m ⟨senza stelo⟩

tummy /'tʌmɪ/ n fam pancia f

tumour /'tjuːmə(r)/ n tumore m

tumult /'tjuːmʌlt/ n tumulto m. ~**uous** /-'mʌltjʊəs/ a tumultuoso

tuna /'tjuːnə/ n tonno m

tune /tjuːn/ n motivo m; **out of** ~ ⟨instrument⟩ scordato/accordato; ⟨person⟩ stonato/intonato; **to the** ~ **of** fam per la modesta somma di ● vt accordare ⟨instrument⟩; sintonizzare ⟨radio, TV⟩; mettere a punto ⟨engine⟩. **tune in** vt sintonizzare ● vi sintonizzarsi ⟨to su⟩. **tune up** vi ⟨orchestra⟩ accordare gli strumenti

tuneful /'tjuːnfl/ a melodioso

tuner /'tjuːnə(r)/ n accordatore,

-trice mf; Radio, TV sintonizzatore m

tunic /'tjuːnɪk/ n tunica f; Mil giacca f; Sch ≈ grembiule m

Tunisia /tjuː'nɪzɪə/ n Tunisia f. ~**n** a & n tunisino, -a mf

tunnel /'tʌnl/ n tunnel m inv ● vi (pt/pp **tunnelled**) scavare un tunnel

turban /'tɜːbən/ n turbante m

turbine /'tɜːbaɪn/ n turbina f

turbulen|ce /'tɜːbjʊləns/ n turbolenza f. ~**t** a turbolento

turf /tɜːf/ n erba f; ⟨segment⟩ zolla f erbosa ● **turf out** vt fam buttar fuori

Turin /tjuː'rɪn/ n Torino f

Turk /tɜːk/ n turco, -a mf

turkey /'tɜːkɪ/ n tacchino m

Turkey n Turchia f. ~**ish** a turco

turmoil /'tɜːmɔɪl/ n tumulto m

turn /tɜːn/ n ⟨rotation, short walk⟩ giro m; ⟨in road⟩ svolta f, curva f; ⟨development⟩ svolta f; Theat numero m; ⟨fam: attack⟩ crisi f inv; ~ **for the better/worse** un miglioramento/peggioramento; **do sb a good** ~ rendere un servizio a qcno; **take** ~ fare a turno; **in** ~ a turno; **out of** ~ ⟨speak⟩ a sproposito; **it's your** ~ tocca a te ● vi girare; voltare ⟨back, eyes⟩; dirigere ⟨gun, attention⟩ ● vi girare; ⟨person⟩ girarsi; ⟨leaves⟩ ingiallire; ⟨become⟩ diventare; ~ **right/left** girare a destra/sinistra; ~ **sour** inacidirsi; ~ **to sb** girarsi verso qcno; fig rivolgersi a qcno. **turn against** vi diventare ostile a ● vt mettere contro. **turn away** vt mandare via ⟨people⟩; girare dall'altra parte ⟨head⟩ ● vi girarsi dall'altra parte. **turn down** vt piegare ⟨collar⟩; abbassare ⟨heat, gas, sound⟩; respingere ⟨person, proposal⟩. **turn in** vt ripiegare in dentro ⟨edges⟩; consegnare ⟨lost object⟩ ● vi ⟨fam: go to bed⟩ andare a letto; ~ **into** vt/i drive entrare nel viale. **turn off** vt spegnere; chiudere ⟨tap, water⟩ ● vi girare;

girare. **turn on** *vt* accendere; aprire ⟨*tap, water*⟩; ⟨*fam: attract*⟩ eccitare ● *vi* ⟨*attack*⟩ attaccare. **turn out** *vt* ⟨*expel*⟩ mandar via; spegnere ⟨*light, gas*⟩; ⟨*produce*⟩ produrre; ⟨*empty*⟩ svuotare ⟨*room, cupboard*⟩ ● *vi* ⟨*transpire*⟩ risultare; ~ **out well/badly** ⟨*cake, dress*⟩: riuscire bene/male; ⟨*situation*:⟩ andare bene/male. **turn over** *vt* girare ● *vi* girarsi; **please ~ over** vedi retro. **turn round** *vt* girare ⟨*car*:⟩ girare. **turn up** *vt* tirare su ⟨*collar*⟩; alzare ⟨*heat, gas, sound, radio*⟩ ● *vi* farsi vedere

turning /'tɜːnɪŋ/ *n* svolta *f*. **~-point** *n* svolta *f* decisiva

turnip /'tɜːnɪp/ *n* rapa *f*

turn-: **~out** *n* ⟨*of people*⟩ affluenza *f*. **~over** *n* Comm giro *m* d'affari; ⟨*of staff*⟩ ricambio *m*. **~pike** *n Am* autostrada *f*. **~stile** *n* cancelletto *m* girevole. **~table** *n* piattaforma *f* girevole; ⟨*on record-player*⟩ piatto *m* ⟨*di giradischi*⟩. **~up** *n* ⟨*of trousers*⟩ risvolto *m*

turpentine /'tɜːpəntam/ *n* trementina *f*

turquoise /'tɜːkwɔɪz/ *a* ⟨*colour*⟩ turchese ● *n* turchese *m*

turret /'tʌrɪt/ *n* torretta *f*

turtle /'tɜːtl/ *n* tartaruga *f* acquatica

tusk /tʌsk/ *n* zanna *f*

tussle /'tʌsl/ *n* zuffa *f* ● *vi* azzuffarsi

tutor /'tjuːtə(r)/ *n* insegnante *mf* privato, -a; *Univ* insegnante *mf* universitario, -a *che segue individualmente un ristretto numero di studenti*. **~ial** /-'tɔːrɪəl/ *n* discussione *f* col tutor

tuxedo /tʌk'siːdəʊ/ *n Am* smoking *m inv*

TV *n abbr* ⟨**television**⟩ tv *f inv*, tivù *f inv*

twaddle /'twɒdl/ *n* scemenze *fpl*

twang /twæŋ/ *n* ⟨*in voice*⟩ suono *m* nasale ● *vt* far vibrare

tweed /twiːd/ *n* tweed *m inv*

tweezers /'twiːzəz/ *npl* pinzette *fpl*

twelfth /twelfθ/ *a* dodicesimo

twelve /twelv/ *a* dodici

twentieth /'twentɪθ/ *a* ventesimo

twenty /'twentɪ/ *a* venti

twerp /twɜːp/ *n fam* stupido, -a *mf*

twice /twaɪs/ *adv* due volte

twiddle /'twɪdl/ *vt* giocherellare con; ~ **one's thumbs** *fig* girarsi i pollici

twig¹ /twɪg/ *n* ramoscello *m*

twig² /twɪg/ *vt/i* ⟨*pt/pp* **twigged**⟩ *fam* intuire

twilight /'twaɪ-/ *n* crepuscolo *m*

twin /twɪn/ *n* gemello, -a *mf* ● *attrib* gemello. ~ **beds** *npl* letti *mpl* gemelli

twine /twaɪn/ *n* spago *m* ● *vi* intrecciarsi; ⟨*plant*:⟩ attorcigliarsi ● *vt* intrecciare

twinge /twɪndʒ/ *n* fitta *f*; ~ **of conscience** rimorso *m* di coscienza

twinkle /'twɪŋkl/ *n* scintillio *m* ● *vi* scintillare

twin 'town *n* città *f inv* gemellata

twirl /twɜːl/ *vt* far roteare ● *vi* volteggiare ● *n* piroetta *f*

twist /twɪst/ *n* torsione *f*; ⟨*curve*⟩ curva *f*; ⟨*in rope*⟩ attorcigliata *f*; ⟨*in book, plot*⟩ colpo *m* di scena ● *vt* attorcigliare ⟨*rope*⟩; torcere ⟨*metal*⟩; girare ⟨*knob, cap*⟩; ⟨*distort*⟩ distorcere; ~ **one's ankle** storcersi la caviglia ● *vi* attorcigliarsi; ⟨*road*:⟩ essere pieno di curve

twit /twɪt/ *n fam* cretino, -a *mf*

twitch /twɪtʃ/ *n* tic *m inv*; ⟨*jerk*⟩ strattone *m* ● *vi* contrarsi

twitter /'twɪtə(r)/ *n* cinguettio *m* ● *vi* cinguettare; ⟨*person*:⟩ cianciare

two /tuː/ *a* due

two-: **~-faced** *a* falso. **~-piece** *a* ⟨*swimsuit*⟩ due pezzi *m inv*; ⟨*suit*⟩ completo *m*. **~some** /-səm/ *n* coppia *f*. **~-way** *a* ⟨*traffic*⟩ a doppio senso di marcia

tycoon /taɪ'kuːn/ *n* magnate *m*

tying /'taɪɪŋ/ *see* **tie**

type /taɪp/ *n* tipo *m*; ⟨*printing*⟩ carattere *m* [tipografico] ● *vt* scrivere a macchina ● *vi* scrivere a macchina. **~writer** *n* macchina *f* da scrivere. **~written** *a* dattiloscritto

typhoid /'taɪfɔɪd/ *n* febbre *f* tifoidea

typical /'tɪpɪkl/ *a* tipico. **~ly** *adv* tipicamente; *(as usual)* come al solito

typify /'tɪpɪfaɪ/ *vt (pt/pp* -ied) essere tipico di

typing /'taɪpɪŋ/ *n* dattilografia *f*

typist /'taɪpɪst/ *n* dattilografo, -a *mf*

typography /taɪ'pɒgrəfɪ/ *n* tipografia *f*

tyrannical /tɪ'rænɪkl/ *a* tirannico

tyranny /'tɪrənɪ/ *n* tirannia *f*

tyrant /'taɪrənt/ *n* tiranno, -a *mf*

tyre /'taɪə(r)/ *n* gomma *f*, pneumatico *m*

Uu

ubiquitous /ju:'bɪkwɪtəs/ *a* onnipresente

udder /'ʌdə(r)/ *n* mammella *f* (*di vacca, capra etc*)

ugliness /'ʌglɪnɪs/ *n* bruttezza *f*. **~y** *a* (**-ier**, **-iest**) brutto

UK *n abbr* **United Kingdom**

ulcer /'ʌlsə(r)/ *n* ulcera *f*

ulterior /ʌl'tɪərɪə(r)/ *a* **~ motive** secondo fine *m*

ultimate /'ʌltɪmət/ *a* definitivo; *(final)* finale; *(fundamental)* fondamentale. **~ly** *adv* alla fine

ultimatum /ʌltɪ'meɪtəm/ *n* ultimatum *m inv*

ultrasound /'ʌltrə-/ *n Med* ecografia *f*

ultra'violet *a* ultravioletto

umbilical /ʌm'bɪlɪkl/ *a* **~ cord** cordone *m* ombelicale

umbrella /ʌm'brelə/ *n* ombrello *m*

umpire /'ʌmpaɪə(r)/ *n* arbitro *m* ● *vt/i* arbitrare

umpteen /ʌmp'ti:n/ *a fam* innumerevole. **~th** *a fam* ennesimo; **for the ~th time** per l'ennesima volta

UN *n abbr* (**United Nations**) ONU *f*

un'able /ʌn-/ *a* **be ~ to do sth** non potere fare qcsa; *(not know how)* non sapere fare qcsa

una'bridged *a* integrale

unac'companied *a* non accompagnato; *(luggage)* incustodito

unac'countable *a* inspiegabile. **~y** *adv* inspiegabilmente

unac'customed *a* insolito; **be ~ to** non essere abituato a

una'dulterated *a (water)* puro; *(wine)* non sofisticato; *fig* assoluto

un'aided *a* senza aiuto

unanimity /ju:nə'nɪmətɪ/ *n* unanimità *f*

unanimous /ju:'nænɪməs/ *a* unanime. **~ly** *adv* all'unanimità

un'armed *a* disarmato; **~ combat** *n* lotta *f* senza armi

unas'suming *a* senza pretese

unat'tached *a* staccato; *(person)* senza legami

unat'tended *a* incustodito

un'authorized *a* non autorizzato

una'voidable *a* inevitabile

una'ware *a* **be ~ of sth** non rendersi conto di qcsa. **~s** /-'eəz/ *adv* **catch sb ~s** prendere qcno alla sprovvista

un'balanced *a* non equilibrato; *(mentally)* squilibrato

un'bearable *a* insopportabile. **~y** *adv* insopportabilmente

unbeatable /ʌn'bi:təbl/ *a* imbattibile. **~en** *a* imbattuto

unbeknown /ʌnbɪ'nəʊn/ *a fam* **~ to me** a mia insaputa

unbe'lievable *a* incredibile

un'bend *vi (pt/pp* -bent) *(relax)* distendersi

un'biased *a* obiettivo

un'block *vt* sbloccare

un'bolt *vt* togliere il chiavistello di

un'breakable *a* infrangibile

un'bridled /ʌn'braɪdld/ *a* sfrenato

un'burden *vt* **~ oneself** *fig* sfogarsi (**to** con)

un'button vt sbottonare

uncalled-for /ʌnkɔːldfɔː(r)/ a fuori luogo

un'canny a sorprendente; ⟨silence, feeling⟩ inquietante

un'ceasing a incessante

uncere'monious a (abrupt) brusco. **~ly** adv senza tante cerimonie

un'certain a incerto; ⟨weather⟩ instabile; **in no ~ terms** senza mezzi termini. **~ty** n incertezza f

un'changed a invariato

un'charitable a duro

uncle /'ʌŋkl/ n zio m

un'comfortable a scomodo; imbarazzante ⟨silence, situation⟩; **feel ~e** fig sentirsi a disagio. **~y** adv ⟨sit⟩ scomodamente; ⟨causing alarm etc⟩ spaventosamente

un'common a insolito

un'compromising a intransigente

uncon'ditional a incondizionato. **~ly** adv incondizionatamente

un'conscious a privo di sensi; (unaware) inconsapevole; **be ~ of sth** non rendersi conto di qcsa. **~ly** adv inconsapevolmente

uncon'ventional a poco convenzionale

unco'operative a poco cooperativo

un'cork vt sturare

uncouth /ʌnˈkuːθ/ a zotico

un'cover vt scoprire; portare alla luce ⟨buried object⟩

unde'cided a indeciso; (not settled) incerto

undeniable /ʌndɪˈnaɪəbl/ a innegabile. **~y** adv innegabilmente

under /'ʌndə(r)/ prep sotto; (less than) al di sotto di; **~ there** lì sotto; **~ repair/construction** in riparazione/costruzione; **~ way** fig in corso ● adv ⟨• water⟩ sott'acqua; (unconscious) sotto anestesia

'undercarriage n Aeron carrello m

'underclothes npl biancheria fsg intima

'undercover a clandestino

'undercurrent n corrente f sottomarina; fig sottofondo m

under'cut vt (pt/pp -cut) Comm vendere a minor prezzo di

'underdog n perdente m

under'done a ⟨meat⟩ al sangue

under'estimate vt sottovalutare

under'fed a denutrito

under'foot adv sotto i piedi; **trample ~** calpestare

under'go vt (pt -went, pp -gone) subire ⟨operation, treatment⟩; **~ repair** essere in riparazione

under'graduate n studente, -tessa mf universitario, -a

'underground¹ adv sottoterra

'underground² a sotterraneo; (secret) clandestino ● n (railway) metropolitana f. **~ car park** n parcheggio m sotterraneo

'undergrowth n sottobosco m

'underhand a subdolo

'underlay n strato m di gomma o feltro posto sotto la moquette

under'lie vt (pt -lay, pp -lain, pres p -lying) fig essere alla base di

under'line vt sottolineare

underling /'ʌndəlɪŋ/ n pej subalterno, -a mf

under'lying a fig fondamentale

under'mine vt fig minare

underneath /ʌndəˈniːθ/ prep sotto; **~ it** sotto ● adv sotto

under'paid a mal pagato

'underpants npl mutande fpl

'underpass n sottopassaggio m

under'privileged a non abbiente

under'rate vt sottovalutare

'underseal n Auto antiruggine m inv

'undershirt n Am maglia f della pelle

under'staffed a a corto di personale

under'stand vt (pt/pp -stood) capire; **I ~ that...** ⟨have heard⟩ mi risulta che... ● vi capire. **~able** /-əbl/ a comprensibile. **~ably** /-əblɪ/ adv comprensibilmente

under'standing a comprensivo

●*n* comprensione *f*; (*agreement*) accordo *m*; **on the ~ that** a condizione che

'understatement *n* understatement *m inv*

'understudy *n Theat* sostituto, -a *mf*

under'take *vt* (*pt* **-took**, *pp* **-taken**) intraprendere; **~ to do sth** impegnarsi a fare qcsa

'undertaker *n* impresario *m* di pompe funebri; **[firm of] ~s** *n* impresa *f* di pompe funebri

under'taking *n* impresa *f*; (*promise*) promessa *f*

'undertone *n fig* sottofondo *m*; **in an ~** sottovoce

under'value *vt* sottovalutare

'underwater[1] *a* subacqueo

under'water[2] *adv* sott'acqua

'underwear *n* biancheria *f* intima

'underweight *a* sotto peso

'underworld *n* (*criminals*) malavita *f*

'underwriter *n* assicuratore *m*

unde'sirable *a* indesiderato; (*person*) poco raccomandabile

'undies /'ʌndɪz/ *npl fam* biancheria *fsg* intima (da donna)

un'dignified *a* non dignitoso

un'do *vt* (*pt* **-did**, *pp* **-done**) disfare; slacciare (*dress, shoes*); sbottonare (*shirt*); *fig, Comput* annullare

un'done *a* (*shirt button*) sbottonato; (*shoes, dress*) slacciato; (*not accomplished*) non fatto; **leave ~** (*job*) tralasciare

un'doubted *a* indubbio. **~ly** *adv* senza dubbio

un'dress *vt* spogliare; **get ~ed** spogliarsi ●*vi* spogliarsi

un'due *a* eccessivo

undulating /'ʌndjʊleɪtɪŋ/ *a* ondulato; (*country*) collinoso

'unduly *adv* eccessivamente

un'dying *a* eterno

un'earth *vt* dissotterrare; *fig* scovare; scoprire (*secret*). **~ly** *a* soprannaturale; **at an ~ly hour** *fam* a un'ora impossibile

un'easje *n* disagio *m*. **~y** *a* a disagio; (*person*) inquieto; (*feeling*) inquietante; (*truce*) precario

un'eatable *a* immangiabile

uneco'nomic *a* poco remunerativo

uneco'nomical *a* poco economico

unem'ployed *a* disoccupato ●*npl* **the ~** i disoccupati

unem'ployment *n* disoccupazione *f*. **~ benefit** *n* sussidio *m* di disoccupazione

un'ending *a* senza fine

un'equal *a* disuguale; (*struggle*) impari; **be ~ to a task** non essere all'altezza di un compito

unequivocal /ʌnɪ'kwɪvəkl/ *a* inequivocabile; (*person*) esplicito

unerring /ʌn'ɜːrɪŋ/ *a* infallibile

un'ethical *a* immorale

un'even *a* irregolare; (*distribution*) ineguale; (*number*) dispari

unex'pected *a* inaspettato. **~ly** *adv* inaspettatamente

un'failing *a* infallibile

un'fair *a* ingiusto. **~ly** *adv* ingiustamente. **~ness** *n* ingiustizia *f*

un'faithful *a* infedele

unfa'miliar *a* sconosciuto; **be ~ with** non conoscere

un'fasten *vt* slacciare; (*detach*) staccare

un'favourable *a* sfavorevole; (*impression*) negativo

un'feeling *a* insensibile

un'finished *a* da finire; (*business*) in sospeso

un'fit *a* inadatto; (*morally*) indegno; *Sport* fuori forma; **~ for work** non in grado di lavorare

un'flinching /ʌn'flɪntʃɪŋ/ *a* risoluto

un'fold *vt* spiegare; (*spread out*) aprire; *fig* rivelare ●*vi* (*view:*) spiegarsi

unfore'seen *a* imprevisto

unfor'gettable /ʌnfə'getəbl/ *a* indimenticabile

unfor'givable /ʌnfə'gɪvəbl/ *a* imperdonabile

un'fortunate *a* sfortunato; (*regret-*

table) spiacevole; ⟨*remark, choice*⟩ infelice. **~ly** *adv* purtroppo

un'founded *a* infondato

unfurl /ʌn'fɜ:l/ *vt* spiegare

un'furnished *a* non ammobiliato

ungainly /ʌn'geɪnlɪ/ *a* sgraziato

ungodly /ʌn'gɒdlɪ/ *a* empio; **~ hour** *fam* ora *f* impossibile

un'grateful *a* ingrato. **~ly** *adv* senza riconoscenza

un'happily *adv* infelicemente; (*unfortunately*) purtroppo. **~ness** *n* infelicità *f*

un'happy *a* infelice; (*not content*) insoddisfatto (**with** di)

un'harmed *a* incolume

un'healthy *a* poco sano; (*insanitary*) malsano

un'hook *vt* sganciare

un'hurt *a* illeso

unhy'gienic *a* non igienico

unification /ju:nɪfɪ'keɪʃn/ *n* unificazione *f*

uniform /'ju:nɪfɔ:m/ *a* uniforme ● *n* uniforme *f*. **~ly** *adv* uniformemente

unify /'ju:nɪfaɪ/ *vt* ⟨*pt/pp* **-ied**⟩ unificare

uni'lateral /ju:nɪ-/ *a* unilaterale

unim'aginable *a* inimmaginabile

unim'portant *a* irrilevante

unin'habited *a* disabitato

unin'tentional *a* involontario. **~ly** *adv* involontariamente

union /'ju:nɪən/ *n* unione *f*; (*trade ~*) sindacato *m*. **U~ Jack** *n* bandiera *f* del Regno Unito

unique /ju:'ni:k/ *a* unico. **~ly** *adv* unicamente

unison /'ju:nɪsn/ *n* **in ~** all'unisono

unit /'ju:nɪt/ *n* unità *f* *inv*; (*department*) reparto *m*; (*of furniture*) elemento *m*

unite /ju:'naɪt/ *vt* unire ● *vi* unirsi

united /ju:'naɪtɪd/ *a* unito. **U~ 'Kingdom** *n* Regno *m* Unito. **U~ 'Nations** *n* [Organizzazione *f* delle] Nazioni Unite *fpl*. **U~ States [of America]** *n* Stati *mpl* Uniti [d'America]

unity /'ju:nətɪ/ *n* unità *f*; (*agreement*) accordo *m*

universal /ju:nɪ'vɜ:sl/ *a* universale. **~ly** *adv* universalmente

universe /'ju:nɪvɜ:s/ *n* universo *m*

university /ju:nɪ'vɜ:sətɪ/ *n* università *f* ● *attrib* universitario

un'just *a* ingiusto

unkempt /ʌn'kempt/ *a* trasandato; ⟨*hair*⟩ arruffato

un'kind *a* scortese. **~ly** *adv* in modo scortese. **~ness** *n* mancanza *f* di gentilezza

un'known *a* sconosciuto

un'lawful *a* illecito, illegale

unleaded /ʌn'ledɪd/ *a* senza piombo

un'leash *vt fig* scatenare

unless /ən'les/ *conj* a meno che; **~ I am mistaken** se non mi sbaglio

un'like *a* (*not the same*) diversi ● *prep* diverso da; **that's ~ him** non è da lui; **~ me, he...** diversamente da me, lui...

un'likely *a* improbabile

un'limited *a* illimitato

un'load *vt* scaricare

un'lock *vt* aprire (*con chiave*)

un'lucky *a* sfortunato; **it's ~ to...** porta sfortuna...

un'manned *a* senza equipaggio

un'married *a* non sposato. **~ 'mother** *n* ragazza *f* madre

un'mask *vt fig* smascherare

unmistakab|le /ʌnmɪ'steɪkəbl/ *a* inconfondibile. **~y** *adv* chiaramente

un'mitigated *a* assoluto

un'natural *a* innaturale; *pej* anormale. **~ly** *adv* in modo innaturale; *pej* in modo anormale

un'necessar|y *a* inutile. **~ily** *adv* inutilmente

un'noticed *a* inosservato

unob'tainable *a* ⟨*product*⟩ introvabile; ⟨*phone number*⟩ non ottenibile

unob'trusive *a* discreto. **~ly** *adv* in modo discreto

unof'ficial *a* non ufficiale. **~ly** *adv* ufficiosamente

un'pack vi disfare le valigie ● vt svuotare (parcel); spacchettare (books); ~ **one's case** disfare la valigia

un'paid a da pagare; (work) non retribuito

un'palatable a sgradevole

un'paralleled a senza pari

un'pick vt disfare

un'pleasant a sgradevole; (person) maleducato. **~ly** adv sgradevolmente; (behave) maleducatamente. **~ness** n (bad feeling) tensioni fpl

un'plug vt (pt/pp -**plugged**) staccare

un'popular a impopolare

un'precedented a senza precedenti

unpre'dictable a imprevedibile

unpre'meditated a involontario

unpre'pared a impreparato

unpre'tentious a senza pretese

un'principled a senza principi; (behaviour) scorretto

unpro'fessional a non professionale; **it's ~** è una mancanza di professionalità

un'profitable a non redditizio

un'qualified a non qualificato; (fig: absolute) assoluto

un'questionable a incontestabile

un'quote vi chiudere le virgolette

unravel /ʌn'rævl/ vt (pt/pp -**ravelled**) districare; (in knitting) disfare

un'real a irreale; fam inverosimile

un'reasonable a irragionevole

unre'lated a (fact) senza rapporto (**to** con); (person) non imparentato (**to** con)

unre'liable a inattendibile; (person) inaffidabile, che non dà affidamento

unre'quited /ʌnrɪ'kwaɪtɪd/ a non corrisposto

unre'servedly /ʌnrɪ'zɜ:vɪdlɪ/ adv senza riserve; (frankly) francamente

un'rest n fermenti mpl

un'rivalled a ineguagliato

un'roll vt srotolare ● vi srotolarsi

unruly /ʌn'ru:lɪ/ a indisciplinato

un'safe a pericoloso

un'said a inespresso

un'salted a non salato

unsatis'factory a poco soddisfacente

un'savoury a equivoco

unscathed /ʌn'skeɪðd/ a illeso

un'screw vt svitare

un'scrupulous a senza scrupoli

un'seemly a indecoroso

un'selfish a disinteressato

un'settled a in agitazione; (weather) variabile; (bill) non saldato

unshakeable /ʌn'ʃeɪkəbl/ a categorico

unshaven /ʌn'ʃeɪvn/ a non rasato

un'sightly a brutto

un'skilled a non specializzato. ~ **worker** n manovale m

un'sociable a scontroso

unso'phisticated a semplice

un'sound a (building, reasoning) poco solido; (advice) poco sensato; **of ~ mind** malato di mente

unspeakable /ʌn'spi:kəbl/ a indicibile

un'stable a instabile; (mentally) squilibrato

un'steady a malsicuro

un'stuck a **come ~** staccarsi; (fam: project) andare a monte

unsuc'cessful a fallimentare; **be ~** (in attempt) non aver successo. **~ly** adv senza successo

un'suitable a (inappropriate) inadatto; (inconvenient) inopportuno

unsu'specting a fiducioso

un'thinkable /ʌn'θɪŋkəbl/ a impensabile

un'tidiness n disordine m

un'tidy a disordinato

un'tie vt slegare

until /ʌn'tɪl/ prep fino a; **not ~** non prima di; ~ **the evening** fino alla sera; ~ **his arrival** fino al suo arrivo ● conj finché, fino a quando; **not ~ you've seen it** non prima che tu l'abbia visto

untimely /ʌn'taɪmlɪ/ a inopportuno; (premature) prematuro

un'tiring a instancabile

un'told a (wealth) incalcolabile; (suffering) indescrivibile; (story) inedito

unto'ward a if nothing ~ happens se non capita un imprevisto

un'true a falso; that's ~ non è vero

unused[1] /ʌn'juːzd/ a non [ancora] usato

unused[2] /ʌn'juːst/ a be ~ to non essere abituato a

un'usual a insolito. ~ly adv insolitamente

un'veil vt scoprire

un'wanted a indesiderato

un'warranted a ingiustificato

un'welcome a sgradito

un'well a indisposto

unwieldy /ʌn'wiːldɪ/ a ingombrante

un'willing a riluttante. ~ly adv malvolentieri

un'wind v (pt/pp **unwound**) ● vt svolgere, srotolare ● vi svolgersi, srotolarsi; (fam: relax) rilassarsi

un'wise a imprudente

unwitting /ʌn'wɪtɪŋ/ a involontario; (victim) inconsapevole. ~ly adv involontariamente

un'worthy a non degno

un'wrap vt (pt/pp **-wrapped**) scartare (present, parcel)

un'written a tacito

up /ʌp/ adv su; (not in bed) alzato; (road) smantellato; (theatre curtain, blinds) alzato; (shelves, tent) montato; (notice) affisso; (building) costruito; prices are up i prezzi sono aumentati; be up for sale essere in vendita; up here quassù/lassù; time's up tempo scaduto; what's up? fam cosa è successo?; up to (as far as) fino a; be up to essere all'altezza di (task); what's he up to? fam cosa sta facendo?; (plotting) cosa sta combinando?; I'm up to page 100 sono arrivato a pagina 100; feel up to it sentirsela; be one up on sb fam essere in vantaggio su qcno; go up salire; lift up alzare; up against fig ale prese con ● prep su; the cat ran/is up the tree il gatto è salito di corsa/è sull'albero; further up this road più avanti su questa strada; row up the river risalire il fiume; go up the stairs salire su per le scale; be up the pub fam essere al pub; be up on or in sth essere bene informato su qcsa ● n ups and downs npl alti mpl e bassi

upbringing n educazione f

up'date[1] vt aggiornare

'update[2] n aggiornamento m

up'grade vt promuovere (person); modernizzare (equipment)

upgradeable /ʌp'greɪdəbl/ a Comput upgradabile

upheaval /ʌp'hiːvl/ n scompiglio m

up'hill a in salita; fig arduo ● adv in salita

up'hold vt (pt/pp **upheld**) sostenere (principle); confermare (verdict)

upholster /ʌp'həʊlstə(r)/ vt tappezzare. ~er n tappezziere, -a mf. ~y n tappezzeria f

'upkeep n mantenimento m

up-'market a di qualità

upon /ə'pɒn/ prep su; ~ arriving home una volta arrivato a casa

upper /'ʌpə(r)/ a superiore ● n (of shoe) tomaia f

upper: ~ circle n seconda galleria f. ~ class n alta borghesia f. ~ hand n have the ~ hand avere il sopravvento. ~most a più alto; that's ~most in my mind è la mia preoccupazione principale

upright a dritto; (piano) verticale; (honest) retto ● n montante m

uprising n rivolta f

uproar n tumulto m; be in an ~ essere in trambusto

up'root vt sradicare

up'set[1] vt (pt/pp **upset**, pres p **upsetting**) rovesciare; sconvolge re ⟨plan⟩; ⟨distress⟩ turbare; **get ~ about sth** prendersela per' qcsa; **be very ~** essere sconvolto; **have an ~ stomach** avere l'intestino disturbato

'**upset**² n scombussolamento m

'**upshot** n risultato m

upside 'down adv sottosopra; **turn ~ ~** capovolgere

up'**stairs**¹ adv [al piano] di sopra

up'**stairs**² a del piano superiore

'**upstart** n arrivato, -a mf

'**upstream** adv controcorrente

'**upsurge** n ⟨in sales⟩ aumento m improvviso; ⟨of enthusiasm, crime⟩ ondata f

'**uptake** n **be slow on the ~** essere lento nel capire; **be quick on the ~** capire le cose al volo

up'**tight** a teso

up-to-'**date** a moderno; ⟨news⟩ ultimo; ⟨records⟩ aggiornato

'**upturn** n ripresa f

'**upward** /'Apwəd/ a verso l'alto, in su; **~ slope** salita f ● adv **~[s]** verso l'alto; **~s of** oltre

u**ranium** /ju'reɪnɪəm/ n uranio m

u**rban** /'3:bən/ a urbano

u**rge** /3:dʒ/ n forte desiderio m ● vt esortare (**to** a); **urge on** spronare

u**rgen|cy** /'3:dʒənsɪ/ n urgenza f. **~t** a urgente

u**rinate** /'jʊərɪneɪt/ vi urinare

u**rine** /'jʊərɪn/ n urina f

u**rn** /3:n/ n ⟨for tea⟩ contenitore m munito di cannella che si trova nei self-service, mense, ecc

us /ʌs/ pron ci; ⟨after prep⟩ noi; **they know us** ci conoscono; **give us the money** dateci i soldi; **give it to us** datecelo; **they showed it to us** ce l'hanno fatto vedere; **they meant us, not you** intendevano noi, non voi; **it's us** siamo noi; **she hates us** ci odia

US[A] n[pl] abbr (**United States**

[of America]) U.S.A. mpl

u**sable** /'ju:zəbl/ a usabile

u**sage** /'ju:sɪdʒ/ n uso m

u**se**¹ /ju:s/ n uso m; **be of ~** essere utile; **be of no ~** essere inutile; **make ~ of** usare; ⟨exploit⟩ sfruttare; **it is no ~** è inutile; **what's the ~?** a che scopo?

u**se**² /ju:z/ vt usare. **use up** vt consumare

u**sed**¹ /ju:zd/ a usato

u**sed**² /ju:st/ pt **be ~ to sth** essere abituato a qcsa; **get ~ to** abituarsi a; **he ~ to live here** viveva qui ~? a che scopo?

u**seful** /'ju:sfl/ a utile. **~ness** n utilità f

u**seless** /'ju:slɪs/ a inutile; ⟨fam: person⟩ incapace

u**ser** /'ju:zə(r)/ n utente mf. **~-'friendly** a facile da usare

u**sher** /'ʌʃə(r)/ n Theat maschera f; Jur usciere m; ⟨at wedding⟩ persona f che accompagna gli invitati ai loro posti in chiesa ● **usher in** vt fare entrare

u**sherette** /ʌʃə'ret/ n maschera f

u**sual** /'ju:ʒʊəl/ a usuale; **as ~** come al solito. **~ly** adv di solito

u**surp** /jʊ'z3:p/ vt usurpare

u**tensil** /ju:'tensl/ n utensile m

u**terus** /'ju:tərəs/ n utero m

u**tilitarian** /jʊtɪlɪ'teərɪən/ a funzionale

u**tility** /ju:'tɪlətɪ/ n servizio m. **~ room** n stanza f in casa privata per il lavaggio, la stiratura dei panni, ecc

u**tilize** /'ju:tɪlaɪz/ vt utilizzare

u**tmost** /'ʌtməʊst/ a estremo ● n **one's ~** tutto il possibile

u**tter**¹ /'ʌtə(r)/ a totale. **~ly** adv completamente

u**tter**² vt emettere ⟨sigh, sound⟩; proferire ⟨word⟩. **~ance** /-əns/ n dichiarazione f

U-'turn /'ju:-/ n Auto inversione f a U, fig marcia f in dietro

Vv

vacan|cy /'veɪk(ə)nsɪ/ *n* ⟨job⟩ posto *m* vacante; ⟨room⟩ stanza *f* disponibile. **~t** *a* libero; ⟨position⟩ vacante; ⟨look⟩ assente

vacate /və'keɪt/ *vt* lasciare libero

vacation /və'keɪʃn/ *n* Univ & Am vacanza *f*

vaccinat|e /'væksɪmeɪt/ *vt* vaccinare. **~ion** /-'neɪʃn/ *n* vaccinazione *f*

vaccine /'væksiːn/ *n* vaccino *m*

vacuum /'vækjʊəm/ *n* vuoto *m* ● *vt* passare l'aspirapolvere in/ su. **~ cleaner** *n* aspirapolvere *m inv*. **~ flask** *n* thermos® *m inv*. **~-packed** *a* confezionato sotto-vuoto

vagabond /'vægəbɒnd/ *n* vagabondo, -a *mf*

vagina /və'dʒaɪnə/ *n* Anat vagina *f*

vagrant /'veɪgrənt/ *n* vagabondo, -a *mf*

vague /veɪg/ *a* vago; ⟨outline⟩ impreciso; ⟨absent-minded⟩ distratto; **I'm still ~ about it** non ho ancora le idee chiare in proposito. **~ly** *adv* vagamente

vain /veɪn/ *a* vanitoso; ⟨hope, attempt⟩ vano; **in ~** invano. **~ly** *adv* vanamente

valentine /'væləntaɪn/ *n* ⟨card⟩ biglietto *m* di San Valentino

valiant /'vælɪənt/ *a* valoroso

valid /'vælɪd/ *a* valido. **~ate** *vt* ⟨confirm⟩ convalidare. **~ity** /və'lɪdətɪ/ *n* validità *f*

valley /'vælɪ/ *n* valle *f*

valour /'vælə(r)/ *n* valore *m*

valuable /'væljʊəbl/ *a* di valore; *fig* prezioso. **~s** *npl* oggetti *mpl* di valore

valuation /væljʊ'eɪʃn/ *n* valutazione *f*

value /'væljuː/ *n* valore *m*; ⟨usefulness⟩ utilità *f* ● *vt* valutare; ⟨cherish⟩ apprezzare. **~ 'added tax** *n* imposta *f* sul valore aggiunto

valve /vælv/ *n* valvola *f*

vampire /'væmpaɪə(r)/ *n* vampiro *m*

van /væn/ *n* furgone *m*

vandal /'vændl/ *n* vandalo, -a *mf*. **~ism** /-ɪzm/ *n* vandalismo *m*. **~ize** *vt* vandalizzare

vanilla /və'nɪlə/ *n* vaniglia *f*

vanish /'vænɪʃ/ *vi* svanire

vanity /'vænətɪ/ *n* vanità *f*. **~ bag** *or* **case** *n* beauty-case *m inv*

vantage-point /'vɑːntɪdʒ-/ *n* punto *m* d'osservazione; *fig* punto *m* di vista

vapour /'veɪpə(r)/ *n* vapore *m*

variable /'veərɪəbl/ *a* variabile; ⟨adjustable⟩ regolabile

variance /'veərɪəns/ *n* **be at ~** essere in disaccordo

variant /'veərɪənt/ *n* variante *f*

variation /veərɪ'eɪʃn/ *n* variazione *f*

varicose /'værɪkəʊs/ *a* **~ veins** vene *fpl* varicose

varied /'veərɪd/ *a* vario; ⟨diet⟩ diversificato; ⟨life⟩ movimentato

variety /və'raɪətɪ/ *n* varietà *f inv*

various /'veərɪəs/ *a* vario

varnish /'vɑːnɪʃ/ *n* vernice *f*; ⟨for nails⟩ smalto *m* ● *vt* verniciare; **one's nails** mettersi lo smalto

vary /'veərɪ/ *vt/i* ⟨pt/pp **-ied**⟩ variare. **~ing** *a* variabile; ⟨different⟩ vario

vase /vɑːz/ *n* vaso *m*

vast /vɑːst/ *a* vasto; ⟨difference, amusement⟩ enorme. **~ly** *adv* ⟨su perior⟩ di gran lunga; ⟨different, amused⟩ enormemente

VAT /viːeɪ'tiː, væt/ *n abbr* ⟨value added tax⟩ I.V.A. *f*

vat /væt/ *n* tino *m*

vault¹ /vɔːlt/ *n* ⟨roof⟩ volta *f*; ⟨in bank⟩ caveau *m inv*; ⟨tomb⟩ cripta *f*

vault² *n* salto *m* ● *vt/i* **~ [over]** saltare

VDU *n abbr* ⟨visual display unit⟩ VDU *m*

veal /viːl/ n carne f di vitello ● attrib di vitello

veer /vɪə(r)/ vi cambiare direzione; Naut, Auto virare

vegetable /ˈvedʒtəbl/ n (food) verdura f; (when growing) ortaggio m ● attrib (oil, fat) vegetale

vegetarian /vedʒɪˈteərɪən/ a & n vegetariano, -a mf

vegetat|e /ˈvedʒɪteɪt/ vi vegetare. **~ion** /-ˈteɪʃn/ n vegetazione f

vehemen|ce /ˈviːəməns/ n veemenza f. **~t** a veemente. **~tly** adv con veemenza

vehicle /ˈviːkl/ n veicolo m; (fig: medium) mezzo m

veil /veɪl/ n velo m ● vt velare

vein /veɪn/ n vena f; (mood) umore m; (manner) tenore m. **~ed** a venato

Velcro® /ˈvelkrəʊ/ n ~ **fastening** chiusura f con velcro®

velocity /vɪˈlɒsɪti/ n velocità f

velvet /ˈvelvɪt/ n velluto m. **~y** a vellutato

vendetta /venˈdetə/ n vendetta f

vending-machine /ˈvendɪŋ-/ n distributore m automatico

veneer /vəˈnɪə(r)/ n impiallacciatura f; fig vernice f. **~ed** a impiallacciato

venereal /vɪˈnɪərɪəl/ a ~ **disease** malattia f venerea

Venetian /vɪˈniːʃn/ a & n veneziano, -a mf. **v~ blind** n persiana f alla veneziana

vengeance /ˈvendʒəns/ n vendetta f; **with a ~** fam a più non posso

Venice /ˈvenɪs/ n Venezia f

venison /ˈvenɪsn/ n Culin carne f di cervo

venom /ˈvenəm/ n veleno m. **~ous** /-əs/ a velenoso

vent¹ /vent/ n presa f d'aria; **give ~ to** fig dar libero sfogo a ● vt fig sfogare (anger)

vent² n (in jacket) spacco m

ventilat|e /ˈventɪleɪt/ vt ventilare. **~ion** /-ˈleɪʃn/ n ventilazione f; (installation) sistema m di ventilazione. **~or** n ventilatore m

ventriloquist /venˈtrɪləkwɪst/ n ventriloquo, -a mf

venture /ˈventʃə(r)/ n impresa f ● vt azzardare ● vi avventurarsi

venue /ˈvenjuː/ n luogo m (di convegno, concerto, ecc.)

veranda /vəˈrændə/ n veranda f

verb /vɜːb/ n verbo m. **~al** a verbale

verbatim /vɜːˈbeɪtɪm/ a letterale ● adv parola per parola

verbose /vɜːˈbəʊs/ a prolisso

verdict /ˈvɜːdɪkt/ n verdetto m; (opinion) parere m

verge /vɜːdʒ/ n orlo m; **be on the ~ of doing sth** essere sul punto di fare qcsa ● **verge on** vt fig rasentare

verger /ˈvɜːdʒə(r)/ n sagrestano m

verify /ˈverɪfaɪ/ vt (pt/pp -ied) verificare; (confirm) confermare

vermin /ˈvɜːmɪn/ n animali mpl nocivi

vermouth /ˈvɜːməθ/ n vermut m

vernacular /vəˈnækjʊlə(r)/ n vernacolo m

versatil|e /ˈvɜːsətaɪl/ a versatile. **~ity** /-ˈtɪlətɪ/ n versatilità f

verse /vɜːs/ n verso m; (of Bible) versetto m; (poetry) versi mpl

versed /vɜːst/ a ~ **in** versato in

version /ˈvɜːʃn/ n versione f

versus /ˈvɜːsəs/ prep contro

vertebra /ˈvɜːtɪbrə/ n (pl -brae /-briː/) Anat vertebra f

vertical /ˈvɜːtɪkl/ a & n verticale m

vertigo /ˈvɜːtɪgəʊ/ n Med vertigine f

verve /vɜːv/ n verve f

very /ˈverɪ/ adv molto; ~ **much** molto; ~ **little** pochissimo; ~ **many** moltissimi; ~ **few** pochissimi; ~ **probably** molto probabilmente; ~ **well** benissimo; **at the ~ most** tutt'al più; **at the ~ latest** al più tardi ● a **the ~ first** il primissimo; **the ~ thing** proprio ciò che ci vuole; **at the ~ end/beginning** proprio alla fine/all'inizio; **that ~ day** proprio quel giorno; **the ~**

thought la sola idea; **only a ~
little** solo un pochino

vessel /'vesl/ n nave f

vest /vest/ n maglia f della pelle;
(Am: waistcoat) gilè m inv. **~ed
interest** n interesse m personale

vestige /'vestɪdʒ/ n (of past) vesti-
gio m

vestment /'vestmənt/ n Relig
paramento m

vestry /'vestri/ n sagrestia f

vet /vet/ n veterinario, -a mf ● vt
(pt/pp vetted) controllare minu-
ziosamente

veteran /'vetərən/ n veterano, -a
mf

veterinary /'vetərinəri/ a veterinario. **~ surgeon** n medico m veterinario

veto /'vi:təʊ/ n (pl -es) veto m ● vt
proibire

vex /veks/ vt irritare. **~ation**
/-'seɪʃn/ n irritazione f. **~ed** a irritato; **~ed question** questione f
controversa

VHF n abbr (very high frequency)
VHF

via /'vaɪə/ prep via; (by means of)
attraverso

viable /'vaɪəbl/ a (life form, relationship, company) in grado di
sopravvivere; (proposition) attua-
bile

viaduct /'vaɪədʌkt/ n viadotto m

vibrat|e /vaɪ'breɪt/ vi vibrare.
~ion /-'breɪʃn/ n vibrazione f

vicar /'vɪkə(r)/ n parroco m (protestante). **~age** /-rɪdʒ/ n casa f parrocchiale

vicarious /vɪ'keərɪəs/ a indiretto

vice¹ /vaɪs/ n vizio m

vice² n Techn morsa f

vice 'chairman n vicepresidente
mf

vice 'president n vicepresidente
mf

vice versa /vaɪs'vɜ:sə/ adv viceversa

vicinity /vɪ'smətɪ/ n vicinanza f; **in
the ~ of** nelle vicinanze di

vicious /'vɪʃəs/ a cattivo; (attack)

brutale; (animal) pericoloso. **~
'circle** n circolo m vizioso. **~ly**
adv (attack) brutalmente

victim /'vɪktɪm/ n vittima f. **~ize**
vt fare delle rappresaglie contro

victor /'vɪktə(r)/ n vincitore m

victor|ious /vɪk'tɔ:rɪəs/ a vittorio-
so. **~y** /'vɪktərɪ/ n vittoria f

video /'vɪdɪəʊ/ n video m; (cassette)
videocassetta f; (recorder) videoregistratore m ● attrib video ● vt
registrare

video: ~ card n Comput scheda f
video. **~ cas'sette** n videocassetta f. **~conference** n videoconfe-
renza f. **~ game** n videogioco m.
~ recorder n videoregistratore
m. **~tape** n videocassetta f

vie /vaɪ/ vi (pres p vying) rivaleggiare

view /vju:/ n vista f; (photo-
graphed, painted) veduta f; (opinion) visione f; **look at the ~**
guardare il panorama; **in my ~**
secondo me; **in ~ of** in considerazione di; **on ~** esposto; **with a ~
to** con l'intenzione di ● vt visitare (house); (consider) considerare ● vi TV guardare. **~er** n TV
telespettatore, -trice mf; Phot
visore m

view: ~finder n Phot mirino m.
~point n punto m di vista

vigil /'vɪdʒɪl/ n veglia f

vigilan|ce /'vɪdʒɪləns/ n vigilanza
f. **~t** a vigile

vigorous /'vɪgərəs/ a vigoroso

vigour /'vɪgə(r)/ n vigore m

vile /vaɪl/ a disgustoso; (weather)
orribile; (temper, mood) pessimo

villa /'vɪlə/ n (for holidays) casa f di
villeggiatura

village /'vɪlɪdʒ/ n paese m. **~r** n pa-
esano, -a mf

villain /'vɪlən/ n furfante m; (in
story) cattivo m

vindicate /'vɪndɪkeɪt/ vt (from
guilt) discolpare; **you are ~d** ti
sei dimostrato nel giusto

vindictive /vɪn'dɪktɪv/ a vendicati-
vo

vine /vaɪn/ n vite f

vinegar /'vɪnɪɡə(r)/ n aceto m

vineyard /'vɪnjɑːd/ n vigneto m

vintage /'vɪntɪdʒ/ a ⟨wine⟩ d'annata ● n ⟨year⟩ annata f

viola /vɪ'əʊlə/ n Mus viola f

violat|e /'vaɪəleɪt/ vt violare. **~ion** /-'leɪʃn/ n violazione f

violen|ce /'vaɪələns/ n violenza f. **~t** a violento

violet /'vaɪələt/ a violetto ● n ⟨flower⟩ violetta f; ⟨colour⟩ violetto m

violin /vaɪə'lɪn/ n violino m. **~ist** n violinista mf

VIP n abbr (**very important person**) vip mf

virgin /'vɜːdʒɪn/ a vergine ● n vergine f. **~ity** /-'dʒɪnətɪ/ n verginità f

Virgo /'vɜːɡəʊ/ n Vergine f

viril|e /'vɪraɪl/ a virile. **~ity** /-'rɪlətɪ/ n virilità f

virtual /'vɜːtjʊəl/ a effettivo. **~ reality** n realtà f virtuale. **~ly** adv praticamente

virtue /'vɜːtjuː/ n virtù f inv; ⟨advantage⟩ vantaggio m; **by** or **in ~ of** a causa di

virtuoso /vɜːtʊ'əʊzəʊ/ n (pl -si /-zi:/) virtuoso m

virtuous /'vɜːtjʊəs/ a virtuoso

virulent /'vɪrʊlənt/ a virulento

virus /'vaɪərəs/ n virus m inv

visa /'viːzə/ n visto m

vis-à-vis /viːzɑː'viː/ prep rispetto a

viscount /'vaɪkaʊnt/ n visconte m

viscous /'vɪskəs/ a vischioso

visibility /vɪzə'bɪlətɪ/ n visibilità f

visib|le /'vɪzəbl/ a visibile. **~y** adv visibilmente

vision /'vɪʒn/ n visione f; ⟨sight⟩ vista f

visit /'vɪzɪt/ n visita f ● vt andare a trovare ⟨person⟩; andare da ⟨doctor etc⟩; visitare ⟨town, building⟩. **~ing hours** npl orario m delle visite. **~or** n ospite mf; ⟨of town, museum⟩ visitatore, -trice mf; ⟨in hotel⟩ cliente mf

visor /'vaɪzə(r)/ n visiera f; Auto parasole m

vista /'vɪstə/ n ⟨view⟩ panorama m

visual /'vɪʒʊəl/ a visivo. **~ aids** npl supporto m visivo. **~ dis'play unit** n visualizzatore m. **~ly** adv visualmente; **~ly handicapped** non vedente

visualize /'vɪʒʊəlaɪz/ vt visualizzare

vital /'vaɪtl/ a vitale. **~ity** /vaɪ'tælətɪ/ n vitalità f. **~ly** /'vaɪtəlɪ/ adv estremamente

vitamin /'vɪtəmɪn/ n vitamina f

vivaci|ous /vɪ'veɪʃəs/ a vivace. **~ty** /-'væsətɪ/ n vivacità f

vivid /'vɪvɪd/ a vivido. **~ly** adv in modo vivido

vocabulary /və'kæbjʊlərɪ/ n vocabolario m; ⟨list⟩ glossario m

vocal /'vəʊkl/ a vocale; ⟨vociferous⟩ eloquente. **~ cords** npl corde fpl vocali

vocalist /'vəʊkəlɪst/ n vocalista mf

vocation /və'keɪʃn/ n vocazione f. **~al** a di orientamento professionale

vociferous /və'sɪfərəs/ a vociante

vodka /'vɒdkə/ n vodka f inv

vogue /vəʊɡ/ n moda f; **in ~** in voga

voice /vɔɪs/ n voce f ● vt esprimere. **~mail** n posta f elettronica vocale

void /vɔɪd/ a ⟨not valid⟩ nullo; **~ of** privo di ● n vuoto m

volatile /'vɒlətaɪl/ a volatile; ⟨person⟩ volubile

volcanic /vɒl'kænɪk/ a vulcanico

volcano /vɒl'keɪnəʊ/ n vulcano m

volition /və'lɪʃn/ n **of his own ~** di sua spontanea volontà

volley /'vɒlɪ/ n ⟨of gunfire⟩ raffica f; Tennis volée f inv

volt /vəʊlt/ n volt m inv. **~age** /-ɪdʒ/ n Electr voltaggio m

volub|le /'vɒljʊbl/ a loquace

volume /'vɒljuːm/ n volume m; ⟨of work, traffic⟩ quantità f inv. **~ control** n volume m

voluntary /'vɒləntərɪ/ a volontario. **~y work** n volontariato m. **~ily** adv volontariamente

volunteer /vɒlənˈtɪə(r)/ n volontario, -a mf ● vt offrire volontariamente ⟨information⟩ ● vi offrirsi volontario; Mil arruolarsi come volontario

voluptuous /vəˈlʌptjʊəs/ a voluttuoso

vomit /ˈvɒmɪt/ n vomito m ● vt/i vomitare

voracious /vəˈreɪʃəs/ a vorace

vot|e /vəʊt/ n voto m; ⟨ballot⟩ votazione f; ⟨right⟩ diritto m di voto; **take a ~e** on votare su ● vi votare ● vt ~ **sb president** eleggere qcno presidente. **~er** n elettore, -trice mf. **~ing** n votazione f

vouch /vaʊtʃ/ vi ~ **for** garantire per. **~er** n buono m

vow /vaʊ/ n voto m ● vt giurare

vowel /ˈvaʊəl/ n vocale f

voyage /ˈvɔɪɪdʒ/ n viaggio m [marittimo]; ⟨in space⟩ viaggio m [nello spazio]

vulgar /ˈvʌlgə(r)/ a volgare. **~ity** /-ˈgærəti/ n volgarità f inv

vulnerable /ˈvʌlnərəbl/ a vulnerabile

vulture /ˈvʌltʃə(r)/ n avvoltoio m

vying /ˈvaɪɪŋ/ see **vie**

Ww

wad /wɒd/ n batuffolo m; ⟨bundle⟩ rotolo m. **~ding** n ovatta f

waddle /ˈwɒdl/ vi camminare ondeggiando

wade /weɪd/ vi guadare; **~ through** fam procedere faticosamente in ⟨book⟩

wafer /ˈweɪfə(r)/ n cialda f, wafer m inv; Relig ostia f

waffle¹ /ˈwɒfl/ vi fam blaterare

waffle² n Culin cialda f

waft /wɒft/ vt trasportare ● vi diffondersi

wag /wæg/ v ⟨pt/pp **wagged**⟩ ● vt agitare ● vi agitarsi

wage¹ /weɪdʒ/ vt dichiarare ⟨war⟩; lanciare ⟨campaign⟩

wage² n, & **~s** pl salario msg. **~ packet** n busta f paga

waggle /ˈwægl/ vt dimenare ● vi dimenarsi

wagon /ˈwægən/ n carro m; Rail vagone m merci

wail /weɪl/ n piagnucolio m; ⟨of wind⟩ lamento m; ⟨of baby⟩ vagito m ● vi piagnucolare; ⟨wind:⟩ lamentarsi; ⟨baby:⟩ vagire

waist /weɪst/ n vita f. **~coat** /ˈweɪskəʊt/ n gilè m inv; ⟨of man's suit⟩ panciotto m. **~line** n vita f

wait /weɪt/ n attesa f; **lie in ~** for appostarsi per sorprendere ● vi aspettare; **~ for** aspettare ● vt ~ **one's turn** aspettare il proprio turno. **wait on** vt servire

waiter /ˈweɪtə(r)/ n cameriere m

waiting: ~-list n lista f d'attesa. **~-room** n sala f d'aspetto

waitress /ˈweɪtrɪs/ n cameriera f

waive /weɪv/ vt rinunciare a ⟨claim⟩; non tener conto di ⟨rule⟩

wake¹ /weɪk/ n veglia f funebre ● v ⟨pt **woke**, pp **woken**⟩ ~ [up] ● vt svegliare ● vi svegliarsi

wake² n Naut scia f; **in the ~ of** fig nella scia di

waken /ˈweɪkn/ vt svegliare ● vi svegliarsi

Wales /weɪlz/ n Galles m

walk /wɔːk/ n passeggiata f; ⟨gait⟩ andatura f; ⟨path⟩ sentiero m; **go for a ~** andare a fare una passeggiata ● vi camminare; ⟨as opposed to drive etc⟩ andare a piedi; ⟨ramble⟩ passeggiare ● vt portare a spasso ⟨dog⟩; percorrere ⟨streets⟩. **walk out** vi ⟨husband, employee:⟩ andarsene; ⟨workers:⟩ scioperare. **walk out on** vt lasciare

walker /ˈwɔːkə(r)/ n camminatore, -trice mf; ⟨rambler⟩ escursionista mf

walking /ˈwɔːkɪŋ/ n camminare m; ⟨rambling⟩ fare delle escursioni. **~-stick** n bastone m da passeggio mf

'**Walkman**® n Walkman® m inv

walk: **~-out** n sciopero m. **~-over** n fig vittoria f facile

wall /wɔːl/ n muro m; go to the ~ fam andare a rotoli; **drive sb up the** ~ fam far diventare matto qcno ● **wall up** vt murare

wallet /'wɒlɪt/ n portafoglio m

wallop /'wɒləp/ n fam colpo m ● vt (pt/pp **walloped**) fam colpire

wallow /'wɒləʊ/ vi sguazzare; (in self-pity, grief) crogiolarsi

'**wallpaper** n tappezzeria f ● vt tappezzare

walnut /'wɔːlnʌt/ n noce f

waltz /wɔːlts/ n valzer m inv ● vi ballare il valzer

wan /wɒn/ a esangue

wand /wɒnd/ n (magic ~) bacchetta f [magica]

wander /'wɒndə(r)/ vi girovagare; (fig: digress) divagare. **wander about** vi andare a spasso

wane /weɪn/ n be on the ~ essere in fase calante ● vi calare

wangle /'wæŋgl/ vt fam rimediare (invitation, holiday)

want /wɒnt/ n (hardship) bisogno m; (lack) mancanza f ● vt volere; (need) aver bisogno di; **~ [to have]** sth volere qcsa; **~ to do** sth voler fare qcsa; **we ~ to stay** vogliamo rimanere; **I ~ you to go** voglio che tu vada; **it ~s painting** ha bisogno d'essere dipinto; **you ~ to learn to swim** dovresti imparare a nuotare ● vi ~ for mancare di. **~ed** a ricercato. **~ing** a be **~ing** mancare; **be ~ing** in mancare di

wanton /'wɒntən/ a (cruelty, neglect) gratuito; (morally) debosciato

war /wɔː(r)/ n guerra f; fig lotta f (on contro); **at** ~ in guerra

ward /wɔːd/ n (in hospital) reparto m; (child) minore m sotto tutela ● **ward off** vt evitare; parare (blow)

warden /'wɔːdn/ n guardiano, -a mf

warder /'wɔːdə(r)/ n guardia f carceraria

wardrobe /'wɔːdrəʊb/ n guardaroba m

warehouse /'weəhaʊs/ n magazzino m

war: ~**fare** n guerra f. ~**head** n testata f

warily /'weərɪlɪ/ adv cautamente

warlike /'wɔːlaɪk/ a bellicoso

warm /wɔːm/ a caldo; (welcome) caloroso; **be** ~ (person:) aver caldo; **it is** ~ (weather:) fa caldo ● vt scaldare. **warm up** vt scaldare ● vi scaldarsi; fig animarsi. ~**-hearted** a espansivo. ~**ly** adv (greet) calorosamente; (dress) in modo pesante

warmth /wɔːmθ/ n calore m

warn /wɔːn/ vt avvertire. ~**ing** n avvertimento m; (advance notice) preavviso m

warp /wɔːp/ vt deformare; fig distorcere ● vi deformarsi

'**war-path** n **on the** ~ sul sentiero di guerra

warped /wɔːpt/ a fig contorto; (sexuality) deviato; (view) distorto

warrant /'wɒrənt/ n (for arrest, search) mandato m. ● vt (justify) giustificare; (guarantee) garantire

warranty /'wɒrəntɪ/ n garanzia f

warring /'wɔːrɪŋ/ a in guerra

warrior /'wɒrɪə(r)/ n guerriero, -a mf

'**warship** n nave f da guerra

wart /wɔːt/ n porro m

'**wartime** n tempo m di guerra

wary /'weərɪ/ a (-ier, -iest) (careful) cauto; (suspicious) diffidente

was /wɒz/ see **be**

wash /wɒʃ/ n lavata f; (clothes) bucato m; (in washing machine) lavaggio m; **have a** ~ darsi una lavata ● vt lavare; (sea:) bagnare; ~ **one's hands** lavarsi le mani ● vi lavarsi. **wash out** vt sciacquare (soap); sciacquarsi (mouth). **wash up** vt lavare ● vi lavare i piatti; Am lavarsi

washable /ˈwɒʃəbl/ a lavabile
wash: ~-**basin** n lavandino m. ~ **cloth** n Am ≈ guanto m da bagno
washed 'out a (faded) scolorito; (tired) spossato
washer /ˈwɒʃə(r)/ n Techn guarnizione f; (machine) lavatrice f
washing /ˈwɒʃɪŋ/ n bucato m. ~-**machine** n lavatrice f. ~-**powder** n detersivo m. ~-'**up** n do the ~-**up** lavare i piatti. ~-'**up liquid** n detersivo m per i piatti
wash: ~-**out** n disastro m. ~-**room** n bagno m
wasp /wɒsp/ n vespa f
wastage /ˈweɪstɪdʒ/ n perdita f
waste /weɪst/ n spreco m; (rubbish) rifiuto m; ~ **of time** perdita f di tempo ● a (product) di scarto; (land) desolato; **lay** ~ devastare ● vt sprecare. **waste away** vi deperire
waste: ~-**di'sposal unit** n eliminatore m di rifiuti. ~-**ful** a dispendioso. ~ '**paper** n carta f straccia. ~-'**paper basket** n cestino m per la carta (straccia)
watch /wɒtʃ/ n guardia f; (period of duty) turno m di guardia; (timepiece) orologio m; **be on the** ~ stare all'erta ● vt guardare (film, match, television); (be careful of, look after) stare attento a ● vi guardare. **watch out** vi (be careful) stare attento (**for** a). **watch out for** vt (look for) fare attenzione all'arrivo di (person)
watch: ~-**dog** n cane m da guardia. ~-**ful** a attento. ~-**maker** n orologiaio, -a mf. ~-**man** n guardiano m. ~-**strap** n cinturino m dell'orologio. ~-**word** n motto m
water /ˈwɔːtə(r)/ n acqua f ● vt annaffiare (garden, plant); (dilute) annacquare ● vi (eyes:) lacrimare; **my mouth was** ~**ing** avevo l'acquolina in bocca. **water down** vt diluire; fig attenuare
water: ~-**colour** n acquerello m. ~**cress** n crescione m. ~**fall** n cascata f

'watering-can n annaffiatoio m
water: ~-**lily** n ninfea f. ~-**logged** a inzuppato. ~-**main** n conduttura f dell'acqua. ~-**polo** n pallanuoto f. ~-**power** n energia f idraulica. ~**proof** a impermeabile. ~**shed** n spartiacque m inv; fig svolta f. ~-**skiing** n sci m nautico. ~**tight** a stagno; fig irrefutabile. ~**way** n canale m navigabile
watery /ˈwɔːtəri/ a acquoso; (eyes) lacrimoso
watt /wɒt/ n watt m inv
wave /weɪv/ n onda f; (gesture) cenno m; fig ondata f ● vt agitare; ~ **one's hand** agitare la mano ● vi far segno; (flag:) sventolare. ~**length** n lunghezza f d'onda
waver /ˈweɪvə(r)/ vi vacillare; (hesitate) esitare
wavy /ˈweɪvi/ a ondulato
wax[1] /wæks/ vi (moon:) crescere; (fig: become) diventare
wax[2] n cera f; (in ear) cerume m ● vt dare la cera a. ~**works** n museo m delle cere
way /weɪ/ n percorso m; (direction) direzione f; (manner, method) modo m; ~**s** pl (customs) abitudini fpl; **be in the** ~ essere in mezzo; **on the** ~ **to Rome** andando a Roma; **I'll do it on the** ~ lo faccio mentre vado; **it's on my** ~ è sul mio percorso; **a long** ~ **off** lontano; **this** ~ da questa parte; (like this) così; **by the** ~ a proposito; **by** ~ **of** come; (via) via; **either** ~ (whatever we do) in un modo o nell'altro; **in some** ~**s** sotto certi aspetti; **in a** ~ in un certo senso; **in a bad** ~ (person) molto grave; **out of the** ~ fuori mano; **under** ~ in corso; **lead the** ~ far strada; fig aprire la strada; **make** ~ far posto (**for** a); **give** ~ Auto dare la precedenza; **go out of one's** ~ fig scomodarsi (**to** per); **get one's [own]** ~ averla vinta ● adv ~ **behind** molto indietro. ● **in** n entrata f
way'lay vt (pt/pp -**laid**) aspettare al varco (person)

way 'out n uscita f; fig via f d'uscita

way-'out a fam eccentrico

wayward /'weɪwəd/ a capriccioso

WC n abbr WC; **the WC** il gabinetto m

we /wiː/ pron noi; **we're the last** siamo gli ultimi; **they're going, but we're not** loro vanno, ma noi no

weak /wiːk/ a debole; (liquid) leggero. **~en** vt indebolire ● vi indebolirsi. **~ling** n smidollato, -a mf. **~ness** n debolezza f; (liking) debole m

wealth /welθ/ n ricchezza f; fig gran quantità f. **~y** a (-ier, -iest) ricco

wean /wiːn/ vt svezzare

weapon /'wepən/ n arma f

wear /weə(r)/ n (clothing) abbigliamento m; **for everyday ~** da portare tutti i giorni; ~ [and tear] usura f ● v (pt wore, pp worn) ● vt portare; (damage) consumare; ~ **a hole in sth** logorare qcsa fino a fare un buco; **what shall I ~?** cosa mi metto? ● vi consumarsi; (last) durare. **wear off** vi scomparire; (effect:) finire. **wear out** vt consumare [fino in fondo]; (exhaust) es. nuare ● vi estenuarsi

wear... /'weərəbl/ a portabile

weary /... / a (-ier, -iest) sfinito ● v (pt/pp ...ried) ● vt sfinire ● vi ~**-y of** stancarsi di. **~ily** adv stancamente

weasel /'wiːzl/ n donnola f

weather /'weðə(r)/ n tempo .. .; **in this ~** con questo tempo; **under the ~** fam giù di corda ● vt sopravvivere a (storm)

weather: **~-beaten** a (face) segnato dalle intemperie. **~cock** n gallo m segnavento. **~ forecast** n previsioni fpl del tempo

weave[1] /wiːv/ vi (pt/pp weaved) (move) zigzagare

weave[2] n tessuto m ● vt (pt wove, pp woven) tessere; intrecciare (flowers etc); intrecciare le fila

di (story etc). **~r** n tessitore, -trice

web /web/ n rete f; (of spider) ragnatela f. **~bed feet** npl piedi mpl palmati. **W~ page** n Comput pagina f web. **W~ site** n Comput sito m web

wed /wed/ vt (pt/pp wedded) sposare ● vi sposarsi. **~ding** n matrimonio m

wedding: ~ **cake** n torta f nuziale. ~ **day** n giorno m del matrimonio. ~ **dress** n vestito m da sposa. **~ring** n fede f

wedge /wedʒ/ n zeppa f; (for splitting wood) cuneo m; (of cheese) fetta f ● vt (fix) fissare

wedlock /'wedlɒk/ n **born out of ~** nato fuori dal matrimonio

Wednesday /'wenzdeɪ/ n mercoledì m inv

wee[1] /wiː/ a fam piccolo

wee[2] vi fam fare la pipì

weed /wiːd/ n erbaccia f; (fam: person) mollusco m ● vt estirpare le erbacce da. **weed out** vt fig eliminare

'weed-killer n erbicida m

weedy /'wiːdɪ/ a fam mingherlino

week /wiːk/ n settimana f. **~day** n giorno m feriale. **~end** n fine settimana m

weekly /'wiːklɪ/ a settimanale ● n settimanale m ● adv settimanalmente

weep /wiːp/ vi (pt/pp wept) piangere

weigh /weɪ/ vt/i pesare; ~ **anchor** levare l'ancora. **weigh down** vt fig piegare. **weigh up** vt fig soppesare; valutare (person)

weight /weɪt/ n peso m; **put on/lose ~** ingrassare/dimagrire. **~ing** n (allowance) indennità f inv

weight: **~essness** n assenza f di gravità. **~lift...** n sollevamento m pesi

weighty /'weɪtɪ/ a (-ier -iest) pesante; (important) di un certo peso

weir /wɪə(r)/ n chiusa f

weird /wɪəd/ a misterioso; (bizarre) bizzarro

614

welcome /'welkəm/ a benvenuto; you're ~! prego!; you're ~ to have it/to come prendilo/vieni pure ● n accoglienza f ● vt accogliere; (appreciate) gradire

weld /weld/ vt saldare. ~er n saldatore m

welfare /'welfeə(r)/ n benessere m; (aid) assistenza f. W~ State n Stato m assistenziale

well¹ /wel/ n pozzo m; (of staircase) tromba f

well² adv (better, best) bene; as ~ anche; as ~ as (in addition) oltre a; ~ done! bravo!; very ~ benissimo ● a he is not ~ non sta bene; get ~ soon! guarisci presto! ● int beh!; ~ I never! ma va!

well: ~-behaved a educato. ~-being n benessere m. ~-bred a beneducato. ~-heeled a fam danaroso

wellingtons /'welɪŋtənz/ npl stivali mpl di gomma

well: ~-known a famoso. ~-meaning a con buone intenzioni. ~-meant a con le migliori intenzioni. ~-off a benestante. ~-read a colto. ~-to-do a ricco

Welsh /welʃ/ a & n gallese; the ~ pl i gallesi. ~man n gallese m. ~ rabbit n toast m inv al formaggio

went /went/ see go

wept /wept/ see weep

were /wə:(r)/ see be

west /west/ n ovest m; to the ~ of a ovest di; the W~ l'Occidente m ● a occidentale ● adv verso occidente; go ~ fam andare in malora. ~erly a verso ovest; occidentale ⟨wind⟩. ~ern a occidentale ● n western m inv

West: ~ 'Germany n Germania f Occidentale. ~ 'Indian a & n antillese mf. ~ 'Indies /'ɪndɪz/ npl Antille fpl

'westward[s] /-wəd[z]/ adv verso ovest

wet /wet/ a (wetter, wettest) bagnato; fresco ⟨paint⟩; (rainy) piovoso; ⟨fam: person⟩ smidollato;

get ~ bagnarsi ● vt (pt/pp wet, wetted) bagnare. ~ 'blanket n guastafeste mf inv

whack /wæk/ n fam colpo m ● vt fam dare un colpo a. ~ed a fam stanco morto. ~ing a (fam: huge) enorme

whale /weil/ n balena f; have a ~ of a time fam divertirsi un sacco

wham /wæm/ int bum

wharf /wɔ:f/ n banchina f

what /wɒt/ pron che, [che] cosa; ~ for? perché?; ~ is that for? a che cosa serve?; ~ is it? (what do you want) cosa c'è?; ~ is it like? com'è?; ~ is your name? come ti chiami?; ~ is the weather like? com'è il tempo?; ~ is the film about? di cosa parla il film?; ~ is he talking about? di cosa sta parlando?; he asked me ~ she had said mi ha chiesto cosa ha detto; ~ about going to the cinema? e se andassimo al cinema?; ~ about the children? (what will they do) e i bambini?; ~ if it rains? e se piove? ● a quale, che; take ~ books you want prendi tutti i libri che vuoi; ~ kind of a che tipo di; at ~ time? a che ora? ● adv che; ~ a lovely day! che bella giornata! ● int ~! [che] cosa!; ~? [che] cosa?

what'ever a qualunque ● pron qualsiasi cosa; ~ is it? cos'è?; he does qualsiasi cosa faccia; ~ happens qualunque cosa succeda; nothing ~ proprio niente

whatso'ever a & pron = whatever

wheat /wi:t/ n grano m, frumento m

wheedle /'wi:d(ə)l/ vt ~ sth out of sb ottenere qcsa da qualcuno con le lusinghe

wheel /wi:l/ n ruota f; (steering ~) volante m; at the ~ al volante ● vt (push) spingere ● vi ⟨circle⟩ ruotare; ~ [round] ruotare

wheel: ~barrow n carriola f ~chair n sedia f a rotelle. ~clamp n ceppo m bloccaruote

wheeze /wi:z/ vi ansimare

when /wen/ *adv & conj* quando; **the day ~** il giorno in cui; **~ swimming/reading** nuotando/leggendo

when'ever *adv & conj* in qualsiasi momento; (*every time that*) ogni volta che; **~ did it happen?** quando è successo?

where /weə(r)/ *adv & conj* dove; **the street ~ I live** la via in cui abito; **~ do you come from?** da dove vieni?

whereabouts¹ /weərə'baʊts/ *adv* dove

'whereabouts² *n* **nobody knows his ~** nessuno sa dove si trova

where'as *conj* dal momento che; (*in contrast*) mentre

where'by *adv* attraverso il quale

whereu'pon *adv* dopo di che

wher'ever *adv & conj* dovunque; **~ is he?** dov'è mai?; **~ possible** dovunque sia possibile

whet /wet/ *vt* (*pt/pp* **whetted**) aguzzare (*appetite*)

whether /'weðə(r)/ *conj* se; **~ you like it or not** che ti piaccia o no

which /wɪtʃ/ *a & pron* quale; **one / quale?**; **~ one of you?** chi di voi?; **~** *pron* (*direction*) in che direzione? **•** *rel pron* (*object*) che; **he does frequently** cosa che fa spesso; **after ~** dopo che; **on/in ~** su/in cui

which'ever *a & pron* qualunque; **~ it is** qualunque sia; **~ of you** chiunque tra voi

whiff /wɪf/ *n* zaffata *f*; **have a ~ of sth** odorare qcsa

while /waɪl/ *n* **a long ~** un bel po'; **a little ~** un po' *conj* mentre; (*as long as*) finché; (*although*) sebbene **• while away** *vt* passare (*time*)

whilst /waɪlst/ *conj see* **while**

whim /wɪm/ *n* capriccio *m*

whimper /'wɪmpə(r)/ *vi* piagnucolare; (*dog:*) mugolare

whimsical /'wɪmzɪkl/ *a* capriccioso; (*story*) fantasioso

whine /waɪn/ *n* lamento *m*; (*of dog*)

guaito *m* **•** *vi* lamentarsi; (*dog:*) guaire

whip /wɪp/ *n* frusta *f*; (*pol: person*) parlamentare *m* incaricato, -a di assicurarsi della presenza dei membri del suo partito alle votazioni **•** *vt* (*pt/pp* **whipped**) frustare; *Culin* sbattere; (*snatch*) afferrare; (*fam: steal*) fregare. **whip up** *vt* (*incite*) stimolare; *fam* improvvisare (*meal*). **~ped 'cream** *n* panna *f* montata

whirl /wɜːl/ *n* (*movement*) rotazione *f*; **my mind's in a ~** ho le idee confuse **•** *vi* girare rapidamente **•** *vt* far girare rapidamente. **~ pool** *n* vortice *m*. **~ wind** *n* turbine *m*

whirr /wɜː(r)/ *vi* ronzare

whisk /wɪsk/ *n* *Culin* frullino *m* **•** *vt* *Culin* frullare. **whisk away** *vt* portare via

whisker /'wɪskə(r)/ *n* **~s** (*of cat*) baffi *mpl*; (*on man's cheek*) basette *fpl*; **by a ~** per un pelo

whisky /'wɪskɪ/ *n* whisky *m inv*

whisper /'wɪspə(r)/ *n* sussurro *m*; (*rumour*) diceria *f* **•** *vt/i* sussurrare

whistle /'wɪsl/ *n* fischio *m*; (*instrument*) fischietto *m* **•** *vt* fischiettare **•** *vi* fischiettare; (*referee:*) fischiare

white /waɪt/ *a* bianco; **go ~** (*pale*) sbiancare **•** *n* bianco *m*; (*of egg*) albume *m*; (*person*) bianco, -a *mf*

white: **~ 'coffee** *n* caffè *m inv* macchiato. **~'collar worker** *n* colletto *m* bianco

White'hall *n* strada *f* di Londra, sede degli uffici del governo britannico; *fig* amministrazione *f* britannica

white 'lie *n* bugia *f* pietosa

whiten /'waɪtn/ *vt* imbiancare **•** *vi* sbiancare

whiteness /'waɪtnɪs/ *n* bianchezza *f*

'whitewash *n* intonaco *m*; *fig* copertura *f* **•** *vt* dare una mano d'intonaco a; *fig* coprire

Whitsun /'wɪtsn/ n Pentecoste f

whittle /'wɪtl/ vt ~ **down** ridurre

whiz[z] /wɪz/ vi (pt/pp whizzed) sibilare. **~-kid** n fam giovane m prodigio

who /hu:/ inter pron chi ● rel pron che; **the children, ~ were all tired,...** i bambini, che erano tutti stanchi,...

who'ever pron chiunque; **~ he is** chiunque sia; **~ can that be?** chi può mai essere?

whole /həʊl/ a tutto; (not broken) intatto; **the ~ truth** tutta la verità; **the ~ world** il mondo intero; **the ~ lot** (everything) tutto; (pl) tutti; **the ~ lot of you** tutti voi ● n tutto m; **as a ~** nell'insieme; **on the ~** tutto considerato; **the ~ of Italy** tutta l'Italia

whole: **~food** n cibo m macrobiotico. **~-'hearted** a di tutto cuore. **~meal** a integrale

'wholesale a & adv all'ingrosso; fig in massa. **~r** n grossista f

wholesome /'həʊlsəm/ a sano

wholly /'həʊli/ adv completamente

whom /hu:m/ rel pron che; **the man ~ I saw** l'uomo che ho visto; **to/with ~** a/con cui ● inter pron chi; **to ~ did you speak?** con chi hai parlato?

whooping cough /'hu:pɪŋ/ n pertosse f

whopping /'wopɪŋ/ a fam enorme

whore /hɔ:(r)/ n puttana f vulg

whose /hu:z/ rel pron il cui; **people ~ name begins with D** le persone i cui nomi cominciano con la D ● inter pron di chi; **~ is that?** di chi è quello? ● a ~ **car did you use?** di chi è la macchina che hai usato?

why /waɪ/ adv (inter) perché; **the reason ~** la ragione per cui; **that's ~** per questo ● int diamine

wick /wɪk/ n stoppino m

wicked /'wɪkɪd/ a cattivo; (mischievous) malizioso

wicker /'wɪkə(r)/ n vimini mpl ● attrib di vimini

wide /waɪd/ a largo; (experience, knowledge) vasto; (difference) profondo; (far from target) lontano; **10 cm ~** largo 10 cm; **how ~ is it?** quanto è largo? ● adv (off target) lontano dal bersaglio; **~ awake** del tutto sveglio; **~ open** spalancato; **far and ~** in lungo e in largo. **~ly** adv largamente; (known, accepted) generalmente; (different) profondamente

widen /'waɪdn/ vt allargare ● vi allargarsi

'widespread a diffuso

widow /'wɪdəʊ/ n vedova f. **~ed** a vedovo. **~er** n vedovo m

width /wɪdθ/ n larghezza f; (of material) altezza f

wield /wi:ld/ vt maneggiare; esercitare (power)

wife /waɪf/ n (pl **wives**) moglie f

wig /wɪg/ n parrucca f

wiggle /'wɪgl/ vi dimenarsi ● vt dimenare

wild /waɪld/ a selvaggio; (animal, flower) selvatico; (furious) furibondo; (applause) fragoroso; (idea) folle; (with joy) pazzo; (guess) azzardato; **be ~ about** (keen on) andare pazzo per ● adv **run ~** crescere senza controllo ● n **in the ~** allo stato naturale; **the ~s** pl le zone fpl sperdute

wilderness /'wɪldənɪs/ n deserto m; (fig: garden) giungla f

'wildfire n **spread like ~** allargarsi a macchia d'olio

wild: **~-'goose chase** n ricerca f inutile. **~-life** n animali mpl selvatici

wilful /'wɪlfl/ a intenzionale; (person, refusal) ostinato. **~ly** adv intenzionalmente; (refuse) ostinatamente

will[1] /wɪl/ v aux he ~ **arrive tomorrow** arriverà domani; **I won't tell him** non glielo dirò; **you ~ be back soon, won't you?** tornerai presto, no?; **he ~ be there, won't he?** sarà là, no?; **she ~ be there by now** sarà là ormai; **~**

you go? (*do you intend to go*) pensi di andare?; **~ you go to the baker's and buy...?** puoi andare dal panettiere a comprare...?; **~ you be quiet!** vuoi stare calmo!; **~ you have some wine?** vuoi del vino?; **the engine won't start** la macchina non parte

will² *n* volontà *f inv*; (*document*) testamento *m*

willing /'wɪlɪŋ/ *a* disposto; (*eager*) volonteroso. **~ly** *adv* volentieri. **~ness** *n* buona volontà *f*

willow /'wɪləʊ/ *n* salice *m*

'will-power *n* forza *f* di volontà

willy-nilly *adv* (*at random*) a casaccio; (*wanting to or not*) volente o nolente

wilt /wɪlt/ *vi* appassire

wily /'waɪlɪ/ *a* (**-ier, -iest**) astuto

wimp /wɪmp/ *n* rammollito, -a *mf*

win /wɪn/ *n* vittoria *f*; **have a ~** riportare una vittoria ● *v* (*pt/pp* **won**; *pres p* **winning**) ● *vt* vincere; conquistare (*fame*) ● *vi* vincere. **win over** *vt* convincere

wince /wɪns/ *vi* contrarre il viso

winch /wɪntʃ/ *n* argano *m*

wind¹ /wɪnd/ *n* vento *m*; (*breath*) fiato *m*; (*fam: flatulence*) aria *f*; **get/have the ~ up** *fam* aver fifa; **get ~ of** aver sentore di; **in the ~** nell'aria ● *vt* ~ **sb** lasciare qcno senza fiato

wind² /waɪnd/ *v* (*pt/pp* **wound**) ● *vt* (*wrap*) avvolgere; (*move by turning*) far girare; (*clock*) caricare ● *vi* (*road*) serpeggiare. **wind up** *vt* caricare (*clock*); concludere (*proceedings*); *fam* prendere in giro (*sb*)

wind /wɪnd/ ~**fall** *n fig* fortuna *f* inaspettata

winding /'waɪndɪŋ/ *a* tortuoso

wind: ~ **instrument** *n* strumento *m* a fiato. ~**mill** *n* mulino *m* a vento

window /'wɪndəʊ/ *n* finestra *f*; (*of car*) finestrino *m*; (*of shop*) vetrina *f*

window: ~**-box** *n* cassetta *f* per

i fiori. ~**-cleaner** *n* (*person*) lavavetri *mf inv*. ~**-dresser** *n* vetrinista *mf*. ~**-dressing** *n* vetrinistica *f*; *fig* fumo *m* negli occhi. ~**-pane** *n* vetro *m*. ~**-shopping** *n*: **go** ~**-shopping** andare in giro a vedere le vetrine. ~**-sill** *n* davanzale *m*

'windscreen *n*, *Am* **'windshield** *n* parabrezza *m inv*. ~ **washer** *n* getto *m* d'acqua. ~**wiper** *n* tergicristallo *m*

wind: ~ **surfing** *n* windsurf *m inv*. ~**-swept** *a* esposto al vento; (*person*) scompigliato

windy /'wɪndɪ/ *a* (**-ier, -iest**) ventoso

wine /waɪn/ *n* vino *m*

wine: ~**-bar** *n* ≈ enoteca *f*. ~**glass** *n* bicchiere *m* da vino. ~**-list** *n* carta *f* dei vini

winery /'waɪnərɪ/ *n* *Am* vigneto *m*

'wine-tasting *n* degustazione *f* di vini

wing /wɪŋ/ *n* ala *f*; *Auto* parafango *m*; ~**s** *pl* *Theat* quinte *fpl*. ~**er** *n* *Sport* ala *f*

wink /wɪŋk/ *n* strizzata *f* d'occhio; **not sleep a ~** non chiudere occhio ● *vi* strizzare l'occhio; (*light*) lampeggiare

winner /'wɪnə(r)/ *n* vincitore, -trice *mf*

winning /'wɪnɪŋ/ *a* vincente; (*smile*) accattivante. ~**-post** *n* linea *f* d'arrivo. ~**s** *npl* vincite *fpl*

winter /'wɪntə(r)/ *n* inverno *m*. ~**ry** *a* invernale

wipe /waɪp/ *n* passata *f*; (*to dry*) asciugata *f* ● *vt* strofinare; (*dry*) asciugare. **wipe off** *vt* asciugare; (*erase*) cancellare. **wipe out** *vt* annientare; eliminare (*village*); estinguere (*debt*). **wipe up** *vt* asciugare (*dishes*)

wire /'waɪə(r)/ *n* fil di ferro; (*electr.*) filo *m* elettrico

wireless /'waɪəlɪs/ *n* radio *f*

wire 'netting *n* rete *f* metallica

wiring /'waɪərɪŋ/ *n* impianto *m* elettrico

wiry /'waɪərɪ/ a (-ier, -iest) ⟨person⟩ dal fisico asciutto; ⟨hair⟩ ispido

wisdom /'wɪzdəm/ n saggezza f; ⟨of action⟩ sensatezza f. ~ **tooth** n dente m del giudizio

wise /waɪz/ a saggio; ⟨prudent⟩ sensato. ~**ly** adv saggiamente; ⟨act⟩ sensatamente

wish /wɪʃ/ n desiderio m; **make a ~** esprimere un desiderio; **with best ~es** con i migliori auguri ● vt desiderare; ~ **sb well** fare tanti auguri a qcno; **I ~ you every success** ti auguro buona fortuna; **I ~ you could stay** vorrei che tu potessi rimanere ● vi ~ **for** sth desiderare qcsa. ~**ful** a ~**ful thinking** illusione f

wishy-washy /'wɪʃɪwɒʃɪ/ a ⟨colour⟩ spento; ⟨personality⟩ insignificante

wisp /wɪsp/ n ⟨of hair⟩ ciocca f; ⟨of smoke⟩ filo m; ⟨of grass⟩ ciuffo m

wistful /'wɪstfl/ a malinconico

wit /wɪt/ n spirito m; ⟨person⟩ persona f di spirito; **be at one's ~s' end** non saper che pesci pigliare

witch /wɪtʃ/ n strega f. ~**craft** n magia f. ~**-hunt** n caccia f alle streghe

with /wɪð/ prep con; ⟨fear, cold, jealousy etc⟩ di; **I'm hot ~ you** I am non ti seguo; **can I leave it ~ you?** ⟨task⟩ puoi occupartene tu?; ~ **no regrets/money** senza rimpianti/soldi; **be ~ it** fam essere al passo coi tempi; ⟨alert⟩ essere concentrato

with·draw v (pt **-drew**, pp **-drawn**) ● vt ritirare; prelevare ⟨money⟩ ● vi ritirarsi. ~**al** n ritiro m; ⟨of money⟩ prelevamento m; ⟨from drugs⟩ crisi f inv di astinenza; Psych chiusura f in se stessi. ~**al symptoms** npl sintomi mpl da crisi di astinenza

with·drawn see **withdraw** ● a ⟨person⟩ chiuso in se stesso

wither /'wɪðə(r)/ vi ⟨flower:⟩ appassire

with·hold vt (pt/pp **-held**) rifiutare ⟨consent⟩ (**from** a); nascondere ⟨information⟩ (**from** a); trattenere ⟨smile⟩

with·in prep in; ⟨before the end of⟩ entro; ~ **the law** legale ● adv all'interno

with·out prep senza; ~ **stopping** senza fermarsi

with·stand vt (pt/pp **-stood**) resistere a

witness /'wɪtnɪs/ n testimone mf ● vt autenticare ⟨signature⟩; essere testimone di ⟨accident⟩. ~**box** n, Am ~**-stand** n banco m dei testimoni

witticism /'wɪtɪsɪzm/ n spiritosaggine f

wittingly /'wɪtɪŋlɪ/ adv consapevolmente

witty /'wɪtɪ/ a (-ier, -iest) spiritoso

wives /waɪvz/ see **wife**

wizard /'wɪzəd/ n mago m. ~**ry** n stregoneria f

wobble /'wɒbl/ vi traballare. ~**ly** a traballante

wodge /wɒdʒ/ n fam mucchio m

woe /wəʊ/ n afflizione f

woke, woken /wəʊk, 'wəʊkn/ see **wake¹**

wolf /wʊlf/ n (pl **wolves** /wʊlvz/) lupo m; ⟨fam: womanizer⟩ donnaiolo m ● vt ~ [**down**] divorare. ~ **whistle** n fischio m ● vi ~**whistle at sb** fischiare dietro a qcno

woman /'wʊmən/ n (pl **women**) donna f. ~**izer** n donnaiolo m. ~**ly** a femmineo

womb /wuːm/ n utero m

women /'wɪmɪn/ see **woman. W~'s Libber** /'lɪbə(r)/ n femminista f. **W~'s Liberation** n movimento m femminista

won /wʌn/ see **win**

wonder /'wʌndə(r)/ n meraviglia f; ⟨surprise⟩ stupore m; **no ~!** non c'è da stupirsi!; **it's a ~ that...** è incredibile che... ● vi restare in ammirazione; ⟨be surprised⟩ essere sorpreso; **I ~** è quello che mi chiedo; **I ~ whether she is ill** mi chiedo se è malata?. **~ful** *a* meraviglioso. **~fully** *adv* meravigliosamente

won't /wəʊnt/ = **will not**

woo /wuː/ *vt* corteggiare; *fig* cercare di accattivarsi ⟨*voters*⟩

wood /wʊd/ *n* legno *m*; ⟨*for burning*⟩ legna *f*; ⟨*forest*⟩ bosco *m*; **out of the ~** *fig* fuori pericolo, **touch ~!** tocca ferro!

wood: **~ed** /-ɪd/ *a* boscoso. **~en** *a* di legno; *fig* legnoso. **~ wind** *n* strumenti *mpl* a fiato. **~work** *n* ⟨*wooden parts*⟩ parti *fpl* in legno; ⟨*craft*⟩ falegnameria *f*. **~worm** *n* tarlo *m*. **~y** *a* legnoso; ⟨*hill*⟩ boscoso

wool /wʊl/ *n* lana *f* ● *attrib* di lana. **~len** *a* di lana. **~lens** /*n*/ capi *mpl* di lana

woolly /ˈwʊlɪ/ *a* (**-ier, -iest**) ⟨*sweater*⟩ di lana; *fig* confuso

word /wɜːd/ *n* parola *f*; ⟨*news*⟩ notizia *f*; **by ~ of mouth** a viva voce; **have a ~** with dire due parole a; **have ~s** bisticciare; **in other ~s** in altre parole. **~ing** *n* parole *fpl*. **~ processor** *n* programma *m* di videoscrittura, word processor *m* *inv*

wore /wɔː(r)/ *see* **wear**

work /wɜːk/ *n* lavoro *m*; ⟨*art*⟩ opera *f*; **~s** *pl* ⟨*factory*⟩ fabbrica *fsg*; ⟨*mechanism*⟩ meccanismo *msg*; **at ~** al lavoro; **out of ~** disoccupato ● *vi* lavorare; ⟨*machine, ruse*⟩ funzionare; ⟨*study*⟩ studiare ● *vt* far funzionare ⟨*machine*⟩; ⟨*employee*⟩ far studiare ⟨*student*⟩. **work off** *vt* sfogare ⟨*anger*⟩; lavorare per estinguere ⟨*debt*⟩; fare spot ⟨*pr*⟩ smaltire ⟨*weight*⟩. **work out** *vt* elaborare ⟨*plan*⟩; risolvere ⟨*problem*⟩; calcolare ⟨*bill*⟩; **I ~ed out how he did it** ho capito come l'ha fatto ● *vi* evolvere. **work up** *vt* **I've ~ed up an appetite** mi è venuto appetito; **don't get ~ed up** ⟨*anxious*⟩ non farti prendere dal panico; ⟨*angry*⟩ non arrabbiarti

workable /ˈwɜːkəbl/ *a* ⟨*feasible*⟩ fattibile

workaholic /wɜːkəˈhɒlɪk/ *n* stacanovista *mf*

worker /ˈwɜːkə(r)/ *n* lavoratore, -trice *mf*; ⟨*manual*⟩ operaio, -a *mf*

working /ˈwɜːkɪŋ/ *a* ⟨*clothes etc*⟩ da lavoro; ⟨*day*⟩ feriale; **in ~ order** funzionante. **~ class** *n* classe *f* operaia. **~-class** *a* operaio

work: **~man** *n* operaio *m*. **~manship** *n* lavorazione *f*. **~out** *n* allenamento *m*. **~shop** *n* officina *f*; ⟨*discussion*⟩ dibattito *m*

world /wɜːld/ *n* mondo *m*; **a ~ of difference** una differenza abissale; **out of this ~** favoloso; **think the ~ of sb** andare matto per qcno. **~ly** *a* materiale; ⟨*person*⟩ materialista. **~wide** *a* mondiale ● *adv* mondialmente

worm /wɜːm/ *n* verme *m* ● *vt* **~ one's way into sb's confidence** conquistarsi la fiducia di qcno in modo subdolo. **~-eaten** *a* tarlato

worn /wɔːn/ *see* **wear** ● *a* sciupato. **~-out** *a* consumato; ⟨*person*⟩ sfinito

worried /ˈwʌrɪd/ *a* preoccupato

worry /ˈwʌrɪ/ *n* preoccupazione *f* ● *v* ⟨*pt/pp* **worried**⟩ ● *vt* preoccupare; ⟨*bother*⟩ disturbare ● *vi* preoccuparsi. **~ing** *a* preoccupante

worse /wɜːs/ *a* peggiore ● *adv* peggio ● *n* peggio *m*

worsen /ˈwɜːsn/ *vt/i* peggiorare

worship /ˈwɜːʃɪp/ *n* culto *m*; ⟨*service*⟩ funzione *f*; **Your/His W~** ⟨*to judge*⟩ signor giudice/il giudice ● *v* ⟨*pt/pp* **-shipped**⟩ ● *vt* venerare ● *vi* andare a messa

worst /wɜːst/ *a* peggiore ● *adv* peggio [di tutti] ● *n* **the ~** il peggio; **get the ~ of it** avere la peggio; **if the ~ comes to the ~** nella peggiore delle ipotesi

worth /wɜːθ/ *n* valore *m*; **£10 ~ of petrol** 10 sterline di benzina ● *a* **be ~** valere; **be ~ it** valerne la pena; **it's ~ trying** vale la pena di provare; **it's ~ my while** fa comodo viene. **~less** *a* senza valore. **~while** *a* che vale la pena; ⟨*cause*⟩ lodevole

worthy /'wɜ:ðɪ/ *a* degno; ⟨*cause*, *motive*⟩ lodevole

would /wʊd/ *v aux* **I ~ do it** lo farei; **~ you go?** andresti?; **~ you mind if I opened the window?** ti dispiace se apro la finestra?; **he ~ come if he could** verrebbe se potesse; **he said he ~n't** ha detto di no; **~ you like a drink?** vuoi qualcosa da bere?; **what ~ you like to drink?** cosa prendi da bere?; **you ~n't, ~ you?** non lo faresti, vero?

wound[1] /wuːnd/ *n* ferita *f* • *vt* ferire

wound[2] /waʊnd/ *see* **wind**

wove, woven /wəʊv, 'wəʊvn/ *see* **weave**

wrangle /'ræŋɡl/ *n* litigio *m* • *vi* litigare

wrap /ræp/ *n* ⟨*shawl*⟩ scialle *m* • *vt* (*pt/pp* **wrapped**) **~ [up]** avvolgere; ⟨*present*⟩ incartare; **be ~ped up in** *fig* essere completamente preso da • *vi* **~ up warmly** coprirsi bene. **~per** *n* ⟨*for sweet*⟩ carta *f* [di caramella]. **~ping** *n* materiale *m* da imballaggio. **~ping paper** *n* carta *f* da pacchi; ⟨*for gift*⟩ carta *f* da regalo

wrath /rɒθ/ *n* ira *f*

wreak /riːk/ *vt* **~ havoc with sth** scombussolare qcsa

wreath /riːθ/ *n* (*pl* **~s** /-ðz/) corona *f*

wreck /rek/ *n* ⟨*of ship*⟩ relitto *m*; ⟨*of car*⟩ carcassa *f*; ⟨*person*⟩ rottame *m* • *vt* far naufragare; demolire ⟨*car*⟩. **~age** /-ɪdʒ/ *n* rottami *mpl*; *fig* brandelli *mpl*

wrench /rentʃ/ *n* ⟨*injury*⟩ slogatura *f*; ⟨*tool*⟩ chiave *f* inglese; ⟨*pull*⟩ strattone *m* • *vt* ⟨*pull*⟩ strappare; slogarsi ⟨*wrist, ankle etc*⟩

wrest /rest/ *vt* strappare (**from** a)

wrestl|e /'resl/ *vi* lottare corpo a corpo; *fig* lottare. **~er** *n* lottatore, -trice *mf*. **~ing** *n* lotta *f* libera; ⟨*all-in*⟩ catch *m*

wretch /retʃ/ *n* disgraziato, -a *mf*. **~ed** /-ɪd/ *a* odioso; ⟨*weather*⟩ orribile; **feel ~ed** ⟨*unhappy*⟩ essere triste; ⟨*ill*⟩ sentirsi malissimo

wriggle /'rɪɡl/ *n* contorsione *f* • *vi* contorcersi; ⟨*move forward*⟩ strisciare; **~ out of sth** *fam* sottrarsi a qcsa

wring /rɪŋ/ *vt* (*pt/pp* **wrung**) torcere ⟨*sb's neck*⟩; strizzare ⟨*clothes*⟩; **~ one's hands** torcersi le mani; **~ing wet** inzuppato

wrinkle /'rɪŋkl/ *n* grinza *f*; ⟨*on skin*⟩ ruga *f* • *vt/i* raggrinzire. **~d** *a* ⟨*skin, face*⟩ rugoso; ⟨*clothes*⟩ raggrinzito

wrist /rɪst/ *n* polso *m*. **~-watch** *n* orologio *m* da polso

writ /rɪt/ *n Jur* mandato *m*

write /raɪt/ *vt/i* (*pt* **wrote**, *pp* **written**, *pres p* **writing**) scrivere. **write down** *vt* annotare. **write off** *vt* cancellare ⟨*debt*⟩; distruggere ⟨*car*⟩

'write-off *n* ⟨*car*⟩ rottame *m*

writer /'raɪtə(r)/ *n* autore, -trice *mf*; **she's a ~** è una scrittrice

'write-up *n* ⟨*review*⟩ recensione *f*

writhe /raɪð/ *vi* contorcersi

writing /'raɪtɪŋ/ *n* ⟨*occupation*⟩ scrivere *m*; ⟨*words*⟩ scritte *fpl*; ⟨*handwriting*⟩ scrittura *f*; **in ~** per iscritto. **~-paper** *n* carta *f* da lettera

written /'rɪtn/ *see* **write**

wrong /rɒŋ/ *a* sbagliato; **be ~** ⟨*person*⟩ sbagliare; **what's ~?** cosa c'è che non va? • *adv* ⟨*spelt*⟩ in modo sbagliato; **go ~** ⟨*person*⟩ sbagliare; ⟨*machine*⟩ funzionare male; ⟨*plan*⟩ andar male • *n* ingiustizia *f*; **in the ~** dalla parte del torto; **know right from ~** distinguere il bene dal male • *vt* fare torto a. **~ful** *a* ingiusto. **~ly** *adv* in modo sbagliato; ⟨*accuse, imagine*⟩ a torto; ⟨*informed*⟩ male

wrote /rəʊt/ *see* **write**

wrought iron /rɔːt-/ *n* ferro *m* battuto • *attrib* di ferro battuto

wrung /rʌŋ/ *see* **wring**

wry /raɪ/ a (-er, -est) ⟨humour, smile⟩ beffardo

Xx

Xmas /'krɪsməs/ n fam Natale m
X-ray n ⟨picture⟩ radiografia f; **have an ~** farsi fare una radiografia ● vt passare ai raggi X

Yy

yacht /jɒt/ n yacht m inv; ⟨for racing⟩ barca f a vela. **~ing** n vela f
Yank n fam americano, -a mf
yank /jæŋk/ vt fam tirare
yap /jæp/ vi (pt/pp yapped) ⟨dog:⟩ guaire
yard¹ /jɑːd/ n cortile m; ⟨for storage⟩ deposito m
yard² n iarda f (= 91,44 cm). **~stick** n fig pietra f di paragone
yarn /jɑːn/ n filo m; ⟨fam: tale⟩ storia f
yawn /jɔːn/ n sbadiglio m ● vi sbadigliare. **~ing** a **~ing gap** enorme divario m
year /jɪə(r)/ n anno m; ⟨of wine⟩ annata f; **for ~s** fam da secoli. **~-book** n annuario m. **~ly** a annuale ● adv annualmente
yearn /jɜːn/ vi struggersi. **~ing** n desiderio m struggente
yeast /jiːst/ n lievito m
yell /jel/ n urlo m ● vi urlare
yellow /'jeləʊ/ a & n giallo m
yelp /jelp/ n ⟨of dog⟩ guaito m ● vi ⟨dog:⟩ guaire
yen /jen/ n forte desiderio m (for di)
yes /jes/ adv sì ● n sì m inv
yesterday /'jestədeɪ/ a & adv ieri

m inv; **~'s paper** il giornale di ieri; **the day before ~** l'altroieri
yet /jet/ adv ancora; **as ~** fino ad ora; **not ~** non ancora; **the best ~** il migliore finora ● conj eppure
yew /juː/ n tasso m ⟨albero⟩
yield /jiːld/ n produzione f; ⟨profit⟩ reddito m ● vt produrre; fruttare ⟨profit⟩ ● vi cedere; Am Auto dare la precedenza
yodel /'jəʊdl/ vi (pt/pp yodelled) cantare jodel
yoga /'jəʊgə/ n yoga m
yoghurt /'jɒgət/ n yogurt m inv
yoke /jəʊk/ n giogo m; ⟨of garment⟩ carré m inv
yokel /'jəʊkl/ n zotico, -a mf
yolk /jəʊk/ n tuorlo m
you /juː/ pron ⟨subject⟩ tu, voi pl; ⟨formal⟩ lei, voi pl; ⟨direct/indirect object⟩ ti, vi pl; ⟨formal: direct object⟩ la; ⟨formal: indirect object⟩ le; ⟨after prep⟩ te, voi pl; ⟨formal: after prep⟩ lei; **~ are very kind** ⟨sg⟩ sei molto gentile; ⟨formal⟩ è molto gentile; ⟨pl & formal pl⟩ siete molto gentili; **~ can stay, but he has to go** ⟨sg⟩ tu puoi rimanere, ma lui deve andarsene; ⟨pl⟩ voi potete rimanere, ma lui deve andarsene; **all of ~** tutti voi; **I'll give ~ the money** ⟨sg⟩ ti darò i soldi; ⟨pl⟩ vi darò i soldi; **I'll give it to ~** ⟨sg⟩ te/⟨pl⟩ ve lo darò; **it was ~!** ⟨sg⟩ eri tu!; ⟨pl⟩ eravate voi!; **~ have to be careful** ⟨one⟩ si deve fare attenzione
young /jʌŋ/ a giovane ● npl ⟨animals⟩ piccoli mpl; **the ~** ⟨people⟩ i giovani mpl. **~ lady** n signorina f. **~ man** n giovanotto. **~ster** n ragazzo, -a mf; ⟨child⟩ bambino, -a mf
your /jɔː(r)/ a il tuo m, la tua f, i tuoi mpl, le tue fpl; ⟨formal⟩ il suo m, la sua f, i suoi mpl, le sue fpl; ⟨pl & formal pl⟩ il vostro m, la vostra f, i vostri mpl, le vostre fpl; **~ mother/father** tua madre/tuo pa-

dre; (*formal*) sua madre/suo padre; (*pl & formal pl*) vostra madre/vostro padre

yours /jɔːz/ *poss pron* il tuo *m*, la tua *f*, i tuoi *mpl*, le tue *fpl*; (*formal*) il suo *m*, la sua *f*, i suoi *mpl*, le sue *fpl*; (*pl & formal pl*) il vostro *m*, la vostra *f*, i vostri *mpl*, le vostre *fpl*; **a friend of ~** un tuo/suo/vostro amico; **friends of ~** dei tuoi/vostri/suoi amici; **that is ~** quello è tuo/vostro/suo; (*as opposed to mine*) quello è il tuo/il vostro/il suo

your·self *pron* (*reflexive*) ti; (*formal*) si; (*emphatic*) te stesso; (*formal*) sé, stesso; **do pour ~ a drink** versati da bere; (*formal*) si versi da bere; **you said so ~** lo hai detto tu stesso; (*formal*) lo ha detto lei stesso; **you can be proud of ~** puoi essere fiero di te/di sé; **by ~** da solo

your·selves *pron* (*reflexive*) vi; (*emphatic*) voi stessi; **do pour ~ a drink** versatevi da bere; **you said so ~** lo avete detto voi stessi; **you can be proud of ~** potete essere fieri di voi; **by ~** da soli

youth /juːθ/ *n* (*pl* youths /-ð:z/) gioventù *f inv*; (*boy*) giovanetto *m*; **the ~** (*young people*) i giovani *mpl*. **~·ful** *a* giovanile. **~ hostel** *n* ostello *m* [della gioventù]

Yugoslav /ˈjuːgəslɑːv/ *a & n* jugoslavo, -a *mf*

Yugoslavia /-ˈslɑːvɪə/ *n* Jugoslavia *f*

crossing *n* passaggio *m* pedonale, zebre *fpl*

zero /ˈzɪərəʊ/ *n* zero *m*

zest /zest/ *n* gusto *m*

zigzag /ˈzɪgzæg/ *n* zigzag *m inv* ● *vi* (*pt/pp* **-zagged**) zigzagare

zilch /zɪltʃ/ *n fam* zero *m* assoluto

zinc /zɪŋk/ *n* zinco *m*

zip /zɪp/ *n* ~ **[fastener]** cerniera *f* [lampo] ● *vt* (*pt/pp* **zipped**) ~ **[up]** chiudere con la cerniera [lampo]

'Zip code *n Am* codice *m* postale

zipper /ˈzɪpə(r)/ *n Am* cerniera *f* [lampo]

zodiac /ˈzəʊdɪæk/ *n* zodiaco *m*

zombie /ˈzɒmbɪ/ *n fam* zombie *mf inv*

zone /zəʊn/ *n* zona *f*

zoo /zuː/ *n* zoo *m inv*

zoolog|ist /zəʊˈɒlədʒɪst/ *n* zoologo, -a *mf*. **~y** zoologia *f*

zoom /zuːm/ *vi* sfrecciare. **~ lens** *n* zoom *m inv*

Zz

zany /ˈzeɪnɪ/ *a* (**-ier, -iest**) demenziale

zeal /ziːl/ *n* zelo *m*

zealous /ˈzeləs/ *a* zelante. **~·ly** *adv* con zelo

zebra /ˈzebrə/ *n* zebra *f*. **~·'**

ITALIAN VERB TABLES

REGULAR VERBS:

1. in **-are** (*eg* compr|are)

   Present ~o, ~i, ~a, ~iamo, ~ate, ~ano
   Imperfect ~avo, ~avi, ~ava, ~avamo, ~avate, ~avano
   Past historic ~ai, ~asti, ~ò, ~ammo, ~aste, ~arono
   Future ~erò, ~erai, ~erà, ~eremo, ~erete, ~eranno
   Present subjunctive ~i, ~i, ~i, ~iamo, ~iate, ~ino
   Past subjunctive ~assi, ~assi, ~asse, ~assimo, ~aste, ~assero
   Present participle ~ando
   Past participle ~ato
   Imperative ~a (*fml* ~i), ~iamo, ~ate
   Conditional ~erei, ~eresti, ~erebbe, ~eremmo, ~ereste, ~erebbero

2. in **-ere** (*eg* vend|ere)

   Pres ~o, ~i, ~e, ~iamo, ~ete, ~ono
   Impf ~evo, ~evi, ~eva, ~evamo, ~evate, ~evano
   Past hist ~ei *or* ~etti, ~esti, ~è *or* ~ette, ~emmo, ~este, ~erono *or* ~ettero
   Fut ~erò, ~erai, ~erà, ~eremo, ~erete, ~eranno
   Pres sub ~a, ~a, ~a, ~iamo, ~iate, ~ano
   Past sub ~essi, ~essi, ~esse, ~essimo, ~este, ~essero
   Pres part ~endo
   Past part ~uto
   Imp ~i (*fml* ~a), ~iamo, ~ete
   Cond ~erei, ~eresti, ~erebbe, ~eremmo, ~ereste, ~erebbero

3. in **-ire** (*eg* dorm|ire)

   Pres ~o, ~i, ~e, ~iamo, ~ite, ~ono
   Impf ~ivo, ~ivi, ~iva, ~ivamo, ~ivate, ~ivano
   Past hist ~ii, ~isti, ~ì, ~immo, ~iste, ~irono
   Fut ~irò, ~irai, ~irà, ~iremo, ~irete, ~iranno
   Pres sub ~a, ~a, ~a, ~iamo, ~iate, ~ano
   Past sub ~issi, ~issi, ~isse, ~issimo, ~iste, ~issero
   Pres part ~endo
   Past part ~ito
   Imp ~i (*fml* ~a), ~iamo, ~ite
   Cond ~irei, ~iresti, ~irebbe, ~iremmo, ~ireste, ~irebbero

Notes

- Many verbs in the third conjugation take *isc* between the stem and the ending in the first, second, and third person singular and in the third person plural of the present, the present subjunctive, and the imperative: fin|ire **Pres** ~isco, ~isci, ~isce, ~iscono. **Pres sub** ~isca, ~iscano **Imp** ~isci.

- The three forms of the imperative are the same as the corresponding forms of the present for the second and third conjugation. In the first conjugation the forms are also the same except for the second person singular: present *compri*, imperative *compra*. The negative form of the second person singular is formed by putting *non* before the infinitive for all conjugations: *non comprare*. In polite forms the third person of the present subjunctive is used instead for all conjugations: *compri*.

IRREGULAR VERBS:

Certain forms of all irregular verbs are regular (except for *essere*). These are: the second person plural of the present, the past subjunctive, and the present participle. All forms not listed below are regular and can be derived from the parts given. Only those irregular verbs considered to be the most useful are shown in the tables.

accadere	*as* cadere
accendere	• **Past hist** accesi, accendesti • **Past part** acceso
affliggere	• **Past hist** afflissi, affliggesti • **Past part** afflitto
ammettere	*as* mettere
andare	• **Pres** vado, vai, va, andiamo, andate, vanno • **Fut** andrò *etc* • **Pres sub** vada, vadano • **Imp** va', vada, vadano
apparire	• **Pres** appaio *or* apparisco, appari *or* apparisci, appare *or* apparisce, appaiono *or* appariscono • **Past hist** apparvi *or* apparsi, apparisti, apparve *or* appari *or* apparse, apparvero *or* apparirono *or* apparsero • **Pres sub** appaia *or* apparisca
aprire	• **Pres** apro • **Past hist** aprii, apristi • **Pres sub** apra • **Past part** aperto

avere
- **Pres** ho, hai, ha, abbiamo, hanno • **Past hist** ebbi, avesti, ebbe, avemmo, aveste, ebbero • **Fut** avrò *etc* • **Pres sub** abbia *etc* • **Imp** abbi, abbia, abbiate, abbiano

bere
- **Pres** bevo *etc* • **Impf** bevevo *etc* • **Past hist** bevvi *or* bevetti, bevesti • **Fut** berrò *etc* • **Pres sub** beva *etc* • **Past sub** bevessi *etc* • **Pres part** bevendo • **Cond** berrei *etc*

cadere
- **Past hist** caddi, cadesti • **Fut** cadrò *etc*

chiedere
- **Past hist** chiesi, chiedesti • **Pres sub** chieda *etc* • **Past part** chiesto *etc*

chiudere
- **Past hist** chiusi, chiudesti • **Past part** chiuso

cogliere
- **Pres** colgo, colgono • **Past hist** colsi, cogliesti • **Pres sub** colga • **Past part** colto

correre
- **Past hist** corsi, corresti • **Past part** corso

crescere
- **Past hist** crebbi • **Past part** cresciuto

cuocere
- **Pres** cuocio, cuociamo, cuociono • **Past hist** cossi, cocesti • **Past part** cotto

dare
- **Pres** do, dai, dà, diamo, danno • **Past hist** diedi *or* detti, desti • **Fut** darò *etc* • **Pres sub** dia *etc* • **Past sub** dessi *etc* • **Imp** da' *(fml* dia)

dire
- **Pres** dico, dici, dice, diciamo, dicono • **Impf** dicevo *etc* • **Past hist** dissi, dicesti • **Fut** dirò *etc* • **Pres sub** dica, diciamo, diciate, dicano • **Past sub** dicessi *etc* • **Pres part** dicendo • **Past part** detto • **Imp** di' *(fml* dica)

dovere
- **Pres** devo *or* debbo, devi, deve, dobbiamo, devono *or* debbono • **Fut** dovrò *etc* • **Pres sub** deva *or* debba, dobbiamo, dobbiate, devano *or* debbano • **Cond** dovrei *etc*

essere
- **Pres** sono, sei, è, siamo, siete, sono • **Impf** ero, eri, era, eravamo, eravate, erano • **Past hist** fui, fosti, fu, fummo, foste, furono • **Fut** sarò *etc* • **Pres sub** sia *etc* • **Past sub** fossi, fossi, fosse, fossimo, foste, fossero • **Past part** stato • **Imp** sii *(fml* sia), siate • **Cond** sarei *etc*

fare
- **Pres** faccio, fai, fa, facciamo, fanno • **Impf** facevo *etc* • **Past hist** feci, facesti • **Fut** farò *etc* • **Pres sub** faccia *etc* • **Past sub** facessi *etc* • **Pres part** facendo • **Past part** fatto • **Imp** fa' *(fml* faccia) • **Cond** farei *etc*

fingere • **Past hist** finsi, fingesti, finsero • **Past part** finto

giungere • **Past hist** giunsi, giungesti, giunsero • **Past part** giunto

leggere • **Past hist** lessi, leggesti • **Past part** letto

mettere • **Past hist** misi, mettesti • **Past part** messo

morire • **Pres** muoio, muori, muore, muoiono • **Fut** morirò or morrò etc • **Pres sub** muoia • **Past part** morto

muovere • **Past hist** mossi, movesti • **Past part** mosso

nascere • **Past hist** nacqui, nascesti • **Past part** nato

offrire • **Past hist** offersi or offrii, offristi • **Pres sub** offra • **Past part** offerto

parere • **Pres** paio, pari, pare, pariamo, paiono • **Past hist** parvi or parsi, paresti • **Fut** parrò etc • **Pres sub** paia, paiamo or pariamo, pariate, paiano • **Past part** parso

piacere • **Pres** piaccio, piaci, piace, piacciamo, piacciono • **Past hist** piacqui, piacesti, piacque, piacemmo, piaceste, piacquero • **Pres sub** piaccia etc • **Past part** piaciuto

porre • **Pres** pongo, poni, pone, poniamo, ponete, pongono • **Impf** ponevo etc • **Past hist** posi, ponesti • **Fut** porrò etc • **Pres sub** ponga, poniamo, poniate, pongano • **Past sub** ponessi etc

potere • **Pres** posso, puoi, può, possiamo, possono • **Fut** potrò etc • **Pres sub** possa, possiamo, possiate, possano • **Cond** potrei etc

prendere • **Past hist** presi, prendesti • **Past part** preso

ridere • **Past hist** risi, ridesti • **Past part** riso

rimanere • **Pres** rimango, rimani, rimane, rimaniamo, rimangono • **Past hist** rimasi, rimanesti • **Fut** rimarrò etc • **Pres sub** rimanga • **Past part** rimasto • **Cond** rimarrei

salire • **Pres** salgo, sali, sale, saliamo, salgono • **Pres sub** salga, saliate, salgono

sapere • **Pres** so, sai, sa, sappiamo, sanno • **Past hist** seppi, sapesti • **Fut** saprò etc • **Pres sub** sappia etc • **Imp** sappi (fml sappia), sappiate • **Cond** saprei etc

scegliere • **Pres** scelgo, scegli, sceglie, scegliamo, scelgono • **Past hist** scelsi, scegliesti *etc* • **Past part** scelto

scrivere • **Past hist** scrissi, scrivesti *etc* • **Past part** scritto

sedere • **Pres** siedo *or* seggo, siedi, siede, siedono • **Pres sub** sieda *or* segga

spegnere • **Pres** spengo, spengono • **Past hist** spensi, spegnesti • **Past part** spento

stare • **Pres** sto, stai, sta, stiamo, stanno • **Past hist** stetti, stesti *etc* • **Fut** starò *etc* • **Pres sub** stia *etc* • **Past sub** stessi *etc* • **Past part** stato • **Imp** sta' (*fml* stia)

tacere • **Pres** taccio, tacciono • **Past hist** tacqui, tacque, tacquero • **Pres sub** taccia

tendere • **Past hist** tesi • **Past part** teso

tenere • **Pres** tengo, tieni, tiene, tengono • **Past hist** tenni, tenesti • **Fut** terrò *etc* • **Pres sub** tenga

togliere • **Pres** tolgo, tolgono • **Past hist** tolsi, tolse, tolsero • **Pres sub** tolga, tolgano • **Past part** tolto • **Imp** *fml* tolga

trarre • **Pres** traggo, trai, trae, traiamo, traete, traggono • **Past hist** trassi, traesti • **Fut** trarrò *etc* • **Pres sub** tragga • **Past sub** traessi *etc* • **Past part** tratto

uscire • **Pres** esco, esci, esce, escono • **Pres sub** esca • **Imp** esci (*fml* esca)

valere • **Pres** valgo, valgono • **Past hist** valsi, valesti • **Fut** varrò *etc* • **Pres sub** valga, valgano • **Past part** valso • **Cond** varrei *etc*

vedere • **Past hist** vidi, vedesti • **Fut** vedrò *etc* • **Past part** visto *or* veduto • **Cond** vedrei *etc*

venire • **Pres** vengo, vieni, viene, vengono • **Past hist** venni, venisti • **Fut** verrò *etc*

vivere • **Past hist** vissi, vivesti • **Fut** vivrò *etc* • **Past part** vissuto • **Cond** vivrei *etc*

volere • **Pres** voglio, vuoi, vuole, vogliamo, volete, vogliono • **Past hist** volli, volesti • **Fut** vorrò *etc* • **Pres sub** voglia *etc* • **Imp** vogliate • **Cond** vorrei *etc*

ENGLISH IRREGULAR VERBS

Infinitive	Past Tense	Past Participle	Infinitive	Past Tense	Past Participle
Infinito	*Passato*	*Participio passato*	*Infinito*	*Passato*	*Participio passato*
arise	arose	arisen	cling	clung	clung
awake	awoke	awoken	come	came	come
be	was	been	cost	cost,	cost,
bear	bore	borne		costed (*vt*)	costed
beat	beat	beaten	creep	crept	crept
become	became	become	cut	cut	cut
begin	began	begun	deal	dealt	dealt
behold	beheld	beheld	dig	dug	dug
bend	bent	bent	do	did	done
beseech	beseeched	beseeched	draw	drew	drawn
	besought	besought	dream	dreamt,	dreamt,
bet	bet,	bet,		dreamed	dreamed
	betted	betted	drink	drank	drunk
bid	bade,	bidden,	drive	drove	driven
	bid	bid	dwell	dwelt	dwelt
bind	bound	bound	eat	ate	eaten
bite	bit	bitten	fall	fell	fallen
bleed	bled	bled	feed	fed	fed
blow	blew	blown	feel	felt	felt
break	broke	broken	fight	fought	fought
breed	bred	bred	find	found	found
bring	brought	brought	flee	fled	fled
build	built	built	fling	flung	flung
burn	burnt,	burnt,	fly	flew	flown
	burned	burned	forbid	forbade	forbidden
burst	burst	burst	forget	forgot	forgotten
bust	busted,	busted,	forgive	forgave	forgiven
	bust	bust	forsake	forsook	forsaken
buy	bought	bought	freeze	froze	frozen
cast	cast	cast	get	got	got,
catch	caught	caught			gotten *Am*
choose	chose	chosen	give	gave	given

Infinitive	Past Tense	Past Participle	Infinitive	Past Tense	Past Participle
Infinito	*Passato*	*Participio passato*	*Infinito*	*Passato*	*Participio passato*
go	went	gone	**mow**	mowed	mown, mowed
grind	ground	ground			
grow	grew	grown	**overhang**	overhung	overhung
hang	hung, hanged (*vt*)	hung, hanged	**pay**	paid	paid
			put	put	put
have	had	had	**quit**	quitted, quit	quitted, quit
hear	heard	heard			
hew	hewed	hewed, hewn	**read** /red/	read /red/	read /red/
			rid	rid	rid
hide	hid	hidden	**ride**	rode	ridden
hit	hit	hit	**ring**	rang	rung
hold	held	held	**rise**	rose	risen
hurt	hurt	hurt	**run**	ran	run
keep	kept	kept	**saw**	sawed	sawn, sawed
kneel	knelt	knelt			
know	knew	known	**say**	said	said
lay	laid	laid	**see**	saw	seen
lead	led	led	**seek**	sought	sought
lean	leaned, leant	leaned, leant	**sell**	sold	sold
			send	sent	sent
leap	leapt, leaped	leapt, leaped	**set**	set	set
			sew	sewed	sewn, sewed
learn	learnt, learned	learnt, learned			
			shake	shook	shaken
leave	left	left	**shear**	sheared	shorn, sheared
lend	lent	lent			
let	let	let	**shed**	shed	shed
lie	lay	lain	**shine**	shone	shone
light	lit, lighted	lit, lighted	**shit**	shit	shit
			shoe	shod	shod
lose	lost	lost	**shoot**	shot	shot
make	made	made	**show**	showed	shown
mean	meant	meant	**shrink**	shrank	shrunk
meet	met	met	**shut**	shut	shut

Infinitive	Past Tense	Past Participle	Infinitive	Past Tense	Past Participle
Infinito	*Passato*	*Participio passato*	*Infinito*	*Passato*	*Participio passato*
sing	sang	sung	stride	strode	stridden
sink	sank	sunk	strike	struck	struck
sit	sat	sat	string	strung	strung
slay	slew	slain	strive	strove	striven
sleep	slept	slept	swear	swore	sworn
slide	slid	slid	sweep	swept	swept
sling	slung	slung	swell	swelled	swollen, swelled
slit	slit	slit	swim	swam	swum
smell	smelt, smelled	smelt, smelled	swing	swung	swung
sow	sowed	sown, sowed	take	took	taken
speak	spoke	spoken	teach	taught	taught
speed	sped, speeded	sped, speeded	tear	tore	torn
			tell	told	told
			think	thought	thought
spell	spelled, spelt	spelled, spelt	thrive	thrived, throve	thrived, thriven
spend	spent	spent	throw	threw	thrown
spill	spilt, spilled	spilt, spilled	thrust	thrust	thrust
			tread	trod	trodden
spin	spun	spun	understand	understood	understood
spit	spat	spat			
split	split	split	undo	undid	undone
spoil	spoilt, spoiled	spoilt, spoiled	wake	woke	woken
			wear	wore	worn
spread	spread	spread	weave	wove	woven
spring	sprang	sprung	weep	wept	wept
stand	stood	stood	wet	wet, wetted	wet, wetted
steal	stole	stolen			
stick	stuck	stuck	win	won	won
sting	stung	stung	wind	wound	wound
stink	stank	stunk	wring	wrung	wrung
strew	strewed	strewn, strewed	write	wrote	written